W9-BYG-316

10. Shipping Terms:

	FOB Shipping Point	FOB Destination
Ownership (title) passes to buyer when merchandise is..................	delivered to freight carrier	delivered to buyer
Transportation costs are paid by	buyer	seller

11. Format for Bank Reconciliation:

Cash balance according to bank statement .... $xxx
Add: Additions by company not on bank
  statement .... $xx
  Bank errors xx   xx
                                                          $xxx
Deduct: Deductions by company not on bank
  statement .... $xx
  Bank errors xx   xx
Adjusted balance.. $xxx

Cash balance according to company's records .... $xxx
Add: Additions by bank not recorded by company .. $xx
  Company errors..................................... xx   xx
                                                          $xxx
Deduct: Deductions by bank not recorded
  by company....................................... $xx
  Company errors..................................... xx   xx
Adjusted balance.. $xxx

12. Inventory Costing Methods:
1. First-in, First-out (FIFO)
2. Last-in, First-out (LIFO)
3. Average Cost

13. Interest Computations:
Interest = Face Amount (or Principal) × Rate × Time

14. Methods of Determining Annual Depreciation:

STRAIGHT-LINE: $\frac{\text{Cost} - \text{Estimated Residual Value}}{\text{Estimated Life}}$

DOUBLE-DECLINING-BALANCE: Rate* × Book Value at Beginning of Period

*Rate is commonly twice the straight-line rate (1/Estimated Life).

15. Adjustments to Net Income (Loss) Using the Indirect Method

	Increase (Decrease)
Net income (loss)	$ XXX
Adjustments to reconcile net income to net cash flow from operating activities:	
Depreciation of fixed assets	XXX
Amortization of intangible assets	XXX
Losses on disposal of assets	XXX
Gains on disposal of assets	(XXX)
Changes in current operating assets and liabilities:	
Increases in noncash current operating assets	(XXX)
Decreases in noncash current operating assets	XXX
Increases in current operating liabilities	XXX
Decreases in current operating liabilities	(XXX)
Net cash flow from operating activities	$ XXX
	or
	$(XXX)

16. Contribution Margin Ratio $= \frac{\text{Sales} - \text{Variable Costs}}{\text{Sales}}$

17. Break-Even Sales (Units) $= \frac{\text{Fixed Costs}}{\text{Unit Contribution Margin}}$

18. Sales (Units) $= \frac{\text{Fixed Costs} + \text{Target Profit}}{\text{Unit Contribution Margin}}$

19. Margin of Safety $= \frac{\text{Sales} - \text{Sales at Break-Even Point}}{\text{Sales}}$

20. Operating Leverage $= \frac{\text{Contribution Margin}}{\text{Income from Operations}}$

21. Variances

$\text{Direct Materials Price Variance} = \left(\text{Actual Price per Unit} - \text{Standard Price}\right) \times \text{Actual Quantity Used}$

$\text{Direct Materials Quantity Variance} = \left(\text{Actual Quantity Used} - \text{Standard Quantity}\right) \times \text{Standard Price per Unit}$

$\text{Direct Labor Rate Variance} = \left(\text{Actual Rate per Hour} - \text{Standard Rate}\right) \times \text{Actual Hours Worked}$

$\text{Direct Labor Time Variance} = \left(\text{Actual Hours Worked} - \text{Standard Hours}\right) \times \text{Standard Rate per Hour}$

$\text{Variable Factory Overhead Controllable Variance} = \text{Actual Factory Overhead} - \text{Budgeted Factory Overhead for Amount Produced}$

$\text{Fixed Factory Overhead Volume Variance} = \text{Budgeted Factory Overhead for Amount Produced} - \text{Applied Factory Overhead}$

22. Rate of Return on Investment (ROI) $= \frac{\text{Income from Operations}}{\text{Invested Assets}}$

Alternative ROI Computation:

$\text{ROI} = \frac{\text{Income from Operations}}{\text{Sales}} \times \frac{\text{Sales}}{\text{Invested Assets}}$

23. Capital Investment Analysis Methods:
1. Methods That Ignore Present Values:
   A. Average Rate of Return Method
   B. Cash Payback Method
2. Methods That Use Present Values:
   A. Net Present Value Method
   B. Internal Rate of Return Method

24. Average Rate of Return $= \frac{\text{Estimated Average Annual Income}}{\text{Average Investment}}$

25. Present Value Index $= \frac{\text{Total Present Value of Net Cash Flow}}{\text{Amount to Be Invested}}$

26. Present Value Factor for an Annuity of $1 $= \frac{\text{Amount to Be Invested}}{\text{Equal Annual Net Cash Flows}}$

WARREN · REEVE · DUCHAC

FINANCIAL
ACCOUNTING

10E

CARL S. WARREN
Professor Emeritus of Accounting
University of Georgia, Athens

JAMES M. REEVE
Professor Emeritus of Accounting
University of Tennessee, Knoxville

JONATHAN E. DUCHAC
Professor of Accounting
Wake Forest University

THOMSON
™
SOUTH-WESTERN

Australia · Brazil · Canada · Mexico · Singapore · Spain · United Kingdom · United States

THOMSON
★
SOUTH-WESTERN

Financial Accounting, 10e
Carl S. Warren, James M. Reeve, Jonathan E. Duchac

VP/Editorial Director:
Jack W. Calhoun

Publisher:
Rob Dewey

Sr. Acquisitions Editor:
Sharon Oblinger

Developmental Editor:
Steven E. Joos

Assistant Editor:
Erin Berger

Marketing Manager:
Robin Farrar

Sr. Content Project Manager:
Cliff Kallemeyn

Manager of Technology, Editorial:
Vicky True

Associate Manager of Technology:
John Barans

Sr. Technology Project Editors:
Sally Nieman and Robin Browning

Manufacturing Coordinator:
Doug Wilke

Editorial Assistant:
Kelly Somers

Production House:
LEAP Publishing Services, Inc.

Compositor:
GGS Book Services, Inc.

Printer:
RR Donnelley
Willard, OH

Art Director:
Bethany Casey

Infographic Illustrations:
Grannan Graphic Design, Ltd.

Internal Designer:
Grannan Graphic Design, Ltd.

Cover Designer:
Grannan Graphic Design, Ltd.

Cover Images:
Max Dereta/Jupiterimages

Photography Manager:
John Hill

Photo Researcher:
Rose Alcorn

Library of Congress Control Number:
2006929459

For more information about our products, contact us at:

Thomson Learning Academic Resource
Center

1-800-423-0563

Thomson Higher Education
5191 Natorp Boulevard
Mason, OH 45040
USA

The Author Team • • • • • • • • • • • • • • • •

Carl S. Warren

Dr. Carl S. Warren is Professor Emeritus of Accounting at the University of Georgia, Athens. For over 25 years, Professor Warren taught all levels of accounting classes. Professor Warren has taught classes at the University of Georgia, University of Iowa, Michigan State University, and University of Chicago. Professor Warren focused his teaching efforts on principles of accounting and auditing. Professor Warren received his doctorate degree (Ph.D.) from Michigan State University and his undergraduate (B.B.A) and masters (M.A.) degrees from the University of Iowa. During his career, Professor Warren published numerous articles in professional journals, including *The Accounting Review, Journal of Accounting Research, Journal of Accountancy, The CPA Journal,* and *Auditing: A Journal of Practice & Theory.* Professor Warren's outside interests include writing short stories and novels, oil painting, playing handball, golfing, skiing, backpacking, and fly-fishing.

James M. Reeve

Dr. James M. Reeve is Professor Emeritus of Accounting and Information Management at the University of Tennessee. Professor Reeve taught on the accounting faculty for 25 years, after graduating with his Ph.D. from Oklahoma State University. His teaching effort focused on undergraduate accounting principles and graduate education in the Master of Accountancy and Senior Executive MBA programs. Beyond this, Professor Reeve is also very active in the Supply Chain Certification program, which is a major executive education and research effort of the College. His research interests are varied and include work in managerial accounting, supply chain management, lean manufacturing, and information management. He has published over 40 articles in academic and professional journals, including the *Journal of Cost Management, Journal of Management Accounting Research, Accounting Review, Management Accounting Quarterly, Supply Chain Management Review,* and *Accounting Horizons.* He has consulted or provided training around the world for a wide variety of organizations, including Boeing, Procter and Gamble, Norfolk Southern, Hershey Foods, Coca-Cola, and Sony. When not writing books, Professor Reeve plays golf and is involved in faith-based activities.

Jonathan E. Duchac

Dr. Jonathan Duchac is the Merrill Lynch and Co. Associate Professor of Accounting Policy and Director of the Program in Enterprise Risk Management at Wake Forest University. He earned his Ph.D. in accounting from the University of Georgia and currently teaches introductory and advanced courses in financial accounting. Dr. Duchac has received a number of awards during his career, including the Wake Forest Graduate Accounting Student Teaching Award, the T.B. Rose award for Instructional Innovation, and the University of Georgia Outstanding Teaching Assistant Award. In addition to his teaching responsibilities, Dr. Duchac serves as Accounting Advisor to Merrill Lynch Equity Research, where he works with research analysts in reviewing and evaluating the financial reporting practices of public companies. He has testified before the U.S. House of Representatives, the Financial Accounting Standards Board, and the Securities and Exchange Commission and has worked with a number of major public companies on financial reporting and accounting policy issues.

Get Connected

For over 75 years, *Accounting* has been used effectively to teach generations of businessmen and women. As the most successful business textbook of all time, it continues to introduce students to accounting through a variety of time-tested ways. With this edition, we continue our quest to explore new ways to connect the modern student to accounting, a discipline that is challenging and rewarding.

With this quest in mind, we came to you, the teachers of accounting, and asked what works, what doesn't, and what needs improvement. For this edition, we employed many new methods to get closer to instructors who teach the course every day. As always, your responses were thorough and insightful, and through reviews, focus groups, and our ground-breaking Blue Sky Workshops, we've created a contemporary and efficient learning system for today's student and instructor. In fact, our Blue Sky Workshops brought together accounting teachers from all over the country to discuss content, chapter pedagogy, book design, and supplements. For the first time, instructors had input on every aspect of the project, and the effect of their input on this edition is clear. By connecting with those who use the book, *Financial Accounting, 10e*, delivers everything students and instructors need, with nothing they don't.

The original author of *Accounting*, James McKinsey, could not have imagined the success and influence this text has enjoyed or that his original vision would continue to lead the market into the twenty-first century. As the current authors, we appreciate the responsibility of protecting and enhancing this vision, while continuing to refine it to meet the changing needs of students and instructors. Always in touch with a tradition of excellence but never satisfied with yesterday's success, this edition enthusiastically embraces a changing environment and continues to proudly lead the way. We sincerely thank our many colleagues who have helped to make it happen.

Carl S. Warren

Jonathan Duchac

"The teaching of accounting is no longer designed to train professional accountants only. With the growing complexity of business and the constantly increasing difficulty of the problems of management, it has become essential that everyone who aspires to a position of responsibility should have a knowledge of the fundamental principles of accounting."

— James O. McKinsey, Author, first edition, 1929

Connect to Course Content

As the clear leader in pedagogical innovation, *Financial Accounting, 10e,* introduces the next step in the evolution of accounting textbooks. Through discussions at the Blue Sky Workshops and other instructor interactions, this edition is closer than ever to becoming the "perfect" accounting text.

(NEW!) **Example Exercise**

Based on extensive market feedback, we've developed new Example Exercises that reinforce concepts and procedures in a bold, new way. Like a teacher in a classroom, students follow the authors' example to see how to complete accounting applications as they are presented in the text. This feature also provides a list of Practice Exercises that parallel the Example Exercises, so students get the practice they need.

See the example of the application being presented.

Example Exercise 1-1   objective (2

On August 25, Gallatin Repair Service extended an offer of $125,000 for land that had been priced for sale at $150,000. On September 3, Gallatin Repair Service accepted the seller's counteroffer of $137,000. On October 20, the land was assessed at a value of $98,000 for property tax purposes. On December 4, Gallatin Repair Service was offered $160,000 for the land by a national retail chain. At what value should the land be recorded in Gallatin Repair Service's records?

Follow My Example 1-1

$137,000. Under the cost concept, the land should be recorded at the cost to Gallatin Repair Service.

For Practice: PE 1-1A, PE 1-1B

Follow along as the authors work through the example exercise.

Try these corresponding end-of-chapter exercises for practice!

Clear Objectives and Key Learning Outcomes

To help guide students, the authors revised and focused the chapter objectives and developed key learning outcomes related to each chapter objective. All aspects of the chapter content and end-of-chapter exercises and problems connect back to these objectives and related outcomes. In doing so, students can test their understanding and quickly locate concepts for review.

NEW! "At a Glance" Chapter Summary

The "At a Glance" summary grid ties everything together and helps students stay on track. First, the Key Points recap the chapter content for each chapter objective. Second, the related Key Learning Outcomes list all of the expected student performance capabilities that come from completing each objective. In case students need further practice on a specific outcome, the last two columns reference related Example Exercises and their corresponding Practice Exercises. Through this intuitive grid, all the chapter pedagogy links together in one cleanly integrated summary.

5. Describe the financial statements of a proprietorship and explain how they interrelate.

Key Points	Key Learning Outcomes	Example Exercises	Practice Exercises
The principal financial statements of a proprietorship are the income statement, the statement of owner's equity, the balance sheet, and the statement of cash flows. The income statement reports a period's net income or net loss, which also appears on the statement of owner's equity. The ending owner's capital reported on the statement of owner's equity is also reported on the balance sheet. The ending cash balance is reported on the balance sheet and the statement of cash flows.	• List and describe the financial statements of a proprietorship. • Prepare an income statement. • Prepare a statement of owner's equity. • Prepare a balance sheet. • Prepare a statement of cash flows. • Explain how the financial statements of a proprietorship are interrelated.	1-4 1-5 1-6 1-7	1-4A, 1-4B 1-5A, 1-5B 1-6A, 1-6B 1-7A, 1-7B

Provides a conceptual review of each objective.

Creates a checklist of skills to help review for a test.

Directs the student to this helpful new feature!

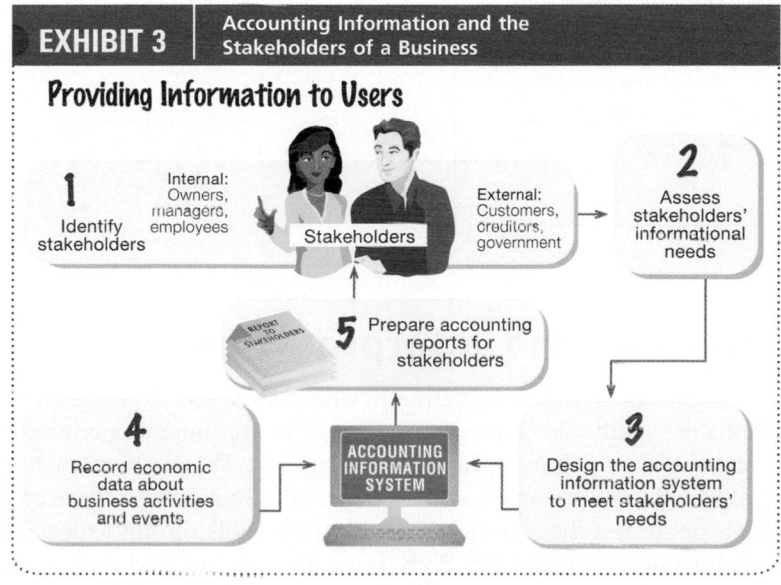

EXHIBIT 3 | Accounting Information and the Stakeholders of a Business

Providing Information to Users

1 Identify stakeholders — Internal: Owners, managers, employees — External: Customers, creditors, government — Stakeholders

2 Assess stakeholders' informational needs

3 Design the accounting information system to meet stakeholders' needs

ACCOUNTING INFORMATION SYSTEM

4 Record economic data about business activities and events

5 Prepare accounting reports for stakeholders

Modern, User-Friendly Design

The internal design has been modified to be both appealing and easy to navigate. Based on student testimonials of what they find most useful, this streamlined presentation includes a wealth of helpful resources without feeling cluttered. To update the look of the material, some Exhibits use computerized spreadsheets to better reflect the changing environment of business. Visual learners will appreciate the generous number of exhibits and illustrations used to convey concepts and procedures.

Always aware of the issues and changes in real world accounting, the colorful and dynamic *Financial Accounting, 10e*, visually highlights coverage that is designed to help students make the connection between accounting concepts and business practices. Accounting doesn't occur in a vacuum, and the new and improved features found in each chapter make the content come to life.

Improved Chapter Openers

Building on the strengths of past editions, these openers continue to relate the accounting and business concepts in the chapter to the student's life. New for this edition, these openers now employ examples of real companies as well providing invaluable insight into real practice. The following companies are among those that have been incorporated into the chapter openers.

- Google
- Gold's Gym
- Marvel Entertainment
- Electronic Arts
- Fatburger
- The North Face

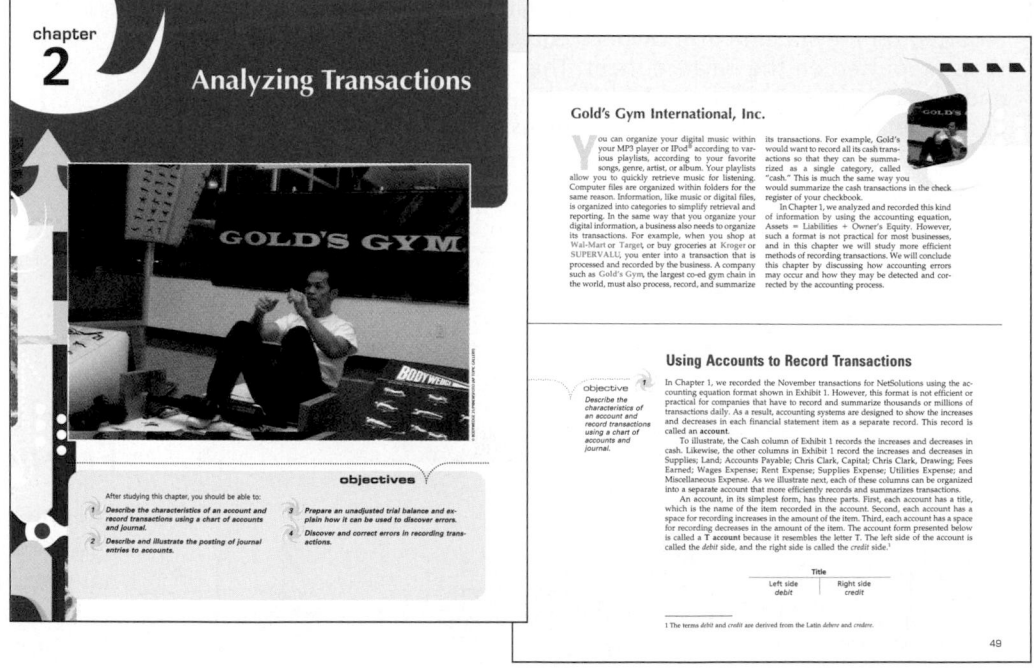

Financial Analysis and Interpretation

The Financial Analysis and Interpretation section in Chapters 6–16 introduces relevant, key ratios throughout the textbook. Students connect with the business environment as they learn how stakeholders will interpret financial reports. This section covers basic analysis tools that students will use again in the Financial Statement Analysis chapter. Furthermore, students get to test their proficiency with these tools through special activities and exercises in the end of the chapter. Both the section and related end-of-chapter material are indicated with a unique icon for a consistent presentation.

World Businesses

Comprehensive Real World Notes

Students get a close-up look at how accounting operates in the marketplace through a variety of items in the margins and in the Business Connections boxed features throughout the book. In addition, a variety of end-of-chapter exercises and problems employ real world data to give students a feel for the material accountants see daily. No matter where they are found, elements that use material from real companies are indicated with a unique icon for a consistent presentation. The following companies are among those highlighted in the text.

- AT&T
- Campbell Soup Co.
- Mercedes-Benz
- J.C. Penney Co.
- Hewlett-Packard
- Delta Air Lines
- Ford Motor Co.
- Gillette
- General Electric

Business Connections

REAL WORLD

RAPID INVENTORY AT COSTCO

Costco Wholesale Corporation operates over 300 membership warehouses that offer members low prices on a limited selection of nationally branded and selected private label products. Costco emphasizes generating high sales volumes and rapid inventory turnover. This enables Costco to operate profitably at significantly lower gross margins than traditional wholesalers, discount retailers, and supermarkets. In addition, Costco's rapid turnover provides it the opportunity to conserve on its cash, as described below.

Because of its high sales volume and rapid inventory turnover, Costco generally has the opportunity to receive cash from the sale of a substantial portion of its inventory at mature warehouse operations before it is required to pay all its merchandise vendors, even though Costco takes advantage of early payment terms to obtain payment dis-

counts. As sales in a given warehouse increase and inventory turnover becomes more rapid, a greater percentage of the inventory is financed through payment terms provided by vendors rather than by working capital (cash).

© DON RYAN/ASSOCIATED PRESS

Integrity, Objectivity, and Ethics in Business

In each chapter, these cases help students develop their ethical compass. Often coupled with related end-of-chapter activities, these cases can be discussed in class or the students can consider them as they read the chapter. These are always indicated with a unique icon for a consistent presentation.

Integrity, Objectivity, and Ethics in Business

ETHICS

THE RESPONSIBLE BOARD

Recent accounting scandals, such as those involving Enron, WorldCom, and Fannie Mae, have highlighted the roles of boards of directors in executing their responsibilities. For example, eighteen of Enron's former directors and their insurance providers have settled shareholder litiga-

tion for $168 million, of which $13 million is to come from the directors' personal assets. Board members are now on notice that their directorship responsibilities are being taken seriously by stockholders.

Though the presentation of this edition includes many new and improved elements, the traditional tools that have helped students for years remain an integral part of the book.

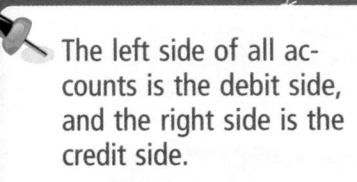 **Continuing Case Study:** Students follow a fictitious company, NetSolutions, throughout Chapters 1–6 as the example company to demonstrate a variety of transactions. To help students connect to the world of accounting, the NetSolutions transactions in Chapters 1 and 2 are often paired with nonbusiness events to which students can easily relate.

Summaries: Within each chapter, these synopses draw special attention to important points and help clarify difficult concepts.

> The left side of all accounts is the debit side, and the right side is the credit side.

In the preceding examples, you should observe that the left side of asset accounts is used for recording increases, and the right side is used for recording decreases. Also, the right side of liability and owner's equity accounts is used to record increases, and the left side of such accounts is used to record decreases. The left side of all accounts, whether asset, liability, or owner's equity, is the debit side, and the right side is the credit side. Thus, a debit may be either an increase or a decrease, depending

Key Terms: At the end of each chapter, this list of key terms provides page numbers for easy reference.

Self-Examination Questions: Five multiple-choice questions, with answers at the end of the chapter, help students review and retain chapter concepts.

Illustrative Problem and Solution: A solved problem models one or more of the chapter's assignment problems, so that students can apply the modeled procedures to end-of-chapter materials.

Illustrative Problem

J. F. Outz, M.D., has been practicing as a cardiologist for three years. During April, 2007, Outz completed the following transactions in her practice of cardiology.

Apr. 1. Paid office rent for April, $800.
3. Purchased equipment on account, $2,100.
5. Received cash on account from patients, $3,150.
8. Purchased X-ray film and other supplies on account, $245.
9. One of the items of equipment purchased on April 3 was defective. It was returned with the permission of the supplier, who agreed to reduce the account for the amount charged for the item, $325.

Dancin Music Continuing Problem

Here's a great opportunity for students to practice what they've learned as they study each step of the accounting cycle. Dancin Music, an imaginary and entrepreneurial company, provides a contemporary example of keen interest to students. As they follow Dancin Music, they examine its transactions and see the effect of those transactions on its financial statements. They can use the Klooster/Allen General Ledger software with this problem as well.

Continuing Problem

✓ 2. Net Income: $730

Kris Payne enjoys listening to all types of music and owns countless CDs and tapes. Over the years, Kris has gained a local reputation for knowledge of music from classical to rap and the ability to put together sets of recordings that appeal to all ages.

During the last several months, Kris served as a guest disc jockey on a local radio station. In addition, Kris has entertained at several friends' parties as the host deejay.

On April 1, 2008, Kris established a proprietorship known as Dancin Music. Using an extensive collection of CDs and tapes, Kris will serve as a disc jockey on a fee basis for weddings, college parties, and other events. During April, Kris entered into the following transactions:

April 1 Deposited $10,000 in a checking account in the name of Dancin Music.
   2. Received $2,500 from a local radio station for serving as the guest disc jockey for April.

In **Chapter 1**, students **analyze the effects of Dancin Music's first month's transactions on the accounting equation.**

Continuing Problem

✓ 4. Total of Debit Column: $37,800

The transactions completed by Dancin Music during April 2008 were described at the end of Chapter 1. The following transactions were completed during May, the second month of the business's operations:

May 1. Kris Payne made an additional investment in Dancin Music by depositing $2,500 in Dancin Music's checking account.
   1. Instead of continuing to share office space with a local real estate agency, Kris decided to rent office space near a local music store. Paid rent for May, $1,600.
   1. Paid a premium of $3,360 for a comprehensive insurance policy covering liability, theft, and fire. The policy covers a one-year period.
   2. Received $1,350 on account.

In **Chapter 2**, students **review debits and credits** by journalizing Dancin Music's second month's transactions.

Continuing Problem

✓ 3. Total of Debit Column: $39,500

The unadjusted trial balance that you prepared for Dancin Music at the end of Chapter 2 should appear as follows:

Dancin Music
Unadjusted Trial Balance
May 31, 2008

	Debit Balances	Credit Balances
Cash	12,085	
Accounts Receivable	2,850	
Supplies	920	
Prepaid Insurance	3,360	
Office Equipment	5,000	
Accounts Payable		5,750
Unearned Revenue		4,800
Kris Payne, Capital		12,500
Kris Payne, Drawing	1,300	
Fees Earned		14,750

In **Chapter 3**, students **review the adjusting process** for Dancin Music.

Continuing Problem

✓ 2. Net income: $4,925

The unadjusted trial balance of Dancin Music as of May 31, 2008, along with the adjustment data for the two months ended May 31, 2008, are shown in Chapter 3.

Based upon the adjustment data, the adjusted trial balance shown at the top of the following page was prepared.

Instructions
1. **Optional.** Using the data from Chapter 3, prepare an end-of-period spreadsheet (work sheet).
2. Prepare an income statement, a statement of owner's equity, and a balance sheet. (*Note:* Kris Payne made investments in Dancin Music on April 1 and May 1, 2008.)

In **Chapter 4**, building on what they've learned in Chapters 1, 2, and 3, students **complete the accounting cycle** for Dancin Music, including **preparing the financial statements.**

Students need to practice accounting in order to understand and use it. To give your students the greatest possible advantages in the real world, *Financial Accounting, 10e*, goes beyond presenting theory and procedure with comprehensive, time-tested, end-of-chapter material.

Eye Openers (formerly Discussion Questions): Contains quick concept review questions and single transaction exercises, which are ideal to help students break down concepts into basic parts, ensuring a solid foundation on which to build.

Example Exercises: For Practice Includes two parallel variations of the Example Exercise in the chapter, allowing students to practice the applications the authors illustrated earlier.

Exercises: Completely revised and accompanied by a general topic and a reference to chapter objective.

Problems Series A and B: Completely revised and accompanied by a general topic and a reference to chapter objective.

Special Activities: Focus on understanding and solving pertinent business and ethical issues. Some are presented as conversations in which students can "observe" and "participate" when they respond to the issue being discussed.

Comprehensive Problems: Located after Chapters 4, 6, 11, and 15 to integrate and summarize chapter concepts and test students' comprehension.

Financial Statement Analysis Problem: Located in Chapter 17, this problem features the Williams-Sonoma, Inc., 2005 Annual Report, which allows students to engage current, real world data.

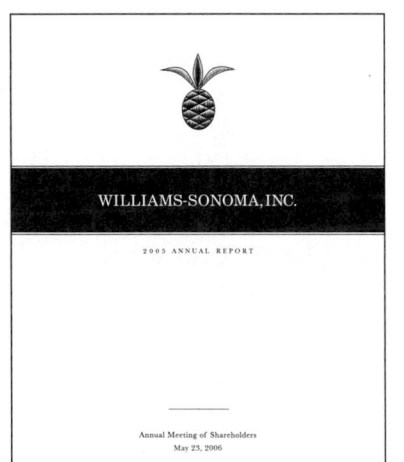

WILLIAMS-SONOMA, INC.

2005 ANNUAL REPORT

Annual Meeting of Shareholders
May 23, 2006

Williams-Sonoma, Inc., Problem

FINANCIAL STATEMENT ANALYSIS

The financial statements for Williams-Sonoma, Inc., are presented in Appendix D at the end of the text. The following additional information (in thousands) is available:

Accounts receivable at February 1, 2004	$ 31,573
Inventories at February 1, 2004	404,100
Total assets at February 1, 2004	1,470,735
Stockholders' equity at February 1, 2004	804,591

Instructions
1. Determine the following measures for the fiscal years ended January 29, 2006 and January 30, 2005, rounding to one decimal place.
   a. Working capital
   b. Current ratio
   c. Quick ratio
   d. Accounts receivable turnover
   e. Number of days' sales in receivables
   f. Inventory turnover
   g. Number of days' sales in inventory

Each chapter's Eye Openers, Example Exercises: For Practice, and Exercises provide those important brief exercises and can be assigned for homework or used as examples in the classroom. Among those sections, you'll find an average of 35 exercises per chapter! In addition, the two full sets of problems can be used as classroom illustrations, assignments, alternate assignments, or as independent study.

While always tied to the chapter content, some of the end-of-chapter material covers special topics like those covered in the book features. Specifically, you'll see

Financial Analysis and Interpretation: After being introduced to key ratios of financial analysis and interpretation in the related section of Chapters 6–16, students get to test their proficiency through special activities and exercises that frequently feature real company data.

Ethical Dilemmas: Often paired with the scenario presented in the Integrity, Objectivity, and Ethics in Business feature, these exercises and activities put the student in the role of a decision maker faced with a problem to solve.

Real World Applications: These exercises and activities encourage students to speculate about the real-world effects of newly learned material.

In addition to content, the versatile end-of-chapter section also indicates

Communication Items: These activities help students develop communication skills that will be essential on the job, regardless of the fields they pursue.

EX 1-2
Professional ethics
obj. 1

A fertilizer manufacturing company wants to relocate to Collier County. A 13-year-old report from a fired researcher at the company says the company's product is releasing toxic by-products. The company has suppressed that report. A second report commissioned by the company shows there is no problem with the fertilizer.

Should the company's chief executive officer reveal the context of the unfavorable report in discussions with Collier County representatives? Discuss.

Internet Projects: These activities acquaint students with the ever-expanding accounting-related areas of the Web.

Team Building: Group Learning Activities let students learn accounting and business concepts while building teamwork skills.

SA 4-4
Compare balance sheets

Group Project

Internet Project

In groups of three or four, compare the balance sheets of two different companies, and present to the class a summary of the similarities and differences of the two companies. You may obtain the balance sheets you need from one of the following sources:

1. Your school or local library.
2. The investor relations department of each company.
3. The company's Web site on the Internet.
4. EDGAR (Electronic Data Gathering, Analysis, and Retrieval), the electronic archives of financial statements filed with the Securities and Exchange Commission.

Your Time
Your Course
Your Way

Just what you need to know and do NOW.

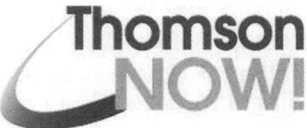

ThomsonNOW for Accounting is a powerful, fully integrated online teaching and learning system that provides you with the ultimate in flexibility, ease of use, and efficient paths to success to deliver the results you want—NOW!

- Select from flexible choices and options to best meet the needs of you and your students.

- Test and grade student results based on AACSB and AICPA or IMA accreditation standards and a special set of principles of accounting course outcomes.

- Teach and reinforce chapter content through integrated eBooks and Personalized Study Plans.

- Save valuable time in planning and managing your course assignments.

- Students stay mobile with Lectures-to-Go. Available in both audio and video formats, these iPod-ready broadcasts can be downloaded for preparation before class or last-minute reviewing for a test.

- Students connect to real businesses through our Business Connections videos. This collection of films on accounting issues brings the subject alive. Most notably, the new Chapter 18, "Introduction to Managerial Accounting," incorporates a video of the manufacturing operation of Washburn Guitars, a producer of instruments used by many popular artists today.

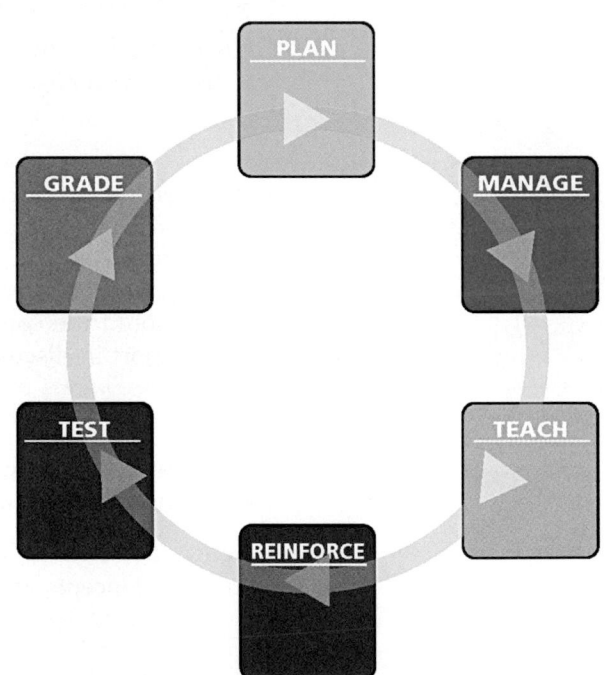

Chapter Changes

1. **Introduction to Accounting and Business**
   - New informational Exhibit 4 on accounting career paths with salary ranges gets students excited about the field.
   - Expanded section on ethical behavior in business accompanied by new Exhibit 2 outlining examples of fraud since 2000 emphasizes the importance of reporting accurate, reliable financial information.
   - A new horizontal format displays how transactions affect each account and facilitates the preparation of the financial statements.
   - New chapter opener features Google.

2. **Analyzing Transactions**
   - Opens with a new transition that ties the horizontal format of Chapter 1 into the use of accounts and the rules of debits and credits. Also, a new section describing how students should analyze and record transactions aids students with their homework.
   - New Exhibit 3 summarizes the rules of debit and credit along with normal balances of accounts so students can see how both guiding principles operate together.
   - New margin labels help guide students through transaction analysis.
   - New chapter opener features Gold's Gym.

3. **The Adjusting Process**
   - All adjusting entries now include explanations.
   - New Exhibits 1 and 2 illustrate the types of adjustments students will encounter as well as the affects of those adjustments on the Income Statement and Balance Sheet. Exhibit 1 focuses on prepaid expense and unearned revenue, and Exhibit 2 focuses on accrued revenue and accrued expense.
   - The terminology has been revised to be consistent with Chapter 2. That is, we now use the terms *prepaid expense* and *unearned revenue* instead of *deferred expense* and *deferred revenue*.
   - Exhibit 6 (formerly Exhibit 5) has been revised with adjusting entries from NetSolutions to clearly summarize the effect of adjustments on the financial statements.
   - New chapter opener features Marvel Entertainment, Inc.
   - New Integrity, Objectivity, and Ethics discusses personal use of office supplies.

4. **Completing the Accounting Cycle**
   - Opens by illustrating the flow of accounting data from the unadjusted trial balance to the adjusted trial balance and financial statements using an end of-period spreadsheet (work sheet). This is followed by the preparation of financial statements and closing entries for NetSolutions.
   - New Exhibit 8 clearly illustrates each step in the accounting cycle and the role of the accountant in the process.
   - New learning objective, Illustration of the Accounting Cycle, reviews and illustrates each step in the accounting cycle for Kelly Consulting. This illustration is a complete review of the accounting cycle and recaps what students have learned in Chapters 1–4.
   - To familiarize students with alternate formats, the end-of-period spreadsheet is presented in a computerized spreadsheet format.
   - Preparation of the end-of-period spreadsheet (work sheet) with acetate layovers is included in an end of the chapter appendix. This appendix uses the NetSolutions chapter illustration. The chapter exercises and problems have been designed so that instructors have the option of requiring students prepare the end-of-period spreadsheet (work sheet).
   - New chapter opener features Electronic Arts, Inc.

5. **Accounting Systems**
   - Internal Controls have been moved to Chapter 8 to allow instructors to focus on special journals and computerized accounting systems.
   - Schedule of accounts receivable is now the customer balance summary report and schedule of accounts payable is now the supplier balance summary report to more accurately reflect titles used in practice.
   - New material on the correction of errors in a computerized environment.
   - New chapter opener features Intuit.

6. **Accounting for Merchandising Businesses**
   - The chart of accounts for a merchandising business is now integrated with the discussion of merchandise transactions early in the chapter to help students transition from service businesses to merchandising business.

Chapter Changes

- Nonbank Credit Card transactions such as American Express transactions are recorded in the same manner as MasterCard and VISA transactions. This better reflects the accounting for American Express transactions used by most retailers.
- Appendix 1, Accounting Systems for Merchandisers, has been revised and updated.
- New Appendix 2 covers periodic inventory in a merchandising business and includes a new exhibit which compares the perpetual and periodic systems. Appendix 2 also includes the closing entries under the periodic system.
- The end-of-chapter exercises and problems have been designed so that instructors can assign exercises and problems using the perpetual system, the periodic inventory, or both systems.
- Transportation Out has been revised as Delivery Expense so that it is easier for students to identify it as an income statement account.
- New chapter opener features Whole Foods Market.

7. **Inventories** (formerly Chapter 9)
   - Based on reviewer and user feedback, inventories are now covered after merchandising businesses.
   - Objectives 3 and 4 now use the same data to draw a better comparison between perpetual (Objective 3) and periodic (Objective 4) inventory systems.
   - The periodic inventory discussion (Objective 4) has been reorganized to better reflect real world practice. Specifically, ending inventory is determined first and is then subtracted from merchandise available for sale to determine the cost of merchandise sold.
   - The prior edition's Objective 2, which focuses on reporting errors of inventory on the financial statements, has been moved to Objective 6 to improve the flow of the chapter. In addition, this discussion has been simplified.
   - New chapter opener features Best Buy.

8. **Sarbanes Oxley, Internal Controls, and Cash** (formerly Chapter 7)
   - The internal controls discussion has been moved from Chapter 5 to Chapter 8. In addition, the chapter begins with a discussion of the Sarbanes-Oxley Act that includes an example of a General Electric internal control report.
   - The coverage of cash now reflects modern banking practices, including new information about cash received by Electronic Funds Transfer, expanded information about bank statements in an electronic environment, and streamlined coverage of vouchers and manual forms.
   - The bank reconciliation form now appears in a vertical format to be consistent with practice. To simplify for students, "company" replaces "depositor" in the bank reconciliation form.
   - Petty Cash coverage is now covered as Special Purpose Cash Funds.
   - New chapter opener features Ebay.
   - Two new Integrity, Objectivity, and Ethics in Business discuss check fraud and bank errors.

9. **Receivables** (formerly Chapter 8)
   - The direct write-off method of accounting for uncollectible receivables now comes before the allowance method, so students can build from simple to complex concepts.
   - A T-account approach is used to illustrate the allowance method.
   - New comparison of the percent of sales and analysis of receivables estimation methods summarizes Objective 4.
   - New Objective 5 compares direct write-off and allowance methods.
   - New chapter opener features FedEx-Kinkos.

10. **Fixed Assets and Intangible Assets**
    - Declining-Balance Depreciation is now Double-Declining-Balance Depreciation.
    - New Exhibit 7 compares depreciation methods.
    - New Exhibit 8 presents revising depreciation estimates graphically.
    - Certain coverage has been streamlined for a clearer presentation. Specifically, capital and revenue expenditure is now covered as part of Objective 1, as is the discussion of leasing fixed assets.
    - Financial Analysis and Interpretation item now covers the Fixed Asset Turnover Ratio, as it is more relevant to the chapter.
    - New chapter opener features Fat Burger.

11. **Current Liabilities and Payroll**
    - Changes to the McGrath withholding table use the universal IRS Percentage Method. This change simplifies the calculation method in the text.
    - New chapter opener features Panera.
    - New Business Connections features a discussion on the condition of Social Security.

12. **Accounting for Partnerships and Limited Liability Companies** (formerly Chapter 13)
   - This chapter is now before the discussion of corporations to better reflect how most instructors teach partnerships and corporations. As a result, the reporting of stockholders' equity has been moved to Chapter 13.
   - New Exhibit 2 illustrates two methods for admitting a partner.
   - New Exhibit 3 illustrates how partner bonuses are determined for existing and newly admitted partners.
   - New Exhibit 4 illustrates the liquidation of a partnership.
   - New chapter opener features Mahanaim Essentials.

13. **Corporations: Organization, Capital Stock Transactions, and Dividends** (formerly Chapter 12)
   - Based upon user and reviewer feedback, this chapter has been reorganized so that dividends are discussed immediately after the accounting for issuing of stock. The accounting for treasury stock, reporting stockholders' equity, and stock splits now follows the discussion of dividends.
   - New Exhibit 2 shows the advantages and disadvantages of corporate forms.
   - The discussion of preferred stock has now been simplified to focus only on nonparticipating preferred stock.
   - New chapter opener features Yankee Candle.
   - New Integrity, Objectivity, and Ethics in Business discusses not-for-profit organizations.

14. **Income Taxes, Unusual Income Items, and Investments in Stocks**
   - New classification scheme for unusual items: those that impact current periods and those that impact prior periods.
   - New section on Retroactive Restatements presented in Objective 2.
   - Cumulative change in accounting principle replaced with the restatement method per SFAS 154.
   - New graphic on three treatments for unusual items.
   - New chapter opener features Gaylord Entertainment, Inc.

15. **Bonds Payable and Investments in Bonds**
   - Objective 2 covers the characteristics and computation of bonds to improve the flow of the chapter.
   - New section covers the payment and redemption of bonds. Sinking funds are now covered here.
   - New chapter opener features Under Armor.
   - Business Connections feature on Bowie Bonds reflects the effect of recent events on these bonds.
   - New Integrity, Objectivity, and Ethics in Business discusses credit quality.

16. **Statement of Cash Flows**
   - Opening section orients the student to the Statement of Cash Flows by building on the discussion in Chapter 1. In addition, new Exhibit 1 examines the Statement of Cash Flows of NetSolutions.
   - New format for the indirect method reflects real world practice.
   - Expanded section on Cash Flows from Operating Activities includes new Exhibit 5 that outlines the adjustment to net income on cash flows and summarizes the affect of changes in current assets and current liabilities on net income as it pertains to cash flows.
   - New chapter opener features Jones Soda Company, as does Exercise 16-16.
   - New Business Connections features Microsoft and Dell's view of cash resources.
   - New Integrity, Objectivity, and Ethics in Business on collecting accounts features Overhill Flowers.
   - Financial, Analysis, and Interpretation item redefines free cash flows to leave out dividends, which could be considered discretionary, to simplify the presentation.

17. **Financial Statement Analysis**
   - Features Williams-Sonoma in the chapter opener and engages Williams-Sonoma's 2005 Annual Report in the end-of-chapter material.
   - Objective 4 on Corporate Annual Reports now discusses internal controls and other auditing issues.
   - New Integrity, Objectivity, and Ethics in Business discusses the results of a CEO survey about corporate ethics.
   - New Business Connections features different investing strategies.

When it comes to supporting instructors, South-Western is unsurpassed. *Financial Accounting, 10e,* **continues the tradition with powerful printed materials along with the latest integrated classroom technology.**

Instructor's Manual: This manual contains a number of resources designed to aid instructors as they prepare lectures, assign homework, and teach in the classroom. For each chapter, the instructor is given a brief synopsis and a list of objectives. Then each objective is explored, including information on Key Terms, Ideas for Class Discussion, Lecture Aids, Demonstration Problems, Group Learning Activities, Exercises and Problems for Reinforcement, and Internet Activities. Also, Suggested Approaches are included that incorporate many of the teaching initiatives being stressed in higher education today, including active learning, collaborative learning, critical thinking, and writing across the curriculum. Other key features are the following:

- New informational grids relate the Key Learning Outcomes from the new At a Glance grid to the exercises and problems found in the end-of-chapter. These helpful resources ensure comprehensive homework assignments.

- Demonstration problems can be used in the classroom to illustrate accounting practices. Working through an accounting problem gives the instructor an opportunity to point out pitfalls that students should avoid.

- Group learning activities provide another opportunity to actively involve students in the learning process. These activities ask students to apply accounting topics by completing an assigned task in small groups of three to five students. Small group work is an excellent way to introduce variety into the accounting classroom and creates a more productive learning environment.

- Writing exercises provide an opportunity for students to develop good written communication skills essential to any businessperson.

- These exercises probe students' knowledge of conceptual issues related to accounting.

- Three to five Accounting Scenarios can be used as handouts.

The Teaching Transparency Masters can be made into acetate transparencies or can be duplicated and used as handouts.

Solutions Manual and Solutions Transparencies: The Solutions Manual contains answers to all exercises, problems, and activities that appear in the text. As always, the solutions are author-written and verified multiple times for numerical accuracy and consistency with the core text. New to this edition, there is an expanded end-of-chapter information chart, which includes correlations to chapter objective, level of difficulty, AACSB outcomes, AICPA or IMA competencies, time to completion and available software. Solutions transparencies are also available.

Test Bank: For each chapter, the Test Bank includes True/False questions, Multiple-Choice questions, and Problems, each marked with a difficulty level, chapter objective association, and a tie-in to standard course outcomes. Along with the normal update and upgrade of the 2,800 test bank questions, variations of the new Example Exercises have been added to this bank for further quizzing and better integration with the textbook. In addition, the bank provides a grid for each chapter that compiles the correlation of each question to the individual chapter's objectives, as well as a ranking of difficulty based on a clearly described categorization. Through this helpful grid, making a test that is comprehensive and well-balanced is a snap! Also included are blank Achievement Tests and Achievement Test Solutions.

ExamView® Pro Testing Software: This intuitive software allows you to easily customize exams, practice tests, and tutorials and deliver them over a network, on the Internet, or in printed form. In addition, ExamView comes with searching capabilities that make sorting the wealth of questions from the printed test bank easy. The software and files are found on the IRCD.

PowerPoint® and Presentation Transparencies: Each presentation, which is included on the IRCD and on the product support site, enhances lectures and simplifies class preparation. Each chapter contains objectives followed by a thorough outline of the chapter that easily provide an entire lecture model. Also, exhibits from the chapter, such as the new Example Exercises, have been recreated as colorful PowerPoint slides to create a powerful, customizable tool. Selections from the PowerPoint presentation are also available on transparency slides.

JoinIn on Turning Point: JoinIn™ on Turning Point™ is interactive PowerPoint® and is simply the best classroom response system available today! This lecture tool makes full use of the Instructor's PowerPoint® presentation but moves it to the next level with interactive questions that provide immediate feedback on the students' understanding of the topic at hand. As students are quizzed using clicker technology, instructors can use this instant feedback to lecture more efficiently. Adding to the already robust PowerPoint® presentation, JoinIn™ integrates 10–20 questions stemming from the textbook's Example Exercises and Eye Openers and includes a variety of newly created questions. Visit http://www.turningpoint.thomsonlearningconnections.com to find out more!

Instructor Excel® Templates: These templates provide the solutions for the problems and exercises that have Enhanced Excel® templates for students. Through these files, instructors can see the solutions in the same format as the students. All problems with accompanying templates are marked in the book with an icon and are listed in the information grid in the solutions manual. These templates are available for download on www.thomsonedu.com/accounting/warren or on the IRCD.

Tutorial and Telecourse Videos: Nothing brings accounting to life like these media-intensive videos. Each chapter comes alive in two half-hour features that reinforce the concepts presented in the text. Based on the Tutorial Videos, the high-broadcast-quality Telecourse Videos are designed for distributed learning courses.

Product Support Web Site: www.thomsonedu.com/accounting/warren Our instructor Web site provides a variety of password-protected, instructor resources. You'll find text-specific and other related resources organized by chapter and topic. Many are also available on the Instructor's Resource CD-ROM.

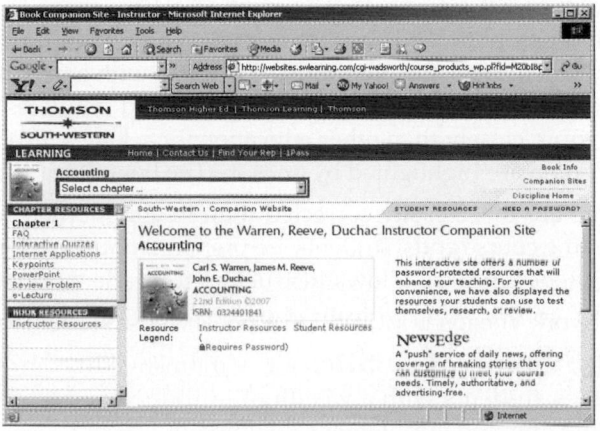

Students come to accounting with a variety of learning needs. *Financial Accounting, 10e,* offers a broad range of supplements in both printed form and easy-to-use technology. We've designed our entire supplement package around the comments instructors have provided about their courses and teaching needs. These comments have made this supplement package the best in the business.

Study Guide: This author-written guide provides students Quiz and Test Hints, Matching questions, Fill-in-the-Blank questions (Parts A & B), Multiple-Choice questions, True/False questions, Exercises, and Problems for each chapter. Designed to assist students in comprehending the concepts and principles in the text, solutions for all of these items are available in the guide for quick reference.

Working Papers for Exercises and Problems: The traditional working papers include problem-specific forms for preparing solutions for Exercises, A & B Problems, the Continuing Problem, and the Comprehensive Problems from the textbook. These forms, with preprinted headings, provide a structure for the problems, which helps students get started and saves them time. Additional blank forms are included.

Working Papers Plus: This alternative to traditional working papers integrates selected Practice Exercises, Exercises, Problems, the Continuing Problem, and the Comprehensive Problems from the text together with the narrative and forms needed to complete the solutions. Because the problem narrative is integrated with the solution, the student's work is easy and quick to review—a real plus when preparing for an exam.

Blank Working Papers: These Working Papers are available for completing exercises and problems either from the text or prepared by the instructor. They have no preprinted headings. A guide at the front of the Working Papers tells students which form they will need for each problem.

Enhanced Excel® Templates: These templates are provided for selected long or complicated end-of-chapter exercises and problems and provide assistance to the student as they set up and work the problem. Certain cells are coded to display a red asterisk when an incorrect answer is entered, which helps students stay on track. Selected problems that can be solved using these templates are designated by an icon.

Klooster & Allen General Ledger Software: *(formerly P.A.S.S)* Prepared by Dale Klooster and Warren Allen, this best-selling, educational, general ledger package introduces students to the world of computerized accounting through a more intuitive, user-friendly system than the commercial software they'll use in the future. In addition, students have access to general ledger files with information based on problems from the textbook and practice sets. This context allows them to see the difference between manual and computerized accounting systems firsthand, while alleviating the stress of an empty screen. Also, the program is enhanced with a problem checker that enables students to determine if their entries are correct and emulates commercial general ledger packages more closely than other educational packages. Problems that can be used with Klooster/Allen are highlighted by an icon. The benefits of using Klooster/Allen are that:

- Errors are more easily corrected than in commercial software.
- After the course ends, students are prepared to use a variety of commercial products.
- The Inspector Disk allows instructors to grade students' work.

A free Network Version is available to schools whose students purchase Klooster/Allen GL.

Product Support Web Site: www.thomsonedu.com/accounting/warren. This site provides students with a wealth of introductory accounting resources, including limited quizzing and supplement downloads.

The textbook plays a vital role in the teaching/learning environment, which makes our collaboration with instructors invaluable. For this edition, accounting teachers discussed with us ways to create a more efficient presentation and connect more with students. The result of these discussions can be seen throughout the textbook.

The following instructors participated in our Blue Sky Workshops in 2005 and 2006.

Gilda M. Agacer
Monmouth University

Rick Andrews
Sinclair Community College

Irene C. Bembenista
Davenport University

Laurel L. Berry
Bryant & Stratton College

Bill Black
Raritan Valley Community College

Gregory Brookins
Santa Monica College

Rebecca Carr
Arkansas State University

James L. Cieslak
Cuyahoga Community College

Sue Cook
Tulsa Community College

Ana M. Cruz
Miami Dade College

Terry Dancer
Arkansas State University

David L. Davis
Tallahassee Community College

Walter DeAguero
Saddleback College

Robert Dunlevy
Montgomery County Community College

Richard Ellison
Middlesex County College

W. Michael Fagan
Raritan Valley Community College

Carol Flowers
Orange Coast College

Linda S. Flowers
Houston Community College

Mike Foland
Southwest Illinois College

Anthony Fortini
Camden Community College

Barbara M. Gershowitz
Nashville State Community College

Angelina Gincel
Middlesex County College

Lori Grady
Bucks County Community College

Joseph R. Guardino
Kingsborough Community College

Amy F. Haas
Kingsborough Community College

Betty Habershon
Prince George's Community College

Patrick A. Haggerty
Lansing Community College

Becky Hancock
El Paso Community College

Paul Harris
Camden County College

Patricia H. Holmes
Des Moines Area Community College

Shirly A. Kleiner
Johnson County Community College

Michael M. Landers
Middlesex College

Phillip Lee
Nashville State Community College

Denise Leggett
Middle Tennessee State University

Lynne Luper
Ocean County College

Maria C. Mari
Miami Dade College

Thomas S. Marsh
Northern Virginia Community College–Annandale

Cynthia McCall
Des Moines Area Community College

Andrea Murowski
Brookdale Community College

Rachel Pernia
Essex County College

Dawn Peters
Southwest Illinois College

Gary J. Pieroni
Diablo Valley College

Debra Prendergast
Northwestern Business College

Renee A. Rigoni
Monroe Community College

Lou Rosamillia
Hudson Valley Community College

Eric Rothenburg
Kingsborough Community College

Richard Sarkisian
Camden Community College

Gerald Savage
Essex Community College

Janice Stoudemire
Midlands Technical College

Linda H. Tarrago
Hillsborough Community College

Judy Toland
Buck Community College

Bob Urell
Irvine Valley College

Carol Welsh
Rowan University

Chris Widmer
Tidewater Community College

Gloria Worthy
Southwest Tennessee Community College

Lynnette Mayne Yerbury
Salt Lake Community College

The following instructors participated in our Adopter Advisory Board.

Lizabeth Austen
East Carolina University

Robert Adkins
Clark State Community College

Candace S. Blankenship
Belmont University

Patrick M. Borja
Citrus College and California State University—Los Angeles

Gary Bower
Community College of Rhode Island

Gregory Brookins
Santa Monica College

Martha Cavalaris
Miami Dade Community College—North Campus

Sue Cook
Tulsa Community College

Leonard Cronin
Rochester Community and Technical College

Bruce England
Massasoit Community College

Robert T. Fahnestock
University of West Florida

Michael J. Farina
Cerritos College

Brenda S. Fowler
Alamance Community College

Mark Fronke
Cerritos College

Marina Grau
Houston Community College

Paul C. Harris Jr.
Camden County College

James L. Haydon
East Los Angeles Community College

Brenda Hester
Volunteer State Community College

Cheryl Honoré
Riverside Community College

Calvin Hoy
County College of Morris

Frank D. Iazzetta
Long Beach City College

Anne C. Kenner
Brevard Community College

Satoshi K. Kojima
East Los Angeles College

Susan Logorda
Lehigh Carbon Community College

Don Lucy
Indian River Community College

Cathy Mallory
San Antonio College

Marjorie A. Marinovic
University of Texas at El Paso

Patricia Norton
Northwest Mississippi Community College

Ken O'Brien
Farmington State University

Craig Pence
Highland Community College

Rachel Pernia
Essex County College

Abe Qastin
Lakeland College

Paul Rivers
Bunker Hill Community College

Patrick D. Rogan
Cosumnes River College

Gary M. Rupp
Farmingdale State University

Richard M. Sarkisian
Camden County College

Debra L. Schmidt
Cerritos Colzlege

Larry L. Simpson
Davenport University, Lansing Campus

Robert K. Smolin
Citrus College

Dawn W. Stevens
Northwest Mississippi Community College

John F. Templeton
Houston Community College

Kathryn Williams
St. Johns River Community College

Karen Wisniewski
County College of Morris

Wayne Yesbick
Darton College

The following instructors partici-pated in the review process and in focus groups.

Heather Albinger
Concordia University

Sylvia Allen
Los Angeles Valley College

Beverley Alleyne
Belmont University

Felix Amenkhienan
Radford University

Sheila Ammons
Austin Community College

Rick Andrews
Sinclair Community College

Joseph Aubert
Bemidji State University

Elenita Ayuyao
Los Angeles City College

Progyan Basu
The University of Georgia

Diane Bechtel
Northwest State Community College

Terry Bechtel
Northwestern State University of Louisiana

Margaret A. Berezewski
Robert Morris College

Bernard Beatty
Wake Forest University

Cynthia Birk
University of Nevada—Reno

Kathy Blondell
St. Johns River Community College

Julio C. Borges
Miami Dade College

Carolyn Bottjer
Lehigh Carbon Community College

Angele Brill
Castleton State College

Rada Brooks
Univeristy of California—Berkeley

Rebecca F. Brown
Des Moines Area Community College

Charles I. Bunn Jr.
Wake Technical Community College

Janet Butler
Texas State University—San Marcos

Robert Carpenter
Eastfield College

Bill Carter
University of Virginia

Fonda L. Carter
Columbus State University

Stanley Chu
Borough of Manhattan Community College

Marilyn G. Ciolino
Delgado Community College

Gretchen Charrier
The University of Texas at Austin

Alexander Clifford
Kennebec Valley Community College

Weldon Terry
Dancer Arkansas State University

Vaun C. Day
Central Arizona College

Stan Deal
Azusa Pacific University

John E. Delaney
Southwestern University

Beatrix DeMott
Park University

Edward Douthett
George Mason University

Richard Dugger
Kilgore College

Carol Dutchover
Eastern New Mexico University, Roswell

Steve Easter
Mineral Area College

Ronald Edward
Camp Trinity Valley Community College

Rafik Z. Elias
California State University—Los Angeles

Carl Essig
Montgomery County Community College

Jack Fatica
Terra Community College

Kathleen Fitzpatrick
University of Toledo

Daniel Fulks
Transylvania University

Thurman Gardner
Harold Washington College

Caroline C. Garrett
The Victoria College

J. Rendall Garrett
Southern Nazarene University

Earl Godfrey
Gardner—Webb University

Saturnino Gonzalez
El Paso Community College

Edward Gordon
Triton College

Thomas Grant
Kutztown University

Barbara Gregorio
Nassau Community College

Jeri W. Griego
Laramie County Community College

Kenneth Haling, Jr.
Gateway Technical College

Carolyn J. Hays
Mount San Jacinto College

Mark Henry
The Victoria College

Aleecia Hibbets
University of Louisiana—Monroe

Linda Hischke
Northeast Wisconsin Technical College

Patricia H. Holmes
Des Moines Area Community College

Anita Hope
Tarrant County College

Allison Hubley
Davenport University

Dawn A. Humburg
Iowa Central Community College

Marianne L. James
California State University—Los Angeles

Bettye Bishop Johnson
Northwest Mississippi Community College

Tara Laken Joliet
Junior College

Becky Knickel
Brookhaven College

Larry W. Koch
Navarro College, Ellis County Campus

Ellen L. Landgraf
Loyola University Chicago

Cathy X. Larson
Middlesex Community College

Brenda Lauer
Davenport University—Kalamazoo Campus

Greg Lauer
North Iowa Area Community College

James Lukawitz
University of Memphis

Terri Lukshaitis
Davenport University

Debbie Luna
El Paso Community College

Diane Marker
University of Toledo

Matthew Maron
University of Bridgeport

John J. Masserwick
Farmingdale State University

Robert McCutcheon
East Texas Baptist University

Andrew M. McKee
North Country Community College

Michael McKittrick
Santa Fe Community College

Yaw Mensah
Rutgers University

Leslie Michie
Big Bend Community College

Nancy Milleman
Central Ohio Technical College

Brian Moore
Davenport University

Carol Moore
Northwest State Community College

Andrew Morgret
University of Memphis

Tim Mulder
Davenport University

Charles Murphy
Bunker Hill Community College

Gary Nelson
Normandale Communiy College

Patricia Norton
Northwest Mississippi Community College

Blanca R. Ortega
Miami Dade College

Kathy Otero
University of Texas at El Paso

Carol Pace
Grayson County College

Vanda Pauwels
Lubbock Christian University

John Perricone
Harper College

Timothy Prindle
Des Moines Area Community College

Paulette Ratliff-Miller
Arkansas State University

Ronald Reed
University of Northern Colordao

John Renza, Jr.
Community College of Rhode Island

Jenny Resnick
Santa Monica College

John C. Roberts, Jr.
St. Johns River Community College

Lawrence A. Roman
Cuyahoga Community College

Gary W. Ross
Harding University

Ann Rowell
Central Piedmont Community College

Charles J. Russo
Bloomsburg University of Pennsylvania

Maria Sanchez
Rider University

Marcia A. Sandvold
Des Moines Area Community College

Tony Scott
Norwalk Community College

Bonnie Scrogham
Sullivan University

Angela Seidel
Cambria-Rowe Business College

Sara Seyedin
Foothill College

Larry L. Simpson
Davenport University, Lansing Campus

Alice Sineath
Forsyth Technical Community College

Kimberly D. Smith
County College of Morris

Roberta Spigle
DuBois Business College

Mary Stevens
University of Texas at El Paso

Norman Sunderman
Angelo State University

Thomas Szczurek
Delaware County Community College

Kathy Tam
Tulsa Community College

Lynette E. Teal
Western Wisconsin Technical College

Wayne Thomas
University of Oklahoma

Bill Townsend
Ferris State University

Robin Turner
Rowan-Cabarrus Community College

Nancy Tyler
Dalton State College

Allan D. Unseth
Norfolk State University

Bob Urell
Irvine Valley College

Michael Van Breda
Southern Methodist University

Peter Vander Weyst
Edmonds Community College

Patricia Walczak
Lansing Community College

Scott Wang
Davenport University

Luke A. Waller
Lindenwood University

Jeffrey Waybright
Spokane Community College

Kimberly Webb
Texas Wesleyan University

Clifford Weeks
Southwestern Michigan College

Karen Williamson
Rochester Community and Technical College

Judith Zander
Grossmont College

Brief Contents

Contents

Practice Set: Puppy Spa and Supply
This set includes payroll transactions for a merchandising business operated as a proprietorship. It includes business documents, and it can be solved manually or with the Klooster/Allen software.

Practice Set: Casa Bella
This set is a service and merchandising business operated as a corporation. It includes narrative for six months of transactions, which are to be recorded in a general journal. The set can be solved manually or with the Klooster/Allen software.

Practice Set: Wizard Computer Sales & Services
This set is a departmentalized merchandising business operated as a corporation. It includes a narrative of transactions, which are to be recorded in special journals. The set can be solved manually or with the Klooster/Allen software.

xxix

WARREN   REEVE   DUCHAC

FINANCIAL
ACCOUNTING

10E

Introduction to Accounting and Business

© PAUL SAKUMA/ASSOCIATED PRESS

objectives

After studying this chapter, you should be able to:

1. **Describe the nature of a business and the role of ethics and accounting in business.**

2. **Summarize the development of accounting principles and relate them to practice.**

3. **State the accounting equation and define each element of the equation.**

4. **Describe and illustrate how business transactions can be recorded in terms of the resulting change in the basic elements of the accounting equation.**

5. **Describe the financial statements of a proprietorship and explain how they interrelate.**

Google™

hen two teams pair up for a game of football, there is often a lot of noise. The band plays, the fans cheer, and fireworks light up the scoreboard. Obviously, the fans are committed and care about the outcome of the game. Just like fans at a football game, the owners of a business want their business to "win" against their competitors in the marketplace. While having our football team win can be a source of pride, winning in the marketplace goes beyond pride and has many tangible benefits. Companies that are winners are better able to serve customers, to provide good jobs for employees, and to make more money for the owners.

One such successful company is Google, one of the most visible companies on the Internet. Many of us cannot visit the Web without first stopping at Google to get a search listing. As one writer said, "Google is the closest thing the Web has to an ultimate answer machine."[1] And yet, Google is a free tool—no one asks for your credit card when you use any of Google's search tools. So, do you think Google has been a successful company? Does it make money? How would you know? Accounting helps to answer these questions. Google's accounting information tells us that Google is a very successful company that makes a lot of money, but not from you and me. Google makes its money from advertisers.

In this textbook, we will introduce you to accounting, the language of business. In this chapter, we begin by discussing what a business is, how it operates, and the role that accounting plays.

Nature of Business and Accounting

objective **1**

Describe the nature of a business and the role of ethics and accounting in business.

You can probably list some examples of companies like Google with which you have recently done business. Your examples might be large companies, such as The Coca-Cola Company, Dell Inc., or Amazon.com. They might be local companies, such as gas stations or grocery stores, or perhaps employers. They might be restaurants, law firms, or medical offices. What do all these examples have in common that identify them as businesses?

In general, a **business**[2] is an organization in which basic resources (inputs), such as materials and labor, are assembled and processed to provide goods or services (outputs) to customers. Businesses come in all sizes, from a local coffee house to a DaimlerChrysler, which sells several billion dollars worth of cars and trucks each year. A business's customers are individuals or other businesses who purchase goods or services in exchange for money or other items of value. In contrast, a church is not a business, because those who receive its services are not legally obligated to pay for them.

The objective of most businesses is to maximize profits. **Profit** is the difference between the amounts received from customers for goods or services provided and the amounts paid for the inputs used to provide the goods or services. Some businesses operate with an objective other than to maximize profits. The objective of such not-for-profit businesses is to provide some benefit to society, such as medical research or conservation of natural resources. In other cases, governmental units such as cities operate water works or sewage treatment plants on a nonprofit basis. We will focus in this text on businesses operating to earn a profit. Keep in mind, though, that many of the same concepts and principles apply to not-for-profit businesses as well.

---

1 As quoted on Google's Web site.
2 A complete glossary of terms appears at the end of the text.

TYPES OF BUSINESSES

There are three different types of businesses that are operated for profit: service, merchandising, and manufacturing businesses. Each type of business has unique characteristics.

Service businesses provide services rather than products to customers. Examples of service businesses and the types of services they offer are shown below.

Service Business	Service
The Walt Disney Company	Entertainment
Delta Air Lines	Transportation
Marriott International, Inc.	Hospitality and lodging
Bank of America Corporation	Financial services
XM Satellite Radio	Satellite radio

Merchandising businesses sell products they purchase from other businesses to customers. In this sense, merchandisers bring products and customers together. Examples of merchandising businesses and some of the products they sell are shown below.

Merchandising Business	Product
Wal-Mart	General merchandise
GameStop Corporation	Video games and accessories
Best Buy	Consumer electronics
Gap Inc.	Apparel
Amazon.com	Internet books, music, videos

Manufacturing businesses change basic inputs into products that are sold to individual customers. Examples of manufacturing businesses and some of their products are as follows:

Manufacturing Business	Product
General Motors Corporation	Cars, trucks, vans
Samsung	Cell phones
Dell Inc.	Personal computers
NIKE	Athletic shoes and apparel
The Coca-Cola Company	Beverages
Sony Corporation	Stereos and televisions

TYPES OF BUSINESS ORGANIZATIONS

The common forms of business organization are proprietorship, partnership, corporation, or limited liability company. Each of these forms and their major characteristics are listed below.

- A **proprietorship** is owned by one individual and
  - Comprises 70% of business organizations in the United States.
  - Cost of organizing is low.
  - Is limited to financial resources of the owner.
  - Is used by small businesses.
- A **partnership** is similar to a proprietorship except that it is owned by two or more individuals and
  - Comprises 10% of business organizations in the United States.
  - Combines the skills and resources of more than one person.
- A **corporation** is organized under state or federal statutes as a separate legal taxable entity and
  - Generates 90% of the total dollars of business receipts received.
  - Comprises 20% of the business organizations in the United States.

- Includes ownership divided into shares of stock, sold to shareholders (stockholders).
- Is able to obtain large amounts of resources by issuing stock.
- Is used by large businesses.

■ A **limited liability company (LLC)** combines attributes of a partnership and a corporation in that it is organized as a corporation. However, an LLC can elect to be taxed as a partnership and

- Is a popular alternative to a partnership.
- Has tax and liability advantages to the owners.

> Service, merchandising, and manufacturing businesses are commonly organized as either proprietorships, partnerships, corporations, or limited liability companies.

The three types of businesses we discussed earlier—service, merchandising, and manufacturing—may be organized as either proprietorships, partnerships, corporations, or limited liability companies. Because of the large amount of resources required to operate a manufacturing business, most manufacturing businesses are corporations. Likewise, most large retailers such as Wal-Mart, Home Depot, and JCPenney are corporations.

BUSINESS STAKEHOLDERS

A **business stakeholder** is a person or entity that has an interest in the economic performance and well-being of a business. For example, owners, suppliers, customers, and employees are all stakeholders in a business. Business stakeholders can be classified into one of the four categories illustrated in Exhibit 1.

Capital market stakeholders provide the major financing for the business in order for the business to begin and continue its operations. Banks and other long-term creditors have an economic interest in recovering the amount they loaned the business plus interest. Owners want to maximize the economic value of their investments and thus also have an economic interest in the business.

Product or service market stakeholders include customers who purchase the business's products or services as well as the vendors who supply inputs to the business. Customers have an economic interest in the continued success of the business. For example, customers who purchase advance tickets from Southwest Airlines Co. have an economic interest in whether Southwest will stay in business. Similarly, suppliers are stakeholders in the continued success of their customers as a source of business.

Government stakeholders have an interest in the economic performance of businesses. As a result, city and state governments often provide incentives for businesses to locate in their jurisdictions. City, county, state, and federal governments collect taxes from businesses within their jurisdictions. In addition, workers are taxed on their wages. The better a business does, the more taxes the government can collect.

Internal stakeholders include individuals employed by the business. The managers are those individuals whom the owners have authorized to operate the business. Managers are primarily evaluated on the economic performance of the business. Thus, managers have an incentive to maximize the economic value of the business. Owners may offer managers salary contracts that are tied directly to how well the business performs. For example, a manager might receive a percentage of the profits or a percentage of the increase in profits. Employees provide services to the company they work for in exchange for pay. Thus, employees have an interest in the economic performance of the business, because their jobs depend upon it.

The state of Alabama offered DaimlerChrysler millions of dollars in incentives to locate a Mercedes plant in Alabama.

ROLE OF ETHICS IN BUSINESS

The moral principles that guide the conduct of individuals are called **ethics**. Unfortunately, business managers can be pressured to violate personal ethics. Such was the case for a number of companies listed in Exhibit 2, on page 6, that engaged in fraudulent business practices and accounting coverups in the early 2000s.

EXHIBIT 1   Business Stakeholders

Business Stakeholder	Interest in the Business	Examples
Capital market stakeholders	Providers of major financing for the business	Banks and owners
Product or service market stakeholders	Buyers of products or services and vendors to the business	Customers and suppliers
Government stakeholders	Collect taxes and fees from the business and its employees	Federal, state, and local governments
Internal stakeholders	Individuals employed by the business	Employees and managers

Stakeholders

Employees/Managers

Customers

Suppliers

Bank and/or Owners

Business

Government

The companies listed in Exhibit 2 were caught in the midst of ethical lapses that led to fines, firings, and criminal and/or civil prosecution. The second column of Exhibit 2 identifies the nature of scandal. The third column of the table identifies some of the results of these events. In most cases, senior and mid-level executives lost their jobs and were sued by upset investors. In some cases, the executives were also criminally prosecuted and are serving prison terms.

What went wrong for these companies and executives? The answer to this question involves the following three factors:

1. Individual character
2. Firm culture
3. Laws and enforcement

Most colleges and universities publish a Student Code of Conduct that sets forth the ethical conduct expected of students.

Individual Character An ethical businessperson displays character by embracing honesty, integrity, and fairness in the face of pressure to hide the truth. Executives often face pressures from senior managers to meet company and analysts' expectations. In many of the cases in Exhibit 2, executives initially justified small violations to avoid such pressures. However, these small lies became big lies as the company's financial problems became worse. By the time the abuses were discovered, the misstatements became sufficient to ruin businesses and wreck lives. For example, David Myers, the former controller

EXHIBIT 2   Accounting and Business Fraud in the 2000s

Company	Nature of Accounting or Business Fraud	Result
Adelphia Communications	Rigas family treated the company assets as their own.	Bankruptcy. Rigas family members found guilty of fraud and lost their investment in the company.
American International Group, Inc. (AIG)	Used sham accounting transactions to inflate performance.	CEO resigned. Executives indicted. AIG paid $126 million in fines.
America Online, Inc. and PurchasePro	Artificially inflated their financial results.	Civil charges filed against senior executives of both companies. $500 million fine.
Computer Associates International, Inc.	Fraudulently inflated its financial results.	CEO and senior executives indicted. Five executives plead guilty. $225 million fine.
Enron	Fraudulently inflated its financial results.	Bankrupcty. Criminal charges against senior executives, over $60 billion in stock market losses.
Fannie Mae	Improperly shifted financial performance between periods.	CEO and CFO fired. Company made a $9 billion correction to previously reported earnings.
HealthSouth	Overstated performance by $4 billion in false entries.	Senior executives criminally indicted.
Qwest Communications International, Inc.	Improperly recognized $3 billion in false receipts.	CEO and six other executives charged with "massive financial fraud." $250 million SEC fine.
Tyco International, Ltd.	Failed to disclose secret loans to executives that were subsequently forgiven.	CEO forced to resign and subjected to frozen asset order and criminal proceedings.
WorldCom	Misstated financial results by nearly $9 billion.	Bankruptcy. Criminal conviction of CEO and CFO. Over $100 billion in stock market losses. Directors forced to pay $18 million.
Xerox Corporation	Recognized $3 billion in revenue prior to when it should have been.	$10 million fine to SEC. Six executives forced to pay $22 million.

of WorldCom, in testifying about his recording of improper transactions stated the following:

> "I didn't think that it was the right thing to do, but I had been asked by Scott (Sullivan, the VP of Finance) to do it. . . ."[3]

Nonetheless, David Myers was criminally convicted and was sentenced to prison.

Firm Culture   By their behavior and attitude, senior managers of a company set the firm culture. As explained by one author, when the leader of a company is put on a pedestal, "they begin to believe they and their organizations are one-of-a-kind, that they're changing the face of the industry. They desire rewards and benefits beyond any other CEOs (chief executive officers)."[4] In most of the firms shown in Exhibit 2, the senior managers created a culture of greed and indifference to the truth. This

---

3 Susan Pulliam, "Crossing the Line: At Center of Fraud, WorldCom Official Sees Life Unravel," *The Wall Street Journal*, March 24, 2005, p. A1.
4 Tim Race, "New Economy Executives Are Smitten, and Undone by Their Own Images," *The New York Times*, July 7, 2002. Quote attributed to Professor Jay A. Conger.

Integrity, Objectivity, and Ethics in Business

DOING THE RIGHT THING

Time Magazine named three women as "Persons of the Year 2002." Each of these not-so-ordinary women had the courage, determination, and integrity to do the right thing. Each risked their personal careers to expose shortcomings in their organizations. Sherron Watkins, an Enron vice president, wrote a letter to Enron's chairman, Kenneth Lay, warning him of improper accounting that eventually led to Enron's collapse. Cynthia Cooper, an internal accountant, informed WorldCom's Board of Directors of phony accounting that allowed WorldCom to cover up over $3 billion in losses and forced WorldCom into bankruptcy. Coleen Rowley, an FBI staff attorney, wrote a memo to FBI Director Robert Mueller, exposing how the Bureau brushed off her pleas to investigate Zacarias Moussaoui, who was indicted as a co-conspirator in the September 11 terrorist attacks.

REAL WORLD

Stanley James Cardiges, the former top U.S. sales representative for American Honda, admitted to receiving $2 million to $5 million in illegal kickbacks from dealers. After being sentenced to five years in prison, he admitted to falling into a pattern of unethical behavior early in his career.

culture flowed down to lower-level managers, creating an environment of short cuts, greed, and lies that ultimately resulted in financial fraud.

Laws and Enforcement Many blamed the lack of laws and enforcement for contributing to the financial reporting abuses described in Exhibit 2. For example, Eliot Spitzer, the attorney general of New York, stated the following:

". . . a key lesson from the recent scandals is that the checks on the system simply have not worked. The honor code among CEOs didn't work. Board oversight didn't work. Self-regulation was a complete failure."[5]

As a result, new laws were enacted by Congress, and enforcement efforts have increased since the early 2000s. For example, the Sarbanes-Oxley Act of 2002 (SOX) was enacted. SOX established a new oversight body for the accounting profession called the Public Company Accounting Oversight Board (PCAOB). In addition, SOX established standards for independence, corporate responsibility, enhanced financial disclosures, and corporate accountability.

THE ROLE OF ACCOUNTING IN BUSINESS

What is the role of accounting in business? The simplest answer to this question is that accounting provides information for managers to use in operating the business. In addition, accounting provides information to other stakeholders to use in assessing the economic performance and condition of the business.

In a general sense, **accounting** can be defined as an information system that provides reports to stakeholders about the economic activities and condition of a business. As we indicated earlier in this chapter, we will focus our discussions on accounting and its role in business. However, many of the concepts in this text apply also to individuals, governments, and other types of organizations.

You may think of accounting as the "language of business." This is because accounting is the means by which business information is communicated to the stakeholders. For example, accounting reports summarizing the profitability of a new product help The Coca-Cola Company's management decide whether to continue selling the product. Likewise, financial analysts use accounting reports in deciding whether to recommend the purchase of Coca-Cola's stock. Banks use accounting reports in determining the amount

> Accounting is an information system that provides reports to stakeholders about the economic activities and condition of a business.

---

5 Eliot Spitzer, "Strong Law Enforcement Is Good for the Economy," *The Wall Street Journal*, April 5, 2005, p. A18.

of credit to extend to Coca-Cola. Suppliers use accounting reports in deciding whether to offer credit for Coca-Cola's purchases of supplies and raw materials. State and federal governments use accounting reports as a basis for assessing taxes on Coca-Cola.

The process by which accounting provides information to business stakeholders is as follows.

1. Identify stakeholders.
2. Assess stakeholders' informational needs.
3. Design the accounting information system to meet stakeholders' needs.
4. Record economic data about business activities and events.
5. Prepare accounting reports for stakeholders.

As illustrated in Exhibit 3, stakeholders use accounting reports as a primary, although not the only, source of information on which they base their decisions. Stakeholders use other information as well. For example, in deciding whether to extend credit to a local retail store, a banker would not only use the store's accounting reports, but might also visit the store and inquire about the owner's reputation in the business community.

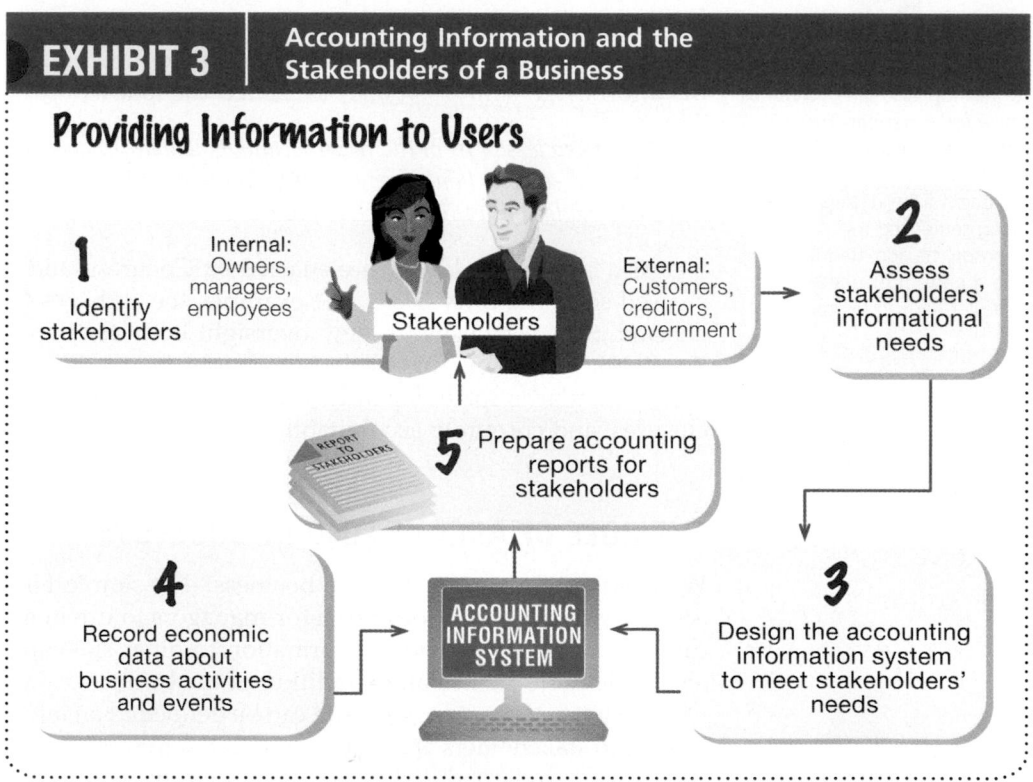

EXHIBIT 3 | **Accounting Information and the Stakeholders of a Business**

PROFESSION OF ACCOUNTING

You may think that all accounting is the same. However, you will find several specialized fields of accounting in practice. The two most common are financial accounting and managerial accounting. Other fields include cost accounting, environmental accounting, tax accounting, accounting systems, international accounting, not-for-profit accounting, and social accounting.

Financial accounting is primarily concerned with the recording and reporting of economic data and activities for a business. Although such reports provide useful information for managers, they are the primary reports for owners, creditors, governmental agencies, and the public. For example, if you wanted to buy some stock in PepsiCo, Inc., American Airlines, or McDonald's, how would you know in which company to invest? One way is to review financial reports and compare the financial performance and condition of each company. The purpose of financial accounting is to provide such reports.

Managerial accounting, or **management accounting**, uses both financial accounting and estimated data to aid management in running day-to-day operations and in planning future operations. Management accountants gather and report information that is relevant and timely to the decision-making needs of management. For example, management might need information on alternative ways to finance the construction of a new building. Alternatively, management might need information on whether to expand its operations into a new product line. Thus, reports to management can differ widely in form and content.

Whether they are engaged in financial accounting or managerial accounting, accountants are employed in either private accounting or public accounting as shown in Exhibit 4. Accountants employed by a business firm or a not-for-profit organization are said to be employed in **private accounting**. Accountants and their staff who provide services on a fee basis are said to be employed in **public accounting**.

Private accountants have a variety of possible career options inside the firm. Some of these career options are shown in Exhibit 4 along with their starting salaries. The phrase "audit services" may be new to you. Individuals who provide audit services, called auditors, verify the accuracy of financial records, accounts, and systems. Several private accounting careers have certification options. The Institute of Management Accountants (IMA) sponsors the **Certified Management Accountant (CMA)** program. The CMA certificate is evidence of competence in management accounting. Becoming a CMA requires a college degree, two years of experience, and successful completion of a two-day examination. Additional certifications in private accounting include the Certified Internal Auditor (CIA), sponsored by The Institute of Internal Auditors, the Certified Information Systems Auditor (CISA), sponsored by the Information Systems Audit and Control Association, and the Certified Payroll Professional (CPP), sponsored by the American Payroll Association.

EXHIBIT 4 Accounting Career Paths and Salaries

Accounting Career Track	Description	Career Options	Annual Starting Salaries[1]	Certification
Private Accounting	Accountants employed by companies, government, and not-for-profit entities.	Bookkeeper	$28,500	
		Payroll clerk	$30,875	Certified Payroll Professional (CPP)
		General accountant	$35,750	
		Budget analyst	$36,750	
		Cost accountant	$37,375	Certified Management Accountant (CMA)
		Internal auditor	$41,500	Certified Internal Auditor (CIA)
		Information technology auditor	$72,500	Certified Information Systems Auditor (CISA)
Public Accounting	Accountants employed individually or within a public accounting firm in tax or audit services.	Local firms	$36,625	Certified Public Accountant (CPA)
		National firms	$44,375	Certified Public Accountant (CPA)

Source: Robert Half 2006 Salary Guide (Finance and Accounting), Robert Half International, Inc.
[1]Median salaries of a reported range. Private accounting salaries are reported for large companies. Information technology auditor salary is for all company sizes and experience levels combined. Salaries may vary by region.

In public accounting, an accountant may practice as an individual or as a member of a public accounting firm. Public accountants who have met a state's education, experience, and examination requirements may become **Certified Public Accountants (CPAs)**. CPAs generally perform general accounting, audit, or tax services. As can be seen in Exhibit 4, CPAs have slightly better starting salaries than private accountants. Career statistics indicate, however, that these salary differences tend to disappear over time.

The requirements for obtaining a CPA certificate differ among the various states. All states require a college education in accounting, and most states require 150 semester hours of college credit. In addition, a candidate must pass an examination prepared by the American Institute of Certified Public Accountants (AICPA). Because all functions within a business use accounting information, experience in private or public accounting provides a solid foundation for a career. Many positions in industry and in government agencies are held by individuals with accounting backgrounds.

Generally Accepted Accounting Principles

objective 2

Summarize the development of accounting principles and relate them to practice.

If a company's management could record and report financial data as it saw fit, comparisons among companies would be difficult, if not impossible. Thus, financial accountants follow **generally accepted accounting principles (GAAP)** in preparing reports. These reports allow investors and other stakeholders to compare one company to another.

To illustrate the importance of generally accepted accounting principles, assume that each sports conference in college football used different rules for counting touchdowns. For example, assume that the Pacific Athletic Conference (PAC 10) counted a touchdown as six points and the Atlantic Coast Conference (ACC) counted a touchdown as two points. It would be difficult to evaluate the teams under such different scoring systems. A standard set of rules and a standard scoring system help fans compare teams across conferences. Likewise, a standard set of generally accepted accounting principles allows for the comparison of financial performance and condition across companies.

Accounting principles and concepts develop from research, accepted accounting practices, and pronouncements of authoritative bodies. Currently, the **Financial Accounting Standards Board (FASB)** is the authoritative body having the primary responsibility for developing accounting principles. The FASB publishes *Statements of Financial Accounting Standards* as well as *Interpretations* of these Standards.

Because generally accepted accounting principles impact how companies report and what they report, all stakeholders are interested in the setting of these principles. Thus, standards are established according to a process that seeks and considers input from all affected parties. The standard-setting activities of the FASB are published and made available at **http://www.fasb.org.**

In this chapter and throughout this text, we emphasize accounting principles and concepts. It is through this emphasis on the "why" of accounting as well as the "how"

Integrity, Objectivity, and Ethics in Business

ETHICS

ACCOUNTING REFORM

The financial accounting and reporting failures of Enron, WorldCom, Tyco, Xerox, and others shocked the investing public. The disclosure that some of the nation's largest and best-known corporations had overstated profits and misled investors raised the question: Where were the CPAs?

In response, Congress passed the Investor Protection, Auditor Reform, and Transparency Act of 2002, called the Sarbanes-Oxley Act. The Act establishes a Public Company Accounting Oversight Board to regulate the portion of the accounting profession that has public companies as clients. In addition, the Act prohibits auditors (CPAs) from providing certain types of nonaudit services, such as investment banking or legal services, to their clients, prohibits employment of auditors by clients for one year after they last audited the client, and increases penalties for the reporting of misleading financial statements.

that you will gain an understanding of the full significance of accounting. In the following paragraphs, we discuss the business entity concept and the cost concept.

BUSINESS ENTITY CONCEPT

The individual business unit is the business entity for which economic data are needed. This entity could be an automobile dealer, a department store, or a grocery store. The business entity must be identified, so that the accountant can determine which economic data should be analyzed, recorded, and summarized in reports.

> Under the business entity concept, the activities of a business are recorded separately from the activities of the stakeholders.

The **business entity concept** is important because it limits the economic data in the accounting system to data related directly to the activities of the business. In other words, the business is viewed as an entity separate from its owners, creditors, or other stakeholders. For example, the accountant for a business with one owner (a proprietorship) would record the activities of the business only, not the personal activities, property, or debts of the owner.

THE COST CONCEPT

If a building is bought for $150,000, that amount should be entered into the buyer's accounting records. The seller may have been asking $170,000 for the building up to the time of the sale. The buyer may have initially offered $130,000 for the building. The building may have been assessed at $125,000 for property tax purposes. The buyer may have received an offer of $175,000 for the building the day after it was acquired. These latter amounts have no effect on the accounting records because they did not result in an exchange of the building from the seller to the buyer. The **cost concept** is the basis for entering the *exchange price, or cost, of $150,000* into the accounting records for the building.

Continuing the illustration, the $175,000 offer received by the buyer the day after the building was acquired indicates that it was a bargain purchase at $150,000. To use $175,000 in the accounting records, however, would record an illusory or unrealized profit. If, after buying the building, the buyer accepts the offer and sells the building for $175,000, a profit of $25,000 is then realized and recorded. The new owner would record $175,000 as the cost of the building.

Using the cost concept involves two other important accounting concepts—objectivity and the unit of measure. The **objectivity concept** requires that the accounting records and reports be based upon objective evidence. In exchanges between a buyer and a seller, both try to get the best price. Only the final agreed-upon amount is objective enough for accounting purposes. If the amounts at which properties were recorded were constantly being revised upward and downward based on offers, appraisals, and opinions, accounting reports could soon become unstable and unreliable.

The **unit of measure concept** requires that economic data be recorded in dollars. Money is a common unit of measurement for reporting uniform financial data and reports.

Example Exercise 1-1   objective 2

On August 25, Gallatin Repair Service extended an offer of $125,000 for land that had been priced for sale at $150,000. On September 3, Gallatin Repair Service accepted the seller's counteroffer of $137,000. On October 20, the land was assessed at a value of $98,000 for property tax purposes. On December 4, Gallatin Repair Service was offered $160,000 for the land by a national retail chain. At what value should the land be recorded in Gallatin Repair Service's records?

Follow My Example 1-1

$137,000. Under the cost concept, the land should be recorded at the cost to Gallatin Repair Service.

For Practice: PE 1-1A, PE 1-1B

The Accounting Equation

The resources owned by a business are its **assets**. Examples of assets include cash, land, buildings, and equipment. The rights or claims to the properties are normally divided into two principal types: (1) the rights of creditors and (2) the rights of owners. The rights of creditors represent debts of the business and are called **liabilities**. The rights of the owners are called **owner's equity**. The relationship between the two may be stated in the form of an equation, as follows:

$$\text{Assets} = \text{Liabilities} + \text{Owner's Equity}$$

This equation is known as the **accounting equation**. Liabilities usually are shown before owner's equity in the accounting equation because creditors have first rights to the assets. The claim of the owners is sometimes given greater emphasis by transposing liabilities to the other side of the equation, which yields:

$$\text{Assets} - \text{Liabilities} = \text{Owner's Equity}$$

To illustrate, if the assets owned by a business amount to $100,000 and the liabilities amount to $30,000, the owner's equity is equal to $70,000, as shown below.

Assets	− Liabilities	= Owner's Equity
$100,000 −	$30,000 =	$70,000

Example Exercise 1-2   objective **3**

John Joos is the owner and operator of You're A Star, a motivational consulting business. At the end of its accounting period, December 31, 2007, You're A Star has assets of $800,000 and liabilities of $350,000. Using the accounting equation, determine the following amounts:

a. Owner's equity, as of December 31, 2007.
b. Owner's equity, as of December 31, 2008, assuming that assets increased by $130,000 and liabilities decreased by $25,000 during 2008.

Follow My Example 1-2

a.   Assets = Liabilities + Owner's Equity
      $800,000 = $350,000 + Owner's Equity
      Owner's Equity = $450,000

b. First, determine the change in Owner's Equity during 2008 as follows:

      Assets = Liabilities + Owner's Equity
      $130,000 = −$25,000 + Owner's Equity
      Owner's Equity = $155,000

Next, add the change in Owner's Equity on December 31, 2007 to arrive at Owner's Equity on December 31, 2008, as shown below:

Owner's Equity on December 31, 2008 =
$605,000 = $450,000 + $155,000

For Practice: PE 1-2A, PE 1-2B

 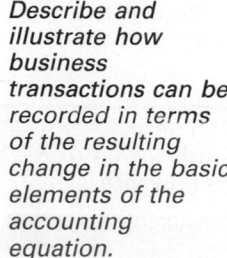
Business Transactions and the Accounting Equation

Paying a monthly telephone bill of $168 affects a business's financial condition because it now has less cash on hand. Such an economic event or condition that directly changes an entity's financial condition or directly affects its results of operations is a **business transaction**. For example, purchasing land for $50,000 is a business transaction. In contrast, a change in a business's credit rating does not directly affect cash or any other element of its financial condition.

Business Connections

THE ACCOUNTING EQUATION

The accounting equation serves as the basic foundation for the accounting systems of all companies. From the smallest business, such as the local convenience store, to the largest business, such as Ford Motor Company, com-panies use the accounting equation. Some examples taken from recent financial reports of well-known companies are shown below.

Company	Assets*	=	Liabilities	+	Owner's Equity
The Coca-Cola Company	$ 31,327	=	$15,392	+	$15,935
Circuit City Stores, Inc.	3,709	=	1,795	+	1,914
Dell Inc.	22,874	=	18,053	+	4,821
eBay Inc.	9,626	=	1,599	+	8,027
Hilton Hospitality, Inc.	8,242	=	5,674	+	2,568
McDonald's	27,844	=	13,328	+	14,516
Microsoft Corporation	71,462	=	23,135	+	48,327
Southwest Airlines Co.	11,337	=	5,813	+	5,524
Wal-Mart	124,765	=	77,044	+	47,721

*Amounts are shown in millions of dollars.

All business transactions can be stated in terms of changes in the elements of the accounting equation. You will see how business transactions affect the accounting equation by studying some typical transactions. As a basis for illustration, we will use a business organized by Chris Clark.

Assume that on November 1, 2007, Chris Clark begins a business that will be known as NetSolutions. The first phase of Chris's business plan is to operate NetSolutions as a service business that provides assistance to individuals and small businesses in developing Web pages and in configuring and installing application soft-ware. Chris expects this initial phase of the business to last one to two years. During this period, Chris will gather information on the software and hardware needs of customers. During the second phase of the business plan, Chris plans to expand NetSolutions into a personalized retailer of software and hardware for individuals and small businesses.

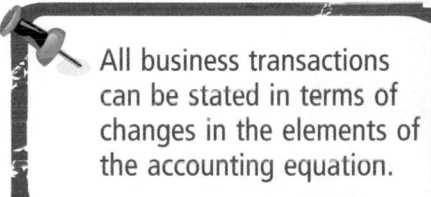

All business transactions can be stated in terms of changes in the elements of the accounting equation.

Each transaction or group of similar transactions during NetSolutions' first month of operations is described in the following paragraphs. The effect of each transaction on the accounting equation is then shown.

Transaction a Chris Clark deposits $25,000 in a bank account in the name of Net-Solutions. The effect of this transaction is to increase the asset cash (on the left side of the equation) by $25,000. To balance the equation, the owner's equity (on the right side of the equation) is increased by the same amount. The equity of the owner is referred to by using the owner's name and "Capital," such as "Chris Clark, Capital." The effect of this transaction on NetSolutions' accounting equation is shown below.

$$\left. \begin{array}{c} \textbf{Assets} \\ \text{Cash} \\ \text{a.} \quad 25{,}000 \end{array} \right\} = \left\{ \begin{array}{c} \textbf{Owner's Equity} \\ \text{Chris Clark, Capital} \\ 25{,}000 \end{array} \right.$$

Note that since Chris Clark is the sole owner, NetSolutions is a proprietorship. Note, too, that the accounting equation shown above relates only to the business, NetSolutions. Under the business entity concept, Chris Clark's personal assets, such as a home or personal bank account, and personal liabilities are excluded from the equation.

Transaction b If you purchased this textbook by paying cash, you entered into a transaction in which you exchanged one asset for another. That is, you exchanged cash for the textbook. Businesses often enter into similar transactions. NetSolutions, for example, exchanged $20,000 cash for land. The land is located in a new business park with convenient access to transportation facilities. Chris Clark plans to rent office space and equipment during the first phase of the business plan. During the second phase, Chris plans to build an office and a warehouse on the land.

The purchase of the land changes the makeup of the assets but does not change the total assets. The items in the equation prior to this transaction and the effect of the transaction are shown next, as well as the new amounts, or *balances*, of the items.

	Assets		=	Owner's Equity
	Cash	+ Land	=	Chris Clark, Capital
Bal.	25,000			25,000
b.	−20,000	+20,000		
Bal.	5,000	20,000		25,000

Transaction c You have probably used a credit card to buy clothing or other merchandise. In this type of transaction, you received clothing for a promise to pay your credit card bill in the future. That is, you received an asset and incurred a liability to pay a future bill. During the month, NetSolutions entered into a similar transaction, buying supplies for $1,350 and agreeing to pay the supplier in the near future. This type of transaction is called a purchase *on account*. The liability created is called an **account payable**. Items such as supplies that will be used in the business in the future are called **prepaid expenses**, which are assets. The effect of this transaction is to increase assets and liabilities by $1,350, as follows:

Other examples of common prepaid expenses include insurance and rent. Businesses often report these assets together as a single item, prepaid expenses.

	Assets			=	Liabilities + Owner's Equity	
					Accounts	Chris Clark,
	Cash	+ Supplies	+ Land	=	Payable	+ Capital
Bal.	5,000		20,000			25,000
c.		+1,350			+1,350	
Bal.	5,000	1,350	20,000		1,350	25,000

Transaction d You may have earned money by painting houses or mowing lawns. If so, you received money for rendering services to a customer. Likewise, a business earns money by selling goods or services to its customers. This amount is called **revenue**.

During its first month of operations, NetSolutions provided services to customers, earning fees of $7,500 and receiving the amount in cash. The receipt of cash increases NetSolutions' assets and also increases Chris Clark's equity in the business. In order to aid in the preparation of financial statements, the revenues of $7,500 are recorded in a separate column to the right of Chris Clark, Capital. This is done so that the effects on owner's capital can be separately identified and summarized. Thus, this transaction is recorded as an increase in Cash and Fees Earned of $7,500 as shown below.

	Assets			=	Liabilities +	Owner's Equity	
					Accounts	Chris Clark,	Fees
	Cash	+ Supplies	+ Land	=	Payable	+ Capital	+ Earned
Bal.	5,000	1,350	20,000		1,350	25,000	
d.	+7,500						+7,500
Bal.	12,500	1,350	20,000		1,350	25,000	7,500

Special terms may be used to describe certain kinds of revenue, such as **sales** for the sale of merchandise. Revenue from providing services is called **fees earned**. For example, a physician would record fees earned for services to patients. Other examples include **rent revenue** (money received for rent) and **interest revenue** (money received for interest).

Instead of requiring the payment of cash at the time services are provided or goods are sold, a business may accept payment at a later date. Such revenues are called *fees on account* or *sales on account*. In such cases, the firm has an **account receivable**, which is a claim against the customer. An account receivable is an asset, and the revenue is earned as if cash had been received. When customers pay their accounts, there is an exchange of one asset for another. Cash increases, while accounts receivable decreases.

Transaction e If you painted houses to earn money, you probably used your own ladders and brushes. NetSolutions also spent cash or used up other assets in earning revenue. The amounts used in this process of earning revenue are called **expenses**. Expenses include supplies used, wages of employees, and other assets and services used in operating the business.

NetSolutions paid the following expenses during the month: wages, $2,125; rent, $800; utilities, $450; and miscellaneous, $275. Miscellaneous expenses include small amounts paid for such items as postage, coffee, and magazine subscriptions. The effect of this group of transactions is the opposite of the effect of revenues. These transactions reduce cash and owner's equity. Like fees earned, the expenses are recorded in separate columns to the right of Chris Clark, Capital. However, since expenses reduce owner's equity, the expenses are entered as negative amounts.

	Assets			=	Liabilities +		Owner's Equity				
					Accounts	Chris Clark,	Fees	Wages	Rent	Utilities	Misc.
	Cash	+ Supplies +	Land		Payable +	Capital	+ Earned −	Expense −	Expense −	Expense −	Expense
Bal.	12,500	1,350	20,000		1,350	25,000	7,500				
e.	−3,650							2,125	−800	−450	−275
Bal.	8,850	1,350	20,000		1,350	25,000	7,500	−2,125	−800	450	−275

Businesses usually record each revenue and expense transaction separately as it occurs. However, to simplify this illustration, we have summarized NetSolutions' revenues and expenses for the month in transactions (d) and (e).

Transaction f When you pay your monthly credit card bill, you decrease the cash in your checking account and also decrease the amount you owe to the credit card company. Likewise, when NetSolutions pays $950 to creditors during the month, it reduces both assets and liabilities, as shown below.

	Assets			=	Liabilities +		Owner's Equity				
					Accounts	Chris Clark,	Fees	Wages	Rent	Utilities	Misc.
	Cash	+ Supplies +	Land		Payable +	Capital	+ Earned −	Expense −	Expense −	Expense −	Expense
Bal.	8,850	1,350	20,000		1,350	25,000	7,500	−2,125	−800	−450	−275
f.	−950				−950						
Bal.	7,900	1,350	20,000		400	25,000	7,500	−2,125	−800	−450	−275

You should note that paying an amount on account is different from paying an amount for an expense. The payment of an expense reduces owner's equity, as illustrated in transaction (e). Paying an amount on account reduces the amount owed on a liability.

Transaction g At the end of the month, the cost of the supplies on hand (not yet used) is $550. The remainder of the supplies ($1,350 − $550) was used in the operations of the business and is treated as an expense. This decrease of $800 in supplies and owner's equity is shown as follows:

	Assets			=	Liabilities +		Owner's Equity						
	Cash +	Supplies +	Land	=	Accounts Payable +	Chris Clark, Capital	+ Fees Earned −	Wages Exp. −	Rent Exp. −	Supplies Exp. −	Utilities Exp. −	Misc. Exp.
Bal.	7,900	1,350	20,000		400	25,000	7,500	−2,125	−800		−450	−275
g.		−800								−800		
Bal.	7,900	550	20,000		400	25,000	7,500	−2,125	−800	−800	−450	−275

Transaction h At the end of the month, Chris Clark withdraws $2,000 in cash from the business for personal use. This transaction is the exact opposite of an investment in the business by the owner. You should be careful not to confuse withdrawals by the owner with expenses. Withdrawals *do not* represent assets or services used in the process of earning revenues. Instead, withdrawals are considered a distribution of capital to the owner. Owner withdrawals are identified by the owner's name followed by *Drawing*. For example, Chris Clark's withdrawal would be identified as Chris Clark, Drawing. Like expenses, withdrawals are recorded in a separate column to the right of Chris Clark, Capital. The effect of the $2,000 withdrawal is shown as follows:

	Assets			=	Liabilities +			Owner's Equity						
	Cash +	Supp. +	Land	=	Accounts Payable +	Chris Clark, Capital −	Chris Clark, Drawing	+ Fees Earned −	Wages Exp. −	Rent Exp. −	Supplies Exp. −	Utilities Exp. −	Misc. Exp.
Bal.	7,900	550	20,000		400	25,000		7,500	−2,125	−800	−800	−450	−275
h.	−2,000						−2,000						
Bal.	5,900	550	20,000		400	25,000	−2,000	7,500	−2,125	−800	−800	−450	−275

Summary The transactions of NetSolutions are summarized as follows. They are identified by letter, and the balance of each item is shown after each transaction.

	Assets			= Liabilities +			Owner's Equity						
	Cash +	Supp. +	Land	= Payable +	Chris Clark, Capital −	Chris Clark, Drawing	+ Fees Earned −	Wages Exp. −	Rent Exp. −	Supplies Exp. −	Utilities Exp. −	Misc. Exp.
a.	+25,000				+25,000							
b.	−20,000		+20,000									
Bal.	5,000		20,000		25,000							
c.		+1,350		+1,350								
Bal.	5,000	1,350	20,000	1,350	25,000							
d.	+ 7,500						+7,500					
Bal.	12,500	1,350	20,000	1,350	25,000		7,500					
e.	− 3,650							−2,125	−800		−450	−275
Bal.	8,850	1,350	20,000	1,350	25,000		7,500	−2,125	−800		−450	−275
f.	− 950			− 950								
Bal.	7,900	1,350	20,000	400	25,000		7,500	−2,125	−800		−450	−275
g.		− 800								−800		
Bal.	7,900	550	20,000	400	25,000		7,500	−2,125	−800	−800	−450	−275
h.	− 2,000					−2,000						
Bal.	5,900	550	20,000	400	25,000	−2,000	7,500	−2,125	−800	−800	−450	−275

In reviewing the preceding summary, you should note the following, which apply to all types of businesses:

1. The effect of every transaction is *an increase or a decrease in one or more of the accounting equation elements.*
2. The two sides of the accounting equation are *always equal.*
3. The owner's equity is *increased by amounts invested by the owner* and is *decreased by withdrawals by the owner.* In addition, the owner's equity is *increased by revenues* and is *decreased by expenses.*

The effects of these four types of transactions on owner's equity are illustrated in Exhibit 5.

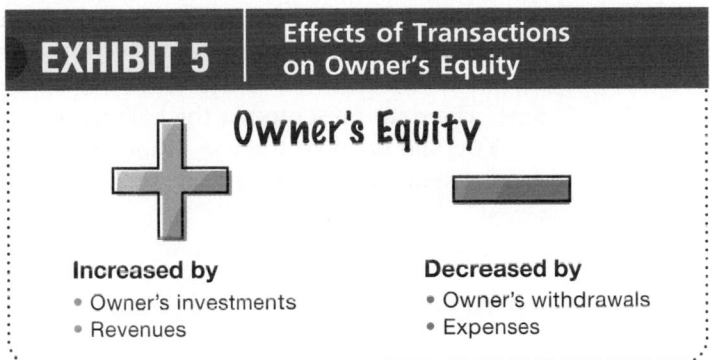

Example Exercise 1-3 objective 4

Salvo Delivery Service is owned and operated by Joel Salvo. The following selected transactions were completed by Salvo Delivery Service during February:

1. Received cash from owner as additional investment, $35,000.
2. Paid creditors on account, $1,800.
3. Billed customers for delivery services on account, $11,250.
4. Received cash from customers on account, $6,740.
5. Paid cash to owner for personal use, $1,000.

Indicate the effect of each transaction on the accounting equation elements (Assets, Liabilities, Owner's Equity, Drawing, Revenue, and Expense) by listing the numbers identifying the transactions, (1) through (5). Also, indicate the specific item within the accounting equation element that is affected. To illustrate, the answer to (1) is shown below.

(1) Asset (Cash) increases by $35,000; Owner's Equity (Joel Salvo, Capital) increases by $35,000.

Follow My Example 1-3

(2) Asset (Cash) decreases by $1,800; Liability (Accounts Payable) decreases by $1,800.
(3) Asset (Accounts Receivable) increases by $11,250; Revenue (Delivery Service Fees) increases by $11,250.
(4) Asset (Cash) increases by $6,740; Asset (Accounts Receivable) decreases by $6,740.
(5) Asset (Cash) decreases by $1,000; Drawing (Joel Salvo, Drawing) increases by $1,000.

For Practice: PE 1-3A, PE 1-3B

Financial Statements

objective 5

Describe the financial statements of a proprietorship and explain how they interrelate.

After transactions have been recorded and summarized, reports are prepared for users. The accounting reports that provide this information are called **financial statements**. The principal financial statements of a proprietorship are the income statement, the statement of owner's equity, the balance sheet, and the statement of cash flows. The order in which the statements are normally prepared and the nature of the data presented in each statement are as follows:

- **Income statement**—A summary of the revenue and expenses *for a specific period of time*, such as a month or a year.
- **Statement of owner's equity**—A summary of the changes in the owner's equity that have occurred *during a specific period of time*, such as a month or a year.
- **Balance sheet**—A list of the assets, liabilities, and owner's equity *as of a specific date*, usually at the close of the last day of a month or a year.
- **Statement of cash flows**—A summary of the cash receipts and cash payments *for a specific period of time*, such as a month or a year.

@netsolutions

The basic features of the four statements and their interrelationships are illustrated in Exhibit 6, on page 20. The data for the statements were taken from the summary of transactions of NetSolutions.

All financial statements should be identified by the name of the business, the title of the statement, and the *date* or *period of time*. The data presented in the income statement, the statement of owner's equity, and the statement of cash flows are for a period of time. The data presented in the balance sheet are for a specific date.

You should note the use of indents, captions, dollar signs, and rulings in the financial statements. They aid the reader by emphasizing the sections of the statements.

When you buy something at a store, you may *match* the cash register total with the amount you paid the cashier and with the amount of change, if any, you received.

INCOME STATEMENT

The income statement reports the revenues and expenses for a period of time, based on the **matching concept**. This concept is applied by *matching* the expenses with the revenue generated during a period by those expenses. The income statement also reports the excess of the revenue over the expenses incurred. This excess of the revenue over the expenses is called **net income** or **net profit**. If the expenses exceed the revenue, the excess is a **net loss**.

The effects of revenue earned and expenses incurred during the month for NetSolutions were shown in the equation as separate increases and decreases in each item. Net income for a period has the effect of increasing owner's equity (capital) for the period, whereas a net loss has the effect of decreasing owner's equity (capital) for the period.

The revenue, expenses, and the net income of $3,050 for NetSolutions are reported in the income statement in Exhibit 6, on page 20. The order in which the expenses are listed in the income statement varies among businesses. One method is to list them in order of size, beginning with the larger items. Miscellaneous expense is usually shown as the last item, regardless of the amount.

Example Exercise 1-4   objective 5

The assets and liabilities of Chickadee Travel Service at April 30, 2008, the end of the current year, and its revenue and expenses for the year are listed below. The capital of the owner, Adam Cellini, was $80,000 at May 1, 2007, the beginning of the current year.

Accounts payable	$ 12,200	Miscellaneous expense	$ 12,950
Accounts receivable	31,350	Office expense	63,000
Cash	53,050	Supplies	3,350
Fees earned	263,200	Wages expense	131,700
Land	80,000		

Prepare an income statement for the current year ended April 30, 2008.

(continued)

Follow My Example 1-4

CHICKADEE TRAVEL SERVICE
INCOME STATEMENT
For the Year Ended April 30, 2008

Fees earned		$263,200
Expenses:		
Wages expense	$131,700	
Office expense	63,000	
Miscellaneous expense	12,950	
Total expenses		207,650
Net income		$ 55,550

For Practice: PE 1-4A, PE 1-4B

STATEMENT OF OWNER'S EQUITY

The statement of owner's equity reports the changes in the owner's equity for a period of time. It is prepared *after* the income statement because the net income or net loss for the period must be reported in this statement. Similarly, it is prepared *before* the balance sheet, since the amount of owner's equity at the end of the period must be reported on the balance sheet. Because of this, the statement of owner's equity is often viewed as the connecting link between the income statement and balance sheet.

Three types of transactions affected owner's equity for NetSolutions during November: (1) the original investment of $25,000, (2) the revenue and expenses that resulted in net income of $3,050 for the month, and (3) a withdrawal of $2,000 by the owner. This information is summarized in the statement of owner's equity in Exhibit 6.

Example Exercise 1-5   objective 5

Using the data for Chickadee Travel Service shown in Example Exercise 1-4, prepare a statement of owner's equity for the current year ended April 30, 2008. Adam Cellini invested an additional $50,000 in the business during the year and withdrew cash of $30,000 for personal use.

Follow My Example 1-5

CHICKADEE TRAVEL SERVICE
STATEMENT OF OWNER'S EQUITY
For the Year Ended April 30, 2008

Adam Cellini, capital, May 1, 2007		$ 80,000
Additional investment by owner during year	$ 50,000	
Net income for the year	55,550	
	$105,550	
Less withdrawals	30,000	
Increase in owner's equity		75,550
Adam Cellini, capital, April 30, 2008		$155,550

For Practice: PE 1-5A, PE 1-5B

EXHIBIT 6

Financial Statements for NetSolutions

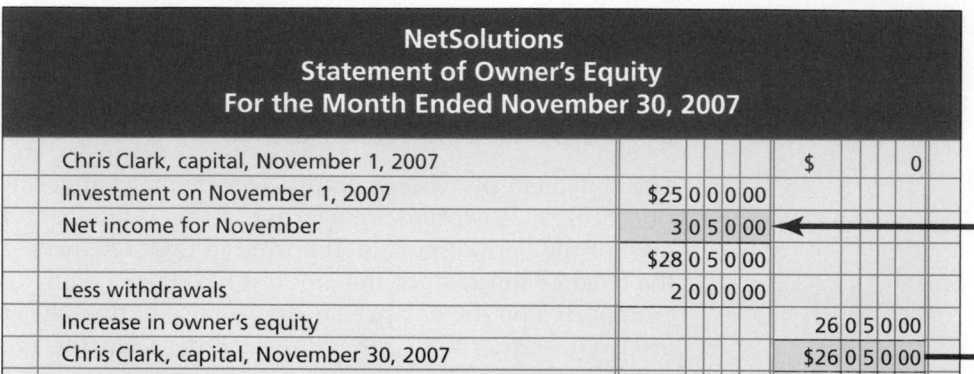

NetSolutions
Income Statement
For the Month Ended November 30, 2007

Fees earned		$7 500 00
Expenses:		
Wages expense	$2 125 00	
Rent expense	800 00	
Supplies expense	800 00	
Utilities expense	450 00	
Miscellaneous expense	275 00	
Total expenses		4 450 00
Net income		$3 050 00

NetSolutions
Statement of Owner's Equity
For the Month Ended November 30, 2007

Chris Clark, capital, November 1, 2007		$ 0
Investment on November 1, 2007	$25 000 00	
Net income for November	3 050 00	
	$28 050 00	
Less withdrawals	2 000 00	
Increase in owner's equity		26 050 00
Chris Clark, capital, November 30, 2007		$26 050 00

NetSolutions
Balance Sheet
November 30, 2007

Assets		Liabilities	
Cash	$ 5 900 00	Accounts payable	$ 400 00
Supplies	550 00	**Owner's Equity**	
Land	20 000 00	Chris Clark, capital	26 050 00
		Total liabilities and	
Total assets	$26 450 00	owner's equity	$26 450 00

NetSolutions
Statement of Cash Flows
For the Month Ended November 30, 2007

Cash flows from operating activities:		
Cash received from customers	$ 7 500 00	
Deduct cash payments for expenses and		
payments to creditors	4 600 00	
Net cash flow from operating activities		$ 2 900 00
Cash flows from investing activities:		
Cash payments for purchase of land		(20 000 00)
Cash flows from financing activities:		
Cash received as owner's investment	$25 000 00	
Deduct cash withdrawal by owner	2 000 00	
Net cash flow from financing activities		23 000 00
Net cash flow and November 30, 2007, cash balance		$ 5 900 00

BALANCE SHEET

The balance sheet in Exhibit 6 reports the amounts of NetSolutions' assets, liabilities, and owner's equity at the end of November. The asset and liability amounts are taken from the last line of the summary of transactions presented earlier. Chris Clark, Capital as of November 30, 2007, is taken from the statement of owner's equity. The form of balance sheet shown in Exhibit 6 is called the **account form** because it resembles the basic format of the accounting equation, with assets on the left side and the liabilities and owner's equity sections on the right side. We illustrate an alternative form of balance sheet, called the **report form**, in a later chapter. It presents the liabilities and owner's equity sections below the assets section.

The assets section of the balance sheet normally presents assets in the order that they will be converted into cash or used in operations. Cash is presented first, followed by receivables, supplies, prepaid insurance, and other assets. The assets of a more permanent nature are shown next, such as land, buildings, and equipment.

In the liabilities section of the balance sheet in Exhibit 6, accounts payable is the only liability. When there are two or more categories of liabilities, each should be listed and the total amount of liabilities presented as follows:

	Liabilities	
Accounts payable	$12,900	
Wages payable	2,570	
Total liabilities		$15,470

Example Exercise 1-6 objective 5

Using the data for Chickadee Travel Service shown in Example Exercises 1-4 and 1-5, prepare the balance sheet as of April 30, 2008.

Follow My Example 1-6

CHICKADEE TRAVEL SERVICE
BALANCE SHEET
April 30, 2008

Assets		Liabilities	
Cash	$ 53,050	Accounts payable	$ 12,200
Accounts receivable	31,350		
Supplies	3,350	**Owner's Equity**	
Land	80,000	Adam Cellini, capital	155,550
Total assets	$167,750	Total liabilities and owner's equity	$167,750

For Practice: PE 1-6A, PE 1-6B

STATEMENT OF CASH FLOWS

The statement of cash flows consists of three sections, as we see in Exhibit 6: (1) operating activities, (2) investing activities, and (3) financing activities. Each of these sections is briefly described below.

Cash Flows from Operating Activities This section reports a summary of cash receipts and cash payments from operations. The net cash flow from operating activities will normally differ from the amount of net income for the period. In Exhibit 6, NetSolutions reported net cash flows from operating activities of $2,900 and net income of $3,050. This difference occurs because revenues and expenses may not be recorded at the same time that cash is received from customers or paid to creditors.

Cash Flows from Investing Activities This section reports the cash transactions for the acquisition and sale of relatively permanent assets. Exhibit 6 reports that NetSolutions paid $20,000 for the purchase of land during November.

Cash Flows from Financing Activities This section reports the cash transactions related to cash investments by the owner, borrowings, and cash withdrawals by the owner. Exhibit 6 shows that Chris Clark invested $25,000 in the business and withdrew $2,000 during November.

Preparing the statement of cash flows requires that each of the November cash transactions for NetSolutions be classified as operating, investing, or financing activities. Using the summary of transactions shown on page 16, the November cash transactions for NetSolutions can be classified as follows:

Transaction	Amount	Cash Flow Activity
a.	$25,000	Financing (Investment by Chris Clark)
b.	−20,000	Investing (Purchase of land)
d.	7,500	Operating (Fees earned)
e.	−3,650	Operating (Payment of expenses)
f.	−950	Operating (Payment of account payable)
h.	−2,000	Financing (Withdrawal by Chris Clark)

Transactions (c) and (g) are not listed above since they did not involve a cash receipt or payment. In additon, the payment of accounts payable in transaction (f) is classified as an operating activity since the account payable arose from the purchase of supplies, which are used in operations. Using the preceding classifications of November cash transactions, the statement of cash flows is prepared as shown in Exhibit 6.[6]

The ending cash balance shown on the statement of cash flows also appears on the balance sheet as of the end of the period. To illustrate, the ending cash of $5,900 reported on the November statement of cash flows in Exhibit 6 also appears as the amount of cash on hand in the November 30, 2007, balance sheet.

Since November is NetSolutions' first period of operations, the net cash flow for November and the November 30, 2007, cash balance are the same amount, $5,900, as shown in Exhibit 6. In subsequent periods, NetSolutions will report in its statement of cash flows a beginning cash balance, an increase or a decrease in cash for the period, and an ending cash balance. For example, assume that for December NetSolutions has a decrease in cash of $3,835. The last three lines of NetSolutions' statement of cash flows for December appear as follows:

Decrease in cash	$3,835
Cash as of December 1, 2007	5,900
Cash as of December 31, 2007	$2,065

Example Exercise 1-7   **objective 5**

A summary of cash flows for Chickadee Travel Service for the year ended April 30, 2008, is shown below.

Cash receipts:
Cash received from customers	$251,000
Cash received from additional investment of owner	50,000

Cash payments:
Cash paid for expenses	210,000
Cash paid for land	80,000
Cash paid to owner for personal use	30,000

The cash balance as of May 1, 2007, was $72,050.

Prepare a statement of cash flows for Chickadee Travel Service for the year ended April 30, 2008.

(continued)

---

6 This method of preparing the statement of cash flows is called the "direct method." This method and the indirect method are discussed further in Chapter 16.

Follow My Example 1-7

CHICKADEE TRAVEL SERVICE
STATEMENT OF CASH FLOWS
For the Year Ended April 30, 2008

Cash flows from operating activities:		
Cash received from customers................................	$251,000	
Deduct cash payments for expenses	210,000	
Net cash flows from operating activities		$ 41,000
Cash flows from investing activities:		
Cash payments for purchase of land		(80,000)
Cash flows from financing activities:		
Cash received from owner as investment	$ 50,000	
Deduct cash withdrawals by owner	30,000	
Net cash flows from financing activities		20,000
Net decrease in cash during year.............................		$(19,000)
Cash as of May 1, 2007		72,050
Cash as of April 30, 2008		$ 53,050

For Practice: PE 1-7A, PE 1-7B

INTERRELATIONSHIPS AMONG FINANCIAL STATEMENTS

As we mentioned earlier, financial statements are prepared in the order of the income statement, statement of owner's equity, balance sheet, and statement of cash flows. Preparing them in this order is important because the financial statements are interrelated. Using the financial statements of NetSolutions as an example, these interrelationships are shown in Exhibit 6 as follows:[7]

1. The income statement and the statement of owner's equity are interrelated. The net income or net loss appears on the income statement and also on the statement of owner's equity as either an addition (net income) to or deduction (net loss) from the beginning owner's equity and any additional investments by the owner during the period. To illustrate, NetSolutions' net income of $3,050 for November is added to Chris Clark's investment of $25,000 in the statement of owner's equity as shown in Exhibit 6.

2. The statement of owner's equity and the balance sheet are interrelated. The owner's capital at the end of the period on the statement of owner's equity also appears on the balance sheet as owner's capital. To illustrate, Chris Clark, Capital of $26,050 as of November 30, 2007, on the statement of owner's equity also appears on the November 30, 2007, balance sheet as shown in Exhibit 6.

3. The balance sheet and the statement of cash flows are interrelated. The cash on the balance sheet also appears as the end-of-period cash on the statement of cash flows. To illustrate, the cash of $5,900 reported on NetSolutions' balance sheet as of November 30, 2007, is also reported on NetSolutions' November statement of cash flows as the end-of-period cash as shown in Exhibit 6.

The preceding interrelationships shown in Exhibit 6 are important in analyzing financial statements and the impact of transactions on a business. In addition, these interrelationships serve as a check on whether the financial statements have been prepared correctly. For example, if the ending cash on the statement of cash flows doesn't agree with the balance sheet cash, then an error has occurred.

---

7 Depending upon the method of preparing the cash flows from operating activities section of the statement of cash flows, net income (or net loss) may also appear on the statement of cash flows. This interrelationship or method of preparing the statement of cash flows, called the "indirect method," is described and illustrated in Chapter 16.

At a Glance

1. Describe the nature of a business and the role of ethics and accounting in business.

Key Points	Key Learning Outcomes	Example Exercises	Practice Exercises
A business provides goods or services (outputs) to customers with the objective of maximizing profits. Service, merchandising, and manufacturing businesses may be organized as proprietorships, partnerships, corporations, and limited liability companies. A business stakeholder is a person or entity (such as an owner, manager, employee, customer, creditor, or the government) who has an interest in the economic performance of the business.	• Distinguish among service, merchandising, and manufacturing businesses. • Describe the characteristics of a proprietorship, partnership, corporation, and limited liability company. • List business stakeholders.		
Ethics are moral principles that guide the conduct of individuals. Good ethical conduct depends upon individual character, firm culture, and laws and enforcement.	• Define ethics and list the three factors affecting good ethical conduct.		
Accounting, called the "language of business," is an information system that provides reports to stakeholders about the economic activities and condition of a business. Accountants are engaged in private accounting or public accounting.	• Describe the role of accounting in business and explain why accounting is called the "language of business." • Describe what private and public accounting means.		

2. Summarize the development of accounting principles and relate them to practice.

Key Points	Key Learning Outcomes	Example Exercises	Practice Exercises
Generally accepted accounting principles (GAAP) are used in preparing financial statements so that stakeholders can compare one company to another. Accounting principles and concepts develop from research, practice, and pronouncements of authoritative bodies such as the Financial Accounting Standards Board (FASB).	• Explain what is meant by generally accepted accounting principles. • Describe how generally accepted accounting principles are developed.		
The business entity concept views the business as an entity separate from its owners, creditors, or other stakeholders. The cost concept requires that properties and services bought by a business be recorded in terms of actual cost. The objectivity concept requires that the accounting records and reports be based upon objective evidence. The unit of measure concept requires that economic data be recorded in dollars.	• Describe and give an example of what is meant by the business entity concept. • Describe and give an example of what is meant by the cost concept. • Describe and give an example of what is meant by the objectivity concept. • Describe and give an example of what is meant by the unit of measure concept.	1-1	1-1A, 1-1B

3. State the accounting equation and define each element of the equation.

Key Points	Key Learning Outcomes	Example Exercises	Practice Exercises
The resources owned by a business and the rights or claims to these resources may be stated in the form of an equation, as follows: Assets = Liabilities + Owner's Equity	• State the accounting equation. • Define assets, liabilities, and owner's equity. • Given two elements of the accounting equation, solve for the third element.	 1-2	 1-2A, 1-2B

4. Describe and illustrate how business transactions can be recorded in terms of the resulting change in the basic elements of the accounting equation.

Key Points	Key Learning Outcomes	Example Exercises	Practice Exercises
All business transactions can be stated in terms of the change in one or more of the three elements of the accounting equation.	• Define a business transaction. • Using the accounting equation as a framework, record transactions.	 1-3	 1-3A, 1-3B

5. Describe the financial statements of a proprietorship and explain how they interrelate.

Key Points	Key Learning Outcomes	Example Exercises	Practice Exercises
The principal financial statements of a proprietorship are the income statement, the statement of owner's equity, the balance sheet, and the statement of cash flows. The income statement reports a period's net income or net loss, which also appears on the statement of owner's equity. The ending owner's capital reported on the statement of owner's equity is also reported on the balance sheet. The ending cash balance is reported on the balance sheet and the statement of cash flows.	• List and describe the financial statements of a proprietorship. • Prepare an income statement. • Prepare a statement of owner's equity. • Prepare a balance sheet. • Prepare a statement of cash flows. • Explain how the financial statements of a proprietorship are interrelated.	 1-4 1-5 1-6 1-7	 1-4A, 1-4B 1-5A, 1-5B 1-6A, 1-6B 1-7A, 1-7B

Key Terms

account form (21)
account payable (14)
account receivable (15)
accounting (7)
accounting equation (12)
assets (12)
balance sheet (18)
business (2)
business entity concept (11)
business stakeholder (4)
business transaction (12)
Certified Management Accountant (CMA) (9)

Certified Public Accountant (CPA) (10)
corporation (3)
cost concept (11)
ethics (4)
expenses (15)
fees earned (15)
financial accounting (8)
Financial Accounting Standards Board (FASB) (10)
financial statements (17)
generally accepted accounting principles (GAAP) (10)

income statement (18)
interest revenue (15)
liabilities (12)
limited liability company (LLC) (4)
management (or managerial) accounting (9)
manufacturing business (3)
matching concept (18)
merchandising business (3)
net income or net profit (18)
net loss (18)
objectivity concept (11)
owner's equity (12)

partnership (3)
prepaid expenses (14)
private accounting (9)
profit (2)
proprietorship (3)

public accounting (9)
rent revenue (15)
report form (21)
revenue (14)
sales (15)

service business (3)
statement of cash flows (18)
statement of owner's equity (18)
unit of measure concept (11)

Illustrative Problem

Cecil Jameson, Attorney-at-Law, is a proprietorship owned and operated by Cecil Jameson. On July 1, 2007, Cecil Jameson, Attorney-at-Law, has the following assets and liabilities: cash, $1,000; accounts receivable, $3,200; supplies, $850; land, $10,000; accounts payable, $1,530. Office space and office equipment are currently being rented, pending the construction of an office complex on land purchased last year. Business transactions during July are summarized as follows:

a. Received cash from clients for services, $3,928.

b. Paid creditors on account, $1,055.

c. Received cash from Cecil Jameson as an additional investment, $3,700.

d. Paid office rent for the month, $1,200.

e. Charged clients for legal services on account, $2,025.

f. Purchased office supplies on account, $245.

g. Received cash from clients on account, $3,000.

h. Received invoice for paralegal services from Legal Aid Inc. for July (to be paid on August 10), $1,635.

i. Paid the following: wages expense, $850; answering service expense, $250; utilities expense, $325; and miscellaneous expense, $75.

j. Determined that the cost of office supplies on hand was $980; therefore, the cost of supplies used during the month was $115.

k. Jameson withdrew $1,000 in cash from the business for personal use.

Instructions

1. Determine the amount of owner's equity (Cecil Jameson's capital) as of July 1, 2007.
2. State the assets, liabilities, and owner's equity as of July 1 in equation form similar to that shown in this chapter. In tabular form below the equation, indicate the increases and decreases resulting from each transaction and the new balances after each transaction.
3. Prepare an income statement for July, a statement of owner's equity for July, and a balance sheet as of July 31, 2007.
4. (Optional). Prepare a statement of cash flows for July.

Solution

1.

$$\text{Assets} - \text{Liabilities} = \text{Owner's Equity (Cecil Jameson, capital)}$$

$$(\$1,000 + \$3,200 + \$850 + \$10,000) - \$1,530 = \text{Owner's Equity (Cecil Jameson, capital)}$$

$$\$15,050 - \$1,530 = \text{Owner's Equity (Cecil Jameson, capital)}$$

$$\$13,520 = \text{Owner's Equity (Cecil Jameson, capital)}$$

2.

	Assets				= Liabilities +		Owner's Equity								
	Cash +	Accts. Rec. +	Supp. +	Land =	Accts. Pay. +	Cecil Jameson, Capital −	Cecil Jameson, Drawing +	Fees Earned −	Paralegal Exp. −	Wages Exp. −	Rent Exp. −	Utilities Exp. −	Answering Service Exp. −	Supp. Exp. −	Misc. Exp.
Bal.	1,000	3,200	850	10,000	1,530	13,520									
a.	+3,928							3,928							
Bal.	4,928	3,200	850	10,000	1,530	13,520									
b.	−1,055				−1,055										
Bal.	3,873	3,200	850	10,000	475	13,520		3,928							
c.	+3,700					+3,700									
Bal.	7,573	3,200	850	10,000	475	17,220		3,928							
d.	−1,200										−1,200				
Bal.	6,373	3,200	850	10,000	475	17,220		3,928			−1,200				
e.		+2,025						+2,025							
Bal.	6,373	5,225	850	10,000	475	17,220		5,953			−1,200				
f.			+ 245		+ 245										
Bal.	6,373	5,225	1,095	10,000	720	17,220		5,953			−1,200				
g.	+3,000	−3,000													
Bal.	9,373	2,225	1,095	10,000	720	17,220		5,953			−1,200				
h.					+1,635				−1,635						
Bal.	9,373	2,225	1,095	10,000	2,355	17,220		5,953	−1,635		−1,200				
i.	−1,500									−850		−325	−250		−75
Bal.	7,873	2,225	1,095	10,000	2,355	17,220		5,953	−1,635	−850	−1,200	−325	−250		−75
j.			− 115											−115	
Bal.	7,873	2,225	980	10,000	2,355	17,220		5,953	−1,635	−850	−1,200	−325	−250	−115	−75
k.	−1,000						−1,000								
Bal.	6,873	2,225	980	10,000	2,355	17,220	−1,000	5,953	−1,635	−850	−1,200	−325	−250	−115	−75

3.

Cecil Jameson, Attorney-at-Law
Income Statement
For the Month Ended July 31, 2007

Fees earned		$5,953
Expenses:		
Paralegal expense	$1,635	
Rent expense	1,200	
Wages expense	850	
Utilities expense	325	
Answering service expense	250	
Supplies expense	115	
Miscellaneous expense	75	
Total expenses		4,450
Net income		$1,503

Cecil Jameson, Attorney-at-Law
Statement of Owner's Equity
For the Month Ended July 31, 2007

Cecil Jameson, capital, July 1, 2007		$13,520
Additional investment by owner	$3,700	
Net income for the month	1,503	
	$5,203	
Less withdrawals	1,000	
Increase in owner's equity		4,203
Cecil Jameson, capital, July 31, 2007		$17,723

(continued)

Cecil Jameson, Attorney-at-Law
Balance Sheet
July 31, 2007

Assets		Liabilities	
Cash	$ 6,873	Accounts payable	$ 2,355
Accounts receivable	2,225	**Owner's Equity**	
Supplies	980	Cecil Jameson, capital	17,723
Land	10,000	Total liabilities and	
Total assets	$20,078	owner's equity	$20,078

4. Optional.

Cecil Jameson, Attorney-at-Law
Statement of Cash Flows
For the Month Ended July 31, 2007

Cash flows from operating activities:		
Cash received from customers	$6,928*	
Deduct cash payments for operating expenses	3,755**	
Net cash flows from operating activities		$3,173
Cash flows from investing activities		—
Cash flows from financing activities:		
Cash received from owner as investment	$3,700	
Deduct cash withdrawals by owner	1,000	
Net cash flows from financing activities		2,700
Net increase in cash during year		$5,873
Cash as of July 1, 2007		1,000
Cash as of July 31, 2007		$6,873

*$6,928 = $3,928 + $3,000
**$3,755 = $1,055 + $1,200 + $1,500

Self-Examination Questions

(Answers at End of Chapter)

1. A profit-making business operating as a separate legal entity and in which ownership is divided into shares of stock is known as a:
   A. proprietorship. C. partnership.
   B. service business. D. corporation.

2. The resources owned by a business are called:
   A. assets. C. the accounting equation.
   B. liabilities. D. owner's equity.

3. A listing of a business entity's assets, liabilities, and owner's equity as of a specific date is a(n):
   A. balance sheet.
   B. income statement.
   C. statement of owner's equity.
   D. statement of cash flows.

4. If total assets increased $20,000 during a period and total liabilities increased $12,000 during the same period, the amount and direction (increase or decrease) of the change in owner's equity for that period is a(n):
   A. $32,000 increase. C. $8,000 increase.
   B. $32,000 decrease. D. $8,000 decrease.

5. If revenue was $45,000, expenses were $37,500, and the owner's withdrawals were $10,000, the amount of net income or net loss would be:
   A. $45,000 net income. C. $37,500 net loss.
   B. $7,500 net income. D. $2,500 net loss.

Eye Openers

1. What is the objective of most businesses?
2. What is the difference between a manufacturing business and a service business? Is a restaurant a manufacturing business, a service business, or both?

3. Why are most large companies like Microsoft, PepsiCo, Caterpillar, and AutoZone organized as corporations?
4. Who are normally included as the stakeholders of a business?
5. What is the role of accounting in business?
6. Rebecca Olson is the owner of Aquarius Delivery Service. Recently, Rebecca paid interest of $1,850 on a personal loan of $30,000 that she used to begin the business. Should Aquarius Delivery Service record the interest payment? Explain.
7. On February 3, Dependable Repair Service extended an offer of $80,000 for land that had been priced for sale at $90,000. On March 6, Dependable Repair Service accepted the seller's counteroffer of $88,000. Describe how Dependable Repair Service should record the land.
8. a. Land with an assessed value of $250,000 for property tax purposes is acquired by a business for $375,000. Seven years later, the plot of land has an assessed value of $400,000 and the business receives an offer of $725,000 for it. Should the monetary amount assigned to the land in the business records now be increased?
   b. Assuming that the land acquired in (a) was sold for $725,000, how would the various elements of the accounting equation be affected?
9. Describe the difference between an account receivable and an account payable.
10. A business had revenues of $420,000 and operating expenses of $565,000. Did the business (a) incur a net loss or (b) realize net income?
11. A business had revenues of $919,500 and operating expenses of $738,600. Did the business (a) incur a net loss or (b) realize net income?
12. What particular item of financial or operating data appears on both the income statement and the statement of owner's equity? What item appears on both the balance sheet and the statement of owner's equity? What item appears on both the balance sheet and the statement of cash flows?

Practice Exercises

PE 1-1A
Cost concept
obj. 2

On November 15, Johnson Repair Service extended an offer of $35,000 for land that had been priced for sale at $43,000. On December 8, Johnson Repair Service accepted the seller's counteroffer of $37,000. On December 30, the land was assessed at a value of $50,000 for property tax purposes. On April 1, Johnson Repair Service was offered $60,000 for the land by a national retail chain. At what value should the land be recorded in Johnson Repair Service's records?

PE 1-1B
Cost concept
obj. 2

On February 2, Duck Repair Service extended an offer of $90,000 for land that had been priced for sale at $115,000. On February 16, Duck Repair Service accepted the seller's counteroffer of $100,000. On April 29, the land was assessed at a value of $110,000 for property tax purposes. On August 30, Duck Repair Service was offered $130,000 for the land by a national retail chain. At what value should the land be recorded in Duck Repair Service's records?

PE 1-2A
Accounting equation
obj. 3

Daryl Wallin is the owner and operator of Pima LLC, a motivational consulting business. At the end of its accounting period, December 31, 2007, Pima has assets of $617,000 and liabilities of $382,000. Using the accounting equation, determine the following amounts:

a. Owner's equity, as of December 31, 2007.
b. Owner's equity, as of December 31, 2008, assuming that assets increased by $114,000 and liabilities decreased by $29,000 during 2008.

PE 1-2B
Accounting equation
obj. 3

Kristen Hagan is the owner and operator of You're Cool, a motivational consulting business. At the end of its accounting period, December 31, 2007, You're Cool has assets of $336,000 and liabilities of $172,500. Using the accounting equation, determine the following amounts:

a. Owner's equity, as of December 31, 2007.
b. Owner's equity, as of December 31, 2008, assuming that assets increased by $75,000 and liabilities increased by $15,000 during 2008.

PE 1-3A
Transactions
obj. 4

Mime Delivery Service is owned and operated by Pamela Kolp. The following selected transactions were completed by Mime Delivery Service during October:

1. Received cash from owner as additional investment, $7,500.
2. Paid creditors on account, $815.
3. Billed customers for delivery services on account, $3,250.
4. Received cash from customers on account, $1,150.
5. Paid cash to owner for personal use, $500.

Indicate the effect of each transaction on the accounting equation elements (Assets, Liabilities, Owner's Equity, Drawing, Revenue, and Expense) by listing the numbers identifying the transactions, (1) through (5). Also, indicate the specific item within the accounting equation element that is affected. To illustrate, the answer to (1) is shown below.

(1) Asset (Cash) increases by $7,500; Owner's Equity (Pamela Kolp, Capital) increases by $7,500.

PE 1-3B
Transactions
obj. 4

Quicken Delivery Service is owned and operated by Zoey Tucker. The following selected transactions were completed by Quicken Delivery Service during July:

1. Received cash from owner as additional investment, $9,000.
2. Paid advertising expense, $674.
3. Purchased supplies on account, $280.
4. Billed customers for delivery services on account, $4,800.
5. Received cash from customers on account, $1,150.

Indicate the effect of each transaction on the accounting equation elements (Assets, Liabilities, Owner's Equity, Drawing, Revenue, and Expense) by listing the numbers identifying the transactions, (1) through (5). Also, indicate the specific item within the accounting equation element that is affected. To illustrate, the answer to (1) is shown below.

(1) Asset (Cash) increases by $9,000; Owner's Equity (Zoey Tucker, Capital) increases by $9,000.

PE 1-4A
Income statement
obj. 5

The assets and liabilities of Herat Travel Service at June 30, 2008, the end of the current year, and its revenue and expenses for the year are listed below. The capital of the owner, Lola Stahn, was $75,000 at July 1, 2007, the beginning of the current year.

Accounts payable	$ 15,300	Miscellaneous expense	$ 3,150
Accounts receivable	24,350	Office expense	91,350
Cash	70,800	Supplies	5,350
Fees earned	378,200	Wages expense	181,500
Land	100,000		

Prepare an income statement for the current year ended June 30, 2008.

PE 1-4B
Income statement
obj. 5

The assets and liabilities of Leotard Travel Service at February 28, 2008, the end of the current year, and its revenue and expenses for the year are listed below. The capital of the owner, Harry Thompson, was $190,000 at March 1, 2007, the beginning of the current year.

Accounts payable	$ 21,000	Miscellaneous expense	$ 6,350
Accounts receivable	37,750	Office expense	156,650
Cash	22,700	Supplies	2,550
Fees earned	377,000	Wages expense	225,000
Land	145,000		

Prepare an income statement for the current year ended February 28, 2008.

PE 1-5A
Statement of owner's equity
obj. 5

Using the data for Herat Travel Service shown in Practice Exercise 1-4A, prepare a statement of owner's equity for the current year ended June 30, 2008. Lola Stahn invested an additional $20,000 in the business during the year and withdrew cash of $12,000 for personal use.

PE 1-5B
Statement of owner's equity
obj. 5

Using the data for Leotard Travel Service shown in Practice Exercise 1-4B, prepare a statement of owner's equity for the current year ended February 28, 2008. Harry Thompson invested an additional $18,000 in the business during the year and withdrew cash of $10,000 for personal use.

PE 1-6A
Balance sheet
obj. 5

Using the data for Herat Travel Service shown in Practice Exercise 1-4A and 1-5A, prepare the balance sheet as of June 30, 2008.

PE 1-6B
Balance sheet
obj. 5

Using the data for Leotard Travel Service shown in Practice Exercise 1-4B and 1-5B, prepare the balance sheet as of February 28, 2008.

PE 1-7A
Statement of cash flows
obj. 5

A summary of cash flows for Herat Travel Service for the year ended June 30, 2008, is shown below.

Cash receipts:
Cash received from customers $350,000
Cash received from additional investment of owner   20,000
Cash payments:
Cash paid for operating expenses 270,000
Cash paid for land   60,000
Cash paid to owner for personal use   12,000

The cash balance as of July 1, 2007, was $42,800.
Prepare a statement of cash flows for Herat Travel Service for the year ended June 30, 2008.

PE 1-7B
Statement of cash flows
obj. 5

A summary of cash flows for Leotard Travel Service for the year ended February 28, 2008, is shown below.

Cash receipts:
Cash received from customers $350,000
Cash received from additional investment of owner   18,000
Cash payments:
Cash paid for operating expenses 365,000
Cash paid for land   27,000
Cash paid to owner for personal use   10,000

The cash balance as of March 1, 2007, was $56,700.
Prepare a statement of cash flows for Leotard Travel Service for the year ended February 28, 2008.

Exercises

EX 1-1
Types of businesses
obj. 1

Indicate whether each of the following companies is primarily a service, merchandise, or manufacturing business. If you are unfamiliar with the company, use the Internet to locate the company's home page or use the finance Web site of Yahoo.com.

1. H&R Block
2. eBay Inc.
3. Wal-Mart Stores, Inc.
4. Ford Motor Company
5. Citigroup
6. Boeing
7. First Union Corporation
8. Alcoa Inc.
9. Procter & Gamble
10. FedEx
11. Gap Inc.
12. Hilton Hospitality, Inc.
13. CVS
14. Caterpillar
15. The Dow Chemical Company

EX 1-2
Professional ethics

obj. 1

ETHICS

A fertilizer manufacturing company wants to relocate to Collier County. A 13-year-old report from a fired researcher at the company says the company's product is releasing toxic by-products. The company has suppressed that report. A second report commissioned by the company shows there is no problem with the fertilizer.

Should the company's chief executive officer reveal the context of the unfavorable report in discussions with Collier County representatives? Discuss.

EX 1-3
Business entity concept

obj. 2

Frontier Sports sells hunting and fishing equipment and provides guided hunting and fishing trips. Frontier Sports is owned and operated by Wally Schnee, a well-known sports enthusiast and hunter. Wally's wife, Helen, owns and operates Blue Sky Boutique, a women's clothing store. Wally and Helen have established a trust fund to finance their children's college education. The trust fund is maintained by First Bank in the name of the children, Anna and Conner.

For each of the following transactions, identify which of the entities listed should record the transaction in its records.

Entities

F	Frontier Sports
B	First Bank Trust Fund
S	Blue Sky Boutique
X	None of the above

1. Wally paid a breeder's fee for an English springer spaniel to be used as a hunting guide dog.
2. Helen paid her dues to the YWCA.
3. Helen purchased two dozen spring dresses from a Denver designer for a special spring sale.
4. Helen deposited a $3,500 personal check in the trust fund at First Bank.
5. Wally paid for an advertisement in a hunters' magazine.
6. Helen authorized the trust fund to purchase mutual fund shares.
7. Wally paid for dinner and a movie to celebrate their tenth wedding anniversary.
8. Helen donated several dresses from inventory for a local charity auction for the benefit of a women's abuse shelter.
9. Wally received a cash advance from customers for a guided hunting trip.
10. Wally paid a local doctor for his annual physical, which was required by the workmen's compensation insurance policy carried by Frontier Sports.

EX 1-4
Accounting equation

obj. 3

REAL WORLD

✓ Coca-Cola, $15,935

The total assets and total liabilities of Coca-Cola and PepsiCo are shown below.

	Coca-Cola (in millions)	PepsiCo (in millions)
Assets	$31,327	$27,987
Liabilities	15,392	14,415

Determine the owners' equity of each company.

EX 1-5
Accounting equation

obj. 3

REAL WORLD

✓ eBay, $6,728

The total assets and total liabilities of eBay and Google are shown below.

	eBay (in millions)	Google (in millions)
Assets	$7,991	$3,313
Liabilities	1,263	384

Determine the owners' equity of each company.

EX 1-6
Accounting equation

obj. 3

✓ *a. $300,600*

Determine the missing amount for each of the following:

	Assets	=	Liabilities	+	Owner's Equity
a.	X	=	$85,000	+	$215,600
b.	$93,500	=	X	+	6,150
c.	42,500	=	11,275	+	X

EX 1-7
Accounting equation

objs. 3, 4

✓ *b. $710,000*

Hector Lopez is the owner and operator of Centillion, a motivational consulting business. At the end of its accounting period, December 31, 2007, Centillion has assets of $950,000 and liabilities of $300,000. Using the accounting equation and considering each case independently, determine the following amounts:

a. Hector Lopez, capital, as of December 31, 2007.
b. Hector Lopez, capital, as of December 31, 2008, assuming that assets increased by $150,000 and liabilities increased by $90,000 during 2008.
c. Hector Lopez, capital, as of December 31, 2008, assuming that assets decreased by $75,000 and liabilities increased by $27,000 during 2008.
d. Hector Lopez, capital, as of December 31, 2008, assuming that assets increased by $125,000 and liabilities decreased by $48,000 during 2008.
e. Net income (or net loss) during 2008, assuming that as of December 31, 2008, assets were $1,200,000, liabilities were $195,000, and there were no additional investments or withdrawals.

EX 1-8
Asset, liability, owner's equity items

obj. 3

Indicate whether each of the following is identified with (1) an asset, (2) a liability, or (3) owner's equity:

a. land
b. wages expense
c. accounts payable
d. fees earned
e. supplies
f. cash

EX 1-9
Effect of transactions on accounting equation

obj. 4

Describe how the following business transactions affect the three elements of the accounting equation.

a. Purchased supplies on account.
b. Purchased supplies for cash.
c. Paid for utilities used in the business.
d. Received cash for services performed.
e. Invested cash in business.

EX 1-10
Effect of transactions on accounting equation

obj. 4

✓ *a. (1) increase $70,000*

a. A vacant lot acquired for $75,000 is sold for $145,000 in cash. What is the effect of the sale on the total amount of the seller's (1) assets, (2) liabilities, and (3) owner's equity?
b. Assume that the seller owes $40,000 on a loan for the land. After receiving the $145,000 cash in (a), the seller pays the $40,000 owed. What is the effect of the payment on the total amount of the seller's (1) assets, (2) liabilities, and (3) owner's equity?

EX 1-11
Effect of transactions on owner's equity

obj. 4

Indicate whether each of the following types of transactions will either (a) increase owner's equity or (b) decrease owner's equity:

1. revenues
2. expenses
3. owner's investments
4. owner's withdrawals

EX 1-12
Transactions

obj. 4

The following selected transactions were completed by Pilgrim Delivery Service during July:

1. Received cash from owner as additional investment, $115,000.
2. Received cash for providing delivery services, $58,000.
3. Paid advertising expense, $2,000.
4. Paid creditors on account, $4,800.
5. Billed customers for delivery services on account, $31,250.
6. Purchased supplies for cash, $800.
7. Paid rent for July, $3,000.

(continued)

8. Received cash from customers on account, $10,740.
9. Determined that the cost of supplies on hand was $135; therefore, $665 of supplies had been used during the month.
10. Paid cash to owner for personal use, $1,500.

Indicate the effect of each transaction on the accounting equation by listing the numbers identifying the transactions, (1) through (10), in a column, and inserting at the right of each number the appropriate letter from the following list:

a. Increase in an asset, decrease in another asset.
b. Increase in an asset, increase in a liability.
c. Increase in an asset, increase in owner's equity.
d. Decrease in an asset, decrease in a liability.
e. Decrease in an asset, decrease in owner's equity.

EX 1-13
Nature of transactions
obj. 4

✓ d. $26,500

Otto Egan operates his own catering service. Summary financial data for August are presented in equation form as follows. Each line designated by a number indicates the effect of a transaction on the equation. Each increase and decrease in owner's equity, except transaction (5), affects net income.

		Assets		=	Liabilities +		Owner's Equity			
	Cash +	Supplies +	Land	=	Accounts Payable +	Otto Egan, Capital −	Otto Egan, Drawing +	Fees Earned −	Expenses
Bal.	27,000	3,000	100,000		15,000	115,000			
1.	+45,000							45,000	
2.	−20,000		+20,000						
3.	−16,000								−16,000
4.		+3,000			+ 3,000				
5.	− 5,000						−5,000		
6.	−12,000				−12,000				
7.		−2,500							−2,500
Bal.	19,000	3,500	120,000		6,000	115,000	−5,000	45,000	−18,500

a. Describe each transaction.
b. What is the amount of net decrease in cash during the month?
c. What is the amount of net increase in owner's equity during the month?
d. What is the amount of the net income for the month?
e. How much of the net income for the month was retained in the business?

EX 1-14
Net income and owner's withdrawals
obj. 5

The income statement of a proprietorship for the month of July indicates a net income of $117,800. During the same period, the owner withdrew $150,000 in cash from the business for personal use.

Would it be correct to say that the business incurred a net loss of $32,200 during the month? Discuss.

EX 1-15
Net income and owner's equity for four businesses
obj. 5

✓ Charlie: Net income, $180,000

Four different proprietorships, Alpha, Bravo, Charlie, and Delta, show the same balance sheet data at the beginning and end of a year. These data, exclusive of the amount of owner's equity, are summarized as follows:

	Total Assets	Total Liabilities
Beginning of the year	$1,350,000	$540,000
End of the year	2,160,000	900,000

On the basis of the above data and the following additional information for the year, determine the net income (or loss) of each company for the year. (*Hint:* First determine the amount of increase or decrease in owner's equity during the year.)

Alpha: The owner had made no additional investments in the business and had made no withdrawals from the business.

Bravo: The owner had made no additional investments in the business but had withdrawn $120,000.

Charlie. The owner had made an additional investment of $270,000 but had made no withdrawals.

Delta: The owner had made an additional investment of $270,000 and had withdrawn $120,000.

EX 1-16
Balance sheet items
obj. 5

From the following list of selected items taken from the records of Maya Appliance Service as of a specific date, identify those that would appear on the balance sheet:

1. Accounts Payable
2. Cash
3. Fees Earned
4. Ishmael Maya, Capital
5. Land

6. Supplies
7. Supplies Expense
8. Utilities Expense
9. Wages Expense
10. Wages Payable

EX 1-17
Income statement items
obj. 5

Based on the data presented in Exercise 1-16, identify those items that would appear on the income statement.

EX 1-18
Statement of owner's equity
obj. 5

✓ *Lynn Jepsen, capital, June 30, 2008: $864,250*

Financial information related to Pickerel Company, a proprietorship, for the month ended June 30, 2008, is as follows:

Net income for June	$196,350
Lynn Jepsen's withdrawals during June	15,000
Lynn Jepsen, capital, June 1, 2008	682,900

Prepare a statement of owner's equity for the month ended June 30, 2008.

EX 1-19
Income statement
obj. 5

✓ *Net income: $91,330*

Giblet Services was organized on February 1, 2008. A summary of the revenue and expense transactions for February follows:

Fees earned	$479,280
Wages expense	310,600
Rent expense	60,000
Supplies expense	6,200
Miscellaneous expense	11,150

Prepare an income statement for the month ended February 28.

EX 1-20
Missing amounts from balance sheet and income statement data
obj. 5

✓ *(a) $117,225*

One item is omitted in each of the following summaries of balance sheet and income statement data for the following four different proprietorships:

	Oscar	Papa	Quebec	Romeo
Beginning of the year:				
Assets	$540,000	$125,000	$200,000	(d)
Liabilities	324,000	65,000	152,000	$120,000
End of the year:				
Assets	670,500	175,000	180,000	248,000
Liabilities	292,500	55,000	160,000	136,000
During the year:				
Additional investment in the business	(a)	25,000	20,000	40,000
Withdrawals from the business	36,000	8,000	(c)	60,000
Revenue	177,975	(b)	230,000	112,000
Expenses	97,200	32,000	245,000	128,000

Determine the missing amounts, identifying them by letter. (*Hint:* First determine the amount of increase or decrease in owner's equity during the year.)

EX 1-21
Balance sheets, net income

obj. 5

✓ b. $54,510

Financial information related to the proprietorship of Burst Interiors for March and April 2008 is as follows:

	March 31, 2008	April 30, 2008
Accounts payable	$18,480	$ 19,920
Accounts receivable	40,800	46,950
Gary Deming, capital	?	?
Cash	72,000	122,400
Supplies	3,600	3,000

a. Prepare balance sheets for Burst Interiors as of March 31 and as of April 30, 2008.
b. Determine the amount of net income for April, assuming that the owner made no additional investments or withdrawals during the month.
c. Determine the amount of net income for April, assuming that the owner made no additional investments but withdrew $15,000 during the month.

EX 1-22
Financial statements

obj. 5

REAL WORLD

Each of the following items is shown in the financial statements of Exxon Mobil Corporation. Identify the financial statement (balance sheet or income statement) in which each item would appear.

a. Accounts payable
b. Cash equivalents
c. Crude oil inventory
d. Equipment
e. Exploration expenses
f. Income taxes payable
g. Investments
h. Long-term debt

i.   Marketable securities
j.   Notes and loans payable
k. Notes receivable
l.   Operating expenses
m. Prepaid taxes
n. Sales
o. Selling expenses

EX 1-23
Statement of cash flows

obj. 5

Indicate whether each of the following activities would be reported on the statement of cash flows as (a) an operating activity, (b) an investing activity, or (c) a financing activity:

1. Cash received as owner's investment
2. Cash received from fees earned
3. Cash paid for land
4. Cash paid for expenses

EX 1-24
Statement of cash flows

obj. 5

A summary of cash flows for Webster Consulting Group for the year ended July 31, 2008, is shown below.

Cash receipts:
    Cash received from customers $495,000
    Cash received from additional investment of owner   20,000
Cash payments:
    Cash paid for operating expenses   371,500
    Cash paid for land   40,000
    Cash paid to owner for personal use   9,000

The cash balance as of August 1, 2007, was $46,750.
    Prepare a statement of cash flows for Webster Consulting Group for the year ended July 31, 2008.

EX 1-25
Financial statements

obj. 5

Galaxy Realty, organized October 1, 2008, is owned and operated by Ora Tasker. How many errors can you find in the following financial statements for Galaxy Realty, prepared after its second month of operations?

✓ *Correct amount of*
total assets is $39,200

Galaxy Realty
Income Statement
November 30, 2008

Sales commissions		$103,800
Expenses:		
Office salaries expense	$64,800	
Rent expense	22,000	
Automobile expense	5,000	
Miscellaneous expense	1,600	
Supplies expense	600	
Total expenses		94,000
Net income		$ 29,800

Ora Tasker
Statement of Owner's Equity
November 30, 2007

Ora Tasker, capital, November 1, 2008	$20,800
Less withdrawals during November	4,000
	$16,800
Additional investment during November	5,000
	$21,800
Net income for the month	29,800
Ora Tasker, capital, November 30, 2008	$51,600

Balance Sheet
For the Month Ended November 30, 2008

Assets			Liabilities		
Cash	$ 6,600		Accounts receivable	$28,600	
Accounts payable	7,600		Supplies	4,000	
			Owner's Equity		
			Ora Tasker, capital	51,600	
Total assets	$14,200		Total liabilities and owner's equity	$84,200	

Problems Series A

PR 1-1A
Transactions

obj. 4

✓ *Cash bal. at end of*
June: $24,620

On June 1 of the current year, Doni Gilmore established a business to manage rental property. She completed the following transactions during June:

a. Opened a business bank account with a deposit of $25,000 from personal funds.
b. Purchased supplies (pens, file folders, and copy paper) on account, $1,150.
c. Received cash from fees earned for managing rental property, $4,500.
d. Paid rent on office and equipment for the month, $1,500.
e. Paid creditors on account, $600.
f. Billed customers for fees earned for managing rental property, $2,250.
g. Paid automobile expenses (including rental charges) for month, $400, and miscellaneous expenses, $180.
h. Paid office salaries, $1,200.
i. Determined that the cost of supplies on hand was $380; therefore, the cost of supplies used was $770.
j. Withdrew cash for personal use, $1,000.

Instructions
1. Indicate the effect of each transaction and the balances after each transaction, using the following tabular headings:

(continued)

Assets			= Liabilities +			Owner's Equity						
Cash	+ Accounts Receivable	+ Supplies	= Accounts Payable	+ Doni Gilmore, Capital	− Doni Gilmore, Drawing	+ Fees Earned	− Rent Expense	− Salaries Expense	− Supplies Expense	− Auto Expense	− Misc. Expense

2. ▬▬▶ Briefly explain why the owner's investment and revenues increased owner's equity, while withdrawals and expenses decreased owner's equity.

PR 1-2A
Financial statements

obj. 5

✓ *1. Net income: $137,500*

Following are the amounts of the assets and liabilities of Pedigree Travel Agency at December 31, 2008, the end of the current year, and its revenue and expenses for the year. The capital of Shiann Ott, owner, was $115,000 on January 1, 2008, the beginning of the current year. During the current year, Shiann withdrew $40,000.

Accounts payable	$ 12,500	Rent expense	$25,000
Accounts receivable	42,300	Supplies	2,700
Cash	180,000	Supplies expense	2,800
Fees earned	250,000	Utilities expense	18,200
Miscellaneous expense	1,500	Wages expense	65,000

Instructions
1. Prepare an income statement for the current year ended December 31, 2008.
2. Prepare a statement of owner's equity for the current year ended December 31, 2008.
3. Prepare a balance sheet as of December 31, 2008.

PR 1-3A
Financial statements

obj. 5

✓ *1. Net income: $23,665*

Barry Kimm established Mariner Financial Services on January 1, 2008. Mariner Financial Services offers financial planning advice to its clients. The effect of each transaction and the balances after each transaction for January are shown at the bottom of the page.

Instructions
1. Prepare an income statement for the month ended January 31, 2008.
2. Prepare a statement of owner's equity for the month ended January 31, 2008.
3. Prepare a balance sheet as of January 31, 2008.
4. (Optional). Prepare a statement of cash flows for the month ending January 31, 2008.

	Assets			= Liabilities +			Owner's Equity						
	Cash	+ Accounts Receivable	+ Supplies	= Accounts Payable	+ Barry Kimm, Capital	− Barry Kimm, Drawing	+ Fees Earned	− Salaries Expense	− Rent Expense	− Auto Expense	− Supplies Expense	− Misc. Expense
a.	+25,000				+25,000							
b.			+1,180	+1,180								
Bal.	25,000		1,180	1,180	25,000							
c.	− 580			− 580								
Bal.	24,420		1,180	600	25,000							
d.	+42,000						+42,000					
Bal.	66,420		1,180	600	25,000		42,000					
e.	− 7,500								−7,500			
Bal.	58,920		1,180	600	25,000		42,000		−7,500			
f.	− 5,780									−4,500		−1,280
Bal.	53,140		1,180	600	25,000		42,000		−7,500	−4,500		−1,280
g.	−15,000							−15,000				
Bal.	38,140		1,180	600	25,000		42,000	−15,000	−7,500	−4,500		−1,280
h.			− 455								−455	
Bal.	38,140		725	600	25,000		42,000	−15,000	−7,500	−4,500	−455	−1,280
i.		+10,400					+10,400					
Bal.	38,140	10,400	725	600	25,000		52,400	−15,000	−7,500	−4,500	−455	−1,280
j.	− 9,000					−9,000						
Bal.	29,140	10,400	725	600	25,000	−9,000	52,400	−15,000	−7,500	−4,500	−455	−1,280

PR 1-4A
Transactions; financial statements
objs. 4, 5

✓2. Net income: $16,850

On March 1, 2008, Ginny Tyler established Seltzer Realty. Ginny completed the following transactions during the month of March:

a. Opened a business bank account with a deposit of $30,000 from personal funds.
b. Purchased supplies (pens, file folders, paper, etc.) on account, $2,650.
c. Paid creditor on account, $1,500.
d. Earned sales commissions, receiving cash, $36,750.
e. Paid rent on office and equipment for the month, $5,200.
f. Withdrew cash for personal use, $8,000.
g. Paid automobile expenses (including rental charge) for month, $2,500, and miscellaneous expenses, $1,200.
h. Paid office salaries, $9,250.
i. Determined that the cost of supplies on hand was $900; therefore, the cost of supplies used was $1,750.

Instructions
1. Indicate the effect of each transaction and the balances after each transaction, using the following tabular headings:

Assets		=	Liabilities	+				Owner's Equity				
Cash	+ Supplies	=	Accounts Payable	+	Ginny Tyler, Capital	− Ginny Tyler, Drawing	+ Sales Commissions	− Office Salaries Expense	− Rent Expense	− Auto Expense	− Supplies Expense	− Misc. Expense

2. Prepare an income statement for March, a statement of owner's equity for March, and a balance sheet as of March 31.

PR 1-5A
Transactions; financial statements
objs. 4, 5

✓3. Net Income: $9,445

Argon Dry Cleaners is owned and operated by Kerry Ulman. A building and equipment are currently being rented, pending expansion to new facilities. The actual work of dry cleaning is done by another company at wholesale rates. The assets and the liabilities of the business on July 1, 2008, are as follows: Cash, $8,500; Accounts Receivable, $15,500; Supplies, $1,600; Land, $18,000; Accounts Payable, $5,200. Business transactions during July are summarized as follows:

a. Kerry Ulman invested additional cash in the business with a deposit of $30,000 in the business bank account.
b. Paid $22,000 for the purchase of land as a future building site.
c. Received cash from cash customers for dry cleaning sales, $17,900.
d. Paid rent for the month, $3,000.
e. Purchased supplies on account, $1,550.
f. Paid creditors on account, $4,950.
g. Charged customers for dry cleaning sales on account, $12,350.
h. Received monthly invoice for dry cleaning expense for July (to be paid on August 10), $7,880.
i. Paid the following: wages expense, $5,100; truck expense, $1,200; utilities expense, $800; miscellaneous expense, $950.
j. Received cash from customers on account, $13,200.
k. Determined that the cost of supplies on hand was $1,275; therefore, the cost of supplies used during the month was $1,875.
l. Withdrew $5,000 cash for personal use.

Instructions
1. Determine the amount of Kerry Ulman's capital as of July 1 of the current year.
2. State the assets, liabilities, and owner's equity as of July 1 in equation form similar to that shown in this chapter. In tabular form below the equation, indicate increases and decreases resulting from each transaction and the new balances after each transaction.
3. Prepare an income statement for July, a statement of owner's equity for July, and a balance sheet as of July 31.
4. (Optional). Prepare a statement of cash flows for July.

PR 1-6A
*Missing amounts from
financial statements*

obj. 5

✓ k. $120,000

The financial statements at the end of Cayenne Realty's first month of operations are shown below.

Cayenne Realty
Income Statement
For the Month Ended June 30, 2008

Fees earned		$ (a)
Expenses:		
Wages expense	$34,000	
Rent expense	12,800	
Supplies expense	(b)	
Utilities expense	7,200	
Miscellaneous expense	4,400	
Total expenses		70,400
Net income		$49,600

Cayenne Realty
Statement of Owner's Equity
For the Month Ended June 30, 2008

Andrea Merkel, capital, June 1, 2008		$ (c)
Investment on June 1, 2008	$160,000	
Net income for June	(d)	
	(e)	
Less withdrawals	24,000	
Increase in owner's equity		(f)
Andrea Merkel, capital, June 30, 2008		(g)

Cayenne Realty
Balance Sheet
June 30, 2008

Assets		Liabilities	
Cash	$ 17,800	Accounts payable	$ 6,400
Supplies	14,200	**Owner's Equity**	
Land	160,000	Andrea Merkel, capital	(i)
		Total liabilities and	
Total assets	(h)	owner's equity	(j)

Cayenne Realty
Statement of Cash Flows
For the Month Ended June 30, 2008

Cash flows from operating activities:		
Cash received from customers	$ (k)	
Deduct cash payments for expenses and		
payments to creditors	78,200	
Net cash flow from operating activities		$ (l)
Cash flows from investing activities:		
Cash payments for acquisition of land		(m)
Cash flows from financing activities:		
Cash received as owner's investment	(n)	
Deduct cash withdrawal by owner	(o)	
Net cash flow from financing activities		(p)
Net cash flow and June 30, 2008, cash balance		(q)

Instructions

By analyzing the interrelationships among the four financial statements, determine the proper amounts for (a) through (q).

Problems Series B

PR 1-1B
Transactions

obj. 4

✓ *Cash bal. at end of March: $37,550*

Ana Urbin established an insurance agency on March 1 of the current year and completed the following transactions during March:

a. Opened a business bank account with a deposit of $40,000 from personal funds.
b. Purchased supplies on account, $1,500.
c. Paid creditors on account, $800.
d. Received cash from fees earned on insurance commissions, $7,250.
e. Paid rent on office and equipment for the month, $2,500.
f. Paid automobile expenses for month, $1,000, and miscellaneous expenses, $400.
g. Paid office salaries, $2,000.
h. Determined that the cost of supplies on hand was $400; therefore, the cost of supplies used was $1,100.
i. Billed insurance companies for sales commissions earned, $9,350.
j. Withdrew cash for personal use, $3,000.

Instructions

1. Indicate the effect of each transaction and the balances after each transaction, using the following tabular headings:

Assets			=	Liabilities	+			Owner's Equity					
Cash	+ Accounts Receivable	+ Supplies	=	Accounts Payable	+	Ana Urbin, Capital	− Ana Urbin, Drawing	+ Fees Earned	− Rent Expense	− Salaries Expense	− Supplies Expense	− Auto Expense	− Misc. Expense

2. ▭━━▷ Briefly explain why the owner's investment and revenues increased owner's equity, while withdrawals and expenses decreased owner's equity.

PR 1-2B
Financial statements

obj. 5

✓ *1. Net income: $130,000*

The amounts of the assets and liabilities of Abyss Travel Service at June 30, 2008, the end of the current year, and its revenue and expenses for the year are listed below. The capital of Megan Koch, owner, was $60,000 at July 1, 2007, the beginning of the current year, and the owner withdrew $50,000 during the current year.

Accounts payable	$ 12,500	Supplies	$ 4,250
Accounts receivable	48,750	Supplies expense	8,250
Cash	99,500	Taxes expense	6,400
Fees earned	375,000	Utilities expense	31,200
Miscellaneous expense	3,150	Wages expense	145,400
Rent expense	50,600		

Instructions

1. Prepare an income statement for the current year ended June 30, 2008.
2. Prepare a statement of owner's equity for the current year ended June 30, 2008.
3. Prepare a balance sheet as of June 30, 2008.

PR 1-3B
Financial statements

obj. 5

✓ *1. Net income: $14,875*

Kelly Cassidy established Firefly Computer Services on May 1, 2008. The effect of each transaction and the balances after each transaction for May are shown at the top of the following page.

Instructions

1. Prepare an income statement for the month ended May 31, 2008.
2. Prepare a statement of owner's equity for the month ended May 31, 2008.
3. Prepare a balance sheet as of May 31, 2008.
4. (Optional). Prepare a statement of cash flows for the month ending May 31, 2008.

(continued)

	Assets			=	Liabilities +		Owner's Equity							
	Cash	+ Accounts Receivable	+ Supplies	=	Accounts Payable	+ Kelly Cassidy, Capital	− Kelly Cassidy, Drawing	+ Fees Earned	− Salaries Expense	− Rent Expense	− Auto Expense	− Supplies Expense	− Misc. Expense
a.	+25,000					+25,000							
b.			+3,600		+3,600								
Bal.	25,000		3,600		3,600	25,000							
c.	+22,500							+22,500					
Bal.	47,500		3,600		3,600	25,000		22,500					
d.	− 9,000									−9,000			
Bal.	38,500		3,600		3,600	25,000		22,500		−9,000			
e.	− 1,250				−1,250								
Bal.	37,250		3,600		2,350	25,000		22,500		−9,000			
f.		+18,750						+18,750					
Bal.	37,250	18,750	3,600		2,350	25,000		41,250		−9,000			
g.	− 5,750										−3,875		−1,875
Bal.	31,500	18,750	3,600		2,350	25,000		41,250		−9,000	−3,875		−1,875
h.	−10,000								−10,000				
Bal.	21,500	18,750	3,600		2,350	25,000		41,250	−10,000	−9,000	−3,875		−1,875
i.			−1,625									−1,625	
Bal.	21,500	18,750	1,975		2,350	25,000		41,250	−10,000	−9,000	−3,875	−1,625	−1,875
j.	− 5,000						−5,000						
Bal.	16,500	18,750	1,975		2,350	25,000	−5,000	41,250	−10,000	−9,000	−3,875	−1,625	−1,875

PR 1-4B
Transactions; financial statements

objs. 4, 5

✓ *2. Net income: $12,990*

On April 1, 2008, Britt Quinn established Uptown Realty. Britt completed the following transactions during the month of April:

a. Opened a business bank account with a deposit of $30,000 from personal funds.
b. Paid rent on office and equipment for the month, $2,200.
c. Paid automobile expenses (including rental charge) for month, $1,200, and miscellaneous expenses, $650.
d. Purchased supplies (pens, file folders, and copy paper) on account, $200.
e. Earned sales commissions, receiving cash, $20,800.
f. Paid creditor on account, $150.
g. Paid office salaries, $3,600.
h. Withdrew cash for personal use, $1,500.
i. Determined that the cost of supplies on hand was $40; therefore, the cost of supplies used was $160.

Instructions

1. Indicate the effect of each transaction and the balances after each transaction, using the following tabular headings:

Assets		=	Liabilities +		Owner's Equity						
Cash	+ Supplies	=	Accounts Payable	+ Britt Quinn, Capital	− Britt Quinn, Drawing	+ Sales Commissions	− Office Salaries Expense	− Rent Expense	− Auto Expense	− Supplies Expense	− Misc. Expense

2. Prepare an income statement for April, a statement of owner's equity for April, and a balance sheet as of April 30.

PR 1-5B
Transactions; financial statements

objs. 4, 5

✓ *3. Net income: $2,320*

Skivvy Dry Cleaners is owned and operated by Jean Potts. A building and equipment are currently being rented, pending expansion to new facilities. The actual work of dry cleaning is done by another company at wholesale rates. The assets and the liabilities of the business on November 1, 2008, are as follows: Cash, $17,200; Accounts Receivable, $19,000; Supplies, $3,750; Land, $30,000; Accounts Payable, $8,200. Business transactions during November are summarized as follows:

a. Jean Potts invested additional cash in the business with a deposit of $50,000 in the business bank account.

b. Purchased land for use as a parking lot, paying cash of $45,000.

c. Paid rent for the month, $4,500.

d. Charged customers for dry cleaning sales on account, $15,250.

e. Paid creditors on account, $5,800.

f. Purchased supplies on account, $3,200.

g. Received cash from cash customers for dry cleaning sales, $22,900.

h. Received cash from customers on account, $17,250.

i. Received monthly invoice for dry cleaning expense for November (to be paid on December 10), $16,380.

j. Paid the following: wages expense, $6,200; truck expense, $1,875; utilities expense, $1,575; miscellaneous expense, $850.

k. Determined that the cost of supplies on hand was $2,500; therefore, the cost of supplies used during the month was $4,450.

l. Withdrew $6,000 for personal use.

Instructions

1. Determine the amount of Jean Potts's capital as of November 1.

2. State the assets, liabilities, and owner's equity as of November 1 in equation form similar to that shown in this chapter. In tabular form below the equation, indicate increases and decreases resulting from each transaction and the new balances after each transaction.

3. Prepare an income statement for November, a statement of owner's equity for November, and a balance sheet as of November 30.

4. (Optional). Prepare a statement of cash flows for November.

PR 1-6B
Missing amounts from financial statements

obj. 5

✓ i. $60,660

The financial statements at the end of Harp Realty's first month of operations are shown below and on the next page.

Harp Realty
Income Statement
For the Month Ended April 30, 2008

Fees earned		$28,200
Expenses:		
Wages expense	$ (a)	
Rent expense	2,880	
Supplies expense	2,400	
Utilities expense	1,620	
Miscellaneous expense	990	
Total expenses		14,340
Net income		(b)

Harp Realty
Statement of Owner's Equity
For the Month Ended April 30, 2008

Iris Sigrist, capital, April 1, 2008		$ (c)
Investment on April 1, 2008	$ (d)	
Net income for April	(e)	
	(f)	
Less withdrawals	(g)	
Increase in owner's equity		(h)
Iris Sigrist, capital, April 30, 2008		(i)

Harp Realty
Balance Sheet
April 30, 2008

Assets		Liabilities	
Cash	$17,700	Accounts payable	$1,440
Supplies	1,200	**Owner's Equity**	
Land	(j)	Iris Sigrist, capital	(l)
		Total liabilities and	
Total assets	(k)	owner's equity	(m)

(continued)

Harp Realty
Statement of Cash Flows
For the Month Ended April 30, 2008

Cash flows from operating activities:			
Cash received from customers		$ (n)	
Deduct cash payments for expenses and			
payments to creditors		14,100	
Net cash flow from operating activities			$ (o)
Cash flows from investing activities:			
Cash payments for acquisition of land			(43,200)
Cash flows from financing activities:			
Cash received as owner's investment		$54,000	
Deduct cash withdrawal by owner		7,200	
Net cash flow from financing activities			(p)
Net cash flow and April 30, 2008, cash balance			(q)

Instructions

By analyzing the interrelationships among the four financial statements, determine the proper amounts for (a) through (q).

Continuing Problem

✓ *2. Net income: $730*

Kris Payne enjoys listening to all types of music and owns countless CDs and tapes. Over the years, Kris has gained a local reputation for knowledge of music from classical to rap and the ability to put together sets of recordings that appeal to all ages.

During the last several months, Kris served as a guest disc jockey on a local radio station. In addition, Kris has entertained at several friends' parties as the host deejay.

On April 1, 2008, Kris established a proprietorship known as Dancin Music. Using an extensive collection of CDs and tapes, Kris will serve as a disc jockey on a fee basis for weddings, college parties, and other events. During April, Kris entered into the following transactions:

April 1. Deposited $10,000 in a checking account in the name of Dancin Music.

2. Received $2,500 from a local radio station for serving as the guest disc jockey for April.

2. Agreed to share office space with a local real estate agency, Cash Realty. Dancin Music will pay one-fourth of the rent. In addition, Dancin Music agreed to pay a portion of the salary of the receptionist and to pay one-fourth of the utilities. Paid $1,000 for the rent of the office.

4. Purchased supplies (blank CDs, poster board, extension cords, etc.) from Richt Office Supply Co. for $350. Agreed to pay $100 within 10 days and the remainder by May 3, 2008.

6. Paid $750 to a local radio station to advertise the services of Dancin Music twice daily for two weeks.

8. Paid $800 to a local electronics store for renting digital recording equipment.

12. Paid $300 (music expense) to Rocket Music for the use of its current music demos to make various music sets.

13. Paid Richt Office Supply Co. $100 on account.

16. Received $350 from a dentist for providing two music sets for the dentist to play for her patients.

22. Served as disc jockey for a wedding party. The father of the bride agreed to pay $1,350 the 1st of May.

25. Received $500 from a friend for serving as the disc jockey for a cancer charity ball hosted by the local hospital.

29. Paid $240 (music expense) to Score Music for the use of its library of music demos.

30. Received $1,000 for serving as disc jockey for a local club's monthly dance.

30. Paid Cash Realty $400 for Dancin Music's share of the receptionist's salary for April.

30. Paid Cash Realty $350 for Dancin Music's share of the utilities for April.
30. Determined that the cost of supplies on hand is $170. Therefore, the cost of supplies used during the month was $180.
30. Paid for miscellaneous expenses, $150.
30. Paid $800 royalties (music expense) to Federated Clearing for use of various artists' music during the month.
30. Withdrew $300 of cash from Dancin Music for personal use.

Instructions

1. Indicate the effect of each transaction and the balances after each transaction, using the following tabular headings:

Assets			=	Liabilities +					Owner's Equity							
Cash	+ Accounts Receivable	+ Supplies	=	Accounts Payable	+ Kris Payne, Capital	− Kris Payne, Drawing	+ Fees Earned	− Music Expense	− Office Rent Expense	− Equipment Rent Expense	− Advertising Expense	− Wages Expense	− Utilities Expense	− Supplies Expense	− Misc. Expense

2. Prepare an income statement for Dancin Music for the month ended April 30, 2008.
3. Prepare a statement of owner's equity for Dancin Music for the month ended April 30, 2008.
4. Prepare a balance sheet for Dancin Music as of April 30, 2008.

Special Activities

SA 1-1
Ethics and professional conduct in business

Group Project

ETHICS

Chester Hunter, president of Jackrabbit Enterprises, applied for a $250,000 loan from Belgrade National Bank. The bank requested financial statements from Jackrabbit Enterprises as a basis for granting the loan. Chester has told his accountant to provide the bank with a balance sheet. Chester has decided to omit the other financial statements because there was a net loss during the past year.

In groups of three or four, discuss the following questions:

1. Is Chester behaving in a professional manner by omitting some of the financial statements?
2. a. What types of information about their businesses would owners be willing to provide bankers? What types of information would owners not be willing to provide?
   b. What types of information about a business would bankers want before extending a loan?
   c. What common interests are shared by bankers and business owners?

SA 1-2
Net income

On July 7, 2007, Dr. Jennifer Dejong established Second Opinion, a medical practice organized as a proprietorship. The following conversation occurred the following January between Dr. Dejong and a former medical school classmate, Dr. James Tomlin, at an American Medical Association convention in Paris.

Dr. Tomlin: Jennifer, good to see you again. Why didn't you call when you were in Chicago? We could have had dinner together.
Dr. Dejong: Actually, I never made it to Chicago this year. My husband and kids went up to our Aspen condo twice, but I got stuck in Boston. I opened a new consulting practice this July and haven't had any time for myself since.
Dr. Tomlin: I heard about it . . . Second . . . something . . . right?
Dr. Dejong: Yes, Second Opinion. My husband chose the name.
Dr. Tomlin: I've thought about doing something like that. Are you making any money? I mean, is it worth your time?
Dr. Dejong: You wouldn't believe it. I started by opening a bank account with $50,000, and my December bank statement has a balance of $140,000. Not bad for six months—all pure profit.
Dr. Tomlin: Maybe I'll try it in Chicago! Let's have breakfast together tomorrow and you can fill me in on the details.

Comment on Dr. Dejong's statement that the difference between the opening bank balance ($50,000) and the December statement balance ($140,000) is pure profit.

SA 1-3
Transactions and financial statements

Kathy Hoss, a junior in college, has been seeking ways to earn extra spending money. As an active sports enthusiast, Kathy plays tennis regularly at the Racquet Club, where her family has a membership. The president of the club recently approached Kathy with the proposal that she manage the club's tennis courts. Kathy's primary duty would be to supervise the operation of the club's four indoor and six outdoor courts, including court reservations.

In return for her services, the club would pay Kathy $150 per week, plus Kathy could keep whatever she earned from lessons and the fees from the use of the ball machine. The club and Kathy agreed to a one-month trial, after which both would consider an arrangement for the remaining two years of Kathy's college career. On this basis, Kathy organized Advantage. During June 2007, Kathy managed the tennis courts and entered into the following transactions:

a. Opened a business account by depositing $1,500.
b. Paid $250 for tennis supplies (practice tennis balls, etc.).
c. Paid $160 for the rental of videotape equipment to be used in offering lessons during June.
d. Arranged for the rental of two ball machines during June for $200. Paid $140 in advance, with the remaining $60 due July 1.
e. Received $1,600 for lessons given during June.
f. Received $350 in fees from the use of the ball machines during June.
g. Paid $600 for salaries of part-time employees who answered the telephone and took reservations while Kathy was giving lessons.
h. Paid $150 for miscellaneous expenses.
i. Received $600 from the club for managing the tennis courts during June.
j. Determined that the cost of supplies on hand at the end of the month totaled $150; therefore, the cost of supplies used was $100.
k. Withdrew $500 for personal use on June 30.

As a friend and accounting student, you have been asked by Kathy to aid her in assessing the venture.

1. Indicate the effect of each transaction and the balances after each transaction, using the following tabular headings:

Assets		= Liabilities +		Owner's Equity					
Cash + Supplies =		Accounts Payable +	Kathy Hoss, Capital –	Kathy Hoss, Drawing +	Service Revenue –	Salary Expense –	Rent Expense –	Supplies Expense –	Misc. Expense

2. Prepare an income statement for June.
3. Prepare a statement of owner's equity for June.
4. Prepare a balance sheet as of June 30.
5. a. Assume that Kathy Hoss could earn $8 per hour working 30 hours a week as a waitress. Evaluate which of the two alternatives, working as a waitress or operating Advantage, would provide Kathy with the most income per month.
   b. Discuss any other factors that you believe Kathy should consider before discussing a long-term arrangement with the Racquet Club.

SA 1-4
Certification requirements for accountants

By satisfying certain specific requirements, accountants may become certified as public accountants (CPAs), management accountants (CMAs), or internal auditors (CIAs). Find the certification requirements for one of these accounting groups by accessing the appropriate Internet site listed below.

Internet Project

Site	Description
http://www.ais-cpa.com	This site lists the address and/or Internet link for each state's board of accountancy. Find your state's requirements.
http://www.imanet.org	This site lists the requirements for becoming a CMA.
http://www.theiia.org	This site lists the requirements for becoming a CIA.

SA 1-5
Cash flows

REAL WORLD

Amazon.com, an Internet retailer, was incorporated and began operation in the mid-90s. On the statement of cash flows, would you expect Amazon.com's net cash flows from operating, investing, and financing activities to be positive or negative for its first three years of operations? Use the following format for your answers, and briefly explain your logic.

	First Year	Second Year	Third Year
Net cash flows from operating activities	negative		
Net cash flows from investing activities			
Net cash flows from financing activities			

SA 1-6
Financial analysis of Enron Corporation

Internet Project

REAL WORLD

The now defunct Enron Corporation, once headquartered in Houston, Texas, provided products and services for natural gas, electricity, and communications to wholesale and retail customers. Enron's operations were conducted through a variety of subsidiaries and affiliates that involved transporting gas through pipelines, transmitting electricity, and managing energy commodities. The following data were taken from Enron's financial statements.

	In millions
Total revenues	$100,789
Total costs and expenses	98,836
Operating income	1,953
Net income	979
Total assets	65,503
Total liabilities	54,033
Total owners' equity	11,470
Net cash flows from operating activities	4,779
Net cash flows from investing activities	(4,264)
Net cash flows from financing activities	571
Net increase in cash	1,086

The market price of Enron's stock was approximately $83 per share when the prior financial statement data were taken. However, eventually Enron's stock was selling for $0.22 per share. Review the preceding financial statement data and search the Internet for articles on Enron Corporation. Briefly explain why Enron's stock dropped so dramatically.

Answers to Self-Examination Questions

1. **D** A corporation, organized in accordance with state or federal statutes, is a separate legal entity in which ownership is divided into shares of stock (answer D). A proprietorship (answer A) is an unincorporated business owned by one individual. A service business (answer B) provides services to its customers. It can be organized as a proprietorship, partnership, corporation, or limited liability company. A partnership (answer C) is an unincorporated business owned by two or more individuals.

2. **A** The resources owned by a business are called assets (answer A). The debts of the business are called liabilities (answer B), and the equity of the owners is called owner's equity (answer D). The relationship between assets, liabilities, and owner's equity is expressed as the accounting equation (answer C).

3. **A** The balance sheet is a listing of the assets, liabilities, and owner's equity of a business at a specific date (answer A). The income statement (answer B) is a summary of the revenue and expenses of a business for a specific period of time. The statement of owner's equity (answer C) summarizes the changes in owner's

equity for a proprietorship or partnership during a specific period of time. The statement of cash flows (answer D) summarizes the cash receipts and cash payments for a specific period of time.

4. **C** The accounting equation is:

Assets = Liabilities + Owner's Equity

Therefore, if assets increased by $20,000 and liabilities increased by $12,000, owner's equity must have increased by $8,000 (answer C), as indicated in the following computation:

Assets	= Liabilities + Owner's Equity
+$20,000	= +$12,000 + Owner's Equity
+$20,000 − $12,000 =	Owner's Equity
$8,000	= Owner's Equity

5. **B** Net income is the excess of revenue over expenses, or $7,500 (answer B). If expenses exceed revenue, the difference is a net loss. Withdrawals by the owner are the opposite of the owner's investing in the business and do not affect the amount of net income or net loss.

chapter
2

Analyzing Transactions

© BODYWEDGE 21/PRNEWSFOTO (AP TOPIC GALLERY)

objectives

After studying this chapter, you should be able to:

1. **Describe the characteristics of an account and record transactions using a chart of accounts and journal.**

2. **Describe and illustrate the posting of journal entries to accounts.**

3. **Prepare an unadjusted trial balance and explain how it can be used to discover errors.**

4. **Discover and correct errors in recording transactions.**

Gold's Gym International, Inc.

You can organize your digital music within your MP3 player or IPod® according to various playlists, according to your favorite songs, genre, artist, or album. Your playlists allow you to quickly retrieve music for listening. Computer files are organized within folders for the same reason. Information, like music or digital files, is organized into categories to simplify retrieval and reporting. In the same way that you organize your digital information, a business also needs to organize its transactions. For example, when you shop at Wal-Mart or Target, or buy groceries at Kroger or SUPERVALU, you enter into a transaction that is processed and recorded by the business. A company such as Gold's Gym, the largest co-ed gym chain in the world, must also process, record, and summarize its transactions. For example, Gold's would want to record all its cash transactions so that they can be summarized as a single category, called "cash." This is much the same way you would summarize the cash transactions in the check register of your checkbook.

In Chapter 1, we analyzed and recorded this kind of information by using the accounting equation, Assets = Liabilities + Owner's Equity. However, such a format is not practical for most businesses, and in this chapter we will study more efficient methods of recording transactions. We will conclude this chapter by discussing how accounting errors may occur and how they may be detected and corrected by the accounting process.

Using Accounts to Record Transactions

In Chapter 1, we recorded the November transactions for NetSolutions using the accounting equation format shown in Exhibit 1. However, this format is not efficient or practical for companies that have to record and summarize thousands or millions of transactions daily. As a result, accounting systems are designed to show the increases and decreases in each financial statement item as a separate record. This record is called an **account**.

To illustrate, the Cash column of Exhibit 1 records the increases and decreases in cash. Likewise, the other columns in Exhibit 1 record the increases and decreases in Supplies; Land; Accounts Payable; Chris Clark, Capital; Chris Clark, Drawing; Fees Earned; Wages Expense; Rent Expense; Supplies Expense; Utilities Expense; and Miscellaneous Expense. As we illustrate next, each of these columns can be organized into a separate account that more efficiently records and summarizes transactions.

An account, in its simplest form, has three parts. First, each account has a title, which is the name of the item recorded in the account. Second, each account has a space for recording increases in the amount of the item. Third, each account has a space for recording decreases in the amount of the item. The account form presented below is called a **T account** because it resembles the letter T. The left side of the account is called the *debit* side, and the right side is called the *credit* side.[1]

Title	
Left side	Right side
debit	*credit*

---

[1] The terms *debit* and *credit* are derived from the Latin *debere* and *credere*.

EXHIBIT 1   NetSolutions November Transactions   @netsolutions

	Assets			= Liabilities +	Owner's Equity							
	Cash	+ Supp.	+ Land	= Accounts Payable +	Chris Clark, Capital −	Chris Clark, Drawing +	Fees Earned −	Wages Exp. −	Rent Exp. −	Supplies Exp. −	Utilities Exp. −	Misc. Exp.
a.	+25,000				+25,000							
b.	−20,000		+20,000									
Bal.	5,000		20,000		25,000							
c.		+1,350		+1,350								
Bal.	5,000	1,350	20,000	1,350	25,000							
d.	+ 7,500						+7,500					
Bal.	12,500	1,350	20,000	1,350	25,000		7,500					
e.	− 3,650							−2,125	−800		−450	−275
Bal.	8,850	1,350	20,000	1,350	25,000		7,500	−2,125	−800		−450	−275
f.	− 950			− 950								
Bal.	7,900	1,350	20,000	400	25,000		7,500	−2,125	−800		−450	−275
g.		− 800								−800		
Bal.	7,900	550	20,000	400	25,000		7,500	−2,125	−800	−800	−450	−275
h.	− 2,000					−2,000						
Bal.	5,900	550	20,000	400	25,000	−2,000	7,500	−2,125	−800	−800	−450	−275

> Amounts entered on the left side of an account are debits, and amounts entered on the right side of an account are credits.

Amounts entered on the left side of an account, regardless of the account title, are called **debits** to the account. When debits are entered in an account, the account is said to be *debited*. Amounts entered on the right side of an account are called **credits**, and the account is said to be *credited*. Debits and credits are sometimes abbreviated as *Dr.* and *Cr.*

The cash account shown below illustrates how NetSolutions' November cash transactions shown in the first column of Exhibit 1 would be recorded in an account. Transactions involving receipts of cash are listed on the debit side of the account. For example, the receipt of $25,000 from Chris Clark in transaction (a) is entered on the debit side of the account. The letter or date of the transaction is also entered into the account. This is done so that if any questions later arise related to the entry, the entry can be traced back to the underlying transaction data. The transactions involving cash payments are listed on the credit side. For example, the payment of $20,000 to purchase land in transaction (b) is entered on the credit side of the account.

If at any time the total of the cash receipts is needed, the entries on the debit side of the account may be added. For NetSolutions, the total receipts is $32,500 ($25,000 + $7,500). Likewise, the total cash payments of $26,600 ($20,000 + $3,650 + $950 + $2,000) may be determined by adding the entries on the credit side of the account. Subtracting the smaller sum from the larger, $32,500 − $26,600, identifies the amount of cash on hand, $5,900. This amount is called the **balance of the account** and is inserted in the

REAL WORLD

Many times when accountants analyze complex transactions, they use T accounts to simplify the thought process. In the same way, you will find T accounts a useful device in this and later accounting courses.

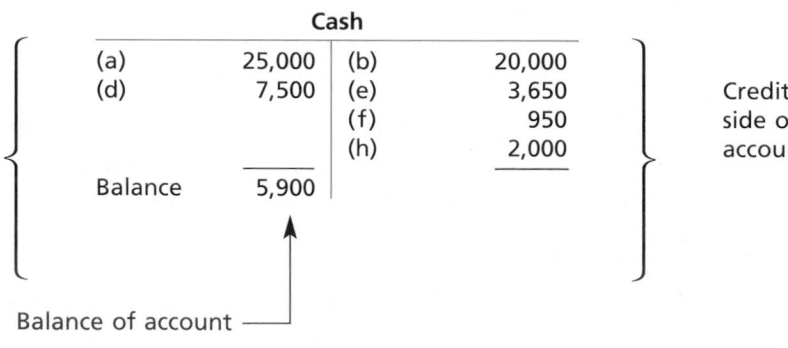

		Cash			
Debit side of account	(a)	25,000	(b)	20,000	Credit side of account
	(d)	7,500	(e)	3,650	
			(f)	950	
			(h)	2,000	
	Balance	5,900			

Balance of account

account, in the debit column. In this way, the balance is identified as a debit balance.[2] This balance is reported on the balance sheet for NetSolutions as of November 30, 2007, shown in Exhibit 6 of Chapter 1. Each of the columns in Exhibit 1 can be converted into an account form in a similar manner as was done for the cash column of Exhibit 1. We illustrate each of these accounts later in this chapter.

CHART OF ACCOUNTS

A group of accounts for a business entity is called a **ledger**. A list of the accounts in the ledger is called a **chart of accounts**. The accounts are normally listed in the order in which they appear in the financial statements. The balance sheet accounts are usually listed first, in the order of assets, liabilities, and owner's equity. The income statement accounts are then listed in the order of revenues and expenses. Each of these major account classifications is briefly described below.

Assets are resources owned by the business entity. These resources can be physical items, such as cash and supplies, or intangibles that have value, such as patent rights. Some other examples of assets include accounts receivable, prepaid expenses (such as insurance), buildings, equipment, and land.

Liabilities are debts owed to outsiders (creditors). Liabilities are often identified on the balance sheet by titles that include the word *payable*. Examples of liabilities include accounts payable, notes payable, and wages payable. Cash received before services are delivered creates a liability to perform the services. These future service commitments are often called *unearned revenues*. Examples of unearned revenues are magazine subscriptions received by a publisher and tuition received by a college at the beginning of a term.

Owner's equity is the owner's right to the assets of the business. For a proprietorship, the owner's equity on the balance sheet is represented by the balance of the owner's *capital* account. A **drawing** account represents the amount of withdrawals made by the owner.

Revenues are increases in owner's equity as a result of selling services or products to customers. Examples of revenues include fees earned, fares earned, commissions revenue, and rent revenue.

Expenses result from using up assets or consuming services in the process of generating revenues. Examples of typical expenses include wages expense, rent expense, utilities expense, supplies expense, and miscellaneous expense.

A chart of accounts is designed to meet the information needs of a company's managers and other users of its financial statements. The accounts within the chart of accounts are numbered for use as references. A flexible numbering system is normally used, so that new accounts can be added without affecting other account numbers.

Exhibit 2 is NetSolutions' chart of accounts that we will be using in this chapter. Additional accounts will be introduced in later chapters. In Exhibit 2, each account number has two digits. The first digit indicates the major classification of the ledger in which the account is located. Accounts beginning with 1 represent assets; 2, liabilities; 3, owner's equity; 4, revenue; and 5, expenses. The second digit indicates the location of the account within its class. You should note that each of the columns in Exhibit 1 has been assigned an account number in the chart of accounts shown in Exhibit 2. In addition, we have added accounts for Accounts Receivable, Prepaid Insurance, Office Equipment, and Unearned Rent. These accounts will be used in recording NetSolutions' December transactions later in this chapter.

ANALYZING AND SUMMARIZING TRANSACTIONS IN ACCOUNTS

Every business transaction affects at least two accounts. To illustrate how transactions are analyzed and summarized in accounts, we will use the NetSolutions transactions from Chapter 1, with dates added. First, we illustrate how transactions (a), (b), (c), and

REAL WORLD

Procter & Gamble's account numbers have over 30 digits to reflect P&G's many different operations and regions.

---

2 The totals of the debit and credit columns may be shown separately in an account. When this is done, these amounts should be identified in some way so that they are not mistaken for entries or the ending balance of the account.

EXHIBIT 2 — Analysis and Recording of Transactions Using Accounts

Balance Sheet Accounts		Income Statement Accounts	
1. Assets		**4. Revenue**	
11	Cash	41	Fees Earned
12	Accounts Receivable		**5. Expenses**
14	Supplies	51	Wages Expense
15	Prepaid Insurance	52	Rent Expense
17	Land	54	Utilities Expense
18	Office Equipment	55	Supplies Expense
	2. Liabilities	59	Miscellaneous Expense
21	Accounts Payable		
23	Unearned Rent		
	3. Owner's Equity		
31	Chris Clark, Capital		
32	Chris Clark, Drawing		

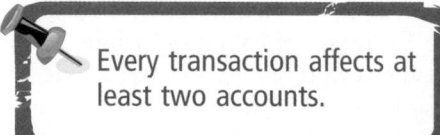

Every transaction affects at least two accounts.

(f) are analyzed and summarized in balance sheet accounts (assets, liabilities, and owner's equity). Next, we illustrate how transactions (d), (e), and (g) are analyzed and summarized in income statement accounts (revenues and expenses). Finally, we illustrate how the withdrawal of cash by Chris Clark, transaction (h), is analyzed and summarized in the accounts.

Balance Sheet Accounts Chris Clark's first transaction, (a), was to deposit $25,000 in a bank account in the name of NetSolutions. The effect of this November 1 transaction on the balance sheet is to increase assets and owner's equity, as shown below.

November 1 Transaction

NetSolutions Balance Sheet November 1, 2007				
Assets		**Owner's Equity**	
Cash	$25 0 0 0 00	Chris Clark, capital	$25 0 0 0 00

This transaction is initially entered in a record called a **journal**. The title of the account to be debited is listed first, followed by the amount to be debited. The title of the account to be credited is listed below and to the right of the debit, followed by the amount to be credited. This process of recording a transaction in the journal is called **journalizing**. This form of recording a transaction is called a **journal entry**.

The journal entry for transaction (a) is shown below.

JOURNAL Page 1

	Date		Description	Post. Ref.	Debit	Credit	
1	2007 Nov.	1	Cash		25 0 0 0 00		1
2			Chris Clark, Capital			25 0 0 0 00	2
3			Invested cash in NetSolutions.				3

A journal can be thought of as being similar to an individual's diary of significant day-to-day life events.

The increase in the asset (Cash), which is reported on the left side of the balance sheet, is debited to the cash account. The increase in owner's equity, which is reported on the right side of the balance sheet, is credited to the Chris Clark, capital account. As other assets are acquired, the increases are also recorded as debits to asset accounts. Likewise, other increases in owner's equity will be recorded as credits to owner's equity accounts.

The effects of this transaction are shown in the accounts by transferring the amount and date of the journal entry to the left (debit) side of Cash and to the right (credit) side of Chris Clark, Capital, as follows:

Cash		Chris Clark, Capital	
Nov. 1 25,000			Nov. 1 25,000

November 5 Transaction On November 5 [transaction (b)], NetSolutions bought land for $20,000, paying cash. This transaction increases one asset account and decreases another. It is entered in the journal as a $20,000 increase (debit) to Land and a $20,000 decrease (credit) to Cash, as shown below.

4				4
5	5	Land	20 00 0 00	5
6		Cash	20 00 0 00	6
7		Purchased land for building site.		7

The effect of this entry is shown in the accounts of NetSolutions as follows:

Cash		Land		Chris Clark, Capital	
Nov. 1 25,000	Nov. 5 20,000	Nov. 5 20,000			Nov. 1 25,000

November 10 Transaction On November 10 [transaction (c)], NetSolutions purchased supplies on account for $1,350. This transaction increases an asset account and increases a liability account. It is entered in the journal as a $1,350 increase (debit) to Supplies and a $1,350 increase (credit) to Accounts Payable, as shown below. To simplify the illustration, the effect of entry (c) and the remaining journal entries for NetSolutions will be shown in the accounts later.

8				8
9	10	Supplies	1 3 5 0 00	9
10		Accounts Payable	1 3 5 0 00	10
11		Purchased supplies on account.		11

November 30 Transaction On November 30 [transaction (f)], NetSolutions paid creditors on account, $950. This transaction decreases a liability account and decreases an asset account. It is entered in the journal as a $950 decrease (debit) to Accounts Payable and a $950 decrease (credit) to Cash, as shown below.

23				23
24	30	Accounts Payable	9 5 0 00	24
25		Cash	9 5 0 00	25
26		Paid creditors on account.		26

The left side of all accounts is the debit side, and the right side is the credit side.

In the preceding examples, you should observe that the left side of asset accounts is used for recording increases, and the right side is used for recording decreases. Also, the right side of liability and owner's equity accounts is used to record increases, and the left side of such accounts is used to record decreases. The left side of all accounts, whether asset, liability, or owner's equity, is the debit side, and the right side is the credit side. Thus, a debit may be either an increase or a decrease, depending on the account affected. Likewise, a credit may be either an increase or a decrease, depending on the account.

The general rules of debit and credit for balance sheet accounts may be stated as follows:

	Debit	Credit
Asset accounts	Increase (+)	Decrease (−)
Liability accounts	Decrease (−)	Increase (+)
Owner's equity (capital) accounts	Decrease (−)	Increase (+)

The rules of debit and credit may also be stated in relationship to the accounting equation, as shown below. The side of the account for recording increases is shown in green.

Balance Sheet Accounts

ASSETS Asset Accounts		=	LIABILITIES Liability Accounts		+	OWNER'S EQUITY Owner's Equity Accounts	
Debit for increases(+)	Credit for decreases(−)		Debit for decreases(−)	Credit for increases(+)		Debit for decreases(−)	Credit for increases(+)

Example Exercise 2-1   objective 1

Prepare a journal entry for the purchase of a truck on June 3 for $42,500, paying $8,500 cash and the remainder on account.

Follow My Example 2-1

June 3	Truck	42,500	
	Cash		8,500
	Accounts Payable		34,000

For Practice: PE 2-1A, PE 2-1B

Income Statement Accounts   The analysis of revenue and expense transactions focuses on how each transaction affects owner's equity. Transactions that increase revenue will increase owner's equity. Just as increases in owner's equity are recorded as credits, so, too, are increases in revenue accounts. Transactions that increase expense will decrease owner's equity. Just as decreases in owner's equity are recorded as debits, increases in expense accounts are recorded as debits.

We will use NetSolutions' transactions (d), (e), and (g) to illustrate the analysis of transactions and the rules of debit and credit for revenue and expense accounts. On **November 18** [transaction (d)], NetSolutions received fees of $7,500 from customers for **Transaction** services provided. This transaction increases an asset account and increases a revenue account. It is entered in the journal as a $7,500 increase (debit) to Cash and a $7,500 increase (credit) to Fees Earned, as shown below [transaction (d)].

12					12
13	18	Cash	7 5 0 0 00		13
14		Fees Earned		7 5 0 0 00	14
15		Received fees from customers.			15

Business Connections

THE HIJACKING RECEIVABLE

A company's chart of accounts should reflect the basic nature of its operations. Occasionally, however, transactions take place that give rise to unusual accounts. The following is a story of one such account.

During the early 1970s, before strict airport security was implemented across the United States, several airlines experienced hijacking incidents. One such incident occurred on November 10, 1972, when a **Southern Airways** DC-9 en route from Memphis to Miami was hijacked during a stopover in Birmingham, Alabama. The three hijackers boarded the plane in Birmingham armed with handguns and hand grenades. At gunpoint, the hijackers took the plane, the plane's crew of four, and 27 passengers to nine American cities, Toronto, and eventually to Havana, Cuba.

During the long flight, the hijackers threatened to crash the plane into the Oak Ridge, Tennessee, nuclear facilities, insisted on talking with President Nixon, and demanded a ransom of $10 million. **Southern Airways**, however, was only able to come up with $2 million. Even-

tually, the pilot talked the hijackers into settling for the $2 million when the plane landed in Chattanooga for refueling.

Upon landing in Havana, the Cuban authorities arrested the hijackers and, after a brief delay, sent the plane, passengers, and crew back to the United States. The hijackers and $2 million stayed in Cuba.

How did Southern Airways account for and report the hijacking payment in its subsequent financial statements? As you might have analyzed, the initial entry credited Cash for $2 million. The debit was to an account entitled "Hijacking Payment." This account was reported as a type of receivable under "other assets" on Southern's balance sheet. The company maintained that it would be able to collect the cash from the Cuban government and that, therefore, a receivable existed. In fact, in August 1975, Southern Airways was repaid $2 million by the Cuban government, which was, at that time, attempting to improve relations with the United States.

November 30 Transaction   Throughout the month, NetSolutions incurred the following expenses: wages, $2,125; rent, $800; utilities, $450; and miscellaneous, $275. To simplify the illustration, the entry to journalize the payment of these expenses is recorded on November 30 [transaction (e)], as shown below. This transaction increases various expense accounts and decreases an asset account.

16					16
17	30	Wages Expense	2 1 2 5 00		17
18		Rent Expense	8 0 0 00		18
19		Utilities Expense	4 5 0 00		19
20		Miscellaneous Expense	2 7 5 00		20
21		Cash		3 6 5 0 00	21
22		Paid expenses.			22

You should note that regardless of the number of accounts, the sum of the debits is always equal to the sum of the credits in a journal entry.

November 30 Transaction   On November 30, NetSolutions recorded the amount of supplies used in the operations during the month [transaction (g)]. This transaction increases an expense account and decreases an asset account. The journal entry for transaction (g) is shown below.

27					27
28	30	Supplies Expense	8 0 0 00		28
29		Supplies		8 0 0 00	29
30		Supplies used during November.			30

The general rules of debit and credit for analyzing transactions affecting income statement accounts are stated as shown at the top of the following page.

	Debit	Credit
Revenue accounts	Decrease (−)	Increase (+)
Expense accounts	Increase (+)	Decrease (−)

The rules of debit and credit for income statement accounts may also be summarized in relationship to the accounting equation, owner's equity accounts, and net income or net loss as shown below.

ASSETS	=	LIABILITIES	+	**OWNER'S EQUITY**

OWNER'S EQUITY
Owner's Equity Accounts

Debit for decreases(−)	Credit for increases(+)

Income Statement Accounts

Revenue Accounts

Debit for decreases(−)	Credit for increases(+)

Less

Expense Accounts

Debit for increases(+)	Credit for decreases(−)

Equals

Net Income
Revenues exceed expenses
Increases owner's equity (capital)

or

Net Loss
Expenses exceed revenues
Decreases owner's equity (capital)

> The sum of the debits must always equal the sum of the credits.

Example Exercise 2-2   objective **1**

Prepare a journal entry on August 7 for the fees earned on account, $115,000.

Follow My Example 2-2

| Aug. 7 | Accounts Receivable | .... | 115,000 | |
| | Fees Earned | .... | | 115,000 |

For Practice: PE 2-2A, PE 2-2B

Drawing Account   The owner of a proprietorship may withdraw cash from the business for personal use. This is common practice for owners devoting full time to the business, since the business may be the owner's main source of income. Such withdrawals have the effect of decreasing owner's equity. Just as decreases in owner's equity are recorded as debits, increases in withdrawals are recorded as debits. Withdrawals are debited to an account with the owner's name followed by *Drawing* or *Personal*.

November 30   In transaction (h), Chris Clark withdrew $2,000 in cash from NetSolutions for per-
Transaction   sonal use. The effect of this transaction is to increase the drawing account and decrease the cash account. The journal entry for transaction (h) is shown on the next page.

	2007						
1	Nov.	30	Chris Clark, Drawing	2 0 0 0 00			1
2			Cash		2 0 0 0 00		2
3			Chris Clark withdrew cash for				3
4			personal use.				4

Example Exercise 2-3 objective

Prepare a journal entry on December 29 for the payment of $12,000 to the owner of Smartstaff Consulting Services, Dominique Walsh, for personal use.

Follow My Example 2-3

| Dec. 29 | Dominique Walsh, Drawing .... | 12,000 | |
| | Cash .... | | 12,000 |

For Practice: PE 2-3A, PE 2-3B

NORMAL BALANCES OF ACCOUNTS

The sum of the increases recorded in an account is usually equal to or greater than the sum of the decreases recorded in the account. For this reason, the normal balances of all accounts are positive rather than negative. For example, the total debits (increases) in an asset account will ordinarily be greater than the total credits (decreases). Thus, asset accounts normally have debit balances.

The rules of debit and credit and the normal balances of the various types of accounts are summarized in Exhibit 3. In Exhibit 3, the side of the account for recording increases and the normal balance is shown in green.

When an account normally having a debit balance actually has a credit balance, or vice versa, an error may have occurred or an unusual situation may exist. For example, a credit balance in the office equipment account could result only from an error. On the other hand, a debit balance in an accounts payable account could result from an overpayment.

Example Exercise 2-4 objective

State for each account whether it is likely to have (a) debit entries only, (b) credit entries only, or (c) both debit and credit entries. Also, indicate its normal balance.

1. Amber Saunders, Drawing
2. Accounts Payable
3. Cash
4. Fees Earned
5. Supplies
6. Utilities Expense

Follow My Example 2-4

1. Debit entries only; normal debit balance
2. Debit and credit entries; normal credit balance
3. Debit and credit entries; normal debit balance
4. Credit entries only; normal credit balance
5. Debit and credit entries; normal debit balance
6. Debit entries only; normal debit balance

For Practice: PE 2-4A, PE 2-4B

Integrity, Objectivity, and Ethics in Business

 ETHICS

WILL JOURNALIZING PREVENT FRAUD?

While journalizing transactions reduces the possibility of fraud, it by no means eliminates it. For example, embezzlement can be hidden within the double-entry bookkeeping system by creating fictitious suppliers to whom checks are issued.

EXHIBIT 3 | Rules of Debit and Credit, Normal Balances of Accounts

Total Debits = Total Credits

Balance Sheet Accounts

ASSETS Asset Accounts		LIABILITIES Liability Accounts		OWNER'S EQUITY Owner's Equity Accounts	
Debit for increases(+)	Credit for decreases(−)	Debit for decreases(−)	Credit for increases(+)	Debit for decreases(−)	Credit for increases(+)

=   +

The side of the account for recording increases and the normal balance is shown in green.

> The sum of the debits is always equal to the sum of the credits for each journal entry.

Income Statement Accounts

Revenue Accounts

Debit for decreases(−)	Credit for increases(+)

Less

Expense Accounts

Debit for increases(+)	Credit for decreases(−)

Equals

Net Income
Revenues exceed expenses
Increases owner's equity (capital)

or

Net Loss
Expenses exceed revenues
Decreases owner's equity (capital)

Drawing Account

Debit for increases(+)	Credit for decreases(−)

Double-Entry Accounting System

In 1494, Luca Pacioli, a Franciscan monk, invented the double-entry accounting system that is still used today.

In the preceding paragraphs, we illustrated the rules of debit and credit for recording transactions in accounts using journal entries. In doing so, the sum of the debits is always equal to the sum of the credits for each journal entry. As shown in Exhibit 3, this equality of debits and credits for each transaction is built into the accounting equation: Assets = Liabilities + Owner's Equity. Because of this double equality, this system of recording transactions is called the **double-entry accounting system**.

As we illustrate in the remainder of this text, the double-entry accounting system is a very powerful tool in analyzing the effects of transactions. Using this system to analyze transactions is summarized below and in Exhibit 4.

1. Carefully read the description of the transaction to determine whether an asset, liability, owner's equity, revenue, expense, or drawing account is affected by the transaction.

EXHIBIT 4 | Recording Transactions Using Double-Entry Accounting

Transaction takes place

1 Determine accounts affected by transaction: asset, liability, owner's equity, revenue, expense, drawing

2 Determine whether accounts affected by transaction increase or decrease

Rules of Debit and Credit

3 Determine whether increases or decreases in account should be recorded as debits or credits

4 Record entry in journal

5 Post entry to ledger

6 Prepare unadjusted trial balance at the end of the period

2. For each account affected by the transaction, determine whether the account increases or decreases.

3. Determine whether each increase or decrease should be recorded as a debit or a credit, following the rules of debit and credit shown in Exhibit 3.

4. Record the transaction using a journal entry.

5. Periodically post journal entries to the accounts in the ledger.

6. Prepare an unadjusted trial balance at the end of the period.

We have described and illustrated steps 1–4 in the preceding paragraphs. In the remainder of this chapter, we describe and illustrate steps 5 and 6.

2
objective

Describe and illustrate the posting of journal entries to accounts.

Posting Journal Entries to Accounts

As we discussed in the preceding section, a transaction is first recorded in a journal. Periodically, the journal entries are transferred to the accounts in the ledger (step 5 in Exhibit 4). The ledger is a history of transactions by account. The process of transferring the debits and credits from the journal entries to the accounts is called **posting**.

In practice, businesses use a variety of formats for recording journal entries. A business may use one all-purpose journal, sometimes called a **two-column journal**, or it may use several journals. In the latter case, each journal is used to record different types of transactions, such as cash receipts or cash payments. The journals may be part of either a manual accounting system or a computerized accounting system.[3]

As a review of the analysis and recording of transactions and to illustrate posting in a manual accounting system, we will use the December transactions of NetSolutions. The first transaction in December occurred on December 1.

---

3 The use of special journals and computerized accounting systems is discussed in Chapter 5, after the basics of accounting systems have been covered.

December 1 Transaction

NetSolutions paid a premium of $2,400 for a comprehensive insurance policy covering liability, theft, and fire. The policy covers a one-year period.

@netsolutions

Analysis   When you purchase insurance for your automobile, you may be required to pay the insurance premium in advance. In this case, your transaction is similar to NetSolutions. Advance payments of expenses such as insurance are prepaid expenses, which are assets. For NetSolutions, the asset acquired for the cash payment is insurance protection for 12 months. The asset Prepaid Insurance increases and is debited for $2,400. The asset Cash decreases and is credited for $2,400. The recording and posting of this transaction is shown in Exhibit 5.

Note where the date of the transaction is recorded in the journal. Also note that the entry is explained as the payment of an insurance premium. Such explanations should be brief. For unusual and complex transactions, such as a long-term rental arrangement, the journal entry explanation may include a reference to the rental agreement or other business document.

You will note that the T account form is not used in this illustration. Although the T account clearly separates debit and credit entries, in practice, the T account is usually replaced with the standard form shown in Exhibit 5.

The debits and credits for each journal entry are posted to the accounts in the order in which they occur in the journal. To illustrate, the debit portion of the December 1 journal entry is posted to the prepaid account in Exhibit 5 using the following four steps:

Step 1: The date (Dec. 1) is entered in the Date Column of Prepaid Insurance;

EXHIBIT 5

Diagram of the Recording and Posting of a Debit and a Credit

Step 2: The amount (2,400) is entered into the Debit Column of Prepaid Insurance;

Step 3: The journal page number (2) is entered in the Posting Reference (Post. Ref.) Column of Prepaid Insurance;

Step 4: The account number (15) is entered in the Posting Reference (Post. Ref.) Column in the journal.

As shown in Exhibit 5, the credit portion of the December 1 journal entry is posted to the cash account in a similar manner.

The remaining December transactions for NetSolutions are analyzed in the following paragraphs. These transactions are posted to the ledger in Exhibit 6, shown later. To simplify and reduce repetition, some of the December transactions are stated in summary form. For example, cash received for services is normally recorded on a daily basis. In this example, however, only summary totals are recorded at the middle and end of the month. Likewise, all fees earned on account during December are recorded at the middle and end of the month. In practice, each fee earned is recorded separately.

December 1 Transaction   NetSolutions paid rent for December, $800. The company from which NetSolutions is renting its store space now requires the payment of rent on the first of each month, rather than at the end of the month.

Analysis   You may pay monthly rent on an apartment on the first of each month. Your rent transaction is similar to NetSolutions. The advance payment of rent is an asset, much like the advance payment of the insurance premium in the preceding transaction. Unlike the insurance premium, this prepaid rent will expire in one month. When an asset that is purchased will be used up in a short period of time, such as a month, it is normal to debit an expense account initially. This avoids having to transfer the balance from an asset account (Prepaid Rent) to an expense account (Rent Expense) at the end of the month. Thus, when the rent for December is prepaid at the beginning of the month, Rent Expense is debited for $800, and Cash is credited for $800.

9						9
10	1	Rent Expense	52	8 0 0 00		10
11		Cash	11		8 0 0 00	11
12		Paid rent for December.				12

December 1 Transaction   NetSolutions received an offer from a local retailer to rent the land purchased on November 5. The retailer plans to use the land as a parking lot for its employees and customers. NetSolutions agreed to rent the land to the retailer for three months, with the rent payable in advance. NetSolutions received $360 for three months' rent beginning December 1.

Analysis   By agreeing to rent the land and accepting the $360, NetSolutions has incurred an obligation (liability) to the retailer. This obligation is to make the land available for use for three months and not to interfere with its use. The liability created by receiving the cash in advance of providing the service is called **unearned revenue**. Thus, the $360 received is an increase in an asset and is debited to Cash. The liability account Unearned Rent increases and is credited for $360. As time passes, the unearned rent liability will decrease and will become revenue.

Magazines that receive subscriptions in advance must record the receipts as unearned revenues. Likewise, airlines that receive ticket payments in advance must record the receipts as unearned revenues until the passengers use the tickets.

13						13
14	1	Cash	11	3 6 0 00		14
15		Unearned Rent	23		3 6 0 00	15
16		Received advance payment for				16
17		three months' rent on land.				17

December 4 Transaction   NetSolutions purchased office equipment on account from Executive Supply Co. for $1,800.

Analysis   The asset account Office Equipment increases and is therefore debited for $1,800. The liability account Accounts Payable increases and is credited for $1,800.

18					18
19	4	Office Equipment	18	1 8 0 0 00	19
20		Accounts Payable	21	1 8 0 0 00	20
21		Purchased office equipment			21
22		on account.			22

December 6 Transaction

NetSolutions paid $180 for a newspaper advertisement.

Analysis   An expense increases and is debited for $180. The asset Cash decreases and is credited for $180. Expense items that are expected to be minor in amount are normally included as part of the miscellaneous expense. Thus, Miscellaneous Expense is debited for $180.

23					23
24	6	Miscellaneous Expense	59	1 8 0 00	24
25		Cash	11	1 8 0 00	25
26		Paid for newspaper ad.			26

December 11 Transaction

NetSolutions paid creditors $400.

Analysis   This payment decreases the liability account Accounts Payable, which is debited for $400. Cash also decreases and is credited for $400.

27					27
28	11	Accounts Payable	21	4 0 0 00	28
29		Cash	11	4 0 0 00	29
30		Paid creditors on account.			30

December 13 Transaction

NetSolutions paid a receptionist and a part-time assistant $950 for two weeks' wages.

Analysis   This transaction is similar to the December 6 transaction, where an expense account is increased and Cash is decreased. Thus, Wages Expense is debited for $950, and Cash is credited for $950.

In computerized accounting systems, some transactions may be automatically authorized and recorded when certain events occur. For example, the wages of employees may be paid automatically at the end of each pay period.

		JOURNAL			Page 3	
	Date	**Description**	**Post. Ref.**	**Debit**	**Credit**	
1	2007 Dec. 13	Wages Expense	51	9 5 0 00		1
2		Cash	11		9 5 0 00	2
3		Paid two weeks' wages.				3

December 16 Transaction

NetSolutions received $3,100 from fees earned for the first half of December.

Analysis   Cash increases and is debited for $3,100. The revenue account Fees Earned increases and is credited for $3,100.

4					4
5	16	Cash	11	3 1 0 0 00	5
6		Fees Earned	41	3 1 0 0 00	6
7		Received fees from customers.			7

December 16
Transaction

Fees earned on account totaled $1,750 for the first half of December.

Analysis Assume that you have agreed to take care of a neighbor's dog for a week for $100. At the end of the week, you agree to wait until the first of the next month to receive the $100. Like NetSolutions, you have provided services on account and thus have a right to receive the payment from your neighbor. When a business agrees that payment for services provided or goods sold can be accepted at a later date, the firm has an **account receivable**, which is a claim against the customer. The account receivable is an asset, and the revenue is earned even though no cash has been received. Thus, Accounts Receivable increases and is debited for $1,750. The revenue account Fees Earned increases and is credited for $1,750.

8					8
9	16	Accounts Receivable	12	1 7 5 0 00	9
10		Fees Earned	41		1 7 5 0 00	10
11		Recorded fees earned on account.			11

December 20
Transaction

NetSolutions paid $900 to Executive Supply Co. on the $1,800 debt owed from the December 4 transaction.

Analysis This is similar to the transaction of December 11.

12					12
13	20	Accounts Payable	21	9 0 0 00	13
14		Cash	11		9 0 0 00	14
15		Paid part of amount owed to			15
16		Executive Supply Co.			16

December 21
Transaction

NetSolutions received $650 from customers in payment of their accounts.

Analysis When customers pay amounts owed for services they have previously received, one asset increases and another asset decreases. Thus, Cash is debited for $650, and Accounts Receivable is credited for $650.

17					17
18	21	Cash	11	6 5 0 00	18
19		Accounts Receivable	12		6 5 0 00	19
20		Received cash from customers			20
21		on account.			21

December 23
Transaction

NetSolutions paid $1,450 for supplies.

Analysis The asset account Supplies increases and is debited for $1,450. The asset account Cash decreases and is credited for $1,450.

22					22
23	23	Supplies	14	1 4 5 0 00	23
24		Cash	11		1 4 5 0 00	24
25		Purchased supplies.			25

December 27
Transaction

NetSolutions paid the receptionist and the part-time assistant $1,200 for two weeks' wages.

Analysis This is similar to the transaction of December 13.

26						26
27		27	Wages Expense	51	1 2 0 0 00		27
28			Cash	11		1 2 0 0 00	28
29			Paid two weeks' wages.				29

December 31 Transaction

NetSolutions paid its $310 telephone bill for the month.

Analysis   You pay a telephone bill each month. Businesses, such as NetSolutions, also must pay monthly utility bills. Such transactions are similar to the transaction of December 6. The expense account Utilities Expense is debited for $310, and Cash is credited for $310.

30							30
31		31	Utilities Expense	54	3 1 0 00		31
32			Cash	11		3 1 0 00	32
33			Paid telephone bill.				33

December 31 Transaction

NetSolutions paid its $225 electric bill for the month.

Analysis   This is similar to the preceding transaction.

		JOURNAL			**Page 4**	
	Date	**Description**	**Post. Ref.**	**Debit**	**Credit**	
1	2007 Dec. 31	Utilities Expense	54	2 2 5 00		1
2		Cash	11		2 2 5 00	2
3		Paid electric bill.				3

December 31 Transaction

NetSolutions received $2,870 from fees earned for the second half of December.

Analysis   This is similar to the transaction of December 16.

4							4
5		31	Cash	11	2 8 7 0 00		5
6			Fees Earned	41		2 8 7 0 00	6
7			Received fees from customers.				7

December 31 Transaction

Fees earned on account totaled $1,120 for the second half of December.

Analysis   This is similar to the transaction of December 16.

8							8
9		31	Accounts Receivable	12	1 1 2 0 00		9
10			Fees Earned	41		1 1 2 0 00	10
11			Recorded fees earned on account.				11

December 31 Transaction

Chris Clark withdrew $2,000 for personal use.

Analysis   This transaction resulted in an increase in the amount of withdrawals and is recorded by a $2,000 debit to Chris Clark, Drawing. The decrease in business cash is recorded by a $2,000 credit to Cash.

12							12
13		31	Chris Clark, Drawing	32	2 0 0 0 00		13
14			Cash	11		2 0 0 0 00	14
15			Chris Clark withdrew cash for				15
16			personal use.				16

Example Exercise 2-5   objective 2

On March 1, the cash account balance was $22,350. During March, cash receipts totaled $241,880 and the March 31 balance was $19,125. Determine the cash payments made during March.

Follow My Example 2-5

Using the following T account, solve for the amount of cash payments (indicated by ? below).

Cash

Mar. 1 Bal.	22,350	?	Cash payments
Cash receipts	241,880		
Mar. 31 Bal.	19,125		

$19,125 = $22,350 + $241,880 − Cash payments
Cash payments = $22,350 + $241,880 − $19,125 = $245,105

For Practice: PE 2-5A, PE 2-5B

The journal for NetSolutions since it was organized on November 1 is shown in Exhibit 6. Exhibit 6 also shows the ledger after the transactions for both November and December have been posted.

EXHIBIT 6

Journal and Ledger—NetSolutions

		JOURNAL			Page 1	
	Date	Description	Post. Ref.	Debit	Credit	
1	2007 Nov. 1	Cash	11	25 0 0 0 00		1
2		Chris Clark, Capital	31		25 0 0 0 00	2
3		Invested cash in NetSolutions.				3
4						4
5	5	Land	17	20 0 0 0 00		5
6		Cash	11		20 0 0 0 00	6
7		Purchased land for building site.				7
8						8
9	10	Supplies	14	1 3 5 0 00		9
10		Accounts Payable	21		1 3 5 0 00	10
11		Purchased supplies on account.				11
12						12
13	18	Cash	11	7 5 0 0 00		13
14		Fees Earned	41		7 5 0 0 00	14
15		Received fees from customers.				15
16						16
17	30	Wages Expense	51	2 1 2 5 00		17
18		Rent Expense	52	8 0 0 00		18
19		Utilities Expense	54	4 5 0 00		19
20		Miscellaneous Expense	59	2 7 5 00		20
21		Cash	11		3 6 5 0 00	21
22		Paid expenses.				22
23						23
24	30	Accounts Payable	21	9 5 0 00		24
25		Cash	11		9 5 0 00	25
26		Paid creditors on account.				26
27						27
28	30	Supplies Expense	55	8 0 0 00		28
29		Supplies	14		8 0 0 00	29
30		Supplies used during November.				30

(continued)

EXHIBIT 6

	Date		Description	Post. Ref.	Debit	Credit	
1	2007 Nov.	30	Chris Clark, Drawing	32	2 0 0 0 00		1
2			Cash	11		2 0 0 0 00	2
3			Chris Clark withdrew cash for				3
4			personal use.				4
5							5
6	Dec.	1	Prepaid Insurance	15	2 4 0 0 00		6
7			Cash	11		2 4 0 0 00	7
8			Paid premium on one-year policy.				8
9							9
10		1	Rent Expense	52	8 0 0 00		10
11			Cash	11		8 0 0 00	11
12			Paid rent for December.				12
13							13
14		1	Cash	11	3 6 0 00		14
15			Unearned Rent	23		3 6 0 00	15
16			Received advance payment for				16
17			three months' rent on land.				17
18							18
19		4	Office Equipment	18	1 8 0 0 00		19
20			Accounts Payable	21		1 8 0 0 00	20
21			Purchased office equipment				21
22			on account.				22
23							23
24		6	Miscellaneous Expense	59	1 8 0 00		24
25			Cash	11		1 8 0 00	25
26			Paid for newspaper ad.				26
27							27
28		11	Accounts Payable	21	4 0 0 00		28
29			Cash	11		4 0 0 00	29
30			Paid creditors on account.				30

JOURNAL   Page 2

(continued)

EXHIBIT 6

	Date		Description	Post. Ref.	Debit	Credit	
1	2007 Dec.	13	Wages Expense	51	9 5 0 00		1
2			Cash	11		9 5 0 00	2
3			Paid two weeks' wages.				3
4							4
5		16	Cash	11	3 1 0 0 00		5
6			Fees Earned	41		3 1 0 0 00	6
7			Received fees from customers.				7
8							8
9		16	Accounts Receivable	12	1 7 5 0 00		9
10			Fees Earned	41		1 7 5 0 00	10
11			Recorded fees earned on account.				11
12							12
13		20	Accounts Payable	21	9 0 0 00		13
14			Cash	11		9 0 0 00	14
15			Paid part of amount owed to				15
16			Executive Supply Co.				16
17							17
18		21	Cash	11	6 5 0 00		18
19			Accounts Receivable	12		6 5 0 00	19
20			Received cash from customers				20
21			on account.				21
22							22
23		23	Supplies	14	1 4 5 0 00		23
24			Cash	11		1 4 5 0 00	24
25			Purchased supplies.				25
26							26
27		27	Wages Expense	51	1 2 0 0 00		27
28			Cash	11		1 2 0 0 00	28
29			Paid two weeks' wages.				29
30							30
31		31	Utilities Expense	54	3 1 0 00		31
32			Cash	11		3 1 0 00	32
33			Paid telephone bill.				33

JOURNAL   Page 3

(continued)

EXHIBIT 6

	JOURNAL				Page 4

	Date		Description	Post. Ref.	Debit	Credit	
1	2007 Dec.	31	Utilities Expense	54	2 2 5 00		1
2			Cash	11		2 2 5 00	2
3			Paid electric bill.				3
4							4
5		31	Cash	11	2 8 7 0 00		5
6			Fees Earned	41		2 8 7 0 00	6
7			Received fees from customers.				7
8							8
9		31	Accounts Receivable	12	1 1 2 0 00		9
10			Fees Earned	41		1 1 2 0 00	10
11			Recorded fees earned on account.				11
12							12
13		31	Chris Clark, Drawing	32	2 0 0 0 00		13
14			Cash	11		2 0 0 0 00	14
15			Chris Clark withdrew cash for				15
16			personal use.				16

		LEDGER					

ACCOUNT *Cash* **ACCOUNT NO.** *11*

Date		Item	Post. Ref.	Debit	Credit	Balance Debit	Balance Credit
2007 Nov.	1		1	25 0 0 0 00		25 0 0 0 00	
	5		1		20 0 0 0 00	5 0 0 0 00	
	18		1	7 5 0 0 00		12 5 0 0 00	
	30		1		3 6 5 0 00	8 8 5 0 00	
	30		1		9 5 0 00	7 9 0 0 00	
	30		2		2 0 0 0 00	5 9 0 0 00	
Dec.	1		2		2 4 0 0 00	3 5 0 0 00	
	1		2		8 0 0 00	2 7 0 0 00	
	1		2	3 6 0 00		3 0 6 0 00	
	6		2		1 8 0 00	2 8 8 0 00	
	11		2		4 0 0 00	2 4 8 0 00	
	13		3		9 5 0 00	1 5 3 0 00	
	16		3	3 1 0 0 00		4 6 3 0 00	
	20		3		9 0 0 00	3 7 3 0 00	
	21		3	6 5 0 00		4 3 8 0 00	
	23		3		1 4 5 0 00	2 9 3 0 00	
	27		3		1 2 0 0 00	1 7 3 0 00	
	31		3		3 1 0 00	1 4 2 0 00	
	31		4		2 2 5 00	1 1 9 5 00	
	31		4	2 8 7 0 00		4 0 6 5 00	
	31		4		2 0 0 0 00	2 0 6 5 00	

(continued)

EXHIBIT 6

ACCOUNT *Accounts Receivable*   **ACCOUNT NO.** *12*

Date	Item	Post. Ref.	Debit	Credit	Balance Debit	Balance Credit
2007 Dec. 16		3	1 7 5 0 00		1 7 5 0 00	
21		3		6 5 0 00	1 1 0 0 00	
31		4	1 1 2 0 00		2 2 2 0 00	

ACCOUNT *Supplies*   **ACCOUNT NO.** *14*

Date	Item	Post. Ref.	Debit	Credit	Balance Debit	Balance Credit
2007 Nov. 10		1	1 3 5 0 00		1 3 5 0 00	
30		1		8 0 0 00	5 5 0 00	
Dec. 23		3	1 4 5 0 00		2 0 0 0 00	

ACCOUNT *Prepaid Insurance*   **ACCOUNT NO.** *15*

Date	Item	Post. Ref.	Debit	Credit	Balance Debit	Balance Credit
2007 Dec. 1		2	2 4 0 0 00		2 4 0 0 00	

ACCOUNT *Land*   **ACCOUNT NO.** *17*

Date	Item	Post. Ref.	Debit	Credit	Balance Debit	Balance Credit
2007 Nov. 5		1	20 0 0 0 00		20 0 0 0 00	

ACCOUNT *Office Equipment*   **ACCOUNT NO.** *18*

Date	Item	Post. Ref.	Debit	Credit	Balance Debit	Balance Credit
2007 Dec. 4		2	1 8 0 0 00		1 8 0 0 00	

(continued)

EXHIBIT 6

ACCOUNT *Accounts Payable*   **ACCOUNT NO.** *21*

Date		Item	Post. Ref.	Debit	Credit	Balance	
						Debit	Credit
2007 Nov.	10		1		1 3 5 0 00		1 3 5 0 00
	30		1	9 5 0 00			4 0 0 00
Dec.	4		2		1 8 0 0 00		2 2 0 0 00
	11		2	4 0 0 00			1 8 0 0 00
	20		3	9 0 0 00			9 0 0 00

ACCOUNT *Unearned Rent*   **ACCOUNT NO.** *23*

Date		Item	Post. Ref.	Debit	Credit	Balance	
						Debit	Credit
2007 Dec.	1		2		3 6 0 00		3 6 0 00

ACCOUNT *Chris Clark, Capital*   **ACCOUNT NO.** *31*

Date		Item	Post. Ref.	Debit	Credit	Balance	
						Debit	Credit
2007 Nov.	1		1		25 0 0 0 00		25 0 0 0 00

ACCOUNT *Chris Clark, Drawing*   **ACCOUNT NO.** *32*

Date		Item	Post. Ref.	Debit	Credit	Balance	
						Debit	Credit
2007 Nov.	30		2	2 0 0 0 00		2 0 0 0 00	
Dec.	31		4	2 0 0 0 00		4 0 0 0 00	

ACCOUNT *Fees Earned*   **ACCOUNT NO.** *41*

Date		Item	Post. Ref.	Debit	Credit	Balance	
						Debit	Credit
2007 Nov.	18		1		7 5 0 0 00		7 5 0 0 00
Dec.	16		3		3 1 0 0 00		10 6 0 0 00
	16		3		1 7 5 0 00		12 3 5 0 00
	31		4		2 8 7 0 00		15 2 2 0 00
	31		4		1 1 2 0 00		16 3 4 0 00

(continued)

EXHIBIT 6

ACCOUNT *Wages Expense*   **ACCOUNT NO.** *51*

Date	Item	Post. Ref.	Debit	Credit	Balance Debit	Balance Credit
2007 Nov. 30		1	2 1 2 5 00		2 1 2 5 00	
Dec. 13		3	9 5 0 00		3 0 7 5 00	
27		3	1 2 0 0 00		4 2 7 5 00	

ACCOUNT *Rent Expense*   **ACCOUNT NO.** *52*

Date	Item	Post. Ref.	Debit	Credit	Balance Debit	Balance Credit
2007 Nov. 30		1	8 0 0 00		8 0 0 00	
Dec. 1		2	8 0 0 00		1 6 0 0 00	

ACCOUNT *Utilities Expense*   **ACCOUNT NO.** *54*

Date	Item	Post. Ref.	Debit	Credit	Balance Debit	Balance Credit
2007 Nov. 30		1	4 5 0 00		4 5 0 00	
Dec. 31		3	3 1 0 00		7 6 0 00	
31		4	2 2 5 00		9 8 5 00	

ACCOUNT *Supplies Expense*   **ACCOUNT NO.** *55*

Date	Item	Post. Ref.	Debit	Credit	Balance Debit	Balance Credit
2007 Nov. 30		1	8 0 0 00		8 0 0 00	

ACCOUNT *Miscellaneous Expense*   **ACCOUNT NO.** *59*

Date	Item	Post. Ref.	Debit	Credit	Balance Debit	Balance Credit
2007 Nov. 30		1	2 7 5 00		2 7 5 00	
Dec. 6		2	1 8 0 00		4 5 5 00	

(concluded)

Trial Balance

objective **3**

Prepare an unadjusted trial balance and explain how it can be used to discover errors.

@netsolutions

How can you be sure that you have not made an error in posting the debits and credits to the ledger? One way is to determine the equality of the debits and credits in the ledger. This equality should be proved at the end of each accounting period, if not more often. Such a proof, called a **trial balance**, may be in the form of a computer printout or in the form shown in Exhibit 7.

The trial balance shown in Exhibit 7 is prepared by first listing the name of the company (NetSolutions), its title (Unadjusted Trial Balance), and the date it is prepared (December 31, 2007). The trial balance shown in Exhibit 7 is titled an unadjusted trial balance. This is to distinguish it from other trial balances that we will be preparing in later chapters. These other trial balances include an adjusted trial balance and a post-closing trial balance.[4]

The account balances in Exhibit 7 are taken from the ledger shown in Exhibit 6. Thus, before the trial balance can be prepared, each account balance in the ledger must be determined. When the standard account form is used, the balance of each account appears in the balance column on the same line as the last posting to the account.

EXHIBIT 7

Trial Balance

NetSolutions Unadjusted Trial Balance December 31, 2007	Debit Balances	Credit Balances
Cash	2 0 6 5 00	
Accounts Receivable	2 2 2 0 00	
Supplies	2 0 0 0 00	
Prepaid Insurance	2 4 0 0 00	
Land	20 0 0 0 00	
Office Equipment	1 8 0 0 00	
Accounts Payable		9 0 0 00
Unearned Rent		3 6 0 00
Chris Clark, Capital		25 0 0 0 00
Chris Clark, Drawing	4 0 0 0 00	
Fees Earned		16 3 4 0 00
Wages Expense	4 2 7 5 00	
Rent Expense	1 6 0 0 00	
Utilities Expense	9 8 5 00	
Supplies Expense	8 0 0 00	
Miscellaneous Expense	4 5 5 00	
	42 6 0 0 00	42 6 0 0 00

The trial balance does not provide complete proof of the accuracy of the ledger. It indicates only that the debits and the credits are equal. This proof is of value, however, because errors often affect the equality of debits and credits. If the two totals of a trial balance are not equal, an error has occurred. In the next section of this chapter, we will discuss procedures for discovering and correcting errors.

---

4 The adjusted trial balance is discussed in Chapter 3, and the post-closing trial balance is discussed in Chapter 4.

Example Exercise 2-6

objective **3**

For each of the following errors, considered individually, indicate whether the error would cause the trial balance totals to be unequal. If the error would cause the trial balance total to be unequal, indicate whether the debit or credit total is higher and by how much.

a. Payment of a cash withdrawal of $5,600 was journalized and posted as a debit of $6,500 to Salary Expense and a credit of $6,500 to Cash.

b. A fee of $2,850 earned from a client was debited to Accounts Receivable for $2,580 and credited to Fees Earned for $2,850.

c. A payment of $3,500 to a creditor was posted as a debit of $3,500 to Accounts Payable and a debit of $3,500 to Cash.

Follow My Example 2-6

a. The totals are equal since both the debit and credit entries were journalized and posted for $6,500.

b. The totals are unequal. The credit total is higher by $270 ($2,850 − $2,580).

c. The totals are unequal. The debit total is higher by $7,000 ($3,500 + $3,500).

For Practice: PE 2-6A, PE 2-6B

Discovery and Correction of Errors

objective **4**

Discover and correct errors in recording transactions.

REAL WORLD

Many large corporations such as Microsoft and Quaker Oats round the figures in their financial statements to millions of dollars.

Errors will sometimes occur in journalizing and posting transactions. In some cases, however, an error might not be significant enough to affect the decisions of management or others. In such cases, the **materiality concept** implies that the error may be treated in the easiest possible way. For example, an error of a few dollars in recording an asset as an expense for a business with millions of dollars in assets would be considered immaterial, and a correction would not be necessary. In the remaining paragraphs, we assume that errors discovered are material and should be corrected.

DISCOVERY OF ERRORS

As mentioned previously, preparing the trial balance is one of the primary ways to discover errors in the ledger. However, it indicates only that the debits and credits are equal. If the two totals of the trial balance are not equal, it is probably due to one or more of the errors described in Exhibit 8.

Among the types of errors that will *not* cause the trial balance totals to be unequal are the following:

1. Failure to record a transaction or to post a transaction.
2. Recording the same erroneous amount for both the debit and the credit parts of a transaction.
3. Recording the same transaction more than once.
4. Posting a part of a transaction correctly as a debit or credit but to the wrong account.

It is obvious that care should be used in recording transactions in the journal and in posting to the accounts. The need for accuracy in determining account balances and reporting them on the trial balance is also evident.

Errors in the accounts may be discovered in various ways: (1) through audit procedures, (2) by looking at the trial balance, or (3) by chance. If the two trial balance totals are not equal, the amount of the difference between the totals should be determined before searching for the error.

EXHIBIT 8 | Errors Causing Unequal Trial Balance

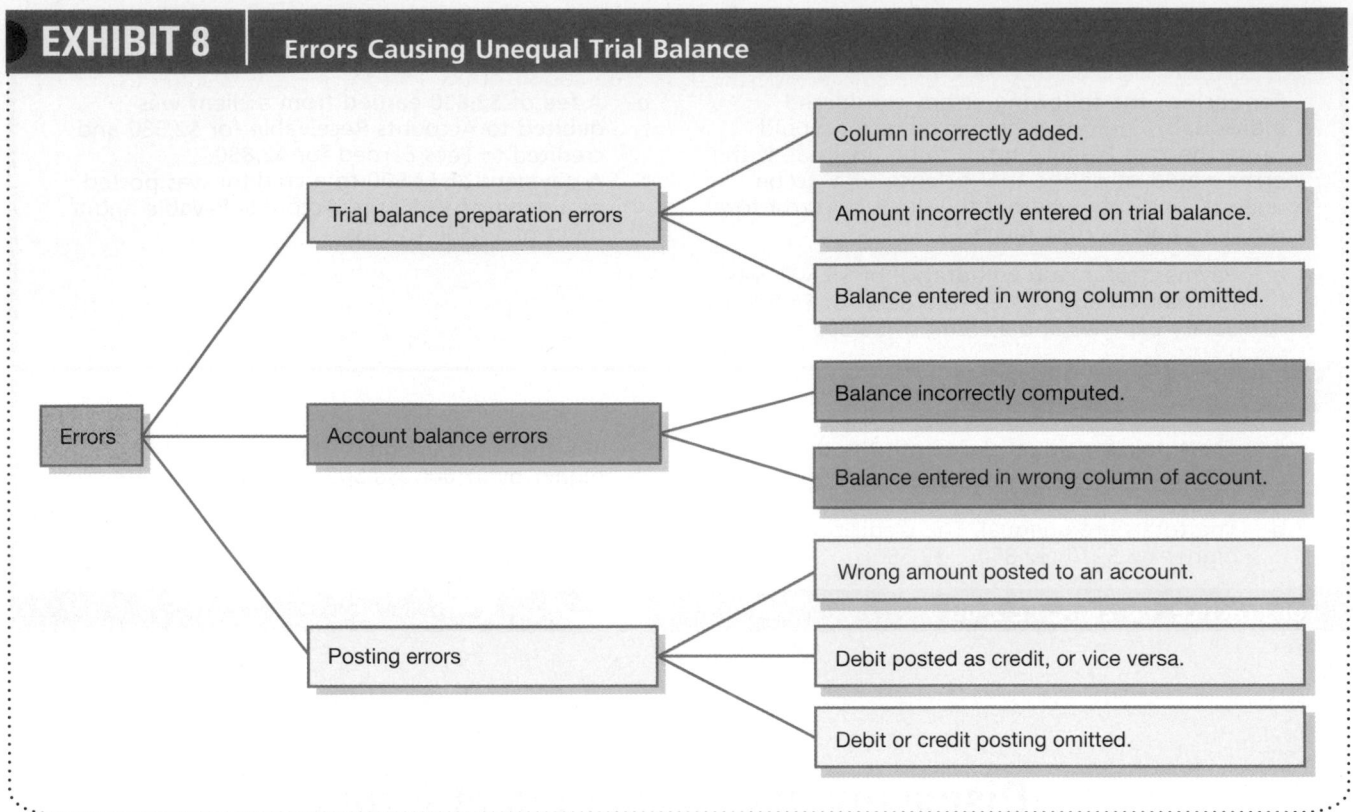

The amount of the difference between the two totals of a trial balance sometimes gives a clue as to the nature of the error or where it occurred. For example, a difference of 10, 100, or 1,000 between two totals is often the result of an error in addition. A difference between totals can also be due to omitting a debit or a credit posting. If the difference can be evenly divided by 2, the error may be due to the posting of a debit as a credit, or vice versa. For example, if the debit total is $20,640 and the credit total is $20,236, the difference of $404 may indicate that a credit posting of $404 was omitted or that a credit of $202 was incorrectly posted as a debit.

Two other common types of errors are known as transpositions and slides. A **transposition** occurs when the order of the digits is changed mistakenly, such as writing $542 as $452 or $524. In a **slide**, the entire number is mistakenly moved one or more spaces to the right or the left, such as writing $542.00 as $54.20 or $5,420.00. If an error of either type has occurred and there are no other errors, the difference between the two trial balance totals can be evenly divided by 9.

If an error is not revealed by the trial balance, the steps in the accounting process must be retraced, beginning with the last step and working back to the entries in the journal. Usually, errors causing the trial balance totals to be unequal will be discovered before all of the steps are retraced.

CORRECTION OF ERRORS

The procedures used to correct an error vary according to the nature of the error, when the error is discovered, and whether a manual or computerized accounting system is used. Oftentimes, an error is discovered as it is being journalized or posted. In such cases, the error is simply corrected. For example, computerized accounting systems automatically verify for each journal entry whether the total debits equal the total credits. If the totals are not equal, an error report is created and the computer program will not proceed until the journal entry is corrected.

Occasionally, however, an error is not discovered until after a journal entry has been recorded and posted to the accounts. Correcting this type of error is more complex. To illustrate, assume that on May 5 a $12,500 purchase of office equipment on account was incorrectly journalized and posted as a debit to Supplies and a credit to Accounts Payable for $12,500. This posting of the incorrect entry is shown in the following T accounts:

	Supplies			Accounts Payable	
Incorrect:	12,500				12,500

Before making a correcting entry, it is best to determine the debit(s) and credit(s) that should have been recorded. These are shown in the following T accounts:

	Office Equipment			Accounts Payable	
Correct:	12,500				12,500

Comparing the two sets of T accounts shows that the incorrect debit to Supplies may be corrected by debiting Office Equipment for $12,500 and crediting Supplies for $12,500. The following correcting entry is then journalized and posted:

Entry to Correct Error:

17						17
18	May	31	Office Equipment	18	12 5 0 0 00	18
19			Supplies	14	12 5 0 0 00	19
20			To correct erroneous debit			20
21			to Supplies on May 5. See invoice			21
22			from Bell Office Equipment Co.			22

Example Exercise 2-7

objective 4

The following errors took place in journalizing and posting transactions:

a. A withdrawal of $6,000 by Cheri Ramey, owner of the business, was recorded as a debit to Office Salaries Expense and a credit to Cash.
b. Utilities Expense of $4,500 paid for the current month was recorded as a debit to Miscellaneous Expense and a credit to Accounts Payable.

Journalize the entries to correct the errors. Omit explanations.

Follow My Example 2-7

a.	Cheri Ramey, Drawing	6,000	
	Office Salaries Expense		6,000
b.	Accounts Payable	4,500	
	Miscellaneous Expense		4,500
	Utilities Expense	4,500	
	Cash		4,500

Note: The first entry in (b) reverses the incorrect entry, and the second entry records the correct entry. These two entries could also be combined into one entry; however, preparing two entries will make it easier for someone later to understand what had happened and why the entries were necessary.

For Practice: PE 2-7A, PE 2-7B

At a Glance

1. Describe the characteristics of an account and record transactions using a chart of accounts and journal.

Key Points	Key Learning Outcomes	Example Exercises	Practice Exercises
The record used for recording individual transactions is an account. A group of accounts is called a ledger. The system of accounts that make up a ledger is called a chart of accounts. Transactions are initially entered in a record called a journal.	• Prepare a chart of accounts for a proprietorship.		
	• Prepare journal entries.	2-1 2-2 2-3	2-1A, 2-1B 2-2A, 2-2B 2-3A, 2-3B
The simplest form of an account, a T account, has three parts: (1) a title; (2) a left side, called the debit side; and (3) a right side, called the credit side. Amounts entered on the left side of an account are called debits to the account. Amounts entered on the right side of an account are called credits. Periodically, the balance of the account is determined.	• Record entries in T accounts.		
The rules of debit and credit for recording increases or decreases in asset, liability, owner's equity, revenue, expense, and drawing accounts are shown in Exhibit 3. Each transaction is recorded so that the sum of the debits is always equal to the sum of the credits. The normal balance of an account is the side of the account (debit or credit) in which increases are recorded.	• List the rules of debit and credit.	2-4	2-4A, 2-4B
	• Determine the normal balance for accounts.	2-4	2-4A, 2-4B

2. Describe and illustrate the posting of journal entries to accounts.

Key Points	Key Learning Outcomes	Example Exercises	Practice Exercises
The debits and credits for each journal entry are periodically posted to the accounts in the order in which they occur in the journal using the steps illustrated in Exhibit 5.	• Post journal entries to a standard account.		
	• Post journal entries to a T account.	2-5	2-5A, 2-5B

3. Prepare an unadjusted trial balance and explain how it can be used to discover errors.

Key Points	Key Learning Outcomes	Example Exercises	Practice Exercises
A trial balance is prepared by listing the accounts from the ledger and their balances. If the two totals of the trial balance are not equal, an error has occurred.	• Prepare an unadjusted trial balance.	2-6	2-6A, 2-6B

4. Discover and correct errors in recording transactions.			
Key Points	**Key Learning Outcomes**	**Example Exercises**	**Practice Exercises**
Errors may be discovered (1) by audit procedures, (2) by looking at the trial balance, or (3) by chance.	• Discover errors in journalizing, posting, or preparing the trial balance. • Prepare correcting entries for errors that have been journalized and posted.	**2-7**	2-7A, 2-7B

Key Terms

account (49)
account receivable (63)
assets (51)
balance of the account (50)
chart of accounts (51)
credits (50)
debits (50)
double-entry accounting
   system (58)

drawing (51)
expenses (51)
journal (52)
journal entry (52)
journalizing (52)
ledger (51)
liabilities (51)
materiality concept (73)
owner's equity (51)

posting (59)
revenues (51)
slide (74)
T account (49)
transposition (74)
trial balance (72)
two-column journal (59)
unearned revenue (61)

Illustrative Problem

J. F. Outz, M.D., has been practicing as a cardiologist for three years. During April, 2007, Outz completed the following transactions in her practice of cardiology.

Apr. 1. Paid office rent for April, $800.
3. Purchased equipment on account, $2,100.
5. Received cash on account from patients, $3,150.
8. Purchased X-ray film and other supplies on account, $245.
9. One of the items of equipment purchased on April 3 was defective. It was returned with the permission of the supplier, who agreed to reduce the account for the amount charged for the item, $325.
12. Paid cash to creditors on account, $1,250.
17. Paid cash for renewal of a six-month property insurance policy, $370.
20. Discovered that the balances of the cash account and the accounts payable account as of April 1 were overstated by $200. A payment of that amount to a creditor in March had not been recorded. Journalize the $200 payment as of April 20.
24. Paid cash for laboratory analysis, $545.
27. Paid cash from business bank account for personal and family expenses, $1,250.
30. Recorded the cash received in payment of services (on a cash basis) to patients during April, $1,720.
30. Paid salaries of receptionist and nurses, $1,725.
30. Paid various utility expenses, $360.
30. Recorded fees charged to patients on account for services performed in April, $5,145.
30. Paid miscellaneous expenses, $132.

Outz's account titles, numbers, and balances as of April 1 (all normal balances) are listed as follows: Cash, 11, $4,123; Accounts Receivable, 12, $6,725; Supplies, 13, $290; Prepaid Insurance, 14, $465; Equipment, 18, $19,745; Accounts Payable, 22, $765; J. F. Outz, Capital, 31, $30,583; J. F. Outz, Drawing, 32; Professional Fees, 41; Salary Expense, 51; Rent Expense, 53; Laboratory Expense, 55; Utilities Expense, 56; Miscellaneous Expense, 59.

Instructions

1. Open a ledger of standard four-column accounts for Dr. Outz as of April 1. Enter the balances in the appropriate balance columns and place a check mark (✔) in the posting reference column. (*Hint:* Verify the equality of the debit and credit balances in the ledger before proceeding with the next instruction.)
2. Journalize each transaction in a two-column journal.
3. Post the journal to the ledger, extending the month-end balances to the appropriate balance columns after each posting.
4. Prepare an unadjusted trial balance as of April 30.

Solution

2. and **3.**

	JOURNAL				Page 27
Date	Description	Post. Ref.	Debit	Credit	
2007 Apr. 1	Rent Expense	53	8 0 0 00		1
	Cash	11		8 0 0 00	2
	Paid office rent for April.				3
					4
3	Equipment	18	2 1 0 0 00		5
	Accounts Payable	22		2 1 0 0 00	6
	Purchased equipment on account.				7
					8
5	Cash	11	3 1 5 0 00		9
	Accounts Receivable	12		3 1 5 0 00	10
	Received cash on account.				11
					12
8	Supplies	13	2 4 5 00		13
	Accounts Payable	22		2 4 5 00	14
	Purchased supplies.				15
					16
9	Accounts Payable	22	3 2 5 00		17
	Equipment	18		3 2 5 00	18
	Returned defective equipment.				19
					20
12	Accounts Payable	22	1 2 5 0 00		21
	Cash	11		1 2 5 0 00	22
	Paid creditors on account.				23
					24
17	Prepaid Insurance	14	3 7 0 00		25
	Cash	11		3 7 0 00	26
	Renewed six-month property policy.				27
					28
20	Accounts Payable	22	2 0 0 00		29
	Cash	11		2 0 0 00	30
	Recorded March payment				31
	to creditor.				32
					33

			JOURNAL				**Page 28**
	Date		Description	Post. Ref.	Debit	Credit	
1	2007 Apr.	24	Laboratory Expense	55	5 4 5 00		1
2			Cash	11		5 4 5 00	2
3			Paid for laboratory analysis.				3
4							4
5		27	J. F. Outz, Drawing	32	1 2 5 0 00		5
6			Cash	11		1 2 5 0 00	6
7			J. F. Outz withdrew cash for				7
8			personal use.				8
9							9
10		30	Cash	11	1 7 2 0 00		10
11			Professional Fees	41		1 7 2 0 00	11
12			Received fees from patients.				12
13							13
14		30	Salary Expense	51	1 7 2 5 00		14
15			Cash	11		1 7 2 5 00	15
16			Paid salaries.				16
17							17
18		30	Utilities Expense	56	3 6 0 00		18
19			Cash	11		3 6 0 00	19
20			Paid utilities.				20
21							21
22		30	Accounts Receivable	12	5 1 4 5 00		22
23			Professional Fees	41		5 1 4 5 00	23
24			Recorded fees earned on account.				24
25							25
26		30	Miscellaneous Expense	59	1 3 2 00		26
27			Cash	11		1 3 2 00	27
28			Paid expenses.				28

1. and **3.**

ACCOUNT Cash							**ACCOUNT NO.** 11		
							Balance		
	Date		Item	Post. Ref.	Debit	Credit	Debit	Credit	
	2007 Apr.	1	Balance	✓			4 1 2 3 00		
		1		27		8 0 0 00	3 3 2 3 00		
		5		27	3 1 5 0 00		6 4 7 3 00		
		12		27		1 2 5 0 00	5 2 2 3 00		
		17		27		3 7 0 00	4 8 5 3 00		
		20		27		2 0 0 00	4 6 5 3 00		
		24		28		5 4 5 00	4 1 0 8 00		
		27		28		1 2 5 0 00	2 8 5 8 00		
		30		28	1 7 2 0 00		4 5 7 8 00		
		30		28		1 7 2 5 00	2 8 5 3 00		
		30		28		3 6 0 00	2 4 9 3 00		
		30		28		1 3 2 00	2 3 6 1 00		

ACCOUNT *Accounts Receivable*   **ACCOUNT NO.** *12*

Date		Item	Post. Ref.	Debit	Credit	Balance Debit	Balance Credit
2007 Apr.	1	Balance	✓			6 7 2 5 00	
	5		27		3 1 5 0 00	3 5 7 5 00	
	30		28	5 1 4 5 00		8 7 2 0 00	

ACCOUNT *Supplies*   **ACCOUNT NO.** *13*

Date		Item	Post. Ref.	Debit	Credit	Balance Debit	Balance Credit
2007 Apr.	1	Balance	✓			2 9 0 00	
	8		27	2 4 5 00		5 3 5 00	

ACCOUNT *Prepaid Insurance*   **ACCOUNT NO.** *14*

Date		Item	Post. Ref.	Debit	Credit	Balance Debit	Balance Credit
2007 Apr.	1	Balance	✓			4 6 5 00	
	17		27	3 7 0 00		8 3 5 00	

ACCOUNT *Equipment*   **ACCOUNT NO.** *18*

Date		Item	Post. Ref.	Debit	Credit	Balance Debit	Balance Credit
2007 Apr.	1	Balance	✓			19 7 4 5 00	
	3		27	2 1 0 0 00		21 8 4 5 00	
	9		27		3 2 5 00	21 5 2 0 00	

ACCOUNT *Accounts Payable*   **ACCOUNT NO.** *22*

Date		Item	Post. Ref.	Debit	Credit	Balance Debit	Balance Credit
2007 Apr.	1	Balance	✓				7 6 5 00
	3		27		2 1 0 0 00		2 8 6 5 00
	8		27		2 4 5 00		3 1 1 0 00
	9		27	3 2 5 00			2 7 8 5 00
	12		27	1 2 5 0 00			1 5 3 5 00
	20		27	2 0 0 00			1 3 3 5 00

ACCOUNT *J. F. Outz, Capital*   **ACCOUNT NO.** *31*

Date		Item	Post. Ref.	Debit	Credit	Balance Debit	Balance Credit
2007 Apr.	1	Balance	✓				3 0 5 8 3 00

ACCOUNT *J. F. Outz, Drawing*   **ACCOUNT NO.** *32*

Date	Item	Post. Ref.	Debit	Credit	Balance Debit	Balance Credit
2007 Apr. 27		28	1 2 5 0 00		1 2 5 0 00	

ACCOUNT *Professional Fees*   **ACCOUNT NO.** *41*

Date	Item	Post. Ref.	Debit	Credit	Balance Debit	Balance Credit
2007 Apr. 30		28		1 7 2 0 00		1 7 2 0 00
30		28		5 1 4 5 00		6 8 6 5 00

ACCOUNT *Salary Expense*   **ACCOUNT NO.** *51*

Date	Item	Post. Ref.	Debit	Credit	Balance Debit	Balance Credit
2007 Apr. 30		28	1 7 2 5 00		1 7 2 5 00	

ACCOUNT *Rent Expense*   **ACCOUNT NO.** *53*

Date	Item	Post. Ref.	Debit	Credit	Balance Debit	Balance Credit
2007 Apr. 1		27	8 0 0 00		8 0 0 00	

ACCOUNT *Laboratory Expense*   **ACCOUNT NO.** *55*

Date	Item	Post. Ref.	Debit	Credit	Balance Debit	Balance Credit
2007 Apr. 24		28	5 4 5 00		5 4 5 00	

ACCOUNT *Utilities Expense*   **ACCOUNT NO.** *56*

Date	Item	Post. Ref.	Debit	Credit	Balance Debit	Balance Credit
2007 Apr. 30		28	3 6 0 00		3 6 0 00	

ACCOUNT *Miscellaneous Expense*   **ACCOUNT NO.** *59*

Date	Item	Post. Ref.	Debit	Credit	Balance Debit	Balance Credit
2007 Apr. 30		28	1 3 2 00		1 3 2 00	

4.

J. F. Outz, M.D.
Unadjusted Trial Balance
April 30, 2007

	Debit Balances	Credit Balances
Cash	2 3 6 1 00	
Accounts Receivable	8 7 2 0 00	
Supplies	5 3 5 00	
Prepaid Insurance	8 3 5 00	
Equipment	21 5 2 0 00	
Accounts Payable		1 3 3 5 00
J. F. Outz, Capital		30 5 8 3 00
J. F. Outz, Drawing	1 2 5 0 00	
Professional Fees		6 8 6 5 00
Salary Expense	1 7 2 5 00	
Rent Expense	8 0 0 00	
Laboratory Expense	5 4 5 00	
Utilities Expense	3 6 0 00	
Miscellaneous Expense	1 3 2 00	
	38 7 8 3 00	38 7 8 3 00

Self-Examination Questions

(Answers at End of Chapter)

1. A debit may signify a(n):
   A. increase in an asset account.
   B. decrease in an asset account.
   C. increase in a liability account.
   D. increase in the owner's capital account.

2. The type of account with a normal credit balance is:
   A. an asset.   C. a revenue.
   B. drawing.   D. an expense.

3. A debit balance in which of the following accounts would indicate a likely error?
   A. Accounts Receivable
   B. Cash
   C. Fees Earned
   D. Miscellaneous Expense

4. The receipt of cash from customers in payment of their accounts would be recorded by:
   A. a debit to Cash and a credit to Accounts Receivable.
   B. a debit to Accounts Receivable and a credit to Cash.
   C. a debit to Cash and a credit to Accounts Payable.
   D. a debit to Accounts Payable and a credit to Cash.

5. The form listing the titles and balances of the accounts in the ledger on a given date is the:
   A. income statement.
   B. balance sheet.
   C. statement of owner's equity.
   D. trial balance.

Eye Openers

1. What is the difference between an account and a ledger?
2. Do the terms *debit* and *credit* signify increase or decrease or can they signify either? Explain.
3. Explain why the rules of debit and credit are the same for liability accounts and owner's equity accounts.

4. What is the effect (increase or decrease) of a debit to an expense account (a) in terms of owner's equity and (b) in terms of expense?
5. What is the effect (increase or decrease) of a credit to a revenue account (a) in terms of owner's equity and (b) in terms of revenue?
6. Rabun Company adheres to a policy of depositing all cash receipts in a bank account and making all payments by check. The cash account as of January 31 has a credit balance of $2,500, and there is no undeposited cash on hand. (a) Assuming no errors occurred during journalizing or posting, what caused this unusual balance? (b) Is the $2,500 credit balance in the cash account an asset, a liability, owner's equity, a revenue, or an expense?
7. Cortes Company performed services in February for a specific customer, for a fee of $6,000. Payment was received the following March. (a) Was the revenue earned in February or March? (b) What accounts should be debited and credited in (1) February and (2) March?
8. What proof is provided by a trial balance?
9. If the two totals of a trial balance are equal, does it mean that there are no errors in the accounting records? Explain.
10. Assume that a trial balance is prepared with an account balance of $21,360 listed as $21,630 and an account balance of $1,500 listed as $15,000. Identify the transposition and the slide.
11. Assume that when a purchase of supplies of $1,380 for cash was recorded, both the debit and the credit were journalized and posted as $1,830. (a) Would this error cause the trial balance to be out of balance? (b) Would the trial balance be out of balance if the $1,380 entry had been journalized correctly but the credit to Cash had been posted as $1,830?
12. Assume that Hahn Consulting erroneously recorded the payment of $5,000 of owner withdrawals as a debit to Salary Expense. (a) How would this error affect the equality of the trial balance? (b) How would this error affect the income statement, statement of owner's equity, and balance sheet?
13. Assume that Hacienda Realty Co. borrowed $80,000 from Clinton Bank and Trust. In recording the transaction, Hacienda erroneously recorded the receipt as a debit to Cash, $80,000, and a credit to Fees Earned, $80,000. (a) How would this error affect the equality of the trial balance? (b) How would this error affect the income statement, statement of owner's equity, and balance sheet?
14. In journalizing and posting the entry to record the purchase of supplies for cash, the accounts payable account was credited in error. What is the preferred procedure to correct this error?
15. Banks rely heavily upon customers' deposits as a source of funds. Demand deposits normally pay interest to the customer, who is entitled to withdraw at any time without prior notice to the bank. Checking and NOW (negotiable order of withdrawal) accounts are the most common form of demand deposits for banks. Assume that Peachtree Storage has a checking account at Buckhead Savings Bank. What type of account (asset, liability, owner's equity, revenue, expense, drawing) does the account balance of $18,750 represent from the viewpoint of (a) Peachtree Storage and (b) Buckhead Savings Bank?

Practice Exercises

PE 2-1A
Journal entry for purchase of office equipment

obj. 1

Prepare a journal entry for the purchase of office equipment on November 23 for $13,750, paying $5,000 cash and the remainder on account.

PE 2-1B
Journal entry for purchase of office supplies
obj. 1

Prepare a journal entry for the purchase of office supplies on March 13 for $6,500, paying $1,300 cash and the remainder on account.

PE 2-2A
Journal entry for fees earned on account
obj. 1

Prepare a journal entry on February 2 for fees earned on account, $6,300.

PE 2-2B
Journal entry for cash received for services rendered
obj. 1

Prepare a journal entry on January 21 for cash received for services rendered, $1,250.

PE 2-3A
Journal entry for owner's withdrawal
obj. 1

Prepare a journal entry on October 31 for the withdrawal of $4,500 by Amy Sykes for personal use.

PE 2-3B
Journal entry for owner's withdrawal
obj. 1

Prepare a journal entry on July 31 for the withdrawal of $7,250 by Paul Wright for personal use.

PE 2-4A
Rules of debit and credit and normal balances
obj. 1

State for each account whether it is likely to have (a) debit entries only, (b) credit entries only, or (c) both debit and credit entries. Also, indicate its normal balance.

1. Notes Payable
2. Accounts Receivable
3. Wages Expense
4. Commissions Earned
5. Unearned Rent
6. Shinya Mylod, Capital

PE 2-4B
Rules of debit and credit and normal balances
obj. 1

State for each account whether it is likely to have (a) debit entries only, (b) credit entries only, or (c) both debit and credit entries. Also, indicate its normal balance.

1. Prepaid Insurance
2. Rent Revenue
3. Li Xu, Drawing
4. Miscellaneous Expense
5. Accounts Payable
6. Cash

PE 2-5A
Determining cash receipts
obj. 2

On April 1, the cash account balance was $18,750. During April, cash payments totaled $219,140, and the April 30 balance was $22,175. Determine the cash receipts during April.

PE 2-5B
Determining supplies expense
obj. 2

On January 1, the supplies account balance was $1,035. During January, supplies of $2,325 were purchased, and $786 of supplies were on hand as of January 31. Determine supplies expense for January.

PE 2-6A
Effect of errors on a trial balance
obj. 3

For each of the following errors, considered individually, indicate whether the error would cause the trial balance totals to be unequal. If the error would cause the trial balance total to be unequal, indicate whether the debit or credit total is higher and by how much.

a. A payment of $468 on account was debited to Accounts Payable for $486 and credited to Cash for $486.
b. A purchase of supplies of $1,130 was debited to Supplies for $1,130 and debited to Accounts Payable for $1,130.
c. The payment of an insurance premium of $2,450 for a two-year policy was debited to Prepaid Insurance for $2,450 and credited to Cash for $2,540.

PE 2-6B
Effect of errors on a trial balance
obj. 3

For each of the following errors, considered individually, indicate whether the error would cause the trial balance totals to be unequal. If the error would cause the trial balance total to be unequal, indicate whether the debit or credit total is higher and by how much.

a. The receipt of cash on account of $1,312 was recorded as a debit to Cash for $1,012 and a credit to Accounts Receivable for $1,312.
b. The payment of cash for the purchase of office equipment of $4,500 was debited to Land for $4,500 and credited to Cash for $4,500.
c. The payment of $1,420 on account was debited to Accounts Payable for $142 and credited to Cash for $1,420.

PE 2-7A
Correction of errors
obj. 4

The following errors took place in journalizing and posting transactions:

a. The payment of $3,125 from a customer on account was recorded as a debit to Cash and a credit to Accounts Payable.
b. Advertising expense of $1,500 paid for the current month was recorded as a debit to Miscellaneous Expense and a credit to Advertising Expense.

Journalize the entries to correct the errors. Omit explanations.

PE 2-7B
Correction of errors
obj. 4

The following errors took place in journalizing and posting transactions:

a. The purchase of supplies of $2,690 on account was recorded as a debit to Office Equipment and a credit to Supplies.
b. The receipt of $3,750 for services rendered was recorded as a debit to Accounts Receivable and a credit to Fees Earned.

Journalize the entries to correct the errors. Omit explanations.

Exercises

EX 2-1
Chart of accounts
obj. 1

The following accounts appeared in recent financial statements of Continental Airlines:

Accounts Payable	Flight Equipment
Air Traffic Liability	Landing Fees
Aircraft Fuel Expense	Passenger Revenue
Cargo and Mail Revenue	Purchase Deposits for Flight Equipment
Commissions	Spare Parts and Supplies

Identify each account as either a balance sheet account or an income statement account. For each balance sheet account, identify it as an asset, a liability, or owner's equity. For each income statement account, identify it as a revenue or an expense.

EX 2-2
Chart of accounts
obj. 1

Mandalay Interiors is owned and operated by Angie Stowe, an interior decorator. In the ledger of Mandalay Interiors, the first digit of the account number indicates its major account classification (1—assets, 2—liabilities, 3—owner's equity, 4—revenues, 5—expenses). The second digit of the account number indicates the specific account within each of the preceding major account classifications.

Match each account number with its most likely account in the list below. The account numbers are 11, 12, 13, 21, 31, 32, 41, 51, 52, and 53.

Accounts Payable	Fees Earned
Accounts Receivable	Land
Angie Stowe, Capital	Miscellaneous Expense
Angie Stowe, Drawing	Supplies Expense
Cash	Wages Expense

EX 2-3
Chart of accounts
obj. 1

Dazzle School is a newly organized business that teaches people how to inspire and influence others. The list of accounts to be opened in the general ledger is as follows:

Accounts Payable	Miscellaneous Expense	Supplies
Accounts Receivable	Prepaid Insurance	Supplies Expense
Cash	Rebecca Wimmer, Capital	Unearned Rent
Equipment	Rebecca Wimmer, Drawing	Wages Expense
Fees Earned	Rent Expense	

List the accounts in the order in which they should appear in the ledger of Dazzle School and assign account numbers. Each account number is to have two digits: the first digit is to indicate the major classification (1 for assets, etc.), and the second digit is to identify the specific account within each major classification (11 for Cash, etc.).

EX 2-4
Identifying transactions
obj. 1

Eos Co. is a travel agency. The nine transactions recorded by Eos during March 2008, its first month of operations, are indicated in the following T accounts:

Cash		Equipment		Tosha Lewis, Drawing	
(1) 30,000	(2) 1,800	(3) 24,000		(8) 2,500	
(7) 10,000	(3) 9,000				
	(4) 3,050				
	(6) 7,500				
	(8) 2,500				

Accounts Receivable		Accounts Payable		Service Revenue	
(5) 15,000	(7) 10,000	(6) 7,500	(3) 15,000		(5) 15,000

Supplies		Tosha Lewis, Capital		Operating Expenses	
(2) 1,800	(9) 1,050		(1) 30,000	(4) 3,050	
				(9) 1,050	

Indicate for each debit and each credit: (a) whether an asset, liability, owner's equity, drawing, revenue, or expense account was affected and (b) whether the account was increased (+) or decreased (−). Present your answers in the following form, with transaction (1) given as an example:

	Account Debited		Account Credited	
Transaction	Type	Effect	Type	Effect
(1)	asset	+	owner's equity	+

EX 2-5
Journal entries
objs. 1, 2

Based upon the T accounts in Exercise 2-4, prepare the nine journal entries from which the postings were made. Journal entry explanations may be omitted.

EX 2-6
Trial balance
obj. 3

✓ *Total Debit Column:*
$52,500

Based upon the data presented in Exercise 2-4, prepare an unadjusted trial balance, listing the accounts in their proper order.

EX 2-7
Normal entries for accounts
obj. 1

During the month, Witherspoon Labs Co. has a substantial number of transactions affecting each of the following accounts. State for each account whether it is likely to have (a) debit entries only, (b) credit entries only, or (c) both debit and credit entries.

1. Accounts Payable
2. Accounts Receivable
3. Cash
4. Fees Earned
5. Insurance Expense
6. Keith Dupree, Drawing
7. Supplies Expense

EX 2-8
Normal balances of accounts
obj. 1

Identify each of the following accounts of Sydney Services Co. as asset, liability, owner's equity, revenue, or expense, and state in each case whether the normal balance is a debit or a credit.

a. Accounts Payable
b. Accounts Receivable
c. Boyd Magnus, Capital
d. Boyd Magnus, Drawing
e. Cash
f. Fees Earned
g. Office Equipment
h. Rent Expense
i. Supplies
j. Wages Expense

EX 2-9
Rules of debit and credit
obj. 1

The following table summarizes the rules of debit and credit. For each of the items (a) through (l), indicate whether the proper answer is a debit or a credit.

	Increase	Decrease	Normal Balance
Balance sheet accounts:			
Asset	(a)	Credit	(b)
Liability	(c)	(d)	Credit
Owner's equity:			
Capital	Credit	(e)	(f)
Drawing	(g)	(h)	Debit
Income statement accounts:			
Revenue	(i)	(j)	(k)
Expense	Debit	(l)	Debit

EX 2-10
Capital account balance
obj. 1

As of January 1, Sarah Bredy, Capital, had a credit balance of $21,800. During the year, withdrawals totaled $1,500, and the business incurred a net loss of $24,000.

a. Calculate the balance of Sarah Bredy, Capital, as of the end of the year.
b. Assuming that there have been no recording errors, will the balance sheet prepared at December 31 balance? Explain.

EX 2-11
Cash account balance
obj. 1

During the month, Harpoon Co. received $479,250 in cash and paid out $312,380 in cash.

a. Do the data indicate that Harpoon Co. earned $166,870 during the month? Explain.
b. If the balance of the cash account is $241,925 at the end of the month, what was the cash balance at the beginning of the month?

EX 2-12
Account balances
obj. 1
✓c. $5,100

a. On June 1, the cash account balance was $11,150. During June, cash receipts totaled $72,300 and the June 30 balance was $15,750. Determine the cash payments made during June.
b. On July 1, the accounts receivable account balance was $25,500. During July, $115,000 was collected from customers on account. Assuming the July 31 balance was $27,500, determine the fees billed to customers on account during July.
c. During December, $60,500 was paid to creditors on account, and purchases on account were $77,700. Assuming the December 31 balance of Accounts Payable was $22,300, determine the account balance on December 1.

EX 2-13
Transactions
objs. 1, 2

The Boa Co. has the following accounts in its ledger: Cash; Accounts Receivable; Supplies; Office Equipment; Accounts Payable; Alfonso Finley, Capital; Alfonso Finley, Drawing; Fees Earned; Rent Expense; Advertising Expense; Utilities Expense; Miscellaneous Expense.
Journalize the following selected transactions for October 2007 in a two-column journal. Journal entry explanations may be omitted.

Oct.   1. Paid rent for the month, $2,500.
       3. Paid advertising expense, $1,100.
       4. Paid cash for supplies, $725.
       6. Purchased office equipment on account, $7,500.
      10. Received cash from customers on account, $3,600.
      12. Paid creditor on account, $600.
      20. Withdrew cash for personal use, $1,000.
      27. Paid cash for repairs to office equipment, $500.
      30. Paid telephone bill for the month, $195.
      31. Fees earned and billed to customers for the month, $20,150.
      31. Paid electricity bill for the month, $315.

EX 2-14
Journalizing and posting
objs. 1, 2

On July 27, 2008, Colorcast Co. purchased $1,875 of supplies on account. In Colorcast Co.'s chart of accounts, the supplies account is No. 15, and the accounts payable account is No. 21.

a. Journalize the July 27, 2008, transaction on page 38 of Colorcast Co.'s two-column journal. Include an explanation of the entry.
b. Prepare a four-column account for Supplies. Enter a debit balance of $735 as of July 1, 2008. Place a check mark (✓) in the Posting Reference column.
c. Prepare a four-column account for Accounts Payable. Enter a credit balance of $11,380 as of July 1, 2008. Place a check mark (✓) in the Posting Reference column.
d. Post the July 27, 2008, transaction to the accounts.

EX 2-15
Transactions and T accounts
objs. 1, 2

The following selected transactions were completed during August of the current year:

1. Billed customers for fees earned, $13,750.
2. Purchased supplies on account, $1,325.
3. Received cash from customers on account, $8,150.
4. Paid creditors on account, $800.

a. Journalize the above transactions in a two-column journal, using the appropriate number to identify the transactions. Journal entry explanations may be omitted.
b. Post the entries prepared in (a) to the following T accounts: Cash, Supplies, Accounts Receivable, Accounts Payable, Fees Earned. To the left of each amount posted in the accounts, place the appropriate number to identify the transactions.

EX 2-16
Trial balance
obj. 3

The accounts in the ledger of Matice Co. as of July 31, 2008, are listed in alphabetical order as follows. All accounts have normal balances. The balance of the cash account has been intentionally omitted.

Accounts Payable	$ 56,130	Notes Payable	$120,000
Accounts Receivable	112,500	Prepaid Insurance	9,000
Cash	?	Rent Expense	180,000
Fees Earned	930,000	Supplies	6,300
Insurance Expense	18,000	Supplies Expense	23,700
Land	255,000	Unearned Rent	27,000
Milton Adair, Capital	259,920	Utilities Expense	124,500
Milton Adair, Drawing	60,000	Wages Expense	525,000
Miscellaneous Expense	26,700		

Prepare an unadjusted trial balance, listing the accounts in their proper order and inserting the missing figure for cash.

EX 2-17
Effect of errors on trial balance

obj. 3

Indicate which of the following errors, each considered individually, would cause the trial balance totals to be unequal:

a. A fee of $2,350 earned and due from a client was not debited to Accounts Receivable or credited to a revenue account, because the cash had not been received.
b. A payment of $1,500 to a creditor was posted as a debit of $1,500 to Accounts Payable and a debit of $1,500 to Cash.
c. A payment of $6,000 for equipment purchased was posted as a debit of $600 to Equipment and a credit of $600 to Cash.
d. Payment of a cash withdrawal of $12,000 was journalized and posted as a debit of $21,000 to Salary Expense and a credit of $12,000 to Cash.
e. A receipt of $750 from an account receivable was journalized and posted as a debit of $750 to Cash and a credit of $750 to Fees Earned.

EX 2-18
Errors in trial balance

obj. 3

✓ *Total of Credit Column: $363,200*

The following preliminary unadjusted trial balance of Awesome Co., a sports ticket agency, does not balance:

Awesome Co.
Unadjusted Trial Balance
December 31, 2008

	Debit Balances	Credit Balances
Cash	94,700	
Accounts Receivable	44,200	
Prepaid Insurance		16,000
Equipment	15,000	
Accounts Payable		25,960
Unearned Rent		5,800
Sean Milner, Capital	164,840	
Sean Milner, Drawing	20,000	
Service Revenue		167,500
Wages Expense		84,000
Advertising Expense	14,400	
Miscellaneous Expense		2,850
	353,140	302,110

When the ledger and other records are reviewed, you discover the following: (1) the debits and credits in the cash account total $94,700 and $67,950, respectively; (2) a billing of $5,000 to a customer on account was not posted to the accounts receivable account; (3) a payment of $3,600 made to a creditor on account was not posted to the accounts payable account; (4) the balance of the unearned rent account is $8,500; (5) the correct balance of the equipment account is $150,000; and (6) each account has a normal balance.
Prepare a corrected unadjusted trial balance.

EX 2-19
Effect of errors on trial balance

obj. 3

The following errors occurred in posting from a two-column journal:

1. A credit of $5,125 to Accounts Payable was not posted.
2. A debit of $675 to Accounts Payable was posted as a credit.
3. A debit of $1,375 to Supplies was posted twice.
4. A debit of $3,575 to Wages Expense was posted as $3,557.
5. An entry debiting Accounts Receivable and crediting Fees Earned for $6,000 was not posted.
6. A credit of $350 to Cash was posted as $530.
7. A debit of $1,000 to Cash was posted to Miscellaneous Expense.

Considering each case individually (i.e., assuming that no other errors had occurred), indicate: (a) by "yes" or "no" whether the trial balance would be out of balance; (b) if answer to (a) is "yes," the amount by which the trial balance totals would differ; and (c) whether the debit or credit column of the trial balance would have the larger total. Answers should be presented in the following form, with error (1) given as an example:

Error	(a) Out of Balance	(b) Difference	(c) Larger Total
1.	yes	$5,125	debit

EX 2-20
Errors in trial balance

obj. 3

✓ *Total of Credit Column: $375,000*

Identify the errors in the following trial balance. All accounts have normal balances.

Hybrid Co.
Unadjusted Trial Balance
For the Month Ending October 31, 2008

	Debit Balances	Credit Balances
Cash	22,500	
Accounts Receivable		49,200
Prepaid Insurance	10,800	
Equipment	150,000	
Accounts Payable	5,550	
Salaries Payable		3,750
Nolan Towns, Capital		129,600
Nolan Towns, Drawing		18,000
Service Revenue		236,100
Salary Expense	98,430	
Advertising Expense		21,600
Miscellaneous Expense	4,470	
	458,250	458,250

EX 2-21
Entries to correct errors

obj. 4

The following errors took place in journalizing and posting transactions:

a. A withdrawal of $20,000 by Joel Goodson, owner of the business, was recorded as a debit to Wages Expense and a credit to Cash.
b. Rent of $3,600 paid for the current month was recorded as a debit to Rent Expense and a credit to Prepaid Rent.

Journalize the entries to correct the errors. Omit explanations.

EX 2-22
Entries to correct errors

obj. 4

The following errors took place in journalizing and posting transactions:

a. A $940 purchase of supplies for cash was recorded as a debit to Supplies Expense and a credit to Accounts Payable.
b. Cash of $2,750 received on account was recorded as a debit to Fees Earned and a credit to Cash.

Journalize the entries to correct the errors. Omit explanations.

Problems Series A

PR 2-1A
*Entries into T accounts
and trial balance*

objs. 1, 2, 3

✓ *3. Total of Debit
Column: $51,200*

Hannah Knox, an architect, opened an office on July 1, 2008. During the month, she completed the following transactions connected with her professional practice:

a. Transferred cash from a personal bank account to an account to be used for the business, $25,000.
b. Paid July rent for office and workroom, $2,000.
c. Purchased used automobile for $16,500, paying $1,500 cash and giving a note payable for the remainder.
d. Purchased office and computer equipment on account, $6,500.
e. Paid cash for supplies, $975.
f. Paid cash for annual insurance policies, $1,200.
g. Received cash from client for plans delivered, $3,750.
h. Paid cash for miscellaneous expenses, $240.
i. Paid cash to creditors on account, $2,500.
j. Paid installment due on note payable, $450.
k. Received invoice for blueprint service, due in August, $750.
l. Recorded fee earned on plans delivered, payment to be received in August, $3,150.
m. Paid salary of assistant, $1,500.
n. Paid gas, oil, and repairs on automobile for July, $280.

Instructions
1. Record the above transactions directly in the following T accounts, without journalizing: Cash; Accounts Receivable; Supplies; Prepaid Insurance; Automobiles; Equipment; Notes Payable; Accounts Payable; Hannah Knox, Capital; Professional Fees; Rent Expense; Salary Expense; Automobile Expense; Blueprint Expense; Miscellaneous Expense. To the left of the amount entered in the accounts, place the appropriate letter to identify the transaction.
2. Determine account balances of the T accounts. Accounts containing a single entry only (such as Prepaid Insurance) do not need a balance.
3. Prepare an unadjusted trial balance for Hannah Knox, Architect, as of July 31, 2008.

PR 2-2A
*Journal entries and trial
balance*

objs. 1, 2, 3

✓ *4. c. $6,425*

On March 1, 2008, Kara Frantz established Mudcat Realty, which completed the following transactions during the month:

a. Kara Frantz transferred cash from a personal bank account to an account to be used for the business, $15,000.
b. Paid rent on office and equipment for the month, $2,500.
c. Purchased supplies on account, $850.
d. Paid creditor on account, $400.
e. Earned sales commissions, receiving cash, $15,750.
f. Paid automobile expenses (including rental charge) for month, $2,400, and miscellaneous expenses, $600.
g. Paid office salaries, $3,250.
h. Determined that the cost of supplies used was $575.
i. Withdrew cash for personal use, $1,000.

Instructions
1. Journalize entries for transactions (a) through (i), using the following account titles: Cash; Supplies; Accounts Payable; Kara Frantz, Capital; Kara Frantz, Drawing; Sales Commissions; Office Salaries Expense; Rent Expense; Automobile Expense; Supplies Expense; Miscellaneous Expense. Explanations may be omitted.
2. Prepare T accounts, using the account titles in (1). Post the journal entries to these accounts, placing the appropriate letter to the left of each amount to identify the transactions. Determine the account balances, after all posting is complete. Accounts containing only a single entry do not need a balance.
3. Prepare an unadjusted trial balance as of March 31, 2008.

(continued)

4. Determine the following:
   a. Amount of total revenue recorded in the ledger.
   b. Amount of total expenses recorded in the ledger.
   c. Amount of net income for March.

PR 2-3A
Journal entries and trial balance

objs. 1, 2, 3

✓ *3. Total of Credit Column: $49,825*

On June 1, 2008, Brooks Dodd established an interior decorating business, Coordinated Designs. During the month, Brooks completed the following transactions related to the business:

June 1. Brooks transferred cash from a personal bank account to an account to be used for the business, $18,000.
      5. Paid rent for period of June 5 to end of month, $2,150.
      6. Purchased office equipment on account, $8,500.
      8. Purchased a used truck for $18,000, paying $10,000 cash and giving a note payable for the remainder.
      10. Purchased supplies for cash, $1,200.
      12. Received cash for job completed, $10,500.
      15. Paid annual premiums on property and casualty insurance, $2,400.
      23. Recorded jobs completed on account and sent invoices to customers, $5,950.
      24. Received an invoice for truck expenses, to be paid in July, $1,000.
      29. Paid utilities expense, $1,200.
      29. Paid miscellaneous expenses, $400.
      30. Received cash from customers on account, $3,200.
      30. Paid wages of employees, $2,900.
      30. Paid creditor a portion of the amount owed for equipment purchased on June 6, $2,125.
      30. Withdrew cash for personal use, $1,750.

Instructions
1. Journalize each transaction in a two-column journal, referring to the following chart of accounts in selecting the accounts to be debited and credited. (Do not insert the account numbers in the journal at this time.) Explanations may be omitted.

11 Cash	31 Brooks Dodd, Capital
12 Accounts Receivable	32 Brooks Dodd, Drawing
13 Supplies	41 Fees Earned
14 Prepaid Insurance	51 Wages Expense
16 Equipment	53 Rent Expense
18 Truck	54 Utilities Expense
21 Notes Payable	55 Truck Expense
22 Accounts Payable	59 Miscellaneous Expense

2. Post the journal to a ledger of four-column accounts, inserting appropriate posting references as each item is posted. Extend the balances to the appropriate balance columns after each transaction is posted.
3. Prepare an unadjusted trial balance for Coordinated Designs as of June 30, 2008.

PR 2-4A
Journal entries and trial balance

objs. 1, 2, 3

✓ *4. Total of Debit Column: $430,650*

Passport Realty acts as an agent in buying, selling, renting, and managing real estate. The unadjusted trial balance on October 31, 2008, is shown at the top of the following page.
   The following business transactions were completed by Passport Realty during November 2008:

Nov. 1. Paid rent on office for month, $5,000.
      2. Purchased office supplies on account, $1,750.
      5. Paid annual insurance premiums, $4,800.
      10. Received cash from clients on account, $52,000.
      15. Purchased land for a future building site for $90,000, paying $10,000 in cash and giving a note payable for the remainder.
      17. Paid creditors on account, $7,750.

Passport Realty
Unadjusted Trial Balance
October 31, 2008

		Debit Balances	Credit Balances
11	Cash	26,300	
12	Accounts Receivable	67,500	
13	Prepaid Insurance	3,000	
14	Office Supplies	1,800	
16	Land	—	
21	Accounts Payable		13,020
22	Unearned Rent		—
23	Notes Payable		—
31	Ashley Carnes, Capital		32,980
32	Ashley Carnes, Drawing	2,000	
41	Fees Earned		260,000
51	Salary and Commission Expense	148,200	
52	Rent Expense	30,000	
53	Advertising Expense	17,800	
54	Automobile Expense	5,500	
59	Miscellaneous Expense	3,900	
		306,000	306,000

Nov. 20. Returned a portion of the office supplies purchased on November 2, receiving
full credit for their cost, $250.
23. Paid advertising expense, $2,100.
27. Discovered an error in computing a commission; received cash from the salesperson for the overpayment, $700.
28. Paid automobile expense (including rental charges for an automobile), $1,500.
29. Paid miscellaneous expenses, $450.
30. Recorded revenue earned and billed to clients during the month, $48,400.
30. Paid salaries and commissions for the month, $25,000.
30. Withdrew cash for personal use, $8,000.
30. Rented land purchased on November 15 to local merchants association for use
as a parking lot in December and January, during a street rebuilding program;
received advance payment of $2,500.

Instructions
1. Record the November 1, 2008, balance of each account in the appropriate balance column of a four-column account, write *Balance* in the item section, and place a check mark
(✓) in the Posting Reference column.
2. Journalize the transactions for November in a two-column journal. Journal entry explanations may be omitted.
3. Post to the ledger, extending the account balance to the appropriate balance column after each posting.
4. Prepare an unadjusted trial balance of the ledger as of November 30, 2008.

PR 2-5A
Errors in trial balance
objs. 3, 4

*✓7. Total of Debit
Column: $43,338.10*

If the working papers correlating with this textbook are not used, omit Problem 2-5A.

The following records of Mainstay TV Repair are presented in the working papers:

- Journal containing entries for the period July 1–31.
- Ledger to which the July entries have been posted.
- Preliminary trial balance as of July 31, which does not balance.

Locate the errors, supply the information requested, and prepare a corrected trial balance
according to the following instructions. The balances recorded in the accounts as of July 1
and the entries in the journal are correctly stated. If it is necessary to correct any posted

amounts in the ledger, a line should be drawn through the erroneous figure and the correct amount inserted above. Corrections or notations may be inserted on the preliminary trial balance in any manner desired. It is not necessary to complete all of the instructions if equal trial balance totals can be obtained earlier. However, the requirements of instructions (6) and (7) should be completed in any event.

Instructions

1. Verify the totals of the preliminary trial balance, inserting the correct amounts in the schedule provided in the working papers.
2. Compute the difference between the trial balance totals.
3. Compare the listings in the trial balance with the balances appearing in the ledger, and list the errors in the space provided in the working papers.
4. Verify the accuracy of the balance of each account in the ledger, and list the errors in the space provided in the working papers.
5. Trace the postings in the ledger back to the journal, using small check marks to identify items traced. Correct any amounts in the ledger that may be necessitated by errors in posting, and list the errors in the space provided in the working papers.
6. Journalize as of July 31 the payment of $125 for advertising expense. The bill had been paid on July 31 but was inadvertently omitted from the journal. Post to the ledger. (Revise any amounts necessitated by posting this entry.)
7. Prepare a new unadjusted trial balance.

PR 2-6A
Corrected trial balance

obj. 3

✔ *1. Total of Debit Column: $200,000*

Iberian Carpet has the following unadjusted trial balance as of March 31, 2008.

Iberian Carpet
Unadjusted Trial Balance
March 31, 2008

	Debit Balances	Credit Balances
Cash	4,300	
Accounts Receivable	11,870	
Supplies	2,320	
Prepaid Insurance	880	
Equipment	56,000	
Notes Payable		26,100
Accounts Payable		7,900
Jose Mendrano, Capital		38,400
Jose Mendrano, Drawing	14,500	
Fees Earned		122,700
Wages Expense	70,000	
Rent Expense	16,600	
Advertising Expense	720	
Miscellaneous Expense	1,450	
	178,640	195,100

The debit and credit totals are not equal as a result of the following errors:

a. The balance of cash was understated by $3,000.
b. A cash receipt of $4,500 was posted as a debit to Cash of $5,400.
c. A debit of $1,850 to Accounts Receivable was not posted.
d. A return of $350 of defective supplies was erroneously posted as a $530 credit to Supplies.
e. An insurance policy acquired at a cost of $175 was posted as a credit to Prepaid Insurance.
f. The balance of Notes Payable was understated by $7,500.
g. A credit of $900 in Accounts Payable was overlooked when determining the balance of the account.
h. A debit of $3,500 for a withdrawal by the owner was posted as a credit to Jose Mendrano, Capital.
i. The balance of $7,200 in Advertising Expense was entered as $720 in the trial balance.
j. Gas, Electricity, and Water Expense, with a balance of $6,900, was omitted from the trial balance.

Instructions
1. Prepare a corrected unadjusted trial balance as of March 31, 2008.
2. ━━━▶ Does the fact that the unadjusted trial balance in (1) is balanced mean that there are no errors in the accounts? Explain.

Problems Series B

PR 2-1B
Entries into T accounts and trial balance
objs. 1, 2, 3

✓ 3. Total of Debit
Column: $47,800

Lynette Moss, an architect, opened an office on April 1, 2008. During the month, she completed the following transactions connected with her professional practice:

a. Transferred cash from a personal bank account to an account to be used for the business, $22,500.
b. Purchased used automobile for $15,300, paying $4,000 cash and giving a note payable for the remainder.
c. Paid April rent for office and workroom, $2,500.
d. Paid cash for supplies, $1,200.
e. Purchased office and computer equipment on account, $5,200.
f. Paid cash for annual insurance policies on automobile and equipment, $1,600.
g. Received cash from a client for plans delivered, $6,500.
h. Paid cash to creditors on account, $1,800.
i. Paid cash for miscellaneous expenses, $300.
j. Received invoice for blueprint service, due in May, $800.
k. Recorded fee earned on plans delivered, payment to be received in May, $3,500.
l. Paid salary of assistant, $1,500.
m. Paid cash for miscellaneous expenses, $210.
n. Paid installment due on note payable, $200.
o. Paid gas, oil, and repairs on automobile for April, $250.

Instructions
1. Record the above transactions directly in the following T accounts, without journalizing: Cash; Accounts Receivable; Supplies; Prepaid Insurance; Automobiles; Equipment; Notes Payable; Accounts Payable; Lynette Moss, Capital; Professional Fees; Rent Expense; Salary Expense; Blueprint Expense; Automobile Expense; Miscellaneous Expense. To the left of each amount entered in the accounts, place the appropriate letter to identify the transaction.
2. Determine account balances of the T accounts. Accounts containing a single entry only (such as Prepaid Insurance) do not need a balance.
3. Prepare an unadjusted trial balance for Lynette Moss, Architect, as of April 30, 2008.

PR 2-2B
Journal entries and trial balance
objs. 1, 2, 3

✓ 4. c. $5,575

On July 1, 2008, Bill Bonds established Genesis Realty, which completed the following transactions during the month:

a. Bill Bonds transferred cash from a personal bank account to an account to be used for the business, $18,000.
b. Purchased supplies on account, $1,000.
c. Earned sales commissions, receiving cash, $14,600.
d. Paid rent on office and equipment for the month, $3,000.
e. Paid creditor on account, $600.
f. Withdrew cash for personal use, $1,500.
g. Paid automobile expenses (including rental charge) for month, $2,000, and miscellaneous expenses, $500.
h. Paid office salaries, $2,800.
i. Determined that the cost of supplies used was $725.

Instructions
1. Journalize entries for transactions (a) through (i), using the following account titles: Cash; Supplies; Accounts Payable; Bill Bonds, Capital; Bill Bonds, Drawing; Sales Commissions; Rent Expense; Office Salaries Expense; Automobile Expense; Supplies Expense; Miscellaneous Expense. Journal entry explanations may be omitted.

(continued)

2. Prepare T accounts, using the account titles in (1). Post the journal entries to these accounts, placing the appropriate letter to the left of each amount to identify the transactions. Determine the account balances, after all posting is complete. Accounts containing only a single entry do not need a balance.

3. Prepare an unadjusted trial balance as of July 31, 2008.

4. Determine the following:

   a. Amount of total revenue recorded in the ledger.

   b. Amount of total expenses recorded in the ledger.

   c. Amount of net income for July.

PR 2-3B

Journal entries and trial balance

objs. 1, 2, 3

✓3. Total of Credit Column: $47,675

On October 1, 2008, Kristy Gomez established an interior decorating business, Ultimate Designs. During the month, Kristy Gomez completed the following transactions related to the business:

Oct. 1. Kristy transferred cash from a personal bank account to an account to be used for the business, $20,000.

   3. Paid rent for period of October 3 to end of month, $1,600.

   10. Purchased a truck for $15,000, paying $5,000 cash and giving a note payable for the remainder.

   13. Purchased equipment on account, $4,500.

   14. Purchased supplies for cash, $1,100.

   15. Paid annual premiums on property and casualty insurance, $2,800.

   15. Received cash for job completed, $6,100.

   21. Paid creditor a portion of the amount owed for equipment purchased on October 13, $2,400.

   24. Recorded jobs completed on account and sent invoices to customers, $8,600.

   26. Received an invoice for truck expenses, to be paid in November, $875.

   27. Paid utilities expense, $900.

   27. Paid miscellaneous expenses, $315.

   29. Received cash from customers on account, $4,100.

   30. Paid wages of employees, $2,500.

   31. Withdrew cash for personal use, $3,000.

Instructions

1. Journalize each transaction in a two-column journal, referring to the following chart of accounts in selecting the accounts to be debited and credited. (Do not insert the account numbers in the journal at this time.) Journal entry explanations may be omitted.

11 Cash	31 Kristy Gomez, Capital
12 Accounts Receivable	32 Kristy Gomez, Drawing
13 Supplies	41 Fees Earned
14 Prepaid Insurance	51 Wages Expense
16 Equipment	53 Rent Expense
18 Truck	54 Utilities Expense
21 Notes Payable	55 Truck Expense
22 Accounts Payable	59 Miscellaneous Expense

2. Post the journal to a ledger of four-column accounts, inserting appropriate posting references as each item is posted. Extend the balances to the appropriate balance columns after each transaction is posted.

3. Prepare an unadjusted trial balance for Ultimate Designs as of October 31, 2008.

PR 2-4B

Journal entries and trial balance

objs. 1, 2, 3

✓4. Total of Debit Column: $375,230

Equity Realty acts as an agent in buying, selling, renting, and managing real estate. The unadjusted trial balance on July 31, 2008, is shown at the top of the following page.

The following business transactions were completed by Equity Realty during August 2008:

Aug. 1. Purchased office supplies on account, $1,500.

   2. Paid rent on office for month, $2,500.

   3. Received cash from clients on account, $28,720.

   5. Paid annual insurance premiums, $3,600.

Equity Realty
Unadjusted Trial Balance
July 31, 2008

		Debit Balances	Credit Balances
11	Cash	21,200	
12	Accounts Receivable	35,750	
13	Prepaid Insurance	4,500	
14	Office Supplies	1,000	
16	Land	—	
21	Accounts Payable		6,200
22	Unearned Rent		—
23	Notes Payable		—
31	Jody Craft, Capital		31,550
32	Jody Craft, Drawing	16,000	
41	Fees Earned		220,000
51	Salary and Commission Expense	140,000	
52	Rent Expense	17,500	
53	Advertising Expense	14,300	
54	Automobile Expense	6,400	
59	Miscellaneous Expense	1,100	
		257,750	257,750

Aug. 9. Returned a portion of the office supplies purchased on August 1, receiving full credit for their cost, $250.

17. Paid advertising expense, $3,450.

23. Paid creditors on account, $2,670.

29. Paid miscellaneous expenses, $500.

30. Paid automobile expense (including rental charges for an automobile), $1,500.

31. Discovered an error in computing a commission; received cash from the salesperson for the overpayment, $1,000.

31. Paid salaries and commissions for the month, $17,400.

31. Recorded revenue earned and billed to clients during the month, $51,900.

31. Purchased land for a future building site for $75,000, paying $10,000 in cash and giving a note payable for the remainder.

31. Withdrew cash for personal use, $5,000.

31. Rented land purchased on August 31 to a local university for use as a parking lot during football season (September, October, and November); received advance payment of $2,000.

Instructions

1. Record the August 1 balance of each account in the appropriate balance column of a four-column account, write *Balance* in the item section, and place a check mark (✔) in the Posting Reference column.

2. Journalize the transactions for August in a two-column journal. Journal entry explanations may be omitted.

3. Post to the ledger, extending the account balance to the appropriate balance column after each posting.

4. Prepare an unadjusted trial balance of the ledger as of August 31, 2008.

PR 2-5B
Errors in trial balance
objs. 3, 4

If the working papers correlating with this textbook are not used, omit Problem 2-5B.

The following records of Mainstay TV Repair are presented in the working papers:

- Journal containing entries for the period July 1–31.
- Ledger to which the July entries have been posted.
- Preliminary trial balance as of July 31, which does not balance.

Locate the errors, supply the information requested, and prepare a corrected trial balance according to the following instructions. The balances recorded in the accounts as of July 1

✓ *7. Total of Credit Column: $43,338.10*

and the entries in the journal are correctly stated. If it is necessary to correct any posted amounts in the ledger, a line should be drawn through the erroneous figure and the correct amount inserted above. Corrections or notations may be inserted on the preliminary trial balance in any manner desired. It is not necessary to complete all of the instructions if equal trial balance totals can be obtained earlier. However, the requirements of instructions (6) and (7) should be completed in any event.

Instructions

1. Verify the totals of the preliminary trial balance, inserting the correct amounts in the schedule provided in the working papers.
2. Compute the difference between the trial balance totals.
3. Compare the listings in the trial balance with the balances appearing in the ledger, and list the errors in the space provided in the working papers.
4. Verify the accuracy of the balance of each account in the ledger, and list the errors in the space provided in the working papers.
5. Trace the postings in the ledger back to the journal, using small check marks to identify items traced. Correct any amounts in the ledger that may be necessitated by errors in posting, and list the errors in the space provided in the working papers.
6. Journalize as of July 31 the payment of $110 for gas and electricity. The bill had been paid on July 31 but was inadvertently omitted from the journal. Post to the ledger. (Revise any amounts necessitated by posting this entry.)
7. Prepare a new unadjusted trial balance.

PR 2-6B
Corrected trial balance

obj. 3

✓ *1. Total of Debit Column: $234,000*

Epic Video has the following unadjusted trial balance as of July 31, 2008:

Epic Video
Unadjusted Trial Balance
July 31, 2008

	Debit Balances	Credit Balances
Cash	6,250	
Accounts Receivable	12,520	
Supplies	2,232	
Prepaid Insurance	710	
Equipment	54,000	
Notes Payable		22,500
Accounts Payable		4,980
Carlton Dey, Capital		30,400
Carlton Dey, Drawing	11,500	
Fees Earned		178,020
Wages Expense	102,000	
Rent Expense	20,850	
Advertising Expense	9,540	
Gas, Electricity, and Water Expense	5,670	
	225,272	235,900

The debit and credit totals are not equal as a result of the following errors:

a. The balance of cash was overstated by $5,000.
b. A cash receipt of $3,200 was posted as a credit to Cash of $2,300.
c. A debit of $2,780 to Accounts Receivable was not posted.
d. A return of $235 of defective supplies was erroneously posted as a $253 credit to Supplies.
e. An insurance policy acquired at a cost of $500 was posted as a credit to Prepaid Insurance.
f. The balance of Notes Payable was overstated by $4,500.
g. A credit of $600 in Accounts Payable was overlooked when the balance of the account was determined.

h. A debit of $2,000 for a withdrawal by the owner was posted as a debit to Carlton Dey, Capital.
i. The balance of $9,450 in Advertising Expense was entered as $9,540 in the trial balance.
j. Miscellaneous Expense, with a balance of $2,520, was omitted from the trial balance.

Instructions

1. Prepare a corrected unadjusted trial balance as of July 31 of the current year.
2. ▬▬▬► Does the fact that the unadjusted trial balance in (1) is balanced mean that there are no errors in the accounts? Explain.

Continuing Problem

✓ *4. Total of Debit Column: $37,800*

The transactions completed by Dancin Music during April 2008 were described at the end of Chapter 1. The following transactions were completed during May, the second month of the business's operations:

May 1. Kris Payne made an additional investment in Dancin Music by depositing $2,500 in Dancin Music's checking account.
  1. Instead of continuing to share office space with a local real estate agency, Kris decided to rent office space near a local music store. Paid rent for May, $1,600.
  1. Paid a premium of $3,360 for a comprehensive insurance policy covering liability, theft, and fire. The policy covers a one-year period.
  2. Received $1,350 on account.
  3. On behalf of Dancin Music, Kris signed a contract with a local radio station, KPRG, to provide guest spots for the next three months. The contract requires Dancin Music to provide a guest disc jockey for 80 hours per month for a monthly fee of $2,400. Any additional hours beyond 80 will be billed to KPRG at $40 per hour. In accordance with the contract, Kris received $4,800 from KPRG as an advance payment for the first two months.
  3. Paid $250 on account.
  4. Paid an attorney $300 for reviewing the May 3rd contract with KPRG. (Record as Miscellaneous Expense.)
  5. Purchased office equipment on account from One-Stop Office Mart, $5,000.
  8. Paid for a newspaper advertisement, $180.
  11. Received $750 for serving as a disc jockey for a college fraternity party.
  13. Paid $500 to a local audio electronics store for rental of digital recording equipment.
  14. Paid wages of $1,000 to receptionist and part-time assistant.
  16. Received $1,500 for serving as a disc jockey for a wedding reception.
  18. Purchased supplies on account, $750.
  21. Paid $325 to Rocket Music for use of its current music demos in making various music sets.
  22. Paid $800 to a local radio station to advertise the services of Dancin Music twice daily for the remainder of May.
  23. Served as disc jockey for a party for $2,500. Received $750, with the remainder due June 4, 2008.
  27. Paid electric bill, $560.
  28. Paid wages of $1,000 to receptionist and part-time assistant.
  29. Paid miscellaneous expenses, $150.
  30. Served as a disc jockey for a charity ball for $1,500. Received $400, with the remainder due on June 9, 2008.
  31. Received $2,800 for serving as a disc jockey for a party.
  31. Paid $900 royalties (music expense) to Federated Clearing for use of various artists' music during May.
  31. Withdrew $1,000 cash from Dancin Music for personal use.

Dancin Music's chart of accounts and the balance of accounts as of May 1, 2008 (all normal balances), are as follows:

11	Cash	$ 9,160	41	Fees Earned	$5,700
12	Accounts Receivable	1,350	50	Wages Expense	400
14	Supplies	170	51	Office Rent Expense	1,000
15	Prepaid Insurance	—	52	Equipment Rent Expense	800
17	Office Equipment	—	53	Utilities Expense	350
21	Accounts Payable	250	54	Music Expense	1,340
23	Unearned Revenue	—	55	Advertising Expense	750
31	Kris Payne, Capital	10,000	56	Supplies Expense	180
32	Kris Payne, Drawing	300	59	Miscellaneous Expense	150

Instructions

1. Enter the May 1, 2008, account balances in the appropriate balance column of a four-column account. Write *Balance* in the Item column, and place a check mark (✓) in the Posting Reference column. (*Hint:* Verify the equality of the debit and credit balances in the ledger before proceeding with the next instruction.)
2. Analyze and journalize each transaction in a two-column journal, omitting journal entry explanations.
3. Post the journal to the ledger, extending the account balance to the appropriate balance column after each posting.
4. Prepare an unadjusted trial balance as of May 31, 2008.

Special Activities

SA 2-1
Ethics and professional conduct in business

ETHICS

At the end of the current month, Tomas Lott prepared a trial balance for AAA Rescue Service. The credit side of the trial balance exceeds the debit side by a significant amount. Tomas has decided to add the difference to the balance of the miscellaneous expense account in order to complete the preparation of the current month's financial statements by a 5 o'clock deadline. Tomas will look for the difference next week when he has more time.

➤ Discuss whether Tomas is behaving in a professional manner.

SA 2-2
Account for revenue

Ennis College requires students to pay tuition each term before classes begin. Students who have not paid their tuition are not allowed to enroll or to attend classes.

What journal entry do you think Ennis College would use to record the receipt of the students' tuition payments? Describe the nature of each account in the entry.

SA 2-3
Record transactions

The following discussion took place between Mary Louden, the office manager of Zoomworks Data Company, and a new accountant, Allen Jarvis.

Allen: I've been thinking about our method of recording entries. It seems that it's inefficient.
Mary: In what way?
Allen: Well—correct me if I'm wrong—it seems like we have unnecessary steps in the process. We could easily develop a trial balance by posting our transactions directly into the ledger and bypassing the journal altogether. In this way, we could combine the recording and posting process into one step and save ourselves a lot of time. What do you think?
Mary: We need to have a talk.

➤ What should Mary say to Allen?

SA 2-4
Debits and credits

Group Project

The following excerpt is from a conversation between Shelley Ryan, the president and chief operating officer of Diamond Construction Company, and her neighbor, Miguel Jimenez.

Miguel: Shelley, I'm taking a course in night school, "Intro to Accounting." I was wondering—could you answer a couple of questions for me?

Shelley: Well, I will if I can.

Miguel: Okay, our instructor says that it's critical we understand the basic concepts of accounting, or we'll never get beyond the first test. My problem is with those rules of debit and credit . . . you know, assets increase with debits, decrease with credits, etc.

Shelley: Yes, pretty basic stuff. You just have to memorize the rules. It shouldn't be too difficult.

Miguel: Sure, I can memorize the rules, but my problem is I want to be sure I understand the basic concepts behind the rules. For example, why can't assets be increased with credits and decreased with debits like revenue? As long as everyone did it that way, why not? It would seem easier if we had the same rules for all increases and decreases in accounts. Also, why is the left side of an account called the debit side? Why couldn't it be called something simple . . . like the "LE" for Left Entry? The right side could be called just "RE" for Right Entry. Finally, why are there just two sides to an entry? Why can't there be three or four sides to an entry?

In a group of four or five, select one person to play the role of Shelley and one person to play the role of Miguel.

1. After listening to the conversation between Shelley and Miguel, help Shelley answer Miguel's questions.
2. What information (other than just debit and credit journal entries) could the accounting system gather that might be useful to Shelley in managing Diamond Construction Company?

SA 2-5
Transactions and income statement

Shane Raburn is planning to manage and operate Birdie Caddy Service at Biloxi Golf and Country Club during June through August 2008. Shane will rent a small maintenance building from the country club for $500 per month and will offer caddy services, including cart rentals, to golfers. Shane has had no formal training in record keeping.

Shane keeps notes of all receipts and expenses in a shoe box. An examination of Shane's shoe box records for June revealed the following:

June 1. Withdrew $2,000 from personal bank account to be used to operate the caddy service.
1. Paid rent to Biloxi Golf and Country Club, $500.
2. Paid for golf supplies (practice balls, etc.), $650.
3. Arranged for the rental of 40 regular (pulling) golf carts and 10 gasoline-driven carts for $1,500 per month. Paid $750 in advance, with the remaining $750 due June 20.
7. Purchased supplies, including gasoline, for the golf carts on account, $350. Biloxi Golf and Country Club has agreed to allow Shane to store the gasoline in one of its fuel tanks at no cost.
15. Received cash for services from June 1–15, $3,150.
17. Paid cash to creditors on account, $350.
20. Paid remaining rental on golf carts, $750.
22. Purchased supplies, including gasoline, on account, $200.
25. Accepted IOUs from customers on account, $850.
28. Paid miscellaneous expenses, $180.
30. Received cash for services from June 16–30, $3,200.
30. Paid telephone and electricity (utilities) expenses, $160.
30. Paid wages of part-time employees, $450.
30. Received cash in payment of IOUs on account, $550.
30. Determined the amount of supplies on hand at the end of June, $390.

Shane has asked you several questions concerning his financial affairs to date, and he has asked you to assist with his record keeping and reporting of financial data.

a. To assist Shane with his record keeping, prepare a chart of accounts that would be appropriate for Birdie Caddy Service.

b. Prepare an income statement for June in order to help Shane assess the profitability of Birdie Caddy Service. For this purpose, the use of T accounts may be helpful in analyzing the effects of each June transaction.

c. Based on Shane's records of receipts and payments, calculate the amount of cash on hand on June 30. For this purpose, a T account for cash may be useful.

d. ▭▭▭▶ A count of the cash on hand on June 30 totaled $4,980. Briefly discuss the possible causes of the difference between the amount of cash computed in (c) and the actual amount of cash on hand.

SA 2-6
Opportunities for accountants

[Internet Project]

The increasing complexity of the current business and regulatory environment has created an increased demand for accountants who can analyze business transactions and interpret their effects on the financial statements. In addition, a basic ability to analyze the effects of transactions is necessary to be successful in all fields of business as well as in other disciplines, such as law. To better understand the importance of accounting in today's environment, search the Internet or your local newspaper for job opportunities. One possible Internet site is **http://www.monster.com**. Then do one of the following:

1. Print a listing of at least two ads for accounting jobs. Alternatively, bring to class at least two newspaper ads for accounting jobs.

2. Print a listing of at least two ads for nonaccounting jobs for which some knowledge of accounting is preferred or necessary. Alternatively, bring to class at least two newspaper ads for such jobs.

Answers to Self-Examination Questions

1. **A** A debit may signify an increase in an asset account (answer A) or a decrease in a liability or owner's capital account. A credit may signify a decrease in an asset account (answer B) or an increase in a liability or owner's capital account (answers C and D).

2. **C** Liability, capital, and revenue (answer C) accounts have normal credit balances. Asset (answer A), drawing (answer B), and expense (answer D) accounts have normal debit balances.

3. **C** Accounts Receivable (answer A), Cash (answer B), and Miscellaneous Expense (answer D) would all normally have debit balances. Fees Earned should normally have a credit balance. Hence, a debit balance in Fees Earned (answer C) would indicate a likely error in the recording process.

4. **A** The receipt of cash from customers on account increases the asset Cash and decreases the asset Accounts Receivable, as indicated by answer A. Answer B has the debit and credit reversed, and answers C and D involve transactions with creditors (accounts payable) and not customers (accounts receivable).

5. **D** The trial balance (answer D) is a listing of the balances and the titles of the accounts in the ledger on a given date, so that the equality of the debits and credits in the ledger can be verified. The income statement (answer A) is a summary of revenue and expenses for a period of time. The balance sheet (answer B) is a presentation of the assets, liabilities, and owner's equity on a given date. The statement of owner's equity (answer C) is a summary of the changes in owner's equity for a period of time.

The Adjusting Process

© JEFF KRAVITZ/ASSOCIATED PRESS

objectives

After studying this chapter, you should be able to:

1 *Describe the nature of the adjusting process.*

2 *Journalize entries for accounts requiring adjustment.*

3 *Summarize the adjustment process.*

4 *Prepare an adjusted trial balance.*

Marvel Entertainment, Inc.

D o you subscribe to any magazines? Most of us subscribe to one or more magazines such as *Cosmopolitan*, *Sports Illustrated*, *Golf Digest*, *Newsweek*, or *Rolling Stone*. Magazines usually require you to prepay the yearly subscription price before you receive any issues. When should the magazine company record revenue from the subscriptions? As we discussed in Chapter 2, sometimes revenues are earned and expenses are incurred at the point cash is received or paid. For transactions such as magazine subscriptions, the revenue is earned when the magazine is delivered, not when the cash is received. Most companies are required to account for revenues and expenses when the benefit is substantially provided or consumed, which may not be when cash is received or paid.

One company that records revenue from subscriptions is Marvel Entertainment, Inc. Marvel be-

gan in 1939 as a comic book publishing company, establishing such popular comic book characters as Spider-Man®, X-Men®, Fantastic Four®, and the Avengers®. From these humble beginnings, Marvel has grown into a full-line, multi-billion-dollar entertainment company. Marvel not only publishes comic books, but it has also added feature films, such as the *Spider-Man* movies, video games, and toys to its product offerings.

Most companies, like Marvel Entertainment, are required to update their accounting records for items such as revenues earned from magazine subscriptions before preparing their financial statements. In this chapter, we describe and illustrate this updating process.

Nature of the Adjusting Process

When accountants prepare financial statements, they assume that the economic life of the business can be divided into time periods. Using this **accounting period concept**, accountants must determine in which period the revenues and expenses of the business should be reported. To determine the proper period, accountants use generally accepted accounting principles, which require the use of the accrual basis of accounting.

Under the **accrual basis of accounting**, revenues are reported in the income statement in the period in which they are earned. For example, revenue is reported when the services are provided to customers. Cash may or may not be received from customers during this period. The accounting concept that supports this reporting of revenues is called the **revenue recognition concept**.

Under the accrual basis, expenses are reported in the same period as the revenues to which they relate. For example, employee wages are reported as an expense in the period in which the employees provided services to customers, and not necessarily when the wages are paid. The accounting concept that supports reporting revenues and related expenses in the same period is called the **matching concept**, or **matching principle**. By matching revenues and expenses, net income or loss for the period will be properly reported on the income statement.

Although generally accepted accounting principles require the accrual basis of accounting, some businesses use the **cash basis of accounting**. Under the cash basis of accounting, revenues and expenses are reported in the income statement in the period in which cash is received or paid. For example, fees are recorded when cash is received from clients, and wages are recorded when cash is paid to employees. The net income (or net loss) is the difference between the cash receipts (revenues) and the cash payments (expenses).

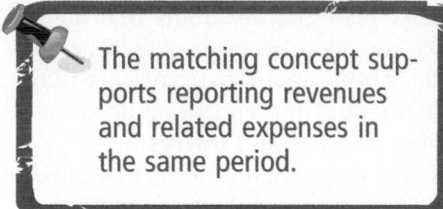

The matching concept supports reporting revenues and related expenses in the same period.

Small service businesses may use the cash basis, because they have few receivables and payables. For example, attorneys, physicians, and real estate agents often use the cash basis. For them, the cash basis will yield financial statements similar to those prepared under the accrual basis. For most large businesses, the cash basis will not provide accurate financial statements for user needs. For this reason, we will emphasize the accrual basis in this text.

THE ADJUSTING PROCESS

At the end of an accounting period, many of the balances of accounts in the ledger can be reported, without change, in the financial statements. For example, the balances of the cash and land accounts are normally the amount reported on the balance sheet.

Under the accrual basis, however, some accounts in the ledger require updating.[1] For example, the balances listed for prepaid expenses are normally overstated because the use of these assets is not recorded on a day-to-day basis. The balance of the supplies account usually represents the cost of supplies at the beginning of the period plus the cost of supplies acquired during the period. To record the daily use of supplies would require many entries with small amounts. In addition, the total amount of supplies is small relative to other assets, and managers usually do not require day-to-day information about supplies.

All adjusting entries affect at least one income statement account and one balance sheet account.

The analysis and updating of accounts at the end of the period before the financial statements are prepared is called the **adjusting process**. The journal entries that bring the accounts up to date at the end of the accounting period are called **adjusting entries**. All adjusting entries affect at least one income statement account and one balance sheet account. Thus, an adjusting entry will *always* involve a revenue or an expense account *and* an asset or a liability account. In the next section, we describe how to determine if an account needs adjusting.

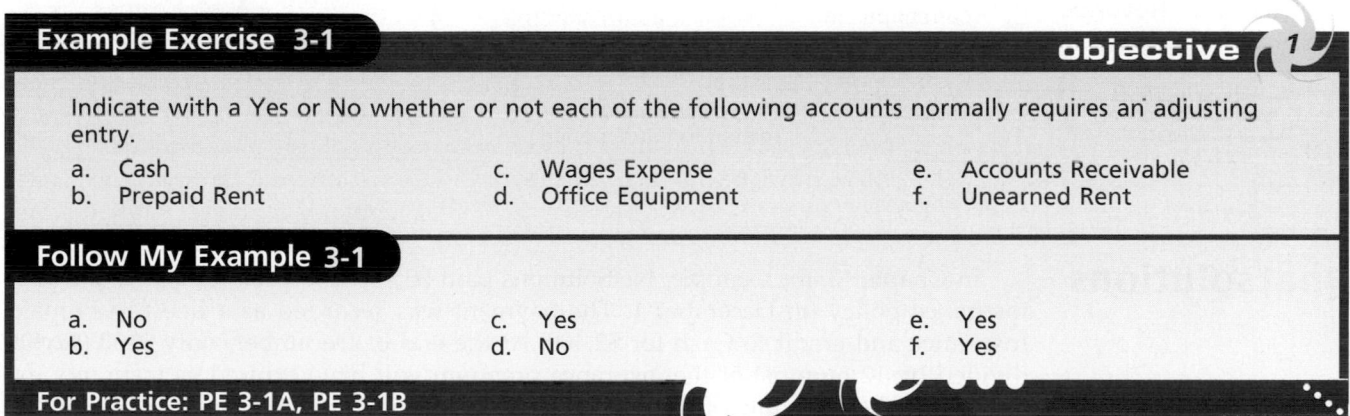

Example Exercise 3-1   objective 1

Indicate with a Yes or No whether or not each of the following accounts normally requires an adjusting entry.

a. Cash
b. Prepaid Rent

c. Wages Expense
d. Office Equipment

e. Accounts Receivable
f. Unearned Rent

Follow My Example 3-1

a. No
b. Yes

c. Yes
d. No

e. Yes
f. Yes

For Practice: PE 3-1A, PE 3-1B

TYPES OF ACCOUNTS REQUIRING ADJUSTMENT

Is there an easy way to know when an adjusting entry is needed? Yes, four basic types of accounts require adjusting entries. These accounts are prepaid expenses, unearned revenues, accrued revenues, and accrued expenses.

---

1 Under the cash basis of accounting, accounts do not require adjusting. This is because transactions are recorded only when cash is received or paid. Thus, the matching concept is not used under the cash basis.

Prepaid expenses, sometimes referred to as *deferred expenses*, are items that have been initially recorded as assets but are expected to become expenses over time or through the normal operations of the business. Supplies and prepaid insurance are two examples of prepaid expenses that may require adjustment at the end of an accounting period. Other examples include prepaid advertising and prepaid interest.

Unearned revenues, sometimes referred to as *deferred revenues*, are items that have been initially recorded as liabilities but are expected to become revenues over time or through the normal operations of the business. An example of unearned revenue is unearned rent. Other examples include tuition received in advance by a school, an annual retainer fee received by an attorney, premiums received in advance by an insurance company, and magazine subscriptions received in advance by a publisher.

Prepaid expenses and unearned revenues are created from transactions that involve the receipt or payment of cash. In both cases, the recording of the related expense or revenue is delayed until the end of the period or to a future period as illustrated in Exhibit 1.

EXHIBIT 1 | Type of Adjustments: Prepaid Expense and Unearned Revenue

@netsolutions

In Chapter 2, for example, NetSolutions paid $2,400 as a premium on a one-year insurance policy on December 1. The payment was recorded as a debit to Prepaid Insurance and credit to Cash for $2,400. At the end of December, only $200 ($2,400 divided by 12 months) of the insurance premium will have expired as insurance expense, and the recording of the remaining $2,200 of insurance expense will be delayed to future periods. As we will see in the next section, the $200 insurance premium expiring in December will be recorded as insurance expense at the end of December, using an adjusting entry.

Accrued revenues, sometimes referred to as *accrued assets*, are revenues that have been earned but have not been recorded in the accounts. An example of an accrued revenue is fees for services that an attorney has provided but hasn't billed to the client at the end of the period. Other examples include unbilled commissions by a travel agent, accrued interest on notes receivable, and accrued rent on property rented to others.

Accrued expenses, sometimes referred to as *accrued liabilities*, are expenses that have been incurred but have not been recorded in the accounts. An example of an accrued expense is accrued wages owed to employees at the end of a period. Other examples include accrued interest on notes payable and accrued taxes.

Accrued revenues and expenses are created by an unrecorded revenue that has been earned or an unrecorded expense that has been incurred. For example, in the next section, we will record accrued revenues and accrued wages expense for NetSolutions at the end of December by using adjusting entries. Prior to recording the adjusting entries, neither accrued revenues nor accrued wages have been recorded. The nature of accrued revenues and expenses is illustrated in Exhibit 2.

| EXHIBIT 2 | Type of Adjustments: Accrued Revenue and Expense |

Example Exercise 3-2 objective 1

Classify the following items as (1) prepaid expense, (2) unearned revenue, (3) accrued expense, or (4) accrued revenue.

a. Wages owed but not yet paid.
b. Supplies on hand.
c. Fees received but not yet earned.
d. Fees earned but not yet received.

Follow My Example 3-2

a. Accrued expense
b. Prepaid expense
c. Unearned revenue
d. Accrued revenue

For Practice: PE 3-2A, PE 3-2B

Recording Adjusting Entries

objective 2

Journalize entries for accounts requiring adjustment.

The examples of adjusting entries in the following paragraphs are based on the ledger of NetSolutions as reported in the December 31, 2007, unadjusted trial balance in Exhibit 3.

An expanded chart of accounts for NetSolutions is shown in Exhibit 4. The additional accounts that will be used in this chapter are shown in color. In addition, the adjusting entries are shown in color in T accounts to separate them from other transactions.

NetSolutions
Unadjusted Trial Balance
December 31, 2007

	Debit Balances	Credit Balances
Cash	2 0 6 5 00	
Accounts Receivable	2 2 2 0 00	
Supplies	2 0 0 0 00	
Prepaid Insurance	2 4 0 0 00	
Land	20 0 0 0 00	
Office Equipment	1 8 0 0 00	
Accounts Payable		9 0 0 00
Unearned Rent		3 6 0 00
Chris Clark, Capital		25 0 0 0 00
Chris Clark, Drawing	4 0 0 0 00	
Fees Earned		16 3 4 0 00
Wages Expense	4 2 7 5 00	
Rent Expense	1 6 0 0 00	
Utilities Expense	9 8 5 00	
Supplies Expense	8 0 0 00	
Miscellaneous Expense	4 5 5 00	
	42 6 0 0 00	42 6 0 0 00

EXHIBIT 4   **Expanded Chart of Accounts for NetSolutions**

Balance Sheet Accounts	Income Statement Accounts
1. Assets	4. Revenue
11 Cash	41 Fees Earned
12 Accounts Receivable	42 Rent Revenue
14 Supplies	5. Expenses
15 Prepaid Insurance	51 Wages Expense
17 Land	52 Rent Expense
18 Office Equipment	53 Depreciation Expense
19 Accumulated Depreciation—Equipment	54 Utilities Expense
2. Liabilities	55 Supplies Expense
21 Accounts Payable	56 Insurance Expense
22 Wages Payable	59 Miscellaneous Expense
23 Unearned Rent	
3. Owner's Equity	
31 Chris Clark, Capital	
32 Chris Clark, Drawing	

PREPAID EXPENSES

The concept of adjusting accounting records was introduced in Chapters 1 and 2 in the illustration for NetSolutions. In that illustration, supplies were purchased on November 10 [transaction (c)]. The supplies used during November were recorded on November 30 [transaction (g)].

The balance in NetSolutions' supplies account on December 31 is $2,000. Some of these supplies (CDs, paper, envelopes, etc.) were used during December, and some are still on hand (not used). If either amount is known, the other can be determined. It is normally easier to determine the cost of the supplies on hand at the end of the month than it is to keep a daily record of those used. Assuming that on December 31 the amount of supplies on hand is $760, the amount to be transferred from the asset account to the expense account is $1,240, computed as follows:

Supplies available during December (balance of account)	$2,000
Supplies on hand, December 31	760
Supplies used (amount of adjustment)	$1,240

As we discussed in Chapter 2, increases in expense accounts are recorded as debits and decreases in asset accounts are recorded as credits. At the end of December, the supplies expense account should be debited for $1,240, and the supplies account should be credited for $1,240 to record the supplies used during December. The adjusting journal entry and T accounts for Supplies and Supplies Expense are as follows:

1					
2	2007 Dec.	31	Supplies Expense	55	1 2 4 0 00
3			Supplies	14	1 2 4 0 00
4			Supplies used ($2,000 − $760).		

Supplies				**Supplies Expense**	
Bal.	2,000	Dec. 31	1,240	Bal.	800
Adj. Bal.	760			Dec. 31	1,240
				Adj. Bal.	2,040

After the adjustment has been recorded and posted, the supplies account has a debit balance of $760. This balance represents an asset that will become an expense in a future period.

The debit balance of $2,400 in NetSolutions' prepaid insurance account represents a December 1 prepayment of insurance for 12 months. At the end of December, the insurance expense account should be increased (debited), and the prepaid insurance account should be decreased (credited) by $200, the insurance for one month. The adjusting journal entry and T accounts for Prepaid Insurance and Insurance Expense are as follows:

5					
6		31	Insurance Expense	56	2 0 0 00
7			Prepaid Insurance	15	2 0 0 00
8			Insurance expired ($2,400/12).		

Prepaid Insurance				**Insurance Expense**	
Bal.	2,400	Dec. 31	200	Dec. 31	200
Adj. Bal.	2,200				

Integrity, Objectivity, and Ethics in Business

FREE ISSUE

Office supplies are often available to employees on a "free issue" basis. This means that employees do not have to "sign" for the release of office supplies but merely obtain the necessary supplies from a local storage area as needed. Just because supplies are easily available, however, doesn't mean they can be taken for personal use. There are many instances where employees have been terminated for taking supplies home for personal use.

> The adjusted balance of a prepaid expense is an asset that will become an expense in a future period.

After the adjustment has been recorded and posted, the prepaid insurance account has a debit balance of $2,200. This balance represents an asset that will become an expense in future periods. The insurance expense account has a debit balance of $200, which is an expense of the current period.

What is the effect of omitting adjusting entries? If the preceding adjustments for supplies ($1,240) and insurance ($200) are not recorded, the financial statements prepared as of December 31 will be misstated. On the income statement, Supplies Expense and Insurance Expense will be understated by a total of $1,440, and net income will be overstated by $1,440. On the balance sheet, Supplies and Prepaid Insurance will be overstated by a total of $1,440. Since net income increases owner's equity, Chris Clark, Capital will also be overstated by $1,440 on the balance sheet. The effects of omitting these adjusting entries on the income statement and balance sheet are as follows:

Arrow (1) indicates the effect of the understated expenses on assets. Arrow (2) indicates the effect of the overstated net income on owner's equity.

Prepayments of expenses are sometimes made at the beginning of the period in which they will be *entirely consumed*. On December 1, for example, NetSolutions paid rent of $800 for the month. On December 1, the rent payment represents the asset prepaid rent. The prepaid rent expires daily, and at the end of December, the entire amount has become an expense (rent expense). In cases such as this, the initial payment is recorded as an expense rather than as an asset. Thus, if the payment is recorded as a debit to Rent Expense, no adjusting entry is needed at the end of the period.[2]

Example Exercise 3-3   **objective 2**

The prepaid insurance account had a beginning balance of $6,400 and was debited for $3,600 of premiums paid during the year. Journalize the adjusting entry required at the end of the year assuming the amount of unexpired insurance related to future periods is $3,250.

Follow My Example 3-3

Insurance Expense   6,750
    Prepaid Insurance   6,750
      Insurance expired ($6,400 + $3,600 − $3,250).

For Practice: PE 3-3A, PE 3-3B

---

2 This alternative treatment of recording the cost of supplies, rent, and other prepayments of expenses is discussed in an appendix that can be downloaded from the book's companion Web site.

UNEARNED REVENUES

According to NetSolutions' trial balance on December 31, the balance in the unearned rent account is $360. This balance represents the receipt of three months' rent on December 1 for December, January, and February. At the end of December, the unearned rent account should be decreased (debited) by $120, and the rent revenue account should be increased (credited) by $120. The $120 represents the rental revenue for one month ($360/3). The adjusting journal entry and T accounts are shown below.

REAL WORLD

Best Buy sells extended warranty contracts with terms between 12 and 36 months. The receipts from sales of these contracts are reported as unearned revenue on Best Buy's balance sheet. Revenue is recorded as the contracts expire.

9						9
10	31	Unearned Rent	23	1 2 0 00		10
11		Rent Revenue	42		1 2 0 00	11
12		Rent earned ($360/3 months).				12

Unearned Rent				**Rent Revenue**	
Dec. 31	120	Bal.	360		Dec. 31	120
		Adj. Bal.	240		

After the adjustment has been recorded and posted, the unearned rent account, which is a liability, has a credit balance of $240. This amount represents a deferral that will become revenue in a future period. The rent revenue account has a balance of $120, which is revenue of the current period.[3]

If the preceding adjustment of unearned rent and rent revenue is not recorded, the financial statements prepared on December 31 will be misstated. On the income statement, Rent Revenue and the net income will be understated by $120. On the balance sheet, Unearned Rent will be overstated by $120, and Chris Clark, Capital will be understated by $120. The effects of omitting this adjusting entry are shown below.

	Amount of Misstatement
Income Statement	
Revenues understated by	$(120)
Expenses correctly stated	XXX
Net income understated by	$(120)
Balance Sheet	
Assets correctly stated	$XXX
Liabilities overstated by	$ 120
Owner's equity understated by	(120)
Total liabilities and owner's equity correctly stated	$XXX

Example Exercise 3-4   objective **2**

The balance in the unearned fees account, before adjustment at the end of the year, is $44,900. Journalize the adjusting entry required if the amount of unearned fees at the end of the year is $22,300.

Follow My Example 3-4

Unearned Fees	....	22,600	
Fees Earned	....		22,600
Fees earned ($44,900 − $22,300).			

For Practice: PE 3-4A, PE 3-4B

---

3 An alternative treatment of recording revenues received in advance of their being earned is discussed in an appendix that can be downloaded from the book's companion Web site (www.thomsonedu.com/accounting/warren).

ACCRUED REVENUES

During an accounting period, some revenues are recorded only when cash is received. Thus, at the end of an accounting period, there may be items of revenue that have been earned *but have not been recorded*. In such cases, the amount of the revenue should be recorded by debiting an asset account and crediting a revenue account.

To illustrate, assume that NetSolutions signed an agreement with Dankner Co. on December 15. The agreement provides that NetSolutions will be on call to answer computer questions and render assistance to Dankner Co.'s employees. The services provided will be billed to Dankner Co. on the fifteenth of each month at a rate of $20 per hour. As of December 31, NetSolutions had provided 25 hours of assistance to Dankner Co. Although the revenue of $500 (25 hours × $20) will be billed and collected in January, NetSolutions earned the revenue in December. The adjusting journal entry and T accounts to record the claim against the customer (an account receivable) and the fees earned in December are shown below.

13					13
14	31	Accounts Receivable	12	5 0 0 00	14
15		Fees Earned	41	5 0 0 00	15
16		Accrued fees (25 hrs. × $20)			16

Accounts Receivable			Fees Earned	
Bal.	2,220		Bal.	16,340
Dec. 31	500		Dec. 31	500
Adj. Bal.	2,720		Adj. Bal.	16,840

If the adjustment for the accrued asset ($500) is not recorded, Fees Earned and the net income will be understated by $500 on the income statement. On the balance sheet, Accounts Receivable and Chris Clark, Capital will be understated by $500. The effects of omitting this adjusting entry are shown below.

	Amount of Misstatement
Income Statement	
Revenues understated by	$(500)
Expenses correctly stated	XXX
Net income understated by	$(500)
Balance Sheet	
Assets understated by	$(500)
Liabilities correctly stated	$XXX
Owner's equity understated by	(500)
Total liabilities and owner's equity understated by	$(500)

Example Exercise 3-5   objective 2

At the end of the current year, $13,680 of fees have been earned but have not been billed to clients. Journalize the adjusting entry to record the accrued fees.

Follow My Example 3-5

Accounts Receivable	13,680	
Fees Earned		13,680
Accrued fees.		

For Practice: PE 3-5A, PE 3-5B

ACCRUED EXPENSES

Some types of services, such as insurance, are normally paid for *before* they are used. These prepayments are deferrals. Other types of services are paid for *after* the service has been performed. For example, wages expense accumulates or *accrues* hour by hour and day by day, but payment may be made only weekly, biweekly, or monthly. The amount of such an accrued but unpaid item at the end of the accounting period is both an expense and a liability. In the case of wages expense, if the last day of a pay period is not the last day of the accounting period, the accrued wages expense and the related liability must be recorded in the accounts by an adjusting entry. This adjusting entry is necessary so that expenses are properly matched to the period in which they were incurred.

At the end of December, accrued wages for NetSolutions were $250. This amount is an additional expense of December and is debited to the wages expense account. It is also a liability as of December 31 and is credited to Wages Payable. The adjusting journal entry and T accounts are as follows:

17					17
18	31	Wages Expense	51	2 5 0 00	18
19		Wages Payable	22	2 5 0 00	19
20		Accrued wages.			20

Wages Expense

Bal.	4,275
Dec. 31	250
Adj. Bal.	4,525

Wages Payable

| | Dec. 31 | 250 |

Callaway Golf Company, a manufacturer of such innovative golf clubs as the "Big Bertha" driver, reports accrued warranty expense on its balance sheet.

After the adjustment has been recorded and posted, the debit balance of the wages expense account is $4,525, which is the wages expense for the two months, November and December. The credit balance of $250 in Wages Payable is the amount of the liability for wages owed as of December 31.

The accrual of the wages expense for NetSolutions is summarized in Exhibit 5, on page 114. Note that NetSolutions paid wages of $950 on December 13 and $1,200 on December 27. These payments covered the biweekly pay periods that ended on those days. The wages of $250 incurred for Monday and Tuesday, December 30 and 31, are accrued at December 31. The wages paid on January 10 totaled $1,275, which included the $250 accrued wages of December 31. The payment of the January 10 wages is recorded by debiting Wages Expense for $1,025, debiting Wages Payable for $250, and crediting Cash for $1,275, as shown below.[4]

21						21
22	Jan.	10	Wages Expense	1 0 2 5 00		22
23			Wages Payable	2 5 0 00		23
24			Cash		1 2 7 5 00	24

What would be the effect on the financial statements if the adjustment for wages ($250) is not recorded? On the income statement, Wages Expense will be understated by $250, and the net income will be overstated by $250. On the balance sheet, Wages

---

4 To simplify the subsequent recording of the following period's transactions, some accountants use what is known as reversing entries for certain types of adjustments. Reversing entries are discussed and illustrated in an appendix at the end of the textbook.

EXHIBIT 5

Accrued Wages

1. Wages are paid on the second and fourth Fridays for the two-week periods ending on those Fridays. The payments were $950 on December 13 and $1,200 on December 27.

2. The wages accrued for Monday and Tuesday, December 30 and 31, are $250.

3. Wages paid on Friday, January 10, total $1,275.

Payable will be understated by $250, and Chris Clark, Capital will be overstated by $250. The effects of omitting this adjusting entry are shown as follows:

	Amount of Misstatement
Income Statement	
Revenues correctly stated	$XXX
Expenses understated by	(250)
Net income overstated by	$ 250
Balance Sheet	
Assets correctly stated	$XXX
Liabilities understated by	$(250)
Owner's equity overstated by	250
Total liabilities and owner's equity correctly stated	$XXX

Example Exercise 3-6   objective 2

Sanregret Realty Co. pays weekly salaries of $12,500 on Friday for a five-day week ending on that day. Journalize the necessary adjusting entry at the end of the accounting period, assuming that the period ends on Thursday.

Follow My Example 3-6

Salaries Expense	10,000	
Salaries Payable		10,000
Accrued salaries [($12,500/5 days) × 4 days].		

For Practice: PE 3-6A, PE 3-6B

DEPRECIATION EXPENSE

Physical resources that are owned and used by a business and are permanent or have a long life are called **fixed assets**, or **plant assets**. In a sense, fixed assets are a type of long-term prepaid expense. Because of their nature and long life, they are discussed separately from other prepaid expenses, such as supplies and prepaid insurance.

NetSolutions' fixed assets include office equipment, which is used much like supplies are used to generate revenue. Unlike supplies, however, there is no visible reduction in the quantity of the equipment. Instead, as time passes, the equipment loses its ability to provide useful services. This decrease in usefulness is called **depreciation**.

All fixed assets, except land, lose their usefulness. Decreases in the usefulness of assets that are used in generating revenue are recorded as expenses. However, such decreases for fixed assets are difficult to measure. For this reason, a portion of the cost of a fixed asset is recorded as an expense each year of its useful life. This periodic expense is called **depreciation expense**. Methods of computing depreciation expense are discussed and illustrated in a later chapter.

The adjusting entry to record depreciation is similar to the adjusting entry for supplies used. The account debited is a depreciation expense account. However, the asset account Office Equipment is not credited because both the original cost of a fixed asset and the amount of depreciation recorded since its purchase are normally reported on the balance sheet. The account credited is an **accumulated depreciation** account. Accumulated depreciation accounts are called **contra accounts**, or **contra asset accounts**, because they are deducted from the related asset accounts on the balance sheet. The normal balance of a contra account is opposite to the account from which it is deducted. Thus, the normal balance for Accumulated Depreciation is a credit.

Lowe's Companies, Inc., reported land, buildings, and store equipment at a cost of over $18 billion and accumulated depreciation of over $4.1 billion.

Normal titles for fixed asset accounts and their related contra asset accounts are as follows:

Fixed Asset	Contra Asset
Land	None—Land is not depreciated.
Buildings	Accumulated Depreciation—Buildings
Store Equipment	Accumulated Depreciation—Store Equipment
Office Equipment	Accumulated Depreciation—Office Equipment

The adjusting entry to record depreciation for December for NetSolutions is illustrated in the following journal entry and T accounts. The estimated amount of depreciation for the month is assumed to be $50.

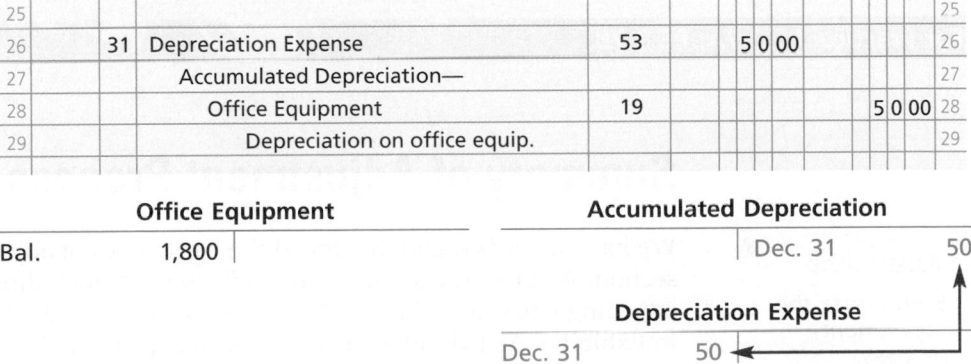

The $50 increase in the accumulated depreciation account is subtracted from the $1,800 cost recorded in the related fixed asset account. The difference between the two balances is the $1,750 cost that has not yet been depreciated. This amount ($1,750) is called the **book value of the asset** (or **net book value**), which may be presented on the balance sheet in the following manner:

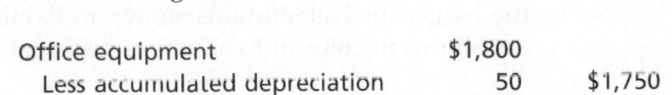

You should note that the market value of a fixed asset usually differs from its book value. This is because depreciation is an *allocation* method, not a *valuation* method. That is, depreciation allocates the cost of a fixed asset to expense over its estimated life. Depreciation does not attempt to measure changes in market values, which may vary significantly from year to year.

If the previous adjustment for depreciation ($50) is not recorded, Depreciation Expense on the income statement will be understated by $50, and the net income will be overstated by $50. On the balance sheet, the book value of Office Equipment and Chris Clark, Capital will be overstated by $50. The effects of omitting the adjustment for depreciation are shown below.

	Amount of Misstatement
Income Statement	
Revenues correctly stated	$XX
Expenses understated by	(50)
Net income overstated by	$ 50
Balance Sheet	
Assets overstated by	$ 50
Liabilities correctly stated	$XX
Owner's equity overstated by	50
Total liabilities and owner's equity overstated by	$ 50

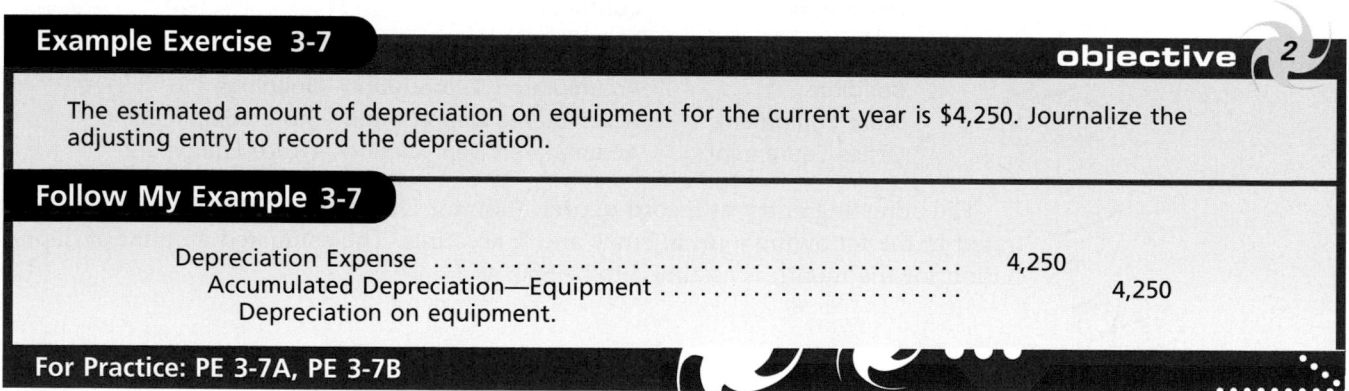

Example Exercise 3-7   objective **2**

The estimated amount of depreciation on equipment for the current year is $4,250. Journalize the adjusting entry to record the depreciation.

Follow My Example 3-7

Depreciation Expense 4,250
    Accumulated Depreciation—Equipment 4,250
    Depreciation on equipment.

For Practice: PE 3-7A, PE 3-7B

Summary of Adjustment Process

objective **3**

Summarize the adjustment process.

@netsolutions

We have described and illustrated the basic types of adjusting entries in the preceding section. A summary of these basic adjustments, including the type of adjustment, the adjusting entry, and the effect of the adjustment on the financial statements, is shown in Exhibit 6. As Exhibit 6 illustrates, each adjustment affects the income statement and balance sheet.

The adjusting entries for NetSolutions that we illustrated in this chapter are shown in Exhibit 7, on page 118. The adjusting entries are dated as of the last day of the period. However, because some time may be needed for collecting the adjustment information, the entries are usually recorded at a later date. Each adjusting entry is normally supported by an explanation. These adjusting entries have been posted to the ledger for NetSolutions shown in Exhibit 8, on pages 119–120. The adjustments are shown in color in Exhibit 8 to distinguish them from other transactions.

EXHIBIT 6   Summary of Adjustments

Financial Statement Effect of Adjustment
Increase (Decrease)

Type of Adjustment	Adjusting Entry		Revenues	− Expenses	= Net Income	Assets	= Liabilities	+ Owner's Equity
Prepaid Expenses								
Supplies	Supplies Exp.	1,240		1,240	(1,240)			
	Supplies		1,240			(1,240)		(1,240)
Prepaid Insurance	Insurance Exp.	200		200	(200)			
	Prepaid Ins.		200			(200)		(200)
Unearned Revenue								
Unearned Rent	Unearned Rent	120					(120)	120
	Rent Revenue		120	120		120		
Accrued Revenue								
Accrued Fees	Accts. Receivable	500				500		500
	Fees Earned		500	500		500		
Accrued Expense								
Accrued Wages	Wages Expense	250			250	(250)		
	Wages Payable		250				250	(250)
Depreciation Expense								
Office Equipment	Depreciation Exp.	50			50	(50)		
	Acc. Dep. —							
	Office Equip.		50			(50)		(50)

Example Exercise 3-8   objective 3

For the year ending December 31, 2008, Mann Medical Co. mistakenly omitted adjusting entries for (1) $8,600 of unearned revenue that was earned, (2) earned revenue that was not billed of $12,500, and (3) accrued wages of $2,900. Indicate the combined effect of the errors on (a) revenues, (b) expenses, and (c) net income for 2008.

Follow My Example 3-8

a. Revenues were understated by $21,100 ($8,600 + $12,500).
b. Expenses were understated by $2,900.
c. Net income was understated by $18,200 ($8,600 + $12,500 − $2,900).

For Practice: PE 3-8A, PE 3-8B

EXHIBIT 7

Adjusting Entries—
NetSolutions

	Date		Description	Post. Ref.	Debit	Credit	
1			Adjusting Entries				1
2	2007 Dec.	31	Supplies Expense	55	1 2 4 0 00		2
3			Supplies	14		1 2 4 0 00	3
4			Supplies used ($2,000 − $760).				4
5							5
6		31	Insurance Expense	56	2 0 0 00		6
7			Prepaid Insurance	15		2 0 0 00	7
8			Insurance expired ($2,400/12 months).				8
9							9
10		31	Unearned Rent	23	1 2 0 00		10
11			Rent Revenue	42		1 2 0 00	11
12			Rent earned ($360/3 months).				12
13							13
14		31	Accounts Receivable	12	5 0 0 00		14
15			Fees Earned	41		5 0 0 00	15
16			Accrued fees (25 hrs. × $20).				16
17							17
18		31	Wages Expense	51	2 5 0 00		18
19			Wages Payable	22		2 5 0 00	19
20			Accrued wages.				20
21							21
22		31	Depreciation Expense	53	5 0 00		22
23			Accum. Depr.—Office Equip.	19		5 0 00	23
24			Depreciation on office equip.				24
25							25

One way for an accountant to check whether all adjustments have been made is to compare the current period's adjustments with those of the prior period.

Business Connections

Microsoft Corporation develops, manufactures, licenses, and supports a wide range of computer software products, including Windows XP®, Windows NT®, Word®, Excel®, and the Xbox® gaming system. When Microsoft sells its products, it incurs an obligation to support its software with technical support and periodic updates. As a result, not all the revenue is earned on the date of sale; some of the revenue on the date of sale is unearned. The portion of revenue related to support services, such as updates and technical support, is earned as time passes and support is provided to customers. Thus, each year Microsoft makes adjusting entries transferring some of its unearned revenue to revenue. The following excerpts were taken from Microsoft's 2005 financial statements.

> The percentage of revenue recorded as unearned . . . ranges from approximately 15% to 25% of the sales price for Windows XP Home, approximately 5% to 15% of the sales price for Windows XP Professional, and approximately 1% to 15% of the sales price for desktop applications . . .
>
> Unearned Revenue:

	June 30, 2005	June 30, 2004
Unearned revenue (in millions)	$9,167	$8,177

During the year ending June 30, 2006, Microsoft expects to record over $7,500 million of unearned revenue as revenue. At the same time, Microsoft will record additional unearned revenue from current period sales.

Source: Taken from Microsoft's June 30, 2005, annual report.

EXHIBIT 8	Ledger with Adjusting Entries—NetSolutions

ACCOUNT *Cash*   **ACCOUNT NO.** *11*

Date	Item	Post. Ref.	Debit	Credit	Balance Debit	Balance Credit
2007 Nov. 1		1	25,000		25,000	
5		1		20,000	5,000	
18		1	7,500		12,500	
30		1		3,650	8,850	
30		1		950	7,900	
30		2		2,000	5,900	
Dec. 1		2		2,400	3,500	
1		2		800	2,700	
1		2	360		3,060	
6		2		180	2,880	
11		2		400	2,480	
13		3		950	1,530	
16		3	3,100		4,630	
20		3		900	3,730	
21		3	650		4,380	
23		3		1,450	2,930	
27		3		1,200	1,730	
31		3		310	1,420	
31		4		225	1,195	
31		4	2,870		4,065	
31		4		2,000	2,065	

ACCOUNT *Accounts Receivable*   **ACCOUNT NO.** *12*

Date	Item	Post. Ref.	Debit	Credit	Balance Debit	Balance Credit
2007 Dec. 16		3	1,750		1,750	
21		3		650	1,100	
31		4	1,120		2,220	
31	Adjusting	5	500		2,720	

ACCOUNT *Supplies*   **ACCOUNT NO.** *14*

Date	Item	Post. Ref.	Debit	Credit	Balance Debit	Balance Credit
2007 Nov. 10		1	1,350		1,350	
30		1		800	550	
Dec. 23		3	1,450		2,000	
31	Adjusting	5		1,240	760	

ACCOUNT *Prepaid Insurance*   **ACCOUNT NO.** *15*

Date	Item	Post. Ref.	Debit	Credit	Balance Debit	Balance Credit
2007 Dec. 1		2	2,400		2,400	
31	Adjusting	5		200	2,200	

ACCOUNT *Land*   **ACCOUNT NO.** *17*

Date	Item	Post. Ref.	Debit	Credit	Balance Debit	Balance Credit
2007 Nov. 5		1	20,000		20,000	

ACCOUNT *Office Equipment*   **ACCOUNT NO.** *18*

Date	Item	Post. Ref.	Debit	Credit	Balance Debit	Balance Credit
2007 Dec. 4		2	1,800		1,800	

ACCOUNT *Acc. Depr.—Equipment*   **ACCOUNT NO.** *19*

Date	Item	Post. Ref.	Debit	Credit	Balance Debit	Balance Credit
2007 Dec. 31	Adjusting	5		50		50

ACCOUNT *Accounts Payable*   **ACCOUNT NO.** *21*

Date	Item	Post. Ref.	Debit	Credit	Balance Debit	Balance Credit
2007 Nov. 10		1		1,350		1,350
30		1	950			400
Dec. 4		2		1,800		2,200
11		2	400			1,800
20		3	900			900

ACCOUNT *Wages Payable*   **ACCOUNT NO.** *22*

Date	Item	Post. Ref.	Debit	Credit	Balance Debit	Balance Credit
2007 Dec. 31	Adjusting	5		250		250

ACCOUNT *Unearned Rent*   **ACCOUNT NO.** *23*

Date	Item	Post. Ref.	Debit	Credit	Balance Debit	Balance Credit
2007 Dec. 1		2		360		360
31	Adjusting	5	120			240

ACCOUNT *Chris Clark, Capital*   **ACCOUNT NO.** *31*

Date	Item	Post. Ref.	Debit	Credit	Balance Debit	Balance Credit
2007 Nov. 1		1		25,000		25,000

(continued)

EXHIBIT 8

ACCOUNT *Chris Clark, Drawing*   **ACCOUNT NO.** *32*

Date	Item	Post. Ref.	Debit	Credit	Balance Debit	Balance Credit
2007 Nov. 30		2	2,000		2,000	
Dec. 31		4	2,000		4,000	

ACCOUNT *Fees Earned*   **ACCOUNT NO.** *41*

Date	Item	Post. Ref.	Debit	Credit	Balance Debit	Balance Credit
2007 Nov. 18		1		7,500		7,500
Dec. 16		3		3,100		10,600
16		3		1,750		12,350
31		4		2,870		15,220
31		4		1,120		16,340
31	Adjusting	5		500		16,840

ACCOUNT *Rent Revenue*   **ACCOUNT NO.** *42*

Date	Item	Post. Ref.	Debit	Credit	Balance Debit	Balance Credit
2007 Dec. 31	Adjusting	5		120		120

ACCOUNT *Wages Expense*   **ACCOUNT NO.** *51*

Date	Item	Post. Ref.	Debit	Credit	Balance Debit	Balance Credit
2007 Nov. 30		1	2,125		2,125	
Dec. 13		3	950		3,075	
27		3	1,200		4,275	
31	Adjusting	5	250		4,525	

ACCOUNT *Rent Expense*   **ACCOUNT NO.** *52*

Date	Item	Post. Ref.	Debit	Credit	Balance Debit	Balance Credit
2007 Nov. 30		1	800		800	
Dec. 1		2	800		1,600	

ACCOUNT *Depreciation Expense*   **ACCOUNT NO.** *53*

Date	Item	Post. Ref.	Debit	Credit	Balance Debit	Balance Credit
2007 Dec. 31	Adjusting	5	50		50	

ACCOUNT *Utilities Expense*   **ACCOUNT NO.** *54*

Date	Item	Post. Ref.	Debit	Credit	Balance Debit	Balance Credit
2007 Nov. 30		1	450		450	
Dec. 31		3	310		760	
31		4	225		985	

ACCOUNT *Supplies Expense*   **ACCOUNT NO.** *55*

Date	Item	Post. Ref.	Debit	Credit	Balance Debit	Balance Credit
2007 Nov. 30		1	800		800	
Dec. 31	Adjusting	5	1,240		2,040	

ACCOUNT *Insurance Expense*   **ACCOUNT NO.** *56*

Date	Item	Post. Ref.	Debit	Credit	Balance Debit	Balance Credit
2007 Dec. 31	Adjusting	5	200		200	

ACCOUNT *Miscellaneous Expense*   **ACCOUNT NO.** *59*

Date	Item	Post. Ref.	Debit	Credit	Balance Debit	Balance Credit
2007 Nov. 30		1	275		275	
Dec. 6		2	180		455	

Adjusted Trial Balance

objective 4

Prepare an adjusted trial balance.

After all the adjusting entries have been posted, another trial balance, called the **adjusted trial balance**, is prepared. The purpose of the adjusted trial balance is to verify the equality of the total debit balances and total credit balances before we prepare the financial statements. If the adjusted trial balance does not balance, an error has occurred. However, as we discussed in Chapter 2, errors may have occurred even though the adjusted trial balance totals agree. For example, the adjusted trial balance totals would agree if an adjusting entry has been omitted.

@netsolutions

Exhibit 9 shows the adjusted trial balance for NetSolutions as of December 31, 2007. In Chapter 4, we discuss how financial statements, including a classified balance sheet, can be prepared from an adjusted trial balance. We also discuss the use of an end-of-period spreadsheet (work sheet) as an aid in summarizing the data for preparing adjusting entries and financial statements.

EXHIBIT 9

Adjusted Trial Balance

NetSolutions Adjusted Trial Balance December 31, 2007	Debit Balances	Credit Balances
Cash	2 0 6 5 00	
Accounts Receivable	2 7 2 0 00	
Supplies	7 6 0 00	
Prepaid Insurance	2 2 0 0 00	
Land	20 0 0 0 00	
Office Equipment	1 8 0 0 00	
Accumulated Depreciation—Equipment		5 0 00
Accounts Payable		9 0 0 00
Wages Payable		2 5 0 00
Unearned Rent		2 4 0 00
Chris Clark, Capital		25 0 0 0 00
Chris Clark, Drawing	4 0 0 0 00	
Fees Earned		16 8 4 0 00
Rent Revenue		1 2 0 00
Wages Expense	4 5 2 5 00	
Rent Expense	1 6 0 0 00	
Depreciation Expense	5 0 00	
Utilities Expense	9 8 5 00	
Supplies Expense	2 0 4 0 00	
Insurance Expense	2 0 0 00	
Miscellaneous Expense	4 5 5 00	
	43 4 0 0 00	43 4 0 0 00

Example Exercise 3-9

 objective **4**

For each of the following errors, considered individually, indicate whether the error would cause the adjusted trial balance totals to be unequal. If the error would cause the adjusted trial balance totals to be unequal, indicate whether the debit or credit total is higher and by how much.

a. The adjustment for accrued fees of $5,340 was journalized as a debit to Accounts Payable for $5,340 and a credit to Fees Earned of $5,340.
b. The adjustment for depreciation of $3,260 was journalized as a debit to Depreciation Expense for $3,620 and a credit to Accumulated Depreciation for $3,260.

Follow My Example 3-9

a. The totals are equal even though the debit should have been to Accounts Receivable instead of Accounts Payable.
b. The totals are unequal. The debit total is higher by $360 ($3,620 − $3,260).

For Practice: PE 3-9A, PE 3-9B

At a Glance

1. Describe the nature of the adjusting process.

Key Points	Key Learning Outcomes	Example Exercises	Practice Exercises
The accrual basis of accounting requires that revenues are reported in the period in which they are earned and expenses matched with the revenues they generate. The updating of accounts at the end of the accounting period is called the adjusting process. Each adjusting entry affects an income statement and balance sheet account. The four types of accounts requiring adjusting entries are prepaid expenses, unearned revenues, accrued revenues, and accrued expenses.	• Explain why accrual accounting requires adjusting entries. • List accounts that do and do NOT require adjusting entries at the end of the accounting period. • Give an example of a prepaid expense, unearned revenue, accrued revenue, and accrued expense.	3-1 3-2	3-1A, 3-1B 3-2A, 3-2B

2. Journalize entries for accounts requiring adjustment.

Key Points	Key Learning Outcomes	Example Exercises	Practice Exercises
Adjusting entries illustrated in this chapter include prepaid expenses, unearned revenues, accrued revenues, and accrued expenses. In addition, the adjusting entry necessary to record depreciation on fixed assets was illustrated.	• Prepare an adjusting entry for a prepaid expense. • Prepare an adjusting entry for an unearned revenue. • Prepare an adjusting entry for an accrued revenue. • Prepare an adjusting entry for an accrued expense. • Prepare an adjusting entry for depreciation expense.	3-3 3-4 3-5 3-6 3-7	3-3A, 3-3B 3-4A, 3-4B 3-5A, 3-5B 3-6A, 3-6B 3-7A, 3-7B

3. Summarize the adjustment process.

Key Points	Key Learning Outcomes	Example Exercises	Practice Exercises
A summary of adjustments, including the type of adjustment, the adjusting entry, and the effect of omitting an adjustment on the financial statements, is shown in Exhibit 6.	• Determine the effect on the income statement and balance sheet of omitting an adjusting entry for prepaid expense, unearned revenue, accrued revenue, accrued expense, and depreciation.	3-8	3-8A, 3-8B

4. Prepare an adjusted trial balance.

Key Points	Key Learning Outcomes	Example Exercises	Practice Exercises
After all the adjusting entries have been posted, the equality of the total debit balances and total credit balances is verified by an adjusted trial balance.	• Prepare an adjusted trial balance. • Determine the effect of errors on the equality of the adjusted trial balance.	3-9	3-9A, 3-9B

Key Terms

accounting period concept (104)
accrual basis of accounting (104)
accrued expenses (106)
accrued revenues (106)
accumulated depreciation (115)
adjusted trial balance (120)
adjusting entries (105)

adjusting process (105)
book value of the asset (or net book value) (115)
cash basis of accounting (104)
contra account (or contra asset account) (115)
depreciation (115)

depreciation expense (115)
fixed assets (or plant assets) (115)
matching concept (or matching principle) (104)
prepaid expenses (106)
revenue recognition concept (104)
unearned revenues (106)

Illustrative Problem

Three years ago, T. Roderick organized Harbor Realty. At July 31, 2008, the end of the current year, the unadjusted trial balance of Harbor Realty appears as shown below.

Harbor Realty
Unadjusted Trial Balance
July 31, 2008

	Debit Balances	Credit Balances
Cash	3 4 2 5 00	
Accounts Receivable	7 0 0 0 00	
Supplies	1 2 7 0 00	
Prepaid Insurance	6 2 0 00	
Office Equipment	51 6 5 0 00	
Accumulated Depreciation		9 7 0 0 00
Accounts Payable		9 2 5 00
Wages Payable		0 00
Unearned Fees		1 2 5 0 00
T. Roderick, Capital		29 0 0 0 00
T. Roderick, Drawing	5 2 0 0 00	
Fees Earned		59 1 2 5 00
Wages Expense	22 4 1 5 00	
Depreciation Expense	0 00	
Rent Expense	4 2 0 0 00	
Utilities Expense	2 7 1 5 00	
Supplies Expense	0 00	
Insurance Expense	0 00	
Miscellaneous Expense	1 5 0 5 00	
	100 0 0 0 00	100 0 0 0 00

The data needed to determine year-end adjustments are as follows:

a. Supplies on hand at July 31, 2008, $380.
b. Insurance premiums expired during the year, $315.
c. Depreciation of equipment during the year, $4,950.
d. Wages accrued but not paid at July 31, 2008, $440.
e. Accrued fees earned but not recorded at July 31, 2008, $1,000.
f. Unearned fees on July 31, 2008, $750.

Instructions
1. Prepare the necessary adjusting journal entries. Include journal entry explanations.
2. Determine the balance of the accounts affected by the adjusting entries, and prepare an adjusted trial balance.

Solution   **1.**

JOURNAL

	Date		Description	Post. Ref.	Debit	Credit	
1	2008 July	31	Supplies Expense		8 9 0 00		1
2			Supplies			8 9 0 00	2
3			Supplies used ($1,270 − $380).				3
4							4
5		31	Insurance Expense		3 1 5 00		5
6			Prepaid Insurance			3 1 5 00	6
7			Insurance expired.				7
8							8
9		31	Depreciation Expense		4 9 5 0 00		9
10			Accumulated Depreciation			4 9 5 0 00	10
11			Depreciation expense.				11
12							12
13		31	Wages Expense		4 4 0 00		13
14			Wages Payable			4 4 0 00	14
15			Accrued wages.				15
16							16
17		31	Accounts Receivable		1 0 0 0 00		17
18			Fees Earned			1 0 0 0 00	18
19			Accrued fees.				19
20							20
21		31	Unearned Fees		5 0 0 00		21
22			Fees Earned			5 0 0 00	22
23			Fees earned ($1,250 − $750).				23

2.

Harbor Realty
Adjusted Trial Balance
July 31, 2008

	Debit Balances	Credit Balances
Cash	3 4 2 5 00	
Accounts Receivable	8 0 0 0 00	
Supplies	3 8 0 00	
Prepaid Insurance	3 0 5 00	
Office Equipment	51 6 5 0 00	
Accumulated Depreciation		14 6 5 0 00
Accounts Payable		9 2 5 00
Wages Payable		4 4 0 00
Unearned Fees		7 5 0 00
T. Roderick, Capital		29 0 0 0 00
T. Roderick, Drawing	5 2 0 0 00	
Fees Earned		60 6 2 5 00
Wages Expense	22 8 5 5 00	
Depreciation Expense	4 9 5 0 00	
Rent Expense	4 2 0 0 00	
Utilities Expense	2 7 1 5 00	
Supplies Expense	8 9 0 00	
Insurance Expense	3 1 5 00	
Miscellaneous Expense	1 5 0 5 00	
	106 3 9 0 00	106 3 9 0 00

Self-Examination Questions

(Answers at End of Chapter)

1. Which of the following items represents a deferral?
   A. Prepaid insurance C. Fees earned
   B. Wages payable D. Accumulated depreciation

2. If the supplies account, before adjustment on May 31, indicated a balance of $2,250, and supplies on hand at May 31 totaled $950, the adjusting entry would be:
   A. debit Supplies, $950; credit Supplies Expense, $950.
   B. debit Supplies, $1,300; credit Supplies Expense, $1,300.
   C. debit Supplies Expense, $950; credit Supplies, $950.
   D. debit Supplies Expense, $1,300; credit Supplies, $1,300.

3. The balance in the unearned rent account for Jones Co. as of December 31 is $1,200. If Jones Co. failed to record the adjusting entry for $600 of rent earned during December, the effect on the balance sheet and income statement for December would be:
   A. assets understated $600; net income overstated $600.
   B. liabilities understated $600; net income understated $600.

   C. liabilities overstated $600; net income understated $600.
   D. liabilities overstated $600; net income overstated $600.

4. If the estimated amount of depreciation on equipment for a period is $2,000, the adjusting entry to record depreciation would be:
   A. debit Depreciation Expense, $2,000; credit Equipment, $2,000.
   B. debit Equipment, $2,000; credit Depreciation Expense, $2,000.
   C. debit Depreciation Expense, $2,000; credit Accumulated Depreciation, $2,000.
   D. debit Accumulated Depreciation, $2,000; credit Depreciation Expense, $2,000.

5. If the equipment account has a balance of $22,500 and its accumulated depreciation account has a balance of $14,000, the book value of the equipment would be:
   A. $36,500. C. $14,000.
   B. $22,500. D. $8,500.

Eye Openers

1. How are revenues and expenses reported on the income statement under (a) the cash basis of accounting and (b) the accrual basis of accounting?
2. Fees for services provided are billed to a customer during 2007. The customer remits the amount owed in 2008. During which year would the revenues be reported on the income statement under (a) the cash basis? (b) the accrual basis?
3. Employees performed services in 2007, but the wages were not paid until 2008. During which year would the wages expense be reported on the income statement under (a) the cash basis? (b) the accrual basis?
4. Is the matching concept related to (a) the cash basis of accounting or (b) the accrual basis of accounting?
5. Is the balance listed for cash on the trial balance, before the accounts have been adjusted, the amount that should normally be reported on the balance sheet? Explain.
6. Is the balance listed for supplies on the trial balance, before the accounts have been adjusted, the amount that should normally be reported on the balance sheet? Explain.
7. Why are adjusting entries needed at the end of an accounting period?
8. What is the difference between *adjusting entries* and *correcting entries*?
9. Identify the four different categories of adjusting entries frequently required at the end of an accounting period.
10. If the effect of the credit portion of an adjusting entry is to increase the balance of a liability account, which of the following statements describes the effect of the debit portion of the entry?
    a. Increases the balance of a revenue account.
    b. Increases the balance of an expense account.
    c. Increases the balance of an asset account.
11. If the effect of the debit portion of an adjusting entry is to increase the balance of an asset account, which of the following statements describes the effect of the credit portion of the entry?
    a. Increases the balance of a revenue account.
    b. Increases the balance of an expense account.
    c. Increases the balance of a liability account.

12. Does every adjusting entry have an effect on determining the amount of net income for a period? Explain.
13. What is the nature of the balance in the prepaid insurance account at the end of the accounting period (a) before adjustment? (b) after adjustment?
14. On October 1 of the current year, a business paid the October rent on the building that it occupies. (a) Do the rights acquired at October 1 represent an asset or an expense? (b) What is the justification for debiting Rent Expense at the time of payment?
15. (a) Explain the purpose of the two accounts: Depreciation Expense and Accumulated Depreciation. (b) What is the normal balance of each account? (c) Is it customary for the balances of the two accounts to be equal in amount? (d) In what financial statements, if any, will each account appear?

Practice Exercises

PE 3-1A
Accounts requiring adjustment
obj. 1

Indicate with a Yes or No whether or not each of the following accounts normally requires an adjusting entry.

a. Salaries Payable   c. Dana Cates, Drawing   e. Unearned Rent
b. Land   d. Accumulated Depreciation   f. Supplies

PE 3-1B
Accounts requiring adjustment
obj. 1

Indicate with a Yes or No whether or not each of the following accounts normally requires an adjusting entry.

a. Mary Elizabeth Rebok, Capital   c. Prepaid Insurance   e. Interest Payable
b. Building   d. Cash   f. Miscellaneous Expense

PE 3-2A
Type of adjustment
obj. 1

Classify the following items as (1) prepaid expense, (2) unearned revenue, (3) accrued revenue, or (4) accrued expense.

a. Cash received for services not yet rendered   c. Insurance paid
b. Salaries owed but not yet paid   d. Rent revenue earned but not received

PE 3-2B
Type of adjustment
obj. 1

Classify the following items as (1) prepaid expense, (2) unearned revenue, (3) accrued revenue, or (4) accrued expense.

a. Rent expense owed but not yet paid   c. Supplies on hand
b. Fees earned but not received   d. Cash received for use of land next month

PE 3-3A
Adjustment for supplies used
obj. 2

The supplies account had a beginning balance of $1,245 and was debited for $2,860 for supplies purchased during the year. Journalize the adjusting entry required at the end of the year assuming the amount of supplies on hand is $1,349.

PE 3-3B
Adjustment for insurance expired
obj. 2

The prepaid insurance account had a beginning balance of $4,800 and was debited for $5,850 of premiums paid during the year. Journalize the adjusting entry required at the end of the year assuming the amount of unexpired insurance related to future periods is $4,125.

PE 3-4A
Adjustment for unearned fees
obj. 2

The balance in the unearned fees account, before adjustment at the end of the year, is $23,676. Journalize the adjusting entry required assuming the amount of unearned fees at the end of the year is $7,388.

PE 3-4B
Adjustment for unearned rent
obj. 2

On August 1, 2007, Myopic Co. received $6,900 for the rent of land for 12 months. Journalize the adjusting entry required for unearned rent on December 31, 2007.

PE 3-5A
Adjustment for accrued fees
obj. 2

At the end of the current year, $7,234 of fees have been earned but have not been billed to clients. Journalize the adjusting entry to record the accrued fees.

PE 3-5B
Adjustment for accrued fees
obj. 2

At the end of the current year, $1,772 of fees have been earned but have not been billed to clients. Journalize the adjusting entry to record the accrued fees.

PE 3-6A
Adjustment for salaries payable
obj. 2

Yarbrough Realty Co. pays weekly salaries of $11,875 on Friday for a five-day workweek ending on that day. Journalize the necessary adjusting entry at the end of the accounting period assuming that the period ends on Tuesday.

PE 3-6B
Adjustment for salaries payable
obj. 2

Hobbs Realty Co. pays weekly salaries of $24,840 on Monday for a six-day workweek ending the preceding Saturday. Journalize the necessary adjusting entry at the end of the accounting period assuming that the period ends on Thursday.

PE 3-7A
Adjustment for depreciation
obj. 2

The estimated amount of depreciation on equipment for the current year is $6,450. Journalize the adjusting entry to record the depreciation.

PE 3-7B
Adjustment for depreciation
obj. 2

The estimated amount of depreciation on equipment for the current year is $1,820. Journalize the adjusting entry to record the depreciation.

PE 3-8A
Effect of omitting adjustments
obj. 3

For the year ending February 28, 2007, Miracle Medical Co. mistakenly omitted adjusting entries for (1) depreciation of $2,276, (2) fees earned that were not billed of $9,638, and (3) accrued wages of $780. Indicate the combined effect of the errors on (a) revenues, (b) expenses, and (c) net income for the year ended February 28, 2007.

PE 3-8B
Effect of omitting adjustments
obj. 3

For the year ending June 30, 2008, Ambulatory Medical Services Co. mistakenly omitted adjusting entries for (1) $1,034 of supplies that were used, (2) unearned revenue of $6,481 that was earned, and (3) insurance of $7,500 that expired. Indicate the combined effect of the errors on (a) revenues, (b) expenses, and (c) net income for the year ended June 30, 2008.

PE 3-9A
Effect of errors on adjusted trial balance
obj. 4

For each of the following errors, considered individually, indicate whether the error would cause the adjusted trial balance totals to be unequal. If the error would cause the adjusted trial balance totals to be unequal, indicate whether the debit or credit total is higher and by how much.

a. The adjustment of depreciation of $3,500 was omitted from the end-of-period adjusting entries.

b. The adjustment of $2,565 for accrued fees earned was journalized as a debit to Accounts Receivable for $2,565 and a credit to Fees Earned for $2,556.

PE 3-9B
Effect of errors on adjusted trial balance
obj. 4

For each of the following errors, considered individually, indicate whether the error would cause the adjusted trial balance totals to be unequal. If the error would cause the adjusted trial balance totals to be unequal, indicate whether the debit or credit total is higher and by how much.

a. The entry for $460 of supplies used during the period was journalized as a debit to Supplies Expense of $460 and a credit to Supplies of $640.

b. The adjustment for accrued wages of $1,240 was journalized as a debit to Wages Expense for $1,240 and a credit to Accounts Payable for $1,240.

Exercises

EX 3-1
Classifying types of adjustments
obj. 1

Classify the following items as (a) prepaid expense, (b) unearned revenue, (c) accrued revenue, or (d) accrued expense.

1. Fees earned but not yet received.
2. Taxes owed but payable in the following period.
3. Utilities owed but not yet paid.
4. Salary owed but not yet paid.
5. Supplies on hand.
6. Fees received but not yet earned.
7. A two-year premium paid on a fire insurance policy.
8. Subscriptions received in advance by a magazine publisher.

EX 3-2
Classifying adjusting entries
obj. 1

The following accounts were taken from the unadjusted trial balance of Hartford Co., a congressional lobbying firm. Indicate whether or not each account would normally require an adjusting entry. If the account normally requires an adjusting entry, use the following notation to indicate the type of adjustment:

AE—Accrued Expense
AR—Accrued Revenue
PE—Prepaid Expense
UR—Unearned Revenue

To illustrate, the answer for the first account is shown below.

Account	Answer
Accounts Receivable	Normally requires adjustment (AR).
Cash	
Charmaine Hollis, Drawing	
Interest Payable	
Interest Receivable	
Land	
Office Equipment	
Prepaid Rent	
Supplies	
Unearned Fees	
Wages Expense	

EX 3-3
Adjusting entry for supplies
obj. 2

The balance in the supplies account, before adjustment at the end of the year, is $2,975. Journalize the adjusting entry required if the amount of supplies on hand at the end of the year is $614.

EX 3-4
Determining supplies purchased
obj. 2

The supplies and supplies expense accounts at December 31, after adjusting entries have been posted at the end of the first year of operations, are shown in the following T accounts:

Supplies		Supplies Expense	
Bal.	279	Bal.	1,261

Determine the amount of supplies purchased during the year.

EX 3-5
Effect of omitting adjusting entry
obj. 2

At December 31, the end of the first month of operations, the usual adjusting entry transferring prepaid insurance expired to an expense account is omitted. Which items will be incorrectly stated, because of the error, on (a) the income statement for December and (b) the balance sheet as of December 31? Also indicate whether the items in error will be overstated or understated.

EX 3-6
Adjusting entries for prepaid insurance
obj. 2

The balance in the prepaid insurance account, before adjustment at the end of the year, is $6,175. Journalize the adjusting entry required under each of the following *alternatives* for determining the amount of the adjustment: (a) the amount of insurance expired during the year is $4,180; (b) the amount of unexpired insurance applicable to future periods is $1,995.

EX 3-7
Adjusting entries for prepaid insurance
obj. 2

The prepaid insurance account had a balance of $3,600 at the beginning of the year. The account was debited for $4,800 for premiums on policies purchased during the year. Journalize the adjusting entry required at the end of the year for each of the following situations: (a) the amount of unexpired insurance applicable to future periods is $2,950; (b) the amount of insurance expired during the year is $5,450.

EX 3-8
Adjusting entries for unearned fees
obj. 2
✓ *Amount of entry: $22,320*

The balance in the unearned fees account, before adjustment at the end of the year, is $49,500. Journalize the adjusting entry required if the amount of unearned fees at the end of the year is $27,180.

EX 3-9
Effect of omitting adjusting entry
obj. 2

At the end of August, the first month of the business year, the usual adjusting entry transferring rent earned to a revenue account from the unearned rent account was omitted. Indicate which items will be incorrectly stated, because of the error, on (a) the income statement for August and (b) the balance sheet as of August 31. Also indicate whether the items in error will be overstated or understated.

EX 3-10
Adjusting entry for accrued fees
obj. 2

At the end of the current year, $17,600 of fees have been earned but have not been billed to clients.

a. Journalize the adjusting entry to record the accrued fees.
b. If the cash basis rather than the accrual basis had been used, would an adjusting entry have been necessary? Explain.

EX 3-11
Adjusting entries for unearned and accrued fees
obj. 2

The balance in the unearned fees account, before adjustment at the end of the year, is $39,750. Of these fees, $12,300 have been earned. In addition, $7,100 of fees have been earned but have not been billed. Journalize the adjusting entries (a) to adjust the unearned fees account and (b) to record the accrued fees.

EX 3-12
Effect on financial statements of omitting adjusting entry
obj. 2

The adjusting entry for accrued fees was omitted at December 31, the end of the current year. Indicate which items will be in error, because of the omission, on (a) the income statement for the current year and (b) the balance sheet as of December 31. Also indicate whether the items in error will be overstated or understated.

EX 3-13
Adjusting entries for accrued salaries
obj. 2
✓ a. Amount of entry: $12,375

Ash Realty Co. pays weekly salaries of $20,625 on Friday for a five-day workweek ending on that day. Journalize the necessary adjusting entry at the end of the accounting period assuming that the period ends (a) on Wednesday and (b) on Thursday.

EX 3-14
Determining wages paid
obj. 2

The wages payable and wages expense accounts at March 31, after adjusting entries have been posted at the end of the first month of operations, are shown in the following T accounts:

Wages Payable			Wages Expense	
	Bal.	6,480	Bal.	72,150

Determine the amount of wages paid during the month.

EX 3-15
Effect of omitting adjusting entry
obj. 2

Accrued salaries of $3,910 owed to employees for December 30 and 31 are not considered in preparing the financial statements for the year ended December 31. Indicate which items will be erroneously stated, because of the error, on (a) the income statement for the year and (b) the balance sheet as of December 31. Also indicate whether the items in error will be overstated or understated.

EX 3-16
Effect of omitting adjusting entry
obj. 2

Assume that the error in Exercise 3-15 was not corrected and that the $3,910 of accrued salaries was included in the first salary payment in January. Indicate which items will be erroneously stated, because of failure to correct the initial error, on (a) the income statement for the month of January and (b) the balance sheet as of January 31.

EX 3-17
Adjusting entries for prepaid and accrued taxes

obj. 2

✓ b. $18,675

Pisces Financial Services was organized on April 1 of the current year. On April 2, Pisces prepaid $3,000 to the city for taxes (license fees) for the *next* 12 months and debited the prepaid taxes account. Pisces is also required to pay in January an annual tax (on property) for the *previous* calendar year. The estimated amount of the property tax for the current year (April 1 to December 31) is $16,425.

a. Journalize the two adjusting entries required to bring the accounts affected by the two taxes up to date as of December 31, the end of the current year.
b. What is the amount of tax expense for the current year?

EX 3-18
Adjustment for depreciation

obj. 2

The estimated amount of depreciation on equipment for the current year is $3,275. Journalize the adjusting entry to record the depreciation.

EX 3-19
Determining fixed asset's book value

obj. 2

The balance in the equipment account is $678,950, and the balance in the accumulated depreciation—equipment account is $262,200.

a. What is the book value of the equipment?
b. Does the balance in the accumulated depreciation account mean that the equipment's loss of value is $262,200? Explain.

EX 3-20
Book value of fixed assets

objs. 2, 3

In a recent balance sheet, Microsoft Corporation reported *Property, Plant, and Equipment* of $6,078 million and *Accumulated Depreciation* of $3,855 million.

a. What was the book value of the fixed assets?
b. Would the book value of Microsoft Corporation's fixed assets normally approximate their fair market values?

EX 3-21
Effects of errors on financial statements

objs. 2, 3

For a recent period, Circuit City Stores, Inc., reported accrued expenses and other current liabilities of $228,966,000. For the same period, Circuit City reported earnings of $95,789,000 before income taxes. If accrued expenses and other current liabilities had not been recorded, what would have been the earnings (loss) before income taxes?

EX 3-22
Effects of errors on financial statements

objs. 2, 3

For a recent year, the balance sheet for The Campbell Soup Company includes accrued liabilities of $606,000,000. The income before taxes for The Campbell Soup Company for the year was $1,030,000,000.

a. If the accruals had not been recorded at the end of the year, by how much would income before taxes have been misstated?
b. What is the percentage of the misstatement in (a) to the reported income of $1,030,000,000? Round to one decimal place.

EX 3-23
Effects of errors on financial statements

objs. 2, 3

The accountant for Cyprus Medical Co., a medical services consulting firm, mistakenly omitted adjusting entries for (a) unearned revenue earned during the year ($12,450) and (b) accrued wages ($7,280). Indicate the effect of each error, considered individually, on the income statement for the current year ended August 31. Also indicate the effect of each error on the August 31 balance sheet. Set up a table similar to the following, and record your

✓1. a. Revenue
understated, $12,450

answers by inserting the dollar amount in the appropriate spaces. Insert a zero if the error does not affect the item.

	Error (a)		Error (b)	
	Over-stated	Under-stated	Over-stated	Under-stated
1. Revenue for the year would be	$ ___	$ ___	$ ___	$ ___
2. Expenses for the year would be	$ ___	$ ___	$ ___	$ ___
3. Net income for the year would be	$ ___	$ ___	$ ___	$ ___
4. Assets at August 31 would be	$ ___	$ ___	$ ___	$ ___
5. Liabilities at August 31 would be	$ ___	$ ___	$ ___	$ ___
6. Owner's equity at August 31 would be	$ ___	$ ___	$ ___	$ ___

EX 3-24
*Effects of errors on
financial statements*

objs. 2, 3

If the net income for the current year had been $262,800 in Exercise 3-23, what would have been the correct net income if the proper adjusting entries had been made?

EX 3-25
*Adjusting entries for
depreciation; effect of
error*

objs. 2, 3

On December 31, a business estimates depreciation on equipment used during the first year of operations to be $18,100.

a. Journalize the adjusting entry required as of December 31.
b. If the adjusting entry in (a) were omitted, which items would be erroneously stated on (1) the income statement for the year and (2) the balance sheet as of December 31?

EX 3-26
*Adjusting entries from
trial balances*

obj. 4

The unadjusted and adjusted trial balances for Tomahawk Services Co. on July 31, 2008, are shown below.

Tomahawk Services Co.
Trial Balance
July 31, 2008

	Unadjusted		Adjusted	
	Debit Balances	Credit Balances	Debit Balances	Credit Balances
Cash	48		48	
Accounts Receivable	114		126	
Supplies	36		27	
Prepaid Insurance	60		36	
Land	78		78	
Equipment	120		120	
Accumulated Depreciation—Equipment		24		39
Accounts Payable		78		78
Wages Payable		0		3
Cleo Dexter, Capital		276		276
Cleo Dexter, Drawing	24		24	
Fees Earned		222		234
Wages Expense	72		75	
Rent Expense	24		24	
Insurance Expense	0		24	
Utilities Expense	12		12	
Depreciation Expense	0		15	
Supplies Expense	0		9	
Miscellaneous Expense	12		12	
	600	600	630	630

Journalize the five entries that adjusted the accounts at July 31, 2008. None of the accounts were affected by more than one adjusting entry.

EX 3-27
Adjusting entries from trial balances
obj. 4

✓ *Corrected trial balance totals, $310,950*

The accountant for Sweetwater Laundry prepared the following unadjusted and adjusted trial balances. Assume that all balances in the unadjusted trial balance and the amounts of the adjustments are correct. Identify the errors in the accountant's adjusting entries.

Sweetwater Laundry
Trial Balance
October 31, 2008

	Unadjusted		Adjusted	
	Debit Balances	Credit Balances	Debit Balances	Credit Balances
Cash	7,500		7,500	
Accounts Receivable	18,250		22,000	
Laundry Supplies	3,750		5,500	
Prepaid Insurance*	5,200		1,400	
Laundry Equipment	140,000		134,000	
Accumulated Depreciation		48,000		48,000
Accounts Payable		9,600		9,600
Wages Payable				1,200
Mattie Ivy, Capital		60,300		60,300
Mattie Ivy, Drawing	28,775		28,775	
Laundry Revenue		182,100		182,100
Wages Expense	49,200		49,200	
Rent Expense	25,575		25,575	
Utilities Expense	18,500		18,500	
Depreciation Expense			6,000	
Laundry Supplies Expense			1,750	
Insurance Expense			800	
Miscellaneous Expense	3,250		3,250	
	300,000	300,000	304,250	301,200

*$3,800 of insurance expired during the year.

Problems Series A

PR 3-1A
Adjusting entries
obj. 2

On July 31, 2008, the following data were accumulated to assist the accountant in preparing the adjusting entries for Fremont Realty:

a. The supplies account balance on July 31 is $1,975. The supplies on hand on July 31 are $625.
b. The unearned rent account balance on July 31 is $3,750, representing the receipt of an advance payment on July 1 of three months' rent from tenants.
c. Wages accrued but not paid at July 31 are $1,000.
d. Fees accrued but unbilled at July 31 are $12,275.
e. Depreciation of office equipment is $850.

Instructions
1. Journalize the adjusting entries required at July 31, 2008.
2. Briefly explain the difference between adjusting entries and entries that would be made to correct errors.

PR 3-2A
Adjusting entries
obj. 2

Selected account balances before adjustment for Foxboro Realty at December 31, 2008, the end of the current year, are as follows:

	Debits	Credits
Accounts Receivable	$18,250	
Equipment	72,500	
Accumulated Depreciation		$ 11,900
Prepaid Rent	7,500	
Supplies	2,050	
Wages Payable		—
Unearned Fees		8,500
Fees Earned		187,950
Wages Expense	60,100	
Rent Expense	—	
Depreciation Expense	—	
Supplies Expense	—	

Data needed for year-end adjustments are as follows:

a. Unbilled fees at December 31, $1,650.
b. Supplies on hand at December 31, $200.
c. Rent expired, $5,000.
d. Depreciation of equipment during year, $1,150.
e. Unearned fees at December 31, $1,500.
f. Wages accrued but not paid at December 31, $3,150.

Instructions
Journalize the six adjusting entries required at December 31, based upon the data presented.

PR 3-3A
Adjusting entries
obj. 2

Iron River Company, an electronics repair store, prepared the unadjusted trial balance at the end of its first year of operations shown below.

Iron River Company
Unadjusted Trial Balance
April 30, 2008

	Debit Balances	Credit Balances
Cash	3,450	
Accounts Receivable	22,500	
Supplies	5,400	
Equipment	113,700	
Accounts Payable		5,250
Unearned Fees		6,000
Walker Kellogg, Capital		78,000
Walker Kellogg, Drawing	4,500	
Fees Earned		135,750
Wages Expense	31,500	
Rent Expense	24,000	
Utilities Expense	17,250	
Miscellaneous Expense	2,700	
	225,000	225,000

For preparing the adjusting entries, the following data were assembled:

a. Fees earned but unbilled on April 30 were $1,775.
b. Supplies on hand on April 30 were $1,200.
c. Depreciation of equipment was estimated to be $4,100 for the year.
d. The balance in unearned fees represented the April 1 receipt in advance for services to be provided. Only $1,750 of the services was provided between April 1 and April 30.
e. Unpaid wages accrued on April 30 were $600.

Instructions
Journalize the adjusting entries necessary on April 30, 2008.

PR 3-4A
Adjusting entries
objs. 2, 3, 4

Danville Company specializes in the repair of music equipment and is owned and operated by Harry Nagel. On April 30, 2008, the end of the current year, the accountant for Danville Company prepared the following trial balances:

Danville Company
Trial Balance
April 30, 2008

	Unadjusted		Adjusted	
	Debit Balances	Credit Balances	Debit Balances	Credit Balances
Cash	12,750		12,750	
Accounts Receivable	36,500		36,500	
Supplies	3,750		900	
Prepaid Insurance	4,750		1,500	
Equipment	120,150		120,150	
Accumulated Depreciation—Equipment		31,500		34,000
Automobiles	36,500		36,500	
Accumulated Depreciation—Automobiles		18,250		20,400
Accounts Payable		8,310		8,800
Salaries Payable		—		2,000
Unearned Service Fees		6,000		2,900
Harry Nagel, Capital		131,340		131,340
Harry Nagel, Drawing	25,000		25,000	
Service Fees Earned		244,600		247,700
Salary Expense	172,300		174,300	
Rent Expense	18,000		18,000	
Supplies Expense	—		2,850	
Depreciation Expense—Equipment	—		2,500	
Depreciation Expense—Automobiles	—		2,150	
Utilities Expense	4,300		4,790	
Taxes Expense	2,725		2,725	
Insurance Expense	—		3,250	
Miscellaneous Expense	3,275		3,275	
	440,000	440,000	447,140	447,140

Instructions
Journalize the seven entries that adjusted the accounts at April 30. None of the accounts were affected by more than one adjusting entry.

PR 3-5A
Adjusting entries and adjusted trial balances
objs. 2, 3, 4

✓ *2. Total of Debit Column: $765,000*

Cambridge Company is a small editorial services company owned and operated by Dave Maier. On December 31, 2008, the end of the current year, Cambridge Company's accounting clerk prepared the unadjusted trial balance shown at the top of the following page.
The data needed to determine year-end adjustments are as follows:

a. Unexpired insurance at December 31, $2,700.
b. Supplies on hand at December 31, $480.
c. Depreciation of building for the year, $1,600.
d. Depreciation of equipment for the year, $4,400.
e. Rent unearned at December 31, $3,250.
f. Accrued salaries and wages at December 31, $2,800.
g. Fees earned but unbilled on December 31, $6,200.

Instructions
1. Journalize the adjusting entries. Add additional accounts as needed.
2. Determine the balances of the accounts affected by the adjusting entries, and prepare an adjusted trial balance.

Cambridge Company
Unadjusted Trial Balance
December 31, 2008

	Debit Balances	Credit Balances
Cash	5,550	
Accounts Receivable	28,350	
Prepaid Insurance	7,200	
Supplies	1,980	
Land	112,500	
Building	212,250	
Accumulated Depreciation—Building		137,550
Equipment	135,300	
Accumulated Depreciation—Equipment		97,950
Accounts Payable		12,150
Unearned Rent		6,750
Dave Maier, Capital		201,000
Dave Maier, Drawing	15,000	
Fees Earned		294,600
Salaries and Wages Expense	143,370	
Utilities Expense	42,375	
Advertising Expense	22,800	
Repairs Expense	17,250	
Miscellaneous Expense	6,075	
	750,000	750,000

PR 3-6A
Adjusting entries and errors

obj. 3

✓ *2. Corrected Net Income: $157,600*

At the end of June, the first month of operations, the following selected data were taken from the financial statements of Teryse Weire, an attorney:

Net income for June	$155,000
Total assets at June 30	350,000
Total liabilities at June 30	120,000
Total owner's equity at June 30	230,000

In preparing the financial statements, adjustments for the following data were overlooked:

a. Supplies used during June, $1,800.
b. Unbilled fees earned at June 30, $11,600.
c. Depreciation of equipment for June, $4,950.
d. Accrued wages at June 30, $2,250.

Instructions

1. Journalize the entries to record the omitted adjustments.
2. Determine the correct amount of net income for June and the total assets, liabilities, and owner's equity at June 30. In addition to indicating the corrected amounts, indicate the effect of each omitted adjustment by setting up and completing a columnar table similar to the following. Adjustment (a) is presented as an example.

	Net Income	Total Assets	Total Liabilities	Total Owner's Equity
Reported amounts	$155,000	$350,000	$120,000	$230,000
Corrections:				
Adjustment (a)	−1,800	−1,800	0	−1,800
Adjustment (b)				
Adjustment (c)				
Adjustment (d)				
Corrected amounts				

Problems Series B

PR 3-1B
Adjusting entries
obj. 2

On October 31, 2008, the following data were accumulated to assist the accountant in preparing the adjusting entries for Twin Bluffs Realty:

a. Fees accrued but unbilled at October 31 are $11,385.
b. The supplies account balance on October 31 is $2,973. The supplies on hand at October 31 are $740.
c. Wages accrued but not paid at October 31 are $1,500.
d. The unearned rent account balance at October 31 is $9,450, representing the receipt of an advance payment on October 1 of three months' rent from tenants.
e. Depreciation of office equipment is $2,650.

Instructions
1. Journalize the adjusting entries required at October 31, 2008.
2. Briefly explain the difference between adjusting entries and entries that would be made to correct errors.

PR 3-2B
Adjusting entries
obj. 2

Selected account balances before adjustment for Green Lake Realty at August 31, 2008, the end of the current year, are shown below.

	Debits	Credits
Accounts Receivable	$38,250	
Accumulated Depreciation		$ 26,900
Depreciation Expense	—	
Equipment	90,500	
Fees Earned		275,500
Prepaid Rent	9,750	
Rent Expense	—	
Supplies	2,145	
Supplies Expense	—	
Unearned Fees		6,175
Wages Expense	81,500	
Wages Payable	—	

Data needed for year-end adjustments are as follows:

a. Supplies on hand at August 31, $500.
b. Depreciation of equipment during year, $1,375.
c. Rent expired during year, $4,525.
d. Wages accrued but not paid at August 31, $2,200.
e. Unearned fees at August 31, $1,500.
f. Unbilled fees at August 31, $6,780.

Instructions
Journalize the six adjusting entries required at August 31, based upon the data presented.

PR 3-3B
Adjusting entries
obj. 2

Lander Outfitters Co., an outfitter store for fishing treks, prepared the unadjusted trial balance shown on the following page at the end of its first year of operations.
    For preparing the adjusting entries, the following data were assembled:

a. Supplies on hand on June 30 were $300.
b. Fees earned but unbilled on June 30 were $2,310.
c. Depreciation of equipment was estimated to be $1,500 for the year.

d. Unpaid wages accrued on June 30 were $475.

e. The balance in unearned fees represented the June 1 receipt in advance for services to be provided. Only $1,000 of the services was provided between June 1 and June 30.

Lander Outfitters Co.
Unadjusted Trial Balance
June 30, 2008

	Debit Balances	Credit Balances
Cash	6,610	
Accounts Receivable	21,900	
Supplies	1,820	
Equipment	37,860	
Accounts Payable		3,050
Unearned Fees		4,800
Tim Hudson, Capital		55,700
Tim Hudson, Drawing	2,500	
Fees Earned		71,450
Wages Expense	38,210	
Rent Expense	13,790	
Utilities Expense	10,050	
Miscellaneous Expense	2,260	
	135,000	135,000

Instructions

Journalize the adjusting entries necessary on June 30.

PR 3-4B
Adjusting entries
objs. 2, 3, 4

Elkton Company specializes in the maintenance and repair of signs, such as billboards. On July 31, 2008, the accountant for Elkton Company prepared the following trial balances.

Elkton Company
Trial Balance
July 31, 2008

	Unadjusted Debit Balances	Unadjusted Credit Balances	Adjusted Debit Balances	Adjusted Credit Balances
Cash	4,750		4,750	
Accounts Receivable	17,400		17,400	
Supplies	3,600		975	
Prepaid Insurance	5,650		1,200	
Land	50,000		50,000	
Buildings	120,000		120,000	
Accumulated Depreciation—Buildings		49,500		53,100
Trucks	75,000		75,000	
Accumulated Depreciation—Trucks		11,800		13,300
Accounts Payable		6,920		7,520
Salaries Payable		—		1,180
Unearned Service Fees		7,400		5,100
Mario Salas, Capital		146,700		146,700
Mario Salas, Drawing	5,000		5,000	
Service Fees Earned		152,680		154,980
Salary Expense	73,600		74,780	
Depreciation Expense—Trucks	—		1,500	
Rent Expense	9,600		9,600	
Supplies Expense	—		2,625	
Utilities Expense	6,200		6,800	
Depreciation Expense—Buildings	—		3,600	
Taxes Expense	1,720		1,720	
Insurance Expense	—		4,450	
Miscellaneous Expense	2,480		2,480	
	375,000	375,000	381,880	381,880

Instructions

Journalize the seven entries that adjusted the accounts at July 31. None of the accounts were affected by more than one adjusting entry.

PR 3-5B
Adjusting entries and adjusted trial balances
objs. 2, 3, 4

✓ 2. Total of Debit Column: $285,150

Lincoln Service Co., which specializes in appliance repair services, is owned and operated by Molly Jordan. Lincoln Service Co.'s accounting clerk prepared the following unadjusted trial balance at December 31, 2008, shown below.

Lincoln Service Co.
Unadjusted Trial Balance
December 31, 2008

	Debit Balances	Credit Balances
Cash	2,100	
Accounts Receivable	10,300	
Prepaid Insurance	3,000	
Supplies	1,725	
Land	50,000	
Building	80,750	
Accumulated Depreciation—Building		37,850
Equipment	44,000	
Accumulated Depreciation—Equipment		17,650
Accounts Payable		3,750
Unearned Rent		3,600
Molly Jordan, Capital		83,550
Molly Jordan, Drawing	2,500	
Fees Earned		128,600
Salaries and Wages Expense	50,900	
Utilities Expense	14,100	
Advertising Expense	7,500	
Repairs Expense	6,100	
Miscellaneous Expense	2,025	
	275,000	275,000

The data needed to determine year-end adjustments are as follows:

a. Depreciation of building for the year, $3,500.
b. Depreciation of equipment for the year, $2,300.
c. Accrued salaries and wages at December 31, $1,100.
d. Unexpired insurance at December 31, $750.
e. Fees earned but unbilled on December 31, $3,250.
f. Supplies on hand at December 31, $525.
g. Rent unearned at December 31, $1,500.

Instructions

1. Journalize the adjusting entries. Add additional accounts as needed.
2. Determine the balances of the accounts affected by the adjusting entries and prepare an adjusted trial balance.

PR 3-6B
Adjusting entries and errors
obj. 3

✓ 2. Corrected Net Income: $97,755

At the end of October, the first month of operations, the following selected data were taken from the financial statements of Lauren Powell, an attorney:

Net income for October	$ 99,480
Total assets at October 31	400,000
Total liabilities at October 31	100,000
Total owner's equity at October 31	300,000

In preparing the financial statements, adjustments for the following data were overlooked:

a. Unbilled fees earned at October 31, $8,000.
b. Depreciation of equipment for October, $5,500.
c. Accrued wages at October 31, $2,500.
d. Supplies used during October, $1,725.

Instructions
1. Journalize the entries to record the omitted adjustments.
2. Determine the correct amount of net income for October and the total assets, liabilities, and owner's equity at October 31. In addition to indicating the corrected amounts, indicate the effect of each omitted adjustment by setting up and completing a columnar table similar to the following. Adjustment (a) is presented as an example.

	Net Income	Total Assets	Total Liabilities	Total Owner's Equity
Reported amounts	$99,480	$400,000	$100,000	$300,000
Corrections:				
Adjustment (a)	+8,000	+8,000	0	+8,000
Adjustment (b)				
Adjustment (c)				
Adjustment (d)				
Corrected amounts				

Continuing Problem

✓3. Total of Debit Column: $39,500

The unadjusted trial balance that you prepared for Dancin Music at the end of Chapter 2 should appear as follows:

Dancin Music
Unadjusted Trial Balance
May 31, 2008

	Debit Balances	Credit Balances
Cash	12,085	
Accounts Receivable	2,850	
Supplies	920	
Prepaid Insurance	3,360	
Office Equipment	5,000	
Accounts Payable		5,750
Unearned Revenue		4,800
Kris Payne, Capital		12,500
Kris Payne, Drawing	1,300	
Fees Earned		14,750
Wages Expense	2,400	
Office Rent Expense	2,600	
Equipment Rent Expense	1,300	
Utilities Expense	910	
Music Expense	2,565	
Advertising Expense	1,730	
Supplies Expense	180	
Miscellaneous Expense	600	
	37,800	37,800

The data needed to determine adjustments for the two-month period ending May 31, 2008, are as follows:

a. During May, Dancin Music provided guest disc jockeys for KPRG for a total of 115 hours. For information on the amount of the accrued revenue to be billed to KPRG, see the contract described in the May 3, 2008, transaction at the end of Chapter 2.
b. Supplies on hand at May 31, $160.
c. The balance of the prepaid insurance account relates to the May 1, 2008, transaction at the end of Chapter 2.
d. Depreciation of the office equipment is $100.

e. The balance of the unearned revenue account relates to the contract between Dancin Music and KPRG, described in the May 3, 2008, transaction at the end of Chapter 2.
f. Accrued wages as of May 31, 2008, were $200.

Instructions

1. Prepare adjusting journal entries. You will need the following additional accounts:

   18 Accumulated Depreciation—Office Equipment
   22 Wages Payable
   57 Insurance Expense
   58 Depreciation Expense

2. Post the adjusting entries, inserting balances in the accounts affected.
3. Prepare an adjusted trial balance.

Special Activities

SA 3-1
Ethics and professional conduct in business

ETHICS

Annette Kagel opened Harre Real Estate Co. on January 1, 2007. At the end of the first year, the business needed additional capital. On behalf of Harre Real Estate, Annette applied to Lake County State Bank for a loan of $200,000. Based on Harre Real Estate's financial statements, which had been prepared on a cash basis, the Lake County State Bank loan officer rejected the loan as too risky.

After receiving the rejection notice, Annette instructed her accountant to prepare the financial statements on an accrual basis. These statements included $31,500 in accounts receivable and $10,200 in accounts payable. Annette then instructed her accountant to record an additional $10,000 of accounts receivable for commissions on property for which a contract had been signed on December 28, 2007, but which would not be formally "closed" and the title transferred until January 5, 2008.

Annette then applied for a $200,000 loan from First National Bank, using the revised financial statements. On this application, Annette indicated that she had not previously been rejected for credit.

Discuss the ethical and professional conduct of Annette Kagel in applying for the loan from First National Bank.

SA 3-2
Accrued expense

REAL WORLD

On December 30, 2008, you buy a Ford Expedition. It comes with a three-year, 36,000-mile warranty. On March 5, 2009, you return the Expedition to the dealership for some basic repairs covered under the warranty. The cost of the repairs to the dealership is $1,560. In what year, 2008 or 2009, should Ford Motor Company recognize the cost of the warranty repairs as an expense?

SA 3-3
Accrued revenue

REAL WORLD

The following is an excerpt from a conversation between Sybil Towns and Greg Gibbs just before they boarded a flight to London on American Airlines. They are going to London to attend their company's annual sales conference.

Sybil: Greg, aren't you taking an introductory accounting course at college?
Greg: Yes, I decided it's about time I learned something about accounting. You know, our annual bonuses are based upon the sales figures that come from the accounting department.
Sybil: I guess I never really thought about it.
Greg: You should think about it! Last year, I placed a $500,000 order on December 28. But when I got my bonus, the $500,000 sale wasn't included. They said it hadn't been shipped until January 3, so it would have to count in next year's bonus.
Sybil: A real bummer!
Greg: Right! I was counting on that bonus including the $500,000 sale.
Sybil: Did you complain?

Greg: Yes, but it didn't do any good. Ashley, the head accountant, said something about matching revenues and expenses. Also, something about not recording revenues until the sale is final. I figure I'd take the accounting course and find out whether she's just jerking me around.

Sybil: I never really thought about it. When do you think American Airlines will record its revenues from this flight?

Greg: Mmm . . . I guess it could record the revenue when it sells the ticket . . . or . . . when the boarding passes are taken at the door . . . or . . . when we get off the plane . . . or when our company pays for the tickets . . . or . . . I don't know. I'll ask my accounting instructor.

Discuss when American Airlines should recognize the revenue from ticket sales to properly match revenues and expenses.

SA 3-4
Adjustments and financial statements

Several years ago, your brother opened Pomona Television Repair. He made a small initial investment and added money from his personal bank account as needed. He withdrew money for living expenses at irregular intervals. As the business grew, he hired an assistant. He is now considering adding more employees, purchasing additional service trucks, and purchasing the building he now rents. To secure funds for the expansion, your brother submitted a loan application to the bank and included the most recent financial statements (shown below) prepared from accounts maintained by a part-time bookkeeper.

Pomona Television Repair
Income Statement
For the Year Ended July 31, 2008

Service revenue		$90,000
Less: Rent paid	$30,000	
Wages paid	28,500	
Supplies paid	5,100	
Utilities paid	3,175	
Insurance paid	2,400	
Miscellaneous payments	3,600	72,775
Net income		$17,225

Pomona Television Repair
Balance Sheet
July 31, 2008

Assets

Cash	$10,600
Amounts due from customers	12,500
Truck	36,900
Total assets	$60,000

Equities

Owner's capital	$60,000

After reviewing the financial statements, the loan officer at the bank asked your brother if he used the accrual basis of accounting for revenues and expenses. Your brother responded that he did and that is why he included an account for "Amounts Due from Customers." The loan officer then asked whether or not the accounts were adjusted prior to the preparation of the statements. Your brother answered that they had not been adjusted.

a. Why do you think the loan officer suspected that the accounts had not been adjusted prior to the preparation of the statements?
b. Indicate possible accounts that might need to be adjusted before an accurate set of financial statements could be prepared.

SA 3-5
Codes of ethics

Group Project

ETHICS

Obtain a copy of your college or university's student code of conduct. In groups of three or four, answer the following question.

1. Compare this code of conduct with the accountant's Codes of Professional Conduct, which is linked to the text Web site at **www.thomsonedu.com/accounting/warren**.
2. One of your classmates asks you for permission to copy your homework, which your instructor will be collecting and grading for part of your overall term grade. Although your instructor has not stated whether one student may or may not copy another student's homework, is it ethical for you to allow your classmate to copy your homework? Is it ethical for your classmate to copy your homework?

Answers to Self-Examination Questions

1. **A** A deferral is the delay in recording an expense already paid, such as prepaid insurance (answer A). Wages payable (answer B) is considered an accrued expense or accrued liability. Fees earned (answer C) is a revenue item. Accumulated depreciation (answer D) is a contra account to a fixed asset.

2. **D** The balance in the supplies account, before adjustment, represents the amount of supplies available. From this amount ($2,250) is subtracted the amount of supplies on hand ($950) to determine the supplies used ($1,300). Since increases in expense accounts are recorded by debits and decreases in asset accounts are recorded by credits, answer D is the correct entry.

3. **C** The failure to record the adjusting entry debiting Unearned Rent, $600, and crediting Rent Revenue, $600, would have the effect of overstating liabilities by $600 and understating net income by $600 (answer C).

4. **C** Since increases in expense accounts (such as depreciation expense) are recorded by debits and it is customary to record the decreases in usefulness of fixed assets as credits to accumulated depreciation accounts, answer C is the correct entry.

5. **D** The book value of a fixed asset is the difference between the balance in the asset account and the balance in the related accumulated depreciation account, or $22,500 − $14,000, as indicated by answer D ($8,500).

Completing the Accounting Cycle

© ERIC RISBERG/ASSOCIATED PRESS

objectives

After studying this chapter, you should be able to:

1 *Describe the flow of accounting information from the unadjusted trial balance into the adjusted trial balance and financial statements.*

2 *Prepare financial statements from adjusted account balances.*

3 *Prepare closing entries.*

4 *Describe the accounting cycle.*

5 *Illustrate the accounting cycle for one period.*

6 *Explain what is meant by the fiscal year and the natural business year.*

Electronic Arts Inc.

Most of us have had to file a personal tax return. At the beginning of the year, you estimate your upcoming income and decide whether you need to increase your payroll tax withholdings or perhaps pay estimated taxes. During the year, you earn income and enter into tax-related transactions, such as making charitable contributions. At the end of the year, your employer sends you a tax withholding information form (W-2) form, and you collect the tax records needed for completing your yearly tax forms. As the next year begins, you start the cycle all over again.

Businesses also go through a cycle of activities. For example, Electronic Arts Inc., the world's largest developer and marketer of electronic game software, begins its cycle by developing new or revised game titles, such as Madden NFL Football®, Need for Speed®, Tiger Woods PGA Tour®, The Sims®, and The Lord of the Rings®. These games are marketed and sold throughout the year. During the year, operating transactions of the business are recorded. For Electronic Arts, such transactions include the salaries for game developers, advertising expenditures, costs for producing and packaging games, and game revenues. At the end of the year, financial statements are prepared that summarize the operating activities for the year. Electronic Arts publishes these statements on its Web site at **http://www.investor.ea.com**. Finally, before the start of the next year, the accounts are readied for recording the operations of the next year.

As we saw in Chapter 1, the initial cycle for NetSolutions began with Chris Clark's investment in the business on November 1, 2007. The cycle continued with recording NetSolutions' transactions for November and December, as we discussed and illustrated in Chapters 1 and 2. In Chapter 3, the cycle continued when the adjusting entries for the two months ending December 31, 2007, were recorded. In this chapter, we complete the cycle for NetSolutions by preparing financial statements and getting the accounts ready for recording transactions of the next period.

Flow of Accounting Information

objective 1

Describe the flow of accounting information from the unadjusted trial balance into the adjusted trial balance and financial statements.

@netsolutions

Many companies use Microsoft's Excel® software to prepare end-of-period spreadsheets (work sheets).

The end-of-period process by which accounts are adjusted and the financial statements are prepared is one of the most important in accounting. Using our illustration of NetSolutions from Chapters 1–3, this process is summarized in spreadsheet form in Exhibit 1.

Exhibit 1 begins with the unadjusted trial balance as of the end of the period. The unadjusted trial balance serves as a control to verify that the total of the debit balances equals the total of the credit balances. If the trial balance totals are unequal, an error has occurred, which must be found and corrected before the end-of-period process can continue.

The adjustments that we explained and illustrated for NetSolutions in Chapter 3 are shown in the Adjustments columns of Exhibit 1. Cross-referencing (by letters) the debit and credit of each adjustment is useful in reviewing the impact of the adjustments on the unadjusted account balances. The order of the adjustments on the spreadsheet is not important, and the adjustments are normally entered in the order in which the data are assembled. When the titles of the accounts to be adjusted do not appear in the unadjusted trial balance, the accounts are inserted in the Account Title column, below the unadjusted trial balance totals. The total of the Adjustments columns is a control to verify the mathematical accuracy of the adjustment data and adjusting entries. The total of the Debit column must equal the total of the Credit column.

The adjustment data are added to or subtracted from the amounts in the Unadjusted Trial Balance columns to arrive at the Adjusted Trial Balance columns. In this way, the Adjusted Trial Balance columns of Exhibit 1 illustrate the impact of the adjusting entries

EXHIBIT 1   End-of-Period Spreadsheet (Work Sheet)

	A	B	C	D	E	F	G	H	I	J	K	
		NetSolutions										
		End-of-Period Spreadsheet (Work Sheet)										
		For the Two Months Ended December 31, 2007										
		Unadjusted Trial Balance		Adjustments		Adjusted Trial Balance		Income Statement		Balance Sheet		
	Account Title	Dr.	Cr.	Dr.	Cr.	Dr.	Cr.	Dr.	Cr.	Dr.	Cr.	
1	Cash	2,065				2,065				2,065		1
2	Accounts Receivable	2,220		(d) 500		2,720				2,720		2
3	Supplies	2,000			(a) 1,240	760				760		3
4	Prepaid Insurance	2,400			(b) 200	2,200				2,200		4
5	Land	20,000				20,000				20,000		5
6	Office Equipment	1,800				1,800				1,800		6
7	Accounts Payable		900				900				900	7
8	Unearned Rent		360	(c) 120			240				240	8
9	Chris Clark, Capital		25,000				25,000				25,000	9
10	Chris Clark, Drawing	4,000				4,000				4,000		10
11	Fees Earned		16,340		(d) 500		16,840		16,840			11
12	Wages Expense	4,275		(e) 250		4,525		4,525				12
13	Rent Expense	1,600				1,600		1,600				13
14	Utilities Expense	985				985		985				14
15	Supplies Expense	800		(a) 1,240		2,040		2,040				15
16	Miscellaneous Expense	455				455		455				16
17		42,600	42,600									17
18	Insurance Expense			(b) 200		200		200				18
19	Rent Revenue				(c) 120		120		120			19
20	Wages Payable				(e) 250		250				250	20
21	Depreciation Expense			(f) 50		50		50				21
22	Accumulated Depreciation				(f) 50		50				50	22
23				2,360	2,360	43,400	43,400	9,855	16,960	33,545	26,440	23
24	Net income							7,105			7,105	24
25								16,960	16,960	33,545	33,545	25

on the unadjusted accounts. The totals of the Adjusted Trial Balance columns prove the equality of the totals of the debit and credit balances after adjustment.

Exhibit 1 also illustrates the flow of the accounts from the adjusted trial balance into the financial statements. The revenue and expense accounts are extended to the Income Statement columns. At the bottom of the Income Statement columns, the net income or net loss for the period is shown. For example, Exhibit 1 shows that NetSolutions had net income of $7,105 for the period. Likewise, the assets, liabilities, owner's capital, and drawing accounts are extended to the Balance Sheet columns. Since net income increases owner's capital, NetSolutions' net income of $7,105 is also shown in the Balance Sheet Cr. column. As we will describe and illustrate in the next section, the financial statements can be prepared directly from Exhibit 1.

To summarize, Exhibit 1 illustrates the end-of-period process by which accounts are adjusted and how the adjusted accounts flow into the financial statements. The spreadsheet shown in Exhibit 1 is not a required part of the accounting process. However, many accountants prepare such a spreadsheet, often called a work sheet, in manual or electronic form, as part of their normal end-of-period process. The primary advantage in doing so is that it allows managers and accountants to see the impact of the adjustments on the financial statements. This is especially useful for adjustments that depend upon estimates. We discuss such estimates and their impact on the financial statements in later chapters.[1]

---

1 The appendix to this chapter describes and illustrates how to prepare the end-of-period spreadsheet (work sheet) shown in Exhibit 1.

Example Exercise 4-1 objective **1**

The balances for the accounts listed below appear in the Adjusted Trial Balance columns of the end-of-period spreadsheet (work sheet). Indicate whether each balance should be extended to (a) an Income Statement column or (b) a Balance Sheet column.

1. Amber Bablock, Drawing
2. Utilities Expense
3. Accumulated Depreciation—Equipment
4. Unearned Rent

5. Fees Earned
6. Accounts Payable
7. Rent Revenue
8. Supplies

Follow My Example 4-1

1. Balance Sheet column
2. Income Statement column
3. Balance Sheet column
4. Balance Sheet column

5. Income Statement column
6. Balance Sheet column
7. Income Statement column
8. Balance Sheet column

For Practice: PE 4-1A, PE 4-1B

Financial Statements

objective **2**

Prepare financial statements from adjusted account balances.

Using Exhibit 1, the financial statements for NetSolutions can be prepared. The income statement, the statement of owner's equity, and the balance sheet are shown in Exhibit 2, on page 148. In the following paragraphs, we discuss each of these financial statements and how they are prepared.

INCOME STATEMENT

@netsolutions

The income statement is prepared directly from the Income Statement or Adjusted Trial Balance columns of Exhibit 1 beginning with fees earned of $16,840. The order of the expenses may change, however, from that listed in Exhibit 1. As we did in Chapter 1, we list the expenses in the income statement in Exhibit 2 in order of size, beginning with the larger items. Miscellaneous expense is the last item, regardless of its amount.

STATEMENT OF OWNER'S EQUITY

The first item presented on the statement of owner's equity is the balance of the owner's capital account at the beginning of the period. In Exhibit 1, however, the

Example Exercise 4-2 objective **2**

In the Balance Sheet columns of the end-of-period spreadsheet (work sheet) for Dimple Consulting Co. for the current year, the Debit column total is $678,450, and the Credit column total is $599,750 before the amount for net income or net loss has been included. In preparing the income statement from the end-of-period spreadsheet (work sheet), what is the amount of net income or net loss?

Follow My Example 4-2

A net income of $78,700 ($678,450 − $599,750) would be reported. When the Debit column of the Balance Sheet columns is more than the Credit column, net income is reported. If the Credit column exceeds the Debit column, a net loss is reported.

For Practice: PE 4-2A, PE 4-2B

EXHIBIT 2   Financial Statements Prepared from Work Sheet

NetSolutions
Income Statement
For the Two Months Ended December 31, 2007

Fees earned	$16 840 00	
Rent revenue	120 00	
Total revenues		$16 960 00
Expenses:		
Wages expense	$ 4 525 00	
Supplies expense	2 040 00	
Rent expense	1 600 00	
Utilities expense	985 00	
Insurance expense	200 00	
Depreciation expense	50 00	
Miscellaneous expense	455 00	
Total expenses		9 855 00
Net income		$ 7 105 00

NetSolutions
Statement of Owner's Equity
For the Two Months Ended December 31, 2007

Chris Clark, capital, November 1, 2007		$ 0
Investment on November 1, 2007	$25 000 00	
Net income for November and December	7 105 00	
	$32 105 00	
Less withdrawals	4 000 00	
Increase in owner's equity		28 105 00
Chris Clark, capital, December 31, 2007		$28 105 00

NetSolutions
Balance Sheet
December 31, 2007

Assets				Liabilities		
Current assets:				Current liabilities:		
Cash	$ 2 065 00			Accounts payable	$900 00	
Accounts receivable	2 720 00			Wages payable	250 00	
Supplies	760 00			Unearned rent	240 00	
Prepaid insurance	2 200 00			Total liabilities		$ 1 390 00
Total current assets		$ 7 745 00				
Property, plant, and equipment:						
Land	$20 000 00					
Office equipment $1,800						
Less accum. depr. 50	1 750 00			**Owner's Equity**		
Total property, plant,				Chris Clark, capital		28 105 00
and equipment		21 750 00		Total liabilities and		
Total assets		$29 495 00		owner's equity		$29 495 00

Integrity, Objectivity, and Ethics in Business

ETHICS

THE ROUND TRIP

A common type of fraud involves artificially inflating revenue. One fraudulent method of inflating revenue is called "round tripping." Under this scheme, a selling company (S) "lends" money to a customer company (C). The money is then used by C to purchase a product from S. Thus, S sells product to C and is paid with the money just loaned to C! This looks like a sale in the accounting records, but in reality, S is shipping free product. The fraud is exposed when it is determined that there was no intent to repay the original loan.

amount listed as owner's capital is not always the account balance at the beginning of the period. The owner may have invested additional assets in the business during the period. Thus, for the beginning balance and any additional investments, it is necessary to refer to the owner's capital account in the ledger. These amounts, along with the net income (or net loss) and the drawing account balance shown on the adjusted trial balance, are used to determine the ending owner's capital account balance.

The basic form of the statement of owner's equity is shown in Exhibit 2. For NetSolutions, the amount of drawings by the owner was less than the net income. If the owner's withdrawals had exceeded the net income, the order of the net income and the withdrawals would have been reversed. The difference between the two items would then be deducted from the beginning capital account balance. Other factors, such as additional investments or a net loss, also require some change in the form, as shown in the following example:

Allan Johnson, capital, January 1, 2007	$39,000	
Additional investment during the year	6,000	
Total		$45,000
Net loss for the year	$ 5,600	
Withdrawals	9,500	
Decrease in owner's equity		15,100
Allan Johnson, capital, December 31, 2007		$29,900

Example Exercise 4-3

objective 2

Zack Gaddis owns and operates Gaddis Employment Services. On January 1, 2007, Zack Gaddis, Capital had a balance of $186,000. During the year, Zack invested an additional $40,000 and withdrew $25,000. For the year ended December 31, 2007, Gaddis Employment Services reported a net income of $18,750. Prepare a statement of owner's equity for the year ended December 31, 2007.

Follow My Example 4-3

GADDIS EMPLOYMENT SERVICES
STATEMENT OF OWNER'S EQUITY
For the Year Ended December 31, 2007

Zack Gaddis, capital, January 1, 2007	$186,000	
Additional investment during 2007	40,000	
Total		$226,000
Withdrawals	$ 25,000	
Less net income	18,750	
Decrease in owner's equity		6,250
Zack Gaddis, capital, December 31, 2007		$219,750

For Practice: PE 4-3A, PE 4-3B

BALANCE SHEET

The balance sheet is prepared directly from the Balance Sheet or Adjusted Trial Balance columns of Exhibit 1 beginning with Cash of $2,065.

The balance sheet in Exhibit 2 was expanded by adding subsections for current assets; property, plant, and equipment; and current liabilities. Such a balance sheet is a *classified balance sheet*. In the following paragraphs, we describe some of the sections and subsections that may be used in a balance sheet. We will introduce additional sections in later chapters.

> Two common classes of assets are current assets and property, plant, and equipment.

Assets   Assets are commonly divided into classes for presentation on the balance sheet. Two of these classes are (1) current assets and (2) property, plant, and equipment.

Current Assets   Cash and other assets that are expected to be converted to cash or sold or used up usually within one year or less, through the normal operations of the business, are called **current assets**. In addition to cash, the current assets usually owned by a service business are notes receivable, accounts receivable, supplies, and other prepaid expenses.

Notes receivable are amounts that customers owe. They are written promises to pay the amount of the note and possibly interest at an agreed rate. Accounts receivable are also amounts customers owe, but they are less formal than notes and do not provide for interest. Accounts receivable normally result from providing services or selling merchandise on account. Notes receivable and accounts receivable are current assets because they will usually be converted to cash within one year or less.

Property, Plant, and Equipment   The property, plant, and equipment section may also be described as **fixed assets** or **plant assets**. These assets include equipment, machinery, buildings, and land. With the exception of land, as we discussed in Chapter 3, fixed assets depreciate over a period of time. The cost, accumulated depreciation, and book value of each major type of fixed asset are normally reported on the balance sheet or in accompanying notes.

> Two common classes of liabilities are current liabilities and long-term liabilities.

Liabilities   Liabilities are the amounts the business owes to creditors. The two most common classes of liabilities are (1) current liabilities and (2) long-term liabilities.

Current Liabilities   Liabilities that will be due within a short time (usually one year or less) and that are to be paid out of current assets are called **current liabilities**. The most common liabilities in this group are notes payable and accounts payable. Other current liability accounts commonly found in the ledger are Wages Payable, Interest Payable, Taxes Payable, and Unearned Fees.

Long-Term Liabilities   Liabilities that will not be due for a long time (usually more than one year) are called **long-term liabilities**. If NetSolutions had long-term liabilities, they would be reported below the current liabilities. As long-term liabilities come due and are to be paid within one year, they are classified as current liabilities. If they are to be renewed rather than paid, they would continue to be classified as long term. When an asset is pledged as security for a liability, the obligation may be called a *mortgage note payable* or a *mortgage payable*.

Owner's Equity   The owner's right to the assets of the business is presented on the balance sheet below the liabilities section. The owner's equity is added to the total liabilities, and this total must be equal to the total assets.

Example Exercise 4-4 objective 2

The following accounts appear in an adjusted trial balance of Hindsight Consulting. Indicate whether each account would be reported in the (a) current asset; (b) property, plant, and equipment; (c) current liability; (d) long-term liability; or (e) owner's equity section of the December 31, 2007, balance sheet of Hindsight Consulting.

1. Jason Corbin, Capital
2. Notes Receivable (due in 6 months)
3. Notes Payable (due in 2009)
4. Land

5. Cash
6. Unearned Rent (3 months)
7. Accumulated Depreciation—Equipment
8. Accounts Payable

Follow My Example 4-4

1. Owner's equity
2. Current asset
3. Long-term liability
4. Property, plant, and equipment

5. Current asset
6. Current liability
7. Property, plant, and equipment
8. Current liability

For Practice: PE 4-4A, PE 4-4B

Business Connections

REAL WORLD

INTERNATIONAL DIFFERENCES

Financial statements prepared under accounting practices in other countries often differ from those prepared under generally accepted accounting principles found in the United States. This is to be expected, since cultures and market structures differ from country to country.

To illustrate, **BMW Group** prepares its financial statements under German law and German accounting principles. In doing so, BMW's balance sheet reports fixed assets first, followed by current assets. It also reports owner's equity before the liabilities. In contrast, balance sheets prepared under U.S. accounting principles report current assets followed by fixed assets and current liabilities followed by long-term liabilities and owner's equity. The U.S.

form of balance sheet is organized to emphasize creditor interpretation and analysis. For example, current assets and current liabilities are presented first to facilitate their interpretation and analysis by creditors. Likewise, to emphasize their importance, liabilities are reported before owner's equity.

Regardless of these differences, the basic principles underlying the accounting equation and the double-entry accounting system are the same in Germany and the United States. Even though differences in recording and reporting exist, the accounting equation holds true: the total assets still equal the total liabilities and owner's equity.

Closing Entries

objective 3

Prepare closing entries.

@netsolutions

As we discussed in Chapter 3, the adjusting entries are recorded in the journal at the end of the accounting period. For NetSolutions, the adjusting entries are shown in Exhibit 7 of Chapter 3.

After the adjusting entries have been posted to NetSolutions' ledger, shown in Exhibit 6 (on pages 155–159), the ledger is in agreement with the data reported on the financial statements. The balances of the accounts reported on the balance sheet are carried forward from year to year. Because they are relatively permanent, these accounts are called **real accounts**. The balances of the accounts reported on the income statement are not carried forward from year to year. Likewise, the balance of the owner's withdrawal account, which is reported on the statement of owner's equity, is

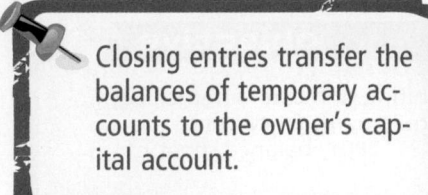

Closing entries transfer the balances of temporary accounts to the owner's capital account.

not carried forward. Because these accounts report amounts for only one period, they are called **temporary accounts** or **nominal accounts**.

To report amounts for only one period, temporary accounts should have zero balances at the beginning of a period. How are these balances converted to zero? The revenue and expense account balances are transferred to an account called **Income Summary**. The balance of Income Summary is then transferred to the owner's capital account. The balance of the owner's drawing account is also transferred to the owner's capital account. The entries that transfer these balances are called **closing entries**. The transfer process is called the **closing process**. Exhibit 3 is a diagram of this process.

EXHIBIT 3 | The Closing Process

2 Expenses are transferred to Income Summary

INCOME SUMMARY

1 Revenues are transferred to Income Summary

3 Net Income or Net Loss is transferred to Owner's Capital

Owner's Capital

4 Drawings are transferred to Owner's Capital

The income summary account does not appear on the financial statements.

You should note that Income Summary is used only at the end of the period. At the beginning of the closing process, Income Summary has no balance. During the closing process, Income Summary will be debited and credited for various amounts. At the end of the closing process, Income Summary will again have no balance. Because Income Summary has the effect of clearing the revenue and expense accounts of their balances, it is sometimes called a **clearing account**. Other titles used for this account include Revenue and Expense Summary, Profit and Loss Summary, and Income and Expense Summary.

It is possible to close the temporary revenue and expense accounts without using a clearing account such as Income Summary. In this case, the balances of the revenue and expense accounts are closed directly to the owner's capital account. This process is automatic in a computerized accounting system. In a manual system, the use of an income summary account aids in detecting and correcting errors.

JOURNALIZING AND POSTING CLOSING ENTRIES

Four closing entries are required at the end of an accounting period, as outlined in Exhibit 3. The account titles and balances needed in preparing these entries may be obtained from the end-of-period spreadsheet (work sheet), the adjusted trial balance, the income statement, the statement of owner's equity, or the ledger.

A flowchart of the closing entries for NetSolutions is shown in Exhibit 4. The balances in the accounts are those shown in the adjusted trial balance columns of the end-of-period spreadsheet (work sheet) shown in Exhibit 1.

EXHIBIT 4 | Flowchart of Closing Entries for NetSolutions

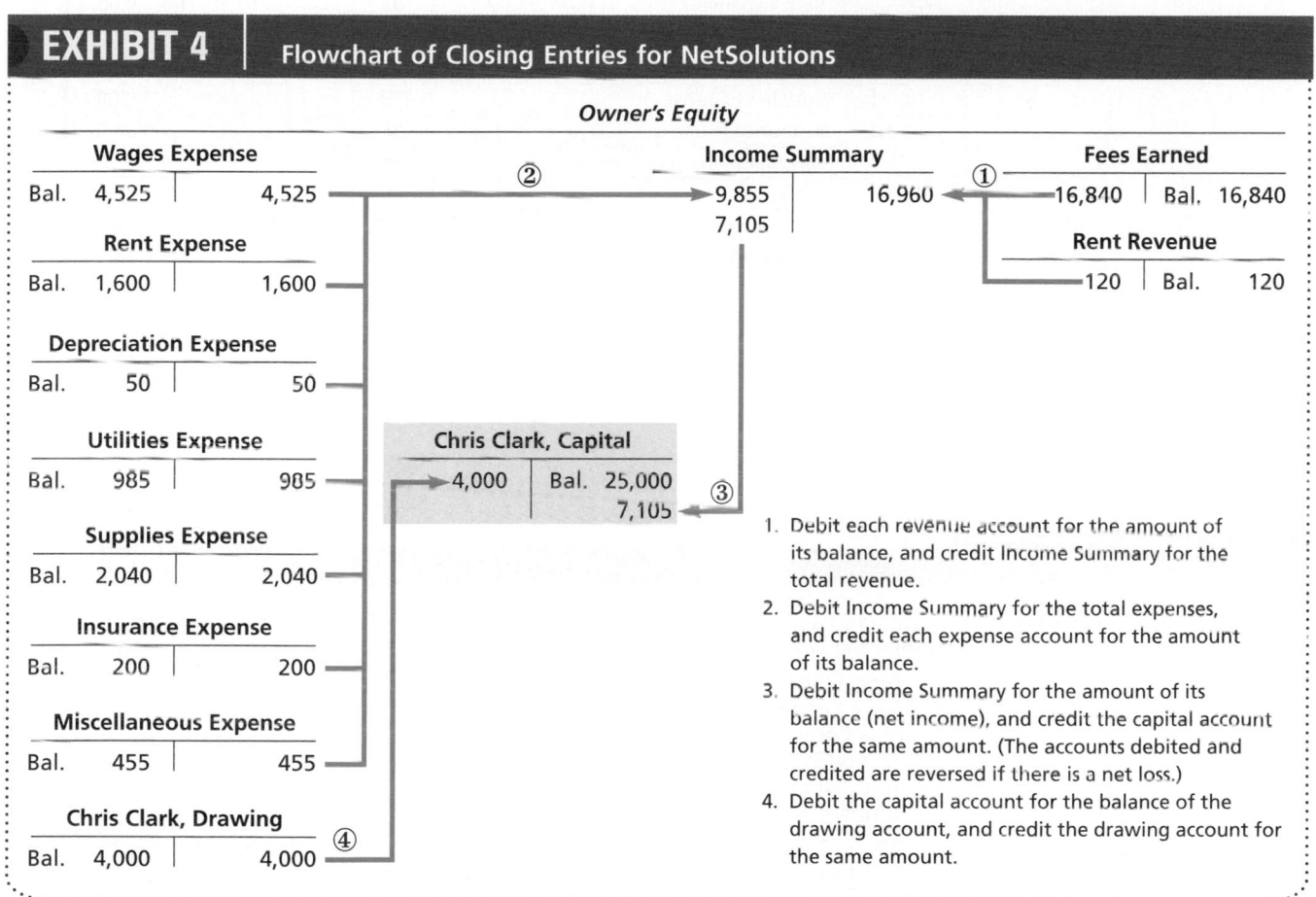

The closing entries for NetSolutions are shown in Exhibit 5. After the closing entries have been posted to the ledger, as shown in Exhibit 6 (on pages 155–159), the balance in the capital account will agree with the amount reported on the statement of owner's equity and the balance sheet. In addition, the revenue, expense, and drawing accounts will have zero balances.

After the entry to close an account has been posted, a line should be inserted in both balance columns opposite the final entry. The next period's transactions for the revenue, expense, and drawing accounts will be posted directly below the closing entry.

EXHIBIT 5

Closing Entries for
NetSolutions

	Date		Description	Post. Ref.	Debit	Credit	
1			Closing Entries				1
2	2007 Dec.	31	Fees Earned	41	16 8 4 0 00		2
3			Rent Revenue	42	1 2 0 00		3
4			Income Summary	33		16 9 6 0 00	4
5							5
6		31	Income Summary	33	9 8 5 5 00		6
7			Wages Expense	51		4 5 2 5 00	7
8			Rent Expense	52		1 6 0 0 00	8
9			Depreciation Expense	53		5 0 00	9
10			Utilities Expense	54		9 8 5 00	10
11			Supplies Expense	55		2 0 4 0 00	11
12			Insurance Expense	56		2 0 0 00	12
13			Miscellaneous Expense	59		4 5 5 00	13
14							14
15		31	Income Summary	33	7 1 0 5 00		15
16			Chris Clark, Capital	31		7 1 0 5 00	16
17							17
18		31	Chris Clark, Capital	31	4 0 0 0 00		18
19			Chris Clark, Drawing	32		4 0 0 0 00	19

JOURNAL Page 6

Example Exercise 4-5 objective 3

After the accounts have been adjusted at July 31, the end of the fiscal year, the following balances are taken from the ledger of Cabriolet Services Co.:

Terry Lambert, Capital	$615,850
Terry Lambert, Drawing	25,000
Fees Earned	380,450
Wages Expense	250,000
Rent Expense	65,000
Supplies Expense	18,250
Miscellaneous Expense	6,200

Journalize the four entries required to close the accounts.

Follow My Example 4-5

July	31	Fees Earned	380,450	
		Income Summary		380,450
	31	Income Summary	339,450	
		Wages Expense		250,000
		Rent Expense		65,000
		Supplies Expense		18,250
		Miscellaneous Expense		6,200
	31	Income Summary	41,000	
		Terry Lambert, Capital		41,000
	31	Terry Lambert, Capital	25,000	
		Terry Lambert, Drawing		25,000

For Practice: PE 4-5A, PE 4-5B

POST-CLOSING TRIAL BALANCE

The last accounting procedure for a period is to prepare a trial balance after the closing entries have been posted. The purpose of the post-closing (after closing) trial balance is to make sure that the ledger is in balance at the beginning of the next period. The accounts and amounts should agree exactly with the accounts and amounts listed on the balance sheet at the end of the period. The post-closing trial balance for NetSolutions is shown in Exhibit 7, on page 159.

Instead of preparing a formal post-closing trial balance, it is possible to list the accounts directly from the ledger, using a computer. The computer printout, in effect, becomes the post-closing trial balance.

EXHIBIT 6

Ledger for NetSolutions

LEDGER

ACCOUNT Cash   **ACCOUNT NO. 11**

Date		Item	Post. Ref.	Debit	Credit	Balance Debit	Balance Credit
2007 Nov.	1		1	25 000 00		25 000 00	
	5		1		20 000 00	5 000 00	
	18		1	7 500 00		12 500 00	
	30		1		3 650 00	8 850 00	
	30		1		950 00	7 900 00	
	30		2		2 000 00	5 900 00	
Dec.	1		2		2 400 00	3 500 00	
	1		2		800 00	2 700 00	
	1		2	360 00		3 060 00	
	6		2		180 00	2 880 00	
	11		2		400 00	2 480 00	
	13		3		950 00	1 530 00	
	16		3	3 100 00		4 630 00	
	20		3		900 00	3 730 00	
	21		3	650 00		4 380 00	
	23		3		1 450 00	2 930 00	
	27		3		1 200 00	1 730 00	
	31		3		310 00	1 420 00	
	31		4		225 00	1 195 00	
	31		4	2 870 00		4 065 00	
	31		4		2 000 00	2 065 00	

ACCOUNT Accounts Receivable   **ACCOUNT NO. 12**

Date		Item	Post. Ref.	Debit	Credit	Balance Debit	Balance Credit
2007 Dec.	16		3	1 750 00		1 750 00	
	21		3		650 00	1 100 00	
	31		4	1 120 00		2 220 00	
	31	Adjusting	5	500 00		2 720 00	

(continued)

EXHIBIT 6

ACCOUNT *Supplies*   **ACCOUNT NO.** *14*

Date	Item	Post. Ref.	Debit	Credit	Balance Debit	Balance Credit
2007 Nov. 10		1	1 3 5 0 00		1 3 5 0 00	
30		1		8 0 0 00	5 5 0 00	
23		3	1 4 5 0 00		2 0 0 0 00	
Dec. 31	Adjusting	5		1 2 4 0 00	7 6 0 00	

ACCOUNT *Prepaid Insurance*   **ACCOUNT NO.** *15*

Date	Item	Post. Ref.	Debit	Credit	Balance Debit	Balance Credit
2007 Dec. 1		2	2 4 0 0 00		2 4 0 0 00	
31	Adjusting	5		2 0 0 00	2 2 0 0 00	

ACCOUNT *Land*   **ACCOUNT NO.** *17*

Date	Item	Post. Ref.	Debit	Credit	Balance Debit	Balance Credit
2007 Nov. 5		1	20 0 0 0 00		20 0 0 0 00	

ACCOUNT *Office Equipment*   **ACCOUNT NO.** *18*

Date	Item	Post. Ref.	Debit	Credit	Balance Debit	Balance Credit
2007 Dec. 4		2	1 8 0 0 00		1 8 0 0 00	

ACCOUNT *Accumulated Depreciation*   **ACCOUNT NO.** *19*

Date	Item	Post. Ref.	Debit	Credit	Balance Debit	Balance Credit
2007 Dec. 31	Adjusting	5		5 0 00		5 0 00

ACCOUNT *Accounts Payable*   **ACCOUNT NO.** *21*

Date	Item	Post. Ref.	Debit	Credit	Balance Debit	Balance Credit
2007 Nov. 10		1		1 3 5 0 00		1 3 5 0 00
30		1	9 5 0 00			4 0 0 00
Dec. 4		2		1 8 0 0 00		2 2 0 0 00
11		2	4 0 0 00			1 8 0 0 00
20		3	9 0 0 00			9 0 0 00

(continued)

EXHIBIT 6

ACCOUNT *Wages Payable* **ACCOUNT NO.** *22*

Date	Item	Post. Ref.	Debit	Credit	Balance Debit	Balance Credit
2007 Dec. 31	Adjusting	5		2 5 0 00		2 5 0 00

ACCOUNT *Unearned Rent* **ACCOUNT NO.** *23*

Date	Item	Post. Ref.	Debit	Credit	Balance Debit	Balance Credit
2007 Dec. 1		2		3 6 0 00		3 6 0 00
31	Adjusting	5	1 2 0 00			2 4 0 00

ACCOUNT *Chris Clark, Capital* **ACCOUNT NO.** *31*

Date	Item	Post. Ref.	Debit	Credit	Balance Debit	Balance Credit
2007 Nov. 1		1		25 0 0 0 00		25 0 0 0 00
Dec. 31	Closing	6		7 1 0 5 00		32 1 0 5 00
31	Closing	6	4 0 0 0 00			28 1 0 5 00

ACCOUNT *Chris Clark, Drawing* **ACCOUNT NO.** *32*

Date	Item	Post. Ref.	Debit	Credit	Balance Debit	Balance Credit
2007 Nov. 30		2	2 0 0 0 00		2 0 0 0 00	
Dec. 31		4	2 0 0 0 00		4 0 0 0 00	
31	Closing	6		4 0 0 0 00	—	—

ACCOUNT *Income Summary* **ACCOUNT NO.** *33*

Date	Item	Post. Ref.	Debit	Credit	Balance Debit	Balance Credit
2007 Dec. 31	Closing	6		16 9 6 0 00		16 9 6 0 00
31	Closing	6	9 8 5 5 00			7 1 0 5 00
31	Closing	6	7 1 0 5 00		—	—

ACCOUNT *Fees Earned* **ACCOUNT NO.** *41*

Date	Item	Post. Ref.	Debit	Credit	Balance Debit	Balance Credit
2007 Nov. 18		1		7 5 0 0 00		7 5 0 0 00
Dec. 16		3		3 1 0 0 00		10 6 0 0 00
16		3		1 7 5 0 00		12 3 5 0 00
31		4		2 8 7 0 00		15 2 2 0 00
31		4		1 1 2 0 00		16 3 4 0 00
31	Adjusting	5		5 0 0 00		16 8 4 0 00
31	Closing	6	16 8 4 0 00		—	—

(continued)

EXHIBIT 6

ACCOUNT *Rent Revenue*　　　　　　　　　　　　　　　　　**ACCOUNT NO.** *42*

Date		Item	Post. Ref.	Debit	Credit	Balance Debit	Balance Credit
2007 Dec.	31	Adjusting	5		1 2 0 00		1 2 0 00
	31	Closing	6	1 2 0 00		—	—

ACCOUNT *Wages Expense*　　　　　　　　　　　　　　　　**ACCOUNT NO.** *51*

Date		Item	Post. Ref.	Debit	Credit	Balance Debit	Balance Credit
2007 Nov.	30		1	2 1 2 5 00		2 1 2 5 00	
Dec.	13		3	9 5 0 00		3 0 7 5 00	
	27		3	1 2 0 0 00		4 2 7 5 00	
	31	Adjusting	5	2 5 0 00		4 5 2 5 00	
	31	Closing	6		4 5 2 5 00	—	—

ACCOUNT *Rent Expense*　　　　　　　　　　　　　　　　**ACCOUNT NO.** *52*

Date		Item	Post. Ref.	Debit	Credit	Balance Debit	Balance Credit
2007 Nov.	30		1	8 0 0 00		8 0 0 00	
Dec.	1		2	8 0 0 00		1 6 0 0 00	
	31	Closing	6		1 6 0 0 00	—	—

ACCOUNT *Depreciation Expense*　　　　　　　　　　　　**ACCOUNT NO.** *53*

Date		Item	Post. Ref.	Debit	Credit	Balance Debit	Balance Credit
2007 Dec.	31	Adjusting	5	5 0 00		5 0 00	
	31	Closing	6		5 0 00	—	—

ACCOUNT *Utilities Expense*　　　　　　　　　　　　　　**ACCOUNT NO.** *54*

Date		Item	Post. Ref.	Debit	Credit	Balance Debit	Balance Credit
2007 Nov.	30		1	4 5 0 00		4 5 0 00	
Dec.	31		3	3 1 0 00		7 6 0 00	
	31		4	2 2 5 00		9 8 5 00	
	31	Closing	6		9 8 5 00	—	—

ACCOUNT *Supplies Expense*　　　　　　　　　　　　　　**ACCOUNT NO.** *55*

Date		Item	Post. Ref.	Debit	Credit	Balance Debit	Balance Credit
2007 Nov.	30		1	8 0 0 00		8 0 0 00	
Dec.	31	Adjusting	5	1 2 4 0 00		2 0 4 0 00	
	31	Closing	6		2 0 4 0 00	—	—

(continued)

EXHIBIT 6

ACCOUNT Insurance Expense						ACCOUNT NO. 56	
		Post. Ref.	Debit	Credit	Balance		
Date	Item				Debit	Credit	
2007 Dec. 31	Adjusting	5	2 0 0 00		2 0 0 00		
31	Closing	6		2 0 0 00	—	—	

ACCOUNT Miscellaneous Expense						ACCOUNT NO. 59	
		Post. Ref.	Debit	Credit	Balance		
Date	Item				Debit	Credit	
2007 Nov. 30		1	2 7 5 00		2 7 5 00		
Dec. 6		2	1 8 0 00		4 5 5 00		
31	Closing	6		4 5 5 00	—	—	

(concluded)

EXHIBIT 7

Post-Closing
Trial Balance

NetSolutions
Post-Closing Trial Balance
December 31, 2007

	Debit Balances	Credit Balances
Cash	2 0 6 5 00	
Accounts Receivable	2 7 2 0 00	
Supplies	7 6 0 00	
Prepaid Insurance	2 2 0 0 00	
Land	20 0 0 0 00	
Office Equipment	1 8 0 0 00	
Accumulated Depreciation		5 0 00
Accounts Payable		9 0 0 00
Wages Payable		2 5 0 00
Unearned Rent		2 4 0 00
Chris Clark, Capital		28 1 0 5 00
	29 5 4 5 00	29 5 4 5 00

Accounting Cycle

objective 4

Describe the accounting cycle.

The accounting process that begins with analyzing and journalizing transactions and ends with preparing the accounting records for the next period's transactions is called the **accounting cycle**. The steps in the accounting cycle are as follows:

1. Transactions are analyzed and recorded in the journal.
2. Transactions are posted to the ledger.
3. An unadjusted trial balance is prepared.
4. Adjustment data are assembled and analyzed.
5. An optional end-of-period spreadsheet (work sheet) is prepared.
6. Adjusting entries are journalized and posted to the ledger.
7. An adjusted trial balance is prepared.
8. Financial statements are prepared.
9. Closing entries are journalized and posted to the ledger.
10. A post-closing trial balance is prepared.[2]

---

2 Some accountants include the journalizing and posting of "reversing entries" as the last step in the accounting cycle. Because reversing entries are not required, we describe and illustrate them in Appendix B at the end of the book.

Exhibit 8 illustrates the accounting cycle in graphic form. In addition, Exhibit 8 illustrates how the accounting data beginning with the source documents for a transaction flow through the accounting system and into the financial statements. In the next section, we illustrate a comprehensive example of the accounting cycle.

EXHIBIT 8 | Accounting Cycle

Accounting Cycle Steps

1 Transactions are analyzed and recorded in the journal.

2 Transactions are posted to the ledger.

3 An unadjusted trial balance is prepared.

4 Adjustment data are assembled and analyzed.

5 An optional end-of-period spreadsheet (work sheet) is prepared.

6 Adjusting entries are journalized and posted to the ledger.

7 An adjusted trial balance is prepared.

8 Financial statements are prepared.

9 Closing entries are journalized and posted to the ledger.

10 A post-closing trial balance is prepared.

Example Exercise 4-6

objective 4

From the following list of steps in the accounting cycle, identify what two steps are missing.

    a. Transactions are analyzed and recorded in the journal.
    b. Transactions are posted to the ledger.
    c. Adjustment data are assembled and analyzed.
    d. An optional end-of-period spreadsheet (work sheet) is prepared.
    e. Adjusting entries are journalized and posted to the ledger.
    f. Financial statements are prepared.
    g. Closing entries are journalized and posted to the ledger.
    h. A post-closing trial balance is prepared.

Follow My Example 4-6

The following two steps are missing: (1) the preparation of an unadjusted trial balance and (2) the preparation of the adjusted trial balance. The unadjusted trial balance should be prepared after step (b). The adjusted trial balance should be prepared after step (e).

For Practice: PE 4-6A, PE 4-6B

Illustration of the Accounting Cycle

objective 5

Illustrate the accounting cycle for one period.

In this section, we will illustrate the complete accounting cycle for one period. We assume that for several years Kelly Pitney has operated a part-time consulting business from her home. As of April 1, 2008, Kelly decided to move to rented quarters and to operate the business, which will be known as Kelly Consulting, on a full-time basis. Kelly Consulting entered into the following transactions during April:

Apr. 1. The following assets were received from Kelly Pitney: cash, $13,100; accounts receivable, $3,000; supplies, $1,400; and office equipment, $12,500. There were no liabilities received.
    1. Paid three months' rent on a lease rental contract, $4,800.
    2. Paid the premiums on property and casualty insurance policies, $1,800.
    4. Received cash from clients as an advance payment for services to be provided and recorded it as unearned fees, $5,000.
    5. Purchased additional office equipment on account from Office Station Co., $2,000.
    6. Received cash from clients on account, $1,800.
    10. Paid cash for a newspaper advertisement, $120.
    12. Paid Office Station Co. for part of the debt incurred on April 5, $1,200.
    12. Recorded services provided on account for the period April 1–12, $4,200.
    14. Paid part-time receptionist for two weeks' salary, $750.
    17. Recorded cash from cash clients for fees earned during the period April 1–16, $6,250.
    18. Paid cash for supplies, $800.
    20. Recorded services provided on account for the period April 13–20, $2,100.
    24. Recorded cash from cash clients for fees earned for the period April 17–24, $3,850.
    26. Received cash from clients on account, $5,600.
    27. Paid part-time receptionist for two weeks' salary, $750.
    29. Paid telephone bill for April, $130.
    30. Paid electricity bill for April, $200.
    30. Recorded cash from cash clients for fees earned for the period April 25–30, $3,050.
    30. Recorded services provided on account for the remainder of April, $1,500.
    30. Kelly withdrew $6,000 for personal use.

STEP 1. ANALYZING AND RECORDING TRANSACTIONS IN THE JOURNAL

The first step in the accounting cycle is to analyze and record transactions in the journal shown in Exhibit 9. As we illustrated in Chapter 2, the double-entry accounting system is a very powerful tool for analyzing transactions. In using this system to analyze transactions, we do the following:

1. Carefully read the description of the transaction to determine whether an asset, liability, owner's equity, revenue, expense, or drawing account is affected by the transaction.
2. For each account affected by the transaction, determine whether the account increases or decreases.
3. Determine whether each increase or decrease should be recorded as a debit or a credit following the rules of debit and credit shown in Exhibit 3 of Chapter 2.
4. Record the transaction using a journal entry.

EXHIBIT 9

Journal Entries
for April,
Kelly Consulting

JOURNAL   Page 1

	Date		Description	Post. Ref.	Debit	Credit	
1	2008 April	1	Cash	11	13 1 0 0 00		1
2			Accounts Receivable	12	3 0 0 0 00		2
3			Supplies	14	1 4 0 0 00		3
4			Office Equipment	18	12 5 0 0 00		4
5			Kelly Pitney, Capital	31		3 0 0 0 0 00	5
6							6
7		1	Prepaid Rent	15	4 8 0 0 00		7
8			Cash	11		4 8 0 0 00	8
9							9
10		2	Prepaid Insurance	16	1 8 0 0 00		10
11			Cash	11		1 8 0 0 00	11
12							12
13		4	Cash	11	5 0 0 0 00		13
14			Unearned Fees	23		5 0 0 0 00	14
15							15
16		5	Office Equipment	18	2 0 0 0 00		16
17			Accounts Payable	21		2 0 0 0 00	17
18							18
19		6	Cash	11	1 8 0 0 00		19
20			Accounts Receivable	12		1 8 0 0 00	20
21							21
22		10	Miscellaneous Expense	59	1 2 0 00		22
23			Cash	11		1 2 0 00	23
24							24
25		12	Accounts Payable	21	1 2 0 0 00		25
26			Cash	11		1 2 0 0 00	26
27							27
28		12	Accounts Receivable	12	4 2 0 0 00		28
29			Fees Earned	41		4 2 0 0 00	29
30							30
31		14	Salary Expense	51	7 5 0 00		31
32			Cash	11		7 5 0 00	32
33							33

(continued)

The company's chart of accounts is useful in determining which accounts are affected by the transaction. The chart of accounts for Kelly Consulting is as follows:

11	Cash	31	Kelly Pitney, Capital
12	Accounts Receivable	32	Kelly Pitney, Drawing
14	Supplies	33	Income Summary
15	Prepaid Rent	41	Fees Earned
16	Prepaid Insurance	51	Salary Expense
18	Office Equipment	52	Rent Expense
19	Accumulated Depreciation	53	Supplies Expense
21	Accounts Payable	54	Depreciation Expense
22	Salaries Payable	55	Insurance Expense
23	Unearned Fees	59	Miscellaneous Expense

After analyzing each of Kelly Consulting's transactions for April, the journal entries are recorded as shown in Exhibit 9.

EXHIBIT 9

Continued

JOURNAL Page 2

	Date		Description	Post. Ref.	Debit	Credit	
1	2008 April	17	Cash	11	6 2 5 0 00		1
2			Fees Earned	41		6 2 5 0 00	2
3							3
4		18	Supplies	14	8 0 0 00		4
5			Cash	11		8 0 0 00	5
6							6
7		20	Accounts Receivable	12	2 1 0 0 00		7
8			Fees Earned	41		2 1 0 0 00	8
9							9
10		24	Cash	11	3 8 5 0 00		10
11			Fees Earned	41		3 8 5 0 00	11
12							12
13		26	Cash	11	5 6 0 0 00		13
14			Accounts Receivable	12		5 6 0 0 00	14
15							15
16		27	Salary Expense	51	7 5 0 00		16
17			Cash	11		7 5 0 00	17
18							18
19		29	Miscellaneous Expense	59	1 3 0 00		19
20			Cash	11		1 3 0 00	20
21							21
22		30	Miscellaneous Expense	59	2 0 0 00		22
23			Cash	11		2 0 0 00	23
24							24
25		30	Cash	11	3 0 5 0 00		25
26			Fees Earned	41		3 0 5 0 00	26
27							27
28		30	Accounts Receivable	12	1 5 0 0 00		28
29			Fees Earned	41		1 5 0 0 00	29
30							30
31		30	Kelly Pitney, Drawing	32	6 0 0 0 00		31
32			Cash	11		6 0 0 0 00	32
33							33

STEP 2. POSTING TRANSACTIONS TO THE LEDGER

Periodically, the transactions recorded in the journal are posted to the accounts in the ledger. As we illustrated in Chapters 2 and 3, the posting process includes recording the date of the transaction, the debit or credit amount, and the journal reference in the account. In addition, account numbers are recorded in the Post Reference column of the journal to indicate that the entry has been posted to the accounts in the ledger. The journal entries for Kelly Consulting have been posted to the ledger shown in Exhibit 17.

STEP 3. PREPARING AN UNADJUSTED TRIAL BALANCE

In order to determine whether any errors have been made in posting the debits and credits to the ledger, an unadjusted trial balance should be prepared. The unadjusted trial balance does not provide complete proof of the accuracy of the ledger. It indicates only that the debits and the credits are equal. This proof is of value, however, because errors often affect the equality of debits and credits. If the two totals of a trial balance are not equal, an error has occurred that must be discovered and corrected.

The unadjusted trial balance for Kelly Consulting is shown in Exhibit 10. The unadjusted account balances shown in Exhibit 10 were taken from Kelly Consulting's ledger shown in Exhibit 17, on pages 170–174, before any adjusting entries were recorded.

EXHIBIT 10

Unadjusted
Trial Balance,
Kelly Consulting

Kelly Consulting
Unadjusted Trial Balance
April 30, 2008

	Debit Balances	Credit Balances
Cash	22 1 0 0 00	
Accounts Receivable	3 4 0 0 00	
Supplies	2 2 0 0 00	
Prepaid Rent	4 8 0 0 00	
Prepaid Insurance	1 8 0 0 00	
Office Equipment	14 5 0 0 00	
Accumulated Depreciation		
Accounts Payable		8 0 0 00
Salaries Payable		
Unearned Fees		5 0 0 0 00
Kelly Pitney, Capital		30 0 0 0 00
Kelly Pitney, Drawing	6 0 0 0 00	
Fees Earned		20 9 5 0 00
Salary Expense	1 5 0 0 00	
Rent Expense		
Supplies Expense		
Depreciation Expense		
Insurance Expense		
Miscellaneous Expense	4 5 0 00	
	56 7 5 0 00	56 7 5 0 00

STEP 4. ASSEMBLING AND ANALYZING ADJUSTMENT DATA

Before the financial statements can be prepared, the accounts must be updated. The four types of accounts that normally require adjustment include prepaid expenses, unearned revenue, accrued revenue, and accrued expenses. In addition, depreciation expense must be recorded for fixed assets other than land. The following data have been assembled on April 30, 2008, for analysis of possible adjustments for Kelly Consulting:

a. Insurance expired during April is $300.
b. Supplies on hand on April 30 are $1,350.
c. Depreciation of office equipment for April is $330.
d. Accrued receptionist salary on April 30 is $120.
e. Rent expired during April is $1,600.
f. Unearned fees on April 30 are $2,500.

STEP 5. PREPARING AN OPTIONAL END-OF-PERIOD SPREADSHEET (WORK SHEET)

Although an end-of-period spreadsheet (work sheet) is not required, it is useful in showing the flow of accounting information from the unadjusted trial balance to the adjusted trial balance and financial statements. In addition, an end-of-period spreadsheet (work sheet) is useful in analyzing the impact of proposed adjustments on the financial statements. The end-of-period spreadsheet (work sheet) for Kelly Consulting is shown in Exhibit 11.

EXHIBIT 11 End-of-Period Spreadsheet (Work Sheet)

Kelly Consulting
End-of-Period Spreadsheet (Work Sheet)
For the Month Ended April 30, 2008

	A	B	C	D	E	F	G	H	I	J	K	
	Account Title	Unadjusted Trial Balance Dr.	Cr.	Adjustments Dr.	Cr.	Adjusted Trial Balance Dr.	Cr.	Income Statement Dr.	Cr.	Balance Sheet Dr.	Cr.	
1	Cash	22,100				22,100				22,100		1
2	Accounts Receivable	3,400				3,400				3,400		2
3	Supplies	2,200			(b) 850	1,350				1,350		3
4	Prepaid Rent	4,800			(e) 1,600	3,200				3,200		4
5	Prepaid Insurance	1,800			(a) 300	1,500				1,500		5
6	Office Equipment	14,500				14,500				14,500		6
7	Accum. Depreciation				(c) 330		330				330	7
8	Accounts Payable		800				800				800	8
9	Salaries Payable				(d) 120		120				120	9
10	Unearned Fees		5,000	(f) 2,500			2,500				2,500	10
11	Kelly Pitney, Capital		30,000				30,000				30,000	11
12	Kelly Pitney, Drawing	6,000				6,000				6,000		12
13	Fees Earned		20,950		(f) 2,500		23,450		23,450			13
14	Salary Expense	1,500		(d) 120		1,620		1,620				14
15	Rent Expense			(e) 1,600		1,600		1,600				15
16	Supplies Expense			(b) 850		850		850				16
17	Depreciation Expense			(c) 330		330		330				17
18	Insurance Expense			(a) 300		300		300				18
19	Miscellaneous Expense	450				450		450				19
20		56,750	56,750	5,700	5,700	57,200	57,200	5,150	23,450	52,050	33,750	20
21	Net income							18,300			18,300	21
22								23,450	23,450	52,050	52,050	22

STEP 6. JOURNALIZNG AND POSTING ADJUSTING ENTRIES

Based upon the adjustment data shown in step 4, adjusting entries for Kelly Consulting are prepared. Each adjusting entry affects at least one income statement account and one balance sheet account. Explanations for each adjustment including any computations are normally included with each adjusting entry. The adjusting entries for Kelly Consulting are shown in Exhibit 12.

Each of the adjusting entries shown in Exhibit 12 is posted to Kelly Consulting's ledger shown in Exhibit 17. The adjusting entries are identified in the ledger as "Adjusting Entry."

EXHIBIT 12

Adjusting Entries, Kelly Consulting

	Date			Post. Ref.	Debit	Credit	
			JOURNAL			**Page 3**	
			Adjusting Entries				
1	2008 Apr.	30	Insurance Expense	55	3 0 0 00		1
2			Prepaid Insurance	16		3 0 0 00	2
3			Expired Insurance.				3
4							4
5		30	Supplies Expense	53	8 5 0 00		5
6			Supplies	14		8 5 0 00	6
7			Supplies used ($2,200 – $1,350).				7
8							8
9		30	Depreciation Expense	54	3 3 0 00		9
10			Accumulated Depreciation	19		3 3 0 00	10
11			Depreciation of office equipment.				11
12							12
13		30	Salary Expense	51	1 2 0 00		13
14			Salaries Payable	22		1 2 0 00	14
15			Accrued salary.				15
16							16
17		30	Rent Expense	52	1 6 0 0 00		17
18			Prepaid Rent	15		1 6 0 0 00	18
19			Rent expired during April.				19
20							20
21		30	Unearned Fees	23	2 5 0 0 00		21
22			Fees Earned	41		2 5 0 0 00	22
23			Fees earned ($5,000 – $2,500).				23

STEP 7. PREPARING AN ADJUSTED TRIAL BALANCE

After the adjustments have been journalized and posted, an adjusted trial balance is prepared to verify the equality of the total of the debit and credit balances. This is the last step before preparing the financial statements, and any errors arising from posting the adjusting entries must be found and corrected. The adjusted trial balance for Kelly Consulting as of April 30, 2008, is shown in Exhibit 13.

STEP 8. PREPARING THE FINANCIAL STATEMENTS

The most important outcome of the accounting cycle is the financial statements. The income statement is prepared first, followed by the statement of owner's equity and then the balance sheet. The statements can be prepared directly from the adjusted trial balance, the end-of-period spreadsheet, or the ledger. The net income or net loss shown on the income statement is reported on the statement of owner's equity along with any additional investments by the owner and any withdrawals. The ending owner's capi-

EXHIBIT 13

Adjusted Trial Balance,
Kelly Consulting

Kelly Consulting Adjusted Trial Balance April 30, 2008	Debit Balances	Credit Balances
Cash	22 1 0 0 00	
Accounts Receivable	3 4 0 0 00	
Supplies	1 3 5 0 00	
Prepaid Rent	3 2 0 0 00	
Prepaid Insurance	1 5 0 0 00	
Office Equipment	14 5 0 0 00	
Accumulated Depreciation		3 3 0 00
Accounts Payable		8 0 0 00
Salaries Payable		1 2 0 00
Unearned Fees		2 5 0 0 00
Kelly Pitney, Capital		30 0 0 0 00
Kelly Pitney, Drawing	6 0 0 0 00	
Fees Earned		23 4 5 0 00
Salary Expense	1 6 2 0 00	
Rent Expense	1 6 0 0 00	
Supplies Expense	8 5 0 00	
Depreciation Expense	3 3 0 00	
Insurance Expense	3 0 0 00	
Miscellaneous Expense	4 5 0 00	
	57 2 0 0 00	57 2 0 0 00

tal is reported on the balance sheet and is added with total liabilities to equal total assets.

The financial statements for Kelly Consulting are shown in Exhibit 14. Kelly Consulting earned net income of $18,300 for April. As of April 30, 2008, Kelly Consulting has total assets of $45,720, total liabilities of $3,420, and total owner's equity of $42,300.

EXHIBIT 14

Financial Statements,
Kelly Consulting

Kelly Consulting Income Statement For the Month Ended April 30, 2008		
Fees earned		$23 4 5 0 00
Expenses:		
Salary expense	$1 6 2 0 00	
Rent expense	1 6 0 0 00	
Supplies expense	8 5 0 00	
Depreciation expense	3 3 0 00	
Insurance expense	3 0 0 00	
Miscellaneous expense	4 5 0 00	
Total expenses		5 1 5 0 00
Net income		$18 3 0 0 00

(continued)

EXHIBIT 14

Kelly Consulting
Statement of Owner's Equity
For the Month Ended April 30, 2008

Kelly Pitney, capital, April 1, 2008		$ 0
Investment during the month	$30 000 00	
Net income for the month	18 300 00	
	$48 300 00	
Less withdrawals	6 000 00	
Increase in owner's equity		42 300 00
Kelly Pitney, capital, April 30, 2008		$42 300 00

Kelly Consulting
Balance Sheet
April 30, 2008

Assets			Liabilities		
Current assets:			Current liabilities:		
Cash	$22 100 00		Accounts payable	$ 800 00	
Accounts receivable	3 400 00		Salaries payable	120 00	
Supplies	1 350 00		Unearned fees	2 500 00	
Prepaid rent	3 200 00		Total liabilities		$ 3 420 00
Prepaid insurance	1 500 00				
Total current assets		$31 550 00			
Property, plant, and equipment:					
Office equipment	$14 500 00				
Less accumulated depr.	330 00		**Owner's Equity**		
Total property, plant,			Kelly Pitney, capital		42 300 00
and equipment		14 170 00	Total liabilities and		
Total assets		$45 720 00	owner's equity		$45 720 00

STEP 9. JOURNALIZING AND POSTING CLOSING ENTRIES

As described earlier in this chapter, four closing entries are required at the end of an accounting period to ready the accounts for the next period. The first closing entry transfers the revenue account balances to Income Summary. The second closing entry transfers the expense account balances to Income Summary. The third entry transfers the balance of Income Summary to the owner's capital account. Finally, the fourth entry transfers any balance in the owner's drawing account to the owner's capital account. The four closing entries for Kelly Consulting are shown in Exhibit 15.

After the closing entries have been posted to the ledger, the balance in owner's capital account will agree with the amount reported on the statement of owner's equity and the balance sheet. For Kelly Consulting, the ending balance of the Kelly Pitney, Capital is $42,300, as shown in Exhibit 17. In addition, as shown in Exhibit 17, after the closing entries are posted, all the revenue, expense, and drawing accounts have zero balances. The closing entries are identified in the ledger as "Closing."

STEP 10. PREPARING A POST-CLOSING TRIAL BALANCE

The last step in the accounting cycle is to prepare a post-closing trial balance. The purpose of the post-closing trial balance is to make sure that the ledger is in balance at the

EXHIBIT 15

Closing Entries,
Kelly Consulting

	Date		Description	Post. Ref.	Debit	Credit	
			Closing Entries				
1	2008 Apr.	30	Fees Earned	41	23 4 5 0 00		1
2			Income Summary	33		23 4 5 0 00	2
3							3
4		30	Income Summary	33	5 1 5 0 00		4
5			Salary Expense	51		1 6 2 0 00	5
6			Rent Expense	52		1 6 0 0 00	6
7			Supplies Expense	53		8 5 0 00	7
8			Depreciation Expense	54		3 3 0 00	8
9			Insurance Expense	55		3 0 0 00	9
10			Miscellaneous Expense	59		4 5 0 00	10
11							11
12		30	Income Summary	33	18 3 0 0 00		12
13			Kelly Pitney, Capital	31		18 3 0 0 00	13
14							14
15		30	Kelly Pitney, Capital	31	6 0 0 0 00		15
16			Kelly Pitney, Drawing	32		6 0 0 0 00	16

JOURNAL Page 4

beginning of the next period. The accounts and amounts in the post-closing trial balance should agree exactly with the accounts and amounts listed on the balance sheet at the end of the period.

The post-closing trial balance for Kelly Consulting is shown in Exhibit 16. The balances shown in the post-closing trial balance are taken from the ending balances in the ledger shown in Exhibit 17. These balances agree with the amounts shown on Kelly Consulting's balance sheet in Exhibit 14.

EXHIBIT 16

Post-Closing
Trial Balance,
Kelly Consulting

Kelly Consulting
Post-Closing Trial Balance
April 30, 2008

	Debit Balances	Credit Balances
Cash	22 1 0 0 00	
Accounts Receivable	3 4 0 0 00	
Supplies	1 3 5 0 00	
Prepaid Rent	3 2 0 0 00	
Prepaid Insurance	1 5 0 0 00	
Office Equipment	14 5 0 0 00	
Accumulated Depreciation		3 3 0 00
Accounts Payable		8 0 0 00
Salaries Payable		1 2 0 00
Unearned Fees		2 5 0 0 00
Kelly Pitney, Capital		42 3 0 0 00
	46 0 5 0 00	46 0 5 0 00

EXHIBIT 17

Ledger,
Kelly Consulting

LEDGER

ACCOUNT *Cash*   **ACCOUNT NO.** *11*

Date		Item	Post. Ref.	Debit	Credit	Balance Debit	Balance Credit
2008 Apr.	1		1	13 1 0 0 00		13 1 0 0 00	
	1		1		4 8 0 0 00	8 3 0 0 00	
	2		1		1 8 0 0 00	6 5 0 0 00	
	4		1	5 0 0 0 00		11 5 0 0 00	
	6		1	1 8 0 0 00		13 3 0 0 00	
	10		1		1 2 0 00	13 1 8 0 00	
	12		1		1 2 0 0 00	11 9 8 0 00	
	14		1		7 5 0 00	11 2 3 0 00	
	17		2	6 2 5 0 00		17 4 8 0 00	
	18		2		8 0 0 00	16 6 8 0 00	
	24		2	3 8 5 0 00		20 5 3 0 00	
	26		2	5 6 0 0 00		26 1 3 0 00	
	27		2		7 5 0 00	25 3 8 0 00	
	29		2		1 3 0 00	25 2 5 0 00	
	30		2		2 0 0 00	25 0 5 0 00	
	30		2	3 0 5 0 00		28 1 0 0 00	
	30		2		6 0 0 0 00	22 1 0 0 00	

ACCOUNT *Accounts Receivable*   **ACCOUNT NO.** *12*

Date		Item	Post. Ref.	Debit	Credit	Balance Debit	Balance Credit
2008 Apr.	1		1	3 0 0 0 00		3 0 0 0 00	
	6		1		1 8 0 0 00	1 2 0 0 00	
	12		1	4 2 0 0 00		5 4 0 0 00	
	20		2	2 1 0 0 00		7 5 0 0 00	
	26		2		5 6 0 0 00	1 9 0 0 00	
	30		2	1 5 0 0 00		3 4 0 0 00	

ACCOUNT *Supplies*   **ACCOUNT NO.** *14*

Date		Item	Post. Ref.	Debit	Credit	Balance Debit	Balance Credit
2008 Apr.	1		1	1 4 0 0 00		1 4 0 0 00	
	18		2	8 0 0 00		2 2 0 0 00	
	30	Adjusting	3		8 5 0 00	1 3 5 0 00	

(continued)

EXHIBIT 17

ACCOUNT *Prepaid Rent*   **ACCOUNT NO.** *15*

Date		Item	Post. Ref.	Debit	Credit	Balance Debit	Balance Credit
2008 Apr.	1		1	4 80 0 00		4 80 0 00	
	30	Adjusting	3		1 60 0 00	3 20 0 00	

ACCOUNT *Prepaid Insurance*   **ACCOUNT NO.** *16*

Date		Item	Post. Ref.	Debit	Credit	Balance Debit	Balance Credit
2008 Apr.	2		1	1 80 0 00		1 80 0 00	
	30	Adjusting	3		3 0 0 00	1 50 0 00	

ACCOUNT *Office Equipment*   **ACCOUNT NO.** *18*

Date		Item	Post. Ref.	Debit	Credit	Balance Debit	Balance Credit
2008 Apr.	1		1	12 50 0 00		12 50 0 00	
	5		1	2 00 0 00		14 50 0 00	

ACCOUNT *Accumulated Depreciation*   **ACCOUNT NO.** *19*

Date		Item	Post. Ref.	Debit	Credit	Balance Debit	Balance Credit
2008 Apr.	30	Adjusting	3		3 3 0 00		3 3 0 00

ACCOUNT *Accounts Payable*   **ACCOUNT NO.** *21*

Date		Item	Post. Ref.	Debit	Credit	Balance Debit	Balance Credit
2008 Apr.	5		1		2 00 0 00		2 00 0 00
	12		1	1 20 0 00			8 0 0 00

(continued)

EXHIBIT 17

ACCOUNT *Salaries Payable*   **ACCOUNT NO.** *22*

Date		Item	Post. Ref.	Debit	Credit	Balance Debit	Balance Credit
2008 Apr.	30	Adjusting	3		1 2 0 00		1 2 0 00

ACCOUNT *Unearned Fees*   **ACCOUNT NO.** *23*

Date		Item	Post. Ref.	Debit	Credit	Balance Debit	Balance Credit
2008 Apr.	4		1		5 0 0 0 00		5 0 0 0 00
	30	Adjusting	3	2 5 0 0 00			2 5 0 0 00

ACCOUNT *Kelly Pitney, Capital*   **ACCOUNT NO.** *31*

Date		Item	Post. Ref.	Debit	Credit	Balance Debit	Balance Credit
2008 Apr.	1		1		30 0 0 0 00		30 0 0 0 00
	30	Closing	4		18 3 0 0 00		48 3 0 0 00
	30	Closing	4	6 0 0 0 00			42 3 0 0 00

ACCOUNT *Kelly Pitney, Drawing*   **ACCOUNT NO.** *32*

Date		Item	Post. Ref.	Debit	Credit	Balance Debit	Balance Credit
2008 Apr.	30		2	6 0 0 0 00		6 0 0 0 00	
	30	Closing	4		6 0 0 0 00	—	—

ACCOUNT *Income Summary*   **ACCOUNT NO.** *33*

Date		Item	Post. Ref.	Debit	Credit	Balance Debit	Balance Credit
2008 Apr.	30	Closing	4		23 4 5 0 00		23 4 5 0 00
	30	Closing	4	5 1 5 0 00			18 3 0 0 00
	30	Closing	4	18 3 0 0 00		—	—

(continued)

EXHIBIT 17

ACCOUNT Fees Earned   ACCOUNT NO. 41

Date		Item	Post. Ref.	Debit	Credit	Balance Debit	Balance Credit
2008 Apr.	12		1		4 2 0 0 00		4 2 0 0 00
	17		2		6 2 5 0 00		10 4 5 0 00
	20		2		2 1 0 0 00		12 5 5 0 00
	24		2		3 8 5 0 00		16 4 0 0 00
	30		2		3 0 5 0 00		19 4 5 0 00
	30		2		1 5 0 0 00		20 9 5 0 00
	30	Adjusting	3		2 5 0 0 00		23 4 5 0 00
	30	Closing	4	23 4 5 0 00		—	—

ACCOUNT Salary Expense   ACCOUNT NO. 51

Date		Item	Post. Ref.	Debit	Credit	Balance Debit	Balance Credit
2008 Apr.	14		1	7 5 0 00		7 5 0 00	
	27		2	7 5 0 00		1 5 0 0 00	
	30	Adjusting	3	1 2 0 00		1 6 2 0 00	
	30	Closing	4		1 6 2 0 00	—	—

ACCOUNT Rent Expense   ACCOUNT NO. 52

Date		Item	Post. Ref.	Debit	Credit	Balance Debit	Balance Credit
2008 Apr.	30	Adjusting	3	1 6 0 0 00		1 6 0 0 00	
	30	Closing	4		1 6 0 0 00	—	—

ACCOUNT Supplies Expense   ACCOUNT NO. 53

Date		Item	Post. Ref.	Debit	Credit	Balance Debit	Balance Credit
2008 Apr.	30	Adjusting	3	8 5 0 00		8 5 0 00	
	30	Closing	4		8 5 0 00	—	—

ACCOUNT Depreciation Expense   ACCOUNT NO. 54

Date		Item	Post. Ref.	Debit	Credit	Balance Debit	Balance Credit
2008 Apr.	30	Adjusting	3	3 3 0 00		3 3 0 00	
	30	Closing	4		3 3 0 00	—	—

(continued)

EXHIBIT 17

ACCOUNT *Insurance Expense*   **ACCOUNT NO.** 55

| | | Post. | | | Balance | |
Date	Item	Ref.	Debit	Credit	Debit	Credit
2008 Apr. 30	Adjusting	3	3 0 0 00		3 0 0 00	
30	Closing	4		3 0 0 00	—	—

ACCOUNT *Miscellaneous Expense*   **ACCOUNT NO.** 59

| | | Post. | | | Balance | |
Date	Item	Ref.	Debit	Credit	Debit	Credit
2008 Apr. 10		1	1 2 0 00		1 2 0 00	
29		2	1 3 0 00		2 5 0 00	
30		2	2 0 0 00		4 5 0 00	
30	Closing	4		4 5 0 00	—	—

(concluded)

Fiscal Year

objective 6

Explain what is meant by the fiscal year and the natural business year.

The annual accounting period adopted by a business is known as its **fiscal year**. Fiscal years begin with the first day of the month selected and end on the last day of the following twelfth month. The period most commonly used is the calendar year. Other periods are not unusual, especially for businesses organized as corporations. For example, a corporation may adopt a fiscal year that ends when business activities have reached the lowest point in its annual operating cycle. Such a fiscal year is called the **natural business year**. At the low point in its operating cycle, a business has more time to analyze the results of operations and to prepare financial statements.

Because companies with fiscal years often have highly seasonal operations, investors and others should be careful in interpreting partial-year reports for such companies. That is, you should expect the results of operations for these companies to vary significantly throughout the fiscal year.

The financial history of a business may be shown by a series of balance sheets and income statements for several fiscal years. If the life of a business is expressed by a line moving from left to right, the series of balance sheets and income statements may be graphed as follows:

REAL WORLD

Percentage of Companies with Fiscal Years Ending in:

January	5%	July	2%
February	1	August	2
March	3	September	7
April	2	October	3
May	3	November	2
June	7	December	63

Source: *Accounting Trends & Techniques,* 59th edition, 2005 (New York: American Institute of Certified Public Accountants).

Financial History of a Business

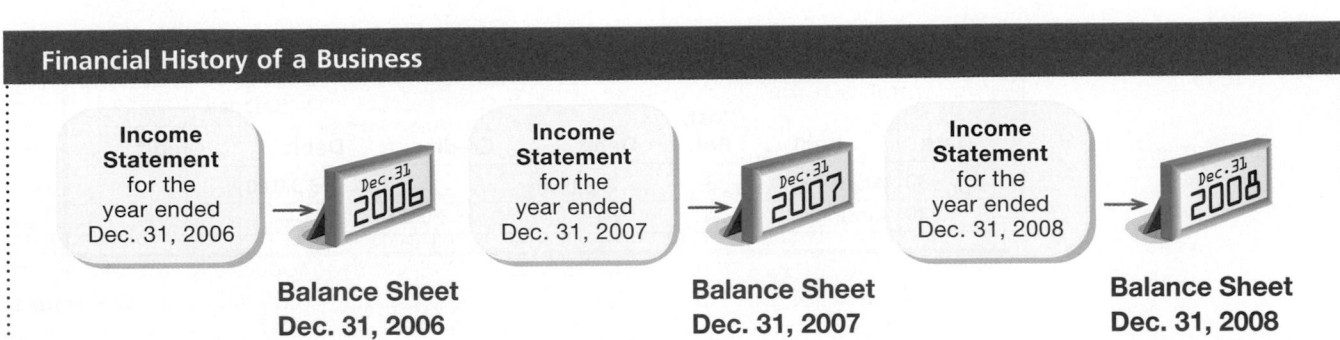

You may think of the income statements, balance sheets, and financial history of a business as similar to the record of a college football team. The final score of each football game is similar to the net income reported on the income statement of a business. The team's season record after each game is similar to the balance sheet. At the end of the season, the final record of the team measures its success or failure. Likewise, at the end of a life of a business, its final balance sheet is a measure of its financial success or failure.

Appendix

End-of-Period Spreadsheet (Work Sheet)

Accountants often use working papers for collecting and summarizing data they need for preparing various analyses and reports. Such working papers are useful tools, but they are not considered a part of the formal accounting records. This is in contrast to the chart of accounts, the journal, and the ledger, which are essential parts of the accounting system. Working papers are usually prepared by using a spreadsheet program on a computer.

The end-of-period spreadsheet (work sheet) shown in Exhibit 1 is a working paper that accountants can use to summarize adjusting entries and the account balances for the financial statements. In small companies with few accounts and adjustments, an end-of-period spreadsheet (work sheet) may not be necessary. For example, the financial statements for NetSolutions can be prepared directly from the adjusted trial balance in Exhibit 1. However, many accountants prefer to use an end-of-period spreadsheet (work sheet) as an aid to analyzing adjustment data and preparing the financial statements. We use Exhibits 18 through 21 on page 176B to describe and illustrate how to prepare this type of end-of-period spreadsheet (work sheet).

@netsolutions

UNADJUSTED TRIAL BALANCE COLUMNS

To begin the spreadsheet (work sheet), enter at the top the name of the business, the type of working paper, and the period of time, as shown in Exhibit 18. Next, enter the unadjusted trial balance directly on the spreadsheet. The spreadsheet in Exhibit 18 shows the unadjusted trial balance for NetSolutions at December 31, 2007.

ADJUSTMENTS COLUMNS

The adjustments that we explained and illustrated for NetSolutions in Chapter 3 are entered in the Adjustments columns, as shown in Exhibit 19. Cross-referencing (by letters) the debit and credit of each adjustment is useful in reviewing the spreadsheet (work sheet). It is also helpful for identifying the adjusting entries that need to be recorded in the journal.

The order in which the adjustments are entered on the spreadsheet (work sheet) is not important. Most accountants enter the adjustments in the order in which the data are assembled. If the titles of some of the accounts to be adjusted do not appear in the trial balance, they should be entered in the Account Title column, below the trial balance totals, as needed.

To review, the entries in the Adjustments columns of the work sheet are:

(a) **Supplies.** The supplies account has a debit balance of $2,000. The cost of the supplies on hand at the end of the period is $760. Therefore, the supplies expense for December is the difference between the two amounts, or $1,240. The adjustment is entered as (1) $1,240 in the Adjustments Debit column on the same line as Supplies Expense and (2) $1,240 in the Adjustments Credit column on the same line as Supplies.

(b) **Prepaid Insurance.** The prepaid insurance account has a debit balance of $2,400, which represents the prepayment of insurance for 12 months beginning December 1. Thus, the insurance expense for December is $200 ($2,400/12). The adjustment is entered as (1) $200 in the Adjustments Debit column on the same line as Insurance Expense and (2) $200 in the Adjustments Credit column on the same line as Prepaid Insurance.

(c) **Unearned Rent.** The unearned rent account has a credit balance of $360, which represents the receipt of three months' rent, beginning with December. Thus, the rent revenue for December is $120. The adjustment is entered as (1) $120 in the Adjustments Debit column on the same line as Unearned Rent and (2) $120 in the Adjustments Credit column on the same line as Rent Revenue.

(d) **Accrued Fees.** Fees accrued at the end of December but not recorded total $500. This amount is an increase in an asset and an increase in revenue. The adjustment is entered as (1) $500 in the Adjustments Debit column on the same line as Accounts Receivable and (2) $500 in the Adjustments Credit column on the same line as Fees Earned.

(e) **Wages.** Wages accrued but not paid at the end of December total $250. This amount is an increase in expenses and an increase in liabilities. The adjustment is entered as (1) $250 in the Adjustments Debit column on the same line as Wages Expense and (2) $250 in the Adjustments Credit column on the same line as Wages Payable.

(f) **Depreciation.** Depreciation of the office equipment is $50 for December. The adjustment is entered as (1) $50 in the Adjustments Debit column on the same line as Depreciation Expense and (2) $50 in the Adjustments Credit column on the same line as Accumulated Depreciation.

Total the Adjustments columns to verify the mathematical accuracy of the adjustment data. The total of the Debit column must equal the total of the Credit column.

ADJUSTED TRIAL BALANCE COLUMNS

The adjustment data are added to or subtracted from the amounts in the Unadjusted Trial Balance columns. The adjusted amounts are then extended to (placed in) the Adjusted Trial Balance columns, as shown in Exhibit 19. For example, the cash amount of $2,065 is extended to the Adjusted Trial Balance Debit column, since no adjustments affected Cash. Accounts Receivable has an initial balance of $2,220 and a debit adjustment (increase) of $500. The amount entered in the Adjusted Trial Balance Debit column is the debit balance of $2,720. The same procedure continues until all account balances are extended to the Adjusted Trial Balance columns. Total the columns of the Adjusted Trial Balance to verify the equality of debits and credits.

INCOME STATEMENT AND BALANCE SHEET COLUMNS

The spreadsheet (work sheet) is completed by extending the adjusted trial balance amounts to the Income Statement and Balance Sheet columns. The amounts for revenues and expenses are extended to the Income Statement columns. The amounts for assets, liabilities, owner's capital, and drawing are extended to the Balance Sheet columns.[3]

In the NetSolutions spreadsheet (work sheet), the first account listed is Cash, and the balance appearing in the Adjusted Trial Balance Debit column is $2,065. Cash is an asset, is listed on the balance sheet, and has a debit balance. Therefore, $2,065 is extended to the Balance Sheet Debit column. The Fees Earned balance of $16,840 is extended to the Income Statement Credit column. The same procedure continues until all account balances have been extended to the proper columns, as shown in Exhibit 20.

---

3 The balances of the capital and drawing accounts are also extended to the Balance Sheet columns because this spreadsheet (work sheet) does not provide for separate Statement of Owner's Equity columns.

After all of the balances have been extended to the four statement columns, total each of these columns, as shown in Exhibit 21. The difference between the two Income Statement column totals is the amount of the net income or the net loss for the period. Likewise, the difference between the two Balance Sheet column totals is also the amount of the net income or net loss for the period.

If the Income Statement Credit column total (representing total revenue) is greater than the Income Statement Debit column total (representing total expenses), the difference is the net income. If the Income Statement Debit column total is greater than the Income Statement Credit column total, the difference is a net loss. For NetSolutions, the computation of net income is as follows:

Total of Credit column (revenues)	$16,960
Total of Debit column (expenses)	9,855
Net income (excess of revenues over expenses)	$ 7,105

As shown in Exhibit 21, enter the amount of the net income, $7,105, in the Income Statement Debit column and the Balance Sheet Credit column. Enter the term *Net income* in the Account Title column. If there was a net loss instead of net income, you would enter the amount in the Income Statement Credit column and the Balance Sheet Debit column and the term *Net loss* in the Account Title column. Entering the net income or net loss in the statement columns on the spreadsheet (work sheet) shows the effect of transferring the net balance of the revenue and expense accounts to the owner's capital account.

After the net income or net loss has been entered on the spreadsheet (work sheet), again total each of the four statement columns. The totals of the two Income Statement columns must now be equal. The totals of the two Balance Sheet columns must also be equal.

The spreadsheet (work sheet) is an aid in preparing the income statement, the statement of owner's equity, and the balance sheet, which are presented in Exhibit 2. The income statement is normally prepared directly from the spreadsheet (work sheet). However, the order of the expenses may be changed. As we did in Chapter 1, we list the expenses in the income statement in Exhibit 2 in order of size, beginning with the larger items. Miscellaneous expense is the last item, regardless of its amount.

The first item normally presented on the statement of owner's equity is the balance of the owner's capital account at the beginning of the period. On the spreadsheet (work sheet), however, the amount listed as capital is not always the account balance at the beginning of the period. The owner may have invested additional assets in the business during the period. Hence, for the beginning balance and any additional investments, it is necessary to refer to the capital account in the ledger. These amounts, along with the net income (or net loss) and the drawing amount shown in the spreadsheet (work sheet), are used to determine the ending capital account balance. The balance sheet can be prepared directly from the spreadsheet (work sheet) columns except for the ending balance of owner's capital, which is taken from the statement of owner's equity.

When a spreadsheet (work sheet) is used, the adjusting and closing entries are normally not journalized or posted until after the spreadsheet and financial statements have been prepared. The data for the adjusting entries are taken from the adjustments columns of the spreadsheet. The data for the first two closing entries are taken from the Income Statement columns of the spreadsheet. The amount for the closing third entry is the net income or net loss appearing at the bottom of the spreadsheet. The amount for the fourth closing entry is the drawing account balance that appears in the Balance Sheet Debit column of the spreadsheet.

EXHIBIT 18   Spreadsheet (Work Sheet) with Unadjusted Trial Balance Entered

	A	B	C	D	E	F	G	H	I	J	K	
		NetSolutions										
		End-of-Period Spreadsheet (Work Sheet)										
		For the Two Months Ended December 31, 2007										
		Unadjusted Trial Balance		Adjustments		Adjusted Trial Balance		Income Statement		Balance Sheet		
	Account Title	Dr.	Cr.	Dr.	Cr.	Dr.	Cr.	Dr.	Cr.	Dr.	Cr.	
1	Cash	2,065										1
2	Accounts Receivable	2,220										2
3	Supplies	2,000										3
4	Prepaid Insurance	2,400										4
5	Land	20,000										5
6	Office Equipment	1,800										6
7	Accounts Payable		900									7
8	Unearned Rent		360									8
9	Chris Clark, Capital		25,000									9
10	Chris Clark, Drawing	4,000										10
11	Fees Earned		16,340									11
12	Wages Expense	4,275										12
13	Rent Expense	1,600										13
14	Utilities Expense	985										14
15	Supplies Expense	800										15
16	Miscellaneous Expense	455										16
17		42,600	42,600									17
18												18
19												19
20												20
21												21
22												22
23												23
24												24
25												25

The spreadsheet (work sheet) is used for summarizing the effects of adjusting entries. It also aids in preparing financial statements.

At a Glance

1. Describe the flow of accounting information from the unadjusted trial balance into the adjusted trial balance and financial statements.

Key Points	Key Learning Outcomes	Example Exercises	Practice Exercises
Exhibit 1 illustrates the end-of-period process by which accounts are adjusted and how the adjusted accounts flow into the financial statements.	• Using an end-of-period spreadsheet (work sheet), describe how the unadjusted trial balance accounts are affected by adjustments and how the adjusted trial balance accounts flow into the income statement and balance sheet.	4-1	4-1A, 4-1B

2. Prepare financial statements from adjusted account balances.

Key Points	Key Learning Outcomes	Example Exercises	Practice Exercises
Using the end-of-period spreadsheet (work sheet) shown in Exhibit 1, the income statement and balance sheet for NetSolutions can be prepared. The statement of owner's equity is prepared by referring to transactions that have been posted to owner's capital accounts in the ledger. A classified balance sheet has sections for current assets; property, plant, and equipment; current liabilities; long-term liabilities; and owner's equity.	• Describe how the net income or net loss from the period can be determined from an end-of-period spreadsheet (work sheet).	4-2	4-2A, 4-2B
	• Prepare an income statement, statement of owner's equity, and a balance sheet.	4-3	4-3A, 4-3B
	• Indicate how accounts would be reported in a classified balance sheet.	4-4	4-4A, 4-4B

3. Prepare closing entries.

Key Points	Key Learning Outcomes	Example Exercises	Practice Exercises
Four entries are required in closing the temporary accounts. The first entry closes the revenue accounts to Income Summary. The second entry closes the expense accounts to Income Summary. The third entry closes the balance of Income Summary (net income or net loss) to the owner's capital account. The fourth entry closes the drawing account to the owner's capital account. After the closing entries have been posted to the ledger, the balance in the capital account agrees with the amount reported on the statement of owner's equity and balance sheet. In addition, the revenue, expense, and drawing accounts will have zero balances.	• Prepare the closing entry for revenues.	4-5	4-5A, 4-5B
	• Prepare the closing entry for expenses.	4-5	4-5A, 4-5B
	• Prepare the closing entry for transferring the balance of Income Summary to the owner's capital account.	4-5	4-5A, 4-5B
	• Prepare the closing entry for the owner's drawing account.	4-5	4-5A, 4-5B

(continued)

4. Describe the accounting cycle.

Key Points	Key Learning Outcomes	Example Exercises	Practice Exercises
The 10 basic steps of the accounting cycle are as follows: 1. Transactions are analyzed and recorded in the journal. 2. Transactions are posted to the ledger. 3. An unadjusted trial balance is prepared. 4. Adjustment data are assembled and analyzed. 5. An optional end-of-period spreadsheet (work sheet) is prepared. 6. Adjusting entries are journalized and posted to the ledger. 7. An adjusted trial balance is prepared. 8. Financial statements are prepared. 9. Closing entries are journalized and posted to the ledger. 10. A post-closing trial balance is prepared.	• List the 10 steps of the accounting cycle. • Determine whether any steps are out of order in a listing of accounting cycle steps. • Determine whether there are any missing steps in a listing of accounting cycle steps.	4-6	4-6A, 4-6B

5. Illustrate the accounting cycle for one period.

Key Points	Key Learning Outcomes	Example Exercises	Practice Exercises
The complete accounting for Kelly Consulting for the month of April is described and illustrated on pages 161–174.	• Complete the accounting cycle for a period from beginning to end.		

6. Explain what is meant by the fiscal year and the natural business year.

Key Points	Key Learning Outcomes	Example Exercises	Practice Exercises
The annual accounting period adopted by a business is its fiscal year. A company's fiscal year that ends when business activities have reached the lowest point in its annual operating cycle is called the natural business year.	• Explain why companies use a fiscal year that is different from the calendar year.		

Key Terms

accounting cycle (159)
clearing account (152)
closing entries (152)
closing process (152)
current assets (150)

current liabilities (150)
fiscal year (174)
fixed (plant) assets (150)
Income Summary (152)
long-term liabilities (150)

natural business year (174)
notes receivable (150)
real accounts (151)
temporary (nominal) accounts (152)

Illustrative Problem

Three years ago, T. Roderick organized Harbor Realty. At July 31, 2008, the end of the current fiscal year, the following end-of-period spreadsheet (work sheet) was prepared:

Harbor Realty
End-of-Period Spreadsheet (Work Sheet)
For the Year Ended July 31, 2008

	A	B	C	D	E	F	G	H	I	J	K	
	Account Title	Unadjusted Trial Balance Dr.	Cr.	Adjustments Dr.	Cr.	Adjusted Trial Balance Dr.	Cr.	Income Statement Dr.	Cr.	Balance Sheet Dr.	Cr.	
1	Cash	3,425				3,425				3,425		1
2	Accounts Receivable	7,000		(e) 1,000		8,000				8,000		2
3	Supplies	1,270			(a) 890	380				380		3
4	Prepaid Insurance	620			(b) 315	305				305		4
5	Office Equipment	51,650				51,650				51,650		5
6	Accum. Depreciation		9,700		(c) 4,950		14,650				14,650	6
7	Accounts Payable		925				925				925	7
8	Unearned Fees		1,250	(f) 500			750				750	8
9	T. Roderick, Capital		29,000				29,000				29,000	9
10	T. Roderick, Drawing	5,200				5,200				5,200		10
11	Fees Earned		59,125		(e) 1,000		60,625		60,625			11
12					(f) 500							12
13	Wages Expense	22,415		(d) 440		22,855		22,855				13
14	Rent Expense	4,200				4,200		4,200				14
15	Utilities Expense	2,715				2,715		2,715				15
16	Miscellaneous Expense	1,505				1,505		1,505				16
17		100,000	100,000									17
18	Supplies Expense			(a) 890		890		890				18
19	Insurance Expense			(b) 315		315		315				19
20	Depreciation Expense			(c) 4,950		4,950		4,950				20
21	Wages Payable				(d) 440		440				440	21
22				8,095	8,095	106,390	106,390	37,430	60,625	68,960	45,765	22
23	Net income							23,195			23,195	23
24								60,625	60,625	68,960	68,960	24

Instructions

1. Prepare an income statement, a statement of owner's equity (no additional investments were made during the year), and a balance sheet.
2. On the basis of the data in the end-of-period spreadsheet (work sheet), journalize the closing entries.

Solution

1.

Harbor Realty
Income Statement
For the Year Ended July 31, 2008

Fees earned		$60 625 00
Expenses:		
Wages expense	$22 855 00	
Depreciation expense	4 950 00	
Rent expense	4 200 00	
Utilities expense	2 715 00	
Supplies expense	890 00	
Insurance expense	315 00	
Miscellaneous expense	1 505 00	
Total expenses		37 430 00
Net income		$23 195 00

(continued)

Harbor Realty
Statement of Owner's Equity
For the Year Ended July 31, 2008

T. Roderick, capital, August 1, 2007		$29 0 0 0 00
Net income for the year	$23 1 9 5 00	
Less withdrawals	5 2 0 0 00	
Increase in owner's equity		17 9 9 5 00
T. Roderick, capital, July 31, 2008		$46 9 9 5 00

Harbor Realty
Balance Sheet
July 31, 2008

Assets			Liabilities		
Current assets:			Current liabilities:		
Cash	$ 3 4 2 5 00		Accounts payable	$ 9 2 5 00	
Accounts receivable	8 0 0 0 00		Unearned fees	7 5 0 00	
Supplies	3 8 0 00		Wages payable	4 4 0 00	
Prepaid insurance	3 0 5 00		Total liabilities		$ 2 1 1 5 00
Total current assets		$12 1 1 0 00			
Property, plant, and equipment:					
Office equipment	$51 6 5 0 00				
Less accumulated depr.	14 6 5 0 00		**Owner's Equity**		
Total property, plant,			T. Roderick, capital		46 9 9 5 00
and equipment		37 0 0 0 00	Total liabilities and		
Total assets		$49 1 1 0 00	owner's equity		$49 1 1 0 00

2.

JOURNAL   Page

	Date		Description	Post. Ref.	Debit	Credit	
1			Closing Entries				1
2	2008 July	31	Fees Earned		60 6 2 5 00		2
3			Income Summary			60 6 2 5 00	3
4							4
5		31	Income Summary		37 4 3 0 00		5
6			Wages Expense			22 8 5 5 00	6
7			Rent Expense			4 2 0 0 00	7
8			Utilities Expense			2 7 1 5 00	8
9			Miscellaneous Expense			1 5 0 5 00	9
10			Supplies Expense			8 9 0 00	10
11			Insurance Expense			3 1 5 00	11
12			Depreciation Expense			4 9 5 0 00	12
13							13
14		31	Income Summary		23 1 9 5 00		14
15			T. Roderick, Capital			23 1 9 5 00	15
16							16
17		31	T. Roderick, Capital		5 2 0 0 00		17
18			T. Roderick, Drawing			5 2 0 0 00	18

Self-Examination Questions

(Answers at End of Chapter)

1. Which of the following accounts in the Adjusted Trial Balance columns of the end-of-period spreadsheet (work sheet) would be extended to the Balance Sheet columns?
   A. Utilities Expense
   B. Rent Revenue
   C. M. E. Jones, Drawing
   D. Miscellaneous Expense

2. Which of the following accounts would be classified as a current asset on the balance sheet?
   A. Office Equipment
   B. Land
   C. Accumulated Depreciation
   D. Accounts Receivable

3. Which of the following entries closes the owner's drawing account at the end of the period?
   A. Debit the drawing account, credit the income summary account.
   B. Debit the owner's capital account, credit the drawing account.
   C. Debit the income summary account, credit the drawing account.
   D. Debit the drawing account, credit the owner's capital account.

4. Which of the following accounts would *not* be closed to the income summary account at the end of a period?
   A. Fees Earned
   B. Wages Expense
   C. Rent Expense
   D. Accumulated Depreciation

5. Which of the following accounts would *not* be included in a post-closing trial balance?
   A. Cash
   B. Fees Earned
   C. Accumulated Depreciation
   D. J. C. Smith, Capital

Eye Openers

1. Why do some accountants prepare an end-of-period spreadsheet (work sheet)?
2. Is the end-of-period spreadsheet (work sheet) a substitute for the financial statements? Discuss.
3. In the Income Statement columns of the end-of-period spreadsheet (work sheet) for Allen Consulting Co. for the current year, the Debit column total is $262,250 and the Credit column total is $323,500 before the amount for net income or net loss has been included. In preparing the income statement from the end-of-period spreadsheet (work sheet), what is the amount of net income or net loss?
4. Describe the nature of the assets that compose the following sections of a balance sheet: (a) current assets, (b) property, plant, and equipment.
5. What is the difference between a current liability and a long-term liability?
6. What types of accounts are referred to as temporary accounts?
7. Why are closing entries required at the end of an accounting period?
8. What is the difference between adjusting entries and closing entries?
9. Describe the four entries that close the temporary accounts.
10. What is the purpose of the post-closing trial balance?
11. (a) What is the most important output of the accounting cycle? (b) Do all companies have an accounting cycle? Explain.
12. What is the natural business year?
13. Why might a department store select a fiscal year ending January 31, rather than a fiscal year ending December 31?
14. The fiscal years for several well-known companies are as follows:

Company	Fiscal Year Ending	Company	Fiscal Year Ending
Kmart	January 30	Toys "R" Us, Inc.	February 3
JCPenney	January 26	Federated Department Stores, Inc.	February 3
Target Corp.	January 28	The Limited, Inc.	February 2

What general characteristic shared by these companies explains why they do not have fiscal years ending December 31?

Practice Exercises

PE 4-1A
Flow of accounts into financial statements
obj. 1

The balances for the accounts listed below appear in the Adjusted Trial Balance columns of the end-of-period spreadsheet (work sheet). Indicate whether each balance should be extended to (a) an Income Statement column or (b) a Balance Sheet column.

1. Supplies Expense
2. Unearned Service Revenue
3. Accounts Payable
4. Rent Revenue

5. Wages Payable
6. Office Equipment
7. Depreciation Expense—Equipment
8. Brandi Gowdy, Capital

PE 4-1B
Flow of accounts into financial statements
obj. 1

The balances for the accounts listed below appear in the Adjusted Trial Balance columns of the end-of-period spreadsheet (work sheet). Indicate whether each balance should be extended to (a) an Income Statement column or (b) a Balance Sheet column.

1. Cash
2. Insurance Expense
3. Prepaid Rent
4. Supplies

5. Commissions Earned
6. Accumulated Depreciation—Equipment
7. Christina Egan, Drawing
8. Wages Expense

PE 4-2A
Determining net income from the end-of-period spreadsheet (work sheet)
obj. 2

In the Balance Sheet columns of the end-of-period spreadsheet (work sheet) for FreeLance Consulting Co. for the current year, the Debit column total is $247,690 and the Credit column total is $278,100 before the amount for net income or net loss has been included. In preparing the income statement from the end-of-period spreadsheet (work sheet), what is the amount of net income or net loss?

PE 4-2B
Determining net income from the end-of-period spreadsheet (work sheet)
obj. 2

In the Income Statement columns of the end-of-period spreadsheet (work sheet) for Irwin Consulting Co. for the current year, the Debit column total is $436,700 and the Credit column total is $523,550 before the amount for net income or net loss has been included. In preparing the income statement from the end-of-period spreadsheet (work sheet), what is the amount of net income or net loss?

PE 4-3A
Statement of owner's equity
obj. 2

Jody Padget owns and operates Padget Advertising Services. On January 1, 2007, Jody Padget, Capital had a balance of $550,600. During the year, Jody invested an additional $50,000 and withdrew $40,000. For the year ended December 31, 2007, Padget Advertising Services reported a net income of $68,150. Prepare a statement of owner's equity for the year ended December 31, 2007.

PE 4-3B
Statement of owner's equity
obj. 2

Ali Khalid owns and operates AAA Delivery Services. On January 1, 2007, Ali Khalid, Capital had a balance of $854,450. During the year, Ali made no additional investments and withdrew $38,400. For the year ended December 31, 2007, AAA Delivery Services reported a net loss of $11,875. Prepare a statement of owner's equity for the year ended December 31, 2007.

PE 4-4A
Reporting accounts on classified balance sheet
obj. 2

The following accounts appear in an adjusted trial balance of Ramrod Consulting. Indicate whether each account would be reported in the (a) current asset; (b) property, plant, and equipment; (c) current liability; (d) long-term liability; or (e) owner's equity section of the December 31, 2007, balance sheet of Ramrod Consulting.

1. Taxes Payable
2. Building
3. Supplies
4. Mortgage Payable (due in 2011)

5. Prepaid Rent
6. Salaries Payable
7. Unearned Service Fees
8. Cecily Renick, Capital

PE 4-4B
Reporting accounts on classified balance sheet
obj. 2

The following accounts appear in an adjusted trial balance of Fastback Consulting. Indicate whether each account would be reported in the (a) current asset; (b) property, plant, and equipment; (c) current liability; (d) long-term liability; or (e) owner's equity section of the December 31, 2007, balance sheet of Fastback Consulting.

1. Accounts Payable
2. Accounts Receivable
3. Glen Moore, Capital
4. Wages Payable
5. Note Payable (due in 2014)
6. Cash
7. Supplies
8. Accumulated Depreciation—Building

PE 4-5A
Closing entries with net loss
obj. 3

After the accounts have been adjusted at October 31, the end of the fiscal year, the following balances were taken from the ledger of Velocity Delivery Services Co.:

Lisa Jordon, Capital	$318,500
Lisa Jordon, Drawing	36,000
Fees Earned	475,150
Wages Expense	390,000
Rent Expense	85,000
Supplies Expense	38,350
Miscellaneous Expense	12,675

Journalize the four entries required to close the accounts.

PE 4-5B
Closing entries with net income
obj. 3

After the accounts have been adjusted at April 30, the end of the fiscal year, the following balances were taken from the ledger of Magnolia Landscaping Co.:

Jayme Carmichael, Capital	$528,900
Jayme Carmichael, Drawing	60,000
Fees Earned	690,500
Wages Expense	410,000
Rent Expense	75,000
Supplies Expense	48,650
Miscellaneous Expense	19,700

Journalize the four entries required to close the accounts.

PE 4-6A
Missing steps in the accounting cycle
obj. 4

From the following list of steps in the accounting cycle, identify what two steps are missing.

a. Transactions are analyzed and recorded in the journal.
b. An unadjusted trial balance is prepared.
c. Adjustment data are assembled and analyzed.
d. An optional end-of-period spreadsheet (work sheet) is prepared.
e. Adjusting entries are journalized and posted to the ledger.
f. An adjusted trial balance is prepared.
g. Closing entries are journalized and posted to the ledger.
h. A post-closing trial balance is prepared.

PE 4-6B
Missing steps in the accounting cycle
obj. 4

From the following list of steps in the accounting cycle, identify what two steps are missing.

a. Transactions are analyzed and recorded in the journal.
b. Transactions are posted to the ledger.
c. An unadjusted trial balance is prepared.
d. An optional end-of-period spreadsheet (work sheet) is prepared.
e. Adjusting entries are journalized and posted to the ledger.
f. An adjusted trial balance is prepared.
g. Financial statements are prepared.
h. A post-closing trial balance is prepared.

Exercises

EX 4-1
Extending account balances in an end-of-period spreadsheet (work sheet)
objs. 1, 2

The balances for the accounts listed below appear in the Adjusted Trial Balance columns of the end-of-period spreadsheet (work sheet). Indicate whether each balance should be extended to (a) an Income Statement column or (b) a Balance Sheet column.

1. Accounts Payable	6. Supplies
2. Accounts Receivable	7. Unearned Fees
3. Beth Posey, Capital	8. Utilities Expense
4. Beth Posey, Drawing	9. Wages Expense
5. Fees Earned	10. Wages Payable

EX 4-2
Classifying accounts
objs. 1, 2

Balances for each of the following accounts appear in an adjusted trial balance. Identify each as (a) asset, (b) liability, (c) revenue, or (d) expense.

1. Accounts Receivable	7. Rent Revenue
2. Fees Earned	8. Salary Expense
3. Insurance Expense	9. Salary Payable
4. Land	10. Supplies
5. Prepaid Advertising	11. Supplies Expense
6. Prepaid Insurance	12. Unearned Rent

EX 4-3
Financial statements from the end-of-period spreadsheet (work sheet)
objs. 1, 2

Sandy Bottom Consulting is a consulting firm owned and operated by Dee Schofield. The end-of-period spreadsheet (work sheet) shown below was prepared for the year ended August 31, 2008.

	A	B	C	D	E	F	G	H	I	J	K	
		Sandy Bottom Consulting										
		End-of-Period Spreadsheet (Work Sheet)										
		For the Year Ended August 31, 2008										
		Unadjusted Trial Balance		Adjustments		Adjusted Trial Balance		Income Statement		Balance Sheet		
	Account Title	Dr.	Cr.	Dr.	Cr.	Dr.	Cr.	Dr.	Cr.	Dr.	Cr.	
1	Cash	10,000				10,000				10,000		1
2	Accounts Receivable	12,500				12,500				12,500		2
3	Supplies	2,200			(a) 1,750	450				450		3
4	Office Equipment	14,500				14,500				14,500		4
5	Accumulated Depreciation		2,500		(b) 1,200		3,700				3,700	5
6	Accounts Payable		6,100				6,100				6,100	6
7	Salaries Payable				(c) 800		800				800	7
8	Dee Schofield, Capital		19,400				19,400				19,400	8
9	Dee Schofield, Drawing	2,700				2,700				2,700		9
10	Fees Earned		32,000				32,000		32,000			10
11	Salary Expense	16,250		(c) 800		17,050		17,050				11
12	Supplies Expense			(a) 1,750		1,750		1,750				12
13	Depreciation Expense			(b) 1,200		1,200		1,200				13
14	Miscellaneous Expense	1,850				1,850		1,850				14
15		60,000	60,000	3,750	3,750	62,000	62,000	21,850	32,000	40,150	30,000	15
16	Net income							10,150			10,150	16
17								32,000	32,000	40,150	40,150	17

Based upon the preceding spreadsheet, prepare an income statement, statement of owner's equity, and balance sheet for Sandy Bottom Consulting.

EX 4-4
Financial statements from the end-of-period spreadsheet (work sheet)
objs. 1, 2

Rectifier Consulting is a consulting firm owned and operated by Adam Beauchamp. The following end-of-period spreadsheet (work sheet) was prepared for the year ended June 30, 2008.

	A	B	C	D	E	F	G	H	I	J	K	
		Rectifier Consulting										
		End-of-Period Spreadsheet (Work Sheet)										
		For the Year Ended June 30, 2008										
		Unadjusted Trial Balance		Adjustments		Adjusted Trial Balance		Income Statement		Balance Sheet		
	Account Title	Dr.	Cr.	Dr.	Cr.	Dr.	Cr.	Dr.	Cr.	Dr.	Cr.	
1	Cash	8,000				8,000				8,000		1
2	Accounts Receivable	15,500				15,500				15,500		2
3	Supplies	2,500			(a) 1,850	650				650		3
4	Office Equipment	24,500				24,500				24,500		4
5	Accumulated Depreciation		4,500		(b) 900		5,400				5,400	5
6	Accounts Payable		3,300				3,300				3,300	6
7	Salaries Payable				(c) 400		400				400	7
8	Adam Beauchamp, Capital		25,200				25,200				25,200	8
9	Adam Beauchamp, Drawing	2,000				2,000				2,000		9
10	Fees Earned		51,750				51,750		51,750			10
11	Salary Expense	30,750		(c) 400		31,150		31,150				11
12	Supplies Expense			(a) 1,850		1,850		1,850				12
13	Depreciation Expense			(b) 900		900		900				13
14	Miscellaneous Expense	1,500				1,500		1,500				14
15		84,750	84,750	3,150	3,150	86,050	86,050	35,400	51,750	50,650	34,300	15
16	Net income							16,350			16,350	16
17								51,750	51,750	50,650	50,650	17

Based upon the preceding spreadsheet, prepare an income statement, statement of owner's equity, and balance sheet for Rectifier Consulting.

EX 4-5
Income statement
obj. 2

✓ *Net income, $184,500*

The following account balances were taken from the adjusted trial balance for Admiral Messenger Service, a delivery service firm, for the current fiscal year ended April 30, 2008:

Depreciation Expense	$ 5,000	Rent Expense	$ 43,400
Fees Earned	375,500	Salaries Expense	125,600
Insurance Expense	1,500	Supplies Expense	2,750
Miscellaneous Expense	1,250	Utilities Expense	11,500

Prepare an income statement.

EX 4-6
Income statement; net loss
obj. 2

✓ *Net loss, $23,300*

The following revenue and expense account balances were taken from the ledger of Cupcake Services Co. after the accounts had been adjusted on October 31, 2008, the end of the current fiscal year:

Depreciation Expense	$10,000	Service Revenue	$163,375
Insurance Expense	6,000	Supplies Expense	2,875
Miscellaneous Expense	4,750	Utilities Expense	18,750
Rent Expense	51,500	Wages Expense	92,800

Prepare an income statement.

EX 4-7
Income statement
obj. 2

Internet Project

✓ *a. Net income: $1,449*

FedEx Corporation had the following revenue and expense account balances (in millions) at its fiscal year-end of May 31, 2005:

Depreciation	$1,462	Purchased Transportation	$ 2,935
Fuel	2,317	Rentals and Landing Fees	2,314
Maintenance and Repairs	1,680	Revenues	29,363
Other Expenses	4,379	Salaries and Employee Benefits	11,963
Provision for Income Taxes	864		

a. Prepare an income statement.
b. ▬▬▶ Compare your income statement with the related income statement that is available at the FedEx Corporation Web site, which is linked to the text's Web site at **www.thomsonedu.com/accounting/warren**. What similarities and differences do you see?

EX 4-8
Statement of owner's equity

obj. 2

✓ *Josh Winfrey, capital, Aug. 31, 2008: $652,750*

Icon Systems Co. offers its services to residents in the Pasadena area. Selected accounts from the ledger of Icon Systems Co. for the current fiscal year ended August 31, 2008, are as follows:

Josh Winfrey, Capital				Josh Winfrey, Drawing			
Aug. 31	16,000	Sept. 1 (2007)	573,750	Nov. 30	4,000	Aug. 31	16,000
		Aug. 31	95,000	Feb. 28	4,000		
				May 31	4,000		
				Aug. 31	4,000		

Income Summary			
Aug. 31	380,000	Aug. 31	475,000
31	95,000		

Prepare a statement of owner's equity for the year.

EX 4-9
Statement of owner's equity; net loss

obj. 2

✓ *Tammy Eddy, capital, June 30, 2008: $128,250*

Selected accounts from the ledger of Aspen Sports for the current fiscal year ended June 30, 2008, are as follows:

Tammy Eddy, Capital				Tammy Eddy, Drawing			
June 30	30,000	July 1 (2007)	190,800	Sept. 30	7,500	June 30	30,000
30	32,550			Dec. 31	7,500		
				May 31	7,500		
				June 30	7,500		

Income Summary			
June 30	348,150	June 30	315,600
		30	32,550

Prepare a statement of owner's equity for the year.

EX 4-10
Classifying assets

obj. 2

Identify each of the following as (a) a current asset or (b) property, plant, and equipment:

1. Accounts receivable
2. Building
3. Cash
4. Equipment
5. Prepaid insurance
6. Supplies

EX 4-11
Balance sheet classification

obj. 2

At the balance sheet date, a business owes a mortgage note payable of $750,000, the terms of which provide for monthly payments of $15,000.

▶ Explain how the liability should be classified on the balance sheet.

EX 4-12
Balance sheet

obj. 2

✓ *Total assets: $375,000*

Healthy & Trim Co. offers personal weight reduction consulting services to individuals. After all the accounts have been closed on November 30, 2008, the end of the current fiscal year, the balances of selected accounts from the ledger of Healthy & Trim Co. are as follows:

Accounts Payable	$ 17,250	Equipment	$350,000
Accounts Receivable	41,560	Prepaid Insurance	9,600
Accumulated Depreciation—		Prepaid Rent	6,000
Equipment	51,950	Salaries Payable	6,750
Cash	?	Supplies	1,040
Cindy DeLoach, Capital	346,000	Unearned Fees	5,000

Prepare a classified balance sheet that includes the correct balance for Cash.

EX 4-13
Balance sheet

obj. 2

List the errors you find in the following balance sheet. Prepare a corrected balance sheet.

Eucalyptus Services Co.
Balance Sheet
For the Year Ended July 31, 2008

Assets			Liabilities		
Current assets:			Current liabilities:		
Cash	$ 5,280		Accounts receivable	$ 13,750	
Accounts payable	6,790		Accum. depr.—building	86,700	
Supplies	1,650		Accum. depr.—equipment	18,480	
Prepaid insurance	4,800		Net income	25,000	
Land	60,000		Total liabilities		$143,930
Total current assets		$ 78,520			
Property, plant, and equipment:			**Owner's Equity**		
Building	$156,700		Wages payable	$ 1,340	
Equipment	43,000		Sydney Kitchel, capital	171,870	
Total property, plant, and equipmet		238,620	Total owner's equity		173,210
Total assets		$317,140	Total liabilities and owner's equity		$317,140

EX 4-14
Identifying accounts to be closed

obj. 3

From the following list, identify the accounts that should be closed to Income Summary at the end of the fiscal year:

a. Accounts Receivable
b. Accumulated Depreciation— Equipment
c. Depreciation Expense—Equipment
d. Equipment
e. Fees Earned
f. Keri Upshaw, Capital
g. Keri Upshaw, Drawing
h. Land
i. Supplies
j. Supplies Expense
k. Wages Expense
l. Wages Payable

EX 4-15
Closing entries

obj. 3

Prior to its closing, Income Summary had total debits of $279,615 and total credits of $392,750.

➤ Briefly explain the purpose served by the income summary account and the nature of the entries that resulted in the $279,615 and the $392,750.

EX 4-16
Closing entries with net income

obj. 3

After all revenue and expense accounts have been closed at the end of the fiscal year, Income Summary has a debit of $218,380 and a credit of $375,000. At the same date, Rachel Bray, Capital has a credit balance of $479,100, and Rachel Bray, Drawing has a balance of $18,000. (a) Journalize the entries required to complete the closing of the accounts. (b) Determine the amount of Rachel Bray, Capital at the end of the period.

EX 4-17
Closing entries with net loss

obj. 3

Firefly Services Co. offers its services to individuals desiring to improve their personal images. After the accounts have been adjusted at October 31, the end of the fiscal year, the following balances were taken from the ledger of Firefly Services Co.

Natalie Wilson, Capital	$554,500	Rent Expense	$65,000
Natalie Wilson, Drawing	20,000	Supplies Expense	3,150
Fees Earned	293,300	Miscellaneous Expense	7,100
Wages Expense	250,000		

Journalize the four entries required to close the accounts.

EX 4-18
Identifying permanent accounts

obj. 3

Which of the following accounts will usually appear in the post-closing trial balance?

a. Accounts Payable
b. Accumulated Depreciation
c. Cash
d. Depreciation Expense
e. Fees Earned
f. Office Equipment
g. Salaries Expense
h. Salaries Payable
i. Stephanie Hamm, Capital
j. Stephanie Hamm, Drawing
k. Supplies

EX 4-19
Post-closing trial balance
obj. 3

✓ *Correct column totals,*
$150,505

An accountant prepared the following post-closing trial balance:

Honest Sam's Repair Co.
Post-Closing Trial Balance
July 31, 2008

	Debit Balances	Credit Balances
Cash	12,915	
Accounts Receivable	46,620	
Supplies		2,770
Equipment		88,200
Accumulated Depreciation—Equipment	27,970	
Accounts Payable	15,750	
Salaries Payable		3,780
Unearned Rent	7,560	
Samantha Marcus, Capital	95,445	
	206,260	94,750

Prepare a corrected post-closing trial balance. Assume that all accounts have normal balances and that the amounts shown are correct.

EX 4-20
Steps in the accounting cycle
obj. 4

Rearrange the following steps in the accounting cycle in proper sequence:

a. An adjusted trial balance is prepared.
b. Financial statements are prepared.
c. A post-closing trial balance is prepared.
d. Transactions are analyzed and recorded in the journal.
e. An optional end-of-period spreadsheet (work sheet) is prepared.
f. Adjustment data are asssembled and analyzed.
g. Transactions are posted to the ledger.
h. Closing entries are journalized and posted to the ledger.
i. An unadjusted trial balance is prepared.
j. Adjusting entries are journalized and posted to the ledger.

EX 4-21
Appendix: Steps in completing an end-of-period spreadsheet (work sheet)

The steps performed in completing an end-of-period spreadsheet (work sheet) are listed below in random order.

a. Extend the adjusted trial balance amounts to the Income Statement columns and the Balance Sheet columns.
b. Enter the adjusting entries into the spreadsheet (work sheet), based upon the adjustment data.
c. Add the Debit and Credit columns of the Unadjusted Trial Balance columns of the spreadsheet (work sheet) to verify that the totals are equal.
d. Enter the amount of net income or net loss for the period in the proper Income Statement column and Balance Sheet column.
e. Add the Debit and Credit columns of the Balance Sheet and Income Statement columns of the spreadsheet (work sheet) to verify that the totals are equal.
f. Enter the unadjusted account balances from the general ledger into the Unadjusted Trial Balance columns of the spreadsheet (work sheet).
g. Add or deduct adjusting entry data to trial balance amounts, and extend amounts to the Adjusted Trial Balance columns.
h. Add the Debit and Credit columns of the Adjustments columns of the spreadsheet (work sheet) to verify that the totals are equal.
i. Add the Debit and Credit columns of the Balance Sheet and Income Statement columns of the spreadsheet (work sheet) to determine the amount of net income or net loss for the period.
j. Add the Debit and Credit columns of the Adjusted Trial Balance columns of the spreadsheet (work sheet) to verify that the totals are equal.

Indicate the order in which the preceding steps would be performed in preparing and completing a spreadsheet (work sheet).

EX 4-22
Appendix: Adjustment data on an end-of-period spreadsheet (work sheet)

✓ *Total debits of Adjustments column: $15*

Dakota Services Co. offers cleaning services to business clients. The trial balance for Dakota Services Co. has been prepared on the end-of-period spreadsheet (work sheet) for the year ended July 31, 2008, shown below.

Dakota Services Co.
End-of-Period Spreadsheet (Work Sheet)
For the Year Ended July 31, 2008

Account Title	Unadjusted Trial Balance Dr.	Cr.	Adjustments Dr.	Cr.	Adjusted Trial Balance Dr.	Cr.
Cash	4					
Accounts Receivable	25					
Supplies	4					
Prepaid Insurance	6					
Land	25					
Equipment	16					
Accum. Depr.—Equipment		1				
Accounts Payable		13				
Wages Payable		0				
Christina Keene, Capital		56				
Christina Keene, Drawing	4					
Fees Earned		30				
Wages Expense	8					
Rent Expense	4					
Insurance Expense	0					
Utilities Expense	3					
Depreciation Expense	0					
Supplies Expense	0					
Miscellaneous Expense	1					
	100	100				

The data for year-end adjustments are as follows:

a. Fees earned, but not yet billed, $5.
b. Supplies on hand, $1.
c. Insurance premiums expired, $4.
d. Depreciation expense, $2.
e. Wages accrued, but not paid, $1.

Enter the adjustment data, and place the balances in the Adjusted Trial Balance columns.

EX 4-23
Appendix: Completing an end-of-period spreadsheet (work sheet)

✓ *Net income: $9*

Dakota Services Co. offers cleaning services to business clients. Complete the following end-of-period spreadsheet (work sheet) for Dakota Services Co.

(continued)

Dakota Services Co.
End-of-Period Spreadsheet (Work Sheet)
For the Year Ended July 31, 2008

Account Title	Adjusted Trial Balance		Income Statement		Balance Sheet	
	Dr.	Cr.	Dr.	Cr.	Dr.	Cr.
Cash	4					
Accounts Receivable	30					
Supplies	1					
Prepaid Insurance	2					
Land	25					
Equipment	16					
Accum. Depr.—Equipment		3				
Accounts Payable		13				
Wages Payable		1				
Christina Keene, Capital		56				
Christina Keene, Drawing	4					
Fees Earned		35				
Wages Expense	9					
Rent Expense	4					
Insurance Expense	4					
Utilities Expense	3					
Depreciation Expense	2					
Supplies Expense	3					
Miscellaneous Expense	1					
	108	108				
Net income (loss)						

EX 4-24
Appendix: Financial statements from an end-of-period spreadsheet (work sheet)

✓ *Christina Keene, capital, July 31, 2008: $61*

Based upon the data in Exercise 4-23, prepare an income statement, statement of owner's equity, and balance sheet for Dakota Services Co.

EX 4-25
Appendix: Adjusting entries from an end-of-period spreadsheet (work sheet)

Based upon the data in Exercise 4-22, prepare the adjusting entries for Dakota Services Co.

EX 4-26
Appendix: Closing entries from an end-of-period spreadsheet (work sheet)

Based upon the data in Exercise 4-23, prepare the closing entries for Dakota Services Co.

Problems Series A

PR 4-1A
Financial statements and closing entries
objs. 1, 2, 3

Blink-On Company maintains and repairs warning lights, such as those found on radio towers and lighthouses. Blink-On Company prepared the end-of-period spreadsheet (work sheet) at the top of the following page at March 31, 2008, the end of the current fiscal year:

	A	B	C	D	E	F	G	H	I	J	K	
		Blink-On Company										
		End-of-Period Spreadsheet (Work Sheet)										
		For the Year Ended March 31, 2008										
		Unadjusted Trial Balance		Adjustments		Adjusted Trial Balance		Income Statement		Balance Sheet		
	Account Title	Dr.	Cr.	Dr.	Cr.	Dr.	Cr.	Dr.	Cr.	Dr.	Cr.	
1	Cash	6,300				6,300				6,300		1
2	Accounts Receivable	18,900		(a) 3,500		22,400				22,400		2
3	Prepaid Insurance	4,200			(b) 2,800	1,400				1,400		3
4	Supplies	2,730			(c) 1,600	1,130				1,130		4
5	Land	98,000				98,000				98,000		5
6	Building	140,000				140,000				140,000		6
7	Acc. Depr.—Building		100,300		(d) 1,400		101,700				101,700	7
8	Equipment	100,500				100,500				100,500		8
9	Acc. Depr.—Equipment		85,100		(e) 3,200		88,300				88,300	9
10	Accounts Payable		5,700				5,700				5,700	10
11	Unearned Rent		2,100	(g) 1,200			900				900	11
12	Amanda Ayers, Capital		78,100				78,100				78,100	12
13	Amanda Ayers, Drawing	5,600				5,600				5,600		13
14	Fees Revenue		253,700		(a) 3,500		257,200		257,200			14
15	Salaries & Wages Expense	102,500		(f) 1,800		104,300		104,300				15
16	Advertising Expense	21,700				21,700		21,700				16
17	Utilities Expense	11,400				11,400		11,400				17
18	Repairs Expense	8,850				8,850		8,850				18
19	Misc. Expense	4,320				4,320		4,320				19
20		525,000	525,000									20
21	Insurance Expense			(b) 2,800		2,800		2,800				21
22	Supplies Expense			(c) 1,600		1,600		1,000				22
23	Depr. Exp.—Building			(d) 1,400		1,400		1,400				23
24	Depr. Exp.—Equipment			(e) 3,200		3,200		3,200				24
25	Salaries & Wages Payable				(f) 1,800		1,800				1,800	25
26	Rent Revenue				(g) 1,200		1,200		1,200			26
27				15,500	15,500	534,900	534,900	159,570	258,400	375,330	276,500	27
28	Net Income							98,830			98,830	28
29								258,400	258,400	375,330	375,330	29

✓ 1. Net income: $98,830

Instructions
1. Prepare an income statement for the year ended March 31.
2. Prepare a statement of owner's equity for the year ended March 31. No additional investments were made during the year.
3. Prepare a balance sheet as of March 31.
4. Based upon the end-of-period spreadsheet (work sheet), journalize the closing entries.
5. Prepare a post-closing trial balance.

PR 4-2A
Financial statements and closing entries
objs. 2, 3

✓ 1. Stacey Vargas, capital, April 30: $152,800

The Nevus Company is an investigative services firm that is owned and operated by Stacey Vargas. On April 30, 2008, the end of the current fiscal year, the accountant for The Nevus Company prepared an end-of-period spreadsheet (work sheet), a part of which is shown at the top of the following page.

Instructions
1. Prepare an income statement, statement of owner's equity (no additional investments were made during the year), and a balance sheet.
2. Journalize the entries that were required to close the accounts at April 30.
3. If Stacey Vargas, Capital decreased $35,000 after the closing entries were posted, and the withdrawals remained the same, what was the amount of net income or net loss?

(continued)

	A		H	I	J	K	
	The Nevus Company						
	End-of-Period Spreadsheet (Work Sheet)						
	For the Year Ended April 30, 2008						
			Income Statement		Balance Sheet		
1	Cash				9,000		1
2	Accounts Receivable				37,200		2
3	Supplies				3,500		3
4	Prepaid Insurance				4,800		4
5	Equipment				169,500		5
6	Accumulated Depreciation—Equipment					55,200	6
7	Accounts Payable					10,500	7
8	Salaries Payable					2,500	8
9	Unearned Rent					3,000	9
10	Stacey Vargas, Capital					142,800	10
11	Stacey Vargas, Drawing				16,000		11
12	Service Fees			363,000			12
13	Rent Revenue			7,000			13
14	Salary Expense		270,000				14
15	Rent Expense		37,000				15
16	Supplies Expense		8,000				16
17	Depreciation Expense—Equipment		7,000				17
18	Utilities Expense		6,400				18
19	Repairs Expense		6,200				19
20	Insurance Expense		4,800				20
21	Miscellaneous Expense		4,600				21
22			344,000	370,000	240,000	214,000	22
23	Net income		26,000			26,000	23
24			370,000	370,000	240,000	240,000	24

PR 4-3A

T accounts, adjusting entries, financial statements, and closing entries; optional end-of-period spreadsheet (work sheet)

objs. 2, 3

✓ *2. Net income: $13,650*

The unadjusted trial balance of Iguana Laundromat at June 30, 2008, the end of the current fiscal year, is shown below.

Iguana Laundromat
Unadjusted Trial Balance
June 30, 2008

	Debit Balances	Credit Balances
Cash	5,500	
Laundry Supplies	9,450	
Prepaid Insurance	4,300	
Laundry Equipment	142,000	
Accumulated Depreciation		75,200
Accounts Payable		4,900
Scott Mathis, Capital		53,800
Scott Mathis, Drawing	4,200	
Laundry Revenue		116,100
Wages Expense	52,000	
Rent Expense	19,650	
Utilities Expense	10,200	
Miscellaneous Expense	2,700	
	250,000	250,000

The data needed to determine year-end adjustments are as follows:

a. Laundry supplies on hand at June 30 are $1,500.
b. Insurance premiums expired during the year are $3,200.
c. Depreciation of equipment during the year is $6,000.
d. Wages accrued but not paid at June 30 are $750.

Instructions

1. For each account listed in the unadjusted trial balance, enter the balance in a T account. Identify the balance as "June 30 Bal." In addition, add T accounts for Wages Payable, Depreciation Expense, Laundry Supplies Expense, Insurance Expense, and Income Summary.
2. **Optional:** Enter the unadjusted trial balance on an end-of-period spreadsheet (work sheet) and complete the spreadsheet. Add the accounts listed in part (1) as needed.
3. Journalize and post the adjusting entries. Identify the adjustments by "Adj." and the new balances as "Adj. Bal."
4. Prepare an adjusted trial balance.
5. Prepare an income statement, a statement of owner's equity (no additional investments were made during the year), and a balance sheet.
6. Journalize and post the closing entries. Identify the closing entries by "Clos."
7. Prepare a post-closing trial balance.

PR 4-4A
Ledger accounts, adjusting entries, financial statements, and closing entries; optional end-of-period spreadsheet (work sheet)

objs. 2, 3

✓ *4. Net income: $24,593*

If the working papers correlating with this textbook are not used, omit Problem 4-4A.

The ledger and trial balance of Wainscot Services Co. as of March 31, 2008, the end of the first month of its current fiscal year, are presented in the working papers.

Data needed to determine the necessary adjusting entries are as follows:

a. Service revenue accrued at March 31 is $1,750.
b. Supplies on hand at March 31 are $400.
c. Insurance premiums expired during March are $250.
d. Depreciation of the building during March is $400.
e. Depreciation of equipment during March is $200.
f. Unearned rent at March 31 is $1,000.
g. Wages accrued at March 31 are $500.

Instructions

1. **Optional:** Complete the end-of-period spreadsheet (work sheet) using the adjustment data shown above.
2. Journalize and post the adjusting entries, inserting balances in the accounts affected.
3. Prepare an adjusted trial balance.
4. Prepare an income statement, a statement of owner's equity, and a balance sheet.
5. Journalize and post the closing entries. Indicate closed accounts by inserting a line in both Balance columns opposite the closing entry. Insert the new balance of the capital account.
6. Prepare a post-closing trial balance.

PR 4-5A
Ledger accounts, adjusting entries, financial statements, and closing entries; optional spreadsheet (work sheet)

objs. 2, 3

✓ *5. Net income: $41,705*

The unadjusted trial balance of Quick Repairs at October 31, 2008, the end of the current year, is shown below.

	Quick Repairs Unadjusted Trial Balance October 31, 2008	Debit Balances	Credit Balances
11	Cash	2,950	
13	Supplies	12,295	
14	Prepaid Insurance	2,735	
16	Equipment	95,650	
17	Accumulated Depreciation—Equipment		21,209
18	Trucks	36,300	
19	Accumulated Depreciation—Trucks		7,400
21	Accounts Payable		4,015
31	Rhonda Salter, Capital		67,426
32	Rhonda Salter, Drawing	6,000	
41	Service Revenue		99,950
51	Wages Expense	26,925	
53	Rent Expense	9,600	
55	Truck Expense	5,350	
59	Miscellaneous Expense	2,195	
		200,000	200,000

The data needed to determine year-end adjustments are as follows:

a. Supplies on hand at October 31 are $7,120.
b. Insurance premiums expired during year are $2,000.
c. Depreciation of equipment during year is $4,200.
d. Depreciation of trucks during year is $2,200.
e. Wages accrued but not paid at October 31 are $600.

Instructions
1. For each account listed in the trial balance, enter the balance in the appropriate Balance column of a four-column account and place a check mark (✓) in the Posting Reference column.
2. **Optional:** Enter the unadjusted trial balance on an end-of-period spreadsheet (work sheet) and complete the spreadsheet. Add the accounts listed in part (3) as needed.
3. Journalize and post the adjusting entries, inserting balances in the accounts affected. The following additional accounts from Quick Repair's chart of accounts should be used: Wages Payable, 22; Supplies Expense, 52; Depreciation Expense—Equipment, 54; Depreciation Expense—Trucks, 56; Insurance Expense, 57.
4. Prepare an adjusted trial balance.
5. Prepare an income statement, a statement of owner's equity (no additional investments were made during the year), and a balance sheet.
6. Journalize and post the closing entries. (Income Summary is account #33 in the chart of accounts.) Indicate closed accounts by inserting a line in both Balance columns opposite the closing entry.
7. Prepare a post-closing trial balance.

PR 4-6A
Complete accounting cycle

objs. 4, 5, 6

✓8. Net income: $17,250

For the past several years, Dawn Lytle has operated a part-time consulting business from her home. As of October 1, 2008, Dawn decided to move to rented quarters and to operate the business, which was to be known as Sky's-The-Limit Consulting, on a full-time basis. Sky's-The-Limit Consulting entered into the following transactions during October:

Oct. 1. The following assets were received from Dawn Lytle: cash, $12,950; accounts receivable, $2,800; supplies, $1,500; and office equipment, $18,750. There were no liabilities received.
1. Paid three months' rent on a lease rental contract, $3,600.
2. Paid the premiums on property and casualty insurance policies, $2,400.
4. Received cash from clients as an advance payment for services to be provided and recorded it as unearned fees, $4,150.
5. Purchased additional office equipment on account from Office Station Co., $2,500.
6. Received cash from clients on account, $1,900.
10. Paid cash for a newspaper advertisement, $325.
12. Paid Office Station Co. for part of the debt incurred on October 5, $1,250.
12. Recorded services provided on account for the period October 1–12, $3,750.
14. Paid part-time receptionist for two weeks' salary, $750.
17. Recorded cash from cash clients for fees earned during the period October 1–17, $6,250.
18. Paid cash for supplies, $600.
20. Recorded services provided on account for the period October 13–20, $2,100.
24. Recorded cash from cash clients for fees earned for the period October 17–24, $3,850.
26. Received cash from clients on account, $4,450.
27. Paid part-time receptionist for two weeks' salary, $750.
29. Paid telephone bill for October, $250.
31. Paid electricity bill for October, $300.
31. Recorded cash from cash clients for fees earned for the period October 25–31, $2,975.
31. Recorded services provided on account for the remainder of October, $1,500.
31. Dawn withdrew $5,000 for personal use.

Instructions
1. Journalize each transaction in a two-column journal, referring to the following chart of accounts in selecting the accounts to be debited and credited. (Do not insert the account numbers in the journal at this time.)

11	Cash	31	Dawn Lytle, Capital
12	Accounts Receivable	32	Dawn Lytle, Drawing
14	Supplies	41	Fees Earned
15	Prepaid Rent	51	Salary Expense
16	Prepaid Insurance	52	Rent Expense
18	Office Equipment	53	Supplies Expense
19	Accumulated Depreciation	54	Depreciation Expense
21	Accounts Payable	55	Insurance Expense
22	Salaries Payable	59	Miscellaneous Expense
23	Unearned Fees		

2. Post the journal to a ledger of four-column accounts.
3. Prepare an unadjusted trial balance.
4. At the end of October, the following adjustment data were assembled. Analyze and use these data to complete parts (5) and (6).
   a. Insurance expired during October is $200.
   b. Supplies on hand on October 31 are $875.
   c. Depreciation of office equipment for October is $675.
   d. Accrued receptionist salary on October 31 is $150.
   e. Rent expired during October is $1,550.
   f. Unearned fees on October 31 are $1,150.
5. **Optional:** Enter the unadjusted trial balance on an end-of-period spreadsheet (work sheet) and complete the spreadsheet.
6. Journalize and post the adjusting entries.
7. Prepare an adjusted trial balance.
8. Prepare an income statement, a statement of owner's equity, and a balance sheet.
9. Prepare and post the closing entries. (Income Summary is account #33 in the chart of accounts.) Indicate closed accounts by inserting a line in both the Balance columns opposite the closing entry.
10. Prepare a post-closing trial balance.

Problems Series B

PR 4-1B
Financial statements and closing entries
objs. 1, 2, 3

✓1. Net loss: $10,900

Last-Chance Company offers legal consulting advice to prison inmates. Last-Chance Company prepared the end-of-period spreadsheet (work sheet) at the top of the following page at November 30, 2008, the end of the current fiscal year.

Instructions
1. Prepare an income statement for the year ended November 30.
2. Prepare a statement of owner's equity for the year ended November 30. No additional investments were made during the year.
3. Prepare a balance sheet as of November 30.
4. On the basis of the end-of-period spreadsheet (work sheet), journalize the closing entries.
5. Prepare a post-closing trial balance.

	A	B	C	D	E	F	G	H	I	J	K	
		\multicolumn{10}{c}{**Last-Chance Company**}									
		\multicolumn{10}{c}{**End-of-Period Spreadsheet (Work Sheet)**}									
		\multicolumn{10}{c}{**For the Year Ended November 30, 2008**}									
		Unadjusted Trial Balance		Adjustments		Adjusted Trial Balance		Income Statement		Balance Sheet		
	Account Title	Dr.	Cr.	Dr.	Cr.	Dr.	Cr.	Dr.	Cr.	Dr.	Cr.	
1	Cash	4,800				4,800				4,800		1
2	Accounts Receivable	15,750		(a) 4,200		19,950				19,950		2
3	Prepaid Insurance	2,700			(b) 1,450	1,250				1,250		3
4	Supplies	2,025			(c) 1,525	500				500		4
5	Land	75,000				75,000				75,000		5
6	Building	205,000				205,000				205,000		6
7	Acc. Depr.—Building		76,000		(d) 2,000		78,000				78,000	7
8	Equipment	139,000				139,000				139,000		8
9	Acc. Depr.—Equipment		54,450		(e) 5,200		59,650				59,650	9
10	Accounts Payable		9,750				9,750				9,750	10
11	Unearned Rent		4,500	(g) 2,000			2,500				2,500	11
12	Corey Evans, Capital		318,800				318,800				318,800	12
13	Corey Evans, Drawing	15,000				15,000				15,000		13
14	Fees Revenue		286,500		(a) 4,200		290,700		290,700			14
15	Salaries & Wages Expense	144,300		(f) 2,700		147,000		147,000				15
16	Advertising Expense	94,800				94,800		94,800				16
17	Utilities Expense	27,000				27,000		27,000				17
18	Travel Expense	18,750				18,750		18,750				18
19	Misc. Expense	5,875				5,875		5,875				19
20		750,000	750,000									20
21	Insurance Expense			(b) 1,450		1,450		1,450				21
22	Supplies Expense			(c) 1,525		1,525		1,525				22
23	Depr. Exp.—Building			(d) 2,000		2,000		2,000				23
24	Depr. Exp.—Equipment			(e) 5,200		5,200		5,200				24
25	Sal. & Wages Payable				(f) 2,700		2,700				2,700	25
26	Rent Revenue				(g) 2,000		2,000		2,000			26
27				19,075	19,075	764,100	764,100	303,600	292,700	460,500	471,400	27
28	Net loss								10,900	10,900		28
29								303,600	303,600	471,400	471,400	29

PR 4-2B

Financial statements and closing entries

objs. 2, 3

✓1. Chad Tillman, capital, July 31: $492,000

The Ultra Services Company is a financial planning services firm owned and operated by Chad Tillman. As of July 31, 2008, the end of the current fiscal year, the accountant for The Ultra Services Company prepared an end-of-period spreadsheet (work sheet), part of which is shown at the top of the next page.

Instructions

1. Prepare an income statement, a statement of owner's equity (no additional investments were made during the year), and a balance sheet.
2. Journalize the entries that were required to close the accounts at July 31.
3. If the balance of Chad Tillman, Capital decreased $40,000 after the closing entries were posted, and the withdrawals remained the same, what was the amount of net income or net loss?

	A	H	I	J	K	
	The Ultra Services Company					
	End-of-Period Spreadsheet (Work Sheet)					
	For the Year Ended July 31, 2008					
		Income Statement		**Balance Sheet**		
1	Cash			13,950		1
2	Accounts Receivable			41,880		2
3	Supplies			8,400		3
4	Prepaid Insurance			7,500		4
5	Land			180,000		5
6	Buildings			360,000		6
7	Accumulated Depreciation—Buildings				217,200	7
8	Equipment			258,270		8
9	Accumulated Depreciation—Equipment				122,700	9
10	Accounts Payable				33,300	10
11	Salaries Payable				3,300	11
12	Unearned Rent				1,500	12
13	Chad Tillman, Capital				340,500	13
14	Chad Tillman, Drawing			30,000		14
15	Service Fees		525,000			15
16	Rent Revenue		4,500			16
17	Salary Expense	219,000				17
18	Depreciation Expense—Equipment	28,500				18
19	Rent Expense	25,500				19
20	Supplies Expense	22,950				20
21	Utilities Expense	15,900				21
22	Depreciation Expense—Buildings	15,600				22
23	Repairs Expense	12,450				23
24	Insurance Expense	3,000				24
25	Miscellaneous Expense	5,100				25
26		348,000	529,500	900,000	718,500	26
27	Net income	181,500			181,500	27
28		529,500	529,500	900,000	900,000	28

PR 4-3B

T accounts, adjusting entries, financial statements, and closing entries; optional end-of-period spreadsheet (work sheet).

objs. **2, 3**

✓ *2. Net income: $12,300*

The unadjusted trial balance of Best Laundry at March 31, 2008, the end of the current fiscal year, is shown below.

Best Laundry
Unadjusted Trial Balance
March 31, 2008

	Debit Balances	Credit Balances
Cash	1,450	
Laundry Supplies	3,750	
Prepaid Insurance	2,400	
Laundry Equipment	54,500	
Accumulated Depreciation		20,500
Accounts Payable		3,100
Ryan Boyle, Capital		18,900
Ryan Boyle, Drawing	1,000	
Laundry Revenue		82,500
Wages Expense	35,750	
Rent Expense	18,000	
Utilities Expense	6,800	
Miscellaneous Expense	1,350	
	125,000	125,000

The data needed to determine year-end adjustments are as follows:

a. Laundry supplies on hand at March 31 are $950.
b. Insurance premiums expired during the year are $2,000.
c. Depreciation of equipment during the year is $2,900.
d. Wages accrued but not paid at March 31 are $600.

Instructions

1. For each account listed in the unadjusted trial balance, enter the balance in a T account. Identify the balance as "Mar. 31 Bal." In addition, add T accounts for Wages Payable, Depreciation Expense, Laundry Supplies Expense, Insurance Expense, and Income Summary.
2. **Optional:** Enter the unadjusted trial balance on an end-of-period spreadsheet (work sheet) and complete the spreadsheet. Add the accounts listed in Part (1) as needed.
3. Journalize and post the adjusting entries. Identify the adjustments by "Adj." and the new balances as "Adj. Bal."
4. Prepare an adjusted trial balance.
5. Prepare an income statement, a statement of owner's equity (no additional investments were made during the year), and a balance sheet.
6. Journalize and post the closing entries. Identify the closing entries by "Clos."
7. Prepare a post-closing trial balance.

PR 4-4B
Ledger accounts, adjusting entries, financial statements, and closing entries; optional end-of-period spreadsheet (work sheet)

objs. 2, 3

✓ *4. Net income: $23,818*

If the working papers correlating with this textbook are not used, omit Problem 4-4B.

The ledger and trial balance of Wainscot Services Co. as of March 31, 2008, the end of the first month of its current fiscal year, are presented in the working papers.

Data needed to determine the necessary adjusting entries are as follows:

a. Service revenue accrued at March 31 is $2,000.
b. Supplies on hand at March 31 are $400.
c. Insurance premiums expired during March are $150.
d. Depreciation of the building during March is $625.
e. Depreciation of equipment during March is $200.
f. Unearned rent at March 31 is $1,800.
g. Wages accrued but not paid at March 31 are $600.

Instructions

1. **Optional:** Complete the end-of-period spreadsheet (work sheet) using the adjustment data shown above.
2. Journalize and post the adjusting entries, inserting balances in the accounts affected.
3. Prepare an adjusted trial balance.
4. Prepare an income statement, a statement of owner's equity, and a balance sheet.
5. Journalize and post the closing entries. Indicate closed accounts by inserting a line in both Balance columns opposite the closing entry. Insert the new balance of the capital account.
6. Prepare a post-closing trial balance.

PR 4-5B
Ledger accounts, adjusting entries, financial statements, and closing entries; optional end-of-period spreadsheet (work sheet).

objs. 2, 3

✓ *5. Net income: $30,175*

The unadjusted trial balance of Reliable Repairs at December 31, 2008, the end of the current year, is shown at the top of the next page. The data needed to determine year-end adjustments are as follows:

a. Supplies on hand at December 31 are $6,500.
b. Insurance premiums expired during the year are $2,500.
c. Depreciation of equipment during the year is $4,800.
d. Depreciation of trucks during the year is $3,500.
e. Wages accrued but not paid at December 31 are $1,000.

Reliable Repairs
Unadjusted Trial Balance
December 31, 2008

		Debit Balances	Credit Balances
11	Cash	2,825	
13	Supplies	10,820	
14	Prepaid Insurance	7,500	
16	Equipment	54,200	
17	Accumulated Depreciation—Equipment		12,050
18	Trucks	50,000	
19	Accumulated Depreciation—Trucks		27,100
21	Accounts Payable		12,015
31	Lee Mendoza, Capital		32,885
32	Lee Mendoza, Drawing	5,000	
41	Service Revenue		90,950
51	Wages Expense	28,010	
53	Rent Expense	8,100	
55	Truck Expense	6,350	
59	Miscellaneous Expense	2,195	
		175,000	175,000

Instructions

1. For each account listed in the unadjusted trial balance, enter the balance in the appropriate Balance column of a four-column account and place a check mark (✓) in the Posting Reference column.
2. **Optional:** Enter the unadjusted trial balance on an end-of-period spreadsheet (work sheet) and complete the spreadsheet. Add the accounts listed in part (3) as needed.
3. Journalize and post the adjusting entries, inserting balances in the accounts affected. The following additional accounts from Reliable's chart of accounts should be used: Wages Payable, 22; Supplies Expense, 52; Depreciation Expense—Equipment, 54; Depreciation Expense—Trucks, 56; Insurance Expense, 57.
4. Prepare an adjusted trial balance.
5. Prepare an income statement, a statement of owner's equity (no additional investments were made during the year), and a balance sheet.
6. Journalize and post the closing entries. (Income Summary is account #33 in the chart of accounts.) Indicate closed accounts by inserting a line in both Balance columns opposite the closing entry.
7. Prepare a post-closing trial balance.

PR 4-6B
Complete accounting cycle
objs. 4, 5, 6

✓ 8. Net income: $10,980

For the past several years, Derrick Epstein has operated a part-time consulting business from his home. As of June 1, 2008, Derrick decided to move to rented quarters and to operate the business, which was to be known as Luminary Consulting, on a full-time basis. Luminary Consulting entered into the following transactions during June:

June 1. The following assets were received from Derrick Epstein: cash, $26,200; accounts receivable, $6,000; supplies, $2,800; and office equipment, $25,000. There were no liabilities received.
　　　1. Paid three months' rent on a lease rental contract, $5,250.
　　　2. Paid the premiums on property and casualty insurance policies, $2,100.
　　　4. Received cash from clients as an advance payment for services to be provided and recorded it as unearned fees, $2,700.
　　　5. Purchased additional office equipment on account from Office Station Co., $5,000.
　　　6. Received cash from clients on account, $3,000.
　　10. Paid cash for a newspaper advertisement, $200.
　　12. Paid Office Station Co. for part of the debt incurred on June 5, $1,000.
　　12. Recorded services provided on account for the period June 1–12, $5,100.
　　14. Paid part-time receptionist for two weeks' salary, $800.
　　17. Recorded cash from cash clients for fees earned during the period June 1–16, $3,500.

(continued)

June 18. Paid cash for supplies, $750.
      20. Recorded services provided on account for the period June 13–20, $1,100.
      24. Recorded cash from cash clients for fees earned for the period June 17–24, $4,150.
      26. Received cash from clients on account, $4,900.
      27. Paid part-time receptionist for two weeks' salary, $800.
      29. Paid telephone bill for June, $150.
      30. Paid electricity bill for June, $400.
      30. Recorded cash from cash clients for fees earned for the period June 25–30, $1,500.
      30. Recorded services provided on account for the remainder of June, $1,000.
      30. Derrick withdrew $8,000 for personal use.

Instructions

1. Journalize each transaction in a two-column journal, referring to the following chart of accounts in selecting the accounts to be debited and credited. (Do not insert the account numbers in the journal at this time.)

11	Cash	
12	Accounts Receivable	
14	Supplies	
15	Prepaid Rent	
16	Prepaid Insurance	
18	Office Equipment	
19	Accumulated Depreciation	
21	Accounts Payable	
22	Salaries Payable	
23	Unearned Fees	

31	Derrick Epstein, Capital
32	Derrick Epstein, Drawing
41	Fees Earned
51	Salary Expense
52	Rent Expense
53	Supplies Expense
54	Depreciation Expense
55	Insurance Expense
59	Miscellaneous Expense

2. Post the journal to a ledger of four-column accounts.
3. Prepare an unadjusted trial balance.
4. At the end of June, the following adjustment data were assembled. Analyze and use these data to complete parts (5) and (6).
   a. Insurance expired during June is $175.
   b. Supplies on hand on June 30 are $2,000.
   c. Depreciation of office equipment for June is $500.
   d. Accrued receptionist salary on June 30 is $120.
   e. Rent expired during June is $1,500.
   f. Unearned fees on June 30 are $1,875.
5. **Optional:** Enter the unadjusted trial balance on an end-of-period spreadsheet (work sheet) and complete the spreadsheet.
6. Journalize and post the adjusting entries.
7. Prepare an adjusted trial balance.
8. Prepare an income statement, a statement of owner's equity, and a balance sheet.
9. Prepare and post the closing entries. (Income Summary is account #33 in the chart of accounts.) Indicate closed accounts by inserting a line in both the Balance columns opposite the closing entry.
10. Prepare a post-closing trial balance.

Continuing Problem

The unadjusted trial balance of Dancin Music as of May 31, 2008, along with the adjustment data for the two months ended May 31, 2008, are shown in Chapter 3.
      Based upon the adjustment data, the adjusted trial balance shown at the top of the following page was prepared.

Instructions

1. **Optional.** Using the data from Chapter 3, prepare an end-of-period spreadsheet (work sheet).
2. Prepare an income statement, a statement of owner's equity, and a balance sheet. (*Note:* Kris Payne made investments in Dancin Music on April 1 and May 1, 2008.)

✓2. Net income: $4,925

Dancin Music
Adjusted Trial Balance
May 31, 2008

	Debit Balances	Credit Balances
Cash	12,085	
Accounts Receivable	4,250	
Supplies	160	
Prepaid Insurance	3,080	
Office Equipment	5,000	
Accumulated Depreciation—Office Equipment		100
Accounts Payable		5,750
Wages Payable		200
Unearned Revenue		2,400
Kris Payne, Capital		12,500
Kris Payne, Drawing	1,300	
Fees Earned		18,550
Wages Expense	2,600	
Office Rent Expense	2,600	
Equipment Rent Expense	1,300	
Utilities Expense	910	
Music Expense	2,565	
Advertising Expense	1,730	
Supplies Expense	940	
Insurance Expense	280	
Depreciation Expense	100	
Miscellaneous Expense	600	
	39,500	39,500

3. Journalize and post the closing entries. The income summary account is #33 in the ledger of Dancin Music. Indicate closed accounts by inserting a line in both Balance columns opposite the closing entry.
4. Prepare a post-closing trial balance.

Comprehensive Problem 1

✓ *8. Net income, $22,160*

Kelly Pitney began her consulting business, Kelly Consulting, on April 1, 2008. The accounting cycle for Kelly Consulting for April, including financial statements, was illustrated on pages 161–174. During May, Kelly Consulting entered into the following transactions:

May 3. Received cash from clients as an advance payment for services to be provided and recorded it as unearned fees, $1,550.
  5. Received cash from clients on account, $1,750.
  9. Paid cash for a newspaper advertisement, $100.
  13. Paid Office Station Co. for part of the debt incurred on April 5, $400.
  15. Recorded services provided on account for the period May 1–15, $5,100.
  16. Paid part-time receptionist for two weeks' salary including the amount owed on April 30, $750.
  17. Recorded cash from cash clients for fees earned during the period May 1–16, $7,380.
  20. Purchased supplies on account, $500.
  21. Recorded services provided on account for the period May 16–20, $2,900.
  25. Recorded cash from cash clients for fees earned for the period May 17–23, $4,200.
  27. Received cash from clients on account, $6,600.
  28. Paid part-time receptionist for two weeks' salary, $750.
  30. Paid telephone bill for May, $150.
  31. Paid electricity bill for May, $225.
  31. Recorded cash from cash clients for fees earned for the period May 26–31, $2,875.
  31. Recorded services provided on account for the remainder of May, $2,200.
  31. Kelly withdrew $7,500 for personal use.

Instructions

1. The chart of accounts for Kelly Consulting is shown on page 163, and the post-closing trial balance as of April 30, 2008, is shown on page 169. For each account in the post-closing trial balance, enter the balance in the appropriate Balance column of a four-column account. Date the balances May 1, 2008, and place a check mark (✓) in the Post Reference column. Journalize each of the May transactions in a two-column journal using Kelly Consulting's chart of accounts. (Do not insert the account numbers in the journal at this time.)

2. Post the journal to a ledger of four-column accounts.

3. Prepare an unadjusted trial balance.

4. At the end of May, the following adjustment data were assembled. Analyze and use these data to complete parts (5) and (6).
   a.   Insurance expired during May is $300.
   b.   Supplies on hand on May 31 are $950.
   c.   Depreciation of office equipment for May is $330.
   d.   Accrued receptionist salary on May 31 is $260.
   e.   Rent expired during May is $1,600.
   f.   Unearned fees on May 31 are $1,300.

5. **Optional:** Enter the unadjusted trial balance on an end-of-period spreadsheet (work sheet) and complete the spreadsheet.

6. Journalize and post the adjusting entries.

7. Prepare an adjusted trial balance.

8. Prepare an income statement, a statement of owner's equity, and a balance sheet.

9. Prepare and post the closing entries. (Income Summary is account #33 in the chart of accounts.) Indicate closed accounts by inserting a line in both the Balance columns opposite the closing entry.

10. Prepare a post-closing trial balance.

Special Activities

SA 4-1
Ethics and professional conduct in business

ETHICS

Fantasy Graphics is a graphics arts design consulting firm. Terri Bierman, its treasurer and vice president of finance, has prepared a classified balance sheet as of January 31, 2008, the end of its fiscal year. This balance sheet will be submitted with Fantasy Graphics' loan application to Booneville Trust & Savings Bank.

In the Current Assets section of the balance sheet, Terri reported a $100,000 receivable from Kent Miles, the president of Fantasy Graphics, as a trade account receivable. Kent borrowed the money from Fantasy Graphics in November 2006 for a down payment on a new home. He has orally assured Terri that he will pay off the account receivable within the next year. Terri reported the $100,000 in the same manner on the preceding year's balance sheet.

▶ Evaluate whether it is acceptable for Terri Bierman to prepare the January 31, 2008, balance sheet in the manner indicated above.

SA 4-2
Financial statements

The following is an excerpt from a telephone conversation between Jan Young, president of Cupboard Supplies Co., and Steve Nisbet, owner of Nisbet Employment Co.

Jan: Steve, you're going to have to do a better job of finding me a new computer programmer. That last guy was great at programming, but he didn't have any common sense.

Steve: What do you mean? The guy had a master's degree with straight A's.

Jan: Yes, well, last month he developed a new financial reporting system. He said we could do away with manually preparing an end-of-period spreadsheet (work sheet) and financial statements. The computer would automatically generate our financial statements with "a push of a button."

Steve: So what's the big deal? Sounds to me like it would save you time and effort.

Jan: Right! The balance sheet showed a minus for supplies!

Steve: Minus supplies? How can that be?

Jan: That's what I asked.

Steve: So, what did he say?

Jan: Well, after he checked the program, he said that it must be right. The minuses were greater than the pluses. . . .

Steve: Didn't he know that Supplies can't have a credit balance—it must have a debit balance?

Jan: He asked me what a debit and credit were.

Steve: I see your point.

1. **━━▶** Comment on (a) the desirability of computerizing Cupboard Supplies Co.'s financial reporting system, (b) the elimination of the end-of-period spreadsheet (work sheet) in a computerized accounting system, and (c) the computer programmer's lack of accounting knowledge.

2. **━━▶** Explain to the programmer why Supplies could not have a credit balance.

SA 4-3
Financial statements

Assume that you recently accepted a position with the First Security Bank as an assistant loan officer. As one of your first duties, you have been assigned the responsibility of evaluating a loan request for $80,000 from DiamondJewelry.com, a small proprietorship. In support of the loan application, Marion Zastrow, owner, submitted a "Statement of Accounts" (trial balance) for the first year of operations ended December 31, 2008.

DiamondJewelry.com
Statement of Accounts
December 31, 2008

Cash	2,050	
Billings Due from Others	15,070	
Supplies (chemicals, etc.)	7,470	
Trucks	26,370	
Equipment	8,090	
Amounts Owed to Others		2,850
Investment in Business		23,500
Service Revenue		73,650
Wages Expense	30,050	
Utilities Expense	7,330	
Rent Expense	2,400	
Insurance Expense	700	
Other Expenses	470	
	100,000	100,000

1. **━━▶** Explain to Marion Zastrow why a set of financial statements (income statement, statement of owner's equity, and balance sheet) would be useful to you in evaluating the loan request.

2. In discussing the "Statement of Accounts" with Marion Zastrow, you discovered that the accounts had not been adjusted at December 31. Analyze the "Statement of Accounts" and indicate possible adjusting entries that might be necessary before an accurate set of financial statements could be prepared.

3. **━━▶** Assuming that an accurate set of financial statements will be submitted by Marion Zastrow in a few days, what other considerations or information would you require before making a decision on the loan request?

SA 4-4
Compare balance sheets

Group Project

Internet Project

In groups of three or four, compare the balance sheets of two different companies, and present to the class a summary of the similarities and differences of the two companies. You may obtain the balance sheets you need from one of the following sources:

1. Your school or local library.
2. The investor relations department of each company.
3. The company's Web site on the Internet.
4. EDGAR (Electronic Data Gathering, Analysis, and Retrieval), the electronic archives of financial statements filed with the Securities and Exchange Commission.

SEC documents can be retrieved using the EdgarScan™ service from Pricewaterhouse-Coopers at **http://edgarscan.pwcglobal.com**. To obtain annual report information, key in a company name in the appropriate space. EdgarScan will list the reports available to you for the company you've selected. Select the most recent annual report filing, identified as a 10-K or 10-K405. EdgarScan provides an outline of the report, including the separate financial statements, which can also be selected in an Excel® spreadsheet.

Answers to Self-Examination Questions

1. **C** The drawing account, M. E. Jones, Drawing (answer C), would be extended to the Balance Sheet columns of the work sheet. Utilities Expense (answer A), Rent Revenue (answer B), and Miscellaneous Expense (answer D) would all be extended to the Income Statement columns of the work sheet.

2. **D** Cash or other assets that are expected to be converted to cash or sold or used up within one year or less, through the normal operations of the business, are classified as current assets on the balance sheet. Accounts Receivable (answer D) is a current asset, since it will normally be converted to cash within one year. Office Equipment (answer A), Land (answer B), and Accumulated Depreciation (answer C) are all reported in the property, plant, and equipment section of the balance sheet.

3. **B** The entry to close the owner's drawing account is to debit the owner's capital account and credit the drawing account (answer B).

4. **D** Since all revenue and expense accounts are closed at the end of the period, Fees Earned (answer A), Wages Expense (answer B), and Rent Expense (answer C) would all be closed to Income Summary. Accumulated Depreciation (answer D) is a contra asset account that is not closed.

5. **B** Since the post-closing trial balance includes only balance sheet accounts (all of the revenue, expense, and drawing accounts are closed), Cash (answer A), Accumulated Depreciation (answer C), and J. C. Smith, Capital (answer D) would appear on the post-closing trial balance. Fees Earned (answer B) is a temporary account that is closed prior to preparing the post-closing trial balance.

Accounting Systems

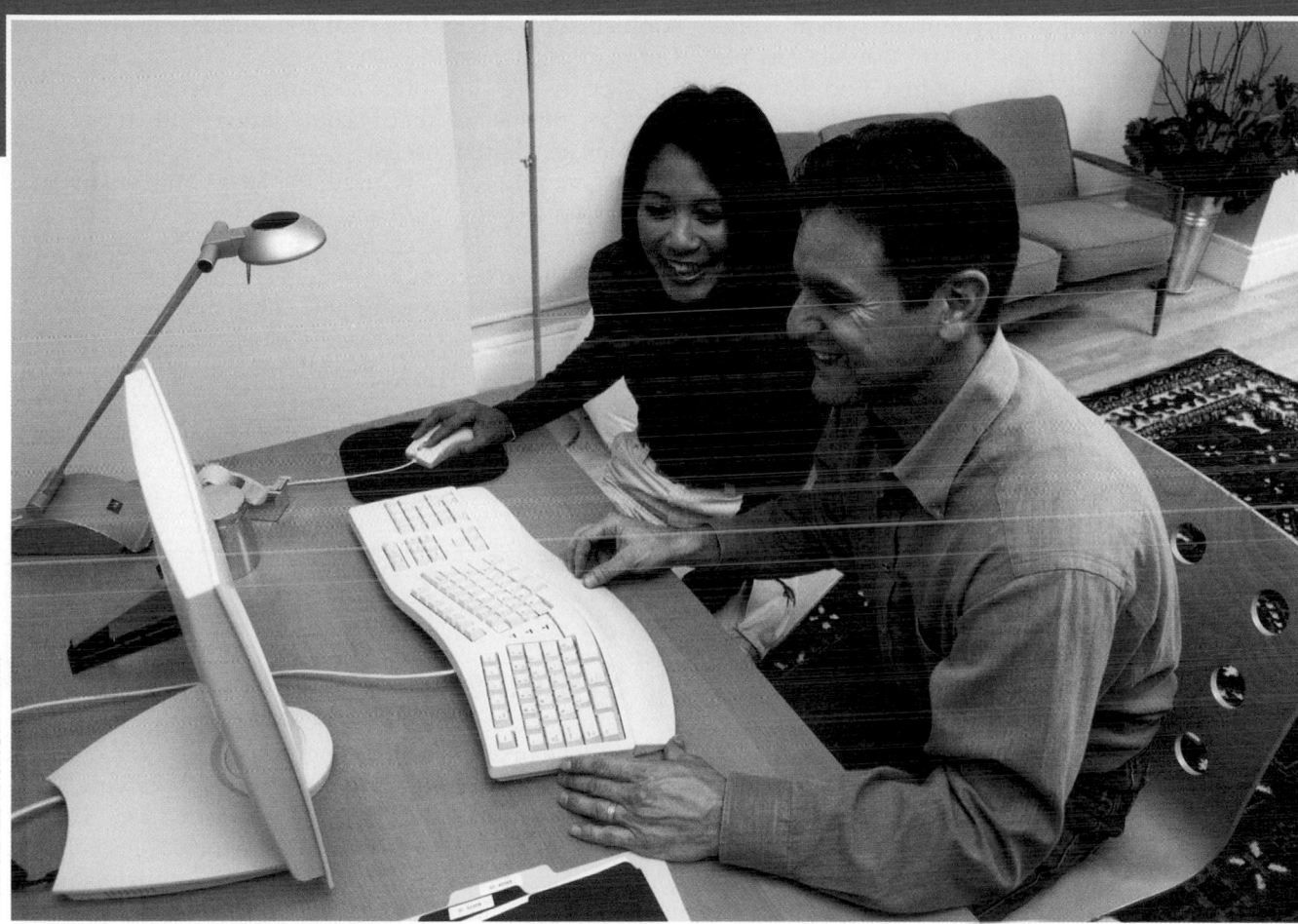

© ADAM CROWLEY/PHOTODISC/GETTY IMAGES

objectives

After studying this chapter, you should be able to:

1 Define an accounting system and describe its implementation.

2 Journalize and post transactions in a manual accounting system that uses subsidiary ledgers and special journals.

3 Describe and give examples of additional subsidiary ledgers and modified special journals.

4 Apply computerized accounting to the revenue and collection cycle.

5 Describe the basic features of e-commerce.

Intuit Inc.

Whether you realize it or not, you likely interact with accounting systems. For example, your checkbook register is a type of accounting system. When you make a deposit, you record an addition to your cash; when you write a check, you record a reduction in your cash. Such a simple accounting system works well for a person with just a few transactions per month. However, over time, you may find that your financial affairs will become more complex and involve many different types of transactions, including investments and loan payments. At this point, a simple checkbook register may not be sufficient for managing your financial affairs. Personal financial planning software, such as Intuit's Quicken®, can be useful when your financial affairs reach this level of complexity.

What happens if you decide to begin a small business? Now the transactions occurring every month have expanded and involve customers, vendors, and employees. As a result, the accounting system will need to grow with this complexity. Thus, many small businesses will use small-business accounting software, such as Intuit's QuickBooks®, as their first accounting system. As a business grows, more sophisticated accounting systems will be needed. Companies such as SAP, Oracle, NetSuite Inc., and Sage Software, Inc. offer accounting system solutions for businesses that become larger with more complex accounting needs.

Accounting systems used by large and small businesses employ the basic principles of the accounting cycle discussed in the previous chapters. However, these accounting systems include features that simplify the recording and summary process. In this chapter, we will discuss these simplifying procedures as they apply to both manual and computerized environments.

Basic Accounting Systems

objective *1*

Define an accounting system and describe its implementation.

@netsolutions

In the four previous chapters, we developed an accounting system for NetSolutions. An **accounting system** is the methods and procedures for collecting, classifying, summarizing, and reporting a business's financial and operating information. The accounting system for most businesses, however, is more complex than NetSolutions'. Accounting systems for large businesses must be able to collect, accumulate, and report many types of transactions. For example, American Airlines' accounting system collects and maintains information on ticket reservations, credit card collections, aircraft maintenance, employee hours, frequent-flier mileage balances, fuel consumption, and travel agent commissions, just to name a few. As you might expect, American Airlines' accounting system has evolved as the company has grown.

Accounting systems evolve through a three-step process as a business grows and changes. The first step in this process is *analysis*, which consists of (1) identifying the needs of those who use the business's financial information and (2) determining how the system should provide this information. For NetSolutions, we determined that Chris Clark would need financial statements for the new business. In the second step, the system is *designed* so that it will meet the users' needs. For NetSolutions, a very basic manual system was designed. This system included a chart of accounts, a two-column journal, and a general ledger. Finally, the system is *implemented* and used. For NetSolutions, the system was used to record transactions and prepare financial statements.

Once a system has been implemented, *feedback*, or input, from the users of the information can be used to analyze and improve the system. For example, in later chapters we will see that NetSolutions will expand its chart of accounts as it becomes a more complex business.

Internal controls and information processing methods are essential in an accounting system. **Internal controls** are the policies and procedures that protect assets from misuse, ensure that business information is accurate, and ensure that laws and regulations are being followed. We will discuss internal controls in more detail in Chapter 8. *Processing methods* are the means by which the system collects, summarizes, and reports accounting information. These methods may be either *manual* or *computerized*. In the following sections, we will first discuss manual accounting systems that use special journals and then computerized accounting systems.

Manual Accounting Systems

objective **2**

Journalize and post transactions in a manual accounting system that uses subsidiary ledgers and special journals.

Accounting systems may be either manual or computerized. Understanding a manual accounting system assists in recognizing the relationships between accounting data and accounting reports. In addition, most computerized systems use principles used in a manual system. Therefore, we illustrate the manual system first.

In preceding chapters, all transactions for NetSolutions were manually recorded in an all-purpose (two-column) journal. The journal entries were then posted individually to the accounts in the ledger. Such manual accounting systems are simple to use and easy to understand. Manually kept records may serve a business reasonably well when the amount of data collected, stored, and used is relatively small. For a large business, such manual processing is too costly and time consuming; thus, a computerized system is preferred. For example, a large company such as Verizon Communications has millions of telephone fees earned on account with millions of customers daily. Each telephone fee on account requires an entry debiting Accounts Receivable and crediting Fees Earned. In addition, a record of each customer's receivable must be kept. Clearly, a simple manual system would not serve the business needs of Verizon Communications.

When a business has a large number of similar transactions, using an all-purpose journal is inefficient and impractical. In such cases, subsidiary ledgers and special journals are useful. As a business becomes more complex, the manual system can be supplemented or replaced by a computerized system. Although we will illustrate the manual use of subsidiary ledgers and special journals, the basic principles described in the following paragraphs also apply to a computerized accounting system.

SUBSIDIARY LEDGERS

An accounting system should be designed to provide information on the amounts due from various customers (accounts receivable) and amounts owed to various creditors (accounts payable). A separate account for each customer and creditor could be added to the ledger. However, as the number of customers and creditors increases, the ledger becomes awkward to use when it includes many customers and creditors.

A large number of individual accounts with a common characteristic can be grouped together in a separate ledger called a **subsidiary ledger**. The primary ledger, which contains all of the balance sheet and income statement accounts, is then called the **general ledger**. Each subsidiary ledger is represented in the general ledger by a summarizing account, called a **controlling account**. The sum of the balances of the accounts in a subsidiary ledger must equal the balance of the related controlling account. Thus, you may think of a subsidiary ledger as a secondary ledger that supports a controlling account in the general ledger.

The individual accounts with customers are arranged in alphabetical order in a subsidiary ledger called the **accounts receivable subsidiary ledger**, or *customers ledger*. The controlling account in the general ledger that summarizes the debits and credits to the individual customer accounts is *Accounts Receivable*. The individual accounts with creditors are arranged in alphabetical order in a subsidiary ledger called the **accounts payable subsidiary ledger**, or *creditors ledger*. The related controlling account in the general ledger is *Accounts Payable*. The relationship between the general ledger and these subsidiary ledgers is illustrated in Exhibit 1.

EXHIBIT 1   General Ledger and Subsidiary Ledgers

SPECIAL JOURNALS

One method of processing data more efficiently in a manual accounting system is to expand the all-purpose two-column journal to a multicolumn journal. Each column in a multicolumn journal is used only for recording transactions that affect a certain account. For example, a special column could be used only for recording debits to the cash account, and another special column could be used only for recording credits to the cash account. The addition of the two special columns would eliminate the writing of *Cash* in the journal for every receipt and every payment of cash. Also, there would be no need to post each individual debit and credit to the cash account. Instead, the *Cash Dr.* and *Cash Cr.* columns could be totaled periodically and only the totals posted. In a similar way, special columns could be added for recording credits to Fees Earned, debits and credits to Accounts Receivable and Accounts Payable, and for other entries that are often repeated.

An all-purpose multicolumn journal may be adequate for a small business that has many transactions of a similar nature. However, a journal that has many columns for recording many different types of transactions is impractical for larger businesses.

> Special journals are a method of summarizing transactions.

The next logical extension of the accounting system is to replace the single multicolumn journal with several **special journals**. Each special journal is designed to be used for recording a single kind of transaction that occurs frequently. For example, since most businesses have many transactions in which cash is paid out, they will likely use a special journal for recording cash payments. Likewise, they will use another special journal for recording cash receipts. Special journals are a method of summarizing transactions, which is a basic feature of any accounting system.

The format and number of special journals that a business uses depends upon the nature of the business. A business that gives credit might use a special journal designed for recording only revenue from services provided on credit. On the other hand, a business that does not give credit would have no need for such a journal. In other cases, record-keeping costs may be reduced by using supporting documents as special journals.

The transactions that occur most often in a small- to medium-size service business and the special journals in which they are recorded are as follows:

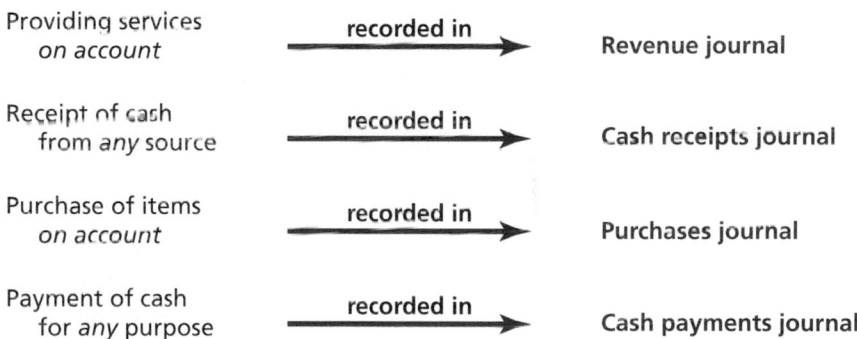

Providing services on account	recorded in	Revenue journal
Receipt of cash from *any* source	recorded in	Cash receipts journal
Purchase of items on account	recorded in	Purchases journal
Payment of cash for *any* purpose	recorded in	Cash payments journal

The all-purpose two-column journal, called the **general journal** or simply the *journal*, can be used for entries that do not fit into any of the special journals. For example, adjusting and closing entries are recorded in the general journal.

@netsolutions

In the following paragraphs, we illustrate special journals and subsidiary ledgers in a manual accounting system for NetSolutions. To simplify the illustration, we will use a minimum number of transactions. We will focus our discussion on two common operating cycles: (1) the revenue and collection cycle and (2) the purchase and payment cycle. We will assume that NetSolutions had the following selected general ledger balances on March 1, 2008:

Account Number	Account	Balance
11	Cash	$6,200
12	Accounts Receivable	3,400
14	Supplies	2,500
18	Office Equipment	2,500
21	Accounts Payable	1,230

MANUAL ACCOUNTING SYSTEM: THE REVENUE AND COLLECTION CYCLE

The *revenue and collection cycle* for NetSolutions consists of providing services on account and collecting cash from customers. Revenues earned on account create a customer receivable and will be recorded in a revenue journal. Customers' accounts receivable are collected and will be recorded in a cash receipts journal.

Internal control is enhanced by separating the function of recording revenue transactions in the revenue journal from recording cash collections in the cash receipts journal. For example, if these duties are separated, it is more difficult for one person to embezzle cash collections and manipulate the accounting records.

Revenue Journal   The **revenue journal** is used only for recording *fees earned on account. Cash fees earned would be recorded in the cash receipts journal.* The sale of products is recorded in a sales journal, which is similar to a *revenue journal*. We will compare the efficiency of using a revenue journal with a general journal by assuming that NetSolutions recorded the following revenue transactions in a general journal:

2008					
Mar.	2	Accounts Receivable—Accessories By Claire	12/✔	2 2 0 0 00	
		Fees Earned	41		2 2 0 0 00
	6	Accounts Receivable—RapZone	12/✔	1 7 5 0 00	
		Fees Earned	41		1 7 5 0 00
	18	Accounts Receivable—Web Cantina	12/✔	2 6 5 0 00	
		Fees Earned	41		2 6 5 0 00
	27	Accounts Receivable—Accessories By Claire	12/✔	3 0 0 0 00	
		Fees Earned	41		3 0 0 0 00

For these four transactions, NetSolutions recorded eight account titles and eight amounts. In addition, NetSolutions made 12 postings to the ledgers—four to Accounts Receivable in the general ledger, four to the accounts receivable subsidiary ledger (indicated by each check mark), and four to Fees Earned in the general ledger. These transactions could be recorded more efficiently in a revenue journal, as shown in Exhibit 2. In each revenue transaction, the amount of the debit to Accounts Receivable is the same as the amount of the credit to Fees Earned. Therefore, only a single amount column is necessary. The date, invoice number, customer name, and amount are entered separately for each transaction.

◗ EXHIBIT 2   Revenue Journal

			REVENUE JOURNAL		Page 35
	Date	Invoice No.	Account Debited	Post. Ref.	Accts. Rec. Dr. Fees Earned Cr.
1	2008 Mar. 2	615	Accessories By Claire		2 2 0 0 00
2	6	616	RapZone		1 7 5 0 00
3	18	617	Web Cantina		2 6 5 0 00
4	27	618	Accessories By Claire		3 0 0 0 00
5	31				9 6 0 0 00

The basic procedure of posting from a revenue journal is shown in Exhibit 3. A single monthly total is posted to Accounts Receivable and Fees Earned in the general ledger. Each transaction, such as the $2,200 debit to Accessories By Claire, must also be posted individually to a customer account in the accounts receivable subsidiary ledger. These postings to customer accounts should be made frequently. In this way, management has information on the current balance of each customer's account. Since the balances in the customer accounts are usually debit balances, the three-column account form shown in the exhibit is often used.

To provide a trail of the entries posted to the subsidiary ledger, the source of these entries is indicated in the *Posting Reference* column of each account by inserting the letter *R* (for revenue journal) and the page number of the revenue journal. A check mark (✔) instead of a number is then inserted in the *Posting Reference* column of the revenue journal, as shown in Exhibit 3.

If a customer's account has a credit balance, that fact should be indicated by an asterisk or parentheses in the *Balance* column. When an account's balance is zero, a line may be drawn in the *Balance* column.

EXHIBIT 3   Revenue Journal Postings to Ledgers

REVENUE JOURNAL   Page 35

	Date	Invoice No.	Account Debited	Post. Ref.	Accts. Rec. Dr. Fees Earned Cr.	
	2008					
1	Mar. 2	615	Accessories By Claire	✔	2,200	1
2	6	616	RapZone	✔	1,750	2
3	18	617	Web Cantina	✔	2,650	3
4	27	618	Accessories By Claire	✔	3,000	4
5	31				9,600	5
6					(12) (41)	6

GENERAL LEDGER

ACCOUNT   Accounts Receivable   Account No. 12

		Post.			Balance	
Date	Item	Ref.	Dr.	Cr.	Dr.	Cr.
2008						
Mar. 1	Balance	✔			3,400	
31		R35	9,600		13,000	

ACCOUNT   Fees Earned   Account No. 41

		Post.			Balance	
Date	Item	Ref.	Dr.	Cr.	Dr.	Cr.
2008						
Mar. 31		R35		9,600		9,600

ACCOUNTS RECEIVABLE SUBSIDIARY LEDGER

NAME: Accessories By Claire

		Post.			
Date	Item	Ref.	Dr.	Cr.	Balance
2008					
Mar. 2		R35	2,200		2,200
27		R35	3,000		5,200

NAME: RapZone

		Post.			
Date	Item	Ref.	Dr.	Cr.	Balance
2008					
Mar. 6		R35	1,750		1,750

NAME: Web Cantina

		Post.			
Date	Item	Ref.	Dr.	Cr.	Balance
2008					
Mar. 1	Balance	✔			3,400
18		R35	2,650		6,050

At the end of each month, the amount column of the revenue journal is totaled. This total is equal to the sum of the month's debits to the individual accounts in the subsidiary ledger. It is posted in the general ledger as a debit to Accounts Receivable and a credit to Fees Earned, as shown in Exhibit 3. The respective account numbers (12 and 41) are then inserted below the total in the revenue journal to indicate that the posting is completed, as shown in Exhibit 3. In this way, all of the transactions for fees earned during the month are posted to the general ledger only once—at the end of the month—greatly simplifying the posting process.

Example Exercise 5-1   objective 2

The following revenue transactions occurred during December:

Dec. 5. Issued Invoice No. 302 to Butler Company for services provided on account, $5,000.
    9. Issued Invoice No. 303 to JoJo Enterprises for services provided on account, $2,100.
  15. Issued Invoice No. 304 to Double D Inc. for services provided on account, $3,250.

Record these transactions in a revenue journal as illustrated in Exhibit 2.

Follow My Example 5-1

REVENUE JOURNAL

Date	Invoice No.	Account Debited	Post. Ref.	Accts. Rec. Dr. Fees Earned Cr.
Dec. 5	302	Butler Company		5,000
9	303	JoJo Enterprises		2,100
15	304	Double D Inc.		3,250

For Practice: PE 5-1A, PE 5-1B

Cash Receipts Journal All transactions that involve the receipt of cash are recorded in a **cash receipts journal**. Thus, the cash receipts journal has a column entitled *Cash Dr.*, as shown in Exhibit 4. All transactions recorded in the cash receipts journal will involve an entry in the *Cash Dr.* column. For example, on March 28 NetSolutions received cash of $2,200 from Accessories by Claire and entered that amount in the *Cash Dr.* column.

The kinds of transactions in which cash is received and how often they occur determine the titles of the other columns. For NetSolutions, the most frequent source of cash is collections from customers. Thus, the cash receipts journal in Exhibit 4 has an *Accounts Receivable Cr.* column. On March 28, when *Accessories By Claire* made a payment on its account, NetSolutions entered *Accessories By Claire* in the *Account Credited* column and entered *2,200* in the *Accounts Receivable Cr.* column.

The *Other Accounts Cr.* column in Exhibit 4 is used for recording credits to any account for which there is no special credit column. For example, NetSolutions received cash on March 1 for rent. Since no special column exists for Rent Revenue, NetSolutions entered *Rent Revenue* in the *Account Credited* column and entered *400* in the *Other Accounts Cr.* column.

Postings from the cash receipts journal to the ledgers of NetSolutions are also shown in Exhibit 4. This posting process is similar to that of the revenue journal. At regular intervals, each amount in the *Other Accounts Cr.* column is posted to the proper account in the general ledger. The posting is indicated by inserting the account number in the *Posting Reference* column of the cash receipts journal. The posting reference *CR* (for cash receipts journal) and the proper page number are inserted in the *Posting Reference* columns of the accounts.

The amounts in the *Accounts Receivable Cr.* column are posted individually to the customer accounts in the accounts receivable subsidiary ledger. These postings should be made frequently. The posting reference *CR* and the proper page number are inserted

REAL WORLD

Invoices that have yet to be collected are often termed *open invoices.*

EXHIBIT 4   Cash Receipts Journal and Postings

CASH RECEIPTS JOURNAL   Page 14

	Date	Account Credited	Post. Ref.	Other Accounts Cr.	Accounts Receivable Cr.	Cash Dr.	
	2008						
1	Mar. 1	Rent Revenue	42	400		400	1
2	19	Web Cantina	✔		3,400	3,400	2
3	28	Accessories by Claire	✔		2,200	2,200	3
4	30	RapZone	✔		1,750	1,750	4
5	31			400	7,350	7,750	5
6				(✔)	(12)	(11)	6

GENERAL LEDGER

ACCOUNT   Rent Revenue   Account No. 42

Date	Item	Post. Ref.	Dr.	Cr.	Balance Dr.	Balance Cr.
2008						
Mar. 1		CR14		400		400

ACCOUNT   Accounts Receivable   Account No. 12

Date	Item	Post. Ref.	Dr.	Cr.	Balance Dr.	Balance Cr.
2008						
Mar. 1	Balance	✔			3,400	
31		R35	9,600		13,000	
31		CR14		7,350	5,650	

ACCOUNT   Cash   Account No. 11

Date	Item	Post. Ref.	Dr.	Cr.	Balance Dr.	Balance Cr.
2008						
Mar. 1	Balance	✔			6,200	
31		CR14	7,750		13,950	

ACCOUNTS RECEIVABLE SUBSIDIARY LEDGER

NAME: Accessories By Claire

Date	Item	Post. Ref.	Dr.	Cr.	Balance
2008					
Mar. 2		R35	2,200		2,200
27		R35	3,000		5,200
28		CR14		2,200	3,000

NAME: RapZone

Date	Item	Post. Ref.	Dr.	Cr.	Balance
2008					
Mar. 6		R35	1,750		1,750
30		CR14		1,750	—

NAME: Web Cantina

Date	Item	Post. Ref.	Dr.	Cr.	Balance
2008					
Mar. 1	Balance	✔			3,400
18		R35	2,650		6,050
19		CR14		3,400	2,650

in the *Posting Reference* column of each customer's account. A check mark is placed in the *Posting Reference* column of the cash receipts journal to show that each amount has been posted. None of the individual amounts in the *Cash Dr.* column is posted separately.

At the end of the month, all of the amount columns are totaled. The debits should equal the credits. Because each amount in the *Other Accounts Cr.* column has been posted individually to a general ledger account, a check mark is inserted below the column total to indicate that no further action is needed. The totals of the *Accounts Receivable Cr.* and *Cash Dr.* columns are posted to the proper accounts in the general ledger, and their account numbers are inserted below the totals to show that the postings have been completed.

Accounts Receivable Control and Subsidiary Ledger   After all posting has been completed for the month, the sum of the balances in the accounts receivable subsidiary ledger should be compared with the balance of the accounts receivable controlling account in the general ledger. If the controlling account and the subsidiary ledger do not agree, the error or errors must be located and corrected. The balances of the individual customer accounts may be summarized in a customer balance summary report. The total of NetSolutions' customer balance summary report, $5,650, agrees with the balance of its accounts receivable control account on March 31, 2008, as shown below.

Accounts Receivable (Control)		NetSolutions Customer Balance Summary March 31, 2008	
Balance, March 1, 2008	$ 3,400	Accessories By Claire	$3,000
Total debits (from revenue journal)	9,600	RapZone	0
Total credits (from cash receipts journal)	(7,350)	Web Cantina	2,650
Balance, March 31, 2008	$ 5,650	Total accounts receivable	$5,650

Example Exercise 5-2

objective **2**

The debits and credits from two transactions are presented in the following customer account:

NAME   *Sweet Tooth Confections*
ADDRESS   *1212 Lombard St.*

Date	Item	Post. Ref.	Debit	Credit	Balance
July 1	Balance				625
7	Invoice 35	R12	86		711
31	Invoice 31	CR4		122	589

Describe each transaction and the source of each posting.

Follow My Example 5-2

July 7. Provided $86 of services on account to Sweet Tooth Confections, itemized on Invoice 35. Amount posted from page 12 of the revenue journal.
     31. Collected cash of $122 from Sweet Tooth Confections (Invoice 31). Amount posted from page 4 of the cash receipts journal.

For Practice: PE 5-2A, PE 5-2B

MANUAL ACCOUNTING SYSTEM: THE PURCHASE AND PAYMENT CYCLE

The *purchase and payment cycle* for NetSolutions consists of purchases on account and payments of cash to suppliers. To make purchases of supplies and other items on account requires establishing a supplier account payable. These transactions will be recorded in a purchases journal. The payments of suppliers' accounts payable will be recorded in the cash payments journal.

Internal control is enhanced by separating the function of recording purchases in the purchases journal from recording cash payments in the cash payments journal. Separating duties in this way prevents an individual from establishing a fictitious supplier and then collecting payments for fictitious purchases from this supplier.

Purchases Journal   The **purchases journal** is designed for recording all *purchases on account. Cash purchases would be recorded in the cash payments* *journal.* The purchases journal has a column entitled *Accounts Payable Cr.* The purchases journal also has special columns for recording debits to the accounts most often affected. Since NetSolutions makes frequent debits to its supplies account, a *Supplies Dr.* column is included for these transactions. For example, as shown in Exhibit 5, NetSolutions recorded the purchase of supplies on March 3 by entering *600* in the *Supplies Dr.* column, *600* in the *Accounts Payable Cr.* column, and *Howard Supplies* in the *Account Credited* column.

The *Other Accounts Dr.* column in Exhibit 5 is used to record purchases, on account, of any item for which there is no special debit column. The title of the account to be

> **EXHIBIT 5** Purchases Journal and Postings

Purchases are often initiated with a request to a vendor, termed a *purchase order*.

debited is entered in the *Other Accounts Dr.* column, and the amount is entered in the *Amount* column. For example, NetSolutions recorded the purchase of office equipment on account on March 12 by entering *Office Equipment* in the *Other Accounts Dr.* column, *2,800* in the *Amount* column, *2,800* in the *Accounts Payable Cr.* column, and *Jewett Business Systems* in the *Account Credited* column.

Postings from the purchases journal to the ledgers of NetSolutions are also shown in Exhibit 5. The principles used in posting the purchases journal are similar to those used in posting the revenue and cash receipts journals. The source of the entries posted to the subsidiary and general ledgers is indicated in the *Posting Reference* column of each account by inserting the letter *P* (for purchases journal) and the page number of the purchases journal. A check mark (✔) is inserted in the *Posting Reference* column of the purchases journal after each credit is posted to a creditor's account in the accounts payable subsidiary ledger.

At regular intervals, the amounts in the *Other Accounts Dr.* column are posted to the accounts in the general ledger. As each amount is posted, the related general ledger account number is inserted in the *Posting Reference* column of the *Other Accounts* section.

At the end of each month, the amount columns in the purchases journal are totaled. The sum of the two debit column totals should equal the sum of the credit column.

The totals of the *Accounts Payable Cr.* and *Supplies Dr.* columns are posted to the appropriate general ledger accounts in the usual manner, with the related account numbers inserted below the column totals. Because each amount in the *Other Accounts Dr.* column was posted individually, a check mark is placed below the $2,800 total to show that no further action is needed.

Example Exercise 5-3   objective

The following purchase transactions occurred during October for Helping Hand Cleaners:

Oct. 11. Purchased cleaning supplies for $235, on account, from General Supplies.
    19. Purchased cleaning supplies for $110, on account, from Hubble Supplies.
    24. Purchased office equipment for $850, on account, from Office Warehouse.

Record these transactions in a purchases journal as illustrated at the top of Exhibit 5.

Follow My Example 5-3

PURCHASES JOURNAL

Date	Account Credited	Post. Ref.	Accounts Payable Cr.	Cleaning Supplies Dr.	Other Accounts Dr.	Post. Ref.	Amount
Oct. 11	General Supplies		235	235			
19	Hubble Supplies		110	110			
24	Office Warehouse		850		Office Equipment	18	850

For Practice: PE 5-3A, PE 5-3B

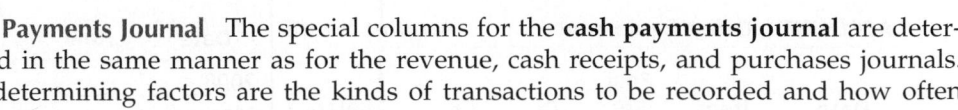

Cash Payments Journal   The special columns for the **cash payments journal** are determined in the same manner as for the revenue, cash receipts, and purchases journals. The determining factors are the kinds of transactions to be recorded and how often they occur.

The cash payments journal has a *Cash Cr.* column, as shown in Exhibit 6. All transactions recorded in the cash payments journal will involve an entry in this column. Payments to creditors on account happen often enough to require an *Accounts Payable Dr.* column. Debits to creditor accounts for invoices paid, often called *bills*, are recorded in the *Accounts Payable Dr.* column. For example, on March 15 NetSolutions paid $1,230 on its account with Grayco Supplies. NetSolutions recorded this transaction by entering *1,230* in the *Accounts Payable Dr.* column, *1,230* in the *Cash Cr.* column, and *Grayco Supplies* in the *Account Debited* column.

EXHIBIT 6 Cash Payments Journal and Postings

CASH PAYMENTS JOURNAL — Page 7

	Date	Ck. No.	Account Debited	Post. Ref.	Other Accounts Dr.	Accounts Payable Dr.	Cash Cr.	
	2008							
1	Mar. 2	150	Rent Expense	52	1,600		1,600	1
2	15	151	Grayco Supplies	✔		1,230	1,230	2
3	21	152	Jewett Business Systems	✔		2,800	2,800	3
4	22	153	Donnelly Supplies	✔		420	420	4
5	30	154	Utilities Expense	54	1,050		1,050	5
6	31	155	Howard Supplies	✔		600	600	6
7	31				2,650	5,050	7,700	7
8					(✔)	(21)	(11)	8

GENERAL LEDGER

ACCOUNT Accounts Payable — Account No. 21

Date	Item	Post. Ref.	Dr.	Cr.	Balance
2008					
Mar. 1	Balance	✔			1,230
31		P11		6,230	7,460
31		CP7	5,050		2,410

ACCOUNT Cash — Account No. 11

Date	Item	Post. Ref.	Dr.	Cr.	Balance
2008					
Mar. 1	Balance	✔			6,200
31		CR14	7,750		13,950
31		CP7		7,700	6,250

ACCOUNT Rent Expense — Account No. 52

Date	Item	Post. Ref.	Dr.	Cr.	Balance
2008					
Mar. 2		CP7	1,600		1,600

ACCOUNT Utilities Expense — Account No. 54

Date	Item	Post. Ref.	Dr.	Cr.	Balance
2008					
Mar. 30		CP7	1,050		1,050

ACCOUNTS PAYABLE SUBSIDIARY LEDGER

NAME: Donnelly Supplies

Date	Item	Post. Ref.	Dr.	Cr.	Balance
2008					
Mar. 7		P11		420	420
19		P11		1,450	1,870
22		CP7	420		1,450

NAME: Grayco Supplies

Date	Item	Post. Ref.	Dr.	Cr.	Balance
2008					
Mar. 1	Balance	✔			1,230
15		CP7	1,230		—

NAME: Howard Supplies

Date	Item	Post. Ref.	Dr.	Cr.	Balance
2008					
Mar. 3		P11		600	600
27		P11		960	1,560
31		CP7	600		960

NAME: Jewett Business Systems

Date	Item	Post. Ref.	Dr.	Cr.	Balance
2008					
Mar. 12		P11		2,800	2,800
21		CP7	2,800		—

NetSolutions makes all payments by check. As each transaction is recorded in the cash payments journal, the related check number is entered in the column at the right of the *Date* column. The check numbers are helpful in controlling cash payments, and they provide a useful cross-reference.

The *Other Accounts Dr.* column is used for recording debits to any account for which there is no special column. For example, NetSolutions paid $1,600 on March 2 for rent. The transaction was recorded by entering *Rent Expense* in the space provided and *1,600* in the *Other Accounts Dr.* and *Cash Cr.* columns.

Postings from the cash payments journal to the ledgers of NetSolutions are also shown in Exhibit 6. The amounts entered in the *Accounts Payable Dr.* column are posted to the individual creditor accounts in the accounts payable subsidiary ledger. These postings should be made frequently. After each posting, *CP* (for cash payments journal) and the page number of the journal are inserted in the *Posting Reference* column of the account. A check mark is placed in the *Posting Reference* column of the cash payments journal to indicate that each amount has been posted.

At regular intervals, each item in the *Other Accounts Dr.* column is also posted individually to an account in the general ledger. The posting is indicated by writing the account number in the *Posting Reference* column of the cash payments journal.

At the end of the month, each of the amount columns in the cash payments journal is totaled. The sum of the two debit totals is compared with the credit total to determine their equality. A check mark is placed below the total of the *Other Accounts Dr.* column to indicate that no further action is needed. When each of the totals of the other two columns is posted to the general ledger, an account number is inserted below each column total.

Accounts Payable Control and Subsidiary Ledger After all posting has been completed for the month, the sum of the balances in the accounts payable subsidiary ledger should be compared with the balance of the accounts payable control account in the general ledger. If the controlling account and the subsidiary ledger do not agree, the error or errors must be located and corrected. The balances of the individual creditor (supplier) accounts may be summarized in a supplier balance summary report. The total of NetSolutions' supplier balance summary report, $2,410, agrees with the balance of the accounts payable control account on March 31, 2008, as shown below.

<table>
<tr><td colspan="2" align="center">**Accounts Payable**
(Control)</td><td colspan="2" align="center">**NetSolutions**
Supplier Balance Summary
March 31, 2008</td></tr>
<tr><td>Balance, March 1, 2008</td><td>$ 1,230</td><td>Donnelly Supplies</td><td>$1,450</td></tr>
<tr><td>Total credits (from purchases journal)</td><td>6,230</td><td>Grayco Supplies</td><td>0</td></tr>
<tr><td>Total debits</td><td></td><td>Howard Supplies</td><td>960</td></tr>
<tr><td> (from cash payments journal)</td><td>(5,050)</td><td>Jewett Business Systems</td><td>0</td></tr>
<tr><td>Balance, March 31, 2008</td><td>$ 2,410</td><td>Total</td><td>$2,410</td></tr>
</table>

Example Exercise 5-4 objective 2

The debits and credits from two transactions are presented in the following creditor's (supplier's) account:

NAME   *Lassiter Services Inc.*
ADDRESS   *301 St. Bonaventure Ave.*

Date	Item	Post. Ref.	Debit	Credit	Balance
Aug. 1	Balance				320
12	Invoice 101	CP36	200		120
22	Invoice 106	P16		140	260

Describe each transaction and the source of each posting.

Follow My Example 5-4

> Aug. 12. Paid $200 to Lassiter Services Inc. on account (Invoice 101). Amount posted from page 36 of the cash payments journal.
>
> 22. Purchased $140 of services on account from Lassiter Services Inc. itemized on Invoice 106. Amount posted from page 16 of the purchases journal.

For Practice: PE 5-4A, PE 5-4B

Adapting Manual Accounting Systems

objective **3**

Describe and give examples of additional subsidiary ledgers and modified special journals.

The preceding sections of this chapter illustrate subsidiary ledgers and special journals that are common for a medium-size business. Many businesses use subsidiary ledgers for other accounts, in addition to Accounts Receivable and Accounts Payable. Also, special journals are often adapted or modified in practice to meet the specific needs of a business. In the following paragraphs, we describe other subsidiary ledgers and modified special journals.

ADDITIONAL SUBSIDIARY LEDGERS

Generally, subsidiary ledgers are used for accounts that consist of a large number of individual items, each of which has unique characteristics. For example, businesses may use a subsidiary equipment ledger to keep track of each item of equipment purchased, its cost, location, and other data. Such ledgers are similar to the accounts receivable and accounts payable subsidiary ledgers that we illustrated in this chapter.

MODIFIED SPECIAL JOURNALS

A business may modify its special journals by adding one or more columns for recording transactions that occur frequently. For example, a business may collect sales taxes that must be remitted periodically to the taxing authorities. Thus, the business may add a special column for *Sales Taxes Payable Cr.* in its revenue journal, as shown below.

	Date	Invoice No.	Account Debited	Post. Ref.	Accts. Rec. Dr.	Fees Earned Cr.	Sales Taxes Payable Cr.	
			REVENUE JOURNAL				**Page 40**	
1	2008 Nov. 2	842	Litten Co.	✔	4 7 7 0 00	4 5 0 0 00	2 7 0 00	1
2	3	843	Kauffman Supply Co.	✔	1 1 6 6 00	1 1 0 0 00	6 6 00	2

Some other examples of how special journals may be modified for a variety of different types of businesses are:

- **Farm**—The purchases journal may be modified to include columns for various types of seeds (corn, wheat), livestock (cows, hogs, sheep), fertilizer, and fuel.
- **Automobile Repair Shop**—The revenue journal may be modified to include columns for each major type of repair service. In addition, columns for warranty repairs, credit card charges, and sales taxes may be added.
- **Hospital**—The cash receipts journal may be modified to include columns for receipts from patients on account, from Blue Cross/Blue Shield or other major insurance reimbursers, and Medicare.

- **Movie Theater**—The cash receipts journal may be modified to include columns for revenues from admissions, gift certificates, and concession sales.
- **Restaurant**—The purchases journal may be modified to include columns for food, linen, silverware and glassware, and kitchen supplies.

Regardless of how a special journal is modified, the basic principles and procedures discussed in this chapter apply. For example, the columns in special journals are normally totaled at periodic intervals. The totals of the debit and credit columns are then compared to verify their equality before the totals are posted to the general ledger accounts.

Example Exercise 5-5   objective 3

The state of Tennessee has a 7% sales tax. Volunteer Services, Inc., a Tennessee company, had two revenue transactions as follows:

Aug. 3. Issued Invoice No. 58 to Helena Company for services provided on account, $1,400, plus sales tax.
    19. Issued Invoice No. 59 to K-Jam Enterprises for services provided on account, $900, plus sales tax.

Record these transactions in a revenue journal as illustrated in this section.

Follow My Example 5-5

REVENUE JOURNAL

Date	Invoice No.	Account Debited	Post. Ref.	Accts. Rec. Dr.	Fees Earned Cr.	Sales Taxes Payable Cr.
Aug. 3	58	Helena Company		1,498	1,400	98
19	59	K-Jam Enterprises		963	900	63

For Practice: PE 5-5A, PE 5-5B

Computerized Accounting Systems

objective 4

Apply computerized accounting to the revenue and collection cycle.

Computerized accounting systems have become more widely used as the cost of hardware and software has declined. In addition, computerized accounting systems have three main advantages over manual systems. *First*, computerized systems simplify the record-keeping process. Transactions are recorded in electronic forms and, at the same time, posted electronically to general and subsidiary ledger accounts. *Second*, computerized systems are generally more accurate than manual systems. *Third*, computerized

---

Business Connections   REAL WORLD

ACCOUNTING SYSTEMS AND PROFIT MEASUREMENT

A Greek restaurant owner in Canada had his own system of accounting. He kept his accounts payable in a cigar box on the left-hand side of his cash register, his daily cash returns in the cash register, and his receipts for paid bills in another cigar box on the right. A truly "manual" system.

When his youngest son graduated as an accountant, he was appalled by his father's primitive methods. "I don't know how you can run a business that way," he said. "How do you know what your profits are?"

"Well, son," the father replied, "when I got off the boat from Greece, I had nothing but the pants I was wearing. Today, your brother is a doctor. You are an accountant. Your sister is a speech therapist. Your mother and I have a nice car, a city house, and a country home. We have a good business, and everything is paid for. . . ."

"So, you add all that together, subtract the pants, and there's your profit!"

systems provide management current account balance information to support decision making, since account balances are posted as the transactions occur.

How do computerized accounting systems work? Exhibit 7 provides a general overview. Many transactions must first be authorized. This means that the transaction is approved by management before it is permitted. For example, most sales and purchase transactions must first be authorized before they are permitted. Without this step, sales may be made to customers that have insufficient credit, or purchases may be made for items that are not needed. Most computerized accounting systems include authorization steps in the software. Once authorized, the transaction can be completed. The completed transaction must be recorded in the accounting system. In computerized accounting systems, details of the specific transaction are input on a computer screen. The computer screen is often tailored to the specific transaction, much the way a special journal is tailored to a specific transaction. Once the computer screen is completed, the transaction is *submitted* into the computer system, often by the click of a button. The submitted transaction updates information in a database. A **database** collects, stores, and organizes information so it can be quickly retrieved. Once transaction details have been submitted to the database, managers are able to create reports from the database to answer questions about the business. Examples would include reports identifying the revenues of a customer, the cash receipts of a customer, or the account summary of a customer.

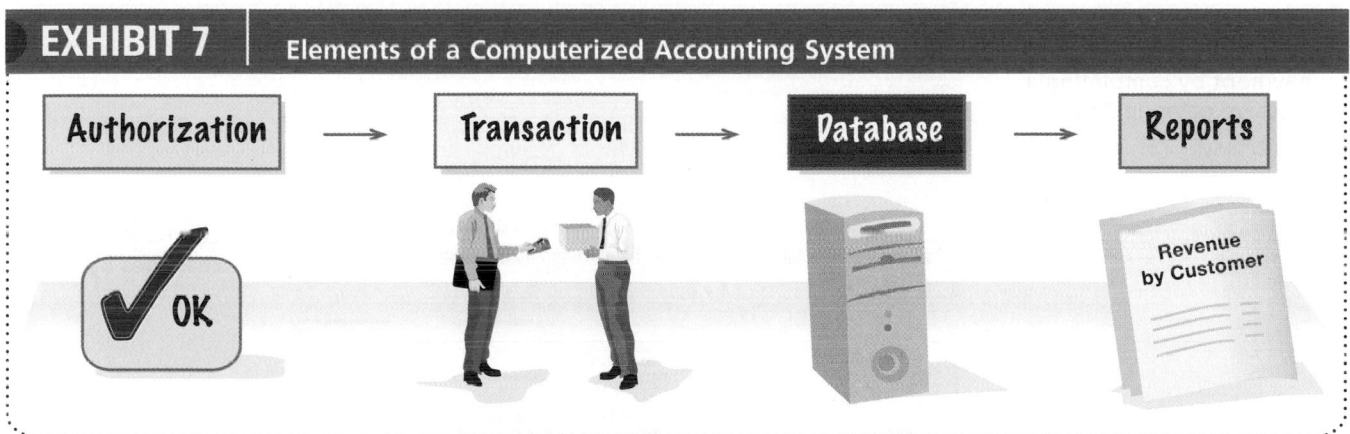

EXHIBIT 7 | Elements of a Computerized Accounting System

@netsolutions   While all accounting systems have these general features, the specific details can vary across accounting software solutions. We will use the popular QuickBooks® accounting software for small to medium-sized businesses to illustrate the revenue and collection cycle for NetSolutions. In this illustration, we will assume the transaction has been authorized, and thus we will focus on the transaction and reporting elements.

As shown in Exhibit 8, the first step in recording revenue in QuickBooks® is to enter the sales and customer information onto the computer screen using an electronic invoice form, as illustrated for the March 2 Accessories By Claire invoice (No. 615). An electronic form is a window that appears like a paper form. The form has spaces, or fields, in which to input information about a particular type of transaction. Many of the information spaces have pull-down lists for easy data entry. When the form is completed, it may be printed out and mailed, or e-mailed, to the customer. In addition, upon submitting the invoice form, the software automatically posts the $2,200 debit to the Accessories By Claire customer account and the credit to Fees Earned.

In step two, the collection from the customer is received. Upon collection, the "receive payment" electronic form is opened and completed. In Exhibit 8, this form indicates that a $2,200 payment was collected from Accessories By Claire on March 28. This amount was applied to Invoice 615, as shown by the check mark next to the March 2 date at the bottom of the form. The March 27 invoice of $3,000 remains uncollected,

EXHIBIT 8   The Revenue and Collection Cycle in QuickBooks®

1. Record fees by completing an electronic invoice form.

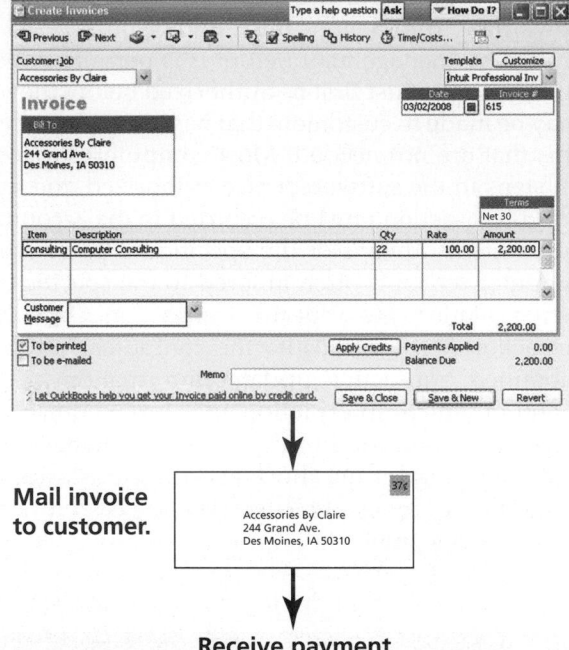

Automatic Postings
Dr. Accounts Receivable—
   Accessories By Claire
   Cr. Fees Earned

Mail invoice to customer.

Receive payment

2. Record collection of payment by completing a "receive payment" form.

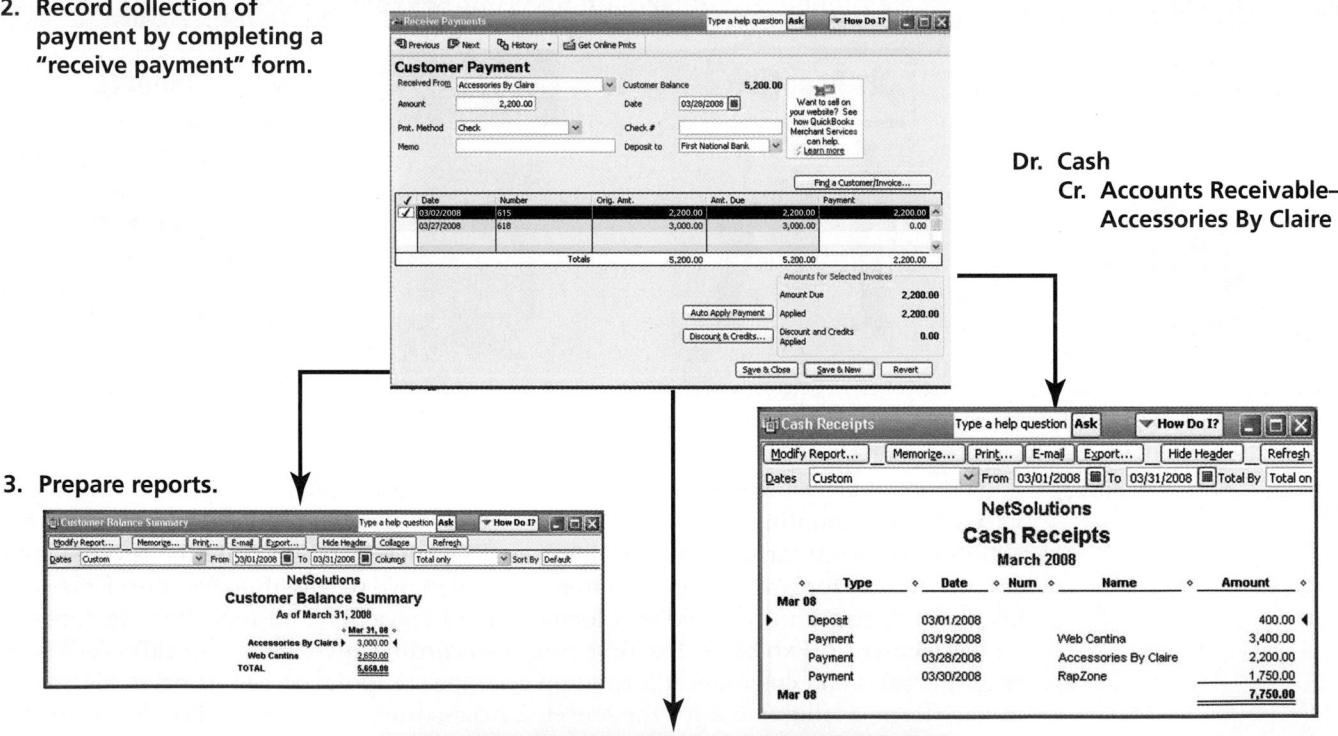

Dr. Cash
   Cr. Accounts Receivable—
      Accessories By Claire

3. Prepare reports.

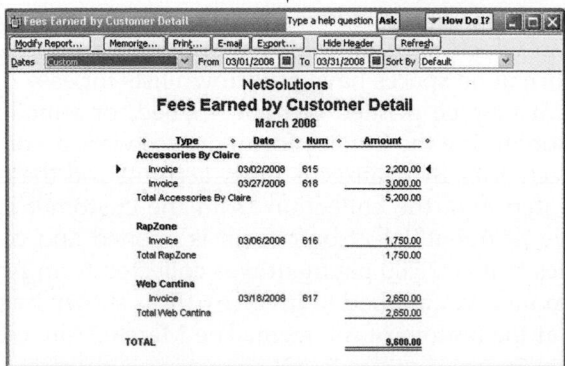

as shown at the bottom of the form. When this screen is completed, a debit of $2,200 is automatically posted to the cash account, and a credit for the same amount is posted to the Accessories By Claire account, causing the balance to be reduced from $5,200 to $3,000.

At any time, managers may request reports from the software. In step three, three such reports are illustrated in Exhibit 8: (1) the customer balance summary, (2) the fees earned by customer detail, and (3) the cash receipts. The reports are shown for March 31, 2008. Notice that the customer balance summary lists the outstanding accounts receivable balances by customer. These are often called the *open invoices*. This is essentially a report providing the details of the accounts receivable subsidiary ledger. It shows the same information as NetSolutions' Customer Balance Summary Report on page 212. The fees earned by customer detail provides a listing of revenue by customer, which is similar to the information listed by the revenue journal in the manual system. This listing is created from the electronic invoice form used in the first step of the cycle. The cash receipts report provides a listing of NetSolutions' cash receipts during the month. This report is similar to the information listed by the cash receipts journal in the manual system.

At the end of the month, the manual system posted revenue journal and cash collection totals to the accounts receivable controlling account. In a computerized system, special journals typically are not used. Instead, transactions are recorded in electronic forms, which are automatically posted to affected accounts at the time the form is completed. In a manual system, the controlling account balance can be reconciled to the sum of the individual customer account balances to identify any posting and mathematical errors. The computer, however, does not make posting and mathematical errors. Thus, there are no month-end postings to controlling accounts. Controlling accounts are simply the sum of the balances of any individual subsidiary account balances.

The discovery and correction of errors are also important in a computerized system. Such errors, however, are not related to mechanical posting procedures or unbalanced journal entries. A computerized accounting system does not allow these types of mechanical and arithmetic errors. Thus, trial balances are not used in a computerized environment to discover posting and mechanical errors, because the debit and credit totals will always be equal in a computerized trial balance. The trial balance can be used to evaluate the reasonableness of the account balances.

Errors can still occur in a computerized system due to errors made in recording the original transaction. Such errors include failing to record a transaction, recording a transaction more than once, using the wrong debit or credit accounts, or entering an incorrect number in both the debit and credit parts of the transaction. The discovery of such errors is often accomplished through audit procedures or objections from parties affected by the incorrect transaction, such as from an employee objecting to a missed or incorrect payroll check. Incorrectly recorded transactions can be corrected in computerized accounting systems by electronically deleting incorrect transactions and replacing them with corrected entries. When a transaction is deleted in a computerized system, the postings to the accounts are automatically deleted as well, thus removing

Integrity, Objectivity, and Ethics in Business

ONLINE FRAUD

Fraud accounted for over $2.8 billion in e-commerce losses in 2005, or approximately 1.6% of all online revenue. As a result, online retailers are using address verification and credit card security codes as additional security measures. Address verification matches the customer's address to the address on file with the credit card company, while the security code is the additional four-digit code designed to reduce fictitious credit card transactions.

Source: 7th Annual CyberSource fraud survey, *CyberSource*, November 9, 2005.

the effect of the incorrect entry from the accounts. Alternatively, correcting entries may also be used as described in Chapter 2.

We have illustrated the revenue and collection cycle to help you understand how a portion of a computerized accounting system works. A similar description could be provided for the purchases and payments cycle. A description of a complete computerized accounting system is beyond our scope. However, a thorough understanding of this chapter provides a solid foundation for applying the accounting system concepts in either a manual or a computerized system.

E-Commerce

The U.S. Census Bureau retail data indicate that e-commerce sales are growing at a rate of 25% per year to over $80 billion in retail sales, representing over 2% of all retail sales.[1] In addition, consumers are using the Internet as a vast information source for researching prices and features for just about anything. Using the Internet to perform business transactions is termed **e-commerce**. When transactions are between a company and a consumer, it is termed B2C (business-to-consumer) e-commerce. Examples of companies engaged in B2C e-commerce include Amazon.com, Priceline.com Inc., and Dell Inc.

The B2C business adds value by allowing the consumer to shop and receive goods at home, rather than going to the store for an item. For example, Whirlpool Corporation allows consumers to use its Web site to order appliances, selecting color and other features. After paying for the appliance online with a credit card, customers can then receive direct delivery from the Whirlpool factory. Thus, the revenue and collection cycle illustrated earlier in the text under the manual system is shortened under e-commerce. For example, Whirlpool receives cash from an Internet transaction *before* the goods are actually shipped.

When transactions are conducted between a company and another company, it is termed B2B (business-to-business) e-commerce. Examples of companies engaged in B2B e-commerce include Cisco Systems, Inc., an Internet equipment manufacturer, and Bristol-Myers Squibb Company (BMS), a pharmaceutical company. BMS, for example, launched an e-procurement solution for purchasing supplies and equipment from its suppliers. The e-procurement solution streamlines the purchase and payment cycle by automating transactions and eliminating paperwork. BMS uses an Internet "market" to request vendor quotes for supplies. Vendors place bids on the Internet market and compete with other vendors for BMS's business. Using an Internet market in this way, called a *reverse auction*, is fast becoming a popular method for purchasing common items. BMS claims over $90 million in savings by placing its purchase/payment cycle on the Internet.

The Internet creates opportunities for improving the speed and efficiency in conducting transactions. Many companies are realizing these benefits of using e-commerce in their revenue/collection and purchase/payment cycles, as illustrated above. In addition, three more advanced areas where the Internet is being used for business purposes are:

1. **Supply chain management (SCM):** Internet applications to plan and coordinate suppliers.
2. **Customer relationship management (CRM):** Internet applications to plan and coordinate marketing and sales effort.
3. **Product life-cycle management (PLM):** Internet applications to plan and coordinate the product development and design process.

E-commerce also provides opportunities for faster business processes that operate at lower costs. New Internet applications are being introduced continuously as the Internet matures into a preferred method of conducting business.

---

1 Estimated Quarterly U.S. Retail Sales: Total and E-commerce, U.S. Census Bureau, November 22, 2005.

At a Glance

1. Define an accounting system and describe its implementation.

Key Points	Key Learning Outcomes	Example Exercises	Practice Exercises
An accounting system is the methods and procedures for collecting, classifying, summarizing, and reporting a business's financial information. The three steps through which an accounting system evolves are: (1) analysis of information needs, (2) design of the system, and (3) implementation of the system design.	• Define an accounting system. • Describe the three steps for designing an accounting system: (1) analysis, (2) design, and (3) implementation.		

2. Journalize and post transactions in a manual accounting system that uses subsidiary ledgers and special journals.

Key Points	Key Learning Outcomes	Example Exercises	Practice Exercises
Subsidiary ledgers may be used to maintain separate records for customers and creditors (vendors). A controlling account summarizes the subsidiary ledger accounts. The sum of the subsidiary ledger must agree with the balance in the related controlling account. Special journals efficiently summarize a large number of similar transactions as follows:	• Define subsidiary ledger accounts for customers and creditors.		
The revenue journal is used to record the sale of services on account.	• Prepare a revenue journal and post services provided on account to individual customer accounts and the accounts receivable control account.	5-1	5-1A, 5-1B
The cash receipts journal is used to record the collection of accounts and other cash receipts.	• Prepare a cash receipts journal and post collections to individual customer accounts and the accounts receivable control account.	5-2	5-2A, 5-2B
The purchases journal is used to record purchases on account.	• Prepare a purchases journal and post amounts owed to individual creditor accounts and the accounts payable control account.	5-3	5-3A, 5-3B
The cash payments journal is used to record the payments of creditor accounts and other cash payments.	• Prepare a cash payments journal and post the amounts paid to individual creditor accounts and the accounts payable control account.	5-4	5-4A, 5-4B

3. Describe and give examples of additional subsidiary ledgers and modified special journals.

Key Points	Key Learning Outcomes	Example Exercises	Practice Exercises
Subsidiary ledgers may be maintained for a variety of accounts, such as fixed assets, accounts receivable, and accounts payable. Special journals may be modified by adding columns for frequently occurring transactions.	• Prepare modified special journals that incorporate additional columns for frequently occurring transactions.	5-5	5-5A, 5-5B

4. Apply computerized accounting to the revenue and collection cycle.

Key Points	Key Learning Outcomes	Example Exercises	Practice Exercises
Computerized accounting systems are similar to manual systems. The main advantages of a computerized accounting system are the simultaneous recording and posting of transactions, high degree of accuracy, and timeliness of reporting.	• Differentiate between a manual and a computerized accounting system. • Illustrate the revenue and collection cycle using QuickBooks®.		

5. Describe the basic features of e-commerce.

Key Points	Key Learning Outcomes	Example Exercises	Practice Exercises
Using the Internet to perform business transactions is termed e-commerce. B2C e-commerce involves Internet transactions between a business and consumer, while B2B e-commerce involves Internet transactions between businesses. More elaborate e-commerce involves planning and coordinating suppliers, customers, and product design.	• Define e-commerce and describe the major trends in e-commerce.		

Key Terms

accounting system (204)
accounts payable subsidiary
   ledger (206)
accounts receivable subsidiary
   ledger (206)
cash payments journal (214)

cash receipts journal (210)
controlling account (206)
database (219)
e-commerce (222)
general journal (207)
general ledger (206)

internal controls (205)
purchases journal (212)
revenue journal (208)
special journals (207)
subsidiary ledger (205)

Illustrative Problem

Selected transactions of O'Malley Co. for the month of May are as follows:

a. May 1. Issued Check No. 1001 in payment of rent for May, $1,200.
b.   2. Purchased office supplies on account from McMillan Co., $3,600.
c.   4. Issued Check No. 1003 in payment of freight charges on the supplies purchased on May 2, $320.
d.   8. Provided services on account to Waller Co., Invoice No. 51, $4,500.
e.   9. Issued Check No. 1005 for office supplies purchased, $450.
f.   10. Received cash for office supplies sold to employees at cost, $120.
g.   11. Purchased office equipment on account from Fender Office Products, $15,000.
h.   12. Issued Check No. 1010 in payment of the supplies purchased from McMillan Co. on May 2, $3,600.
i.   16. Provided services on account to Riese Co., Invoice No. 58, $8,000.
j.   18. Received $4,500 from Waller Co. in payment of May 8 invoice.
k.   20. Invested additional cash in the business, $10,000.

l.   May 25. Provided services for cash, $15,900.
m.   30. Issued Check No. 1040 for withdrawal of cash for personal use, $1,000.
n.   30. Issued Check No. 1041 in payment of electricity and water invoices, $690.
o.   30. Issued Check No. 1042 in payment of office and sales salaries for May, $15,800.
p.   31. Journalized adjusting entries from the work sheet prepared for the fiscal year ended May 31.

O'Malley Co. maintains a revenue journal, a cash receipts journal, a purchases journal, a cash payments journal, and a general journal. In addition, accounts receivable and accounts payable subsidiary ledgers are used.

Instructions

1. Indicate the journal in which each of the preceding transactions, (a) through (p), would be recorded.
2. Indicate whether an account in the accounts receivable or accounts payable subsidiary ledgers would be affected for each of the preceding transactions.
3. Journalize transactions (b), (c), (d), (h), and (j) in the appropriate journals.

Solution

1.	Journal	2.	Subsidiary Ledger
a.	Cash payments journal		
b.	Purchases journal		Accounts payable ledger
c.	Cash payments journal		
d.	Revenue journal		Accounts receivable ledger
e.	Cash payments journal		
f.	Cash receipts journal		
g.	Purchases journal		Accounts payable ledger
h.	Cash payments journal		Accounts payable ledger
i.	Revenue journal		Accounts receivable ledger
j.	Cash receipts journal		Accounts receivable ledger
k.	Cash receipts journal		
l.	Cash receipts journal		
m.	Cash payments journal		
n.	Cash payments journal		
o.	Cash payments journal		
p.	General journal		

3.

Transaction (b):

PURCHASES JOURNAL

Date	Account Credited	Post. Ref.	Accounts Payable Cr.	Office Supplies Dr.	Other Accounts Dr.	Post. Ref.	Amount
May 2	McMillan Co.		3 6 0 0 00	3 6 0 0 00			

Transactions (c) and (h):

CASH PAYMENTS JOURNAL

Date	Ck. No.	Account Debited	Post. Ref.	Other Accounts Dr.	Accounts Payable Dr.	Cash Cr.
May 4	1003	Freight Expense		3 2 0 00		3 2 0 00
12	1010	McMillan Co.			3 6 0 0 00	3 6 0 0 00

Transaction (d):

REVENUE JOURNAL					
Date	Invoice No.	Account Debited	Post. Ref.	Accts. Rec. Dr. Fees Earned Cr.	
May 8	51	Waller Co.		4 5 0 0 00	

Transaction (j):

CASH RECEIPTS JOURNAL					
Date	Account Credited	Post. Ref.	Other Accounts Cr.	Accounts Receivable Cr.	Cash Dr.
May 18	Waller Co.			4 5 0 0 00	4 5 0 0 00

Self-Examination Questions

(Answers at End of Chapter)

1. The initial step in the process of developing an accounting system is called:
   A. analysis.
   B. design.
   C. implementation.
   D. feedback.

2. The policies and procedures used by management to protect assets from misuse, ensure accurate business information, and ensure compliance with laws and regulations are called:
   A. internal controls.
   B. systems analysis.
   C. systems design.
   D. systems implementation.

3. A payment of cash for the purchase of services should be recorded in the:
   A. purchases journal.
   B. cash payments journal.
   C. revenue journal.
   D. cash receipts journal.

4. When there are a large number of individual accounts with a common characteristic, it is common to place them in a separate ledger called a(n):
   A. subsidiary ledger.
   B. creditors ledger.
   C. accounts payable ledger.
   D. accounts receivable ledger.

5. Which of the following would be used in a computerized accounting system?
   A. Special journals
   B. Accounts receivable control accounts
   C. Electronic invoice form
   D. Month-end postings to the general ledger

Eye Openers

1. Why would a company maintain separate accounts receivable ledgers for each customer, as opposed to maintaining a single accounts receivable ledger for all customers?
2. What are the major advantages of the use of special journals?
3. In recording 250 fees earned on account during a single month, how many times will it be necessary to write Fees Earned (a) if each transaction, including fees earned, is recorded individually in a two-column general journal; (b) if each transaction for fees earned is recorded in a revenue journal?

4. How many postings to Fees Earned for the month would be needed in Eye Opener 3 if the procedure described in (a) had been used; if the procedure described in (b) had been used?

5. During the current month, the following errors occurred in recording transactions in the purchases journal or in posting from it.
   a. An invoice for $900 of supplies from Collins Co. was recorded as having been received from Collings Co., another supplier.
   b. A credit of $840 to Tanner Company was posted as $480 in the subsidiary ledger.
   c. An invoice for equipment of $6,500 was recorded as $5,500.
   d. The Accounts Payable column of the purchases journal was overstated by $2,000.
   How will each error come to the bookkeeper's attention, other than by chance discovery?

6. The Accounts Payable and Cash columns in the cash payments journal were unknowingly overstated by $100 at the end of the month. (a) Assuming no other errors in recording or posting, will the error cause the trial balance totals to be unequal? (b) Will the creditors ledger agree with the accounts payable control account?

7. Assuming the use of a two-column general journal, a purchases journal, and a cash payments journal as illustrated in this chapter, indicate the journal in which each of the following transactions should be recorded:
   a. Purchase of office supplies on account.
   b. Purchase of supplies for cash.
   c. Purchase of store equipment on account.
   d. Payment of cash on account to creditor.
   e. Payment of cash for office supplies.

8. What is the role of a database in a computerized accounting system?

9. What is an electronic form, and how is it used in a computerized accounting system?

10. Do computerized systems use controlling accounts to verify the accuracy of the subsidiary accounts?

11. What happens to the special journal in a computerized accounting system that uses electronic forms?

12. How would e-commerce improve the revenue/collection cycle?

Practice Exercises

PE 5-1A
Prepare journal entries in a revenue journal
obj. 2

The following revenue transactions occurred during March:

Mar. 3. Issued Invoice No. 78 to Langley Co. for services provided on account, $450.
   12. Issued Invoice No. 79 to Hitchcock Inc. for services provided on account, $215.
   28. Issued Invoice No. 80 to Sunshine Inc. for services provided on account, $685.

Record these three transactions into the following revenue journal format:

REVENUE JOURNAL

Date	Invoice No.	Account Debited	Post. Ref.	Accts. Rec. Dr. Fees Earned Cr.

PE 5-1B
Prepare journal entries in a revenue journal
obj. 2

The following revenue transactions occurred during September:

Sept. 9. Issued Invoice No. 121 to Barney Co. for services provided on account, $6,780.
   20. Issued Invoice No. 122 to Triple A Inc. for services provided on account, $5,240.
   24. Issued Invoice No. 123 to Connors Co. for services provided on account, $2,890.

Record these three transactions into the following revenue journal format:

REVENUE JOURNAL

Date	Invoice No.	Account Debited	Post. Ref.	Accts. Rec. Dr. Fees Earned Cr.

PE 5-2A
Identify transactions in an accounts receivable ledger
obj. 2

The debits and credits from two transactions are presented in the following customer account:

NAME   New Generation Products Inc.
ADDRESS   46 W. Elm St.

Date	Item	Post. Ref.	Debit	Credit	Balance
Jan. 1	Balance	✔			1,450
10	Invoice 345	R45	895		2,345
19	Invoice 329	CR78		1,080	1,265

Describe each transaction and the source of each posting.

PE 5-2B
Identify transactions in an accounts receivable ledger
obj. 2

The debits and credits from two transactions are presented in the following customer account:

NAME   Hopewell Communications Inc.
ADDRESS   76 Oak Ridge Rd.

Date	Item	Post. Ref.	Debit	Credit	Balance
Apr. 1	Balance	✔			255
14	Invoice 962	CR315		140	115
25	Invoice 976	R240	85		200

Describe each transaction and the source of each posting.

PE 5-3A
Prepare journal entries in a purchases journal
obj. 2

The following purchase transactions occurred during June for Mahanaim Inc.:

June   4. Purchased office supplies for $85, on account from Office-to-Go Inc.
     19. Purchased office equipment for $3,890, on account from Bell Computer Inc.
     23. Purchased office supplies for $145, on account from Paper Warehouse Inc.

Record these transactions in the following purchases journal format:

PURCHASES JOURNAL

Date	Account Credited	Post. Ref.	Accounts Payable Cr.	Office Supplies Dr.	Other Accounts Dr.	Post. Ref.	Amount

PE 5-3B
Prepare journal entries in a purchases journal
obj. 2

The following purchase transactions occurred during May for Joan's Catering Service:

Oct. 11. Purchased party supplies for $445, on account from Celebration Supplies Inc.
     19. Purchased party supplies for $230, on account from Party Time Supplies Inc.
     24. Purchased office furniture for $2,570, on account from Office Space Inc.

Record these transactions in the following purchases journal format:

PURCHASES JOURNAL

Date	Account Credited	Post. Ref.	Accounts Payable Cr.	Party Supplies Dr.	Other Accounts Dr.	Post. Ref.	Amount

PE 5-4A
Identify transactions in an accounts payable ledger
obj. 2

The debits and credits from two transactions are presented in the following supplier's (creditor's) account:

NAME   *Xavier Inc.*
ADDRESS   *5000 Grand Ave.*

Date	Item	Post. Ref.	Debit	Credit	Balance
Dec. 1	Balance				78
9	Invoice 456	CP55	54		24
18	Invoice 475	P89		94	118

Describe each transaction and the source of each posting.

PE 5-4B
Identify transactions in an accounts payable ledger
obj. 2

The debits and credits from two transactions are presented in the following supplier's (creditor's) account:

NAME   *Bonitelli Computer Services Inc.*
ADDRESS   *301 St. Bonaventure Ave.*

Date	Item	Post. Ref.	Debit	Credit	Balance
Feb. 1	Balance				8,400
19	Invoice 45	P16		4,250	12,650
26	Invoice 39	CP36	6,700		5,950

Describe each transaction and the source of each posting.

PE 5-5A
Prepare journal entries in a modified revenue Journal
obj. 3

The state of Iowa has a 5% sales tax. Hawkeye Services Inc., an Iowa company, had two revenue transactions as follows:

May   8.   Issued Invoice No. 112 to Howerton Inc. for services provided on account, $4,200, plus sales tax.
      20.   Issued Invoice No. 113 to Tel Optics Inc. for services provided on account, $5,780, plus sales tax.

Record these transactions in a revenue journal using the following format:

REVENUE JOURNAL

Date	Invoice No.	Account Debited	Post. Ref.	Accts. Rec. Dr.	Fees Earned Cr.	Sales Tax Payable Cr.

PE 5-5B
Prepare journal entries in a modified revenue journal
obj. 3

Guardian Security Services Inc. provides both commercial and residential security services on account. Two transactions are identified below.

Mar.   1.   Issued Invoice No. 919 to Matrix Inc. for security services provided on account, $350.
       1.   Issued Invoice No. 920 to James King, a residential customer, for services provided on account, $75.

Record these transactions in a revenue journal using the following format:

REVENUE JOURNAL

Date	Invoice No.	Account Debited	Post. Ref.	Accts. Rec. Dr.	Fees Earned— Commercial Cr.	Fees Earned— Residential Cr.

Exercises

EX 5-1
Identify postings from revenue journal
obj. 2

Using the following revenue journal for Omega Services Inc., identify each of the posting references, indicated by a letter, as representing (1) posting to general ledger accounts or (2) posting to subsidiary ledger accounts.

REVENUE JOURNAL

Date	Invoice No.	Account Debited	Post. Ref.	Accounts Receivable Dr. Fees Earned Cr.
2008				
Sept. 1	772	Environmental Safety Co.	(a)	$2,625
10	773	Greenberg Co.	(b)	1,050
20	774	Eco-Systems	(c)	1,400
27	775	SSC Corp.	(d)	965
30				$6,040
				(e)

EX 5-2
Accounts receivable ledger
obj. 2

✓d. Total accounts receivable, $6,580

Based upon the data presented in Exercise 5-1, assume that the beginning balances for the customer accounts were zero, except for SSC Corp., which had a $540 beginning balance. In addition, there were no collections during the period.

a. Set up a T account for Accounts Receivable and T accounts for the four accounts needed in the customer ledger.
b. Post to the T accounts.
c. Determine the balance in the accounts.
d. Prepare a customer balance summary report at September 30, 2008.

EX 5-3
Identify journals
obj. 2

Assuming the use of a two-column (all-purpose) general journal, a revenue journal, and a cash receipts journal as illustrated in this chapter, indicate the journal in which each of the following transactions should be recorded:

a. Receipt of cash for rent.
b. Receipt of cash refund from overpayment of taxes.
c. Closing of drawing account at the end of the year.
d. Sale of office supplies on account, at cost, to a neighboring business.
e. Receipt of cash from sale of office equipment.
f. Providing services for cash.
g. Adjustment to record accrued salaries at the end of the year.
h. Receipt of cash on account from a customer.
i. Providing services on account.
j. Investment of additional cash in the business by the owner.

EX 5-4
Identify journals
obj. 2

Assuming the use of a two-column (all-purpose) general journal, a purchases journal, and a cash payments journal as illustrated in this chapter, indicate the journal in which each of the following transactions should be recorded:

a. Adjustment to prepaid insurance at the end of the month.
b. Adjustment to prepaid rent at the end of the month.
c. Purchase of office supplies for cash.
d. Purchase of office supplies on account.
e. Payment of six months' rent in advance.
f. Purchase of services on account.
g. Adjustment to record depreciation at the end of the month.
h. Adjustment to record accrued salaries at the end of the period.
i. Advance payment of a one-year fire insurance policy on the office.
j. Purchase of an office computer on account.
k. Purchase of office equipment for cash.

EX 5-5
Identify transactions in accounts receivable ledger
obj. 2

The debits and credits from three related transactions are presented in the following customer's account taken from the accounts receivable subsidiary ledger.

NAME *Impact Graphic Design*
ADDRESS *1319 Elm Street*

Date	Item	Post. Ref.	Debit	Credit	Balance
2008					
Dec. 3		R50	680		680
9		J9		70	610
13		CR38		610	—

Describe each transaction, and identify the source of each posting.

EX 5-6
Prepare journal entries in a revenue journal
obj. 2

Gaylord Services Company had the following transactions during the month of May:

May 2. Issued Invoice No. 201 to Townley Corp. for services rendered on account, $320.
    3. Issued Invoice No. 202 to Mid States Inc. for services rendered on account, $450.
    12. Issued Invoice No. 203 to Townley Corp. for services rendered on account, $165.
    24. Issued Invoice No. 204 to Parker Co. for services rendered on account, $665.
    28. Collected Invoice No. 201 from Townley Corp.

a. Prepare a revenue journal with the following headings to record the May revenue transactions for Gaylord Services Company.

REVENUE JOURNAL

Date	Invoice No.	Account Debited	Post. Ref.	Accts. Rec. Dr. Fees Earned Cr.

b. What is the total amount posted to the accounts receivable control and fees earned accounts from the revenue journal for May?
c. What is the May 31 balance of the Townley Corp. customer account assuming a zero balance on May 1?

EX 5-7
Posting a revenue journal
obj. 2

The revenue journal for Tri Star Consulting Inc. is shown below. The accounts receivable control account has a May 1, 2008, balance of $1,200 consisting of an amount due from Ayres Co. There were no collections during May.

REVENUE JOURNAL   Page 12

Date	Invoice No.	Account Debited	Post. Ref.	Accts. Rec. Dr. Fees Earned Cr.
2008				
May 4	355	Brown Co.		2,250
9	356	Life Star Inc.		3,640
14	357	Ayres Co.		1,890
22	359	Brown Co.		2,820
				10,600

a. Prepare a T account for the accounts receivable customer accounts.
b. Post the transactions from the revenue journal to the customer accounts, and determine their ending balances.
c. Prepare T accounts for the accounts receivable control and fees earned accounts. Post control totals to the two accounts, and determine the ending balances.
d. Verify the equality of the sum of the customer account balances and the accounts receivable control account balance.

EX 5-8
Customer balance summary report
obj. 2

The revenue and cash receipts journals for Star Productions Inc. are shown on the next page. The accounts receivable control account has a September 1, 2008, balance of $5,060, consisting of an amount due from Blockbuster Studios Inc.

✓ *Accounts Receivable balance, September 30, $6,300*

		REVENUE JOURNAL			Page 16
Date	Invoice No.	Account Debited	Post. Ref.		Accounts Rec. Dr. Fees Earned Cr.
2008					
Sept. 6	1	Central States Broadcasting Co.	✓		1,500
14	2	Gold Coast Media Inc.	✓		6,100
22	3	Central States Broadcasting Co.	✓		2,450
27	4	Blockbuster Studios Inc.	✓		1,410
28	5	Alpha Communications Inc.	✓		2,440
30					13,900
					(12) (41)

		CASH RECEIPTS JOURNAL				Page 36
Date	Account Credited		Post. Ref.	Fees Earned Cr.	Accts. Rec. Cr.	Cash Dr.
2008						
Sept. 6	Blockbuster Studios Inc.		✓	—	5,060	5,060
11	Fees Earned			3,400		3,400
18	Central States Broadcasting Co.		✓	—	1,500	1,500
28	Gold Coast Media Inc.		✓	—	6,100	6,100
30				3,400	12,660	16,060
				(41)	(12)	(11)

Prepare the customer balance summary report, and determine that the total agrees with the ending balance of the accounts receivable control account.

EX 5-9
Revenue and cash receipts journals

obj. 2

Transactions related to revenue and cash receipts completed by Fine Tune Inc. during the month of October 2008 are as follows:

Oct. 2. Issued Invoice No. 512 to Bellows Co., $870.
4. Received cash from CMI Inc., on account, for $210.
8. Issued Invoice No. 513 to Gabriel Co., $275.
12. Issued Invoice No. 514 to Drake Inc., $730.
19. Received cash from Drake Inc., on account, $670.
22. Issued Invoice No. 515 to Electronic Central Inc., $180.
27. Received cash from Marshall Inc. for services provided, $105.
29. Received cash from Bellows Co. for invoice of October 2.
31. Received cash from McCleary Co. for services provided, $80.

Prepare a single-column revenue journal and a cash receipts journal to record these transactions. Use the following column headings for the cash receipts journal: Fees Earned, Accounts Receivable, and Cash. Place a check mark (✓) in the Post. Ref. column to indicate when the Accounts Receivable subsidiary ledger should be posted.

EX 5-10
Revenue and cash receipts journals

obj. 2

✓ *Revenue Journal total, $11,880*

Orion Corp. has $2,490 in the August 1 balance of the accounts receivable account consisting of $1,030 from Dunn Co. and $1,460 from Townley Co. Transactions related to revenue and cash receipts completed by Orion Corp. during the month of August 2008 are as follows:

Aug. 3. Issued Invoice No. 622 for services provided to Phillips Corp., $2,340.
5. Received cash from Dunn Co., on account, for $1,030.
10. Issued Invoice No. 623 for services provided to Sunstream Aviation Inc., $4,260.
15. Received cash from Townley Co., on account, for $1,460.
18. Issued Invoice No. 624 for services provided to Amex Services Inc., $2,900.
23. Received cash from Phillips Corp. for Invoice No. 622.
28. Issued Invoice No. 625 to Townley Co., on account, for $2,380.
30. Received cash from Rogers Co. for services provided, $60.

a. Prepare a single-column revenue journal and a cash receipts journal to record these transactions. Use the following column headings for the cash receipts journal: Fees Earned, Accounts Receivable, and Cash. Place a check mark (✓) in the Post. Ref. column to indicate when the Accounts Receivable subsidiary ledger should be posted.
b. Prepare a customer balance summary report on August 31, 2008. Verify that the total of the customer balance summary report equals the balance of the accounts receivable control account on August 31, 2008.

EX 5-11
Identify postings from purchases journal
obj. 2

Using the following purchases journal, identify each of the posting references, indicated by a letter, as representing (1) a posting to a general ledger account, (2) a posting to a subsidiary ledger account, or (3) that no posting is required.

PURCHASES JOURNAL — Page 49

Date	Account Credited	Post. Ref.	Accounts Payable Cr.	Store Supplies Dr.	Office Supplies Dr.	Account	Post. Ref.	Amount
2008								
June 4	Corter Supply Co.	(a)	4,200		4,200			
6	Coastal Insurance Co.	(b)	5,325			Prepaid Insurance	(c)	5,325
11	Office To Go	(d)	2,000			Office Equipment	(e)	2,000
13	Taylor Products	(f)	1,675	1,400	275			
20	Office To Go	(g)	5,500			Store Equipment	(h)	5,500
27	Miller Supply Co.	(i)	2,740	2,740				
30			21,440	4,140	4,475			12,825
			(j)	(k)	(l)			(m)

EX 5-12
Identify postings from cash payments journal
obj. 2

Using the following cash payments journal, identify each of the posting references, indicated by a letter, as representing (1) a posting to a general ledger account, (2) a posting to a subsidiary ledger account, or (3) that no posting is required.

CASH PAYMENTS JOURNAL — Page 46

Date	Ck. No.	Account Debited	Post. Ref.	Other Accounts Dr.	Accounts Payable Dr.	Cash Cr.
2008						
Oct. 3	611	Aquatic Systems Co.	(a)		4,000	4,000
5	612	Utilities Expense	(b)	325		325
10	613	Prepaid Rent	(c)	3,200		3,200
17	614	Advertising Expense	(d)	640		640
20	615	Derby Co.	(e)		1,450	1,450
22	616	Office Equipment	(f)	3,900		3,900
25	617	Office Supplies	(g)	250		250
27	618	Evans Co.	(h)		5,500	5,500
31	619	Salaries Expense	(i)	1,750		1,750
31				10,065	10,950	21,015
				(j)	(k)	(l)

EX 5-13
Identify transactions in accounts payable ledger account
obj. 2

The debits and credits from three related transactions are presented in the following creditor's account taken from the accounts payable ledger.

NAME   *Moore Co.*
ADDRESS   *101 W. Stratford Ave.*

Date	Item	Post. Ref.	Debit	Credit	Balance
2008					
Mar. 6		P34		12,200	12,200
10		J10	300		11,900
16		CP37	11,900		—

Describe each transaction, and identify the source of each posting.

EX 5-14
Prepare journal entries in a purchases journal

obj. 2

High Tower Security Company had the following transactions during the month of April:

Apr. 4. Purchased office supplies from Office Helper Inc. on account, $420.
8. Purchased office equipment on account from Best Equipment, Inc., $1,800.
12. Purchased office supplies from Office Helper Inc. on account, $120.
21. Purchased office supplies from Paper-to-Go Inc. on account, $185.
27. Paid invoice on April 4 purchase from Office Helper Inc.

a. Prepare a purchases journal with the following headings to record the April purchase transactions for High Tower Security Company.

PURCHASES JOURNAL

Date	Account Credited	Post. Ref.	Accts. Payable Cr.	Office Supplies Dr.	Other Accounts Dr.	Post. Ref.	Amount

b. What is the total amount posted to the accounts payable control and office supplies accounts from the purchases journal for April?
c. What is the April 30 balance of the Office Helper Inc. creditor account assuming a zero balance on April 1?

EX 5-15
Posting a purchases journal

obj. 2

✓ d. Total, $4,605

The purchases journal for Keep Kleen Window Cleaners Inc. is shown below. The accounts payable control account has a January 1, 2008, balance of $265 of an amount due from Lawson Co. There were no payments made on creditor invoices during January.

PURCHASES JOURNAL   Page 16

Date	Account Credited	Post. Ref.	Accts. Payable Cr.	Cleaning Supplies Dr.	Other Accounts Dr.	Post. Ref.	Amount
2008							
Jan. 4	Best Cleaning Supplies Inc.		345	345			
15	Lawson Co.		285	285			
21	Office Mate Inc.		3,400		Office Equipment		3,400
26	Best Cleaning Supplies Inc.		310	310			
31			4,340	940			3,400

a. Prepare a T account for the accounts payable creditor accounts.
b. Post the transactions from the purchases journal to the creditor accounts, and determine their ending balances.
c. Prepare T accounts for the accounts payable control and cleaning supplies accounts. Post control totals to the two accounts, and determine their ending balances.
d. Verify the equality of the sum of the creditor account balances and the accounts payable control account balance.

EX 5-16
*Supplier balance
summary report*

obj. 2

✓ *Accts. Pay., June 30,
$11,060*

The cash payments and purchases journals for Silver Spring Landscaping Co. are shown below. The accounts payable control account has a June 1, 2008 balance of $2,940, consisting of an amount owed to Augusta Sod Co.

CASH PAYMENTS JOURNAL Page 31

Date	Ck. No.	Account Debited	Post. Ref.	Other Accounts Dr.	Accounts Payable Dr.	Cash Cr.
2008						
June 4	203	Augusta Sod Co.	✓		2,940	2,940
5	204	Utilities Expense	54	325		325
15	205	Kimble Lumber Co.	✓		5,920	5,920
27	206	Schott's Fertilizer	✓		970	970
30				325	9,830	10,155
				(✓)	(21)	(11)

PURCHASES JOURNAL Page 22

Date	Account Credited	Post. Ref.	Accounts Payable Cr.	Landscaping Supplies Dr.	Other Accounts Dr.	Post. Ref.	Amount
2008							
June 3	Kimble Lumber Co.	✓	5,920	5,920			
7	Gibraltar Insurance Co.	✓	1,100		Prepaid Insurance	17	1,100
14	Schott's Fertilizer	✓	970	970			
24	Augusta Sod Co.	✓	6,310	6,310			
29	Kimble Lumber Co.	✓	3,650	3,650			
30			17,950	16,850			1,100
			(21)	(14)			(✓)

Prepare the supplier balance summary report, and determine that the total agrees with the ending balance of the accounts payable control account.

EX 5-17
*Purchases and cash
payments journals*

obj. 2

✓ *Accts. Pay., Total, $660*

Transactions related to purchases and cash payments completed by Winston Cleaning Services Inc. during the month of December 2008 are as follows:

Dec. 1. Issued Check No. 57 to Liquid Klean Supplies Inc. in payment of account, $205.
  3. Purchased cleaning supplies on account from Industrial Products Inc., $130.
  8. Issued Check No. 58 to purchase equipment from Jefferson Equipment Sales, $2,600.
  12. Purchased cleaning supplies on account from Purcell Products Inc., $190.
  15. Issued Check No. 59 to Maryville Laundry Service in payment of account, $100.
  17. Purchased supplies on account from Liquid Klean Supplies Inc., $245.
  20. Purchased laundry services from Maryville Laundry Service on account, $95.
  25. Issued Check No. 60 to Industrial Products Inc. in payment of December 3rd invoice.
  31. Issued Check No. 61 in payment of salaries, $4,100.

Prepare a purchases journal and a cash payments journal to record these transactions. The forms of the journals are similar to those illustrated in the text. Place a check mark (✓) in the Post. Ref. column to indicate when the Accounts Payable subsidiary ledger should be posted. Winston Cleaning Services Inc. uses the following accounts:

Cleaning Supplies	14
Equipment	18
Salary Expense	51
Laundry Service Expense	53

EX 5-18
Purchases and cash payments journals

obj. 2

Pet Groom Inc. has $685 in the May 1 balance of the accounts payable control account. Transactions related to purchases and cash payments completed by Pet Groom Inc. during the month of May 2008 are as follows:

May 4. Purchased pet supplies from Best Friend Supplies Inc. on account, $265.
6. Issued Check No. 345 to Larrimore Inc. in payment of account, $455.
11. Purchased pet supplies from Poodle Pals Inc., $675.
18. Issued Check No. 346 to Pets Mart Inc. in payment of account, $230.
19. Purchased office equipment from Office Helper Inc. on account, $2,400.
23. Issued Check No. 347 to Best Friend Supplies Inc. in payment of account from purchase made on May 4.
27. Purchased pet supplies from Pets Mart Inc. on account, $410.
30. Issued Check No. 348 to Sanders Inc. for cleaning expenses, $45.

a. Prepare a purchases journal and a cash payments journal to record these transactions. The forms of the journals are similar to those used in the text. Place a check mark (✓) in the Post. Ref. column to indicate when the Accounts Payable subsidiary ledger should be posted. Pet Groom Inc. uses the following accounts:

Office Equipment	13
Pet Supplies	14
Cleaning Expense	54

b. Prepare a supplier balance summary report on May 31, 2008. Verify that the total of the supplier balance summary report equals the balance of the accounts payable control account on May 31, 2008.

EX 5-19
Error in accounts payable ledger and supplier balance summary report

obj. 2

✓ *b. Total accounts payable, $37,450*

After Western Assay Services Inc. had completed all postings for October in the current year (2008), the sum of the balances in the following accounts payable ledger did not agree with the $37,450 balance of the controlling account in the general ledger.

NAME   *C. D. Greer and Son*
ADDRESS   *972 S. Tenth Street*

Date	Item	Post. Ref.	Debit	Credit	Balance
2008					
Oct. 17		P30		3,750	3,750
27		P31		10,000	13,750

NAME   *Cheyenne Minerals Inc.*
ADDRESS   *1170 Mattis Avenue*

Date	Item	Post. Ref.	Debit	Credit	Balance
2008					
Oct. 1	Balance	✓			8,300
7		P30		5,900	14,300
12		J7	300		14,000
20		CP23	5,500		8,500

NAME   *Cutler and Powell*
ADDRESS   *717 Elm Street*

Date	Item	Post. Ref.	Debit	Credit	Balance
2008					
Oct. 1	Balance	✓			6,100
18		CP23	6,100		—
29		P31		9,100	9,100

NAME   *Martinez Mining Co.*
ADDRESS   *1240 W. Main Street*

Date	Item	Post. Ref.	Debit	Credit	Balance
2008					
Oct. 1	Balance	✓			4,750
10		CP22	4,750		—
17		P30		3,900	3,900
25		J7	850		2,050

NAME   *Valley Power*
ADDRESS   *915 E. Walnut Street*

Date	Item	Post. Ref.	Debit	Credit	Balance
2008					
Oct. 5		P30		3,150	3,150

Assuming that the controlling account balance of $37,450 has been verified as correct, (a) determine the error(s) in the preceding accounts and (b) prepare a supplier balance summary report from the corrected accounts payable subsidiary ledger.

EX 5-20
Identify postings from special journals
obj. 2

Ready Solutions Consulting Company makes most of its sales and purchases on credit. It uses the five journals described in this chapter (revenue, cash receipts, purchases, cash payments, and general journals). Identify the journal most likely used in recording the postings for selected transactions indicated by letter in the following T accounts:

	Cash		
a.	11,190	b.	9,280

	Prepaid Rent	
	c.	400

	Accounts Receivable		
d.	12,410	e.	10,500

	Accounts Payable		
f.	7,600	g.	6,500

	Office Supplies	
h.	6,500	

	Fees Earned	
	i.	12,410

	Rent Expense	
j.	400	

EX 5-21
Cash receipts journal
obj. 2

The following cash receipts journal headings have been suggested for a small service firm. List the errors you find in the headings.

			CASH RECEIPTS JOURNAL			Page 12
Date	Account Credited	Post. Ref.	Fees Earned Cr.	Accts. Rec. Cr.	Cash Cr.	Other Accounts Dr.

EX 5-22
Modified special journals
objs. 2, 3
✓ c. 2. $1,218

Lee Technical Services Inc. was established on June 15, 2008. The clients for whom Lee provided technical services during the remainder of June are listed below. These clients pay Lee the amount indicated plus a 5% sales tax.

June 16. Issued Invoice No. 1 to A. Sommerfeld for $400 plus tax on account.
     19. Issued Invoice No. 2 to R. Mendoza for $180 plus tax.
     21. Issued Invoice No. 3 to J. Koss for $100 plus tax.
     22. Issued Invoice No. 4 to D. Jeffries for $160 plus tax.

June 24. Provided services to K. Sallinger, in exchange for office supplies having a value of $100, plus tax.
    26. Issued Invoice No. 5 to J. Koss for $280 plus tax.
    28. Issued Invoice No. 6 to R. Mendoza for $40 plus tax.

a. Journalize the transactions for June, using a three-column revenue journal and a two-column general journal. Post the customer accounts in the accounts receivable subsidiary ledger, and insert the balance immediately after recording each entry.

b. Post the general journal and the revenue journal to the following general ledger accounts, inserting account balances only after the last postings:

12	Accounts Receivable
14	Office Supplies
22	Sales Tax Payable
41	Fees Earned

c. 1. What is the sum of the balances in the accounts receivable subsidiary ledger at June 30?
   2. What is the balance of the controlling account at June 30?

EX 5-23
Computerized accounting systems

obj. 4

Most computerized accounting systems use electronic forms to record transaction information, such as the invoice form illustrated at the top of Exhibit 8.

a. Identify the key input fields (spaces) in an electronic invoice form.
b. What accounts are posted from an electronic invoice form?
c. Why aren't special journal totals posted to control accounts at the end of the month in an electronic accounting system?

EX 5-24
E-commerce

obj. 5

For each of the following companies, determine if their e-commerce strategy is primarily business-to-consumer (B2C), business-to-business (B2B), or both. Use the Internet to investigate each company's site in conducting your research.

a. Amazon.com
b. Dell Inc.
c. W.W. Grainger, Inc.
d. L.L. Bean, Inc.
e. Smurfit-Stone Container Corporation
f. Intuit Inc.

Problems Series A

PR 5-1A
Revenue journal; accounts receivable and general ledgers

obj. 2

✓ *1. Revenue journal, total fees earned, $1,060*

A-Plus Learning Centers was established on March 20, 2008, to provide educational services. The services provided during the remainder of the month are as follows:

Mar. 21. Issued Invoice No. 1 to J. Dunlop for $70 on account.
    22. Issued Invoice No. 2 to K. Thorne for $310 on account.
    24. Issued Invoice No. 3 to T. Morris for $95 on account.
    25. Provided educational services, $125, to K. Thorne in exchange for educational supplies.
    27. Issued Invoice No. 4 to F. Mintz for $190 on account.
    28. Issued Invoice No. 5 to D. Bennett for $175 on account.
    30. Issued Invoice No. 6 to K. Thorne for $105 on account.
    31. Issued Invoice No. 7 to T. Morris for $115 on account.

Instructions
1. Journalize the transactions for March, using a single-column revenue journal and a two-column general journal. Post to the following customer accounts in the accounts receivable ledger, and insert the balance immediately after recording each entry: D. Bennett; J. Dunlop; F. Mintz; T. Morris; K. Thorne.

2. Post the revenue journal and the general journal to the following accounts in the general ledger, inserting the account balances only after the last postings:

12	Accounts Receivable
13	Supplies
41	Fees Earned

3. a. What is the sum of the balances of the accounts in the subsidiary ledger at March 31?
   b. What is the balance of the controlling account at March 31?
4. Assume that on April 1, the state in which A-Plus operates begins requiring that sales tax be collected on educational services. Briefly explain how the revenue journal may be modified to accommodate sales of services on account that require the collection of a state sales tax.

PR 5-2A

Revenue and cash receipts journals; accounts receivable and general ledgers

obj. 2

✓ *3. Total cash receipts, $34,680*

Transactions related to revenue and cash receipts completed by Palm Beach Architects Co. during the period September 2–30, 2008, are as follows:

Sept. 2. Issued Invoice No. 793 to Morton Co., $5,400.
         5. Received cash from Mendez Co. for the balance owed on its account.
         6. Issued Invoice No. 794 to Quest Co., $1,980.
        13. Issued Invoice No. 795 to Shilo Co., $2,950.
             Post revenue and collections to the accounts receivable subsidiary ledger.
        15. Received cash from Quest Co. for the balance owed on September 1.
        16. Issued Invoice No. 796 to Quest Co., $6,100.
             Post revenue and collections to the accounts receivable subsidiary ledger.
        19. Received cash from Morton Co. for the balance due on invoice of September 2.
        20. Received cash from Quest Co. for invoice of September 6.
        22. Issued Invoice No. 797 to Mendez Co., $8,020.
        25. Received $2,000 note receivable in partial settlement of the balance due on the Shilo Co. account.
        30. Recorded cash fees earned, $11,930.
             Post revenue and collections to the accounts receivable subsidiary ledger.

Instructions

1. Insert the following balances in the general ledger as of September 1:

11	Cash	$13,650
12	Accounts Receivable	15,370
14	Notes Receivable	5,000
41	Fees Earned	—

2. Insert the following balances in the accounts receivable subsidiary ledger as of September 1:

Mendez Co.	$8,960
Morton Co.	—
Quest Co.	6,410
Shilo Co.	—

3. Prepare a single-column revenue journal and a cash receipts journal. Use the following column headings for the cash receipts journal: Fees Earned, Accounts Receivable, and Cash. The Fees Earned column is used to record cash fees. Insert a check mark (✓) in the Post. Ref. column.
4. Using the two special journals and the two-column general journal, journalize the transactions for September. Post to the accounts receivable subsidiary ledger, and insert the balances at the points indicated in the narrative of transactions. Determine the balance in the customer's account before recording a cash receipt.
5. Total each of the columns of the special journals, and post the individual entries and totals to the general ledger. Insert account balances after the last posting.
6. Determine that the subsidiary ledger agrees with the controlling account in the general ledger.

PR 5-3A
Purchases, accounts payable account, and accounts payable ledger

objs. 2, 3

KLOOSTER
& ALLEN

✓3. Total accounts payable credit, $16,500

Forever Spring Landscaping designs and installs landscaping. The landscape designers and office staff use office supplies, while field supplies (rock, bark, etc.) are used in the actual landscaping. Purchases on account completed by Forever Spring Landscaping during May 2008 are as follows:

May 2. Purchased office supplies on account from Lawson Co., $360.
     5. Purchased office equipment on account from Peach Computers Co., $5,150.
     9. Purchased office supplies on account from Executive Office Supply Co., $305.
    13. Purchased field supplies on account from Yee Co., $1,360.
    14. Purchased field supplies on account from Nelson Co., $2,940.
    17. Purchased field supplies on account from Yee Co., $1,345.
    24. Purchased field supplies on account from Nelson Co., $3,810.
    29. Purchased office supplies on account from Executive Office Supply Co., $225.
    31. Purchased field supplies on account from Nelson Co., $1,005.

Instructions
1. Insert the following balances in the general ledger as of May 1:

14	Field Supplies	$ 6,310
15	Office Supplies	830
18	Office Equipment	14,300
21	Accounts Payable	1,105

2. Insert the following balances in the accounts payable subsidiary ledger as of May 1:

Executive Office Supply	$365
Lawson Co.	740
Nelson Co.	—
Peach Computers Co.	—
Yee Co.	—

3. Journalize the transactions for May, using a purchases journal similar to the one illustrated in this chapter. Prepare the purchases journal with columns for Accounts Payable, Field Supplies, Office Supplies, and Other Accounts. Post to the creditor accounts in the accounts payable subsidiary ledger immediately after each entry.
4. Post the purchases journal to the accounts in the general ledger.
5. a. What is the sum of the balances in the subsidiary ledger at May 31?
   b. What is the balance of the controlling account at May 31?

PR 5-4A
Purchases and cash payments journals; accounts payable and general ledgers

objs. 2, 3

KLOOSTER
& ALLEN

✓1. Total cash payments, $81,160

Artesian Springs Water Testing Service was established on September 16, 2008. Artesian uses field equipment and field supplies (chemicals and other supplies) to analyze water for unsafe contaminants in streams, lakes, and ponds. Transactions related to purchases and cash payments during the remainder of September are as follows:

Sept. 16. Issued Check No. 1 in payment of rent for the remainder of September, $1,500.
      16. Purchased field supplies on account from Heath Supply Co., $4,360.
      16. Purchased field equipment on account from Test-Rite Equipment Co., $15,900.
      17. Purchased office supplies on account from Baker Supply Co., $280.
      19. Issued Check No. 2 in payment of field supplies, $2,420, and office supplies, $300.
          Post the journals to the accounts payable subsidiary ledger.
      23. Purchased office supplies on account from Baker Supply Co., $410.
      23. Issued Check No. 3 to purchase land, $35,000.
      24. Issued Check No. 4 to Heath Supply Co. in payment of invoice, $4,360.
      26. Issued Check No. 5 to Test-Rite Equipment Co. in payment of invoice, $15,900.
          Post the journals to the accounts payable subsidiary ledger.
      30. Acquired land in exchange for field equipment having a cost of $7,000.
      30. Purchased field supplies on account from Heath Supply Co., $5,300.
      30. Issued Check No. 6 to Baker Supply Co. in payment of invoice, $280.
      30. Purchased the following from Test-Rite Equipment Co. on account: field supplies, $700, and field equipment, $3,600.
      30. Issued Check No. 7 in payment of salaries, $21,400.
          Post the journals to the accounts payable subsidiary ledger.

Instructions

1. Journalize the transactions for September. Use a purchases journal and a cash payments journal, similar to those illustrated in this chapter, and a two-column general journal. Use debit columns for Field Supplies, Office Supplies, and Other Accounts in the purchases journal. Refer to the following partial chart of accounts:

11	Cash	19	Land
14	Field Supplies	21	Accounts Payable
15	Office Supplies	61	Salary Expense
17	Field Equipment	71	Rent Expense

At the points indicated in the narrative of transactions, post to the following accounts in the accounts payable subsidiary ledger:

Baker Supply Co.
Heath Supply Co.
Test-Rite Equipment Co.

2. Post the individual entries (Other Accounts columns of the purchases journal and the cash payments journal and both columns of the general journal) to the appropriate general ledger accounts.
3. Total each of the columns of the purchases journal and the cash payments journal, and post the appropriate totals to the general ledger. (Because the problem does not include transactions related to cash receipts, the cash account in the ledger will have a credit balance.)
4. Prepare a supplier balance summary report.

PR 5-5A
All journals and general ledger; trial balance

objs. 2, 3

✓ *2. Total cash receipts, $52,560*

The transactions completed by Lightening Express Delivery Company during July 2008, the first month of the fiscal year, were as follows:

July 1 Issued Check No. 610 for July rent, $6,400.
    2. Issued Invoice No. 940 to Capps Co., $2,420.
    3. Received check for $5,400 from Perkins Co. in payment of account.
    5. Purchased a vehicle on account from Browning Transportation, $31,600.
    6. Purchased office equipment on account from Bell Computer Co., $4,200.
    6. Issued Invoice No. 941 to Darr Co., $5,920.
    9. Issued Check No. 611 for fuel expense, $850.
   10. Received check from Shingo Co. in payment of $4,050 invoice.
   10. Issued Check No. 612 for $905 to Office To Go Inc. in payment of invoice.
   10. Issued Invoice No. 942 to Joy Co., $1,260.
   11. Issued Check No. 613 for $3,605 to Crowne Supply Co. in payment of account.
   11. Issued Check No. 614 for $805 to Porter Co. in payment of account.
   12. Received check from Capps Co. in payment of $2,420 invoice.
   13. Issued Check No. 615 to Browning Transportation in payment of $31,600 balance.
   16. Issued Check No. 616 for $38,900 for cash purchase of a vehicle.
   16. Cash fees earned for July 1–16, $17,800.
   17. Issued Check No. 617 for miscellaneous administrative expense, $260.
   18. Purchased maintenance supplies on account from Crowne Supply Co., $1,730.
   19. Purchased the following on account from McClain Co.: maintenance supplies, $1,980; office supplies, $430.
   20. Issued Check No. 618 in payment of advertising expense, $1,700.
   20. Used $3,500 maintenance supplies to repair delivery vehicles.
   23. Purchased office supplies on account from Office To Go Inc., $600.
   24. Issued Invoice No. 943 to Shingo Co., $5,070.
   24. Issued Check No. 619 to K. Rivera as a personal withdrawal, $3,000.
   25. Issued Invoice No. 944 to Darr Co., $6,200.
   25. Received check for $3,950 from Perkins Co. in payment of balance.
   26. Issued Check No. 620 to Bell Computer Co. in payment of $4,200 invoice of July 6.
   30. Issued Check No. 621 for monthly salaries as follows: driver salaries, $16,500; office salaries, $8,200.
   31. Cash fees earned for July 17–31, $18,940.
   31. Issued Check No. 622 in payment for office supplies, $800.

Instructions

1. Enter the following account balances in the general ledger as of July 1:

11	Cash	$158,965	32	K. Rivera, Drawing	—
12	Accounts Receivable	13,400	41	Fees Earned	—
14	Maintenance Supplies	9,300	51	Driver Salaries Expense	—
15	Office Supplies	4,500	52	Maintenance Supplies	
16	Office Equipment	24,300		Expense	—
17	Accumulated Depreciation		53	Fuel Expense	—
	—Office Equipment	4,500	61	Office Salaries Expense	—
18	Vehicles	84,600	62	Rent Expense	—
19	Accumulated Depreciation		63	Advertising Expense	—
	—Vehicles	12,300	64	Miscellaneous Adminis-	
21	Accounts Payable	5,315		trative Expense	—
31	K. Rivera, Capital	272,950			

2. Journalize the transactions for July 2008, using the following journals similar to those illustrated in this chapter: cash receipts journal, purchases journal (with columns for Accounts Payable, Maintenance Supplies, Office Supplies, and Other Accounts), single-column revenue journal, cash payments journal, and two-column general journal. Assume that the daily postings to the individual accounts in the accounts payable ledger and the accounts receivable ledger have been made.
3. Post the appropriate individual entries to the general ledger.
4. Total each of the columns of the special journals, and post the appropriate totals to the general ledger; insert the account balances.
5. Prepare a trial balance.
6. Verify the agreement of each subsidiary ledger with its control account. The sum of the balances of the accounts in the subsidiary ledgers as of July 31 are:

Accounts Receivable	$18,450
Accounts Payable	4,740

Problems Series B

PR 5-1B
*Revenue journal;
accounts receivable and
general ledgers*

obj. 2

✓1. Revenue journal,
total fees earned, $2,140

Sentinel Security Services was established on August 15, 2008, to provide security services. The services provided during the remainder of the month are listed below.

Aug. 18. Issued Invoice No. 1 to Jacob Co. for $340 on account.
  20. Issued Invoice No. 2 to Qwik-Mart Co. for $275 on account.
  22. Issued Invoice No. 3 to Great Northern Co. for $580 on account.
  27. Issued Invoice No. 4 to Carson Co. for $465 on account.
  28. Issued Invoice No. 5 to Bower Co. for $105 on account.
  28. Provided security services, $90, to Qwik-Mart Co. in exchange for supplies.
  30. Issued Invoice No. 6 to Qwik-Mart Co. for $135 on account.
  31. Issued Invoice No. 7 to Great Northern Co. for $240 on account.

Instructions

1. Journalize the transactions for August, using a single-column revenue journal and a two-column general journal. Post to the following customer accounts in the accounts receivable ledger, and insert the balance immediately after recording each entry: Bower Co.; Carson Co.; Great Northern Co.; Jacob Co.; Qwik-Mart Co.
2. Post the revenue journal to the following accounts in the general ledger, inserting the account balances only after the last postings:

12	Accounts Receivable
14	Supplies
41	Fees Earned

3. a. What is the sum of the balances of the accounts in the subsidiary ledger at August 31?
 b. What is the balance of the controlling account at August 31?
4. Assume that on September 1, the state in which Sentinel operates begins requiring that sales tax be collected on accounting services. Briefly explain how the revenue journal

may be modified to accommodate sales of services on account requiring the collection of a state sales tax.

PR 5-2B
Revenue and cash receipts journals; accounts receivable and general ledgers

obj. 2

✓ *3. Total cash receipts, $7,040*

Transactions related to revenue and cash receipts completed by Elite Engineering Services during the period November 2–30, 2008, are as follows:

Nov. 2. Issued Invoice No. 717 to Yamura Co., $850.
   3. Received cash from AGI Co. for the balance owed on its account.
   7. Issued Invoice No. 718 to Phoenix Development Co., $430.
   10. Issued Invoice No. 719 to Ross and Son, $2,010.
       Post revenue and collections to the accounts receivable subsidiary ledger.
   14. Received cash from Phoenix Development Co. for the balance owed on November 1.
   16. Issued Invoice No. 720 to Phoenix Development Co., $295.
       Post revenue and collections to the accounts receivable subsidiary ledger.
   19. Received cash from Yamura Co. for the balance due on invoice of November 2.
   20. Received cash from Phoenix Development Co. for invoice of November 7.
   23. Issued Invoice No. 721 to AGI Co., $695.
   30. Recorded cash fees earned, $3,510.
   30. Received office equipment of $1,600 in partial settlement of balance due on the Ross and Son account.
       Post revenue and collections to the accounts receivable subsidiary ledger.

Instructions
1. Insert the following balances in the general ledger as of November 1:

11	Cash	$18,940
12	Accounts Receivable	2,250
18	Office Equipment	32,600
41	Fees Earned	—

2. Insert the following balances in the accounts receivable subsidiary ledger as of November 1:

AGI Co.	$1,490
Phoenix Development Co.	760
Ross and Son	—
Yamura Co.	—

3. Prepare a single-column revenue journal and a cash receipts journal. Use the following column headings for the cash receipts journal: Fees Earned, Accounts Receivable, and Cash. The Fees Earned column is used to record cash fees. Insert a check mark (✓) in the Post. Ref. column.
4. Using the two special journals and the two-column general journal, journalize the transactions for November. Post to the accounts receivable subsidiary ledger, and insert the balances at the points indicated in the narrative of transactions. Determine the balance in the customer's account before recording a cash receipt.
5. Total each of the columns of the special journals, and post the individual entries and totals to the general ledger. Insert account balances after the last posting.
6. Determine that the subsidiary ledger agrees with the controlling account in the general ledger.

PR 5-3B
Purchases, accounts payable account, and accounts payable ledger

objs. 2, 3

Washington Surveyors provides survey work for construction projects. The office staff use office supplies, while surveying crews use field supplies. Purchases on account completed by Washington Surveyors during October 2008 are as follows:

Oct. 1. Purchased field supplies on account from Wendell Co., $2,540.
   3. Purchased office supplies on account from Lassiter Co., $280.
   8. Purchased field supplies on account from Precision Supplies, $3,640.
   12. Purchased field supplies on account from Wendell Co., $3,000.
   15. Purchased office supplies on account from J-Mart Co., $390.
   19. Purchased office equipment on account from Eskew Co., $7,000.

✓ *3. Total accounts payable credit, $21,625*

Oct. 23. Purchased field supplies on account from Precision Supplies, $1,940.
　　26. Purchased office supplies on account from J-Mart Co., $185.
　　30. Purchased field supplies on account from Precision Supplies, $2,650.

Instructions
1. Insert the following balances in the general ledger as of October 1:

14	Field Supplies	$ 5,300
15	Office Supplies	1,230
18	Office Equipment	18,400
21	Accounts Payable	4,540

2. Insert the following balances in the accounts payable subsidiary ledger as of October 1:

Eskew Co.	$3,500
J-Mart Co.	620
Lassiter Co.	420
Precision Supplies	—
Wendell Co.	—

3. Journalize the transactions for October, using a purchases journal similar to the one illustrated in this chapter. Prepare the purchases journal with columns for Accounts Payable, Field Supplies, Office Supplies, and Other Accounts. Post to the creditor accounts in the accounts payable ledger immediately after each entry.
4. Post the purchases journal to the accounts in the general ledger.
5. a. What is the sum of the balances in the subsidiary ledger at October 31?
　 b. What is the balance of the controlling account at October 31?

PR 5-4B
Purchases and cash payments journals; accounts payable and general ledgers

objs. 2, 3

✓ *1. Total cash payments, $235,140*

Texas Tea Exploration Co. was established on March 15, 2008, to provide oil-drilling services. Texas Tea uses field equipment (rigs and pipe) and field supplies (drill bits and lubricants) in its operations. Transactions related to purchases and cash payments during the remainder of March are as follows:

Mar. 16. Issued Check No. 1 in payment of rent for the remainder of March, $4,800.
　　16. Purchased field equipment on account from PMI Sales Inc., $28,500.
　　17. Purchased field supplies on account from Culver Supply Co., $8,740.
　　18. Issued Check No. 2 in payment of field supplies, $2,150, and office supplies, $390.
　　20. Purchased office supplies on account from Castle Office Supply Co., $1,060.
　　　 Post the journals to the accounts payable subsidiary ledger.
　　24. Issued Check No. 3 to PMI Sales Inc., in payment of March 16 invoice.
　　26. Issued Check No. 4 to Culver Supply Co. in payment of March 17 invoice.
　　28. Issued Check No. 5 to purchase land, $165,000.
　　28. Purchased office supplies on account from Castle Office Supply Co., $2,570.
　　　 Post the journals to the accounts payable subsidiary ledger.
　　30. Purchased the following from PMI Sales Inc. on account: field supplies, $21,380, and office equipment, $12,200.
　　30. Issued Check No. 6 to Castle Office Supply Co. in payment of March 20 invoice.
　　30. Purchased field supplies on account from Culver Supply Co., $11,100.
　　31. Issued Check No. 7 in payment of salaries, $24,500.
　　31. Rented building for one year in exchange for field equipment having a cost of $12,400.
　　　 Post the journals to the accounts payable subsidiary ledger.

Instructions
1. Journalize the transactions for March. Use a purchases journal and a cash payments journal, similar to those illustrated in this chapter, and a two-column general journal. Set debit columns for Field Supplies, Office Supplies, and Other Accounts in the purchases journal. Refer to the following partial chart of accounts:

11	Cash		18	Office Equipment
14	Field Supplies		19	Land
15	Office Supplies		21	Accounts Payable
16	Prepaid Rent		61	Salary Expense
17	Field Equipment		71	Rent Expense

At the points indicated in the narrative of transactions, post to the following accounts in the accounts payable ledger:

Castle Office Supply Co.
Culver Supply Co.
PMI Sales Inc.

2. Post the individual entries (Other Accounts columns of the purchases journal and the cash payments journal; both columns of the general journal) to the appropriate general ledger accounts.
3. Total each of the columns of the purchases journal and the cash payments journal, and post the appropriate totals to the general ledger. (Because the problem does not include transactions related to cash receipts, the cash account in the ledger will have a credit balance.)
4. Prepare a supplier balance summary report.

PR 5-5B
All journals and general ledger; trial balance

obj. 2

✓ 2. Total cash receipts,
$65,430

The transactions completed by One Day Courier Company during May 2008, the first month of the fiscal year, were as follows:

May 1. Issued Check No. 205 for May rent, $800.
  2. Purchased a vehicle on account from McIntyre Sales Co., $21,700.
  3. Purchased office equipment on account from Office Mate Inc., $470.
  5. Issued Invoice No. 91 to Martin Co., $4,700.
  6. Received check for $5,240 from Baker Co. in payment of invoice.
  7. Issued Invoice No. 92 to Trent Co., $7,900.
  9. Issued Check No. 206 for fuel expense, $590.
  10. Received check for $7,490 from Sing Co. in payment of invoice.
  10. Issued Check No. 207 to Office City in payment of $440 invoice.
  10. Issued Check No. 208 to Bastille Co. in payment of $1,250 invoice.
  11. Issued Invoice No. 93 to Jarvis Co., $6,300.
  11. Issued Check No. 209 to Porter Co. in payment of $290 invoice.
  12. Received check for $4,700 from Martin Co. in payment of invoice.
  13. Issued Check No. 210 to McIntyre Sales Co. in payment of $21,700 invoice.
  16. Cash fees earned for May 1–16, $16,800.
  16. Issued Check No. 211 for purchase of a vehicle, $21,800.
  17. Issued Check No. 212 for miscellaneous administrative expense, $3,700.
  18. Purchased maintenance supplies on account from Bastille Co., $1,590.
  18. Received check for rent revenue on office space, $1,000.
  19. Purchased the following on account from Master Supply Co.: maintenance supplies, $1,950, and office supplies, $1,550.
  20. Issued Check No. 213 in payment of advertising expense, $6,900.
  20. Used maintenance supplies with a cost of $2,200 to repair vehicles.
  21. Purchased office supplies on account from Office City, $630.
  24. Issued Invoice No. 94 to Sing Co., $7,590.
  25. Received check for $11,700 from Baker Co. in payment of invoice.
  25. Issued Invoice No. 95 to Trent Co., $4,870.
  26. Issued Check No. 214 to Office Mate Inc. in payment of $470 invoice.
  27. Issued Check No. 215 to F. Desai as a personal withdrawal, $3,000.
  30. Issued Check No. 216 in payment of driver salaries, $26,900.
  31. Issued Check No. 217 in payment of office salaries, $16,800.
  31. Issued Check No. 218 for office supplies, $300.
  31. Cash fees earned for May 17–31, $18,500.

Instructions
1. Enter the following account balances in the general ledger as of May 1:

11	Cash	$ 57,900	18	Vehicles	$ 48,000
12	Accounts Receivable	24,430	19	Accumulated Depreciation	
14	Maintenance Supplies	6,150		—Vehicles	13,590
15	Office Supplies	2,580	21	Accounts Payable	1,980
16	Office Equipment	14,370	31	F. Desai, Capital	135,280
17	Accumulated Depreciation		32	F. Desai, Drawing	—
	—Office Equipment	2,580	41	Fees Earned	—

(continued)

42	Rent Revenue	—	61	Office Salaries Expense	—
51	Driver Salaries Expense	—	62	Rent Expense	—
52	Maintenance Supplies		63	Advertising Expense	—
	Expense	—	64	Miscellaneous Adminis-	
53	Fuel Expense	—		trative Expense	—

2. Journalize the transactions for May 2008, using the following journals similar to those illustrated in this chapter: single-column revenue journal, cash receipts journal, purchases journal (with columns for Accounts Payable, Maintenance Supplies, Office Supplies, and Other Accounts), cash payments journal, and two-column general journal. Assume that the daily postings to the individual accounts in the accounts payable ledger and the accounts receivable ledger have been made.
3. Post the appropriate individual entries to the general ledger.
4. Total each of the columns of the special journals, and post the appropriate totals to the general ledger; insert the account balances.
5. Prepare a trial balance.
6. Verify the agreement of each subsidiary ledger with its controlling account. The sum of the balances of the accounts in the subsidiary ledgers as of May 31 are as follows:

Accounts Receivable	$26,660
Accounts Payable	5,720

Special Activities

SA 5-1
Ethics and professional conduct in business

ETHICS

Sharon Els sells security systems for Guardsman Security Co. Els has a monthly sales quota of $40,000. If Els exceeds this quota, she is awarded a bonus. In measuring the quota, a sale is credited to the salesperson when a customer signs a contract for installation of a security system. Through the 25th of the current month, Els has sold $30,000 in security systems.

Vortex Co., a business rumored to be on the verge of bankruptcy, contacted Els on the 26th of the month about having a security system installed. Els estimates that the contract would yield about $14,000 worth of business for Guardsman Security Co. In addition, this contract would be large enough to put Els "over the top" for a bonus in the current month. However, Els is concerned that Vortex Co. will not be able to make the contract payment after the security system is installed. In fact, Els has heard rumors that a competing security services company refused to install a system for Vortex Co. because of these concerns.

Upon further consideration, Els concluded that her job is to sell security systems and that it's someone else's problem to collect the resulting accounts receivable. Thus, Els wrote the contract with Vortex Co. and received a bonus for the month.

a.   Discuss whether Sharon Els was acting in an ethical manner.
b.   How might Guardsman Security Co. prevent this scenario from occurring?

SA 5-2
Manual vs. computerized accounting systems

The following conversation took place between Merit Construction Co.'s bookkeeper, Todd Monroe, and the accounting supervisor, Kim Hargrove.

Kim: Todd, I'm thinking about bringing in a new computerized accounting system to replace our manual system. I guess this will mean that you will need to learn how to do computerized accounting.

Todd: What does computerized accounting mean?

Kim: I'm not sure, but you'll need to prepare for this new way of doing business.

Todd: I'm not so sure we need a computerized system. I've been looking at some of the sample reports from the software vendor. It looks to me as if the computer will not add much to what we are already doing.

Kim: What do you mean?

Todd: Well, look at these reports. This Sales by Customer Report looks like our revenue journal, and the Deposit Detail Report looks like our cash receipts journal. Granted, the computer types them, so they look much neater than my special journals, but I don't see that we're gaining much from this change.

Kim: Well, surely there's more to it than nice-looking reports. I've got to believe that a computerized system will save us time and effort someplace.

Todd: I don't see how. We still need to key in transactions into the computer. If anything, there may be more work when it's all said and done.

▭▭▷ Do you agree with Todd? Why might a computerized environment be preferred over the manual system?

SA 5-3
Accounts receivable and accounts payable

Like most businesses, when Eagle Company renders services to another business, it is typical that the service is rendered "on account," rather than as a cash transaction. As a result, Eagle Company has an account receivable for the service provided. Likewise, the company receiving the service has an account payable for the amount owed for services received. At a later date, Eagle Company will receive cash from the customer to satisfy the accounts receivable balance. However, when individuals conduct transactions with each other, it is common for the transaction to be for cash. For example, when you buy a pizza, you often pay with cash.

▭▭▷ Why is it unusual for businesses such as Eagle Company to engage in cash transactions, while for individuals it is more common?

SA 5-4
The virtual close

Internet Project

Cisco Systems, Inc., pioneered the concept of a "virtual close" of the financial records. A virtual close is described as follows:

> The traditional practice of closing a company's books on a monthly, quarterly, or annual basis is out of sync with the dynamics of the new economy. In the past, the financial close and subsequent report generation was a static, scheduled event. It consumed days, weeks, and months and was based on a "thick black book." The new paradigm is driven by dynamic information accessible anytime and anywhere. Web-based reporting tools allow for real-time access to the very latest data and make interaction, summary to detail drill downs, and various data views possible. The result is fast, intuitive, on-the-fly creation of information views targeted for a specific analytical need to answer a specific question.
>
> **Source:** *Virtual Close—A Financial Management Solution*, Cisco Systems, Inc., and Bearingpoint Consulting Solutions Brief, 2001.

Additional information about the virtual close can be found at Cisco's Web site, which is linked to the text's Web site at **www.thomsonedu.com/accounting/warren**.

a. ▭▭▷ How is a virtual close different from traditional practice?
b. ▭▭▷ How does the virtual close impact the decision-making ability of Cisco's management.

SA 5-5
Design of accounting systems

For the past few years, your client, Freemont Medical Group (FMG), has operated a small medical practice. FMG's current annual revenues are $420,000. Because the accountant has been spending more and more time each month recording all transactions in a two-column journal and preparing the financial statements, FMG is considering improving the accounting system by adding special journals and subsidiary ledgers. FMG has asked you to help with this project and has compiled the following information:

Type of Transaction	Estimated Frequency per Month
Fees earned on account	240
Purchase of medical supplies on account	190
Cash receipts from patients on account	175
Cash payments on account	160
Cash receipts from patients at time services provided	120
Purchase of office supplies on account	35
Purchase of magazine subscriptions on account	5
Purchase of medical equipment on account	4
Cash payments for office salaries	3
Cash payments for utilities expense	3

A local sales tax is collected on all patient invoices, and monthly financial statements are prepared.

1. ▬▬► Briefly discuss the circumstances under which special journals would be used in place of a two-column (all-purpose) journal. Include in your answer your recommendations for FMG's medical practice.
2. Assume that FMG has decided to use a revenue journal and a purchases journal. Design the format for each journal, giving special consideration to the needs of the medical practice.
3. Which subsidiary ledgers would you recommend for the medical practice?

SA 5-6
Web-based accounting systems

[Internet Project]

Web-based application software is a recent trend in business computing. Major software firms such as Oracle, SAP, and NetSuites are running their core products on the Web. NetSuite Inc. is one of the most popular small business Web-based accounting systems. ▬▬► Go to the text's Web site at **www.thomsonedu.com/accounting/warren** and click on the link to the NetSuite Inc. site. Read about the product from the site, and prepare a memo to management, defining Web-based accounting. Also, outline the advantages and disadvantages of Web-based accounting compared to running software on a company's internal computer network.

SA 5-7
SCM and CRM

[Group Project]

[Internet Project]

The two leading software application providers for supply chain management (SCM) and customer relationship management (CRM) software are Manugistics and Salesforce.com, respectively. In groups of two or three, go to the Web site for each company (linked to the text's Web site at **www.thomsonedu.com/accounting/warren**) and list the functions provided by each company's application.

Answers to Self-Examination Questions

1. **A** Analysis (answer A) is the initial step of determining the informational needs and how the system provides this information. Design (answer B) is the step in which proposals for changes are developed. Implementation (answer C) is the final step involving carrying out or implementing the proposals for changes. Feedback (answer D) is not a separate step but is considered part of the systems implementation.
2. **A** The policies and procedures that are established to safeguard assets, ensure accurate business information, and ensure compliance with laws and regulations are called internal controls (answer A). The three steps in setting up an accounting system are (1) analysis (answer B), (2) design (answer C), and (3) implementation (answer D).
3. **B** All payments of cash for any purpose are recorded in the cash payments journal (answer B). Only purchases of services or other items on account are recorded in the purchases journal (answer A). All sales of services on account are recorded in the revenue journal (answer C), and all receipts of cash are recorded in the cash receipts journal (answer D).

4. **A** The general term used to describe the type of separate ledger that contains a large number of individual accounts with a common characteristic is a subsidiary ledger (answer A). The creditors ledger (answer B), sometimes called the accounts payable ledger (answer C), is a specific subsidiary ledger containing only individual accounts with creditors. Likewise, the accounts receivable ledger (answer D), also called the customers ledger, is a specific subsidiary ledger containing only individual accounts with customers.
5. **C** Both special journals (answer A) and accounts receivable control accounts (answer B) are generally not used in a computerized accounting system. Rather, electronic forms, such as an electronic invoice form (answer C), are used to record original transactions. The computer automatically posts transactions from electronic forms to the general ledger and individual accounts at the time the transactions are recorded. Therefore, month-end postings to the general ledger (answer D) are not necessary in a computerized accounting system.

Accounting for Merchandising Businesses

© JOSE JUAREZ/ASSOCIATED PRESS

objectives

After studying this chapter, you should be able to:

1 *Distinguish between the activities and financial statements of service and merchandising businesses.*

2 *Describe and illustrate the financial statements of a merchandising business.*

3 *Describe and illustrate the accounting for merchandise transactions including:*
- *sale of merchandise*
- *purchase of merchandise*
- *transportation costs, sales taxes, and trade discounts*
- *dual nature of merchandising transactions*

4 *Describe the adjusting and closing process for a merchandising business.*

Whole Foods Market

When you buy groceries, textbooks, school supplies, or an automobile, you are doing business with either a retail or a merchandising business. One such merchandising business is Whole Foods Market, the world's leading retailer of natural and organic foods. Whole Foods obtains its products locally and around the world, with a unique commitment to sustainable agriculture. In addition, Whole Foods has distinguished itself by placing 15th on the Fortune ®100 Best Companies to Work For.

Assume you bought groceries at Whole Foods Market and received the receipt such as shown below.

```
           WHÕLE
           FOODS
           M A R K E T

*     365  FRENCH ROAST 2      9.99 B
****  TAX   .39    BAL         10.38

      Cash                     20.00

      CHANGE                    9.62

TOTAL NUMBER OF ITEMS SOLD = 1
 2/24/06   3:32 PM 0713 10 0064 706

      Your cashier today is MAX
    Thank You For Shopping at
  Whole Foods Buckhead 404-324-4100
```

This receipt indicates that one item was purchased totaling $9.99, the sales tax was $0.39 (4%), the total due was $10.38, the clerk was given $20.00, and change of $9.62 was given back to the customer. The receipt also indicates that the sale was made by Buckhead Store of the Whole Foods Market chain, located in Atlanta, Georgia. The date and time of the sale and other data used internally by the store are also indicated.

As you may have guessed from the preceding receipt, the accounting for a merchandising business is more complex than that for a service business. For example, the accounting system for a merchandiser must be designed to record the receipt of goods for resale, keep track of the goods available for sale, and record the sale and cost of the merchandise sold.

In this chapter, we will focus on the accounting principles and concepts for merchandising businesses. We begin our discussion by highlighting the basic differences between the activities of merchandise and service businesses. We then describe and illustrate financial statements for merchandising businesses and purchases and sales transactions.

Nature of Merchandising Businesses

objective **1**

Distinguish between the activities and financial statements of service and merchandising businesses.

@netsolutions

How do the activities of NetSolutions, an attorney, and an architect, which are service businesses, differ from those of Wal-Mart or Best Buy, which are merchandising businesses? These differences are best illustrated by focusing on the revenues and expenses in the following condensed income statements:

Service Business		Merchandising Business	
Fees earned	$XXX	Sales	$XXX
Operating expenses	−XXX	Cost of merchandise sold	−XXX
Net income	$XXX	Gross profit	$XXX
		Operating expenses	−XXX
		Net income	$XXX

The revenue activities of a service business involve providing services to customers. On the income statement for a service business, the revenues from services are reported as *fees earned*. The operating expenses incurred in providing the services are subtracted from the fees earned to arrive at *net income*.

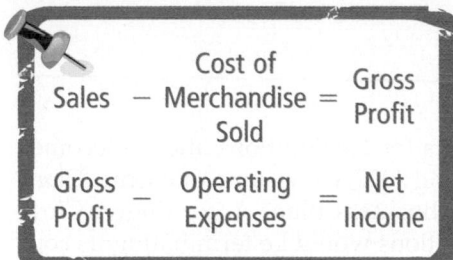

$$\text{Sales} - \begin{matrix}\text{Cost of}\\\text{Merchandise}\\\text{Sold}\end{matrix} = \begin{matrix}\text{Gross}\\\text{Profit}\end{matrix}$$

$$\begin{matrix}\text{Gross}\\\text{Profit}\end{matrix} - \begin{matrix}\text{Operating}\\\text{Expenses}\end{matrix} = \begin{matrix}\text{Net}\\\text{Income}\end{matrix}$$

In contrast, the revenue activities of a merchandising business involve the buying and selling of merchandise. A merchandising business must first purchase merchandise to sell to its customers. When this merchandise is sold, the revenue is reported as sales, and its cost is recognized as an expense called the **cost of merchandise sold**. The cost of merchandise sold is subtracted from sales to arrive at gross profit. This amount is called **gross profit** because it is the profit *before* deducting operating expenses.

Merchandise on hand (not sold) at the end of an accounting period is called **merchandise inventory**. Merchandise inventory is reported as a current asset on the balance sheet.

In the remainder of this chapter, we illustrate merchandiser financial statements and transactions that affect the income statement (sales, cost of merchandise sold, and gross profit) and the balance sheet (merchandise inventory).

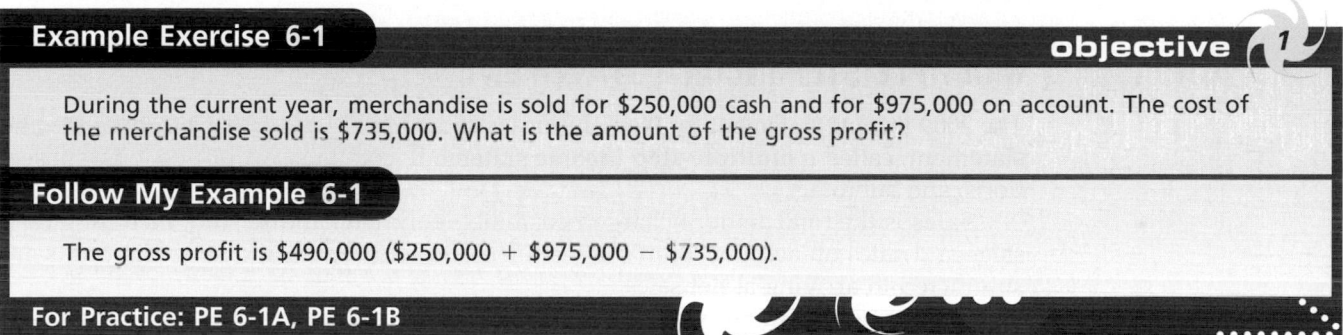

Example Exercise 6-1

objective 1

During the current year, merchandise is sold for $250,000 cash and for $975,000 on account. The cost of the merchandise sold is $735,000. What is the amount of the gross profit?

Follow My Example 6-1

The gross profit is $490,000 ($250,000 + $975,000 − $735,000).

For Practice: PE 6-1A, PE 6-1B

THE OPERATING CYCLE

The operations of a merchandising business involve the purchase of merchandise for sale (purchasing activity), the sale and distribution of the products to customers (sales activity), and the receipt of cash from customers (collection activity). This overall process is referred to as the *operating cycle*. Thus, the operating cycle begins with spending cash, and it ends with receiving cash from customers. The operating cycle for a merchandising business is shown below.

Operating cycles differ, depending upon the nature of the business and its operations. For example, the operating cycles for tobacco, distillery, and lumber industries are much longer than the operating cycles of the automobile, consumer electronics, and home furnishings industries. Likewise, the operating cycles for retailers are usually shorter than for manufacturers because retailers purchase goods in a form ready for sale to the customer. Of course, some retailers will have shorter operating cycles than others because of the nature of their products. For example, a jewelry store or an automobile dealer normally has a longer operating cycle than a consumer electronics store or a grocery store.

Businesses with longer operating cycles normally have higher profit margins on their products than businesses with shorter operating cycles. For example, it is not unusual for jewelry stores to price their jewelry at 30%–50% above cost. In contrast, grocery stores operate on very small profit margins, often below 5%. Grocery stores make up the difference by selling their products more quickly.

Financial Statements for a Merchandising Business

In this section, we illustrate the financial statements for NetSolutions after it becomes a retailer of computer hardware and software. During 2007, we assume that Chris Clark implemented the second phase of NetSolutions' business plan. Accordingly, Chris notified clients that beginning July 1, 2008, NetSolutions would be terminating its consulting services. Instead, it would become a personalized retailer.

NetSolutions' business strategy is to focus on offering personalized service to individuals and small businesses who are upgrading or purchasing new computer systems. NetSolutions' personal service before the sale will include a no-obligation, on-site assessment of the customer's computer needs. By providing tailor-made solutions, personalized service, and follow-up, Chris feels that NetSolutions can compete effectively against larger retailers, such as Best Buy or Office Depot, Inc.

MULTIPLE-STEP INCOME STATEMENT

The 2009 income statement for NetSolutions is shown in Exhibit 1.[1] This form of income statement, called a **multiple-step income statement**, contains several sections, subsections, and subtotals.

Sales is the total amount charged customers for merchandise sold, including cash sales and sales on account. Both sales returns and allowances and sales discounts are subtracted in arriving at net sales.

Sales returns and allowances are granted by the seller to customers for damaged or defective merchandise. For example, rather than have a buyer return merchandise, a seller may offer a $500 allowance to the customer as compensation for damaged merchandise. Sales returns and allowances are recorded when the merchandise is returned or when the allowance is granted by the seller.

Sales discounts are granted by the seller to customers for early payment of amounts owed. For example, a seller may offer a customer a 2% discount on a sale of $10,000 if the customer pays within 10 days. If the customer pays within the 10-day period, the seller receives cash of $9,800 and the buyer receives a discount of $200 ($10,000 × 2%). Sales discounts are recorded when the customer pays the bill.

Net sales is determined by subtracting sales returns and allowances and sales discounts from sales. Rather than reporting sales, sales returns and allowances, and sales discounts as shown in Exhibit 1, many companies report only net sales.

Cost of merchandise sold is the cost of the merchandise sold to customers. To illustrate the determination of the cost of merchandise sold, assume that NetSolutions purchased $340,000 of merchandise during the last half of 2008. If the inventory at December 31, 2008, the end of the year, is $59,700, the cost of the merchandise sold during 2007 is $280,300.

For many merchandising businesses, the cost of merchandise sold is usually the largest expense. For example, the approximate percentage of cost of merchandise sold to sales is 61% for JCPenney and 67% for The Home Depot.

Purchases	$340,000
Less merchandise inventory, December 31, 2008	59,700
Cost of merchandise sold	$280,300

As we discussed in the preceding paragraphs, sellers may offer customers sales discounts for early payment of their bills. Such discounts are referred to as **purchases discounts** by the buyer. Purchase discounts reduce the cost of merchandise. A buyer may return merchandise to the seller (a **purchase return**), or the buyer may receive a reduction in the initial price at which the merchandise was purchased (a **purchase allowance**). Like purchase discounts, purchases returns and allowances reduce the cost

---

1 We use the NetSolutions income statement for 2009 as a basis for illustration because, as will be shown, it allows us to better illustrate the computation of the cost of merchandise sold.

EXHIBIT 1   Multiple-Step Income Statement

NetSolutions Income Statement For the Year Ended December 31, 2009				
Revenue from sales:				
Sales		$720 185 00		
Less: Sales returns and allowances	$ 6 14 0 00			
Sales discounts	5 79 0 00	11 93 0 00		
Net sales			$708 25 5 00	
Cost of merchandise sold			525 30 5 00	
Gross profit			$182 95 0 00	
Operating expenses:				
Selling expenses:				
Sales salaries expense	$53 43 0 00			
Advertising expense	10 86 0 00			
Depr. expense—store equipment	3 10 0 00			
Delivery expense	2 80 0 00			
Miscellaneous selling expense	6 3 0 00			
Total selling expenses		$ 70 82 0 00		
Administrative expenses:				
Office salaries expense	$21 02 0 00			
Rent expense	8 10 0 00			
Depr. expense—office equipment	2 49 0 00			
Insurance expense	1 91 0 00			
Office supplies expense	6 1 0 00			
Misc. administrative expense	7 6 0 00			
Total administrative expenses		34 89 0 00		
Total operating expenses			105 71 0 00	
Income from operations			$ 77 24 0 00	
Other income and expense:				
Rent revenue		$ 6 0 0 00		
Interest expense		(2 44 0 00)	(1 84 0 00)	
Net income			$ 75 40 0 00	

of merchandise purchased during a period. In addition, transportation costs paid by the buyer for merchandise also increase the cost of merchandise purchased.

To continue the illustration, assume that during 2009 NetSolutions purchased additional merchandise of $521,980. It received credit for purchases returns and allowances of $9,100, took purchases discounts of $2,525, and paid transportation costs of $17,400. The purchases returns and allowances and the purchases discounts are deducted from the total purchases to yield the **net purchases**. The transportation costs, termed **transportation in**, are added to the net purchases to yield the **cost of merchandise purchased** of $527,755, as shown below.

Purchases		$521,980
Less: Purchases returns and allowances	$9,100	
Purchases discounts	2,525	11,625
Net purchases		$510,355
Add transportation in		17,400
Cost of merchandise purchased		$527,755

The ending inventory of NetSolutions on December 31, 2008, $59,700, becomes the beginning inventory for 2009. This beginning inventory is added to the cost of merchandise purchased to yield **merchandise available for sale**. The ending inventory, which is assumed to be $62,150, is then subtracted from the merchandise available for sale to yield the cost of merchandise sold of $525,305, as shown in Exhibit 2.

EXHIBIT 2   Cost of Merchandise Sold

Merchandise inventory, January 1, 2009			$ 59,700
Purchases		$521,980	
Less: Purchases returns and allowances	$9,100		
Purchases discounts	2,525	11,625	
Net purchases		$510,355	
Add transportation in		17,400	
Cost of merchandise purchased			527,755
Merchandise available for sale			$587,455
Less merchandise inventory, December 31, 2009 . .			62,150
Cost of merchandise sold			$525,305

The cost of merchandise sold was determined by deducting the merchandise on hand at the end of the period from the merchandise available for sale during the period. The merchandise on hand at the end of the period is determined by taking a physical count of inventory on hand. This method of determining the cost of merchandise sold and the amount of merchandise on hand is called the **periodic system** of accounting for merchandise inventory. Under the periodic system, the inventory records do not show the amount available for sale or the amount sold during the period. In contrast, under the **perpetual system** of accounting for merchandise inventory, each purchase and sale of merchandise is recorded in the inventory and the cost of merchandise sold accounts. As a result, the amount of merchandise available for sale and the amount sold are continuously (perpetually) disclosed in the inventory records.

Most large retailers and many small merchandising businesses use computerized perpetual inventory systems. Such systems normally use bar codes, such as the one on the back of this textbook. An optical scanner reads the bar code to record merchandise purchased and sold. Merchandise businesses using a perpetual inventory system report the cost of merchandise sold as a single line on the income statement, as shown in Exhibit 1 for NetSolutions. Merchandise businesses using the periodic inventory system report the cost of merchandise sold by using the format shown in Exhibit 2. Because of its wide use, we will use the perpetual inventory system throughout the remainder of this chapter. The periodic inventory system is described and illustrated in Appendix 2 of this chapter.

Gross profit is determined by subtracting the cost of merchandise sold from net sales. Exhibit 1 shows that NetSolutions reported gross profit of $182,950 in 2009. *Operating income*, sometimes called **income from operations**, is determined by subtracting operating expenses from gross profit. Most merchandising businesses classify operating expenses as either selling expenses or administrative expenses. Expenses that are incurred directly in the selling of merchandise are **selling expenses**. They include such expenses as salespersons' salaries, store supplies used, depreciation of store equipment, delivery expense, and advertising. Expenses incurred in the administration or general operations of the business are **administrative expenses** or *general expenses*. Examples of these expenses are office salaries, depreciation of office equipment, and office supplies used. Credit card expense is also normally classified as an administrative expense. Although selling and administrative expenses may be reported separately, many companies report operating expenses as a single item.

Retailers, such as Best Buy, Sears Holding Corporation, and Wal-Mart, and grocery store chains, such as Winn-Dixie Stores, Inc. and Kroger, use bar codes and optical scanners as part of their computerized inventory systems.

Other income and expense is reported on NetSolutions' income statement in Exhibit 1. Revenue from sources other than the primary operating activity of a business is classified as **other income**. In a merchandising business, these items include income from interest, rent, and gains resulting from the sale of fixed assets.

Expenses that cannot be traced directly to operations are identified as **other expense**. Interest expense that results from financing activities and losses incurred in the disposal of fixed assets are examples of these items.

Other income and other expense are offset against each other on the income statement, as shown in Exhibit 1. If the total of other income exceeds the total of other expense, the difference is added to income from operations to determine net income. If the reverse is true, the difference is subtracted from income from operations.

Example Exercise 6-2   objective ➁

Based upon the following data, determine the cost of merchandise sold for May. Follow the format used in Exhibit 2.

Merchandise inventory, May 1	$121,200
Merchandise inventory, May 31	142,000
Purchases	985,000
Purchases returns and allowances	23,500
Purchases discounts	21,000
Transportation in	11,300

Follow My Example 6-2

Cost of merchandise sold:

Merchandise inventory, May 1			$ 121,200
Purchases		$985,000	
Less: Purchases returns and allowances	$23,500		
Purchases discounts	21,000	44,500	
Net purchases		$940,500	
Add transportation in		11,300	
Cost of merchandise purchased			951,800
Merchandise available for sale			$1,073,000
Less merchandise inventory, May 31			142,000
Cost of merchandise sold			$ 931,000

For Practice: PE 6-2A, PE 6-2B

SINGLE-STEP INCOME STATEMENT

An alternate form of income statement is the **single-step income statement**. As shown in Exhibit 3, the income statement for NetSolutions deducts the total of all expenses *in one step* from the total of all revenues.

The single-step form emphasizes total revenues and total expenses as the factors that determine net income. A criticism of the single-step form is that such amounts as gross profit and income from operations are not readily available for analysis.

STATEMENT OF OWNER'S EQUITY

The statement of owner's equity for NetSolutions is shown in Exhibit 4. This statement is prepared in the same manner that we described previously for a service business.

BALANCE SHEET

As we discussed and illustrated in previous chapters, the balance sheet may be presented with assets on the left-hand side and the liabilities and owner's equity on the

EXHIBIT 3

Single-Step Income
Statement

NetSolutions Income Statement For the Year Ended December 31, 2009			
Revenues:			
Net sales			$708 255 00
Rent revenue			6 000 00
Total revenues			$708 855 00
Expenses:			
Cost of merchandise sold	$525 305 00		
Selling expenses	70 820 00		
Administrative expenses	34 890 00		
Interest expense	2 440 00		
Total expenses			633 455 00
Net income			$ 75 400 00

EXHIBIT 4

Statement of
Owner's Equity for
Merchandising
Business

NetSolutions Statement of Owner's Equity For the Year Ended December 31, 2009			
Chris Clark, capital, January 1, 2009			$153 800 00
Net income for year	$75 400 00		
Less withdrawals	18 000 00		
Increase in owner's equity			57 400 00
Chris Clark, capital, December 31, 2009			$211 200 00

Business Connections

H&R BLOCK VERSUS THE HOME DEPOT

H&R Block is a service business that primarily offers tax planning and preparation to its customers. The Home Depot is the world's largest home improvement retailer and the second largest merchandise business in the United States. The differences in the operations of a service and merchandise business are illustrated in their income statements, as shown below.

As will be discussed in a later chapter, corporations are subject to income taxes. Thus, the income statements of H&R Block and Home Depot report "income taxes" as a deduction from "income before income taxes" in arriving at net income. This is in contrast to a proprietorship such as NetSolutions, which is not subject to income taxes.

H&R Block
Condensed Income Statement
For the Year Ending April 30, 2005
(in millions)

Revenue	$4,420
Operating expenses	3,368
Operating income	$1,052
Other income (expense)	(34)
Income before taxes	$1,018
Income taxes	382
Net income	$ 636

The Home Depot
Condensed Income Statement
For the Year Ending January 30, 2005
(in millions)

Net sales	$73,094
Cost of merchandise sold	48,664
Gross profit	$24,430
Operating expenses	16,504
Operating income	$ 7,926
Other income (expense)	(14)
Income before taxes	$ 7,912
Income taxes	2,911
Net income	$ 5,001

right-hand side. This form of the balance sheet is called the **account form**. The balance sheet may also be presented in a downward sequence in three sections. This form of balance sheet is called the **report form**. The report form of balance sheet for NetSolutions is shown in Exhibit 5. In this balance sheet, note that merchandise inventory at the end of the period is reported as a current asset and that the current portion of the note payable is $5,000.

EXHIBIT 5

Report Form of Balance Sheet

NetSolutions Balance Sheet December 31, 2009			
Assets			
Current assets:			
Cash		$52 9 5 0 00	
Accounts receivable		91 0 8 0 00	
Merchandise inventory		62 1 5 0 00	
Office supplies		4 8 0 00	
Prepaid insurance		2 6 5 0 00	
Total current assets			$209 3 1 0 00
Property, plant, and equipment:			
Land		$20 0 0 0 00	
Store equipment	$27 1 0 0 00		
Less accumulated depreciation	5 7 0 0 00	21 4 0 0 00	
Office equipment	$15 5 7 0 00		
Less accumulated depreciation	4 7 2 0 00	10 8 5 0 00	
Total property, plant, and equipment			52 2 5 0 00
Total assets			$261 5 6 0 00
Liabilities			
Current liabilities:			
Accounts payable		$22 4 2 0 00	
Note payable (current portion)		5 0 0 0 00	
Salaries payable		1 1 4 0 00	
Unearned rent		1 8 0 0 00	
Total current liabilities			$ 30 3 6 0 00
Long-term liabilities:			
Note payable (final payment due 2019)			20 0 0 0 00
Total liabilities			$ 50 3 6 0 00
Owner's Equity			
Chris Clark, capital			211 2 0 0 00
Total liabilities and owner's equity			$261 5 6 0 00

objective *3*

Describe and illustrate the accounting for merchandise transactions including:
- *sale of merchandise*
- *purchase of merchandise*
- *transportation costs, sales taxes, and trade discounts*
- *dual nature of merchandising transactions*

Merchandising Transactions

In the preceding section, we described and illustrated the financial statements of a merchandising business, NetSolutions. In this section, we describe and illustrate the recording of merchandise transactions including sales, purchases, transportation costs, and sales taxes. We also discuss trade discounts and the dual nature of merchandising transactions. As a basis for recording merchandise transactions, we begin by describing the chart of accounts for a merchandising business.

CHART OF ACCOUNTS FOR A MERCHANDISING BUSINESS

The chart of accounts for a merchandising business should reflect the elements of the financial statements we described and illustrated in the preceding section. The chart of

EXHIBIT 6

Chart of Accounts for NetSolutions Merchandising Business

Balance Sheet Accounts		Income Statement Accounts	
	100 Assets		**400 Revenues**
110	Cash	410	Sales
112	Accounts Receivable	411	Sales Returns and Allowances
115	Merchandise Inventory	412	Sales Discounts
116	Office Supplies		**500 Costs and Expenses**
117	Prepaid Insurance	510	Cost of Merchandise Sold
120	Land	520	Sales Salaries Expense
123	Store Equipment	521	Advertising Expense
124	Accumulated Depreciation— Store Equipment	522	Depreciation Expense—Store Equipment
125	Office Equipment	523	Delivery Expense
126	Accumulated Depreciation— Office Equipment	529	Miscellaneous Selling Expense
		530	Office Salaries Expense
	200 Liabilities	531	Rent Expense
210	Accounts Payable	532	Depreciation Expense—Office Equipment
211	Salaries Payable	533	Insurance Expense
212	Unearned Rent	534	Office Supplies Expense
215	Notes Payable	539	Misc. Administrative Expense
	300 Owner's Equity		**600 Other Income**
310	Chris Clark, Capital	610	Rent Revenue
311	Chris Clark, Drawing		
312	Income Summary		**700 Other Expense**
		710	Interest Expense

@netsolutions

accounts for NetSolutions is shown in Exhibit 6. The accounts related to merchandising transactions are shown in color.

NetSolutions is now using three-digit account numbers, which permits it to add new accounts as they are needed. The first digit indicates the major financial statement classification (1 for assets, 2 for liabilities, and so on). The second digit indicates the subclassification (e.g., 11 for current assets, 12 for noncurrent assets). The third digit identifies the specific account (e.g., 110 for Cash, 123 for Store Equipment).

NetSolutions is using a more complex numbering system because it has a greater variety of transactions. In addition, its growth creates a need for more detailed information for use in managing it. For example, a wages expense account was adequate for NetSolutions when it was a small service business with few employees. However, as a merchandising business, NetSolutions now uses two payroll accounts, one for Sales Salaries Expense and one for Office Salaries Expense. In the following paragraphs, we use the accounts appearing in Exhibit 6 to record various merchandising transactions of NetSolutions.

SALES TRANSACTIONS

Merchandise transactions are recorded in the accounts, using the rules of debit and credit that we described and illustrated in earlier chapters. Special journals may be used, or transactions may be entered, recorded, and posted to the accounts electronically. Although journal entries may not be manually prepared, we will use a two-column general journal format in this chapter in order to simplify the discussion.[2]

Cash Sales A business may sell merchandise for cash. Cash sales are normally rung up (entered) on a cash register and recorded in the accounts. To illustrate, assume that

---

2 Special journals and computerized accounting systems for merchandising businesses are described in Appendix 1 at the end of this chapter.

on January 3, NetSolutions sells merchandise for $1,800. These cash sales can be recorded as follows:

		JOURNAL			Page 25
Date		**Description**	**Post. Ref.**	**Debit**	**Credit**
2009 Jan.	3	Cash		1 8 0 0 00	
		Sales			1 8 0 0 00
		To record cash sales.			

Under the perpetual inventory system, the cost of merchandise sold and the reduction in merchandise inventory should also be recorded. In this way, the merchandise inventory account will indicate the amount of merchandise on hand (not sold). To illustrate, assume that the cost of merchandise sold on January 3 was $1,200. The entry to record the cost of merchandise sold and the reduction in the merchandise inventory is as follows:

Jan.	3	Cost of Merchandise Sold		1 2 0 0 00	
		Merchandise Inventory			1 2 0 0 00
		To record the cost of merch. sold.			

In recent years, a large percentage of retail sales have been made to customers who use credit cards such as MasterCard or VISA. How do retailers record sales made with the use of credit cards? Such sales are recorded as cash sales. This is because the retailer normally receives payment within a few days of making the sale. Specifically, such sales are normally processed by a clearing-house that contacts the bank that issued the card. The issuing bank then electronically transfers cash directly to the retailer's bank account.[3] Thus, if the customers in the preceding sales had used MasterCards to pay for their purchases, the sales would be recorded exactly as shown above. Any processing fees charged by the clearing-house or issuing bank are periodically recorded as an expense as shown below.

Jan.	31	Credit Card Expense		4 8 00	
		Cash			4 8 00
		To record service charges on credit			
		card sales for the month.			

Instead of using MasterCard or VISA, a customer may use a credit card that is not issued by a bank, such as American Express or Discover. If the seller uses a clearing-house, the clearing-house will collect the receivable and transfer the cash to the retailer's bank account similar to the way it would have if the customer had used MasterCard or VISA. Large businesses, however, may not use a clearing-house. In such cases, nonbank credit card sales must first be reported to the card company before cash is received. Thus, a receivable is created with the nonbank credit card company.

---

3 CyberSource is one of the major credit card clearing-houses. For a more detailed description of how credit card sales are processed, see the following CyberSource web page:
http://www.cybersource.com/products_and_services/electronic_payments/credit_card_processing/howitworks.xml.

However, since most retailers use clearing-houses to process both bank and nonbank credit cards, we will record all credit card sales as cash sales.

Sales on Account   A business may sell merchandise on account. The seller records such sales as a debit to Accounts Receivable and a credit to Sales. An example of an entry for a NetSolutions sale on account of $510 follows. The cost of merchandise sold was $280.

Jan.	12	Accounts Receivable—Sims Co.	5 1 0 00	
		Sales		5 1 0 00
		Invoice No. 7172.		
	12	Cost of Merchandise Sold	2 8 0 00	
		Merchandise Inventory		2 8 0 00
		Cost of merch. sold on Invoice No. 7172.		

Sales Discounts   The terms of a sale are normally indicated on the **invoice** or bill that the seller sends to the buyer. An example of a sales invoice for NetSolutions is shown in Exhibit 7.

EXHIBIT 7   Invoice

The terms for when payments for merchandise are to be made, agreed on by the buyer and the seller, are called the **credit terms**. If payment is required on delivery, the terms are *cash* or *net cash*. Otherwise, the buyer is allowed an amount of time, known as the **credit period**, in which to pay.

The credit period usually begins with the date of the sale as shown on the invoice. If payment is due within a stated number of days after the date of the invoice, such as 30 days, the terms are *net 30 days*. These terms may be written as *n/30*.[4] If payment is due by the end of the month in which the sale was made, the terms are written as *n/eom*.

---

4 The word *net* as used here does not have the usual meaning of a number after deductions have been subtracted, as in *net income*.

As a means of encouraging the buyer to pay before the end of the credit period, the seller may offer a discount. For example, a seller may offer a 2% discount if the buyer pays within 10 days of the invoice date. If the buyer does not take the discount, the total amount is due within 30 days. These terms are expressed as *2/10, n/30* and are read as *2% discount if paid within 10 days, net amount due within 30 days*. The credit terms of 2/10, n/30 are summarized in Exhibit 8, using the information from the invoice in Exhibit 7.

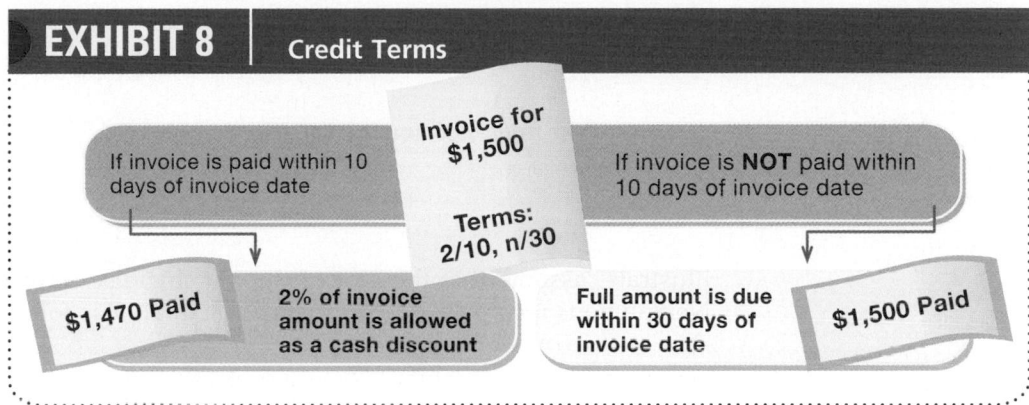

EXHIBIT 8 | **Credit Terms**

Invoice for $1,500

Terms: 2/10, n/30

If invoice is paid within 10 days of invoice date → **$1,470 Paid** — 2% of invoice amount is allowed as a cash discount

If invoice is **NOT** paid within 10 days of invoice date → Full amount is due within 30 days of invoice date — **$1,500 Paid**

Discounts taken by the buyer for early payment are recorded as sales discounts by the seller. Since managers may want to know the amount of the sales discounts for a period, the seller normally records the sales discounts in a separate account. The sales discounts account is a *contra* (or *offsetting*) account to Sales. To illustrate, assume that cash is received within the discount period (10 days) from the credit sale of $1,500, shown on the invoice in Exhibit 7. NetSolutions would record the receipt of the cash as follows:

Jan.	22	Cash		1 4 7 0 00	
		Sales Discounts		3 0 00	
		Accounts Receivable—Omega Tech.			1 5 0 0 00
		Collection on Invoice No. 106-8, less			
		2% discount.			

Sales Returns and Allowances   Merchandise sold may be returned to the seller (**sales return**). In addition, because of defects or for other reasons, the seller may reduce the initial price at which the goods were sold (**sales allowance**). If the return or allowance is for a sale on account, the seller usually issues the buyer a **credit memorandum**. This memorandum shows the amount of and the reason for the seller's credit to an account receivable. A credit memorandum issued by NetSolutions is illustrated in Exhibit 9.

Like sales discounts, sales returns and allowances reduce sales revenue. They also result in additional shipping and other expenses. Since managers often want to know the amount of returns and allowances for a period, the seller records sales returns and allowances in a separate account. Sales Returns and Allowances is a *contra* (or *offsetting*) account to Sales.

The seller debits Sales Returns and Allowances for the amount of the return or allowance. If the original sale was on account, the seller credits Accounts Receivable. Since the merchandise inventory is kept up to date in a perpetual system, the seller adds the cost of the returned merchandise to the merchandise inventory account. The seller must also credit the cost of returned merchandise to the cost of merchandise sold account, since this account was debited when the original sale was recorded. To

REAL WORLD

Book publishers often experience large returns if a book is not immediately successful. For example, 35% of adult hardcover books shipped to retailers are returned to publishers, according to the Association of American Publishers.

EXHIBIT 9	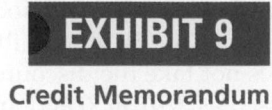 No. 32

EXHIBIT 9

Credit Memorandum

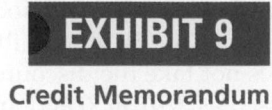

@netsolutions   No. 32
5101 Washington Ave.
Cincinnati, OH 45227–5101

CREDIT MEMORANDUM

TO	DATE
Krier Company	January 13, 2009
7608 Melton Avenue	
Los Angeles, CA 90025-3942	

WE CREDIT YOUR ACCOUNT AS FOLLOWS

1 Controller Kit	225.00

illustrate, assume that the cost of the merchandise returned in Exhibit 9 was $140. NetSolutions records the credit memo in Exhibit 9 as follows:

Jan.	13	Sales Returns and Allowances		2 2 5 00	
		Accounts Receivable—Krier Company			2 2 5 00
		Credit Memo No. 32.			

Jan.	13	Merchandise Inventory		1 4 0 00	
		Cost of Merchandise Sold			1 4 0 00
		Cost of merchandise returned, Credit			
		Memo No. 32.			

What if the buyer pays for the merchandise and the merchandise is later returned? In this case, the seller may issue a credit and apply it against other accounts receivable owed by the buyer, or the cash may be refunded. If the credit is applied against the buyer's other receivables, the seller records entries similar to those preceding. If cash is refunded for merchandise returned or for an allowance, the seller debits Sales Returns and Allowances and credits Cash.

Example Exercise 6-3   objective **3**

Journalize the following merchandise transactions:

a.   Sold merchandise on account, $7,500 with terms 2/10, n/30. The cost of the merchandise sold was $5,625.
b.   Received payment less the discount.

Follow My Example 6-3

a.   Accounts Receivable   7,500
          Sales   7,500
     Cost of Merchandise Sold   5,625
          Merchandise Inventory   5,625

b.   Cash   7,350
     Sales Discounts   150
          Accounts Receivable   7,500

For Practice: PE 6-3A, PE 6-3B

Integrity, Objectivity, and Ethics in Business

THE CASE OF THE FRAUDULENT PRICE TAGS

One of the challenges for a retailer is policing its sales return policy. There are many ways in which customers can unethically or illegally abuse such policies. In one case, a couple was accused of attaching Marshalls' store price tags to cheaper merchandise bought or obtained else-where. The couple then returned the cheaper goods and received the substantially higher refund amount. Company security officials discovered the fraud and had the couple arrested after they had allegedly bilked the company for over $1 million.

PURCHASE TRANSACTIONS

As we indicated earlier in this chapter, most large retailers and many small merchandising businesses use computerized perpetual inventory systems. Under the perpetual inventory system, cash purchases of merchandise are recorded as follows:

JOURNAL   Page 24

Date		Description	Post. Ref.	Debit	Credit
2009 Jan.	3	Merchandise Inventory		2 5 1 0 00	
		Cash			2 5 1 0 00
		Purchased inventory from Bowen Co.			

Purchases of merchandise on account are recorded as follows:

Jan.	4	Merchandise Inventory		9 2 5 0 00	
		Accounts Payable—Thomas Corporation			9 2 5 0 00
		Purchased inventory on account.			

Purchases Discounts   Purchases discounts taken by the buyer for early payment of an invoice reduce the cost of the merchandise purchased. Most businesses design their accounting systems so that all available discounts are taken. Even if the buyer has to borrow to make the payment within a discount period, it is normally to the buyer's advantage to do so. To illustrate, assume that Alpha Technologies issues an invoice for $3,000 to NetSolutions, dated March 12, with terms 2/10, n/30. The last day of the discount period in which the $60 discount can be taken is March 22. Assume that in order to pay the invoice on March 22, NetSolutions borrows the money for the remaining 20 days of the credit period. If we assume an annual interest rate of 6% and a 360-day year, the interest on the loan of $2,940 ($3,000 − $60) is $9.80 ($2,940 × 6% × 20/360). The net savings to NetSolutions is $50.20, computed as follows:

Discount of 2% on $3,000	$60.00
Interest for 20 days at rate of 6% on $2,940	−9.80
Savings from borrowing	$50.20

The savings can also be seen by comparing the interest rate on the money *saved* by taking the discount and the interest rate on the money *borrowed* to take the discount. For NetSolutions, the interest rate on the money saved in this example is estimated by converting 2% for 20 days to a yearly rate, as follows:

$$2\% \times \frac{360 \text{ days}}{20 \text{ days}} = 2\% \times 18 = 36\%$$

If NetSolutions borrows the money to take the discount, it *pays* interest of 6%. If NetSolutions does not take the discount, it *pays* estimated interest of 36% for using the $2,940 for an additional 20 days.

Under the perpetual inventory system, the buyer initially debits the merchandise inventory account for the amount of the invoice. When paying the invoice, the buyer credits the merchandise inventory account for the amount of the discount. In this way, the merchandise inventory shows the *net* cost to the buyer. For example, NetSolutions would record the Alpha Technologies invoice and its payment at the end of the discount period as follows:

Mar.	12	Merchandise Inventory	3 0 0 0 00	
		Accounts Payable—Alpha Technologies		3 0 0 0 00
	22	Accounts Payable—Alpha Technologies	3 0 0 0 00	
		Cash		2 9 4 0 00
		Merchandise Inventory		6 0 00

If NetSolutions does not take the discount because it does not pay the invoice until April 11, it would record the payment as follows:

Apr.	11	Accounts Payable—Alpha Technologies	3 0 0 0 00	
		Cash		3 0 0 0 00

Purchases Returns and Allowances   When merchandise is returned (**purchases return**) or a price adjustment is requested (**purchases allowance**), the buyer (debtor) usually sends the seller a letter or a debit memorandum. A **debit memorandum**, shown in Exhibit 10, informs the seller of the amount the buyer proposes to *debit* to the account payable due the seller. It also states the reasons for the return or the request for a price reduction.

The buyer may use a copy of the debit memorandum as the basis for recording the return or allowance or wait for approval from the seller (creditor). In either case, the buyer must debit Accounts Payable and credit Merchandise Inventory. To illustrate,

EXHIBIT 10

Debit Memorandum

@netsolutions
5101 Washington Ave.
Cincinnati, OH 45227–5101

No. 18

DEBIT MEMORANDUM

TO	DATE
Maxim Systems	March 7, 2009
7519 East Willson Ave.	
Seattle, WA 98101–7519	

WE DEBIT YOUR ACCOUNT AS FOLLOWS

10 Server Network Interface Cards,   @ 90.00   900.00
     your Invoice No. 7291, are
     being returned via parcel post.
     Our order specified No. 825X.

NetSolutions records the return of the merchandise indicated in the debit memo in Exhibit 10 as follows:

Mar.	7	Accounts Payable—Maxim Systems	9 0 0 00	
		Merchandise Inventory		9 0 0 00
		Debit Memo No. 18.		

When a buyer returns merchandise or has been granted an allowance prior to paying the invoice, the amount of the debit memorandum is deducted from the invoice amount. The amount is deducted before the purchase discount is computed. For example, assume that on May 2, NetSolutions purchases $5,000 of merchandise from Delta Data Link, subject to terms 2/10, n/30. On May 4, NetSolutions returns $3,000 of the merchandise, and on May 12, NetSolutions pays the original invoice less the return. NetSolutions would record these transactions as follows:

May	2	Merchandise Inventory	5 0 0 0 00	
		Accounts Payable—Delta Data Link		5 0 0 0 00
		Purchased merchandise.		
	4	Accounts Payable—Delta Data Link	3 0 0 0 00	
		Merchandise Inventory		3 0 0 0 00
		Returned portion of merch. purchased.		
	12	Accounts Payable—Delta Data Link	2 0 0 0 00	
		Cash		1 9 6 0 00
		Merchandise Inventory		4 0 00
		Paid invoice [($5,000 − $3,000) × 2%		
		= $40; $2,000 − $40 = $1,960].		

Example Exercise 6-4   objective 3

Rofles Company purchased merchandise on account from a supplier for $11,500, terms 2/10, n/30. Rofles Company returned $3,000 of the merchandise and received full credit.

a. If Rofles Company pays the invoice within the discount period, what is the amount of cash required for the payment?
b. Under a perpetual inventory system, what account is credited by Rofles Company to record the return?

Follow My Example 6-4

a. $8,330. Purchase of $11,500 less the return of $3,000 less the discount of $170 [($11,500 − $3,000) × 2%].
b. Merchandise Inventory

For Practice: PE 6-4A, PE 6-4B

TRANSPORTATION COSTS, SALES TAXES, AND TRADE DISCOUNTS

In the preceding two sections, we described and illustrated merchandise transactions involving sales and purchases. In this section, we discuss merchandise transactions involving transportation costs, sales taxes, and trade discounts.

> The buyer bears the transportation costs if the shipping terms are FOB shipping point.

REAL WORLD

Sometimes FOB shipping point and FOB destination are expressed in terms of the location at which the title to the merchandise passes to the buyer. For example, if Toyota Motor Corporation's assembly plant in Osaka, Japan, sells automobiles to a dealer in Chicago, FOB shipping point could be expressed as FOB Osaka. Likewise, FOB destination could be expressed as FOB Chicago.

Transportation Costs   The terms of a sale should indicate when the ownership (title) of the merchandise passes to the buyer. This point determines which party, the buyer or the seller, must pay the transportation costs.[5]

The ownership of the merchandise may pass to the buyer when the seller delivers the merchandise to the transportation company or freight carrier. For example, DaimlerChrysler records the sale and the transfer of ownership of its vehicles to dealers when the vehicles are shipped from the factory. In this case, the terms are said to be **FOB (free on board) shipping point**. This term means that the dealer pays the transportation costs from the shipping point (factory) to the final destination. Such costs are part of the dealer's total cost of purchasing inventory and should be added to the cost of the inventory by debiting Merchandise Inventory.

To illustrate, assume that on June 10, NetSolutions buys merchandise from Magna Data on account, $900, terms FOB shipping point, and pays the transportation cost of $50. NetSolutions records these two transactions as follows:

June	10	Merchandise Inventory		9 0 0 00	
		Accounts Payable—Magna Data			9 0 0 00
		Purchased merchandise, terms FOB			
		shipping point.			
	10	Merchandise Inventory		5 0 00	
		Cash			5 0 00
		Paid shipping cost on merchandise			
		purchased.			

The ownership of the merchandise may pass to the buyer when the buyer receives the merchandise. In this case, the terms are said to be **FOB (free on board) destination**. This term means that the seller delivers the merchandise to the buyer's final destination, free of transportation charges to the buyer. The seller thus pays the transportation costs to the final destination. The seller debits Delivery Expense or Transportation Out, which is reported on the seller's income statement as an expense.

> The seller bears the transportation costs if the shipping terms are FOB destination.

To illustrate, assume that on June 15, NetSolutions sells merchandise to Kranz Company on account, $700, terms FOB destination. The cost of the merchandise sold is $480, and NetSolutions pays the transportation cost of $40. NetSolutions records the sale, the cost of the sale, and the transportation cost as follows:

June	15	Accounts Receivable—Kranz Company		7 0 0 00	
		Sales			7 0 0 00
		Sold merchandise, terms FOB			
		destination.			
	15	Cost of Merchandise Sold		4 8 0 00	
		Merchandise Inventory			4 8 0 00
		Recorded cost of merchandise sold to			
		Kranz Company.			
	15	Delivery Expense		4 0 00	
		Cash			4 0 00
		Paid shipping cost on merch. sold.			

---

5 The passage of title also determines whether the buyer or seller must pay other costs, such as the cost of insurance, while the merchandise is in transit.

As a convenience to the buyer, the seller may prepay the transportation costs, even though the terms are FOB shipping point. The seller will then add the transportation costs to the invoice. The buyer will debit Merchandise Inventory for the total amount of the invoice, including the transportation costs. Any discount terms would not apply to the prepaid transportation costs.

To illustrate, assume that on June 20, NetSolutions sells merchandise to Planter Company on account, $800, terms FOB shipping point. NetSolutions pays the transportation cost of $45 and adds it to the invoice. The cost of the merchandise sold is $360. NetSolutions records these transactions as follows:

June	20	Accounts Receivable—Planter Company		80000	
		Sales			80000
		Sold merch., terms FOB shipping point.			
	20	Cost of Merchandise Sold		36000	
		Merchandise Inventory			36000
		Recorded cost of merchandise sold to			
		Planter Company.			
	20	Accounts Receivable—Planter Company		4500	
		Cash			4500
		Prepaid shipping cost on merch. sold.			

Shipping terms, the passage of title, and whether the buyer or seller is to pay the transportation costs are summarized in Exhibit 11.

Example Exercise 6-5

objective 3

Determine the amount to be paid in full settlement of each of invoices (a) and (b), assuming that credit for returns and allowances was received prior to payment and that all invoices were paid within the discount period.

	Merchandise	Transportation Paid by Seller	Transportation Terms	Returns and Allowances
a.	$4,500	$200	FOB shipping point, 1/10, n/30	$ 800
b.	5,000	60	FOB destination, 2/10, n/30	2,500

Follow My Example 6-5

a. $3,863. Purchase of $4,500 less return of $800 less the discount of $37 [($4,500 − $800) × 1%] plus $200 of shipping.
b. $2,450. Purchase of $5,000 less return of $2,500 less the discount of $50 [($5,000 − $2,500) × 2%].

For Practice: PE 6-5A, PE 6-5B

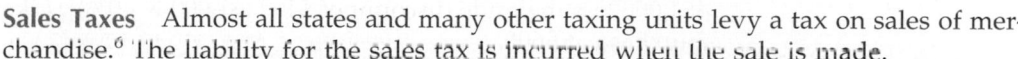

Sales Taxes Almost all states and many other taxing units levy a tax on sales of merchandise.[6] The liability for the sales tax is incurred when the sale is made.

At the time of a cash sale, the seller collects the sales tax. When a sale is made on account, the seller charges the tax to the buyer by debiting Accounts Receivable. The seller credits the sales account for the amount of the sale and credits the tax to Sales

---

6 Businesses that purchase merchandise for resale to others are normally exempt from paying sales taxes on their purchases. Only final buyers of merchandise normally pay sales taxes.

EXHIBIT 11 | **Transportation Terms**

The six states with the highest sales tax are Mississippi, Rhode Island, Tennessee, Minnesota, Nevada, and Washington. Some states have no sales tax, including Alaska, Delaware, Montana, New Hampshire, and Oregon.

Business collects sales tax from customers

Customer

Business remits sales tax to state

State

Tax Payable. For example, the seller would record a sale of $100 on account, subject to a tax of 6%, as follows:

Aug.	12	Accounts Receivable—Lemon Co.		1 0 6 00	
		Sales			1 0 0 00
		Sales Tax Payable			6 00
		Invoice No. 339.			

Normally on a regular basis, the seller pays to the taxing unit the amount of the sales tax collected. The seller records such a payment as follows:

Sept.	15	Sales Tax Payable		2 9 0 0 00	
		Cash			2 9 0 0 00
		Payment for sales taxes collected			
		during August.			

Trade Discounts   Wholesalers are businesses that sell merchandise to other businesses rather than to the general public. Many wholesalers publish catalogs. Rather than updating their catalogs frequently, wholesalers often publish price updates, which may involve large discounts from the list prices in their catalogs. In addition, wholesalers may offer special discounts to certain classes of buyers, such as government agencies or businesses that order large quantities. Such discounts are called **trade discounts**.

Sellers and buyers do not normally record the list prices of merchandise and the related trade discounts in their accounts. For example, assume that an item has a list price of $1,000 and a 40% trade discount. The seller records the sale of the item at $600 [$1,000 less the trade discount of $400 ($1,000 × 40%)]. Likewise, the buyer records the purchase at $600.

DUAL NATURE OF MERCHANDISE TRANSACTIONS

Each merchandising transaction affects a buyer and a seller. In the illustration on the next page, we show how the same transactions would be recorded by both the seller and the buyer. In this example, the seller is Scully Company and the buyer is Burton Co.

Transaction	Scully Company (Seller)			Burton Co. (Buyer)		

July 1. Scully Company sold merchandise on account to Burton Co., $7,500, terms FOB shipping point, n/45. The cost of the merchandise sold was $4,500.	Accounts Receivable—Burton Co.
	  Sales
	
	Cost of Merchandise Sold
	  Merchandise Inventory
		7,500
		
		4,500
			7,500
			
			4,500
				Merchandise Inventory
				  Accounts Payable—Scully Co.
					7,500	7,500

July 2. Burton Co. paid transportation charges of $150 on July 1 purchase from Scully Company.	No entry.			Merchandise Inventory Cash	150	150

July 5. Scully Company sold merchandise on account to Burton Co., $5,000, terms FOB destination, n/30. The cost of the merchandise sold was $3,500.	Accounts Receivable—Burton Co.
	  Sales
	
	Cost of Merchandise Sold
	  Merchandise Inventory
		5,000
		
		3,500
			5,000
			
			3,500
				Merchandise Inventory
				  Accounts Payable—Scully Co.
					5,000	5,000

July 7. Scully Company paid transportation costs of $250 for delivery of merchandise sold to Burton Co. on July 5.	Delivery Expense Cash	250	250	No entry.		

July 13. Scully Company issued Burton Co. a credit memorandum for merchandise returned, $1,000. The merchandise had been purchased by Burton Co. on account on July 5. The cost of the merchandise returned was $700.	Sales Returns and Allowances
	  Accounts Receivable—Burton Co.
	
	Merchandise Inventory
	  Cost of Merchandise Sold
		1,000
		
		700
			1,000
			
			700
				Accounts Payable—Scully Co.
				  Merchandise Inventory
					1,000	1,000

July 15. Scully Company received payment from Burton Co. for purchase of July 5.	Cash
	  Accounts Receivable—Burton Co.
		4,000	4,000	Accounts Payable—Scully Co.
				  Cash
					4,000	4,000

July 18. Scully Company sold merchandise on account to Burton Co., $12,000, terms FOB shipping point, 2/10, n/eom. Scully Company prepaid transportation costs of $500, which were added to the invoice. The cost of the merchandise sold was $7,200.	Accounts Receivable—Burton Co.
	  Sales
	
	Accounts Receivable—Burton Co.
	  Cash
	
	Cost of Merchandise Sold
	  Merchandise Inventory
		12,000
		
		500
		
		7,200
			12,000
			
			500
			
			7,200
				Merchandise Inventory
				  Accounts Payable—Scully Co.
					12,500	12,500

July 28. Scully Company received payment from Burton Co. for purchase of July 18, less discount (2% × $12,000).	Cash
	Sales Discounts
	  Accounts Receivable—Burton Co.
		12,260
		240
			12,500	Accounts Payable—Scully Co.
				  Merchandise Inventory
				  Cash
					12,500	240
						12,260

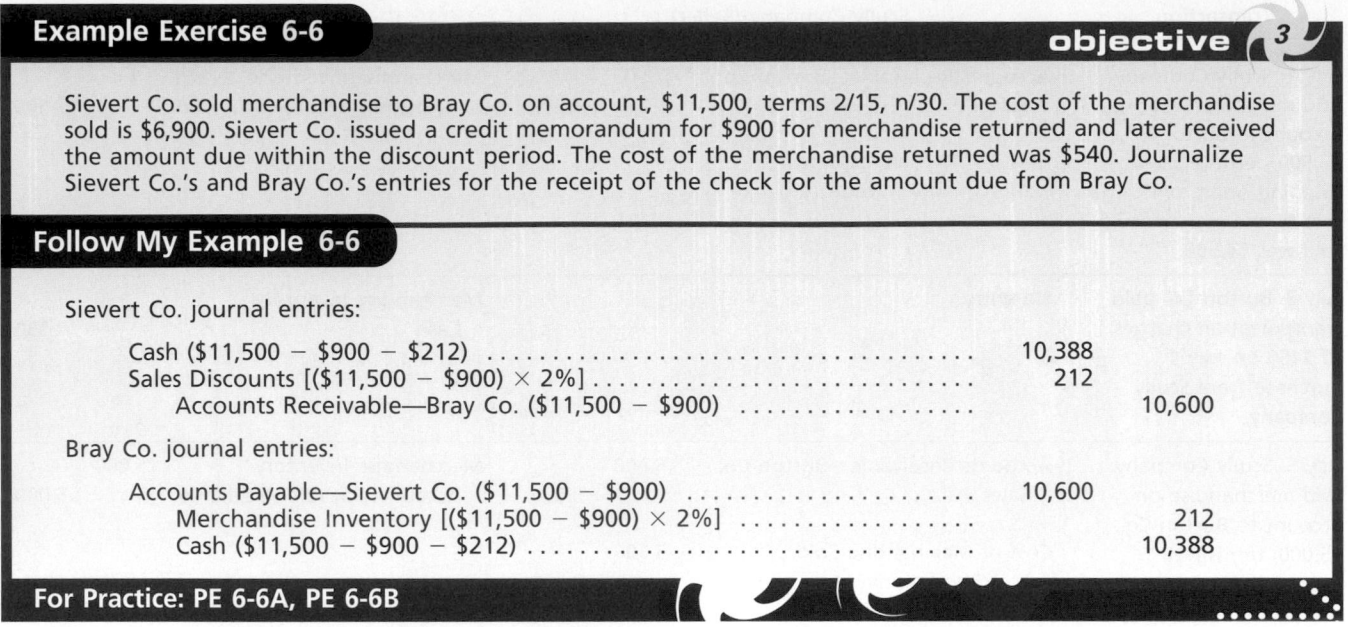

Example Exercise 6-6   objective 3

Sievert Co. sold merchandise to Bray Co. on account, $11,500, terms 2/15, n/30. The cost of the merchandise sold is $6,900. Sievert Co. issued a credit memorandum for $900 for merchandise returned and later received the amount due within the discount period. The cost of the merchandise returned was $540. Journalize Sievert Co.'s and Bray Co.'s entries for the receipt of the check for the amount due from Bray Co.

Follow My Example 6-6

Sievert Co. journal entries:

Cash ($11,500 − $900 − $212)	10,388	
Sales Discounts [($11,500 − $900) × 2%]	212	
Accounts Receivable—Bray Co. ($11,500 − $900)		10,600

Bray Co. journal entries:

Accounts Payable—Sievert Co. ($11,500 − $900)	10,600	
Merchandise Inventory [($11,500 − $900) × 2%]		212
Cash ($11,500 − $900 − $212)		10,388

For Practice: PE 6-6A, PE 6-6B

The Adjusting and Closing Process

objective 4

Describe the adjusting and closing process for a merchandising business.

We have described and illustrated the chart of accounts and the analysis and recording of transactions for a merchandising business. We have also illustrated the preparation of financial statements for a merchandiser, NetSolutions. In the remainder of this chapter, we describe the adjusting and closing process for a merchandising business. In this discussion, we will focus primarily on the elements of the accounting cycle that are likely to differ from those of a service business.

@netsolutions

ADJUSTING ENTRY FOR INVENTORY SHRINKAGE

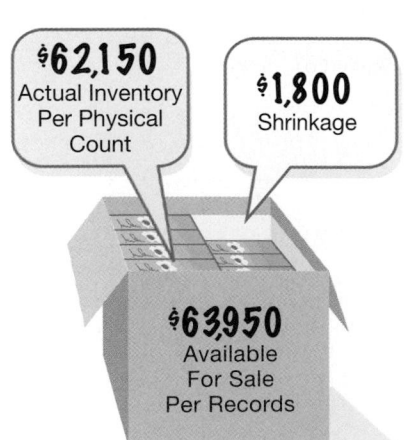

$62,150
Actual Inventory
Per Physical
Count

$1,800
Shrinkage

$63,950
Available
For Sale
Per Records

Under the perpetual inventory system, a separate merchandise inventory account is maintained in the ledger. During the accounting period, this account shows the amount of merchandise for sale at any time. However, merchandising businesses may experience some loss of inventory due to shoplifting, employee theft, or errors in recording or counting inventory. As a result, the physical inventory taken at the end of the accounting period may differ from the amount of inventory shown in the inventory records. Normally, the amount of merchandise for sale, as indicated by the balance of the merchandise inventory account, is larger than the total amount of merchandise counted during the physical inventory. For this reason, the difference is often called **inventory shrinkage** or *inventory shortage*.

To illustrate, NetSolutions' inventory records indicate that $63,950 of merchandise should be available for sale on December 31, 2009. The physical inventory taken on December 31, 2009, however, indicates that only $62,150 of merchandise is actually available. Thus, the inventory shrinkage for the year ending December 31, 2009, is $1,800 ($63,950 − $62,150), as shown at the left. This amount is recorded by the following adjusting entry:

		Adjusting Entry		
Dec.	31	Cost of Merchandise Sold	1 8 0 0 00	
		Merchandise Inventory		1 8 0 0 00
		Inv. shrinkage ($63,950 − $62,150).		

Retailers lose an estimated $30 billion to inventory shrinkage. The primary causes of the shrinkage are employee theft and shoplifting.

After this entry has been recorded, the accounting records agree with the actual physical inventory at the end of the period. Since no system of procedures and safeguards can totally eliminate it, inventory shrinkage is often considered a normal cost of operations. If the amount of the shrinkage is abnormally large, it may be disclosed separately on the income statement. In such cases, the shrinkage may be recorded in a separate account, such as Loss from Merchandise Inventory Shrinkage.[7]

CLOSING ENTRIES

The closing entries for a merchandising business are similar to those for a service business. The first entry closes the temporary accounts with credit balances, such as Sales, to the income summary account. The second entry closes the temporary accounts with debit balances, including Sales Returns and Allowances, Sales Discounts, and Cost of Merchandise Sold, to the income summary account. The third entry closes the balance of the income summary account to the owner's capital account. The fourth entry closes the owner's drawing account to the owner's capital account. The closing entries for NetSolutions are shown below.

	Date	Item	Post. Ref.	Debit	Credit	
1	2009	Closing Entries				1
2	Dec. 31	Sales	410	720 1 8 5 00		2
3		Rent Revenue	610	6 0 0 00		3
4		Income Summary	312		720 7 8 5 00	4
5						5
6	31	Income Summary	312	645 3 8 5 00		6
7		Sales Returns and Allowances	411		6 1 4 0 00	7
8		Sales Discounts	412		5 7 9 0 00	8
9		Cost of Merchandise Sold	510		525 3 0 5 00	9
10		Sales Salaries Expense	520		53 4 3 0 00	10
11		Advertising Expense	521		10 8 6 0 00	11
12		Depr. Expense—Store Equipment	522		3 1 0 0 00	12
13		Delivery Expense	523		2 8 0 0 00	13
14		Miscellaneous Selling Expense	529		6 3 0 00	14
15		Office Salaries Expense	530		21 0 2 0 00	15
16		Rent Expense	531		8 1 0 0 00	16
17		Depr. Expense—Office Equipment	532		2 4 9 0 00	17
18		Insurance Expense	533		1 9 1 0 00	18
19		Office Supplies Expense	534		6 1 0 00	19
20		Misc. Administrative Expense	539		7 6 0 00	20
21		Interest Expense	710		2 4 4 0 00	21
22						22
23	31	Income Summary	312	75 4 0 0 00		23
24		Chris Clark, Capital	310		75 4 0 0 00	24
25						25
26	31	Chris Clark, Capital	310	18 0 0 0 00		26
27		Chris Clark, Drawing	311		18 0 0 0 00	27

The balance of Income Summary, after the first two closing entries have been posted, is the net income or net loss for the period. The third closing entry transfers

---

7 The adjusting process for a merchandising business may be aided by preparing an end-of-period spreadsheet (work sheet). An end-of-period spreadsheet (work sheet) for a merchandising business is described and illustrated in Appendix C.

this balance to the owner's capital account. NetSolutions' income summary account after the closing entries have been posted is as follows:

ACCOUNT *Income Summary*						ACCOUNT NO. *312*	
		Post. Ref.	Debit	Credit		**Balance**	
Date	Item					Debit	Credit
2009 Dec. 31	Revenues	29		720 7 8 5 00			720 7 8 5 00
31	Expenses	29	645 3 8 5 00				75 4 0 0 00
31	Net income	29	75 4 0 0 00			—	—

After the closing entries have been prepared and posted to the accounts, a post-closing trial balance may be prepared to verify the debit-credit equality. The only accounts that should appear on the post-closing trial balance are the asset, contra asset, liability, and owner's capital accounts with balances. These are the same accounts that appear on the end-of-period balance sheet.

Example Exercise 6-7   objective ④

Pulmonary Company's perpetual inventory records indicate that $382,800 of merchandise should be on hand on March 31, 2008. The physical inventory indicates that $371,250 of merchandise is actually on hand. Journalize the adjusting entry for the inventory shrinkage for Pulmonary Company for the year ended March 31, 2008.

Follow My Example 6-7

Mar. 31	Cost of Merchandise Sold	11,550	
	Merchandise Inventory		11,550
	Inventory shrinkage ($382,800 − $371,250).		

For Practice: PE 6-7A, PE 6-7B

FINANCIAL ANALYSIS AND INTERPRETATION

The ratio of net sales to assets measures how effectively a business is using its assets to generate sales. A high ratio indicates an effective use of assets. The assets used in computing the ratio may be the total assets at the end of the year, the average of the total assets at the beginning and end of the year, or the average of the monthly assets. For our purposes, we will use the average of the total assets at the beginning and end of the year. The ratio is computed as follows:

$$\text{Ratio of Net Sales to Assets} = \frac{\text{Net Sales}}{\text{Average Total Assets}}$$

To illustrate the use of this ratio, the following data (in millions) are taken from annual reports of Sears Holding Corporation and JCPenney:

	Sears	JCPenney
Total revenues (net sales)	$19,701	$18,424
Total assets:		
Beginning of year	6,074	18,300
End of year	8,651	14,127

The ratio of net sales to assets for each company is as follows:

	Sears	JCPenney
Ratio of net sales to assets	2.68*	1.14**

*$19,701/[($6,074 + $8,651)/2]
**$18,424/[($18,300 + $14,127)/2]

Based on these ratios, Sears appears better than JCPenney in utilizing its assets to generate sales. Comparing this ratio over time for both Sears and JCPenney, as well as comparing it with industry averages, would provide a better basis for interpreting the financial performance of each company.

Integrity, Objectivity, and Ethics in Business

ETHICS

THE COST OF EMPLOYEE THEFT

One survey reported that the 27 largest U.S. retail store chains have lost over $4.7 billion to shoplifting and employee theft. Of this amount, only 2.74% of the losses resulted in any recovery. The stores apprehended over 750,000 shoplifters and dishonest employees. Approximately 1 out of every 28 employees was apprehended for theft from his or her employer. Each dishonest employee stole approximately 6.6 times the amount stolen by shoplifters ($671 vs. $102).

Source: Jack L. Hayes International, 17th Annual Retail Theft Survey, 2004.

Appendix 1

Accounting Systems for Merchandisers

Merchandising companies may use either manual or computerized accounting systems, similar to those used by service businesses. In this appendix, we describe and illustrate special journals and electronic forms that merchandise businesses may use in these systems.

MANUAL ACCOUNTING SYSTEM

In a manual accounting system, a merchandise business normally uses four special journals: sales journal (for sales on account), purchases journal (for purchases on account), cash receipts journal, and cash payments journal. These journals can be adapted from the special journals that we illustrated in Chapter 5 for a service business.

@netsolutions

Exhibit 12 illustrates NetSolutions' sales journal, which is modified from a revenue journal. In a sales journal, each transaction is recorded by entering the sales amount in the *Accounts Receivable Dr./Sales Cr.* column and entering the cost of the merchandise sold amount in the *Cost of Merchandise Sold Dr./Merchandise Inventory Cr.* column. The totals of the two columns would be posted to the four general ledger accounts. The inventory and accounts receivable subsidiary ledgers would be updated when each transaction is recorded.

EXHIBIT 12

Sales Journal for a Merchandising Business

			SALES JOURNAL			Page 35	
	Date	Invoice No.	Account Debited	Post. Ref.	Accts. Rec. Dr. Sales Cr.	Cost of Merchandise Sold Dr. Merchandise Inventory Cr.	
1	2009 Mar. 2	810	Berry Co.	✔	2 7 5 0 00	2 0 0 0 00	1
2	14	811	Handler Co.	✔	4 2 6 0 00	3 4 7 0 00	2
3	19	812	Jordan Co.	✔	5 8 0 0 00	4 6 5 0 00	3
4	26	813	Kenner Co.	✔	4 5 0 0 00	3 8 4 0 00	4
5					17 3 1 0 00	13 9 6 0 00	5
6					(112) (410)	(510) (115)	6

Exhibit 13 illustrates a purchases journal for NetSolutions' merchandising business. This journal is similar to the purchases journal for NetSolutions' service business that we illustrated previously. It includes an *Accounts Payable Cr.* column and a *Merchandise Inventory Dr.* column, rather than a *Supplies Dr.* column. At the end of the month,

EXHIBIT 13   Purchases Journal for a Merchandising Business

	Date	Account Credited	Post. Ref.	Accounts Payable Cr.	Merchandise Inventory Dr.	Other Accounts Dr.	Post. Ref.	Amount	
				PURCHASES JOURNAL				Page 11	
1	2009 Mar. 4	Compu-Tek	✔	13 88 0 00	13 88 0 00				1
2	7	Omega Technologies	✔	4 65 0 00	4 65 0 00				2
3	15	Dale Furniture Co.	✔	5 70 0 00		Store Equipment	123	5 70 0 00	3
4	22	Delta Data Link	✔	3 84 0 00	3 84 0 00				4
5	29	Power Electronics	✔	3 20 0 00	3 20 0 00				5
6				31 27 0 00	25 57 0 00			5 70 0 00	6
7				(210)	(115)			(✔)	7

these two column totals would be posted to the general ledger controlling accounts, Accounts Payable and Merchandise Inventory. The amounts in *Other Accounts Dr.* would be posted individually. The inventory and accounts payable subsidiary ledgers would be updated when each transaction is recorded.

Exhibit 14 illustrates a portion of NetSolutions' cash receipts journal. In this journal, cash sales are recorded in a *Sales Cr.* column rather than a *Fees Earned Cr.* column. In addition, the cost of merchandise sold for cash is recorded in a *Cost of Merchandise Sold Dr./Merchandise Inventory Cr.* column. Each entry in this column is posted to the inventory subsidiary ledger at the time the transaction is recorded. Sales discounts are recorded in a *Sales Discounts Dr.* column. At the end of the month, all the column totals except for *Other Accounts Cr.* are posted to the general ledger.

EXHIBIT 14   Cash Receipts Journal for Merchandising Business

	Date	Account Credited	Post. Ref.	Other Accounts Cr.	Cost of Merchandise Sold Dr. Merchandise Inventory Cr.	Sales Cr.	Accounts Receivable Cr.	Sales Discounts Dr.	Cash Dr.	
					CASH RECEIPTS JOURNAL				Page 14	
1	2009 Mar. 3	Sales	✔		4 0 0 00	6 0 0 00			6 0 0 00	1
2	12	Berry Co.	✔				2 75 0 00	5 5 00	2 69 5 00	2

Exhibit 15 illustrates a portion of the cash payments journal for NetSolutions. This journal is modified for a merchandising business by adding a *Merchandise Inventory Cr.* column for recording discounts on purchases paid within the discount period. Each entry in this column is posted to the inventory subsidiary ledger at the time the transaction is recorded. At the end of the month, all the column totals except for *Other Accounts Dr.* are posted to the general ledger.

COMPUTERIZED ACCOUNTING SYSTEMS

In computerized accounting systems, special journals may be replaced by electronic forms. Electronic forms collect information that is used by software for making computerized entries. In QuickBooks®, for example, the transactions for purchases and sales can be accomplished using electronic bill and invoice forms.

EXHIBIT 15 Cash Payments Journal for Merchandising Business

CASH PAYMENTS JOURNAL   Page 7

	Date	Ck. No.	Account Debited	Post. Ref.	Other Accounts Dr.	Accounts Payable Dr.	Merchandise Inventory Cr.	Cash Cr.	
1	2009 Mar. 16	210	Compu-Tek	✔		13 88 0 00		13 88 0 00	1
2	17	211	Omega Technologies	✔		4 65 0 00	9 3 00	4 55 7 00	2

To illustrate, NetSolutions first purchases four LT-1000 servers for $13,880 on March 4, 2009 from Compu-Tek. This transaction was illustrated previously in the purchases journal in Exhibit 13. We will use the "Enter Bills" form, shown in Exhibit 16, to record the purchase. The form shows the following:

■ The vendor: Compu-Tek
■ The item purchased: LT-1000 network server
■ The number of LT-1000s purchased: 4
■ The cost per unit: $3,470
■ The total amount of the purchase: $13,880

After the Enter Bills form has been completed and submitted (Save), the software debits the cost of four LT-1000s to NetSolutions' Inventory and credits Accounts Payable to Compu-Tek for $13,880.

EXHIBIT 16

Enter Bills Form

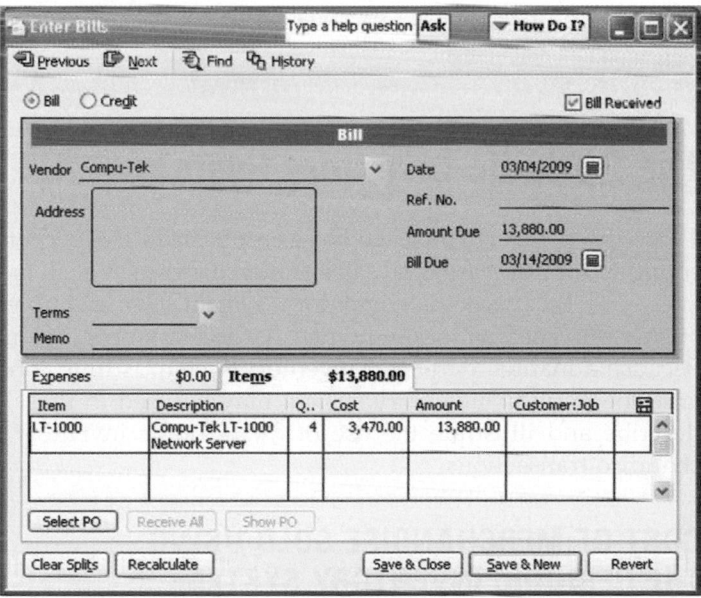

Next, assume that on March 14, 2009 NetSolutions invoices Handler Co. for the sale of one of these network servers, as illustrated previously in the sales journal in Exhibit 12. The sale can be entered in QuickBooks® using the "Create Invoices" form in QuickBooks®, as shown in Exhibit 17. The form shows:

■ The customer: Handler Co
■ The item sold: Compu-Tek LT-1000 network server
■ The quantity sold: 1
■ The price per item: $4,260
■ The total invoice amount of the sale, $4,260

EXHIBIT 17

Create Invoice Form

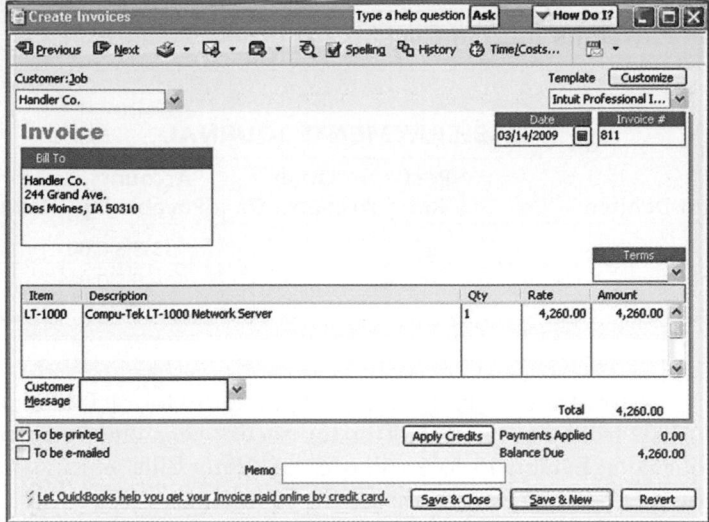

Once this form has been submitted to the system, the computer debits Accounts Receivable for Handler Co. and credits Sales for $4,260. In addition, the software debits Cost of Goods Sold and credits Inventory for the $3,470 value of one LT-1000. This latter transaction is recorded automatically and is not shown on the Create Invoices form.

An income statement prepared after these forms have been completed would show sales of $4,260, cost of goods sold of $3,470, and gross profit of $790. A balance sheet would show accounts receivable of $4,260, inventory of $10,410 (3 units × $3,470), accounts payable of $13,880, and retained earnings of $790.

Appendix 2

The Periodic Inventory System

Throughout this chapter, we have emphasized the perpetual inventory system of accounting for purchases and sales of merchandise. Not all merchandise businesses, however, use the perpetual inventory system. For example, some small merchandise businesses, such as locally owned hardware stores, use manual accounting systems. Because a manual perpetual inventory system is time consuming and costly to maintain, the periodic inventory system may be used in these cases. In this appendix, we describe and illustrate the use of the periodic inventory system for recording merchandise transactions.

COST OF MERCHANDISE SOLD USING THE PERIODIC INVENTORY SYSTEM

@netsolutions

Using the periodic inventory system, the revenues from sales are recorded when sales are made in the same manner as in the perpetual inventory system. However, no attempt is made on the date of sale to record the cost of the merchandise sold. Instead, as we illustrated earlier in this chapter for NetSolutions, cost of merchandise sold is determined as shown in Exhibit 18.

CHART OF ACCOUNTS UNDER THE PERIODIC INVENTORY SYSTEM

The chart of accounts under a periodic inventory system is shown in Exhibit 19. The accounts used to record transactions under the periodic inventory system are highlighted in Exhibit 19. We describe and illustrate how these accounts are used to record transactions under the periodic inventory system next.

EXHIBIT 18

Determining Cost of
Merchandise Sold
Using the Periodic
System

Merchandise inventory, January 1, 2009 . . .			$ 59,700
Purchases		$521,980	
Less: Purchases returns and allowances	$9,100		
Purchases discounts	2,525	11,625	
Net purchases		$510,355	
Add transportation in		17,400	
Cost of merchandise purchased			527,755
Merchandise available for sale			$587,455
Less merchandise inventory,			
December 31, 2009			62,150
Cost of merchandise sold			$525,305

EXHIBIT 19

Chart of Accounts
Under the Periodic
Inventory System

Balance Sheet Accounts		Income Statement Accounts	
	100 Assets		400 Revenues
110	Cash	410	Sales
111	Notes Receivable	411	Sales Returns and Allowances
112	Accounts Receivable	412	Sales Discounts
115	Merchandise Inventory		
116	Office Supplies		500 Costs and Expenses
117	Prepaid Insurance	510	Purchases
120	Land	511	Purchases Returns and
123	Store Equipment		Allowances
124	Accumulated Depreciation—	512	Purchases Discounts
	Store Equipment	513	Transportation In
125	Office Equipment	520	Sales Salaries Expense
126	Accumulated Depreciation—	521	Advertising Expense
	Office Equipment	522	Depreciation Expense—Store
			Equipment
	200 Liabilities	523	Delivery Expense
210	Accounts Payable	529	Miscellaneous Selling Expense
211	Salaries Payable	530	Office Salaries Expense
212	Unearned Rent	531	Rent Expense
215	Notes Payable	532	Depreciation Expense—Office
			Equipment
	300 Owner's Equity	533	Insurance Expense
310	Chris Clark, Capital	534	Office Supplies Expense
311	Chris Clark, Drawing	539	Misc. Administrative Expense
312	Income Summary		
			600 Other Income
		610	Rent Revenue
			700 Other Expense
		710	Interest Expense

RECORDING MERCHANDISE TRANSACTIONS UNDER THE PERIODIC INVENTORY SYSTEM

Using the periodic inventory system, purchases of inventory are recorded in a *purchases* account rather than in a merchandise inventory account. No attempt is made to keep a detailed record of the amount of inventory on hand at any given time. Instead, at the end of the period, a physical count of merchandise inventory is taken. This physical count is then used to determine the cost of merchandise sold as shown in Exhibit 18.

The purchases account is debited for the amount of the invoice before considering any purchases discounts. Purchases discounts are normally recorded in a separate *purchases discounts* account. The balance of this account is reported as a deduction from the amount initially recorded in Purchases for the period. Thus, the purchases discounts account is viewed as a contra (or offsetting) account to Purchases.

Purchases returns and allowances are recorded in a similar manner as purchases discounts. A separate *purchases returns and allowances* account is used to keep a record of the amount of returns and allowances during a period. Purchases returns and allowances are reported as a deduction from the amount initially recorded as Purchases. Like Purchases Discounts, the purchases returns and allowances account is a contra (or offsetting) account to Purchases.

When merchandise is purchased FOB shipping point, the buyer is responsible for paying the freight charges. Under the periodic inventory system, freight charges paid when purchasing merchandise FOB shipping point are debited to *Transportation In*, Freight In, or a similarly titled account.

The preceding periodic inventory accounts and their effect on the cost of merchandise purchased are summarized below.

Account	Entry to Increase (Decrease)	Normal Balance	Effect on Cost of Merchandise Purchased
Purchases	Debit	Debit	Increases
Purchases Discounts	Credit	Credit	Decreases
Purchases Returns and Allowances	Credit	Credit	Decreases
Transportation In	Debit	Debit	Increases

Exhibit 20 illustrates the recording of merchandise transactions using the periodic system. As a review, Exhibit 20 also illustrates how each transaction would have been recorded using the perpetual system.

ADJUSTING PROCESS UNDER THE PERIODIC INVENTORY SYSTEM

The adjusting process is the same under the periodic and perpetual inventory systems except for the inventory shrinkage adjustment. Under both the periodic and perpetual inventory systems the ending merchandise inventory is determined by a physical count. Under the perpetual inventory system the ending inventory physical count is then compared to the amounts in the inventory ledger and the amount of inventory shrinkage is determined. This inventory shrinkage is recorded as a debit to Cost of Merchandise Sold and a credit to Merchandise Inventory.

Under the periodic inventory system, a separate inventory ledger is not maintained during the year. Instead, purchases of inventory are recorded in the *purchases* account. As a result, the inventory shrinkage cannot be directly determined, but is included indirectly in the cost of merchandise sold computation shown in Exhibit 18. This is done at the end of the year when the merchandise inventory account is increased or decreased to the ending physical merchandise inventory, which we will describe later. A primary disadvantage of the periodic inventory system is that the amount of inventory shrinkage is not separately determined.

FINANCIAL STATEMENTS UNDER THE PERIODIC INVENTORY SYSTEM

The financial statements are essentially the same under both the perpetual and periodic inventory systems. When a multiple-step income statement is reported, cost of merchandise sold may be reported as shown in Exhibit 18.

EXHIBIT 20	Transactions Using the Periodic and Perpetual Inventory Systems					
Transaction	**Periodic Inventory System**			**Perpetual Inventory System**		

June 5. Purchased $30,000 of merchandise on account, terms 2/10, n/30.	Purchases
	   Accounts Payable
		30,000	30,000	Merchandise Inventory
				   Accounts Payable
					30,000	30,000

June 8. Returned merchandise purchased on account on June 5, $500.	Accounts Payable
	   Purchases Returns and Allowances
		500	500	Accounts Payable
				   Merchandise Inventory
					500	500

June 15. Paid for purchase of June 5, less return of $500 and discount of $590 [($30,000 − 500) × 2%].	Accounts Payable
	   Cash
	   Purchases Discounts
		29,500	28,910
			590
				Accounts Payable
				   Cash
				   Merchandise Inventory
					29,500	28,910
						590

June 18. Sold merchandise on account, $12,500, 1/10, n/30. The cost of the merchandise sold was $9,000.	Accounts Receivable
	   Sales
		12,500	12,500	Accounts Receivable
				   Sales
				Cost of Merchandise Sold
				   Merchandise Inventory
					12,500
					
					9,000
						12,500
						
						9,000

June 21. Received merchandise returned on account, $4,000. The cost of the merchandise returned was $2,800.	Sales Returns and Allowances
	   Accounts Receivable
		4,000	4,000	Sales Returns and Allowances
				   Accounts Receivable
				Merchandise Inventory
				   Cost of Merchandise Sold
					4,000
					
					2,800
						4,000
						
						2,800

June 22. Purchased merchandise, $15,000, terms FOB shipping point, 2/15, n/30, with prepaid transportation charges of $750 added to the invoice.	Purchases
	Transportation In
	   Accounts Payable
		15,000
		750
			15,750	Merchandise Inventory
				   Accounts Payable
					15,750	15,750

June 28. Received $8,415 as payment on account from June 18 sale less return of June 21 and less discount of $85 [($12,500 − $4,000) × 1%].	Cash
	Sales Discounts
	   Accounts Receivable
		8,415
		85
			8,500	Cash
				Sales Discounts
				   Accounts Receivable
					8,415
					85
						8,500

June 29. Received $19,600 from cash sales. The cost of the merchandise sold was $13,800.	Cash
	   Sales
		19,600	19,600	Cash
				   Sales
				Cost of Merchandise Sold
				   Merchandise Inventory
					19,600
					
					13,800
						19,600
						
						13,800

CLOSING ENTRIES UNDER THE PERIODIC INVENTORY SYSTEM

The closing entries differ in the periodic inventory system in that there is no cost of merchandise sold account to be closed to Income Summary. Instead, the purchases, purchases discounts, purchases returns and allowances, and transportation in accounts are closed to Income Summary. In addition, the merchandise inventory account is adjusted to the physical inventory count through the closing process. To illustrate, the closing entries for NetSolutions under the periodic inventory system are shown at the top of the following page.

JOURNAL

	Date		Item	Post. Ref.	Debit	Credit	
1	2009		Closing Entries				1
2	Dec.	31	Merchandise Inventory	115	62 1 5 0 00		2
3			Sales	410	720 1 8 5 00		3
4			Purchases Returns and Allowances	511	9 1 0 0 00		4
5			Purchases Discounts	512	2 5 2 5 00		5
6			Rent Revenue	610	6 0 0 00		6
7			Income Summary			794 5 6 0 00	7
8							8
9		31	Income Summary		719 1 6 0 00		9
10			Merchandise Inventory	115		59 7 0 0 00	10
11			Sales Returns and Allowances	411		6 1 4 0 00	11
12			Sales Discounts	412		5 7 9 0 00	12
13			Purchases	510		521 9 8 0 00	13
14			Transportation In	513		17 4 0 0 00	14
15			Sales Salaries Expense	520		53 4 3 0 00	15
16			Advertising Expense	521		10 8 6 0 00	16
17			Depreciation Expense—Store Equipment	522		3 1 0 0 00	17
18			Delivery Expense	523		2 8 0 0 00	18
19			Miscellaneous Selling Expense	529		6 3 0 00	19
20			Office Salaries Expense	530		21 0 2 0 00	20
21			Rent Expense	531		8 1 0 0 00	21
22			Depreciation Expense—Office Equipment	532		2 4 9 0 00	22
23			Insurance Expense	533		1 9 1 0 00	23
24			Office Supplies Expense	534		6 1 0 00	24
25			Miscellaneous Administrative Expense	539		7 6 0 00	25
26			Interest Expense	710		2 4 4 0 00	26
27							27
28		31	Income Summary	312	75 4 0 0 00		28
29			Chris Clark, Capital	310		75 4 0 0 00	29
30							30
31		31	Chris Clark, Capital	310	18 0 0 0 00		31
32			Chris Clark, Drawing	311		18 0 0 0 00	32

In the preceding closing entries, the periodic accounts are highlighted. Under the perpetual inventory system, these highlighted periodic inventory accounts are replaced by the cost of merchandise sold account. Also, you should note that in the first closing entry Merchandise Inventory is debited for $62,150 to increase it to the ending physical inventory count on December 31, 2009. In the second closing entry, Merchandise Inventory is credited for its January 1, 2009, balance of $59,700. Including beginning and ending balances of Merchandise Inventory in both entries highlights its importance in determining cost of merchandise sold as shown in Exhibit 18. After the closing entries are posted, Merchandise Inventory will have a balance of $62,150, which is the amount reported on the December 31, 2009, balance sheet.

At a Glance

1. Distinguish between the activities and financial statements of service and merchandising businesses.

Key Points	Key Learning Outcomes	Example Exercises	Practice Exercises
The primary differences between a service business and a merchandising business relate to revenue activities. Merchandising businesses purchase merchandise for selling to customers. On a merchandising business's income statement, revenue from selling merchandise is reported as sales. The cost of the merchandise sold is subtracted from sales to arrive at gross profit. The operating expenses are subtracted from gross profit to arrive at net income. Merchandise inventory, which is merchandise not sold, is reported as a current asset on the balance sheet.	• Describe how the activities of a service and a merchandising business differ. • Describe the differences between the income statements of a service and a merchandising business. • Compute gross profit. • Describe how merchandise inventory is reported on the balance sheet.	6-1	6-1A, 6-1B

2. Describe and illustrate the financial statements of a merchandising business.

Key Points	Key Learning Outcomes	Example Exercises	Practice Exercises
The multiple-step income statement of a merchandiser reports sales, sales returns and allowances, sales discounts, and net sales. The cost of the merchandise sold is subtracted from net sales to determine the gross profit. The cost of merchandise sold is determined by using either the periodic or perpetual system. Operating income is determined by subtracting operating expenses from gross profit. Operating expenses are normally classified as selling or administrative expenses. Net income is determined by adding or subtracting the net of other income and expense. The income statement may also be reported in a single-step form. The statement of owner's equity is similar to that for a service business. The balance sheet reports merchandise inventory at the end of the period as a current asset.	• Prepare a multiple-step income statement for a merchandising business. • Describe how cost of merchandise sold is determined under a periodic inventory system. • Compute cost of merchandise sold under a periodic inventory system as shown in Exhibit 2. • Prepare a single-step income statement. • Prepare a statement of owner's equity for a merchandising business. • Prepare a balance sheet for a merchandising business.	6-2	6-2A, 6-2B

3. Describe and illustrate the accounting for merchandise transactions including:
- sale of merchandise
- purchase of merchandise
- transportation costs, sales taxes, and trade discounts
- dual nature of merchandising transactions

Key Points	Key Learning Outcomes	Example Exercises	Practice Exercises
Sales of merchandise for cash or on account are recorded by crediting Sales. Under the perpetual inventory system, the cost of merchandise sold and the reduction in merchandise inventory are also recorded for the sale. For sales of merchandise on account, the credit terms may allow discounts for early payment. Such discounts are recorded by the seller as a debit to Sales Discounts. Sales discounts are reported as a deduction from the amount initially recorded in Sales. Likewise, when merchandise is returned or a price adjustment is granted, the seller debits Sales Returns and Allowances.	• Prepare journal entries to record sales of merchandise for cash or using a credit card.		
	• Prepare journal entries to record sales of merchandise on account.	6-3	6-3A, 6-3B
	• Prepare journal entries to record sales discounts and sales returns and allowances.	6-3	6-3A, 6-3B
Purchases of merchandise for cash or on account are recorded by debiting Merchandise Inventory. For purchases of merchandise on account, the credit terms may allow cash discounts for early payment. Such purchases discounts are viewed as a reduction in the cost of the merchandise purchased. When merchandise is returned or a price adjustment is granted, the buyer credits Merchandise Inventory.	• Prepare journal entries to record the purchase of merchandise for cash.		
	• Prepare journal entries to record the purchase of merchandise on account.	6-4	6-4A, 6-4B
	• Prepare journal entries to record purchases discounts and purchases returns and allowances.	6-4	6-4A, 6-4B
When merchandise is shipped FOB shipping point, the buyer pays the transportation costs and debits Merchandise Inventory. When merchandise is shipped FOB destination, the seller pays the transportation costs and debits Transportation Out or Delivery Expense. If the seller prepays transportation costs as a convenience to the buyer, the seller debits Accounts Receivable for the costs.	• Prepare journal entries for transportation costs from the point of view of the buyer and seller.		
	• Determine the total cost of the purchase of merchandise under differing transportation terms.	6-5	6-5A, 6-5B
The liability for sales tax is incurred when the sale is made and is recorded by the seller as a credit to the sales tax payable account. When the amount of the sales tax is paid to the taxing unit, Sales Tax Payable is debited and Cash is credited.	• Prepare journal entries for the collection and payment of sales taxes by the seller.		
Many wholesalers offer trade discounts, which are discounts off the list prices of merchandise. Normally, neither the seller nor the buyer records the list price and the related trade discount in the accounts.	• Determine the cost of merchandise purchased when a trade discount is offered by the seller.		
Each merchandising transaction affects a buyer and a seller. The illustration in this chapter shows how the same transactions would be recorded by both.	• Record the same merchandise transactions for the buyer and seller.	6-6	6-6A, 6-6B

4. Describe the adjusting and closing process for a merchandising business.			
Key Points	**Key Learning Outcomes**	Example Exercises	Practice Exercises
The accounting cycle for a merchandising business is similar to that of a service business. However, a merchandiser is likely to experience inventory shrinkage, which must be recorded. The normal adjusting entry is to debit Cost of Merchandise Sold and credit Merchandise Inventory for the amount of the shrinkage.	• Prepare the adjusting journal entry for inventory shrinkage.	6-7	6-7A, 6-7B
The closing entries for a merchandise business are similar to those for a service business. The first entry closes sales and other revenue to Income Summary. The second entry closes cost of merchandise sold, sales discounts, sales returns and allowances, and other expenses to Income Summary. The third entry closes the balance of Income Summary (the net income or net loss) to the owner's capital account. The fourth entry closes the owner's drawing account to the owner's capital account.	• Prepare the closing entries for a merchandise business.		

Key Terms

account form (257)
administrative expenses (general expenses) (254)
cost of merchandise purchased (253)
cost of merchandise sold (251)
credit memorandum (261)
credit period (260)
credit terms (260)
debit memorandum (264)
FOB (free on board) destination (266)
FOB (free on board) shipping point (266)

gross profit (251)
income from operations (operating income) (254)
inventory shrinkage (270)
invoice (260)
merchandise available for sale (254)
merchandise inventory (251)
multiple-step income statement (252)
net purchases (253)
net sales (252)
other expense (255)
other income (255)

periodic system (254)
perpetual system (254)
purchase return or allowance (252)
purchases discounts (252)
report form (257)
sales (252)
sales discounts (252)
sales returns and allowances (252)
selling expenses (254)
single-step income statement (255)
trade discounts (268)
transportation in (253)

Illustrative Problem

The following transactions were completed by Montrose Company during May of the current year. Montrose Company uses a perpetual inventory system.

May 3. Purchased merchandise on account from Floyd Co., $4,000, terms FOB shipping point, 2/10, n/30, with prepaid transportation costs of $120 added to the invoice.

   5. Purchased merchandise on account from Kramer Co., $8,500, terms FOB destination, 1/10, n/30.

   6. Sold merchandise on account to C. F. Howell Co., list price $4,000, trade discount 30%, terms 2/10, n/30. The cost of the merchandise sold was $1,125.

May 8. Purchased office supplies for cash, $150.
     10. Returned merchandise purchased on May 5 from Kramer Co., $1,300.
     13. Paid Floyd Co. on account for purchase of May 3, less discount.
     14. Purchased merchandise for cash, $10,500.
     15. Paid Kramer Co. on account for purchase of May 5, less return of May 10 and discount.
     16. Received cash on account from sale of May 6 to C. F. Howell Co., less discount.
     19. Sold merchandise on MasterCard credit cards, $2,450. The cost of the merchandise sold was $980.
     22. Sold merchandise on account to Comer Co., $3,480, terms 2/10, n/30. The cost of the merchandise sold was $1,400.
     24. Sold merchandise for cash, $4,350. The cost of the merchandise sold was $1,750.
     25. Received merchandise returned by Comer Co. from sale on May 22, $1,480. The cost of the returned merchandise was $600.
     31. Paid a service processing fee of $140 for MasterCard sales.

Instructions

1. Journalize the preceding transactions.
2. Journalize the adjusting entry for merchandise inventory shrinkage, $3,750.

Solution

1.

May	3	Merchandise Inventory		4,120	
		Accounts Payable—Floyd Co.			4,120
	5	Merchandise Inventory		8,500	
		Accounts Payable—Kramer Co.			8,500
	6	Accounts Receivable—C. F. Howell Co.		2,800	
		Sales			2,800
		[$4,000 − (30% × $4,000)].			
	6	Cost of Merchandise Sold		1,125	
		Merchandise Inventory			1,125
	8	Office Supplies		150	
		Cash			150
	10	Accounts Payable—Kramer Co.		1,300	
		Merchandise Inventory			1,300
	13	Accounts Payable—Floyd Co.		4,120	
		Merchandise Inventory			80
		Cash			4,040
		[$4,000 − (2% × $4,000) + $120].			
	14	Merchandise Inventory		10,500	
		Cash			10,500
	15	Accounts Payable—Kramer Co.		7,200	
		Merchandise Inventory			72
		Cash			7,128
		[($8,500 − $1,300) × 1% = $72; $8,500 − $1,300 − $72 = $7,128].			
	16	Cash		2,744	
		Sales Discounts		56	
		Accounts Receivable—C. F. Howell Co.			2,800
	19	Cash		2,450	
		Sales			2,450
	19	Cost of Merchandise Sold		980	
		Merchandise Inventory			980
	22	Accounts Receivable—Comer Co.		3,480	
		Sales			3,480
	22	Cost of Merchandise Sold		1,400	
		Merchandise Inventory			1,400
	24	Cash		4,350	
		Sales			4,350
	24	Cost of Merchandise Sold		1,750	
		Merchandise Inventory			1,750

May 25		Sales Returns and Allowances		1,480	
		Accounts Receivable—Comer Co.			1,480
	25	Merchandise Inventory		600	
		Cost of Merchandise Sold			600
	31	Credit Card Expense		140	
		Cash			140
2.	May 31	Cost of Merchandise Sold		3,750	
		Merchandise Inventory			3,750
		Inventory shrinkage.			

Self-Examination Questions   (Answers at End of Chapter)

1. If merchandise purchased on account is returned, the buyer may inform the seller of the details by issuing a(n):
   A. debit memorandum.
   B. credit memorandum.
   C. invoice.
   D. bill.

2. If merchandise is sold on account to a customer for $1,000, terms FOB shipping point, 1/10, n/30, and the seller prepays $50 in transportation costs, the amount of the discount for early payment would be:
   A. $0.   C. $10.00.
   B. $5.00.   D. $10.50.

3. The income statement in which the total of all expenses is deducted from the total of all revenues is termed the:
   A. multiple-step form.   C. account form.
   B. single-step form.   D. report form.

4. On a multiple-step income statement, the excess of net sales over the cost of merchandise sold is called:
   A. operating income.
   B. income from operations.
   C. gross profit.
   D. net income.

5. Which of the following expenses would normally be classified as other expense on a multiple-step income statement?
   A. Depreciation expense—office equipment
   B. Sales salaries expense
   C. Insurance expense
   D. Interest expense

Eye Openers

1. What distinguishes a merchandising business from a service business?
2. Can a business earn a gross profit but incur a net loss? Explain.
3. In computing the cost of merchandise sold, does each of the following items increase or decrease that cost? (a) transportation costs, (b) beginning merchandise inventory, (c) purchase discounts, (d) ending merchandise inventory.
4. Describe how the periodic system differs from the perpetual system of accounting for merchandise inventory.
5. Differentiate between the multiple-step and the single-step forms of the income statement.
6. What are the major advantages and disadvantages of the single-step form of income statement compared to the multiple-step statement?
7. What type of revenue is reported in the other income section of the multiple-step income statement?
8. Name at least three accounts that would normally appear in the chart of accounts of a merchandising business but would not appear in the chart of accounts of a service business.
9. How are sales to customers using MasterCard and VISA recorded?
10. The credit period during which the buyer of merchandise is allowed to pay usually begins with what date?
11. What is the meaning of (a) 2/10, n/60; (b) n/30; (c) n/eom?
12. What is the nature of (a) a credit memorandum issued by the seller of merchandise, (b) a debit memorandum issued by the buyer of merchandise?

13. Who bears the transportation costs when the terms of sale are (a) FOB shipping point, (b) FOB destination?
14. Pembroke Office Equipment, which uses a perpetual inventory system, experienced a normal inventory shrinkage of $13,762. What accounts would be debited and credited to record the adjustment for the inventory shrinkage at the end of the accounting period?
15. Assume that Pembroke Office Equipment in Eye Opener 14 experienced an abnormal inventory shrinkage of $215,650. Pembroke Office Equipment has decided to record the abnormal inventory shrinkage so that it would be separately disclosed on the income statement. What account would be debited for the abnormal inventory shrinkage?

Practice Exercises

PE 6-1A
Determine gross profit
obj. 1

During the current year, merchandise is sold for $127,500 cash and $435,600 on account. The cost of the merchandise sold is $422,325. What is the amount of the gross profit?

PE 6-1B
Determine gross profit
obj. 1

During the current year, merchandise is sold for $17,500 cash and $141,750 on account. The cost of the merchandise sold is $127,400. What is the amount of the gross profit?

PE 6-2A
Computing cost of merchandise sold
obj. 2

Based upon the following data, determine the cost of merchandise sold for July:

Merchandise inventory, July 1	$ 88,370
Merchandise inventory, July 31	92,120
Purchases	681,400
Purchases returns and allowances	9,250
Purchases discounts	7,000
Transportation in	3,180

PE 6-2B
Computing cost of merchandise sold
obj. 2

Based upon the following data, determine the cost of merchandise sold for April:

Merchandise inventory, April 1	$128,120
Merchandise inventory, April 30	140,500
Purchases	983,400
Purchases returns and allowances	10,250
Purchases discounts	8,000
Transportation in	5,680

PE 6-3A
Entries for sales transactions
obj. 3

Journalize the following merchandise transactions:

a. Sold merchandise on account, $12,250 with terms 2/10, n/30. The cost of the merchandise sold was $7,400.
b. Received payment less the discount.

PE 6-3B
Entries for sales transactions
obj. 3

Journalize the following merchandise transactions:

a. Sold merchandise on account, $22,500 with terms 1/10, n/30. The cost of the merchandise sold was $14,150.
b. Received payment less the discount.

PE 6-4A
Purchase transactions
obj. 3

Wilder Company purchased merchandise on account from a supplier for $7,500, terms 2/10, n/30. Wilder Company returned $1,500 of the merchandise and received full credit.

a. If Wilder Company pays the invoice within the discount period, what is the amount of cash required for the payment?
b. Under a perpetual inventory system, what account is credited by Wilder Company to record the return?

PE 6-4B
Purchase transactions
obj. 3

Gupta Company purchased merchandise on account from a supplier for $13,200, terms 1/10, n/30. Gupta Company returned $1,700 of the merchandise and received full credit.

a. If Gupta Company pays the invoice within the discount period, what is the amount of cash required for the payment?
b. Under a perpetual inventory system, what account is debited by Gupta Company to record the return?

PE 6-5A
Payments under different transportation terms
obj. 3

Determine the amount to be paid in full settlement of each of invoices (a) and (b), assuming that credit for returns and allowances was received prior to payment and that all invoices were paid within the discount period.

	Merchandise	Transportation Paid by Seller	Transportation Terms	Returns and Allowances
a.	$6,000	$400	FOB shipping point, 1/10, n/30	$1,000
b.	2,500	150	FOB destination, 2/10, n/30	900

PE 6-5B
Payments under different transportation terms
obj. 3

Determine the amount to be paid in full settlement of each of invoices (a) and (b), assuming that credit for returns and allowances was received prior to payment and that all invoices were paid within the discount period.

	Merchandise	Transportation Paid by Seller	Transportation Terms	Returns and Allowances
a.	$ 8,150	$200	FOB destination, 2/10, n/30	$1,300
b.	12,750	625	FOB shipping point, 2/10, n/30	3,000

PE 6-6A
Recording transactions for buyer and seller
obj. 3

Stuckey Co. sold merchandise to Bullock Co. on account, $5,250, terms 2/15, n/30. The cost of the merchandise sold is $3,150. Stuckey Co. issued a credit memorandum for $650 for merchandise returned and later received the amount due within the discount period. The cost of the merchandise returned was $390. Journalize Stuckey Co.'s and Bullock Co.'s entries for the receipt of the check for the amount due from Bullock Co.

PE 6-6B
Recording transactions for buyer and seller
obj. 3

Sparks Co. sold merchandise to Boyt Co. on account, $8,500, terms FOB shipping point, 2/10, n/30. The cost of the merchandise sold is $5,100. Sparks Co. paid transportation charges of $225 and later received the amount due within the discount period. Journalize Sparks Co.'s and Boyt Co.'s entries for the receipt of the check for the amount due from Boyt Co.

PE 6-7A
Entry for inventory shrinkage
obj. 4

Triangle Company's perpetual inventory records indicate that $111,500 of merchandise should be on hand on September 30, 2008. The physical inventory indicates that $107,400 of merchandise is actually on hand. Journalize the adjusting entry for the inventory shrinkage for Triangle Company for the year ended September 30, 2008.

PE 6-7B
Entry for inventory shrinkage
obj. 4

Three Turtles Company's perpetual inventory records indicate that $543,735 of merchandise should be on hand on August 31, 2008. The physical inventory indicates that $520,250 of merchandise is actually on hand. Journalize the adjusting entry for the inventory shrinkage for Three Turtles Company for the year ended August 31, 2008.

Exercises

EX 6-1
Determining gross profit
obj. 1

During the current year, merchandise is sold for $2,850,750. The cost of the merchandise sold is $1,995,525.

a. What is the amount of the gross profit?
b. Compute the gross profit percentage (gross profit divided by sales).
c. ➤ Will the income statement necessarily report a net income? Explain.

EX 6-2
Determining cost of merchandise sold
obj. 1

In 2005, Best Buy reported revenue of $27,433 million. Its gross profit was $6,495 million. What was the amount of Best Buy's cost of merchandise sold?

EX 6-3
Identify items missing in determining cost of merchandise sold
obj. 2

For (a) through (d), identify the items designated by "X" and "Y."

a. Purchases − (X + Y) = Net purchases.
b. Net purchases + X = Cost of merchandise purchased.
c. Merchandise inventory (beginning) + Cost of merchandise purchased = X.
d. Merchandise available for sale − X = Cost of merchandise sold.

EX 6-4
Cost of merchandise sold and related items
obj. 2

✓ a. Cost of merchandise sold, $1,218,300

The following data were extracted from the accounting records of Meniscus Company for the year ended June 30, 2008:

Merchandise inventory, July 1, 2007	$ 183,250
Merchandise inventory, June 30, 2008	200,100
Purchases	1,279,600
Purchases returns and allowances	41,200
Purchases discounts	20,500
Sales	1,800,000
Transportation in	17,250

a. Prepare the cost of merchandise sold section of the income statement for the year ended June 30, 2008, using the periodic inventory system.
b. Determine the gross profit to be reported on the income statement for the year ended June 30, 2008.

EX 6-5
Cost of merchandise sold
obj. 2

✓ Correct cost of merchandise sold, $820,500

Identify the errors in the following schedule of cost of merchandise sold for the current year ended March 31, 2008:

Cost of merchandise sold:			
Merchandise inventory, March 31, 2008			$135,750
Purchases		$852,100	
Plus: Purchases returns and allowances	$10,500		
Purchases discounts	8,000	18,500	
Gross purchases		$870,600	
Less transportation in		7,500	
Cost of merchandise purchased			863,100
Merchandise available for sale			$998,850
Less merchandise inventory, April 1, 2007			115,150
Cost of merchandise sold			$883,700

EX 6-6
Income statement for merchandiser
obj. 2

For the fiscal year, sales were $4,125,800, sales discounts were $380,000, sales returns and allowances were $186,750, and the cost of merchandise sold was $2,475,500.

a. What was the amount of net sales?
b. What was the amount of gross profit?

EX 6-7
Income statement for merchandiser
obj. 2

The following expenses were incurred by a merchandising business during the year. In which expense section of the income statement should each be reported: (a) selling, (b) administrative, or (c) other?

1. Advertising expense.
2. Depreciation expense on store equipment.
3. Insurance expense on office equipment.
4. Interest expense on notes payable.
5. Rent expense on office building.
6. Salaries of office personnel.
7. Salary of sales manager.
8. Sales supplies used.

EX 6-8
Single-step income statement
obj. 2
✓*Net income: $451,450*

Summary operating data for The Voodoo Company during the current year ended November 30, 2008, are as follows: cost of merchandise sold, $2,175,350; administrative expenses, $500,000; interest expense, $23,200; rent revenue, $30,000; net sales, $4,000,000; and selling expenses, $880,000. Prepare a single-step income statement.

EX 6-9
Multiple-step income statement
obj. 2

Identify the errors in the following income statement:

The Euclidian Company
Income Statement
For the Year Ended March 31, 2008

Revenue from sales:			
Sales			$7,127,500
Add: Sales returns and allowances	$112,300		
Sales discounts	60,000	172,300	
Gross sales			$7,299,800
Cost of merchandise sold			4,175,100
Income from operations			$3,124,700
Expenses:			
Selling expenses		$ 710,000	
Administrative expenses		525,000	
Delivery expense		18,100	
Total expenses			1,253,100
			$1,871,600
Other expense:			
Interest revenue			80,000
Gross profit			$1,791,600

EX 6-10
Determining amounts for items omitted from income statement
obj. 2
✓*a. $30,000*
✓*h. $690,000*

Two items are omitted in each of the following four lists of income statement data. Determine the amounts of the missing items, identifying them by letter.

Sales	$400,000	$500,000	$1,000,000	$ (g)
Sales returns and allowances	(a)	15,000	(e)	30,500
Sales discounts	20,000	8,000	40,000	37,000
Net sales	350,000	(c)	910,000	(h)
Cost of merchandise sold	(b)	285,000	(f)	540,000
Gross profit	200,000	(d)	286,500	150,000

EX 6-11
Multiple-step income statement
obj. 2

✓ *a. Net income: $137,500*

On August 31, 2008, the balances of the accounts appearing in the ledger of The Bent Needle Company, a furniture wholesaler, are as follows:

Administrative Expenses	$125,000	Notes Payable	$ 25,000
Building	512,500	Office Supplies	10,600
Cash	48,500	Salaries Payable	3,220
Cost of Merchandise Sold	700,000	Sales	1,275,000
Interest Expense	7,500	Sales Discounts	20,000
Jason Ritchie, Capital	568,580	Sales Returns and Allowances	80,000
Jason Ritchie, Drawing	25,000	Selling Expenses	205,000
Merchandise Inventory	130,000	Store Supplies	7,700

a. Prepare a multiple-step income statement for the year ended August 31, 2008.
b. Compare the major advantages and disadvantages of the multiple-step and single-step forms of income statements.

EX 6-12
Chart of accounts
obj. 3

Gemini Co. is a newly organized business with a list of accounts arranged in alphabetical order below.

Accounts Payable
Accounts Receivable
Accumulated Depreciation—Office Equipment
Accumulated Depreciation—Store Equipment
Advertising Expense
Cash
Cost of Merchandise Sold
Delivery Expense
Depreciation Expense—Office Equipment
Depreciation Expense—Store Equipment
Income Summary
Insurance Expense
Interest Expense
Jung Qiang, Capital
Jung Qiang, Drawing
Land
Merchandise Inventory

Miscellaneous Administrative Expense
Miscellaneous Selling Expense
Notes Payable
Office Equipment
Office Salaries Expense
Office Supplies
Office Supplies Expense
Prepaid Insurance
Rent Expense
Salaries Payable
Sales
Sales Discounts
Sales Returns and Allowances
Sales Salaries Expense
Store Equipment
Store Supplies
Store Supplies Expense

Construct a chart of accounts, assigning account numbers and arranging the accounts in balance sheet and income statement order, as illustrated in Exhibit 6. Each account number is three digits: the first digit is to indicate the major classification ("1" for assets, and so on); the second digit is to indicate the subclassification ("11" for current assets, and so on); and the third digit is to identify the specific account ("110" for Cash, and so on).

EX 6-13
Sales-related transactions, including the use of credit cards
obj. 3

Journalize the entries for the following transactions:

a. Sold merchandise for cash, $12,150. The cost of the merchandise sold was $9,100.
b. Sold merchandise on account, $6,000. The cost of the merchandise sold was $4,000.
c. Sold merchandise to customers who used MasterCard and VISA, $30,780. The cost of the merchandise sold was $20,000.
d. Sold merchandise to customers who used American Express, $17,650. The cost of the merchandise sold was $10,500.
e. Received an invoice from National Credit Co. for $1,900, representing a service fee paid for processing MasterCard, VISA, and American Express sales.

EX 6-14
Sales returns and allowances
obj. 3

During the year, sales returns and allowances totaled $172,100. The cost of the merchandise returned was $100,300. The accountant recorded all the returns and allowances by debiting the sales account and crediting Cost of Merchandise Sold for $172,100.

▭▭▭▶ Was the accountant's method of recording returns acceptable? Explain. In your explanation, include the advantages of using a sales returns and allowances account.

EX 6-15
Sales-related transactions
obj. 3

After the amount due on a sale of $18,500, terms 2/10, n/eom, is received from a customer within the discount period, the seller consents to the return of the entire shipment. The cost of the merchandise returned was $11,100. (a) What is the amount of the refund owed to the customer? (b) Journalize the entries made by the seller to record the return and the refund.

EX 6-16
Sales-related transactions
obj. 3

The debits and credits for three related transactions are presented in the following T accounts. Describe each transaction.

Cash				Sales		
(5)	9,310				(1)	11,750

Accounts Receivable				Sales Discounts		
(1)	11,750	(3)	2,250	(5)	190	
		(5)	9,500			

Merchandise Inventory				Sales Returns and Allowances		
(4)	1,350	(2)	6,900	(3)	2,250	

Cost of Merchandise Sold		
(2)	6,900	(4)	1,350

EX 6-17
Sales-related transactions
obj. 3
✓d. $9,654

Merchandise is sold on account to a customer for $9,200, terms FOB shipping point, 2/10, n/30. The seller paid the transportation costs of $638. Determine the following: (a) amount of the sale, (b) amount debited to Accounts Receivable, (c) amount of the discount for early payment, and (d) amount due within the discount period.

EX 6-18
Purchase-related transaction
obj. 3

Hushpuppy Company purchased merchandise on account from a supplier for $6,750, terms 2/10, n/30. Hushpuppy Company returned $1,500 of the merchandise and received full credit.

a. If Hushpuppy Company pays the invoice within the discount period, what is the amount of cash required for the payment?
b. Under a perpetual inventory system, what account is credited by Hushpuppy Company to record the return?

EX 6-19
Purchase-related transactions
obj. 3

A retailer is considering the purchase of 100 units of a specific item from either of two suppliers. Their offers are as follows:

A: $375 a unit, total of $37,500, 2/10, n/30, plus transportation costs of $1,050.
B: $380 a unit, total of $38,000, 1/10, n/30, no charge for transportation.

Which of the two offers, A or B, yields the lower price?

EX 6-20
Purchase-related transactions
obj. 3

The debits and credits from four related transactions are presented in the following T accounts. Describe each transaction.

Cash				Accounts Payable		
		(2)	450	(3)	500	(1)	11,500
		(4)	10,780	(4)	11,000		

Merchandise Inventory			
(1)	11,500	(3)	500
(2)	450	(4)	220

EX 6-21
Purchase-related
transactions

obj. 3

✓ *(c) Cash, cr. $7,350*

Madamé Co., a women's clothing store, purchased $10,000 of merchandise from a supplier on account, terms FOB destination, 2/10, n/30. Madamé Co. returned $2,500 of the merchandise, receiving a credit memorandum, and then paid the amount due within the discount period. Journalize Madamé Co.'s entries to record (a) the purchase, (b) the merchandise return, and (c) the payment.

EX 6-22
Purchase-related
transactions

obj. 3

✓ *(e) Cash, dr. $1,410*

Journalize entries for the following related transactions of La Paz Company:

a. Purchased $18,400 of merchandise from Harbin Co. on account, terms 2/10, n/30.
b. Paid the amount owed on the invoice within the discount period.
c. Discovered that $4,500 of the merchandise was defective and returned items, receiving credit.
d. Purchased $3,000 of merchandise from Harbin Co. on account, terms n/30.
e. Received a check for the balance owed from the return in (c), after deducting for the purchase in (d).

EX 6-23
Determining amounts to
be paid on invoices

obj. 3

✓ *a. $6,435*

Determine the amount to be paid in full settlement of each of the following invoices, assuming that credit for returns and allowances was received prior to payment and that all invoices were paid within the discount period.

	Merchandise	Transportation Paid by Seller		Returns and Allowances
a.	$ 8,000	—	FOB shipping point, 1/10, n/30	$1,500
b.	2,900	$125	FOB shipping point, 2/10, n/30	400
c.	3,850	—	FOB destination, 2/10, n/30	—
d.	15,000	—	FOB destination, n/30	2,500
e.	5,000	275	FOB shipping point, 2/10, n/30	1,000

EX 6-24
Sales tax

obj. 3

✓ *c. $12,932*

A sale of merchandise on account for $12,200 is subject to a 6% sales tax. (a) Should the sales tax be recorded at the time of sale or when payment is received? (b) What is the amount of the sale? (c) What is the amount debited to Accounts Receivable? (d) What is the title of the account to which the $732 ($12,200 × 6%) is credited?

EX 6-25
Sales tax transactions

obj. 3

Journalize the entries to record the following selected transactions:

a. Sold $15,750 of merchandise on account, subject to a sales tax of 8%. The cost of the merchandise sold was $9,450.
b. Paid $29,183 to the state sales tax department for taxes collected.

EX 6-26
Sale related transactions

obj. 3

Sellers Co., a furniture wholesaler, sells merchandise to Beyer Co. on account, $14,500, terms 2/10, n/30. The cost of the merchandise sold is $8,800. Sellers Co. issues a credit memorandum for $3,750 for merchandise returned and subsequently receives the amount due within the discount period. The cost of the merchandise returned is $2,100. Journalize Sellers Co.'s entries for (a) the sale, including the cost of the merchandise sold, (b) the credit memorandum, including the cost of the returned merchandise, and (c) the receipt of the check for the amount due from Beyer Co.

EX 6-27
Purchase-related
transactions

obj. 3

Based on the data presented in Exercise 6-26, journalize Beyer Co.'s entries for (a) the purchase, (b) the return of the merchandise for credit, and (c) the payment of the invoice within the discount period.

EX 6-28
Normal balances of merchandise accounts
obj. 3

What is the normal balance of the following accounts: (a) Sales, (b) Sales Discounts, (c) Sales Returns and Allowances, (d) Cost of Merchandise Sold, (e) Delivery Expense, (f) Merchandise Inventory, (g) Sales Tax Payable?

EX 6-29
Adjusting entry for merchandise inventory shrinkage
obj. 4

Teramycin Inc.'s perpetual inventory records indicate that $715,275 of merchandise should be on hand on January 31, 2008. The physical inventory indicates that $698,150 of merchandise is actually on hand. Journalize the adjusting entry for the inventory shrinkage for Teramycin Inc. for the year ended January 31, 2008.

EX 6-30
Closing the accounts of a merchandiser
obj. 4

From the following list, identify the accounts that should be closed to Income Summary at the end of the fiscal year under a perpetual inventory system: (a) Accounts Payable, (b) Advertising Expense, (c) Cost of Merchandise Sold, (d) Merchandise Inventory, (e) Sales, (f) Sales Discounts, (g) Sales Returns and Allowances, (h) Supplies, (i) Supplies Expense, (j) Terry Weaver, Drawing, (k) Wages Payable.

EX 6-31
Closing entries; net income
obj. 4

Based on the data presented in Exercise 6-11, journalize the closing entries.

EX 6-32
Closing entries
obj. 4

On October 31, 2008, the balances of the accounts appearing in the ledger of Kavanaugh Company, a furniture wholesaler, are as follows:

Accumulated Dep.—Building	$152,300	Notes Payable	$ 120,000
Administrative Expenses	326,500	Salaries Payable	3,400
Building	278,400	Sales	1,567,700
Cash	44,200	Sales Discounts	90,000
Cost of Merchandise Sold	940,000	Sales Returns and Allow.	60,000
Interest Expense	9,600	Sales Tax Payable	24,500
Lillian Kavanaugh, Capital	705,775	Selling Expenses	620,000
Lillian Kavanaugh, Drawing	39,750	Store Supplies	22,900
Merchandise Inventory	130,000	Store Supplies Exp.	12,325

Prepare the October 31, 2008, closing entries for Kavanaugh Company.

EX 6-33
Ratio of net sales to total assets

The Home Depot reported the following data (in millions) in its financial statements for 2005 and 2004:

	2005	2004
Net sales	$73,094	$64,816
Total assets at the end of the year	38,907	34,437
Total assets at the beginning of the year	34,437	30,011

a. Determine the ratio of net sales to average total assets for The Home Depot for 2005 and 2004. Round to two decimal places.
b. What conclusions can be drawn from these ratios concerning the trend in the ability of The Home Depot to effectively use its assets to generate sales?

EX 6-34
Ratio of net sales to total assets

Kroger, a national supermarket chain, reported the following data (in millions) in its financial statements for 2005:

Total revenue	$56,434
Total assets at end of year	20,491
Total assets at beginning of year	20,763

a. Compute the ratio of net sales to assets for 2005. Round to two decimal places.
b. ▬▬▶ Would you expect the ratio of net sales to assets for Kroger to be similar to or different from that of Tiffany & Co.? Tiffany is the large North American retailer of jewelry, with a ratio of net sales to average total assets of 0.87.

APPENDIX 1
EX 6-35
Merchandising special journals

✓ d. $62,500

Patel Rug Company had the following credit sales transactions during March 2008:

Date	Customer	Quantity	Rug Style	Sales
Mar. 3	Samantha McGill	1	10 by 8 Chinese	$14,750
8	L. Smith	1	8 by 12 Persian	10,000
19	Paula Larkin	1	8 by 10 Indian	11,500
26	Amy Pugh	1	10 by 12 Persian	21,000

The March 1 inventory was $26,000, consisting of:

Quantity	Style	Cost per Rug	Total Cost
2	10 by 8 Chinese	$7,500	$15,000
2	8 by 12 Persian	5,500	11,000

During March, Patel Rug Company purchased the following rugs from Lee Rug Importers:

Date	Quantity	Rug Style	Cost per Rug	Amount
Mar. 10	2	8 by 10 Indian	$ 6,000	$12,000
12	1	10 by 8 Chinese	10,500	10,500
21	3	10 by 12 Persian	16,500	49,500

The general ledger includes the following accounts:

Account Number	Account
11	Accounts Receivable
12	Merchandise Inventory
21	Accounts Payable
41	Sales
51	Cost of Merchandise Sold

a. Record the sales in a two-column sales journal. Use the sales journal form shown in Appendix 1 at the end of this chapter. Begin with Invoice No. 80.
b. Record the purchases in a purchases journal. Use the purchases journal form shown in Appendix 1 at the end of this chapter.
c. Assume that you have posted the journal entries to the appropriate ledgers. Insert the correct posting references in the sales and purchases journals.
d. Determine the March 31 balance of Merchandise Inventory.

APPENDIX 2
EX 6-36
Accounts for periodic and perpetual inventory systems

Indicate which of the following accounts would be included in the chart of accounts of a merchandising company using either the (a) periodic inventory system or (b) perpetual inventory system. If the account would be included in the chart of accounts of a company using the periodic and perpetual systems, indicate (c) for both.

(1) Cost of Merchandise Sold
(2) Purchases Discounts
(3) Sales
(4) Merchandise Inventory
(5) Sales Discounts
(6) Purchases Returns and Allowances
(7) Delivery Expense
(8) Sales Returns and Allowances
(9) Transportation In
(10) Purchases

APPENDIX 2
EX 6-37
Rules of debit and credit for periodic inventory accounts

Complete the following table by indicating for (a) through (g) whether the proper answer is debit or credit.

Account	Increase	Decrease	Normal Balance
Purchases	(a)	credit	(b)
Purchases Discounts	credit	debit	(c)
Purchases Returns and Allowances	(d)	(e)	credit
Transportation In	(f)	credit	(g)

APPENDIX 2
EX 6-38
Journal entries using the periodic inventory system

The following selected transactions were completed by Lorimer Company during August of the current year. Lorimer Company uses the periodic inventory system.

Aug. 3. Purchased $24,500 of merchandise on account, FOB shipping point, terms 2/10, n/30.
     4. Paid transportation costs of $475 on the August 3 purchase.
     7. Returned $4,000 of the merchandise purchased on August 3.
   11. Sold merchandise on account, $12,700, FOB destination, 2/15, n/30. The cost of merchandise sold was $7,600.
   12. Paid transportation costs of $300 for the merchandise sold on August 11.
   13. Paid for the purchase of August 3 less the return and discount.
   26. Received payment on account for the sale of August 11 less the discount.

Journalize the entries to record the transactions of Lorimer Company.

APPENDIX 2
EX 6-39
Journal entries using perpetual inventory system

Using the data shown in Exercise 6-38, journalize the entries for the transactions assuming that Lorimer Company uses the perpetual inventory system.

APPENDIX 2
EX 6-40
Closing entries using periodic inventory system

Greenway Company is a small rug retailer owned and operated by Lorene Greenway. After the accounts have been adjusted on March 31, the following account balances were taken from the ledger:

Advertising Expense	$ 25,800
Depreciation Expense	5,100
Lorene Greenway, Drawing	50,000
Merchandise Inventory, March 1	34,500
Merchandise Inventory, March 31	42,150
Miscellaneous Expense	6,350
Purchases	480,000
Purchases Discounts	2,000
Purchases Returns and Allowances	9,000
Sales	925,000
Sales Discounts	4,000
Sales Returns and Allowances	8,000
Salaries Expense	76,300
Transportation In	15,400

Journalize the closing entries on March 31.

Problems Series A

PR 6-1A
Multiple-step income statement and report form of balance sheet

obj. 2

✓ 1. Net income: $120,000

The following selected accounts and their current balances appear in the ledger of Magic Vinyl Co. for the fiscal year ended March 31, 2008:

Cash	$ 184,500	Sales Returns and Allowances	$ 27,720
Accounts Receivable	145,200	Sales Discounts	26,280
Merchandise Inventory	210,000	Cost of Merchandise Sold	930,000
Office Supplies	6,720	Sales Salaries Expense	207,840
Prepaid Insurance	4,080	Advertising Expense	52,560
Office Equipment	102,000	Depreciation Expense—	
Accumulated Depreciation—		Store Equipment	7,680
Office Equipment	15,360	Miscellaneous Selling Expense	1,920
Store Equipment	183,600	Office Salaries Expense	100,980
Accumulated Depreciation—		Rent Expense	37,620
Store Equipment	41,040	Depreciation Expense—	
Accounts Payable	66,720	Office Equipment	15,240
Salaries Payable	2,880	Insurance Expense	4,680
Note Payable		Office Supplies Expense	1,560
(final payment due 2018)	67,200	Miscellaneous Administrative	
Tiffany Garland, Capital	564,900	Expense	1,920
Tiffany Garland, Drawing	42,000	Interest Expense	6,000
Sales	1,542,000		

Instructions
1. Prepare a multiple-step income statement.
2. Prepare a statement of owner's equity.
3. Prepare a report form of balance sheet, assuming that the current portion of the note payable is $9,000.
4. Briefly explain (a) how multiple-step and single-step income statements differ and (b) how report-form and account-form balance sheets differ.

PR 6-2A
Single-step income statement and account form of balance sheet

objs. 2, 4

✓ 3. Total assets: $779,700

Selected accounts and related amounts for Magic Vinyl Co. for the fiscal year ended March 31, 2008, are presented in Problem 6-1A.

Instructions
1. Prepare a single-step income statement in the format shown in Exhibit 3.
2. Prepare a statement of owner's equity.
3. Prepare an account form of balance sheet, assuming that the current portion of the note payable is $9,000.
4. Prepare closing entries as of March 31, 2008.

PR 6-3A
Sales-related transactions

obj. 3

The following selected transactions were completed by Cardroom Supply Co., which sells office supplies primarily to wholesalers and occasionally to retail customers.

Jan. 2. Sold merchandise on account to Kibler Co., $10,000, terms FOB destination, 1/10, n/30. The cost of the merchandise sold was $6,500.
   3. Sold merchandise for $12,000 plus 8% sales tax to cash customers. The cost of merchandise sold was $9,000.
   4. Sold merchandise on account to Glickman Co., $5,600, terms FOB shipping point, n/eom. The cost of merchandise sold was $3,100.
   5. Sold merchandise for $8,000 plus 8% sales tax to customers who used Master-Card. The cost of merchandise sold was $6,000.
   12. Received check for amount due from Kibler Co. for sale on January 2.
   14. Sold merchandise to customers who used American Express cards, $15,000. The cost of merchandise sold was $9,200.
   16. Sold merchandise on account to Bryan Co., $12,000, terms FOB shipping point, 1/10, n/30. The cost of merchandise sold was $7,200.

Jan. 18. Issued credit memorandum for $3,000 to Bryan Co. for merchandise returned from sale on January 16. The cost of the merchandise returned was $1,800.

19. Sold merchandise on account to Cooney Co., $15,750, terms FOB shipping point, 2/10, n/30. Added $400 to the invoice for transportation costs prepaid. The cost of merchandise sold was $9,500.

26. Received check for amount due from Bryan Co. for sale on January 16 less credit memorandum of January 18 and discount.

28. Received check for amount due from Cooney Co. for sale of January 19.

31. Received check for amount due from Glickman Co. for sale of January 4.

31. Paid Speedy Delivery Service $1,875 for merchandise delivered during January to customers under shipping terms of FOB destination.

Feb. 3. Paid First State Bank $1,150 for service fees for handling MasterCard and American Express sales during January.

15. Paid $1,600 to state sales tax division for taxes owed on sales.

Instructions

Journalize the entries to record the transactions of Cardroom Supply Co.

PR 6-4A
Purchase-related transactions

obj. 3

The following selected transactions were completed by Scat Trak Company during July of the current year:

July 1. Purchased merchandise from Kermit Co., $18,750, terms FOB destination, n/30.

3. Purchased merchandise from Basaway Co., $12,150, terms FOB shipping point, 2/10, n/eom. Prepaid transportation costs of $180 were added to the invoice.

4. Purchased merchandise from Phillips Co., $13,800, terms FOB destination, 2/10, n/30.

6. Issued debit memorandum to Phillips Co. for $1,900 of merchandise returned from purchase on July 4.

13. Paid Basaway Co. for invoice of July 3, less discount.

14. Paid Phillips Co. for invoice of July 4, less debit memorandum of July 6 and discount.

19. Purchased merchandise from Cleghorne Co., $18,000, terms FOB shipping point, n/eom.

19. Paid transportation charges of $500 on July 19 purchase from Cleghorne Co.

20. Purchased merchandise from Graham Co., $9,000, terms FOB destination, 1/10, n/30.

30. Paid Graham Co. for invoice of July 20, less discount.

31. Paid Kermit Co. for invoice of July 1.

31. Paid Cleghorne Co. for invoice of July 19.

Instructions

Journalize the entries to record the transactions of Scat Trak Company for July.

PR 6-5A
Sales-related and purchase-related transactions

obj. 3

The following were selected from among the transactions completed by Southmont Company during April of the current year:

Apr. 3. Purchased merchandise on account from Mandell Co., list price $30,000, trade discount 40%, terms FOB destination, 2/10, n/30.

4. Sold merchandise for cash, $12,800. The cost of the merchandise sold was $7,600.

5. Purchased merchandise on account from Quinn Co., $18,750, terms FOB shipping point, 2/10, n/30, with prepaid transportation costs of $715 added to the invoice.

6. Returned $3,500 of merchandise purchased on April 3 from Mandell Co.

11. Sold merchandise on account to Campo Co., list price $6,000, trade discount 20%, terms 1/10, n/30. The cost of the merchandise sold was $3,200.

13. Paid Mandell Co. on account for purchase of April 3, less return of April 6 and discount.

14. Sold merchandise on VISA, $52,700. The cost of the merchandise sold was $31,500.

15. Paid Quinn Co. on account for purchase of April 5, less discount.

Apr. 21. Received cash on account from sale of April 11 to Campo Co., less discount.
24. Sold merchandise on account to Elkins Co., $8,150, terms 1/10, n/30. The cost of the merchandise sold was $4,500.
28. Paid VISA service fee of $1,500.
30. Received merchandise returned by Elkins Co. from sale on April 24, $1,200. The cost of the returned merchandise was $900.

Instructions
Journalize the transactions.

PR 6-6A
Sales-related and purchase-related transactions for seller and buyer
obj. 3

The following selected transactions were completed during August between Sellars Company and Beyer Co.:

Aug. 1. Sellars Company sold merchandise on account to Beyer Co., $17,850, terms FOB destination, 2/15, n/eom. The cost of the merchandise sold was $10,700.
2. Sellars Company paid transportation costs of $140 for delivery of merchandise sold to Beyer Co. on August 1.
5. Sellars Company sold merchandise on account to Beyer Co., $27,550, terms FOB shipping point, n/eom. The cost of the merchandise sold was $16,500.
6. Beyer Co. returned $1,800 of merchandise purchased on account on August 1 from Sellars Company. The cost of the merchandise returned was $1,050.
9. Beyer Co. paid transportation charges of $165 on August 5 purchase from Sellars Company.
15. Sellars Company sold merchandise on account to Beyer Co., $32,000, terms FOB shipping point, 1/10, n/30. Sellars Company paid transportation costs of $1,243, which were added to the invoice. The cost of the merchandise sold was $19,200.
16. Beyer Co. paid Sellars Company for purchase of August 1, less discount and less return of August 6.
25. Beyer Co. paid Sellars Company on account for purchase of August 15, less discount.
31. Beyer Co. paid Sellars Company on account for purchase of August 5.

Instructions
Journalize the August transactions for (1) Sellars Company and (2) Beyer Co.

APPENDIX 2
PR 6-7A
Purchase-related transactions using periodic inventory system

Selected transactions for Scat Trak Company during July of the current year are listed in Problem 6-4A.

Instructions
Journalize the entries to record the transactions of Scat Trak Company for July using the periodic inventory system.

APPENDIX 2
PR 6-8A
Sales-related and purchase-related transactions using periodic inventory system

Selected transactions for Southmont Company during April of the current year are listed in Problem 6-5A.

Instructions
Journalize the entries to record the transactions of Southmont Company for April using the periodic inventory system.

APPENDIX 2
PR 6-9A
Sales-related and purchase-related transactions for buyer and seller using periodic inventory system

Selected transactions during August between Sellars Company and Beyer Co. are listed in Problem 6-6A.

Instructions
Journalize the entries to record the transactions for (1) Sellars Company and (2) Beyers Co. assuming that both companies use the periodic inventory system.

APPENDIX 2
PR 6-10A
Periodic inventory accounts, multiple-step income statement, closing entries

✔ *2. Net income, $725,200*

On July 31, 2008, the balances of the accounts appearing in the ledger of Odell Company are as follows:

Cash	$ 73,200	Sales Discounts	$ 37,500
Accounts Receivable	288,500	Purchases	2,146,000
Merchandise Inventory, Aug. 1, 2007	350,900	Purchases Returns and Allowances	24,000
Office Supplies	12,100	Purchases Discounts	18,000
Prepaid Insurance	18,000	Transportation In	43,600
Land	140,000	Sales Salaries Expense	625,000
Store Equipment	683,100	Advertising Expense	220,000
Accumulated Depreciation—		Delivery Expense	36,000
Store Equipment	223,600	Depreciation Expense—Store	
Office Equipment	314,000	Equipment	23,600
Accumulated Depreciation—		Miscellaneous Selling Expense	42,800
Office Equipment	65,000	Office Salaries Expense	400,000
Accounts Payable	111,300	Rent Expense	125,000
Salaries Payable	11,800	Insurance Expense	12,000
Unearned Rent	33,200	Office Supplies Expense	9,200
Notes Payable	50,000	Depreciation Expense—	
Marcus Odell, Capital	760,200	Office Equipment	6,000
Marcus Odell, Drawing	75,000	Miscellaneous Administrative Expense	23,400
Sales	4,425,800	Rent Revenue	25,000
Sales Returns and Allowances	40,000	Interest Expense	3,000

Instructions
1. Does Odell Company use the periodic or perpetual inventory system? Explain.
2. Prepare a multiple-step income statement for Odell Company for the year ended July 31, 2008. The merchandise inventory as of July 31, 2008, was $376,400.
3. Prepare the closing entries for Odell Company as of July 31, 2008.

Problems Series B

PR 6-1B
Multiple-step income statement and report form of balance sheet

obj. 2

✔ *1. Net income: $61,200*

The following selected accounts and their current balances appear in the ledger of Hobbs' Co. for the fiscal year ended June 30, 2008:

Cash	$ 68,850	Sales Returns and Allowances	$ 18,900
Accounts Receivable	55,800	Sales Discounts	9,900
Merchandise Inventory	90,000	Cost of Merchandise Sold	963,000
Office Supplies	2,340	Sales Salaries Expense	189,000
Prepaid Insurance	6,120	Advertising Expense	25,470
Office Equipment	57,600	Depreciation Expense—	
Accumulated Depreciation—		Store Equipment	4,140
Office Equipment	9,720	Miscellaneous Selling Expense	990
Store Equipment	105,750	Office Salaries Expense	36,900
Accumulated Depreciation—		Rent Expense	19,935
Store Equipment	43,740	Insurance Expense	11,475
Accounts Payable	24,300	Depreciation Expense—	
Salaries Payable	1,800	Office Equipment	8,100
Note Payable		Office Supplies Expense	810
(final payment due 2018)	27,000	Miscellaneous Administrative	
Jeremiah Hobbs, Capital	241,200	Expense	1,080
Jeremiah Hobbs, Drawing	22,500	Interest Expense	900
Sales	1,351,800		

Instructions
1. Prepare a multiple-step income statement.
2. Prepare a statement of owner's equity.
3. Prepare a report form of balance sheet, assuming that the current portion of the note payable is $2,250.
4. Briefly explain (a) how multiple-step and single-step income statements differ and (b) how report-form and account-form balance sheets differ.

PR 6-2B

Single-step income statement and account form of balance sheet

objs. 2, 4

✓ *3. Total assets: $333,000*

Selected accounts and related amounts for Hobbs' Co. for the fiscal year ended June 30, 2008, are presented in Problem 6-1B.

Instructions

1. Prepare a single-step income statement in the format shown in Exhibit 3.
2. Prepare a statement of owner's equity.
3. Prepare an account form of balance sheet, assuming that the current portion of the note payable is $2,250.
4. Prepare closing entries as of June 30, 2008.

PR 6-3B

Sales-related transactions

obj. 3

The following selected transactions were completed by Water Tech Supplies Co., which sells irrigation supplies primarily to wholesalers and occasionally to retail customers.

July 1. Sold merchandise on account to Upshaw Co., $8,000, terms FOB shipping point, n/eom. The cost of merchandise sold was $4,800.
   2. Sold merchandise for $15,000 plus 7% sales tax to cash customers. The cost of merchandise sold was $8,800.
   5. Sold merchandise on account to Westone Company, $16,000, terms FOB destination, 1/10, n/30. The cost of merchandise sold was $10,500.
   8. Sold merchandise for $11,500 plus 7% sales tax to customers who used VISA cards. The cost of merchandise sold was $7,000.
   13. Sold merchandise to customers who used MasterCard cards, $8,000. The cost of merchandise sold was $4,750.
   14. Sold merchandise on account to Tyler Co., $7,500, terms FOB shipping point, 1/10, n/30. The cost of merchandise sold was $4,000.
   15. Received check for amount due from Westone Company for sale on July 5.
   16. Issued credit memorandum for $800 to Tyler Co. for merchandise returned from sale on July 14. The cost of the merchandise returned was $360.
   18. Sold merchandise on account to Horton Company, $6,850, terms FOB shipping point, 2/10, n/30. Paid $210 for transportation costs and added them to the invoice. The cost of merchandise sold was $4,100.
   24. Received check for amount due from Tyler Co. for sale on July 14 less credit memorandum of July 16 and discount.
   28. Received check for amount due from Horton Company for sale of July 18.
   31. Paid Uptown Delivery Service $3,100 for merchandise delivered during July to customers under shipping terms of FOB destination.
   31. Received check for amount due from Upshaw Co. for sale of July 1.
Aug. 3. Paid First National Bank $780 for service fees for handling MasterCard and VISA sales during July.
   10. Paid $1,855 to state sales tax division for taxes owed on sales.

Instructions

Journalize the entries to record the transactions of Water Tech Supplies Co.

PR 6-4B

Purchase-related transactions

obj. 3

The following selected transactions were completed by Bodyworks Co. during October of the current year:

Oct. 1. Purchased merchandise from Mantooth Co., $11,800, terms FOB shipping point, 2/10, n/eom. Prepaid transportation costs of $325 were added to the invoice.
   5. Purchased merchandise from Hauck Co., $17,500, terms FOB destination, n/30.
   10. Paid Mantooth Co. for invoice of October 1, less discount.
   13. Purchased merchandise from Lieu Co., $7,500, terms FOB destination, 1/10, n/30.
   14. Issued debit memorandum to Lieu Co. for $2,500 of merchandise returned from purchase on October 13.
   18. Purchased merchandise from Fowler Company, $9,600, terms FOB shipping point, n/eom.

Oct. 18. Paid transportation charges of $150 on October 18 purchase from Fowler Company.

19. Purchased merchandise from Hatcher Co., $9,750, terms FOB destination, 2/10, n/30.

23. Paid Lieu Co. for invoice of October 13, less debit memorandum of October 14 and discount.

29. Paid Hatcher Co. for invoice of October 19, less discount.

31. Paid Fowler Company for invoice of October 18.

31. Paid Hauck Co. for invoice of October 5.

Instructions

Journalize the entries to record the transactions of Bodyworks Co. for October.

PR 6-5B
Sales-related and purchase-related transactions

obj. 3

The following were selected from among the transactions completed by Theisen Company during December of the current year:

Dec. 3. Purchased merchandise on account from Shipley Co., list price $24,000, trade discount 25%, terms FOB shipping point, 2/10, n/30, with prepaid transportation costs of $615 added to the invoice.

5. Purchased merchandise on account from Kirch Co., $10,250, terms FOB destination, 2/10, n/30.

6. Sold merchandise on account to Murdock Co., list price $18,000, trade discount 35%, terms 2/10, n/30. The cost of the merchandise sold was $8,250.

7. Returned $1,800 of merchandise purchased on December 5 from Kirch Co.

13. Paid Shipley Co. on account for purchase of December 3, less discount.

15. Paid Kirch Co. on account for purchase of December 5, less return of December 7 and discount.

16. Received cash on account from sale of December 6 to Murdock Co., less discount.

19. Sold merchandise on MasterCard, $39,500. The cost of the merchandise sold was $23,700.

22. Sold merchandise on account to Milk River Co., $11,300, terms 2/10, n/30. The cost of the merchandise sold was $6,700.

23. Sold merchandise for cash, $17,680. The cost of the merchandise sold was $9,100.

28. Received merchandise returned by Milk River Co. from sale on December 22, $2,000. The cost of the returned merchandise was $1,100.

31. Paid MasterCard service fee of $1,050.

Instructions

Journalize the transactions.

PR 6-6B
Sales-related and purchase-related transactions for seller and buyer

obj. 3

The following selected transactions were completed during November between Sallis Company and Byce Company:

Nov. 2. Sallis Company sold merchandise on account to Byce Company, $12,500, terms FOB shipping point, 2/10, n/30. Sallis Company paid transportation costs of $425, which were added to the invoice. The cost of the merchandise sold was $7,500.

8. Sallis Company sold merchandise on account to Byce Company, $21,600, terms FOB destination, 1/15, n/eom. The cost of the merchandise sold was $13,000.

8. Sallis Company paid transportation costs of $879 for delivery of merchandise sold to Byce Company on November 8.

12. Byce Company returned $5,000 of merchandise purchased on account on November 8 from Sallis Company. The cost of the merchandise returned was $2,900.

12. Byce Company paid Sallis Company for purchase of November 2, less discount.

23. Byce Company paid Sallis Company for purchase of November 8, less discount and less return of November 12.

Nov. 24. Sallis Company sold merchandise on account to Byce Company, $15,000, terms FOB shipping point, n/eom. The cost of the merchandise sold was $9,000.

26. Byce Company paid transportation charges of $400 on November 24 purchase from Sallis Company.

30. Byce Company paid Sallis Company on account for purchase of November 24.

Instructions
Journalize the November transactions for (1) Sallis Company and (2) Byce Company.

APPENDIX 2
PR 6-7B
Purchase-related transactions using periodic inventory system

Selected transactions for Bodyworks Co. during October of the current year are listed in Problem 6-4B.

Instructions
Journalize the entries to record the transactions of Bodyworks Co. for October using the periodic inventory system.

APPENDIX 2
PR 6-8B
Sales-related and purchase-related transactions using periodic inventory system

Selected transactions for Theisen Company during December of the current year are listed in Problem 6-5B.

Instructions
Journalize the entries to record the transactions of Theisen Company for December using the periodic inventory system.

APPENDIX 2
PR 6-9B
Sales-related and purchase-related transactions for buyer and seller using periodic inventory system

Selected transactions during November between Sallis Company and Byce Company are listed in Problem 6-6B.

Instructions
Journalize the entries to record the transactions for (1) Sallis Company and (2) Byce Company assuming that both companies use the periodic inventory system.

APPENDIX 2
PR 6-10B
Periodic inventory accounts, multiple-step income statement, closing entries

✓ *2. Net income, $181,300*

On April 30, 2008, the balances of the accounts appearing in the ledger of Headwinds Company are as follows:

Cash	$ 18,300	Sales Discounts	$ 9,375
Accounts Receivable	72,125	Purchases	536,500
Merchandise Inventory, May 1, 2007	87,725	Purchases Returns and Allowances	6,000
Office Supplies	3,025	Purchases Discounts	4,500
Prepaid Insurance	4,500	Transportation In	10,900
Land	35,000	Sales Salaries Expense	156,250
Store Equipment	170,775	Advertising Expense	55,000
Accumulated Depreciation—		Delivery Expense	9,000
Store Equipment	55,900	Depreciation Expense—	
Office Equipment	78,500	Store Equipment	5,900
Accumulated Depreciation—		Miscellaneous Selling Expense	10,700
Office Equipment	16,250	Office Salaries Expense	100,000
Accounts Payable	27,825	Rent Expense	31,250
Salaries Payable	2,950	Insurance Expense	3,000
Unearned Rent	8,300	Office Supplies Expense	2,300
Notes Payable	12,500	Depreciation Expense—	
Kasey Kurtz, Capital	190,050	Office Equipment	1,500
Kasey Kurtz, Drawing	18,750	Miscellaneous Administrative Expense	5,850
Sales	1,106,450	Rent Revenue	6,250
Sales Returns and Allowances	10,000	Interest Expense	750

Instructions

1. Does Headwinds Company use a periodic or perpetual inventory system? Explain.
2. Prepare a multiple-step income statement for Headwinds Company for the year ended April 30, 2008. The merchandise inventory as of April 30, 2008, was $94,100.
3. Prepare the closing entries for Headwinds Company as of April 30, 2008.

Comprehensive Problem 2

✓8. Net income:
$231,962

World Boards Co. is a merchandising business. The account balances for World Boards Co. as of March 1, 2008 (unless otherwise indicated), are as follows:

110	Cash	$ 21,200
112	Accounts Receivable	51,300
115	Merchandise Inventory	200,800
116	Prepaid Insurance	5,600
117	Store Supplies	3,800
123	Store Equipment	156,500
124	Accumulated Depreciation—Store Equipment	18,900
210	Accounts Payable	32,200
211	Salaries Payable	—
310	Evan Raskind, Capital, April 1, 2007	185,100
311	Evan Raskind, Drawing	45,000
312	Income Summary	—
410	Sales	1,073,700
411	Sales Returns and Allowances	30,900
412	Sales Discounts	19,800
510	Cost of Merchandise Sold	541,000
520	Sales Salaries Expense	111,600
521	Advertising Expense	27,000
522	Depreciation Expense	—
523	Store Supplies Expense	—
529	Miscellaneous Selling Expense	4,200
530	Office Salaries Expense	60,700
531	Rent Expense	27,900
532	Insurance Expense	—
539	Miscellaneous Administrative Expense	2,600

During March, the last month of the fiscal year, the following transactions were completed:

Mar. 1. Paid rent for March, $2,400.
   3. Purchased merchandise on account from Huisman Co., terms 2/10, n/30, FOB shipping point, $21,600.
   4. Paid transportation charges on purchase of March 3, $500.
   6. Sold merchandise on account to Hillcrest Co., terms 2/10, n/30, FOB shipping point, $8,500. The cost of the merchandise sold was $5,000.
   7. Received $8,900 cash from Foley Co. on account, no discount.
   10. Sold merchandise for cash, $27,200. The cost of the merchandise sold was $16,000.
   13. Paid for merchandise purchased on March 3, less discount.
   14. Received merchandise returned on sale of March 6, $1,500. The cost of the merchandise returned was $900.
   15. Paid advertising expense for last half of March, $2,600.
   16. Received cash from sale of March 6, less return of March 14 and discount.
   19. Purchased merchandise for cash, $11,800.
   19. Paid $9,000 to Bakke Co. on account, no discount.
   20. Sold merchandise on account to Wilts Co., terms 1/10, n/30, FOB shipping point, $22,300. The cost of the merchandise sold was $13,200.

Mar. 21. For the convenience of the customer, paid shipping charges on sale of March 20, $1,100.

21. Received $17,600 cash from Owen Co. on account, no discount.

21. Purchased merchandise on account from Nye Co., terms 1/10, n/30, FOB destination, $19,900.

24. Returned $2,000 of damaged merchandise purchased on March 21, receiving credit from the seller.

26. Refunded cash on sales made for cash, $1,200. The cost of the merchandise returned was $700.

28. Paid sales salaries of $7,600 and office salaries of $4,800.

29. Purchased store supplies for cash, $800.

30. Sold merchandise on account to Whitetail Co., terms 2/10, n/30, FOB shipping point, $18,750. The cost of the merchandise sold was $11,250.

30. Received cash from sale of March 20, less discount, plus transportation paid on March 21.

31. Paid for purchase of March 21, less return of March 24 and discount.

Instructions

1. Enter the balances of each of the accounts in the appropriate balance column of a four-column account. Write *Balance* in the item section, and place a check mark (✓) in the Posting Reference column. Journalize the transactions for March.

2. Post the journal to the general ledger, extending the month-end balances to the appropriate balance columns after all posting is completed. In this problem, you are not required to update or post to the accounts receivable and accounts payable subsidiary ledgers.

3. Prepare an unadjusted trial balance.

4. At the end of March, the following adjustment data were assembled. Analyze and use these data to complete (5) and (6).

a.	Merchandise inventory on March 31		$196,139
b.	Insurance expired during the year		1,875
c.	Store supplies on hand on March 31		1,500
d.	Depreciation for the current year		9,500
e.	Accrued salaries on March 31:		
	Sales salaries	$1,200	
	Office salaries	800	2,000

5. **Optional:** Enter the unadjusted trial balance on a 10-column end-of-period spreadsheet (work sheet), and complete the spreadsheet. See Appendix C for how to prepare an end-of-period spreadsheet (work sheet) for a merchandising business.

6. Journalize and post the adjusting entries.

7. Prepare an adjusted trial balance.

8. Prepare an income statement, a statement of owner's equity, and a balance sheet.

9. Prepare and post the closing entries. Indicate closed accounts by inserting a line in both the Balance columns opposite the closing entry. Insert the new balance in the owner's capital account.

10. Prepare a post-closing trial balance.

Special Activities

SA 6-1

Ethics and professional conduct in business

ETHICS

On February 24, 2008, Lawn Ranger Company, a garden retailer, purchased $40,000 of corn seed, terms 2/10, n/30, from Nebraska Farm Co. Even though the discount period had expired, Corey Gilbert subtracted the discount of $800 when he processed the documents for payment on March 25, 2008.

➤ Discuss whether Corey Gilbert behaved in a professional manner by subtracting the discount, even though the discount period had expired.

SA 6-2
Purchases discounts and accounts payable

The Eclipse Video Store Co. is owned and operated by Jared Helms. The following is an excerpt from a conversation between Jared Helms and Allison Fain, the chief accountant for The Eclipse Video Store.

Jared: Allison, I've got a question about this recent balance sheet.
Allison: Sure, what's your question?
Jared: Well, as you know, I'm applying for a bank loan to finance our new store in Winterville, and I noticed that the accounts payable are listed as $85,000.
Allison: That's right. Approximately $78,000 of that represents amounts due our suppliers, and the remainder is miscellaneous payables to creditors for utilities, office equipment, supplies, etc.
Jared: That's what I thought. But as you know, we normally receive a 2% discount from our suppliers for earlier payment, and we always try to take the discount.
Allison: That's right. I can't remember the last time we missed a discount.
Jared: Well, in that case, it seems to me the accounts payable should be listed minus the 2% discount. Let's list the accounts payable due suppliers as $76,440, rather than $78,000. Every little bit helps. You never know. It might make the difference between getting the loan and not.

➤ How would you respond to Jared Helms' request?

SA 6-3
Determining cost of purchase

The following is an excerpt from a conversation between Kate Fleming and Bob Dent. Kate is debating whether to buy a stereo system from Design Sound, a locally owned electronics store, or Big Sound Electronics, an online electronics company.

Kate: Bob, I don't know what to do about buying my new stereo.
Bob: What's the problem?
Kate: Well, I can buy it locally at Design Sound for $580.00. However, Big Sound Electronics has the same system listed for $599.99.
Bob: So what's the big deal? Buy it from Design Sound.
Kate: It's not quite that simple. Big Sound said something about not having to pay sales tax, since I was out-of-state.
Bob: Yes, that's a good point. If you buy it at Design Sound, they'll charge you 8% sales tax.
Kate: But Big Sound Electronics charges $18.99 for shipping and handling. If I have them send it next-day air, it'll cost $24.99 for shipping and handling.
Bob: I guess it is a little confusing.
Kate: That's not all. Design Sound will give an additional 1% discount if I pay cash. Otherwise, they will let me use my VISA, or I can pay it off in three monthly installments.
Bob: Anything else???
Kate: Well . . . Big Sound says I have to charge it on my VISA. They don't accept checks.
Bob: I am not surprised. Many online stores don't accept checks.
Kate: I give up. What would you do?

1. Assuming that Big Sound Electronics doesn't charge sales tax on the sale to Kate, which company is offering the best buy?
2. ➤ What might be some considerations other than price that might influence Kate's decision on where to buy the stereo system?

SA 6-4
Sales discounts

Your sister operates Emigrant Parts Company, an online boat parts distributorship that is in its third year of operation. The income statement is shown at the top of the following page and was recently prepared for the year ended July 31, 2008.

Your sister is considering a proposal to increase net income by offering sales discounts of 2/15, n/30, and by shipping all merchandise FOB shipping point. Currently, no sales discounts are allowed and merchandise is shipped FOB destination. It is estimated that these credit terms will increase net sales by 15%. The ratio of the cost of merchandise sold to net sales is expected to be 65%. All selling and administrative expenses are expected to remain unchanged, except for store supplies, miscellaneous selling, office supplies, and miscellaneous administrative expenses, which are expected to increase proportionately with

Emigrant Parts Company
Income Statement
For the Year Ended July 31, 2008

Revenues:		
Net sales		$800,000
Interest revenue		10,000
Total revenues		$810,000
Expenses:		
Cost of merchandise sold	$520,000	
Selling expenses	90,000	
Administrative expenses	48,550	
Interest expense	15,000	
Total expenses		673,550
Net income		$136,450

increased net sales. The amounts of these preceding items for the year ended July 31, 2008, were as follows:

Store supplies expense	$12,000
Miscellaneous selling expense	3,000
Office supplies expense	2,000
Miscellaneous administrative expense	1,000

The other income and other expense items will remain unchanged. The shipment of all merchandise FOB shipping point will eliminate all delivery expense, which for the year ended July 31, 2008, were $18,750.

1. Prepare a projected single-step income statement for the year ending July 31, 2009, based on the proposal. Assume all sales are collected within the discount period.
2. a. Based on the projected income statement in (1), would you recommend the implementation of the proposed changes?
   b. Describe any possible concerns you may have related to the proposed changes described in (1).

SA 6-5
Shopping for a television

Group Project

Assume that you are planning to purchase a 50-inch Plasma television. In groups of three or four, determine the lowest cost for the television, considering the available alternatives and the advantages and disadvantages of each alternative. For example, you could purchase locally, through mail order, or through an Internet shopping service. Consider such factors as delivery charges, interest-free financing, discounts, coupons, and availability of warranty services. Prepare a report for presentation to the class.

Answers to Self-Examination Questions

1. **A** A debit memorandum (answer A), issued by the buyer, indicates the amount the buyer proposes to debit to the accounts payable account. A credit memorandum (answer B), issued by the seller, indicates the amount the seller proposes to credit to the accounts receivable account. An invoice (answer C) or a bill (answer D), issued by the seller, indicates the amount and terms of the sale.
2. **C** The amount of discount for early payment is $10 (answer C), or 1% of $1,000. Although the $50 of transportation costs paid by the seller is debited to the customer's account, the customer is not entitled to a discount on that amount.
3. **B** The single-step form of income statement (answer B) is so named because the total of all expenses is deducted in one step from the total of all revenues. The multiple-step form (answer A) includes numerous sections and subsections with several subtotals. The ac-

count form (answer C) and the report form (answer D) are two common forms of the balance sheet.
4. **C** Gross profit (answer C) is the excess of net sales over the cost of merchandise sold. Operating income (answer A) or income from operations (answer B) is the excess of gross profit over operating expenses. Net income (answer D) is the final figure on the income statement after all revenues and expenses have been reported.
5. **D** Expenses such as interest expense (answer D) that cannot be associated directly with operations are identified as *other expense* or *nonoperating expense*. Depreciation expense—office equipment (answer A) is an administrative expense. Sales salaries expense (answer B) is a selling expense. Insurance expense (answer C) is a mixed expense with elements of both selling expense and administrative expense. For small businesses, insurance expense is usually reported as an administrative expense.

Inventories

© RYAN MCVAY/PHOTODISC/GETTY IMAGES

objectives

After studying this chapter, you should be able to:

1 **Describe the importance of control over inventory.**

2 **Describe three inventory cost flow assumptions and how they impact the income statement and balance sheet.**

3 **Determine the cost of inventory under the perpetual inventory system, using the FIFO, LIFO, and average cost methods.**

4 **Determine the cost of inventory under the periodic inventory system, using the FIFO, LIFO, and average cost methods.**

5 **Compare and contrast the use of the three inventory costing methods.**

6 **Describe and illustrate the reporting of merchandise inventory in the financial statements.**

7 **Estimate the cost of inventory, using the retail method and the gross profit method.**

Best Buy

Assume that in September you purchased a Philips HDTV plasma television from Best Buy. At the same time, you purchased a Sony surround sound system for $299.99. You liked your surround sound so well that in November you purchased an identical Sony system on sale for $249.99 for your bedroom TV. Over the holidays, you moved to a new apartment and in the process of unpacking discovered that one of the Sony surround sound systems was missing. Luckily, your renters/homeowners insurance policy will cover the theft, but the insurance company needs to know the cost of the system that was stolen.

The Sony systems were identical. However, to respond to the insurance company, you will need to identify which system was stolen. Was it the first system, which cost $299.99, or was it the second system, which cost $249.99? Whichever assumption you make may determine the amount that you receive from the insurance company.

Merchandising businesses such as Best Buy make similar assumptions when identical merchandise is purchased at different costs. For example, Best Buy may have purchased thousands of Sony surround sound systems over the past year at different costs. At the end of a period, some of the Sony systems will still be in inventory, and some will have been sold. But which costs relate to the sold systems, and which costs relate to the Sony systems still in inventory? Best Buy's assumption about inventory costs can involve large dollar amounts and, thus, can have a significant impact on the financial statements. For example, Best Buy reported $2,851,000,000 of inventory and net income of $984,000,000 for the year ending February 26, 2005.

In this chapter, we will discuss such issues as how to determine the cost of merchandise in inventory and the cost of merchandise sold. However, we begin this chapter by discussing the importance of control over inventory.

Control of Inventory

objective 1

Describe the importance of control over inventory.

REAL WORLD

Best Buy uses scanners to screen customers as they leave the store for merchandise that has not been purchased. In addition, Best Buy stations greeters at the store's entrance to keep customers from bringing in bags that can be used to shoplift merchandise.

For companies such as Best Buy, good control over inventory must be maintained. Two primary objectives of control over inventory are safeguarding the inventory and properly reporting it in the financial statements.[1]

Control over inventory should begin as soon as the inventory is received. A *receiving report* should be completed by the company's receiving department in order to establish initial accountability for the inventory. To make sure the inventory received is what was ordered, the receiving report should agree with the company's original *purchase order* for the merchandise. A purchase order authorizes the purchase of an item from a vendor. Likewise, the price at which the inventory was ordered, as shown on the purchase order, should be compared to the price at which the vendor billed the company, as shown on the *vendor's invoice*. After the receiving report, purchase order, and vendor's invoice have been reconciled, the company should record the inventory and related account payable in the accounting records.

Controls for safeguarding inventory include developing and using security measures to prevent inventory damage or customer or employee theft. For example, inventory should be stored in a warehouse or other area to which access is restricted to authorized employees. When shopping, you may have noticed how retail stores protect inventory from customer theft. Retail stores often use such devices as two-way mirrors, cameras, and security guards. High-priced items are often displayed in locked cabinets. Retail clothing stores often place plastic alarm tags on valuable items such as leather coats. Sensors at the exit doors set off alarms if the tags have not been removed by the clerk. These controls are designed to prevent customers from shoplifting.

---

1 Additional controls used by businesses are described and illustrated in Chapter 8, "Sarbanes-Oxley, Internal Controls, and Cash."

Using a perpetual inventory system for merchandise also provides an effective means of control over inventory. The amount of each type of merchandise is always readily available in a subsidiary *inventory ledger*. In addition, the subsidiary ledger can be an aid in maintaining inventory quantities at proper levels. Frequently, comparing balances with predetermined maximum and minimum levels allows for the timely re-ordering of merchandise and prevents the ordering of excess inventory.

To ensure the accuracy of the amount of inventory reported in the financial statements, a merchandising business should take a **physical inventory** (i.e., count the merchandise). In a perpetual inventory system, the physical inventory is compared to the recorded inventory in order to determine the amount of shrinkage or shortage. If the inventory shrinkage is unusually large, management can investigate further and take any necessary corrective action. Knowing that a physical inventory will be taken also helps prevent employee thefts or misuses of inventory.

Most companies take their physical inventories when their inventory levels are the lowest. For example, most retailers take their physical inventories in late January or early February, which is after the holiday selling season but before restocking for spring.

objective 2

Describe three inventory cost flow assumptions and how they impact the income statement and balance sheet.

Inventory Cost Flow Assumptions

A major accounting issue arises when identical units of merchandise are acquired at different unit costs during a period. In such cases, when an item is sold, it is necessary to determine its unit cost using a cost flow assumption so that the proper accounting entry can be recorded. There are three common cost flow assumptions used in business. Each of these assumptions is identified with an inventory costing method, as shown below.

Cost Flow Assumption

| 1. Cost flow is in the order in which the costs were incurred. | 2. Cost flow is in the reverse order in which the costs were incurred. | 3. Cost flow is an average of the costs. |

Inventory Costing Method

| First-in, First-out (FIFO) | Last-in, First-out (LIFO) | Average Cost |

To illustrate, assume that three identical units of Item X are purchased during May, as shown at the top of page 310. Assume that one unit is sold on May 30 for $20. If this unit can be identified with a specific purchase, the *specific identification method* can be used to determine the cost of the unit sold. For example, if the unit sold was purchased on May 18, the cost assigned to the unit is $13 and the gross profit is $7 ($20 − $13). If, however, the unit sold was purchased on May 10, the cost assigned to the unit is $9 and the gross profit is $11 ($20 − $9).

	Item X	Units	Cost
May 10	Purchase	1	$ 9
18	Purchase	1	13
24	Purchase	1	14
	Total	3	$36
	Average cost per unit		$12

REAL WORLD

The specific identification method is normally used by automobile dealerships, jewelry stores, and art galleries.

The specific identification method is not practical unless each unit can be identified accurately. An automobile dealer, for example, may be able to use this method, since each automobile has a unique serial number. For many businesses, however, identical units cannot be separately identified, and a cost flow must be assumed. That is, which units have been sold and which units are still in inventory must be assumed using the first-in, first-out; last-in, first-out; or average cost method.

When the **first-in, first-out (FIFO) method** is used, the ending inventory is made up of the most recent costs. When the **last-in, first-out (LIFO) method** is used, the ending inventory is made up of the earliest costs. When the **average cost method** is used, the cost of the units in inventory is an average of the purchase costs.

To illustrate, we use the preceding example to prepare the income statement for May and the balance sheet as of May 31 for each of the cost flow methods, again assuming that one unit is sold. These financial statements are shown in Exhibit 1.

EXHIBIT 1 | **Effect of Inventory Costing Methods on Financial Statements**

Purchases

Balance Sheet

FIFO Method

Income Statement

Sales . . . . $ 20
Cost of merchandise sold . . . 9
Gross profit . . . . $ 11

May 10 $9   **May 18** $13   **May 24** $14

May 31
Merchandise Inventory
$27

LIFO Method

Income Statement

Sales . . . . $ 20
Cost of merchandise sold . . . 14
Gross profit . . . . $ 6

$9 $13 $14

Merchandise Inventory
$22

Average Cost Method

Income Statement

Sales . . . . $ 20
Cost of merchandise sold . . . 12
Gross profit . . . . $ 8

$9 $13 $14

Merchandise Inventory
$24

$36/3 = $12;
$12 x 2 = $24

As you can see, the selection of an inventory costing method can have a significant impact on the financial statements. For this reason, the selection has important implications for managers and others in analyzing and interpreting the financial statements. The chart in Exhibit 2 shows the frequency with which FIFO, LIFO, and the average methods are used in practice.

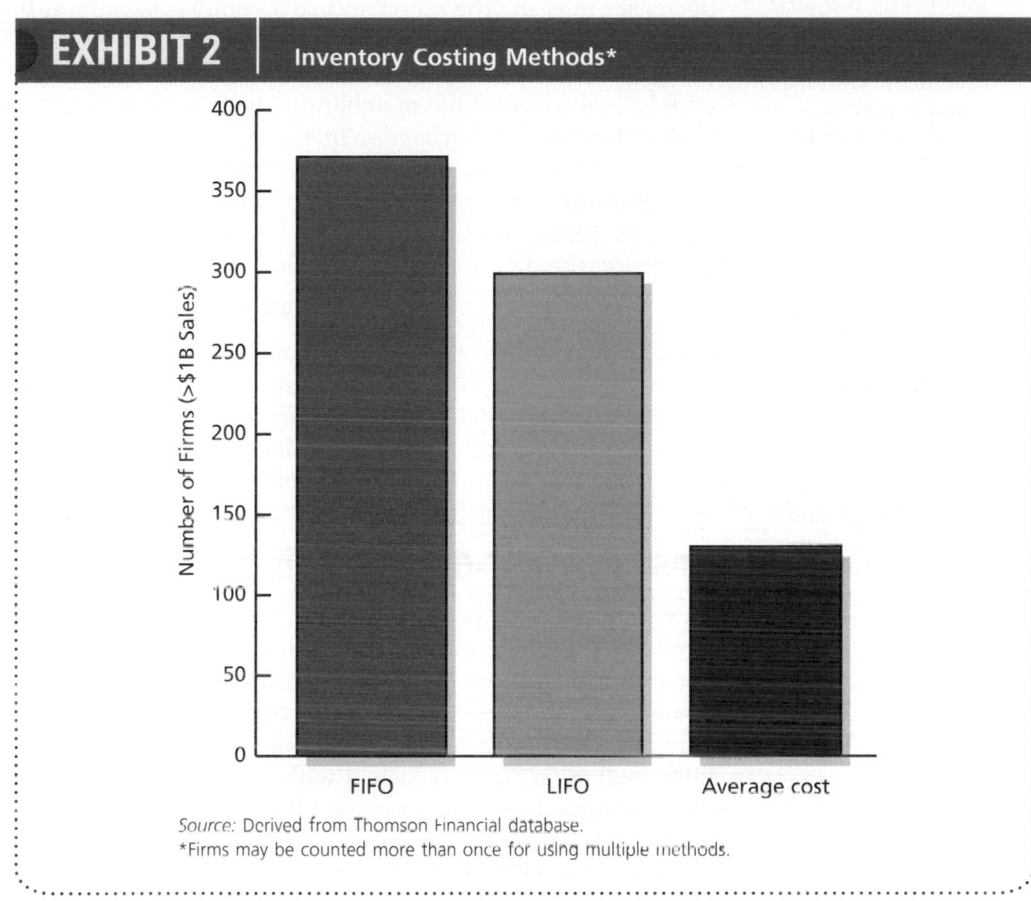

EXHIBIT 2 | **Inventory Costing Methods***

Source: Derived from Thomson Financial database.
*Firms may be counted more than once for using multiple methods.

Example Exercise 7-1
objective **2**

Three identical units of Item QBM are purchased during February, as shown below.

	Item QBM	Units	Cost
Feb. 8	Purchase	1	$ 45
15	Purchase	1	48
26	Purchase	1	51
	Total	3	$144
	Average cost per unit		$ 48 ($144/3 units)

Assume that one unit is sold on February 27 for $70.
   Determine the gross profit for February and ending inventory on February 28 using the (a) first-in, first-out (FIFO); (b) last-in, first-out (LIFO); and (c) average cost methods.

Follow My Example 7-1

		Gross Profit	Ending Inventory
a.	First-in, first-out (FIFO)	$25 ($70 − $45)	$99 ($48 + $51)
b.	Last-in, first-out (LIFO)	$19 ($70 − $51)	$93 ($45 + $48)
c.	Average cost	$22 ($70 − $48)	$96 ($48 × 2)

For Practice: PE 7-1A, PE 7-1B

Inventory Costing Methods Under a Perpetual Inventory System

In a perpetual inventory system, as we discussed in Chapter 6, all merchandise increases and decreases are recorded in a manner similar to recording increases and decreases in cash. The merchandise inventory account at the beginning of an accounting period indicates the merchandise in stock on that date. Purchases are recorded by debiting *Merchandise Inventory* and crediting *Cash* or *Accounts Payable*. On the date of each sale, the cost of the merchandise sold is recorded by debiting *Cost of Merchandise Sold* and crediting *Merchandise Inventory*.

As we illustrated in the preceding section, when identical units of an item are purchased at different unit costs during a period, a cost flow must be assumed. In such cases, the FIFO, LIFO, or average cost method is used. We illustrate each of these methods, using the data for Item 127B, shown below.

Item 127B		Units	Cost
Jan. 1	Inventory	100	$20
4	Sale	70	
10	Purchase	80	21
22	Sale	40	
28	Sale	20	
30	Purchase	100	22

FIRST-IN, FIRST-OUT METHOD

Most businesses dispose of goods in the order in which the goods are purchased. This would be especially true of perishables and goods whose styles or models often change. For example, grocery stores shelve their milk products by expiration dates. Likewise, men's and women's clothing stores display clothes by season. At the end of a season, they often have sales to clear their stores of off-season or out-of-style clothing. Thus, the FIFO method is often consistent with the *physical flow* or movement of merchandise. To the extent that this is the case, the FIFO method provides results that are about the same as those obtained by identifying the specific costs of each item sold and in inventory.

When the FIFO method of costing inventory is used, costs are included in the cost of merchandise sold in the order in which they were incurred. To illustrate, Exhibit 3

EXHIBIT 3   Entries and Perpetual Inventory Account (FIFO)

Jan. 4	Accounts Receivable	2,100	
	Sales		2,100
4	Cost of Merchandise Sold	1,400	
	Merchandise Inventory		1,400

10	Merchandise Inventory	1,680	
	Accounts Payable		1,680

22	Accounts Receivable	1,200	
	Sales		1,200
22	Cost of Merchandise Sold	810	
	Merchandise Inventory		810

28	Accounts Receivable	600	
	Sales		600
28	Cost of Merchandise Sold	420	
	Merchandise Inventory		420

30	Merchandise Inventory	2,200	
	Accounts Payable		2,200

Item 127B

	Purchases			Cost of Merchandise Sold			Inventory		
Date	Quantity	Unit Cost	Total Cost	Quantity	Unit Cost	Total Cost	Quantity	Unit Cost	Total Cost
Jan. 1							100	20	2,000
4				70	20	1,400	30	20	600
10	80	21	1,680				30	20	600
							80	21	1,680
22				30	20	600			
				10	21	210	70	21	1,470
28				20	21	420	50	21	1,050
30	100	22	2,200				50	21	1,050
							100	22	2,200
31	Balances					2,630			3,250

Cost of merchandise sold

January 31, inventory

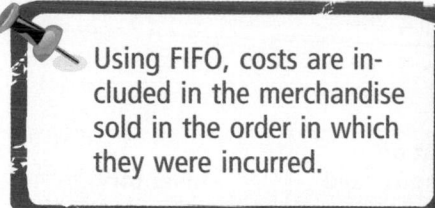

Using FIFO, costs are included in the merchandise sold in the order in which they were incurred.

shows the journal entries for purchases and sales and the inventory subsidiary ledger account for Item 127B. The number of units in inventory after each transaction, together with total costs and unit costs, are shown in the account. We assume that the units are sold on account for $30 each.

You should note that after the 70 units were sold on January 4, there was an inventory of 30 units at $20 each. The 80 units purchased on January 10 were acquired at a unit cost of $21, instead of $20. Therefore, the inventory after the January 10 purchase is reported on two lines, 30 units at $20 each and 80 units at $21 each. Next, note that the $810 cost of the 40 units sold on January 22 is made up of the remaining 30 units at $20 each and 10 unit at $21. At this point, 70 units are in inventory at a cost of $21 per unit. The remainder of the illustration is explained in a similar manner.

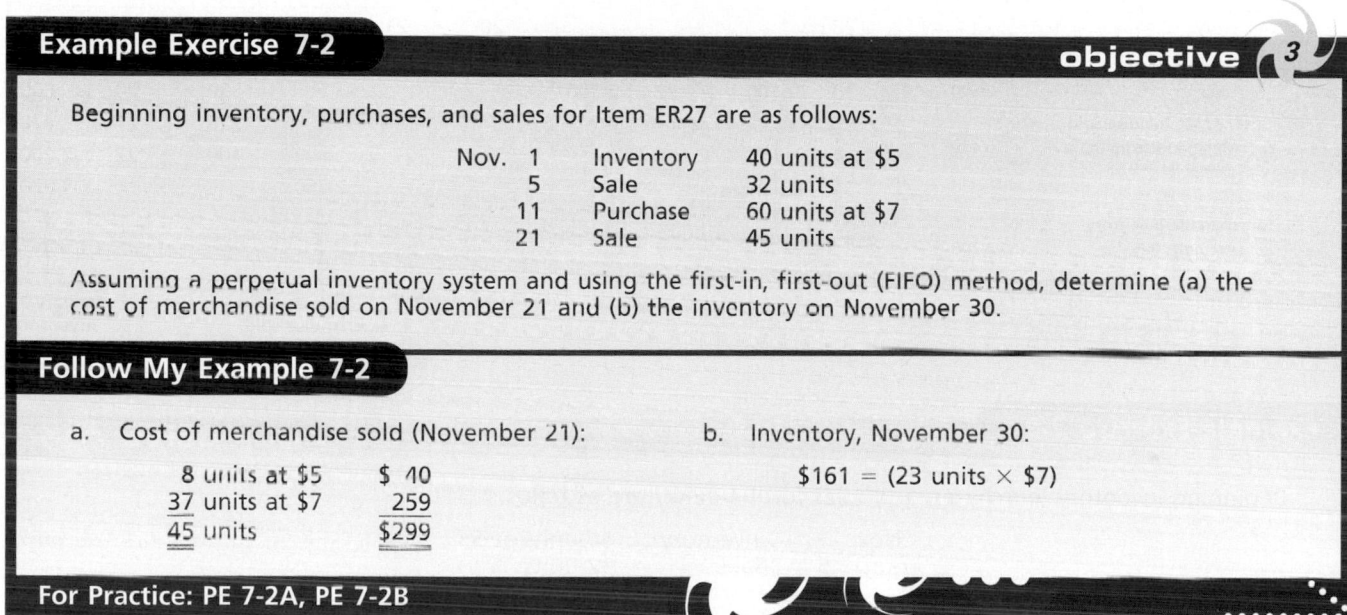

Example Exercise 7-2   objective **3**

Beginning inventory, purchases, and sales for Item ER27 are as follows:

Nov.	1	Inventory	40 units at $5
	5	Sale	32 units
	11	Purchase	60 units at $7
	21	Sale	45 units

Assuming a perpetual inventory system and using the first-in, first-out (FIFO) method, determine (a) the cost of merchandise sold on November 21 and (b) the inventory on November 30.

Follow My Example 7-2

a. Cost of merchandise sold (November 21):

    8 units at $5 $ 40
   37 units at $7   259
   45 units $299

b. Inventory, November 30:

      $161 = (23 units × $7)

For Practice: PE 7-2A, PE 7-2B

LAST-IN, FIRST-OUT METHOD

When the LIFO method is used in a perpetual inventory system, the cost of the units sold is the cost of the most recent purchases. To illustrate, Exhibit 4 shows the journal entries for purchases and sales and the subsidiary ledger account for Item 127B, prepared on a LIFO basis.

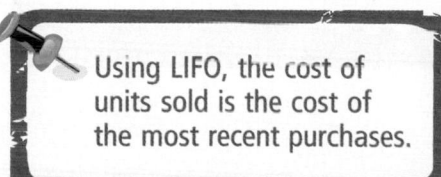

Using LIFO, the cost of units sold is the cost of the most recent purchases.

If you compare the ledger accounts for the FIFO perpetual system and the LIFO perpetual system, you should discover that the accounts are the same through the January 10 purchase. Using LIFO, however, the cost of the 40 units sold on January 22 is the cost of the units from the January 10 purchase ($21 per unit). The cost of the 70 units in inventory after the sale on January 22 is the cost of the 30 units remaining from the beginning inventory and the cost of the 40 units remaining from the January 10 purchase. The remainder of the LIFO illustration is explained in a similar manner.

When the LIFO method is used, the inventory ledger is sometimes maintained in units only. The units are converted to dollars when the financial statements are prepared at the end of the period.

The use of the LIFO method was originally limited to rare situations in which the units sold were taken from the most recently acquired goods. For tax reasons, which we will discuss later, its use has greatly increased during the past few decades. LIFO is now often used even when it does not represent the physical flow of goods.

EXHIBIT 4   Entries and Perpetual Inventory Account (LIFO)

Jan. 4	Accounts Receivable	2,100	
	Sales		2,100
4	Cost of Merchandise Sold	1,400	
	Merchandise Inventory		1,400
10	Merchandise Inventory	1,680	
	Accounts Payable		1,680
22	Accounts Receivable	1,200	
	Sales		1,200
22	Cost of Merchandise Sold	840	
	Merchandise Inventory		840
28	Accounts Receivable	600	
	Sales		600
28	Cost of Merchandise Sold	420	
	Merchandise Inventory		420
30	Merchandise Inventory	2,200	
	Accounts Payable		2,200

Item 127B

	Purchases			Cost of Merchandise Sold			Inventory		
Date	Quantity	Unit Cost	Total Cost	Quantity	Unit Cost	Total Cost	Quantity	Unit Cost	Total Cost
Jan. 1							100	20	2,000
4				70	20	1,400	30	20	600
10	80	21	1,680				30	20	600
							80	21	1,680
22				40	21	840	30	20	600
							40	21	840
28				20	21	420	30	20	600
							20	21	420
30	100	22	2,200				30	20	600
							20	21	420
							100	22	2,200
31	Balances					2,660			3,220

Cost of merchandise sold

January 31, inventory

Example Exercise 7-3   objective 3

Beginning inventory, purchases, and sales for Item ER27 are as follows:

Nov.	1	Inventory	40 units at $5
	5	Sale	32 units
	11	Purchase	60 units at $7
	21	Sale	45 units

Assuming a perpetual inventory system and using the last-in, first-out (LIFO) method, determine (a) the cost of the merchandise sold on November 21 and (b) the inventory on November 30.

Follow My Example 7-3

a. Cost of merchandise sold (November 21):

$315 = (45 units × $7)

b. Inventory, November 30:

8 units at $5	$ 40
15 units at $7	105
23 units	$145

For Practice: PE 7-3A, PE 7-3B

The FIFO, LIFO, and average cost flow assumptions also apply to other areas of business. For example, individuals and businesses often purchase marketable securities at different costs per share. When such investments are sold, the investor must either specifically identify which shares are sold or use the FIFO cost flow assumption.

AVERAGE COST METHOD

When the average cost method is used in a perpetual inventory system, an average unit cost for each type of item is computed each time a purchase is made. This unit cost is then used to determine the cost of each sale until another purchase is made and a new average is computed. This averaging technique is called a *moving average*. Since the average cost method is rarely used in a perpetual inventory system, we do not illustrate it in this chapter.

COMPUTERIZED PERPETUAL INVENTORY SYSTEMS

The records for a perpetual inventory system may be maintained manually. However, such a system is costly and time consuming for businesses with a large number of inventory items with many purchase and sales transactions. In most cases, the record keeping for perpetual inventory systems is computerized.

An example of using computers in maintaining perpetual inventory records for retail stores follows.

1. The relevant details for each inventory item, such as a description, quantity, and unit size, are stored in an inventory record. The individual inventory records make up the computerized inventory file, the total of which agrees with the balance of the inventory ledger account.
2. Each time an item is purchased or returned by a customer, the inventory data are entered into the computer's inventory records and files.
3. Each time an item is sold, a salesclerk scans the item's bar code with an optical scanner. The scanner reads the magnetic code and rings up the sale on the cash register. The inventory records and files are then updated for the cost of goods sold.
4. After a physical inventory is taken, the inventory count data are entered into the computer. These data are compared with the current balances, and a listing of the overages and shortages is printed. The inventory balances are then adjusted to the quantities determined by the physical count.

Wal-Mart, Target, and other retailers use bar code scanners as part of their perpetual inventory systems.

Such systems can be extended to aid managers in controlling and managing inventory quantities. For example, items that are selling fast can be reordered before the stock is depleted. Past sales patterns can be analyzed to determine when to mark down merchandise for sales and when to restock seasonal merchandise. In addition, such systems can provide managers with data for developing and fine-tuning their marketing strategies. For example, such data can be used to evaluate the effectiveness of advertising campaigns and sales promotions.

Inventory Costing Methods Under a Periodic Inventory System

objective 4

Determine the cost of inventory under the periodic inventory system, using the FIFO, LIFO, and average cost methods.

When the periodic inventory system is used, only revenue is recorded each time a sale is made. No entry is made at the time of the sale to record the cost of the merchandise sold. At the end of the accounting period, a physical inventory is taken to determine the cost of the inventory and the cost of the merchandise sold.[2]

Like the perpetual inventory system, a cost flow assumption must be made when identical units are acquired at different unit costs during a period. In such cases, the FIFO, LIFO, or average cost method is used.

FIRST-IN, FIRST-OUT METHOD

To illustrate the use of the FIFO method in a periodic inventory system, we use the same data for Item 127B as in the perpetual inventory example. The beginning inventory entry and purchases of Item 127B in January are as follows:

Jan. 1	Inventory:	100 units at	$20	$2,000
10	Purchase:	80 units at	21	1,680
30	Purchase:	100 units at	22	2,200
Available for sale during month		280		$5,880

---

2 Determining the cost of merchandise sold using the periodic system was illustrated in Chapter 6.

The physical count on January 31 shows that 150 units are on hand. Using the FIFO method, the cost of the merchandise on hand at the end of the period is made up of the most recent costs. The cost of the 150 units in ending inventory on January 31 is determined as follows:

Most recent costs, January 30 purchase	100 units at	$22	$2,200
Next most recent costs, January 10 purchase	50 units at	$21	1,050
Inventory, January 31	150 units		$3,250

Deducting the cost of the January 31 inventory of $3,250 from the cost of merchandise available for sale of $5,880 yields the cost of merchandise sold of $2,630, as shown below.

Beginning inventory, January 1	$2,000
Purchases ($1,680 + $2,200)	3,880
Cost of merchandise available for sale in January	$5,880
Ending inventory, January 31	3,250
Cost of merchandise sold	$2,630

The $3,250 cost of the ending merchandise inventory on January 31 is made up of the most recent costs. The $2,630 cost of merchandise sold is made up of the beginning inventory and the earliest costs. Exhibit 5 shows the relationship of the cost of merchandise sold for January and the ending inventory on January 31.

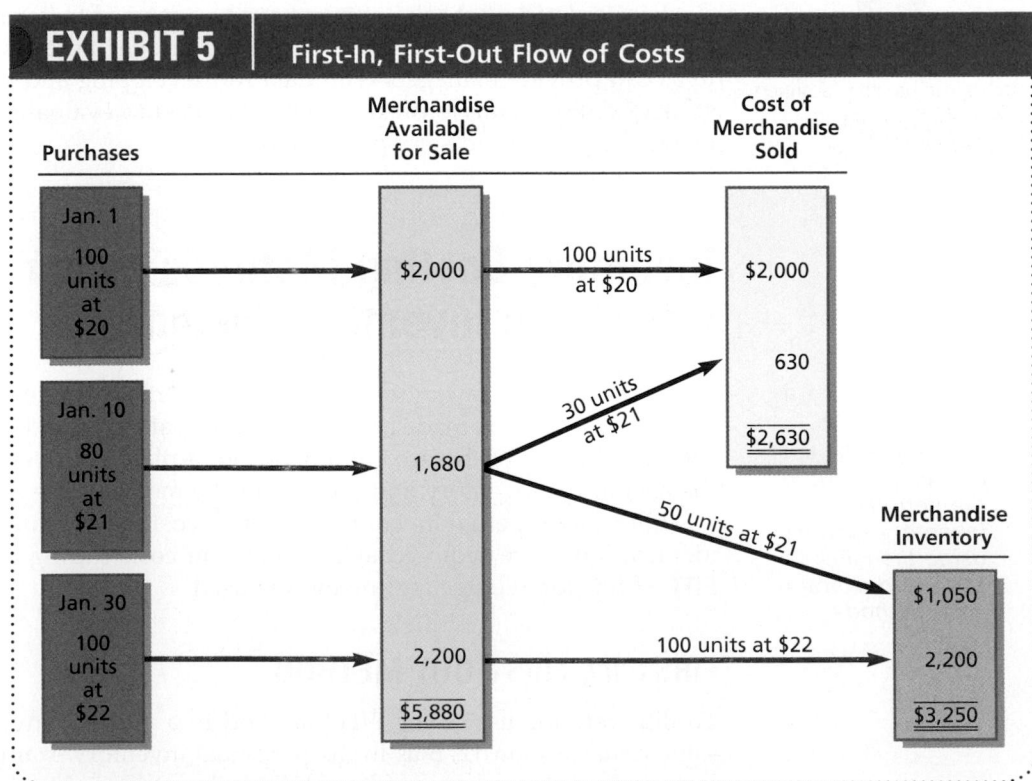

EXHIBIT 5 | First-In, First-Out Flow of Costs

LAST-IN, FIRST-OUT METHOD

When the LIFO method is used, the cost of merchandise on hand at the end of the period is made up of the earliest costs. Based upon the same data as in the FIFO example, the cost of the 150 units in ending inventory on January 31 is determined as follows:

Beginning inventory, January 1	100 units at	$20	$2,000
Next earliest costs, January 10	50 units at	$21	1,050
Inventory, January 31	150 units		$3,050

Deducting the cost of the January 31 inventory of $3,050 from the cost of merchandise available for sale of $5,880 yields the cost of merchandise sold of $2,830, as shown below.

Beginning inventory, January 1	$2,000
Purchases ($1,680 + $2,200)	3,880
Cost of merchandise available for sale in January	$5,880
Ending inventory, January 31	3,050
Cost of merchandise sold	$2,830

The $3,050 cost of the ending merchandise inventory on January 31 is made up of the earliest costs. The $2,830 cost of merchandise sold is made up of the most recent costs. Exhibit 6 shows the relationship of the cost of merchandise sold for January and the ending inventory on January 31.

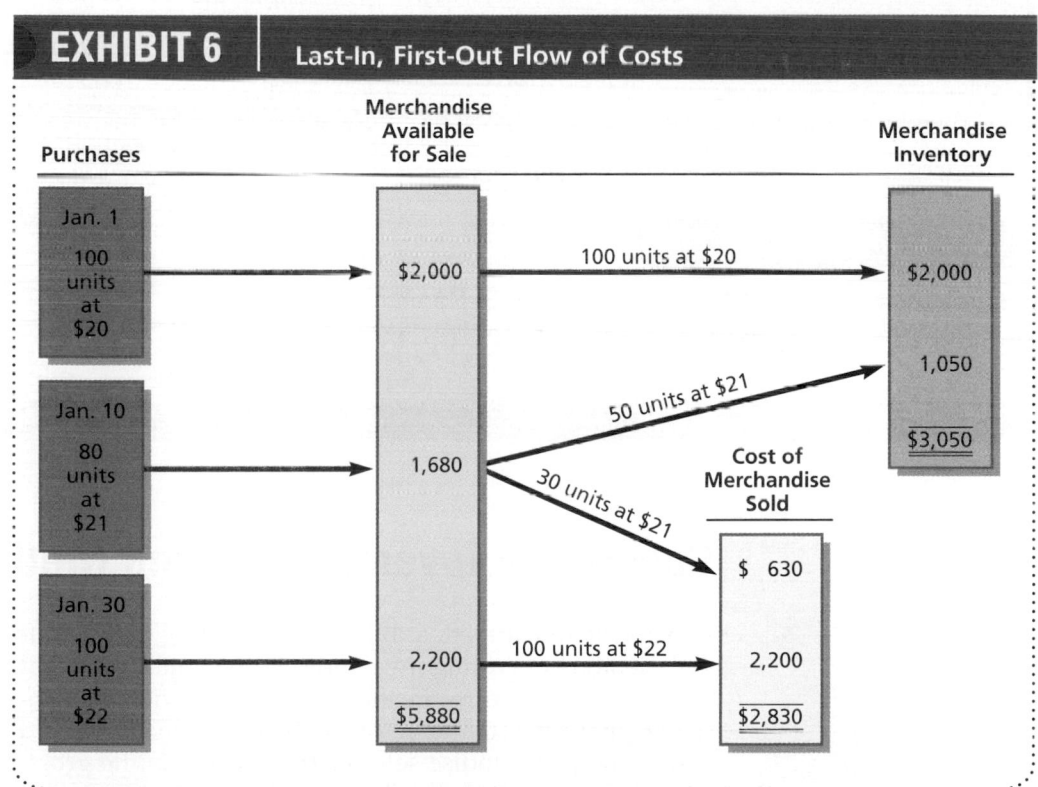

EXHIBIT 6 | **Last-In, First-Out Flow of Costs**

AVERAGE COST METHOD

The average cost method is sometimes called the *weighted average method*. When this method is used, costs are matched against revenue according to an average of the unit costs of the goods sold. The same weighted average unit costs are used in determining the cost of the merchandise inventory at the end of the period. For businesses in which merchandise sales may be made up of various purchases of identical units, the average cost method approximates the physical flow of goods.

The weighted average unit cost is determined by dividing the total cost of the units of each item available for sale during the period by the related number of units of that item. Using the same cost data as in the FIFO and LIFO examples, the average cost of the 280 units, $21, and the cost of 150 units in ending inventory, are determined as follows:

Average unit cost: $5,880/280 units = $21
Inventory, January 31: 150 units at $21 = $3,150

Deducting the cost of the January 31 inventory of $3,150 from the cost of merchandise available for sale of $5,880 yields the cost of merchandise sold of $2,730, as shown below.

Beginning inventory, January 1	$2,000
Purchases ($1,680 + $2,200)	3,880
Cost of merchandise available for sale in January	$5,880
Ending inventory, January 31	3,150
Cost of merchandise sold	$2,730

Example Exercise 7-4

objective 4

The units of an item available for sale during the year were as follows:

Jan. 1	Inventory	6 units at $50		$ 300
Mar. 20	Purchase	14 units at $55		770
Oct. 30	Purchase	20 units at $62		1,240
	Available for sale	40 units		$2,310

There are 16 units of the item in the physical inventory at December 31. The periodic inventory system is used. Determine the inventory cost using (a) the first-in, first-out (FIFO) method, (b) the last-in, first-out (LIFO) method, and (c) the average cost method.

Follow My Example 7-4

a. First-in, first-out (FIFO) method: $992 = (16 units × $62)
b. Last-in, first-out (LIFO) method: $850 = (6 units × $50) + (10 units × $55)
c. Average cost method: $924 (16 units × $57.75), where average cost = $57.75 = $2,310/40 units

For Practice: PE 7-4A, PE 7-4B

Comparing Inventory Costing Methods

objective 5

Compare and contrast the use of the three inventory costing methods.

As we have illustrated, a different cost flow is assumed for each of the three alternative methods of costing inventories. You should note that if the cost of units had remained stable, all three methods would have yielded the same results. Since prices do change, however, the three methods will normally yield different amounts for (1) the cost of the merchandise sold for the period, (2) the gross profit (and net income) for the period, and (3) the ending inventory. Using the preceding examples for the periodic inventory system and sales of $3,900 (130 units × $30), the partial income statements, shown on page 319, indicate the effects of each method when prices are rising.[3]

As shown in the partial income statements, the FIFO method yielded the lowest amount for the cost of merchandise sold and the highest amount for gross profit (and net income). It also yielded the highest amount for the ending inventory. On the other hand, the LIFO method yielded the highest amount for the cost of merchandise sold, the lowest amount for gross profit (and net income), and the lowest amount for ending inventory. The average cost method yielded results that were between those of FIFO and LIFO.

---

3 Similar results would also occur when comparing inventory costing methods under a perpetual inventory system.

Ford Motor Company disclosed in a recent annual report that its inventories would have been over $1 billion higher if FIFO had been used instead of LIFO.

Partial Income Statements

	First-In, First-Out		Average Cost		Last-In, First-Out	
Net sales		$3,900		$3,900		$3,900
Cost of merchandise sold:						
Beginning inventory	$2,000		$2,000		$2,000	
Purchases	3,880		3,880		3,880	
Merchandise available for sale	$5,880		$5,880		$5,880	
Less ending inventory	3,250		3,150		3,050	
Cost of merchandise sold		2,630		2,730		2,830
Gross profit		$1,270		$1,170		$1,070

USE OF THE FIRST-IN, FIRST-OUT METHOD

When the FIFO method is used during a period of inflation or rising prices, the earlier unit costs are lower than the more recent unit costs, as shown in the preceding FIFO example. Thus, FIFO will show a larger gross profit. However, the inventory must be replaced at prices higher than indicated by the cost of merchandise sold. In fact, the balance sheet will report the ending merchandise inventory at an amount that is about the same as its current replacement cost. When the rate of inflation reaches double digits, as it did during the 1970s, the larger gross profits that result from the FIFO method are often called *inventory profits* or *illusory profits*. You should note that in a period of deflation or declining prices, the effect is just the opposite.

USE OF THE LAST-IN, FIRST-OUT METHOD

DaimlerChrysler's reason for changing from the FIFO method to the LIFO method was stated in the following note that accompanied its financial statements: *DaimlerChrysler changed its method of accounting from first-in, first-out (FIFO) to last-in, first-out (LIFO) for substantially all of its domestic productive inventories. The change to LIFO was made to more accurately match current costs with current revenues.*

When the LIFO method is used during a period of inflation or rising prices, the results are opposite those of the other two methods. As shown in the preceding example, the LIFO method will yield a higher amount of cost of merchandise sold, a lower amount of gross profit, and a lower amount of inventory at the end of the period than the other two methods. The reason for these effects is that the cost of the most recently acquired units is about the same as the cost of their replacement. In a period of inflation, the more recent unit costs are higher than the earlier unit costs. Thus, it can be argued that the LIFO method more nearly matches current costs with current revenues.

During periods of rising prices, using LIFO offers an income tax savings. The income tax savings results because LIFO reports the lowest amount of net income of the three methods. During the double-digit inflationary period of the 1970s, many businesses changed from FIFO to LIFO for the tax savings. However, the ending inventory on the balance sheet may be quite different from its current replacement cost. In such cases, the financial statements normally include a note that states the estimated difference between the LIFO inventory and the inventory if FIFO had been used. Again, you should note that in a period of deflation or falling price levels, the effects are just the opposite.

USE OF THE AVERAGE COST METHOD

As you might have already reasoned, the average cost method of inventory costing is, in a sense, a compromise between FIFO and LIFO. The effect of price trends is averaged in determining the cost of merchandise sold and the ending inventory. For a series of purchases, the average cost will be the same, regardless of the direction of price trends. For example, a complete reversal of the sequence of unit costs presented in the preceding illustration would not affect the reported cost of merchandise sold, gross profit, or ending inventory.

Integrity, Objectivity, and Ethics in Business

WHERE'S THE BONUS?

Managers are often given bonuses based on reported earnings numbers. This can create a conflict. LIFO can improve the value of the company through lower taxes. However, LIFO also produces a lower earnings number and, therefore, lower management bonuses. Ethically, managers should select accounting procedures that will maximize the value of the firm, rather than their own compensation. Compensation specialists can help avoid this ethical dilemma by adjusting the bonus plan for the accounting procedure differences.

Reporting Merchandise Inventory in the Financial Statements

objective 6

Describe and illustrate the reporting of merchandise inventory in the financial statements.

Dell Inc. recorded over $39.3 million of charges (expenses) in writing down its inventory of notebook computers. The remaining inventories of computers were then sold at significantly reduced prices.

As we indicated earlier, cost is the primary basis for valuing inventories. In some cases, however, inventory is valued at other than cost. Two such cases arise when (1) the cost of replacing items in inventory is below the recorded cost and (2) the inventory is not salable at normal sales prices. This latter case may be due to imperfections, shop wear, style changes, or other causes.

VALUATION AT LOWER OF COST OR MARKET

If the cost of replacing an item in inventory is lower than the original purchase cost, the **lower-of-cost-or-market (LCM) method** is used to value the inventory. *Market*, as used in *lower of cost or market*, is the cost to replace the merchandise on the inventory date. This market value is based on quantities normally purchased from the usual source of supply. In businesses where inflation is the norm, market prices rarely decline. In businesses where technology changes rapidly (e.g., microcomputers and televisions), market declines are common. The primary advantage of the lower-of-cost-or-market method is that gross profit (and net income) is reduced in the period in which the market decline occurred.

In applying the lower-of-cost-or-market method, the cost and replacement cost can be determined in one of three ways. Cost and replacement cost can be determined for (1) each item in the inventory, (2) major classes or categories of inventory, or (3) the inventory as a whole. In practice, the cost and replacement cost of each item are usually determined.

To illustrate, assume that there are 400 identical units of Item A in inventory, acquired at a unit cost of $10.25 each. If at the inventory date the item would cost $10.50 to replace, the cost price of $10.25 would be multiplied by 400 to determine the inventory value. On the other hand, if the item could be replaced at $9.50 a unit, the replacement cost of $9.50 would be used for valuation purposes.

Exhibit 7 illustrates a method of organizing inventory data and applying the lower-of-cost-or-market method to each inventory item. The amount of the market decline, $450 ($15,520 − $15,070), may be reported as a separate item on the income statement

EXHIBIT 7

Determining Inventory at Lower of Cost or Market

	A	B	C	D	E	F	G	
			Unit	Unit		Total		
		Inventory	Cost	Market			Lower	
	Commodity	Quantity	Price	Price	Cost	Market	of C or M	
1	A	400	$10.25	$ 9.50	$ 4,100	$ 3,800	$ 3,800	1
2	B	120	22.50	24.10	2,700	2,892	2,700	2
3	C	600	8.00	7.75	4,800	4,650	4,650	3
4	D	280	14.00	14.75	3,920	4,130	3,920	4
5	Total				$15,520	$15,472	$15,070	5

or included in the cost of merchandise sold. Regardless, net income will be reduced by the amount of the market decline.

Example Exercise 7-5   objective **6**

On the basis of the following data, determine the value of the inventory at the lower of cost or market. Apply lower of cost or market to each inventory item as shown in Exhibit 7.

Commodity	Inventory Quantity	Unit Cost Price	Unit Market Price
C17Y	10	$ 39	$40
B563	7	110	98

Follow My Example 7-5

	A	B	C	D	E	F	G	
			Unit	Unit		Total		
		Inventory	Cost	Market			Lower	
	Commodity	Quantity	Price	Price	Cost	Market	of C or M	
1	C17Y	10	$ 39	$ 40	$ 390	$ 400	$ 390	1
2	B563	7	110	98	770	686	686	2
3	Total				$1,160	$1,086	$1,076	3

For Practice: PE 7-5A, PE 7-5B

VALUATION AT NET REALIZABLE VALUE

REAL WORLD

Out-of-date merchandise is a major problem for many types of retailers. For example, you may have noticed the shelf-life dates of grocery products, such as milk, eggs, canned goods, and meat. Grocery stores often mark down the prices of products nearing the end of their shelf life to avoid having to dispose of the products as waste.

As you would expect, merchandise that is out of date, spoiled, or damaged or that can be sold only at prices below cost should be written down. Such merchandise should be valued at net realizable value. **Net realizable value** is the estimated selling price less any direct cost of disposal, such as sales commissions. For example, assume that damaged merchandise costing $1,000 can be sold for only $800, and direct selling expenses are estimated to be $150. This inventory should be valued at $650 ($800 − $150), which is its net realizable value.

For example, Digital Theater Systems Inc. provides digital entertainment technologies, products, and services to the motion picture, consumer electronics, and professional audio industries. In the notes to its recent financial statements, Digital Theater reported the following write-downs of its monochrome projector inventory:

Inventories are stated at the lower of cost or market. Cost is determined using the first-in, first-out method. The Company evaluates its ending inventories for estimated excess quantities and obsolescence. The Company's evaluation includes the analysis of future sales demand by product, within specific time horizons. Inventories in excess of projected future demand are written down to net realizable value. In addition, the Company assesses the impact of changing technology on inventory balances and writes down inventories that are considered obsolete. The Company recorded an inventory write-down of $3,871 (thousands) related to its monochrome projector inventory during the year ended December 31, 2004 due to declines in future demand and technological obsolescence.

REAL WORLD

General Motors Corporation uses the last-in, first-out (LIFO) method to account for all U.S. inventories other than those of Saturn Corporation. The cost of non-U.S., Saturn inventories is determined by using either first-in, first-out (FIFO) or average cost.

MERCHANDISE INVENTORY ON THE BALANCE SHEET

Merchandise inventory is usually presented in the Current Assets section of the balance sheet, following receivables. Both the method of determining the cost of the inventory (FIFO, LIFO, or average) and the method of valuing the inventory (cost or the lower of cost or market) should be shown. It is not unusual for large businesses with varied activities to use different costing methods for different segments of their inventories.

The details may be disclosed in parentheses on the balance sheet or in a note to the financial statements. Exhibit 8 shows how parentheses may be used.

A company may change its inventory costing methods for a valid reason. In such cases, the effect of the change and the reason for the change should be disclosed in the financial statements for the period in which the change occurred.

EXHIBIT 8	Merchandise Inventory on the Balance Sheet

Metro Arts
Balance Sheet
December 31, 2008

Assets		
Current assets:		
Cash		$ 19 4 0 0 00
Accounts receivable	$80 0 0 0 00	
Less allowance for doubtful accounts	3 0 0 0 00	77 0 0 0 00
Merchandise inventory—at lower of cost (first-in,		
first-out method) or market		216 3 0 0 00

EFFECT OF INVENTORY ERRORS ON THE FINANCIAL STATEMENTS

Any errors in the merchandise inventory will affect both the balance sheet and the income statement. For example, an error in the physical inventory will misstate the ending inventory, current assets, and total assets on the balance sheet. In addition, an error in inventory will also affect the cost of merchandise sold and gross profit on the income statement.

To illustrate the effect of inventory errors on the financial statements, we use the following partial income statement of SysExpress Company. We will illustrate the effect of inventory errors using the periodic system. This is because it is easier to see the impact of inventory errors on the income statement using the periodic system.[4]

SysExpress Company
Income Statement
For the Year Ended December 31, 2008

Net sales		$980,000
Merchandise inventory, January 1, 2008	$ 55,000	
Purchases	650,000	
Merchandise available for sale	$705,000	
Less merchandise inventory, December 31, 2008	60,000	
Cost of merchandise sold		645,000
Gross profit		$335,000

Assume that in taking the physical inventory on December 31, 2008, SysExpress incorrectly records its physical inventory as $57,500 instead of the correct amount of $60,000. As a result, the merchandise inventory, current assets, and total assets reported on the December 31, 2008, balance sheet would be understated by $2,500 ($60,000 − $57,500). Because the ending physical inventory is understated, the cost of merchandise sold will be overstated by $2,500. Thus, the gross profit and the net income for the year will be understated by $2,500. Since the net income is closed to owner's equity (capital) at the end of the period, the owner's equity on the December 31, 2008, balance sheet will also be understated by $2,500. These effects on SysExpress's financial statements are summarized as follows:

---

4 The effect of inventory errors would be the same under the perpetual inventory system.

	Amount of Misstatement
Balance Sheet:	
Merchandise inventory understated	➤ $(2,500)
Current assets understated	(2,500)
Total assets understated	(2,500)
Owner's equity understated	(2,500) ◄
Income Statement:	
Cost of merchandise sold overstated	↳➤ $ 2,500
Gross profit understated	(2,500)
Net income understated	(2,500) ◄

Now assume that in the preceding example the physical inventory had been overstated on December 31, 2008, by $2,500. That is, SysExpress erroneously recorded its inventory as $62,500. In this case, the effects on the balance sheet and income statement would be just the opposite of those indicated above.

Inventory errors often arise from shipping terms and inventory held on consignment. As we discussed in Chapter 6, shipping terms determine when the title to merchandise passes. When goods are purchased or sold *FOB shipping point*, title passes to the buyer when the goods are shipped. When the terms are *FOB destination*, title passes to the buyer when the goods are delivered.

To illustrate inventory errors arising from shipping terms, assume that SysExpress orders $8,300 of merchandise FOB shipping point on December 27. Assume also that the supplier ships the merchandise on December 30. When SysExpress counts its physical inventory on December 31, the merchandise is still in transit. In such cases, it would be easy for SysExpress to overlook the inventory in transit and not include it in the December 31 physical inventory. Likewise, merchandise *sold* by SysExpress FOB destination is still SysExpress's inventory even if it is still in transit to the buyer on December 31.

Inventory errors also arise frequently from consigned inventory. Manufacturers sometimes ship merchandise to retailers who act as the manufacturer's agent when selling the merchandise. The manufacturer, called the *consignor*, retains title until the goods are sold. Such merchandise is said to be shipped on consignment to the retailer, called the *consignee*. The unsold merchandise is a part of the manufacturer's (consignor's) inventory, even though the merchandise is in the hands of the retailer (consignee). In taking its year-end physical inventory, the retailer (consignee) must be careful to not include any consigned inventory on hand as part of its physical inventory. Likewise, the manufacturer (consignor) must be careful to include consigned inventory in its physical inventory even though the inventory is not on hand.

Example Exercise 7-6   objective 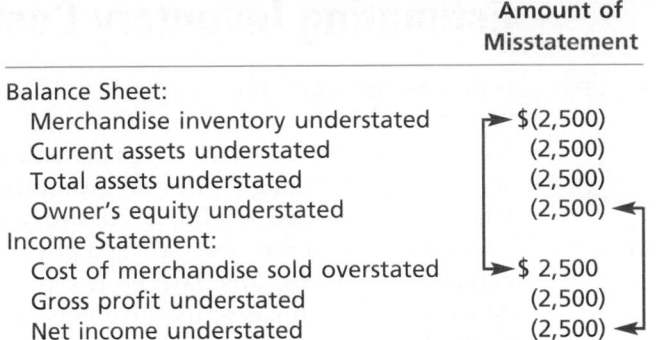 6

Zula Repair Shop incorrectly counted its December 31, 2008, inventory as $250,000 instead of the correct amount of $220,000. Indicate the effect of the misstatement on Zula's December 31, 2008, balance sheet and income statement for the year ended December 31, 2008.

Follow My Example 7-6

	Amount of Misstatement Overstatement (Understatement)
Balance Sheet:	
Merchandise inventory overstated	$ 30,000
Current assets overstated	30,000
Total assets overstated	30,000
Owner's equity overstated	30,000
Income Statement:	
Cost of merchandise sold understated	$(30,000)
Gross profit overstated	30,000
Net income overstated	30,000

For Practice: PE 7-6A, PE 7-6B

Estimating Inventory Cost

It may be necessary for a business to know the amount of inventory when perpetual inventory records are not maintained and it is impractical to take a physical inventory. For example, a business that uses a periodic inventory system may need monthly income statements, but taking a physical inventory each month may be too costly. Moreover, when a disaster such as a fire has destroyed the inventory, the amount of the loss must be determined. In this case, taking a physical inventory is impossible, and even if perpetual inventory records have been kept, the accounting records may also have been destroyed. In such cases, the inventory cost can be estimated by using (1) the retail method or (2) the gross profit method.

RETAIL METHOD OF INVENTORY COSTING

The **retail inventory method** of estimating inventory cost is based on the relationship of the cost of merchandise available for sale to the retail price of the same merchandise. To use this method, the retail prices of all merchandise are maintained and totaled. Next, the inventory at retail is determined by deducting sales for the period from the retail price of the goods that were available for sale during the period. The estimated inventory cost is then computed by multiplying the inventory at retail by the ratio of cost to selling (retail) price for the merchandise available for sale, as illustrated in Exhibit 9.

EXHIBIT 9

Determining Inventory by the Retail Method

	A	B Cost	C Retail	
1	Merchandise inventory, January 1	$19,400	$ 36,000	1
2	Purchases in January (net)	42,600	64,000	2
3	Merchandise available for sale	$62,000	$100,000	3
4	Ratio of cost to retail price: $\frac{\$62,000}{\$100,000} = 62\%$			4
5	Sales for January (net)		70,000	5
6	Merchandise inventory, January 31, at retail		$ 30,000	6
7	Merchandise inventory, January 31, at estimated cost			7
8	($30,000 × 62%)		$ 18,600	8

When estimating the percent of cost to selling price, we assume that the mix of the items in the ending inventory is the same as the entire stock of merchandise available for sale. In Exhibit 9, for example, it is unlikely that the retail price of every item was made up of exactly 62% cost and 38% gross profit. We assume, however, that the weighted average of the cost percentages of the merchandise in the inventory ($30,000) is the same as in the merchandise available for sale ($100,000).

When the inventory is made up of different classes of merchandise with very different gross profit rates, the cost percentages and the inventory should be developed for each class of inventory.

One of the major advantages of the retail method is that it provides inventory figures for preparing monthly or quarterly statements when the periodic system is used. Department stores and similar merchandisers like to determine gross profit and operating income each month but may take a physical inventory only once or twice a year. In addition, comparing the estimated ending inventory with the physical ending inventory, both at retail prices, will help identify inventory shortages resulting from shoplifting and other causes. Management can then take appropriate actions.

The retail method may also be used as an aid in taking a physical inventory. In this case, the items counted are recorded on the inventory sheets at their retail (selling) prices instead of their cost prices. The physical inventory at selling price is then converted to cost by applying the ratio of cost to selling (retail) price for the merchandise available for sale.

To illustrate, assume that the data in Exhibit 9 are for an entire fiscal year rather than for only January. If the physical inventory taken at the end of the year totaled $29,000, priced at retail, this amount rather than the $30,000 would be converted to cost. Thus, the inventory at cost would be $17,980 ($29,000 × 62%) instead of $18,600 ($30,000 × 62%). The $17,980 would be used for the year-end financial statements and for income tax purposes.

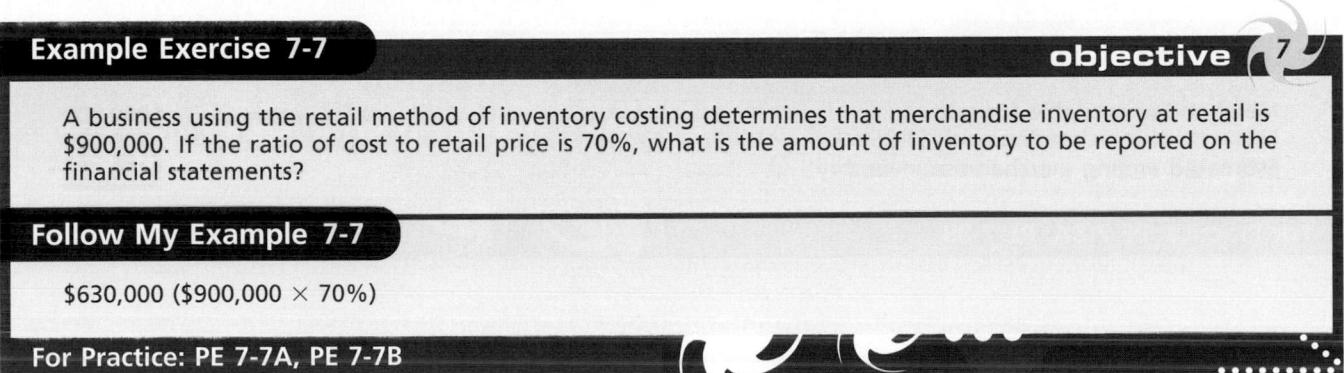

Example Exercise 7-7   **objective** 7

A business using the retail method of inventory costing determines that merchandise inventory at retail is $900,000. If the ratio of cost to retail price is 70%, what is the amount of inventory to be reported on the financial statements?

Follow My Example 7-7

$630,000 ($900,000 × 70%)

For Practice: PE 7-7A, PE 7-7B

GROSS PROFIT METHOD OF ESTIMATING INVENTORIES

The **gross profit method** uses the estimated gross profit for the period to estimate the inventory at the end of the period. The gross profit is usually estimated from the actual rate for the preceding year, adjusted for any changes made in the cost and sales prices during the current period. By using the gross profit rate, the dollar amount of sales for a period can be divided into its two components: (1) gross profit and (2) cost of merchandise sold. The latter amount may then be deducted from the cost of merchandise available for sale to yield the estimated cost of the inventory.

Exhibit 10 illustrates the gross profit method for estimating a company's inventory on January 31. In this example, the inventory on January 1 is assumed to be $57,000, the net purchases during the month are $180,000, and the net sales during the month are $250,000. In addition, the historical gross profit was 30% of net sales.

EXHIBIT 10

Estimating Inventory by Gross Profit Method

	A	B	C	
		Cost	Retail	
1	Merchandise inventory, January 1		$ 57,000	1
2	Purchases in January (net)		180,000	2
3	Merchandise available for sale		$237,000	3
4	Sales for January (net)	$250,000		4
5	Less estimated gross profit ($250,000 × 30%)	75,000		5
6	Estimated cost of merchandise sold		175,000	6
7	Estimated merchandise inventory, January 31		$ 62,000	7

The gross profit method is useful for estimating inventories for monthly or quarterly financial statements in a periodic inventory system. It is also useful in estimating the cost of merchandise destroyed by fire or other disasters.

Example Exercise 7-8   objective 7

Based upon the following data, estimate the cost of ending merchandise inventory:

Sales (net)	$1,250,000
Estimated gross profit rate	40%
Beginning merchandise inventory	$100,000
Purchases (net)	800,000
Merchandise available for sale	$900,000

Follow My Example 7-8

Merchandise available for sale	$900,000
Less cost of merchandise sold [$1,250,000 × (100% − 40%)]	750,000
Estimated ending merchandise inventory	$150,000

For Practice: PE 7-8A, PE 7-8B

Financial Analysis and Interpretation

A merchandising business should keep enough inventory on hand to meet the needs of its customers. A failure to do so may result in lost sales. At the same time, too much inventory reduces solvency by tying up funds that could be better used to expand or improve operations. In addition, excess inventory increases expenses such as storage, insurance, and property taxes. Finally, excess inventory increases the risk of losses due to price declines, damage, or changes in customers' buying patterns.

As with many types of financial analyses, it is possible to use more than one measure to analyze the efficiency and effectiveness by which a business manages its inventory. Two such measures are the inventory turnover and the number of days' sales in inventory.

Inventory turnover measures the relationship between the volume of goods (merchandise) sold and the amount of inventory carried during the period. It is computed as follows:

$$\text{Inventory Turnover} = \frac{\text{Cost of Merchandise Sold}}{\text{Average Inventory}}$$

To illustrate, the following data have been taken from recent annual reports for SUPERVALU Inc. and Zale Corporation:

	SUPERVALU	Zale
Cost of merchandise sold	$16,681,472,000	$1,157,226,000
Inventories:		
Beginning of year	$1,078,343,000	$826,824,000
End of year	$1,032,034,000	$853,580,000
Average	$1,055,188,500	$840,202,000
Inventory turnover	15.8	1.4

The inventory turnover is 15.8 for SUPERVALU and 1.4 for Zale. Generally, the larger the inventory turnover, the more efficient and effective the management of inventory. However, differences in companies and industries may be too great to allow specific statements as to what is a good inventory turnover. For example, SUPERVALU is a leading food distributor and the tenth largest food retailer in the United States. Because SUPERVALU's inventory is perishable, we would expect it to have a high inventory turnover. In contrast, Zale Corporation is the largest speciality retailer of fine jewelry in the United States. Thus, we would expect Zale to have a lower inventory turnover than SUPERVALU.

The **number of days' sales in inventory** is a rough measure of the length of time it takes to acquire, sell, and replace the inventory. It is computed as follows:

$$\text{Number of Days' Sales in Inventory} = \frac{\text{Average Inventory}}{\text{Average Daily Cost of Merchandise Sold}}$$

The average daily cost of merchandise sold is determined by dividing the cost of merchandise sold by 365. The number of days' sales in inventory for SUPERVALU and Zale is computed as shown below.

	SUPERVALU	Zale
Average daily cost of merchandise sold:		
$16,681,472,000/365	$45,702,663	
$1,157,226,000/365		$3,170,482
Average inventory	$1,055,188,500	$840,202,000
Number of days' sales in inventory	23.1 days	265.0 days

Generally, the lower the number of days' sales in inventory, the better. As with inventory turnover, we should expect differences among industries, such as those for SUPERVALU and Zale.

Business Connections

REAL WORLD

RAPID INVENTORY AT COSTCO

Costco Wholesale Corporation operates over 300 membership warehouses that offer members low prices on a limited selection of nationally branded and selected private label products. Costco emphasizes generating high sales volumes and rapid inventory turnover. This enables Costco to operate profitably at significantly lower gross margins than traditional wholesalers, discount retailers, and supermarkets. In addition, Costco's rapid turnover provides it the opportunity to conserve on its cash, as described below.

Because of its high sales volume and rapid inventory turnover, Costco generally has the opportunity to receive cash from the sale of a substantial portion of its inventory at mature warehouse operations before it is required to pay all its merchandise vendors, even though Costco takes advantage of early payment terms to obtain payment dis-

counts. As sales in a given warehouse increase and inventory turnover becomes more rapid, a greater percentage of the inventory is financed through payment terms provided by vendors rather than by working capital (cash).

© DON RYAN/ASSOCIATED PRESS

At a Glance

1. Describe the importance of control over inventory.

Key Points	Key Learning Outcomes	Example Exercises	Practice Exercises
Two primary objectives of control over inventory are safeguarding the inventory and properly reporting it in the financial statements. The perpetual inventory system enhances control over inventory. In addition, a physical inventory count should be taken periodically to detect shortages as well as to deter employee thefts.	• Describe controls for safeguarding inventory. • Describe how a perpetual inventory system enhances control over inventory. • Describe why taking a physical inventory enhances control over inventory.		

2. Describe three inventory cost flow assumptions and how they impact the income statement and balance sheet.

Key Points	Key Learning Outcomes	Example Exercises	Practice Exercises
The three common cost flow assumptions used in business are the (1) first-in, first-out method (FIFO); (2) last-in, first-out method (LIFO); and (3) average cost method. The choice of a cost flow assumption directly affects the income statement and balance sheet.	• Describe the FIFO, LIFO, and average cost flow methods. • Describe how choice of a cost flow method affects the income statement and balance sheet.	7-1	7-1A, 7-1B

3. Determine the cost of inventory under the perpetual inventory system, using the FIFO, LIFO, and average cost methods.

Key Points	Key Learning Outcomes	Example Exercises	Practice Exercises
In a perpetual inventory system, the number of units and the cost of each type of merchandise are recorded in a subsidiary inventory ledger, with a separate account for each type of merchandise.	• Determine the cost of inventory and cost of merchandise sold using a perpetual inventory system under the FIFO method.	7-2	7-2A, 7-2B
	• Determine the cost of inventory and cost of merchandise sold using a perpetual inventory system under the LIFO method.	7-3	7-3A, 7-3B

4. Determine the cost of inventory under the periodic inventory system, using the FIFO, LIFO, and average cost methods.

Key Points	Key Learning Outcomes	Example Exercises	Practice Exercises
In a periodic inventory system, a physical inventory is taken to determine the cost of the inventory and the cost of merchandise sold.	• Determine the cost of inventory and cost of merchandise sold using a periodic inventory system under the FIFO method.	7-4	7-4A, 7-4B
	• Determine the cost of inventory and cost of merchandise sold using a periodic inventory system under the LIFO method.	7-4	7-4A, 7-4B
	• Determine the cost of inventory and cost of merchandise sold using a periodic inventory system under the average cost method.	7-4	7-4A, 7-4B

5. Compare and contrast the use of the three inventory costing methods.

Key Points	Key Learning Outcomes	Example Exercises	Practice Exercises
The three inventory costing methods will normally yield different amounts for (1) the ending inventory, (2) the cost of merchandise sold for the period, and (3) the gross profit (and net income) for the period.	• Indicate which inventory cost flow method will yield the highest and lowest ending inventory and net income under periods of increasing prices. • Indicate which inventory cost flow method will yield the highest and lowest ending inventory and net income under periods of decreasing prices.		

6. Describe and illustrate the reporting of merchandise inventory in the financial statements.

Key Points	Key Learning Outcomes	Example Exercises	Practice Exercises
The lower of cost or market is used to value inventory. Inventory that is out of date, spoiled, or damaged is valued at its net realizable value. 　Merchandise inventory is usually presented in the Current Assets section of the balance sheet, following receivables. The method of determining the cost and valuing the inventory is reported. 　Errors in reporting inventory based upon the physical inventory will affect the balance sheet and income statement.	• Determine inventory using lower of cost or market. • Illustrate the use of net realizable value for spoiled or damaged inventory. • Prepare the Current Assets section of the balance sheet that includes inventory. • Determine the effect of inventory errors on the balance sheet and income statement.	7-5 7-6	7-5A, 7-5B 7-6A, 7-6B

7. Estimate the cost of inventory, using the retail method and the gross profit method.

Key Points	Key Learning Outcomes	Example Exercises	Practice Exercises
The retail method of estimating inventory determines inventory at retail prices and then converts it to cost using the ratio of cost to selling (retail) price. 　The gross profit method of estimating inventory deducts gross profit from the sales to determine the cost of merchandise sold. This amount is then deducted from the cost of merchandise available for sale to determine the ending inventory.	• Estimate ending inventory using the retail method. • Estimate ending inventory using the gross profit method.	7-7 7-8	7-7A, 7-7B 7-8A, 7-8B

Key Terms

average cost method (310)
first-in, first-out (FIFO) method
    (310)
gross profit method (325)
inventory turnover (326)

last-in, first-out (LIFO) method
    (310)
lower-of-cost-or-market (LCM)
    method (320)
net realizable value (321)

number of days' sales in
    inventory (326)
physical inventory (309)
retail inventory method (324)

Illustrative Problem

Stewart Co.'s beginning inventory and purchases during the year ended December 31, 2008, were as follows:

		Units	Unit Cost	Total Cost
January 1	Inventory	1,000	$50.00	$ 50,000
March 10	Purchase	1,200	52.50	63,000
June 25	Sold 800 units			
August 30	Purchase	800	55.00	44,000
October 5	Sold 1,500 units			
November 26	Purchase	2,000	56.00	112,000
December 31	Sold 1,000 units			
Total		5,000		$269,000

Instructions

1. Determine the cost of inventory on December 31, 2008, using the perpetual inventory system and each of the following inventory costing methods:
   a.   first-in, first-out
   b.   last-in, first-out
2. Determine the cost of inventory on December 31, 2008, using the periodic inventory system and each of the following inventory costing methods:
   a.   first-in, first-out
   b.   last-in, first-out
   c.   average cost
3. Assume that during the fiscal year ended December 31, 2008, sales were $290,000 and the estimated gross profit rate was 40%. Estimate the ending inventory at December 31, 2008, using the gross profit method.

Solution

1. a. First-in, first-out method: $95,200 (shown on page 331)
   b. Last-in, first-out method: $91,000 ($35,000 + $56,000) (shown on page 331)
2. a. First-in, first-out method:
      1,700 units at $56 = $95,200
   b. Last-in, first-out method:

1,000 units at $50.00	$50,000
700 units at $52.50	36,750
1,700 units	$86,750

1. a. First-in, first-out method: $95,200

Date	Purchases			Cost of Merchandise Sold			Inventory		
	Quantity	Unit Cost	Total Cost	Quantity	Unit Cost	Total Cost	Quantity	Unit Cost	Total Cost
2008 Jan. 1							1,000	50.00	50,000
Mar. 10	1,200	52.50	63,000				1,000	50.00	50,000
							1,200	52.50	63,000
June 25				800	50.00	40,000	200	50.00	10,000
							1,200	52.50	63,000
Aug. 30	800	55.00	44,000				200	50.00	10,000
							1,200	52.50	63,000
							800	55.00	44,000
Oct. 5				200	50.00	10,000	700	55.00	38,500
				1,200	52.50	63,000			
				100	55.00	5,500			
Nov. 26	2,000	56.00	112,000				700	55.00	38,500
							2,000	56.00	112,000
Dec. 31				700	55.00	38,500	1,700	56.00	95,200
				300	56.00	16,800			
Balances						173,800			95,200

b. Last-in, first-out method: $91,000 ($35,000 + $56,000)

Date	Purchases			Cost of Merchandise Sold			Inventory		
	Quantity	Unit Cost	Total Cost	Quantity	Unit Cost	Total Cost	Quantity	Unit Cost	Total Cost
2008 Jan. 1							1,000	50.00	50,000
Mar. 10	1,200	52.50	63,000				1,000	50.00	50,000
							1,200	52.50	63,000
June 25				800	52.50	42,000	1,000	50.00	50,000
							400	52.50	21,000
Aug. 30	800	55.00	44,000				1,000	50.00	50,000
							400	52.50	21,000
							800	55.00	44,000
Oct. 5				800	55.00	44,000	700	50.00	35,000
				400	52.50	21,000			
				300	50.00	15,000			
Nov. 26	2,000	56.00	112,000				700	50.00	35,000
							2,000	56.00	112,000
Dec. 31				1,000	56.00	56,000	700	50.00	35,000
							1,000	56.00	56,000
Balances						178,000			91,000

c. Average cost method:

Average cost per unit: $269,000/5,000 units = $53.80
Inventory, December 31, 2008: 1,700 units at $53.80 = $91,460

3. Merchandise inventory, January 1, 2008 .... $ 50,000
Purchases (net) 219,000
Merchandise available for sale $269,000
Sales (net) $290,000
Less estimated gross profit ($290,000 × 40%) 116,000
Estimated cost of merchandise sold 174,000
Estimated merchandise inventory, December 31, 2008 .... $ 95,000

Self-Examination Questions

(Answers at End of Chapter)

1. The inventory costing method that is based on the assumption that costs should be charged against revenue in the order in which they were incurred is:
   - A. FIFO.
   - B. LIFO.
   - C. average cost.
   - D. perpetual inventory.

2. The following units of a particular item were purchased and sold during the period:

Beginning inventory	40 units at $20
First purchase	50 units at $21
Second purchase	50 units at $22
First sale	110 units
Third purchase	50 units at $23
Second sale	45 units

   What is the cost of the 35 units on hand at the end of the period as determined under the perpetual inventory system by the LIFO costing method?
   - A. $715
   - B. $705
   - C. $700
   - D. $805

3. The following units of a particular item were available for sale during the period:

Beginning inventory	40 units at $20
First purchase	50 units at $21
Second purchase	50 units at $22
Third purchase	50 units at $23

   What is the unit cost of the 35 units on hand at the end of the period as determined under the periodic inventory system by the FIFO costing method?
   - A. $20
   - B. $21
   - C. $22
   - D. $23

4. If merchandise inventory is being valued at cost and the price level is steadily rising, the method of costing that will yield the highest net income is:
   - A. LIFO.
   - B. FIFO.
   - C. average.
   - D. periodic.

5. If the inventory at the end of the year is understated by $7,500, the error will cause an:
   - A. understatement of cost of merchandise sold for the year by $7,500.
   - B. overstatement of gross profit for the year by $7,500.
   - C. overstatement of merchandise inventory for the year by $7,500.
   - D. understatement of net income for the year by $7,500.

Eye Openers

1. Before inventory purchases are recorded, the receiving report should be reconciled to what documents?
2. What security measures may be used by retailers to protect merchandise inventory from customer theft?
3. Which inventory system provides the more effective means of controlling inventories (perpetual or periodic)? Why?
4. Why is it important to periodically take a physical inventory if the perpetual system is used?
5. Do the terms *FIFO* and *LIFO* refer to techniques used in determining quantities of the various classes of merchandise on hand? Explain.
6. Does the term *last-in* in the LIFO method mean that the items in the inventory are assumed to be the most recent (last) acquisitions? Explain.
7. If merchandise inventory is being valued at cost and the price level is steadily rising, which of the three methods of costing—FIFO, LIFO, or average cost—will yield (a) the highest inventory cost, (b) the lowest inventory cost, (c) the highest gross profit, and (d) the lowest gross profit?
8. Which of the three methods of inventory costing—FIFO, LIFO, or average cost—will in general yield an inventory cost most nearly approximating current replacement cost?
9. If inventory is being valued at cost and the price level is steadily rising, which of the three methods of costing—FIFO, LIFO, or average cost—will yield the lowest annual income tax expense? Explain.
10. Can a company change its method of costing inventory? Explain.
11. Because of imperfections, an item of merchandise cannot be sold at its normal selling price. How should this item be valued for financial statement purposes?
12. How is the method of determining the cost of the inventory and the method of valuing it disclosed in the financial statements?

13. The inventory at the end of the year was understated by $8,750. (a) Did the error cause an overstatement or an understatement of the gross profit for the year? (b) Which items on the balance sheet at the end of the year were overstated or understated as a result of the error?
14. Fargo Co. sold merchandise to Keepsakes Company on December 31, FOB shipping point. If the merchandise is in transit on December 31, the end of the fiscal year, which company would report it in its financial statements? Explain.
15. A manufacturer shipped merchandise to a retailer on a consignment basis. If the merchandise is unsold at the end of the period, in whose inventory should the merchandise be included?
16. What uses can be made of the estimate of the cost of inventory determined by the gross profit method?

Practice Exercises

PE 7-1A
Cost flow methods, gross profit, and ending inventory

obj. 2

Three identical units of Item T4W are purchased during July, as shown below.

Item T4W		Units	Cost
July 6	Purchase	1	$115
19	Purchase	1	118
24	Purchase	1	121
Total		3	$354
Average cost per unit			$118 ($354/3 units)

Assume that one unit is sold on July 28 for $150.
Determine the gross profit for July and ending inventory on July 31 using the (a) first-in, first-out (FIFO); (b) last-in, first-out (LIFO); and (c) average cost methods.

PE 7-1B
Cost flow methods, gross profit, and ending inventory

obj. 2

Three identical units of Item S77 are purchased during October, as shown below.

Item S77		Units	Cost
Oct. 6	Purchase	1	$ 88
19	Purchase	1	85
24	Purchase	1	82
Total		3	$255
Average cost per unit			$ 85 ($255/3 units)

Assume that one unit is sold on October 26 for $100.
Determine the gross profit for October and ending inventory on October 31 using the (a) first-in, first-out (FIFO); (b) last-in, first-out (LIFO); and (c) average cost methods.

PE 7-2A
Perpetual inventory using FIFO method

obj. 3

Beginning inventory, purchases, and sales for Item SJ68 are as follows:

Aug. 1	Inventory	28 units at $34
8	Sale	15 units
15	Purchase	22 units at $38
30	Sale	20 units

Assuming a perpetual inventory system and using the first-in, first-out (FIFO) method, determine (a) the cost of merchandise sold on August 30 and (b) the inventory on August 31.

PE 7-2B
Perpetual inventory using FIFO method
obj. 3

Beginning inventory, purchases, and sales for Item FC33 are as follows:

Mar.	1	Inventory	23 units at $10
	8	Sale	18 units
	15	Purchase	57 units at $14
	29	Sale	40 units

Assuming a perpetual inventory system and using the first-in, first-out (FIFO) method, determine (a) the cost of merchandise sold on March 29 and (b) the inventory on March 31.

PE 7-3A
Perpetual inventory using LIFO method
obj. 3

Beginning inventory, purchases, and sales for Item SJ68 are as follows:

Aug.	1	Inventory	28 units at $34
	8	Sale	15 units
	15	Purchase	22 units at $38
	30	Sale	20 units

Assuming a perpetual inventory system and using the last-in, first-out (LIFO) method, determine (a) the cost of merchandise sold on August 30 and (b) the inventory on August 31.

PE 7-3B
Perpetual inventory using LIFO method
obj. 3

Beginning inventory, purchases, and sales for Item FC33 are as follows:

Mar.	1	Inventory	23 units at $10
	8	Sale	18 units
	15	Purchase	57 units at $14
	29	Sale	40 units

Assuming a perpetual inventory system and using the last-in, first-out (LIFO) method, determine (a) the cost of merchandise sold on March 29 and (b) the inventory on March 31.

PE 7-4A
Periodic inventory using FIFO, LIFO, average cost methods
obj. 4

The units of an item available for sale during the year were as follows:

Jan. 1	Inventory	12 units at $25	$ 300
Apr. 20	Purchase	28 units at $30	840
Nov. 30	Purchase	40 units at $36	1,440
	Available for sale	80 units	$2,580

There are 20 units of the item in the physical inventory at December 31. The periodic inventory system is used. Determine the inventory cost using (a) the first-in, first-out (FIFO) method; (b) the last-in, first-out (LIFO) method; and (c) the average cost method.

PE 7-4B
Periodic inventory using FIFO, LIFO, average cost methods
obj. 4

The units of an item available for sale during the year were as follows:

Jan. 1	Inventory	18 units at $300	$ 5,400
Apr. 20	Purchase	46 units at $275	12,650
Nov. 30	Purchase	36 units at $250	9,000
	Available for sale	100 units	$27,050

There are 38 units of the item in the physical inventory at December 31. The periodic inventory system is used. Determine the inventory cost using (a) the first-in, first-out (FIFO) method; (b) the last-in, first-out (LIFO) method; and (c) the average cost method.

PE 7-5A
Lower of cost or market
obj. 6

On the basis of the following data, determine the value of the inventory at the lower of cost or market. Apply lower of cost or market to each inventory item as shown in Exhibit 7.

Commodity	Inventory Quantity	Unit Cost Price	Unit Market Price
TRP4	96	$29	$18
V555	200	13	14

PE 7-5B
Lower of cost or market
obj. 6

On the basis of the following data, determine the value of the inventory at the lower of cost or market. Apply lower of cost or market to each inventory item as shown in Exhibit 7

Commodity	Inventory Quantity	Unit Cost Price	Unit Market Price
E662	215	$30	$28
C11R	741	22	26

PE 7-6A
Effect of inventory errors
obj. 6

During the taking of its physical inventory on December 31, 2008, Genesis Company incorrectly counted its inventory as $126,000 instead of the correct amount of $135,000. Indicate the effect of the misstatement on Genesis's December 31, 2008, balance sheet and income statement for the year ended December 31, 2008.

PE 7-6B
Effect of inventory errors
obj. 6

During the taking of its physical inventory on December 31, 2008, Poindexter Company incorrectly counted its inventory as $769,000 instead of the correct amount of $740,000. Indicate the effect of the misstatement on Poindexter's December 31, 2008, balance sheet and income statement for the year ended December 31, 2008.

PE 7-7A
Retail inventory method
obj. 7

A business using the retail method of inventory costing determines that merchandise inventory at retail is $675,000. If the ratio of cost to retail price is 80%, what is the amount of inventory to be reported on the financial statements?

PE 7-7B
Retail inventory method
obj. 7

A business using the retail method of inventory costing determines that merchandise inventory at retail is $280,000. If the ratio of cost to retail price is 65%, what is the amount of inventory to be reported on the financial statements?

PE 7-8A
Gross profit method
obj. 7

Based upon the following data, estimate the cost of ending merchandise inventory:

Sales (net)	$1,500,000
Estimated gross profit rate	35%
Beginning merchandise inventory	$ 180,000
Purchases (net)	1,200,000
Merchandise available for sale	$1,380,000

PE 7-8B
Gross profit method
obj. 7

Based upon the following data, estimate the cost of ending merchandise inventory:

Sales (net)	$800,000
Estimated gross profit rate	36%
Beginning merchandise inventory	$ 75,000
Purchases (net)	625,000
Merchandise available for sale	$700,000

Exercises

EX 7-1
Control of inventories
obj. 1

Handy Hardware Store currently uses a periodic inventory system. Peggy Yang, the owner, is considering the purchase of a computer system that would make it feasible to switch to a perpetual inventory system.

Peggy is unhappy with the periodic inventory system because it does not provide timely information on inventory levels. Peggy has noticed on several occasions that the store runs out of good-selling items, while too many poor-selling items are on hand.

Peggy is also concerned about lost sales while a physical inventory is being taken. Handy Hardware currently takes a physical inventory twice a year. To minimize distractions, the store is closed on the day inventory is taken. Peggy believes that closing the store is the only way to get an accurate inventory count.

→ Will switching to a perpetual inventory system strengthen Handy Hardware's control over inventory items? Will switching to a perpetual inventory system eliminate the need for a physical inventory count? Explain.

EX 7-2
Control of inventories
obj. 1

PacTec Luggage Shop is a small retail establishment located in a large shopping mall. This shop has implemented the following procedures regarding inventory items:

a. Since the display area of the store is limited, only a sample of each piece of luggage is kept on the selling floor. Whenever a customer selects a piece of luggage, the salesclerk gets the appropriate piece from the store's stockroom. Since all salesclerks need access to the stockroom, it is not locked. The stockroom is adjacent to the break room used by all mall employees.

b. Whenever PacTec receives a shipment of new inventory, the items are taken directly to the stockroom. PacTec's accountant uses the vendor's invoice to record the amount of inventory received.

c. Since the shop carries mostly high-quality, designer luggage, all inventory items are tagged with a control device that activates an alarm if a tagged item is removed from the store.

→ State whether each of these procedures is appropriate or inappropriate. If it is inappropriate, state why.

EX 7-3
Perpetual inventory using FIFO
objs. 2, 3

✓*Inventory balance, November 30, $1,302*

Beginning inventory, purchases, and sales data for portable MP3 players are as follows:

Nov.	1	Inventory	70 units at $40
	5	Sale	52 units
	16	Purchase	30 units at $42
	21	Sale	24 units
	24	Sale	8 units
	30	Purchase	14 units at $45

The business maintains a perpetual inventory system, costing by the first-in, first-out method. Determine the cost of the merchandise sold for each sale and the inventory balance after each sale, presenting the data in the form illustrated in Exhibit 3.

EX 7-4
Perpetual inventory using LIFO
objs. 2, 3

✓*Inventory balance, November 30, $1,270*

Assume that the business in Exercise 7-3 maintains a perpetual inventory system, costing by the last-in, first-out method. Determine the cost of merchandise sold for each sale and the inventory balance after each sale, presenting the data in the form illustrated in Exhibit 4.

EX 7-5
Perpetual inventory using LIFO
objs. 2, 3

✓*Inventory balance, July 31, $1,764*

Beginning inventory, purchases, and sales data for cell phones for July are as follows:

Inventory		Purchases		Sales	
July 1	100 units at $30	July 3	80 units at $32	July 7	72 units
		21	60 units at $33	13	80 units
				31	32 units

Assuming that the perpetual inventory system is used, costing by the LIFO method, determine the cost of merchandise sold for each sale and the inventory balance after each sale, presenting the data in the form illustrated in Exhibit 4.

EX 7-6
Perpetual inventory using FIFO
objs. 2, 3

✓ *Inventory balance, July 31, $1,848*

Assume that the business in Exercise 7-5 maintains a perpetual inventory system, costing by the first-in, first-out method. Determine the cost of merchandise sold for each sale and the inventory balance after each sale, presenting the data in the form illustrated in Exhibit 3.

EX 7-7
FIFO, LIFO costs under perpetual inventory system
objs. 2, 3
✓ *a. $5,040*

The following units of a particular item were available for sale during the year:

Beginning inventory	100 units at $60
Sale	75 units at $112
First purchase	155 units at $65
Sale	135 units at $112
Second purchase	200 units at $72
Sale	175 units at $112

The firm uses the perpetual inventory system, and there are 70 units of the item on hand at the end of the year. What is the total cost of the ending inventory according to (a) FIFO, (b) LIFO?

EX 7-8
Periodic inventory by three methods
objs. 2, 4
✓ *b. $1,410*

The units of an item available for sale during the year were as follows:

Jan. 1	Inventory	18 units at $40
Feb. 26	Purchase	36 units at $46
June 18	Purchase	42 units at $52
Dec. 29	Purchase	24 units at $55

There are 33 units of the item in the physical inventory at December 31. The periodic inventory system is used. Determine the inventory cost by (a) the first-in, first out method, (b) the last-in, first-out method, and (c) the average cost method.

EX 7-9
Periodic inventory by three methods; cost of merchandise sold
objs. 2, 4

✓ *a. Inventory, $9,760*

The units of an item available for sale during the year were as follows:

Jan. 1	Inventory	168 units at $60
Apr. 15	Purchase	232 units at $65
Sept. 3	Purchase	80 units at $68
Nov. 23	Purchase	120 units at $70

There are 140 units of the item in the physical inventory at December 31. The periodic inventory system is used. Determine the inventory cost and the cost of merchandise sold by three methods, presenting your answers in the following form:

	Cost	
Inventory Method	**Merchandise Inventory**	**Merchandise Sold**
a. First-in, first-out	$	$
b. Last-in, first-out		
c. Average cost		

EX 7-10
Comparing inventory methods
obj. 5

Assume that a firm separately determined inventory under FIFO and LIFO and then compared the results.

1. In each space below, place the correct sign [less than (<), greater than (>), or equal (=)] for each comparison, assuming periods of rising prices.

a. FIFO inventory	_____	LIFO inventory
b. FIFO cost of goods sold	_____	LIFO cost of goods sold
c. FIFO net income	_____	LIFO net income
d. FIFO income tax	_____	LIFO income tax

2. Why would management prefer to use LIFO over FIFO in periods of rising prices?

EX 7-11
Lower-of-cost-or-market inventory
obj. 6

✓ LCM: $10,473

On the basis of the following data, determine the value of the inventory at the lower of cost or market. Assemble the data in the form illustrated in Exhibit 7.

Commodity	Inventory Quantity	Unit Cost Price	Unit Market Price
62CF3	10	$120	$131
41DH2	35	80	75
O3MQ3	10	275	260
23FH6	16	40	28
10KT4	40	90	94

EX 7-12
Merchandise inventory on the balance sheet
obj. 6

Based on the data in Exercise 7-11 and assuming that cost was determined by the FIFO method, show how the merchandise inventory would appear on the balance sheet.

EX 7-13
Effect of errors in physical inventory
obj. 6

Morena White Water Co. sells canoes, kayaks, whitewater rafts, and other boating supplies. During the taking of its physical inventory on December 31, 2008, Morena White Water incorrectly counted its inventory as $279,150 instead of the correct amount of $285,780.

a. State the effect of the error on the December 31, 2008, balance sheet of Morena White Water.
b. State the effect of the error on the income statement of Morena White Water for the year ended December 31, 2008.

EX 7-14
Effect of errors in physical inventory
obj. 6

Megan's Motorcycle Shop sells motorcycles, jet skis, and other related supplies and accessories. During the taking of its physical inventory on December 31, 2008, Megan's Motorcycle Shop incorrectly counted its inventory as $315,200 instead of the correct amount of $300,750.

a. State the effect of the error on the December 31, 2008, balance sheet of Megan's Motorcycle Shop.
b. State the effect of the error on the income statement of Megan's Motorcycle Shop for the year ended December 31, 2008.

EX 7-15
Error in inventory
obj. 6

During 2008, the accountant discovered that the physical inventory at the end of 2007 had been understated by $8,175. Instead of correcting the error, however, the accountant assumed that an $8,175 overstatement of the physical inventory in 2008 would balance out the error.

➤ Are there any flaws in the accountant's assumption? Explain.

EX 7-16
Retail inventory method
obj. 7

A business using the retail method of inventory costing determines that merchandise inventory at retail is $1,260,000. If the ratio of cost to retail price is 74%, what is the amount of inventory to be reported on the financial statements?

EX 7-17
Retail inventory method
obj. 7

✓ Inventory, September 30: $173,400

On the basis of the following data, estimate the cost of the merchandise inventory at September 30 by the retail method:

		Cost	Retail
September 1	Merchandise inventory	$ 220,000	$ 320,000
September 1–30	Purchases (net)	1,718,000	2,530,000
September 1–30	Sales (net)		2,595,000

EX 7-18
Gross profit inventory method

obj. 7

The merchandise inventory was destroyed by fire on August 19. The following data were obtained from the accounting records:

Jan. 1	Merchandise inventory	$ 360,000
Jan. 1–Aug. 19	Purchases (net)	3,200,000
	Sales (net)	5,200,000
	Estimated gross profit rate	36%

a. Estimate the cost of the merchandise destroyed.
b. Briefly describe the situations in which the gross profit method is useful.

EX 7-19
Inventory turnover

The following data were taken from recent annual reports of Apple Computer, Inc., a manufacturer of personal computers and related products, and American Greetings Corporation, a manufacturer and distributor of greeting cards and related products:

	Apple	American Greetings
Cost of goods sold	$9,888,000,000	$905,201,000
Inventory, end of year	165,000,000	222,874,000
Inventory, beginning of the year	101,000,000	246,171,000

a. Determine the inventory turnover for Apple and American Greetings. Round to one decimal place.
b. Would you expect American Greetings' inventory turnover to be higher or lower than Apple's? Why?

EX 7-20
Inventory turnover and number of days' sales in inventory

✓a. Albertson's, 40 days' sales in inventory

Kroger, Albertson's, Inc., and Safeway Inc. are the three largest grocery chains in the United States. Inventory management is an important aspect of the grocery retail business. Recent balance sheets for these three companies indicated the following merchandise inventory information:

	Merchandise Inventory	
	End of Year (in millions)	Beginning of Year (in millions)
Albertson's	$3,162	$3,104
Kroger	4,356	4,169
Safeway	2,741	2,642

The cost of goods sold for each company were:

	Cost of Goods Sold (in millions)
Albertson's	$28,711
Kroger	42,140
Safeway	25,228

a. Determine the number of days' sales in inventory and inventory turnover for the three companies. Round to the nearest day and one decimal place.
b. Interpret your results in (a).
c. If Albertson's had Kroger's number of days' sales in inventory, how much additional cash flow would have been generated from the smaller inventory relative to its actual average inventory position?

Problems Series A

PR 7-1A
FIFO perpetual inventory

The beginning inventory at Continental Office Supplies and data on purchases and sales for a three-month period are as follows:

objs. 2, 3

✓ 3. $11,420

Date		Transaction	Number of Units	Per Unit	Total
Jan.	1	Inventory	50	$20.00	$1,000
	7	Purchase	200	22.00	4,400
	20	Sale	90	40.00	3,600
	30	Sale	110	40.00	4,400
Feb.	8	Sale	20	44.00	880
	10	Purchase	130	23.00	2,990
	27	Sale	90	42.00	3,780
	28	Sale	50	45.00	2,250
Mar.	5	Purchase	180	24.00	4,320
	13	Sale	90	50.00	4,500
	23	Purchase	100	26.00	2,600
	30	Sale	80	50.00	4,000

Instructions
1. Record the inventory, purchases, and cost of merchandise sold data in a perpetual inventory record similar to the one illustrated in Exhibit 3, using the first-in, first-out method.
2. Determine the total sales and the total cost of merchandise sold for the period. Journalize the entries in the sales and cost of merchandise sold accounts. Assume that all sales were on account.
3. Determine the gross profit from sales for the period.
4. Determine the ending inventory cost.

PR 7-2A
LIFO perpetual inventory
objs. 2, 3

✓ 2. Gross profit, $11,180

The beginning inventory at Continental Office Supplies and data on purchases and sales for a three-month period are shown in Problem 7-1A.

Instructions
1. Record the inventory, purchases, and cost of merchandise sold data in a perpetual inventory record similar to the one illustrated in Exhibit 4, using the last-in, first-out method.
2. Determine the total sales, the total cost of merchandise sold, and the gross profit from sales for the period.
3. Determine the ending inventory cost.

PR 7-3A
Periodic inventory by three methods
objs. 2, 4

✓ 1. $6,863

Del Mar Appliances uses the periodic inventory system. Details regarding the inventory of appliances at August 1, 2007, purchases invoices during the year, and the inventory count at July 31, 2008, are summarized as follows:

Model	Inventory, August 1	Purchases Invoices 1st	2nd	3rd	Inventory Count, July 31
T742	2 at $125	2 at $130	4 at $135	2 at $140	5
PM18	7 at 242	6 at 250	5 at 260	10 at 259	9
K21G	6 at 80	5 at 82	8 at 89	8 at 90	6
H60W	2 at 108	2 at 110	3 at 128	3 at 130	5
B153Z	8 at 88	4 at 79	3 at 85	6 at 92	8
J600T	5 at 160	4 at 170	4 at 175	7 at 180	8
C273W	—	4 at 75	4 at 100	4 at 101	5

Instructions
1. Determine the cost of the inventory on July 31, 2008, by the first-in, first-out method. Present data in columnar form, using the following headings:

Model	Quantity	Unit Cost	Total Cost

If the inventory of a particular model comprises one entire purchase plus a portion of another purchase acquired at a different unit cost, use a separate line for each purchase.
2. Determine the cost of the inventory on July 31, 2008, by the last-in, first-out method, following the procedures indicated in (1).

3. Determine the cost of the inventory on July 31, 2008, by the average cost method, using the columnar headings indicated in (1).
4. ➤ Discuss which method (FIFO or LIFO) would be preferred for income tax purposes in periods of (a) rising prices and (b) declining prices.

PR 7-4A
Lower-of-cost-or-market inventory
obj. 6
✓ *Total LCM, $43,703*

If the working papers correlating with this textbook are not used, omit Problem 7-4A.

Data on the physical inventory of Exchange Company as of December 31, 2008, are presented in the working papers. The quantity of each commodity on hand has been determined and recorded on the inventory sheet. Unit market prices have also been determined as of December 31 and recorded on the sheet. The inventory is to be determined at cost and also at the lower of cost or market, using the first-in, first-out method. Quantity and cost data from the last purchases invoice of the year and the next-to-the-last purchases invoice are summarized as follows:

	Last Purchases Invoice		Next-to-the-Last Purchases Invoice	
Description	Quantity Purchased	Unit Cost	Quantity Purchased	Unit Cost
AC172	25	$ 60	30	$ 58
BE43	35	175	20	180
CJ9	18	130	25	128
E34	150	25	100	24
F17	10	565	10	560
G68	100	15	100	14
K41	10	385	5	384
Q79	500	6	500	6
RZ13	80	22	50	21
S60	5	250	4	260
W21	100	20	75	19
XR90	9	750	9	740

Instructions
Record the appropriate unit costs on the inventory sheet, and complete the pricing of the inventory. When there are two different unit costs applicable to an item, proceed as follows:

1. Draw a line through the quantity, and insert the quantity and unit cost of the last purchase.
2. On the following line, insert the quantity and unit cost of the next-to-the-last purchase.
3. Total the cost and market columns and insert the lower of the two totals in the Lower of C or M column. The first item on the inventory sheet has been completed as an example.

PR 7-5A
Retail method; gross profit method
obj. 7
✓ *1. $306,000*

Selected data on merchandise inventory, purchases, and sales for Hacienda Co. and San Lucas Co. are as follows:

	Cost	Retail
Hacienda Co.		
Merchandise inventory, June 1	$ 200,000	$ 290,000
Transactions during June:		
Purchases (net)	2,086,000	2,885,000
Sales		2,780,000
Sales returns and allowances		30,000
San Lucas Co.		
Merchandise inventory, November 1	$ 225,000	
Transactions during November and December:		
Purchases (net)	1,685,000	
Sales	2,815,000	
Sales returns and allowances	85,000	
Estimated gross profit rate	40%	

Instructions

1. Determine the estimated cost of the merchandise inventory of Hacienda Co. on June 30 by the retail method, presenting details of the computations.

2. a. Estimate the cost of the merchandise inventory of San Lucas Co. on December 31 by the gross profit method, presenting details of the computations.

   b. Assume that San Lucas Co. took a physical inventory on December 31 and discovered that $269,250 of merchandise was on hand. What was the estimated loss of inventory due to theft or damage during November and December?

Problems Series B

PR 7-1B
FIFO perpetual inventory
objs. 2, 3

✓3. $1,560,000

The beginning inventory of merchandise at Citrine Co. and data on purchases and sales for a three-month period are as follows:

Date		Transaction	Number of Units	Per Unit	Total
March	1	Inventory	132	$1,500	$198,000
	8	Purchase	108	2,000	216,000
	11	Sale	72	4,800	345,600
	22	Sale	66	4,800	316,800
April	3	Purchase	96	2,300	220,800
	10	Sale	60	5,000	300,000
	21	Sale	30	5,000	150,000
	30	Purchase	120	2,350	282,000
May	5	Sale	120	5,250	630,000
	13	Sale	72	5,250	378,000
	21	Purchase	180	2,400	432,000
	28	Sale	90	5,400	486,000

Instructions

1. Record the inventory, purchases, and cost of merchandise sold data in a perpetual inventory record similar to the one illustrated in Exhibit 3, using the first-in, first-out method.

2. Determine the total sales and the total cost of merchandise sold for the period. Journalize the entries in the sales and cost of merchandise sold accounts. Assume that all sales were on account.

3. Determine the gross profit from sales for the period.

4. Determine the ending inventory cost.

PR 7-2B
LIFO perpetual inventory
objs. 2, 3

✓2. Gross profit,
$1,527,600

The beginning inventory and data on purchases and sales for a three-month period are shown in Problem 7-1B.

Instructions

1. Record the inventory, purchases, and cost of merchandise sold data in a perpetual inventory record similar to the one illustrated in Exhibit 4, using the last-in, first-out method.

2. Determine the total sales, the total cost of merchandise sold, and the gross profit from sales for the period.

3. Determine the ending inventory cost.

PR 7-3B
Periodic inventory by three methods

Concord Appliances uses the periodic inventory system. Details regarding the inventory of appliances at January 1, 2008, purchases invoices during the year, and the inventory count at December 31, 2008, are summarized as follows:

objs. 2, 4

✓ 1. $11,108

Model	Inventory, January 1	Purchases Invoices 1st	2nd	3rd	Inventory Count, December 31
F10	5 at $ 60	6 at $ 65	2 at $ 65	2 at $ 70	3
J64	6 at 305	3 at 310	3 at 316	4 at 317	4
M13	2 at 520	2 at 527	2 at 530	2 at 535	4
Q73	6 at 520	8 at 531	4 at 549	6 at 542	7
144Z	9 at 213	7 at 215	6 at 222	6 at 225	11
Z120	—	4 at 222	4 at 232	—	2
W941	4 at 140	6 at 144	8 at 148	7 at 156	5

Instructions

1. Determine the cost of the inventory on December 31, 2008, by the first-in, first-out method. Present data in columnar form, using the following headings:

Model	Quantity	Unit Cost	Total Cost

If the inventory of a particular model comprises one entire purchase plus a portion of another purchase acquired at a different unit cost, use a separate line for each purchase.
2. Determine the cost of the inventory on December 31, 2008, by the last-in, first-out method, following the procedures indicated in (1).
3. Determine the cost of the inventory on December 31, 2008, by the average cost method, using the columnar headings indicated in (1).
4. Discuss which method (FIFO or LIFO) would be preferred for income tax purposes in periods of (a) rising prices and (b) declining prices.

PR 7-4B
Lower-of-cost-or-market inventory
obj. 6
✓ Total LCM, $43,548

If the working papers correlating with this textbook are not used, omit Problem 7-4B.

Data on the physical inventory of Satchell Co. as of December 31, 2008, are presented in the working papers. The quantity of each commodity on hand has been determined and recorded on the inventory sheet. Unit market prices have also been determined as of December 31 and recorded on the sheet. The inventory is to be determined at cost and also at the lower of cost or market, using the first-in, first-out method. Quantity and cost data from the last purchases invoice of the year and the next-to-the-last purchases invoice are summarized as follows:

Description	Last Purchases Invoice Quantity Purchased	Unit Cost	Next-to-the-Last Purchases Invoice Quantity Purchased	Unit Cost
AC172	30	$ 60	40	$ 59
BE43	25	175	15	180
CJ9	20	130	15	128
E34	150	25	100	27
F17	6	550	15	540
G68	75	14	100	13
K41	8	400	4	398
Q79	500	6	500	7
RZ13	65	22	50	21
S60	5	250	4	260
W21	120	20	115	17
XR90	10	750	8	740

Instructions
Record the appropriate unit costs on the inventory sheet, and complete the pricing of the inventory. When there are two different unit costs applicable to an item:

1. Draw a line through the quantity, and insert the quantity and unit cost of the last purchase.
2. On the following line, insert the quantity and unit cost of the next-to-the-last purchase.
3. Total the cost and market columns and insert the lower of the two totals in the Lower of C or M column. The first item on the inventory sheet has been completed as an example.

PR 7-5B
Retail method; gross profit method

obj. 7

✓1. $187,000

Selected data on merchandise inventory, purchases, and sales for Miramar Co. and Boyar's Co. are as follows:

	Cost	Retail
Miramar Co.		
Merchandise inventory, March 1	$ 185,000	$ 280,000
Transactions during March:		
Purchases (net)	2,246,000	3,295,000
Sales		3,360,000
Sales returns and allowances		60,000
Boyar's Co.		
Merchandise inventory, August 1	$ 425,000	
Transactions during August and September:		
Purchases (net)	2,980,000	
Sales	5,075,000	
Sales returns and allowances	75,000	
Estimated gross profit rate	40%	

Instructions

1. Determine the estimated cost of the merchandise inventory of Miramar Co. on March 31 by the retail method, presenting details of the computations.
2. a. Estimate the cost of the merchandise inventory of Boyar's Co. on September 30 by the gross profit method, presenting details of the computations.
   b. Assume that Boyar's Co. took a physical inventory on September 30 and discovered that $398,250 of merchandise was on hand. What was the estimated loss of inventory due to theft or damage during August and September?

Special Activities

SA 7-1
Ethics and professional conduct in business

ETHICS

Beeson Co. is experiencing a decrease in sales and operating income for the fiscal year ending December 31, 2008. Julia Faure, controller of Beeson Co., has suggested that all orders received before the end of the fiscal year be shipped by midnight, December 31, 2008, even if the shipping department must work overtime. Since Beeson Co. ships all merchandise FOB shipping point, it would record all such shipments as sales for the year ending December 31, 2008, thereby offsetting some of the decreases in sales and operating income.

➤ Discuss whether Julia Faure is behaving in a professional manner.

SA 7-2
LIFO and inventory flow

The following is an excerpt from a conversation between Jack O'Brien, the warehouse manager for Murrieta Wholesale Co., and its accountant, Carole Timmons. Murrieta Wholesale operates a large regional warehouse that supplies produce and other grocery products to grocery stores in smaller communities.

Jack: Carole, can you explain what's going on here with these monthly statements?
Carole: Sure, Jack. How can I help you?
Jack: I don't understand this last-in, first-out inventory procedure. It just doesn't make sense.
Carole: Well, what it means is that we assume that the last goods we receive are the first ones sold. So the inventory is made up of the items we purchased first.
Jack: Yes, but that's my problem. It doesn't work that way! We always distribute the oldest produce first. Some of that produce is perishable! We can't keep any of it very long or it'll spoil.
Carole: Jack, you don't understand. We only *assume* that the products we distribute are the last ones received. We don't actually have to distribute the goods in this way.
Jack: I always thought that accounting was supposed to show what really happened. It all sounds like "make believe" to me! Why not report what really happens?

➤ Respond to Jack's concerns.

SA 7-3
Costing inventory

Kowalski Company began operations in 2007 by selling a single product. Data on purchases and sales for the year were as follows:

Purchases:

Date	Units Purchased	Unit Cost	Total Cost
April 6	3,875	$12.20	$ 47,275
May 18	4,125	13.00	53,625
June 6	5,000	13.20	66,000
July 10	5,000	14.00	70,000
August 10	3,400	14.25	48,450
October 25	1,600	14.50	23,200
November 4	1,000	14.95	14,950
December 10	1,000	16.00	16,000
	25,000		$339,500

Sales:

April	2,000 units
May	2,000
June	2,500
July	3,000
August	3,500
September	3,500
October	2,250
November	1,250
December	1,000
Total units	21,000
Total sales	$325,000

On January 6, 2008, the president of the company, Jolly Zondra, asked for your advice on costing the 4,000-unit physical inventory that was taken on December 31, 2007. Moreover, since the firm plans to expand its product line, she asked for your advice on the use of a perpetual inventory system in the future.

1. Determine the cost of the December 31, 2007, inventory under the periodic system, using the (a) first-in, first-out method, (b) last-in, first-out method, and (c) average cost method.
2. Determine the gross profit for the year under each of the three methods in (1).
3. a. ▭▭▶ Explain varying viewpoints why each of the three inventory costing methods may best reflect the results of operations for 2007.
   b. ▭▭▶ Which of the three inventory costing methods may best reflect the replacement cost of the inventory on the balance sheet as of December 31, 2007?
   c. ▭▭▶ Which inventory costing method would you choose to use for income tax purposes? Why?
   d. ▭▭▶ Discuss the advantages and disadvantages of using a perpetual inventory system. From the data presented in this case, is there any indication of the adequacy of inventory levels during the year?

SA 7-4
Inventory ratios for Dell and HP

Dell Inc. and Hewlett-Packard Development Company, L.P. (HP) are both manufacturers of computer equipment and peripherals. However, the two companies follow two different strategies. Dell follows a build-to-order strategy, where the consumer orders the computer from a Web page. The order is then manufactured and shipped to the customer within days of the order. In contrast, HP follows a build-to-stock strategy, where the computer is first built for inventory, then sold from inventory to retailers, such as Best Buy. The two strategies can be seen in the difference between the inventory turnover and number of days' sales in inventory ratios for the two companies. The following financial statement information is provided for Dell and HP for a recent fiscal year (in millions):

	Dell	HP
Inventory, beginning of period	$ 327	$ 7,071
Inventory, end of period	459	6,877
Cost of goods sold	40,190	66,224

a. Determine the inventory turnover ratio and number of days' sales in inventory ratio for each company. Round to one decimal place.
b. ▭▭▶ Interpret the difference between the ratios for the two companies.

SA 7-5
Comparing inventory ratios for two companies

The Neiman Marcus Group, Inc., is a high-end specialty retailer, while Amazon.com uses its e-commerce services, features, and technologies to sell its products through the Internet. Recent balance sheet inventory disclosures for Neiman Marcus and Amazon.com are as follows:

	End-of-Period Inventory	Beginning-of-Period Inventory
Neiman Marcus Group, Inc.	$720,277,000	$687,062,000
Amazon.com	479,709,000	293,917,000

The cost of merchandise sold reported by each company was as follows:

	Neiman Marcus Group, Inc.	Amazon.com
Cost of merchandise sold	$2,321,110,000	$5,319,127,000

a. Determine the inventory turnover and number of days' sales in inventory for Neiman Marcus and Amazon.com.
b. Interpret your results.

SA 7-6
Comparing inventory ratios for three companies

The general merchandise retail industry has a number of segments represented by the following companies:

Company Name	Merchandise Concept
Costco Wholesale Corporation	Membership warehouse
Wal-Mart	Discount general merchandise
JCPenney	Department store

For a recent year, the following cost of merchandise sold and beginning and ending inventories have been provided from corporate annual reports for these three companies:

	Costco	Wal-Mart	JCPenney
Cost of merchandise sold	$42,092	$219,793	$11,285
Merchandise inventory, beginning	3,339	26,612	3,156
Merchandise inventory, ending	3,644	29,447	3,169

a. Determine the inventory turnover ratio for all three companies. Round to one decimal place.
b. Determine the number of days' sales in inventory for all three companies. Round to one decimal place.
c. Interpret these results based upon each company's merchandise concept.

Answers to Self-Examination Questions

1. **A** The FIFO method (answer A) is based on the assumption that costs are charged against revenue in the order in which they were incurred. The LIFO method (answer B) charges the most recent costs incurred against revenue, and the average cost method (answer C) charges a weighted average of unit costs of items sold against revenue. The perpetual inventory system (answer D) is a system and not a method of costing.

2. **A** The LIFO method of costing is based on the assumption that costs should be charged against revenue in the reverse order in which costs were incurred. Thus, the oldest costs are assigned to inventory. Thirty of the 35 units would be assigned a unit cost of $20 (since 10 of the beginning inventory units were sold on the first sale), and the remaining 5 units would be assigned a cost of $23, for a total of $715 (answer A).

3. **D** The FIFO method of costing is based on the assumption that costs should be charged against revenue in the order in which they were incurred (first-in, first-out). Thus, the most recent costs are assigned to inventory. The 35 units would be assigned a unit cost of $23 (answer D).

4. **B** When the price level is steadily rising, the earlier unit costs are lower than recent unit costs. Under the FIFO method (answer B), these earlier costs are matched against revenue to yield the highest possible net income. The periodic inventory system (answer D) is a system and not a method of costing.

5. **D** The understatement of inventory by $7,500 at the end of the year will cause the cost of merchandise sold for the year to be overstated by $7,500, the gross profit for the year to be understated by $7,500, the merchandise inventory to be understated by $7,500, and the net income for the year to be understated by $7,500 (answer D).

Sarbanes-Oxley, Internal Control, and Cash

© KEMIE GUAIDA/ISTOCKPHOTO INC.

objectives

After studying this chapter, you should be able to:

1 **Describe the Sarbanes-Oxley Act of 2002 and its impact on internal controls and financial reporting.**

2 **Describe and illustrate the objectives and elements of internal control.**

3 **Describe and illustrate the application of internal controls to cash.**

4 **Describe the nature of a bank account and its use in controlling cash.**

5 **Describe and illustrate the use of a bank reconciliation in controlling cash.**

6 **Describe the accounting for special-purpose cash funds.**

7 **Describe and illustrate the reporting of cash and cash equivalents in the financial statements.**

eBay Inc.

Controls are a part of your everyday life. At one extreme, laws are used to limit your behavior. For example, the speed limit is a control on your driving, designed for traffic safety. In addition, you are also affected by many nonlegal controls. For example, you can keep credit card receipts in order to compare your transactions to the monthly credit card statement. Comparing receipts to the monthly statement is a control designed to catch mistakes made by the credit card company. Likewise, recording checks in your checkbook is a control that you can use at the end of the month to verify the accuracy of your bank statement. In addition, banks give you a personal identification number (PIN) as a control against unauthorized access to your cash if you lose your automated teller machine (ATM) card. Dairies use freshness dating on their milk containers as a control to prevent the purchase or sale of soured milk. As you can see, you use and encounter controls every day.

Just as there are many examples of controls throughout society, businesses must also implement controls to help guide the behavior of their managers, employees, and customers. For example, eBay Inc. maintains an Internet-based marketplace for the sale of goods and services. Using eBay's online platform, buyers and sellers can browse, buy, and sell a wide variety of items including antiques and used cars. However, in order to maintain the integrity and trust of its buyers and sellers, eBay must have controls to ensure that buyers pay for their items and sellers don't misrepresent their items or fail to deliver sales. One such control that eBay uses is the buyer's or seller's reputation based upon feedback from past transactions of the member. A prospective buyer or seller can view the member's reputation and feedback comments before completing a transaction. Dishonest or unfair trading can lead to a negative reputation and even suspension or cancellation of the member's ability to trade on eBay.

In this chapter, we will discuss controls that can be included in accounting systems to provide reasonable assurance that the financial statements are reliable. We also discuss controls over cash that you can use to determine whether your bank has made any errors in your account. We begin this chapter by discussing the Sarbanes-Oxley Act of 2002 and its impact on controls and financial reporting.

Sarbanes-Oxley Act of 2002

During the Enron, WorldCom, Tyco International, Ltd., Adelphia Communications, and other financial scandals of the early 2000s, stockholders, creditors, and other investors lost millions and in some cases billions of dollars.[1] The resulting public outcry led Congress to pass the **Sarbanes-Oxley Act of 2002**. This act, referred to simply as *Sarbanes-Oxley*, is considered one of the most important and significant laws affecting publicly held companies in recent history. Although Sarbanes-Oxley applies only to companies whose stock is traded on public exchanges, referred to as *publicly held companies*, it has highlighted the need to assess the financial controls and reporting of all companies.

Sarbanes-Oxley's purpose is to restore public confidence and trust in the financial statements of companies. In doing so, Sarbanes-Oxley emphasizes the importance of effective internal control.[2] **Internal control** is broadly defined as the procedures and processes used by a company to safeguard its assets, process information accurately, and ensure compliance with laws and regulations.

---

1 Exhibit 2 in Chapter 1 briefly summarizes these scandals.
2 Sarbanes-Oxley also has important implications for corporate governance and the regulation of the public accounting profession. In this chapter, we focus on the internal control implications of Sarbanes-Oxley.

Sarbanes-Oxley requires companies to maintain strong and effective internal controls over the recording of transactions and the preparing of financial statements. Such controls are important because they deter fraud and prevent misleading financial statements as shown in the following illustration:

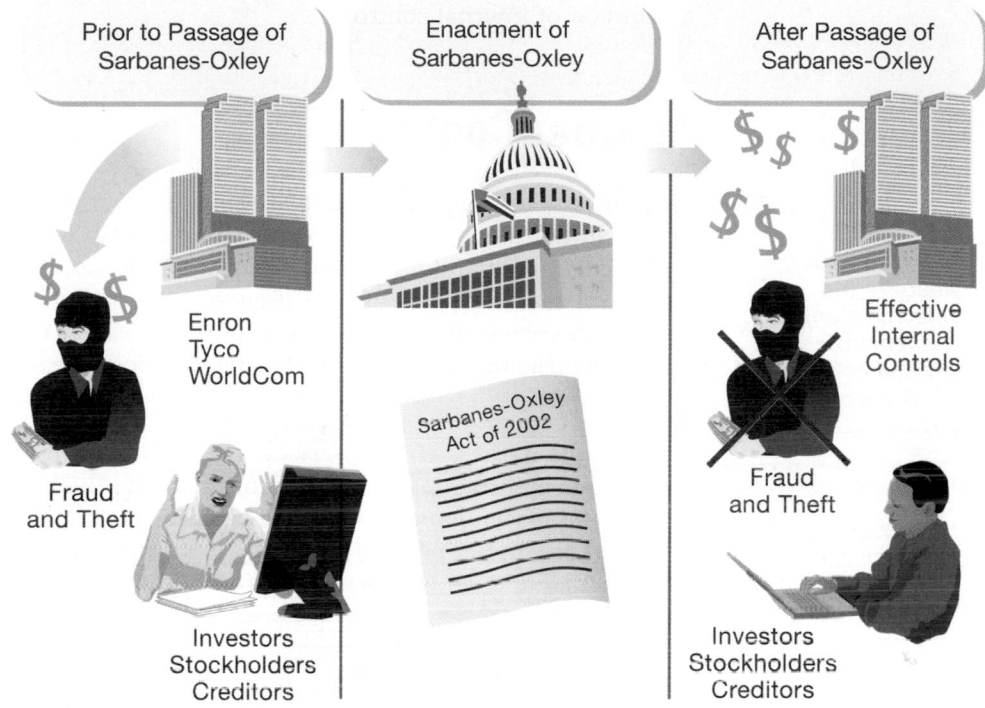

Prior to Passage of Sarbanes-Oxley

Enron
Tyco
WorldCom

Fraud
and Theft

Investors
Stockholders
Creditors

Enactment of Sarbanes-Oxley

Sarbanes-Oxley
Act of 2002

After Passage of Sarbanes-Oxley

Effective
Internal
Controls

Fraud
and Theft

Investors
Stockholders
Creditors

REAL WORLD

It is estimated that companies spend millions each year to comply with the requirements of Sarbanes-Oxley.

Sarbanes-Oxley not only requires companies to maintain strong and effective internal controls, but it also requires companies and their independent accountants to report on the effectiveness of the company's internal controls.[3] These reports are required to be filed with the company's annual 10-K report with the Securities and Exchange Commission. The act also encourages companies to include these reports in their annual reports to stockholders. An example of such a report by the management of General Electric Company (GE) is shown in Exhibit 1.

EXHIBIT 1

**Sarbanes-Oxley Report
General Electric
Company**

Management's Annual Report on Internal Control over Financial Reporting

The management of General Electric Company is responsible for establishing and maintaining adequate internal control over financial reporting for the company. With the participation of the Chief Executive Officer and the Chief Financial Officer, our management conducted an evaluation of the effectiveness of our internal control over financial reporting based on the framework and criteria established in *Internal Control—Integrated Framework*, issued by the Committee of Sponsoring Organizations. . . . Based on this evaluation . . . our management has concluded that our internal control over financial reporting was effective. . . .

General Electric Company's independent [accountant] auditor, KPMG LLP, a registered public accounting firm, has [also] issued an audit report on our management's assessment of our internal control over financial reporting.

JEFFREY R. IMMELT
Chairman of the Board
and Chief Executive Officer

KEITH S. SHERIN
Senior Vice President, Finance
and Chief Financial Officer

---

3 These reporting requirements are required under Section 404 of the act. As a result, these requirements and reports are often referred to as 404 requirements and 404 reports.

GE based its assessment and evaluation of internal controls upon *Internal Control—Integrated Framework,* which was issued by the Committee of Sponsoring Organizations (COSO) of the Treadway Commission. This framework is the widely accepted standard by which companies design, analyze, and evaluate internal controls. For this reason, we use this framework in the next section of this chapter as a basis for our discussion of internal controls.

Internal Control

objective   2

Describe and illustrate the objectives and elements of internal control.

As indicated in the prior section, effective internal controls are required by Sarbanes-Oxley. In addition, effective internal controls help businesses guide their operations and prevent theft and other abuses. For example, assume that you own and manage a lawn care service. Your business uses several employee teams, and you provide each team with vehicle and lawn equipment. What issues might you face as a manager in controlling the operations of this business? Below are some examples.

- Lawn care must be provided on time.
- The quality of lawn care services must meet customer expectations.
- Employees must provide work for the hours they are paid.
- Lawn care equipment should be used for business purposes only.
- Vehicles should be used for business purposes only.
- Customers must be billed and payments collected for services rendered.

How would you address these issues? You could, for example, develop a schedule at the beginning of each day and then inspect the work at the end of the day to verify that it was completed according to quality standards. You could have "surprise" inspections by arriving on site at random times to verify that the teams are working according to schedule. You could require employees to "clock in" at the beginning of the day and "clock out" at the end of the day to make sure that they are paid for hours worked. You could require the work teams to return the vehicles and equipment to a central location to prevent unauthorized use. You could keep a log of odometer readings at the end of each day to verify that the vehicles have not been used for "joy riding." You could bill customers after you have inspected the work and then monitor the collection of all receivables. All of these are examples of internal control.

In this section, we describe and illustrate internal control using the framework developed by the Committee of Sponsoring Organizations (COSO), which was formed by five major business associations. The committee's deliberations were published in *Internal Control—Integrated Framework.*[4] This framework, cited by GE in Exhibit 1, has become the standard by which companies design, analyze, and evaluate internal control. We describe and illustrate the framework by first describing the objectives of internal control and then showing how these objectives can be achieved through the five elements of internal control.

Information on *Internal Control—Integrated Framework* can be found on COSO's Web site at **http://www.coso.org/**.

OBJECTIVES OF INTERNAL CONTROL

The objectives of internal control are to provide reasonable assurance that (1) assets are safeguarded and used for business purposes, (2) business information is accurate, and (3) employees comply with laws and regulations. These objectives are illustrated on the following page.

Internal control can safeguard assets by preventing theft, fraud, misuse, or misplacement. One of the most serious breaches of internal control is employee fraud. **Employee fraud** is the intentional act of deceiving an employer for personal gain.

---

4 *Internal Control—Integrated Framework* by the Committee of Sponsoring Organizations of the Treadway Commission, 1992.

Objectives of Internal Control

Safeguarded Assets · Accurate Information · Compliance with Laws and Regulations

The Association of Certified Fraud Examiners has estimated that businesses will lose over $660 billion, or around 6% of revenue, to employee fraud.

Source: *2004 Report to the Nation: Occupational Fraud and Abuse*, Association of Certified Fraud Examiners.

Such deception may range from purposely overstating expenses on a travel expense report to embezzling millions of dollars through complex schemes.

Accurate information is necessary for operating a business successfully. The safeguarding of assets and accurate information often go hand-in-hand. The reason is that employees attempting to defraud a business will also need to adjust the accounting records in order to hide the fraud.

Businesses must comply with applicable laws, regulations, and financial reporting standards. Examples of such standards and laws include environmental regulations, contract terms, safety regulations, and generally accepted accounting principles (GAAP).

ELEMENTS OF INTERNAL CONTROL

How does management achieve its internal control objectives? Management is responsible for designing and applying five **elements of internal control** to meet the three internal control objectives. These elements are (1) the control environment, (2) risk assessment, (3) control procedures, (4) monitoring, and (5) information and communication.[5]

The elements of internal control are illustrated in Exhibit 2. In this exhibit, these elements form an umbrella over the business to protect it from control threats. The

EXHIBIT 2 | Elements of Internal Control

Control Threats

Monitoring · Risk Assessment Control Procedure · Control Environment

Information and Communication

Management · Business

5 Ibid., 12–14.

business's control environment is represented by the size of the umbrella. Risk assessment, control procedures, and monitoring are the fabric that keeps the umbrella from leaking. Information and communication link the umbrella to management. In the following paragraphs, we discuss each of these elements.

CONTROL ENVIRONMENT

A business's control environment is the overall attitude of management and employees about the importance of controls. One of the factors that influences the control environment is *management's philosophy and operating style*. A management that overemphasizes operating goals and deviates from control policies may indirectly encourage employees to ignore controls. For example, the pressure to achieve revenue targets may encourage employees to fraudulently record sham sales. On the other hand, a management that emphasizes the importance of controls and encourages adherence to control policies will create an effective control environment.

Control Environment

CEO

Employees

Management's Philosophy
and Operating Style

Organizational Structure

Personnel Policies

How do companies discover fraud? Most fraud is discovered from tips by employees, customers, suppliers, or anonymous sources.

The business's *organizational structure*, which is the framework for planning and controlling operations, also influences the control environment. For example, a department store chain might organize each of its stores as separate business units. Each store manager has full authority over pricing and other operating activities. In such a structure, each store manager has the responsibility for establishing an effective control environment.

Personnel policies also affect the control environment. Personnel policies involve the hiring, training, evaluation, compensation, and promotion of employees. In addition, job descriptions, employee codes of ethics, and conflict-of-interest policies are part of the personnel policies. Such policies can enhance the internal control environment if they provide reasonable assurance that only competent, honest employees are hired and retained.

To illustrate the importance of the control environment, consider the case where the head of a bank's loan department perpetrated a fraud by accepting bribes from customers with poor credit ratings. As a result, the bank lost thousands of dollars from bad loans. After discovering the fraud, the bank president improved the bank's control environment by implementing a program that allowed employees to report suspicious conduct anonymously. In addition to encouraging employees to report suspicious conduct, the employees were warned that employee fraud might occur anywhere and involve anyone.

RISK ASSESSMENT

All organizations face risks. Examples of risk include changes in customer requirements, competitive threats, regulatory changes, changes in economic factors such as interest rates, and employee violations of company policies and procedures. Management should assess these risks and take necessary actions to control them, so that the objectives of internal control can be achieved.

Once risks are identified, they can be analyzed to estimate their significance, to assess their likelihood of occurring, and to determine actions that will minimize them. For example, the manager of a warehouse operation may analyze the risk of employee back injuries, which might give rise to lawsuits. If the manager determines that the risk is significant, the company may purchase back support braces for its warehouse employees and require them to wear the braces.

CONTROL PROCEDURES

Control procedures are established to provide reasonable assurance that business goals will be achieved, including the prevention of fraud. In the following paragraphs, we will briefly discuss control procedures that can be integrated throughout the accounting system. These procedures are listed in Exhibit 3.

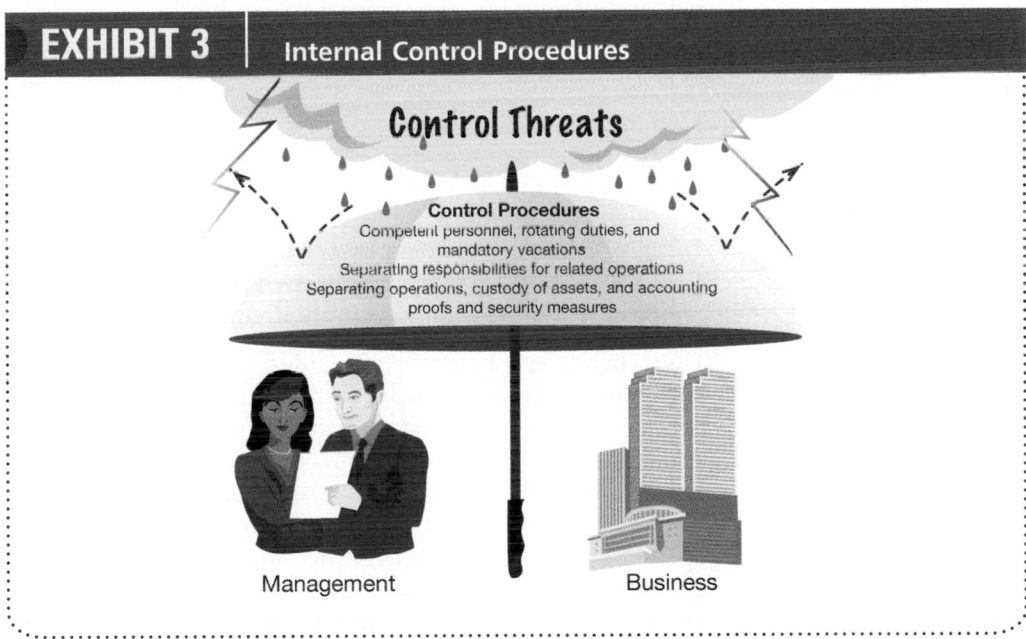

EXHIBIT 3 | Internal Control Procedures

Control Threats

Control Procedures
Competent personnel, rotating duties, and mandatory vacations
Separating responsibilities for related operations
Separating operations, custody of assets, and accounting
proofs and security measures

Management   Business

Competent Personnel, Rotating Duties, and Mandatory Vacations The successful operation of an accounting system requires procedures to ensure that people are able to perform the duties to which they are assigned. Hence, it is necessary that all accounting employees be adequately trained and supervised in performing their jobs. It may also be advisable to rotate duties of clerical personnel and mandate vacations for nonclerical personnel. These policies encourage employees to adhere to prescribed procedures. In addition, existing errors or fraud may be detected. For example, numerous cases of employee fraud have been discovered after a long-term employee, who never took vacations, missed work because of an illness or other unavoidable reasons.

To illustrate, consider the case where a bank officer who was not required to take vacations stole approximately $5 million over 16 years by printing fake certificates of deposit. The officer would then issue the fake certificate to the customer and pocket the customer's money. After discovering the theft, the bank began requiring all employees to take vacations.

Integrity, Objectivity, and Ethics in Business

ETHICS

TIPS ON PREVENTING EMPLOYEE FRAUD IN SMALL COMPANIES

- Do not have the same employee write company checks and keep the books. Look for payments to vendors you don't know or payments to vendors whose names appear to be misspelled.
- If your business has a computer system, restrict access to accounting files as much as possible. Also, keep a backup copy of your accounting files and store it at an off-site location.
- Be wary of anybody working in finance that declines to take vacations. They may be afraid that a replacement will uncover fraud.

- Require and monitor supporting documentation (such as vendor invoices) before signing checks.
- Track the number of credit card bills you sign monthly.
- Limit and monitor access to important documents and supplies, such as blank checks and signature stamps.
- Check W-2 forms against your payroll annually to make sure you're not carrying any fictitious employees.
- Rely on yourself, not on your accountant, to spot fraud.

Source: Steve Kaufman, "Embezzlement Common at Small Companies," Knight-Ridder Newspapers, reported in *Athens Daily News/Athens Banner-Herald*, March 10, 1996, p. 4D.

Separating Responsibilities for Related Operations   To decrease the possibility of inefficiency, errors, and fraud, the responsibility for related operations should be divided among two or more persons. For example, the responsibilities for purchasing, receiving, and paying for computer supplies should be divided among three persons or departments. If the same person orders supplies, verifies the receipt of the supplies, and pays the supplier, the following abuses are possible:

Many companies have "fraud hotlines" where employees can anonymously report suspicious or fraudulent activities.

1. Orders may be placed on the basis of friendship with a supplier, rather than on price, quality, and other objective factors.
2. The quantity and quality of supplies received may not be verified, thus causing payment for supplies not received or poor-quality supplies.
3. Supplies may be stolen by the employee.
4. The validity and accuracy of invoices may be verified carelessly, thus causing the payment of false or inaccurate invoices.

The "checks and balances" provided by dividing responsibilities among various departments requires no duplication of effort. The business documents prepared by one department are designed to coordinate with and support those prepared by other departments.

To illustrate, consider the case where an accounts payable clerk created false invoices and submitted them for payment. The clerk obtained the resulting checks, opened a bank account, and cashed the checks under an assumed name. The clerk was able to steal thousands of dollars because no one was required to approve the payments other than the accounts payable clerk.

An accounting clerk for the Grant County (Washington) Alcoholism Program was in charge of collecting money, making deposits, and keeping the records. While the clerk was away on maternity leave, the replacement clerk discovered a fraud: $17,800 in fees had been collected but had been hidden for personal gain.

Separating Operations, Custody of Assets, and Accounting   Control policies should establish the responsibilities for various business activities. To reduce the possibility of errors and fraud, the responsibilities for operations, custody of assets, and accounting should be separated. The accounting records then serve as an independent check on the individuals who have custody of the assets and who engage in the business operations. For example, the employees entrusted with handling cash receipts from credit customers should not record cash receipts in the accounting records. To do so would allow employees to borrow or steal cash and hide the theft in the records. Likewise, if those engaged in operating activities also record the results of operations, they could distort the accounting reports to show favorable results. For example, a store manager whose year-end bonus is based upon operating profits might be tempted to record fictitious sales in order to receive a larger bonus.

To illustrate, consider the case where a payroll clerk was responsible for preparing the payroll and distributing the payroll checks. The clerk stole almost $40,000 over two months by preparing duplicate payroll checks and checks for fictitious part-time employees. After the theft was detected, the duties of preparing payroll checks and distributing payroll checks were assigned to separate employees.

Proofs and Security Measures   Proofs and security measures should be used to safeguard assets and ensure reliable accounting data. This control procedure applies to many different techniques, such as authorization, approval, and reconciliation procedures. For example, employees who travel on company business may be required to obtain a department manager's approval on a travel request form.

Other examples of control procedures include the use of bank accounts and other measures to ensure the safety of cash and valuable documents. A cash register that displays the amount recorded for each sale and provides the customer a printed receipt can be an effective part of the internal control structure. An all-night convenience store could use the following security measures to deter robberies:

1. Locate the cash register near the door, so that it is fully visible from outside the store; have two employees work late hours; employ a security guard.
2. Deposit cash in the bank daily, before 5 p.m.
3. Keep only small amounts of cash on hand after 5 p.m. by depositing excess cash in a store safe that can't be opened by employees on duty.
4. Install cameras and alarm systems.

To illustrate, consider the case where someone stole thousands of dollars in parking fines from a small town. Citizens would pay their parking fines by placing money in ticket envelopes and putting them in a locked box outside the town hall. The key to the locked box was not safeguarded and was readily available to a variety of people. As a result, the person who stole the money was never discovered. The town later gave one person the responsibility of safeguarding the key and emptying the locked box.

MONITORING

Monitoring the internal control system locates weaknesses and improves control effectiveness. The internal control system can be monitored through either ongoing efforts by management or by separate evaluations. Ongoing monitoring efforts may include observing both employee behavior and warning signs from the accounting system. The indicators shown in Exhibit 4 may be clues to internal control problems.[6]

Separate monitoring evaluations are generally performed when there are major changes in strategy, senior management, business structure, or operations. In large businesses, internal auditors who are independent of operations normally are responsible for monitoring the internal control system. Internal auditors can report issues and concerns to an audit committee of the board of directors, who are independent of management. In addition, external auditors also evaluate internal control as a normal part of their annual financial statement audit.

INFORMATION AND COMMUNICATION

Information and communication are essential elements of internal control. Information about the control environment, risk assessment, control procedures, and monitoring is needed by management to guide operations and ensure compliance with reporting, legal, and regulatory requirements. Management can also use external information to assess events and conditions that impact decision making and external reporting. For example, management uses information from the Financial Accounting Standards Board (FASB) to assess the impact of possible changes in reporting standards.

---

6 Edwin C. Bliss, "Employee Theft," *Boardroom Reports*, July 15, 1994, pp. 5–6.

EXHIBIT 4 | Warning Signs of Internal Control Problems

Warning signs with regard to people

1. Abrupt change in lifestyle (without winning the lottery).
2. Close social relationships with suppliers.
3. Refusing to take a vacation.
4. Frequent borrowing from other employees.
5. Excessive use of alcohol or drugs.

Warning signs from the accounting system

1. Missing documents or gaps in transaction numbers (could mean documents are being used for fraudulent transactions).
2. An unusual increase in customer refunds (refunds may be phony).
3. Differences between daily cash receipts and bank deposits (could mean receipts are being pocketed before being deposited).
4. Sudden increase in slow payments (employee may be pocketing the payment).
5. Backlog in recording transactions (possibly an attempt to delay detection of fraud).

Example Exercise 8-1
objective 2

Identify each of the following as relating to (a) the control environment, (b) risk assessment, or (c) control procedures.

1. Mandatory vacations
2. Personnel policies
3. Report of outside consultants on future market changes

Follow My Example 8-1

1. (c) control procedures
2. (a) the control environment
3. (b) risk assessment

For Practice: PE 8-1A, PE 8-1B

Cash Controls Over Receipts and Payments

Cash includes coins, currency (paper money), checks, money orders, and money on deposit that is available for unrestricted withdrawal from banks and other financial institutions. Normally, you can think of cash as anything that a bank would accept for deposit in your account. For example, a check made payable to you could normally be deposited in a bank and thus is considered cash.

We will assume in this chapter that a business maintains only *one* bank account, represented in the ledger as *Cash*. In practice, however, a business may have several bank accounts, such as one for general cash payments and another for payroll. For each of its bank accounts, the business will maintain a ledger account, one of which may be called *Cash in Bank—First Bank*, for example. It will also maintain separate ledger accounts for special-purpose cash funds, such as travel reimbursements. We will introduce some of these other cash accounts later in this chapter.

Because of the ease with which money can be transferred, cash is the asset most likely to be diverted and used improperly by employees. In addition, many transactions either directly or indirectly affect the receipt or the payment of cash. Businesses must therefore design and use controls that safeguard cash and control the authorization of cash transactions. In the following paragraphs, we will discuss these controls.

CONTROL OF CASH RECEIPTS

To protect cash from theft and misuse, a business must control cash from the time it is received until it is deposited in a bank. Businesses normally receive cash from two main sources: (1) customers purchasing products or services and (2) customers making payments on account. For example, fast-food restaurants, such as McDonald's, Wendy's International Inc., and Burger King Corporation, receive cash primarily from over-the-counter sales to customers. Mail-order and Internet retailers, such as Lands' End Inc., The Orvis Company, Inc., L.L. Bean, Inc., and Amazon.com, receive cash primarily through electronic funds transfers from credit card companies.

Cash Received from Cash Sales Regardless of the source of cash receipts, every business must properly safeguard and record its cash receipts. One of the most important controls to protect cash received in over-the-counter sales is a cash register. When a clerk (cashier) enters the amount of a sale, the cash register normally displays the amount. This is a control to ensure that the clerk has charged you the correct amount. You also receive a receipt to verify the accuracy of the amount.

At the beginning of a work shift, each cash register clerk is given a cash drawer that contains a predetermined amount of cash for making change for customers. The amount in each drawer is sometimes called a *change fund*. At the end of the shift, the clerk and the supervisor count the cash in that clerk's cash drawer. The amount of cash in each drawer should equal the beginning amount of cash plus the cash sales for the day. However, errors in recording cash sales or errors in making change cause the amount of cash on hand to differ from this amount. Such differences are recorded in a **cash short and over account**.

At the end of the accounting period, a debit balance in the cash short and over account is included in Miscellaneous Expense in the income statement. A credit balance is included in the Other Income section. If a clerk consistently has significant cash short and over amounts, the supervisor may require the clerk to take additional training.

After a cash register clerk's cash has been counted and recorded on a memorandum form, the cash is then placed in a store safe in the Cashier's Department until it can be deposited in the bank. The supervisor forwards the clerk's cash register receipts to the Accounting Department, where they serve as the basis for recording the transactions for the day as shown on the following page.

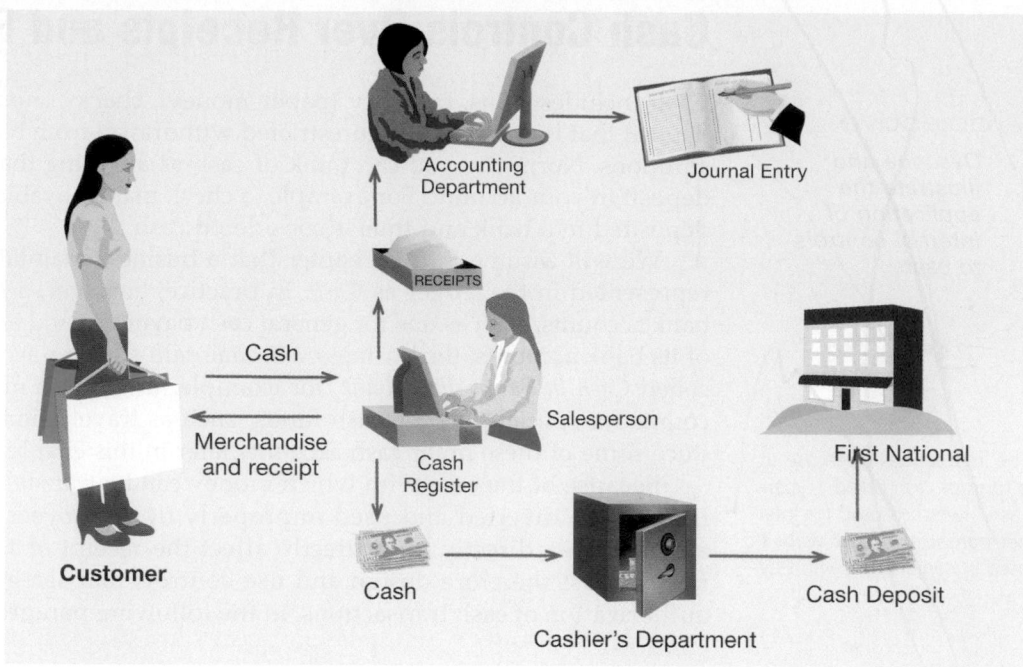

Some retail companies use debit card systems to transfer and record the receipt of cash. In a debit card system, a customer pays for goods at the time of purchase by presenting a plastic card. The card authorizes the electronic transfer of cash from the customer's checking account to the retailer's bank account.

Cash Received in the Mail   Cash is received in the mail when customers pay their bills. This cash is usually in the form of checks and money orders. Most companies' invoices are designed so that customers return a portion of the invoice, called a *remittance advice*, with their payment. The employee who opens the incoming mail should initially compare the amount of cash received with the amount shown on the remittance advice. If a customer does not return a remittance advice, an employee prepares one. Like the cash register, the remittance advice serves as a record of cash initially received. It also helps ensure that the posting to the customer's account is accurate. Finally, as a control, the employee opening the mail normally also stamps checks and money orders "For Deposit Only" in the bank account of the business.

All cash received in the mail is sent to the Cashier's Department. An employee there combines it with the receipts from cash sales and prepares a bank deposit ticket. The remittance advices and their summary totals are delivered to the Accounting Department. An accounting clerk then prepares the records of the transactions and posts them to the customer accounts.

When cash is deposited in the bank, the bank normally stamps a duplicate copy of the deposit ticket with the amount received. This bank receipt is returned to the Accounting Department, where a clerk compares the receipt with the total amount that should have been deposited. This control helps ensure that all the cash is deposited and that no cash is lost or stolen on the way to the bank. Any shortages are thus promptly detected.

Separating the duties of the Cashier's Department, which handles cash, and the Accounting Department, which records cash, is a control. If Accounting Department employees both handle and record cash, an employee could steal cash and change the accounting records to hide the theft.

Cash Received by EFT   Cash may also be received from customers through **electronic funds transfers (EFT)**. For example, customers may authorize automatic electronic transfers from their checking accounts to pay monthly bills for such items as cell phone, cable, Internet, and electric services. In such cases, the company sends the customer's bank a signed form from the customer authorizing the monthly electronic transfers from the customer's checking account to the company's bank account. Each month, the company electronically notifies the customer's bank of the amount of the transfer and the date the transfer should take place. On the due date, the company records the electronic transfer as a receipt of cash to its bank account and posts the amount paid to the customer's account.

Most companies encourage automatic electronic transfers by customers for several reasons. First, electronic transfers are less costly than receiving cash payments through the mail since the employee handling of cash is eliminated. Second, electronic transfers enhance internal controls over cash since the cash is received directly by the bank without the handling of cash by employees. Thus, potential theft of cash is eliminated. Finally, electronic transfers reduce late payments from customers and speed up the processing of cash receipts.

CONTROL OF CASH PAYMENTS

Howard Schultz & Associates (HS&A) specializes in reviewing cash payments for its clients. HS&A searches for errors, such as duplicate payments, failures to take discounts, and inaccurate computations. Amounts recovered for clients ranged from thousands to millions of dollars.

The control of cash payments should provide reasonable assurance that payments are made for only authorized transactions. In addition, controls should ensure that cash is used efficiently. For example, controls should ensure that all available discounts, such as purchase discounts, are taken.

In a small business, an owner/manager may authorize payments based upon personal knowledge of goods and services purchased. In a large business, however, the duties of purchasing goods, inspecting the goods received, and verifying the invoices are usually performed by different employees. These duties must be coordinated to ensure that checks for proper payments are made to creditors. One system used for this purpose is the voucher system.

Voucher System   A **voucher system** is a set of procedures for authorizing and recording liabilities and cash payments. A **voucher** is any document that serves as proof of authority to pay cash or issue an electronic funds transfer. For example, an invoice properly approved for payment could be considered a voucher. In many businesses, however, a voucher is a special form for recording relevant data about a liability and the details of its payment.

A voucher system may be either manual or computerized. In a manual system, a voucher is normally prepared after all necessary supporting documents have been received. For example, when a voucher is prepared for the purchase of goods, the voucher should be supported by the supplier's invoice, a purchase order, and a receiving report. After a voucher is prepared, it is submitted to the proper manager for approval. Once approved, the voucher is recorded in the accounts and filed by due date. Upon payment, the voucher is recorded in the same manner as the payment of an account payable.

In a computerized system, properly approved supporting documents (such as purchase orders and receiving reports) would be entered directly into computer files. At the due date, the checks would be automatically generated and mailed to creditors. At that time, the voucher would be electronically transferred to a paid voucher file.

Cash Paid by EFT   Cash can also be paid by electronic funds transfer systems by using computers rather than paper money or checks. For example, a company may pay its employees by means of EFT. Under such a system, employees may authorize the deposit of their payroll checks directly into checking accounts. Each pay period, the business electronically transfers the employees' net pay to their checking accounts through the use of computer systems and networks. Likewise, many companies are using EFT systems to pay their suppliers and other vendors.

Bank Accounts

Most of you are familiar with bank accounts. You probably have a checking account at a local bank, credit union, savings and loan association, or other financial institution. In this section, we discuss the use of bank accounts by businesses. We then discuss the use of bank accounts as an additional control over cash.

USE OF BANK ACCOUNTS

A business often maintains several bank accounts. For example, a business with several branches or retail outlets such as Sears Holdings, Inc. or Gap Inc. will often maintain a bank account for each location. In addition, businesses usually maintain a separate bank account for payroll and other special purposes.

A major reason that businesses use bank accounts is for control purposes. Use of bank accounts reduces the amount of cash on hand at any one time. For example, many merchandise businesses deposit cash receipts twice daily to reduce the amount of cash on hand that is susceptible to theft. Likewise, using a payroll account allows for paying employees by check or electronic funds transfer rather than by distributing a large amount of cash each payroll period.

In addition to reducing the amount of cash on hand, bank accounts provide an independent recording of cash transactions that can be used as a verification of the business's recording of transactions. That is, the use of bank accounts provides a double recording of cash transactions. The company's cash account corresponds to the bank's liability (deposit) account for the company. As we will discuss and illustrate in the next section, this double recording of cash transactions allows for a reconciliation of the cash account on the company's records with the cash balance recorded by the bank.

Finally, the use of bank accounts facilitates the transfer of funds. For example, electronic funds transfer systems require bank accounts for the transfer of funds between companies. Within a company, cash can be transferred between bank accounts through the use of wire transfers. In addition, online banking allows companies to transfer funds and pay bills electronically as well as monitor their cash balances on a real-time basis.

BANK STATEMENT

Banks usually maintain a record of all checking account transactions. A summary of all transactions, called a **bank statement**, is mailed to the depositor or made available online, usually each month. Like any account with a customer or a creditor, the bank statement shows the beginning balance, additions, deductions, and the balance at the end of the period. A typical bank statement is shown in Exhibit 5.

The depositor's checks or copies of the checks received by the bank during the period may accompany the bank statement, arranged in order of payment. If paid checks are returned, they are stamped "Paid," together with the date of payment. Many banks no longer return checks or check copies with bank statements. Instead, the check payment information is available online. Other entries that the bank has made in the depositor's account are described as debit or credit memorandums on the statement.

The depositor's checking account balance *in the bank records* is a liability; thus, in the bank's records, the depositor's account has a credit balance. Since the bank statement is prepared from the bank's point of view, a credit memorandum entry on the bank statement indicates an increase (a credit) in the depositor's account. Likewise, a debit memorandum entry on the bank statement indicates a decrease (a debit) in the depositor's account. This relationship is shown at the bottom of page 361.

A bank makes credit entries (issues credit memoranda) for deposits made by electronic funds transfer, for collections of note receivable for the depositor, for proceeds for a loan to the depositor, for interest earned on the depositor's account, and to correct bank errors. A bank makes debit entries (issues debit memoranda) for payments made by electronic funds transfer, for service charges, for customers' checks returned for not sufficient funds, and to correct bank errors.

EXHIBIT 5

Bank Statement

MEMBER FDIC

**VALLEY NATIONAL BANK
OF LOS ANGELES**

LOS ANGELES, CA 90020-4253   (310)555-5151

POWER NETWORKING
1000 Belkin Street
Los Angeles, CA 90014 -1000

		PAGE 1
ACCOUNT NUMBER	1627042	
FROM 6/30/07	TO 7/31/07	
BALANCE		4,218.60
22 DEPOSITS		13,749.75
52 WITHDRAWALS		14,698.57
3 OTHER DEBITS AND CREDITS		90.00CR
NEW BALANCE		3,359.78

* - - CHECKS AND OTHER DEBITS - - - *			- - DEPOSITS - - *	- - DATE - - *	- - BALANCE - - *
819.40	122.54		585.75	07/01	3,862.41
369.50	732.26	20.15	421.53	07/02	3,162.03
600.00	190.70	52.50	781.30	07/03	3,100.13
25.93	160.00		662.50	07/05	3,576.70
921.20	NSF 300.00		503.18	07/07	2,858.68

32.26	535.09		ACH 932.00	07/29	3,404.40
21.10	126.20		705.21	07/30	3,962.31
	SC 18.00		MS 408.00	07/30	4,353.31
26.12	ACH 1,615.13		648.72	07/31	3,359.78

EC — ERROR CORRECTION   ACH — AUTOMATED CLEARING HOUSE
MS — MISCELLANEOUS
NSF — NOT SUFFICIENT FUNDS   SC — SERVICE CHARGE

* * *   * * *   * * *

THE RECONCILEMENT OF THIS STATEMENT WITH YOUR RECORDS IS ESSENTIAL.
ANY ERROR OR EXCEPTION SHOULD BE REPORTED IMMEDIATELY.

Customers' checks returned for not sufficient funds, called *NSF checks*, are checks that were initially deposited, but were not paid when they were presented to the customer's bank for payment. Since the bank initially credited the check to the depositor's account when it was deposited, the bank debits (issues a debit memorandum) when the check is returned without payment. We discuss the accounting for NSF checks later in this chapter.

The reason for a credit or debit memorandum entry is indicated on the bank statement. For example, Exhibit 5 identifies the following types of credit and debit memorandum entries:

    EC: Error correction to correct bank error.
   NSF: Not sufficient funds check.
    SC: Service charge.
   ACH: Automated Clearing House entry for electronic funds transfer.
    MS: Miscellaneous item such as collection of a note receivable on behalf of
         the depositor or receipt of loan proceeds by the depositor from the bank.

In the preceding list, we have included the notation "ACH" for electronic funds transfers. ACH is a network for clearing electronic funds transfers among individuals, companies, and banks.[7] Because electronic funds transfers may be either deposits or payments, ACH entries may indicate either a debit or credit entry to the depositor's account. Likewise, entries to correct bank errors and miscellaneous items may indicate a debit or credit entry to the depositor's account.

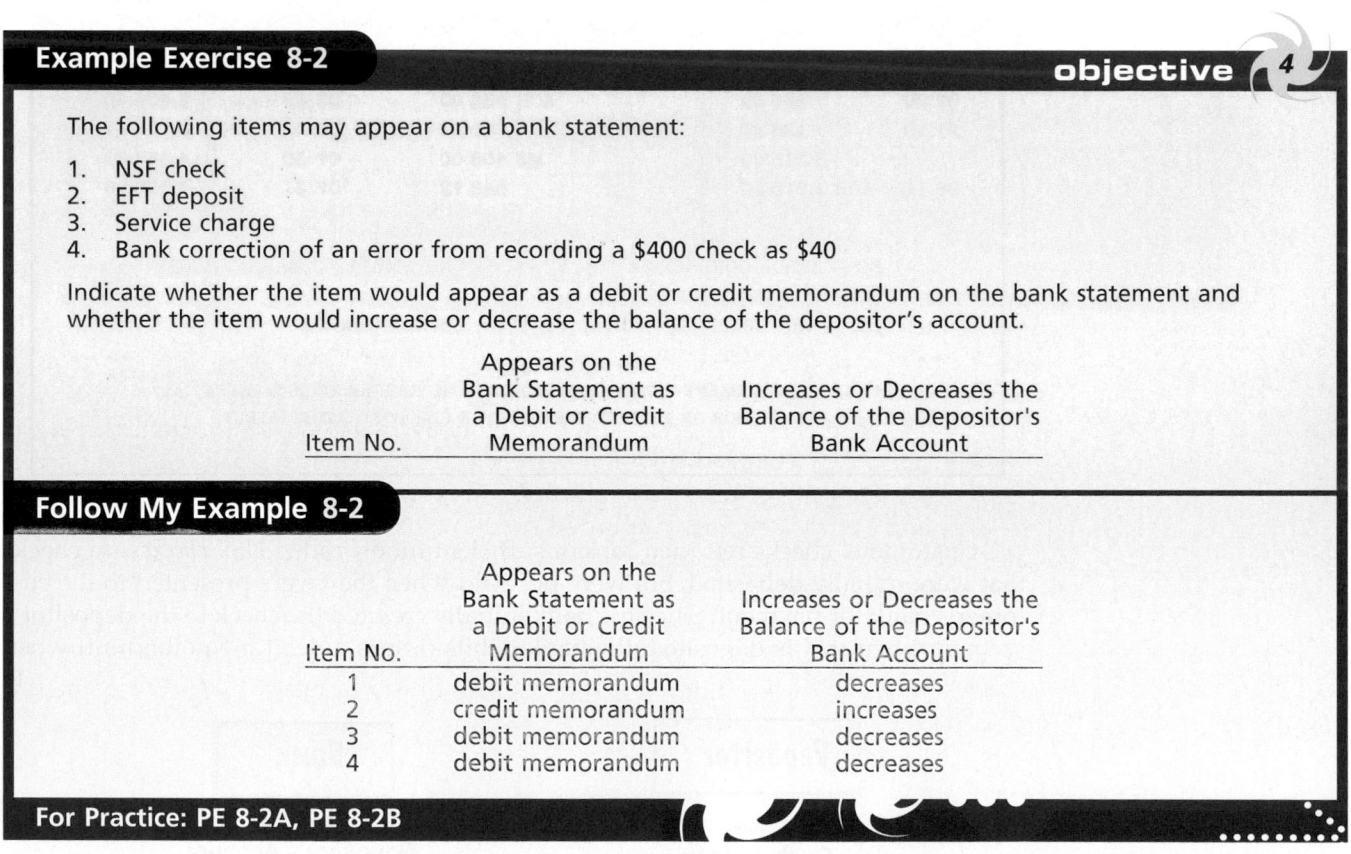

Example Exercise 8-2   objective **4**

The following items may appear on a bank statement:

1. NSF check
2. EFT deposit
3. Service charge
4. Bank correction of an error from recording a $400 check as $40

Indicate whether the item would appear as a debit or credit memorandum on the bank statement and whether the item would increase or decrease the balance of the depositor's account.

Item No.	Appears on the Bank Statement as a Debit or Credit Memorandum	Increases or Decreases the Balance of the Depositor's Bank Account

Follow My Example 8-2

Item No.	Appears on the Bank Statement as a Debit or Credit Memorandum	Increases or Decreases the Balance of the Depositor's Bank Account
1	debit memorandum	decreases
2	credit memorandum	increases
3	debit memorandum	decreases
4	debit memorandum	decreases

For Practice: PE 8-2A, PE 8-2B

BANK ACCOUNTS AS A CONTROL OVER CASH

As we mentioned earlier, a bank account is one of the primary tools a company uses to control cash. For example, companies often require that all cash receipts be initially deposited in a bank account. Likewise, companies usually use checks or bank account

---

7 For further information on ACH, go to **http://www.nacha.org**/. Click on "About Us," and then click on "What is ACH?"

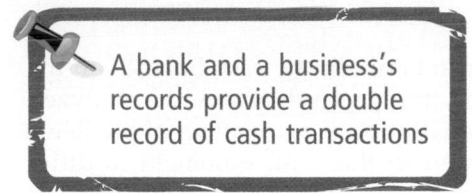

A bank and a business's records provide a double record of cash transactions

transfers to make all cash payments, except for very small amounts. When such a system is used, there is a double record of cash transactions—one by the company and the other by the bank.

A company can use a bank statement to compare the cash transactions recorded in its accounting records to those recorded by the bank. The cash balance shown by a bank statement is usually different from the cash balance shown in the accounting records of the company, as shown in Exhibit 6.

EXHIBIT 6

Power Networking's Records and Bank Statement

Bank Statement		
Beginning balance		$ 4,218.60
Additions:		
Deposits	$13,749.75	
Miscellaneous	408.00	14,157.75
Deductions:		
Checks	$14,698.57	
NSF check	300.00	
Service charge	18.00	15,016.57
Ending balance		$ 3,359.78

Power Networking Records	
Beginning balance	$ 4,227.60
Deposits	14,565.95
Checks	16,243.56
Ending balance	$ 2,549.99

Power Networking should determine the reason for the difference in these two amounts.

This difference may be the result of a delay by either party in recording transactions. For example, there is a time lag of one day or more between the date a check is written and the date that it is presented to the bank for payment. If the company mails deposits to the bank or uses the night depository, a time lag between the date of the deposit and the date that it is recorded by the bank is also probable. The bank may also debit or credit the company's account for transactions about which the company will not be informed until later.

The difference may be the result of errors made by either the company or the bank in recording transactions. For example, the company may incorrectly post to Cash a check written for $4,500 as $450. Likewise, a bank may incorrectly record the amount of a check.

Integrity, Objectivity, and Ethics in Business

ETHICS

CHECK FRAUD

Check fraud involves counterfeiting, altering, or otherwise manipulating the information on checks in order to fraudulently cash a check. According to the National Check Fraud Center, check fraud and counterfeiting are among the fastest growing problems affecting the financial system, generating over $10 billion in losses annually. Criminals perpetrate the fraud by taking blank checks from your checkbook, finding a canceled check in the garbage, or removing a check you have mailed to pay bills. Consumers can prevent check fraud by carefully storing blank checks, placing outgoing mail in postal mailboxes, and shredding canceled checks.

Bank Reconciliation

objective   **5**

Describe and illustrate the use of a bank reconciliation in controlling cash.

For effective control, the reasons for the difference between the cash balance on the bank statement and the cash balance in the accounting records should be analyzed by preparing a bank reconciliation. A **bank reconciliation** is an analysis of the items and amounts that cause the cash balance reported in the bank statement to differ from the balance of the cash account in the ledger in order to determine the adjusted cash balance.

A bank reconciliation is usually divided into two sections. The first section, referred to as the bank section, begins with the cash balance according to the bank statement and ends with the adjusted balance. The second section, referred to as the company section, begins with the cash balance according to the company's records and ends with the adjusted balance. The two amounts designated as the adjusted balance must be equal. The content of the bank reconciliation is shown below.

The following steps are useful in finding the reconciling items and determining the adjusted balance of Cash:

1. Compare each deposit listed on the bank statement with unrecorded deposits appearing in the preceding period's reconciliation and with the current period's deposits. *Add deposits not recorded by the bank to the balance according to the bank statement.*
2. Compare paid checks with outstanding checks appearing on the preceding period's reconciliation and with recorded checks. *Deduct checks outstanding that have not been paid by the bank from the balance according to the bank statement.*
3. Compare bank credit memorandums to entries in the journal. For example, a bank would issue a credit memorandum for a note receivable and interest that it collected for a company. *Add credit memorandums that have not been recorded to the balance according to the company's records.*
4. Compare bank debit memorandums to entries recording cash payments. For example, a bank normally issues debit memorandums for service charges and check printing charges. A bank also issues debit memorandums for not sufficient funds checks. NSF checks are normally charged back to the customer as an account receivable. *Deduct debit memorandums that have not been recorded from the balance according to the company's records.*
5. List any errors discovered during the preceding steps. For example, if an amount has been recorded incorrectly by the company, the amount of the error should be added to or deducted from the cash balance according to the company's records. Similarly, errors by the bank should be added to or deducted from the cash balance according to the bank statement.

To illustrate a bank reconciliation, we will use the bank statement for Power Networking in Exhibit 5. This bank statement shows a balance of $3,359.78 as of July 31. The cash balance in Power Networking's ledger as of the same date is $2,549.99. The following reconciling items are revealed by using the steps outlined above:

Deposit of July 31, not recorded on bank statement	$ 816.20
Checks outstanding: No. 812, $1,061.00; No. 878, $435.39;	
No. 883, $48.60	1,544.99
Note plus interest of $8 collected by bank (credit memorandum), not	
recorded in the journal	408.00
Check from customer (Thomas Ivey) returned by bank because of	
insufficient funds (NSF)	300.00
Bank service charges (debit memorandum), not recorded in the journal	18.00
Check No. 879 for $732.26 to Taylor Co. on account, recorded	
in the journal as $723.26	9.00

The bank reconciliation, based on the bank statement and the reconciling items, is shown in Exhibit 7.

EXHIBIT 7

Bank Reconciliation for Power Networking

Power Networking
Bank Reconciliation
July 31, 2007

Cash balance according to bank statement			$3 3 5 9 78
Add deposit of July 31, not recorded by bank			8 1 6 20
			$4 1 7 5 98
Deduct outstanding checks:			
No. 812	$1 0 6 1 00		
No. 878	4 3 5 39		
No. 883	4 8 60	1 5 4 4 99	
Adjusted balance			$2 6 3 0 99
Cash balance according to Power Networking records			$2 5 4 9 99
Add note and interest collected by bank			4 0 8 00
			$2 9 5 7 99
Deduct: Check returned because of insufficient funds	$ 3 0 0 00		
Bank service charge	1 8 00		
Error in recording Check No. 879	9 00	3 2 7 00	
Adjusted balance			$2 6 3 0 99

No entries are necessary on the company's records as a result of the information included in the bank section of the reconciliation. This section begins with the cash balance according to the bank statement. However, the bank should be notified of any errors that need to be corrected on its records.

Any items in the company's section of the bank reconciliation must be recorded in the company's accounts. For example, journal entries should be made for any unrecorded bank memorandums and any company errors. The journal entries for Power Networking, based on the preceding bank reconciliation, are as follows:

July	31	Cash			4 0 8 00		
		Notes Receivable				4 0 0 00	
		Interest Revenue				8 00	
	31	Accounts Receivable—Thomas Ivey			3 0 0 00		
		Miscellaneous Expense			1 8 00		
		Accounts Payable—Taylor Co.			9 00		
		Cash				3 2 7 00	

After the entries above have been posted, the cash account will have a debit balance of $2,630.99. This balance agrees with the adjusted cash balance shown on the bank reconciliation. This is the amount of cash available as of July 31 and the amount that would be reported on Power Networking's July 31 balance sheet.

Although businesses may reconcile their bank accounts in a slightly different format from what we described above, the objective is the same: to control cash by reconciling the company's records to the records of an independent outside source, the bank. In doing so, any errors or misuse of cash may be detected.

For effective control, the bank reconciliation should be prepared by an employee who does not take part in or record cash transactions. When these duties are not properly separated, mistakes are likely to occur, and it is more likely that cash will be stolen or otherwise misapplied. For example, an employee who takes part in all of these duties could prepare and cash an unauthorized check, omit it from the accounts, and omit it from the reconciliation.

A bank reconciliation is also appropriate in a computerized environment where the deposits and checks are stored in electronic files and records. In some systems, the computer determines the difference between the ending bank balance and the balance per the company's records and then adjusts for deposits in transit and outstanding checks. Any remaining differences are reported for further analysis.

Example Exercise 8-3   objective 5

The following data were gathered to use in reconciling the bank account of Photo Op.

Balance per bank	$14,500
Balance per company records	13,875
Bank service charges	75
Deposit in transit	3,750
NSF check	800
Outstanding checks	5,250

a. What is the adjusted balance on the bank reconciliation?
b. Journalize any necessary entries for Photo Op based upon the bank reconciliation.

Follow My Example 8-3

a. $13,000, as shown below.

Bank section of reconciliation: $14,500 + $3,750 − $5,250 = $13,000
Company section of reconciliation: $13,875 − $75 − $800 = $13,000

b. Accounts Receivable 800
    Miscellaneous Expense 75
       Cash 875

For Practice: PE 8-3A, PE 8-3B

Special-Purpose Cash Funds

objective **6**

Describe the accounting for special-purpose cash funds.

It is usually not practical for a business to write checks to pay small amounts, such as postage. Yet, these small payments may occur often enough to add up to a significant total amount. Thus, it is desirable to control such payments. For this purpose, a special cash fund, called a **petty cash fund**, is used.

A petty cash fund is established by first estimating the amount of cash needed for payments from the fund during a period, such as a week or a month. After necessary approvals, a check is written and cashed for this amount. The money obtained from cashing the check is then given to an employee, called the petty cash custodian, who is authorized to disburse monies from the fund. For control purposes, the company may place restrictions on the maximum amount and the types of payments that can be made from the fund. Each time monies are paid from petty cash, the custodian records the details of the payment on a petty cash receipt form.

The petty cash fund is normally replenished at periodic intervals or when it is depleted or reaches a minimum amount. When a petty cash fund is replenished, the accounts debited are determined by summarizing the petty cash receipts. A check is then written for this amount, payable to petty cash.

To illustrate normal petty cash fund entries, assume that a petty cash fund of $500 is established on August 1. The entry to record this transaction is as follows:

Aug.	1	Petty Cash	5 0 0 00	
		Cash		5 0 0 00

At the end of August, the petty cash receipts indicate expenditures for the following items: office supplies, $380; postage (office supplies), $22; store supplies, $35; and miscellaneous administrative expense, $30. The entry to replenish the petty cash fund on August 31 is as follows:

Aug.	31	Office Supplies	4 0 2 00	
		Store Supplies	3 5 00	
		Miscellaneous Administrative Expense	3 0 00	
		Cash		4 6 7 00

Replenishing the petty cash fund restores it to its original amount of $500. You should note that there is no entry in Petty Cash when the fund is replenished. Petty Cash is debited only when the fund is initially set up or when the amount of the fund is increased at a later time. Petty Cash is credited if it is being decreased.

In addition, businesses often use other cash funds to meet special needs, such as payroll or travel expenses for salespersons. Such funds are called **special-purpose**

funds. For example, each salesperson might be given $200 for travel-related expenses. Periodically, the salesperson submits a detailed expense report and the travel funds are replenished. Also, as we discussed earlier in this chapter, retail businesses use change funds for making change for customers. Finally, most businesses use a payroll bank account to pay employees.

A special-purpose cash fund is initially established by first estimating the amount of cash needed for payments from the fund during a period, such as a week or a month. After necessary approvals, cash is transferred to the special-purpose fund. The employee responsible for disbursing monies from the fund, called the custodian, approves all diburements from the fund. For control purposes, the company may place restrictions on the maximum amount and types of payments that can be made from the fund. Periodically, an independent employee reviews disbursements from the fund, the disbursements are recorded, and the fund is replenished.

Example Exercise 8-4   objective 6

Prepare journal entries for each of the following:

a. Issued a check to establish a petty cash fund of $500.
b. The amount of cash in the petty cash fund is $120. Issued a check to replenish the fund, based on the following summary of petty cash receipts: office supplies, $300 and miscellaneous administrative expense, $75. Record any missing funds in the cash short and over account.

Follow My Example 8-4

a.	Petty Cash	500	
	Cash		500
b.	Office Supplies	300	
	Miscellaneous Administrative Expense	75	
	Cash Short and Over	5	
	Cash		380

For Practice: PE 8-4A, PE 8-4B

Financial Statement Reporting of Cash

objective 7

Describe and illustrate the reporting of cash and cash equivalents in the financial statements.

Cash is the most liquid asset, and therefore it is listed as the first asset in the Current Assets section of the balance sheet. Most companies present only a single cash amount on the balance sheet by combining all their bank and cash fund accounts.

A company may have cash in excess of its operating needs. In such cases, the company normally invests in highly liquid investments in order to earn interest. These investments are called **cash equivalents**.[8] Examples of cash equivalents include U.S. Treasury Bills, notes issued by major corporations (referred to as commercial paper), and money market funds. Companies that have invested excess cash in cash equivalents usually report *Cash and cash equivalents* as one amount on the balance sheet.

Banks may require depositors to maintain minimum cash balances in their bank accounts. Such a balance is called a **compensating balance**. This requirement is often imposed by the

REAL WORLD

In the United Kingdom, the statement of cash flows is prepared using a narrower definition of "cash" than in the United States. Specifically, the United Kingdom does not include cash equivalents, such as certificates of deposit, in its definition of cash as does the United States.

---

8 To be classified a cash equivalent, according to FASB Statement 95, the investment is expected to be converted to cash within 90 days.

bank as a part of a loan agreement or line of credit. A *line of credit* is a preapproved amount the bank is willing to lend to a customer upon request. Compensating balance requirements should be disclosed in notes to the financial statements.

Business Connections

REAL WORLD

MICROSOFT CORPORATION

Microsoft Corporation develops, manufactures, licenses, and supports software products for computing devices. Microsoft software products include computer operating systems, such as Windows, and application software, such as Microsoft Word™ and Excel.™ Microsoft is actively in-volved in the video game market through its Xbox and is also involved in online products and services.

Microsoft is known for its strong cash position. Microsoft's June 30, 2005 balance sheet reported almost $38 billion of cash and short-term investments, as shown below.

Balance Sheet June 30, 2005 (In millions) Assets	
Current assets:	
Cash and equivalents	$ 4,851
Short-term investments	32,900
Total cash and short-term investments	$37,751

The cash and cash equivalents of $4,851 million are further described in the notes to the financial statements, as shown below.

Cash and equivalents:	
Cash	$1,911
Commercial paper	1,570
Certificates of deposit	453
Money market mutual funds	817
Corporate notes and bonds	80
Municipal securities	20
Total cash and equivalents	$4,851

Financial Analysis and Interpretation

For companies that are either starting up or in financial distress, cash is critical for their survival. In their first few years of operations, startup companies often report losses and negative net cash flows. In these cases, the ratio of cash to monthly cash expenses (negative cash flow for operating activities) is useful for assessing how long a company can continue to operate without additional financing or without generating positive cash flows from operations. Likewise, this ratio can be used to assess how long a business may continue to operate when experiencing financial distress. In computing cash to monthly cash expenses, the amount of cash on hand can be taken from the balance sheet, while the monthly cash expenses can be estimated from the operating activities section of the statement of cash flows.

The ratio of cash to monthly cash expenses is computed by first determining the monthly cash expenses. The monthly cash expenses are determined as follows:

$$\text{Monthly Cash Expenses} = \frac{\text{Negative Cash Flows from Operations}}{12}$$

The ratio of cash to monthly cash expenses can then be computed as follows:

$$\text{Ratio of Cash to Monthly Cash Expenses} = \frac{\text{Cash and Cash Equivalents as of Year-End}}{\text{Monthly Cash Expenses}}$$

To illustrate these ratios, we use Northwest Airlines Corporation, a major carrier of passengers and cargo with service to approximately 900 cities in 160 countries. For the year ending December 31, 2005, Northwest Airlines reported the following data (in millions):

Negative cash flows from operations	$ (436)
Cash and cash equivalents as of December 31, 2005	1,284

Based upon the preceding data, the monthly cash expenses, sometimes referred to as cash burn, were $36.3 million per month ($436/12). Thus, as of December 31, 2005, the cash to monthly cash expenses ratio was 35.4 ($1,284/$36.3). That is, as of December 31, 2005, Northwest would run out of cash in less than three years unless it changes its operations, sells investments, or raises additional financing. In September 2005, Northwest Airlines filed for voluntary reorganization under Chapter 11 of the U.S. Bankruptcy Code.

At a Glance

1. Describe the Sarbanes-Oxley Act of 2002 and its impact on internal controls and financial reporting.

Key Points	Key Learning Outcomes	Example Exercises	Practice Exercises
The purpose of the Sarbanes-Oxley Act of 2002 is to restore public confidence and trust in the financial statements of companies. Sarbanes-Oxley requires companies to maintain strong and effective internal controls and to report on the effectiveness of the internal controls.	• Describe why Congress passed Sarbanes-Oxley. • Describe the purpose of Sarbanes-Oxley. • Define *internal control*.		

2. Describe and illustrate the objectives and elements of internal control.

Key Points	Key Learning Outcomes	Example Exercises	Practice Exercises
The objectives of internal control are to provide reasonable assurance that (1) assets are safeguarded and used for business purposes, (2) business information is accurate, and (3) laws and regulations are complied with. The elements of internal control are the control environment, risk assessment, control procedures, monitoring, and information and communication.	• List the objectives of internal control. • List the elements of internal control. • Describe each element of internal control and factors influencing each element.	8-1	8-1A, 8-1B

3. Describe and illustrate the application of internal controls to cash.

Key Points	Key Learning Outcomes	Example Exercises	Practice Exercises
A cash register is one of the most important controls to protect cash received in over-the-counter sales. A remittance advice is a control for cash received through the mail. Separating the duties of handling cash and recording cash is also a control. A voucher system is a control system for cash payments that uses a set of procedures for authorizing and recording liabilities and cash payments. Many companies use electronic funds transfers to enhance their control over cash receipts and cash payments.	• Describe and give examples of controls for cash received from cash sales, cash received in the mail, and cash received by EFT. • Describe and give examples of controls for cash payments made using a voucher system and cash payments made by EFT.		

4. Describe the nature of a bank account and its use in controlling cash.

Key Points	Key Learning Outcomes	Example Exercises	Practice Exercises
Bank accounts help control cash by reducing the amount of cash on hand and facilitating the transfer of cash between businesses and locations. In addition, the bank statement allows a business to reconcile the cash transactions recorded in the accounting records to those recorded by the bank.	• Describe how the use of bank accounts helps control cash. • Describe a bank statement and provide examples of items that appear on a bank statement as debit and credit memoranda.	8-2	8-2A, 8-2B

(continued)

5. Describe and illustrate the use of a bank reconciliation in controlling cash.

Key Points	Key Learning Outcomes	Example Exercises	Practice Exercises
The bank reconciliation begins with the cash balance according to the bank statement. This balance is adjusted for the company's changes in cash that do not appear on the bank statement and for any bank errors. The second section begins with the cash balance according to the company's records. This balance is adjusted for the bank's changes in cash that do not appear on the company's records and for any company errors. The adjusted balances for the two sections must be equal. The items in the company section must be journalized on the company's records.	• Describe a bank reconciliation. • Prepare a bank reconciliation. • Journalize any necessary entries on the company's records based upon the bank reconciliation.	8-3 8-3 8-3	8-3A, 8-3B 8-3A, 8-3B 8-3A, 8-3B

6. Describe the accounting for special-purpose cash funds.

Key Points	Key Learning Outcomes	Example Exercises	Practice Exercises
Special-purpose cash funds, such as a petty cash fund or travel funds, are used by businesses to meet specific needs. Each fund is established by cashing a check for the amount of cash needed. At periodic intervals, the fund is replenished and the disbursements recorded.	• Describe the use of special-purpose cash funds. • Journalize the entry to establish a petty cash fund. • Journalize the entry to replenish a petty cash fund.	8-4 8-4	8-4A, 8-4B 8-4A, 8-4B

7. Describe and illustrate the reporting of cash and cash equivalents in the financial statements.

Key Points	Key Learning Outcomes	Example Exercises	Practice Exercises
Cash is listed as the first asset in the Current Assets section of the balance sheet. Companies that have invested excess cash in highly liquid investments usually report *Cash and cash equivalents* on the balance sheet.	• Describe the reporting of cash and cash equivalents in the financial statements. • Illustrate the reporting of cash and cash equivalents in the financial statements.		

Key Terms

Bank reconciliation (364)
Bank statement (360)
Cash (357)
Cash equivalents (368)
Cash short and over account (357)
Compensating balance (368)

Electronic funds transfer (EFT) (358)
Elements of internal control (351)
Employee fraud (350)
Internal controls (348)
Petty cash fund (367)

Sarbanes-Oxley Act of 2002 (348)
Special-purpose fund (367)
Voucher (359)
Voucher system (359)

Illustrative Problem

The bank statement for Urethane Company for June 30, 2007, indicates a balance of $9,143.11. All cash receipts are deposited each evening in a night depository, after banking hours. The accounting records indicate the following summary data for cash receipts and payments for June:

Cash balance as of June 1	$ 3,943.50
Total cash receipts for June	28,971.60
Total amount of checks issued in June	28,388.85

Comparing the bank statement and the accompanying canceled checks and memoranda with the records reveals the following reconciling items:

a. The bank had collected for Urethane Company $1,030 on a note left for collection. The face amount of the note was $1,000.
b. A deposit of $1,852.21, representing receipts of June 30, had been made too late to appear on the bank statement.
c. Checks outstanding totaled $5,265.27.
d. A check drawn for $139 had been incorrectly charged by the bank as $157.
e. A check for $30 returned with the statement had been recorded in the company's records as $240. The check was for the payment of an obligation to Avery Equipment Company for the purchase of office supplies on account.
f. Bank service charges for June amounted to $18.20.

Instructions

1. Prepare a bank reconciliation for June.
2. Journalize the entries that should be made by Urethane Company.

Solution

1.

Urethane Company Bank Reconciliation June 30, 2007			
Cash balance according to bank statement			$ 9 1 4 3 11
Add: Deposit of June 30 not recorded by bank	$1 8 5 2 21		
Bank error in charging check as $157			
instead of $139		1 8 00	1 8 7 0 21
			$11 0 1 3 32
Deduct: Outstanding checks			5 2 6 5 27
Adjusted balance			$ 5 7 4 8 05
Cash balance according to company's records			$ 4 5 2 6 25 *
Add: Proceeds of note collected by bank,			
including $30 interest	$1 0 3 0 00		
Error in recording check		2 1 0 00	1 2 4 0 00
			$ 5 7 6 6 25
Deduct: Bank service charges			1 8 20
Adjusted balance			$ 5 7 4 8 05
*$3,943.50 + $28,971.60 − $28,388.85			

(continued)

2.

June	30	Cash		1 2 4 0 00	
		Notes Receivable			1 0 0 0 00
		Interest Revenue			3 0 00
		Accounts Payable—Avery Equipment Company			2 1 0 00
	30	Miscellaneous Administrative Expense		1 8 20	
		Cash			1 8 20

Self-Examination Questions

(Answers at End of Chapter)

1. Which of the following is *not* an element of internal control?
   A. Control environment
   B. Monitoring
   C. Compliance with laws and regulations
   D. Control procedures

2. The bank erroneously charged Tropical Services' account for $450.50 for a check that was correctly written and recorded by Tropical Services as $540.50. To reconcile the bank account of Tropical Services at the end of the month, you would:
   A. add $90 to the cash balance according to the bank statement.
   B. add $90 to the cash balance according to Tropical Services' records.
   C. deduct $90 from the cash balance according to the bank statement.
   D. deduct $90 from the cash balance according to Tropical Services' records.

3. In preparing a bank reconciliation, the amount of checks outstanding would be:
   A. added to the cash balance according to the bank statement.

   B. deducted from the cash balance according to the bank statement.
   C. added to the cash balance according to the company's records.
   D. deducted from the cash balance according to the company's records.

4. Journal entries based on the bank reconciliation are required for:
   A. additions to the cash balance according to the company's records.
   B. deductions from the cash balance according to the company's records.
   C. both A and B.
   D. neither A nor B.

5. A petty cash fund is:
   A. used to pay relatively small amounts.
   B. established by estimating the amount of cash needed for disbursements of relatively small amounts during a specified period.
   C. reimbursed when the amount of money in the fund is reduced to a predetermined minimum amount.
   D. all of the above.

Eye Openers

1. (a) Why did Congress pass the Sarbanes-Oxley Act of 2002? (b) What was the purpose of the Sarbanes-Oxley Act of 2002?
2. Define *internal control*.
3. (a) Name and describe the five elements of internal control. (b) Is any one element of internal control more important than another?
4. How does a policy of rotating clerical employees from job to job aid in strengthening the control procedures within the control environment? Explain.
5. Why should the responsibility for a sequence of related operations be divided among different persons? Explain.
6. Why should the employee who handles cash receipts not have the responsibility for maintaining the accounts receivable records? Explain.
7. In an attempt to improve operating efficiency, one employee was made responsible for all purchasing, receiving, and storing of supplies. Is this organizational change wise from an internal control standpoint? Explain.
8. The ticket seller at a movie theater doubles as a ticket taker for a few minutes each day while the ticket taker is on a break. Which control procedure of a business's system of internal control is violated in this situation?

9. Why should the responsibility for maintaining the accounting records be separated from the responsibility for operations? Explain.
10. Assume that Julee Shiver, accounts payable clerk for Galaxy Inc., stole $110,000 by paying fictitious invoices for goods that were never received. The clerk set up accounts in the names of the fictitious companies and cashed the checks at a local bank. Describe a control procedure that would have prevented or detected the fraud.
11. Before a voucher for the purchase of merchandise is approved for payment, supporting documents should be compared to verify the accuracy of the liability. Give an example of supporting documents for the purchase of merchandise.
12. The accounting clerk pays all obligations by prenumbered checks. What are the strengths and weaknesses in the internal control over cash payments in this situation?
13. The balance of Cash is likely to differ from the bank statement balance. What two factors are likely to be responsible for the difference?
14. What is the purpose of preparing a bank reconciliation?
15. Do items reported as credits on the bank statement represent (a) additions made by the bank to the company's balance or (b) deductions made by the bank from the company's balance? Explain.
16. Spectacle Inc. has a petty cash fund of $2,000. (a) Since the petty cash fund is only $2,000, should Spectacle Inc. implement controls over petty cash? (b) What controls, if any, could be used for the petty cash fund?
17. (a) How are cash equivalents reported in the financial statements? (b) What are some examples of cash equivalents?

Practice Exercises

PE 8-1A
Internal control elements
obj. 2

Identify each of the following as relating to (a) the control environment, (b) control procedures, or (c) information and communication.

1. Separating related operations
2. Report of internal auditors
3. Management's philosophy and operating style

PE 8-1B
Internal control elements
obj. 2

Identify each of the following as relating to (a) the control environment, (b) control procedures, or (c) monitoring.

1. Personnel policies
2. Safeguarding inventory in a locked warehouse
3. Hiring of external auditors to review the adequacy of controls

PE 8-2A
Effect of items on depositor's bank account
obj. 4

The following items may appear on a bank statement:

1. Service charge
2. Note collected for depositor
3. Bank correction of an error from recording a $2,100 deposit as $1,200
4. EFT payment

Using the format shown below, indicate whether each item would appear as a debit or credit memorandum on the bank statement and whether the item would increase or decrease the balance of your account.

Item No.	Appears on the Bank Statement as a Debit or Credit Memorandum	Increases or Decreases the Balance of the Depositor's Bank Account

PE 8-2B
Effect of items on depositor's bank account
obj. 4

The following items may appear on a bank statement:

1. Bank correction of an error from posting another customer's check to your account
2. Loan proceeds
3. NSF check
4. EFT deposit

Using the format shown below, indicate whether each item would appear as a debit or credit memorandum on the bank statement and whether the item would increase or decrease the balance of your account.

Item No.	Appears on the Bank Statement as a Debit or Credit Memorandum	Increases or Decreases the Balance of the Depositor's Bank Account

PE 8-3A
Adjusted balance and entries from bank account reconciliation

obj. 5

The following data were gathered to use in reconciling the bank account of Cards Company.

Balance per bank	$9,200
Balance per company records	9,335
Bank service charges	40
Deposit in transit	2,800
NSF check	475
Outstanding checks	3,180

a. What is the adjusted balance on the bank reconciliation?
b. Journalize any necessary entries for Cards Company based upon the bank reconciliation.

PE 8-3B
Adjusted balance and entries from bank account reconciliation

obj. 5

The following data were gathered to use in reconciling the bank account of DRW Company.

Balance per bank	$28,100
Balance per company records	9,155
Bank service charges	80
Deposit in transit	3,100
Note collected by bank with $225 interest	15,225
Outstanding checks	6,900

a. What is the adjusted balance on the bank reconciliation?
b. Journalize any necessary entries for DRW Company based upon the bank reconciliation.

PE 8-4A
Entries for petty cash fund

obj. 6

Prepare journal entries for each of the following:

a. Issued a check to establish a petty cash fund of $600.
b. The amount of cash in the petty cash fund is $175. Issued a check to replenish the fund, based on the following summary of petty cash receipts: repair expense, $350 and miscellaneous selling expense, $55. Record any missing funds in the cash short and over account.

PE 8-4B
Entries for petty cash fund

obj. 6

Prepare journal entries for each of the following:

a. Issued a check to establish a petty cash fund of $400.
b. The amount of cash in the petty cash fund is $85. Issued a check to replenish the fund, based on the following summary of petty cash receipts: store supplies, $180 and miscellaneous selling expense, $110. Record any missing funds in the cash short and over account.

Exercises

EX 8-1
Sarbanes-Oxley internal control report

obj. 1

Using the **http://www.google.com** Advanced Search feature, enter "Sarbanes-Oxley" and click on Google Search. Click on "Summary of Sarbanes-Oxley Act of 2002" that appears as part of the aipca.org Web site. Scan the summary of the act and read Section 404.
　　　　　　 What does Section 404 require of management's internal control report?

EX 8-2
Internal controls
objs. 2, 3

Tyler Kirsch has recently been hired as the manager of Dark Canyon Coffee. Dark Canyon Coffee is a national chain of franchised coffee shops. During his first month as store manager, Tyler encountered the following internal control situations:

a. Dark Canyon Coffee has one cash register. Prior to Tyler's joining the coffee shop, each employee working on a shift would take a customer order, accept payment, and then prepare the order. Tyler made one employee on each shift responsible for taking orders and accepting the customer's payment. Other employees prepare the orders.

b. Since only one employee uses the cash register, that employee is responsible for counting the cash at the end of the shift and verifying that the cash in the drawer matches the amount of cash sales recorded by the cash register. Tyler expects each cashier to balance the drawer to the penny *every* time—no exceptions.

c. Tyler caught an employee putting a box of 100 single-serving tea bags in his car. Not wanting to create a scene, Tyler smiled and said, "I don't think you're putting those tea bags on the right shelf. Don't they belong inside the coffee shop?" The employee returned the tea bags to the stockroom.

State whether you agree or disagree with Tyler's method of handling each situation and explain your answer.

EX 8-3
Internal controls
objs. 2, 3

Rare Earth Clothing is a retail store specializing in women's clothing. The store has established a liberal return policy for the holiday season in order to encourage gift purchases. Any item purchased during November and December may be returned through January 31, with a receipt, for cash or exchange. If the customer does not have a receipt, cash will still be refunded for any item under $100. If the item is more than $100, a check is mailed to the customer.

Whenever an item is returned, a store clerk completes a return slip, which the customer signs. The return slip is placed in a special box. The store manager visits the return counter approximately once every two hours to authorize the return slips. Clerks are instructed to place the returned merchandise on the proper rack on the selling floor as soon as possible.

This year, returns at Rare Earth Clothing have reached an all-time high. There are a large number of returns under $100 without receipts.

a. How can sales clerks employed at Rare Earth Clothing use the store's return policy to steal money from the cash register?

b. What internal control weaknesses do you see in the return policy that make cash thefts easier?

c. Would issuing a store credit in place of a cash refund for all merchandise returned without a receipt reduce the possibility of theft? List some advantages and disadvantages of issuing a store credit in place of a cash refund.

d. Assume that Rare Earth Clothing is committed to the current policy of issuing cash refunds without a receipt. What changes could be made in the store's procedures regarding customer refunds in order to improve internal control?

EX 8-4
Internal controls for bank lending
objs. 2, 3

First Capone Bank provides loans to businesses in the community through its Commercial Lending Department. Small loans (less than $125,000) may be approved by an individual loan officer, while larger loans (greater than $125,000) must be approved by a board of loan officers. Once a loan is approved, the funds are made available to the loan applicant under agreed-upon terms. The president of First Capone Bank has instituted a policy whereby she has the individual authority to approve loans up to $4,000,000. The president believes that this policy will allow flexibility to approve loans to valued clients much quicker than under the previous policy.

As an internal auditor of First Capone Bank, how would you respond to this change in policy?

EX 8-5
Internal controls
objs. 2, 3

One of the largest fraud losses in history involved a securities trader for the Singapore office of Barings Bank, a British merchant bank. The trader established an unauthorized account number that was used to hide $1.4 billion in losses. Even after Barings' internal auditors noted that the trader both executed trades and recorded them, management did not take action. As a result, a lone individual in a remote office bankrupted an internationally recognized firm overnight.

What general weaknesses in Barings' internal controls contributed to the occurrence and size of the fraud?

EX 8-6
Internal controls
objs. 2, 3

An employee of JHT Holdings, Inc., a trucking company, was responsible for resolving roadway accident claims under $25,000. The employee created fake accident claims and wrote settlement checks of between $5,000 and $25,000 to friends or acquaintances acting as phony "victims." One friend recruited subordinates at his place of work to cash some of the checks. Beyond this, the JHT employee also recruited lawyers, who he paid to represent both the trucking company and the fake victims in the bogus accident settlements. When the lawyers cashed the checks, they allegedly split the money with the corrupt JHT employee. This fraud went undetected for two years.

Why would it take so long to discover such a fraud?

EX 8-7
Internal controls
objs. 2, 3

Quality Sound Co. discovered a fraud whereby one of its front office administrative employees used company funds to purchase goods, such as computers, digital cameras, compact disk players, and other electronic items for her own use. The fraud was discovered when employees noticed an increase in delivery frequency from vendors and the use of unusual vendors. After some investigation, it was discovered that the employee would alter the description or change the quantity on an invoice in order to explain the cost on the bill.

What general internal control weaknesses contributed to this fraud?

EX 8-8
Financial statement fraud
objs. 2, 3

A former chairman, CFO, and controller of Donnkenny, Inc., an apparel company that makes sportswear for Pierre Cardin and Victoria Jones, pleaded guilty to financial statement fraud. These managers used false journal entries to record fictitious sales, hid inventory in public warehouses so that it could be recorded as "sold," and required sales orders to be backdated so that the sale could be moved back to an earlier period. The combined effect of these actions caused $25 million out of $40 million in quarterly sales to be phony.

a. Why might control procedures listed in this chapter be insufficient in stopping this type of fraud?
b. How could this type of fraud be stopped?

EX 8-9
Internal control of cash receipts
objs. 2, 3

The procedures used for over-the-counter receipts are as follows. At the close of each day's business, the sales clerks count the cash in their respective cash drawers, after which they determine the amount recorded by the cash register and prepare the memorandum cash form, noting any discrepancies. An employee from the cashier's office counts the cash, compares the total with the memorandum, and takes the cash to the cashier's office.

a. Indicate the weak link in internal control.
b. How can the weakness be corrected?

EX 8-10
Internal control of cash receipts
objs. 2, 3

Amber Meehan works at the drive-through window of Jackpot Burgers. Occasionally, when a drive-through customer orders, Amber fills the order and pockets the customer's money. She does not ring up the order on the cash register.

Identify the internal control weaknesses that exist at Jackpot Burgers, and discuss what can be done to prevent this theft.

EX 8-11
Internal control of cash receipts
objs. 2, 3

The mailroom employees send all remittances and remittance advices to the cashier. The cashier deposits the cash in the bank and forwards the remittance advices and duplicate deposit slips to the Accounting Department.

a. Indicate the weak link in internal control in the handling of cash receipts.
b. How can the weakness be corrected?

EX 8-12
Entry for cash sales; cash short
objs. 2, 3

The actual cash received from cash sales was $21,099.75, and the amount indicated by the cash register total was $21,114.26. Journalize the entry to record the cash receipts and cash sales.

EX 8-13
Entry for cash sales; cash over
objs. 2, 3

The actual cash received from cash sales was $8,374.58, and the amount indicated by the cash register total was $8,351.14. Journalize the entry to record the cash receipts and cash sales.

EX 8-14
Internal control of cash payments
objs. 2, 3

Paul's Rama Co. is a medium-size merchandising company. An investigation revealed that in spite of a sufficient bank balance, a significant amount of available cash discounts had been lost because of failure to make timely payments. In addition, it was discovered that the invoices for several purchases had been paid twice.

Outline procedures for the payment of vendors' invoices, so that the possibilities of losing available cash discounts and of paying an invoice a second time will be minimized.

EX 8-15
Internal control of cash payments
objs. 2, 3

Clear Voice Company, a communications equipment manufacturer, recently fell victim to a fraud scheme developed by one of its employees. To understand the scheme, it is necessary to review Clear Voice's procedures for the purchase of services.

The purchasing agent is responsible for ordering services (such as repairs to a photocopy machine or office cleaning) after receiving a service requisition from an authorized manager. However, since no tangible goods are delivered, a receiving report is not prepared. When the Accounting Department receives an invoice billing Clear Voice for a service call, the accounts payable clerk calls the manager who requested the service in order to verify that it was performed.

The fraud scheme involves Dana Foley, the manager of plant and facilities. Dana arranged for her uncle's company, Foley Industrial Supply and Service, to be placed on Clear Voice's approved vendor list. Dana did not disclose the family relationship.

On several occasions, Dana would submit a requisition for services to be provided by Foley Industrial Supply and Service. However, the service requested was really not needed, and it was never performed. Foley would bill Clear Voice for the service and then split the cash payment with Dana.

Explain what changes should be made to Clear Voice's procedures for ordering and paying for services in order to prevent such occurrences in the future.

EX 8-16
Bank reconciliation
obj. 5

Identify each of the following reconciling items as: (a) an addition to the cash balance according to the bank statement, (b) a deduction from the cash balance according to the bank statement, (c) an addition to the cash balance according to the company's records, or (d) a deduction from the cash balance according to the company's records. (None of the transactions reported by bank debit and credit memoranda have been recorded by the company.)

1. Bank service charges, $48.
2. Outstanding checks, $8,125.50.
3. Deposit in transit, $12,200.
4. Note collected by bank, $8,750.
5. Check drawn by company for $150 but incorrectly recorded as $510.
6. Check for $200 incorrectly charged by bank as $2,000.
7. Check of a customer returned by bank to company because of insufficient funds, $1,200.

EX 8-17
Entries based on bank reconciliation
obj. 5

Which of the reconciling items listed in Exercise 8-16 require an entry in the company's accounts?

EX 8-18

Bank reconciliation

obj. 5

✓ *Adjusted balance:*
$8,506.50

The following data were accumulated for use in reconciling the bank account of Spectrum Co. for July:

a. Cash balance according to the company's records at July 31, $8,346.50.
b. Cash balance according to the bank statement at July 31, $9,066.35.
c. Checks outstanding, $3,175.25.
d. Deposit in transit, not recorded by bank, $2,615.40.
e. A check for $240 in payment of an account was erroneously recorded in the check register as $420.
f. Bank debit memorandum for service charges, $20.00.

Prepare a bank reconciliation, using the format shown in Exhibit 7.

EX 8-19

Entries for bank reconciliation

obj. 5

Using the data presented in Exercise 8-18, journalize the entry or entries that should be made by the company.

EX 8-20

Entries for note collected by bank

obj. 5

Accompanying a bank statement for Bionics Company is a credit memorandum for $17,750, representing the principal ($15,000) and interest ($2,750) on a note that had been collected by the bank. The depositor had been notified by the bank at the time of the collection, but had made no entries. Journalize the entry that should be made by the depositor to bring the accounting records up to date.

EX 8-21

Bank reconciliation

obj. 5

✓ *Adjusted balance:*
$15,175.60

An accounting clerk for Lock-It Co. prepared the following bank reconciliation:

Lock-It Co.
Bank Reconciliation
October 31, 2008

Cash balance according to company's records		$ 9,305.60
Add: Outstanding checks	$ 7,115.35	
Error by Lock-It Co. in recording Check		
No. 1007 as $4,715 instead of $4,175	540.00	
Note for $5,000 collected by bank, including interest	5,375.00	13,030.35
		$22,335.95
Deduct: Deposit in transit on October 31	$13,690.45	
Bank service charges	45.00	13,735.45
Cash balance according to bank statement		$ 8,600.50

a. From the data in the above bank reconciliation, prepare a new bank reconciliation for Lock-It Co., using the format shown in the illustrative problem.
b. If a balance sheet were prepared for Lock-It Co. on October 31, 2008, what amount should be reported for cash?

EX 8-22

Bank reconciliation

obj. 5

✓ *Corrected adjusted balance: $9,000.00*

Identify the errors in the following bank reconciliation:

Mkabe Co.
Bank Reconciliation
For the Month Ended June 30, 2008

Cash balance according to bank statement		$ 7,560.14
Add outstanding checks:		
No. 315	$ 717.42	
360	617.11	
364	906.15	
365	1,501.50	3,742.18
		$11,302.32
Deduct deposit of June 30, not recorded by bank		5,182.04
Adjusted balance		$ 7,120.28

(continued)

Cash balance according to company's records		$ 3,735.70
Add: Proceeds of note collected by bank:		
Principal $6,000.00		
Interest 180.00	$6,180.00	
Service charges	27.00	6,207.00
		$ 9,942.70
Deduct: Check returned because of		
insufficient funds	$1,158.70	
Error in recording June 15		
deposit of $3,960 as $3,690	270.00	1,428.70
Adjusted balance		$ 8,514.00

EX 8-23
Using bank reconciliation to determine cash receipts stolen
obj. 5

Argonaut Co. records all cash receipts on the basis of its cash register tapes. Argonaut Co. discovered during November 2008 that one of its sales clerks had stolen an undetermined amount of cash receipts when she took the daily deposits to the bank. The following data have been gathered for November:

Cash in bank according to the general ledger	$12,510.45
Cash according to the November 30, 2008 bank statement	22,060.65
Outstanding checks as of November 30, 2008	6,381.42
Bank service charge for November	35.00
Note receivable, including interest collected by bank in November	7,140.00

No deposits were in transit on November 30, which fell on a Sunday.

a. Determine the amount of cash receipts stolen by the sales clerk.
b. ➤ What accounting controls would have prevented or detected this theft?

EX 8-24
Petty cash fund entries
obj. 6

Journalize the entries to record the following:

a. Check No. 6172 is issued to establish a petty cash fund of $1,000.
b. The amount of cash in the petty cash fund is now $239.16. Check No. 6319 is issued to replenish the fund, based on the following summary of petty cash receipts: office supplies, $379.10; miscellaneous selling expense, $216.25; miscellaneous administrative expense, $143.06. (Since the amount of the check to replenish the fund plus the balance in the fund do not equal $1,000, record the discrepancy in the cash short and over account.)

EX 8-25
Variation in cash flows
obj. 7

REAL WORLD

Mattel, Inc. designs, manufactures, and markets toy products worldwide. Mattel's toys include Barbie™ fashion dolls and accessories, Hot Wheels™, and Fisher-Price brands. For a recent year, Mattel reported the following net cash flows from operating activities (in thousands):

First quarter ending March 31, 2005	$(374,933)
Second quarter ending June 30, 2005	(551,080)
Third quarter ending September 30, 2005	(629,006)
Year ending December 31, 2005	466,677

➤ Explain how Mattel can report negative net cash flows from operating activities during the first three quarters yet report net positive cash flows on December 31.

EX 8-26
Cash to monthly cash expenses ratio

During 2007, Kinetic Inc. has monthly cash expenses of $175,000. On December 31, 2007, the cash balance is $1,575,000.

a. Compute the ratio of cash to monthly cash expenses.
b. ➤ Based upon (a), what are the implications for Kinetic Inc.?

EX 8-27
Cash to monthly cash expenses ratio

Delta Air Lines is one of the major airlines in the United States and the world. It provides passengers and cargo services for over 200 domestic U.S. cities as well as 70 international cities. It operates a fleet of over 800 aircraft and is headquartered in Atlanta, Georgia.

Delta reported the following financial data (in millions) for the year ended December 31, 2004:

Net cash flows from operating activities	$(1,123)
Cash, December 31, 2004	1,811

a. Determine the monthly cash expenses. Round to one decimal place.
b. Determine the ratio of cash to monthly expenses. Round to one decimal place.
c. ▭▭▭▶ Based upon your analysis, do you believe that Delta will remain in business?

EX 8-28

Cash to monthly cash expenses ratio

Hyperspace Communications, Inc., engages in the development, manufacture, and marketing of network acceleration and data compression software worldwide. Its software products speed up the delivery of information over computer networks, including the Internet, wireless, broadband, private, and dial-up networks. Hyperspace reported the following data (in thousands) for the years ending December 31:

	2005	2004
Net cash flows from operating activities	$(7,827)	$(2,558)
Cash, December 31	3,897	5,875

a. Determine the monthly cash expenses for 2005 and 2004. Round to one decimal place.
b. Determine the ratio of cash to monthly expenses for December 31, 2005 and 2004. Round to one decimal place.
c. ▭▭▭▶ Based upon (a) and (b), what are the implications for Hyperspace?

Problems Series A

PR 8-1A

Evaluating internal control of cash

objs. 2, 3

The following procedures were recently installed by Sacha's Company:

a. The accounts payable clerk prepares a voucher for each disbursement. The voucher along with the supporting documentation is forwarded to the treasurer's office for approval.
b. After necessary approvals have been obtained for the payment of a voucher, the treasurer signs and mails the check. The treasurer then stamps the voucher and supporting documentation as paid and returns the voucher and supporting documentation to the accounts payable clerk for filing.
c. Along with petty cash expense receipts for postage, office supplies, etc., several post-dated employee checks are in the petty cash fund.
d. At the end of the day, cash register clerks are required to use their own funds to make up any cash shortages in their registers.
e. All mail is opened by the mail clerk, who forwards all cash remittances to the cashier. The cashier prepares a listing of the cash receipts and forwards a copy of the list to the accounts receivable clerk for recording in the accounts.
f. At the end of each day, any deposited cash receipts are placed in the bank's night depository.
g. At the end of each day, an accounting clerk compares the duplicate copy of the daily cash deposit slip with the deposit receipt obtained from the bank.
h. The bank reconciliation is prepared by the cashier, who works under the supervision of the treasurer.

Instructions

▭▭▭▶ Indicate whether each of the procedures of internal control over cash represents (1) a strength or (2) a weakness. For each weakness, indicate why it exists.

PR 8-2A

Transactions for petty cash, cash short and over

objs. 3, 6

Ivan's Restoration Company completed the following selected transactions during October 2008:

Oct. 1. Established a petty cash fund of $750.
   15. The cash sales for the day, according to the cash register records, totaled $9,702.38. The actual cash received from cash sales was $9,752.38.
   31. Petty cash on hand was $40.75. Replenished the petty cash fund for the following disbursements, each evidenced by a petty cash receipt:

   Oct. 4. Store supplies, $217.30.
        8. Express charges on merchandise sold, $150 (Delivery Expense).
        9. Office supplies, $13.75.
       18. Office supplies, $27.80.
       19. Postage stamps, $11.70 (Office Supplies).
       21. Repair to office file cabinet lock, $50.00 (Miscellaneous Administrative Expense).
       23. Postage due on special delivery letter, $21.95 (Miscellaneous Administrative Expense).
       24. Express charges on merchandise sold, $165 (Delivery Expense).
       29. Office supplies, $26.85.
   31. The cash sales for the day, according to the cash register records, totaled $10,125.95. The actual cash received from cash sales was $10,123.05.
   31. Increased the petty cash fund by $150.

Instructions
Journalize the transactions.

PR 8-3A

Bank reconciliation and entries

obj. 5

✓ 1. Adjusted balance: $12,110.30

The cash account for Bonita Medical Co. at September 30, 2008, indicated a balance of $5,335.30. The bank statement indicated a balance of $5,604.60 on September 30, 2008. Comparing the bank statement and the accompanying canceled checks and memoranda with the records revealed the following reconciling items:

a. Checks outstanding totaled $4,790.45.
b. A deposit of $9,226.15, representing receipts of September 30, had been made too late to appear on the bank statement.
c. The bank had collected $7,725 on a note left for collection. The face of the note was $7,500.
d. A check for $4,315 returned with the statement had been incorrectly recorded by Bonita Medical Co. as $3,415. The check was for the payment of an obligation to Rowe Co. for the purchase of office equipment on account.
e. A check drawn for $230 had been erroneously charged by the bank as $2,300.
f. Bank service charges for September amounted to $50.

Instructions
1. Prepare a bank reconciliation.
2. Journalize the necessary entries. The accounts have not been closed.

PR 8-4A

Bank reconciliation and entries

obj. 5

✓ 1. Adjusted balance: $9,175.15

The cash account for Cabrillo Co. at March 1, 2008, indicated a balance of $10,676.67. During March, the total cash deposited was $39,146.38, and checks written totaled $42,918.40. The bank statement indicated a balance of $10,960.06 on March 31. Comparing the bank statement, the canceled checks, and the accompanying memoranda with the records revealed the following reconciling items:

a. Checks outstanding totaled $11,008.25.
b. A deposit of $8,773.34, representing receipts of March 31, had been made too late to appear on the bank statement.
c. The bank had collected for Cabrillo Co. $3,710 on a note left for collection. The face of the note was $3,500.
d. A check for $380 returned with the statement had been incorrectly charged by the bank as $830.

e. A check for $419 returned with the statement had been recorded by Cabrillo Co. as $149. The check was for the payment of an obligation to Graven Co. on account.

f. Bank service charges for March amounted to $40.

g. A check for $1,129.50 from Kane-Miller Co. was returned by the bank because of insufficient funds.

Instructions

1. Prepare a bank reconciliation as of March 31.
2. Journalize the necessary entries. The accounts have not been closed.

PR 8-5A
Bank reconciliation and entries

obj. 5

✓ *1. Adjusted balance: $12,822.02*

Pacific Furniture Company deposits all cash receipts each Wednesday and Friday in a night depository, after banking hours. The data required to reconcile the bank statement as of June 30 have been taken from various documents and records and are reproduced as follows. The sources of the data are printed in capital letters. All checks were written for payments on account.

JUNE BANK STATEMENT:

		MEMBER FDIC			PAGE 1

AMERICAN NATIONAL BANK OF DETROIT
DETROIT, MI 48201-2500   (313)933-8547

ACCOUNT NUMBER
FROM 6/01/20–   TO 6/30/20–

BALANCE		9,447.20
9 DEPOSITS		8,691.77
20 WITHDRAWALS		7,345.91
4 OTHER DEBITS AND CREDITS		2,298.70CR
NEW BALANCE		13,091.76

PACIFIC FURNITURE COMPANY

--- CHECKS AND OTHER DEBITS ---		*-- DEPOSITS --*	*- DATE -*	*-- BALANCE--*
No.731 162.15	No.738 251.40	690.25	6/01	9,723.90
No.739 60.55	No.740 237.50	1,080.50	6/02	10,506.35
No.741 495.15	No.742 501.90	854.17	6/04	10,363.47
No.743 671.30	No.744 506.88	840.50	6/09	10,025.79
No.745 117.25	No.746 298.66	MS 2,500.00	6/09	12,109.88
No.748 450.90	No.749 640.13	MS 125.00	6/09	11,143.85
No.750 276.77	No.751 299.37	896.61	6/11	11,464.32
No.752 537.01	No.753 380.95	882.95	6/16	11,429.31
No.754 449.75	No.756 113.95	1,606.74	6/18	12,472.35
No.757 407.95	No.760 486.39	897.34	6/23	12,475.35
		942.71	6/25	13,418.06
	NSF 291.90		6/28	13,126.16
	SC 34.40		6/30	13,091.76

EC — ERROR CORRECTION	OD — OVERDRAFT
MS — MISCELLANEOUS	PS — PAYMENT STOPPED
NSF — NOT SUFFICIENT FUNDS	SC — SERVICE CHARGE

* * *   * * *   * * *

THE RECONCILEMENT OF THIS STATEMENT WITH YOUR RECORDS IS ESSENTIAL.
ANY ERROR OR EXCEPTION SHOULD BE REPORTED IMMEDIATELY.

CASH ACCOUNT:
Balance as of June 1 $9,317.40

CASH RECEIPTS FOR MONTH OF JUNE $9,565.31

DUPLICATE DEPOSIT TICKETS:
Date and amount of each deposit in June:

Date	Amount	Date	Amount	Date	Amount
June 1	$1,080.50	June 10	$ 896.61	June 22	$ 897.34
3	854.17	15	882.95	24	942.71
8	840.50	17	1,660.47	30	1,510.06

CHECKS WRITTEN:
Number and amount of each check issued in June:

Check No.	Amount	Check No.	Amount	Check No.	Amount
740	$237.50	747	Void	754	$ 449.75
741	495.15	748	$450.90	755	272.75
742	501.90	749	640.31	756	113.95
743	671.30	750	276.77	757	407.95
744	506.88	751	299.37	758	259.60
745	117.25	752	537.01	759	901.50
746	298.66	753	380.95	760	486.39

Total amount of checks issued in June $8,305.84

BANK RECONCILIATION FOR PRECEDING MONTH:

Pacific Furniture Company
Bank Reconciliation
May 31, 20—

Cash balance according to bank statement		$ 9,447.20
Add deposit for May 31, not recorded by bank		690.25
		$10,137.45
Deduct outstanding checks:		
No. 731	$162.15	
736	345.95	
738	251.40	
739	60.55	820.05
Adjusted balance		$ 9,317.40
Cash balance according to depositor's records		$ 9,352.50
Deduct service charges		35.10
Adjusted balance		$ 9,317.40

Instructions

1. Prepare a bank reconciliation as of June 30. If errors in recording deposits or checks are discovered, assume that the errors were made by the company. Assume that all deposits are from cash sales. All checks are written to satisfy accounts payable.
2. Journalize the necessary entries. The accounts have not been closed.
3. What is the amount of Cash that should appear on the balance sheet as of June 30?
4. ▬▬▶ Assume that a canceled check for $390 has been incorrectly recorded by the bank as $930. Briefly explain how the error would be included in a bank reconciliation and how it should be corrected.

Problems Series B

PR 8-1B
Evaluate internal control of cash
objs. 2, 3

The following procedures were recently installed by The Insideout Company:

a. All sales are rung up on the cash register, and a receipt is given to the customer. All sales are recorded on a record locked inside the cash register.
b. Vouchers and all supporting documents are perforated with a PAID designation after being paid by the treasurer.

c. Checks received through the mail are given daily to the accounts receivable clerk for recording collections on account and for depositing in the bank.

d. At the end of a shift, each cashier counts the cash in his or her cash register, unlocks the cash register record, and compares the amount of cash with the amount on the record to determine cash shortages and overages.

e. Each cashier is assigned a separate cash register drawer to which no other cashier has access.

f. Disbursements are made from the petty cash fund only after a petty cash receipt has been completed and signed by the payee.

g. The bank reconciliation is prepared by the accountant.

Instructions

➤ Indicate whether each of the procedures of internal control over cash represents (1) a strength or (2) a weakness. For each weakness, indicate why it exists.

PR 8-2B
Transactions for petty cash, cash short and over
objs. 3, 6

Avalanche Company completed the following selected transactions during April 2008:

Apr. 1. Established a petty cash fund of $900.

4. The cash sales for the day, according to the cash register records, totaled $12,099.69. The actual cash received from cash sales was $12,115.42.

30. Petty cash on hand was $118.40. Replenished the petty cash fund for the following disbursements, each evidenced by a petty cash receipt:

April 4. Store supplies, $62.18.

9. Express charges on merchandise purchased, $116.30 (Merchandise Inventory).

12. Office supplies, $42.80.

15. Office supplies, $119.82.

19. Postage stamps, $78.00 (Office Supplies).

20. Repair to fax, $205.00 (Miscellaneous Administrative Expense).

21. Repair to office door lock, $51.50 (Miscellaneous Administrative Expense).

22. Postage due on special delivery letter, $24.10 (Miscellaneous Administrative Expense).

27. Express charges on merchandise purchased, $75.40 (Merchandise Inventory).

30. The cash sales for the day, according to the cash register records, totaled $13,800.60. The actual cash received from cash sales was $13,774.90.

30. Decreased the petty cash fund by $100.

Instructions
Journalize the transactions.

PR 8-3B
Bank reconciliation and entries
obj. 5

✓ *1. Adjusted balance: $19,278.13*

The cash account for Turbocharged Systems at February 29, 2008, indicated a balance of $8,608.13. The bank statement indicated a balance of $17,877.63 on February 29, 2008. Comparing the bank statement and the accompanying canceled checks and memoranda with the records reveals the following reconciling items:

a. Checks outstanding totaled $9,652.40.

b. A deposit of $11,322.90, representing receipts of February 29, had been made too late to appear on the bank statement.

c. The bank had collected $10,250 on a note left for collection. The face of the note was $10,000.

d. A check for $2,380 returned with the statement had been incorrectly recorded by Turbocharged Systems as $2,830. The check was for the payment of an obligation to Yanni Co. for the purchase of office supplies on account.

e. A check drawn for $960 had been incorrectly charged by the bank as $690.

f. Bank service charges for February amounted to $30.

Instructions
1. Prepare a bank reconciliation.
2. Journalize the necessary entries. The accounts have not been closed.

PR 8-4B
Bank reconciliation and entries
obj. 5

✓1. *Adjusted balance:*
$29,615.50

The cash account for Black Diamond Sports Co. on November 1, 2008, indicated a balance of $23,326.69. During November, the total cash deposited was $118,125.41, and checks written totaled $115,650.10. The bank statement indicated a balance of $24,226.75 on November 30, 2008. Comparing the bank statement, the canceled checks, and the accompanying memoranda with the records revealed the following reconciling items:

a. Checks outstanding totaled $12,673.40.
b. A deposit of $18,332.15, representing receipts of November 30, had been made too late to appear on the bank statement.
c. A check for $850 had been incorrectly charged by the bank as $580.
d. A check for $39.30 returned with the statement had been recorded by Black Diamond Sports Co. as $393.00. The check was for the payment of an obligation to Locke & Son on account.
e. The bank had collected for Black Diamond Sports Co. $4,590 on a note left for collection. The face of the note was $4,500.
f. Bank service charges for November amounted to $50.
g. A check for $1,080.20 from Kalina Co. was returned by the bank because of insufficient funds.

Instructions
1. Prepare a bank reconciliation as of November 30.
2. Journalize the necessary entries. The accounts have not been closed.

PR 8-5B
Bank reconciliation and entries
obj. 5

✓1. *Adjusted balance:*
$12,644.09

Vintage Interiors deposits all cash receipts each Wednesday and Friday in a night depository, after banking hours. The data required to reconcile the bank statement as of July 31 have been taken from various documents and records and are reproduced as follows. The sources of the data are printed in capital letters. All checks were written for payments on account.

BANK RECONCILIATION FOR PRECEDING MONTH (DATED JUNE 30):

Cash balance according to bank statement		$ 9,422.80
Add deposit of June 30, not recorded by bank		780.80
		$10,203.60
Deduct outstanding checks:		
No. 580	$310.10	
No. 602	85.50	
No. 612	92.50	
No. 613	137.50	625.60
Adjusted balance		$ 9,578.00
Cash balance according to company's records		$ 9,605.70
Deduct service charges		27.70
Adjusted balance		$ 9,578.00

CASH ACCOUNT:

Balance as of July 1	$9,578.00

CHECKS WRITTEN:
Number and amount of each check issued in July:

Check No.	Amount	Check No.	Amount	Check No.	Amount
614	$243.50	621	$309.50	628	$ 837.70
615	350.10	622	Void	629	329.90
616	279.90	623	Void	630	882.80
617	395.50	624	707.01	631	1,081.56
618	435.40	625	518.63	632	62.40
619	320.10	626	550.03	633	310.08
620	238.87	627	318.73	634	503.30

Total amount of checks issued in July	$8,675.01

JULY BANK STATEMENT:

				MEMBER FDIC		PAGE 1

AMERICAN NATIONAL BANK OF DETROIT

DETROIT, MI 48201-2500　(313)933-8547

VINTAGE INTERIORS

ACCOUNT NUMBER

FROM 7/01/20– TO 7/31/20–	
BALANCE	9,422.80
9 DEPOSITS	6,086.35
20 WITHDRAWALS	7,514.11
4 OTHER DEBITS AND CREDITS	5,150.50CR
NEW BALANCE	13,145.54

– – – – – CHECKS AND OTHER DEBITS – – – – –– DEPOSITS –*– DATE –*– BALANCE–*

No.580	310.10	No.612	92.50	780.80	07/01	9,801.00
No.613	137.50	No.614	243.50	569.50	07/03	9,989.50
No.615	350.10	No.616	279.90	701.80	07/06	10,061.30
No.617	395.50	No.618	435.40	819.24	07/11	10,049.64
No.619	320.10	No.620	238.87	580.70	07/13	10,071.37
No.621	309.50	No.624	707.01	MS 5,000.00	07/14	14,054.86
No.625	158.63	No.626	550.03	MS 400.00	07/14	13,746.20
No.627	318.73	No.629	329.90	600.10	07/17	13,697.67
No.630	882.80	No.631	1,081.56 NSF 225.40		07/20	11,507.91
No.632	62.40	No.633	310.08	701.26	07/21	11,836.69
				731.45	07/24	12,568.14
				601.50	07/28	13,169.64
		SC	24.10		07/31	13,145.54

EC — ERROR CORRECTION　　　　OD — OVERDRAFT
MS — MISCELLANEOUS　　　　　　PS — PAYMENT STOPPED
NSF — NOT SUFFICIENT FUNDS　　SC — SERVICE CHARGE

* * *　　　　　　　　　* * *　　　　　　　　　* * *

THE RECONCILEMENT OF THIS STATEMENT WITH YOUR RECORDS IS ESSENTIAL.
ANY ERROR OR EXCEPTION SHOULD BE REPORTED IMMEDIATELY.

CASH RECEIPTS FOR MONTH OF JULY　　　　　　　　　　　　　　　　6,230.10

DUPLICATE DEPOSIT TICKETS:
　Date and amount of each deposit in July:

Date	Amount	Date	Amount	Date	Amount
July 2	$569.50	July 12	$580.70	July 23	$731.45
5	701.80	16	600.10	26	601.00
9	819.24	19	701.26	31	925.05

Instructions

1. Prepare a bank reconciliation as of July 31. If errors in recording deposits or checks are discovered, assume that the errors were made by the company. Assume that all deposits are from cash sales. All checks are written to satisfy accounts payable.
2. Journalize the necessary entries. The accounts have not been closed.
3. What is the amount of Cash that should appear on the balance sheet as of July 31?
4. ━━━▶ Assume that a canceled check for $2,680 has been incorrectly recorded by the bank as $6,280. Briefly explain how the error would be included in a bank reconciliation and how it should be corrected.

Special Activities

SA 8-1
Ethics and professional conduct in business

ETHICS

During the preparation of the bank reconciliation for Colonial Co., Javier Frailey, the assistant controller, discovered that El Camino National Bank incorrectly recorded an $819 check written by Colonial Co. as $189. Javier has decided not to notify the bank but wait for the bank to detect the error. Javier plans to record the $630 error as Other Income if the bank fails to detect the error within the next three months.

➤ Discuss whether Javier is behaving in a professional manner.

SA 8-2
Internal controls

The following is an excerpt from a conversation between two sales clerks, Fred Loya and Steph Gillespie. Both Fred and Steph are employed by Wireless Electronics, a locally owned and operated electronics retail store.

Fred: Did you hear the news?
Steph: What news?
Fred: Alice and John were both arrested this morning.
Steph: What? Arrested? You're putting me on!
Fred: No, really! The police arrested them first thing this morning. Put them in handcuffs, read them their rights—the whole works. It was unreal!
Steph: What did they do?
Fred: Well, apparently they were filling out merchandise refund forms for fictitious customers and then taking the cash.
Steph: I guess I never thought of that. How did they catch them?
Fred: The store manager noticed that returns were twice that of last year and seemed to be increasing. When he confronted Alice, she became flustered and admitted to taking the cash, apparently over $5,000 in just three months. They're going over the last six months' transactions to try to determine how much John stole. He apparently started stealing first.

➤ Suggest appropriate control procedures that would have prevented or detected the theft of cash.

SA 8-3
Internal controls

The following is an excerpt from a conversation between the store manager of Trader Sam's Grocery Stores, Jennings Maloy, and Sam Burley, president of Trader Sam's Grocery Stores.

Sam: Jennings, I'm concerned about this new scanning system.
Jennings: What's the problem?
Sam: Well, how do we know the clerks are ringing up all the merchandise?
Jennings: That's one of the strong points about the system. The scanner automatically rings up each item, based on its bar code. We update the prices daily, so we're sure that the sale is rung up for the right price.
Sam: That's not my concern. What keeps a clerk from pretending to scan items and then simply not charging his friends? If his friends were buying 10-15 items, it would be easy for the clerk to pass through several items with his finger over the bar code or just pass the merchandise through the scanner with the wrong side showing. It would look normal for anyone observing. In the old days, we at least could hear the cash register ringing up each sale.
Jennings: I see your point.

➤ Suggest ways that Trader Sam's Grocery Stores could prevent or detect the theft of merchandise as described.

SA 8-4
Ethics and professional conduct in business

ETHICS

Pete Harsh and Sara Alper are both cash register clerks for Farmers' Markets. Gina Majed is the store manager for Farmers' Markets. The following is an excerpt of a conversation between Pete and Sara:

Pete: Sara, how long have you been working for Farmers' Markets?
Sara: Almost five years this July. You just started two weeks ago . . . right?

Pete: Yes. Do you mind if I ask you a question?

Sara: No, go ahead.

Pete: What I want to know is, have they always had this rule that if your cash register is short at the end of the day, you have to make up the shortage out of your own pocket?

Sara: Yes, as long as I've been working here.

Pete: Well, it's the pits. Last week I had to pay in almost $50.

Sara: It's not that big a deal. I just make sure that I'm not short at the end of the day.

Pete: How do you do that?

Sara: I just short-change a few customers early in the day. There are a few jerks that deserve it anyway. Most of the time, their attention is elsewhere and they don't think to check their change.

Pete: What happens if you're over at the end of the day?

Sara: Majed lets me keep it as long as it doesn't get to be too large. I've not been short in over a year. I usually clear about $50 to $80 extra per day.

➤ Discuss this case from the viewpoint of proper controls and professional behavior.

SA 8-5
Bank reconciliation and internal control

The records of Filippi's Company indicate a March 31 cash balance of $10,806.05, which includes undeposited receipts for March 30 and 31. The cash balance on the bank statement as of March 31 is $7,004.95. This balance includes a note of $3,000 plus $120 interest collected by the bank but not recorded in the journal. Checks outstanding on March 31 were as follows: No. 670, $1,129.16; No. 679, $830; No. 690, $525.90; No. 2148, $127.40; No. 2149, $520; and No. 2151, $851.50.

On March 3, the cashier resigned, effective at the end of the month. Before leaving on March 31, the cashier prepared the following bank reconciliation:

Cash balance per books, March 31		$10,806.05
Add outstanding checks:		
No. 2148	$127.40	
2149	520.00	
2151	851.50	1,198.90
		$12,004.95
Less undeposited receipts		5,000.00
Cash balance per bank, March 31		$ 7,004.95
Deduct unrecorded note with interest		3,120.00
True cash, March 31		$ 3,884.95

```
Calculator Tape of Outstanding Checks:
         0.00 *
       127.40 +
       520.00 +
       851.50 +
     1,198.90 *
```

Subsequently, the owner of Filippi's Company discovered that the cashier had stolen an unknown amount of undeposited receipts, leaving only $5,000 to be deposited on March 31. The owner, a close family friend, has asked your help in determining the amount that the former cashier has stolen.

1. Determine the amount the cashier stole from Filippi's. Show your computations in good form.
2. How did the cashier attempt to conceal the theft?
3. a. Identify two major weaknesses in internal controls, which allowed the cashier to steal the undeposited cash receipts.
   b. ➤ Recommend improvements in internal controls, so that similar types of thefts of undeposited cash receipts can be prevented.

SA 8-6
Observe internal controls over cash

Group Project

Select a business in your community and observe its internal controls over cash receipts and cash payments. The business could be a bank or a bookstore, restaurant, department store, or other retailer. In groups of three or four, identify and discuss the similarities and differences in each business's cash internal controls.

SA 8-7
Cash to monthly cash expenses ratio

OccuLogix, Inc., provides treatments for eye diseases, including age-related macular degeneration (AMD). The company's treatment system, called the RHEO system, consists of an Octonova pump and disposable treatment sets that improve microcirculation in the eye by filtering high molecular weight proteins and other macromolecules from the patient's plasma. OccuLogix reported the following data (in thousands) for the years ending December 31, 2005, 2004, and 2003:

	2005	2004	2003
Cash as of December 31*	$41,268	$60,040	$ 1,239
Net cash flows from operating activities	(18,710)	(5,382)	(2,375)

*Includes cash equivalents and short-term investments.

1. Determine the monthly cash expenses for 2005, 2004, and 2003. Round to one decimal place.
2. Determine the ratio of cash to monthly expenses as of December 31, 2005, 2004, and 2003. Round to one decimal place.
3. ➤ Based upon (1) and (2), comment on OccuLogix's ratio of cash to monthly operating expenses for 2005, 2004, and 2003.

SA 8-8
Cash to monthly cash expenses ratio

Acusphere, Inc., is a specialty pharmaceutical company that develops new drugs and improved formulations of existing drugs using its proprietary microparticle technology. Currently, the company has three products in development in the areas of cardiology, oncology, and asthma. Acusphere reported the following data (in thousands) for the years ending December 31, 2005, 2004, and 2003.

	2005	2004	2003
Cash as of December 31^	$ 51,112	$ 45,180	$ 54,562
Net cash flows from operating activities	(30,683)	(19,319)	(15,507)

*Includes cash equivalents and short-term investments.

1. Determine the monthly cash expenses for 2005, 2004, and 2003. Round to one decimal place.
2. Determine the ratio of cash to monthly expenses as of December 31, 2005, 2004, and 2003. Round to one decimal place.
3. ➤ Based upon (1) and (2), comment on Acusphere's ratio of cash to monthly operating expenses for 2005, 2004, and 2003.

Answers to Self-Examination Questions

1. **C** Compliance with laws and regulations (answer C) is an objective, not an element, of internal control. The control environment (answer A), monitoring (answer B), control procedures (answer D), risk assessment, and information and communication are the five elements of internal control.
2. **C** The error was made by the bank, so the cash balance according to the bank statement needs to be adjusted.

Since the bank deducted $90 ($540.50 − $450.50) too little, the error of $90 should be deducted from the cash balance according to the bank statement (answer C).

3. **B** On any specific date, the cash account in a company's ledger may not agree with the account in the bank's ledger because of delays and/or errors by either party in recording transactions. The purpose of a bank reconciliation, therefore, is to determine the reasons for

any differences between the two account balances. All errors should then be corrected by the company or the bank, as appropriate. In arriving at the adjusted cash balance according to the bank statement, outstanding checks must be deducted (answer B) to adjust for checks that have been written by the company but that have not yet been presented to the bank for payment.

4. **C** All reconciling items that are added to and deducted from the cash balance according to the company's records on the bank reconciliation (answer C) require that journal entries be made by the company to correct errors made in recording transactions or to bring the cash account up to date for delays in recording transactions.

5. **D** To avoid the delay, annoyance, and expense that is associated with paying all obligations by check, relatively small amounts (answer A) are paid from a petty cash fund. The fund is established by estimating the amount of cash needed to pay these small amounts during a specified period (answer B), and it is then reimbursed when the amount of money in the fund is reduced to a predetermined minimum amount (answer C).

Receivables

objectives

After studying this chapter, you should be able to:

1. **Describe the common classifications of receivables.**

2. **Describe the nature of and the accounting for uncollectible receivables.**

3. **Describe the direct write-off method of accounting for uncollectible receivables.**

4. **Describe the allowance method of accounting for uncollectible receivables.**

5. **Compare the direct write-off and allowance methods of accounting for uncollectible accounts.**

6. **Describe the nature, characteristics, and accounting for notes receivable.**

7. **Describe the reporting of receivables on the balance sheet.**

FedEx Kinko's

The sale and purchase of merchandise involves the exchange of goods for money. The point at which the merchandise and the money changes hands, however, can vary depending on the transaction. Consider transactions with FedEx Kinko's, a division of FedEx consisting of a nationwide chain of copy shops. If you were to purchase class notes or other copy services, you would pay at the same time they are received. FedEx Kinko's also provides services to businesses prior to receiving payment. Because FedEx Kinko's has a history with its business partners, it allows these customers to purchase goods and services "on account." In the same way, you, as an individual, might be able to purchase goods or services on account with some businesses, such as a copy store, coffee shop, or bar, after establishing trust from a history of cash basis transactions.

Trust is a large part of business. Trust allows companies to avoid cash transactions and use trade credit. Trade credit gives rise to accounts receivable for the seller, which is often a significant current asset for many businesses. In this chapter, we will discuss common classifications of receivables, how to account for uncollectible receivables, and the reporting of receivables on the balance sheet.

Classification of Receivables

objective **1**

Describe the common classifications of receivables.

Many companies sell on credit in order to sell more services or products. The receivables that result from such sales are normally classified as accounts receivable or notes receivable. The term **receivables** includes all money claims against other entities, including people, business firms, and other organizations. These receivables are usually a significant portion of the total current assets.

ACCOUNTS RECEIVABLE

The most common transaction creating a receivable is selling merchandise or services on credit. The receivable is recorded as a debit to the accounts receivable account. Such **accounts receivable** are normally expected to be collected within a relatively short period, such as 30 or 60 days. They are classified on the balance sheet as a current asset.

NOTES RECEIVABLE

Notes receivable are amounts that customers owe for which a formal, written instrument of credit has been issued. As long as notes receivable are expected to be collected within a year, they are normally classified on the balance sheet as a current asset.

Notes are often used for credit periods of more than 60 days. For example, a furniture dealer may require a down payment at the time of sale and accept a note or a series of notes for the remainder. Such arrangements usually provide for monthly payments. For example, if you have purchased furniture on credit, you probably signed a note. From your viewpoint, the note is a note payable. From the creditor's viewpoint, the note is a note receivable.

Notes may be used to settle a customer's account receivable. Notes and accounts receivable that result from sales transactions are sometimes called *trade receivables*. Unless stated otherwise, we will assume that all notes and accounts receivable in this chapter are from sales transactions.

OTHER RECEIVABLES

Other receivables are normally listed separately on the balance sheet. If they are expected to be collected within one year, they are classified as current assets. If collection is expected beyond one year, they are classified as noncurrent assets and reported under the caption *Investments*. *Other receivables* include interest receivable, taxes receivable, and receivables from officers or employees.

Uncollectible Receivables

objective **2**

Describe the nature of and the accounting for uncollectible receivables.

In addition to their own credit departments, many businesses use external credit agencies, such as Dun & Bradstreet, to evaluate credit customers.

Adams, Stevens & Bradley, Ltd. is a collection agency that operates on a contingency basis. That is, its fees are based upon what it collects.

In prior chapters, we described and illustrated the accounting for transactions involving sales of merchandise or services on credit. A major issue that we have not yet discussed is that some customers will not pay their accounts. That is, some accounts receivable will be uncollectible.

Many retail businesses may shift the risk of uncollectible receivables to other companies. For example, some retailers do not accept sales on account, but will only accept cash or credit cards. Such policies shift the risk to the credit card companies.

Companies may also sell their receivables to other companies. This is often the case when a company issues its own credit card. For example, Macy's, Sears Holdings Corp., and JCPenney issue their own credit cards. Selling receivables is called *factoring* the receivables, and the buyer of the receivables is called a *factor*. An advantage of factoring is that the company selling its receivables receives immediate cash for operating and other needs. In addition, depending upon the factoring agreement, some of the risk of uncollectible accounts may be shifted to the factor.

Regardless of the care used in granting credit and the collection procedures used, a part of the credit sales will not be collectible. The operating expense recorded from uncollectible receivables is called **Bad debt expense**, *Uncollectible accounts expense*, or *Doubtful accounts expense*.

When does an account or a note become uncollectible? There is no general rule for determining when an account is uncollectible. Once a receivable is past due, a company should first notify the customer and try to collect the account. If after repeated attempts the customer doesn't pay, the company may turn the account over to a collection agency. After the collection agency attempts collection, any remaining balance in the account is considered worthless. One of the most significant indications of partial or complete uncollectibility occurs when the debtor goes into bankruptcy. Other indications include the closing of the customer's business and an inability to locate or contact the customer.

There are two methods of accounting for receivables that appear to be uncollectible: the direct write-off method and the allowance method. The **direct write-off method** records bad debt expense only when an account is judged to be worthless. The **allowance method** records bad debt expense by estimating uncollectible accounts at the end of the accounting period.

In the next sections of this chapter, we describe and illustrate the accounting for bad debt expense using the direct write-off method and the allowance method. We begin by describing and illustrating the direct write-off method since it is simpler and easier to understand. The direct write-off method is used by smaller companies and by companies with few receivables.[1] Generally accepted accounting principles, however, require companies with a large amount of receivables to use the allowance method.

---

1 The direct write-off method is also required for federal income tax purposes.

Direct Write-Off Method for Uncollectible Accounts

Under the direct write-off method, Bad Debt Expense is not recorded until the customer's account is determined to be worthless. At that time, the customer's account receivable is written off. To illustrate, assume that a $4,200 account receivable from D. L. Ross has been determined to be uncollectible. The entry to write off the account is as follows:

May	10	Bad Debt Expense	4 2 0 0 00	
		Accounts Receivable—D. L. Ross		4 2 0 0 00

What happens if an account receivable that has been written off is later collected? In such cases, the account is reinstated by an entry that reverses the write-off entry. The cash received in payment is then recorded as a receipt on account.

To illustrate, assume that the D. L. Ross account of $4,200 written off on May 10 in the preceding entry is later collected on November 21. The reinstatement and receipt of cash is recorded as follows:

Nov.	21	Accounts Receivable—D. L. Ross	4 2 0 0 00	
		Bad Debt Expense		4 2 0 0 00
	21	Cash	4 2 0 0 00	
		Accounts Receivable—D. L. Ross		4 2 0 0 00

The direct write-off method is used by businesses that sell most of their goods or services for cash and accept only MasterCard or VISA, which are recorded as cash sales. In such cases, receivables are a small part of the current assets and any bad debt expense would be small. Examples of such businesses are a restaurant, a convenience store, and a small retail store.

Example Exercise 9-1   objective 3

Journalize the following transactions using the direct write-off method of accounting for uncollectible receivables:

July 9.   Received $1,200 from Jay Burke and wrote off the remainder owed of $3,900 as uncollectible.
Oct. 11.   Reinstated the account of Jay Burke and received $3,900 cash in full payment.

Follow My Example 9-1

July 9	Cash	1,200	
	Bad Debt Expense	3,900	
	Accounts Receivable—Jay Burke		5,100
Oct. 11	Accounts Receivable—Jay Burke	3,900	
	Bad Debt Expense		3,900
11	Cash	3,900	
	Accounts Receivable—Jay Burke		3,900

For Practice: PE 9-1A, PE 9-1B

Allowance Method for Uncollectible Accounts

As we mentioned earlier, the allowance method is required by generally accepted accounting principles for companies with large accounts receivable. As a result, most well-known companies such as General Electric Company, PepsiCo, Inc., Intel Corporation, and FedEx use the allowance method.

As discussed in the preceding section, the direct write-off method records bad debt expense only when an account is determined to be worthless. In contrast, the allowance method estimates the accounts receivable that will not be collected and records bad debt expense for this estimate at the end of each accounting period. Based upon this estimate, Bad Debt Expense is then recorded by an adjusting entry.

To illustrate, assume that ExTone Company began operations in August and chose to use the calendar year as its fiscal year. As of December 31, 2007, ExTone Company has an accounts receivable balance of $1,000,000 that includes some accounts that are past due. However, ExTone doesn't know which customer accounts will be uncollectible. Based upon industry data, ExTone estimates that $40,000 of its accounts receivable will be uncollectible. Using this estimate, the following adjusting entry is made on December 31:

Dec.	31	Bad Debt Expense	40 0 0 0 00	
		Allowance for Doubtful Accounts		40 0 0 0 00
		Uncollectible accounts estimate.		

The adjusting entry reduces receivables to their net realizable value and matches the uncollectible expense with revenues.

Since the $40,000 reduction in accounts receivable is an estimate, specific customer accounts cannot be reduced or credited. Instead, a contra asset account entitled **Allowance for Doubtful Accounts** is credited.

As with all adjustments, the preceding adjusting entry affects the balance sheet and income statement. First, the adjusting entry records $40,000 of Bad Debt Expense, which will be matched against the related revenues of the period on the income statement. Second, the adjusting entry reduces the value of the receivables to the amount of cash expected to be realized in the future. This amount, $960,000 ($1,000,000 − $40,000), is called the **net realizable value** of the receivables. The net realizable value of the receivables is reported on the balance sheet.

You should note that after the preceding adjusting entry has been recorded, Accounts Receivable still has a debit balance of $1,000,000. This balance represents the total amount owed by customers on account and is supported by the individual customer accounts in the accounts receivable subsidiary ledger. The accounts receivable contra account, Allowance for Doubtful Accounts, has a credit balance of $40,000.

Integrity, Objectivity, and Ethics in Business

ETHICS

SELLER BEWARE

A company in financial distress will still try to purchase goods and services on account. In these cases, rather than "buyer beware," it is more like "seller beware." Sellers must be careful in advancing credit to such companies, because trade creditors have low priority for cash payments in the event of bankruptcy. To help suppliers, third-party services specialize in evaluating financially distressed customers. These services analyze credit risk for these firms by evaluating recent management payment decisions (who is getting paid and when), court actions (if in bankruptcy), and other supplier credit tightening or suspension actions. Such information helps a supplier monitor and tune trade credit amounts and terms with the financially distressed customer.

WRITE-OFFS TO THE ALLOWANCE ACCOUNT

When a customer's account is identified as uncollectible, it is written off against the allowance account. This requires the company to remove the specific accounts receivable and an equal amount from the allowance account. For example, on January 21, 2008, John Parker's account of $6,000 with ExTone Company is written off as follows:

Jan.	21	Allowance for Doubtful Accounts		6 0 0 0 00	
		Accounts Receivable—John Parker			6 0 0 0 00

At the end of a period, the Allowance for Doubtful Accounts will normally have a balance. This is because the Allowance for Doubtful Accounts is based upon an estimate. As a result, the total write-offs to the allowance account during the period will rarely equal the balance of the account at the beginning of the period. The allowance account will have a credit balance at the end of the period if the write-offs during the period are less than the beginning balance. It will have a debit balance if the write-offs exceed the beginning balance.

The Allowance Method

Adjusting Entry

Adjusting entry fills the bucket

Allowance for DOUBTFUL Accounts

Writing off accounts empties the bucket

Allowance for DOUBTFUL Accounts

To illustrate, assume that during 2008 ExTone Company writes off $36,750 of uncollectible accounts, including the $6,000 account of John Parker recorded on January 21. The Allowance for Doubtful Accounts will have a credit balance of $3,250 ($40,000 − $36,750), as shown below.

ALLOWANCE FOR DOUBTFUL ACCOUNTS

	Jan. 21	6,000	Jan. 1, 2008	Balance	40,000
Total accounts	Feb. 2	3,900			
written off $36,750	.	.			
	.	.			
			Dec. 31, 2008	Unadjusted balance	3,250

If ExTone Company had written off $44,100 in accounts receivable during 2008, the Allowance for Doubtful Accounts would have a debit balance of $4,100, as shown below.

ALLOWANCE FOR DOUBTFUL ACCOUNTS

	Jan. 21	6,000	Jan. 1, 2008 Balance	40,000
Total accounts	Feb. 2	3,900		
written off $44,100	.	.		
	.	.		
Dec. 31, 2008 Unadjusted balance	4,100			

You should note that the allowance account balances (credit balance of $3,250 and debit balance of $4,100) in the preceding illustrations are *before* the end-of-period adjusting entry. After the end-of-period adjusting entry is recorded, Allowance for Doubtful Accounts should always have a credit balance.

What happens if an account receivable that has been written off against the allowance account is later collected? Like the direct write-off method, the account is reinstated by an entry that reverses the write-off entry. The cash received in payment is then recorded as a receipt on account.

To illustrate, assume that Nancy Smith's account of $5,000 which was written off on April 2 is later collected on June 10. ExTone Company records the reinstatement and the collection as follows:

June	10	Accounts Receivable—Nancy Smith	5 0 0 0 00	
		Allowance for Doubtful Accounts		5 0 0 0 00
	10	Cash	5 0 0 0 00	
		Accounts Receivable—Nancy Smith		5 0 0 0 00

Example Exercise 9-2   objective 4

Journalize the following transactions using the allowance method of accounting for uncollectible receivables.

July 9. Received $1,200 from Jay Burke and wrote off the remainder owed of $3,900 as uncollectible.
Oct. 11. Reinstated the account of Jay Burke and received $3,900 cash in full payment.

Follow My Example 9-2

July 9	Cash	1,200	
	Allowance for Doubtful Accounts	3,900	
	Accounts Receivable—Jay Burke		5,100
Oct. 11	Accounts Receivable—Jay Burke	3,900	
	Allowance for Doubtful Accounts		3,900
11	Cash	3,900	
	Accounts Receivable—Jay Burke		3,900

For Practice: PE 9-2A, PE 9-2B

ESTIMATING UNCOLLECTIBLES

As we indicated earlier in this section, the allowance method estimates bad debt expense at the end of the period. How is the amount of uncollectible accounts estimated? The estimate of uncollectibles at the end of a fiscal period is based on past experience and forecasts of the future. When the general economy is doing well, the estimate of bad debt expense is normally less than it would be when the economy is doing poorly.

Two methods are commonly used to estimate uncollectible accounts receivable at the end of the period. The estimate may be based upon (1) a percent of sales or (2) an analysis of the receivables. We describe and illustrate each method next.

Estimate Based on Percent of Sales   Since accounts receivable are created by credit sales, bad debt expense can be estimated as a percent of credit sales. To illustrate, assume that on December 31, 2008, the Allowance for Doubtful Accounts for ExTone Company has a credit balance of $3,250. In addition, ExTone estimates that 1½% of 2008 credit sales will be uncollectible. If credit sales for the year are $3,000,000, the adjusting entry for uncollectible accounts on December 31 is as follows:

The percentage of uncollectible accounts will vary across companies and industries. For example, in their recent annual reports, JCPenney reported 1.7% of its receivables as uncollectible, Deere & Company (manufacturer of John Deere tractors, etc.) reported only 1.0% of its dealer receivables as uncollectible, and HCA Inc., a hospital management company, reported 42% of its receivables as uncollectible.

Dec.	31	Bad Debt Expense	45 0 0 0 00	
		Allowance for Doubtful Accounts		45 0 0 0 00
		Uncollectible accounts estimate.		
		($3,000,000 × 0.015 = $45,000)		

After the preceding adjusting entry is posted to the ledger, Bad Debt Expense will have a balance of $45,000, and the Allowance for Doubtful Accounts will have a balance of $48,250, as shown below.

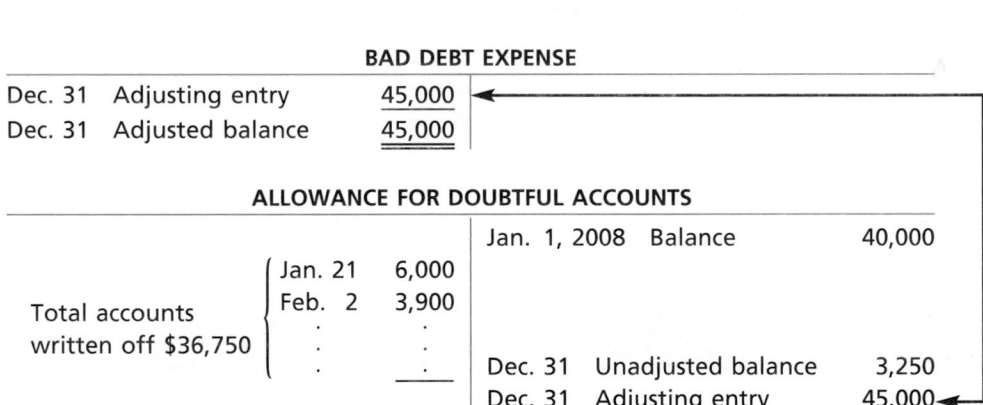

BAD DEBT EXPENSE

Dec. 31	Adjusting entry	45,000
Dec. 31	Adjusted balance	45,000

ALLOWANCE FOR DOUBTFUL ACCOUNTS

			Jan. 1, 2008	Balance	40,000
	Jan. 21	6,000			
Total accounts	Feb. 2	3,900			
written off $36,750	.	.			
	.	.	Dec. 31	Unadjusted balance	3,250
			Dec. 31	Adjusting entry	45,000
			Dec. 31	Adjusted balance	48,250

As shown above, after the adjusting entry is recorded, the Allowance for Doubtful Accounts has a credit balance of $48,250. If there had been a debit balance of $4,100 in the allowance account before the year-end adjustment, the amount of the adjustment would still have been $45,000. However, the December 31 ending balance of the allowance account would have been $40,900 ($45,000 − $4,100). In other words, under the percent of sales method, the amount of the adjusting entry for Bad Debt Expense is credited to whatever balance exists in the Allowance for Doubtful Accounts.

> The estimate based on sales is added to any balance in Allowance for Doubtful Accounts.

Example Exercise 9-3   objective 4

At the end of the current year, Accounts Receivable has a balance of $800,000; Allowance for Doubtful Accounts has a credit balance of $7,500; and net sales for the year total $3,500,000. Bad debt expense is estimated at ½ of 1% of net sales.

Determine (a) the amount of the adjusting entry for uncollectible accounts; (b) the adjusted balances of Accounts Receivable, Allowance for Doubtful Accounts, and Bad Debt Expense; and (c) the net realizable value of accounts receivable.

(continued)

Follow My Example 9-3

a. $17,500 ($3,500,000 × 0.005)

		Adjusted Balance
b.	Accounts Receivable	$800,000
	Allowance for Doubtful Accounts ($7,500 + $17,500)	25,000
	Bad Debt Expense	17,500

c. $775,000 ($800,000 − $25,000)

For Practice: PE 9-3A, PE 9-3B

Estimate Based on Analysis of Receivables The longer an account receivable is outstanding, the less likely that it will be collected. Thus, we can base the estimate of uncollectible accounts on how long specific accounts have been outstanding. For this purpose, we can use a process called **aging the receivables**.

Receivables are aged by preparing a schedule that classifies each customer's receivable by its due date. The number of days an account is past due is the number of days between the due date of the account and the date the aging schedule is prepared. To illustrate, assume that Rodriguez Company is preparing an aging schedule for its accounts receivable of $86,300 as of August 31, 2008. The $160 account receivable for Saxon Woods Company was due on May 29. As of August 31, Saxon's account is 94 days past due, as shown below.

Number of days past due in May	2 days	(31 − 29)
Number of days past due in June	30 days	
Number of days past due in July	31 days	
Number of days past due in August	31 days	
Total number of days past due	94 days	

A portion of the aging schedule for Rodriguez Company is shown in Exhibit 1. The schedule shows the total amount of receivables in each aging class.

EXHIBIT 1

Aging of Accounts Receivable

	A	B	C	D	E	F	G	H	I	
			Not			Days Past Due				
			Past						Over	
	Customer	Balance	Due	1–30	31–60	61–90	91–180	181–365	365	
1	Ashby & Co.	$ 150			$ 150					1
2	B. T. Barr	610					$ 350	$260		2
3	Brock Co.	470	$ 470							3
21										21
22	Saxon Woods Co.	160					160			22
23	Total	$86,300	$75,000	$4,000	$3,100	$1,900	$1,200	$800	$300	23

The estimate based on receivables is compared to the balance in the allowance account to determine the amount of the adjusting entry.

Rodriguez Company uses a sliding scale of percentages, based on industry or company experience, to estimate the amount of uncollectibles in each aging class. As shown in Exhibit 2, the percent estimated as uncollectible increases the longer the account is past due. For accounts not past due, the percent is 2%, while for accounts over 365 days past due the percent is 80%. The total of these amounts is the desired end-of-period balance for the Allowance for Doubtful Accounts. For Rodriguez Company, the desired August 31 balance of the Allowance for Doubtful Accounts is $3,390.

Comparing the estimate of $3,390 with the unadjusted balance of the allowance account determines the amount of the adjustment for Bad Debt

EXHIBIT 2

Estimate of
Uncollectible
Accounts

	A	B	C	D	
			Estimated Uncollectible Accounts		
	Age Interval	Balance	Percent	Amount	
1	Not past due	$75,000	2%	$1,500	1
2	1–30 days past due	4,000	5	200	2
3	31–60 days past due	3,100	10	310	3
4	61–90 days past due	1,900	20	380	4
5	91–180 days past due	1,200	30	360	5
6	181–365 days past due	800	50	400	6
7	Over 365 days past due	300	80	240	7
8	Total	$86,300		$3,390	8

Expense. For example, assume that the unadjusted balance of the allowance account is a credit balance of $510. The amount to be added to this balance is therefore $2,880 ($3,390 − $510), and the adjusting entry is as follows:

Aug.	31	Bad Debt Expense		2 8 8 0 00	
		Allowance for Doubtful Accounts			2 8 8 0 00
		Uncollectible accounts estimate.			
		($3,390 − $510)			

After the preceding adjusting entry is posted to the ledger, Bad Debt Expense will have a balance of $2,880, and the Allowance for Doubtful Accounts will have a balance of $3,390, as shown below.

BAD DEBT EXPENSE

Aug. 31	Adjusting entry	2,880
Aug. 31	Adjusted balance	2,880

ALLOWANCE FOR DOUBTFUL ACCOUNTS

	Aug. 31	Unadusted balance	510
	Aug. 31	Adjusting entry	2,880
	Aug. 31	Adjusted balance	3,390

The Commercial Collection Agency Section of the Commercial Law League of America reported the following collection rates by number of months past due:

As shown above, after the adjustment is recorded, the balance of the bad debt expense account is $2,880, and the balance of the allowance account is $3,390. The net realizable value of the receivables is $82,910 ($86,300 − $3,390).

If the unadjusted balance of the allowance account had been a debit balance of $300, the amount of the adjustment would have been $3,690 ($3,390 + $300). In this case, the bad debt expense account would have a $3,690 balance, but the balance of the allowance account would still have been $3,390, as shown below.

BAD DEBT EXPENSE

Aug. 31	Adjusting entry	3,690
Aug. 31	Adjusted balance	3,690

ALLOWANCE FOR DOUBTFUL ACCOUNTS

Aug. 31	Unadjusted balance	300				
			Aug. 31	Adjusting entry	3,690
			Aug. 31	Adjusted balance	3,390

Example Exercise 9-4

objective 4

At the end of the current year, Accounts Receivable has a balance of $800,000; Allowance for Doubtful Accounts has a credit balance of $7,500; and net sales for the year total $3,500,000. Using the aging method, the balance of Allowance for Doubtful Accounts is estimated as $30,000.

   Determine (a) the amount of the adjusting entry for uncollectible accounts; (b) the adjusted balances of Accounts Receivable, Allowance for Doubtful Accounts, and Bad Debt Expense; and (c) the net realizable value of accounts receivable.

Follow My Example 9-4

a. $22,500 ($30,000 − $7,500)

		Adjusted Balance
b.	Accounts Receivable	$800,000
	Allowance for Doubtful Accounts	30,000
	Bad Debt Expense	22,500

c. $770,000 ($800,000 − $30,000)

For Practice: PE 9-4A, PE 9-4B

Comparing Estimation Methods   The percent of sales and analysis of receivables methods of estimating uncollectible accounts can be compared in two different ways. First, the methods can be compared based on their financial statement emphasis. Second, the methods can be compared based on whether Bad Debt Expense or the Allowance for Doubtful Accounts is the focus of the estimate.

   The percent of sales method emphasizes the matching of bad debt expense with the related credit sales of the period. In doing so, the percent of sales method places more emphasis on the income statement. The analysis of receivables method emphasizes the end-of-period net realizable value of the receivables and the related balance of the allowance account. Thus, the analysis of receivables method places more emphasis on the balance sheet.

   Under the percent of sales method, Bad Debt Expense is the focus of the estimation process. In other words, the percent of sales method emphasizes obtaining the best estimate for Bad Debt Expense for the period. The ending balance for Allowance for Doubtful Accounts is the result of estimating bad debt expense. For example, in the ExTone Company illustration, bad debt expense was estimated as $45,000 ($3,000,000 × 1½%) and thus, $45,000 was credited to the Allowance for Doubtful Accounts. Since the Allowance for Doubtful Accounts had an unadjusted credit balance of $3,250, its ending balance became a credit balance of $48,250.

   Under the analysis of receivables method, Allowance for Doubtful Accounts is the focus of the estimation process. Bad Debt Expense becomes the end result of estimating Allowance for Doubtful Accounts. For example, in the Rodriguez Company illustration, the adjusted balance for the Allowance for Doubtful Accounts was estimated using the aging method as $3,390. Since the Allowance for Doubtful Accounts had an unadjusted credit balance of $510, it was credited for $2,880 ($3,390 − $510). The related debit of $2,880 was to Bad Debt Expense. Thus, the ending balance of Bad Debt Expense became $2,880.

   The following table summarizes the differences between the percent of sales and the analysis of receivables methods.

	Percent of Sales Method	Analysis of Receivables Method
Financial statement emphasis	Income statement	Balance sheet
Focus of estimate	Bad Debt Expense	Allowance for Doubtful Accounts
End result of estimate	Allowance for Doubtful Accounts	Bad Debt Expense

Comparing Direct Write-Off and Allowance Methods

objective   **5**

Compare the direct write-off and allowance methods of accounting for uncollectible accounts.

In this section, we will illustrate and compare the journal entries for the direct write-off and allowance methods. As a basis for our illustration, we will use the following selected transactions, taken from the records of Hobbs Company for the year ending December 31, 2007:

Mar. 1.   Wrote off account of C. York, $3,650.
Apr. 12. Received $2,250 as partial payment on the $5,500 account of Cary Bradshaw. Wrote off the remaining balance as uncollectible.
June 22. Received the $3,650 from C. York, which had been written off on March 1. Reinstated the account and recorded the cash receipt.
Sept. 7. Wrote off the following accounts as uncollectible (record as one journal entry):

Jason Bigg	$1,100	Stanford Noonan	$1,360
Steve Bradey	2,220	Aiden Wyman	990
Samantha Neeley	775		

Dec. 31. Hobbs Company uses the percent of credit sales method of estimating uncollectible expenses. Based upon past history and industry averages, 1.25% of credit sales are expected to be uncollectible. Hobbs recorded $3,400,000 of credit sales during 2007.

Exhibit 3 illustrates the journal entries that would have been recorded for Hobbs Company using the direct write-off method and the allowance method. Using the direct write-off method, there is no adjusting entry on December 31 for uncollectible accounts. In contrast, the allowance method records an adjusting entry for estimated uncollectible accounts of $42,500.

EXHIBIT 3   Comparing Direct Write-Off and Allowance Methods

	Direct Write-Off Method			Allowance Method		
Mar. 1	Bad Debt Expense	3,650		Allowance for Doubtful Accounts	3,650	
	Accounts Receivable—C. York		3,650	Accounts Receivable—C. York		3,650
Apr. 12	Cash	2,250		Cash	2,250	
	Bad Debt Expense	3,250		Allowance for Doubtful Accounts	3,250	
	Accounts Receivable—Cary Bradshaw		5,500	Accounts Receivable—Cary Bradshaw		5,500
June 22	Accounts Receivable—C. York	3,650		Accounts Receivable—C. York	3,650	
	Bad Debt Expense		3,650	Allowance for Doubtful Accounts		3,650
22	Cash	3,650		Cash	3,650	
	Accounts Receivable—C. York		3,650	Accounts Receivable—C. York		3,650
Sept. 7	Bad Debt Expense	6,445		Allowance for Doubtful Accounts	6,445	
	Accounts Receivable—Jason Bigg		1,100	Accounts Receivable—Jason Bigg		1,100
	Accounts Receivable—Steve Bradey		2,220	Accounts Receivable—Steve Bradey		2,220
	Accounts Receivable—Samantha Neeley		775	Accounts Receivable—Samantha Neeley		775
	Accounts Receivable—Stanford Noonan		1,360	Accounts Receivable—Stanford Noonan		1,360
	Accounts Receivable—Aiden Wyman		990	Accounts Receivable—Aiden Wyman		990
Dec. 31	No Entry			Bad Debt Expense	42,500	
				Allowance for Doubtful Accounts		42,500
				Uncollectible accounts estimate.		
				($3,400,000 × 0.0125 = $42,500)		

The primary differences between these two methods are summarized in the table below.

COMPARING THE DIRECT WRITE-OFF AND ALLOWANCE METHODS

	Direct Write-Off Method	Allowance Method
Amount of bad debt expense recorded	When the actual accounts receivable are determined to be uncollectible.	Using estimate based on either (1) a percent of sales or (2) an analysis of receivables.
Allowance account	No allowance account is used.	The allowance account is used.
Primary users	Small companies and companies with relatively few receivables.	Large companies and those with a large amount of receivables.

Integrity, Objectivity, and Ethics in Business

RECEIVABLES FRAUD

Financial reporting frauds are often tied to accounts receivable, because receivables allow companies to record revenue before cash is received. Take, for example, the case of entrepreneur Michael Weinstein, who acquired Coated Sales, Inc. with the dream of growing the small specialty company into a major corporation. To acquire funding that would facilitate this growth, Weinstein had to artificially boost the company's sales. He accomplished this by adding millions in false accounts receivable to existing customer accounts.

The company's auditors began to sense a problem when they called one of the company's customers to confirm a large order. When the customer denied placing the order, the auditors began to investigate the company's receivables more closely. Their analysis revealed a fraud which overstated profits by $55 million and forced the company into bankruptcy, costing investors and creditors over $160 million.

Source: Joseph T. Wells, "Follow Fraud to the Likely Perpetrator," *The Journal of Accountancy*, March 2001.

Notes Receivable

objective 6

Describe the nature, characteristics, and accounting for notes receivable.

A claim supported by a note has some advantages over a claim in the form of an account receivable. By signing a note, the debtor recognizes the debt and agrees to pay it according to the terms listed. A note is thus a stronger legal claim.

CHARACTERISTICS OF NOTES RECEIVABLE

A note receivable, or promissory note, is a written promise to pay a sum of money (face amount) on demand or at a definite time. It can be payable either to an individual or a business, or to the bearer or holder of the note. It is signed by the person or firm that makes the promise. The one to whose order the note is payable is called the *payee*, and the one making the promise is called the *maker*.

The date a note is to be paid is called the *due date* or *maturity date*. The period of time between the issuance date and the due date of a short-term note may be stated in either days or months. When the term of a note is stated in days, the due date is the specified number of days after its issuance. To illustrate, the due date of a 90-day note dated March 16 is June 14, as shown at the top of the following page.

The term of a note may be stated as a certain number of months after the issuance date. In such cases, the due date is determined by counting the number of months from the issuance date. For example, a three-month note dated June 5 would be due on September 5. A two-month note dated July 31 would be due on September 30.

Due Date of 90-Day Note

MARCH 16-31	APRIL 1-30	MAY 1-31	JUNE 1-14
15 days	+ 30 days	+ 31 days	+ 14 days

Mar. 16   **Total of 90 days**   Jun. 14

Your credit card balances that are not paid at the end of the month incur an interest charge expressed as a percent per month. Interest charges of 1½% per month are common. Such charges approximate an annual interest rate of 18% per year (1½% × 12). Thus, if you can borrow money at less than 18%, you are better off borrowing the money to pay off the credit card balance.

A note normally specifies that interest be paid for the period between the issuance date and the due date.[2] Notes covering a period of time longer than one year normally provide for interest to be paid annually, semiannually, quarterly, or monthly. When the term of the note is less than one year, the interest is usually payable at the time the note is paid.

The interest rate on notes is normally stated in terms of a year, regardless of the actual period of time involved. Thus, the interest on $2,000 for one year at 12% is $240 (12% × $2,000). The interest on $2,000 for 90 days at 12% is $60 ($2,000 × 12% × 90/360). To simplify computations, we will use 360 days per year. In practice, companies such as banks and mortgage companies use the exact number of days in a year, 365.

The amount that is due at the maturity or due date of a note receivable is its **maturity value**. The maturity value of a note is the sum of the face amount and the interest. For example, the maturity value of a $25,000, 9%, 120-day note receivable is $25,750 [$25,000 + ($25,000 × 9% × 120/360)].

ACCOUNTING FOR NOTES RECEIVABLE

A customer may use a note to replace an account receivable. To illustrate, assume that a company accepts a 30-day, 12% note dated November 21, 2008, in settlement of the account of W. A. Bunn Co., which is past due and has a balance of $6,000. The company records the receipt of the note as follows:

Nov.	21	Notes Receivable—W. A. Bunn Co.	6 0 0 0 00	
		Accounts Receivable—W. A. Bunn Co.		6 0 0 0 00

When the note matures, the company records the receipt of $6,060 ($6,000 principal plus $60 interest) as follows:

Dec.	21	Cash	6 0 6 0 00	
		Notes Receivable—W. A. Bunn Co.		6 0 0 0 00
		Interest Revenue		6 0 00

If the maker of a note fails to pay the debt on the due date, the note is a **dishonored note receivable**. A company that holds a dishonored note transfers the face value of the note plus any interest due back to an accounts receivable account. For example, assume that the $6,000, 30-day, 12% note received from W. A. Bunn Co. and recorded on November 21 is dishonored at maturity. The company holding the note transfers the note and interest back to the customer's account as follows:

---

2 You may occasionally see references to non-interest-bearing notes receivable. Such notes are not widely used and carry an assumed or implicit interest rate.

	Dec.	21	Accounts Receivable—W. A. Bunn Co.	6 0 6 0 00	
			Notes Receivable—W. A. Bunn Co.		6 0 0 0 00
			Interest Revenue		6 0 00

The company has earned the interest of $60, even though the note is dishonored. If the account receivable is uncollectible, the company will write off $6,060 against the Allowance for Doubtful Accounts.

If a note matures in a later fiscal period, the company holding the note records an adjustment for the interest accrued in the period in which the note is received. For example, assume that Crawford Company uses a 90-day, 12% note dated December 1, 2008, to settle its account, which has a balance of $4,000. Assuming that the accounting period ends on December 31, the holder of the note records the transactions as follows:

2008 Dec.	1	Notes Receivable—Crawford Company	4 0 0 0 00	
		Accounts Receivable—Crawford Company		4 0 0 0 00
	31	Interest Receivable	4 0 00	
		Interest Revenue		4 0 00
		Accrued interest		
		($4,000 × 12% × 30/360).		
2009 Mar.	1	Cash	4 1 2 0 00	
		Notes Receivable—Crawford Company		4 0 0 0 00
		Interest Receivable		4 0 00
		Interest Revenue		8 0 00
		Total interest of $120		
		($4,000 × 12% × 90/360).		

The interest revenue account is closed at the end of each accounting period. The amount of interest revenue is normally reported in the Other Income section of the income statement.

Example Exercise 9-5   objective 6

Same Day Surgery Center received a 120-day, 6% note for $40,000, dated March 14 from a patient on account.

a. Determine the due date of the note.
b. Determine the maturity value of the note.
c. Journalize the entry to record the receipt of the payment of the note at maturity.

Follow My Example 9-5

a. The due date of the note is July 12, determined as follows:

March	17 days (31 – 14)	
April	30 days	
May	31 days	
June	30 days	
July	12 days	
Total	120 days	

b. $40,800 [$40,000 + ($40,000 × 6% × 120/360)]

c. July 12   Cash   40,800
                    Note Receivable   40,000
                    Interest Revenue   800

For Practice: PE 9-5A, PE 9-5B

Reporting Receivables on the Balance Sheet

objective 7

Describe the reporting of receivables on the balance sheet.

All receivables that are expected to be realized in cash within a year are presented in the Current Assets section of the balance sheet. It is normal to list the assets in the order of their liquidity. This is the order in which they are expected to be converted to cash during normal operations. An example of the presentation of receivables is shown in the partial balance sheet for Crabtree Co. in Exhibit 4.

EXHIBIT 4

Receivables on Balance Sheet

Crabtree Co. Balance Sheet December 31, 2008			
Assets			
Current assets:			
Cash			$119 5 0 0 00
Notes receivable			250 0 0 0 00
Accounts receivable	$445 0 0 0 00		
Less allowance for doubtful accounts	15 0 0 0 00	430 0 0 0 00	
Interest receivable		14 5 0 0 00	

The balances of Crabtree's notes receivable, accounts receivable, and interest receivable accounts are reported in Exhibit 4. The allowance for doubtful accounts is subtracted from the accounts receivable. Alternatively, the accounts receivable may be listed on the balance sheet at its net realizable value of $430,000, with a note showing the amount of the allowance. If the allowance account includes provisions for doubtful notes as well as accounts, it should be deducted from the total of Notes Receivable and Accounts Receivable.

Other disclosures related to receivables are presented either on the face of the financial statements or in the accompanying notes. Such disclosures include the market (fair) value of the receivables. In addition, if unusual credit risks exist within the receivables, the nature of the risks should be disclosed. For example, if the majority of

Business Connections

REAL WORLD

DELTA AIR LINES

Delta Air Lines is a major air carrier that services over 144 cities in 47 states within the United States and 59 cities in 41 countries throughout the world. In its operations, Delta generates accounts receivable as reported in the following note to its financial statements:

© RIC FELD/ASSOCIATED PRESS

Our accounts receivable are generated largely from the sale of passenger airline tickets and cargo transportation services. The majority of these sales are processed through major credit card companies, resulting in accounts receivable which are generally short-term in duration. We also have receivables from the sale of mileage credits to partners, such as credit card com-panies, hotels and car rental agencies, that participate in our SkyMiles program. We believe that the credit risk associated with these receivables is minimal and that the allowance for uncollectible accounts that we have provided is appropriate.

In its December 31, 2004, balance sheet, Delta reported the following accounts receivable (in millions):

	2005	2004
Current Assets:		
. . .		
Accounts receivable, net of an allowance for uncollectible accounts of $41 at 12/31/05 and 12/31/04	819	696

the receivables are due from one customer or are due from customers located in one area of the country or one industry, these facts should be disclosed.[3]

Financial Analysis and Interpretation

Two financial measures that are especially useful in evaluating efficiency in collecting receivables are (1) the accounts receivable turnover and (2) the number of days' sales in receivables.

The **accounts receivable turnover** measures how frequently during the year the accounts receivable are being converted to cash. For example, with credit terms of 2/10, n/30, the accounts receivable should turn over more than 12 times per year. The accounts receivable turnover is computed as follows:[4]

$$\text{Accounts Receivable Turnover} = \frac{\text{Net Sales}}{\text{Average Accounts Receivable}}$$

The average accounts receivable can be determined by using monthly data or by simply adding the beginning and ending accounts receivable balances and dividing by two. For example, using the following financial data (in millions) for FedEx, the 2005 and 2004 accounts receivable turnover is computed as 7.5 and 7.4, respectively.

	2005	**2004**	**2003**
Net sales	$19,364	$17,383	—
Accounts receivable	2,703	2,475	$2,199
Average accounts receivable	2,589 [($2,703 + $2,475)/2]	2,337 [($2,475 + $2,199)/2]	
Accounts receivable turnover	7.5 ($19,364/$2,589)	7.4 ($17,383/$2,337)	

Comparing 2005 and 2004 indicates that the accounts receivable turnover has increased from 7.4 to 7.5. Thus, FedEx's management of accounts receivable has improved slightly in 2005.

The **number of days' sales in receivables** is an estimate of the length of time the accounts receivable have been outstanding. With credit terms of 2/10, n/30, the number of days' sales in receivables should be less than 20 days. It is computed as follows:

$$\text{Number of Days' Sales in Receivables} = \frac{\text{Average Accounts Receivable}}{\text{Average Daily Sales}}$$

Average daily sales are determined by dividing net sales by 365 days. For example, using the preceding data for FedEx, the number of days' sales in receivables is 48.8 and 49.1 for 2005 and 2004, respectively, as shown below.

	2005	**2004**
Net sales	$19,364	$17,383
Average accounts receivable	2,589 [($2,703 + $2,475)/2]	2,337 [($2,475 + $2,199)/2]
Average daily sales	53.1 ($19,364/365)	47.6 ($17,383/365)
Days' sales in receivables	48.8 ($2,589/53.1)	49.1 ($2,337/47.6)

The number of days' sales in receivables confirms a slight improvement in managing accounts receivable during 2005. That is, the efficiency in collecting accounts receivable has improved when the number of days' sales in receivables decreases. However, these measures should also be compared with similar companies within the industry.

---

3 *Statement of Financial Accounting Standards No. 105*, "Disclosures of Information about Financial Instruments with Off-Balance Sheet Risk and Financial Instruments with Concentrations of Credit Risk," and *No. 107*, "Disclosures about Fair Value of Financial Instruments" (Norwalk, CT: Financial Accounting Standards Board).

4 If known, credit sales can be used in the numerator. However, because credit sales are not normally disclosed to external users, most analysts use net sales in the numerator.

Discounting Notes Receivable

Although it is not a common transaction, a company may endorse its notes receivable by transferring them to a bank in return for cash. The bank transfers cash (the *proceeds*) to the company after deducting a *discount* (interest) that is computed on the maturity value of the note for the discount period. The discount period is the time that the bank must hold the note before it becomes due.

To illustrate, assume that a 90-day, 12%, $1,800 note receivable from Pryor & Co., dated April 8, is discounted at the payee's bank on May 3 at the rate of 14%. The data used in determining the effect of the transaction are as follows:

Face value of note dated April 8	$1,800.00
Interest on note (90 days at 12%)	54.00
Maturity value of note due July 7	$1,854.00
Discount on maturity value (65 days from May 3 to July 7, at 14%)	46.87
Proceeds	$1,807.13

The endorser records as interest revenue the excess of the proceeds from discounting the note, $1,807.13, over its face value, $1,800, as follows:

May	3	Cash		1 8 0 7 13	
		Notes Receivable			1 8 0 0 00
		Interest Revenue			7 13
		Discounted $1,800, 90-day, 12% note			
		at 14%.			

What if the proceeds from discounting a note receivable are less than the face value? When this situation occurs, the endorser records the excess of the face value over the proceeds as interest expense. The length of the discount period and the difference between the interest rate and the discount rate determine whether interest expense or interest revenue will result from discounting.

Without a statement limiting responsibility, the endorser of a note is committed to paying the note if the maker defaults. This potential liability is called a *contingent liability*. Thus, the endorser of a note that has been discounted has a contingent liability until the due date. If the maker pays the promised amount at maturity, the contingent liability is removed without any action on the part of the endorser. If, on the other hand, the maker dishonors the note and the endorser is notified according to legal requirements, the endorser's liability becomes an actual one.

When a discounted note receivable is dishonored, the bank notifies the endorser and asks for payment. In some cases, the bank may charge a *protest fee* for notifying the endorser that a note has been dishonored. The entire amount paid to the bank by the endorser, including the interest and protest fee, should be debited to the account receivable of the maker. For example, assume that the $1,800, 90-day, 12% note discounted on May 3 is dishonored at maturity by the maker, Pryor & Co. The bank charges a protest fee of $12. The endorser's entry to record the payment to the bank is as follows:

July	7	Accounts Receivable—Pryor & Co.		1 8 6 6 00	
		Cash			1 8 6 6 00
		Paid dishonored, discounted note			
		(maturity value of $1,854 plus protest			
		fee of $12).			

At a Glance

1. Describe the common classifications of receivables.

Key Points	Key Learning Outcomes	Example Exercises	Practice Exercises
The term *receivables* includes all money claims against other entities, including people, business firms, and other organizations. Receivables are normally classified as accounts receivable, notes receivable, or other receivables.	• Define the term *receivables*. • List some common classifications of receivables.		

2. Describe the nature of and the accounting for uncollectible receivables.

Key Points	Key Learning Outcomes	Example Exercises	Practice Exercises
Regardless of the care used in granting credit and the collection procedures used, a part of the credit sales will not be collectible. The operating expense recorded from uncollectible receivables is called *bad debt expense*. The two methods of accounting for uncollectible receivables are the direct write-off method and the allowance method.	• Describe how a company may shift the risk of uncollectible receivables to other companies. • List factors that indicate an account receivable is uncollectible. • Describe two methods of accounting for uncollectible accounts receivable.		

3. Describe the direct write-off method of accounting for uncollectible receivables.

Key Points	Key Learning Outcomes	Example Exercises	Practice Exercises
Under the direct write-off method, the entry to write off an account debits Bad Debt Expense and credits Accounts Receivable. Neither an allowance account nor an adjusting entry is needed at the end of the period.	• Prepare journal entries to write off an account using the direct method. • Prepare journal entries for the reinstatement and collection of an account previously written off.	9-1 9-1	9-1A, 9-1B 9-1A, 9-1B

(continued)

4. Describe the allowance method of accounting for uncollectible receivables.

Key Points	Key Learning Outcomes	Example Exercises	Practice Exercises
Under the allowance method, an adjusting entry is made for uncollectible accounts. When an account is determined to be uncollectible, it is written off against the allowance account. The allowance account normally has a credit balance after the adjusting entry has been posted and is a contra asset account. The estimate of uncollectibles may be based on a percent of sales or an analysis of receivables. Using the percent of sales, the adjusting entry is made without regard to the balance of the allowance account. Using the analysis of receivables, the adjusting entry is made so that the balance of the allowance account will equal the estimated uncollectibles at the end of the period.	• Prepare journal entries to write off an account using the allowance method.	9-2	9-2A, 9-2B
	• Prepare journal entries for the reinstatement and collection of an account previously written off.	9-2	9-2A, 9-2B
	• Determine the adjustment, bad debt expense, and net realizable value of accounts receivable using the percent of sales method.	9-3	9-3A, 9-3B
	• Determine the adjustment, bad debt expense, and net realizable value of accounts receivable using the analysis of receivables.	9-4	9-4A, 9-4B

5. Compare the direct write-off and allowance methods of accounting for uncollectible accounts.

Key Points	Key Learning Outcomes	Example Exercises	Practice Exercises
The direct write-off and allowance methods of accounting for uncollectible accounts are recorded differently in the accounts and presented differently in the financial statements. Exhibit 3 illustrates both methods of accounting for uncollectible accounts.	• Describe the differences in accounting for uncollectible accounts under the direct write-off and allowance methods. • Record journal entries using the direct write-off and allowance methods.		

6. Describe the nature, characteristics, and accounting for notes receivable.

Key Points	Key Learning Outcomes	Example Exercises	Practice Exercises
A note received in settlement of an account receivable is recorded as a debit to Notes Receivable and a credit to Accounts Receivable. When a note matures, Cash is debited, Notes Receivable is credited, and Interest Revenue is credited. If the maker of a note fails to pay the debt on the due date, the dishonored note is recorded by debiting an accounts receivable account for the amount of the claim against the maker of the note.	• Describe the characteristics of a note receivable.		
	• Determine the due date and maturity value of a note receivable.	9-5	9-5A, 9-5B
	• Prepare journal entries for the receipt of the payment of a note receivable.	9-5	9-5A, 9-5B
	• Prepare a journal entry for the dishonored note receivable.		

7. **Describe the reporting of receivables on the balance sheet.**

Key Points	Key Learning Outcomes	Example Exercises	Practice Exercises
All receivables that are expected to be realized in cash within a year are reported in the Current Assets section of the balance sheet in the order in which they can be converted to cash in normal operations. In addition to the allowance for doubtful accounts, additional receivable disclosures include the market (fair) value and unusual credit risks.	• Describe how receivables are reported in the Current Assets section of the balance sheet. • Describe disclosures related to receivables that should be reported in the financial statements.		

Key Terms

Accounts receivable (394)
Accounts receivable turnover (409)
Aging the receivables (401)
Allowance for Doubtful Accounts (397)

Allowance method (395)
Bad Debt Expense (395)
Direct write-off method (395)
Dishonored note receivable (406)
Maturity value (406)

Net realizable value (397)
Notes receivable (394)
Number of days' sales in receivables (409)
Receivables (394)

Illustrative Problem

Ditzler Company, a construction supply company, uses the allowance method of accounting for uncollectible accounts receivable. Selected transactions completed by Ditzler Company are as follows:

Feb. 1 Sold merchandise on account to Ames Co., $8,000. The cost of the merchandise sold was $4,500.
Mar. 15 Accepted a 60-day, 12% note for $8,000 from Ames Co. on account.
Apr. 9 Wrote off a $2,500 account from Dorset Co. as uncollectible.
      21 Loaned $7,500 cash to Jill Klein, receiving a 90-day, 14% note.
May 14 Received the interest due from Ames Co. and a new 90-day, 14% note as a renewal of the loan. (Record both the debit and the credit to the notes receivable account.)
June 13 Reinstated the account of Dorset Co., written off on April 9, and received $2,500 in full payment.
July 20 Jill Klein dishonored her note.
Aug. 12 Received from Ames Co. the amount due on its note of May 14.
      19 Received from Jill Klein the amount owed on the dishonored note, plus interest for 30 days at 15%, computed on the maturity value of the note.
Dec. 16 Accepted a 60-day, 12% note for $12,000 from Global Company on account.
      31 It is estimated that 3% of the credit sales of $1,375,000 for the year ended December 31 will be uncollectible.

Instructions
1. Journalize the transactions.
2. Journalize the adjusting entry to record the accrued interest on December 31 on the Global Company note.

Solution

1.

Date		Description	Debit	Credit
Feb.	1	Accounts Receivable—Ames Co.	8 0 0 0 00	
		Sales		8 0 0 0 00
	1	Cost of Merchandise Sold	4 5 0 0 00	
		Merchandise Inventory		4 5 0 0 00
Mar.	15	Notes Receivable—Ames Co.	8 0 0 0 00	
		Accounts Receivable—Ames Co.		8 0 0 0 00
Apr.	9	Allowance for Doubtful Accounts	2 5 0 0 00	
		Accounts Receivable—Dorset Co.		2 5 0 0 00
	21	Notes Receivable—Jill Klein	7 5 0 0 00	
		Cash		7 5 0 0 00
May	14	Notes Receivable—Ames Co.	8 0 0 0 00	
		Cash	1 6 0 00	
		Notes Receivable—Ames Co.		8 0 0 0 00
		Interest Revenue		1 6 0 00
June	13	Accounts Receivable—Dorset Co.	2 5 0 0 00	
		Allowance for Doubtful Accounts		2 5 0 0 00
	13	Cash	2 5 0 0 00	
		Accounts Receivable—Dorset Co.		2 5 0 0 00
July	20	Accounts Receivable—Jill Klein	7 7 6 2 50	
		Notes Receivable—Jill Klein		7 5 0 0 00
		Interest Revenue		2 6 2 50
Aug.	12	Cash	8 2 8 0 00	
		Notes Receivable—Ames Co.		8 0 0 0 00
		Interest Revenue		2 8 0 00
Aug.	19	Cash	7 8 5 9 53	
		Accounts Receivable—Jill Klein		7 7 6 2 50
		Interest Revenue		9 7 03
		($7,762.50 × 15% × 30/360).		
Dec.	16	Notes Receivable—Global Company	12 0 0 0 00	
		Accounts Receivable—Global Company		12 0 0 0 00
	31	Bad Debt Expense	41 2 5 0 00	
		Allowance for Doubtful Accounts		41 2 5 0 00
		Uncollectible accounts estimate.		
		($1,375,000 × 3%)		

2.

Date		Description	Debit	Credit
Dec.	31	Interest Receivable	6 0 00	
		Interest Revenue		6 0 00
		Accrued interest		
		($12,000 × 12% × 15/360).		

Self-Examination Questions

(Answers at End of Chapter)

1. At the end of the fiscal year, before the accounts are adjusted, Accounts Receivable has a balance of $200,000 and Allowance for Doubtful Accounts has a credit balance of $2,500. If the estimate of uncollectible accounts determined by aging the receivables is $8,500, the amount of bad debt expense is:
   A. $2,500.   C. $8,500.
   B. $6,000.   D. $11,000.

2. At the end of the fiscal year, Accounts Receivable has a balance of $100,000 and Allowance for Doubtful Accounts has a balance of $7,000. The expected net realizable value of the accounts receivable is:
   A. $7,000.   C. $100,000.
   B. $93,000.   D. $107,000.

3. What is the maturity value of a 90-day, 12% note for $10,000?
   A. $8,800   C. $10,300
   B. $10,000   D. $11,200

4. What is the due date of a $12,000, 90-day, 8% note receivable dated August 5?
   A. October 31   C. November 3
   B. November 2   D. November 4

5. When a note receivable is dishonored, Accounts Receivable is debited for what amount?
   A. The face value of the note
   B. The maturity value of the note
   C. The maturity value of the note less accrued interest
   D. The maturity value of the note plus accrued interest

Eye Openers

1. What are the three classifications of receivables?
2. What types of transactions give rise to accounts receivable?
3. In what section of the balance sheet should a note receivable be listed if its term is (a) 120 days, (b) six years?
4. Give two examples of other receivables.
5. Wilson's Hardware is a small hardware store in the rural township of Struggleville that rarely extends credit to its customers in the form of an account receivable. The few customers that are allowed to carry accounts receivable are long-time residents of Struggleville and have a history of doing business at Wilson's. What method of accounting for uncollectible receivables should Wilson's Hardware use? Why?
6. Which of the two methods of accounting for uncollectible accounts provides for the recognition of the expense at the earlier date?
7. What kind of an account (asset, liability, etc.) is Allowance for Doubtful Accounts, and is its normal balance a debit or a credit?
8. After the accounts are adjusted and closed at the end of the fiscal year, Accounts Receivable has a balance of $783,150 and Allowance for Doubtful Accounts has a balance of $41,694. Describe how the accounts receivable and the allowance for doubtful accounts are reported on the balance sheet.
9. A firm has consistently adjusted its allowance account at the end of the fiscal year by adding a fixed percent of the period's net sales on account. After five years, the balance in Allowance for Doubtful Accounts has become very large in relationship to the balance in Accounts Receivable. Give two possible explanations.
10. Which of the two methods of estimating uncollectibles provides for the most accurate estimate of the current net realizable value of the receivables?
11. For a business, what are the advantages of a note receivable in comparison to an account receivable?
12. Tecan Company issued a note receivable to Bauer Company. (a) Who is the payee? (b) What is the title of the account used by Bauer Company in recording the note?
13. If a note provides for payment of principal of $75,000 and interest at the rate of 8%, will the interest amount to $6,000? Explain.
14. The maker of a $6,000, 10%, 120-day note receivable failed to pay the note on the due date of April 30. What accounts should be debited and credited by the payee to record the dishonored note receivable?
15. The note receivable dishonored in Eye Opener 14 is paid on May 30 by the maker, plus interest for 30 days, 9%. What entry should be made to record the receipt of the payment?
16. Under what section should accounts receivable be reported on the balance sheet?

Practice Exercises

PE 9-1A
Entries for uncollectible accounts using direct write-off method
obj. 3

Journalize the following transactions using the direct write-off method of accounting for uncollectible receivables:

Feb. 12. Received $750 from Manning Wingard and wrote off the remainder owed of $2,000 as uncollectible.

June 30. Reinstated the account of Manning Wingard and received $2,000 cash in full payment.

PE 9-1B
Entries for uncollectible accounts using direct write-off method
obj. 3

Journalize the following transactions using the direct write-off method of accounting for uncollectible receivables:

Aug. 7. Received $175 from Roosevelt McLair and wrote off the remainder owed of $400 as uncollectible.

Nov. 23. Reinstated the account of Roosevelt McLair and received $400 cash in full payment.

PE 9-2A
Entries for uncollectible accounts using allowance method
obj. 4

Journalize the following transactions using the allowance method of accounting for uncollectible receivables:

Feb. 12. Received $750 from Manning Wingard and wrote off the remainder owed of $2,000 as uncollectible.

June 30. Reinstated the account of Manning Wingard and received $2,000 cash in full payment.

PE 9-2B
Entries for uncollectible accounts using allowance method
obj. 4

Journalize the following transactions using the allowance method of accounting for uncollectible receivables:

Aug. 7. Received $175 from Roosevelt McLair and wrote off the remainder owed of $400 as uncollectible.

Nov. 23. Reinstated the account of Roosevelt McLair and received $400 cash in full payment.

PE 9-3A
Percent of sales method of estimating uncollectible accounts
obj. 4

At the end of the current year, Accounts Receivable has a balance of $500,000; Allowance for Doubtful Accounts has a credit balance of $4,000; and net sales for the year total $2,800,000. Bad debt expense is estimated at 1/4 of 1% of net sales.

Determine (1) the amount of the adjusting entry for uncollectible accounts; (2) the adjusted balances of Accounts Receivable, Allowance for Doubtful Accounts, and Bad Debt Expense; and (3) the net realizable value of accounts receivable.

PE 9-3B
Percent of sales method of estimating uncollectible accounts
obj. 4

At the end of the current year, Accounts Receivable has a balance of $1,200,000; Allowance for Doubtful Accounts has a debit balance of $5,000; and net sales for the year total $6,200,000. Bad debt expense is estimated at 1/2 of 1% of net sales.

Determine (1) the amount of the adjusting entry for uncollectible accounts; (2) the adjusted balances of Accounts Receivable, Allowance for Doubtful Accounts, and Bad Debt Expense; and (3) the net realizable value of accounts receivable.

PE 9-4A
Aging method of estimating uncollectible accounts
obj. 4

At the end of the current year, Accounts Receivable has a balance of $500,000; Allowance for Doubtful Accounts has a credit balance of $4,000; and net sales for the year total $2,800,000. Using the aging method, the balance of Allowance for Doubtful Accounts is estimated as $16,000.

Determine (1) the amount of the adjusting entry for uncollectible accounts; (2) the adjusted balances of Accounts Receivable, Allowance for Doubtful Accounts, and Bad Debt Expense; and (3) the net realizable value of accounts receivable.

PE 9-4B
Aging method of estimating uncollectible accounts
obj. 4

At the end of the current year, Accounts Receivable has a balance of $1,200,000; Allowance for Doubtful Accounts has a debit balance of $5,000; and net sales for the year total $6,200,000. Using the aging method, the balance of Allowance for Doubtful Accounts is estimated as $34,500.

Determine (1) the amount of the adjusting entry for uncollectible accounts; (2) the adjusted balances of Accounts Receivable, Allowance for Doubtful Accounts, and Bad Debt Expense; and (3) the net realizable value of accounts receivable.

PE 9-5A
Note receivable due date, maturity value, and entry
obj. 6

Mountain Supply received a 90-day, 8% note for $25,000, dated August 10 from a customer on account.

a. Determine the due date of the note.
b. Determine the maturity value of the note.
c. Journalize the entry to record the receipt of the payment of the note at maturity.

PE 9-5B
Note receivable due date, maturity value, and entry
obj. 6

Mountain Supply received a 60-day, 7% note for $120,000, dated April 2 from a customer on account.

a. Determine the due date of the note.
b. Determine the maturity value of the note.
c. Journalize the entry to record the receipt of the payment of the note at maturity.

Exercises

EX 9-1
Classifications of receivables
obj. 1

Boeing is one of the world's major aerospace firms, with operations involving commercial aircraft, military aircraft, missiles, satellite systems, and information and battle management systems. As of December 31, 2005, Boeing had $2,620 million of receivables involving U.S. government contracts and $1,155 million of receivables involving commercial aircraft customers, such as Delta Air Lines and United Airlines.

Should Boeing report these receivables separately in the financial statements, or combine them into one overall accounts receivable amount? Explain.

EX 9-2
Nature of uncollectible accounts
obj. 2

✓ a. 5.4%

Mandalay Resort Group owns and operates casinos at several of its hotels, located primarily in Nevada. At the end of one fiscal year, the following accounts and notes receivable were reported (in thousands):

Hotel accounts and notes receivable	$31,724	
Less: Allowance for doubtful accounts	1,699	
		$30,025
Casino accounts receivable	$44,139	
Less: Allowance for doubtful accounts	12,300	
		31,839

a. Compute the percentage of the allowance for doubtful accounts to the gross hotel accounts and notes receivable for the end of the fiscal year.
b. Compute the percentage of the allowance for doubtful accounts to the gross casino accounts receivable for the end of the fiscal year.
c. Discuss possible reasons for the difference in the two ratios computed in (a) and (b).

EX 9-3
Entries for uncollectible accounts, using direct write-off method
obj. 3

Journalize the following transactions in the accounts of Simmons Co., a medical equipment company that uses the direct write-off method of accounting for uncollectible receivables:

Feb. 10. Sold merchandise on account to Dr. Pete Baker, $21,400. The cost of the merchandise sold was $12,600.
July 9. Received $13,000 from Dr. Pete Baker and wrote off the remainder owed on the sale of February 10 as uncollectible.
Oct. 27. Reinstated the account of Dr. Pete Baker that had been written off on July 9 and received $8,400 cash in full payment.

EX 9-4

Entries for uncollectible receivables, using allowance method

obj. 4

Journalize the following transactions in the accounts of Simply Yummy Company, a restaurant supply company that uses the allowance method of accounting for uncollectible receivables:

June 2. Sold merchandise on account to Lynn Berry, $16,000. The cost of the merchandise sold was $9,400.

Oct. 15. Received $4,000 from Lynn Berry and wrote off the remainder owed on the sale of June 2 as uncollectible.

Dec. 30. Reinstated the account of Lynn Berry that had been written off on October 15 and received $12,000 cash in full payment.

EX 9-5

Entries to write off accounts receivable

objs. 3, 4

Jadelis Resources, a computer consulting firm, has decided to write off the $12,500 balance of an account owed by a customer. Journalize the entry to record the write-off, assuming that (a) the direct write-off method is used and (b) the allowance method is used.

EX 9-6

Providing for doubtful accounts

obj. 4

✓ a. $13,750

✓ b. $12,900

At the end of the current year, the accounts receivable account has a debit balance of $650,000, and net sales for the year total $5,500,000. Determine the amount of the adjusting entry to provide for doubtful accounts under each of the following assumptions:

a. The allowance account before adjustment has a credit balance of $3,175. Bad debt expense is estimated at ¼ of 1% of net sales.

b. The allowance account before adjustment has a credit balance of $4,600. An aging of the accounts in the customer ledger indicates estimated doubtful accounts of $17,500.

c. The allowance account before adjustment has a debit balance of $8,100. Bad debt expense is estimated at ½ of 1% of net sales.

d. The allowance account before adjustment has a debit balance of $8,100. An aging of the accounts in the customer ledger indicates estimated doubtful accounts of $24,650.

EX 9-7

Number of days past due

obj. 4

✓ Ben's Pickup Shop, 52 days

Chuck's Auto Supply distributes new and used automobile parts to local dealers throughout the Southeast. Chuck's credit terms are n/30. As of the end of business on July 31, the following accounts receivable were past due:

Account	Due Date	Amount
Ben's Pickup Shop	June 9	$5,000
Bumper Auto	July 10	4,500
Downtown Repair	March 18	2,000
Jake's Auto Repair	May 19	1,800
Like New	June 18	750
Sally's	April 12	2,800
Uptown Auto	May 8	1,500
Yellowstone Repair & Tow	April 15	3,100

Determine the number of days each account is past due.

EX 9-8

Aging-of-receivables schedule

obj. 4

The accounts receivable clerk for Vandalay Industries prepared the following partially completed aging-of-receivables schedule as of the end of business on November 30.

	A	B	C	D	E	F	G	
			Not		**Days Past Due**			
			Past				**Over**	
	Customer	**Balance**	**Due**	**1–30**	**31–60**	**61–90**	**90**	
1	Aaron Brothers Inc.	2,000	2,000					1
2	Abell Company	1,500		1,500				2
								3
21	Zollo Company	5,000			5,000			21
22	Subtotals	772,500	440,000	180,000	78,500	42,300	31,700	22

The following accounts were unintentionally omitted from the aging schedule and not included in the subtotals above:

Customer	Balance	Due Date
Tamika Industries	$25,000	August 24
Ruppert Company	8,500	September 3
Welborne Inc.	35,000	October 17
Kristi Company	6,500	November 5
Simrill Company	12,000	December 3

a. Determine the number of days past due for each of the preceding accounts.
b. Complete the aging-of-receivables schedule by including the omitted accounts.

EX 9-9
Estimating allowance for doubtful accounts
obj. 4

✓ *$75,290*

Vandalay Industries has a past history of uncollectible accounts, as shown below. Estimate the allowance for doubtful accounts, based on the aging-of-receivables schedule you completed in Exercise 9-8.

Age Class	Percent Uncollectible
Not past due	3%
1–30 days past due	5
31–60 days past due	15
61–90 days past due	25
Over 90 days past due	40

EX 9-10
Adjustment for uncollectible accounts
obj. 4

Using data in Exercise 9-8, assume that the allowance for doubtful accounts for Vandalay Industries has a credit balance of $6,150 before adjustment on November 30. Journalize the adjusting entry for uncollectible accounts as of November 30.

EX 9-11
Estimating doubtful accounts
obj. 4

Renegade Co. is a wholesaler of motorcycle supplies. An aging of the company's accounts receivable on December 31, 2008, and a historical analysis of the percentage of uncollectible accounts in each age category are as follows:

Age Interval	Balance	Percent Uncollectible
Not past due	$400,000	1%
1–30 days past due	80,000	2
31–60 days past due	18,000	5
61–90 days past due	12,500	10
91–180 days past due	6,000	70
Over 180 days past due	2,500	90
	$519,000	

Estimate what the proper balance of the allowance for doubtful accounts should be as of December 31, 2008.

EX 9-12
Entry for uncollectible accounts
obj. 4

Using the data in Exercise 9-11, assume that the allowance for doubtful accounts for Renegade Co. had a debit balance of $3,500 as of December 31, 2008.
Journalize the adjusting entry for uncollectible accounts as of December 31, 2008.

EX 9-13
Entries for bad debt expense under the direct write-off and allowance methods
obj. 5

The following selected transactions were taken from the records of Shaw Company for the first year of its operations ending December 31, 2008:

Jan. 31. Wrote off account of B. Roberts, $2,400.
Mar. 26. Received $1,500 as partial payment on the $3,500 account of Carol Castellino. Wrote off the remaining balance as uncollectible.

(continued)

July 7. Received $2,400 from B. Roberts, which had been written off on January 31. Reinstated the account and recorded the cash receipt.

Oct. 12. Wrote off the following accounts as uncollectible (record as one journal entry):

Julie Lindley	$1,350
Mark Black	950
Jennifer Kerlin	525
Beth Chalhoub	1,125
Allison Fain	725

Dec. 31. Shaw Company uses the percent of credit sales method of estimating uncollectible accounts expense. Based upon past history and industry averages, 2% of credit sales are expected to be uncollectible. Shaw recorded $750,000 of credit sales during 2008.

a. Journalize the transactions for 2008 under the direct write-off method.
b. Journalize the transactions for 2008 under the allowance method.
c. How much higher (lower) would Shaw's 2008 net income have been under the direct write-off method than under the allowance method?

EX 9-14
Entries for bad debt expense under the direct write-off and allowance methods
obj. 5

✓c. $3,675 higher

The following selected transactions were taken from the records of Kemper Company for the year ending December 31, 2008:

Feb. 2. Wrote off account of L. Armstrong, $7,250.
May 10. Received $4,150 as partial payment on the $8,500 account of Jill Knapp. Wrote off the remaining balance as uncollectible.
Aug. 12. Received the $7,250 from L. Armstrong, which had been written off on February 2. Reinstated the account and recorded the cash receipt.
Sept. 27. Wrote off the following accounts as uncollectible (record as one journal entry):

Kim Whalen	$4,400
Brad Johnson	2,210
Angelina Quan	1,375
Tammy Newsome	2,850
Donna Short	1,690

Dec. 31. The company prepared the following aging schedule for its accounts receivable:

Aging Class (Number of Days Past Due)	Receivables Balance on December 31	Estimated Percent of Uncollectible Accounts
0–30 days	$160,000	3%
31–60 days	40,000	10
61–90 days	18,000	20
91–120 days	11,000	40
More than 120 days	6,500	75
Total receivables	$235,500	

a. Journalize the transactions for 2008 under the direct write-off method.
b. Journalize the transactions for 2008 under the allowance method, assuming that the allowance account had a beginning balance of $18,000 on January 1, 2008, and the company uses the analysis of receivables method.
c. How much higher (lower) would Kemper's 2008 net income have been under the direct write-off method than under the allowance method?

EX 9-15
Effect of doubtful accounts on net income
obj. 5

During its first year of operations, West Plumbing Supply Co. had net sales of $1,800,000, wrote off $51,000 of accounts as uncollectible using the direct write-off method, and reported net income of $125,000. Determine what the net income would have been if the allowance method had been used, and the company estimated that 3% of net sales would be uncollectible.

EX 9-16
Effect of doubtful accounts on net income

obj. 5

✓ b. $7,500 credit balance

Using the data in Exercise 9-15, assume that during the second year of operations West Plumbing Supply Co. had net sales of $2,200,000, wrote off $61,500 of accounts as uncollectible using the direct write-off method, and reported net income of $143,500.

a. Determine what net income would have been in the second year if the allowance method (using 3% of net sales) had been used in both the first and second years.
b. Determine what the balance of the allowance for doubtful accounts would have been at the end of the second year if the allowance method had been used in both the first and second years.

EX 9-17
Entries for bad debt expense under the direct write-off and allowance methods

obj. 5

✓ c. $15,000 higher

Becker Company wrote off the following accounts receivable as uncollectible for the first year of its operations ending December 31, 2008:

Customer	Amount
Skip Simon	$20,000
Clarence Watson	13,500
Bill Jacks	7,300
Matt Putnam	4,200
Total	$45,000

a. Journalize the write-offs for 2008 under the direct write-off method.
b. Journalize the write-offs for 2008 under the allowance method. Also, journalize the adjusting entry for uncollectible accounts. The company recorded $2,000,000 of credit sales during 2008. Based on past history and industry averages, 3% of credit sales are expected to be uncollectible.
c. How much higher (lower) would Becker Company's 2008 net income have been under the direct write-off method than under the allowance method?

EX 9-18
Entries for bad debt expense under the direct write-off and allowance methods

obj. 5

Hazard Company wrote off the following accounts receivable as uncollectible for the year ending December 31, 2008:

Customer	Amount
Boss Hogg	$ 5,000
Daisy Duke	3,500
Bo Duke	6,300
Luke Duke	4,200
Total	$19,000

The company prepared the following aging schedule for its accounts receivable on December 31, 2008:

Aging Class (Number of Days Past Due)	Receivables Balance on December 31	Estimated Percent of Uncollectible Accounts
0–30 days	$380,000	2%
31–60 days	70,000	5
61–90 days	30,000	15
91–120 days	25,000	25
More than 120 days	10,000	50
Total receivables	$515,000	

a. Journalize the write-offs for 2008 under the direct write-off method.
b. Journalize the write-offs and the year-end adjusting entry for 2008 under the allowance method, assuming that the allowance account had a beginning balance of $18,000 on January 1, 2008, and the company uses the analysis of receivables method.

EX 9-19

Determine due date and interest on notes

obj. 6

✓ *a. May 5, $225*

Determine the due date and the amount of interest due at maturity on the following notes:

	Date of Note	Face Amount	Interest Rate	Term of Note
a.	March 6	$15,000	9%	60 days
b.	May 20	8,000	10	60 days
c.	June 2	5,000	12	90 days
d.	August 30	18,000	10	120 days
e.	October 1	10,500	12	60 days

EX 9-20

Entries for notes receivable

obj. 6

✓ *b. $30,675*

Holsten Interior Decorators issued a 90-day, 9% note for $30,000, dated May 20, to Maderia Furniture Company on account.

a. Determine the due date of the note.

b. Determine the maturity value of the note.

c. Journalize the entries to record the following: (1) receipt of the note by Maderia Furniture and (2) receipt of payment of the note at maturity.

EX 9-21

Entries for notes receivable

obj. 6

The series of seven transactions recorded in the following T-accounts were related to a sale to a customer on account and the receipt of the amount owed. Briefly describe each transaction.

CASH		
(7)	26,446	

NOTES RECEIVABLE		
(5)	26,000	(6) 26,000

ACCOUNTS RECEIVABLE		
(1)	29,500	(3) 3,500
(6)	26,226	(5) 26,000
		(7) 26,226

SALES RETURNS AND ALLOWANCES		
(3)	3,500	

MERCHANDISE INVENTORY		
(4)	2,100	(2) 17,700

COST OF MERCHANDISE SOLD		
(2)	17,700	(4) 2,100

SALES		
		(1) 29,500

INTEREST REVENUE		
		(6) 226
		(7) 220

EX 9-22

Entries for notes receivable, including year-end entries

obj. 6

The following selected transactions were completed by Cactus Co., a supplier of velcro for clothing:

2007

Dec. 13. Received from Lady Ann's Co., on account, a $60,000, 90-day, 9% note dated December 13.

31. Recorded an adjusting entry for accrued interest on the note of December 13.

2008

Mar. 12. Received payment of note and interest from Lady Ann's Co.

Journalize the transactions.

EX 9-23

Entries for receipt and dishonor of note receivable

obj. 6

Journalize the following transactions of Theres Productions:

May 3. Received a $150,000, 90-day, 8% note dated May 3 from Xpedx Company on account.

Aug. 1. The note is dishonored by Xpedx Company.

31. Received the amount due on the dishonored note plus interest for 30 days at 10% on the total amount charged to Xpedx Company on August 1.

EX 9-24
Entries for receipt and dishonor of notes receivable

objs. 4, 6

Journalize the following transactions in the accounts of Powerplay Co., which operates a riverboat casino:

Mar. 1. Received a $45,000, 60-day, 6% note dated March 1 from Pynn Co. on account.
     18. Received a $24,000, 60-day, 9% note dated March 18 from Abode Co. on account.
Apr. 30. The note dated March 1 from Pynn Co. is dishonored, and the customer's account is charged for the note, including interest.
May 17. The note dated March 18 from Abode Co. is dishonored, and the customer's account is charged for the note, including interest.
July 29. Cash is received for the amount due on the dishonored note dated March 1 plus interest for 90 days at 8% on the total amount debited to Pynn Co. on April 30.
Aug. 23. Wrote off against the allowance account the amount charged to Abode Co. on May 16 for the dishonored note dated March 18.

EX 9-25
Receivables on the balance sheet

obj. 7

List any errors you can find in the following partial balance sheet.

Mishkie Company
Balance Sheet
December 31, 2008

	Assets		
Current assets:			
Cash			$127,500
Notes receivable		$400,000	
Less interest receivable		24,000	376,000
Accounts receivable		$529,200	
Plus allowance for doubtful accounts		42,000	571,200

EX 9-26
Accounts receivable turnover and days' sales in receivables

✓ a. 2005: 6.6

Polo Ralph Lauren Corporation designs, markets, and distributes a variety of apparel, home decor, accessory, and fragrance products. The company's products include such brands as Polo by Ralph Lauren, Ralph Lauren Purple Label, Ralph Lauren, Polo Jeans Co., and Chaps. Polo Ralph Lauren reported the following (in thousands):

	For the Period Ending	
	April 2, 2005	**April 3, 2004**
Net sales	$3,305,415	$2,649,654
Accounts receivable	530,503	463,289

Assume that accounts receivable (in millions) were $391,558 at the beginning of the 2004 fiscal year.

a. Compute the accounts receivable turnover for 2005 and 2004. Round to one decimal place.
b. Compute the days' sales in receivables for 2005 and 2004. Round to one decimal place.
c. ━━▶ What conclusions can be drawn from these analyses regarding Ralph Lauren's efficiency in collecting receivables?

EX 9-27
Accounts receivable turnover and days' sales in receivables

✓ a. 2005: 8.2

H.J. Heinz Company was founded in 1869 at Sharpsburg, Pennsylvania, by Henry J. Heinz. The company manufactures and markets food products throughout the world, including ketchup, condiments and sauces, frozen food, pet food, soups, and tuna. For the fiscal years 2005 and 2004, H.J. Heinz reported the following (in thousands):

	Year Ending	
	April 27, 2005	**April 28, 2004**
Net sales	$8,912,297	$8,414,538
Account receivable	1,092,394	1,093,155

Assume that the accounts receivable (in thousands) were $1,165,460 at the beginning of 2004.

a. Compute the accounts receivable turnover for 2005 and 2004. Round to one decimal place.
b. Compute the days' sales in receivables at the end of 2005 and 2004. Round to one decimal place.
c. ▭▭▶ What conclusions can be drawn from these analyses regarding Heinz's efficiency in collecting receivables?

EX 9-28
Accounts receivable turnover and days' sales in receivables

The Limited, Inc., sells women's and men's clothing through specialty retail stores, including The Limited, Express, and Lane Bryant. The Limited sells women's intimate apparel and personal care products through Victoria's Secret and Bath & Body Works stores. The Limited reported the following (in millions):

	For the Period Ending	
	Jan. 31, 2006	Jan. 29, 2005
Net sales	$9,699	$9,408
Accounts receivable	182	128

Assume that accounts receivable (in millions) were $110 on February 1, 2004.

a. Compute the accounts receivable turnover for 2006 and 2005. Round to one decimal place.
b. Compute the day's sales in receivables for 2006 and 2005. Round to one decimal place.
c. ▭▭▶ What conclusions can be drawn from these analyses regarding The Limited's efficiency in collecting receivables?

EX 9-29
Accounts receivable turnover

Use the data in Exercises 9-27 and 9-28 to analyze the accounts receivable turnover ratios of H.J. Heinz Company and The Limited, Inc.

a. Compute the average accounts receivable turnover ratio for The Limited, Inc., and H.J. Heinz Company for the years shown in Exercises 9-27 and 9-28.
b. ▭▭▶ Does The Limited or H.J. Heinz Company have the higher average accounts receivable turnover ratio?
c. ▭▭▶ Explain the logic underlying your answer in (b).

APPENDIX EX 9-30
Discounting notes receivable

✓ a. $82,400

Alpine Co., a building construction company, holds a 120-day, 9% note for $80,000, dated July 23, which was received from a customer on account. On September 21, the note is discounted at the bank at the rate of 12%.

a. Determine the maturity value of the note.
b. Determine the number of days in the discount period.
c. Determine the amount of the discount.
d. Determine the amount of the proceeds.
e. Journalize the entry to record the discounting of the note on September 21.

APPENDIX EX 9-31
Entries for receipt and discounting of note receivable and dishonored notes

Journalize the following transactions in the accounts of Monarch Theater Productions:

Aug. 1. Received a $100,000, 90-day, 8% note dated August 1 from Elk Horn Company on account.
Sept. 1. Discounted the note at National Credit Bank at 10%.
Oct. 30. The note is dishonored by Elk Horn Company; paid the bank the amount due on the note, plus a protest fee of $500.
Nov. 29. Received the amount due on the dishonored note plus interest for 30 days at 12% on the total amount charged to Elk Horn Company on October 30.

Problems Series A

PR 9-1A
Entries related to uncollectible accounts

obj. 4

KLOOSTER & ALLEN

✓3. $798,490

The following transactions were completed by Clark Management Company during the current fiscal year ended December 31:

July 5. Received 70% of the $21,000 balance owed by Dockins Co., a bankrupt business, and wrote off the remainder as uncollectible.

Sept. 21. Reinstated the account of Bart Tiffany, which had been written off in the preceding year as uncollectible. Journalized the receipt of $4,875 cash in full payment of Tiffany's account.

Oct. 19. Wrote off the $6,275 balance owed by Ski Time Co., which has no assets.

Nov. 6. Reinstated the account of Kirby Co., which had been written off in the preceding year as uncollectible. Journalized the receipt of $4,750 cash in full payment of the account.

Dec. 31. Wrote off the following accounts as uncollectible (compound entry): Maxie Co., $2,150; Kommers Co., $3,600; Helena Distributors, $5,500; Ed Ballantyne, $1,750.

31. Based on an analysis of the $815,240 of accounts receivable, it was estimated that $16,750 will be uncollectible. Journalized the adjusting entry.

Instructions

1. Record the January 1 credit balance of $12,550 in a T-account for Allowance for Doubtful Accounts.

2. Journalize the transactions. Post each entry that affects the following selected T-accounts and determine the new balances:

> Allowance for Doubtful Accounts
> Bad Debt Expense

3. Determine the expected net realizable value of the accounts receivable as of December 31.

4. Assuming that instead of basing the provision for uncollectible accounts on an analysis of receivables, the adjusting entry on December 31 had been based on an estimated expense of $\frac{1}{4}$ of 1% of the net sales of $7,126,000 for the year, determine the following:

a. Bad debt expense for the year.

b. Balance in the allowance account after the adjustment of December 31.

c. Expected net realizable value of the accounts receivable as of December 31.

PR 9-2A
Aging of receivables; estimating allowance for doubtful accounts

obj. 4

✓3. $76,171

Steelhead Company supplies flies and fishing gear to sporting goods stores and outfitters throughout the western United States. The accounts receivable clerk for Steelhead prepared the following partially completed aging-of-receivables schedule as of the end of business on December 31, 2007:

	A	B	C	D	E	F	G	H	
			Not		Days Past Due				
			Past						
	Customer	Balance	Due	1–30	31–60	61–90	91–120	Over 120	
1	Alexandra Fishery	15,000	15,000						1
2	Cutthroat Sports	5,500			5,500				2
3									3
30	Yellowstone Sports	2,900		2,900					30
31	Subtotals	880,000	448,600	247,250	98,750	33,300	29,950	22,150	31

The following accounts were unintentionally omitted from the aging schedule.

Customer	Due Date	Balance
Baitfish Sports & Flies	June 21, 2007	$1,750
Kiwi Flies	Sept. 9, 2007	650
Adams Co.	Sept. 30, 2007	1,500
Bailey Sports	Oct. 17, 2007	600
Prince Sports	Nov. 18, 2007	950
Cahill Co.	Nov. 28, 2007	2,000
Wintson Company	Dec. 1, 2007	2,250
Goofus Bug Sports	Jan. 6, 2008	6,200

Steelhead Company has a past history of uncollectible accounts by age category, as follows:

Age Class	Percent Uncollectible
Not past due	2%
1–30 days past due	5
31–60 days past due	10
61–90 days past due	25
91–120 days past due	45
Over 120 days past due	90

Instructions
1. Determine the number of days past due for each of the preceding accounts.
2. Complete the aging-of-receivables schedule.
3. Estimate the allowance for doubtful accounts, based on the aging-of-receivables schedule.
4. Assume that the allowance for doubtful accounts for Steelhead Company has a debit balance of $3,199 before adjustment on December 31, 2007. Journalize the adjusting entry for uncollectible accounts.

PR 9-3A
Compare two methods of accounting for uncollectible receivables

objs. 3, 4, 5

✓ *1. Year 4: Balance of allowance account, end of year, $17,150*

Pegasus Company, a telephone service and supply company, has just completed its fourth year of operations. The direct write-off method of recording bad debt expense has been used during the entire period. Because of substantial increases in sales volume and the amount of uncollectible accounts, the firm is considering changing to the allowance method. Information is requested as to the effect that an annual provision of $\frac{3}{4}$% of sales would have had on the amount of bad debt expense reported for each of the past four years. It is also considered desirable to know what the balance of Allowance for Doubtful Accounts would have been at the end of each year. The following data have been obtained from the accounts:

Year	Sales	Uncollectible Accounts Written Off	1st	2nd	3rd	4th
				Year of Origin of Accounts Receivable Written Off as Uncollectible		
1st	$ 910,000	$ 3,500	$3,500			
2nd	1,064,000	4,130	2,660	$1,470		
3rd	1,330,000	7,980	980	5,600	$1,400	
4th	2,520,000	10,920		1,680	3,570	$5,670

Instructions
1. Assemble the desired data, using the following column headings:

	Bad Debt Expense			
Year	Expense Actually Reported	Expense Based on Estimate	Increase (Decrease) in Amount of Expense	Balance of Allowance Account, End of Year

2. ▬▬▶ Experience during the first four years of operations indicated that the receivables were either collected within two years or had to be written off as uncollectible. Does the estimate of $\frac{3}{4}$% of sales appear to be reasonably close to the actual experience with uncollectible accounts originating during the first two years? Explain.

PR 9-4A
Details of notes receivable and related entries

obj. 6

✓ *1. Note 2: Due date, July 15; Interest due at maturity, $190*

Gentry Co. wholesales bathroom fixtures. During the current fiscal year, Gentry Co. received the following notes:

	Date	Face Amount	Term	Interest Rate
1.	Mar. 3	$27,000	60 days	8%
2.	June 15	19,000	30 days	12
3.	Aug. 20	10,800	120 days	6
4.	Oct. 31	36,000	60 days	9
5.	Nov. 23	15,000	60 days	6
6.	Dec. 27	27,000	30 days	12

Instructions
1. Determine for each note (a) the due date and (b) the amount of interest due at maturity, identifying each note by number.
2. Journalize the entry to record the dishonor of Note (3) on its due date.
3. Journalize the adjusting entry to record the accrued interest on Notes (5) and (6) on December 31.
4. Journalize the entries to record the receipt of the amounts due on Notes (5) and (6) in January.

PR 9-5A
Notes receivable entries

obj. 6

The following data relate to notes receivable and interest for Generic Optic Co., a cable manufacturer and supplier. (All notes are dated as of the day they are received.)

June 12. Received a $20,000, 9%, 60-day note on account.
July 13. Received a $36,000, 10%, 120-day note on account.
Aug. 11. Received $20,300 on note of June 12.
Sept. 4. Received a $15,000, 9%, 60-day note on account.
Nov. 3. Received $15,225 on note of September 4.
 5. Received a $24,000, 7%, 30-day note on account.
 10. Received $37,200 on note of July 13.
 30. Received a $15,000, 10%, 30-day note on account.
Dec. 5. Received $24,140 on note of November 5.
 30. Received $15,125 on note of November 30.

Instructions
Journalize entries to record the transactions.

PR 9-6A
Sales and notes receivable transactions

obj. 6

The following were selected from among the transactions completed by Hunter Co. during the current year. Hunter Co. sells and installs home and business security systems.

Jan. 15. Loaned $6,000 cash to Dan Hough, receiving a 90-day, 8% note.
Feb. 6. Sold merchandise on account to Kent and Son, $16,000. The cost of the merchandise sold was $9,000.
 13. Sold merchandise on account to Centennial Co., $30,000. The cost of merchandise sold was $15,750.
Mar. 5. Accepted a 60-day, 6% note for $16,000 from Kent and Son on account.
 14. Accepted a 60-day, 12% note for $30,000 from Centennial Co. on account.
Apr. 15. Received the interest due from Dan Hough and a new 90-day, 10% note as a renewal of the loan of January 15. (Record both the debit and the credit to the notes receivable account.)
May 4. Received from Kent and Son the amount due on the note of March 5.
 13. Centennial Co. dishonored its note dated March 14.
June 12. Received from Centennial Co. the amount owed on the dishonored note, plus interest for 30 days at 12% computed on the maturity value of the note.
July 14. Received from Dan Hough the amount due on his note of April 15.
Aug. 10. Sold merchandise on account to Conover Co., $10,000. The cost of the merchandise sold was $6,500.
 20. Received from Conover Co. the amount of the invoice of August 10, less 1% discount.

Instructions
Journalize the transactions.

Problems Series B

PR 9-1B
Entries related to uncollectible accounts

obj. 4

KLOOSTER & ALLEN

✓ *3. $842,750*

The following transactions were completed by The Corion Gallery during the current fiscal year ended December 31:

Mar. 21. Reinstated the account of Tony Marshal, which had been written off in the preceding year as uncollectible. Journalized the receipt of $4,050 cash in full payment of Marshal's account.

Apr. 18. Wrote off the $5,500 balance owed by Crossroads Co., which is bankrupt.

Aug. 17. Received 25% of the $10,000 balance owed by Raven Co., a bankrupt business, and wrote off the remainder as uncollectible.

Oct. 10. Reinstated the account of Elden Hickman, which had been written off two years earlier as uncollectible. Recorded the receipt of $2,400 cash in full payment.

Dec. 31. Wrote off the following accounts as uncollectible (compound entry): Buffalo Co., $13,275; Combs Co., $4,000; Nash Furniture, $6,150; Tony DePuy, $1,720.

31. Based on an analysis of the $900,750 of accounts receivable, it was estimated that $58,000 will be uncollectible. Journalized the adjusting entry.

Instructions

1. Record the January 1 credit balance of $41,500 in a T-account for Allowance for Doubtful Accounts.

2. Journalize the transactions. Post each entry that affects the following T-accounts and determine the new balances:

   Allowance for Doubtful Accounts
   Bad Debt Expense

3. Determine the expected net realizable value of the accounts receivable as of December 31.

4. Assuming that instead of basing the provision for uncollectible accounts on an analysis of receivables, the adjusting entry on December 31 had been based on an estimated expense of ½ of 1% of the net sales of $10,380,000 for the year, determine the following:

   a. Bad debt expense for the year.

   b. Balance in the allowance account after the adjustment of December 31.

   c. Expected net realizable value of the accounts receivable as of December 31.

PR 9-2B
Aging of receivables; estimating allowance for doubtful accounts

obj. 4

✓ *3. $61,266*

Looks Good Wigs Company supplies wigs and hair care products to beauty salons throughout California and the Pacific Northwest. The accounts receivable clerk for Looks Good prepared the following partially completed aging-of-receivables schedule as of the end of business on December 31, 2007:

	A	B	C	D	E	F	G	H	
			Not		**Days Past Due**				
			Past						
	Customer	**Balance**	**Due**	**1–30**	**31–60**	**61–90**	**91–120**	**Over 120**	
1	Daytime Beauty	20,000	20,000						1
2	Blount Wigs	11,000			11,000				2
~									3
30	Zabka's	2,900		2,900					30
31	Subtotals	780,000	398,600	197,250	98,750	33,300	29,950	22,150	31

The following accounts were unintentionally omitted from the aging schedule:

Customer	Due Date	Balance
Uniquely Yours	July 1, 2007	$1,200
Paradise Beauty Store	Sept. 29, 2007	1,050
Morgan's Hair Products	Oct. 17, 2007	800
Hairy's Hair Care	Oct. 31, 2007	2,000
Superior Images	Nov. 18, 2007	700
Oh The Hair	Nov. 30, 2007	3,500
Mountain Coatings	Dec. 1, 2007	1,000
Theatrical Images	Jan. 3, 2008	6,200

Looks Good Wigs has a past history of uncollectible accounts by age category, as follows:

Age Class	Percent Uncollectible
Not past due	2%
1–30 days past due	4
31–60 days past due	10
61–90 days past due	15
91–120 days past due	35
Over 120 days past due	80

Instructions
1. Determine the number of days past due for each of the preceding accounts.
2. Complete the aging-of-receivables schedule.
3. Estimate the allowance for doubtful accounts, based on the aging-of-receivables schedule.
4. Assume that the allowance for doubtful accounts for Looks Good Wigs has a credit balance of $9,550 before adjustment on December 31, 2007. Journalize the adjustment for uncollectible accounts.

PR 9-3B
Compare two methods of accounting for uncollectible receivables
objs. 3, 4, 5

✓ *1. Year 4: Balance of allowance account, end of year, $5,050*

Baron Company, which operates a chain of 30 electronics supply stores, has just completed its fourth year of operations. The direct write-off method of recording bad debt expense has been used during the entire period. Because of substantial increases in sales volume and the amount of uncollectible accounts, the firm is considering changing to the allowance method. Information is requested as to the effect that an annual provision of ½% of sales would have had on the amount of bad debt expense reported for each of the past four years. It is also considered desirable to know what the balance of Allowance for Doubtful Accounts would have been at the end of each year. The following data have been obtained from the accounts:

Year	Sales	Uncollectible Accounts Written Off	Year of Origin of Accounts Receivable Written Off as Uncollectible			
			1st	2nd	3rd	4th
1st	$ 500,000	$ 600	$ 600			
2nd	750,000	1,500	700	$ 800		
3rd	1,150,000	6,500	1,900	1,500	$3,100	
4th	2,100,000	8,850		2,000	3,050	$3,800

Instructions
1. Assemble the desired data, using the following column headings:

	Bad Debt Expense			
Year	Expense Actually Reported	Expense Based on Estimate	Increase (Decrease) in Amount of Expense	Balance of Allowance Account, End of Year

2. ▬▬▶ Experience during the first four years of operations indicated that the receivables were either collected within two years or had to be written off as uncollectible.

(continued)

Does the estimate of ½% of sales appear to be reasonably close to the actual experience with uncollectible accounts originating during the first two years? Explain.

PR 9-4B
Details of notes receivable and related entries
obj. 6

✓1. Note 2: Due date, Sept. 7; Interest due at maturity, $200

Abdou Co. produces advertising videos. During the last six months of the current fiscal year, Abdou Co. received the following notes:

	Date	Face Amount	Term	Interest Rate
1.	May 17	$12,000	45 days	9%
2.	July 9	15,000	60 days	8
3.	Aug. 1	18,000	90 days	7
4.	Sept. 4	20,000	90 days	6
5.	Nov. 26	54,000	60 days	8
6.	Dec. 16	36,000	60 days	13

Instructions
1. Determine for each note (a) the due date and (b) the amount of interest due at maturity, identifying each note by number.
2. Journalize the entry to record the dishonor of Note (3) on its due date.
3. Journalize the adjusting entry to record the accrued interest on Notes (5) and (6) on December 31.
4. Journalize the entries to record the receipt of the amounts due on Notes (5) and (6) in January and February.

PR 9-5B
Notes receivable entries
obj. 6

The following data relate to notes receivable and interest for Vidovich Co., a financial services company. (All notes are dated as of the day they are received.)

Mar. 6. Received an $18,000, 9%, 60-day note on account.
     25. Received a $10,000, 8%, 90-day note on account.
May   5. Received $18,270 on note of March 6.
     16. Received a $40,000, 7%, 90-day note on account.
     31. Received a $12,000, 8%, 30-day note on account.
June 23. Received $10,200 on note of March 25.
     30. Received $12,080 on note of May 31.
July 1. Received a $5,000, 12%, 30-day note on account.
     31. Received $5,050 on note of July 1.
Aug. 14. Received $40,700 on note of May 16.

Instructions
Journalize the entries to record the transactions.

PR 9-6B
Sales and notes receivable transactions
obj. 6

The following were selected from among the transactions completed during the current year by Hackworth Co., an appliance wholesale company:

Jan. 12. Sold merchandise on account to Dewit Co., $12,300. The cost of merchandise sold was $6,800.
Mar. 12. Accepted a 60-day, 8% note for $12,300 from Dewit Co. on account.
May 11. Received from Dewit Co. the amount due on the note of March 12.
June 3. Sold merchandise on account to Kihl's for $15,000. The cost of merchandise sold was $10,750.
      5. Loaned $18,000 cash to Michele Hobson, receiving a 30-day, 6% note.
     13. Received from Kihl's the amount due on the invoice of June 3, less 2% discount.
July 5. Received the interest due from Michele Hobson and a new 60-day, 9% note as a renewal of the loan of June 5. (Record both the debit and the credit to the notes receivable account.)
Sept. 3. Received from Michele Hobson the amount due on her note of July 5.
     17. Sold merchandise on account to Wood Co., $9,000. The cost of merchandise sold was $6,250.
Oct. 4. Accepted a 60-day, 6% note for $9,000 from Wood Co. on account.

Dec. 3. Wood Co. dishonored the note dated October 4.
　　29. Received from Wood Co. the amount owed on the dishonored note, plus interest for 26 days at 6% computed on the maturity value of the note.

Instructions
Journalize the transactions.

Special Activities

SA 9-1
Ethics and professional conduct in business

ETHICS

Neka Kiser, vice president of operations for Mountain National Bank, has instructed the bank's computer programmer to use a 365-day year to compute interest on depository accounts (payables). Neka also instructed the programmer to use a 360-day year to compute interest on loans (receivables).

　　Discuss whether Neka is behaving in a professional manner.

SA 9-2
Estimate uncollectible accounts

For several years, sales have been on a "cash only" basis. On January 1, 2005, however, Litespeed Co. began offering credit on terms of n/30. The amount of the adjusting entry to record the estimated uncollectible receivables at the end of each year has been ¼ of 1% of credit sales, which is the rate reported as the average for the industry. Credit sales and the year-end credit balances in Allowance for Doubtful Accounts for the past four years are as follows:

Year	Credit Sales	Allowance for Doubtful Accounts
2005	$8,160,000	$ 8,520
2006	8,400,000	15,840
2007	8,520,000	22,680
2008	8,700,000	32,820

　　Ursula Sykes, president of Litespeed Co., is concerned that the method used to account for and write off uncollectible receivables is unsatisfactory. She has asked for your advice in the analysis of past operations in this area and for recommendations for change.

1. Determine the amount of (a) the addition to Allowance for Doubtful Accounts and (b) the accounts written off for each of the four years.
2. a. 　　 Advise Ursula Sykes as to whether the estimate of ¼ of 1% of credit sales appears reasonable.
　 b. 　　 Assume that after discussing (a) with Ursula Sykes, she asked you what action might be taken to determine what the balance of Allowance for Doubtful Accounts should be at December 31, 2008, and what possible changes, if any, you might recommend in accounting for uncollectible receivables. How would you respond?

SA 9-3
Accounts receivable turnover and days' sales in receivables

REAL WORLD

FAI

Best Buy is a specialty retailer of consumer electronics, including personal computers, entertainment software, and appliances. Best Buy operates retail stores in addition to the Best Buy, Media Play, On Cue, and Magnolia Hi Fi Web sites. For the years ending February 26, 2005, and February 28, 2004, Best Buy reported the following (in millions):

	Year Ending	
	Feb. 26, 2005	**Feb. 28, 2004**
Net sales	$27,433	$24,548
Accounts receivable at end of year	375	343

　　Assume that the accounts receivable (in millions) were $312 at the beginning of the year ending February 28, 2004.

1. Compute the accounts receivable turnover for 2005 and 2004. Round to one decimal place.
2. Compute the days' sales in receivables at the end of 2005 and 2004.

(continued)

3. ◖▬▬▶ What conclusions can be drawn from (1) and (2) regarding Best Buy's efficiency in collecting receivables?
4. ◖▬▬▶ For its years ending in 2005 and 2004, Circuit City Stores, Inc., has an accounts receivable turnover of 61.0 and 56.3, respectively. Compare Best Buy's efficiency in collecting receivables with that of Circuit City.
5. ◖▬▬▶ What assumption did we make about sales for the Circuit City and Best Buy ratio computations that might distort the two company ratios and therefore cause the ratios not to be comparable?

SA 9-4
Accounts receivable turnover and days' sales in receivables

Apple Computer, Inc., designs, manufactures, and markets personal computers and related personal computing and communicating solutions for sale primarily to education, creative, consumer, and business customers. Substantially all of the company's net sales over the last five years are from sales of its Apple Macintosh line of personal computers and related software and peripherals. For the fiscal years ending September 24, 2005 and September 25, 2004, Apple reported the following (in millions):

	Year Ending	
	Sept. 24, 2005	Sept. 25, 2004
Net sales	$13,931	$8,279
Accounts receivable at end of year	895	774

Assume that the accounts receivable (in millions) were $766 at the beginning of 2004.

1. Compute the accounts receivable turnover for 2005 and 2004. Round to one decimal place.
2. Compute the days' sales in receivables at the end of 2005 and 2004.
3. ◖▬▬▶ What conclusions can be drawn from (1) and (2) regarding Apple's efficiency in collecting receivables?
4. ◖▬▬▶ Using the Internet, access the Apple September 25, 2004, 10-K filing with the Securities and Exchange Commission. You can use the PricewaterhouseCoopers Web site at **http://edgarscan.pwcglobal.com** to search for company filings by name. Search the 10-K filing for the term "receivable." Identify one company that had accounts receivable with Apple at the end of fiscal years 2005 and 2004.

SA 9-5
Accounts receivable turnover and days' sales in receivables

EarthLink, Inc., is a nationwide Internet Service Provider (ISP). Earthlink provides a variety of services to its customers, including narrowband access, broadband or high-speed access, and Web hosting services. For the years ending December 31, 2005 and 2004, Earthlink reported the following (in thousands):

	Year Ending	
	Dec. 31, 2005	Dec. 31, 2004
Net sales	$1,290,072	$1,382,202
Accounts receivable at end of year	36,033	30,733

Assume that the accounts receivable (in thousands) were $35,585 at January 1, 2004.

1. Compute the accounts receivable turnover for 2005 and 2004. Round to one decimal place.
2. Compute the days' sales in receivables at the end of 2005 and 2004.
3. ◖▬▬▶ What conclusions can be drawn from (1) and (2) regarding EarthLink's efficiency in collecting receivables?
4. ◖▬▬▶ Given the nature of EarthLink's operations, do you believe EarthLink's accounts receivable turnover ratio would be higher or lower than a typical manufacturing company, such as Boeing or Kellogg Company? Explain.

SA 9-6
Accounts receivable turnover

The accounts receivable turnover ratio will vary across companies, depending upon the nature of the company's operations. For example, an accounts receivable turnover of 6 for an Internet Services Provider is unacceptable but might be excellent for a manufacturer of specialty milling equipment. A list of well-known companies follows.

Alcoa Inc.   The Coca-Cola Company   Kroger
AutoZone, Inc.   Delta Air Lines   Procter & Gamble
Barnes & Noble, Inc.   The Home Depot   Wal-Mart
Caterpillar   IBM   Whirlpool Corporation

1. Using the PricewaterhouseCoopers Web site, **http://edgarscan.pwcglobal.com**, look up each company by entering its name. Click on each company's name and then scroll down to the bottom of the page to "Set Preferences." Select "Receivables Turnover" in the Ratios list. Then click "Save Preferences."
2. Categorize each of the preceding companies as to whether its turnover ratio is above or below 15.
3. Based upon (2), identify a characteristic of companies with accounts receivable turnover ratios above 15.

Answers to Self-Examination Questions

1. **B** The estimate of uncollectible accounts, $8,500 (answer C), is the amount of the desired balance of Allowance for Doubtful Accounts after adjustment. The amount of the current provision to be made for uncollectible accounts expense is thus $6,000 (answer B), which is the amount that must be added to the Allowance for Doubtful Accounts credit balance of $2,500 (answer A) so that the account will have the desired balance of $8,500.

2. **B** The amount expected to be realized from accounts receivable is the balance of Accounts Receivable, $100,000, less the balance of Allowance for Doubtful Accounts, $7,000, or $93,000 (answer B).

3. **C** Maturity value is the amount that is due at the maturity or due date. The maturity value of $10,300 (answer C) is determined as follows:

Face amount of note ... $10,000
Plus interest ($10,000 × 0.12 × 90/360) ... 300
Maturity value of note ... $10,300

4. **C** November 3 is the due date of a $12,000, 90-day, 8% note receivable dated August 5 [26 days in August (31 days − 5 days) + 30 days in September + 31 days in October + 3 days in November].

5. **B** If a note is dishonored, Accounts Receivable is debited for the maturity value of the note (answer B). The maturity value of the note is its face value (answer A) plus the accrued interest. The maturity value of the note less accrued interest (answer C) is equal to the face value of the note. The maturity value of the note plus accrued interest (answer D) is incorrect, since the interest would be added twice.

chapter

10

Fixed Assets and Intangible Assets

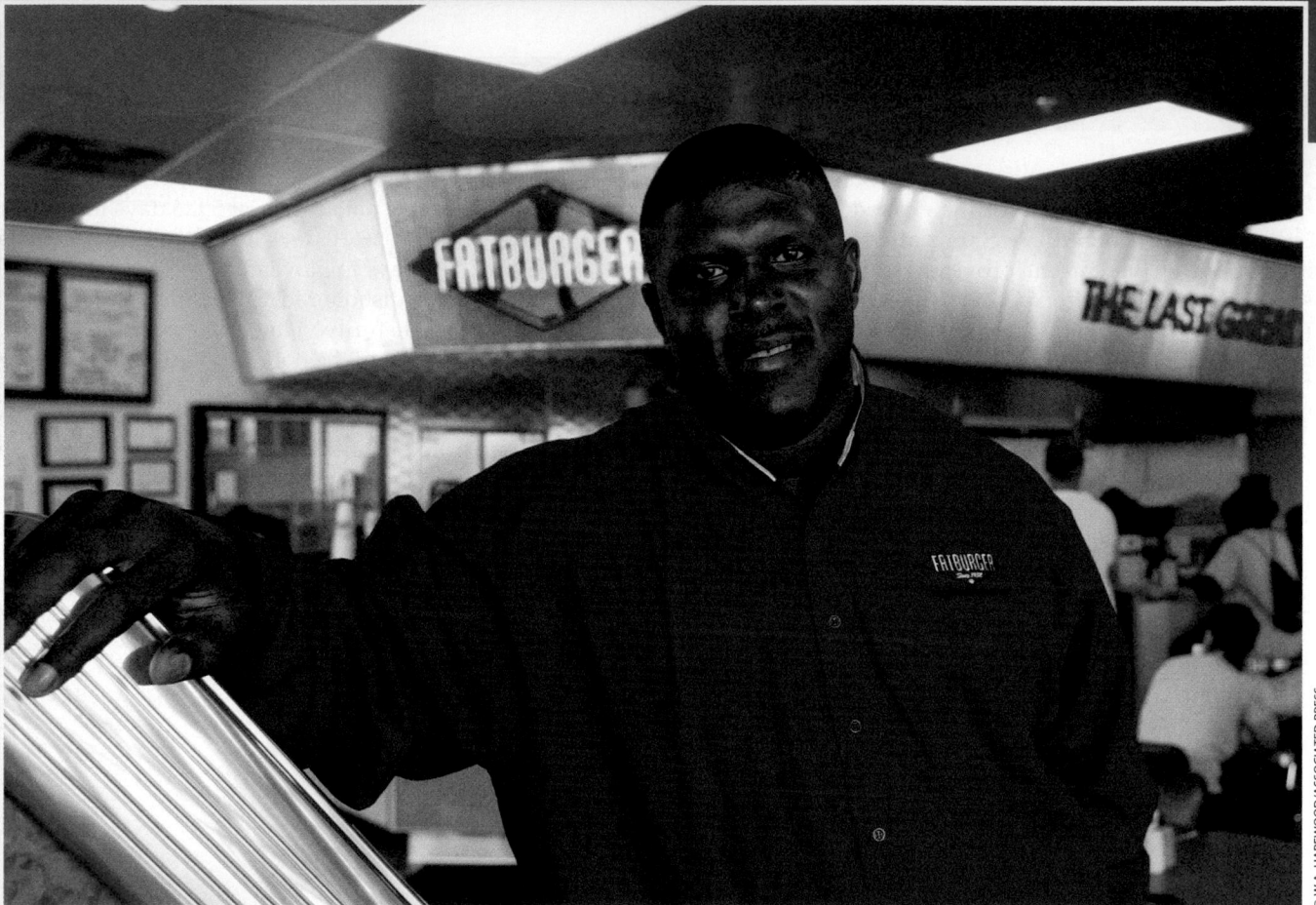

© W.A. HAREWOOD/ASSOCIATED PRESS

objectives

After studying this chapter, you should be able to:

1 *Define, classify, and account for the cost of fixed assets.*

2 *Compute depreciation, using the following methods: straight-line method, units-of-production method, and double-declining-balance method.*

3 *Journalize entries for the disposal of fixed assets.*

4 *Compute depletion and journalize the entry for depletion.*

5 *Describe the accounting for intangible assets, such as patents, copyrights, and goodwill.*

6 *Describe how depreciation expense is reported in an income statement and prepare a balance sheet that includes fixed assets and intangible assets.*

FATBURGER Corporation

Do you remember purchasing your first car? You probably didn't buy your first car like you would buy a CD. A used or new car is expensive and will affect your life for years to come. Typically, you would spend hours considering different makes and models, safety ratings, warranties, and operating costs before deciding on the final purchase.

Like buying her first car, Lovie Yancey spent a lot of time before deciding to open her first restaurant. In 1952, she created the biggest, juiciest hamburger that anyone had ever seen. She called it a Fatburger. The restaurant initially started as a 24-hour operation to cater to the schedules of professional musicians. As a fan of popular music and its performers, Yancey played rhythm and blues, jazz, and blues recordings for her customers. Fatburger's popularity with entertainers was illustrated when its name was used in a 1992 rap by Ice Cube. "Two in the mornin' got the Fatburger," Cube said, in "It Was a Good Day," a track on his *Predator* album.

The demand for this incredible burger was such that, in 1980, Ms. Yancey decided to offer Fatburger franchise opportunities. In 1990, with the goal of expanding Fatburger throughout the world, the Fatburger Corporation purchased the business from Ms. Yancey. Today, Fatburger has grown to a multi-restaurant chain with owners and investors such as talk show host Montel Williams, Cincinnati Bengal's tackle Willie Anderson, comedian David Spade, and musicians Cher, Janet Jackson, and Pharrell.

So, how much would it cost you to open a Fatburger restaurant? The total investment ranges from $491,500 to $818,000 per restaurant. Thus, in starting a Fatburger restaurant, you would be making a significant investment that would affect your life for years to come. In this chapter, we discuss the accounting for investments in fixed assets such as those used to open a Fatburger restaurant. We also explain how to determine the portion of the fixed asset that becomes an expense over time. Finally, we discuss the accounting for the disposal of fixed assets and accounting for intangible assets such as patents and copyrights.

http://www.fatburger.net

Nature of Fixed Assets

objective 1

Define, classify, and account for the cost of fixed assets.

Businesses purchase and use a variety of fixed assets, such as equipment, furniture, tools, machinery, buildings, and land. **Fixed assets** are long-term or relatively permanent assets. They are *tangible assets* because they exist physically. They are owned and used by the business and are not offered for sale as part of normal operations. Other descriptive titles for these assets are *plant assets* or *property, plant, and equipment*.

The fixed assets of a business can be a significant part of the total assets. Exhibit 1 shows the percent of fixed assets to total assets for some select companies, divided between service, manufacturing, and merchandising firms. As you can see, the fixed assets for most firms comprise a significant proportion of their total assets. In contrast, Computer Associates International, Inc., is a consulting firm that relies less on fixed assets to deliver value to customers.

CLASSIFYING COSTS

Exhibit 2 displays questions that help classify costs. If the purchased item is long-lived, then it should be *capitalized*, which means it should appear on the balance sheet as an asset. Otherwise, the cost should be reported as an expense on the income statement. Capitalized costs are normally expected to last more than a year. If the asset is also used for a productive purpose, which involves a repeated use or benefit, then it should

EXHIBIT 1

Fixed Assets as a Percent of Total Assets—Selected Companies

	Fixed Assets as a Percent of Total Assets
Service Firms:	
Computer Associates International, Inc.	6%
Marriott International, Inc.	31
Verizon Communications	45
Manufacturing Firms:	
Alcoa Inc.	40%
Ford Motor Company	35
ExxonMobil Corporation	60
Merchandising Firms:	
Kroger	55%
Walgreen Co.	46
Wal-Mart	53

be classified as a fixed asset, such as land, buildings, or equipment. An asset does not need to be used regularly to be a fixed asset. For example, standby equipment for use in the event of a breakdown of regular equipment or for use only during peak periods is included in fixed assets. Fixed assets that have been abandoned or are no longer used should not be classified as fixed assets.

EXHIBIT 2

Classifying Costs

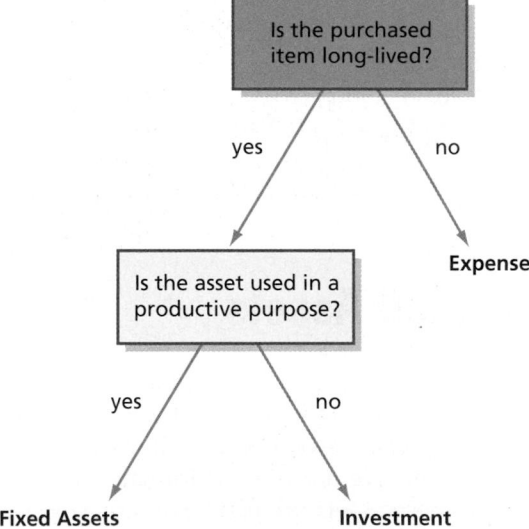

Fixed assets are owned and used by the business and are not offered for resale. Long-lived assets held for resale are not classified as fixed assets, but should be listed on the balance sheet in a section entitled *Investments*. For example, undeveloped land acquired as an investment for resale would be classified as an investment, not land.

REAL WORLD

Intel Corporation recently reported almost $2 billion of construction in progress, which was 5% of its total fixed assets.

THE COST OF FIXED ASSETS

The costs of acquiring fixed assets include all amounts spent to get the asset in place and ready for use. For example, freight costs and the costs of installing equipment are included as part of the asset's total cost. The direct costs associated with new construction, such as labor and materials, should be debited to a "construction in progress" asset account. When the construction is complete, the costs should be reclassified by crediting the construction in progress account and debiting the appropriate fixed asset account. For growing companies, construction in progress can be significant.

Exhibit 3 summarizes some of the common costs of acquiring fixed assets. These costs should be recorded by debiting the related fixed asset account, such as Land,[1] Building, Land Improvements, or Machinery and Equipment.

EXHIBIT 3 | Costs of Acquiring Fixed Assets

Building
- Architects' fees
- Engineers' fees
- Insurance costs incurred during construction
- Interest on money borrowed to finance construction
- Walkways to and around the building
- Sales taxes
- Repairs (purchase of existing building)
- Reconditioning (purchase of existing building)
- Modifying for use
- Permits from government agencies

Machinery & Equipment
- Sales taxes
- Freight
- Installation
- Repairs (purchase of used equipment)
- Reconditioning (purchase of used equipment)
- Insurance while in transit
- Assembly
- Modifying for use
- Testing for use
- Permits from government agencies

Land
- Purchase price
- Sales taxes
- Permits from government agencies
- Broker's commissions
- Title fees
- Surveying fees
- Delinquent real estate taxes
- Razing or removing unwanted buildings, less any salvage
- Grading and leveling
- Paving a public street bordering the land

Land Improvements
- Trees and shrubs
- Fences
- Outdoor lighting
- Paved parking areas

Only costs necessary for preparing a long-lived asset for use should be included as a cost of the asset. Unnecessary costs that do not increase the asset's usefulness are recorded as an expense. For example, the following costs are included as an expense:

- Vandalism
- Mistakes in installation
- Uninsured theft
- Damage during unpacking and installing
- Fines for not obtaining proper permits from governmental agencies

CAPITAL AND REVENUE EXPENDITURES

Once a fixed asset has been acquired and placed in service, expenditures may be incurred for ordinary maintenance and repairs. In addition, expenditures may be incurred

---

1 As discussed here, land is assumed to be used only as a location or site and not for its mineral deposits or other natural resources.

for improving an asset or for extraordinary repairs that extend the asset's useful life. Expenditures that benefit only the current period are called **revenue expenditures**. Expenditures that improve the asset or extend its useful life are **capital expenditures**.

Ordinary Maintenance and Repairs Expenditures related to the ordinary maintenance and repairs of a fixed asset are recorded as an expense of the current period. Such expenditures are *revenue expenditures* and are recorded as increases to Repairs and Maintenance Expense. For example, $300 paid for a tune-up of a delivery truck would be recorded as follows:

	Repairs and Maintenance Expense		3 0 0 00		
	Cash				3 0 0 00

Asset Improvements After a fixed asset has been placed in service, expenditures may be incurred to improve an asset. For example, the service value of a delivery truck might be improved by adding a $5,500 hydraulic lift to allow for easier and quicker loading of heavy cargo. Such expenditures are *capital expenditures* and are recorded as increases to the fixed asset account. In the case of the hydraulic lift, the expenditure is recorded as follows:

	Delivery Truck		5 5 0 0 00		
	Cash				5 5 0 0 00

Because the cost of the delivery truck has increased, depreciation for the truck would also change over its remaining useful life.

Extraordinary Repairs After a fixed asset has been placed in service, expenditures may be incurred to extend the asset's useful life. For example, the engine of a forklift that is near the end of its useful life may be overhauled at a cost of $4,500, which would extend its useful life by eight years. Such expenditures are *capital expenditures* and are recorded as a decrease in an accumulated depreciation account. In the case of the forklift, the expenditure is recorded as follows:

	Accumulated Depreciation—Forklift		4 5 0 0 00		
	Cash				4 5 0 0 00

Because the forklift's remaining useful life has changed, depreciation for the forklift would also change based upon the new book value of the forklift.

Integrity, Objectivity, and Ethics in Business

ETHICS

CAPITAL CRIME

One of the largest alleged accounting frauds in history involved the improper accounting for capital expenditures. WorldCom, the second largest telecommunications company in the United States, improperly treated maintenance expenditures on its telecommunications network as capital expenditures. As a result, the company had to restate its prior years' earnings downward by nearly $4 billion to correct this error. The company declared bankruptcy within months of disclosing the error, and the CEO was sentenced to 25 years in prison.

The accounting for revenue and capital expenditures is summarized below.

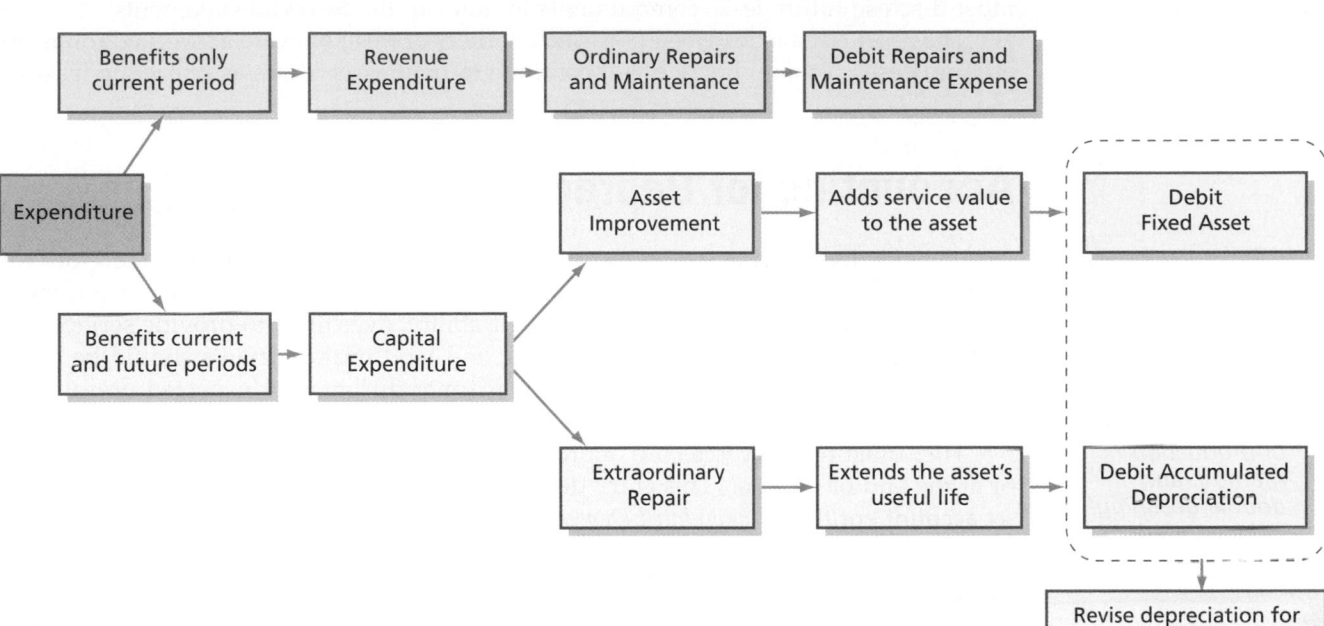

Example Exercise 10-1   objective 1

On June 18, GTS Co. paid $1,200 to upgrade a hydraulic lift and $45 for an oil change for one of its delivery trucks. Journalize the entries for the hydraulic lift upgrade and oil change expenditures.

Follow My Example 10-1

June 18	Delivery Truck	1,200	
	Cash		1,200
18	Repairs and Maintenance Expense	45	
	Cash		45

For Practice: PE 10-1A, PE 10-1B

LEASING FIXED ASSETS

You are probably familiar with leases. A *lease* is a contract for the use of an asset for a stated period of time. Leases are frequently used in business. For example, automobiles, computers, medical equipment, buildings, and airplanes are often leased.

The two parties to a lease contract are the lessor and the lessee. The *lessor* is the party who owns the asset. The *lessee* is the party to whom the rights to use the asset are granted by the lessor. The lessee is obligated to make periodic rent payments for the lease term. All leases are classified by the lessee as either capital leases or operating leases.

A **capital lease** is accounted for as if the lessee has, in fact, purchased the asset. The lessee debits an asset account for the fair market value of the asset and credits a long-term lease liability account. The asset is then written off as expense (amortized) over the life of the capital lease. The accounting for capital leases and the criteria that a capital lease must satisfy are discussed in more advanced accounting texts.

A lease that is not classified as a capital lease for accounting purposes is classified as an **operating lease**. The lessee records the payments under an operating lease by debiting *Rent Expense* and crediting *Cash*. Neither future lease obligations nor the

On December 31, 2004, Delta Air Lines operated 297 aircraft under operating leases and 48 aircraft under capital leases with future lease commitments of over $10 billion.

future rights to use the leased asset are recognized in the accounts. However, the lessee must disclose future lease commitments in notes to the financial statements.

The asset rentals described in earlier chapters of this text were accounted for as operating leases. To simplify, we will continue to treat asset leases as operating leases.

Accounting for Depreciation

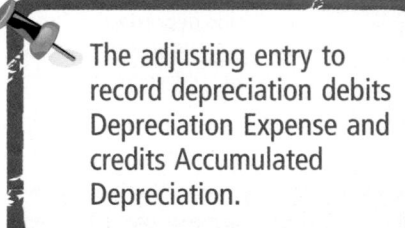

objective **2**

Compute depreciation, using the following methods: straight-line method, units-of-production method, and double-declining-balance method.

As we have discussed in earlier chapters, land has an unlimited life and therefore can provide unlimited services. On the other hand, other fixed assets such as equipment, buildings, and land improvements lose their ability, over time, to provide services. As a result, the costs of equipment, buildings, and land improvements should be transferred to expense accounts in a systematic manner during their expected useful lives. This periodic transfer of cost to expense is called **depreciation**.

The adjusting entry to record depreciation is usually made at the end of each month or at the end of the year. This entry debits *Depreciation Expense* and credits a *contra asset* account entitled *Accumulated Depreciation* or *Allowance for Depreciation*. The use of a contra asset account allows the original cost to remain unchanged in the fixed asset account.

Factors that cause a decline in the ability of a fixed asset to provide services may be identified as physical depreciation or functional depreciation. *Physical depreciation* occurs from wear and tear while in use and from the action of the weather. *Functional depreciation* occurs when a fixed asset is no longer able to provide services at the level for which it was intended. For example, a personal computer made in the 1980s would not be able to provide an Internet connection. Such advances in technology during this century have made functional depreciation an increasingly important cause of depreciation.

> The adjusting entry to record depreciation debits Depreciation Expense and credits Accumulated Depreciation.

The term *depreciation* as used in accounting is often misunderstood because the same term is also used in business to mean a decline in the market value of an asset. However, the amount of a fixed asset's unexpired cost reported in the balance sheet usually does not agree with the amount that could be realized from its sale. Fixed assets are held for use in a business rather than for sale. It is assumed that the business will continue as a going concern. Thus, a decision to dispose of a fixed asset is based mainly on the usefulness of the asset to the business and not on its market value.

REAL WORLD

Would you have more cash if you depreciated your car? The answer is no. Depreciation does not affect your cash flows. Likewise, depreciation does not affect the cash flows of a business. However, depreciation is subtracted in determining net income.

Another common misunderstanding is that accounting for depreciation provides cash needed to replace fixed assets as they wear out. This misunderstanding probably occurs because depreciation, unlike most expenses, does not require an outlay of cash in the period in which it is recorded. The cash account is neither increased nor decreased by the periodic entries that transfer the cost of fixed assets to depreciation expense accounts.

FACTORS IN COMPUTING DEPRECIATION EXPENSE

Three factors are considered in determining the amount of depreciation expense to be recognized each period. These three factors are (a) the fixed asset's initial cost, (b) its expected useful life, and (c) its estimated value at the end of its useful life. This third factor is called the *residual value, scrap value, salvage value,* or *trade-in value*.

A fixed asset's **residual value** at the end of its expected useful life must be estimated at the time the asset is placed in service. If a fixed asset is expected to have little or no residual value when it is taken out of service, then its initial cost should be spread over its expected useful life as depreciation expense. If, however, a fixed asset is expected to have a significant residual value, the difference between its initial cost and its residual value, called the asset's *depreciable cost*, is the amount that is spread over the asset's useful life as depreciation expense. Exhibit 4 shows the relationship among the three factors and the periodic depreciation expense.

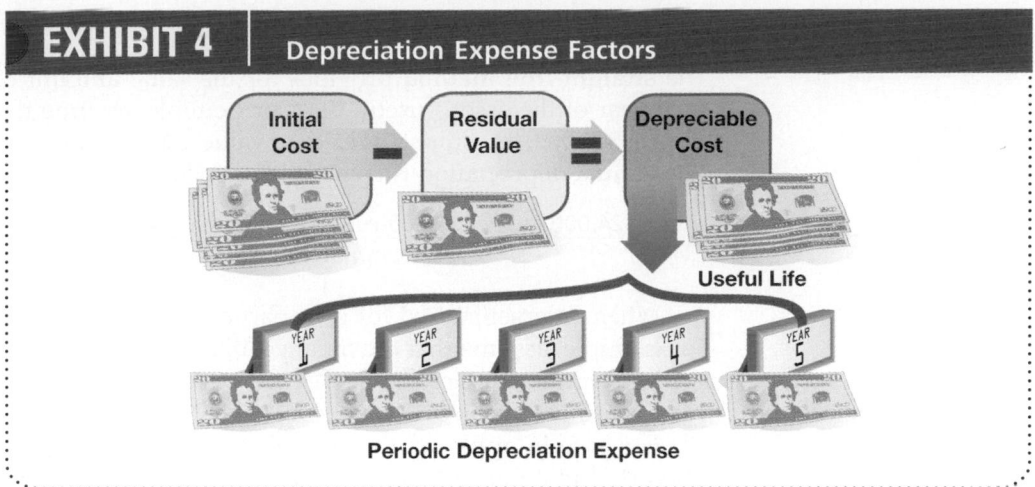

EXHIBIT 4 | **Depreciation Expense Factors**

JCPenney depreciates buildings over 50 years, while Tandy Corporation depreciates buildings over 10–40 years.

The Internal Revenue Service guideline for the useful life of automobiles and light-duty trucks is five years, while the designated life for most machinery and equipment is seven years.

A fixed asset's *expected useful life* must also be estimated at the time the asset is placed in service. Estimates of expected useful lives are available from various trade associations and other publications. For federal income tax purposes, the Internal Revenue Service has established guidelines for useful lives. These guidelines may also be helpful in determining depreciation for financial reporting purposes. However, it is common for different companies to use a different useful life for similar assets.

In practice, many businesses use the guideline that all assets placed in or taken out of service during the first half of a month are treated as if the event occurred on the first day of *that* month. That is, these businesses compute depreciation on these assets for the entire month. Likewise, all fixed asset additions and deductions during the second half of a month are treated as if the event occurred on the first day of the *next* month. We will follow this practice in this chapter.

It is not necessary that a business use a single method of computing depreciation for all its depreciable assets. The methods used in the accounts and financial statements may also differ from the methods used in determining income taxes and property taxes. The three methods used most often are (1) straight-line, (2) units-of-production, and (3) double-declining-balance.[2] Exhibit 5 shows the extent of the use of these methods in financial statements.

EXHIBIT 5

Use of Depreciation Methods

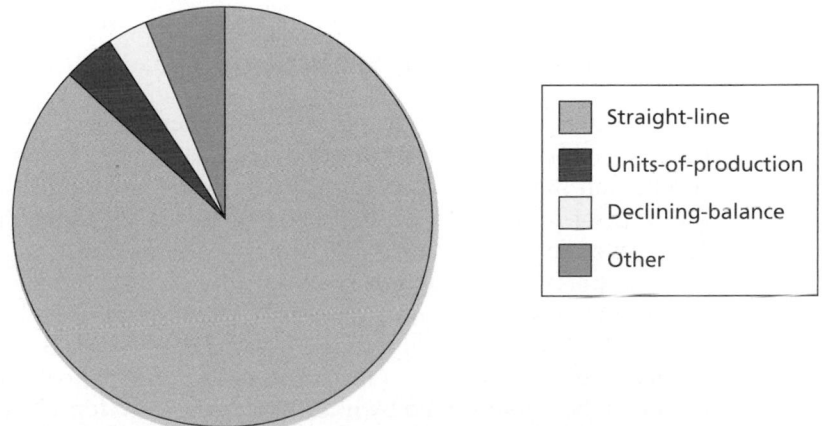

Legend:
- Straight-line
- Units-of-production
- Declining-balance
- Other

Source: Accounting Trends & Techniques, 59th ed., American Institute of Certified Public Accountants, New York, 2005.

---

2 Another method not often used today, called the *sum-of-the-years-digits method*, is described and illustrated in the appendix at the end of this chapter.

STRAIGHT-LINE METHOD

The **straight-line method** provides for the same amount of depreciation expense for each year of the asset's useful life. For example, assume that the cost of a depreciable asset is $24,000, its estimated residual value is $2,000, and its estimated life is five years. The annual depreciation is computed as follows:

$$\frac{\$24,000 \text{ cost} - \$2,000 \text{ estimated residual value}}{5 \text{ years estimated life}} = \$4,400 \text{ annual depreciation}$$

When an asset is used for only part of a year, the annual depreciation is prorated. For example, assume that the fiscal year ends on December 31 and that the asset in the above example is placed in service on October 1. The depreciation for the first fiscal year of use would be $1,100 ($4,400 × 3/12).

For ease in applying the straight-line method, the annual depreciation may be converted to a percentage of the depreciable cost. This percentage is determined by dividing 100% by the number of years of useful life. For example, a useful life of 20 years converts to a 5% rate (100%/20), 8 years converts to a 12.5% rate (100%/8), and so on.[3] In the above example, the annual depreciation of $4,400 can be computed by multiplying the depreciable cost of $22,000 by 20% (100%/5).

The straight-line method is simple and is widely used. It provides a reasonable transfer of costs to periodic expense when the asset's use and the related revenues from its use are about the same from period to period.

Example Exercise 10-2

objective 2

Equipment acquired at the beginning of the year at a cost of $125,000 has an estimated residual value of $5,000 and an estimated useful life of 10 years. Determine (a) the depreciable cost, (b) the straight-line rate, and (c) the annual straight-line depreciation.

Follow My Example 10-2

a. $120,000 ($125,000 − $5,000)
b. 10% = 1/10
c. $12,000 ($120,000 × 10%), or ($120,000/10 years)

For Practice: PE 10-2A, PE 10-2B

UNITS-OF-PRODUCTION METHOD

How would you depreciate a fixed asset when its service is related to use rather than time? When the amount of use of a fixed asset varies from year to year, the units-of-production method is more appropriate than the straight-line method. In such cases, the units-of-production method better matches the depreciation expense with the related revenue.

The **units-of-production method** provides for the same amount of depreciation expense for each unit produced or each unit of capacity used by the asset. To apply this method, the useful life of the asset is expressed in terms of units of productive capacity such as hours or miles. The total depreciation expense for each accounting period is then determined by multiplying the unit depreciation by the number of units produced or used during the period. For example, assume that a machine with a cost of $24,000 and an estimated residual value of $2,000 is expected to have an estimated

Norfolk Southern Corporation depreciates its train engines based upon hours of operation.

---

3 The depreciation rate may also be expressed as a fraction. For example, the annual straight-line rate for an asset with a three-year useful life is 1/3.

life of 10,000 operating hours. The depreciation for a unit of one hour is computed as follows:

$$\frac{\$24,000 \text{ cost} - \$2,000 \text{ estimated residual value}}{10,000 \text{ estimated hours}} = \$2.20 \text{ hourly depreciation}$$

Assuming that the machine was in operation for 2,100 hours during a year, the depreciation for that year would be $4,620 ($2.20 × 2,100 hours).

Example Exercise 10-3   objective **2**

Equipment acquired at a cost of $180,000 has an estimated residual value of $10,000, has an estimated useful life of 40,000 hours, and was operated 3,600 hours during the year. Determine (a) the depreciable cost, (b) the depreciation rate, and (c) the units-of-production depreciation for the year.

Follow My Example 10-3

a. $170,000 ($180,000 − $10,000)
b. $4.25 per hour ($170,000/40,000 hours)
c. $15,300 (3,600 hours × $4.25)

For Practice: PE 10-3A, PE 10-3B

DOUBLE-DECLINING-BALANCE METHOD

The **double-declining-balance method** provides for a declining periodic expense over the estimated useful life of the asset. In using this method, a double-declining-balance rate is determined by doubling the straight-line rate. To illustrate, assume that an asset has a useful life of five years. The double-declining-balance rate of 40% is determined as shown below.

$$\text{Double-Declining-Balance Rate} = \text{Straight-Line Rate} \times 2$$
$$= (1/5) \times 2 = 20\% \times 2$$
$$= 40\%$$

For the first year of use, the cost of the asset is multiplied by the double-declining-balance rate. After the first year, the declining **book value** (cost minus accumulated depreciation) of the asset is multiplied by this rate. To illustrate, the annual double-declining-balance depreciation for an asset with an estimated five-year life and a cost of $24,000 is shown below.

Year	Cost	Accum. Depr. at Beginning of Year	Book Value at Beginning of Year		Double-Declining Balance Rate	Depreciation for Year	Book Value at End of Year
1	$24,000		$24,000.00	×	40%	$9,600.00	$14,400.00
2	24,000	$ 9,600.00	14,400.00	×	40%	5,760.00	8,640.00
3	24,000	15,360.00	8,640.00	×	40%	3,456.00	5,184.00
4	24,000	18,816.00	5,184.00	×	40%	2,073.60	3,110.40
5	24,000	20,889.60	3,110.40		—	1,110.40	2,000.00

You should note that when the double-declining-balance method is used, the estimated residual value is *not* considered in determining the depreciation rate. It is also ignored in computing the periodic depreciation. However, the asset should not be depreciated below its estimated residual value. In the above example, the estimated residual value was $2,000. Therefore, the depreciation for the fifth year is $1,110.40 ($3,110.40 − $2,000.00) instead of $1,244.16 (40% × $3,110.40).

In the example, we assumed that the first use of the asset occurred at the beginning of the fiscal year. This is normally not the case in practice, however, and depreciation for the first partial year of use must be computed. For example, assume that the asset above was in service at the end of the *third* month of the fiscal year. In this case, only a portion (9/12) of the first full year's depreciation of $9,600 is allocated to the first fiscal year. Thus, depreciation of $7,200 (9/12 × $9,600) is allocated to the first partial year of use. The depreciation for the second fiscal year would then be $6,720 [40% × ($24,000 − $7,200)].

Example Exercise 10-4   objective 2

Equipment acquired at the beginning of the year at a cost of $125,000 has an estimated residual value of $5,000 and an estimated useful life of 10 years. Determine (a) the depreciable cost, (b) the double-declining-balance rate, and (c) the double-declining-balance depreciation for the first year.

Follow My Example 10-4

   a. $120,000 ($125,000 − $5,000)
   b. 20% [(1/10) × 2]
   c. $25,000 ($125,000 × 20%)

For Practice: PE 10-4A, PE 10-4B

COMPARING DEPRECIATION METHODS

The differences among the three depreciation methods are summarized in Exhibit 6. All three methods assign a portion of the total cost of an asset to an accounting period, while never depreciating an asset below its residual value.

EXHIBIT 6

Summary of Depreciation Methods

Method	Useful Life	Depreciable Cost	Depreciation Rate	Depreciation Expense
Straight-line	Years	Cost less residual value	Straight-line rate*	Constant
Units-of-production	Total estimated units of production	Cost less residual value	(Cost − Residual value)/Total estimated units of production	Variable
Double-declining-balance	Years	Declining book value, but not below residual value	Straight-line rate* × 2	Declining

*Straight-line rate = (1/Useful life)

The straight-line method provides for the same periodic amounts of depreciation expense over the life of the asset. The units-of-production method provides for periodic amounts of depreciation expense that vary, depending upon the amount the asset is used.

The double-declining-balance method provides for a higher depreciation amount in the first year of the asset's use, followed by a gradually declining amount. For this reason, the double-declining-balance method is called an **accelerated depreciation method**. It is most appropriate when the decline in an asset's productivity or earning power is greater in the early years of its use than in later years. Further, using this method is often justified because repairs tend to increase with the age of an asset. The reduced amounts of depreciation in later years are thus offset to some extent by increased repair expenses.

The periodic depreciation amounts for the straight-line method and the double-declining-balance method are compared in Exhibit 7. This comparison is based on an asset cost of $24,000, an estimated life of five years, and an estimated residual value of $2,000.

EXHIBIT 7

Comparing Depreciation Methods

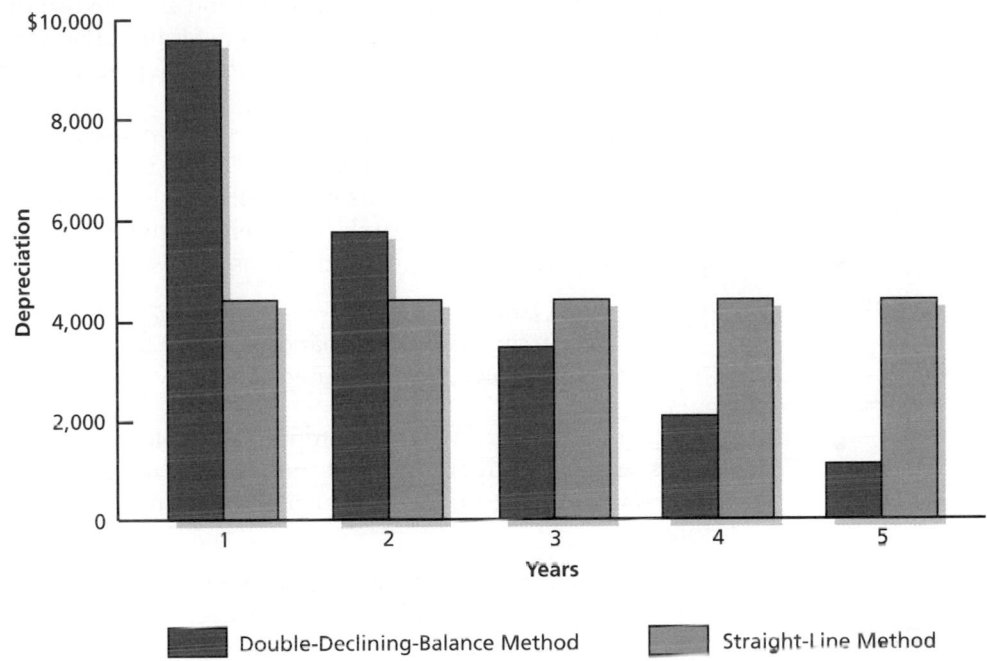

Double-Declining-Balance Method   Straight-Line Method

DEPRECIATION FOR FEDERAL INCOME TAX

Tax Code Section 179 allows a business to deduct up to $100,000 of the cost of qualified property in the year it is placed in service.

The Internal Revenue Code specifies the *Modified Accelerated Cost Recovery System (MACRS)* for use by businesses in computing depreciation for tax purposes. MACRS specifies eight classes of useful life and depreciation rates for each class. The two most common classes, other than real estate, are the five-year class and the seven-year class.[4] The five-year class includes automobiles and light-duty trucks, and the seven-year class includes most machinery and equipment. The depreciation deduction for these two classes is similar to that computed using the double-declining-balance method.

In using the MACRS rates, residual value is ignored, and all fixed assets are assumed to be put in and taken out of service in the middle of the year. For the five-year-class assets, depreciation is spread over six years, as shown in the following MACRS schedule of depreciation rates:

Year	5-Year-Class Depreciation Rates
1	20.0%
2	32.0
3	19.2
4	11.5
5	11.5
6	5.8
	100.0%

---

4 Real estate is in either a $27\frac{1}{2}$ year or a $31\frac{1}{2}$ year class and is depreciated by the straight-line method.

To simplify its record keeping, a business will sometimes use the MACRS method for both financial statement and tax purposes. This is acceptable if MACRS does not result in significantly different amounts than would have been reported using one of the three depreciation methods discussed earlier in this chapter.

REVISING DEPRECIATION ESTIMATES

Revising the estimates of the residual value and the useful life is normal. When these estimates are revised, they are used to determine the depreciation expense in future periods. They do not affect the amounts of depreciation expense recorded in earlier years.[5]

To illustrate, assume that a fixed asset purchased for $140,000 was originally estimated to have a useful life of five years and a residual value of $10,000. The asset has been depreciated for two years by the straight-line method at a rate of $26,000 per year [($140,000 − $10,000)/5 years]. At the end of two years, the asset's book value (undepreciated cost) is $88,000, determined as follows:

Asset cost	$140,000
Less accumulated depreciation ($26,000 per year × 2 years)	52,000
Book value (undepreciated cost), end of second year	$ 88,000

During the third year, the company estimates that the remaining useful life is eight years (instead of three) and that the residual value is $8,000 (instead of $10,000). The depreciation expense for each of the remaining eight years is $10,000, computed as follows:

Book value (undepreciated cost), end of second year	$88,000
Less revised estimated residual value	8,000
Revised remaining depreciable cost	$80,000
Revised annual depreciation expense ($80,000 ÷ 8 years)	$10,000

Exhibit 8 shows the book value of the asset over its original and revised lives. Notice that the book value declines at a slower rate beginning at the end of year 2 and continuing until it reaches the residual value of $8,000 at the end of year 10, which is the revised end of the asset's useful life.

EXHIBIT 8

Book Value of Asset with Change in Estimate

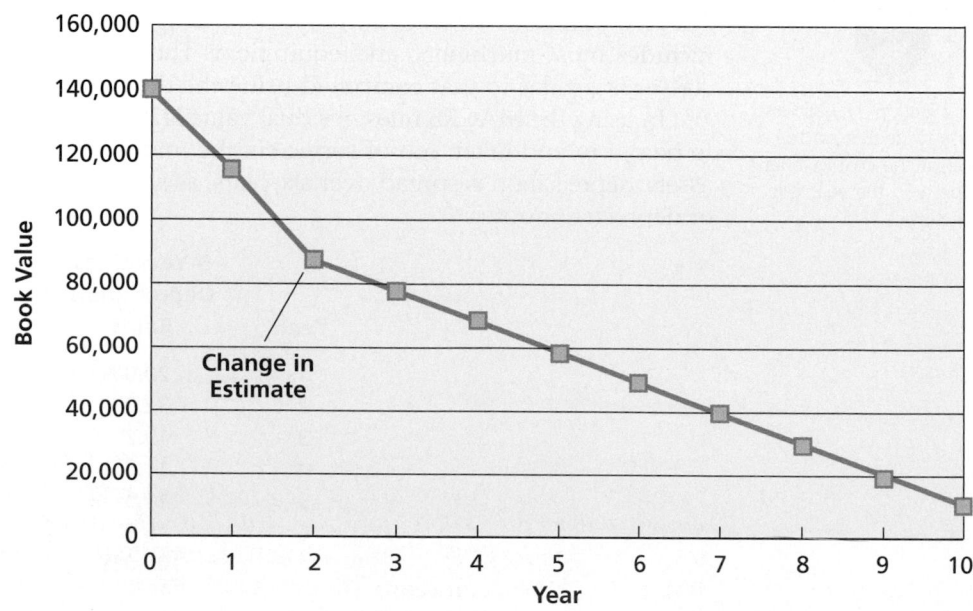

5 *Statement of Financial Accounting Standards No. 154*, "Accounting Changes and Error Corrections" (Financial Accounting Standards Board, Norwalk, CT: 2005).

Example Exercise 10-5

objective 2

A warehouse with a cost of $500,000 has an estimated residual value of $120,000, has an estimated useful life of 40 years, and is depreciated by the straight-line method. (a) Determine the amount of the annual depreciation. (b) Determine the book value at the end of the twentieth year of use. (c) Assuming that at the start of the twenty-first year the remaining life is estimated to be 25 years and the residual value is estimated to be $150,000, determine the depreciation expense for each of the remaining 25 years.

Follow My Example 10-5

a. $9,500 [($500,000 − $120,000)/40]
b. $310,000 [$500,000 − ($9,500 × 20)]
c. $6,400 [($310,000 − $150,000)/25]

For Practice: PE 10-5A, PE 10-5B

Disposal of Fixed Assets

objective 3

Journalize entries for the disposal of fixed assets.

Fixed assets that are no longer useful may be discarded, sold, or traded for other fixed assets. The details of the entry to record a disposal will vary. In all cases, however, the book value of the asset must be removed from the accounts. The entry for this purpose debits the asset's accumulated depreciation account for its balance on the date of disposal and credits the asset account for the cost of the asset.

A fixed asset should not be removed from the accounts only because it has been fully depreciated. If the asset is still used by the business, the cost and accumulated depreciation should remain in the ledger. This maintains accountability for the asset in the ledger. If the book value of the asset was removed from the ledger, the accounts would contain no evidence of the continued existence of the asset. In addition, the cost and the accumulated depreciation data on such assets are often needed for property tax and income tax reports.

The entry to record the disposal of a fixed asset removes the cost of the asset and its accumulated depreciation from the accounts.

DISCARDING FIXED ASSETS

When fixed assets are no longer useful to the business and have no residual or market value, they are discarded. To illustrate, assume that an item of equipment acquired at a cost of $25,000 is fully depreciated at December 31, the end of the preceding fiscal year. On February 14, the equipment is discarded. The entry to record this is as follows:

Feb.	14	Accumulated Depreciation—Equipment		25 0 0 0 00	
		Equipment			25 0 0 0 00
		To write off equipment discarded.			

If an asset has not been fully depreciated, depreciation should be recorded prior to removing it from service and from the accounting records. To illustrate, assume that equipment costing $6,000 with no estimated residual value is depreciated at an annual straight-line rate of 10%. In addition, assume that on December 31 of the preceding fiscal year, the accumulated depreciation balance, after adjusting entries, is $4,750. Finally, assume that the asset is removed from service on the following March 24. The entry to record the depreciation for the three months of the current period prior to the asset's removal from service is as follows:

Mar.	24	Depreciation Expense—Equipment		1 5 0 00	
		Accumulated Depreciation—Equipment			1 5 0 00
		To record current depreciation on			
		equipment discarded ($600 × 3/12).			

The discarding of the equipment is then recorded by the following entry:

Mar.	24	Accumulated Depreciation—Equipment		4 9 0 0 00	
		Loss on Disposal of Fixed Assets		1 1 0 0 00	
		Equipment			6 0 0 0 00
		To write off equipment discarded.			

The loss of $1,100 is recorded because the balance of the accumulated depreciation account ($4,900) is less than the balance in the equipment account ($6,000). Losses on the discarding of fixed assets are nonoperating items and are normally reported in the Other Expense section of the income statement.

SELLING FIXED ASSETS

The entry to record the sale of a fixed asset is similar to the entries illustrated above, except that the cash or other asset received must also be recorded. If the selling price is more than the book value of the asset, the transaction results in a gain. If the selling price is less than the book value, there is a loss.

To illustrate, assume that equipment is acquired at a cost of $10,000 with no estimated residual value and is depreciated at an annual straight-line rate of 10%. The equipment is sold for cash on October 12 of the eighth year of its use. The balance of the accumulated depreciation account as of the preceding December 31 is $7,000. The entry to update the depreciation for the nine months of the current year is as follows:

Oct.	12	Depreciation Expense—Equipment		7 5 0 00	
		Accumulated Depreciation—Equipment			7 5 0 00
		To record current depreciation on			
		equipment sold ($10,000 × ¾ × 10%).			

After the current depreciation is recorded, the book value of the asset is $2,250 ($10,000 − $7,750). The entries to record the sale, assuming three different selling prices, are as follows:

Sold at book value, for $2,250. No gain or loss.

Oct.	12	Cash		2 2 5 0 00	
		Accumulated Depreciation—Equipment		7 7 5 0 00	
		Equipment			10 0 0 0 00

Sold below book value, for $1,000. Loss of $1,250.

Oct.	12	Cash		1 0 0 0 00	
		Accumulated Depreciation—Equipment		7 7 5 0 00	
		Loss on Disposal of Fixed Assets		1 2 5 0 00	
		Equipment			10 0 0 0 00

Sold above book value, for $2,800. Gain of $550.

Oct.	12	Cash		2 8 0 0 00	
		Accumulated Depreciation—Equipment		7 7 5 0 00	
		Equipment			10 0 0 0 00
		Gain on Disposal of Fixed Assets			5 5 0 00

Example Exercise 10-6

objective **3**

Equipment was acquired at the beginning of the year at a cost of $91,000. The equipment was depreciated using the straight-line method based upon an estimated useful life of nine years and an estimated residual value of $10,000.

a. What was the depreciation for the first year?
b. Assuming the equipment was sold at the end of the second year for $78,000, determine the gain or loss on sale of the equipment.
c. Journalize the entry to record the sale.

Follow My Example 10-6

a. $9,000 [($91,000 − $10,000)/9]
b. $5,000 gain {$78,000 − [$91,000 − ($9,000 × 2)]}

c. Cash 78,000
   Accumulated Depreciation—Equipment 18,000
        Equipment 91,000
        Gain on Sale of Equipment 5,000

For Practice: PE 10-6A, PE 10-6B

EXCHANGING SIMILAR FIXED ASSETS

Old equipment is often traded in for new equipment having a similar use. In such cases, the seller allows the buyer an amount for the old equipment traded in.[6] This amount, called the **trade-in allowance**, may be either greater or less than the book value of the old equipment. The remaining balance—the amount owed—is either paid in cash or recorded as a liability. It is normally called **boot**, which is its tax name.

Gains on exchanges of similar fixed assets are also not recognized for federal income tax purposes.

Gains on Exchanges   Gains on exchanges of similar fixed assets are not recognized for financial reporting purposes.[7] This is based on the theory that revenue occurs from the production and sale of goods produced by fixed assets and not from the exchange of similar fixed assets.

When the trade-in allowance exceeds the book value of an asset traded in and no gain is recognized, the cost recorded for the new asset can be determined in either of two ways:

1. Cost of new asset = List price of new asset − Unrecognized gain

or

2. Cost of new asset = Cash given (or liability assumed) + Book value of old asset

---

6 We assume that exchanges of equipment having similar use will not significantly change the company's future cash flows. As a result, such exchanges are said be to lacking in commercial substance as defined by *Statement of Financial Accounting Standards* No. 153, "Exchanges of Nonmonetary Assets" (Financial Accounting Standards Board, Norwalk, CT: 2004).
7 Gains on exchanges of similar fixed assets are recognized if cash (boot) is received. This topic is discussed in advanced accounting texts.

To illustrate, assume the following exchange:

Similar equipment acquired (new):

List price of new equipment	$5,000
Trade-in allowance on old equipment	1,100
Cash paid at June 19, date of exchange	$3,900

Equipment traded in (old):

Cost of old equipment	$4,000
Accumulated depreciation at date of exchange	3,200
Book value at June 19, date of exchange	$ 800

Recorded cost of new equipment:

Method One:

List price of new equipment		$5,000
Trade-in allowance	$1,100	
Book value of old equipment	800	
Unrecognized gain on exchange		(300)
Cost of new equipment		$4,700

Method Two:

Book value of old equipment	$ 800
Cash paid at date of exchange	3,900
Cost of new equipment	$4,700

The entry to record this exchange and the payment of cash is as follows:

June	19	Accumulated Depreciation—Equipment	3 2 0 0 00		
		Equipment (new equipment)	4 7 0 0 00		
		Equipment (old equipment)		4 0 0 0 00	
		Cash		3 9 0 0 00	
		To record exchange of equipment.			

Not recognizing the $300 gain ($1,100 trade-in allowance minus $800 book value) at the time of the exchange reduces future depreciation expense. That is, the depreciation expense for the new asset is based on a cost of $4,700 rather than on the list price of $5,000. In effect, the unrecognized gain of $300 reduces the total amount of depreciation taken during the life of the equipment by $300.

Losses on Exchanges For financial reporting purposes, losses are recognized on exchanges of similar fixed assets if the trade-in allowance is less than the book value of the old equipment. When there is a loss, the cost recorded for the new asset should be the market (list) price. To illustrate, assume the following exchange:

Similar equipment acquired (new):

List price of new equipment	$10,000
Trade-in allowance on old equipment	2,000
Cash paid at September 7, date of exchange	$ 8,000

Equipment traded in (old):

Cost of old equipment	$ 7,000
Accumulated depreciation at date of exchange	4,600
Book value at September 7, date of exchange	$ 2,400
Trade-in allowance on old equipment	2,000
Loss on exchange	$ 400

The entry to record the exchange is as follows:

Sept.	7	Accumulated Depreciation—Equipment	4 6 0 0 00		
		Equipment	10 0 0 0 00		
		Loss on Disposal of Fixed Assets	4 0 0 00		
		Equipment			7 0 0 0 00
		Cash			8 0 0 0 00
		To record exchange of equipment,			
		with loss.			

Review of Accounting for Exchanges of Similar Fixed Assets   Exhibit 9 reviews the accounting for exchanges of similar fixed assets, using the following data:

List price of new equipment acquired	$15,000
Cost of old equipment traded in	$12,500
Accumulated depreciation at date of exchange	10,100
Book value at date of exchange	$ 2,400

EXHIBIT 9

Summary
Illustration—
Accounting for
Exchanges of Similar
Fixed Assets

CASE ONE (GAIN): Trade-in allowance is more than book value of asset traded in.

Trade-in allowance, $3,000; cash paid, $12,000 ($15,000 − $3,000)

Cost of new asset	List price of new asset acquired, less unrecognized gain: $14,400 [$15,000 − ($3,000 − $2,400)]
	or
	Cash paid plus book value of asset traded in: $14,400 ($12,000 + $2,400)
Gain recognized	None
Entry	Equipment 14,400
	Accumulated Depreciation 10,100
	Equipment 12,500
	Cash 12,000

CASE TWO (LOSS): Trade-in allowance is less than book value of asset traded in.

Trade-in allowance, $2,000; cash paid, $13,000 ($15,000 − $2,000)

Cost of new asset	List price of new asset acquired: $15,000
Loss recognized	$400
Entry	Equipment 15,000
	Accumulated Depreciation 10,100
	Loss on Disposal of Fixed Assets 400
	Equipment 12,500
	Cash 13,000

Example Exercise 10-7

objective 3

On the first day of the fiscal year, a delivery truck with a list price of $75,000 was acquired in exchange for an old delivery truck and $63,000 cash. The old truck had a cost of $50,000 and accumulated depreciation of $39,500.

a.   Determine the cost of the new truck for financial reporting purposes.
b.   Journalize the entry to record the exchange.

(continued)

Follow My Example 10-7

a. $73,500

List price of new truck		$75,000
Trade-in allowance on old truck ($75,000 − $63,000)	$12,000	
Book value of old truck ($50,000 − $39,500)	10,500	
Unrecognized gain on exchange		(1,500)
Cost of new truck		$73,500

or

Book value of old truck ($50,000 − $39,500)	$10,500
Plus cash paid at date of exchange	63,000
Cost of new truck	$73,500

b.

Truck (new)	73,500	
Accumulated Depreciation—Truck (old)	39,500	
Truck (old)		50,000
Cash		63,000

For Practice: PE 10-7A, PE 10-7B

Natural Resources

objective 4

Compute depletion and journalize the entry for depletion.

The fixed assets of some businesses include timber, metal ores, minerals, or other natural resources. As these businesses harvest or mine and then sell these resources, a portion of the cost of acquiring them must be debited to an expense account. This process of transferring the cost of natural resources to an expense account is called **depletion**. The amount of depletion is determined by multiplying the quantity extracted during the period by the depletion rate. This rate is computed by dividing the cost of the mineral deposit by its estimated size.

Computing depletion is similar to computing units-of-production depreciation. To illustrate, assume that a business paid $400,000 for the mining rights to a mineral deposit estimated at 1,000,000 tons of ore. The depletion rate is $0.40 per ton ($400,000/1,000,000 tons). If 90,000 tons are mined during the year, the periodic depletion is $36,000 (90,000 tons × $0.40). The adjusting entry to record the depletion is shown below.

Dec.	31	Depletion Expense	36 0 0 0 00	
		Accumulated Depletion		36 0 0 0 00
		Depletion of mineral deposit.		

Like the accumulated depreciation account, Accumulated Depletion is a *contra asset* account. It is reported on the balance sheet as a deduction from the cost of the mineral deposit.

Example Exercise 10-8

objective 4

Earth's Treasures Mining Co. acquired mineral rights for $45,000,000. The mineral deposit is estimated at 50,000,000 tons. During the current year, 12,600,000 tons were mined and sold.

a. Determine the depletion rate.
b. Determine the amount of depletion expense for the current year.
c. Journalize the adjusting entry on December 31 to recognize the depletion expense.

Intangible Assets

objective 5

Describe the accounting for intangible assets, such as patents, copyrights, and goodwill.

Patents, copyrights, trademarks, and goodwill are long-lived assets that are useful in the operations of a business and are not held for sale. These assets are called **intangible assets** because they do not exist physically.

The basic principles of accounting for intangible assets are like those described earlier for fixed assets. The major concerns are determining (1) the initial cost and (2) the **amortization**—the amount of cost to transfer to expense. Amortization results from the passage of time or a decline in the usefulness of the intangible asset.

PATENTS

Apple Computer, Inc., amortizes intangible assets over 3–10 years.

Manufacturers may acquire exclusive rights to produce and sell goods with one or more unique features. Such rights are granted by **patents**, which the federal government issues to inventors. These rights continue in effect for 20 years. A business may purchase patent rights from others, or it may obtain patents developed by its own research and development efforts.

The initial cost of a purchased patent, including any related legal fees, is debited to an asset account. This cost is written off, or amortized, over the years of the patent's expected usefulness. This period of time may be less than the remaining legal life of the patent. The estimated useful life of the patent may also change as technology or consumer tastes change.

The straight-line method is normally used to determine the periodic amortization. When the amortization is recorded, it is debited to an expense account and credited directly to the patents account. A separate contra asset account is usually *not* used for intangible assets.

To illustrate, assume that at the beginning of its fiscal year, a business acquires patent rights for $100,000. The patent had been granted six years earlier by the Federal Patent Office. Although the patent will not expire for 14 years, its remaining useful life is estimated as five years. The adjusting entry to amortize the patent at the end of the year is as follows:

Dec.	31	Amortization Expense—Patents	20 0 0 0 00	
		Patents		20 0 0 0 00
		Patent amortization ($100,000/5).		

Rather than purchase patent rights, a business may incur significant costs in developing patents through its own research and development efforts. Such *research and development costs* are usually accounted for as current operating expenses in the period in which they are incurred. Expensing research and development costs is justified because the future benefits from research and development efforts are highly uncertain.

COPYRIGHTS AND TRADEMARKS

The exclusive right to publish and sell a literary, artistic, or musical composition is granted by a **copyright**. Copyrights are issued by the federal government and extend for 70 years beyond the author's death. The costs of a copyright include all costs of creating the work plus any administrative or legal costs of obtaining the copyright. A copyright that is purchased from another should be recorded at the price paid for it. Copyrights are amortized over their estimated useful lives. For example, Sony Corporation of America states the following amortization policy with respect to its artistic and music intangible assets:

> *Intangibles, which mainly consist of artist contracts and music catalogs, are being amortized on a straight-line basis principally over 16 years and 21 years, respectively.*

Coke® is one of the world's most recognizable trademarks. As stated in *LIFE*, "Two-thirds of the earth is covered by water; the rest is covered by Coke. If the French are known for wine and the Germans for beer, America achieved global beverage dominance with fizzy water and caramel color."

A **trademark** is a name, term, or symbol used to identify a business and its products. For example, The Coca-Cola Company's distinctive red-and-white Coke logo is an example of a trademark. Most businesses identify their trademarks with ® in their advertisements and on their products. Under federal law, businesses can protect against others using their trademarks by registering them for 10 years and renewing the registration for 10-year periods thereafter. Like a copyright, the legal costs of registering a trademark with the federal government are recorded as an asset. Thus, even though the Coca-Cola trademarks are extremely valuable, they are not shown on the balance sheet, because the legal costs for establishing these trademarks are immaterial. If, however, a trademark is purchased from another business, the cost of its purchase is recorded as an asset. The cost of a trademark is in most cases considered to have an indefinite useful life. Thus, trademarks are not amortized over a useful life, as are the previously discussed intangible assets. Rather, trademarks should be tested periodically for impaired value. When a trademark is impaired from competitive threats or other circumstances, the trademark should be written down and a loss recognized.

Integrity, Objectivity, and Ethics in Business

ETHICS

21ST CENTURY PIRATES

Pirated software is a major concern of software companies. For example, during a recent global sweep, Microsoft Corporation seized nearly five million units of counterfeit Microsoft software with an estimated retail value of $1.7 billion. U.S. copyright laws and practices are sometimes ignored or disputed in other parts of the world.

Businesses must honor the copyrights held by software companies by eliminating pirated software from corporate computers. The Business Software Alliance (BSA) represents the largest software companies in campaigns to investigate illegal use of unlicensed software by businesses. The BSA estimates software industry losses of nearly $12 billion annually from software piracy. Employees using pirated software on business assets risk bringing legal penalties to themselves and their employers.

GOODWILL

In business, **goodwill** refers to an intangible asset of a business that is created from such favorable factors as location, product quality, reputation, and managerial skill. Goodwill allows a business to earn a rate of return on its investment that is often in excess of the normal rate for other firms in the same business.

Generally accepted accounting principles permit goodwill to be recorded in the accounts only if it is objectively determined by a transaction. An example of such a transaction is the purchase of a business at a price in excess of the net assets (assets − liabilities) of the acquired business. The excess is recorded as goodwill and reported as an intangible asset. Unlike patents and copyrights, goodwill is not amortized. However, a loss should be recorded if the business prospects of the acquired firm become significantly impaired. This loss would normally be disclosed in the Other Expense section of the income statement. To illustrate, Time Warner recorded one of the largest losses in corporate history (nearly $54 billion) for the write-down of goodwill associated with the AOL and Time Warner merger. The entry is recorded as follows:

	Loss from Impaired Goodwill	54 0 0 0 0 0 0 0 0 0 00		
	Goodwill		54 0 0 0 0 0 0 0 0 0 00
	Impaired goodwill.		

Exhibit 10 shows the frequency of intangible asset disclosures for a sample of 600 large firms. As you can see, goodwill is the most frequently reported intangible asset. This is because goodwill arises from merger transactions, which are common.

EXHIBIT 10

Frequency of Intangible Asset Disclosures for 600 Firms

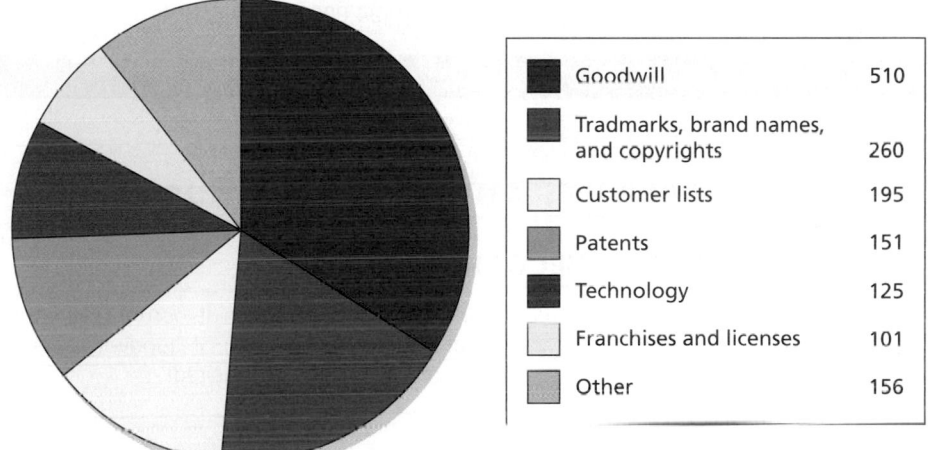

Goodwill	510
Trademarks, brand names, and copyrights	260
Customer lists	195
Patents	151
Technology	125
Franchises and licenses	101
Other	156

Source. Accounting Trends & Techniques, 59th ed., American Institute of Certified Public Accountants, New York, 2005.
Note: Some firms have multiple disclosures.

Exhibit 11 summarizes the characteristics of intangible assets discussed in this section. Patents and copyrights are examples of intangible assets with finite lives and are thus subject to periodic amortization based upon their estimated useful lives. Trademarks and goodwill are examples of intangible assets with indefinite lives and are thus not subject to periodic amortization. Rather, intangible assets with indefinite lives are tested periodically for impairment. If the intangible asset is impaired, then the intangible asset's carrying value is written down, and an impairment loss is recognized for the period.

EXHIBIT 11

Comparison of Intangible Assets

Intangible Asset	Description	Amortization Period	Periodic Expense
Patent	Exclusive right to benefit from an innovation.	Estimated useful life not to exceed legal life.	Amortization expense.
Copyright	Exclusive right to benefit from a literary, artistic, or musical composition.	Estimated useful life not to exceed legal life.	Amortization expense.
Trademark	Exclusive use of a name, term, or symbol.	None	Impairment loss if fair value less than carrying value (impaired).
Goodwill	Excess of purchase price of a business over its net assets.	None	Impairment loss if fair value less than carrying value (impaired).

Example Exercise 10-9

On December 31, it was estimated that goodwill of $40,000 was impaired. In addition, a patent with an estimated useful economic life of 12 years was acquired for $84,000 on July 1.

a.   Journalize the adjusting entry on December 31 for the impaired goodwill.
b.   Journalize the adjusting entry on December 31 for the amortization of the patent rights.

Follow My Example 10-9

a.	Dec. 31	Loss from Impaired Goodwill	40,000	
		Goodwill		40,000
		Impaired goodwill.		
b.	Dec. 31	Amortization Expense—Patents	3,500	
		Patents		3,500
		Amortized patent rights [($84,000/12) × (6/12)].		

For Practice: PE 10-9A, PE 10-9B

Integrity, Objectivity, and Ethics in Business

ETHICS

WHEN DOES GOODWILL BECOME WORTHLESS?

The timing and amount of goodwill write-offs can be very subjective. Managers and their accountants should fairly estimate the value of goodwill and record goodwill impairment when it occurs. It would be unethical to delay a write-down of goodwill when it is determined that the asset is impaired.

Financial Reporting for Fixed Assets and Intangible Assets

objective 6

Describe how depreciation expense is reported in an income statement and prepare a balance sheet that includes fixed assets and intangible assets.

How should fixed assets and intangible assets be reported in the financial statements? The amount of depreciation and amortization expense of a period should be reported separately in the income statement or disclosed in a note. A general description of the method or methods used in computing depreciation should also be reported.

The amount of each major class of fixed assets should be disclosed in the balance sheet or in notes. The related accumulated depreciation should also be disclosed, either by major class or in total. The fixed assets may be shown at their *book value* (cost less accumulated depreciation), which can also be described as their *net* amount. To illustrate, the net book value of office equipment originally costing $125,750 with accumulated depreciation of $86,300 is shown below.

Office equipment	$125,750
Less accumulated depreciation	86,300
Net book value	$ 39,450

If there are too many classes of fixed assets, a single amount may be presented in the balance sheet, supported by a separate detailed listing. Fixed assets are normally presented under the more descriptive caption of *property, plant, and equipment*.

The cost of mineral rights or ore deposits is normally shown as part of the Fixed Assets section of the balance sheet. The related accumulated depletion should also be disclosed. In some cases, the mineral rights are shown net of depletion on the face of the balance sheet, accompanied by a note that discloses the amount of the accumulated depletion.

Intangible assets are usually reported in the balance sheet in a separate section immediately following fixed assets. The balance of each major class of intangible assets should be disclosed at an amount net of amortization taken to date. Exhibit 12 is a partial balance sheet that shows the reporting of fixed assets and intangible assets.

EXHIBIT 12

Fixed Assets and Intangible Assets in the Balance Sheet

Discovery Mining Co.
Balance Sheet
December 31, 2008

Assets

	Cost	Accum. Depr.	Book Value	
Total current assets				$ 462,500
Property, plant, and equipment:				
Land	$ 30,000	—	$ 30,000	
Buildings	110,000	$ 26,000	84,000	
Factory equipment	650,000	192,000	458,000	
Office equipment	120,000	13,000	107,000	
	$ 910,000	$ 231,000		$679,000

	Cost	Accum. Depl.	Book Value	
Mineral deposits:				
Alaska deposit	$1,200,000	$ 800,000	$400,000	
Wyoming deposit	750,000	200,000	550,000	
	$1,950,000	$1,000,000		950,000
Total property, plant, and equipment				1,629,000
Intangible assets:				
Patents			$ 75,000	
Goodwill			50,000	
Total intangible assets				125,000

Business Connections

REAL WORLD

HUB-AND-SPOKE OR POINT-TO-POINT?

Southwest Airlines Co. uses a simple fare structure, featuring low, unrestricted, unlimited, everyday coach fares. These fares are made possible by Southwest's use of a point-to-point, rather than hub-and-spoke, business approach. United Airlines, Inc., Delta Air Lines, and American Airlines employ a hub-and-spoke approach in which an airline establishes major hubs that serve as connecting links to other cities. For example, Delta has established major connecting hubs in Atlanta, Cincinnati, and Salt Lake City. In contrast, Southwest focuses on point-to-point service between selected cities with over 300 one-way, nonstop city pairs with an average length of 500 miles and average fly-

ing time of 1.5 hours. As a result, Southwest minimizes connections, delays, and total trip time. Southwest also focuses on serving conveniently located satellite or downtown airports, such as Dallas Love Field, Houston Hobby, and Chicago Midway. Because these airports are normally less congested than hub airports, Southwest is better able to maintain high employee productivity and reliable ontime performance. This operating approach permits the company to achieve high utilization of its fixed assets, such as its 737 aircraft. For example, aircraft are scheduled to spend only 25 minutes at the gate, thereby reducing the number of aircraft and gate facilities that would otherwise be required.

© MATT SLOCUM/ASSOCIATED PRESS

Financial Analysis and Interpretation

Fixed assets can be evaluated by their ability to generate revenue. One measure of the revenue-generating efficiency of fixed assets is the fixed asset turnover ratio. The **fixed asset turnover ratio** measures the number of dollars of revenue earned per dollar of fixed assets and is computed as follows:

$$\text{Fixed Asset Turnover Ratio} = \frac{\text{Revenue}}{\text{Average Book Value of Fixed Assets}}$$

To illustrate, the following fixed asset balance sheet information is used for Marriott International, Inc.:

	December 31, 2005 (in millions)	January 2, 2005 (in millions)
Property and equipment (net)	$2,341	$2,389

Marriott reported revenue of $11,550 million for 2005. Thus, the fixed asset turnover ratio is calculated as follows:

$$\text{Fixed Asset Turnover Ratio} = \frac{\$11,550}{(\$2,341 + \$2,389)/2} = 4.88$$

For every dollar of fixed assets, Marriott earns $4.88 of revenue. The larger this ratio, the more efficiently a business is using its fixed assets. This ratio can be compared across time within a single firm or to other companies in the industry to evaluate overall fixed asset turnover performance. For example, the fixed asset turnover ratios for Starwood Hotels & Resorts Worldwide, Inc. and Choice Hotels International, Inc. are 0.76 and 8.4, respectively. Marriott is operating its hotel assets at an efficiency level between that of Starwood and Choice.

The fixed asset turnover ratio for a number of different businesses is shown below. The smaller ratios are associated with companies that require large fixed asset investments. The larger fixed asset turnover ratios are associated with firms that are more labor-intensive and require smaller fixed asset investments.

Company (industry)	Fixed Asset Turnover Ratio
Comcast Corporation (cable)	1.00
Computer Associates International, Inc. (consulting)	5.00
Google (Internet)	12.15
Manpower Inc. (temporary employment)	65.15
Norfolk Southern Corporation (railroad)	0.35
Ruby Tuesday, Inc. (restaurant)	1.47
Southwest Airlines Co. (airline)	0.84

Appendix

Sum-of-the-Years-Digits Depreciation

A recent edition of *Accounting Trends & Techniques* reported that only 1%–2% of the surveyed companies now use this method for financial reporting purposes.

At one time, the sum-of-the-years-digits method of depreciation was used by many businesses. However, tax law changes limited its use for tax purposes.

Under the *sum-of-the-years-digits method*, depreciation expense is determined by multiplying the original cost of the asset less its estimated residual value by a smaller fraction each year. Thus, the sum-of-the-years-digits method is similar to the double-declining-balance method in that the depreciation expense declines each year.

The denominator of the fraction used in determining the depreciation expense is the sum of the digits of the years of the asset's useful life. For example, an asset with a useful life of five years would have a denominator of 15 (5 + 4 + 3 + 2 + 1).[8] The

8 The denominator can also be determined from the following formula: $S = N[(N + 1)/2]$, where S = sum of the digits and N = number of years of estimated life.

numerator of the fraction is the number of years of useful life remaining at the beginning of each year for which depreciation is being computed. Thus, the numerator decreases each year by 1. For a useful life of five years, the numerator is 5 the first year, 4 the second year, 3 the third year, and so on.

The following depreciation schedule illustrates the sum-of-the-years-digits method for an asset with a cost of $24,000, an estimated residual value of $2,000, and an estimated useful life of five years:

Year	Cost Less Residual Value	Rate	Depreciation for Year	Accum. Depr. at End of Year	Book Value at End of Year
1	$22,000	$5/15$	$7,333.33	$ 7,333.33	$16,666.67
2	22,000	$4/15$	5,866.67	13,200.00	10,800.00
3	22,000	$3/15$	4,400.00	17,600.00	6,400.00
4	22,000	$2/15$	2,933.33	20,533.33	3,466.67
5	22,000	$1/15$	1,466.67	22,000.00	2,000.00

What if the fixed asset is not placed in service at the beginning of the year? When the date an asset is first put into service is not the beginning of a fiscal year, each full year's depreciation must be allocated between the two fiscal years benefited. To illustrate, assume that the asset in the above example was put into service at the beginning of the fourth month of the first fiscal year. The depreciation for that year would be $5,500 (9/12 × 5/15 × $22,000). The depreciation for the second year would be $6,233.33, computed as follows:

$3/12 × 5/15 × $22,000	$1,833.33
$9/12 × 4/15 × $22,000	4,400.00
Total depreciation for second fiscal year	$6,233.33

At a Glance

1. Define, classify, and account for the cost of fixed assets.

Key Points	Key Learning Outcomes	Example Exercises	Practice Exercises
Fixed assets are long-term tangible assets that are owned by the business and are used in the normal operations of the business such as equipment, buildings, and land. The initial cost of a fixed asset includes all amounts spent to get the asset in place and ready for use. Once an asset is placed into service, revenue and capital expenditures may be incurred. Revenue expenditures include ordinary repairs and maintenance. Capital expenditures include asset improvements and extraordinary repairs. Fixed assets may also be leased and accounted for as capital or operating leases.	• Define *fixed assets*. • List types of costs that should and should not be included in the cost of a fixed asset. • Provide examples of ordinary repairs, asset improvements, and extraordinary repairs. • Prepare journal entries for ordinary repairs, asset improvements, and extraordinary repairs.	10-1	10-1A, 10-1B

(continued)

2. Compute depreciation, using the following methods: straight-line method, units-of-production method, and double-declining-balance method.

Key Points	Key Learning Outcomes	Example Exercises	Practice Exercises
All fixed assets except land lose their ability to provide services and should be depreciated over time. Three factors are considered in determining depreciation: (1) the fixed asset's initial cost, (2) the useful life of the asset, and (3) the residual value of the asset.	• Define and describe *depreciation*. • List the factors used in determining depreciation.		
The straight-line method spreads the initial cost less the residual value equally over the useful life. The units-of-production method spreads the initial cost less the residual value equally over the units expected to be produced by the asset during its useful life. The double-declining-balance method is applied by multiplying the declining book value of the asset by twice the straight-line rate.	• Compute straight-line depreciation. • Compute units-of-production depreciation. • Compute double-declining-balance depreciation.	10-2 10-3 10-4	10-2A, 10-2B 10-3A, 10-3B 10-4A, 10-4B
Depreciation may be revised for changes in an asset's useful life or residual value. Such changes affect future depreciation.	• Compute revised depreciation for a change in an asset's useful life and residual value.	10-5	10-5A, 10-5B

3. Journalize entries for the disposal of fixed assets.

Key Points	Key Learning Outcomes	Example Exercises	Practice Exercises
To record disposals of fixed assets, any depreciation for the current period should be recorded, and the book value of the asset is then removed from the accounts. For assets discarded from service, a loss may be recorded for any remaining book value of the asset.	• Prepare the journal entry for discarding a fixed asset.		
When a fixed asset is sold, the book value is removed, and the cash or other asset received is recorded. If the selling price is more than the book value of the asset, the transaction results in a gain. If the selling price is less than the book value, there is a loss.	• Prepare journal entries for the sale of a fixed asset.	10-6	10-6A, 10-6B
When a fixed asset is exchanged for another of similar nature, no gain is recognized on the exchange. The acquired asset's cost is adjusted for any gains. A loss on an exchange of similar assets is recorded.	• Prepare journal entries for the exchange of similar fixed assets.	10-7	10-7A, 10-7B

4. Compute depletion and journalize the entry for depletion.

Key Points	Key Learning Outcomes	Example Exercises	Practice Exercises
The amount of periodic depletion is computed by multiplying the quantity of minerals extracted during the period by a depletion rate. The depletion rate is computed by dividing the cost of the mineral deposit by its estimated size. The entry to record depletion debits a depletion expense account and credits an accumulated depletion account.	• Define and describe *depletion*. • Compute a depletion rate. • Prepare the journal entry to record depletion.	 10-8 10-8	 10-8A, 10-8B 10-8A, 10-8B

5. Describe the accounting for intangible assets, such as patents, copyrights, and goodwill.

Key Points	Key Learning Outcomes	Example Exercises	Practice Exercises
Long-term assets such as patents, copyrights, trademarks, and goodwill that are without physical attributes but are used in the business are intangible assets. The initial cost of an intangible asset should be debited to an asset account. The cost of patents and copyrights should be amortized over the years of the asset's expected usefulness by debiting an expense account and crediting the intangible asset account. Trademarks and goodwill are not amortized, but are written down only upon impairment.	• Define, describe, and provide examples of intangible assets. • Prepare a journal entry for the purchase of an intangible asset. • Prepare a journal entry to amortize the costs of patents and copyrights. • Prepare the journal entry to record the impairment of goodwill.	**10-9** **10-9**	10-9A, 10-9B 10-9A, 10-9B

6. Describe how depreciation expense is reported in an income statement and prepare a balance sheet that includes fixed assets and intangible assets.

Key Points	Key Learning Outcomes	Example Exercises	Practice Exercises
The amount of depreciation expense and the method or methods used in computing depreciation should be disclosed in the financial statements. In addition, each major class of fixed assets should be disclosed, along with the related accumulated depreciation. Intangible assets are usually presented in the balance sheet in a separate section immediately following fixed assets. Each major class of intangible assets should be disclosed at an amount net of the amortization recorded to date.	• Describe and illustrate how fixed assets are reported on the income statement and balance sheet. • Describe and illustrate how intangible assets are reported on the income statement and balance sheet.		

Key Terms

accelerated depreciation method (444)
amortization (453)
book value (443)
boot (449)
capital expenditures (438)
capital lease (439)
copyright (454)

depletion (452)
depreciation (440)
double-declining-balance method (443)
fixed asset turnover ratio (458)
fixed assets (435)
goodwill (454)
intangible assets (453)

operating lease (439)
patents (453)
residual value (440)
revenue expenditures (438)
straight-line method (442)
trade-in allowance (449)
trademark (454)
units-of-production method (442)

Illustrative Problem

McCollum Company, a furniture wholesaler, acquired new equipment at a cost of $150,000 at the beginning of the fiscal year. The equipment has an estimated life of five years and an estimated residual value of $12,000. Ellen McCollum, the president, has requested information regarding alternative depreciation methods.

Instructions

1. Determine the annual depreciation for each of the five years of estimated useful life of the equipment, the accumulated depreciation at the end of each year, and the book value of the equipment at the end of each year by (a) the straight-line method and (b) the double-declining-balance method.

2. Assume that the equipment was depreciated under the double-declining-balance method. In the first week of the fifth year, the equipment was traded in for similar equipment priced at $175,000. The trade-in allowance on the old equipment was $10,000, and cash was paid for the balance. Journalize the entry to record the exchange.

Solution

1.

	Year	Depreciation Expense	Accumulated Depreciation, End of Year	Book Value, End of Year
a.	1	$27,600*	$ 27,600	$122,400
	2	27,600	55,200	94,800
	3	27,600	82,800	67,200
	4	27,600	110,400	39,600
	5	27,600	138,000	12,000

*$27,600 = ($150,000 − $12,000) ÷ 5

	Year	Depreciation Expense	Accumulated Depreciation, End of Year	Book Value, End of Year
b.	1	$60,000**	$ 60,000	$ 90,000
	2	36,000	96,000	54,000
	3	21,600	117,600	32,400
	4	12,960	130,560	19,440
	5	7,440***	138,000	12,000

**$60,000 = $150,000 × 40%
***The asset is not depreciated below the estimated residual value of $12,000.

2.

Accumulated Depreciation—Equipment		130 5 6 0 00		
Equipment		175 0 0 0 00		
Loss on Disposal of Fixed Assets		9 4 4 0 00		
Equipment			150 0 0 0 00	
Cash			165 0 0 0 00	

Self-Examination Questions   (Answers at End of Chapter)

1. Which of the following expenditures incurred in connection with acquiring machinery is a proper charge to the asset account?
   A. Freight
   B. Installation costs
   C. Both A and B
   D. Neither A nor B

2. What is the amount of depreciation, using the double-declining-balance method for the second year of use for equipment costing $9,000, with an estimated residual value of $600 and an estimated life of three years?
   A. $6,000
   B. $3,000
   C. $2,000
   D. $400

3. An example of an accelerated depreciation method is:
   A. straight-line.
   B. double-declining-balance.
   C. units-of-production.
   D. depletion.

4. A fixed asset priced at $100,000 is acquired by trading in a similar asset that has a book value of $25,000. Assuming that the trade-in allowance is $30,000 and that $70,000 cash is paid for the new asset, what is the cost of the new asset for financial reporting purposes?
   A. $100,000
   B. $95,000
   C. $70,000
   D. $30,000

5. Which of the following is an example of an intangible asset?
   A. Patents
   B. Goodwill
   C. Copyrights
   D. All of the above

Eye Openers

1. Which of the following qualities are characteristic of fixed assets? (a) tangible, (b) capable of repeated use in the operations of the business, (c) held for sale in the normal course of business, (d) used rarely in the operations of the business, (e) long-lived.

2. Office Outfitters Co. has a fleet of automobiles and trucks for use by salespersons and for delivery of office supplies and equipment. Westgate Auto Sales Co. has automobiles and trucks for sale. Under what caption would the automobiles and trucks be reported on the balance sheet of (a) Office Outfitters Co., (b) Westgate Auto Sales Co.?

3. Design Space Co. acquired an adjacent vacant lot with the hope of selling it in the future at a gain. The lot is not intended to be used in Design Space's business operations. Where should such real estate be listed in the balance sheet?

4. Triplent Company solicited bids from several contractors to construct an addition to its office building. The lowest bid received was for $750,000. Triplent Company decided to construct the addition itself at a cost of $590,000. What amount should be recorded in the building account?

5. Distinguish between the accounting for capital expenditures and revenue expenditures.

6. Immediately after a used truck is acquired, a new motor is installed and the tires are replaced at a total cost of $4,150. Is this a capital expenditure or a revenue expenditure?

7. How does the accounting for a capital lease differ from the accounting for an operating lease?

8. Are the amounts at which fixed assets are reported in the balance sheet their approximate market values as of the balance sheet date? Discuss.

9. a. Does the recognition of depreciation in the accounts provide a special cash fund for the replacement of fixed assets? Explain.
   b. Describe the nature of depreciation as the term is used in accounting.

10. Emporium Company purchased a machine that has a manufacturer's suggested life of 20 years. The company plans to use the machine on a special project that will last 13 years. At the completion of the project, the machine will be sold. Over how many years should the machine be depreciated?

11. Is it necessary for a business to use the same method of computing depreciation (a) for all classes of its depreciable assets, (b) in the financial statements and in determining income taxes?

12. a. Under what conditions is the use of an accelerated depreciation method most appropriate?
    b. Why is an accelerated depreciation method often used for income tax purposes?
    c. What is the Modified Accelerated Cost Recovery System (MACRS), and under what conditions is it used?

13. A company revised the estimated useful lives of its fixed assets, which resulted in an increase in the remaining lives of several assets. Can the company include, as income of the current period, the cumulative effect of the changes, which reduces the depreciation expense of past periods? Discuss.

14. For some of the fixed assets of a business, the balance in Accumulated Depreciation is exactly equal to the cost of the asset. (a) Is it permissible to record additional depreciation on the assets if they are still useful to the business? Explain. (b) When should an entry be made to remove the cost and the accumulated depreciation from the accounts?

15. a. Over what period of time should the cost of a patent acquired by purchase be amortized?
    b. In general, what is the required accounting treatment for research and development costs?
    c. How should goodwill be amortized?

Practice Exercises

PE 10-1A
Capital and revenue expenditure entries
obj. 1

On February 13, Scandia Co. paid $1,650 to install a hydraulic lift and $25 for an air filter for one of its delivery trucks. Journalize the entries for the new lift and air filter expenditures.

PE 10-1B
Capital and revenue expenditure entries
obj. 1

On August 30, Stop Shop Co. paid $1,325 to repair the transmission on one of its delivery vans. In addition, Stop Shop paid $1,100 to install a GPS system in its van. Journalize the entries for the transmission and GPS system expenditures.

PE 10-2A
Straight-line depreciation
obj. 2

Equipment acquired at the beginning of the year at a cost of $88,000 has an estimated residual value of $6,000 and an estimated useful life of five years. Determine (a) the depreciable cost, (b) the straight-line rate, and (c) the annual straight-line depreciation.

PE 10-2B
Straight-line depreciation
obj. 2

A building acquired at the beginning of the year at a cost of $316,000 has an estimated residual value of $48,000 and an estimated useful life of 40 years. Determine (a) the depreciable cost, (b) the straight-line rate, and (c) the annual straight-line depreciation.

PE 10-3A
Units-of-production depreciation
obj. 2

A tractor acquired at a cost of $120,000 has an estimated residual value of $5,000, has an estimated useful life of 50,000 hours, and was operated 4,200 hours during the year. Determine (a) the depreciable cost, (b) the depreciation rate, and (c) the units-of-production depreciation for the year.

PE 10-3B
Units-of-production depreciation
obj. 2

A truck acquired at a cost of $90,000 has an estimated residual value of $18,000, has an estimated useful life of 200,000 miles, and was driven 40,000 miles during the year. Determine (a) the depreciable cost, (b) the depreciation rate, and (c) the units-of-production depreciation for the year.

PE 10-4A
Double-declining-balance depreciation
obj. 2

Equipment acquired at the beginning of the year at a cost of $88,000 has an estimated residual value of $6,000 and an estimated useful life of five years. Determine (a) the depreciable cost, (b) the double-declining-balance rate, and (c) the double-declining-balance depreciation for the first year.

PE 10-4B
Double-declining-balance depreciation
obj. 2

A building acquired at the beginning of the year at a cost of $316,000 has an estimated residual value of $48,000 and an estimated useful life of 40 years. Determine (a) the depreciable cost, (b) the double-declining-balance rate, and (c) the double-declining-balance depreciation for the first year.

PE 10-5A
Revision of depreciation estimates
obj. 2

A truck with a cost of $90,000 has an estimated residual value of $15,000, has an estimated useful life of eight years, and is depreciated by the straight-line method. (a) Determine the amount of the annual depreciation. (b) Determine the book value at the end of the fourth year of use. (c) Assuming that at the start of the fifth year the remaining life is estimated to be five years and the residual value is estimated to be $12,500, determine the depreciation expense for each of the remaining five years.

PE 10-5B
Revision of depreciation estimates
obj. 2

Equipment with a cost of $189,000 has an estimated residual value of $24,000, has an estimated useful life of 15 years, and is depreciated by the straight-line method. (a) Determine the amount of the annual depreciation. (b) Determine the book value at the end of the ninth year of use. (c) Assuming that at the start of the tenth year the remaining life is estimated to be eight years and the residual value is estimated to be $6,000, determine the depreciation expense for each of the remaining eight years.

PE 10-6A
Sale of equipment
obj. 3

Equipment was acquired at the beginning of the year at a cost of $158,000. The equipment was depreciated using the straight-line method based upon an estimated useful life of 10 years and an estimated residual value of $28,000.

a. What was the depreciation for the first year?
b. Assuming the equipment was sold at the end of the fifth year for $86,000, determine the gain or loss on the sale of the equipment.
c. Journalize the entry to record the sale.

PE 10-6B
Sale of equipment
obj. 3

Equipment was acquired at the beginning of the year at a cost of $250,000. The equipment was depreciated using the double-declining-balance method based upon an estimated useful life of 10 years and an estimated residual value of $45,000.

a. What was the depreciation for the first year?
b. Assuming the equipment was sold at the end of the second year for $142,000, determine the gain or loss on the sale of the equipment.
c. Journalize the entry to record the sale.

PE 10-7A
Exchange of similar fixed assets
obj. 3

On the first day of the fiscal year, equipment with a list price of $160,000 was acquired in exchange for similar equipment and $136,000 cash. The old equipment had a cost of $99,000 and accumulated depreciation of $79,000.

a. Determine the cost of the new truck for financial reporting purposes.
b. Journalize the entry to record the exchange.

PE 10-7B
Exchange of similar fixed assets
obj. 3

On the first day of the fiscal year, a delivery truck with a list price of $90,000 was acquired in exchange for an old delivery truck and $74,500 cash. The old truck had a cost of $60,000 and accumulated depreciation of $42,000.

a. Determine the cost of the new truck for financial reporting purposes.
b. Journalize the entry to record the exchange.

PE 10-8A
Entry for depletion of mineral rights
obj. 4

Butte Mining Co. acquired mineral rights for $36,000,000. The mineral deposit is estimated at 75,000,000 tons. During the current year, 29,350,000 tons were mined and sold.

a. Determine the depletion rate.
b. Determine the amount of depletion expense for the current year.
c. Journalize the adjusting entry on December 31 to recognize the depletion expense.

PE 10-8B
Entry for depletion of mineral rights
obj. 4

Rocky Mountain Mining Co. acquired mineral rights for $88,000,000. The mineral deposit is estimated at 110,000,000 tons. During the current year, 33,800,000 tons were mined and sold.

a. Determine the depletion rate.
b. Determine the amount of depletion expense for the current year.
c. Journalize the adjusting entry on December 31 to recognize the depletion expense.

PE 10-9A
Entries for impaired goodwill and amortization of patent
obj. 5

On December 31, it was estimated that goodwill of $100,000 was impaired. In addition, a patent with an estimated useful economic life of 12 years was acquired for $450,000 on June 1.

a. Journalize the adjusting entry on December 31 for the impaired goodwill.
b. Journalize the adjusting entry on December 31 for the amortization of the patent rights.

PE 10-9B
Entries for impaired goodwill and amortization of patent
obj. 5

On December 31, it was estimated that goodwill of $375,000 was impaired. In addition, a patent with an estimated useful economic life of 10 years was acquired for $600,000 on October 1.

a. Journalize the adjusting entry on December 31 for the impaired goodwill.
b. Journalize the adjusting entry on December 31 for the amortization of the patent rights.

Exercises

EX 10-1
Costs of acquiring fixed assets
obj. 1

Kelly Melnik owns and operates Aaladin Print Co. During July, Aaladin Print Co. incurred the following costs in acquiring two printing presses. One printing press was new, and the other was used by a business that recently filed for bankruptcy.

Costs related to new printing press:

1. Sales tax on purchase price
2. Insurance while in transit
3. Freight
4. Special foundation
5. Fee paid to factory representative for installation
6. New parts to replace those damaged in unloading

Costs related to used printing press:

7. Fees paid to attorney to review purchase agreement
8. Installation
9. Repair of vandalism during installation
10. Replacement of worn-out parts
11. Freight
12. Repair of damage incurred in reconditioning the press

a. Indicate which costs incurred in acquiring the new printing press should be debited to the asset account.
b. Indicate which costs incurred in acquiring the used printing press should be debited to the asset account.

EX 10-2
Determine cost of land
obj. 1

Serenity Ski Co. has developed a tract of land into a ski resort. The company has cut the trees, cleared and graded the land and hills, and constructed ski lifts. (a) Should the tree cutting, land clearing, and grading costs of constructing the ski slopes be debited to the land account? (b) If such costs are debited to Land, should they be depreciated?

EX 10-3
Determine cost of land
obj. 1
✓ $224,650

Next Day Delivery Company acquired an adjacent lot to construct a new warehouse, paying $25,000 and giving a short-term note for $175,000. Legal fees paid were $1,200, delinquent taxes assumed were $10,850, and fees paid to remove an old building from the land were $15,000. Materials salvaged from the demolition of the building were sold for $2,400. A contractor was paid $760,000 to construct a new warehouse. Determine the cost of the land to be reported on the balance sheet.

EX 10-4
Capital and revenue expenditures
obj. 1

Thare Co. incurred the following costs related to trucks and vans used in operating its delivery service:

1. Changed the oil and greased the joints of all the trucks and vans.
2. Installed security systems on four of the newer trucks.
3. Changed the radiator fluid on a truck that had been in service for the past four years.
4. Installed a hydraulic lift to a van.
5. Removed a two-way radio from one of the trucks and installed a new radio with a greater range of communication.
6. Overhauled the engine on one of the trucks that had been purchased three years ago.
7. Tinted the back and side windows of one of the vans to discourage theft of contents.
8. Repaired a flat tire on one of the vans.
9. Rebuilt the transmission on one of the vans that had been driven 40,000 miles. The van was no longer under warranty.
10. Replaced the trucks' suspension system with a new suspension system that allows for the delivery of heavier loads.

Classify each of the costs as a capital expenditure or a revenue expenditure.

EX 10-5
Capital and revenue expenditures
obj. 1

Felix Little owns and operates Big Sky Transport Co. During the past year, Felix incurred the following costs related to his 18-wheel truck:

1. Replaced a headlight that had burned out.
2. Replaced fog and cab light bulbs.
3. Installed a television in the sleeping compartment of the truck.
4. Removed the old CB radio and replaced it with a newer model with a greater range.
5. Replaced a shock absorber that had worn out.
6. Installed a wind deflector on top of the cab to increase fuel mileage.
7. Replaced the old radar detector with a newer model that detects the KA frequencies now used by many of the state patrol radar guns. The detector is wired directly into the cab, so that it is partially hidden. In addition, Felix fastened the detector to the truck with a locking device that prevents its removal.
8. Changed engine oil.
9. Replaced the hydraulic brake system that had begun to fail during his latest trip through the Rocky Mountains.
10. Modified the factory-installed turbo charger with a special-order kit designed to add 50 more horsepower to the engine performance.

Classify each of the costs as a capital expenditure or a revenue expenditure.

EX 10-6
Capital and revenue expenditures
obj. 1

Load All Company made the following expenditures on one of its delivery trucks:

Feb. 22. Replaced transmission at a cost of $2,300.
Mar. 20. Paid $900 for installation of a hydraulic lift.
Nov. 2. Paid $67 to change the oil and air filter.

Prepare journal entries for each expenditure.

EX 10-7
Nature of depreciation
obj. 2

Armored Metal Co. reported $975,600 for equipment and $600,000 for accumulated depreciation—equipment on its balance sheet.
➤ Does this mean (a) that the replacement cost of the equipment is $975,600 and (b) that $600,000 is set aside in a special fund for the replacement of the equipment? Explain.

EX 10-8
Straight-line depreciation rates
obj. 2
✓ a. 50%

Convert each of the following estimates of useful life to a straight-line depreciation rate, stated as a percentage, assuming that the residual value of the fixed asset is to be ignored: (a) 2 years, (b) 8 years, (c) 10 years, (d) 20 years, (e) 25 years, (f) 40 years, (g) 50 years.

EX 10-9
Straight-line depreciation
obj. 2
✓ $11,200

A refrigerator used by a meat processor has a cost of $198,500, an estimated residual value of $30,500, and an estimated useful life of 15 years. What is the amount of the annual depreciation computed by the straight-line method?

EX 10-10
Depreciation by units-of-production method
obj. 2
✓ $893

A diesel-powered tractor with a cost of $215,000 and estimated residual value of $27,000 is expected to have a useful operating life of 80,000 hours. During October, the generator was operated 380 hours. Determine the depreciation for the month.

EX 10-11
Depreciation by units-of-production method
obj. 2

Prior to adjustment at the end of the year, the balance in Trucks is $225,900 and the balance in Accumulated Depreciation—Trucks is $87,010. Details of the subsidiary ledger are as follows:

✓a. Truck #1, credit
Accumulated
Depreciation, $15,120

Truck No.	Cost	Estimated Residual Value	Estimated Useful Life	Accumulated Depreciation at Beginning of Year	Miles Operated During Year
1	$75,000	$12,000	150,000 miles	$19,110	36,000 miles
2	72,900	9,900	300,000	59,850	18,000
3	38,000	3,000	200,000	8,050	36,000
4	40,000	4,000	120,000	—	16,000

a. Determine the depreciation rates per mile and the amount to be credited to the accumulated depreciation section of each of the subsidiary accounts for the miles operated during the current year.
b. Journalize the entry to record depreciation for the year.

EX 10-12
Depreciation by two methods
obj. 2
✓a. $2,800

A John Deere tractor acquired on January 5 at a cost of $44,800 has an estimated useful life of 16 years. Assuming that it will have no residual value, determine the depreciation for each of the first two years (a) by the straight-line method and (b) by the double-declining-balance method. Round to the nearest dollar.

EX 10-13
Depreciation by two methods
obj. 2
✓a. $9,500

A storage tank acquired at the beginning of the fiscal year at a cost of $86,000 has an estimated residual value of $10,000 and an estimated useful life of eight years. Determine the following: (a) the amount of annual depreciation by the straight-line method and (b) the amount of depreciation for the first and second year computed by the double-declining-balance method.

EX 10-14
Partial-year depreciation
obj. 2
✓a. First year, $1,250

Sandblasting equipment acquired at a cost of $68,000 has an estimated residual value of $18,000 and an estimated useful life of 10 years. It was placed in service on October 1 of the current fiscal year, which ends on December 31. Determine the depreciation for the current fiscal year and for the following fiscal year by (a) the straight-line method and (b) the double-declining-balance method.

EX 10-15
Revision of depreciation
obj. 2
✓a. $12,500

A building with a cost of $750,000 has an estimated residual value of $300,000, has an estimated useful life of 36 years, and is depreciated by the straight-line method. (a) What is the amount of the annual depreciation? (b) What is the book value at the end of the twentieth year of use? (c) If at the start of the twenty-first year it is estimated that the remaining life is 20 years and that the residual value is $200,000, what is the depreciation expense for each of the remaining 20 years?

EX 10-16
Capital expenditure and depreciation
objs. 1, 2
✓b. Depreciation Expense, $2,400

Sime Company purchased and installed carpet in its new general offices on March 29 for a total cost of $48,000. The carpet is estimated to have a 15-year useful life and no residual value.

a. Prepare the journal entries necessary for recording the purchase of the new carpet.
b. Record the December 31 adjusting entry for the partial-year depreciation expense for the carpet, assuming that Sime Company uses the straight-line method.

EX 10-17
Entries for sale of fixed asset
obj. 3

Equipment acquired on January 3, 2005, at a cost of $360,000, has an estimated useful life of 12 years, has an estimated residual value of $30,000, and is depreciated by the straight-line method.

a. What was the book value of the equipment at December 31, 2008, the end of the year?
b. Assuming that the equipment was sold on April 1, 2009, for $220,000, journalize the entries to record (1) depreciation for the three months until the sale date, and (2) the sale of the equipment.

EX 10-18
Disposal of fixed asset
obj. 3
✓ b. $98,750

Equipment acquired on January 3, 2005, at a cost of $147,500, has an estimated useful life of eight years and an estimated residual value of $17,500.

a. What was the annual amount of depreciation for the years 2005, 2006, and 2007, using the straight-line method of depreciation?
b. What was the book value of the equipment on January 1, 2008?
c. Assuming that the equipment was sold on January 2, 2008, for $95,000, journalize the entry to record the sale.
d. Assuming that the equipment had been sold on January 2, 2008, for $100,000 instead of $95,000, journalize the entry to record the sale.

EX 10-19
Asset traded for similar asset
obj. 3
✓ a. $200,000

A printing press priced at $280,000 is acquired by trading in a similar press and paying cash for the difference between the trade-in allowance and the price of the new press.

a. Assuming that the trade-in allowance is $80,000, what is the amount of cash given?
b. Assuming that the book value of the press traded in is $78,750, what is the cost of the new press for financial reporting purposes?

EX 10-20
Asset traded for similar asset
obj. 3
✓ a. $200,000

Assume the same facts as in Exercise 10-19, except that the book value of the press traded in is $103,250. (a) What is the amount of cash given? (b) What is the cost of the new press for financial reporting purposes?

EX 10-21
Entries for trade of fixed asset
obj. 3

On October 1, Clear Spring Co., a water distiller, acquired new bottling equipment with a list price of $288,750. Clear Springs received a trade-in allowance of $60,000 on the old equipment of a similar type, paid cash of $28,750, and gave a series of five notes payable for the remainder. The following information about the old equipment is obtained from the account in the equipment ledger: cost, $210,000; accumulated depreciation on December 31, the end of the preceding fiscal year, $137,500; annual depreciation, $12,500. Journalize the entries to record (a) the current depreciation of the old equipment to the date of trade-in and (b) the exchange transaction on October 1 for financial reporting purposes.

EX 10-22
Entries for trade of fixed asset
obj. 3

On April 1, Senorita's Delivery Services acquired a new truck with a list price of $75,000. Senorita's received a trade-in allowance of $15,000 on an old truck of similar type, paid cash of $10,000, and gave a series of five notes payable for the remainder. The following information about the old truck is obtained from the account in the equipment ledger: cost, $48,000; accumulated depreciation on December 31, the end of the preceding fiscal year, $32,000; annual depreciation, $8,000. Journalize the entries to record (a) the current depreciation of the old truck to the date of trade-in and (b) the transaction on April 1 for financial reporting purposes.

EX 10-23
Depreciable cost of asset acquired by exchange
obj. 3

On the first day of the fiscal year, a delivery truck with a list price of $86,500 was acquired in exchange for an old delivery truck and $75,000 cash. The old truck had a book value of $15,675 at the date of the exchange.

a. Determine the depreciable cost for financial reporting purposes.
b. Assuming that the book value of the old delivery truck was $6,000, determine the depreciable cost for financial reporting purposes.

EX 10-24
Depletion entries
obj. 4
✓ a. $4,500,000

Rainbow Mining Co. acquired mineral rights for $30,000,000. The mineral deposit is estimated at 75,000,000 tons. During the current year, 11,250,000 tons were mined and sold.

a. Determine the amount of depletion expense for the current year.
b. Journalize the adjusting entry to recognize the depletion expense.

EX 10-25
Amortization entries
obj. 5

✓ a. $52,850

Venture Company acquired patent rights on January 3, 2005, for $661,500. The patent has a useful life equal to its legal life of 15 years. On January 5, 2008, Venture successfully defended the patent in a lawsuit at a cost of $105,000.

a. Determine the patent amortization expense for the current year ended December 31, 2008.
b. Journalize the adjusting entry to recognize the amortization.

EX 10-26
Book value of fixed assets
obj. 6

Apple Computer, Inc., designs, manufactures, and markets personal computers and related software. Apple also manufactures and distributes music players (Ipod) along with related accessories and services including the online distribution of third-party music. The following information was taken from a recent annual report of Apple:

Property, Plant, and Equipment (in millions):

	Current Year	Preceding Year
Land and buildings	$361	$351
Machinery, equipment, and internal-use software	494	422
Office furniture and equipment	81	79
Other fixed assets related to leases	545	446
Accumulated depreciation and amortization	664	591

a. Compute the book value of the fixed assets for the current year and the preceding year and explain the differences, if any.
b. 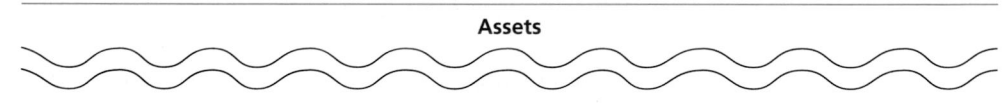 Would you normally expect the book value of fixed assets to increase or decrease during the year?

EX 10-27
Balance sheet presentation
obj. 6

List the errors you find in the following partial balance sheet:

Planet Bronze Company
Balance Sheet
December 31, 2008

Assets

Total current assets $478,000

Property, plant, and equipment:	Replacement Cost	Accumulated Depreciation	Book Value
Land	$ 80,000	$ 16,000	$ 64,000
Buildings	208,000	60,800	147,200
Factory equipment	440,000	233,600	206,400
Office equipment	96,000	64,000	32,000
Patents	64,000	—	64,000
Goodwill	36,000	4,000	32,000
Total property, plant, and equipment	$924,000	$378,400	545,600

EX 10-28
Fixed asset turnover ratio

Verizon Communications is a major telecommunications company in the United States. Verizon's balance sheet disclosed the following information regarding fixed assets:

	Dec. 31, 2005 (in millions)	Dec. 31, 2004 (in millions)
Plant, property, and equipment	$193,610	$185,522
Less accumulated depreciation	118,305	111,398
	$ 75,305	$ 74,124

Verizon's revenue for 2005 was $75,112 million. The fixed asset turnover for the telecommunications industry averages 1.10.

a. Determine Verizon's fixed asset turnover ratio. Round to two decimal places.
b. ▬▬▬▶ Interpret Verizon's fixed asset turnover ratio.

EX 10-29
Fixed asset turnover ratio

The following table shows the revenue and average net fixed assets (in millions) for a recent fiscal year for Best Buy and Circuit City Stores, Inc.:

	Revenue	Average Net Fixed Assets
Best Buy	$27,433	$2,354
Circuit City Stores, Inc.	10,472	662

a Compute the fixed asset turnover for each company. Round to two decimal places.
b. ▬▬▬▶ Which company uses its fixed assets more efficiently? Explain.

APPENDIX EX 10-30
Sum-of-the-years-digits depreciation

✓ *First year: $5,271*

Based on the data in Exercise 10-12, determine the depreciation for the Bobcat for each of the first two years, using the sum-of-the-years-digits depreciation method. Round to the nearest dollar.

APPENDIX EX 10-31
Sum-of-the-years-digits depreciation

✓ *First year: $16,889*

Based on the data in Exercise 10-13, determine the depreciation for the storage tank for each of the first two years, using the sum-of-the-years-digits depreciation method. Round to the nearest dollar.

APPENDIX EX 10-32
Partial-year depreciation

✓ *First year: $2,273*

Based on the data in Exercise 10-14, determine the depreciation for the sandblasting equipment for each of the first two years, using the sum-of-the-years-digits depreciation method. Round to the nearest dollar.

Problems Series A

PR 10-1A
Allocate payments and receipts to fixed asset accounts

obj. 1

✓ *Land $443,200*

The following payments and receipts are related to land, land improvements, and buildings acquired for use in a wholesale ceramic business. The receipts are identified by an asterisk.

a. Fee paid to attorney for title search	$ 3,000
b. Cost of real estate acquired as a plant site: Land	325,000
Building	75,000
c. Delinquent real estate taxes on property, assumed by purchaser	10,000
d. Special assessment paid to city for extension of water main to the property	12,800
e. Cost of razing and removing building	3,900
f. Proceeds from sale of salvage materials from old building	4,000*
g. Cost of filling and grading land	17,500
h. Architect's and engineer's fees for plans and supervision	40,000
i. Premium on one-year insurance policy during construction	4,800
j. Cost of trees and shrubbery planted	9,000
k. Money borrowed to pay building contractor	800,000*
l. Cost of paving parking lot to be used by customers	15,000
m. Cost of repairing windstorm damage during construction	2,000

(continued)

n. Cost of repairing vandalism damage during construction . . . . $ 2,500
o. Cost of floodlights installed on parking lot 1,100
p. Interest incurred on building loan during construction 42,000
q. Payment to building contractor for new building 915,000
r. Proceeds from insurance company for windstorm and vandalism damage . . 4,000*
s. Refund of premium on insurance policy (i) canceled after 11 months 400*

Instructions
1. Assign each payment and receipt to Land (unlimited life), Land Improvements (limited life), Building, or Other Accounts. Indicate receipts by an asterisk. Identify each item by letter and list the amounts in columnar form, as follows:

Item	Land	Land Improvements	Building	Other Accounts

2. Determine the amount debited to Land, Land Improvements, and Building.
3. ▭▶ The costs assigned to the land, which is used as a plant site, will not be depreciated, while the costs assigned to land improvements will be depreciated. Explain this seemingly contradictory application of the concept of depreciation.

PR 10-2A
Compare three depreciation methods
obj. 2

✓ *a. 2006: straight-line depreciation, $28,000*

Air Pack Company purchased packaging equipment on January 3, 2006, for $90,000. The equipment was expected to have a useful life of three years, or 21,000 operating hours, and a residual value of $6,000. The equipment was used for 8,000 hours during 2006, 7,500 hours in 2007, and 5,500 hours in 2008.

Instructions
Determine the amount of depreciation expense for the years ended December 31, 2006, 2007, and 2008, by (a) the straight-line method, (b) the units-of-production method, and (c) the double-declining-balance method. Also determine the total depreciation expense for the three years by each method. The following columnar headings are suggested for recording the depreciation expense amounts:

	Depreciation Expense		
Year	Straight-Line Method	Units-of-Production Method	Double-Declining-Balance Method

---

PR 10-3A
Depreciation by three methods; partial years
obj. 2

✓ *a. 2006: $1,255*

Covershot Company purchased plastic laminating equipment on July 1, 2006, for $7,830. The equipment was expected to have a useful life of three years, or 10,040 operating hours, and a residual value of $300. The equipment was used for 1,600 hours during 2006, 3,800 hours in 2007, 3,400 hours in 2008, and 1,240 hours in 2009.

Instructions
Determine the amount of depreciation expense for the years ended December 31, 2006, 2007, 2008, and 2009, by (a) the straight-line method, (b) the units-of-production method, and (c) the double-declining-balance method. Round to the nearest dollar.

PR 10-4A
Depreciation by two methods; trade of fixed asset
objs. 2, 3

✓ *1. b. Year 1: $70,000 depreciation expense*
✓ *2. $237,680*

New lithographic equipment, acquired at a cost of $175,000 at the beginning of a fiscal year, has an estimated useful life of five years and an estimated residual value of $15,000. The manager requested information regarding the effect of alternative methods on the amount of depreciation expense each year. On the basis of the data presented to the manager, the double-declining-balance method was selected.

In the first week of the fifth year, the equipment was traded in for similar equipment priced at $240,000. The trade-in allowance on the old equipment was $25,000, cash of $15,000 was paid, and a note payable was issued for the balance.

Instructions
1. Determine the annual depreciation expense for each of the estimated five years of use, the accumulated depreciation at the end of each year, and the book value of the equipment at the end of each year by (a) the straight-line method and (b) the double-declining-balance method. The following columnar headings are suggested for each schedule:

Year	Depreciation Expense	Accumulated Depreciation, End of Year	Book Value, End of Year

2. For financial reporting purposes, determine the cost of the new equipment acquired in the exchange.
3. Journalize the entry to record the exchange.
4. Journalize the entry to record the exchange, assuming that the trade-in allowance was $18,000 instead of $25,000.

PR 10-5A
Transactions for fixed assets, including trade
objs. 1, 2, 3

KLOOSTER & ALLEN

The following transactions, adjusting entries, and closing entries were completed by Willow Run Furniture Co. during a three-year period. All are related to the use of delivery equipment. The double-declining-balance method of depreciation is used.

2006
Jan.   9. Purchased a used delivery truck for $32,000, paying cash.
Sept. 24. Paid garage $470 for miscellaneous repairs to the truck.
Dec. 31. Recorded depreciation on the truck for the year. The estimated useful life of the truck is four years, with a residual value of $4,500 for the truck.

2007
Jan.   1. Purchased a new truck for $57,500, paying cash.
June 30. Sold the used truck for $13,500. (Record depreciation to date in 2007 for the truck.)
Nov. 23. Paid garage $550 for miscellaneous repairs to the truck.
Dec. 31. Recorded depreciation on the truck. It has an estimated residual value of $12,000 and an estimated life of five years.

2008
July   1. Purchased a new truck for $60,000, paying cash.
Oct.   1. Sold the truck purchased January 1, 2007, for $22,000. (Record depreciation for the year.)
Dec. 31. Recorded depreciation on the remaining truck. It has an estimated residual value of $15,000 and an estimated useful life of eight years.

Instructions
Journalize the transactions and the adjusting entries.

PR 10-6A
Amortization and depletion entries
objs. 4, 5
✓1. a. $216,000

Data related to the acquisition of timber rights and intangible assets during the current year ended December 31 are as follows:

a. Timber rights on a tract of land were purchased for $648,000 on July 5. The stand of timber is estimated at 3,600,000 board feet. During the current year, 1,200,000 board feet of timber were cut and sold.
b. Goodwill in the amount of $27,000,000 was purchased on January 7.
c. Governmental and legal costs of $780,000 were incurred on October 4 in obtaining a patent with an estimated economic life of 12 years. Amortization is to be for one-fourth year.

Instructions
1. Determine the amount of the amortization or depletion expense for the current year for each of the foregoing items.
2. Journalize the adjusting entries required to record the amortization or depletion for each item.

Problems Series B

PR 10-1B
Allocate payments and receipts to fixed asset accounts

obj. 1

✓ *Land: $322,400*

The following payments and receipts are related to land, land improvements, and buildings acquired for use in a wholesale apparel business. The receipts are identified by an asterisk.

a.	Finder's fee paid to real estate agency	$ 7,500
b.	Cost of real estate acquired as a plant site: Land	210,000
	Building	50,000
c.	Fee paid to attorney for title search	2,500
d.	Delinquent real estate taxes on property, assumed by purchaser	20,650
e.	Cost of razing and removing building	16,250
f.	Cost of filling and grading land	12,500
g.	Proceeds from sale of salvage materials from old building	5,000*
h.	Architect's and engineer's fees for plans and supervision	36,000
i.	Special assessment paid to city for extension of water main to the property	8,000
j.	Premium on one-year insurance policy during construction	3,600
k.	Money borrowed to pay building contractor	900,000*
l.	Cost of trees and shrubbery planted	18,000
m.	Cost of repairing windstorm damage during construction	3,000
n.	Cost of repairing vandalism damage during construction	4,200
o.	Cost of paving parking lot to be used by customers	15,000
p.	Proceeds from insurance company for windstorm and vandalism damage	7,000*
q.	Interest incurred on building loan during construction	54,000
r.	Payment to building contractor for new building	1,000,000
s.	Refund of premium on insurance policy (j) canceled after 10 months	600*

Instructions

1. Assign each payment and receipt to Land (unlimited life), Land Improvements (limited life), Building, or Other Accounts. Indicate receipts by an asterisk. Identify each item by letter and list the amounts in columnar form, as follows:

Item	Land	Land Improvements	Building	Other Accounts

2. Determine the amount debited to Land, Land Improvements, and Building.
3. ⬤▭▭▭▶ The costs assigned to the land, which is used as a plant site, will not be depreciated, while the costs assigned to land improvements will be depreciated. Explain this seemingly contradictory application of the concept of depreciation.

PR 10-2B
Compare three depreciation methods

obj. 2

✓ *a. 2007: straight-line depreciation, $107,500*

Seal Coatings Company purchased waterproofing equipment on January 2, 2007, for $475,000. The equipment was expected to have a useful life of four years, or 21,500 operating hours, and a residual value of $45,000. The equipment was used for 7,600 hours during 2007, 6,800 hours in 2008, 5,100 hours in 2009, and 2,000 hours in 2010.

Instructions

Determine the amount of depreciation expense for the years ended December 31, 2007, 2008, 2009, and 2010, by (a) the straight-line method, (b) the units-of-production method, and (c) the double-declining-balance method. Also determine the total depreciation expense for the four years by each method. The following columnar headings are suggested for recording the depreciation expense amounts:

	Depreciation Expense		
Year	Straight-Line Method	Units-of-Production Method	Double-Declining-Balance Method

PR 10-3B
Depreciation by three methods; partial years

obj. 2

✓ *a. 2006, $15,200*

E-Sharp Company purchased tool sharpening equipment on July 1, 2006, for $97,200. The equipment was expected to have a useful life of three years, or 22,800 operating hours, and a residual value of $6,000. The equipment was used for 3,650 hours during 2006, 8,000 hours in 2007, 7,850 hours in 2008, and 3,300 hours in 2009.

Instructions
Determine the amount of depreciation expense for the years ended December 31, 2006, 2007, 2008, and 2009, by (a) the straight-line method, (b) the units-of-production method, and (c) the double-declining-balance method.

PR 10-4B
Depreciation by two methods; trade of fixed asset

objs. 2, 3

✓ *1. b. Year 1, $120,000 depreciation expense*

✓ *2. $310,000*

New tire retreading equipment, acquired at a cost of $240,000 at the beginning of a fiscal year, has an estimated useful life of four years and an estimated residual value of $18,000. The manager requested information regarding the effect of alternative methods on the amount of depreciation expense each year. On the basis of the data presented to the manager, the double-declining-balance method was selected.

In the first week of the fourth year, the equipment was traded in for similar equipment priced at $325,000. The trade-in allowance on the old equipment was $45,000, cash of $10,000 was paid, and a note payable was issued for the balance.

Instructions
1. Determine the annual depreciation expense for each of the estimated four years of use, the accumulated depreciation at the end of each year, and the book value of the equipment at the end of each year by (a) the straight-line method and (b) the double-declining-balance method. The following columnar headings are suggested for each schedule:

Year	Depreciation Expense	Accumulated Depreciation, End of Year	Book Value, End of Year

2. For financial reporting purposes, determine the cost of the new equipment acquired in the exchange.
3. Journalize the entry to record the exchange.
4. Journalize the entry to record the exchange, assuming that the trade-in allowance was $25,000 instead of $45,000.

PR 10-5B
Transactions for fixed assets, including trade

objs. 1, 2, 3

The following transactions, adjusting entries, and closing entries were completed by Crown Furniture Co. during a three-year period. All are related to the use of delivery equipment. The double-declining-balance method of depreciation is used.

2006
Jan.   9. Purchased a used delivery truck for $38,000, paying cash.
Mar. 15. Paid garage $180 for changing the oil, replacing the oil filter, and tuning the engine on the delivery truck.
Dec. 31. Recorded depreciation on the truck for the fiscal year. The estimated useful life of the truck is eight years, with a residual value of $7,000 for the truck.

2007
Jan.   3. Purchased a new truck for $62,500, paying cash.
Feb. 20. Paid garage $150 to tune the engine and make other minor repairs on the used truck.
Apr. 30. Sold the used truck for $25,000. (Record depreciation to date in 2007 for the truck.)
Dec. 31. Recorded depreciation on the truck. It has an estimated trade-in value of $12,000 and an estimated life of 10 years.

2008
July   1. Purchased a new truck for $70,000, paying cash.
Oct.   6. Sold the truck purchased January 3, 2007, for $43,900. (Record depreciation for the year.)
Dec. 31. Recorded depreciation on the remaining truck. It has an estimated residual value of $4,500 and an estimated useful life of 10 years.

Instructions
Journalize the transactions and the adjusting entries.

PR 10-6B
Amortization and depletion entries
objs. 4, 5
✓ *1. b. $23,750*

Data related to the acquisition of timber rights and intangible assets during the current year ended December 31 are as follows:

a. Goodwill in the amount of $15,000,000 was purchased on January 11.
b. Governmental and legal costs of $475,000 were incurred on June 30 in obtaining a patent with an estimated economic life of 10 years. Amortization is to be for one-half year.
c. Timber rights on a tract of land were purchased for $900,000 on April 6. The stand of timber is estimated at 6,000,000 board feet. During the current year, 800,000 board feet of timber were cut and sold.

Instructions
1. Determine the amount of the amortization or depletion expense for the current year for each of the foregoing items.
2. Journalize the adjusting entries to record the amortization or depletion expense for each item.

Special Activities

SA 10-1
Ethics and professional conduct in business

ETHICS

Leah Corbin, CPA, is an assistant to the controller of Beartooth Consulting Co. In her spare time, Leah also prepares tax returns and performs general accounting services for clients. Frequently, Leah performs these services after her normal working hours, using Beartooth Consulting Co.'s computers and laser printers. Occasionally, Leah's clients will call her at the office during regular working hours.

➤ Discuss whether Leah is performing in a professional manner.

SA 10-2
Financial vs. tax depreciation

The following is an excerpt from a conversation between two employees of Resource Technologies, Haley Eubanks and Clay Hamon. Haley is the accounts payable clerk, and Clay is the cashier.

Haley: Clay, could I get your opinion on something?
Clay: Sure, Haley.
Haley: Do you know Amber, the fixed assets clerk?
Clay: I know who she is, but I don't know her real well. Why?
Haley: Well, I was talking to her at lunch last Monday about how she liked her job, etc. You know, the usual . . . and she mentioned something about having to keep two sets of books . . . one for taxes and one for the financial statements. That can't be good accounting, can it? What do you think?
Clay: Two sets of books? It doesn't sound right.
Haley: It doesn't seem right to me either. I was always taught that you had to use generally accepted accounting principles. How can there be two sets of books? What can be the difference between the two?

➤ How would you respond to Clay and Haley if you were Amber?

SA 10-3
Effect of depreciation on net income

Cowboy Construction Co. specializes in building replicas of historic houses. Tom Askew, president of Cowboy Construction, is considering the purchase of various items of equipment on July 1, 2006, for $150,000. The equipment would have a useful life of five years and no residual value. In the past, all equipment has been leased. For tax purposes, Tom is considering depreciating the equipment by the straight-line method. He discussed the matter with his CPA and learned that, although the straight-line method could be elected, it was to his advantage to use the Modified Accelerated Cost Recovery System (MACRS) for tax purposes. He asked for your advice as to which method to use for tax purposes.

1. Compute depreciation for each of the years (2006, 2007, 2008, 2009, 2010, and 2011) of useful life by (a) the straight-line method and (b) MACRS. In using the straight-line method, one-half year's depreciation should be computed for 2006 and 2011. Use the MACRS rates presented in the chapter.

2. Assuming that income before depreciation and income tax is estimated to be $300,000 uniformly per year and that the income tax rate is 30%, compute the net income for each of the years 2006, 2007, 2008, 2009, 2010, and 2011, if (a) the straight-line method is used and (b) MACRS is used.

3. ▭▭▶ What factors would you present for Tom's consideration in the selection of a depreciation method?

SA 10-4
Shopping for a delivery truck

Group Project

You are planning to acquire a delivery truck for use in your business for three years. In groups of three or four, explore a local dealer's purchase and leasing options for the truck. Summarize the costs of purchasing versus leasing, and list other factors that might help you decide whether to buy or lease the truck.

SA 10-5
Applying for patents, copyrights, and trademarks

Internet Project

Go to the Internet and review the procedures for applying for a patent, a copyright, and a trademark. One Internet site that is useful for this purpose is **idresearch.com**, which is linked to the text's Web site at **http://www.thomsonedu.com/accounting/warren**. Prepare a written summary of these procedures.

SA 10-6
Fixed asset turnover: three industries

The following table shows the revenues and average net fixed assets for a recent fiscal year for three different companies from three different industries: retailing, manufacturing, and communications.

	Revenues (in millions)	Average Net Fixed Assets (in millions)
Wal-Mart	$258,681	$51,686
Alcoa Inc.	21,504	12,333
Comcast Corporation	18,348	18,427

a. For each company, determine the fixed asset turnover ratio. Round to two decimal places.
b. Explain Wal-Mart's ratio relative to the other two companies.

Answers to Self-Examination Questions

1. **C** All amounts spent to get a fixed asset (such as machinery) in place and ready for use are proper charges to the asset account. In the case of machinery acquired, the freight (answer A) and the installation costs (answer B) are both (answer C) proper charges to the machinery account.

2. **C** The periodic charge for depreciation under the double-declining-balance method for the second year is determined by first computing the depreciation charge for the first year. The depreciation for the first year of $6,000 (answer A) is computed by multiplying the cost of the equipment, $9,000, by 2/3 (the straight-line rate of 1/3 multiplied by 2). The depreciation for the second year of $2,000 (answer C) is then determined by multiplying the book value at the end of the first year, $3,000 (the cost of $9,000 minus the first-year depreciation of $6,000), by 2/3. The third year's depreciation is $400 (answer D). It is determined by multiplying the book value at the end of the second year, $1,000, by 2/3, thus yielding $667. However, the equipment cannot be depreciated below its residual value

of $600; thus, the third-year depreciation is $400 ($1,000 − $600).

3. **B** A depreciation method that provides for a higher depreciation amount in the first year of the use of an asset and a gradually declining periodic amount thereafter is called an accelerated depreciation method. The double-declining-balance method (answer B) is an example of such a method.

4. **B** The acceptable method of accounting for an exchange of similar assets in which the trade-in allowance ($30,000) exceeds the book value of the old asset ($25,000) requires that the cost of the new asset be determined by adding the amount of cash given ($70,000) to the book value of the old asset ($25,000), which totals $95,000. Alternatively, the unrecognized gain ($5,000) can be subtracted from the list price ($100,000).

5. **D** Long-lived assets that are useful in operations, not held for sale, and without physical qualities are called intangible assets. Patents, goodwill, and copyrights are examples of intangible assets (answer D).

Current Liabilities and Payroll

© TOM GANNAM/ASSOCIATED PRESS

objectives

After studying this chapter, you should be able to:

1 *Describe and illustrate current liabilities related to accounts payable, current portion of long-term debt, and notes payable.*

2 *Determine employer liabilities for payroll, including liabilities arising from employee earnings and deductions from earnings.*

3 *Describe payroll accounting systems that use a payroll register, employee earnings records, and a general journal.*

4 *Journalize entries for employee fringe benefits, including vacation pay and pensions.*

5 *Describe the accounting treatment for contingent liabilities and journalize entries for product warranties.*

Panera Bread

Banks and other financial institutions provide loans or credit to buyers for purchases of various items. Using credit to purchase items is probably as old as commerce itself. In fact, the Babylonians were lending money to support trade as early as 1300 B.C. The use of credit provides *individuals* convenience and buying power. Credit cards provide individuals convenience over writing checks and make purchasing over the Internet easier. Credit cards also provide individuals control over cash by providing documentation of their purchases through receipt of monthly credit card statements and by allowing them to avoid carrying large amounts of cash and purchase items before they are paid.

Short-term credit is also used by *businesses* to provide convenience in purchasing items for manufacture or resale. More importantly, short-term credit gives a business control over the payment for goods and services. For example, Panera Bread, a chain of bakery-cafés located throughout the United States, uses short-term trade credit, or accounts payable, to purchase ingredients for making bread products in its bakeries. Short-term trade credit gives Panera control over cash payments by separating the purchase function from the payment function. Thus, the employee responsible for purchasing the bakery ingredients is separated from the employee responsible for paying for the purchase. This separation of duties can help prevent unauthorized purchases or payments.

In addition to accounts payable, a business like Panera Bread can also have current liabilities related to payroll, payroll taxes, employee benefits, short-term notes, unearned revenue, and contingencies. We will discuss each of these types of current liabilities in this chapter.

Current Liabilities

objective 1

Describe and illustrate current liabilities related to accounts payable, current portion of long-term debt, and notes payable.

When a business or a bank advances *credit*, it is making a loan. In these circumstances, it is called a *creditor* (or *lender*). Individuals or businesses that receive the credit are called *debtors* (or *borrowers*). Debt is an obligation that is recorded as a liability. *Long-term liabilities* are obligations due for a period of time greater than one year. Thus, a 30-year mortgage taken out to purchase property would be an example of a long-term liability. In contrast, *current liabilities* are obligations that will be paid out of current assets and are due within a short time, usually within one year.

Three types of current liabilities will be discussed in this section—accounts payable, current portion of long-term debt, and notes payable.

ACCOUNTS PAYABLE

Accounts payable arise from purchasing goods or services for use in a company's operations or for purchasing merchandise for resale. We have described and illustrated accounts payable transactions in earlier chapters. For most businesses, this is often the largest current liability. Exhibit 1 illustrates the size of the accounts payable balance as a percent of total current liabilities for a number of different companies. The average percent of accounts payable to total current liabilities for large companies is 35.7%.[1]

---

1 Determined from analysis of public companies exceeding $10 billion in sales.

Accounts Payable as a Percent of Total Current Liabilities

Company	Accounts Payable as a Percent of Total Current Liabilities
Alcoa Inc.	39%
BellSouth Corp.	16
Gap Inc.	47
IBM	22
Nissan Motor Co. Ltd.	25
Rite Aid Corp.	51
ChevronTexaco	54

CURRENT PORTION OF LONG-TERM DEBT

Long-term liabilities are often paid back in periodic payments, called *installments*, much like a car loan. Long-term liability installments that are due *within* the coming year must be classified as a current liability. The total amount of the installments due *after* the coming year is classified as a long-term liability. To illustrate, Starbucks Corporation reported the following scheduled debt payments in the notes to its September 30, 2005, annual report to shareholders:

Fiscal year ending	
2006	$ 748,000
2007	762,000
2008	775,000
2009	790,000
2010	337,000
Thereafter	206,000
Total principal payments	$3,618,000

The debt of $748,000 due in 2006 would be reported as a current liability on the September 30, 2005, balance sheet. The remaining debt of $2,870,000 ($3,618,000 − $748,000) would be reported as a long-term liability on the balance sheet, which we will discuss in a later chapter.

SHORT-TERM NOTES PAYABLE

Notes may be issued when merchandise or other assets are purchased. They may also be issued to creditors to temporarily satisfy an account payable created earlier. For example, assume that a business issues a 90-day, 12% note for $1,000, dated August 1, 2007, to Murray Co. for a $1,000 overdue account. The entry to record the issuance of the note is as follows:

Aug.	1	Accounts Payable—Murray Co.		1 0 0 0 00	
		Notes Payable			1 0 0 0 00
		Issued a 90-day, 12% note on account.			

When the note matures, the entry to record the payment of $1,000 principal plus $30 interest ($1,000 × 12% × 90/360) is as follows:

Oct.	30	Notes Payable		1 0 0 0 00	
		Interest Expense		3 0 00	
		Cash			1 0 3 0 00
		Paid principal and interest due on note.			

The interest expense is reported in the Other expense section of the income statement for the year ended December 31, 2007. The interest expense account is closed at December 31.

The preceding entries for notes payable are similar to those we discussed in Chapter 9 for notes receivable. Notes payable entries are presented from the viewpoint of the borrower, while notes receivable entries are presented from the viewpoint of the creditor or lender. To illustrate, the following entries are journalized for a borrower (Bowden Co.), who issues a note payable to a creditor (Coker Co.):

	Bowden Co. (Borrower)			Coker Co. (Creditor)		

May 1. Bowden Co. purchased merchandise on account from Coker Co., $10,000, 2/10, n/30. The merchandise cost Coker Co. $7,500.	Merchandise Inventory
	  Accounts Payable
		10,000	10,000	Accounts Receivable
				  Sales
				
				Cost of Merchandise Sold
				  Merchandise Inventory
					10,000
					
					7,500
						10,000
						
						7,500

May 31. Bowden Co. issued a 60-day, 12% note for $10,000 to Coker Co. on account.	Accounts Payable
	  Notes Payable
		10,000	10,000	Notes Receivable
				  Accounts Receivable
					10,000	10,000

July 30. Bowden Co. paid Coker Co. the amount due on the note of May 31. Interest: $10,000 × 12% × 60/360.	Notes Payable
	Interest Expense
	  Cash
		10,000
		200
			10,200	Cash
				  Interest Revenue
				  Notes Receivable
					10,200	200
						10,000

Notes may also be issued when money is borrowed from banks. Although the terms may vary, many banks would accept from the borrower an interest-bearing note for the amount of the loan. For example, assume that on September 19 a firm borrows $4,000 from First National Bank by giving the bank a 90-day, 15% note. The entry to record the receipt of cash and the issuance of the note is as follows:

Sept.	19	Cash		4 0 0 0 00	
		Notes Payable			4 0 0 0 00
		Issued a 90-day, 15% note to the bank.			

On the due date of the note (December 18), the borrower owes $4,000, the principal of the note, plus interest of $150 ($4,000 × 15% × 90/360). The entry to record the payment of the note is as follows:

Dec.	18	Notes Payable		4 0 0 0 00	
		Interest Expense		1 5 0 00	
		Cash			4 1 5 0 00
		Paid principal and interest due on note.			

The U.S. Treasury issues short-term treasury bills to investors at a discount.

Sometimes a borrower will issue a discounted note rather than an interest-bearing note. Although such a note does not specify an interest rate, the creditor sets a rate of interest and deducts the interest from the face amount of the note. This interest is called the **discount**. The rate used in computing the discount is called the **discount rate**. The borrower is given the remainder, called the **proceeds**.

To illustrate, assume that on August 10, Cary Company issues a $20,000, 90-day note to Rock Company in exchange for inventory. Rock discounts the note at a rate of 15%. The amount of the discount, $750, is debited to *Interest Expense*. The proceeds, $19,250, are debited to *Merchandise Inventory*. *Notes Payable* is credited for the face amount of the note, which is also its maturity value. The entry for Cary Company is shown at the top of the following page.

Aug.	10	Merchandise Inventory		19 2 5 0 00		
		Interest Expense		7 5 0 00		
		Notes Payable			20 0 0 0 00	
		Issued a 90-day note to Rock Company,				
		discounted at 15%.				

When the note is paid, the following entry is recorded:[2]

Nov.	8	Notes Payable		20 0 0 0 00		
		Cash			20 0 0 0 00	
		Paid note due.				

Additional current liabilities include accrued expenses, unearned revenue, and interest payable, which we have discussed in previous chapters. We have also discussed wages and salaries payable earlier. However, the accounting for wages and salaries, termed *payroll accounting,* is important to every business. Thus, we will discuss payroll accounting in detail in the next two sections.

Example Exercise 11-1 | objective 1

On July 1, Bella Salon Company issued a 60-day note with a face amount of $60,000 to Delilah Hair Products Company for merchandise inventory.

    a.   Determine the proceeds of the note, assuming the note carries an interest rate of 6%.
    b.   Determine the proceeds of the note, assuming the note is discounted at 6%.

Follow My Example 11-1

    a. $60,000.
    b. $59,400. [$60,000 − ($60,000 × 6% × 60/360)]

For Practice: PE 11-1A, PE 11-1B

Payroll and Payroll Taxes

objective 2

Determine employer liabilities for payroll, including liabilities arising from employee earnings and deductions from earnings.

We are all familiar with the term *payroll.* In accounting, the term **payroll** refers to the amount paid to employees for the services they provide during a period. A business's payroll is usually significant for several reasons. First, employees are sensitive to payroll errors and irregularities. Maintaining good employee morale requires that the payroll be paid on a timely, accurate basis. Second, the payroll is subject to various federal and state regulations. Finally, the payroll and related payroll taxes have a significant effect on the net income of most businesses. Although the amount of such expenses varies widely, it is not unusual for a business's payroll and payroll-related expenses to equal nearly one-third of its revenue.

---

2 If the accounting period ends before a discounted note is paid, an adjusting entry should record the prepaid (deferred) interest that is not yet an expense. This deferred interest would be deducted from Notes Payable in the Current Liabilities section of the balance sheet.

LIABILITY FOR EMPLOYEE EARNINGS

Salaries and wages paid to employees are an employer's labor expenses. The term *salary* usually refers to payment for managerial, administrative, or similar services. The rate of salary is normally expressed in terms of a month or a year. The term *wages* usually refers to payment for manual labor, both skilled and unskilled. The rate of wages is normally stated on an hourly or a weekly basis. In practice, the terms salary and wages are often used interchangeably.

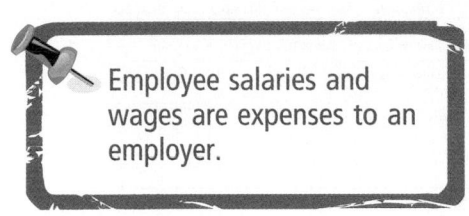

Employee salaries and wages are expenses to an employer.

The basic salary or wage of an employee may be increased by commissions, profit sharing, or cost-of-living adjustments. Many businesses pay managers an annual bonus in addition to a basic salary. The amount of the bonus is often based on some measure of productivity, such as income or profit of the business. Although payment is usually made by check or in cash, it may be in the form of securities, notes, lodging, or other property or services. Generally, the form of payment has no effect on how salaries and wages are treated by either the employer or the employee.

Salary and wage rates are determined by agreement between the employer and the employees. Businesses engaged in interstate commerce must follow the requirements of the Fair Labor Standards Act. Employers covered by this legislation, which is commonly called the Federal Wage and Hour Law, are required to pay a minimum rate of $1\frac{1}{2}$ times the regular rate for all hours worked in excess of 40 hours per week. Exemptions are provided for executive, administrative, and certain supervisory positions. Premium rates for overtime or for working at night, holidays, or other less desirable times are fairly common, even when not required by law. In some cases, the premium rates may be as much as twice the base rate.

Information on average salaries for a variety of professions can be found at the *Economic Research Institute's* Web site, which is **http://www.erieri.com**.

To illustrate computing an employee's earnings, assume that John T. McGrath is a salesperson employed by McDermott Supply Co. at the rate of $34 per hour. Any hours in excess of 40 hours per week are paid at a rate of $1\frac{1}{2}$ times the normal rate, or $51 ($34 + $17) per hour. For the week ended December 27, McGrath's time card indicates that he worked 42 hours. His earnings for that week are computed as follows:

Earnings at base rate (40 × $34)	$1,360
Earnings at overtime rate (2 × $51)	102
Total earnings	$1,462

DEDUCTIONS FROM EMPLOYEE EARNINGS

Professional athletes must pay local taxes in each location in which they play their sport.

The total earnings of an employee for a payroll period, including bonuses and overtime pay, are called **gross pay**. From this amount is subtracted one or more *deductions* to arrive at the net pay. **Net pay** is the amount the employer must pay the employee. The deductions for federal taxes are usually the largest deduction. Deductions may also be required for state or local income taxes. Other deductions may be made for medical insurance, contributions to pensions, and for items authorized by individual employees.

Income Taxes Except for certain types of employment, all employers must withhold a portion of employee earnings for payment of the employees' federal income tax. As a basis for determining the amount to be withheld, each employee completes and submits to the employer an "Employee's Withholding Allowance Certificate," often called a W-4. Exhibit 2 is an example of a completed W-4 form.

You may recall filling out a W-4 form. On the W-4, an employee indicates marital status, the number of withholding allowances, and whether any additional withholdings are authorized. A single employee may claim one withholding allowance. A married employee may claim an additional allowance for a spouse. An employee may also claim an allowance for each dependent other than a spouse. Each allowance claimed reduces the amount of federal income tax withheld from the employee's check.

Cut here and give Form W-4 to your employer. Keep the top part for your records. ---

Form **W-4**	**Employee's Withholding Allowance Certificate**	OMB No. 1545-0074
Department of the Treasury Internal Revenue Service	▶ Whether you are entitled to claim a certain number of allowances or exemption from withholding is subject to review by the IRS. Your employer may be required to send a copy of this form to the IRS.	**2006**

1 Type or print your first name and middle initial. John T.	Last name McGrath	2 Your social security number 381 :48: 9120

Home address (number and street or rural route) 1830 4th Street	3 ☒ Single ☐ Married ☐ Married, but withhold at higher Single rate. Note. If married, but legally separated, or spouse is a nonresident alien, check the "Single" box.
City or town, state, and ZIP code Clinton, Iowa 52732-6142	4 If your last name differs from that shown on your social security card, check here. You must call 1-800-772-1213 for a new card. ▶ ☐

5 Total number of allowances you are claiming (from line **H** above **or** from the applicable worksheet on page 2) . . | 5 | 1

6 Additional amount, if any, you want withheld from each paycheck . . . . | 6 | $

7 I claim exemption from withholding for **2006**, and I certify that I meet **both** of the following conditions for exemption.
 • Last year I had a right to a refund of **all** federal income tax withheld because I had **no** tax liability **and**
 • This year I expect a refund of **all** federal income tax withheld because I expect to have **no** tax liability.
 If you meet both conditions, write "Exempt" here . . . . ▶ | 7 |

Under penalties of perjury, I declare that I have examined this certificate and to the best of my knowledge and belief, it is true, correct, and complete.

Employee's signature
(Form is not valid
unless you sign it.) ▶ *John T. McGrath*   Date ▶ June 2, 2006

8 Employer's name and address (Employer: Complete lines 8 and 10 only if sending to the IRS.) | 9 Office code (optional) | 10 Employer identification number (EIN)

Cat. No. 10220Q   Form **W-4** (2006)

The amount that must be withheld for income tax differs, depending upon each employee's gross pay and completed W-4. Most employers use wage bracket withholding tables furnished by the Internal Revenue Service (IRS) to determine the amount to be withheld.

Exhibit 3 is an example of an IRS wage bracket withholding table for a single person who is paid weekly.[3] Each row represents a person's wages after subtracting a standard IRS withholding allowance. The standard IRS withholding allowance is determined annually by the IRS. For a single person paid weekly, we assume the standard withholding allowance is $63.[4]

To illustrate, John T. McGrath made $1,462 for the week ended December 27. Thus, the wages used in determining McGrath's withholding for the week are $1,399 ($1,462 − $63). If McGrath had declared two withholding allowances, the total amount deducted would have been $126, and the wages used in determining McGrath's withholding for the week would have been $1,336 ($1,462 − $126).

**Table for Percentage Method of Withholding
WEEKLY Payroll Period**

(a) SINGLE person (including head of household)—

If the amount of wages (after subtracting withholding allowances) is:	The amount of income tax to withhold is:
Not over $51.	$0

Over—	But not over—			of excess over—
$51	—$192	. .	10%	—$51
$192	—$620	. .	$14.10 plus 15%	—$192
$620	—$1,409	. .	$78.30 plus 25%	—$620	◀— McGrath wage bracket
$1,409	—$3,013	. .	$275.55 plus 28%	—$1,409
$3,013	—$6,508	. .	$724.67 plus 33%	—$3,013
$6,508	. . . . .	. .	$1,878.02 plus 35%	—$6,508

Source: Publication 15, *Employer's Tax Guide,* Internal Revenue Service, 2006.

After the person's withholding wage bracket has been computed, the amount of federal income tax withheld is determined using Exhibit 3 as follows:

1. Locate the proper withholding wage bracket. Since McGrath's wages after deducting one standard IRS withholding allowance is $1,399, the proper wage bracket for McGrath is $620 − $1,409.

---

3 IRS withholding tables are also available for married employees and for pay periods other than weekly.
4 The actual IRS standard withholding allowance changes every year and was $63.46 for 2006.

2. Compute the withholding for the proper wage bracket using the directions in the two right-hand columns of Exhibit 3. For McGrath's wage bracket, Exhibit 3 indicates that the withholding should be "$78.30 plus 25% of the excess over $620." Thus, the withholding for McGrath is $273.05, as shown below.

Initial withholding from wage bracket in Exhibit 3	$ 78.30
Plus additional withholding: 25% of excess over $620	194.75*
Total withholding	$273.05

*($1,399 − $620) × 25%

In addition to the federal income tax, employees may also be required to pay a state income tax and a city income tax. State and city taxes are withheld from employees' earnings and paid to state and city governments.

Example Exercise 11-2   objective 2

Karen Dunn's weekly gross earnings for the present week were $2,250. Dunn has two exemptions. Using the wage bracket withholding table in Exhibit 3 with a $63 standard withholding allowance for each exemption, what is Dunn's federal income tax withholding?

Follow My Example 11-2

Total wage payment		$2,250
One allowance (provided by IRS)	$63	
Multiplied by allowances claimed on Form W-4	× 2	126
Amount subject to withholding		$2,124
Initial withholding from wage bracket in Exhibit 3		$275.55
Plus additional withholding: 28% of excess over $1,409		200.20*
Federal income tax withholding		$475.75

*28% × ($2,124 − $1,409)

For Practice: PE 11-2A, PE 11-2B

FICA Tax Most of us have FICA tax withheld from our payroll checks by our employers. Employers are required by the Federal Insurance Contributions Act (FICA) to withhold a portion of the earnings of each of the employees. The amount of **FICA tax** withheld is the employees' contribution to two federal programs. Tax is withheld separately under each program. The first program, called *social security*, is for old age, survivors, and disability insurance (OASDI). The second program, called *Medicare*, is health insurance for senior citizens.

The amount of tax that employers are required to withhold from each employee is normally based on the amount of earnings paid in the *calendar* year. Although both the schedule of future tax rates and the maximum amount subject to tax are revised often by Congress, such changes have little effect on the basic payroll system. In this text, we will use a social security rate of 6% on the first $100,000 of annual earnings and a Medicare rate of 1.5% on all annual earnings.

To illustrate, assume that John T. McGrath's annual earnings prior to the current payroll period total $99,038. Assume also that the current period earnings are $1,462. The total FICA tax of $79.65 is determined as follows:

Earnings subject to 6% social security tax		
($100,000 − $99,038)	$ 962	
Social security tax rate	× 6%	
Social security tax		$57.72
Earnings subject to 1.5% Medicare tax	$1,462	
Medicare tax rate	× 1.5%	
Medicare tax		21.93
Total FICA tax		$79.65

Other Deductions   Neither the employer nor the employee has any choice in deducting taxes from gross earnings. However, employees may choose to have additional amounts deducted for other purposes. For example, you as an employee may authorize deductions for retirement savings, for contributions to charitable organizations, or for premiums on employee insurance. A union contract may also require the deduction of union dues.

COMPUTING EMPLOYEE NET PAY

Gross earnings less payroll deductions equals the amount to be paid to an employee for the payroll period. This amount is the *net pay*, which is often called the *take-home pay*. Assuming that John T. McGrath authorized deductions for retirement savings and for a United Fund contribution, the amount to be paid McGrath for the week ended December 27 is $1,084.30, as shown below.

Gross earnings for the week		$1,462.00
Deductions:		
Social security tax	$ 57.72	
Medicare tax	21.93	
Federal income tax	273.05	
Retirement savings	20.00	
United Fund	5.00	
Total deductions		377.70
Net pay		$1,084.30

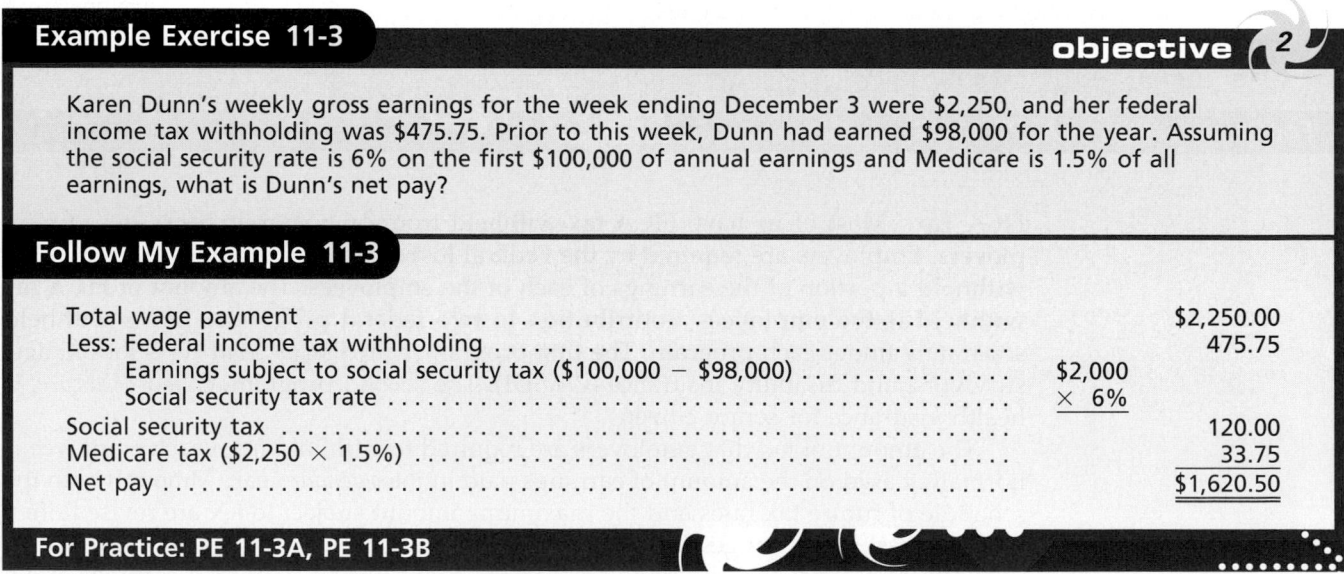

Example Exercise 11-3   **objective** 2

Karen Dunn's weekly gross earnings for the week ending December 3 were $2,250, and her federal income tax withholding was $475.75. Prior to this week, Dunn had earned $98,000 for the year. Assuming the social security rate is 6% on the first $100,000 of annual earnings and Medicare is 1.5% of all earnings, what is Dunn's net pay?

Follow My Example 11-3

Total wage payment		$2,250.00
Less: Federal income tax withholding		475.75
Earnings subject to social security tax ($100,000 − $98,000)	$2,000	
Social security tax rate	× 6%	
Social security tax		120.00
Medicare tax ($2,250 × 1.5%)		33.75
Net pay		$1,620.50

For Practice: PE 11-3A, PE 11-3B

LIABILITY FOR EMPLOYER'S PAYROLL TAXES

So far, we have discussed the payroll taxes that are withheld from the employees' earnings. Most employers are also subject to federal and state payroll taxes based on the amount paid their employees. Such taxes are an operating expense of the business. Exhibit 4 summarizes the responsibility for employee and employer payroll taxes.

FICA Tax   Employers are required to contribute to the social security and Medicare programs for each employee. The employer must match the employee's contribution to each program.

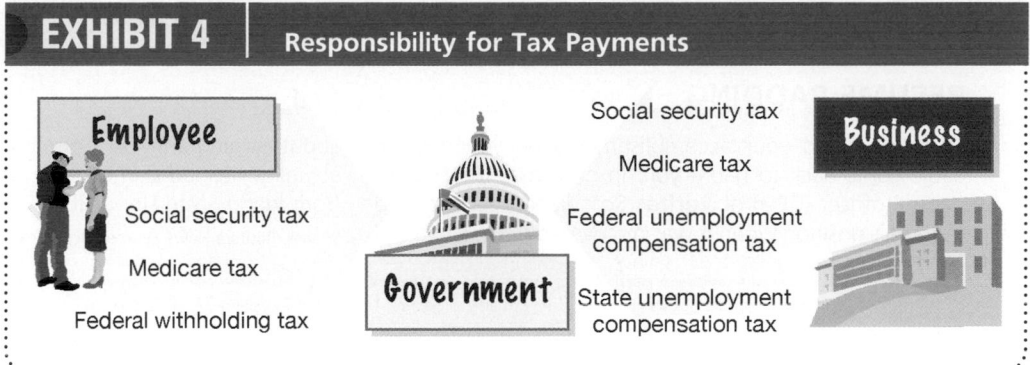

EXHIBIT 4 | Responsibility for Tax Payments

Federal Unemployment Compensation Tax The Federal Unemployment Tax Act (FUTA) provides for temporary payments to those who become unemployed as a result of layoffs due to economic causes beyond their control. Types of employment subject to this program are similar to those covered by FICA taxes. A tax of 6.2% is levied on employers only, rather than on both employers and employees.[5] It is applied to only the first $7,000 of the earnings of each covered employee during a calendar year. Congress often revises the rate and maximum earnings subject to federal unemployment compensation tax. The funds collected by the federal government are not paid directly to the unemployed but are allocated among the states for use in state programs.

State Unemployment Compensation Tax State Unemployment Tax Acts (SUTA) also provide for payments to unemployed workers. The amounts paid as benefits are obtained, for the most part, from a tax levied upon employers only. A few states require employee contributions also. The rates of tax and the tax bases vary. In most states, employers who provide stable employment for their employees are granted reduced rates. The employment experience and the status of each employer's tax account are reviewed annually, and the tax rates are adjusted accordingly.[6]

Business Connections

REAL WORLD

THE MOST YOU WILL EVER PAY

In 1936, the Social Security Board described how the tax was expected to affect a worker's pay, as follows:

The taxes called for in this law will be paid both by your employer and by you. For the next 3 years you will pay maybe 15 cents a week, maybe 25 cents a week, maybe 30 cents or more, according to what you earn. That is to say, during the next 3 years, beginning January 1, 1937, you will pay 1 cent for every dollar you earn, and at the same time your employer will pay 1 cent for every dollar you earn, up to $3,000 a year. . . .

. . . Beginning in 1940 you will pay, and your employer will pay, 1¹/₂ cents for each dollar you earn, up to $3,000 a year . . . and then beginning in 1943, you will

pay 2 cents, and so will your employer, for every dollar you earn for the next three years. After that, you and your employer will each pay half a cent more for 3 years, and finally, beginning in 1949, . . . you and your employer will each pay 3 cents on each dollar you earn, up to $3,000 a year. That is the most you will ever pay.

The rate on January 1, 2006, was 7.65 cents per dollar earned (7.65%). The social security portion was 6.20% on the first $94,200 of earnings. The Medicare portion was 1.45% on all earnings.

Source: Arthur Lodge, "That Is the Most You Will Ever Pay," *Journal of Accountancy*, October 1985, p. 44.

---

5 This rate may be reduced to 0.8% for credits for state unemployment compensation tax.
6 As of January 1, 2006, the maximum state rate credited against the federal unemployment rate was 5.4% of the first $7,000 of each employee's earnings during a calendar year.

Integrity, Objectivity, and Ethics in Business

RESUMÉ PADDING

Misrepresenting your accomplishments on your resumé could come back to haunt you. In one case, the chief financial officer (CFO) of Veritas Software was forced to resign his position when it was discovered that he had lied about earning an MBA from Stanford University, when in actuality he had earned only an undergraduate degree from Idaho State University.

Source: Reuters News Service, October 4, 2002.

Accounting Systems for Payroll and Payroll Taxes

objective **3**

Describe payroll accounting systems that use a payroll register, employee earnings records, and a general journal.

In designing payroll systems, the requirements of various federal, state, and local agencies for payroll data are considered. Payroll data must also be maintained accurately for each payroll period and for each employee. Periodic reports using payroll data must be submitted to government agencies. The payroll data itself must be retained for possible inspection by the various agencies.

Payroll systems must be designed to pay employees on a timely basis. Payroll systems should also be designed to provide useful data for management decision-making needs. Such needs might include settling employee grievances and negotiating retirement or other benefits with employees.

Although payroll systems differ among businesses, the major elements common to most payroll systems are the payroll register, employee's earnings record, and payroll checks. We discuss and illustrate each of these elements next. We have kept the illustrations relatively simple, and they may be modified in practice to meet the needs of each individual business.

PAYROLL REGISTER

The **payroll register** is a multicolumn report used for summarizing the data for each payroll period. Its design varies according to the number and classes of employees and the extent to which computers are used. Exhibit 5 illustrates a payroll register suitable for a small number of employees.

The nature of the data appearing in the payroll register is evident from the column headings. The number of hours worked and the earnings and deduction data are inserted in their proper columns. The sum of the deductions for each employee is then

EXHIBIT 5

Payroll Register

	Employee Name	Total Hours	Earnings			
			Regular	Overtime	Total	
1	Abrams, Julie S.	40	500.00		500.00	1
2	Elrod, Fred G.	44	392.00	58.80	450.80	2
3	Gomez, Jose C.	40	840.00		840.00	3
4	**McGrath, John T.**	42	1,360.00	102.00	1,462.00	4
25	Wilkes, Glenn K.	40	480.00		480.00	25
26	Zumpano, Michael W.	40	600.00		600.00	26
27	Total		13,328.00	574.00	13,902.00	27
28						28

subtracted from the total earnings to yield the amount to be paid. The check numbers are recorded in the payroll register as evidence of payment.

The last two columns of the payroll register are used to accumulate the total wages or salaries to be debited to the various expense accounts. This process is usually called *payroll distribution*.

Recording Employees' Earnings The column totals of the payroll register support the journal entry for payroll. The entry based on the payroll register in Exhibit 5 follows.

Dec.	27	Sales Salaries Expense	11 1 2 2 00	
		Office Salaries Expense	2 7 8 0 00	
		Social Security Tax Payable		6 4 3 07
		Medicare Tax Payable		2 0 8 53
		Employees Federal Income Tax Payable		3 3 3 2 00
		Retirement Savings Deductions Payable		6 8 0 00
		United Fund Deductions Payable		4 7 0 00
		Accounts Receivable—Fred G. Elrod (emp.)		5 0 00
		Salaries Payable		8 5 1 8 40
		Payroll for week ended December 27.		

Example Exercise 11-4

objective 3

The payroll register of Chen Engineering Services indicates $900 of social security withheld and $225 of Medicare tax withheld on total salaries of $15,000 for the period. Federal withholding for the period totaled $2,925.

Provide the journal entry for the period's payroll.

Follow My Example 11-4

Salaries Expense	15,000	
Social Security Tax Payable		900
Medicare Tax Payable		225
Employees Federal Withholding Tax Payable		2,925
Salaries Payable		10,950

For Practice: PE 11-4A, PE 11-4B

EXHIBIT 5 (Concluded)

	Deductions						Paid		Accounts Debited		
	Social Security Tax	Medicare Tax	Federal Income Tax	Retirement Savings	Misc.	Total	Net Amount	Check No.	Sales Salaries Expense	Office Salaries Expense	
1	30.00	7.50	74.00	20.00	UF 10.00	141.50	358.50	6857	500.00		1
2	27.05	6.76	62.00		AR 50.00	145.81	304.99	6858		450.80	2
3	50.40	12.60	131.00	25.00	UF 10.00	229.00	611.00	6859	840.00		3
4	57.72	21.93	273.05	20.00	UF 5.00	377.70	1,084.30	6860	1,462.00		4
25	28.80	7.20	69.00	10.00		115.00	365.00	6880	480.00		25
26	36.00	9.00	79.00	5.00	UF 2.00	131.00	469.00	6881		600.00	26
27	643.07	208.53	3,332.00	680.00	UF 470.00	5,383.60	8,518.40		11,122.00	2,780.00	27
28					AR 50.00						28

Miscellaneous Deductions: UF—United Fund; AR—Accounts Receivable

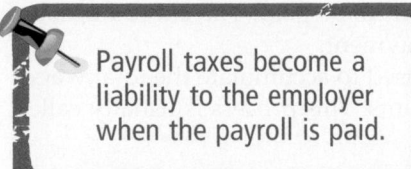

Payroll taxes become a liability to the employer when the payroll is paid.

Recording and Paying Payroll Taxes   The employer's payroll taxes become liabilities when the related payroll is *paid* to employees. In addition, employers are required to compute and report payroll taxes on a *calendar-year* basis, even if a different fiscal year is used for financial reporting and income tax purposes.

To illustrate, assume that Everson Company's fiscal year ends on April 30. Also, assume that Everson Company owes its employees $26,000 of wages on December 31. The following portions of the $26,000 of wages are subject to payroll taxes on December 31:

	Earnings Subject to Payroll Taxes
Social security tax (6.0%)	$18,000
Medicare tax (1.5%)	26,000
State and federal unemployment compensation tax	1,000

If the payroll is paid on December 31, the payroll taxes will be based on the preceding amounts. If the payroll is paid on January 2, however, the *entire* $26,000 will be subject to *all* payroll taxes. This is because the maximum earnings limitation for determining social security and unemployment taxes will not be exceeded at the beginning of the calendar year.

The payroll register for McDermott Supply Co. in Exhibit 5 indicates that the amount of social security tax withheld is $643.07 and Medicare tax withheld is $208.53. Since the employer must match the employees' FICA contributions, the employer's social security payroll tax will also be $643.07, and the Medicare tax will be $208.53. Further, assume that the earnings subject to state and federal unemployment compensation taxes are $2,710. Multiplying this amount by the state (5.4%) and federal (0.8%) rates yields the unemployment compensation taxes shown in the following payroll tax computation:

Social security tax	$ 643.07
Medicare tax	208.53
State unemployment compensation tax (5.4% × $2,710)	146.34
Federal unemployment compensation tax (0.8% × $2,710)	21.68
Total payroll tax expense	$1,019.62

The entry to journalize the payroll tax expense for the week and the liability for the taxes accrued is shown below.

Dec.	27	Payroll Tax Expense	1 0 1 9 62	
		Social Security Tax Payable		6 4 3 07
		Medicare Tax Payable		2 0 8 53
		State Unemployment Tax Payable		1 4 6 34
		Federal Unemployment Tax Payable		2 1 68
		Payroll taxes for week ended		
		December 27.		

Example Exercise 11-5   objective 3

The payroll register of Chen Engineering Services indicates $900 of social security withheld and $225 of Medicare tax withheld on total salaries of $15,000 for the period. Assume earnings subject to state and federal unemployment compensation taxes are $5,250, at the federal rate of 0.8% and the state rate of 5.4%.

Provide the journal entry to record the payroll tax expense for the period.

(continued)

Follow My Example 11-5

Payroll Tax Expense	1,450.50	
Social Security Tax Payable		900.00
Medicare Tax Payable		225.00
State Unemployment Tax Payable		283.50*
Federal Unemployment Tax Payable		42.00**

*$5,250 × 5.4%
**$5,250 × 0.8%

For Practice: PE 11-5A, PE 11-5B

EMPLOYEE'S EARNINGS RECORD

The amount of each employee's earnings to date must be available at the end of each payroll period. This cumulative amount is required in order to compute each employee's social security and Medicare tax withholding and the employer's payroll taxes. It is essential, therefore, that a detailed payroll record be maintained for each employee. This record is called an **employee's earnings record**.

Exhibit 6, on the following pages, shows a portion of the employee's earnings record for John T. McGrath. The relationship between this record and the payroll register can be seen by tracing the amounts entered on McGrath's earnings record for December 27 back to its source—the fourth line of the payroll register in Exhibit 5.

In addition to spaces for recording data for each payroll period and the cumulative total of earnings, the employee's earnings record has spaces for quarterly totals and the yearly total. These totals are used in various reports for tax, insurance, and other purposes. One such report is the Wage and Tax Statement, commonly called a *Form W-2*. You may recall receiving a W-2 form for use in preparing your individual tax return. This form must be provided annually to each employee as well as to the Social Security Administration. The amounts reported in the Form W-2 shown below were taken from McGrath's employee's earnings record.

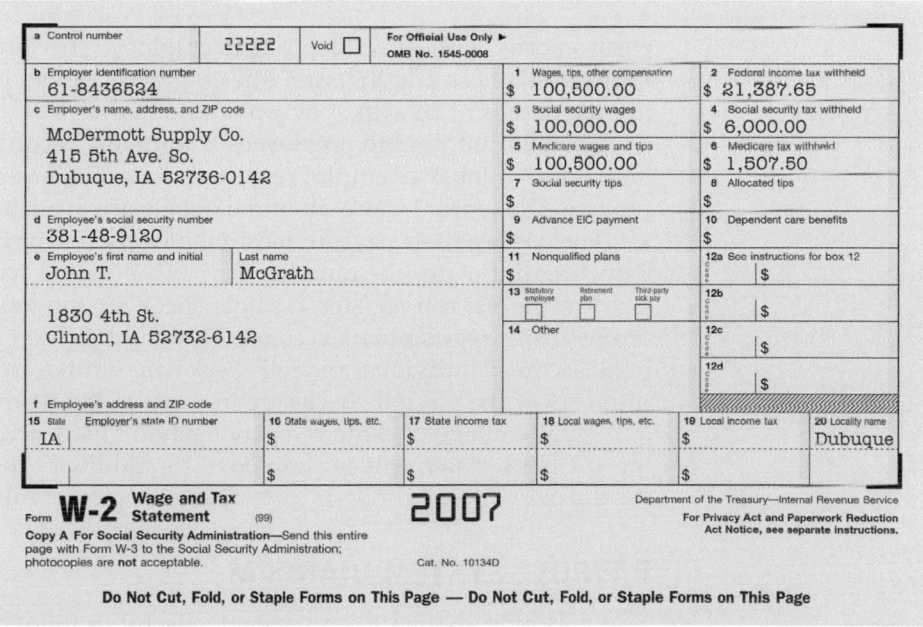

PAYROLL CHECKS

At the end of each pay period, *payroll checks* are prepared. Each check includes a detachable statement showing the details of how the net pay was computed. Exhibit 7, on page 494, is a payroll check for John T. McGrath. Many businesses pay their employees

EXHIBIT 6   Employee's Earnings Record

John T. McGrath
1830 4th Street
Clinton, IA 52732-6142   PHONE: 555-3148

SINGLE	NUMBER OF WITHHOLDING ALLOWANCES: 1	PAY RATE:	$1,360.00 Per Week
OCCUPATION: Salesperson		EQUIVALENT HOURLY RATE: $34	

	Period Ending	Total Hours	Regular Earnings	Overtime Earnings	Total Earnings	Cumulative Total	
				Earnings			
42	SEP. 27	53	1,360.00	663.00	2,023.00	75,565.00	42
43	THIRD QUARTER		17,680.00	7,605.00	25,285.00		43
44	OCT. 4	51	1,360.00	561.00	1,921.00	77,486.00	44
50	NOV. 15	50	1,360.00	510.00	1,870.00	89,382.00	50
51	NOV. 22	53	1,360.00	663.00	2,023.00	91,405.00	51
52	NOV. 29	47	1,360.00	357.00	1,717.00	93,122.00	52
53	DEC. 6	53	1,360.00	663.00	2,023.00	95,145.00	53
54	DEC.13	52	1,360.00	612.00	1,972.00	97,117.00	54
55	DEC. 20	51	1,360.00	561.00	1,921.00	99,038.00	55
56	DEC. 27	42	1,360.00	102.00	1,462.00	100,500.00	56
57	FOURTH QUARTER		17,680.00	7,255.00	24,935.00		57
58	YEARLY TOTAL		70,720.00	29,780.00	100,500.00		58

electronically with direct deposits to employee checking accounts, rather than preparing payroll checks. In this case, the employee will still receive a statement summarizing the details of how the pay was computed.

The amount paid to employees is normally recorded as a single amount, regardless of the number of employees. There is no need to record each payroll check separately in the journal, since all of the details are available in the payroll register.

For paying their payroll, most employers use payroll checks drawn on a special bank account. After the data for the payroll period have been recorded and summarized in the payroll register, a single check for the total amount to be paid is written on the firm's regular bank account. This check is then deposited in the special payroll bank account. Individual payroll checks are written from the payroll account, and the numbers of the payroll checks are inserted in the payroll register.

An advantage of using a separate payroll bank account is that the task of reconciling the bank statements is simplified. In addition, a payroll bank account establishes control over payroll checks by preventing the theft or misuse of uncashed payroll checks.

PAYROLL SYSTEM DIAGRAM

You may find Exhibit 8, on page 494, useful in following the flow of data within the payroll segment of an accounting system. The diagram indicates the relationships among the primary components of the payroll system we described in this chapter.

Our focus in the preceding discussion has been on the outputs of a payroll system: the payroll register, payroll checks, the employees' earnings records, and tax and other reports. As shown in the diagram in Exhibit 8, the inputs into a payroll system may be classified as either constants or variables.

EXHIBIT 6 (Concluded)

SOC. SEC. NO.: 381-48-9120   EMPLOYEE NO.: 814

DATE OF BIRTH: February 15, 1982

DATE EMPLOYMENT TERMINATED:

	Deductions						Paid		
	Social Security Tax	Medicare Tax	Federal Income Tax	Retirement Savings	Other		Total	Net Amount	Check No.
42	121.38	30.35	429.83	20.00			601.56	1,421.44	6175
43	1,517.10	379.28	5,391.71	260.00	UF	40.00	7,588.09	17,696.91	
44	115.26	28.82	401.27	20.00			565.35	1,355.65	6225
50	112.20	28.05	386.99	20.00			547.24	1,322.76	6530
51	121.38	30.35	429.83	20.00			601.56	1,421.44	6582
52	103.02	25.76	344.15	20.00			492.93	1,224.07	6640
53	121.38	30.35	429.83	20.00	UF	5.00	606.56	1,416.44	6688
54	118.32	29.58	415.55	20.00			583.45	1,388.55	6743
55	115.26	28.82	401.27	20.00			565.35	1,355.65	6801
56	57.72	21.93	273.05	20.00	UF	5.00	377.70	1,084.30	6860
57	1,466.10	374.03	5,293.71	260.00	UF	15.00	7,408.84	17,526.16	
58	6,000.00	1,507.50	21,387.65	1,040.00	UF	100.00	30,035.15	70,464.85	

Constants are data that remain unchanged from payroll to payroll and thus do not need to be entered into the system each pay period. Examples of constants include such data as each employee's name and social security number, marital status, number of income tax withholding allowances, rate of pay, payroll category (office, sales, etc.), and department where employed. The FICA tax rates and various tax tables are also constants that apply to all employees. In a computerized accounting system, constants are stored within a payroll file.

Variables are data that change from payroll to payroll and thus must be entered into the system each pay period. Examples of variables include such data as the number of hours or days worked for each employee during the payroll period, days of sick leave with pay, vacation credits, and cumulative earnings and taxes withheld. If salespersons are paid commissions, the amount of their sales would also vary from period to period.

Most companies use computerized payroll systems that maintain an electronic payroll register and employee earnings record, similar to those discussed in this section. Payroll system outputs, such as employee checks and tax records, are automatically produced by the software.

INTERNAL CONTROLS FOR PAYROLL SYSTEMS

Payroll processing, as we discussed above, requires the input of a large amount of data, along with numerous and sometimes complex computations. These factors, combined with the large dollar amounts involved, require controls to ensure that payroll payments are timely and accurate. In addition, the system must also provide adequate safeguards against theft or other misuse of funds.

EXHIBIT 7

Payroll Check

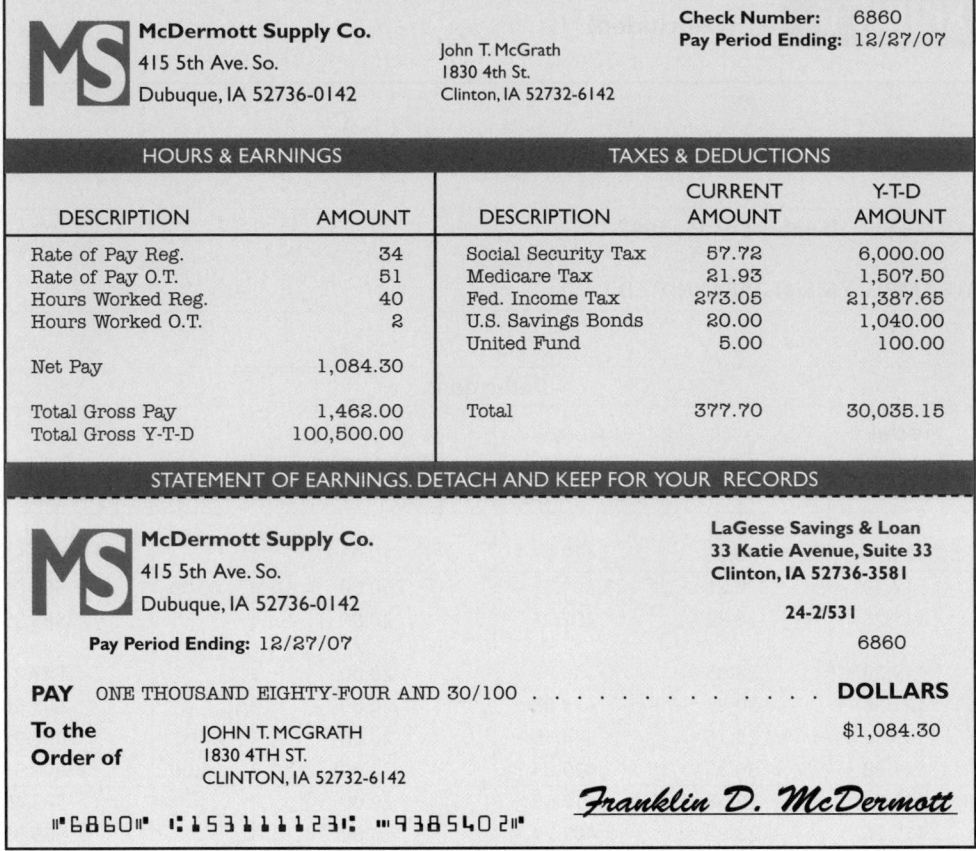

HOURS & EARNINGS		TAXES & DEDUCTIONS		
DESCRIPTION	AMOUNT	DESCRIPTION	CURRENT AMOUNT	Y-T-D AMOUNT
Rate of Pay Reg.	34	Social Security Tax	57.72	6,000.00
Rate of Pay O.T.	51	Medicare Tax	21.93	1,507.50
Hours Worked Reg.	40	Fed. Income Tax	273.05	21,387.65
Hours Worked O.T.	2	U.S. Savings Bonds	20.00	1,040.00
		United Fund	5.00	100.00
Net Pay	1,084.30			
Total Gross Pay	1,462.00	Total	377.70	30,035.15
Total Gross Y-T-D	100,500.00			

McDermott Supply Co.
415 5th Ave. So.
Dubuque, IA 52736-0142

Check Number: 6860
Pay Period Ending: 12/27/07

John T. McGrath
1830 4th St.
Clinton, IA 52732-6142

STATEMENT OF EARNINGS. DETACH AND KEEP FOR YOUR RECORDS

McDermott Supply Co.
415 5th Ave. So.
Dubuque, IA 52736-0142

Pay Period Ending: 12/27/07

LaGesse Savings & Loan
33 Katie Avenue, Suite 33
Clinton, IA 52736-3581

24-2/531

6860

PAY   ONE THOUSAND EIGHTY-FOUR AND 30/100 . . . . **DOLLARS**

To the Order of   JOHN T. MCGRATH
1830 4TH ST.
CLINTON, IA 52732-6142 $1,084.30

Franklin D. McDermott

⑈6860⑈ ⑊153111123⑊ ⑊938540 2⑈

The cash payment controls we discussed in the cash chapter also apply to payrolls. Thus, it is normally desirable to use a system that includes procedures for proper authorization and approval of payroll. When a check-signing machine is used, it is

EXHIBIT 8 | Flow of Data in a Payroll System

important that blank payroll checks and access to the machine be carefully controlled to prevent the theft or misuse of payroll funds.

It is especially important to authorize and approve in writing employee additions and deletions and changes in pay rates. For example, numerous payroll frauds have involved a supervisor adding fictitious employees to the payroll. The supervisor then cashes the fictitious employees' checks. Similar frauds have occurred where employees have been fired but the Payroll Department is not notified. As a result, payroll checks to the fired employees are prepared and cashed by a supervisor.

To prevent or detect frauds such as those we described above, employees' attendance records should be controlled. For example, employee arrival and departure times for computing pay are often determined from a time clock stamp or from the scan of an employee identification card or badge. A Payroll Department employee may be stationed near the time clock or scanning device to verify that authorized employees are "clocking in" only once and only for themselves. When payroll checks are distributed, employee identification cards may be used to deter one employee from picking up another's check.

Other controls include verifying and approving all payroll rate changes. In addition, in a computerized system, all program changes should be properly approved and tested by employees who are independent of the payroll system. The use of a special payroll bank account, as we discussed earlier in this chapter, also enhances control over payroll.

Integrity, Objectivity, and Ethics in Business

ETHICS

$8 MILLION FOR 18 MINUTES OF WORK

Computer system controls can be very important in issuing payroll checks. In one case, a Detroit schoolteacher was paid $4,015,625 after deducting $3,884,375 in payroll deductions for 18 minutes of overtime work. The error was caused by a computer glitch when the teacher's employee identification number was substituted incorrectly in the "hourly wage" field and wasn't caught by the payroll software. After six days, the error was discovered and the money was returned. "One of the things that came with (the software) is a fail-safe that prevents that. It doesn't work," a financial officer said. The district has since installed a program to flag any paycheck exceeding $10,000

Source: Associated Press, September 27, 2002.

Employees' Fringe Benefits

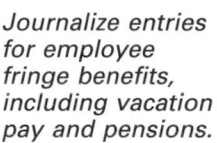

objective 4

Journalize entries for employee fringe benefits, including vacation pay and pensions.

Many companies provide their employees a variety of benefits in addition to salary and wages earned. Such **fringe benefits** may take many forms, including vacations, medical, and postretirement benefits, such as pension plans. The U.S. Chamber of Commerce has estimated that fringe benefits, excluding FICA, average approximately 33% of gross wages. Exhibit 9 shows the three major categories of fringe benefits as a percent of total payroll costs as reported from the same survey.[7]

When the employer pays part or all of the cost of the fringe benefits, these costs must be recognized as expenses. To properly match revenues and expenses, the estimated cost of these benefits should be recorded as an expense during the period in which the employee earns the benefit, as we will illustrate in the next section for vacation pay.

VACATION PAY

Most employers grant vacation rights, sometimes called *compensated absences*, to their employees. Such rights give rise to a liability. The liability for employees' vacation

---

7 *2005 Employee Benefits Study*, U.S. Chamber of Commerce, 2006.

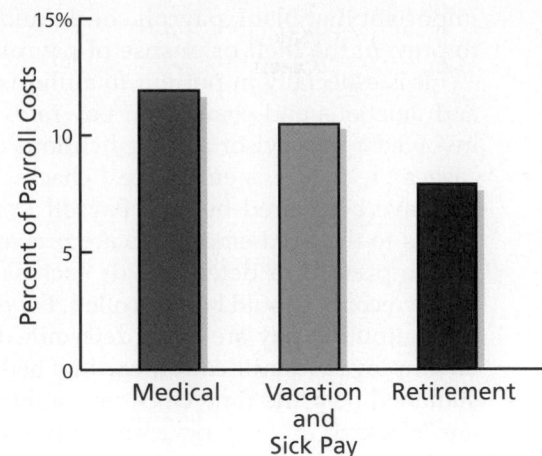

EXHIBIT 9

Benefit Dollars as a
Percent of Payroll
Costs

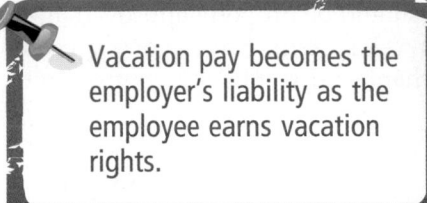

Vacation pay becomes the
employer's liability as the
employee earns vacation
rights.

pay should be accrued as a liability as the vacation rights are earned. The entry to accrue vacation pay may be recorded in total at the end of each fiscal year, or it may be recorded at the end of each pay period. To illustrate this latter case, assume that employees earn one day of vacation for each month worked during the year. Assume also that the estimated vacation pay for the payroll period ending May 5 is $2,000. The entry to record the accrued vacation pay for this pay period is shown as follows:

May	5	Vacation Pay Expense	2 0 0 0 00		
		Vacation Pay Payable		2 0 0 0 00	
		Vacation pay for week ended May 5.			

If employees are required to take all their vacation time within one year, the vacation pay payable is reported on the balance sheet as a current liability. If employees are allowed to accumulate their vacation time, the estimated vacation pay liability that is applicable to time that will *not* be taken within one year is a long-term liability.

When payroll is prepared for the period in which employees have taken vacations, the vacation pay payable is reduced. The entry debits *Vacation Pay Payable* and credits *Salaries Payable* and the other related accounts for taxes and withholdings.

PENSIONS

A *pension* represents a cash payment to retired employees. Rights to pension payments are earned by employees during their working years, based on the pension plan established by the employer. One of the fundamental characteristics of such a plan is whether it is a defined contribution plan or a defined benefit plan.

Investment professionals advise
employees to diversify their
401k investments and avoid
concentrating investments in
their employer's common stock
so that they won't risk losing
their retirement savings if their
employer enters bankruptcy.

Defined Contribution Plan   In a **defined contribution plan**, a fixed amount of money is invested on the employee's behalf during the employee's working years. It is common for the employee and employer to make contributions. There is no promise of future pension benefit payments. The amount of the final pension depends on the total contributions and investment returns earned on those contributions over the employee's working years. The employee bears the investment risk under defined contribution plans.

One of the more popular defined contribution plans is the 401k plan. Under this plan, employees may contribute a limited part of their income to investments, such as mutual funds. A 401k plan offers employees two advantages: (1) the contribution is deducted, before taxes, from current period income, and (2) the contributions and future investment earnings are tax deferred until withdrawn at retirement. In addition, in 90% of the

401k plans, the employer matches some portion of the employee's contribution. These advantages are why nearly 70% of eligible employees elect to enroll in a 401k.[8]

The employer's cost of a defined contribution plan is debited to *Pension Expense.* To illustrate, assume that the pension plan of Heaven Scent Perfumes Company requires an employer contribution of 10% of employee monthly salaries, paid at the end of the month to the employee's plan administrator. The journal entry to record the transaction, assuming $500,000 of monthly salaries, is as follows:

Dec.	31	Pension Expense	50 0 0 0 00	
		Cash		50 0 0 0 00
		Contributed 10% of monthly salaries to		
		pension plan.		

Defined Benefit Plan Employers may choose to promise employees a fixed annual pension benefit at retirement, based on years of service and compensation levels. An example would be a promise to pay an annual pension based on a formula, such as the following:

1.5% × Years of Service × Average Salary for Most Recent 3 Years Prior to Retirement

Pension benefits based on a formula are termed a **defined benefit plan**. Unlike a defined contribution plan, the employer bears the investment risk in funding a future retirement income benefit. As a result, many companies are replacing their defined benefit plans with defined contribution plans.

The accounting for defined benefit plans is usually very complex due to the uncertainties of projecting future pension obligations. These obligations depend upon such factors as employee life expectancies, employee turnover, expected employee compensation levels, and investment income on pension contributions.

The pension cost of a defined benefit plan is debited to *Pension Expense.* The amount funded is credited to *Cash.* Any unfunded amount is credited to *Unfunded Pension Liability.* For example, assume that the pension plan of Hinkle Co. requires an annual pension cost of $80,000, based on an estimate of the future benefit obligation. Further assume that Hinkle Co. pays $60,000 to the pension fund. The entry to record this transaction is as follows:

Dec.	31	Pension Expense	80 0 0 0 00	
		Cash		60 0 0 0 00
		Unfunded Pension Liability		20 0 0 0 00
		To record annual pension cost and		
		contribution to pension plan.		

If the unfunded pension liability is to be paid within one year, it will be classified as a current liability. That portion of the liability to be paid beyond one year is a long-term liability.

Example Exercise 11-6   objective 4

Manfield Services Company provides its employees vacation benefits and a defined contribution pension plan. Employees earned vacation pay of $44,000 for the period. The pension plan requires a contribution to the plan administrator equal to 8% of employee salaries. Salaries were $450,000 during the period. Provide the journal entry for the (a) vacation pay and (b) pension benefit.

(continued)

---

8 "Employees Sluggish in Interacting with 401k Plans," Hewitt Associates, December 26, 2005.

Follow My Example 11-6

a.	Vacation Pay Expense	44,000	
	Vacation Pay Payable		44,000
	Vacation pay accrued for the period.		
b.	Pension Expense	36,000	
	Cash		36,000
	Pension contribution, 8% of $450,000 salary.		

For Practice: PE 11-6A, PE 11-6B

REAL WORLD

Twenty-one percent of private industry uses defined benefit plans, while 42% uses defined contribution plans.

Source: Bureau of Labor Statistics, "Employee Benefits in Private Industry," 2005.

POSTRETIREMENT BENEFITS OTHER THAN PENSIONS

In addition to the pension benefits described above, employees may earn rights to other *postretirement benefits* from their employer. Such benefits may include dental care, eye care, medical care, life insurance, tuition assistance, tax services, and legal services for employees or their dependents. The amount of the annual benefits expense is based upon health statistics of the workforce. This amount is recorded by debiting *Postretirement Benefits Expense. Cash* is credited for the same amount if the benefits are fully funded. If the benefits are not fully funded, a postretirement benefits plan liability account is credited. Thus, the accounting for postretirement health benefits is very similar to that of defined benefit pension plans.

A business's financial statements should fully disclose the nature of its postretirement benefit obligations. These disclosures are usually included as notes to the financial statements. The complex nature of accounting for postretirement benefits is described in more advanced accounting courses.

Contingent Liabilities

objective **5**

Describe the accounting treatment for contingent liabilities and journalize entries for product warranties.

Some past transactions will result in liabilities if certain events occur in the future. These potential obligations are called *contingent liabilities*. For example, Ford Motor Company would have a contingent liability for the estimated costs associated with warranty work on new car sales. The obligation is contingent upon a *future event*, namely, a customer requiring warranty work on a vehicle. The obligation is the result of a *past transaction*, which is the original sale of the vehicle.

If a contingent liability is *probable* and the amount of the liability can be *reasonably estimated*, it should be recorded in the accounts. Ford Motor Company's vehicle warranty costs are an example of a *recordable* contingent liability. The warranty costs are *probable* because it is known that warranty repairs will be required on some vehicles. In addition, the costs can be *estimated* from past warranty experience.

To illustrate, assume that during June a company sells a product for $60,000 on which there is a 36-month warranty for repairing defects. Past experience indicates that the average cost to repair defects is 5% of the sales price over the warranty period. The entry to record the estimated product warranty expense for June is as follows:

June	30	Product Warranty Expense		3 0 0 0 00	
		Product Warranty Payable			3 0 0 0 00
		Warranty expense for June, 5% × $60,000.			

This transaction matches revenues and expenses properly by recording warranty costs in the same period in which the sale is recorded. When the defective product is

DO YOU WANT TO BE A MILLIONAIRE?

A recent survey found that 66% of individuals believe that their standard of living at retirement will be the same or higher than during their current working years. Yet, nearly 30% of these respondents don't have a formal savings plan for retirement. One-fourth of these respondents believe that they will need to save only $100,000 in order to maintain their lifestyle in retirement. However, experts believe that today's 25-year-old will need savings of $750,000 to $1 million to support a basic retirement, given increased life expectancies and inflation. How do you save this much money? The two keys to savings success are (1) save regularly, such as monthly or quarterly, even if it's a small amount, and (2) start early. For example, to have the same retirement income as a 25-year-old saving $100 per month, a 30-year-old would need to save $200 per month. Waiting until you are 35 years old would require saving $400 per month. Every five years of delay requires doubling the necessary contribution. This is the power of compound interest. Therefore, the worst strategy is to begin retirement saving at middle age.

So how much would a 25-year-old need to save monthly to reach the $1 million mark? There are many assumptions that go into such a calculation. Let's assume that an individual begins saving $150 per month at the age of 25, earns 8% on these savings, increases the amount contributed by 5% per year (to match salary increases), and retires at the age of 65. Under these assumptions, the individual would accumulate $975,000 by age 65.

repaired, the repair costs are recorded by debiting *Product Warranty Payable* and crediting *Cash, Supplies, Wages Payable,* or other appropriate accounts. Thus, if a customer required a $200 part replacement on August 16, the entry would be as follows:

Aug.	16	Product Warranty Payable	2 0 0 00	
		Supplies		2 0 0 00
		Replaced defective part under warranty.		

If a contingent liability is probable but cannot be *reasonably estimated* or is only *possible,* then the nature of the contingent liability should be disclosed in the notes to the financial statements. Professional judgment is required in distinguishing between contingent liabilities that are probable versus those that are only possible.

Common examples of contingent liabilities disclosed in notes to the financial statements are litigation, environmental matters, guarantees, and contingencies from the sale of receivables. The following is an example of a contingency disclosure related to litigation from a recent annual report of Google Inc., the popular Internet search engine provider:

Certain entities have also filed copyright claims against us, alleging that certain of our products, including Google Web Search, Google News, Google Image Search, and Google Book Search, infringe their rights. Adverse results in these lawsuits may include awards of damages and may also result in, or even compel, a change in our business practices, which could result in a loss of revenue for us or otherwise harm our business.

Although the results of litigation and claims cannot be predicted with certainty, we believe that the final outcome of the matters discussed above will not have a material adverse effect on our business. . . .

The accounting treatment of contingent liabilities is summarized in Exhibit 10.

EXHIBIT 10   Accounting Treatment of Contingent Liabilities

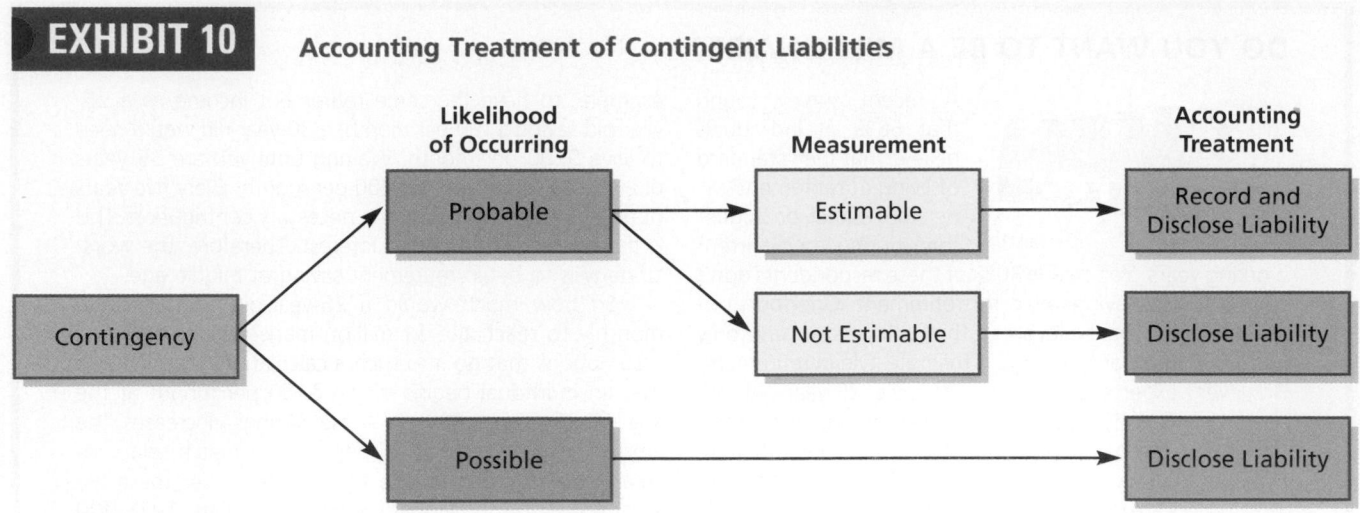

Example Exercise 11-7   objective 5

Cook-Rite Co. sold $140,000 of kitchen appliances during August under a six-month warranty. The cost to repair defects under the warranty is estimated at 6% of the sales price. On September 11, a customer required a $200 part replacement, plus $90 of labor under the warranty.

Provide the journal entry for (a) the estimated warranty expense on August 31 and (b) the September 11 warranty work.

Follow My Example 11-7

a.	Product Warranty Expense	8,400	
	Product Warranty Payable		8,400
	To record warranty expense for August, 6% × $140,000.		
b.	Product Warranty Payable	290	
	Supplies		200
	Wages Payable		90
	Replaced defective part under warranty.		

For Practice: PE 11-7A, PE 11-7B

Integrity, Objectivity, and Ethics in Business

ETHICS

TODAY'S MISTAKES CAN BE TOMORROW'S LIABILITY

Environmental and public health claims are quickly growing into some of the largest contingent liabilities facing companies. For example, tobacco, asbestos, and environmental cleanup claims have reached billions of dollars and have led to a number of corporate bankruptcies. Managers must be careful that today's decisions do not become tomorrow's nightmare.

Financial Analysis and Interpretation

The Current Assets and Current Liabilities sections of the balance sheet for Noble Co. and Hart Co. are illustrated as follows:

	Noble Co.	Hart Co.
Current assets:		
Cash	$147,000	$120,000
Accounts receivable (net)	84,000	472,000
Inventory	150,000	200,000
Total	$381,000	$792,000
Current liabilities:		
Accounts payable	$ 75,000	$227,000
Wages payable	30,000	193,000
Notes payable	115,000	320,000
Total	$220,000	$740,000

We can use this information to evaluate Noble's and Hart's ability to pay their current liabilities within a short period of time, using the **quick ratio** or *acid-test ratio*. The quick ratio is computed as follows:

$$\text{Quick Ratio} = \frac{\text{Quick Assets}}{\text{Current Liabilities}}$$

The quick ratio measures the "instant" debt-paying ability of a company, using quick assets. **Quick assets** are cash, receivables, and other current assets that can quickly be converted into cash. It is often considered desirable to have a quick ratio exceeding 1.0. A ratio less than 1.0 would indicate that current liabilities cannot be covered by cash and "near cash" assets.

To illustrate, the quick ratios for both companies would be:

$$\text{Noble Co: } \frac{\$147,000 + \$84,000}{\$220,000} = 1.05$$

$$\text{Hart Co: } \frac{\$120,000 + \$472,000}{\$740,000} = 0.80$$

As you can see, Noble Co. has quick assets in excess of current liabilities, or a quick ratio of 1.05. The ratio exceeds 1.0, indicating that the quick assets should be sufficient to meet current liabilities. Hart Co., however, has a quick ratio of 0.8. Its quick assets will not be sufficient to cover the current liabilities. Hart could solve this problem by working with a bank to convert its short-term debt of $320,000 into a long-term obligation. This would remove the notes payable from current liabilities. If Hart did this, then its quick ratio would improve to 1.4 ($592,000/$420,000), which would be sufficient for quick assets to cover current liabilities.

At a Glance

1. Describe and illustrate current liabilities related to accounts payable, current portion of long-term debt, and notes payable.

Key Points	Key Learning Outcomes	Example Exercises	Practice Exercises
Current liabilities are obligations that are to be paid out of current assets and are due within a short time, usually within one year. The three primary types of current liabilities are accounts payable, notes payable, and current portion of long-term debt.	• Identify and define the most frequently reported current liabilities on the balance sheet. • Determine the interest from interest-bearing and discounted notes payable.	**11-1**	11-1A, 11-1B

2. Determine employer liabilities for payroll, including liabilities arising from employee earnings and deductions from earnings.

Key Points	Key Learning Outcomes	Example Exercises	Practice Exercises
An employer's liability for payroll is determined from employee total earnings, including overtime pay. From this amount, employee deductions are subtracted to arrive at the net pay to be paid to each employee. Most employers also incur liabilities for payroll taxes, such as social security tax, Medicare tax, federal unemployment compensation tax, and state unemployment compensation tax.	• Calculate the federal withholding tax from a wage bracket withholding table. • Compute employee net pay, including deductions for social security and Medicare tax.	**11-2** **11-3**	11-2A, 11-2B 11-3A, 11-3B

3. Describe payroll accounting systems that use a payroll register, employee earnings records, and a general journal.

Key Points	Key Learning Outcomes	Example Exercises	Practice Exercises
The payroll register is used in assembling and summarizing the data needed for each payroll period. The payroll register is supported by a detailed payroll record for each employee, called an *employee's earnings record*.	• Journalize the employee's earnings, net pay, and payroll liabilities from the payroll register. • Journalize the payroll tax expense. • Describe elements of a payroll system, including the employee's earnings record, payroll checks, and internal controls.	**11-4** **11-5**	11-4A, 11-4B 11-5A, 11-5B

4. Journalize entries for employee fringe benefits, including vacation pay and pensions.

Key Points	Key Learning Outcomes	Example Exercises	Practice Exercises
Fringe benefits are expenses of the period in which the employees earn the benefits. Fringe benefits are recorded by debiting an expense account and crediting a liability account.	• Journalize vacation pay. • Distinguish and journalize defined contribution and defined benefit pension plans.	**11-6** **11-6**	11-6A, 11-6B 11-6A, 11-6B

5. Describe the accounting treatment for contingent liabilities and journalize entries for product warranties.			
Key Points	**Key Learning Outcomes**	Example Exercises	Practice Exercises
A contingent liability is a potential obligation that results from a past transaction but depends on a future event. If the contingent liability is both probable and estimable, the liability should be recorded.	• Describe the accounting for contingent liabilities. • Journalize estimated warranty obligations and services granted under warranty.	11-7	11-7A, 11-7B

Key Terms

defined benefit plan (497)
defined contribution plan (496)
discount (481)
discount rate (481)
employee's earnings record (491)

FICA tax (485)
fringe benefits (495)
gross pay (483)
net pay (483)
payroll (482)

payroll register (488)
proceeds (481)
quick assets (501)
quick ratio (501)

Illustrative Problem

Selected transactions of Taylor Company, completed during the fiscal year ended December 31, are as follows:

Mar. 1. Purchased merchandise on account from Kelvin Co., $20,000.
Apr. 10. Issued a 60-day, 12% note for $20,000 to Kelvin Co. on account.
June 9. Paid Kelvin Co. the amount owed on the note of April 10.
Aug. 1. Issued a $50,000, 90-day note to Harold Co. in exchange for a building. Harold Co. discounted the note at 15%.
Oct. 30. Paid Harold Co. the amount due on the note of August 1.
Dec. 27. Journalized the entry to record the biweekly payroll. A summary of the payroll record follows:

Salary distribution:		
Sales	$63,400	
Officers	36,600	
Office	10,000	$110,000
Deductions:		
Social security tax	$ 5,050	
Medicare tax	1,650	
Federal income tax withheld	17,600	
State income tax withheld	4,950	
Savings bond deductions	850	
Medical insurance deductions	1,120	31,220
Net amount		$ 78,780

27. Journalized the entry to record payroll taxes for social security and Medicare from the biweekly payroll.
30. Issued a check in payment of liabilities for employees' federal income tax of $17,600, social security tax of $10,100, and Medicare tax of $3,300.
31. Issued a check for $9,500 to the pension fund trustee to fully fund the pension cost for December.

(continued)

Dec. 31. Journalized an entry to record the employees' accrued vacation pay, $36,100.
　　 31. Journalized an entry to record the estimated accrued product warranty liability, $37,240.

Instructions

Journalize the preceding transactions.

Solution

Date		Account	Debit	Credit
Mar.	1	Merchandise Inventory	20 0 0 0 00	
		Accounts Payable—Kelvin Co.		20 0 0 0 00
Apr.	10	Accounts Payable—Kelvin Co.	20 0 0 0 00	
		Notes Payable		20 0 0 0 00
June	9	Notes Payable	20 0 0 0 00	
		Interest Expense	4 0 0 00	
		Cash		20 4 0 0 00
Aug.	1	Building	48 1 2 5 00	
		Interest Expense	1 8 7 5 00	
		Notes Payable		50 0 0 0 00
Oct.	30	Notes Payable	50 0 0 0 00	
		Cash		50 0 0 0 00
Dec.	27	Sales Salaries Expense	63 4 0 0 00	
		Officers Salaries Expense	36 6 0 0 00	
		Office Salaries Expense	10 0 0 0 00	
		Social Security Tax Payable		5 0 5 0 00
		Medicare Tax Payable		1 6 5 0 00
		Employees Federal Income Tax Payable		17 6 0 0 00
		Employees State Income Tax Payable		4 9 5 0 00
		Bond Deductions Payable		8 5 0 00
		Medical Insurance Payable		1 1 2 0 00
		Salaries Payable		78 7 8 0 00
	27	Payroll Tax Expense	6 7 0 0 00	
		Social Security Tax Payable		5 0 5 0 00
		Medicare Tax Payable		1 6 5 0 00
	30	Employees Federal Income Tax Payable	17 6 0 0 00	
		Social Security Tax Payable	10 1 0 0 00	
		Medicare Tax Payable	3 3 0 0 00	
		Cash		31 0 0 0 00
	31	Pension Expense	9 5 0 0 00	
		Cash		9 5 0 0 00
	31	Vacation Pay Expense	36 1 0 0 00	
		Vacation Pay Payable		36 1 0 0 00
	31	Product Warranty Expense	37 2 4 0 00	
		Product Warranty Payable		37 2 4 0 00

Self-Examination Questions (Answers at End of Chapter)

1. A business issued a $5,000, 60-day, 12% note to the bank. The amount due at maturity is:
   A. $4,900. C. $5,100.
   B. $5,000. D. $5,600.

2. A business issued a $5,000, 60-day note to a supplier, which discounted the note at 12%. The proceeds are:
   A. $4,400. C. $5,000.
   B. $4,900. D. $5,100.

3. Which of the following taxes are employers usually not required to withhold from employees?
   A. Federal income tax
   B. Federal unemployment compensation tax
   C. Medicare tax
   D. State and local income tax

4. An employee's rate of pay is $40 per hour, with time and a half for all hours worked in excess of 40 during a week. The social security rate is 6.0% on the first $100,000 of annual earnings, and the Medicare rate is 1.5% on all earnings. The following additional data are available:

Hours worked during current week	45
Year's cumulative earnings prior to current week	$99,400
Federal income tax withheld	$450

Based on these data, the amount of the employee's net pay for the current week is:
   A. $1,307.50. C. $1,450.00.
   B. $1,405.00. D. $1,385.50.

5. Within limitations on the maximum earnings subject to the tax, employers do not incur an expense for which of the following payroll taxes?
   A. Social security tax
   B. Federal unemployment compensation tax
   C. State unemployment compensation tax
   D. Employees' federal income tax

Eye Openers

1. Does a discounted note payable provide credit without interest? Discuss.
2. Employees are subject to taxes withheld from their paychecks.
   a. List the federal taxes withheld from most employee paychecks.
   b. Give the title of the accounts credited by amounts withheld.
3. For each of the following payroll-related taxes, indicate whether there is a ceiling on the annual earnings subject to the tax: (a) federal income tax, (b) Medicare tax, (c) social security tax, (d) federal unemployment compensation tax.
4. Why are deductions from employees' earnings classified as liabilities for the employer?
5. Taylor Company, with 20 employees, is expanding operations. It is trying to decide whether to hire one full-time employee for $25,000 or two part-time employees for a total of $25,000. Would any of the employer's payroll taxes discussed in this chapter have a bearing on this decision? Explain.
6. For each of the following payroll-related taxes, indicate whether they generally apply to (a) employees only, (b) employers only, or (c) both employees and employers:
   1. Federal income tax
   2. Medicare tax
   3. Social security tax
   4. Federal unemployment compensation tax
   5. State unemployment compensation tax
7. What are the principal reasons for using a special payroll checking account?
8. In a payroll system, what types of input data are referred to as (a) constants and (b) variables?
9. Explain how a payroll system that is properly designed and operated tends to ensure that (a) wages paid are based on hours actually worked and (b) payroll checks are not issued to fictitious employees.
10. To match revenues and expenses properly, should the expense for employee vacation pay be recorded in the period during which the vacation privilege is earned or during the period in which the vacation is taken? Discuss.
11. Identify several factors that influence the future pension obligation of an employer under a defined benefit pension plan.

12. When should the liability associated with a product warranty be recorded? Discuss.
13. General Motors Corporation reported $8.8 billion of product warranties in the Current Liabilities section of a recent balance sheet. How would costs of repairing a defective product be recorded?
14. The "Questions and Answers Technical Hotline" in the *Journal of Accountancy* included the following question:

    Several years ago, Company B instituted legal action against Company A. Under a memorandum of settlement and agreement, Company A agreed to pay Company B a total of $17,500 in three installments—$5,000 on March 1, $7,500 on July 1, and the remaining $5,000 on December 31. Company A paid the first two installments during its fiscal year ended September 30. Should the unpaid amount of $5,000 be presented as a current liability at September 30?

    How would you answer this question?

Practice Exercises

PE 11-1A
Calculate proceeds from notes payable
obj. 1

On September 1, Klondike Co. issued a 90-day note with a face amount of $120,000 to Arctic Apparel Co. for merchandise inventory.

a. Determine the proceeds of the note, assuming the note carries an interest rate of 8%.
b. Determine the proceeds of the note, assuming the note is discounted at 8%.

PE 11-1B
Calculate proceeds from notes payable
obj. 1

On February 1, Electronic Warehouse Co. issued a 30-day note with a face amount of $50,000 to Yamura Products Co. for cash.

a. Determine the proceeds of the note, assuming the note carries an interest rate of 6%.
b. Determine the proceeds of the note, assuming the note is discounted at 6%.

PE 11-2A
Calculate federal income tax withholding
obj. 2

Don Truett's weekly gross earnings for the present week were $1,680. Truett has three exemptions. Using the wage bracket withholding table in Exhibit 3 with a $63 standard withholding allowance for each exemption, what is Truett's federal income tax withholding?

PE 11-2B
Calculate federal income tax withholding
obj. 2

Leah Wilson's weekly gross earnings for the present week were $600. Wilson has one exemption. Using the wage bracket withholding table in Exhibit 3 with a $63 standard withholding allowance for each exemption, what is Wilson's federal income tax withholding?

PE 11-3A
Calculate employee net pay
obj. 2

Don Truett's weekly gross earnings for the week ending December 18 were $1,680, and his federal income tax withholding was $298.51. Prior to this week, Truett had earned $99,000 for the year. Assuming the social security rate is 6% on the first $100,000 of annual earnings and Medicare is 1.5% of all earnings, what is Truett's net pay?

PE 11-3B
Calculate employee net pay
obj. 2

Leah Wilson's weekly gross earnings for the week ending September 5 were $600, and her federal income tax withholding was $65.85. Prior to this week, Wilson had earned $21,500 for the year. Assuming the social security rate is 6% on the first $100,000 of annual earnings and Medicare is 1.5% of all earnings, what is Wilson's net pay?

PE 11-4A
Journalize period payroll
obj. 3

The payroll register of Lowry Landscaping Co. indicates $1,260 of social security withheld and $315 of Medicare tax withheld on total salaries of $21,000 for the period. Federal withholding for the period totaled $3,822.

Provide the journal entry for the period's payroll.

PE 11-4B
Journalize period payroll
obj. 3

The payroll register of Tri-State Construction Co. indicates $25,650 of social security withheld and $6,750 of Medicare tax withheld on total salaries of $450,000 for the period. Retirement savings withheld from employee paychecks were $27,000 for the period. Federal withholding for the period totaled $89,100.

Provide the journal entry for the period's payroll.

PE 11-5A
Journalize period payroll tax
obj. 3

The payroll register of Lowry Landscaping Co. indicates $1,260 of social security withheld and $315 of Medicare tax withheld on total salaries of $21,000 for the period. Assume earnings subject to state and federal unemployment compensation taxes are $6,540, at the federal rate of 0.8% and the state rate of 5.4%.

Provide the journal entry to record the payroll tax expense for the period.

PE 11-5B
Journalize period payroll tax
obj. 3

The payroll register of Tri-State Construction Co. indicates $25,650 of social security withheld and $6,750 of Medicare tax withheld on total salaries of $450,000 for the period. Assume earnings subject to state and federal unemployment compensation taxes are $12,550, at the federal rate of 0.8% and the state rate of 5.4%.

Provide the journal entry to record the payroll tax expense for the period.

PE 11-6A
Journalize vacation pay and pension benefits
obj. 4

Kirby Company provides its employees with vacation benefits and a defined contribution pension plan. Employees earned vacation pay of $17,500 for the period. The pension plan requires a contribution to the plan administrator equal to 7% of employee salaries. Salaries were $180,000 during the period.

Provide the journal entry for the (a) vacation pay and (b) pension benefit.

PE 11-6B
Journalize vacation pay and pension benefits
obj. 4

Lyon Capital Company provides its employees vacation benefits and a defined benefit pension plan. Employees earned vacation pay of $52,300 for the period. The pension formula calculated a pension cost of $123,000. Only $100,000 was contributed to the pension plan administrator.

Provide the journal entry for the (a) vacation pay and (b) pension benefit.

PE 11-7A
Journalize estimated warranty liability
obj. 5

EZ Equipment Co. sold $870,000 of equipment during March under a one-year warranty. The cost to repair defects under the warranty is estimated at 4.5% of the sales price. On October 4, a customer required a $420 part replacement, plus $100 of labor under the warranty.

Provide the journal entry for (a) the estimated warranty expense on March 31 and (b) the October 4 warranty work.

PE 11-7B
Journalize estimated warranty liability
obj. 5

Tower Electronics sold $480,000 of consumer electronics during June under a nine-month warranty. The cost to repair defects under the warranty is estimated at 5% of the sales price. On August 16, a customer was given $90 cash under terms of the warranty.

Provide the journal entry for (a) the estimated warranty expense on June 30 and (b) the August 16 cash payment.

Exercises

EX 11-1
Current liabilities
obj. 1

✓ *Total current liabilities, $348,250*

Rock On Magazine Co. sold 11,400 annual subscriptions of *Rock On* for $35 during December 2008. These new subscribers will receive monthly issues, beginning in January 2009. In addition, the business had taxable income of $140,000 during the first calendar quarter of 2009. The federal tax rate is 35%. A quarterly tax payment will be made on April 7, 2009.

Prepare the Current Liabilities section of the balance sheet for Rock On Magazine Co. on March 31, 2009.

EX 11-2
Entries for discounting notes payable
obj. 1

Home Center Warehouse issues a 90-day note for $250,000 to Gem Lighting Co. for merchandise inventory. Gem Lighting Co. discounts the note at 5%.

a. Journalize Home Center Warehouse's entries to record:
  1. the issuance of the note.
  2. the payment of the note at maturity.
b. Journalize Gem Lighting Co.'s entries to record:
  1. the receipt of the note.
  2. the receipt of the payment of the note at maturity.

EX 11-3
Evaluate alternative notes
obj. 1

A borrower has two alternatives for a loan: (1) issue a $120,000, 90-day, 6% note or (2) issue a $120,000, 90-day note that the creditor discounts at 6%.

a. Calculate the amount of the interest expense for each option.
b. Determine the proceeds received by the borrower in each situation.
c. Which alternative is more favorable to the borrower? Explain.

EX 11-4
Entries for notes payable
obj. 1

A business issued a 60-day, 7% note for $15,000 to a creditor on account. Journalize the entries to record (a) the issuance of the note and (b) the payment of the note at maturity, including interest.

EX 11-5
Entries for discounted note payable
obj. 1

A business issued a 90-day note for $80,000 to a creditor on account. The note was discounted at 8%. Journalize the entries to record (a) the issuance of the note and (b) the payment of the note at maturity.

EX 11-6
Fixed asset purchases with note
obj. 1

On June 30, Mystic Mountain Game Company purchased land for $250,000 and a building for $690,000, paying $240,000 cash and issuing an 8% note for the balance, secured by a mortgage on the property. The terms of the note provide for 20 semiannual payments of $35,000 on the principal plus the interest accrued from the date of the preceding payment. Journalize the entry to record (a) the transaction on June 30, (b) the payment of the first installment on December 31, and (c) the payment of the second installment the following June 30.

EX 11-7
Current portion of long-term debt
obj. 1

REAL WORLD

WD-40 Company, the manufacturer and marketer of WD-40® lubricant, reported the following information about its long-term debt in the notes to a recent financial statement:

Long-term debt is comprised of the following:

	August 31,	
	2005	2004
Notes payable	$75,000,000	$85,000,000
Less current portion	(10,714,000)	(10,000,000)
Long-term debt	$64,286,000	$75,000,000

a. How much of the notes payable was disclosed as a current liability on the August 31, 2005, balance sheet?
b. How much did the total current liabilities change between 2004 and 2005 as a result of the current portion of long-term debt?
c. If WD-40 did not issue additional notes payable during 2006, what would be the total notes payable on August 31, 2006?

EX 11-8
Calculate payroll
obj. 2

An employee earns $22 per hour and 1½ times that rate for all hours in excess of 40 hours per week. Assume that the employee worked 50 hours during the week, and that the gross pay prior to the current week totaled $42,710. Assume further that the social security tax

✓ b. Net pay, $883.25   rate was 6.0% (on earnings up to $100,000), the Medicare tax rate was 1.5%, and federal income tax to be withheld was $236.

a. Determine the gross pay for the week.
b. Determine the net pay for the week.

EX 11-9
Calculate payroll
obj. 2

✓ *Administrator net pay, $829.32*

Strategem Business Consultants has three employees—a consultant, a computer programmer, and an administrator. The following payroll information is available for each employee:

	Consultant	Computer Programmer	Administrator
Regular earnings rate	$2,400 per week	$40 per hour	$22 per hour
Overtime earnings rate	Not applicable	1½ times hourly rate	1½ times hourly rate
Gross pay prior to current pay period	$115,200	$98,600	$43,100
Number of withholding allowances	1	0	3

For the current pay period, the computer programmer worked 48 hours and the administrator worked 45 hours. The federal income tax withheld for all three employees, who are single, can be determined from the wage bracket withholding table in Exhibit 3 in the chapter. Assume further that the social security tax rate was 6.0% on the first $100,000 of annual earnings, the Medicare tax rate was 1.5%, and one withholding allowance is $63.

Determine the gross pay and the net pay for each of the three employees for the current pay period.

EX 11-10
Summary payroll data
objs. 2, 3

✓ *a. (3) Total earnings, $260,000*

In the following summary of data for a payroll period, some amounts have been intentionally omitted:

Earnings:	
1. At regular rate	?
2. At overtime rate	$ 39,480
3. Total earnings	?
Deductions:	
4. Social security tax	15,250
5. Medicare tax	3,900
6. Income tax withheld	46,590
7. Medical insurance	7,775
8. Union dues	?
9. Total deductions	76,000
10. Net amount paid	184,000
Accounts debited:	
11. Factory Wages	138,900
12. Sales Salaries	?
13. Office Salaries	59,200

a. Calculate the amounts omitted in lines (1), (3), (8), and (12).
b. Journalize the entry to record the payroll accrual.
c. Journalize the entry to record the payment of the payroll.
d. ▭▭▶ From the data given in this exercise and your answer to (a), would you conclude that this payroll was paid sometime during the first few weeks of the calendar year? Explain.

EX 11-11
Payroll tax entries
obj. 3

According to a summary of the payroll of Glitz Publishing Co., $350,000 was subject to the 6.0% social security tax and $420,000 was subject to the 1.5% Medicare tax. Also, $14,000 was subject to state and federal unemployment taxes.

a. Calculate the employer's payroll taxes, using the following rates: state unemployment, 4.3%; federal unemployment, 0.8%.
b. Journalize the entry to record the accrual of payroll taxes.

EX 11-12
Payroll entries
obj. 3

The payroll register for Hillsdale Company for the week ended December 14 indicated the following:

Salaries	$690,000
Social security tax withheld	32,700
Medicare tax withheld	10,350
Federal income tax withheld	138,700

In addition, state and federal unemployment taxes were calculated at the rate of 0.8% and 5.2%, respectively, on $26,000 of salaries.

a. Journalize the entry to record the payroll for the week of December 14.
b. Journalize the entry to record the payroll tax expense incurred for the week of December 14.

EX 11-13
Payroll entries
obj. 3

Dowling Company had gross wages of $356,000 during the week ended December 6. The amount of wages subject to social security tax was $285,000, while the amount of wages subject to federal and state unemployment taxes was $18,000. Tax rates are as follows:

Social security	6.0%
Medicare	1.5%
State unemployment	5.4%
Federal unemployment	0.8%

The total amount withheld from employee wages for federal taxes was $66,900.

a. Journalize the entry to record the payroll for the week of December 6.
b. Journalize the entry to record the payroll tax expense incurred for the week of December 6.

EX 11-14
Payroll internal control procedures
obj. 3

Nashville Sounds is a retail store specializing in the sale of country music. The store employs 3 full-time and 10 part-time workers. The store's weekly payroll averages $2,500 for all 13 workers.

Nashville Sounds uses a personal computer to assist in preparing paychecks. Each week, the store's accountant collects employee time cards and enters the hours worked into the payroll program. The payroll program calculates each employee's pay and prints a paycheck. The accountant uses a check-signing machine to sign the paychecks. Next, the store's owner authorizes the transfer of funds from the store's regular bank account to the payroll account.

For the week of May 10, the accountant accidentally recorded 400 hours worked instead of 40 hours for one of the full-time employees.

Does Nashville Sounds have internal controls in place to catch this error? If so, how will this error be detected?

EX 11-15
Internal control procedures
obj. 3

Handyman's Helper is a small manufacturer of home workshop power tools. The company employs 30 production workers and 10 administrative persons. The following procedures are used to process the company's weekly payroll:

a. All employees are required to record their hours worked by clocking in and out on a time clock. Employees must clock out for lunch break. Due to congestion around the time clock area at lunch time, management has not objected to having one employee clock in and out for an entire department.
b. Whenever a salaried employee is terminated, Personnel authorizes Payroll to remove the employee from the payroll system. However, this procedure is not required when an hourly worker is terminated. Hourly employees only receive a paycheck if their time cards show hours worked. The computer automatically drops an employee from the payroll system when that employee has six consecutive weeks with no hours worked.
c. Whenever an employee receives a pay raise, the supervisor must fill out a wage adjustment form, which is signed by the company president. This form is used to change the employee's wage rate in the payroll system.

d. Handyman's Helper maintains a separate checking account for payroll checks. Each week, the total net pay for all employees is transferred from the company's regular bank account to the payroll account.

e. Paychecks are signed by using a check-signing machine. This machine is located in the main office so that it can be easily accessed by anyone needing a check signed.

State whether each of the procedures is appropriate or inappropriate after considering the principles of internal control. If a procedure is inappropriate, describe the appropriate procedure.

EX 11-16
Payroll procedures
obj. 3

The fiscal year for Super Sale Stores Co. ends on June 30. In addition, the company computes and reports payroll taxes on a fiscal-year basis. Thus, it applies social security and FUTA maximum earnings limitations to the fiscal-year payroll.

What is wrong with these procedures for accounting for payroll taxes?

EX 11-17
Accrued vacation pay
obj. 4

A business provides its employees with varying amounts of vacation per year, depending on the length of employment. The estimated amount of the current year's vacation pay is $54,960. Journalize the adjusting entry required on January 31, the end of the first month of the current year, to record the accrued vacation pay.

EX 11-18
Pension plan entries
obj. 4

Precious Images Co. operates a chain of photography stores. The company maintains a defined contribution pension plan for its employees. The plan requires quarterly installments to be paid to the funding agent, Safeguard Funds, by the fifteenth of the month following the end of each quarter. Assuming that the pension cost is $87,500 for the quarter ended December 31, journalize entries to record (a) the accrued pension liability on December 31 and (b) the payment to the funding agent on January 15.

EX 11-19
Defined benefit pension plan terms
obj. 4

In a recent year's financial statements, Procter & Gamble showed an unfunded pension liability of $2,096 million and a periodic pension cost of $268 million.

Explain the meaning of the $2,096 million unfunded pension liability and the $268 million periodic pension cost.

EX 11-20
Accrued product warranty
obj. 5

Audio-Wave Company warrants its products for one year. The estimated product warranty is 2% of sales. Assume that sales were $85,000 for January. In February, a customer received warranty repairs requiring $210 of parts and $135 of labor.

a. Journalize the adjusting entry required at January 31, the end of the first month of the current year, to record the accrued product warranty.

b. Journalize the entry to record the warranty work provided in February.

EX 11-21
Accrued product warranty
obj. 5

Ford Motor Company disclosed estimated product warranty payable for comparative years as follows.

	(in millions)	
	12/31/05	12/31/04
Current estimated product warranty payable	$12,953	$14,082
Noncurrent estimated product warranty payable	7,359	7,728
Total	$20,312	$21,810

Ford's sales were $147,128 million in 2004 and increased to $153,503 million in 2005. Assume that the total paid on warranty claims during 2005 was $12,000 million.

a. Why are short- and long-term estimated warranty liabilities separately disclosed?

b. Provide the journal entry for the 2005 product warranty expense.

EX 11-22
Contingent liabilities
obj. 5

Several months ago, Rainbow Paint Company experienced a hazardous materials spill at one of its plants. As a result, the Environmental Protection Agency (EPA) fined the company $560,000. The company is contesting the fine. In addition, an employee is seeking $275,000 damages related to the spill. Lastly, a homeowner has sued the company for $190,000. The homeowner lives 25 miles from the plant, but believes that the incident has reduced the home's resale value by $190,000.

Rainbow's legal counsel believes that it is probable that the EPA fine will stand. In addition, counsel indicates that an out-of-court settlement of $150,000 has recently been reached with the employee. The final papers will be signed next week. Counsel believes that the homeowner's case is much weaker and will be decided in favor of Rainbow. Other litigation related to the spill is possible, but the damage amounts are uncertain.

a. Journalize the contingent liabilities associated with the hazardous materials spill. Use the account "Damage Awards and Fines" to recognize the expense for the period.
b. ▣▶ Prepare a note disclosure relating to this incident.

EX 11-23
Quick ratio

✓ *a. 2008: 1.0*

Urban-Wear Clothes Co. had the following current assets and liabilities for two comparative years:

	Dec. 31, 2008	Dec. 31, 2007
Current assets:		
Cash	$140,000	$205,000
Accounts receivable	250,000	245,000
Inventory	300,000	180,000
Total current assets	$690,000	$630,000
Current liabilities:		
Current portion of long-term debt	$ 50,000	$ 50,000
Accounts payable	200,000	190,000
Accrued expenses payable	140,000	135,000
Total current liabilities	$390,000	$375,000

a. Determine the quick ratio for December 31, 2008 and 2007.
b. ▣▶ Interpret the change in the quick ratio between the two balance sheet dates.

EX 11-24
Quick ratio

The current assets and current liabilities for Apple Computer, Inc., and Dell Inc. are shown as follows at the end of a recent fiscal period:

	Apple Computer, Inc. (In millions) Sept. 24, 2005	Dell Inc. (In millions) Feb. 3, 2006
Current assets:		
Cash and cash equivalents	$ 3,491	$ 7,042
Short-term investments	4,770	2,016
Accounts receivable	895	4,089
Inventories	165	576
Other current assets*	979	3,983
Total current assets	$10,300	$17,706
Current liabilities:		
Accounts payable	$ 1,779	$ 9,840
Accrued and other current liabilities	1,705	6,087
Total current liabilities	$ 3,484	$15,927

*These represent prepaid expense and other nonquick current assets.

a. Determine the quick ratio for both companies.
b. ▣▶ Interpret the quick ratio difference between the two companies.

Problems Series A

PR 11-1A
Liability transactions
objs. 1, 5

The following items were selected from among the transactions completed by Sounds and Sight Stores during the current year:

Apr.   7. Borrowed $36,000 from First Financial Company, issuing a 60-day, 8% note for that amount.

May 10. Purchased equipment by issuing a $125,000, 120-day note to Milford Equipment Co., which discounted the note at the rate of 6%.

June   6. Paid First Financial Company the interest due on the note of April 7 and renewed the loan by issuing a new 30-day, 9% note for $36,000. (Record both the debit and credit to the notes payable account.)

July   6. Paid First Financial Company the amount due on the note of June 6.

Aug.   3. Purchased merchandise on account from Hamilton Co., $15,000, terms, n/30.

Sept.   2. Issued a 60-day, 6% note for $15,000 to Hamilton Co., on account.

        7. Paid Milford Equipment Co. the amount due on the note of May 10.

Nov.   1. Paid Hamilton Co. the amount owed on the note of September 2.

    15. Purchased store equipment from Merchandising Systems Co. for $150,000, paying $55,500 and issuing a series of seven 8% notes for $13,500 each, coming due at 30-day intervals.

Dec. 15. Paid the amount due Merchandising Systems Co. on the first note in the series issued on November 15.

    21. Settled a personal injury lawsuit with a customer for $30,000, to be paid in January. Sounds and Sight Stores accrued the loss in a litigation claims payable account.

Instructions

1. Journalize the transactions.
2. Journalize the adjusting entry for each of the following accrued expenses at the end of the current year:
   a. Product warranty cost, $8,400.
   b. Interest on the six remaining notes owed to Merchandising Systems Co.

PR 11-2A
Entries for payroll and payroll taxes
objs. 2, 3

✓ 1. (b) Dr. Payroll Tax
Expense, $37,650

The following information about the payroll for the week ended December 30 was obtained from the records of Greenfield Co.:

Salaries:		Deductions:	
Sales salaries	$320,000	Income tax withheld	$109,760
Warehouse salaries	84,500	Social security tax withheld	28,560
Office salaries	155,500	Medicare tax withheld	8,400
	$560,000	U.S. savings bonds	16,400
		Group insurance	24,690
			$187,810

Tax rates assumed:
   Social security, 6% on first $100,000 of employee annual earnings
   Medicare, 1.5%
   State unemployment (employer only), 3.8%
   Federal unemployment (employer only), 0.8%

Instructions

1. Assuming that the payroll for the last week of the year is to be paid on December 31, journalize the following entries:
   a. December 30, to record the payroll.
   b. December 30, to record the employer's payroll taxes on the payroll to be paid on December 31. Of the total payroll for the last week of the year, $15,000 is subject to unemployment compensation taxes.
2. Assuming that the payroll for the last week of the year is to be paid on January 4 of the following fiscal year, journalize the following entries:
   a. December 30, to record the payroll.
   b. January 4, to record the employer's payroll taxes on the payroll to be paid on January 4.

PR 11-3A
Wage and tax statement data and employer FICA tax

objs. 2, 3

✓2. (e) $30,987.60

Bristol Distribution Company began business on January 2, 2007. Salaries were paid to employees on the last day of each month, and social security tax, Medicare tax, and federal income tax were withheld in the required amounts. An employee who is hired in the middle of the month receives half the monthly salary for that month. All required payroll tax reports were filed, and the correct amount of payroll taxes was remitted by the company for the calendar year. Early in 2008, before the Wage and Tax Statements (Form W-2) could be prepared for distribution to employees and for filing with the Social Security Administration, the employees' earnings records were inadvertently destroyed.

None of the employees resigned or were discharged during the year, and there were no changes in salary rates. The social security tax was withheld at the rate of 6.0% on the first $100,000 of salary and Medicare tax at the rate of 1.5% on salary. Data on dates of employment, salary rates, and employees' income taxes withheld, which are summarized as follows, were obtained from personnel records and payroll records.

Employee	Date First Employed	Monthly Salary	Monthly Income Tax Withheld
Arnold	June 2	$6,400	$1,408
Charles	Jan. 2	8,600	2,064
Gillam	Mar. 1	5,000	950
Nelson	Jan. 2	3,800	684
Quinn	Nov. 15	4,400	814
Ramirez	Apr. 15	3,200	560
Wu	Jan. 16	9,200	2,300

Instructions
1. Calculate the amounts to be reported on each employee's Wage and Tax Statement (Form W-2) for 2007, arranging the data in the following form:

Employee	Gross Earnings	Federal Income Tax Withheld	Social Security Tax Withheld	Medicare Tax Withheld

2. Calculate the following employer payroll taxes for the year: (a) social security; (b) Medicare; (c) state unemployment compensation at 3.8% on the first $9,000 of each employee's earnings; (d) federal unemployment compensation at 0.8% on the first $9,000 of each employee's earnings; (e) total.

PR 11-4A
Payroll register

objs. 2, 3

✓3. Dr. Payroll Tax Expense, $664.92

If the working papers correlating with this textbook are not used, omit Problem 11-4A.

The payroll register for Govi Guitar Co. for the week ended December 12, 2008, is presented in the working papers.

Instructions
1. Journalize the entry to record the payroll for the week.
2. Journalize the entry to record the issuance of the checks to employees.
3. Journalize the entry to record the employer's payroll taxes for the week. Assume the following tax rates: state unemployment, 3.2%; federal unemployment, 0.8%. Of the earnings, $1,200 is subject to unemployment taxes.
4. Journalize the entry to record a check issued on December 15 to Second National Bank in payment of employees' income taxes, $1,402.06, social security taxes, $987.06, and Medicare taxes, $246.78.

PR 11-5A
Payroll register

objs. 2, 3

The following data for Iris Publishing Co. relate to the payroll for the week ended December 7, 2008:

✓1. Total net amount payable, $6,508.96

Employee	Hours Worked	Hourly Rate	Weekly Salary	Federal Income Tax	U.S. Savings Bonds	Accumulated Earnings, Nov. 30
A	38	$16		$109.44		$ 29,184
B	44	25		241.50	$20	47,400
C	46	30		338.10	20	70,800
D	40	12		81.60	35	30,700
E	30	10		36.00	10	14,400
F			$1,100.00	242.00		4,400
G	41	24		199.20		41,500
H			2,200.00	550.00	90	105,600
I	48	18		187.20	10	43,200

Employees F and H are office staff, and all of the other employees are sales personnel. All sales personnel are paid 1½ times the regular rate for all hours in excess of 40 hours per week. The social security tax rate is 6.0% on the first $100,000 of each employee's annual earnings, and Medicare tax is 1.5% of each employee's annual earnings. The next payroll check to be used is No. 981.

Instructions

1. Prepare a payroll register for Iris Publishing Co. for the week ended December 7, 2008. Use the following columns for the payroll register: Total Hours Worked, Regular Hours, Overtime Hours, Social Security Tax, Medicare Tax, Federal Income Tax, U.S. Savings Bonds, Total Deductions, Net Pay, Ck. No., Salaries Expense, and Office Salaries Expense.
2. Journalize the entry to record the payroll for the week.

PR 11-6A
Payroll accounts and year-end entries

objs. 2, 3, 4

The following accounts, with the balances indicated, appear in the ledger of Yosemite Outdoor Equipment Company on December 1 of the current year:

211	Salaries Payable	—	218	Bond Deductions Payable	$ 2,000
212	Social Security Tax Payable	$5,888	219	Medical Insurance Payable	2,400
213	Medicare Tax Payable	1,550	611	Sales Salaries Expense	685,900
214	Employees Federal Income Tax Payable	9,555	711	Officers Salaries Expense	326,400
215	Employees State Income Tax Payable	9,297	712	Office Salaries Expense	124,000
216	State Unemployment Tax Payable	1,000	719	Payroll Tax Expense	88,858
217	Federal Unemployment Tax Payable	280			

The following transactions relating to payroll, payroll deductions, and payroll taxes occurred during December:

Dec. 1. Issued Check No. 728 to Pico Insurance Company for $2,400, in payment of the semiannual premium on the group medical insurance policy.

2. Issued Check No. 729 to First National Bank for $16,993, in payment for $5,888 of social security tax, $1,550 of Medicare tax, and $9,555 of employees' federal income tax due.

3. Issued Check No. 730 for $2,000 to First National Bank to purchase U.S. savings bonds for employees.

14. Journalized the entry to record the biweekly payroll. A summary of the payroll record follows:

Salary distribution:		
Sales	$31,000	
Officers	14,800	
Office	5,600	$51,400
Deductions:		
Social security tax	$ 2,827	
Medicare tax	771	
Federal income tax withheld	9,149	
State income tax withheld	2,313	
Savings bond deductions	1,000	
Medical insurance deductions	400	16,460
Net amount		$34,940

(continued)

Dec. 14. Issued Check No. 738 in payment of the net amount of the biweekly payroll.

14. Journalized the entry to record payroll taxes on employees' earnings of December 14: social security tax, $2,827; Medicare tax, $771; state unemployment tax, $250; federal unemployment tax, $55.

17. Issued Check No. 744 to First National Bank for $16,345, in payment for $5,654 of social security tax, $1,542 of Medicare tax, and $9,149 of employees' federal income tax due.

28. Journalized the entry to record the biweekly payroll. A summary of the payroll record follows:

Salary distribution:		
Sales	$31,500	
Officers	15,000	
Office	5,500	$52,000
Deductions:		
Social security tax	$ 2,808	
Medicare tax	780	
Federal income tax withheld	9,256	
State income tax withheld	2,340	
Savings bond deductions	1,000	16,184
Net amount		$35,816

28. Issued Check No. 782 for the net amount of the biweekly payroll.

28. Journalized the entry to record payroll taxes on employees' earnings of December 28: social security tax, $2,808; Medicare tax, $780; state unemployment tax, $120; federal unemployment tax, $30.

30. Issued Check No. 791 for $13,950 to First National Bank, in payment of employees' state income tax due on December 31.

30. Issued Check No. 792 to First National Bank for $2,000 to purchase U.S. savings bonds for employees.

31. Paid $55,700 to the employee pension plan. The annual pension cost is $65,000. (Record both the payment and the unfunded pension liability.)

Instructions

1. Journalize the transactions.
2. Journalize the following adjusting entries on December 31:
   a. Salaries accrued: sales salaries, $3,150; officers salaries, $1,500; office salaries, $550. The payroll taxes are immaterial and are not accrued.
   b. Vacation pay, $13,200.

Problems Series B

PR 11-1B
Liability transactions
objs. 1, 5

The following items were selected from among the transactions completed by Silver Mountain Stores Co. during the current year:

Feb. 15. Purchased merchandise on account from Ranier Co., $120,000, terms n/30.

Mar. 17. Issued a 30-day, 5% note for $120,000 to Ranier Co., on account.

Apr. 16. Paid Ranier Co. the amount owed on the note of March 17.

July 15. Borrowed $180,000 from United Bank, issuing a 90-day, 6% note.

25. Purchased tools by issuing a $135,000, 120-day note to Sun Supply Co., which discounted the note at the rate of 7%.

Oct. 13. Paid United Bank the interest due on the note of July 15 and renewed the loan by issuing a new 30-day, 9% note for $180,000. (Journalize both the debit and credit to the notes payable account.)

Nov. 12. Paid United Bank the amount due on the note of October 13.

22. Paid Sun Supply Co. the amount due on the note of July 25.

Dec. 1. Purchased office equipment from Valley Equipment Co. for $40,000, paying $10,000 and issuing a series of ten 6% notes for $3,000 each, coming due at 30-day intervals.

17. Settled a product liability lawsuit with a customer for $56,000, payable in January. Silver Mountain accrued the loss in a litigation claims payable account.

Dec. 31. Paid the amount due Valley Equipment Co. on the first note in the series issued on December 1.

Instructions

1. Journalize the transactions.
2. Journalize the adjusting entry for each of the following accrued expenses at the end of the current year: (a) product warranty cost, $21,410; (b) interest on the nine remaining notes owed to Valley Equipment Co.

PR 11-2B
Entries for payroll and payroll taxes
objs. 2, 3

✓1. (b) Dr. Payroll Tax
Expense, $21,450

The following information about the payroll for the week ended December 30 was obtained from the records of Plumb Line Supply Co.:

Salaries:		Deductions:	
Sales salaries	$162,400	Income tax withheld	$52,800
Warehouse salaries	54,200	Social security tax withheld	16,200
Office salaries	83,400	Medicare tax withheld	4,500
	$300,000	U.S. savings bonds	6,500
		Group insurance	5,600
			$85,600

Tax rates assumed:
Social security, 6% on first $100,000 of employee annual earnings
Medicare, 1.5%
State unemployment (employer only), 4.2%
Federal unemployment (employer only), 0.8%

Instructions

1. Assuming that the payroll for the last week of the year is to be paid on December 31, journalize the following entries:
   a. December 30, to record the payroll.
   b. December 30, to record the employer's payroll taxes on the payroll to be paid on December 31. Of the total payroll for the last week of the year, $15,000 is subject to unemployment compensation taxes.
2. Assuming that the payroll for the last week of the year is to be paid on January 5 of the following fiscal year, journalize the following entries:
   a. December 30, to record the payroll.
   b. January 5, to record the employer's payroll taxes on the payroll to be paid on January 5.

PR 11-3B
Wage and tax statement data on employer FICA tax
objs. 2, 3

✓2. (e) $27,397

Daisy Dairy Co. began business on January 2, 2007. Salaries were paid to employees on the last day of each month, and social security tax, Medicare tax, and federal income tax were withheld in the required amounts. An employee who is hired in the middle of the month receives half the monthly salary for that month. All required payroll tax reports were filed, and the correct amount of payroll taxes was remitted by the company for the calendar year. Early in 2008, before the Wage and Tax Statements (Form W-2) could be prepared for distribution to employees and for filing with the Social Security Administration, the employees' earnings records were inadvertently destroyed.

None of the employees resigned or were discharged during the year, and there were no changes in salary rates. The social security tax was withheld at the rate of 6.0% on the first $100,000 of salary and Medicare tax at the rate of 1.5% on salary. Data on dates of employment, salary rates, and employees' income taxes withheld, which are summarized as follows, were obtained from personnel records and payroll records.

Employee	Date First Employed	Monthly Salary	Monthly Income Tax Withheld
Alvarez	Jan. 16	$9,600	$2,400
Collins	Nov. 1	2,500	375
Felix	Jan. 2	3,000	480
Lydall	July 16	4,400	792
Penn	Jan. 2	8,800	2,112
Song	May 1	5,100	918
Walker	Feb. 16	2,000	240

Instructions

1. Calculate the amounts to be reported on each employee's Wage and Tax Statement (Form W-2) for 2007, arranging the data in the following form:

Employee	Gross Earnings	Federal Income Tax Withheld	Social Security Tax Withheld	Medicare Tax Withheld

2. Calculate the following employer payroll taxes for the year: (a) social security; (b) Medicare; (c) state unemployment compensation at 4.8% on the first $7,000 of each employee's earnings; (d) federal unemployment compensation at 0.8% on the first $7,000 of each employee's earnings; (e) total.

PR 11-4B
Payroll register

objs. 2, 3

✓ 3. Dr. Payroll Tax
Expense, $654.32

If the working papers correlating with this textbook are not used, omit Problem 11-4B.

The payroll register for Irish Heritage Stores Co. for the week ended December 12, 2008, is presented in the working papers.

Instructions

1. Journalize the entry to record the payroll for the week.
2. Journalize the entry to record the issuance of the checks to employees.
3. Journalize the entry to record the employer's payroll taxes for the week. Assume the following tax rates: state unemployment, 3.6%; federal unemployment, 0.8%. Of the earnings, $850 is subject to unemployment taxes.
4. Journalize the entry to record a check issued on December 15 to Second National Bank in payment of employees' income taxes, $1,402.06, social security taxes, $987.06, and Medicare taxes, $246.78.

PR 11-5B
Payroll register

objs. 2, 3

✓ 1. Total net amount
payable, $7,503.36

The following data for Center Pointe Co. relate to the payroll for the week ended December 7, 2008:

Employee	Hours Worked	Hourly Rate	Weekly Salary	Federal Income Tax	U.S. Savings Bonds	Accumulated Earnings, Nov. 30
M	52	$36.00		$480.24	$50	$ 82,600
N			$1,200.00	258.00		57,600
O	38	16.00		115.52	25	29,184
P	44	18.50		178.71		38,700
Q	40	20.00		168.00	15	40,500
R			2,400.00	576.00	100	115,200
S	32	22.00		105.60		12,600
T	46	28.00		301.84	40	64,200
U	40	18.00		144.00	20	35,600

Employees N and R are office staff, and all of the other employees are sales personnel. All sales personnel are paid 1½ times the regular rate for all hours in excess of 40 hours per week. The social security tax rate is 6.0% on the first $100,000 of each employee's annual earnings, and Medicare tax is 1.5% of each employee's annual earnings. The next payroll check to be used is No. 818.

Instructions

1. Prepare a payroll register for Center Pointe Co. for the week ended December 7, 2008. Use the following columns for the payroll register: Total Hours Worked, Regular Hours, Overtime Hours, Social Security Tax, Medicare Tax, Federal Income Tax, U.S. Savings Bonds, Total Deductions, Net Pay, Ck. No., Salaries Expense, and Office Salaries Expense.
2. Journalize the entry to record the payroll for the week.

PR 11-6B
Payroll accounts and year-end entries

objs. 2, 3, 4

The following accounts, with the balances indicated, appear in the ledger of Bonnie's Gifts Co. on December 1 of the current year:

211	Salaries Payable	—	218	Bond Deductions Payable	$ 3,000
212	Social Security Tax Payable	$ 8,032	219	Medical Insurance Payable	24,000
213	Medicare Tax Payable	2,114	611	Operations Salaries Expense	850,000
214	Employees Federal Income Tax Payable	13,035	711	Officers Salaries Expense	560,000
215	Employees State Income Tax Payable	12,682	712	Office Salaries Expense	140,000
216	State Unemployment Tax Payable	1,400	719	Payroll Tax Expense	121,506
217	Federal Unemployment Tax Payable	400			

The following transactions relating to payroll, payroll deductions, and payroll taxes occurred during December:

Dec. 2. Issued Check No. 728 for $3,000 to First National Bank to purchase U.S. savings bonds for employees.

3. Issued Check No. 729 to First National Bank for $23,181, in payment of $8,032 of social security tax, $2,114 of Medicare tax, and $13,035 of employees' federal income tax due.

14. Journalized the entry to record the biweekly payroll. A summary of the payroll record follows:

Salary distribution:		
Operations	$38,500	
Officers	25,500	
Office	6,200	$70,200
Deductions:		
Social security tax	$ 3,931	
Medicare tax	1,053	
Federal income tax withheld	12,496	
State income tax withheld	3,159	
Savings bond deductions	1,500	
Medical insurance deductions	4,000	26,139
Net amount		$44,061

14. Issued Check No. 738 in payment of the net amount of the biweekly payroll.

14. Journalized the entry to record payroll taxes on employees' earnings of December 14: social security tax, $3,931; Medicare tax, $1,053; state unemployment tax, $290; federal unemployment tax, $84.

17. Issued Check No. 744 to First National Bank for $22,464, in payment of $7,862 of social security tax, $2,106 of Medicare tax, and $12,496 of employees' federal income tax due.

18. Issued Check No. 750 to Pico Insurance Company for $24,000, in payment of the semiannual premium on the group medical insurance policy.

28. Journalized the entry to record the biweekly payroll. A summary of the payroll record follows:

Salary distribution:		
Operations	$39,000	
Officers	26,000	
Office	6,400	$71,400
Deductions:		
Social security tax	$ 3,856	
Medicare tax	1,071	
Federal income tax withheld	12,709	
State income tax withheld	3,213	
Savings bond deductions	1,500	22,349
Net amount		$49,051

28. Issued Check No. 782 in payment of the net amount of the biweekly payroll.

(continued)

Dec. 28. Journalized the entry to record payroll taxes on employees' earnings of December 28: social security tax, $3,856; Medicare tax, $1,071; state unemployment tax, $155; federal unemployment tax, $38.

30. Issued Check No. 791 to First National Bank for $3,000 to purchase U.S. savings bonds for employees.

30. Issued Check No. 792 for $19,054 to First National Bank in payment of employees' state income tax due on December 31.

31. Paid $43,000 to the employee pension plan. The annual pension cost is $45,000. (Record both the payment and unfunded pension liability.)

Instructions

1. Journalize the transactions.
2. Journalize the following adjusting entries on December 31:
   a. Salaries accrued: operations salaries, $3,900; officers salaries, $2,600; office salaries, $640. The payroll taxes are immaterial and are not accrued.
   b. Vacation pay, $12,650.

Comprehensive Problem 3

✓ 5. Total assets,
$1,423,535

Selected transactions completed by Hirata Company during its first fiscal year ending December 31 were as follows:

Jan. 2. Issued a check to establish a petty cash fund of $1,400.

Mar. 1. Replenished the petty cash fund, based on the following summary of petty cash receipts: office supplies, $678; miscellaneous selling expense, $389; miscellaneous administrative expense, $245.

Apr. 5. Purchased $12,000 of merchandise on account, terms 1/10, n/30. The perpetual inventory system is used to account for inventory.

May 5. Paid the invoice of April 5 after the discount period had passed.

10. Received cash from daily cash sales for $7,755. The amount indicated by the cash register was $7,775.

June 2. Received a 60-day, 8.4% note for $60,000 on the Stevens account.

Aug. 1. Received amount owed on June 2 note, plus interest at the maturity date.

3. Received $2,300 on the Jacobs account and wrote off the remainder owed on a $2,500 accounts receivable balance. (The allowance method is used in accounting for uncollectible receivables.)

28. Reinstated the Jacobs account written off on August 3 and received $200 cash in full payment.

Sept. 2. Purchased land by issuing a $250,000, 90-day note to Ace Development Co., which discounted it at 8%.

Oct. 2. Sold office equipment in exchange for $55,000 cash plus receipt of a $25,000, 120-day, 6% note. The equipment had cost $96,000 and had accumulated depreciation of $10,000 as of October 1.

Nov. 30. Journalized the monthly payroll for November, based on the following data:

Salaries		Deductions	
Sales salaries	$58,200	Income tax withheld	$15,804
Office salaries	29,600	Social security tax	
	$87,800	withheld	5,120
		Medicare tax withheld	1,317

Unemployment tax rates:	
State unemployment	3.8%
Federal unemployment	0.8%
Amount subject to unemployment taxes:	
State unemployment	$2,000
Federal unemployment	2,000

Nov. 30. Journalized the employer's payroll taxes on the payroll.
Dec.   1. Journalized the payment of the September 2 note at maturity.
      30. The pension cost for the year was $65,000, of which $57,450 was paid to the pension plan trustee.

Instructions

1. Journalize the selected transactions.
2. Based on the following data, prepare a bank reconciliation for December of the current year:
   a. Balance according to the bank statement at December 31, $123,200.
   b. Balance according to the ledger at December 31, $108,680.
   c. Checks outstanding at December 31, $27,450.
   d. Deposit in transit, not recorded by bank, $12,450.
   e. Bank debit memorandum for service charges, $280.
   f. A check for $330 in payment of an invoice was incorrectly recorded in the accounts as $130.
3. Based on the bank reconciliation prepared in (2), journalize the entry or entries to be made by Hirata Company.
4. Based on the following selected data, journalize the adjusting entries as of December 31 of the current year:
   a. Estimated uncollectible accounts at December 31, $6,490, based on an aging of accounts receivable. The balance of Allowance for Doubtful Accounts at December 31 was $600 (debit).
   b. The physical inventory on December 31 indicated an inventory shrinkage of $1,320.
   c. Prepaid insurance expired during the year, $9,850.
   d. Office supplies used during the year, $1,580.
   e. Depreciation is computed as follows:

Asset	Cost	Residual Value	Acquisition Date	Useful Life In Years	Depreciation Method Used
Buildings	$380,000	$ 0	January 2	50	Straight-line
Office Equip.	90,000	14,000	October 2	5	Straight-line
Store Equip.	45,000	10,000	January 3	8	Double-declining-balance (at twice the straight-line rate)

   f. A patent costing $18,600 when acquired on January 2 has a remaining legal life of nine years and is expected to have value for six years.
   g. The cost of mineral rights was $185,000. Of the estimated deposit of 333,000 tons of ore, 22,500 tons were mined during the year.
   h. Vacation pay expense for December, $4,400.
   i. A product warranty was granted beginning December 1 and covering a one-year period. The estimated cost is 2.5% of sales, which totaled $796,000 in December.
   j. Interest was accrued on the note receivable received on October 2.
5. Based on the following information and the post-closing trial balance shown on the following page, prepare a balance sheet in report form at December 31 of the current year.

The merchandise inventory is stated at cost by the LIFO method.

The product warranty payable is a current liability.

Vacation pay payable:
   Current liability $3,000
   Long-term liability   1,400

The unfunded pension liability is a long-term liability.

Notes payable:
   Current liability $25,000
   Long-term liability   75,000

Hirata Company
Post-Closing Trial Balance
December 31, 2007

	Debit Balances	Credit Balances
Petty Cash	1,400	
Cash	108,200	
Notes Receivable	25,000	
Accounts Receivable	202,300	
Allowance for Doubtful Accounts		6,490
Merchandise Inventory	140,600	
Interest Receivable	375	
Prepaid Insurance	19,700	
Office Supplies	7,100	
Land	245,000	
Buildings	380,000	
Accumulated Depreciation—Buildings		7,600
Office Equipment	90,000	
Accumulated Depreciation—Office Equipment		3,800
Store Equipment	45,000	
Accumulated Depreciation—Store Equipment		11,250
Mineral Rights	185,000	
Accumulated Depletion		12,500
Patents	15,500	
Social Security Tax Payable		9,910
Medicare Tax Payable		2,700
Employees Federal Income Tax Payable		15,887
State Unemployment Tax Payable		42
Federal Unemployment Tax Payable		9
Salaries Payable		90,000
Accounts Payable		125,300
Interest Payable		3,000
Product Warranty Payable		19,900
Vacation Pay Payable		4,400
Unfunded Pension Liability		7,550
Notes Payable		100,000
J. Goll, Capital		1,044,837
	1,465,175	1,465,175

6. On February 7 of the following year, the merchandise inventory was destroyed by fire. Based on the following data obtained from the accounting records, estimate the cost of the merchandise destroyed:

Jan. 1 Merchandise inventory	$140,600
Jan. 1–Feb. 7 Purchases (net)	38,000
Jan. 1–Feb. 7 Sales (net)	68,000
Estimated gross profit rate	40%

Special Activities

SA 11-1
Ethics and professional conduct in business

ETHICS

Dan Lanier is a certified public accountant (CPA) and staff accountant for Baker and Lin, a local CPA firm. It had been the policy of the firm to provide a holiday bonus equal to two weeks' salary to all employees. The firm's new management team announced on November 25 that a bonus equal to only one week's salary would be made available to employees this year. Dan thought that this policy was unfair because he and his coworkers planned on the full two-week bonus. The two-week bonus had been given for 10 straight years, so it seemed as though the firm had breached an implied commitment. Thus, Dan decided that he would make up the lost bonus week by working an extra six hours of overtime per week over the next five weeks until the end of the year. Baker and Lin's policy is to pay overtime at 150% of straight time.

Dan's supervisor was surprised to see overtime being reported, since there is generally very little additional or unusual client service demands at the end of the calendar year. However, the overtime was not questioned, since firm employees are on the "honor system" in reporting their overtime.

➤ Discuss whether the firm is acting in an ethical manner by changing the bonus. Is Dan behaving in an ethical manner?

SA 11-2 *Recognizing pension expense*	The annual examination of Eclipse Company's financial statements by its external public accounting firm (auditors) is nearing completion. The following conversation took place between the controller of Eclipse Company (Greg) and the audit manager from the public accounting firm (Latiffah).

Latiffah: You know, Greg, we are about to wrap up our audit for this fiscal year. Yet, there is one item still to be resolved.

Greg: What's that?

Latiffah: Well, as you know, at the beginning of the year, Eclipse began a defined benefit pension plan. This plan promises your employees an annual payment when they retire, using a formula based on their salaries at retirement and their years of service. I believe that a pension expense should be recognized this year, equal to the amount of pension earned by your employees.

Greg: Wait a minute. I think you have it all wrong. The company doesn't have a pension expense until it actually pays the pension in cash when the employee retires. After all, some of these employees may not reach retirement, and if they don't, the company doesn't owe them anything.

Latiffah: You're not really seeing this the right way. The pension is earned by your employees during their working years. You actually make the payment much later—when they retire. It's like one long accrual—much like incurring wages in one period and paying them in the next. Thus, I think that you should recognize the expense in the period the pension is earned by the employees.

Greg: Let me see if I've got this straight. I should recognize an expense this period for something that may or may not be paid to the employees in 20 or 30 years, when they finally retire. How am I supposed to determine what the expense is for the current year? The amount of the final retirement depends on many uncertainties: salary levels, employee longevity, mortality rates, and interest earned on investments to fund the pension. I don't think that an amount can be determined, even if I accepted your arguments.

➤ Evaluate Latiffah's position. Is she right or is Greg correct?

SA 11-3 *Executive bonuses and accounting methods*	Troy Rogers, the owner of Rogers Trucking Company, initiated an executive bonus plan for his chief executive officer (CEO). The new plan provides a bonus to the CEO equal to 3% of the income before taxes. Upon learning of the new bonus arrangement, the CEO issued instructions to change the company's accounting for trucks. The CEO has asked the controller to make the following two changes:

a. Change from the double-declining-balance method to the straight-line method of depreciation.
b. Add 50% to the useful lives of all trucks.

➤ Why did the CEO ask for these changes? How would you respond to the CEO's request?

SA 11-4 *Ethics and professional conduct in business* ETHICS	Connor Lang was discussing summer employment with Jarrod McIntyre, president of Azalea Landscaping Service:

Jarrod: I'm glad that you're thinking about joining us for the summer. We could certainly use the help.

(continued)

Connor: Sounds good. I enjoy outdoor work, and I could use the money to help with next year's school expenses.

Jarrod: I've got a plan that can help you out on that. As you know, I'll pay you $12 per hour, but in addition, I'd like to pay you with cash. Since you're only working for the summer, it really doesn't make sense for me to go to the trouble of formally putting you on our payroll system. In fact, I do some jobs for my clients on a strictly cash basis, so it would be easy to just pay you that way.

Connor: Well, that's a bit unusual, but I guess money is money.

Jarrod: Yeah, not only that, it's tax-free!

Connor: What do you mean?

Jarrod: Didn't you know? Any money that you receive in cash is not reported to the IRS on a W-2 form; therefore, the IRS doesn't know about the income—hence, it's the same as tax-free earnings.

a. Why does Jarrod McIntyre want to conduct business transactions using cash (not check or credit card)?

b. How should Connor respond to Jarrod's suggestion?

SA 11-5
Payroll forms

Group Project

Internet Project

Payroll accounting involves the use of government-supplied forms to account for payroll taxes. Three common forms are the W-2, Form 940, and Form 941. Form a team with three of your classmates and retrieve copies of each of these forms. They may be obtained from a local IRS office, a library, or downloaded from the Internet at **http://www.irs.gov** (go to forms and publications).

Briefly describe the purpose of each of the three forms.

SA 11-6
Contingent liabilities

Internet Project

Altria Group, Inc., has over eight pages dedicated to describing contingent liabilities in the notes to recent financial statements. These pages include extensive descriptions of multiple contingent liabilities. Use the Internet to research Altria Group, Inc., at **http://www.altria.com**.

a. What are the major business units of Altria Group?

b. Based on your understanding of this company, why would Altria Group require eight pages of contingency disclosure?

Answers to Self-Examination Questions

1. C The maturity value is $5,100, determined as follows:

Face amount of note	$5,000
Plus interest ($5,000 × 12% × 60/360)	100
Maturity value	$5,100

2. B The net amount available to a borrower from discounting a note payable is called the proceeds. The proceeds of $4,900 (answer B) is determined as follows:

Face amount of note	$5,000
Less discount ($5,000 × 12% × 60/360)	100
Proceeds	$4,900

3. B Employers are usually required to withhold a portion of their employees' earnings for payment of federal income taxes (answer A), Medicare tax (answer C), and state and local income taxes (answer D). Generally, federal unemployment compensation taxes (answer B) are levied against the employer only and thus are not deducted from employee earnings.

4. D The amount of net pay of $1,385.50 (answer D) is determined as follows:

Gross pay:			
40 hours at $40	$1,600.00		
5 hours at $60	300.00	$1,900.00	
Deductions:			
Federal income tax withheld		$ 450.00	
FICA:			
Social security tax ($600 × 0.06)	$36.00		
Medicare tax ($1,900 × 0.015)	28.50	64.50	514.50
			$1,385.50

5. D The employer incurs an expense for social security tax (answer A), federal unemployment compensation tax (answer B), and state unemployment compensation tax (answer C). The employees' federal income tax (answer D) is not an expense of the employer. It is withheld from the employees' earnings.

Accounting for Partnerships and Limited Liability Companies

objectives

After studying this chapter, you should be able to:

1 *Describe the basic characteristics of proprietorships, partnerships, and limited liability companies.*

2 *Describe and illustrate the accounting for forming a partnership and for dividing the net income and net loss of a partnership.*

3 *Describe and illustrate the accounting for partner admission and withdrawal.*

4 *Describe and illustrate the accounting for liquidating a partnership.*

5 *Prepare the statement of partnership equity.*

Mahanaim Essentials LLC

f you were to start up any type of business, you would want to separate the business's affairs from your personal affairs. Keeping business transactions separate from personal transactions aids business analysis and simplifies tax reporting. For example, Tressa Bennick, the founder of Mahanaim Essentials LLC, began her business in her home, making hand lotion in her kitchen and selling the product to friends and family. Even when she operated as a simple sole proprietorship, Tressa maintained a separate business checking account for depositing receipts from sales and writing checks for expenses. Thus, at the end of the year, she would have the information necessary for determining the earnings of the business and completing tax returns.

As a business grows and becomes more complex, the form of the business entity becomes an important consideration. For example, as Tressa's home-based personal care products business grew, she needed a partner to help fund the purchase of manufacturing equipment for blending and filling hand lotions. Thus was born Mahanaim Essentials LLC. The "LLC" means limited liability company and is a business form that frequently involves more than a single person as an owner.

The entity form has an important impact on the owners' legal liability, taxation, and the ability to raise money. The four major forms of business entities that are discussed in this text are the proprietorship, partnership, limited liability company, and corporation. We have already introduced the proprietorship. Partnerships and limited liability companies will be discussed in this chapter, and corporations will be introduced in the next chapter.

Proprietorships, Partnerships, and Limited Liability Companies

objective   **1**

Describe the basic characteristics of proprietorships, partnerships, and limited liability companies.

A variety of legal forms exists for forming and operating a business. The four most common legal forms are proprietorships, corporations, partnerships, and limited liability companies. In this section, we describe the characteristics of proprietorships, partnerships, and limited liability companies. The characteristics of corporations are discussed in the next chapter.

PROPRIETORSHIPS

As we discussed in Chapter 1, a proprietorship is a business enterprise owned by a single individual. Internal Revenue Service (IRS) data indicate that proprietorships comprise 70% of the business tax returns filed but only earn 5% of all business revenues. This statistic suggests that proprietorships, although numerous, consist mostly of small businesses. The most common type of proprietorships are professional service providers, such as lawyers, architects, realtors, and physicians.

A proprietorship is simple to form. Indeed, you may already be a proprietor. For example, a person providing child-care services for friends of the family is a proprietor. There are no legal restrictions or forms to file in forming a proprietorship. The ease of forming a proprietorship is one of its main advantages. In addition, the individual owner can usually make business decisions without consulting others. This ability to be one's own boss is a major reason why many individuals organize their businesses as proprietorships.

A proprietorship is a separate entity for accounting purposes, and when the owner dies or retires, the proprietorship ceases to exist. For federal income tax purposes, however, the proprietorship is not treated as a separate taxable entity. The income or loss is said to "pass through" to the owner's individual income tax return.[1] Thus, the income from a proprietorship is taxed only at the individual level.

A primary disadvantage of a proprietorship is the difficulty in raising large amounts of capital. Investment in the business is limited to the amounts that the owner can provide from personal resources, plus any additional amounts that can be raised through borrowing. In addition, the owner is personally liable for any debts or legal claims against the business. In other words, if the business fails, creditors have rights to the personal assets of the owner, regardless of the amount of the owner's actual investment in the enterprise.

PARTNERSHIPS

A **partnership** is an association of two or more persons who own and manage a business for profit.[2] Partnerships have several characteristics with accounting implications.

A partnership has a *limited life*. A partnership dissolves whenever a partner ceases to be a member of the firm. For example, a partnership is dissolved if a partner withdraws due to bankruptcy, incapacity, or death. Likewise, admitting a new partner dissolves the old partnership. When a partnership is dissolved, the remaining partners must form a new partnership if operations of the business are to continue.

In most partnerships, the partners have *unlimited liability*. That is, each partner is individually liable to creditors for debts incurred by the partnership. Thus, if a partnership becomes insolvent, the partners must contribute sufficient personal assets to settle the debts of the partnership.

Partners have *co-ownership of partnership property*. The property invested in a partnership by a partner becomes the joint property of all the partners. When a partnership is dissolved, the partners' claims against the assets are measured by the amount of the balances in their capital accounts.

Another characteristic of a partnership is *mutual agency*. This means that each partner is an agent of the partnership. The acts of each partner commit the entire partnership and become the obligations of all partners. For example, any partner can enter into a contract on behalf of all the members of the partnership. This is why partnerships should be formed only with people you trust.

An important right of partners is *participation in income* of the partnership. Net income and net loss are distributed among the partners according to their agreement.

A partnership, like a proprietorship, is a *nontaxable entity* and thus does not pay federal income taxes. However, revenue and expense and other results of partnership operations must be reported annually to the Internal Revenue Service. The partners must, in turn, report their share of partnership income on their personal tax returns.

> A partnership is a non-taxable entity that has a limited life and unlimited liability, and it is committed by the actions of each partner.

A partnership is created by a contract, known as the **partnership agreement** or *articles of partnership*. It should include statements regarding such matters as amounts to be invested, limits on withdrawals, distributions of income and losses, and admission and withdrawal of partners.

A variant of the regular partnership is a limited partnership. A *limited partnership* is a unique legal form that allows partners who are not involved in the operations of the partnership to retain limited liability. In such a form, at least one general partner must operate the partnership and retain unlimited liability. The remaining partners are considered limited partners.

---

1 The proprietor's statement of income is included on Schedule C of the individual 1040 tax return.
2 The definition of a partnership is included in the Uniform Partnership Act, which has been adopted by most states.

Integrity, Objectivity, and Ethics in Business

WE ARE FAM-I-LY

Partnership agreements often have limitations on "related party transactions." A related party transaction can give rise to a conflict of interest. For example, most agree-ments would want to limit or disclose partnership trans-actions with other entities owned by a partner.

Companies commonly use partnerships and LLCs in form-ing joint ventures. Joint ven-tures are used to spread risk or expand expertise in operat-ing identifiable businesses or projects. For example, CBS Corp. uses regionally placed joint venture partners to broadcast MTV, VH1, Nick-elodeon, and TV Land around the world. CBS's joint venture partners bring local customs, language, and culture to the broadcast offerings.

The partnership form is less widely used than the proprietorship and corporate forms. However, a partnership has the advantage of bringing together more capital, managerial skills, and experience than does a proprietorship. A partnership is relatively easy and inexpensive to organize, requiring only an agreement between two or more persons. In addition, like a proprietorship, a partnership is a nontaxable entity.

A major disadvantage of the partnership is the unlimited liability feature for part-ners. Other disadvantages of a partnership are that its life is limited, and one partner can bind the partnership to contracts. Also, raising large amounts of capital is more difficult for a partnership than for a corporation. To overcome these limitations, other hybrid forms of organization, such as limited liability companies (LLCs), have been replacing partnerships as a means of organization.

LIMITED LIABILITY COMPANIES

A **limited liability company (LLC)** is a relatively new business entity form that over-comes some of the disadvantages of the partnership form while retaining some of its advantages. For example, similar to partnerships, LLCs must be authorized by state governments through the filing of "articles of organization." The owners of an LLC are termed "members" rather than "partners." The members must create an *operating agree-ment*, which is similar to a partnership agreement. For example, the operating agree-ment normally indicates how income is to be distributed to the members. This distribution is negotiated between the members and is often based upon members' con-tribution of time, money, and talents.

For tax purposes, an LLC may elect to be treated as a partnership. In this way, in-come passes through the LLC and is taxed on the individual members' tax return.[3]

Most operating agreements specify continuity of life for the LLC, even when a member withdraws. In addition, the members may elect to operate the LLC as a "member-managed" entity, which allows individual members to legally bind the LLC, like partners bind a partnership. Alternatively, the LLC may elect to be "manager-managed." In a manager-managed structure, only authorized individuals may legally bind the LLC. This allows members to share in the income of the LLC without concern for managing the business.

One of the most important features of an LLC is to provide limited liability for the members, even if they are active participants in the business. *Limited liability* means that the members' personal assets are legally protected against creditor claims made against the LLC. Such claims may arise from default, bankruptcy, or court actions.

As a result of limited liability and the manager-managed election, LLCs can be used to access capital from a larger number of individuals than will typically be the case in a partnership. Because of these advantages, LLCs have been widely used in small busi-ness formation.

---

3 LLCs may also be taxed as a separate entity, although this election would remove any "pass-through" benefits. Thus, this is a less common election.

COMPARING PROPRIETORSHIPS, PARTNERSHIPS, AND LIMITED LIABILITY COMPANIES

Exhibit 1 summarizes proprietorships, partnerships, and limited liability companies. The columns of Exhibit 1 represent the distinguishing characteristics of these organizational forms: ease of formation, legal liability, taxation, limitation on life of entity, and access to capital. As one expert who has been involved in a number of startup businesses replied when asked what structure makes the most sense: "It depends. Each situation I've been involved with has been different. You can't just make an assumption that one form is better than another."[4]

EXHIBIT 1 — Characteristics of Proprietorships, Partnerships, and Limited Liability Companies

Organizational Form	Ease of Formation	Legal Liability	Taxation	Limitation on Life of Entity	Access to Capital
Proprietorship	Simple	No limitation	Nontaxable (pass-through) entity	Yes	Limited
Partnership	Moderate	No limitation	Nontaxable (pass-through) entity	Yes	Limited
Limited Liability Company	Moderate	Limited liability	Nontaxable (pass-through) entity by election	No	Average

Business Connections

REAL WORLD

ORGANIZATIONAL FORMS IN THE ACCOUNTING AND CONSULTING INDUSTRY

The four major accounting firms, KPMG LLP, Ernst & Young, PricewaterhouseCoopers, and Deloitte & Touche, all began as partnerships. This form was legally required due to the theory of mutual agency. That is, the partnership form was thought to create public trust by requiring all partners to be jointly liable and responsible for each other's judgments. Each partner's personal assets were backing up every partner's judgment. The partnership form also restricted investment to the professionals that actually provide the service in the public trust. Thus, the partnership prevented outside investors from influencing professional decisions from a purely profit motive.

As these firms grew and the risk increased, all of these firms were allowed to change, by law, to limited liability partner-

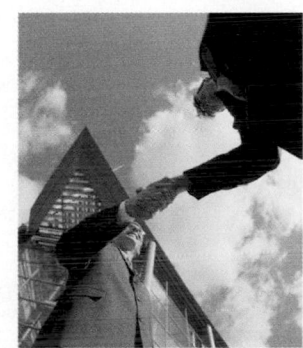

ships (LLPs). Thus, while remaining a partnership, the liability of the partners was limited to their investment in the firm. For example, the partners of Arthur Andersen LLP, while losing most of their investment in the firm due to the Enron fiasco, were protected against most additional claims on their personal assets due to the LLP structure.

Very few of the large consulting firms have remained as partnerships, due to the limitations of this organizational form. One of the few exceptions is McKinsey & Company, a strategy-consulting firm. In the future, we might expect to see new consulting firms use the emerging limited liability company (LLC) form of organization, since it retains attractive features of both partnerships and corporations.

---

4 Laura Tiffany, "Choose Your Business Structure," *Entrepreneur*, March 19, 2001.

Forming and Dividing Income of a Partnership

Describe and illustrate the accounting for forming a partnership and for dividing the net income and net loss of a partnership.

Most of the day-to-day accounting for a partnership or an LLC is the same as the accounting for any other form of business organization. The accounting system described in previous chapters may, with minimal changes, be used by a partnership or an LLC. However, the formation, division of net income or net loss, dissolution, and liquidation of partnerships and LLCs give rise to unique transactions.

In the following sections of this chapter, we will discuss and illustrate these unique transactions for a partnership. An LLC is treated in the same manner as a partnership, except that the terms "member" and "members' equity" are used rather than "partner" or "owners' capital." Because of the similarity of the accounting for LLCs and partnerships, we show the parallel journal entries for an LLC alongside the partnership entries.

FORMING A PARTNERSHIP

In forming a partnership, the investments of each partner are recorded in separate entries. The assets contributed by a partner are debited to the partnership asset accounts. If liabilities are assumed by the partnership, the partnership liability accounts are credited. The partner's capital account is credited for the net amount.

To illustrate, assume that Joseph Stevens and Earl Foster, owners of competing hardware stores, agree to combine their businesses in a partnership. Each is to contribute certain amounts of cash and other assets. Stevens and Foster also agree that the partnership is to assume the liabilities of the separate businesses. The entry to record the assets contributed and the liabilities transferred by Stevens is as follows:

LLC Alternative

Cash	7,200	
Accounts Receivable	16,300	
Merchandise Inventory	28,700	
Store Equipment	5,400	
Office Equipment	1,500	
Allowance for Doubtful Accounts		1,500
Accounts Payable		2,600
Joseph Stevens, Member Equity		55,000

				Debit	Credit
Apr.	1	Cash		7 2 0 0 00	
		Accounts Receivable		16 3 0 0 00	
		Merchandise Inventory		28 7 0 0 00	
		Store Equipment		5 4 0 0 00	
		Office Equipment		1 5 0 0 00	
		Allowance for Doubtful Accounts			1 5 0 0 00
		Accounts Payable			2 6 0 0 00
		Joseph Stevens, Capital			55 0 0 0 00

A similar entry would record the assets contributed and the liabilities transferred by Foster. In each entry, the noncash assets are recorded at values agreed upon by the partners. These values normally represent current market values and thus usually differ from the book values of the assets in the records of the separate businesses. For example, the store equipment recorded at $5,400 in the preceding entry may have had a book value of $3,500 in Stevens' ledger (cost of $10,000 less accumulated depreciation of $6,500). As a further example, receivables contributed to the partnership are recorded at their face amount. Only accounts that are likely to be collected are normally transferred to the partnership.

Example Exercise 12-1

objective 2

Reese Howell contributed equipment, inventory, and $34,000 cash to a partnership. The equipment had a book value of $23,000 and a market value of $29,000. The inventory had a book value of $60,000, but only had a market value of $15,000, due to obsolescence. The partnership also assumed a $12,000 note payable owed by Howell that was used originally to purchase the equipment.

Provide the journal entry for Howell's contribution to the partnership.

(continued)

DIVIDING INCOME

Many partnerships have been dissolved because partners could not agree on how to distribute income equitably. Therefore, the method of dividing partnership income should be stated in the partnership agreement. In the absence of any agreement or if the agreement is silent on dividing net income or net losses, all partners share equally. However, if one partner contributes a larger portion of capital than the others, then net income should be divided to reflect the unequal capital contributions. Likewise, if the services rendered by one partner are more important than those of the others, net income should be divided to reflect the unequal service contributions. In the following paragraphs, we illustrate partnership agreements that recognize these differences.

Dividing Income—Services of Partners One method of recognizing differences in partners' ability and in the amount of time devoted to the partnership is by providing for salary allowances to partners. Since partners are legally not employees of the partnership, such allowances are treated as divisions of the net income and are credited to the partners' capital accounts.

To illustrate, assume that the partnership agreement of Jennifer Stone and Crystal Mills provides for monthly salary allowances. Stone is to receive a monthly allowance of $5,000 ($60,000 annually), and Mills is to receive $4,000 a month ($48,000 annually). Any net income remaining after the salary allowances is to be divided equally. Assume also that the net income for the year is $150,000.

A report of the division of net income may be presented as a separate statement to accompany the balance sheet and the income statement or disclosed within the statement of partnership capital. Another format is to add the division to the bottom of the income statement. If the latter format is used, the lower part of the income statement would appear as follows:

Net income $150,000

Division of net income:

	J. Stone	C. Mills	Total
Annual salary allowance	$60,000	$48,000	$108,000
Remaining income	21,000	21,000	42,000
Net income	$81,000	$69,000	$150,000

The net income division is recorded as a closing entry, even if the partners do not actually withdraw the amounts of their salary allowances. The entry for dividing net income is as follows:

LLC Alternative

Income Summary	*150,000*	
Jennifer Stone, Member Equity		*81,000*
Crystal Mills, Member Equity		*69,000*

Dec.	31	Income Summary	150 0 0 0 00	
		Jennifer Stone, Capital		81 0 0 0 00
		Crystal Mills, Capital		69 0 0 0 00

If Stone and Mills had withdrawn their salary allowances monthly, the withdrawals would have been debited to their drawing accounts during the year. At the end of the year, the debit balances of $60,000 and $48,000 in their drawing accounts would be transferred as reductions to their capital accounts.

Accountants should be careful to distinguish between salary allowances and partner withdrawals. The amount of net income distributed to each partner's capital account at the end of the year may differ from the amount the partner withdraws during the year. In some cases, the partnership agreement may limit the amount of withdrawals a partner may make during a period.

Dividing Income—Services of Partners and Investments Partners may agree that the most equitable plan of dividing income is to provide for (1) salary allowances and (2) interest on capital investments. Any remaining net income is then divided as agreed upon. For example, assume that the partnership agreement for Stone and Mills divides income as follows:

1. Monthly salary allowances of $5,000 for Stone and $4,000 for Mills.
2. Interest of 12% on each partner's capital balance on January 1.
3. Any remaining net income divided equally between the partners.

Stone had a credit balance of $160,000 in her capital account on January 1 of the current fiscal year, and Mills had a credit balance of $120,000 in her capital account. The $150,000 net income for the year is divided per the following schedule:

Net income	....	$150,000

Division of net income:

	J. Stone	C. Mills	Total
Annual salary allowance	$60,000	$48,000	$108,000
Interest allowance	19,200[1]	14,400[2]	33,600
Remaining income	4,200	4,200	8,400
Net income	$83,400	$66,600	$150,000

[1]12% × $160,000
[2]12% × $120,000

For the above example, the entry to close the income summary account is shown below.

LLC Alternative	
Income Summary	*150,000*
Jennifer Stone, Member Equity	*83,400*
Crystal Mills, Member Equity	*66,600*

Dec.	31	Income Summary	150 0 0 0 00		
		Jennifer Stone, Capital			83 4 0 0 00
		Crystal Mills, Capital			66 6 0 0 00

Integrity, Objectivity, and Ethics in Business ETHICS

TYRANNY OF THE MAJORITY

Some partnerships involve the contribution of money by one partner and the contribution of effort and expertise by another. This can create a conflict between the two partners, since one works and the other doesn't. Without a properly developed partnership agreement, the working partner could take income in the form of salary allowance, leaving little for the investor partner. Thus, partnership agreements often require all partners to agree on salary allowances provided to working partners.

Dividing Income—Allowances Exceed Net Income   In the preceding example, the net income exceeded the total of the salary and interest allowances. If the net income is less than the total of the allowances, the remaining balance will be a negative amount. This amount must be divided among the partners as though it were a net loss.

To illustrate, assume the same salary and interest allowances as in the preceding example but that the net income is $100,000. The salary and interest allowances total $79,200 for Stone and $62,400 for Mills. The sum of these amounts, $141,600, exceeds the net income of $100,000 by $41,600. This $41,600 excess must be divided between Stone and Mills. Under the partnership agreement, any net income or net loss remaining after deducting the allowances is divided equally between Stone and Mills. Thus, each partner is allocated one-half of the $41,600, and $20,800 is deducted from each partner's share of the allowances. The final division of net income between Stone and Mills is shown below.

Net income $100,000

Division of net income:

	J. Stone	C. Mills	Total
Annual salary allowance	$60,000	$48,000	$108,000
Interest allowance	19,200	14,400	33,600
Total	$79,200	$62,400	$141,600
Deduct excess of allowances over income	20,800	20,800	41,600
Net income	$58,400	$41,600	$100,000

In closing Income Summary at the end of the year, $58,400 would be credited to Jennifer Stone, Capital, and $41,600 would be credited to Crystal Mills, Capital.[5]

Example Exercise 12-2   objective 2

Steve Prince and Chelsy Bernard formed a partnership, dividing income as follows:

1.   Annual salary allowance to Prince of $42,000.
2.   Interest of 9% on each partner's capital balance on January 1.
3.   Any remaining net income divided equally.

Prince and Bernard had $20,000 and $150,000 in their January 1 capital balances, respectively. Net income for the year was $240,000.
How much net income should be distributed to Prince?

Follow My Example 12-2

Annual salary .... $ 42,000
Interest (9% × $20,000) 1,800
Remaining income 91,350*
Total distributed to Prince $135,150

*[$240,000 − $42,000 − $1,800 − (9% × $150,000)] × 50%

For Practice: PE 12-2A, PE 12-2B

---

5 In the event of a net loss, the amount deducted from the total allowances would be the "excess of allowances over loss" or the sum of the net loss and the allowances, divided according to the sharing ratio.

Partner Admission and Withdrawal

When a partnership dissolves, its affairs are not necessarily finished. For example, a partnership of two partners may admit a third partner. Or if one of the partners in a business withdraws, the remaining partners may continue to operate the business. In such cases, a new partnership is formed and a new partnership agreement should be prepared. Many partnerships provide for the admission of new partners and partner withdrawals in the partnership agreement so that the partnership may continue operations by amending an existing agreement, without having to execute a new agreement.

ADMITTING A PARTNER

A person may be admitted to a partnership only with the consent of all the current partners by:

1. Purchasing an interest from one or more of the current partners.
2. Contributing assets to the partnership.

These two methods are illustrated in Exhibit 2. When the first method is used, the equity of the incoming partner is obtained from the current partners. Thus, *neither the total assets nor the total owners' equity of the business is affected.* This is illustrated in Exhibit 2 when Carr acquires Able's interest. When the second method is used, *both the total assets and the total owners' equity of the business are increased.* This is illustrated in Exhibit 2 when Duncan acquires an interest in the partnership. In the following paragraphs, we will discuss each of these methods.

EXHIBIT 2 | **Two Methods for Admitting a Partner**

Purchasing an Interest
from an Existing Partner

Contributing Assets to a Partnership

Able   Carr
$
Ownership Interest

Duncan   Able & Baker
$
Ownership Interest

Purchasing an Interest in a Partnership   The purchase and sale of a partnership interest occurs between the new partner and the existing partners acting as individuals. The only entry needed is to transfer owners' equity amounts from the capital accounts of the selling partners to the capital account established for the incoming partner.

As an example, assume that partners Tom Andrews and Nathan Bell have capital balances of $50,000 each. On June 1, each sells one-fifth of his equity to Joe Canter for $10,000 in cash. The exchange of cash is not a partnership transaction and thus is not recorded by the partnership. The only entry required in the partnership accounts is as follows:

LLC Alternative

Tom Andrews, Member Equity	*10,000*
Nathan Bell, Member Equity	*10,000*
Joe Canter, Member Equity	*20,000*

June	1	Tom Andrews, Capital	10 0 0 0 00	
		Nathan Bell, Capital	10 0 0 0 00	
		Joe Canter, Capital		20 0 0 0 00

The effect of the transaction on the partnership accounts is presented in the following diagram:

Partnership Accounts

The preceding entry is not affected by the amount paid by Canter for the one-fifth interest. Any gain or loss on the sale of the partnership interest accrues to the selling partners as individuals, not to the partnership. Thus, in either case, the entry to transfer the capital interests is the same as shown above.

After Canter is admitted to the partnership, the total owners' equity of the firm is still $100,000. Canter now has a one-fifth interest, or a $20,000 capital balance. However, Canter may not be entitled to a one-fifth share of the partnership net income. The division of the net income or net loss will be made according to the new or amended partnership agreement.

Contributing Assets to a Partnership When a new partner is admitted by contributing assets to the partnership, both the assets and the owners' equity of the firm increase. For example, assume that Donald Lewis and Gerald Morton are partners with capital accounts of $35,000 and $25,000. On June 1, Sharon Nelson invests $20,000 cash in the business for ownership equity of $20,000. The entry to record this transaction is as follows:

LLC Alternative		
Cash	*20,000*	
Sharon Nelson, Member Equity		*20,000*

June	1	Cash		20 0 0 0 00	
		Sharon Nelson, Capital			20 0 0 0 00

The major difference between admitting Nelson and admitting Canter in the preceding example may be observed by comparing the following diagram with the preceding diagram.

Partnership Accounts

By admitting Nelson, the total owners' equity of the new partnership becomes $80,000, of which Nelson has a one-fourth interest, or $20,000. The extent of Nelson's share in partnership net income will be determined by the partnership agreement.

Revaluation of Assets A partnership's asset account balances should be stated at current values when a new partner is admitted. If the accounts do not approximate current market values, the accounts should be adjusted. The net adjustment (increase or decrease) in asset values is divided among the capital accounts of the existing partners according to their income-sharing ratio. Failure to adjust the accounts for current values may result in the new partner sharing in asset gains or losses that arose in prior periods.

To illustrate, assume that in the preceding example for the Lewis and Morton partnership, the balance of the merchandise inventory account is $14,000 and the current replacement value is $17,000. Assuming that Lewis and Morton share net income equally, the revaluation is recorded as follows:

LLC Alternative

Merchandise Inventory	*3,000*	
Donald Lewis, Member Equity		*1,500*
Gerald Morton, Member Equity		*1,500*

June	1	Merchandise Inventory	3 0 0 0 00	
		Donald Lewis, Capital		1 5 0 0 00
		Gerald Morton, Capital		1 5 0 0 00

Example Exercise 12-3 objective 3

Blake Nelson invested $45,000 in the Lawrence & Kerry partnership for ownership equity of $45,000. Prior to the investment, land was revalued to a market value of $260,000 from a book value of $200,000. Lynne Lawrence and Tim Kerry share net income in a 1:2 ratio.

a. Provide the journal entry for the revaluation of land.
b. Provide the journal entry to admit Nelson.

Follow My Example 12-3

a.	Land	60,000	
	Lynne Lawrence, Capital		20,000[1]
	Tim Kerry, Capital		40,000[2]

1. $60,000 × 1/3
2. $60,000 × 2/3

b.	Cash	45,000	
	Blake Nelson, Capital		45,000

For Practice: PE 12-3A, PE 12-3B

Partner Bonuses   When a new partner is admitted to a partnership, the incoming partner may pay a bonus to the existing partners for the privilege of joining the partnership. Such a bonus is usually paid expecting high partnership profits in the future due to the contributions of the existing partners. Alternatively, the existing partners may pay the incoming partner a bonus to join the partnership. In this case, the bonus is usually paid recognizing special qualities or skills that the incoming partner is bringing to the partnership. For example, celebrities such as actors, musicians, or sports figures often provide name recognition that is expected to increase partnership profits in the future.

Partner bonuses are illustrated in Exhibit 3. Existing partners receive a bonus when the ownership interest received by the admitted partner is less than the amount paid. In contrast, the admitted partner receives a bonus when the ownership interest received by the admitted partner is greater than the amount paid.

To illustrate, assume that on March 1 the partnership of Marsha Jenkins and Helen Kramer is considering admitting a new partner, Alex Diaz. After the assets of the partnership have been adjusted to current market values, the capital balance of Jenkins is $20,000 and the capital balance of Kramer is $24,000. Jenkins and Kramer agree to admit Diaz to the partnership for $31,000. In return, Diaz will receive a one-third equity in

EXHIBIT 3 | Partner Bonuses

the partnership and will share equally with Jenkins and Kramer in partnership income or losses.

In this case, Diaz is paying Jenkins and Kramer a $6,000 bonus to join the partnership. This bonus is computed as follows:

Equity of Jenkins	$20,000
Equity of Kramer	24,000
Diaz's contribution	31,000
Total equity after admitting Diaz	$75,000
Diaz's equity interest after admission	× 1/3
Diaz's equity after admission	$25,000
Diaz's contribution	$31,000
Diaz's equity after admission	25,000
Bonus paid to Jenkins and Kramer	$ 6,000

The bonus is distributed to Jenkins and Kramer according to their income-sharing ratio.[6] Assuming that Jenkins and Kramer share profits and losses equally, the entry to record the admission of Diaz to the partnership is as follows:

LLC Alternative

Cash	31,000	
Alex Diaz, Member Equity		25,000
Marsha Jenkins, Member Equity		3,000
Helen Kramer, Member Equity		3,000

Mar.	1	Cash	31 0 0 0 00	
		Alex Diaz, Capital		25 0 0 0 00
		Marsha Jenkins, Capital		3 0 0 0 00
		Helen Kramer, Capital		3 0 0 0 00

If a new partner possesses unique qualities or skills, the existing partners may agree to pay the new partner a bonus to join the partnership. To illustrate, assume that after adjusting assets to market values, the capital balance of Janice Cowen is $80,000 and the capital balance of Steve Dodd is $40,000. Cowen and Dodd agree to admit Ellen Chou to the partnership on June 1 for an investment of $30,000. In return, Chou will receive a one-fourth equity interest in the partnership and will share in one-fourth of the profits and losses. In this case, Cowen and Dodd are paying Chou a $7,500 bonus to join the partnership. This bonus is computed at the top of the following page.

---

6 Another method used to record the admission of partners attributes goodwill rather than a bonus to the partners. This method is discussed in advanced accounting textbooks.

Equity of Cowen	$ 80,000
Equity of Dodd	40,000
Chou's contribution	30,000
Total equity after admitting Chou	$150,000
Chou's equity interest after admission	× 25%
Chou's equity after admission	$ 37,500
Chou's contribution	30,000
Bonus paid to Chou	$ 7,500

Assuming that the income-sharing ratio of Cowen and Dodd was 2:1 before the admission of Chou, the entry to record the bonus and admission of Chou to the partnership is as follows:

LLC Alternative

Cash	30,000	
Janice Cowen, Member Equity	5,000[1]	
Steve Dodd, Member Equity	2,500[2]	
Ellen Chou, Member Equity		37,500

June	1	Cash	30 0 0 0 00	
		Janice Cowen, Capital	5 0 0 0 00[1]	
		Steve Dodd, Capital	2 5 0 0 00[2]	
		Ellen Chou, Capital		37 5 0 0 00

1. $7,500 × 2/3
2. $7,500 × 1/3

Example Exercise 12-4   objective 3

Lowman has a capital balance of $45,000 after adjusting assets to fair market value. Conrad contributes $26,000 to receive a 30% interest in a new partnership with Lowman.
Determine the amount and recipient of the partner bonus.

Follow My Example 12-4

Equity of Lowman	$45,000
Conrad's contribution	26,000
Total equity after admitting Conrad	$71,000
Conrad's equity interest	× 30%
Conrad's equity after admission	$21,300
Conrad's contribution	$26,000
Conrad's equity after admission	21,300
Bonus paid to Lowman	$ 4,700

For Practice: PE 12-4A, PE 12-4B

WITHDRAWAL OF A PARTNER

A partner generally cannot withdraw without permission of the remaining partners, nor can a partner be forced to withdraw by the other partners. In this sense, a partnership is like a marriage, "for better or for worse."

When a partner retires or withdraws from a partnership, one or more of the remaining partners may buy the withdrawing partner's interest. The firm may then continue its operations uninterrupted. In such cases, the purchase and sale of the partnership interest is between the partners as individuals. The only entry on the partnership's records is to debit the capital account of the partner withdrawing and to credit the capital account of the partner or partners buying the additional interest.

If the withdrawing partner sells the interest directly to the partnership, both the assets and the owners' equity of the partnership are reduced. Before the sale, the asset accounts should be adjusted to current values, so that the withdrawing partner's equity may be accurately determined. The net amount of the adjustment should be divided among the capital accounts of the partners according to their income-sharing ratio. If not enough partnership cash or other assets are available to pay the withdrawing partner, a liability may be created (credited) for the amount owed the withdrawing partner.

DEATH OF A PARTNER

When a partner dies, the accounts should be closed as of the date of death. The net income for the current year should be determined and divided among the partners' capital accounts. The balance in the capital account of the deceased partner is then transferred to a liability account with the deceased's estate. The remaining partner or partners may continue the business or terminate it. If the partnership continues in business, the procedures for settling with the estate are the same as those discussed for the withdrawal of a partner.

Liquidating Partnerships

When a partnership goes out of business, it usually sells the assets, pays the creditors, and distributes the remaining cash or other assets to the partners. This winding-up process is called the **liquidation** of the partnership. Although *liquidating* refers to the payment of liabilities, it often includes the entire winding-up process.

When the partnership goes out of business and the normal operations are discontinued, the accounts should be adjusted and closed. The only accounts remaining open will be the asset, contra asset, liability, and owners' equity accounts.

The liquidation process is illustrated in Exhibit 4. The steps are as follows:

In liquidation, cash is distributed to partners according to their capital balances.

1. Sell the partnership assets. This step is called **realization**.
2. Distribute any gains or losses from realization to the partners based upon their income-sharing ratio.
3. Pay the claims of creditors using the cash from step 1 realization.
4. Distribute the remaining cash after satisfying creditors to the partners based upon the balances in their capital accounts.

EXHIBIT 4	Steps in Liquidating a Partnership

1 Sale of Assets — Realization →

2 Division of Gain or Loss → Gain or Loss on Realization → Income-Sharing Ratio

3 Payment of Liabilities → → BANK

4 Distribution to Partners → → Capital Account Balances

The liquidating process may extend over a long period of time as individual assets are sold. This delays the distribution of cash to partners but does not affect the amount each partner will receive.

To illustrate, assume that Farley, Greene, and Hall share income and losses in a ratio of 5:3:2 (5/10, 3/10, 2/10). On April 9, after discontinuing business operations of the partnership and closing the accounts, the following trial balance in summary form was prepared:

Cash	11,000	
Noncash Assets	64,000	
Liabilities		9,000
Jean Farley, Capital		22,000
Brad Greene, Capital		22,000
Alice Hall, Capital		22,000
	75,000	75,000

Based on these facts, we show the accounting for liquidating the partnership by using three different selling prices for the noncash assets. To simplify, we assume that all noncash assets are sold in a single transaction and that all liabilities are paid at one time. In addition, Noncash Assets and Liabilities will be used as account titles in place of the various asset, contra asset, and liability accounts.

GAIN ON REALIZATION

Between April 10 and April 30 of the current year, Farley, Greene, and Hall sell all non-cash assets for $72,000. Thus, a gain of $8,000 ($72,000 − $64,000) is realized. The gain is divided among the capital accounts in the income-sharing ratio of 5:3:2. The liabilities are paid, and the remaining cash is distributed to the partners. *The cash is distributed to the partners based on the balances in their capital accounts.* A **statement of partnership liquidation**, which summarizes the liquidation process, is shown in Exhibit 5.

EXHIBIT 5	Gain on Realization

Farley, Greene, and Hall
Statement of Partnership Liquidation
For Period April 10–30, 2008

	Cash	+	Noncash Assets	=	Liabilities	+	Capital Farley (50%)	+	Greene (30%)	+	Hall (20%)
Balances before realization	$ 11 000 00		$ 64 000 00		$ 9 000 00		$ 22 000 00		$ 22 000 00		$ 22 000 00
Sale of assets and division of gain	+ 72 000 00		− 64 000 00		—		+ 4 000 00		+ 2 400 00		+ 1 600 00
Balances after realization	$ 83 000 00		$ 0		$ 9 000 00		$ 26 000 00		$ 24 400 00		$ 23 600 00
Payment of liabilities	− 9 000 00		—		− 9 000 00		—		—		—
Balances after payment of liabilities	$ 74 000 00		$ 0		$ 0		$ 26 000 00		$ 24 400 00		$ 23 600 00
Cash distributed to partners	− 74 000 00		—		—		− 26 000 00		− 24 400 00		− 23 600 00
Final balances	$ 0		$ 0		$ 0		$ 0		$ 0		$ 0

The entries to record the steps in the liquidating process are as follows:

Sale of assets:

LLC Alternative

Cash	72,000	
Noncash Assets		64,000
Gain on Realization		8,000

Cash	72 000 00	
Noncash Assets		64 000 00
Gain on Realization		8 000 00

Division of gain:

LLC Alternative

Gain on Realization	8,000	
Jean Farley, Member Equity		4,000
Brad Greene, Member Equity		2,400
Alice Hall, Member Equity		1,600

Gain on Realization	8 0 0 0 00	
Jean Farley, Capital		4 0 0 0 00
Brad Greene, Capital		2 4 0 0 00
Alice Hall, Capital		1 6 0 0 00

Payment of liabilities:

LLC Alternative

Liabilities	9,000	
Cash		9,000

Liabilities	9 0 0 0 00	
Cash		9 0 0 0 00

Distribution of cash to partners:

LLC Alternative

Jean Farley, Member Equity	26,000	
Brad Greene, Member Equity	24,400	
Alice Hall, Member Equity	23,600	
Cash		74,000

Jean Farley, Capital	26 0 0 0 00	
Brad Greene, Capital	24 4 0 0 00	
Alice Hall, Capital	23 6 0 0 00	
Cash		74 0 0 0 00

As shown in Exhibit 5, the cash is distributed to the partners based on the balances of their capital accounts. These balances are determined after the gain on realization has been divided among the partners. *The income-sharing ratio should not be used as a basis for distributing the cash to partners.*

LOSS ON REALIZATION

Assume that in the preceding example, Farley, Greene, and Hall dispose of all noncash assets for $44,000. A loss of $20,000 ($64,000 − $44,000) is realized. The steps in liquidating the partnership are summarized in Exhibit 6.

EXHIBIT 6 **Loss on Realization**

Farley, Greene, and Hall
Statement of Partnership Liquidation
For Period April 10–30, 2008

	Cash +	Noncash Assets =	Liabilities +	Capital Farley (50%) +	Greene (30%) +	Hall (20%)
Balances before realization	$ 11 000 00	$ 64 000 00	$ 9 000 00	$ 22 000 00	$ 22 000 00	$ 22 000 00
Sale of assets and division of loss	+ 44 000 00	− 64 000 00	—	− 10 000 00	− 6 000 00	− 4 000 00
Balances after realization	$ 55 000 00	$ 0	$ 9 000 00	$ 12 000 00	$ 16 000 00	$ 18 000 00
Payment of liabilities	− 9 000 00	—	− 9 000 00			
Balances after payment of liabilities	$ 46 000 00	$ 0	$ 0	$ 12 000 00	$ 16 000 00	$ 18 000 00
Cash distributed to partners	− 46 000 00	—	—	− 12 000 00	− 16 000 00	− 18 000 00
Final balances	$ 0	$ 0	$ 0	$ 0	$ 0	$ 0

The entries to liquidate the partnership are as follows:

Sale of assets:

LLC Alternative

Cash	44,000
Loss on Realization	20,000
Noncash Assets	64,000

Cash	44 0 0 0 00	
Loss on Realization	20 0 0 0 00	
Noncash Assets		64 0 0 0 00

Division of loss:

LLC Alternative

Jean Farley, Member Equity	10,000
Brad Greene, Member Equity	6,000
Alice Hall, Member Equity	4,000
Loss on Realization	20,000

Jean Farley, Capital	10 0 0 0 00	
Brad Greene, Capital	6 0 0 0 00	
Alice Hall, Capital	4 0 0 0 00	
Loss on Realization		20 0 0 0 00

Payment of liabilities:

LLC Alternative

Liabilities	9,000
Cash	9,000

Liabilities	9 0 0 0 00	
Cash		9 0 0 0 00

Distribution of cash to partners:

LLC Alternative

Jean Farley, Member Equity	12,000
Brad Greene, Member Equity	16,000
Alice Hall, Member Equity	18,000
Cash	46,000

Jean Farley, Capital	12 0 0 0 00	
Brad Greene, Capital	16 0 0 0 00	
Alice Hall, Capital	18 0 0 0 00	
Cash		46 0 0 0 00

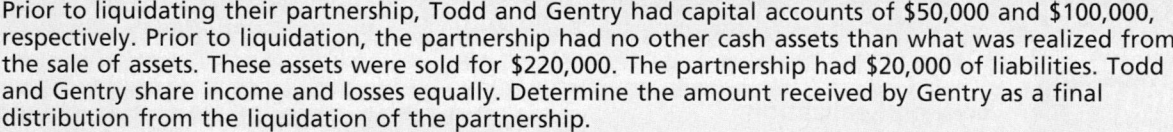

Example Exercise 12-5   objective 4

Prior to liquidating their partnership, Todd and Gentry had capital accounts of $50,000 and $100,000, respectively. Prior to liquidation, the partnership had no other cash assets than what was realized from the sale of assets. These assets were sold for $220,000. The partnership had $20,000 of liabilities. Todd and Gentry share income and losses equally. Determine the amount received by Gentry as a final distribution from the liquidation of the partnership.

Follow My Example 12-5

Gentry's equity prior to liquidation		$100,000
Realization of asset sale	$220,000	
Book value of assets ($50,000 + $100,000 + $20,000)	170,000	
Gain on liquidation	$ 50,000	
Gentry's share of gain (50% × $50,000)		25,000
Gentry's cash distribution		$125,000

For Practice: PE 12-5A, PE 12-5B

LOSS ON REALIZATION—CAPITAL DEFICIENCY

In the preceding example, the capital account of each partner was large enough to absorb the partner's share of the loss from realization. The partners received cash to the extent of the remaining balances in their capital accounts. The share of loss on realization may exceed, however, the balance in the partner's capital account. The resulting debit balance in the capital account is called a **deficiency**. It represents a claim of the partnership against the partner.

To illustrate, assume that Farley, Greene, and Hall sell all of the noncash assets for $10,000. A loss of $54,000 ($64,000 − $10,000) is realized. The share of the loss allocated to Farley, $27,000 (50% of $54,000), exceeds the $22,000 balance in her capital account. This $5,000 deficiency represents an amount that Farley owes the partnership. Assuming that Farley pays the entire deficiency to the partnership, sufficient cash is available to distribute to the remaining partners according to their capital balances. The steps in liquidating the partnership in this case are summarized in Exhibit 7.

EXHIBIT 7   Loss on Realization—Capital Deficiency

Farley, Greene, and Hall
Statement of Partnership Liquidation
For Period April 10–30, 2008

	Cash +	Noncash Assets =	Liabilities +	Capital Farley (50%) +	Greene (30%) +	Hall (20%)
Balances before realization	$ 11 000 00	$ 64 000 00	$ 9 000 00	$ 22 000 00	$ 22 000 00	$ 22 000 00
Sale of assets and division of loss	+ 10 000 00	− 64 000 00	—	− 27 000 00	− 16 200 00	− 10 800 00
Balances after realization	$ 21 000 00	$ 0	$ 9 000 00	$ (5 000 00)	$ 5 800 00	$ 11 200 00
Payment of liabilities	− 9 000 00	—	− 9 000 00	—	—	—
Balances after payment of liabilities	$ 12 000 00	$ 0	$ 0	$ (5 000 00)	$ 5 800 00	$ 11 200 00
Receipt of deficiency	+ 5 000 00	—	—	+ 5 000 00	—	—
Balances	$ 17 000 00	$ 0	$ 0	$ 0	$ 5 800 00	$ 11 200 00
Cash distributed to partners	− 17 000 00	—	—	—	− 5 800 00	− 11 200 00
Final balances	$ 0	$ 0	$ 0	$ 0	$ 0	$ 0

The entries to record the liquidation are as follows:

Sale of assets:

LLC Alternative		
Cash	10,000	
Loss on Realization	54,000	
Noncash Assets		64,000

Cash		10 000 00	
Loss on Realization		54 000 00	
Noncash Assets			64 000 00

Division of loss:

LLC Alternative		
Jean Farley, Member Equity	27,000	
Brad Greene, Member Equity	16,200	
Alice Hall, Member Equity	10,800	
Loss on Realization		54,000

Jean Farley, Capital		27 000 00	
Brad Greene, Capital		16 200 00	
Alice Hall, Capital		10 800 00	
Loss on Realization			54 000 00

Payment of liabilities:

LLC Alternative		
Liabilities	9,000	
Cash		9,000

Liabilities		9 000 00	
Cash			9 000 00

Receipt of deficiency:

LLC Alternative		
Cash	5,000	
Jean Farley, Member Equity		5,000

	Cash		5 0 0 0 00	
	Jean Farley, Capital			5 0 0 0 00

Distribution of cash to partners:

LLC Alternative		
Brad Greene, Member Equity	5,800	
Alice Hall, Member Equity	11,200	
Cash		17,000

	Brad Greene, Capital		5 8 0 0 00	
	Alice Hall, Capital		11 2 0 0 00	
	Cash			17 0 0 0 00

If cash is not collected from a deficient partner, the partnership cash will not be large enough to pay the other partners in full. Any uncollected deficiency becomes a loss to the partnership and is divided among the remaining partners' capital balances, based on their income-sharing ratio. The cash balance will then equal the sum of the capital account balances. Cash is then distributed to the remaining partners, based on the balances of their capital accounts.[7]

ERRORS IN LIQUIDATION

The most common error that occurs in liquidating a partnership is making an improper distribution of cash to the partners. Such an error occurs because the distribution of cash to partners in liquidation is confused with the division of gains and losses on realization.

Gains and losses on realization result from the disposal of assets to outsiders. *Realized gains and losses should be divided among the partner capital accounts in the same manner as the net income or net loss from normal business operations—using the income-sharing ratio.* On the other hand, the distribution of cash (or other assets) to the partners in liquidation is not directly related to the income-sharing ratio. The distribution of assets to the partners in liquidation is the exact reverse of the contribution of assets by the partners at the time the partnership was established. *The distribution of assets to partners in liquidation is equal to the credit balances in their capital accounts after all gains and losses on realization have been divided and allowances have been made for any partner deficiencies.*

Example Exercise 12-6

Prior to liquidating their partnership, Short and Bain had capital accounts of $20,000 and $80,000, respectively. The partnership assets were sold for $40,000. The partnership had no liabilities. Short and Bain share income and losses equally.

a. Determine the amount of Short's deficiency.
b. Determine the amount distributed to Bain, assuming Short is unable to satisfy the deficiency.

(continued)

---

7 The accounting for uncollectible deficiencies is discussed and illustrated in advanced accounting texts.

Follow My Example 12-6

a. Short's equity prior to liquidation		$ 20,000
Realization of asset sale	$ 40,000	
Book value of assets ($20,000 + $80,000)	100,000	
Loss on liquidation	$ 60,000	
Short's share of loss (50% × $60,000)		30,000
Short's deficiency		$(10,000)

b. $40,000. $80,000 − $30,000 share of loss − $10,000 Short deficiency, also equals the amount realized from asset sales.

For Practice: PE 12-6A, PE 12-6B

Statement of Partnership Equity

objective 5

Prepare the statement of partnership equity.

Reporting changes in partnership capital accounts is similar to that for a proprietorship, except that there is an owner's capital account for each partner. The change in the owners' capital accounts for a period of time is reported in a **statement of partnership equity**. Exhibit 8 illustrates the disclosure for Investors Associates, a partnership of Dan Cross and Kelly Baker. The statement of partnership equity discloses each partner's capital account in the columns and the reasons for the change in capital in the rows. The capital account for each partner can change due to capital additions, net income, or withdrawals, as illustrated previously in this chapter. Note that the net income distributed to the partners need not be withdrawn. Net income that is not withdrawn remains a permanent part of the partner's capital until withdrawn at a later date, sold, or liquidated.

EXHIBIT 8

Statement of Partnership Equity

	Investors Associates Statement of Partnership Equity For the Year Ended December 31, 2008		
	Dan Cross, Capital	Kelly Baker, Capital	Total Partnership Capital
Balance, January 1, 2008	$245 0 0 0	$365 0 0 0	$610 0 0 0
Capital additions	50 0 0 0		50 0 0 0
Net income for the year	40 0 0 0	80 0 0 0	120 0 0 0
Less partner withdrawals	(5 0 0 0)	(45 0 0 0)	(50 0 0 0)
Balance, December 31, 2008	$330 0 0 0	$400 0 0 0	$730 0 0 0

The equity reporting for an LLC is similar to that of a partnership. Instead of a statement of partnership capital, a statement of members' equity is prepared. The **statement of members' equity** discloses the changes in member equity for a period. The disclosure would be very similar to Exhibit 8, except that the columns would be the members of the LLC rather than partners.

Financial Analysis and Interpretation

Some partnerships (LLCs) are service-oriented enterprises. This is the case for some professions, such as accounting. The performance of such firms can be measured by the amount of net income per partner, as illustrated in this chapter. Another measure used to assess the performance of service-oriented partnerships (LLCs) is *revenue per employee*. The definition of "employee" can be adjusted to suit the analysis, but often includes the partners of the firm. Revenue per employee may be used as a measure of partnership (LLC) efficiency. Revenues are a measure of "outcomes." The number of people in a service firm is a measure of the critical "effort" in earning those revenues. Thus, the ratio of the two is a type of outcome-effort, or efficiency, ratio. To illustrate, assume that Washburn & Lovett, CPAs, had the following information for the last two years:

	2008	2007
Revenues	$220,000,000	$180,000,000
Number of employees	1,600	1,500

For Washburn & Lovett, this ratio can be computed for 2008 and 2007 as follows:

$$\text{Revenue per employee, 2008:} \quad \frac{\$220,000,000}{1,600} = \$137,500$$

$$\text{Revenue per employee, 2007:} \quad \frac{\$180,000,000}{1,500} = \$120,000$$

Washburn & Lovett improved revenues from $180 million in 2007, to $220 million in 2008. The revenue per employee showed improvement, from $120,000 to $137,500 per employee. This suggests that the firm increased employees at a slower rate than the increase in revenues. Thus, each employee is producing more revenues in 2008 than in 2007, which may indicate improved productivity. Overall, it appears that the firm is properly managing the growth in staff.

At a Glance

1. Describe the basic characteristics of proprietorships, partnerships, and limited liability companies.

Key Points	Key Learning Outcomes	Example Exercises	Practice Exercises
The advantages and disadvantages of proprietorships, partnerships, and limited liability companies with regard to ease of formation, legal liability, taxation, limitation on life of entity, and access to capital were identified in Exhibit 1.	• Identify the advantages and disadvantages of proprietorships, partnerships, and limited liability companies.		

2. Describe and illustrate the accounting for forming a partnership and for dividing the net income and net loss of a partnership.

Key Points	Key Learning Outcomes	Example Exercises	Practice Exercises
When a partnership is formed, accounts are debited for contributed assets and credited for assumed liabilities, and the partner's capital account is credited for the net amount. The net income of a partnership may be divided among the partners on the basis of services rendered, interest earned on the capital account balance, and the income-sharing ratio.	• Journalize the initial formation of a partnership and establish partner capital.	**12-1**	12-1A, 12-1B
	• Determine and journalize the income distributed to each partner.	**12-2**	12-2A, 12-2B

3. Describe and illustrate the accounting for partner admission and withdrawal.

Key Points	Key Learning Outcomes	Example Exercises	Practice Exercises
Partnership assets should be restated to current values prior to admission or withdrawal of a partner. A new partner may be admitted into a partnership by either purchasing an interest from an existing partner or by purchasing an interest directly from the partnership.	• Prepare for partner admission by revaluing assets to approximate current values.	**12-3**	12-3A, 12-3B
	• Distinguish between partner admission through purchase from an existing partner or purchase from the partnership.		
	• Determine partner bonuses.	**12-4**	12-4A, 12-4B

4. Describe and illustrate the accounting for liquidating a partnership.

Key Points	Key Learning Outcomes	Example Exercises	Practice Exercises
A partnership is liquidated by the (1) sale of partnership assets (realization), (2) distribution of gain or loss on realization to the partners, (3) payments to creditors, and (4) distribution of the remaining cash to partners according to their capital account balances. A partner may be deficient when the amount of loss distribution exceeds the capital balance.	• Apply the four steps of liquidating a partnership for either gain or loss upon realization.	**12-5**	12-5A, 12-5B
	• Apply the steps of partnership liquidation when there is a partner deficiency.	**12-6**	12-6A, 12-6B

5. Prepare the statement of partnership equity.

Key Points	Key Learning Outcomes	Example Exercises	Practice Exercises
A statement of partnership equity reports the changes in partnership equity from capital additions, net income, and withdrawals. Net income is added based upon the income distribution method identified in the partnership agreement, regardless of whether or not the net income is distributed in cash.	• Prepare a statement of partnership equity.		

Key Terms

deficiency (543)
limited liability company (LLC)
   (528)
liquidation (539)
partnership (527)

partnership agreement (527)
realization (539)
statement of members' equity
   (545)

statement of partnership equity
   (545)
statement of partnership
   liquidation (540)

Illustrative Problem

Radcliffe, Sonders, and Towers, who share in income and losses in the ratio of 2:3:5, decided to discontinue operations as of April 30 and liquidate their partnership. After the accounts were closed on April 30, the following trial balance was prepared:

Cash	5,900	
Noncash Assets	109,900	
Liabilities		26,800
Radcliffe, Capital		14,600
Sonders, Capital		27,900
Towers, Capital		46,500
	115,800	115,800

Between May 1 and May 18, the noncash assets were sold for $27,400, and the liabilities were paid.

Instructions

1. Assuming that the partner with the capital deficiency pays the entire amount owed to the partnership, prepare a statement of partnership liquidation.
2. Journalize the entries to record (a) the sale of the assets, (b) the division of loss on the sale of the assets, (c) the payment of the liabilities, (d) the receipt of the deficiency, and (e) the distribution of cash to the partners.

Solution

1.

Radcliff, Sonders, and Towers
Statement of Partnership Liquidation
For Period May 1–18, 2008

	Cash	+	Noncash Assets	=	Liabilities	+	Capital Radcliff (20%)	+	Sonders (30%)	+	Towers (50%)
Balances before realization	$ 5,900.00		$ 109,900.00		$ 26,800.00		$ 14,600.00		$ 27,900.00		$ 46,500.00
Sale of assets and division of loss	+ 27,400.00		– 109,900.00		—		– 16,500.00		– 24,750.00		– 41,250.00
Balances after realization	$ 33,300.00		$		$ 26,800.00 0		$ (1,900.00)		$ 3,150.00		$ 5,250.00
Payment of liabilities	– 26,800.00				— – 26,800.00		—		—		—
Balances after payment of liabilities	$ 6,500.00		$ 0		$ 0		$ (1,900.00)		$ 3,150.00		$ 5,250.00
Receipt of deficiency	+ 1,900.00		—		—		+ 1,900.00		—		—
Balances	$ 8,400.00		$ 0		$ 0		$ 0		$ 3,150.00		$ 5,250.00
Cash distributed to partners	– 8,400.00		—		—		—		– 3,150.00		– 5,250.00
Final balances	$ 0		$ 0		$ 0		$ 0		$ 0		$ 0

2. a.

Cash		27 4 0 0 00	
Loss on Realization		82 5 0 0 00	
Noncash Assets			109 9 0 0 00

b.

Radcliffe, Capital		16 5 0 0 00	
Sonders, Capital		24 7 5 0 00	
Towers, Capital		41 2 5 0 00	
Loss on Realization			82 5 0 0 00

c.

Liabilities		26 8 0 0 00	
Cash			26 8 0 0 00

d.

Cash		1 9 0 0 00	
Radcliffe, Capital			1 9 0 0 00

e.

Sonders, Capital		3 1 5 0 00	
Towers, Capital		5 2 5 0 00	
Cash			8 4 0 0 00

Self-Examination Questions

(Answers at End of Chapter)

1. As part of the initial investment, a partner contributes office equipment that had cost $20,000 and on which accumulated depreciation of $12,500 had been recorded. If the partners agree on a valuation of $9,000 for the equipment, what amount should be debited to the office equipment account?
   A. $7,500   C. $12,500
   B. $9,000   D. $20,000

2. Chip and Dale agree to form a partnership. Chip is to contribute $50,000 in assets and to devote one-half time to the partnership. Dale is to contribute $20,000 and to devote full time to the partnership. How will Chip and Dale share in the division of net income or net loss?
   A. 5:2   C. 1:1
   B. 1:2   D. 2.5:1

3. Tracey and Hepburn invest $100,000 and $50,000, respectively, in a partnership and agree to a division of net income that provides for an allowance of interest at 10% on original investments, salary allowances of $12,000 and $24,000, respectively, with the remainder divided equally. What would be Tracey's share of a net income of $45,000?
   A. $22,500   C. $19,000
   B. $22,000   D. $10,000

4. Lee and Stills are partners who share income in the ratio of 2:1 and who have capital balances of $65,000 and $35,000, respectively. If Morr, with the consent of Stills, acquired one-half of Lee's interest for $40,000, for what amount would Morr's capital account be credited?
   A. $32,500   C. $50,000
   B. $40,000   D. $72,500

5. Pavin and Abdel share gains and losses in the ratio of 2:1. After selling all assets for cash, dividing the losses on realization, and paying liabilities, the balances in the capital accounts were as follows: Pavin, $10,000 Cr.; Abdel, $2,000 Cr. How much of the cash of $12,000 would be distributed to Pavin?
   A. $2,000   C. $10,000
   B. $8,000   D. $12,000

Eye Openers

1. What are the main advantages of (a) proprietorships, (b) partnerships, and (c) limited liability companies?
2. What are the disadvantages of a partnership over a limited liability company form of organization for a profit-making business?
3. Emilio Álvarez and Graciela Zavala joined together to form a partnership. Is it possible for them to lose a greater amount than the amount of their investment in the partnership? Explain.
4. What are the major features of a partnership agreement for a partnership, or an operating agreement for a limited liability company?
5. In the absence of an agreement, how will the net income be distributed between Ethan Arnold and Tessa Winthrop, partners in the firm of A and W Environmental Engineering?
6. Josiah Barlow, Patty DuMont, and Owen Maholic are contemplating the formation of a partnership. According to the partnership agreement, Barlow is to invest $60,000 and devote one-half time, DuMont is to invest $40,000 and devote three-fourths time, and Maholic is to make no investment and devote full time. Would Maholic be correct in assuming that, since he is not contributing any assets to the firm, he is risking nothing? Explain.
7. As a part of the initial investment, a partner contributes delivery equipment that had originally cost $50,000 and on which accumulated depreciation of $37,500 had been recorded. The partners agree on a valuation of $10,000. How should the delivery equipment be recorded in the accounts of the partnership?
8. All partners agree that $150,000 of accounts receivable invested by a partner will be collectible to the extent of 90%. How should the accounts receivable be recorded in the general ledger of the partnership?
9. During the current year, Marsha Engles withdrew $4,000 monthly from the partnership of Engles and Cox Water Management Consultants. Is it possible that her share of partnership net income for the current year might be more or less than $48,000? Explain.
10. a. What accounts are debited and credited to record a partner's cash withdrawal in lieu of salary?
    b. The articles of partnership provide for a salary allowance of $6,000 per month to partner C. If C withdrew only $4,000 per month, would this affect the division of the partnership net income?
    c. At the end of the fiscal year, what accounts are debited and credited to record the division of net income among partners?
11. Explain the difference between the admission of a new partner to a partnership (a) by purchase of an interest from another partner and (b) by contribution of assets to the partnership.
12. Why is it important to state all partnership assets in terms of current prices at the time of the admission of a new partner?
13. Why might a partnership pay a bonus to a newly admitted partner?
14. In the liquidation process, (a) how are losses and gains on realization divided among the partners, and (b) how is cash distributed among the partners?
15. How is the statement of members' equity similar to the statement of partners' equity?

Practice Exercises

PE 12-1A
*Journalize partner's
original investment*

obj. 2

Conway Shelton contributed land, inventory, and $58,000 cash to a partnership. The land had a book value of $40,000 and a market value of $68,000. The inventory had a book value of $50,000 and a market value of $45,000. The partnership also assumed a $20,000 note payable owed by Shelton that was used originally to purchase the land.

Provide the journal entry for Shelton's contribution to the partnership.

PE 12-1B
Journalize partner's original investment
obj. 2

Ashley Wells contributed a patent, accounts receivable, and $15,000 cash to a partnership. The patent had a book value of $35,000. However, the technology covered by the patent appeared to have significant market potential. Thus, the patent was appraised at $280,000. The accounts receivable control account was $22,000, with an allowance for doubtful accounts of $1,000. The partnership also assumed an $8,000 account payable from Wells.
    Provide the journal entry for Wells's contribution to the partnership.

PE 12-2A
Dividing partnership net income
obj. 2

Blaine Pierce and Meg Adkins formed a partnership, dividing income as follows:

1. Annual salary allowance to Adkins of $49,000.
2. Interest of 12% on each partner's capital balance on January 1.
3. Any remaining net income divided equally.

Pierce and Adkins had $40,000 and $120,000, respectively, in their January 1 capital balances. Net income for the year was $180,000.
    How much net income should be distributed to Adkins?

PE 12-2B
Dividing partnership net income
obj. 2

Kenny Lodge and Lisa Lane formed a partnership, dividing income as follows:

1. Annual salary allowance to Lodge of $54,000.
2. Interest of 10% on each partner's capital balance on January 1.
3. Any remaining net income divided to Lodge and Lane, 2:1.

Lodge and Lane had $100,000 and $200,000, respectively, in their January 1 capital balances. Net income for the year was $60,000.
    How much net income should be distributed to Lodge?

PE 12-3A
Revalue assets and contribute assets to a partnership
obj. 3

Devin Morris invested $28,000 in the Townley and Starr partnership for ownership equity of $28,000. Prior to the investment, equipment was revalued to a market value of $100,000 from a book value of $85,000. Stuart Townley and Ayesha Starr share net income in a 2:1 ratio.

a. Provide the journal entry for the revaluation of equipment.
b. Provide the journal entry to admit Morris.

PE 12-3B
Revalue assets and purchase an interest in a partnership
obj. 3

Lane Tway purchased one-half of Craig Little's interest in the Browne and Little partnership for $18,000. Prior to the investment, land was revalued to a market value of $140,000 from a book value of $115,000. Leon Browne and Craig Little share net income equally. Little had a capital balance of $18,000 prior to these transactions.

a. Provide the journal entry for the revaluation of land.
b. Provide the journal entry to admit Tway.

PE 12-4A
Partner bonus
obj. 3

Masterson has a capital balance of $90,000 after adjusting assets to fair market value. Nutley contributes $50,000 to receive a 40% interest in a new partnership with Masterson.
    Determine the amount and recipient of the partner bonus.

PE 12-4B
Partner bonus
obj. 3

Porter has a capital balance of $420,000 after adjusting assets to fair market value. Billings contributes $200,000 to receive a 30% interest in a new partnership with Porter.
    Determine the amount and recipient of the partner bonus.

PE 12-5A
Liquidating partnerships—gain
obj. 4

Prior to liquidating their partnership, Chow and Wilder had capital accounts of $18,000 and $25,000, respectively. Prior to liquidation, the partnership had no cash assets other than what was realized from the sale of those assets. These partnership assets were sold for $46,000. The partnership had $1,000 of liabilities. Chow and Wilder share income and losses equally. Determine the amount received by Chow as a final distribution from liquidation of the partnership.

PE 12-5B
Liquidating partnerships—loss
obj. 4

Prior to liquidating their partnership, Dickens and Thomas had capital accounts of $55,000 and $45,000, respectively. Prior to liquidation, the partnership had no cash assets other than what was realized from the sale of those assets. These partnership assets were sold for $75,000. The partnership had $10,000 of liabilities. Dickens and Thomas share income and losses equally. Determine the amount received by Dickens as a final distribution from liquidation of the partnership.

PE 12-6A
Liquidating partnerships—deficiency
obj. 4

Prior to liquidating their partnership, Martin and Abbott had capital accounts of $8,000 and $20,000, respectively. The partnership assets were sold for $5,000. The partnership had no liabilities. Martin and Abbott share income and losses equally.

a. Determine the amount of Martin's deficiency.
b. Determine the amount distributed to Abbott, assuming Martin is unable to satisfy the deficiency.

PE 12-6B
Liquidating partnerships—deficiency
obj. 4

Prior to liquidating their partnership, Knight and Mee had capital accounts of $120,000 and $40,000, respectively. The partnership assets were sold for $50,000. The partnership had no liabilities. Knight and Mee share income and losses equally.

a. Determine the amount of Mee's deficiency.
b. Determine the amount distributed to Knight, assuming Mee is unable to satisfy the deficiency.

Exercises

EX 12-1
Record partner's original investment
obj. 2

Lamar Kline and Kevin Lambert decide to form a partnership by combining the assets of their separate businesses. Kline contributes the following assets to the partnership: cash, $10,000; accounts receivable with a face amount of $123,000 and an allowance for doubtful accounts of $7,300; merchandise inventory with a cost of $85,000; and equipment with a cost of $140,000 and accumulated depreciation of $90,000.

The partners agree that $5,000 of the accounts receivable are completely worthless and are not to be accepted by the partnership, that $8,100 is a reasonable allowance for the uncollectibility of the remaining accounts, that the merchandise inventory is to be recorded at the current market price of $74,300, and that the equipment is to be valued at $67,000.

Journalize the partnership's entry to record Kline's investment.

EX 12-2
Record partner's original investment
obj. 2

Ron Maples and Mei Cui form a partnership by combining assets of their former businesses. The following balance sheet information is provided by Maples, sole proprietorship:

Cash		$ 30,000
Accounts receivable	$65,000	
Less: Allowance for doubtful accounts	3,200	61,800
Land		120,000
Equipment	$60,000	
Less: Accumulated depreciation—equipment	36,000	24,000
Total assets		$235,800
Accounts payable		$ 18,000
Notes payable		45,000
Ron Maples, capital		172,800
Total liabilities and owner's equity		$235,800

Maples obtained appraised values for the land and equipment as follows:

Land	$165,000
Equipment	10,000

An analysis of the accounts receivable indicated that the allowance for doubtful accounts should be increased to $5,000.

Journalize the partnership's entry for Maples's investment.

EX 12-3
Dividing partnership income
obj. 2
✓ b. Haley, $112,500

Gale Haley and Leah Manos formed a partnership, investing $180,000 and $60,000 respectively. Determine their participation in the year's net income of $150,000 under each of the following independent assumptions: (a) no agreement concerning division of net income; (b) divided in the ratio of original capital investment; (c) interest at the rate of 10% allowed on original investments and the remainder divided in the ratio of 2:3; (d) salary allowances of $45,000 and $60,000 respectively, and the balance divided equally; (e) allowance of interest at the rate of 10% on original investments, salary allowances of $45,000 and $60,000 respectively, and the remainder divided equally.

EX 12-4
Dividing partnership income
obj. 2
✓ c. Haley, $104,400

Determine the income participation of Haley and Manos, according to each of the five assumptions as to income division listed in Exercise 12-3 if the year's net income is $240,000.

EX 12-5
Dividing partnership net loss
obj. 2

Curt Kelly and Greg Kaufman formed a partnership in which the partnership agreement provided for salary allowances of $45,000 and $30,000, respectively. Determine the division of a $25,000 net loss for the current year.

EX 12-6
Negotiating income-sharing ratio
obj. 2

Sixty-year-old Jan Howard retired from her computer consulting business in Boston and moved to Florida. There she met 27-year-old Tami Galyon, who had just graduated from Eldon Community College with an associate degree in computer science. Jan and Tami formed a partnership called H&G Computer Consultants. Jan contributed $25,000 for startup costs and devoted one-half time to the business. Tami devoted full time to the business. The monthly drawings were $1,500 for Jan and $3,000 for Tami.

At the end of the first year of operations, the two partners disagreed on the division of net income. Jan reasoned that the division should be equal. Although she devoted only one-half time to the business, she contributed all of the startup funds. Tami reasoned that the income-sharing ratio should be 2:1 in her favor because she devoted full time to the business and her monthly drawings were twice those of Jan.

Can you identify any flaws in the partners' reasoning regarding the income-sharing ratio?

EX 12-7
Dividing LLC income
obj. 2
✓ a. Gardner, $77,200

LaToya Gardner and Lamar Ross formed a limited liability company (LLC) with an operating agreement that provided a salary allowance of $58,000 and $42,000 to each member, respectively. In addition, the operating agreement specified an income-sharing ratio of 3:2. The two members withdrew amounts equal to their salary allowances.

a. Determine the division of $132,000 net income for the year.
b. Provide journal entries to close the (1) income summary and (2) drawing accounts for the two members.

EX 12-8
Dividing LLC net income and statement of members' equity
objs. 2, 5
✓ a. Sizemore, $261,500

Media Properties, LLC, has three members: KXT Radio Partners, Rachel Sizemore, and Daily Sun Newspaper, LLC. On January 1, 2008, the three members had equity of $240,000, $40,000, and $160,000, respectively. KXT Radio Partners contributed an additional $50,000 to Media Properties, LLC, on June 1, 2008. Rachel Sizemore received an annual salary allowance of $139,800 during 2008. The members' equity accounts are also credited with 8% interest on each member's January 1 capital balance. Any remaining income is to be shared in the ratio of 4:3:3 among the three members. The net income for Media

Properties, LLC, for 2008 was $570,000. The salary and interest allowances were distributed to the members.

a. Determine the division of income among the three members.
b. Prepare the journal entry to close the net income and withdrawals to the individual member equity accounts.
c. Prepare a statement of members' equity for 2008.

EX 12-9
Partner income and withdrawal journal entries
objs. 2, 3

The notes to the annual report for KPMG LLP (U.K.) indicated the following policies regarding the partners' capital:

The allocation of profits to those who were partners during the financial year occurs following the finalization of the annual financial statements. During the year, partners receive monthly drawings and, from time to time, additional profit distributions. Both the monthly drawings and profit distributions represent payments on account of current-year profits and are reclaimable from partners until profits have been allocated.

Assume that the partners draw £25,000 million per month for 2008 and the net income for the year is £350 million. Journalize the partner capital and partner drawing control accounts in the following requirements.

a. Provide the journal entry for the monthly partner drawing for January.
b. Provide the journal entry to close the income summary account at the end of the year.
c. Provide the journal entry to close the drawing account at the end of the year.

EX 12-10
Admitting new partners
obj. 3

Charles Shivers and Gong Zhao are partners who share in the income equally and have capital balances of $120,000 and $62,500, respectively. Shivers, with the consent of Zhao, sells one-third of his interest to Theresa Pepin. What entry is required by the partnership if the sales price is (a) $30,000? (b) $50,000?

EX 12-11
Admitting new partners
obj. 3

The public accounting firm of Grant Thornton LLP disclosed global revenues of $2.45 billion for a recent year. The revenues were attributable to 2,090 active partners.

a. What was the average revenue per partner? Round to the nearest $1,000.
b. Assuming that the total partners' capital is $360,000,000 and that it approximates the fair market value of the firm's net assets, what would be considered a minimum contribution for admitting a new partner to the firm, assuming no bonus is paid to the new partner? Round to the nearest $1,000.
c. Why might the amount to be contributed by a new partner for admission to the firm exceed the amount determined in (b)?

EX 12-12
Admitting new partners who buy an interest and contribute assets
obj. 3
✓ b. Perry, $80,000

The capital accounts of Kris Perry and Melvin Newman have balances of $100,000 and $90,000, respectively. Paul Lester and Steve Hurd are to be admitted to the partnership. Lester buys one-fifth of Perry's interest for $30,000 and one-fourth of Newman's interest for $15,000. Hurd contributes $40,000 cash to the partnership, for which he is to receive an ownership equity of $40,000.

a. Journalize the entries to record the admission of (1) Lester and (2) Hurd.
b. What are the capital balances of each partner after the admission of the new partners?

EX 12-13
Admitting new partner who contributes assets
obj. 3
✓ b. Estavez, $62,000

After the tangible assets have been adjusted to current market prices, the capital accounts of Mike Heil and Alan Delong have balances of $75,000 and $85,000, respectively. Felix Estavez is to be admitted to the partnership, contributing $50,000 cash to the partnership, for which he is to receive an ownership equity of $62,000. All partners share equally in income.

a. Journalize the entry to record the admission of Estavez, who is to receive a bonus of $12,000.
b. What are the capital balances of each partner after the admission of the new partner?

EX 12-14
Admitting a new LLC member

obj. 3

✓ *b. (2) Bonus paid to Kopp, $30,000*

Health Source Medical, LLC, consists of two doctors, Dobbs and Fox, who share in all income and losses according to a 2:3 income-sharing ratio. Dr. Lindsey Kopp has been asked to join the LLC. Prior to admitting Kopp, the assets of Health Source were revalued to reflect their current market values. The revaluation resulted in medical equipment being increased by $20,000. Prior to the revaluation, the equity balances for Dobbs and Fox were $300,000 and $325,000, respectively.

a. Provide the journal entry for the asset revaluation.
b. Provide the journal entry for the bonus under the following independent situations:
    1. Kopp purchased a 30% interest in Health Source Medical, LLC, for $310,000.
    2. Kopp purchased a 25% interest in Health Source Medical, LLC, for $175,000.

EX 12-15
Admitting new partner with bonus

obj. 3

b. (1) Bonus paid to Holden, $6,800

J. Trifilio and K. Graham are partners in Enviro-Tek Consultants. Trifilio and Graham share income equally. L. Holden will be admitted to the partnership. Prior to the admission, equipment was revalued downward by $6,000. The capital balances of each partner are $90,000 and $150,000, respectively, prior to the revaluation.

a. Provide the journal entry for the asset revaluation.
b. Provide the journal entry for Holden's admission under the following independent situations:
    1. Holden purchased a 20% interest for $50,000.
    2. Holden purchased a 30% interest for $125,000.

EX 12-16
Partner bonuses, statement of partners' equity

objs. 2, 3, 5

✓ *Strous capital, Dec. 31, 2008, $74,800*

The partnership of Angel Investor Associates began operations on January 1, 2008, with contributions from two partners as follows:

Jan Strous	$36,000
Lisa Lankford	84,000

    The following additional partner transactions took place during the year:

1. In early January, Sarah Rogers is admitted to the partnership by contributing $30,000 cash for a 20% interest.
2. Net income of $140,000 was earned in 2008. In addition, Jan Strous received a salary allowance of $25,000 for the year. The three partners agree to an income-sharing ratio equal to their capital balances after admitting Rogers.
3. The partners' withdrawals are equal to half of the increase in their capital balances resulting from income remaining after salary allowances.

    Prepare a statement of partnership equity for the year ended December 31, 2008.

EX 12-17
Withdrawal of partner

obj. 3

Glenn Powell is to retire from the partnership of Powell and Associates as of March 31, the end of the current fiscal year. After closing the accounts, the capital balances of the partners are as follows: Glenn Powell, $260,000; Tammie Sawyer, $125,000; and Joe Patel, $140,000. They have shared net income and net losses in the ratio of 3:2:2. The partners agree that the merchandise inventory should be increased by $30,000, and the allowance for doubtful accounts should be increased by $6,200. Powell agrees to accept a note for $165,000 in partial settlement of his ownership equity. The remainder of his claim is to be paid in cash. Sawyer and Patel are to share equally in the net income or net loss of the new partnership.

    Journalize the entries to record (a) the adjustment of the assets to bring them into agreement with current market prices and (b) the withdrawal of Powell from the partnership.

EX 12-18
Statement of members' equity, admitting new member

objs. 2, 3, 5

The statement of members' equity for Aztec Mines, LLC, is shown at the top of the following page.

✓ *a. 1:3*

Aztec Mines, LLC
Statement of Members' Equity
For the Years Ended December 31, 2007 and 2008

	Utah Properties, LLC, Member Equity	Aztec Holdings, Ltd., Member Equity	Cleveland Porter, Member Equity	Total Members' Equity
Members' equity, January 1, 2007	$460,000	$310,000		$ 770,000
Net income	70,000	210,000		280,000
Members' equity, December 31, 2007	$530,000	$520,000		$1,050,000
Porter contribution	5,000	15,000	$267,500	287,500
Net income	78,400	254,800	58,800	392,000
Less member withdrawals	(32,000)	(48,000)	(50,000)	(130,000)
Members' equity, December 31, 2008	$581,400	$741,800	$276,300	$1,599,500

a. What was the income-sharing ratio in 2007?

b. What was the income-sharing ratio in 2008?

c. How much cash did Cleveland Porter contribute to Aztec Mines, LLC, for his interest?

d. Why do the member equity accounts of Utah Properties, LLC, and Aztec Holdings, Ltd., have positive entries for Cleveland Porter's contribution?

e. What percentage interest of Aztec Mines did Cleveland Porter acquire?

EX 12-19
Distribution of cash upon liquidation
obj. 4
✓ *a. $11,000 loss*

Pitt and Leon are partners, sharing gains and losses equally. They decide to terminate their partnership. Prior to realization, their capital balances are $15,000 and $20,000, respectively. After all noncash assets are sold and all liabilities are paid, there is a cash balance of $24,000.

a. What is the amount of a gain or loss on realization?

b. How should the gain or loss be divided between Pitt and Leon?

c. How should the cash be divided between Pitt and Leon?

EX 12-20
Distribution of cash upon liquidation
obj. 4
✓ *Boling, $31,000*

Jacob Boling and Harlan Bishop, with capital balances of $43,000 and $57,000, respectively, decide to liquidate their partnership. After selling the noncash assets and paying the liabilities, there is $76,000 of cash remaining. If the partners share income and losses equally, how should the cash be distributed?

EX 12-21
Liquidating partnerships—capital deficiency
obj. 4
✓ *b. $64,000*

Mawby, White, and Shelby share equally in net income and net losses. After the partnership sells all assets for cash, divides the losses on realization, and pays the liabilities, the balances in the capital accounts are as follows: Mawby, $21,000 Cr.; White, $57,500 Cr.; Shelby, $14,500 Dr.

a. What term is applied to the debit balance in Shelby's capital account?

b. What is the amount of cash on hand?

c. Journalize the transaction that must take place for Mawby and White to receive cash in the liquidation process equal to their capital account balances.

EX 12-22
Distribution of cash upon liquidation
obj. 4
✓ *a. Seth, $425*

Allyn Seth, Jim Kerr, and Laura Driver arranged to import and sell orchid corsages for a university dance. They agreed to share equally the net income or net loss of the venture. Seth and Kerr advanced $225 and $150 of their own respective funds to pay for advertising and other expenses. After collecting for all sales and paying creditors, the partnership has $975 in cash.

a. How should the money be distributed?

b. Assuming that the partnership has only $255 instead of $975, do any of the three partners have a capital deficiency? If so, how much?

EX 12-23
Liquidating partnerships—capital deficiency

obj. 4

Heinz, Dicer, and Ho are partners sharing income 3:2:1. After the firm's loss from liquidation is distributed, the capital account balances were: Heinz, $18,000 Dr.; Dicer, $70,000 Cr.; and Ho, $45,000 Cr. If Heinz is personally bankrupt and unable to pay any of the $18,000, what will be the amount of cash received by Dicer and Ho upon liquidation?

EX 12-24
Statement of partnership liquidation

obj. 4

After closing the accounts on July 1, prior to liquidating the partnership, the capital account balances of Dills, Gordon, and Chavez are $32,000, $40,000, and $15,000, respectively. Cash, noncash assets, and liabilities total $42,000, $90,000, and $45,000, respectively. Between July 1 and July 29, the noncash assets are sold for $66,000, the liabilities are paid, and the remaining cash is distributed to the partners. The partners share net income and loss in the ratio of 3:2:1. Prepare a statement of partnership liquidation for the period July 1–29.

EX 12-25
Statement of LLC liquidation

obj. 4

Gilley, Hughes, and Moussa are members of City Signs, LLC, sharing income and losses in the ratio of 2:2:1, respectively. The members decide to liquidate the limited liability company (LLC). The members' equity prior to liquidation and asset realization on March 1, 2008, are as follows:

Gilley	$ 19,000
Hughes	54,000
Moussa	32,000
Total	$105,000

In winding up operations during the month of March, noncash assets with a book value of $126,000 are sold for $146,000, and liabilities of $35,000 are satisfied. Prior to realization, City Signs has a cash balance of $14,000.

a. Prepare a statement of LLC liquidation.
b. Provide the journal entry for the final cash distribution to members.

EX 12-26
Partnership entries and statement of partners' equity

objs. 2, 5

✓ *b. Polivka, capital, Dec. 31, $145,000*

The capital accounts of Dal Polivka and Amanda Pratt have balances of $105,000 and $135,000, respectively, on January 1, 2008, the beginning of the current fiscal year. On April 10, Polivka invested an additional $15,000. During the year, Polivka and Pratt withdrew $65,000 and $76,000, respectively, and net income for the year was $180,000. The articles of partnership make no reference to the division of net income.

a. Journalize the entries to close (1) the income summary account and (2) the drawing accounts.
b. Prepare a statement of partners' equity for the current year for the partnership of Polivka and Pratt.

EX 12-27
Revenue per professional staff

The accounting firm of Deloitte & Touche is the largest international accounting firm in the world as ranked by total revenues. For the last two years, Deloitte & Touche reported the following for its U.S. operations:

	2005	2004
Revenues (in millions)	$ 7,814	$ 6,876
Number of professional staff (including partners)	26,401	22,841

a. For 2004 and 2005, determine the revenue per professional staff. Round to the nearest thousand dollars.
b. Interpret the trend between the two years.

EX 12-28
Revenue per employee

Crystal Clean Services, LLC, provides cleaning services for office buildings. The firm has 10 members in the LLC, which did not change between 2007 and 2008. During 2008, the business expanded into four new cities. The following revenue and employee information is provided:

	2008	2007
Revenues (in thousands)	$38,000	$32,500
Number of employees (excluding members)	380	260

a. For 2007 and 2008, determine the revenue per employee.
b. Interpret the trend between the two years.

Problems Series A

PR 12-1A
Entries and balance sheet for partnership
obj. 2

✓3. Polles net income, $35,000

On May 1, 2007, Crystal Polles and Doug Kovac form a partnership. Polles agrees to invest $16,500 in cash and merchandise inventory valued at $43,500. Kovac invests certain business assets at valuations agreed upon, transfers business liabilities, and contributes sufficient cash to bring his total capital to $50,000. Details regarding the book values of the business assets and liabilities, and the agreed valuations, follow:

	Kovac's Ledger Balance	Agreed-Upon Valuation
Accounts Receivable	$22,600	$19,100
Allowance for Doubtful Accounts	1,100	1,400
Equipment	86,400	53,300
Accumulated Depreciation—Equipment	29,300	
Accounts Payable	14,000	14,000
Notes Payable	20,000	20,000

The partnership agreement includes the following provisions regarding the division of net income: interest on original investments at 10%, salary allowances of $20,000 and $25,000, respectively, and the remainder equally.

Instructions
1. Journalize the entries to record the investments of Polles and Kovac in the partnership accounts.
2. Prepare a balance sheet as of May 1, 2007, the date of formation of the partnership of Polles and Kovac.
3. After adjustments and the closing of revenue and expense accounts at April 30, 2008, the end of the first full year of operations, the income summary account has a credit balance of $74,000, and the drawing accounts have debit balances of $22,000 (Polles) and $28,000 (Kovac). Journalize the entries to close the income summary account and the drawing accounts at April 30.

PR 12-2A
Dividing partnership income
obj. 2

✓1. f. Lange net income, $48,200

Lange and Lopez have decided to form a partnership. They have agreed that Lange is to invest $240,000 and that Lopez is to invest $80,000. Lange is to devote one-half time to the business and Lopez is to devote full time. The following plans for the division of income are being considered:

a. Equal division.
b. In the ratio of original investments.
c. In the ratio of time devoted to the business.
d. Interest of 12% on original investments and the remainder equally.
e. Interest of 12% on original investments, salary allowances of $35,000 to Lange and $70,000 to Lopez, and the remainder equally.

f. Plan (e), except that Lopez is also to be allowed a bonus equal to 20% of the amount by which net income exceeds the salary allowances.

Instructions

For each plan, determine the division of the net income under each of the following assumptions: (1) net income of $114,000 and (2) net income of $210,000. Present the data in tabular form, using the following columnar headings:

	$114,000		$210,000	
Plan	Lange	Lopez	Lange	Lopez

PR 12-3A
Financial statements for partnership

objs. 2, 5

✓ *2. Dec. 31 capital—Koening, $63,100*

The ledger of Peter Sato and May Koening, attorneys-at-law, contains the following accounts and balances after adjustments have been recorded on December 31, 2008:

	Debit Balances	Credit Balances
Cash	30,000	
Accounts Receivable	38,900	
Supplies	1,900	
Land	25,000	
Building	130,000	
Accumulated Depreciation—Building		69,200
Office Equipment	39,000	
Accumulated Depreciation—Office Equipment		21,500
Accounts Payable		2,100
Salaries Payable		2,000
Peter Sato, Capital		95,000
Peter Sato, Drawing	50,000	
May Koening, Capital		65,000
May Koening, Drawing	70,000	
Professional Fees		297,450
Salary Expense	132,300	
Depreciation Expense—Building	10,500	
Property Tax Expense	7,000	
Heating and Lighting Expense	6,300	
Supplies Expense	2,850	
Depreciation Expense—Office Equipment	2,800	
Miscellaneous Expense	5,700	
	552,250	552,250

The balance in Koening's capital account includes an additional investment of $8,000 made on August 10, 2008.

Instructions

1. Prepare an income statement for 2008, indicating the division of net income. The articles of partnership provide for salary allowances of $40,000 to Sato and $50,000 to Koening, allowances of 10% on each partner's capital balance at the beginning of the fiscal year, and equal division of the remaining net income or net loss.
2. Prepare a statement of partners' equity for 2008.
3. Prepare a balance sheet as of the end of 2008.

PR 12-4A
Admitting new partner

obj. 3

✓ *3. Total assets, $364,000*

Prad Kumar and Carol Grigg have operated a successful firm for many years, sharing net income and net losses equally. Sara Culver is to be admitted to the partnership on May 1 of the current year, in accordance with the following agreement:

a. Assets and liabilities of the old partnership are to be valued at their book values as of April 30, except for the following:
   • Accounts receivable amounting to $2,400 are to be written off, and the allowance for doubtful accounts is to be increased to 5% of the remaining accounts.
   • Merchandise inventory is to be valued at $60,000.
   • Equipment is to be valued at $240,080.

b. Culver is to purchase $55,000 of the ownership interest of Grigg for $60,000 cash and to contribute another $25,000 cash to the partnership for a total ownership equity of $80,000.

c. The income-sharing ratio of Kumar, Grigg, and Culver is to be 2:1:1.

The post-closing trial balance of Kumar and Grigg as of April 30 is as follows:

Kumar and Grigg
Post-Closing Trial Balance
April 30, 2008

	Debit Balances	Credit Balances
Cash	6,800	
Accounts Receivable	34,000	
Allowance for Doubtful Accounts		900
Merchandise Inventory	63,000	
Prepaid Insurance	2,100	
Equipment	180,000	
Accumulated Depreciation—Equipment		80,000
Accounts Payable		12,000
Notes Payable		20,000
Prad Kumar, Capital		100,000
Carol Grigg, Capital		73,000
	285,900	285,900

Instructions

1. Journalize the entries as of April 30 to record the revaluations, using a temporary account entitled Asset Revaluations. The balance in the accumulated depreciation account is to be eliminated.
2. Journalize the additional entries to record the remaining transactions relating to the formation of the new partnership. Assume that all transactions occur on May 1.
3. Present a balance sheet for the new partnership as of May 1, 2008.

PR 12-5A
Statement of partnership liquidation
obj. 4

After the accounts are closed on July 3, 2008, prior to liquidating the partnership, the capital accounts of Ann Daniels, Harold Burton, and Carla Ramariz are $27,000, $4,500, and $32,000, respectively. Cash and noncash assets total $9,500 and $84,000, respectively. Amounts owed to creditors total $30,000. The partners share income and losses in the ratio of 2:1:1. Between July 3 and July 29, the noncash assets are sold for $54,000, the partner with the capital deficiency pays his deficiency to the partnership, and the liabilities are paid.

Instructions

1. Prepare a statement of partnership liquidation, indicating (a) the sale of assets and division of loss, (b) the payment of liabilities, (c) the receipt of the deficiency (from the appropriate partner), and (d) the distribution of cash.
2. ▶ If the partner with the capital deficiency declares bankruptcy and is unable to pay the deficiency, explain how the deficiency would be divided between the partners.

PR 12-6A
Statement of partnership liquidation
obj. 4

On October 1, 2008, the firm of Allen, Dee, and Ito decided to liquidate their partnership. The partners have capital balances of $55,000, $75,000, and $12,000, respectively. The cash balance is $13,000, the book values of noncash assets total $179,000, and liabilities total $50,000. The partners share income and losses in the ratio of 2:2:1.

Instructions

Prepare a statement of partnership liquidation, covering the period October 1 through October 30 for each of the following independent assumptions:

1. All of the noncash assets are sold for $224,000 in cash, the creditors are paid, and the remaining cash is distributed to the partners.
2. All of the noncash assets are sold for $109,000 in cash, the creditors are paid, the partner with the debit capital balance pays the amount owed to the firm, and the remaining cash is distributed to the partners.

Problems Series B

PR 12-1B
Entries and balance sheet for partnership
obj. 2

✓ 3. Hoffman net income, $58,000

On November 1, 2007, E. Hoffman and Mark Torres form a partnership. Hoffman agrees to invest $9,000 cash and merchandise inventory valued at $16,000. Torres invests certain business assets at valuations agreed upon, transfers business liabilities, and contributes sufficient cash to bring his total capital to $90,000. Details regarding the book values of the business assets and liabilities, and the agreed valuations, follow:

	Torres' Ledger Balance	Agreed-Upon Valuation
Accounts Receivable	$23,500	$22,000
Allowance for Doubtful Accounts	600	900
Merchandise Inventory	25,600	31,000
Equipment	40,000	38,000
Accumulated Depreciation—Equipment	14,000	
Accounts Payable	7,300	7,300
Notes Payable	3,400	3,400

The partnership agreement includes the following provisions regarding the division of net income: interest of 10% on original investments, salary allowances of $48,000 and $21,000, respectively, and the remainder equally.

Instructions
1. Journalize the entries to record the investments of Hoffman and Torres in the partnership accounts.
2. Prepare a balance sheet as of November 1, 2007, the date of formation of the partnership of Hoffman and Torres.
3. After adjustments and the closing of revenue and expense accounts at October 31, 2008, the end of the first full year of operations, the income summary account has a credit balance of $95,500, and the drawing accounts have debit balances of $20,000 (Hoffman) and $12,000 (Torres). Journalize the entries to close the income summary account and the drawing accounts at October 31.

PR 12-2B
Dividing partnership income
obj. 2

✓ 1. f. LaRue net income, $83,600

Phil LaRue and Russ Small have decided to form a partnership. They have agreed that LaRue is to invest $16,000 and that Small is to invest $24,000. LaRue is to devote full time to the business, and Small is to devote one-half time. The following plans for the division of income are being considered:

a. Equal division.
b. In the ratio of original investments.
c. In the ratio of time devoted to the business.
d. Interest of 10% on original investments and the remainder in the ratio of 3:2.
e. Interest of 10% on original investments, salary allowances of $30,000 to LaRu and $15,000 to Small, and the remainder equally.
f. Plan (e), except that LaRue is also to be allowed a bonus equal to 20% of the amount by which net income exceeds the salary allowances.

Instructions
For each plan, determine the division of the net income under each of the following assumptions: (1) net income of $135,000 and (2) net income of $60,000. Present the data in tabular form, using the following columnar headings:

	$135,000		$60,000	
Plan	LaRue	Small	LaRue	Small

PR 12-3B
Financial statements for partnerships

objs. 2, 5

✓2. Dec. 31 capital—
Murphy, $161,500

The ledger of Dan Warrick and Ron Murphy, attorneys-at-law, contains the following accounts and balances after adjustments have been recorded on December 31, 2008:

	Debit Balances	Credit Balances
Cash	12,500	
Accounts Receivable	31,800	
Supplies	1,400	
Land	140,000	
Building	110,000	
Accumulated Depreciation—Building		46,900
Office Equipment	46,000	
Accumulated Depreciation—Office Equipment		19,200
Accounts Payable		1,600
Salaries Payable		4,000
Dan Warrick, Capital		95,000
Dan Warrick, Drawing	45,000	
Ron Murphy, Capital		140,000
Ron Murphy, Drawing	50,000	
Professional Fees		465,000
Salary Expense	305,800	
Depreciation Expense—Building	6,800	
Property Tax Expense	2,400	
Heating and Lighting Expense	9,400	
Supplies Expense	2,100	
Depreciation Expense—Office Equipment	4,200	
Miscellaneous Expense	4,300	
	771,700	771,700

The balance in Murphy's capital account includes an additional investment of $20,000 made on April 5, 2008.

Instructions
1. Prepare an income statement for the current fiscal year, indicating the division of net income. The articles of partnership provide for salary allowances of $40,000 to Warrick and $50,000 to Murphy, allowances of 12% on each partner's capital balance at the beginning of the fiscal year, and equal division of the remaining net income or net loss.
2. Prepare a statement of partners' equity for 2008.
3. Prepare a balance sheet as of the end of 2008.

PR 12-4B
Admitting new partner

obj. 3

✓3. Total assets, $301,300

Adrian Knox and Lisa Oaks have operated a successful firm for many years, sharing net income and net losses equally. Todd Aguero is to be admitted to the partnership on June 1 of the current year, in accordance with the following agreement:

a. Assets and liabilities of the old partnership are to be valued at their book values as of May 31, except for the following:
  • Accounts receivable amounting to $2,500 are to be written off, and the allowance for doubtful accounts is to be increased to 5% of the remaining accounts.
  • Merchandise inventory is to be valued at $98,000.
  • Equipment is to be valued at $124,000.
b. Aguero is to purchase $30,000 of the ownership interest of Oaks for $37,500 cash and to contribute $40,000 cash to the partnership for a total ownership equity of $70,000.
c. The income-sharing ratio of Knox, Oaks, and Aguero is to be 2:1:1.

The post-closing trial balance of Knox and Oaks as of May 31 follows.

Knox and Oaks
Post-Closing Trial Balance
May 31, 2008

	Debit Balances	Credit Balances
Cash	12,300	
Accounts Receivable	26,500	
Allowance for Doubtful Accounts		400
Merchandise Inventory	89,000	
Prepaid Insurance	4,200	
Equipment	126,000	
Accumulated Depreciation—Equipment		34,200
Accounts Payable		34,400
Notes Payable		30,000
Adrian Knox, Capital		85,000
Lisa Oaks, Capital		74,000
	258,000	258,000

Instructions
1. Journalize the entries as of May 31 to record the revaluations, using a temporary account entitled Asset Revaluations. The balance in the accumulated depreciation account is to be eliminated.
2. Journalize the additional entries to record the remaining transactions relating to the formation of the new partnership. Assume that all transactions occur on June 1.
3. Present a balance sheet for the new partnership as of June 1, 2008.

PR 12-5B
Statement of partnership liquidation
obj. 4

After the accounts are closed on September 10, 2008, prior to liquidating the partnership, the capital accounts of Mark Nichols, Donna Newby, and Janice Patel are $32,200, $5,400, and $28,400, respectively. Cash and noncash assets total $4,300 and $73,700, respectively. Amounts owed to creditors total $12,000. The partners share income and losses in the ratio of 1:1:2. Between September 10 and September 30, the noncash assets are sold for $47,300, the partner with the capital deficiency pays his or her deficiency to the partnership, and the liabilities are paid.

Instructions
1. Prepare a statement of partnership liquidation, indicating (a) the sale of assets and division of loss, (b) the payment of liabilities, (c) the receipt of the deficiency (from the appropriate partner), and (d) the distribution of cash.
2. ▬▬▶ If the partner with the capital deficiency declares bankruptcy and is unable to pay the deficiency, explain how the deficiency would be divided between the partners.

PR 12-6B
Statement of partnership liquidation
obj. 4

On June 3, 2008, the firm of Street, Rhodes, and Flynn decided to liquidate their partnership. The partners have capital balances of $16,000, $78,000, and $123,000, respectively. The cash balance is $43,000, the book values of noncash assets total $234,000, and liabilities total $60,000. The partners share income and losses in the ratio of 1:2:2.

Instructions
Prepare a statement of partnership liquidation, covering the period June 3 through June 29 for each of the following independent assumptions:

1. All of the noncash assets are sold for $300,000 in cash, the creditors are paid, and the remaining cash is distributed to the partners.
2. All of the noncash assets are sold for $106,000 in cash, the creditors are paid, the partner with the debit capital balance pays the amount owed to the firm, and the remaining cash is distributed to the partners.

Special Activities

SA 12-1
Partnership agreement

ETHICS

Ted Crowe, M.D., and Glen Tate, M.D., are sole owners of two medical practices that operate in the same medical building. The two doctors agree to combine assets and liabilities of the two businesses to form a partnership. The partnership agreement calls for dividing income equally between the two doctors. After several months, the following conversation takes place between the two doctors:

Crowe: I've noticed that your patient load has dropped over the last couple of months. When we formed our partnership, we were seeing about the same number of patients per week. However, now our patient records show that you have been seeing about half as many patients as I have. Are there any issues that I should be aware of?

Tate: There's nothing going on. When I was working on my own, I was really putting in the hours. One of the reasons I formed this partnership was to enjoy life a little more and scale back a little bit.

Crowe: I see. Well, I find that I'm working as hard as I did when I was on my own, yet making less than I did previously. Essentially, you're sharing in half of my billings and I'm sharing in half of yours. Since you are working much less than I am, I end up on the short end of the bargain.

Tate: Well, I don't know what to say. An agreement is an agreement. The partnership is based on a 50/50 split. That's what a partnership is all about.

Crowe: If that's so, then it applies equally well on the effort end of the equation as on the income end.

➤ Discuss whether Tate is acting in an ethical manner. How could Crowe rewrite the partnership agreement to avoid this dispute?

SA 12-2
Dividing partnership income

John Wise and Raul Sanchez decide to form a partnership. Wise will contribute $300,000 to the partnership, while Sanchez will contribute only $30,000. However, Sanchez will be responsible for running the day-to-day operations of the partnership, which are anticipated to require about 45 hours per week. In contrast, Wise will only work five hours per week for the partnership. The two partners are attempting to determine a formula for dividing partnership net income. Wise believes the partners should divide income in the ratio of 7:3, favoring Wise, since Wise provides the majority of the capital. Sanchez believes the income should be divided 7:3, favoring Sanchez, since Sanchez provides the majority of effort in running the partnership business.

➤ How would you advise the partners in developing a method for dividing income?

SA 12-3
Revenue per employee

The following table shows key operating statistics for the four largest public accounting firms:

	U.S. Net Revenues (in millions)	No. of Partners	No. of Professional Staff	Accounting and Auditing	Tax	Management Advisory Services (MAS)
					Revenue Split	
Deloitte & Touche	$6,876	2,568	20,273	40%	26%	34%
Ernst & Young	5,511	2,000	16,489	67	30	3
PricewaterhouseCoopers	5,189	2,200	21,210	65	30	5
KPMG LLP	4,115	1,585	11,866	72	28	0

Source: The 2005 *Accounting Today* Top 100 Firms.

a. Determine the revenue per partner and revenue per professional staff for each firm. Round to the nearest dollar.
b. Interpret the differences between the firms in terms of your answer in (a) and the table information.

SA 12-4
Revenue per employee

The partnership of Willis and Diaz, CPAs, has 200 partners and 1,500 staff professionals. Each partner shares equally in partnership income. Assume that the average income for partners in CPA firms across the country is $260,000 per year, and the average income for staff professionals is $75,000 per year. The partnership income statement for the year is as follows:

Revenues		$200,000,000
Staff professional salaries	$120,000,000	
Nonprofessional salaries	18,000,000	
Supplies	1,000,000	
Travel	2,000,000	
Litigation losses	15,000,000	156,000,000
Net income		$ 44,000,000

The total partnership capital balance is $20,000,000 for 200 partners or $100,000 per partner.

a. ▬▬▶ Evaluate the financial performance of the partnership from a partner's perspective. That is, if you were a partner in this firm, would you be satisfied or dissatisfied with partnership performance? Support your answer.

b. ▬▬▶ What are some explanations for the partnership's performance.

SA 12-5
Partnership agreement

Dave Lester has agreed to invest $200,000 into an LLC with Alicia Knowles and Brian Kim. Knowles and Kim will not invest any money, but will provide effort and expertise to the LLC. Knowles and Kim have agreed that the net income of the LLC should be divided so that Lester is to receive a 10% preferred return on his capital investment prior to any remaining income being divided equally among the partners. In addition, Knowles and Kim have suggested that the operating agreement be written so that all matters are settled by majority vote, with each partner having a one-third voting interest in the LLC.

▬▬▶ If you were providing Dave Lester counsel, what might you suggest in forming the final agreement?

Answers to Self-Examination Questions

1. **B** Noncash assets contributed to a partnership should be recorded at the amounts agreed upon by the partners. The preferred practice is to record the office equipment at $9,000 (answer B).

2. **C** Net income and net loss are divided among the partners in accordance with their agreement. In the absence of any agreement, all partners share equally (answer C).

3. **C** Tracey's share of the $45,000 of net income is $19,000 (answer C), determined as follows:

	Tracey	Hepburn	Total
Interest allowance	$10,000	$ 5,000	$15,000
Salary allowance	12,000	24,000	36,000
Total	$22,000	$29,000	$51,000
Excess of allowances over income	3,000	3,000	6,000
Net income distribution	$19,000	$26,000	$45,000

4. **A** When an additional person is admitted to a partnership by purchasing an interest from one or more of the partners, the purchase price is paid directly to the selling partner(s). The amount of capital transferred from the capital account(s) of the selling partner(s) to the capital account of the incoming partner is the capital interest acquired from the selling partner(s). In the question, the amount is $32,500 (answer A), which is one-half of Lee's capital balance of $65,000.

5. **C** Partnership cash would be distributed in accordance with the credit balances in the partners' capital accounts. Therefore, $10,000 (answer C) would be distributed to Pavin (Pavin's $10,000 capital balance).

Corporations: Organization, Stock Transactions, and Dividends

© MATTHEW CAVANAUGH/ASSOCIATED PRESS

objectives

After studying this chapter, you should be able to:

1 Describe the nature of the corporate form of organization.

2 Describe the two main sources of stockholders' equity.

3 Describe and illustrate the characteristics of stock, classes of stock, and entries for issuing stock.

4 Journalize the entries for cash dividends and stock dividends.

5 Journalize the entries for treasury stock transactions.

6 Describe and illustrate the reporting of stockholders' equity.

7 Describe the effect of stock splits on corporate financial statements.

The Yankee Candle Company, Inc.

I f you purchased 100 shares of The Yankee Candle Company, Inc., you would own a small interest in the company. Thus, you would own a small amount of the future financial prospects of a company that makes and sells over 80 million candles each year. Yankee's candle products come in hundreds of fragrances, styles, and sizes, including Housewarmer® jar candles, Samplers® votive candles, Tarts® wax potpourri, designer pillars, tapers, and scented tea lights.

How did Yankee Candle begin? Yankee Candle began in 1969 when teenager Mike Kittredge made his first candle with melted crayons in his South Hadley, Massachusetts, family home as a Christmas gift for his mother. A neighbor saw the candle, wanted to buy it, and Yankee Candle was born. Family, friends, and neighbors raved about Mike's candles and kept buying them as fast as he could make them. Mike operated first out of his parent's kitchen, basement, and garage. In 1971, Mike opened his first retail store; in 1974, he moved his candle making to an abandoned mill building; in 1994, Mike moved Yankee Candle to a 294,000-square-foot manufacturing plant in South Deerfield, Massachusetts. In 1998, Mike sold Yankee Candle, which today is traded on the New York Stock Exchange (symbol YCC) with sales of over $550 million and net income of over $82 million.

Before buying your 100 shares of Yankee Candle, you would want to study the financial statements and management's plans for the future. You would want to know whether management planned to issue additional shares of stock that might impact the value of your stock. You would want to know whether Yankee Candle planned to continue paying its semiannual cash dividend of $0.125. You might visit Yankee Candle's Web site (http://www.yankeecandle.com). Finally, you would explore other sources of investor information, such as whether financial analysts recommend Yankee Candle stock as a buy or sell.

In this chapter, we describe and illustrate the nature of corporations including the accounting for stock and dividends. This discussion will aid you in making decisions such as whether or not to buy Yankee Candle stock.

Nature of a Corporation

In the preceding chapters, we used the proprietorship in illustrations. As we mentioned in a previous chapter, more than 70% of all businesses are proprietorships and 10% are partnerships. Most of these businesses are small businesses. The remaining 20% of businesses are corporations. Many corporations are large and, as a result, they generate more than 90% of the total business dollars in the United States.

CHARACTERISTICS OF A CORPORATION

A corporation was defined in the Dartmouth College case of 1819, in which Chief Justice Marshall of the United States Supreme Court stated: "A corporation is an artificial being, invisible, intangible, and existing only in contemplation of the law."

A *corporation* is a legal entity, distinct and separate from the individuals who create and operate it. As a legal entity, a corporation may acquire, own, and dispose of property in its own name. It may also incur liabilities and enter into contracts. Most importantly, it can sell shares of ownership, called **stock**. This characteristic gives corporations the ability to raise large amounts of capital.

The **stockholders** or *shareholders* who own the stock own the corporation. They can buy and sell stock without affecting the corporation's operations or continued existence. Corporations whose shares of stock are traded in public markets are called *public corporations*. Corporations whose shares are not traded publicly are usually owned by a small group of investors and are called *nonpublic* or *private corporations*.

The stockholders of a corporation have *limited liability*. This means that a corporation's creditors usually may not go beyond the assets of the corporation to satisfy their claims. Thus, the financial loss that a stockholder may suffer is limited to the amount invested. This feature has contributed to the rapid growth of the corporate form of business.

The stockholders control a corporation by electing a *board of directors*. This board meets periodically to establish corporate policies. It also selects the chief executive officer (CEO) and other major officers to manage the corporation's day-to-day affairs. Exhibit 1 shows the organizational structure of a corporation.

EXHIBIT 1 | Organizational Structure of a Corporation

Stockholders → Board of Directors → Officers → Employees

Corporations have a separate legal existence, transferable units of ownership, and limited stockholder liability.

As a separate entity, a corporation is subject to taxes. For example, corporations must pay federal income taxes on their income.[1] Thus, corporate income that is distributed to stockholders in the form of *dividends* has already been taxed. In turn, stockholders must pay income taxes on the dividends they receive. This *double taxation* of corporate earnings is a major disadvantage of the corporate form.[2] The advantages and disadvantages of the corporate form are listed in Exhibit 2.

Integrity, Objectivity, and Ethics in Business

ETHICS

THE RESPONSIBLE BOARD

Recent accounting scandals, such as those involving Enron, WorldCom, and Fannie Mae, have highlighted the roles of boards of directors in executing their responsibilities. For example, eighteen of Enron's former directors and their insurance providers have settled shareholder litiga-tion for $168 million, of which $13 million is to come from the directors' personal assets. Board members are now on notice that their directorship responsibilities are being taken seriously by stockholders.

FORMING A CORPORATION

The first step in forming a corporation is to file an *application of incorporation* with the state. State incorporation laws differ, and corporations often organize in those states with the more favorable laws. For this reason, more than half of the largest companies

---

1 A majority of states also require corporations to pay income taxes.
2 Dividends presently receive a preferential individual tax rate of 15% to reduce the impact of double taxation.

EXHIBIT 2	Advantages and Disadvantages of the Corporate Form

Advantages	Explanation
Separate legal existence	A corporation exists separately from its owners.
Continuous life	A corporation's life is separate from its owners; therefore, it exists indefinitely.
Raising large amounts of capital	The corporate form is suited for raising large amounts of money from shareholders.
Ownership rights are easily transferable	A corporation sells shares of ownership, called *stock*. The stockholders of a public company can transfer their shares of stock to other stockholders through stock markets, such as the New York Stock Exchange.
Limited liability	A corporation's creditors usually may not go beyond the assets of the corporation to satisfy their claims. Thus, the financial loss that a stockholder may suffer is limited to the amount invested.
Disadvantages	
Owner is separate from management	Stockholders control management through a board of directors. The board of directors should represent shareholder interests; however, when the board is not sufficiently independent of management, it is possible that the board of directors and management may not always behave in the best interests of stockholders.
Double taxation of dividends	As a separate legal entity, a corporation is subject to taxation. Thus, net income distributed as dividends will be taxed once at the corporation level, and then again at the individual level.
Regulatory costs	Corporations must satisfy many requirements such as those required by the Sarbanes-Oxley Act of 2002.

A Financial Executives International survey estimated that Sarbanes-Oxley costs the average public company over $3 million per year.

are incorporated in Delaware. Exhibit 3 lists some corporations that you may be familiar with, their states of incorporation, and the location of their headquarters.

After the application of incorporation has been approved, the state grants a *charter* or *articles of incorporation*. The articles of incorporation formally create the corporation.[3] The corporate management and board of directors then prepare a set of *bylaws*, which are the rules and procedures for conducting the corporation's affairs.

EXHIBIT 3	Examples of Corporations and Their States of Incorporation

Corporation	State of Incorporation	Headquarters
Caterpillar	Delaware	Peoria, Ill.
Delta Air Lines	Delaware	Atlanta, Ga.
The Dow Chemical Company	Delaware	Midland, Mich.
General Electric Company	New York	Fairfield, Conn.
The Home Depot	Delaware	Atlanta, Ga.
Kellogg Company	Delaware	Battle Creek, Mich.
3M	Delaware	St. Paul, Minn.
R.J. Reynolds Tobacco Company	Delaware	Winston-Salem, N.C.
Starbucks Corporation	Washington	Seattle, Wash.
Sun Microsystems, Inc.	Delaware	Palo Alto, Calif.
The Washington Post Company	Delaware	Washington, D.C.
Whirlpool Corporation	Delaware	Benton Harbor, Mich.

---

3 The articles of incorporation may also restrict a corporation's activities in certain areas, such as owning certain types of real estate, conducting certain types of business activities, or purchasing its own stock.

Costs may be incurred in organizing a corporation. These costs include legal fees, taxes, state incorporation fees, license fees, and promotional costs. Such costs are debited to an expense account entitled *Organizational Expenses*. To illustrate, the recording of a corporation's organizing costs of $8,500 on January 5 is shown below.

Jan.	5	Organizational Expenses	8 5 0 0 00	
		Cash		8 5 0 0 00
		Paid costs of organizing the corporation.		

Integrity, Objectivity, and Ethics in Business

ETHICS

NOT-FOR-PROFIT, OR NOT?

Corporations can be formed for not-for-profit purposes by making a request to the Internal Revenue Service under *Internal Revenue Code* section 501(c)3. Such corporations, such as the Sierra Club and the National Audubon Society, are exempt from federal taxes. Forming businesses inside a 501(c)3 exempt organization that competes with profit-making (and hence, tax-paying) businesses is very controversial. For example, should the local YMCA receive a tax exemption for providing similar services as the local health club business? The IRS is now challenging such businesses and is withholding 501(c)3 status to many organizations due to this issue.

Stockholders' Equity

objective 2

Describe the two main sources of stockholders' equity.

The owners' equity in a corporation is commonly called **stockholders' equity**, *share holders' equity, shareholders' investment,* or *capital*. In a corporation balance sheet, the Stockholders' Equity section reports the amount of each of the two main sources of stockholders' equity. The first source is capital contributed to the corporation by the stockholders and others, called **paid-in capital** or *contributed capital*. The second source is net income retained in the business, called **retained earnings**.

An example of a Stockholders' Equity section of a corporation balance sheet is shown below.[4]

Stockholders' Equity		
Paid-in capital:		
Common stock	$330,000	
Retained earnings	80,000	
Total stockholders' equity		$410,000

The paid-in capital contributed by the stockholders is recorded in separate accounts for each class of stock. If there is only one class of stock, the account is entitled *Common Stock* or *Capital Stock*.

Retained earnings are generated from operations. Net income increases retained earnings, while dividends decrease retained earnings. Thus, retained earnings represents a corporation's accumulated net income that has not been distributed to stockholders as dividends.

The balance of the retained earnings account at the end of the fiscal year is created by closing entries. First, the balance in the income summary account (the net income or net loss) is transferred to Retained Earnings. Second, the balance of the dividends account, which is similar to the drawing account for a proprietorship, is transferred to Retained Earnings.

---

4 The reporting of stockholders' equity is further discussed and illustrated later in this chapter.

Stockholders' Equity

Paid-In Capital · Retained Earnings

Stockholder investments · Reinvested earnings

Other terms that may be used to identify retained earnings in the financial statements include *earnings retained for use in the business* and *earnings reinvested in the business*. A debit balance in Retained Earnings is called a **deficit**. Such a balance results from accumulated net losses. In the Stockholders' Equity section, a deficit is deducted from paid-in capital in determining total stockholders' equity.

The balance of Retained Earnings should not be interpreted as representing surplus cash or cash left over for dividends. The reason for this is that earnings retained in the business and the related cash generated from these earnings are normally used by management to improve or expand operations. As cash is used to expand or improve operations, its balance decreases. However, the balance of the retained earnings account is unaffected. As a result, over time the balance of the retained earnings account normally becomes less and less related to the balance of the cash account.

Paid-In Capital From Issuing Stock

objective **3**

Describe and illustrate the characteristics of stock, classes of stock, and entries for issuing stock.

As we mentioned in the preceding section, the two main sources of stockholders' equity are paid-in capital (or contributed capital) and retained earnings. The main source of paid-in capital is from issuing stock. In the following paragraphs, we discuss the characteristics of stock, the classes of stock, and entries for recording the issuance of stock.

CHARACTERISTICS OF STOCK

The number of shares of stock that a corporation is *authorized* to issue is stated in its charter. The term *issued* refers to the shares issued to the stockholders. A corporation may, under circumstances we discuss later in this chapter, reacquire some of the stock that it has issued. The stock remaining in the hands of stockholders is then called **outstanding stock**. The relationship between authorized, issued, and outstanding stock is shown in the graphic at the left.

Shares of stock are often assigned a monetary amount, called **par**. Corporations may issue *stock certificates* to stockholders to document their ownership. Printed on a stock certificate is the par value of the stock, the name of the stockholder, and the number of shares owned. Stock may also be issued without par, in which case it is called *no-par stock*. Some states require the board of directors to assign a **stated value** to no-par stock.

Because corporations have limited liability, creditors have no claim against the personal assets of stockholders. However, some state laws require that corporations maintain a minimum stockholder contribution to protect creditors. This minimum amount is called *legal capital*. The amount of required legal capital varies among the states, but it usually includes the amount of par or stated value of the shares of stock issued.

Authorized · Issued · Outstanding

Number of shares authorized, issued, and outstanding

The major rights that accompany ownership of a share of stock are as follows:

1. The right to vote in matters concerning the corporation.
2. The right to share in distributions of earnings.
3. The right to share in assets on liquidation.

As we discuss next, these stock rights normally vary with the class of stock.

CLASSES OF STOCK

When only one class of stock is issued, it is called **common stock**. In this case, each share of common stock has equal rights. To appeal to a broader investment market, a

The two primary classes of paid-in capital are common stock and preferred stock.

corporation may issue one or more classes of stock with various preference rights. A common example of such a right is the preference to dividends. Such a stock is generally called a **preferred stock**.

The dividend rights of preferred stock are usually stated in monetary terms or as a percent of par. For example, $4 *preferred stock* has a right to an annual $4 per share dividend. If the par value of the preferred stock were $50, the same right to dividends could be stated as *8% ($4/$50) preferred stock*.[5]

The board of directors of a corporation has the sole authority to distribute dividends to the stockholders. When such action is taken, the directors are said to *declare* a dividend. Since dividends are normally based on earnings, a corporation cannot guarantee dividends even to preferred stockholders. However, because they have first rights to any dividends, the preferred stockholders have a greater chance of receiving regular dividends than do the common stockholders.

To illustrate, assume that a corporation has 1,000 shares of $4 preferred stock and 4,000 shares of common stock outstanding. Also assume that the net income, amount of earnings retained, and the amount of earnings distributed by the board of directors for the first three years of operations are as follows:

	2006	2007	2008
Net income	$20,000	$9,000	$62,000
Amount retained	10,000	6,000	40,000
Amount distributed	$10,000	$3,000	$22,000

Exhibit 4 shows the earnings distributed each year to the preferred stock and the common stock. In this example, the preferred stockholders received dividends of $4, $3, and $4 per share. In contrast, common stockholders received dividends of $1.50 per share in 2006, no dividends in 2007, and $4.50 per share in 2008. You should note that although preferred stockholders have a greater chance of receiving a regular dividend, common stockholders have a greater chance of receiving larger dividends than do the preferred stockholders.[6]

EXHIBIT 4

Dividends to Preferred and Common Stock

	2006	2007	2008
Amount distributed	$10,000	$3,000	$22,000
Preferred dividend (1,000 shares)	4,000	3,000	4,000
Common dividend (4,000 shares)	$ 6,000	$ 0	$18,000
Dividends per share:			
Preferred stock	$ 4.00	$ 3.00	$ 4.00
Common stock	$ 1.50	none	$ 4.50

In addition to dividend preference, preferred stock may be given preferences to assets if the corporation goes out of business and is liquidated. However, claims of creditors must be satisfied first. Preferred stockholders are next in line to receive any remaining assets, followed by the common stockholders.

---

5 In some cases, preferred stock may receive additional dividends if certain conditions are met. Such stock, called *participating preferred stock*, is not often used.
6 In some cases, preferred stock has the right to receive regular dividends that were not paid (not declared) in prior years before any common stock dividends are paid. Such preferred stock, called *cumulative preferred stock*, is described and illustrated in intermediate accounting textbooks.

Example Exercise 13-1

objective **3**

Sandpiper Company has 20,000 shares of 1% preferred stock of $100 par and 100,000 shares of $50 par common stock. The following amounts were distributed as dividends:

Year 1 $10,000
Year 2 25,000
Year 3 80,000

Determine the dividends per share for preferred and common stock for each year.

Follow My Example 13-1

	Year 1	Year 2	Year 3
Amount distributed	$10,000	$25,000	$80,000
Preferred dividend (20,000 shares)	10,000	20,000	20,000
Common dividend (100,000 shares)	$ 0	$ 5,000	$60,000
Dividends per share:			
Preferred stock	$0.50	$1.00	$1.00
Common stock	None	$0.05	$0.60

For Practice: PE 13-1A, PE 13-1B

ISSUING STOCK

A separate account is used for recording the amount of each class of stock issued to investors in a corporation. For example, assume that a corporation is authorized to issue 10,000 shares of $100 par preferred stock and 100,000 shares of $20 par common stock. One-half of each class of authorized shares is issued at par for cash. The corporation's entry to record the stock issue is as follows:[7]

	Cash			1,500 0 0 0 00	
	Preferred Stock				500 0 0 0 00
	Common Stock				1,000 0 0 0 00
	Issued preferred stock and common				
	stock at par for cash.				

Stock is often issued by a corporation at a price other than its par. This is because the par value of a stock is simply its legal capital. The price at which stock can be sold by a corporation depends on a variety of factors, such as:

1. The financial condition, earnings record, and dividend record of the corporation.
2. Investor expectations of the corporation's potential earning power.
3. General business and economic conditions and prospects.

When stock is issued for a price that is more than its par, the stock has sold at a **premium**. When stock is issued for a price that is less than its par, the stock has sold at a **discount**. Thus, if stock with a par of $50 is issued for a price of $60, the stock has sold at a premium of $10. If the same stock is issued for a price of $45, the stock has sold at a discount of $5. Many states do not permit stock to be issued at a discount. In others, it may be done only under unusual conditions. Since issuing stock at a discount is rare, we will not illustrate it.

---

[7] The accounting for investments in stocks from the point of view of the investor is discussed in a later chapter.

The following stock quotation for Wal-Mart is taken from *The Wall Street Journal* from May 12, 2006:

NEW YORK STOCK EXCHANGE									
52 Weeks					Yld		Vol		Net
Hi	Lo	Stock	Sym	Div	%	PE	100s	Close	Chg
50.87	42.31	WalMart	WMT	.67	1.4	18	108,765	47.25	–.53

The preceding quotation is interpreted as follows:

Hi	Highest price during the past 52 weeks
Lo	Lowest price during the past 52 weeks
Stock	Name of the company
Sym	Stock exchange symbol (WMT for Wal-Mart)
Div	Dividends paid per share during the past year
Yld %	Annual dividend yield per share based on the closing price (Wal-Mart's 1.4% yield on common stock is computed as $0.67/$47.25)
PE	Price-earnings ratio on common stock (price/earnings per share)
Vol	The volume of stock traded in 100s
Close	Closing price for the day
Net Chg	The net change in price from the previous day

A corporation issuing stock must maintain records of the stockholders in order to issue dividend checks and distribute financial statements and other reports. Large public corporations normally use a financial institution, such as a bank, for this purpose.[8] In such cases, the financial institution is referred to as a *transfer agent* or *registrar*. For example, the transfer agent and registrar for The Coca-Cola Company is First Chicago Trust Company of New York.

PREMIUM ON STOCK

When stock is issued at a premium, Cash or other asset accounts are debited for the amount received. Common Stock or Preferred Stock is then credited for the par amount. The excess of the amount paid over par is a part of the total investment of the stockholders in the corporation. Therefore, such an amount in excess of par should be classified as a part of the paid-in capital. An account entitled *Paid-In Capital in Excess of Par* is usually credited for this amount.

To illustrate, assume that Caldwell Company issues 2,000 shares of $50 par preferred stock for cash at $55. The entry to record this transaction is as follows:

Cash		110 0 0 0 00	
Preferred Stock			100 0 0 0 00
Paid-In Capital in Excess of Par—			
Preferred Stock			10 0 0 0 00
Issued $50 par preferred stock at $55.			

When stock is issued in exchange for assets other than cash, such as land, buildings, and equipment, the assets acquired should be recorded at their fair market value. If this value cannot be objectively determined, the fair market price of the stock issued may be used.

To illustrate, assume that a corporation acquired land for which the fair market value cannot be determined. In exchange, the corporation issued 10,000 shares of its $10 par common. Assuming that the stock has a current market price of $12 per share, this transaction is recorded as follows:

Land		120 0 0 0 00	
Common Stock			100 0 0 0 00
Paid-In Capital in Excess of Par			20 0 0 0 00
Issued $10 par common stock, valued			
at $12 per share, for land.			

---

[8] Small corporations may use a subsidiary ledger, called a *stockholders ledger*. In this case, the stock accounts (Preferred Stock and Common Stock) are controlling accounts for the subsidiary ledger.

Business Connections

REAL WORLD

CISCO SYSTEMS, INC.

Cisco Systems, Inc., manufactures and sells networking and communications products worldwide.

The company's technology products include home networking products, which enable users to share Internet access, printers, music, movies, and games. Cisco Systems is incorporated in California and has its headquarters in San Jose, California. Some excerpts from its bylaws are shown below.

© CISCO SYSTEMS, INC.

ARTICLE 2
SHAREHOLDERS' MEETINGS
Section 2.01 Annual Meetings. The annual meeting of the shareholders of the Corporation . . . shall be held each year on the second Thursday in November at 10:00 a.m. . .

ARTICLE 3
BOARD OF DIRECTORS
Section 3.02 Number and Qualification of Directors. The number of authorized directors of this Corporation shall be not less than eight (8) nor more than fifteen (15), the exact number of directors to be (determined) by a . . . resolution of the Board of Directors or shareholders.

Section 3.04 Special Meetings. Special meetings of the Board of Directors may be called at any time by the Chairman of the Board, the President of the Corporation or any two (2) directors.

Section 3.11 Removal. The Board of Directors may declare vacant the office of a director who has been declared of unsound mind by an order of court or who has been convicted of a felony.

ARTICLE 4
OFFICERS
Section 4.01 Number and Term. The officers of the Corporation shall include a President, a Secretary and a Chief Financial Officer, all of which shall be chosen by the Board of Directors. . . .

Section 4.03 Removal and Resignation. Any officer chosen by the Board of Directors may be removed at any time, with or without cause, by the affirmative vote of a majority of all the members of the Board of Directors.

Section 4.05 Chairman of the Board. The Chairman of the Board shall preside at all meetings of the Board of Directors.

Section 4.06 President. The President shall be the general manager and chief executive officer of the Corporation, subject to the control of the Board of Directors, . . . shall preside at all meetings of shareholders, shall have general supervision of the affairs of the Corporation. . . .

Section 4.08 Secretary. The Secretary shall see that notices for all meetings are given in accordance with the provisions of these Bylaws and as required by law, shall keep minutes of all meetings, shall have charge of the seal and the corporate books, and shall have all such other authority . . . as may be delegated or assigned from time to time by the President or by the Board of Directors.

Section 4.10 Treasurer. The Treasurer shall have custody of all moneys and securities of the Corporation and shall keep regular books of account. . . .

Section 4.13 Approval of Loans to Directors and Officers. The Corporation may, upon the approval of the Board of Directors alone, make loans of money or property to, or guarantee the obligations of, any director or officer of the Corporation or its parent or subsidiary, ... provided that (i) the Board of Directors determines that such a loan or guaranty or plan may reasonably be expected to benefit the Corporation . . . and (iii) the approval of the Board of Directors is by a vote sufficient without counting the vote of any interested director or directors.

Section 5.04 Fiscal Year. The fiscal year of the Corporation shall end on the last Saturday of July.

NO-PAR STOCK

In most states, both preferred and common stock may be issued without a par value. When no-par stock is issued, the entire proceeds are credited to the stock account. This is true even though the issue price varies from time to time. For example, assume that a corporation issues 10,000 shares of no-par common stock at $40 a share and at a later date issues 1,000 additional shares at $36. The entries to record the no-par stock are as follows:

		Cash	400 0 0 0 00	
		Common Stock		400 0 0 0 00
		Issued 10,000 shares of no-par		
		common at $40.		
		Cash	36 0 0 0 00	
		Common Stock		36 0 0 0 00
		Issued 1,000 shares of no-par		
		common at $36.		

Some states require that the entire proceeds from the issue of no-par stock be recorded as legal capital. In this case, the preceding entries would be proper. In other states, no-par stock may be assigned a *stated value per share*. The stated value is recorded like a par value, and the excess of the proceeds over the stated value. To illustrate, assume that in the preceding example the no-par common stock is assigned a stated value of $25. The issuance of the stock would be recorded as follows:

		Cash	400 0 0 0 00	
		Common Stock		250 0 0 0 00
		Paid-In Capital in Excess of Stated Value		150 0 0 0 00
		Issued 10,000 shares of no-par common		
		at $40; stated value, $25.		
		Cash	36 0 0 0 00	
		Common Stock		25 0 0 0 00
		Paid-In Capital in Excess of Stated Value		11 0 0 0 00
		Issued 1,000 shares of no-par common		
		at $36; stated value, $25.		

Example Exercise 13-2

objective 3

On March 6, Limerick Corporation issued for cash 15,000 shares of no-par common stock at $30. On April 13, Limerick issued at par 1,000 shares of 4%, $40 par preferred stock for cash. On May 19, Limerick issued for cash 15,000 shares of 4%, $40 par preferred stock at $42.

Journalize the entries to record the March 6, April 13, and May 19 transactions.

Follow My Example 13-2

Mar. 6	Cash	450,000	
	Common Stock		450,000
	(15,000 shares × $30).		
Apr. 13	Cash	40,000	
	Preferred Stock		40,000
	(1,000 shares × $40).		
May 19	Cash	630,000	
	Preferred Stock		600,000
	Paid-In Capital in Excess of Par		30,000
	(15,000 shares × $42)		

For Practice: PE 13-2A, PE 13-2B

Accounting for Dividends

objective 4

Journalize the entries for cash dividends and stock dividends.

When a board of directors declares a cash dividend, it authorizes the distribution of a portion of the corporation's cash to stockholders. When a board of directors declares a stock dividend, it authorizes the distribution of a portion of its stock. In both cases, the declaration of a dividend reduces the retained earnings of the corporation.[9]

CASH DIVIDENDS

A cash distribution of earnings by a corporation to its shareholders is called a **cash dividend**. Although dividends may be paid in the form of other assets, cash dividends are the most common form.

There are usually three conditions that a corporation must meet to pay a cash dividend:

1. Sufficient retained earnings
2. Sufficient cash
3. Formal action by the board of directors

A large amount of retained earnings does not always mean that a corporation is able to pay dividends. As we indicated earlier in the chapter, the balances of the cash and retained earnings accounts are often unrelated. Thus, a large retained earnings account does not mean that there is cash available to pay dividends.

A corporation's board of directors is not required by law to declare dividends. This is true even if both retained earnings and cash are large enough to justify a dividend. However, many corporations try to maintain a stable dividend record in order to make their stock attractive to investors. Although dividends may be paid once a year or semiannually, most corporations pay dividends quarterly. In years of high profits, a corporation may declare a *special* or *extra* dividend.

You may have seen announcements of dividend declarations in financial newspapers or investor services. An example of such an announcement is shown below.

Date of Declaration — Board of Directors takes action to declare dividends.
ENTRY: Debit *Cash Dividends*
Credit *Cash Dividends Payable*

Date of Record — Ownership of shares determines who receives dividend (no entry required).

Date of Payment — Dividend is paid.
ENTRY: Debit *Cash Dividends Payable*
Credit *Cash*

On June 26, the board of directors of The Campbell Soup Company *declared a quarterly cash dividend of $0.225 per common share to stockholders of record as of the close of business on July 8, payable on July 31.*

This announcement includes three important dates: the *date of declaration* (June 26), the *date of record* (July 8), and the *date of payment* (July 31). During the period of time between the record date and the payment date, the stock price is usually quoted as selling *ex-dividends*. This means that since the date of record has passed, a new investor will not receive the dividend.

To illustrate, assume that on *December 1* the board of directors of Hiber Corporation declares the following quarterly cash dividends. The date of record is *December 10*, and the date of payment is *January 2*.

	Dividend per Share	Total Dividends
Preferred stock, $100 par, 5,000 shares outstanding	$2.50	$12,500
Common stock, $10 par, 100,000 shares outstanding	$0.30	30,000
Total		$42,500

9 In rare cases, when a corporation is reducing its operations or going out of business, a dividend may be a distribution of paid-in capital. Such a dividend is called a *liquidating dividend*.

Hiber Corporation records the $42,500 liability for the dividends on December 1, the declaration date, as follows:

Dec.	1	Cash Dividends	42 5 0 0 00	
		Cash Dividends Payable		42 5 0 0 00
		Declared cash dividend.		

No entry is required on the date of record, December 10, since this date merely determines which stockholders will receive the dividend. On the date of payment, January 2, the corporation records the $42,500 payment of the dividends as follows:

Jan.	2	Cash Dividends Payable	42 5 0 0 00	
		Cash		42 5 0 0 00
		Paid cash dividend.		

If Hiber Corporation's fiscal year ends December 31, the balance in Cash Dividends will be transferred to Retained Earnings as a part of the closing process by debiting Retained Earnings and crediting Cash Dividends. Cash Dividends Payable will be listed on the December 31 balance sheet as a current liability.

Example Exercise 13-3   objective 4

The important dates in connection with a cash dividend of $75,000 on a corporation's common stock are February 26, March 30, and April 2. Journalize the entries required on each date.

Follow My Example 13-3

Feb. 26	Cash Dividends	75,000
	Cash Dividends Payable	75,000
Mar. 30	No entry required.	
Apr. 2	Cash Dividends Payable	75,000
	Cash	75,000

For Practice: PE 13-3A, PE 13-3B

Integrity, Objectivity, and Ethics in Business

THE PROFESSOR WHO KNEW TOO MUCH

A major Midwestern university released a quarterly "American Customer Satisfaction Index" based upon its research of customers of popular U.S. products and services. Before the release of the index to the public, the professor in charge of the research bought and sold stocks of some of the companies being reported upon. The professor was quoted as saying that he thought it was important to test his theories of customer satisfaction with "real" [his own] money.

Is this proper or ethical? Apparently, the dean of the Business School didn't think so. In a statement to the press,

the dean stated: "I have instructed anyone affiliated with the (index) not to make personal use of information gathered in the course of producing the quarterly index, prior to the index's release to the general public, and they [the researchers] have agreed."

Sources: Jon E. Hilsenrath and Dan Morse, "Researcher Uses Index to Buy, Short Stocks," *The Wall Street Journal,* February 18, 2003; and Jon E. Hilsenrath, "Satisfaction Theory: Mixed Results," *The Wall Street Journal,* February 19, 2003.

STOCK DIVIDENDS

A distribution of shares of stock to stockholders is called a **stock dividend**. Usually, such distributions are in common stock and are issued to holders of common stock. Stock dividends are different from cash dividends in that there is no distribution of cash or other assets to stockholders.

The effect of a stock dividend on the stockholders' equity of the issuing corporation is to transfer retained earnings to paid-in capital. For public corporations, the amount transferred from retained earnings to paid-in capital is normally the *fair value* (market price) of the shares issued in the stock dividend.[10] To illustrate, assume that the stockholders' equity accounts of Hendrix Corporation as of December 15 are as follows:

Common Stock, $20 par (2,000,000 shares issued)	$40,000,000
Paid-In Capital in Excess of Par—Common Stock	9,000,000
Retained Earnings	26,600,000

On December 15, the board of directors declares a stock dividend of 5% or 100,000 shares (2,000,000 shares × 5%) to be issued on January 10 to stockholders of record on December 31. The market price of the stock on the declaration date is $31 a share. The entry to record the declaration is as follows:

Dec.	15	Stock Dividends		3,100 0 0 0 00	
		Stock Dividends Distributable			2,000 0 0 0 00
		Paid-In Capital in Excess of Par—			
		Common Stock			1,100 0 0 0 00
		Declared 5% (100,000 share) stock			
		dividend on $20 par common stock			
		with a market price of $31 per share.			

The $3,100,000 balance in Stock Dividends is closed to Retained Earnings on December 31. The stock dividends distributable account is listed in the Paid-In Capital section of the balance sheet. Thus, the effect of the stock dividend is to transfer $3,100,000 of retained earnings to paid-in capital.

On January 10, the number of shares outstanding is increased by 100,000 by the following entry to record the issue of the stock:

Jan.	10	Stock Dividends Distributable		2,000 0 0 0 00	
		Common Stock			2,000 0 0 0 00
		Issued stock for the stock dividend.			

A stock dividend does not change the assets, liabilities, or total stockholders' equity of the corporation. Likewise, it does not change a stockholder's proportionate interest (equity) in the corporation. For example, if a stockholder owned 1,000 of a corporation's 10,000 shares outstanding, the stockholder owns 10% (1,000/10,000) of the corporation. After declaring a 6% stock dividend, the corporation will issue 600 additional shares (10,000 shares × 6%), and the total shares outstanding will be 10,600. The stockholder of 1,000 shares will receive 60 additional shares and will now own 1,060 shares, which is still a 10% equity interest.

---

10 The use of fair market value is justified as long as the number of shares issued for the stock dividend is small (less than 25% of the shares outstanding).

Example Exercise 13-4   objective 4

Vienna Highlights Corporation has 150,000 shares of $100 par common stock outstanding. On June 14, Vienna Highlights declared a 4% stock dividend to be issued August 15 to stockholders of record on July 1. The market price of the stock was $110 per share on June 14.
  Journalize the entries required on June 14, July 1, and August 15.

Follow My Example 13-4

June 14	Stock Dividends (150,000 × 4% × $110)	660,000	
	Stock Dividends Distributable (6,000 × $100)		600,000
	Paid-In Capital in Excess of Par—Common Stock		
	($660,000 − $600,000)		60,000
July 1	No entry required.		
Aug. 15	Stock Dividends Distributable	600,000	
	Common Stock		600,000

For Practice: PE 13-4A, PE 13-4B

Treasury Stock Transactions

objective **5**

Journalize the entries for treasury stock transactions.

The 2005 edition of *Accounting Trends & Techniques* indicated that over 66% of the companies surveyed reported treasury stock.

A corporation may buy its own stock to provide shares for resale to employees, for reissuing as a bonus to employees, or for supporting the market price of the stock. For example, General Motors Corporation bought back its common stock and stated that two primary uses of this stock would be for incentive compensation plans and employee savings plans. Such stock that a corporation has once issued and then reacquires is called **treasury stock**.

A commonly used method of accounting for the purchase and resale of treasury stock is the *cost method*.[11] When the stock is purchased by the corporation, paid-in capital is reduced by debiting *Treasury Stock* for its cost (the price paid for it). The par value and the price at which the stock was originally issued are ignored. In addition, no dividends are paid on stock held as treasury stock. To do so would place the corporation in the position of earning income through dealing with itself.

When the stock is resold, Treasury Stock is credited for its cost, and any difference between the cost and the selling price is normally debited or credited to *Paid-In Capital from Sale of Treasury Stock*.

To illustrate, assume that the paid-in capital of a corporation is as follows:

Common stock, $25 par (20,000 shares authorized and issued)	$500,000	
Excess of issue price over par	150,000	$650,000

The purchase and sale of the treasury stock are recorded as follows:

Treasury Stock	45 0 0 0 00	
Cash		45 0 0 0 00
Purchased 1,000 shares of treasury		
stock at $45.		

(continued)

---

11 Another method that is infrequently used, called the *par value method*, is discussed in advanced accounting texts.

Cash		12 0 0 0 00	
Treasury Stock			9 0 0 0 00
Paid-In Capital from Sale of Treasury Stock			3 0 0 0 00
Sold 200 shares of treasury stock at $60.			
Cash		8 0 0 0 00	
Paid-In Capital from Sale of Treasury Stock		1 0 0 0 00	
Treasury Stock			9 0 0 0 00
Sold 200 shares of treasury stock at $40.			

As shown above, a sale of treasury stock may result in a decrease in paid-in capital. To the extent that Paid-In Capital from Sale of Treasury Stock has a credit balance, it should be debited for any decrease. Any remaining decrease should then be debited to the retained earnings account.

Example Exercise 13-5   objective 5

On May 3, Buzz Off Corporation reacquired 3,200 shares of its common stock at $42 per share. On July 22, Buzz Off sold 2,000 of the reacquired shares at $47 per share. On August 30, Buzz Off sold the remaining shares at $40 per share.
   Journalize the transactions of May 3, July 22, and August 30.

Follow My Example 13-5

May 3	Treasury Stock (3,200 × $42)	134,400	
	Cash		134,400
July 22	Cash (2,000 × $47)	94,000	
	Treasury Stock (2,000 × $42)		84,000
	Paid-In Capital from Sale of Treasury Stock		
	[2,000 × ($47 − $42)]		10,000
Aug. 30	Cash (1,200 × $40)	48,000	
	Paid-In Capital from Sale of Treasury Stock [1,200 × ($42 − $40)]	2,400	
	Treasury Stock (1,200 × $42)		50,400

For Practice: PE 13-5A, PE 13-5B

Reporting Stockholders' Equity

objective **6**

Describe and illustrate the reporting of stockholders' equity.

We illustrated the Stockholders' Equity section of the balance sheet earlier in this chapter. However, as with other sections of the balance sheet, alternative terms and formats may be used in reporting stockholders' equity. In addition, the significant changes in the sources of stockholders' equity—retained earnings and paid-in capital—may be reported in separate statements or notes that support the balance sheet.

STOCKHOLDERS' EQUITY IN THE BALANCE SHEET

Two alternatives for reporting stockholders' equity for the December 31, 2008, balance sheet for Telex Inc. are shown in Exhibit 5. In the first example, each class of stock is listed first, followed by its related paid-in capital accounts. In the second example, the stock accounts are listed first. The other paid-in capital accounts are listed as a single item described as *Additional paid-in capital*. These combined accounts could also be described as *Capital in excess of par (or stated value) of shares* or a similar title.

EXHIBIT 5

Stockholders' Equity
Section of a Balance
Sheet

Telex Inc.
Balance Sheet
December 31, 2008

Stockholders' Equity

Paid-in capital:			
Preferred 10% stock,			
$50 par (2,000 shares			
authorized and issued)	$100,000		
Excess of issue price over par	10,000	$ 110,000	
Common stock, $20 par			
(50,000 shares authorized,			
45,000 shares issued)	$900,000		
Excess of issue price over par	190,000	1,090,000	
From sale of treasury stock		2,000	
Total paid-in capital			$1,202,000
Retained earnings			350,000
Total			$1,552,000
Deduct treasury stock (600 shares at cost)			27,000
Total stockholders' equity			$1,525,000

Telex Inc.
Balance Sheet
December 31, 2008

Stockholders' Equity

Contributed capital:		
Preferred 10% stock,		
$50 par (2,000 shares		
authorized and issued)	$100,000	
Common stock, $20 par		
(50,000 shares authorized,		
45,000 shares issued)	900,000	
Additional paid-in capital	202,000	
Total contributed capital		$1,202,000
Retained earnings		350,000
Total		$1,552,000
Deduct treasury stock (600 shares at cost)		27,000
Total stockholders' equity		$1,525,000

Significant changes in stockholders' equity during a period may be presented either in a *statement of stockholders' equity* or in notes to the financial statements. We illustrate the statement of stockholders' equity later in this section. In addition, relevant rights and privileges of the various classes of stock outstanding must be disclosed.[12] Examples of types of information that must be disclosed include dividend and liquidation preferences, conversion rights, and redemption rights. Such information may be disclosed on the face of the balance sheet or in the accompanying notes.

---

12 *Statement of Financial Accounting Standards No. 129,* "Disclosure Information about Capital Structure" (Financial Accounting Standards Board, Norwalk, CT: 1997).

Example Exercise 13-6   objective **6**

Using the following accounts and balances, prepare the Stockholders' Equity section of the balance sheet. Forty thousand shares of common stock are authorized, and 5,000 shares have been reacquired.

Common Stock, $50 par	$1,500,000
Paid-In Capital in Excess of Par	160,000
Paid-In Capital from Sale of Treasury Stock	44,000
Retained Earnings	4,395,000
Treasury Stock	120,000

Follow My Example 13-6

Stockholders' Equity

Paid-in capital:		
Common stock, $50 par		
(40,000 shares authorized, 30,000 shares issued)	$1,500,000	
Excess of issue price over par	160,000	$1,660,000
From sale of treasury stock		44,000
Total paid-in capital		$1,704,000
Retained earnings		4,395,000
Total		$6,099,000
Deduct treasury stock (5,000 shares at cost)		120,000
Total stockholders' equity		$5,979,000

For Practice: PE 13-6A, PE 13-6B

The 2005 edition of *Accounting Trends & Techniques* indicated that 0.8% of the companies surveyed presented a separate statement of retained earnings, 0.5% presented a combined income and retained earnings statement, and 1.3% presented changes in retained earnings in the notes to the financial statements. The other 97% of the companies presented changes in retained earnings in a statement of stockholders' equity.

REPORTING RETAINED EARNINGS

A corporation may report changes in retained earnings by preparing a separate retained earnings statement, a combined income and retained earnings statement, or a statement of stockholders' equity.

When a separate **retained earnings statement** is prepared, the beginning balance of retained earnings is reported. The net income is then added (or net loss is subtracted) and any dividends are subtracted to arrive at the ending retained earnings for the period. An example of a such a statement for Telex Inc. is shown in Exhibit 6.

An alternative format for presenting the retained earnings statement is to combine it with the income statement. An advantage of the combined format is that it emphasizes net income as the connecting link between the income statement and the retained earnings portion of stockholders' equity. Since the combined form is not often used, we do not illustrate it.

Restrictions   The retained earnings available for use as dividends may be limited by action of a corporation's board of directors. These amounts, called **restrictions** or

---

EXHIBIT 6

Retained Earnings Statement

Telex Inc. Retained Earnings Statement For the Year Ended December 31, 2008			
Retained earnings, January 1, 2008			$245,000
Net income		$180,000	
Less dividends:			
Preferred stock	$10,000		
Common stock	65,000	75,000	
Increase in retained earnings			105,000
Retained earnings, December 31, 2008			$350,000

appropriations, remain part of the retained earnings. However, they must be disclosed, usually in the notes to the financial statements.

Restrictions may be classified as either legal, contractual, or discretionary. The board of directors may be legally required to restrict retained earnings because of state laws. For example, some state laws require that retained earnings be restricted by the amount of treasury stock purchased, so that legal capital will not be used for dividends. The board may also be required to restrict retained earnings because of contractual requirements. For example, the terms of a bank loan may require restrictions, so that money for repaying the loan will not be used for dividends. Finally, the board may restrict retained earnings voluntarily. For example, the board may limit dividend distributions so that more money is available for expanding the business.

Prior Period Adjustments Material errors in a prior period's net income may arise from mathematical mistakes and from mistakes in applying accounting principles. The effect of material errors that are not discovered within the same fiscal period in which they occurred should not be included in determining net income for the current period. Instead, corrections of such errors, called **prior period adjustments**, are reported in the retained earnings statement. These adjustments are reported as an adjustment to the retained earnings balance at the beginning of the period in which the error is discovered and corrected.[13]

Example Exercise 13-7

objective 6

Dry Creek Cameras Inc. reported the following results for the year ending March 31, 2008:

Retained earnings, April 1, 2007	$3,338,500
Net income	461,500
Cash dividends declared	80,000
Stock dividends declared	120,000

Prepare a retained earnings statement for the fiscal year ended March 31, 2008.

Follow My Example 13-7

DRY CREEK CAMERAS INC.
RETAINED EARNINGS STATEMENT
For the Year Ended March 31, 2008

Retained earnings, April 1, 2007		$3,338,500
Net income	$461,500	
Less dividends declared	200,000	
Increase in retained earnings		261,500
Retained earnings, March 31, 2008		$3,600,000

For Practice: PE 13-7A, PE 13-7B

STATEMENT OF STOCKHOLDERS' EQUITY

Significant changes in stockholders' equity should be reported for the period in which they occur. When the only change in stockholders' equity is due to net income or net loss and dividends, a retained earnings statement is sufficient. However, when a corporation also has changes in stock and other paid-in capital accounts, a **statement of stockholders' equity** is normally prepared. This statement is often prepared in a columnar format, where each column represents a major stockholders' equity classification. Changes in each classification are then described in the left-hand column. Exhibit 7 illustrates a statement of stockholders' equity for Telex Inc.

---

13 Prior period adjustments are illustrated in advanced texts.

EXHIBIT 7   **Statement of Stockholders' Equity**

	Preferred Stock	Common Stock	Additional Paid-In Capital	Retained Earnings	Treasury Stock	Total
Telex Inc. Statement of Stockholders' Equity For the Year Ended December 31, 2008						
Balance, January 1, 2008	$100,000	$850,000	$177,000	$245,000	$(17,000)	$1,355,000
Net income				180,000		180,000
Dividends on preferred stock				(10,000)		(10,000)
Dividends on common stock				(65,000)		(65,000)
Issuance of additional common stock		50,000	25,000			75,000
Purchase of treasury stock					(10,000)	(10,000)
Balance, December 31, 2008	$100,000	$900,000	$202,000	$350,000	$(27,000)	$1,525,000

Stock Splits

Corporations sometimes reduce the par or stated value of their common stock and issue a proportionate number of additional shares. When this is done, a corporation is said to have *split* its stock, and the process is called a **stock split**.

When stock is split, the reduction in par or stated value applies to all shares, including the unissued, issued, and treasury shares. A major objective of a stock split is to reduce the market price per share of the stock. This, in turn, should attract more investors to enter the market for the stock and broaden the types and numbers of stockholders.

To illustrate a stock split, assume that Rojek Corporation has 10,000 shares of $100 par common stock outstanding with a current market price of $150 per share. The board of directors declares a 5-for-1 stock split, reduces the par to $20, and increases the number of shares to 50,000. The amount of common stock outstanding is $1,000,000 both before and after the stock split. Only the number of shares and the par per share are changed. Each Rojek Corporation shareholder owns the same total par amount of stock before and after the stock split. For example, a stockholder who owned 4 shares of $100 par stock before the split (total par of $400) would own 20 shares of $20 par stock after the split (total par of $400).

Since there are more shares outstanding after the stock split, we would expect that the market price of the stock would fall. For example, in the preceding example, there would be 5 times as many shares outstanding after the split. Thus, we would expect the market price of the stock to fall from $150 to approximately $30 ($150/5).

Before Stock Split	After 5:1 Stock Split
4 shares, $100 par	20 shares, $20 par
$400 total par value	$400 total par value

A stock split does not require a journal entry.

Since a stock split changes only the par or stated value and the number of shares outstanding, it is not recorded by a journal entry. Although the accounts are not affected, the details of stock splits are normally disclosed in the notes to the financial statements.

Financial Analysis and Interpretation

The **dividend yield** indicates the rate of return to stockholders in terms of cash dividend distributions. Although the dividend yield can be computed for both preferred and common stock, it is most often computed for common stock. This is because most preferred stock has a stated dividend rate or amount. In contrast, the amount of common stock dividends normally varies with the profitability of the corporation.

The dividend yield is computed by dividing the annual dividends paid per share of common stock by the market price per share at a specific date, as shown below.

$$\text{Dividend Yield} = \frac{\text{Dividends per Share of Common Stock}}{\text{Market Price per Share of Common Stock}}$$

To illustrate, the market price of Mattel, Inc., common stock was $18.89 as of the close of business, January 10, 2005. During the past year, Mattel had paid dividends of $0.45 per share. Thus, the dividend yield of Mattel's common stock is 2.38% ($0.45/$18.89). Because the market price of a corporation's stock will vary from day to day, its dividend yield will also vary from day to day. Fortunately, the dividend yield is provided with newspaper listings of market prices and most Internet quotation services, such as from Yahoo's Finance Web site.

The recent dividend yields for some selected companies are as follows:

Company	Dividend Yield (%)
AT&T Corporation	5.06
Duke Energy Corporation	4.46
General Motors Corporation	8.10
Hewlett-Packard Development Company, LP	1.05
The Home Depot	0.82
Oracle	None
The Coca-Cola Company	1.00

As can be seen, the dividend yield varies widely across firms. Growth companies often do not pay dividends, but instead, reinvest their earnings in research and development, such as with Oracle.

At a Glance

1. Describe the nature of the corporate form of organization.

Key Points	Key Learning Outcomes	Example Exercises	Practice Exercises
Corporations have a separate legal existence, transferable units of stock, unlimited life, and limited stockholders' liability. The advantages and disadvantages of the corporate form are summarized in Exhibit 2. Costs incurred in organizing a corporation are debited to Organizational Expense.	• Describe the characteristics of corporations. • List the advantages and disadvantages of the corporate form. • Prepare a journal entry for the costs of organizing a corporation.		

2. Describe the two main sources of stockholders' equity.

Key Points	Key Learning Outcomes	Example Exercises	Practice Exercises
The two main sources of stockholders' equity are (1) capital contributed by the stockholders and others, called *paid-in capital*, and (2) net income retained in the business, called *retained earnings*. Stockholders' equity is reported in a corporation balance sheet according to these two sources.	• Describe what is meant by paid-in capital. • Describe what is meant by net income retained in the business. • Prepare a simple Stockholders' Equity section of the balance sheet.		

3. Describe and illustrate the characteristics of stock, classes of stock, and entries for issuing stock.

Key Points	Key Learning Outcomes	Example Exercises	Practice Exercises
The main source of paid-in capital is from issuing common and preferred stock. Stock issued at par is recorded by debiting Cash and crediting the class of stock issued for its par amount. Stock issued for more than par is recorded by debiting Cash and crediting Paid-In Capital in Excess of Par for the difference between the cash received and the par value of the stock. When stock is issued in exchange for assets other than cash, the assets acquired are recorded at their fair market value. When no-par stock is issued, the entire proceeds are credited to the stock account. No-par stock may be assigned a stated value per share, and the excess of the proceeds over the stated value may be credited to Paid-In Capital in Excess of Stated Value.	• Describe the characteristics of common and preferred stock including rights to dividends. • Journalize the entry for common and preferred stock issued at par. • Journalize the entry for common and preferred stock issued at more than par. • Journalize the entry for issuing no-par stock.	13-1 13-2 13-2 13-2	13-1A, 13-1B 13-2A, 13-2B 13-2A, 13-2B 13-2A, 13-2B

4. Journalize the entries for cash dividends and stock dividends.

Key Points	Key Learning Outcomes	Example Exercises	Practice Exercises
The entry to record a declaration of cash dividends debits Dividends and credits Dividends Payable. When a stock dividend is declared, Stock Dividends is debited for the fair value of the stock to be issued. Stock Dividends Distributable is credited for the par or stated value of the common stock to be issued. The difference between the fair value of the stock and its par or stated value is credited to Paid-In Capital in Excess of Par—Common Stock. When the stock is issued on the date of payment, Stock Dividends Distributable is debited and Common Stock is credited for the par or stated value of the stock issued.	• Journalize the entries for the declaration and payment of cash dividends. • Journalize the entries for the declaration and payment of stock dividends.	13-3 13-4	13-3A, 13-3B 13-4A, 13-4B

5. Journalize the entries for treasury stock transactions.

Key Points	Key Learning Outcomes	Example Exercises	Practice Exercises
When a corporation buys its own stock, the cost method of accounting is normally used. Treasury Stock is debited for its cost, and Cash is credited. If the stock is resold, Treasury Stock is credited for its cost and any difference between the cost and the selling price is normally debited or credited to Paid-In Capital from Sale of Treasury Stock.	• Define *treasury stock*. • Describe the accounting for treasury stock. • Journalize entries for the purchase and sale of treasury stock.	13-5	13-5A, 13-5B

6. Describe and illustrate the reporting of stockholders' equity.

Key Points	Key Learning Outcomes	Example Exercises	Practice Exercises
Two alternatives for reporting stockholders' equity are shown in Exhibit 5. Changes in retained earnings are reported in a retained earnings statement, as shown in Exhibit 6. Restrictions to retained earnings should be disclosed. Any prior period adjustments are reported in the retained earnings statement. Changes in stockholders' equity may be reported on a statement of stockholders' equity, as shown in Exhibit 7.	• Prepare the Stockholders' Equity section of the balance sheet. • Prepare a retained earnings statement. • Describe retained earnings restrictions and prior period adjustments. • Prepare a statement of stockholders' equity.	13-6 13-7	13-6A, 13-6B 13-7A, 13-7B

7. Describe the effect of stock splits on corporate financial statements.

Key Points	Key Learning Outcomes	Example Exercises	Practice Exercises
When a corporation reduces the par or stated value of its common stock and issues a proportionate number of additional shares, a stock split has occurred. There are no changes in the balances of any accounts, and no entry is required for a stock split.	• Define and give an example of a stock split. • Describe the accounting for and effects of a stock split on the financial statements.		

Key Terms

cash dividend (578)
common stock (572)
deficit (572)
discount (574)
dividend yield (587)
outstanding stock (572)
paid-in capital (571)
par (572)
preferred stock (573)

premium (574)
prior period adjustments (585)
restrictions (584)
retained earnings (571)
retained earnings statement (584)
stated value (572)
statement of stockholders' equity (585)
stock (568)

stock dividend (580)
stock split (586)
stockholders (568)
stockholders' equity (571)
treasury stock (581)

Illustrative Problem

Altenburg Inc. is a lighting fixture wholesaler located in Arizona. During its current fiscal year, ended December 31, 2008, Altenburg Inc. completed the following selected transactions:

Feb. 3. Purchased 2,500 shares of its own common stock at $26, recording the stock at cost. (Prior to the purchase, there were 40,000 shares of $20 par common stock outstanding.)

May 1. Declared a semiannual dividend of $1 on the 10,000 shares of preferred stock and a 30¢ dividend on the common stock to stockholders of record on May 31, payable on June 15.

June 15. Paid the cash dividends.

Sept. 23. Sold 1,000 shares of treasury stock at $28, receiving cash.

Nov. 1. Declared semiannual dividends of $1 on the preferred stock and 30¢ on the common stock. In addition, a 5% common stock dividend was declared on the common stock outstanding, to be capitalized at the fair market value of the common stock, which is estimated at $30.

Dec. 1. Paid the cash dividends and issued the certificates for the common stock dividend.

Instructions

Journalize the entries to record the transactions for Altenburg Inc.

Solution

2008					
Feb.	3	Treasury Stock		65 0 0 0 00	
		Cash			65 0 0 0 00
May	1	Cash Dividends		21 2 5 0 00	
		Cash Dividends Payable			21 2 5 0 00
		(10,000 × $1) + [(40,000 − 2,500)			
		× $0.30].			
June	15	Cash Dividends Payable		21 2 5 0 00	
		Cash			21 2 5 0 00
Sept.	23	Cash		28 0 0 0 00	
		Treasury Stock			26 0 0 0 00
		Paid-In Capital from Sale of Treasury Stock			2 0 0 0 00
Nov.	1	Cash Dividends		21 5 5 0 00	
		Cash Dividends Payable			21 5 5 0 00
		(10,000 × $1) + [(40,000 − 1,500)			
		× $0.30].			
	1	Stock Dividends		57 7 5 0 00*	
		Stock Dividends Distributable			38 5 0 0 00
		Paid-In Capital in Excess of			
		Par—Common Stock			19 2 5 0 00
		*(40,000 − 1,500) × 5% × $30.			
Dec.	1	Cash Dividends Payable		21 5 5 0 00	
		Stock Dividends Distributable		38 5 0 0 00	
		Cash			21 5 5 0 00
		Common Stock			38 5 0 0 00

Self-Examination Questions

(Answers at End of Chapter)

1. Which of the following is a disadvantage of the corporate form of organization?
   A. Limited liability
   B. Continuous life
   C. Owner is separate from management
   D. Ability to raise capital

2. Paid-in capital for a corporation may arise from which of the following sources?
   A. Issuing preferred stock
   B. Issuing common stock
   C. Selling the corporation's treasury stock
   D. All of the above

3. The Stockholders' Equity section of the balance sheet may include:
   A. Common Stock.
   B. Stock Dividends Distributable.
   C. Preferred Stock.
   D. All of the above.

4. If a corporation reacquires its own stock, the stock is listed on the balance sheet in the:
   A. Current Assets section.
   B. Long-Term Liabilities section.
   C. Stockholders' Equity section.
   D. Investments section.

5. A corporation has issued 25,000 shares of $100 par common stock and holds 3,000 of these shares as treasury stock. If the corporation declares a $2 per share cash dividend, what amount will be recorded as cash dividends?
   A. $22,000   C. $44,000
   B. $25,000   D. $50,000

Eye Openers

1. Describe the stockholders' liability to creditors of a corporation.
2. Why are most large businesses organized as corporations?
3. Of two corporations organized at approximately the same time and engaged in competing businesses, one issued $150 par common stock, and the other issued $1 par common stock. Do the par designations provide any indication as to which stock is preferable as an investment? Explain.
4. A stockbroker advises a client to "buy preferred stock. . . . With that type of stock, . . . [you] will never have to worry about losing the dividends." Is the broker right?
5. What are some of the factors that influence the market price of a corporation's stock?
6. When a corporation issues stock at a premium, is the premium income? Explain.
7. (a) What are the three conditions for the declaration and the payment of a cash dividend? (b) The dates in connection with the declaration of a cash dividend are February 6, March 9, and April 5. Identify each date.
8. A corporation with both preferred stock and common stock outstanding has a substantial credit balance in its retained earnings account at the beginning of the current fiscal year. Although net income for the current year is sufficient to pay the preferred dividend of $250,000 each quarter and a common dividend of $610,000 each quarter, the board of directors declares dividends only on the preferred stock. Suggest possible reasons for passing the dividends on the common stock.
9. An owner of 200 shares of Felt Company common stock receives a stock dividend of 4 shares. (a) What is the effect of the stock dividend on the stockholder's proportionate interest (equity) in the corporation? (b) How does the total equity of 204 shares compare with the total equity of 200 shares before the stock dividend?
10. a. Where should a declared but unpaid cash dividend be reported on the balance sheet?
    b. Where should a declared but unissued stock dividend be reported on the balance sheet?
11. a. In what respect does treasury stock differ from unissued stock?
    b. How should treasury stock be presented on the balance sheet?
12. A corporation reacquires 8,000 shares of its own $10 par common stock for $120,000, recording it at cost. (a) What effect does this transaction have on revenue or expense of the period? (b) What effect does it have on stockholders' equity?

13. The treasury stock in Eye Opener 12 is resold for $158,000. (a) What is the effect on the corporation's revenue of the period? (b) What is the effect on stockholders' equity?
14. What is the primary advantage of combining the retained earnings statement with the income statement?
15. What are the three classifications of restrictions of retained earnings, and how are such restrictions normally reported in the financial statements?
16. Indicate how prior period adjustments would be reported on the financial statements presented only for the current period.
17. When is a statement of stockholders' equity normally prepared?
18. What is the primary purpose of a stock split?

Practice Exercises

PE 13-1A
Dividends per share
obj. 3

Golf-Easy Company has 10,000 shares of 3% preferred stock of $50 par and 25,000 shares of $100 par common stock. The following amounts were distributed as dividends:

Year 1	$ 40,000
Year 2	10,000
Year 3	120,000

Determine the dividends per share for preferred and common stock for each year.

PE 13-1B
Dividends per share
obj. 3

Marsala Company has 5,000 shares of 2% preferred stock of $75 par and 10,000 shares of $150 par common stock. The following amounts were distributed as dividends:

Year 1	$20,000
Year 2	4,000
Year 3	40,000

Determine the dividends per share for preferred and common stock for each year.

PE 13-2A
Entries for issuing stock
obj. 3

On August 3, Waterways Corporation issued for cash 45,000 shares of no-par common stock (with a stated value of $100) at $128. On September 22, Waterways issued at par 2,000 shares of 1%, $75 par preferred stock for cash. On November 4, Waterways issued for cash 3,000 shares of 1%, $75 par preferred stock at $80.

Journalize the entries to record the August 3, September 22, and November 4 transactions.

PE 13-2B
Entries for issuing stock
obj. 3

On July 6, Istanbul Artifacts Corporation issued for cash 800,000 shares of no-par common stock at $1.20. On August 30, Istanbul Artifacts issued at par 10,000 shares of 2%, $50 par preferred stock for cash. On October 14, Istanbul Artifacts issued for cash 7,500 shares of 2%, $50 par preferred stock at $54.

Journalize the entries to record the July 6, August 30, and October 14 transactions.

PE 13-3A
Entries for cash dividends
obj. 4

The important dates in connection with a cash dividend of $48,000 on a corporation's common stock are July 16, August 15, and September 30. Journalize the entries required on each date.

PE 13-3B
Entries for cash dividends
obj. 4

The important dates in connection with a cash dividend of $90,000 on a corporation's common stock are October 1, November 1, and December 24. Journalize the entries required on each date.

PE 13-4A
Entries for stock dividends
obj. 4

Stonehenge Corporation has 300,000 shares of $40 par common stock outstanding. On February 13, Stonehenge Corporation declared a 3% stock dividend to be issued April 30 to stockholders of record on March 14. The market price of the stock was $63 per share on February 13.

Journalize the entries required on February 13, March 14, and April 30.

PE 13-4B
Entries for stock dividends
obj. 4

Big Ben Corporation has 250,000 shares of $50 par common stock outstanding. On May 10, Big Ben Corporation declared a 2% stock dividend to be issued August 1 to stockholders of record on June 9. The market price of the stock was $60 per share on May 10.

Journalize the entries required on May 10, June 9, and August 1.

PE 13-5A
Entries for treasury stock
obj. 5

On January 24, Thunderstorm Inc. reacquired 6,000 shares of its common stock at $18 per share. On March 15, Thunderstorm sold 4,500 of the reacquired shares at $21 per share. On June 2, Thunderstorm sold the remaining shares at $17 per share.

Journalize the transactions of January 24, March 15, and June 2.

PE 13-5B
Entries for treasury stock
obj. 5

On October 2, Baja Clothing Inc. reacquired 12,000 shares of its common stock at $6 per share. On November 15, Baja Clothing sold 8,400 of the reacquired shares at $9 per share. On December 22, Baja Clothing sold the remaining shares at $5 per share.

Journalize the transactions of October 2, November 15, and December 22.

PE 13-6A
Stockholders' Equity section of balance sheet
obj. 6

Using the following accounts and balances, prepare the Stockholders' Equity section of the balance sheet. Thirty thousand shares of common stock are authorized, and 2,000 shares have been reacquired.

Common Stock, $80 par	$2,000,000
Paid-In Capital in Excess of Par	315,000
Paid-In Capital from Sale of Treasury Stock	33,000
Retained Earnings	1,112,000
Treasury Stock	180,000

PE 13-6B
Stockholders' Equity section of balance sheet
obj. 6

Using the following accounts and balances, prepare the Stockholders' Equity section of the balance sheet. Fifty thousand shares of common stock are authorized, and 5,000 shares have been reacquired.

Common Stock, $75 par	$3,375,000
Paid-In Capital in Excess of Par	485,000
Paid-In Capital from Sale of Treasury Stock	18,000
Retained Earnings	1,452,000
Treasury Stock	420,000

PE 13-7A
Retained earnings statement
obj. 6

Dynamic Leaders Inc. reported the following results for the year ending July 31, 2008:

Retained earnings, August 1, 2007	$988,500
Net income	325,000
Cash dividends declared	35,000
Stock dividends declared	90,000

Prepare a retained earnings statement for the fiscal year ended July 31, 2008.

PE 13-7B
Retained earnings statement
obj. 6

Maxima Retractors Inc. reported the following results for the year ending October 31, 2008:

Retained earnings, November 1, 2007	$2,906,000
Net income	553,000
Cash dividends declared	100,000
Stock dividends declared	200,000

Prepare a retained earnings statement for the fiscal year ended October 31, 2008.

Exercises

EX 13-1
Dividends per share
obj. 3

✓ *Preferred stock,*
1st year: $0.80

Electro-Rad Inc., a developer of radiology equipment, has stock outstanding as follows: 50,000 shares of 2%, preferred stock of $50 par, and 100,000 shares of $25 par common. During its first four years of operations, the following amounts were distributed as dividends: first year, $40,000; second year, $98,000; third year, $120,000; fourth year, $195,000. Calculate the dividends per share on each class of stock for each of the four years.

EX 13-2
Dividends per share
obj. 3

✓ *Preferred stock,*
1st year: $0.15

CompuLead Inc., a software development firm, has stock outstanding as follows: 40,000 shares of 1%, preferred stock of $25 par, and 50,000 shares of $75 par common. During its first four years of operations, the following amounts were distributed as dividends: first year, $6,000; second year, $26,000; third year, $4,000; fourth year, $60,000. Calculate the dividends per share on each class of stock for each of the four years.

EX 13-3
Entries for issuing par stock
obj. 3

On February 4, Cinderella Rocks Inc., a marble contractor, issued for cash 30,000 shares of $20 par common stock at $64, and on March 31, it issued for cash 18,000 shares of $75 par preferred stock at $90.

a. Journalize the entries for February 4 and March 31.
b. What is the total amount invested (total paid-in capital) by all stockholders as of March 31?

EX 13-4
Entries for issuing no-par stock
obj. 3

On July 17, America Carpet Inc., a carpet wholesaler, issued for cash 150,000 shares of no-par common stock (with a stated value of $5) at $36, and on September 20, it issued for cash 10,000 shares of $50 par preferred stock at $80.

a. Journalize the entries for July 17 and September 20, assuming that the common stock is to be credited with the stated value.
b. What is the total amount invested (total paid-in capital) by all stockholders as of September 20?

EX 13-5
Issuing stock for assets other than cash
obj. 3

On November 10, Craddock's Corporation, a wholesaler of hydraulic lifts, acquired land in exchange for 15,000 shares of $8 par common stock with a current market price of $32. Journalize the entry to record the transaction.

EX 13-6
Selected stock transactions
obj. 3

Country Sounds Corp., an electric guitar retailer, was organized by Julie Arnold, Joe Harris, and Scott Pickens. The charter authorized 500,000 shares of common stock with a par of $12. The following transactions affecting stockholders' equity were completed during the first year of operations:

a. Issued 20,000 shares of stock at par to Julie Arnold for cash.
b. Issued 500 shares of stock at par to Scott Pickens for promotional services provided in connection with the organization of the corporation, and issued 18,000 shares of stock at par to Scott Pickens for cash.
c. Purchased land and a building from Joe Harris. The building is mortgaged for $200,000 for 25 years at 7%, and there is accrued interest of $2,200 on the mortgage note at the time of the purchase. It is agreed that the land is to be priced at $75,000 and the building at $240,000, and that Joe Harris's equity will be exchanged for stock at par. The corporation agreed to assume responsibility for paying the mortgage note and the accrued interest.

Journalize the entries to record the transactions.

EX 13-7
Issuing stock
obj. 3

Angel Creek Nursey, with an authorization of 40,000 shares of preferred stock and 150,000 shares of common stock, completed several transactions involving its stock on August 15, the first day of operations. The trial balance at the close of the day follows:

Cash	450,000	
Land	100,000	
Buildings	80,000	
Preferred 2% Stock, $80 par		160,000
Paid-In Capital in Excess of Par—Preferred Stock		20,000
Common Stock, $50 par		400,000
Paid-In Capital in Excess of Par—Common Stock		50,000
	630,000	630,000

All shares within each class of stock were sold at the same price. The preferred stock was issued in exchange for the land and buildings.

Journalize the two entries to record the transactions summarized in the trial balance.

EX 13-8
Issuing stock
obj. 3

Heritage Products Inc., a wholesaler of office products, was organized on February 19 of the current year, with an authorization of 60,000 shares of 3% preferred stock, $40 par and 300,000 shares of $75 par common stock. The following selected transactions were completed during the first year of operations:

Feb. 19. Issued 20,000 shares of common stock at par for cash.
　　27. Issued 100 shares of common stock at par to an attorney in payment of legal fees for organizing the corporation.
Mar. 13. Issued 6,000 shares of common stock in exchange for land, buildings, and equipment with fair market prices of $80,000, $350,000, and $45,000, respectively.
May　6. Issued 5,000 shares of preferred stock at $46 for cash.

Journalize the transactions.

EX 13-9
Entries for cash dividends
obj. 4

The dates of importance in connection with a cash dividend of $275,000 on a corporation's common stock are July 2, August 1, and September 1. Journalize the entries required on each date.

EX 13-10
Entries for stock dividends
obj. 4

✓b. (1) $34,500,000
　　(3) $85,100,000

Earthworks Health Co. is an HMO for 12 businesses in the St. Louis area. The following account balances appear on the balance sheet of Earthworks Health Co.: Common stock (400,000 shares authorized), $100 par, $30,000,000; Paid-in capital in excess of par—common stock, $4,500,000; and Retained earnings, $50,600,000. The board of directors declared a 2% stock dividend when the market price of the stock was $120 a share. Earthworks Health Co. reported no income or loss for the current year.

a. Journalize the entries to record (1) the declaration of the dividend, capitalizing an amount equal to market value, and (2) the issuance of the stock certificates.
b. Determine the following amounts before the stock dividend was declared: (1) total paid-in capital, (2) total retained earnings, and (3) total stockholders' equity.
c. Determine the following amounts after the stock dividend was declared and closing entries were recorded at the end of the year: (1) total paid-in capital, (2) total retained earnings, and (3) total stockholders' equity.

EX 13-11
Treasury stock transactions
obj. 5

✓b. $9,000 credit

Mountain Springs Inc. bottles and distributes spring water. On May 2 of the current year, Mountain Springs reacquired 3,000 shares of its common stock at $72 per share. On August 14, Mountain Springs sold 2,500 of the reacquired shares at $76 per share. The remaining 500 shares were sold at $70 per share on November 7.

a. Journalize the transactions of May 2, August 14, and November 7.
b. What is the balance in Paid-In Capital from Sale of Treasury Stock on December 31 of the current year?
c. ▭▭▭ For what reasons might Mountain Springs have purchased the treasury stock?

EX 13-12
Treasury stock transactions
objs. 5, 6

✓ *b. $36,900 credit*

Azalea Gardens Inc. develops and produces spraying equipment for lawn maintenance and industrial uses. On September 9 of the current year, Azalea Gardens Inc. reacquired 12,000 shares of its common stock at $89 per share. On October 31, 10,500 of the reacquired shares were sold at $92 per share, and on December 4, 900 of the reacquired shares were sold at $95.

a. Journalize the transactions of September 9, October 31, and December 4.
b. What is the balance in Paid-In Capital from Sale of Treasury Stock on December 31 of the current year?
c. What is the balance in Treasury Stock on December 31 of the current year?
d. How will the balance in Treasury Stock be reported on the balance sheet?

EX 13-13
Treasury stock transactions
objs. 5, 6

✓ *b. $12,000 credit*

Tacoma Inc. bottles and distributes spring water. On June 12 of the current year, Tacoma Inc. reacquired 15,000 shares of its common stock at $48 per share. On August 10, Tacoma Inc. sold 9,000 of the reacquired shares at $50 per share. The remaining 6,000 shares were sold at $47 per share on December 20.

a. Journalize the transactions of June 12, August 10, and December 20.
b. What is the balance in Paid-In Capital from Sale of Treasury Stock on December 31 of the current year?
c. Where will the balance in Paid-In Capital from Sale of Treasury Stock be reported on the balance sheet?
d. ▭▬▶ For what reasons might Tacoma Inc. have purchased the treasury stock?

EX 13-14
Reporting paid-in capital
obj. 6

✓ *Total paid-in capital, $2,494,500*

The following accounts and their balances were selected from the unadjusted trial balance of Sailors Inc., a freight forwarder, at August 31, the end of the current fiscal year:

Preferred 3% Stock, $100 par	$1,500,000
Paid-In Capital in Excess of Par—Preferred Stock	180,000
Common Stock, no par, $10 stated value	675,000
Paid-In Capital in Excess of Stated Value—Common Stock	125,000
Paid-In Capital from Sale of Treasury Stock	14,500
Retained Earnings	2,106,500

Prepare the Paid-In Capital portion of the Stockholders' Equity section of the balance sheet. There are 500,000 shares of common stock authorized and 50,000 shares of preferred stock authorized.

EX 13-15
Stockholders' Equity section of balance sheet
obj. 6

✓ *Total stockholders' equity, $4,020,000*

The following accounts and their balances appear in the ledger of Heart and Saul Inc. on April 30 of the current year:

Common Stock, $50 par	$ 900,000
Paid-In Capital in Excess of Par	110,000
Paid-In Capital from Sale of Treasury Stock	42,000
Retained Earnings	3,178,000
Treasury Stock	210,000

Prepare the Stockholders' Equity section of the balance sheet as of April 30. Twenty-five thousand shares of common stock are authorized, and 3,500 shares have been reacquired.

EX 13-16
Stockholders' Equity section of balance sheet
obj. 6

✓ *Total stockholders' equity, $4,726,500*

Sports Car Inc. retails racing products for BMWs, Porsches, and Ferraris. The following accounts and their balances appear in the ledger of Sports Car Inc. on November 30, the end of the current year:

Common Stock, $5 par	$ 875,000
Paid-In Capital in Excess of Par—Common Stock	700,000
Paid-In Capital in Excess of Par—Preferred Stock	25,000
Paid-In Capital from Sale of Treasury Stock—Common	16,000
Preferred 3% Stock, $75 par	937,500
Retained Earnings	2,338,000
Treasury Stock—Common	165,000

Twenty thousand shares of preferred and 400,000 shares of common stock are authorized. There are 22,000 shares of common stock held as treasury stock.

Prepare the Stockholders' Equity section of the balance sheet as of November 30, the end of the current year.

EX 13-17
Retained earnings statement
obj. 6

✓ *Retained earnings, August 31, $1,950,000*

Stillwater Corporation, a manufacturer of industrial pumps, reports the following results for the year ending August 31, 2008:

Retained earnings, September 1, 2007	$1,752,000
Net income	378,000
Cash dividends declared	80,000
Stock dividends declared	100,000

Prepare a retained earnings statement for the fiscal year ended August 31, 2008.

EX 13-18
Stockholders' Equity section of balance sheet
obj. 6

✓ *Corrected total stockholders' equity, $5,439,000*

List the errors in the following Stockholders' Equity section of the balance sheet prepared as of the end of the current year.

Stockholders' Equity

Paid-in capital:		
Preferred 1% stock, $75 par		
(8,000 shares authorized and issued)	$ 600,000	
Excess of issue price over par	56,000	$ 656,000
Retained earnings		1,278,000
Treasury stock (4,000 shares at cost)		320,000
Dividends payable		18,000
Total paid-in capital		$2,272,000
Common stock, $50 par (100,000 shares		
authorized, 60,000 shares issued)		3,900,000
Organizing costs		75,000
Total stockholders' equity		$6,247,000

EX 13-19
Statement of stockholders' equity
obj. 6

✓ *Total stockholders' equity, Dec. 31, $3,529,000*

The stockholders' equity T accounts of Family Greeting Cards Inc. for the current fiscal year ended December 31, 2008, are as follows. Prepare a statement of stockholders' equity for the fiscal year ended December 31, 2008.

COMMON STOCK

	Jan. 1	Balance	600,000
	Apr. 9	Issued	
		50,000 shares	150,000
	Dec. 31	Balance	750,000

PAID-IN CAPITAL IN EXCESS OF PAR

	Jan. 1	Balance	350,000
	Apr. 9	Issued	
		50,000 shares	100,000
	Dec. 31	Balance	450,000

TREASURY STOCK

Aug. 7 Purchased		
6,000 shares	24,000	

RETAINED EARNINGS

June 30	Dividend	40,000	Jan. 1	Balance	2,108,000
Dec. 30	Dividend	40,000	Dec. 31	Closing	
				(net income)	325,000
			Dec. 31	Balance	2,353,000

EX 13-20
Effect of stock split
obj. 7

Rolling Pin Corporation wholesales ovens and ranges to restaurants throughout the Midwest. Rolling Pin Corporation, which had 50,000 shares of common stock outstanding, declared a 3-for-1 stock split (2 additional shares for each share issued).

a. What will be the number of shares outstanding after the split?
b. If the common stock had a market price of $180 per share before the stock split, what would be an approximate market price per share after the split?

EX 13-21
Effect of cash dividend and stock split
objs. 4, 7

Indicate whether the following actions would (+) increase, (−) decrease, or (0) not affect Indigo Inc.'s total assets, liabilities, and stockholders' equity:

	Assets	Liabilities	Stockholders' Equity
(1) Declaring a cash dividend	_____	_____	_____
(2) Paying the cash dividend declared in (1)	_____	_____	_____
(3) Authorizing and issuing stock certificates in a stock split	_____	_____	_____
(4) Declaring a stock dividend	_____	_____	_____
(5) Issuing stock certificates for the stock dividend declared in (4)	_____	_____	_____

EX 13-22
Selected dividend transactions, stock split
objs. 4, 7

Selected transactions completed by NuCraft Boating Supply Corporation during the current fiscal year are as follows:

Mar. 5. Split the common stock 4 for 1 and reduced the par from $100 to $25 per share. After the split, there were 800,000 common shares outstanding.
May 15. Declared semiannual dividends of $2 on 15,000 shares of preferred stock and $0.12 on the common stock to stockholders of record on June 14, payable on July 14.
July 14. Paid the cash dividends.
Nov. 15. Declared semiannual dividends of $2 on the preferred stock and $0.14 on the common stock (before the stock dividend). In addition, a 1% common stock dividend was declared on the common stock outstanding. The fair market value of the common stock is estimated at $30.
Dec. 15. Paid the cash dividends and issued the certificates for the common stock dividend.

Journalize the transactions.

EX 13-23
Dividend yield

At the market close on May 12, 2006, Bank of America Corporation had a closing stock price of $49.69. In addition, Bank of America had earnings per share of $4.05 and dividend per share was $1.95. Determine Bank of America's dividend yield. Round to one decimal place.

EX 13-24
Dividend yield

General Electric Company had earnings per share of $1.72 for 2005 and $1.56 for 2004. In addition, the dividends per share were $0.91 for 2005 and $0.82 for 2004. The market price of GE's stock closed at $35.05 and $36.50 on December 31, 2005 and 2004, respectively.

a. Determine the dividend yield for General Electric on December 31, 2005 and 2004. Round percentages to two decimal places.
b. ▬▬▶ Interpret these measures.

EX 13-25
Dividend yield

eBay Inc. developed a Web-based marketplace at **http://www.ebay.com**, in which individuals can buy and sell a variety of items. eBay also acquired PayPal, an online payments system that allows businesses and individuals to send and receive online payments securely. In a recent annual report, eBay published the following dividend policy:

We have never paid cash dividends on our stock, and currently anticipate that we will continue to retain any future earnings to finance the growth of our business.

➤ Given eBay's dividend policy, why would an investor be attracted to its stock?

Problems Series A

PR 13-1A
Dividends on preferred and common stock
obj. 3

✓ 1. Common dividends
in 2004: $20,000

Olympic Theatre Inc. owns and operates movie theaters throughout Texas and California. Olympic Theatre has declared the following annual dividends over a six-year period: 2003, $21,000; 2004, $50,000; 2005, $15,000; 2006, $80,000; 2007, $90,000; and 2008, $140,000. During the entire period, the outstanding stock of the company was composed of 10,000 shares of 4% preferred stock, $75 par, and 100,000 shares of common stock, $10 par.

Instructions
1. Calculate the total dividends and the per-share dividends declared on each class of stock for each of the six years. Summarize the data in tabular form, using the following column headings:

Year	Total Dividends	Preferred Dividends		Common Dividends	
		Total	Per Share	Total	Per Share
2003	$ 21,000				
2004	50,000				
2005	15,000				
2006	80,000				
2007	90,000				
2008	140,000				

2. Calculate the average annual dividend per share for each class of stock for the six-year period.
3. Assuming that the preferred stock was sold at $80 and common stock was sold at par at the beginning of the six-year period, calculate the average annual percentage return on initial shareholders' investment, based on the average annual dividend per share (a) for preferred stock and (b) for common stock.

PR 13-2A
Stock transactions for corporate expansion
obj. 3

On January 31 of the current year, the following accounts and their balances appear in the ledger of Gargantuan Corp., a meat processor:

Preferred 3% Stock, $25 par (50,000 shares authorized, 30,000 shares issued)	$ 750,000
Paid-In Capital in Excess of Par—Preferred Stock	90,000
Common Stock, $30 par (400,000 shares authorized, 120,000 shares issued)	3,600,000
Paid-In Capital in Excess of Par—Common Stock	300,000
Retained Earnings	5,794,000

At the annual stockholders' meeting on April 2, the board of directors presented a plan for modernizing and expanding plant operations at a cost of approximately $2,550,000. The plan provided (a) that a building, valued at $1,200,000, and the land on which it is located, valued at $300,000, be acquired in accordance with preliminary negotiations by the issuance of 45,000 shares of common stock, (b) that 15,000 shares of the unissued preferred stock be issued through an underwriter, and (c) that the corporation borrow $500,000. The plan was approved by the stockholders and accomplished by the following transactions:

June   6. Issued 45,000 shares of common stock in exchange for land and a building, according to the plan.
    14. Issued 15,000 shares of preferred stock, receiving $36 per share in cash.
    30. Borrowed $500,000 from Mt. Baker National Bank, giving a 7% mortgage note.

No other transactions occurred during June.

Instructions
Journalize the entries to record the foregoing transactions.

PR 13-3A
*Selected stock
transactions*

objs. 3, 4, 5

f. Cash dividends, $86,500

The following selected accounts appear in the ledger of Clear Skies Environmental Corporation on July 1, 2008, the beginning of the current fiscal year:

Preferred 2% Stock, $100 par (25,000 shares authorized,	
18,000 shares issued)	$1,800,000
Paid-In Capital in Excess of Par—Preferred Stock	216,000
Common Stock, $40 par (100,000 shares authorized,	
70,000 shares issued)	2,800,000
Paid-In Capital in Excess of Par—Common Stock	700,000
Retained Earnings	3,200,000

During the year, the corporation completed a number of transactions affecting the stockholders' equity. They are summarized as follows:

a. Issued 12,000 shares of common stock at $62, receiving cash.
b. Sold 5,000 shares of preferred 2% stock at $124.
c. Purchased 10,000 shares of treasury common for $580,000.
d. Sold 7,500 shares of treasury common for $457,500.
e. Sold 1,500 shares of treasury common for $82,500.
f. Declared cash dividends of $2 per share on preferred stock and $0.50 per share on common stock.
g. Paid the cash dividends.

Instructions
Journalize the entries to record the transactions. Identify each entry by letter.

PR 13-4A
*Entries for selected
corporate transactions*

objs. 3, 4, 5, 6

✓*4. Total stockholders'
equity, $9,869,000*

Eureka Enterprises Inc. manufactures bathroom fixtures. The stockholders' equity accounts of Eureka Enterprises Inc., with balances on January 1, 2008, are as follows:

Common Stock, $10 stated value (500,000 shares authorized,	
380,000 shares issued)	$3,800,000
Paid-In Capital in Excess of Stated Value	760,000
Retained Earnings	4,390,000
Treasury Stock (25,000 shares, at cost)	500,000

The following selected transactions occurred during the year:

Jan. 10. Paid cash dividends of $0.20 per share on the common stock. The dividend had been properly recorded when declared on December 30 of the preceding fiscal year for $71,000.
Mar. 3. Issued 20,000 shares of common stock for $460,000.
May 21. Sold all of the treasury stock for $650,000.
July 1. Declared a 3% stock dividend on common stock, to be capitalized at the market price of the stock, which is $30 per share.
Aug. 15. Issued the certificates for the dividend declared on July 1.
Sept. 30. Purchased 10,000 shares of treasury stock for $230,000.
Dec. 27. Declared a $0.25-per-share dividend on common stock.
31. Closed the credit balance of the income summary account, $639,500.
31. Closed the two dividends accounts to Retained Earnings.

Instructions
1. Enter the January 1 balances in T accounts for the stockholders' equity accounts listed. Also prepare T accounts for the following: Paid-In Capital from Sale of Treasury Stock; Stock Dividends Distributable; Stock Dividends; Cash Dividends.
2. Journalize the entries to record the transactions, and post to the eight selected accounts.
3. Prepare a retained earnings statement for the year ended December 31, 2008.
4. Prepare the Stockholders' Equity section of the December 31, 2008, balance sheet.

PR 13-5A
Entries for selected corporate transactions
objs. 3, 4, 5, 7

✓ *Nov. 15, cash dividends, $82,800*

Selected transactions completed by Oceano Boating Corporation during the current fiscal year are as follows:

Jan. 3. Split the common stock 2 for 1 and reduced the par from $50 to $25 per share. After the split, there were 400,000 common shares outstanding.

Feb. 20. Purchased 50,000 shares of the corporation's own common stock at $32, recording the stock at cost.

May 1. Declared semiannual dividends of $0.80 on 30,000 shares of preferred stock and $0.14 on the common stock to stockholders of record on May 15, payable on June 1.

June 1. Paid the cash dividends.

Aug. 5. Sold 42,000 shares of treasury stock at $39, receiving cash.

Nov. 15. Declared semiannual dividends of $0.80 on the preferred stock and $0.15 on the common stock (before the stock dividend). In addition, a 2% common stock dividend was declared on the common stock outstanding. The fair market value of the common stock is estimated at $40.

Dec. 31. Paid the cash dividends and issued the certificates for the common stock dividend.

Instructions
Journalize the transactions.

Problems Series B

PR 13-1B
Dividends on preferred and common stock
obj. 3

✓ *1. Common dividends in 2003: $40,000*

Rainer Bike Corp. manufactures mountain bikes and distributes them through retail outlets in Oregon and Washington. Rainer Bike Corp. has declared the following annual dividends over a six-year period: 2003, $60,000; 2004, $8,000; 2005, $30,000; 2006, $40,000; 2007, $80,000; and 2008, $115,000. During the entire period, the outstanding stock of the company was composed of 40,000 shares of 2% preferred stock, $25 par, and 50,000 shares of common stock, $1 par.

Instructions

1. Determine the total dividends and the per-share dividends declared on each class of stock for each of the six years. Summarize the data in tabular form, using the following column headings:

Year	Total Dividends	Preferred Dividends		Common Dividends	
		Total	Per Share	Total	Per Share
2003	$ 60,000				
2004	8,000				
2005	30,000				
2006	40,000				
2007	80,000				
2008	115,000				

2. Determine the average annual dividend per share for each class of stock for the six-year period.

3. Assuming that the preferred stock was sold at par and common stock was sold at $18.75 at the beginning of the six-year period, calculate the average annual percentage return on initial shareholders' investment, based on the average annual dividend per share (a) for preferred stock and (b) for common stock.

PR 13-2B
Stock transaction for corporate expansion
obj. 3

I-Can-See Optics produces medical lasers for use in hospitals. The accounts and their balances appear in the ledger of I-Can-See Optics on November 30 of the current year at the top of the following page.

Preferred 2% Stock, $80 par (40,000 shares authorized,	
25,000 shares issued)	$ 2,000,000
Paid-In Capital in Excess of Par—Preferred Stock	120,000
Common Stock, $100 par (500,000 shares authorized,	
50,000 shares issued)	5,000,000
Paid-In Capital in Excess of Par—Common Stock	300,000
Retained Earnings	12,794,000

At the annual stockholders' meeting on December 10, the board of directors presented a plan for modernizing and expanding plant operations at a cost of approximately $3,800,000. The plan provided (a) that the corporation borrow $900,000, (b) that 10,000 shares of the un-issued preferred stock be issued through an underwriter, and (c) that a building, valued at $1,675,000, and the land on which it is located, valued at $250,000, be acquired in accordance with preliminary negotiations by the issuance of 16,000 shares of common stock. The plan was approved by the stockholders and accomplished by the following transactions:

Jan.   6.   Borrowed $900,000 from City National Bank, giving a 6% mortgage note.
          15.   Issued 10,000 shares of preferred stock, receiving $95 per share in cash.
          31.   Issued 16,000 shares of common stock in exchange for land and a building, according to the plan.

No other transactions occurred during January.

Instructions
Journalize the entries to record the foregoing transactions.

PR 13-3B
Selected stock transactions
objs. 3, 4, 5

✓ *f. Cash dividends, $123,900*

Buellton Welding Corporation sells and services pipe welding equipment in California. The following selected accounts appear in the ledger of Buellton Welding Corporation on January 1, 2008, the beginning of the current fiscal year:

Preferred 2% Stock, $50 par (100,000 shares authorized,	
50,000 shares issued)	$ 2,500,000
Paid-In Capital in Excess of Par—Preferred Stock	180,000
Common Stock, $15 par (900,000 shares authorized,	
600,000 shares issued)	9,000,000
Paid-In Capital in Excess of Par—Common Stock	1,500,000
Retained Earnings	13,100,000

During the year, the corporation completed a number of transactions affecting the stock-holders' equity. They are summarized as follows:

a. Purchased 25,000 shares of treasury common for $650,000.
b. Sold 18,000 shares of treasury common for $576,000.
c. Sold 10,000 shares of preferred 2% stock at $80.
d. Issued 40,000 shares of common stock at $30, receiving cash.
e. Sold 6,000 shares of treasury common for $150,000.
f. Declared cash dividends of $1 per share on preferred stock and $0.10 per share on common stock.
g. Paid the cash dividends.

Instructions
Journalize the entries to record the transactions. Identify each entry by letter.

PR 13-4B
Entries for selected corporate transactions
objs. 3, 4, 5, 6

✓ *4. Total stockholders' equity, $11,160,300*

GPS Enterprises Inc. produces aeronautical navigation equipment. The stockholders' equity accounts of GPS Enterprises Inc., with balances on January 1, 2008, are as follows:

Common Stock, $20 stated value (250,000 shares authorized,	
150,000 shares issued)	$3,000,000
Paid-In Capital in Excess of Stated Value	600,000
Retained Earnings	6,175,000
Treasury Stock (10,000 shares, at cost)	280,000

The following selected transactions occurred during the year:

Jan. 12. Paid cash dividends of $0.25 per share on the common stock. The dividend had been properly recorded when declared on December 28 of the preceding fiscal year for $35,000.
Feb. 19. Sold all of the treasury stock for $360,000.
Apr. 3. Issued 40,000 shares of common stock for $1,600,000.
July 30. Declared a 2% stock dividend on common stock, to be capitalized at the market price of the stock, which is $45 per share.
Aug. 30. Issued the certificates for the dividend declared on July 30.
Nov. 7. Purchased 15,000 shares of treasury stock for $600,000.
Dec. 30. Declared a $0.25-per-share dividend on common stock.
       31. Closed the credit balance of the income summary account, $350,000.
       31. Closed the two dividends accounts to Retained Earnings.

Instructions

1. Enter the January 1 balances in T accounts for the stockholders' equity accounts listed. Also prepare T accounts for the following: Paid-In Capital from Sale of Treasury Stock; Stock Dividends Distributable; Stock Dividends; Cash Dividends.
2. Journalize the entries to record the transactions, and post to the eight selected accounts.
3. Prepare a retained earnings statement for the year ended December 31, 2008.
4. Prepare the Stockholders' Equity section of the December 31, 2008, balance sheet.

PR 13-5B
Entries for selected corporate transactions

objs. 3, 4, 5, 7

✓ *Sept. 1, Cash dividends, $169,100*

Moro Bay Corporation manufactures and distributes leisure clothing. Selected transactions completed by Moro Bay during the current fiscal year are as follows:

Jan. 10. Split the common stock 4 for 1 and reduced the par from $20 to $5 per share. After the split, there were 500,000 common shares outstanding.
Mar. 1. Declared semiannual dividends of $1 on 125,000 shares of preferred stock and $0.12 on the 500,000 shares of $5 par common stock to stockholders of record on March 31, payable on April 30.
Apr. 30. Paid the cash dividends.
July 9. Purchased 40,000 shares of the corporation's own common stock at $16, recording the stock at cost.
Aug. 29. Sold 30,000 shares of treasury stock at $21, receiving cash.
Sept. 1. Declared semiannual dividends of $1 on the preferred stock and $0.09 on the common stock (before the stock dividend). In addition, a 1% common stock dividend was declared on the common stock outstanding, to be capitalized at the fair market value of the common stock, which is estimated at $22.
Oct. 31. Paid the cash dividends and issued the certificates for the common stock dividend.

Instructions
Journalize the transactions.

Special Activities

SA 13-1
Board of directors' actions

Bernie Ebbers, the CEO of WorldCom, a major telecommunications company, was having personal financial troubles. Ebbers pledged a large stake of his WorldCom stock as security for some personal loans. As the price of WorldCom stock sank, Ebbers' bankers threatened to sell his stock in order to protect their loans. To avoid having his stock sold, Ebbers asked the board of directors of WorldCom to loan him nearly $400 million of corporate assets at 2.5% interest to pay off his bankers. The board agreed to lend him the money.

➤ Comment on the decision of the board of directors in this situation.

SA 13-2
Ethics and professional conduct in business

ETHICS

Gigi Liken and Ron Bobo are organizing Gold Unlimited Inc. to undertake a high-risk gold-mining venture in Canada. Gigi and Ron tentatively plan to request authorization for 75,000,000 shares of common stock to be sold to the general public. Gigi and Ron have decided to establish par of $1 per share in order to appeal to a wide variety of potential investors. Gigi and Ron feel that investors would be more willing to invest in the company if they received a large quantity of shares for what might appear to be a "bargain" price.

▶ Discuss whether Gigi and Ron are behaving in a professional manner.

SA 13-3
Issuing stock

Las Animas Inc. began operations on January 2, 2008, with the issuance of 100,000 shares of $50 par common stock. The sole stockholders of Las Animas Inc. are Cindy Stern and Dr. Kassay Heyen, who organized Las Animas Inc. with the objective of developing a new flu vaccine. Dr. Heyen claims that the flu vaccine, which is nearing the final development stage, will protect individuals against 80% of the flu types that have been medically identified. To complete the project, Las Animas Inc. needs $5,000,000 of additional funds. The local banks have been unwilling to loan the funds because of the lack of sufficient collateral and the riskiness of the business.

The following is a conversation between Cindy Stern, the chief executive officer of Las Animas Inc., and Dr. Kassay Heyen, the leading researcher.

Stern: What are we going to do? The banks won't loan us any more money, and we've got to have $5 million to complete the project. We are so close! It would be a disaster to quit now. The only thing I can think of is to issue additional stock. Do you have any suggestions?

Heyen: I guess you're right. But if the banks won't loan us any more money, how do you think we can find any investors to buy stock?

Stern: I've been thinking about that. What if we promise the investors that we will pay them 2% of net sales until they have received an amount equal to what they paid for the stock?

Heyen: What happens when we pay back the $5 million? Do the investors get to keep the stock? If they do, it'll dilute our ownership.

Stern: How about, if after we pay back the $5 million, we make them turn in their stock for $100 per share? That's twice what they paid for it, plus they would have already gotten all their money back. That's a $100 profit per share for the investors.

Heyen: It could work. We get our money, but don't have to pay any interest, dividends, or the $50 until we start generating net sales. At the same time, the investors could get their money back plus $50 per share.

Stern: We'll need current financial statements for the new investors. I'll get our accountant working on them and contact our attorney to draw up a legally binding contract for the new investors. Yes, this could work.

In late 2008, the attorney and the various regulatory authorities approved the new stock offering, and 100,000 shares of common stock were privately sold to new investors at the stock's par of $50.

In preparing financial statements for 2008, Cindy Stern and Debra Allen, the controller for Las Animas Inc., have the following conversation.

Allen: Cindy, I've got a problem.

Stern: What's that, Debra?

Allen: Issuing common stock to raise that additional $5 million was a great idea. But . . .

Stern: But what?

Allen: I've got to prepare the 2008 annual financial statements, and I am not sure how to classify the common stock.

Stern: What do you mean? It's common stock.

Allen: I'm not so sure. I called the auditor and explained how we are contractually obligated to pay the new stockholders 2% of net sales until $50 per share is paid. Then, we may be obligated to pay them $100 per share.

Stern: So . . .

Allen: So the auditor thinks that we should classify the additional issuance of $5 million as debt, not stock! And, if we put the $5 million on the balance sheet as debt, we will violate our other loan agreements with the banks. And, if these agreements are violated, the banks may call in all our debt immediately. If they do that, we are in deep trouble. We'll probably have to file for bankruptcy. We just don't have the cash to pay off the banks.

1. ▬▬▶ Discuss the arguments for and against classifying the issuance of the $5 million of stock as debt.
2. ▬▬▶ What do you think might be a practical solution to this classification problem?

SA 13-4
Interpret stock exchange listing

The Wall Street Journal reported the following stock exchange information for General Electric Company (GE) on May 12, 2006:

52 Weeks		Stock	Sym	Div	Yld%	PE	Vol 100s	LAST	Net Chg
Hi	Lo								
37^{34}	32^{21}	GenElec	GE	1.00	2.9	22	227,456	34^{51}	−.19

a. If you owned 500 shares of GE, what amount would you receive as a quarterly dividend?
b. Calculate and prove the dividend yield. Round to two decimal places.
c. What is GE's percentage change in market price from the May 10, 2006, close? Round to one decimal place.
d. If you bought 500 shares of GE at the close price on May 11, 2006, how much would it cost, and who gets the money?

SA 13-5
Dividends

Sentinel Inc. has paid quarterly cash dividends since 1995. These dividends have steadily increased from $0.05 per share to the latest dividend declaration of $0.40 per share. The board of directors would like to continue this trend and is hesitant to suspend or decrease the amount of quarterly dividends. Unfortunately, sales dropped sharply in the fourth quarter of 2008 because of worsening economic conditions and increased competition. As a result, the board is uncertain as to whether it should declare a dividend for the last quarter of 2008.

On November 1, 2008, Sentinel Inc. borrowed $800,000 from American National Bank to use in modernizing its retail stores and to expand its product line in reaction to its competition. The terms of the 10-year, 6% loan require Sentinel Inc. to:

a. Pay monthly interest on the last day of the month.
b. Pay $80,000 of the principal each November 1, beginning in 2009.
c. Maintain a current ratio (current assets/current liabilities) of 2.
d. Maintain a minimum balance (a compensating balance) of $40,000 in its American National Bank account.

On December 31, 2008, $200,000 of the $800,000 loan had been disbursed in modernization of the retail stores and in expansion of the product line. Sentinel Inc.'s balance sheet as of December 31, 2008, is shown at the top of the following page.

The board of directors is scheduled to meet January 6, 2009, to discuss the results of operations for 2008 and to consider the declaration of dividends for the fourth quarter of 2008. The chairman of the board has asked for your advice on the declaration of dividends.

1. ▬▬▶ What factors should the board consider in deciding whether to declare a cash dividend?
2. ▬▬▶ The board is considering the declaration of a stock dividend instead of a cash dividend. Discuss the issuance of a stock dividend from the point of view of (a) a stockholder and (b) the board of directors.

(continued)

Sentinel Inc.
Balance Sheet
December 31, 2008

Assets

Current assets:			
Cash		$ 64,000	
Marketable securities		600,000	
Accounts receivable	$ 146,400		
Less allowance for doubtful accounts	10,400	136,000	
Merchandise inventory		200,000	
Prepaid expenses		7,200	
Total current assets			$1,007,200
Property, plant, and equipment:			
Land		$ 240,000	
Buildings	$1,520,000		
Less accumulated depreciation	344,000	1,176,000	
Equipment	$ 736,000		
Less accumulated depreciation	176,000	560,000	
Total property, plant, and equipment			1,976,000
Total assets			$2,983,200

Liabilities

Current liabilities:			
Accounts payable	$ 114,880		
Notes payable (American National Bank)	80,000		
Salaries payable	5,120		
Total current liabilities		$ 200,000	
Long-term liabilities:			
Notes payable (American National Bank)		720,000	
Total liabilities			$ 920,000

Stockholders' Equity

Paid-in capital:			
Common stock, $20 par (50,000 shares authorized, 40,000 shares issued)	$ 800,000		
Excess of issue price over par	64,000		
Total paid-in capital		$ 864,000	
Retained earnings		1,199,200	
Total stockholders' equity			2,063,200
Total liabilities and stockholders' equity			$2,983,200

SA 13-6
Profiling a corporation

Group Project

Internet Project

Select a public corporation you are familiar with or which interests you. Using the Internet, your school library, and other sources, develop a short (1 to 2 pages) profile of the corporation. Include in your profile the following information:

1. Name of the corporation.
2. State of incorporation.
3. Nature of its operations.
4. Total assets for the most recent balance sheet.
5. Total revenues for the most recent income statement.
6. Net income for the most recent income statement.
7. Classes of stock outstanding.
8. Market price of the stock outstanding.
9. High and low price of the stock for the past year.
10. Dividends paid for each share of stock during the past year.

In groups of three or four, discuss each corporate profile. Select one of the corporations, assuming that your group has $100,000 to invest in its stock. Summarize why your group selected the corporation it did and how financial accounting information may have affected your decision. Keep track of the performance of your corporation's stock for the remainder of the term.

Note: Most major corporations maintain "home pages" on the Internet. This home page provides a variety of information on the corporation and often includes the corporation's financial statements. In addition, the New York Stock Exchange Web site (**http://www.nyse .com**) includes links to the home pages of many listed companies. Financial statements can also be accessed using EDGAR, the electronic archives of financial statements filed with the Securities and Exchange Commission (SEC).

SEC documents can also be retrieved using the EdgarScan™ service from PricewaterhouseCoopers at **http://edgarscan.pwcglobal.com**. To obtain annual report information, key in a company name in the appropriate space. EdgarScan will list the reports available to you for the company you've selected. Select the most recent annual report filing, identified as a 10-K or 10-K405. EdgarScan provides an outline of the report, including the separate financial statements, which can also be selected in an Excel® spreadsheet.

Answers to Self-Examination Questions

1. **C** The separation of the owner from management (answer C) is a disadvantage of the corporate form of organization. This is because management may not always behave in the best interests of the owners. Limited liability (answer A), continuous life (answer B), and the ability to raise capital (answer D) are all advantages of the corporate form of organization.

2. **D** Paid-in capital is one of the two major subdivisions of the stockholders' equity of a corporation. It may result from many sources, including the issuance of preferred stock (answer A), issuing common stock (answer B), or the sale of a corporation's treasury stock (answer C).

3. **D** The Stockholders' Equity section of corporate balance sheets is divided into two principal subsections: (1) investments contributed by the stockholders and others and (2) net income retained in the business.

Included as part of the investments by stockholders and others is the par of common stock (answer A), stock dividends distributable (answer B), and the par of preferred stock (answer C).

4. **C** Reacquired stock, known as *treasury stock,* should be listed in the Stockholders' Equity section (answer C) of the balance sheet. The price paid for the treasury stock is deducted from the total of all the stockholders' equity accounts.

5. **C** If a corporation that holds treasury stock declares a cash dividend, the dividends are not paid on the treasury shares. To do so would place the corporation in the position of earning income through dealing with itself. Thus, the corporation will record $44,000 (answer C) as cash dividends [(25,000 shares issued less 3,000 shares held as treasury stock) × $2 per share dividend].

chapter 14

Income Taxes, Unusual Income Items, and Investments in Stocks

© NEIL BRAKE/ASSOCIATED PRESS

objectives

After studying this chapter, you should be able to:

1 Journalize the entries for corporate income taxes, including deferred income taxes.

2 Describe and illustrate the reporting of unusual items on the income statement.

3 Prepare an income statement reporting earnings per share data.

4 Describe the concept and the reporting of comprehensive income.

5 Describe the accounting for investments in stocks.

Gaylord Entertainment Co.

I f you apply for a bank loan, you will be required to list your assets and liabilities on a loan application. In addition, you will be asked to indicate your monthly income. Assume that the day you fill out the application, you win $4,000 in the state lottery. The $4,000 lottery winnings increase your assets by $4,000. Should you also show your lottery winnings as part of your monthly income?

The answer, of course, is no. Winning the lottery is an unusual event and, for most of us, a nonrecurring event. In determining whether to grant the loan, the bank is interested in your ability to make monthly loan payments. Such payments depend upon your recurring monthly income.

Businesses also experience unusual and nonrecurring events that affect their financial statements. Such events should be clearly disclosed in the financial statements so that stakeholders in the business will not misinterpret the financial effects of the events.

Gaylord Entertainment Co. is an example of such a company. Gaylord has pioneered the self-contained "all-in-one-place" hotel and resort concept, with the Gaylord Opryland, Gaylord Texan, and Gaylord Palms resorts. In addition, Gaylord owns ResortQuest and Ryman Auditorim (the original Grand Ole Opry) in Nashville, Tennessee. While Gaylord's operating income is positive, it has continued to report net losses over a number of recent years, due to losses from discontinued operations. Such unusual items are identified on Gaylord's income statement to alert users of the nonrecurring nature of some of its activities.

In this chapter, we discuss unusual items that affect income statements, such as those for Gaylord Entertainment, and illustrate how such items should be reported. We also discuss other specialized accounting and reporting topics, including accounting for income taxes, comprehensive income, and investments.

Corporate Income Taxes

objective *1*

Journalize the entries for corporate income taxes, including deferred income taxes.

Under the U.S. tax code, corporations are taxable entities that must pay federal income taxes.[1] Depending upon where it is located, a corporation may also be required to pay state and local income taxes. Although we limit our discussion to federal income taxes, the basic concepts also apply to other income taxes.

PAYMENT OF INCOME TAXES

Individuals pay quarterly estimated taxes if the amount of tax withholding is not sufficient to pay their taxes at the end of the year. This usually occurs when a significant portion of an individual's income is from self-employment, rent, dividends, or interest.

Most corporations are required to pay estimated federal income taxes in four installments throughout the year. For example, assume that a corporation with a calendar-year accounting period estimates its income tax expense for the year as $84,000. The entry to record the first of the four estimated tax payments of $21,000 (1/4 of $84,000) is as follows:

Apr.	15	Income Tax Expense	21 0 0 0 00	
		Cash		21 0 0 0 00

---

1 Limited liability companies (LLCs) are not separate taxable entities and thus are not subject to federal (and most state) income taxes. For this reason, the material in this section would not generally apply to an LLC.

At year-end, the actual taxable income and the related tax are determined.[2] If additional taxes are owed, the additional liability is recorded. If the total estimated tax payments are greater than the tax liability based on actual taxable income, the overpayment should be debited to a receivable account and credited to *Income Tax Expense*.[3]

Income taxes are normally disclosed as a deduction at the bottom of the income statement in determining net income, as shown below, in an excerpt from an income statement for Procter & Gamble.

Year Ended June 30, 2005	(Amounts in Millions)
Net Sales	**$56,741**
Cost of products sold	27,804
Marketing, research, and administrative expenses	18,010
Income from Operations	**$10,927**
Interest expense	(834)
Other income, net	346
Earnings Before Income Taxes	**$10,439**
Income taxes	3,182
Net Earnings	**$ 7,257**

The ratio of reported income tax expense to earnings before taxes is shown for selected industries, as follows:

Industry	Percent of Reported Income Tax Expense to Earnings before Taxes
Automobiles	33%
Banking	35
Computers	23
Food	35
Integrated oil	39
Pharmaceuticals	30
Retail	39
Telecommunication	37
Transportation	38

As you can see, the reported income tax expense is normally between 30%–40% of earnings before tax. Therefore, taxes are a significant expense for most companies and must be considered when analyzing a company. Differences in tax rates between industries can be due to tax regulations unique to certain industries.

ALLOCATING INCOME TAXES

The **taxable income** of a corporation is determined according to the tax laws and is reported to taxing authorities on the corporation's tax return.[4] It is often different from the income before income taxes reported in the income statement according to

---

2 A corporation's income tax returns and supporting records are subject to audits by taxing authorities, who may assess additional taxes. Because of this possibility, the liability for income taxes is sometimes described in the balance sheet as *Estimated income tax payable*.

3 Another common term used for income taxes on the income statement and note disclosures is *Provision for income taxes*.

4 Accounting for deferred income taxes is a complex topic that is treated in greater detail in advanced accounting texts. The treatment here provides a general overview and conceptual understanding of the topic.

generally accepted accounting principles. As a result, the *income tax based on taxable income* usually differs from the *income tax based on income before taxes*. This difference may need to be allocated between various financial statement periods, depending on the nature of the items causing the differences.

Some differences between taxable income and income before income taxes are created because items are recognized in one period for tax purposes and in another period for income statement purposes. Such differences, called **temporary differences**, reverse or turn around in later years. Some examples of items that create temporary differences are listed below.

1. *Revenues or gains are taxed **after** they are reported in the income statement.* Example: In some cases, companies that make sales under an installment plan recognize revenue for financial reporting purposes when a sale is made but defer recognizing revenue for tax purposes until cash is collected.
2. *Expenses or losses are deducted in determining taxable income **after** they are reported in the income statement.* Example: Product warranty expense estimated and reported in the year of the sale for financial statement reporting is deducted for tax reporting when paid.
3. *Revenues or gains are taxed **before** they are reported in the income statement.* Example: Cash received in advance for magazine subscriptions is included in taxable income when received but included in the income statement only when earned in a future period.
4. *Expenses or losses are deducted in determining taxable income **before** they are reported in the income statement.* Example: MACRS depreciation is used for tax purposes, and the straight-line method is used for financial reporting purposes.

Since temporary differences reverse in later years, they do not change or reduce the total amount of taxable income over the life of a business. Exhibit 1 illustrates the reversing nature of temporary differences in which a business uses MACRS depreciation for tax purposes and straight-line depreciation for financial statement purposes. Exhibit 1 assumes that MACRS recognizes more depreciation in the early years and less depreciation in the later years. The total depreciation expense is the same for both methods over the life of the asset.

As Exhibit 1 illustrates, temporary differences affect only the timing of when revenues and expenses are recognized for tax purposes. As a result, the total amount of taxes paid does not change. Only the timing of the payment of taxes is affected. As shown in Exhibit 1, most managers use tax-planning techniques so that temporary differences delay or defer the payment of taxes to later years. As a result, at the end of

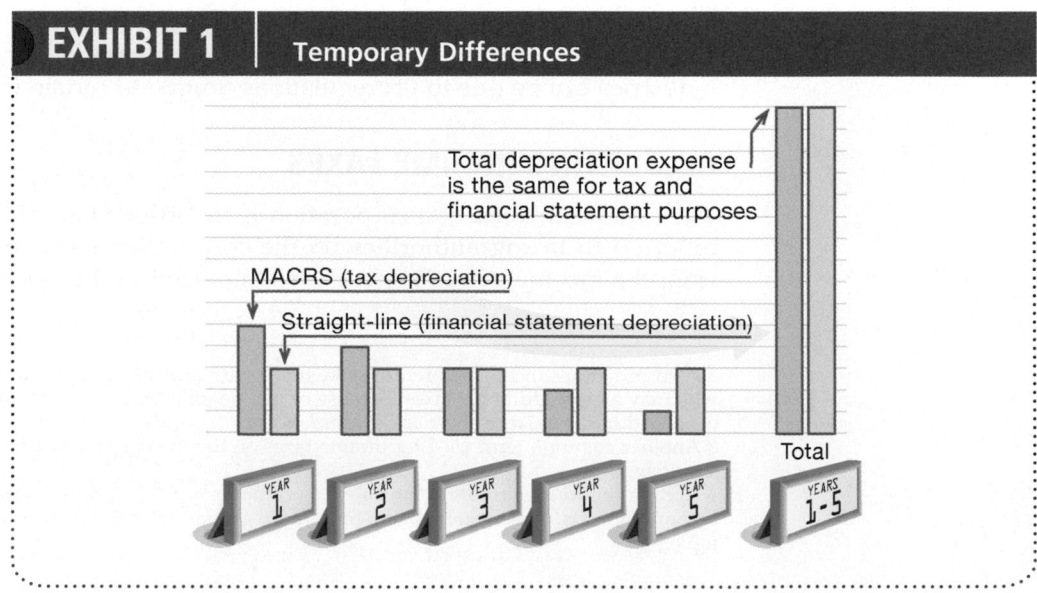

EXHIBIT 1　　**Temporary Differences**

Total depreciation expense is the same for tax and financial statement purposes

MACRS (tax depreciation)

Straight-line (financial statement depreciation)

Total

YEAR 1　YEAR 2　YEAR 3　YEAR 4　YEAR 5　YEARS 1-5

each year the amount of the current tax liability and the postponed (deferred) liability must be recorded.

To illustrate, assume that at the end of the first year of operations a corporation reports $300,000 income before income taxes on its income statement. If we assume an income tax rate of 40%, the income tax expense reported on the income statement is $120,000 ($300,000 × 40%).[5] However, to reduce the amount owed for current income taxes, the corporation uses tax planning to reduce the taxable income to $100,000. Thus, the income tax actually due for the year is only $40,000 ($100,000 × 40%). The $80,000 ($120,000 − $40,000) difference between the two tax amounts is created by temporary differences in recognizing revenue. This amount is deferred to future years. The example is summarized below.

Income tax expense based on $300,000 reported income at 40%	$120,000
Income tax payable based on $100,000 taxable income at 40%	40,000
Income tax deferred to future years	$ 80,000

To match the current year's expenses (including income tax) against the current year's revenue on the income statement, income tax is allocated between periods, using the following journal entry:

Income Tax Expense		120 0 0 0 00	
Income Tax Payable			40 0 0 0 00
Deferred Income Tax Payable			80 0 0 0 00

The income tax expense reported on the income statement is the total tax, $120,000, expected to be paid on the income for the year. In future years, the $80,000 in *Deferred Income Tax Payable* will be transferred to *Income Tax Payable* as the temporary differences reverse and the taxes become due. For example, if $48,000 of the deferred tax reverses and becomes due in the second year, the following journal entry would be made in the second year:

Deferred Income Tax Payable		48 0 0 0 00	
Income Tax Payable			48 0 0 0 00

REPORTING AND ANALYZING TAXES

The balance of *Deferred Income Tax Payable* at the end of a year is reported as a liability.[6] The amount due within one year is classified as a current liability. The remainder is classified as a long-term liability or reported in a Deferred Credits section following the Long-Term Liabilities section.[7]

Differences between taxable income and income (before taxes) reported on the income statement may also arise because certain revenues are exempt from tax and certain expenses are not deductible in determining taxable income. Such differences, which will not reverse with the passage of time, are sometimes called **permanent differences**. For example, interest income on municipal bonds may be exempt from taxation. Such differences create no special financial reporting problems, since the amount of income tax determined according to the tax laws is the *same* amount reported on the income statement.

Interest from investments in municipal bonds is also tax exempt for individual taxpayers.

---

5 For purposes of illustration, the 40% rate is assumed to include all federal, state, and local income taxes.
6 In some cases, a deferred tax asset may arise for tax benefits to be received in the future. Such deferred tax assets are reported as either current or long-term assets, depending on when the benefits are expected to be realized.
7 Additional note disclosures for deferred income taxes are also required. These are discussed in advanced accounting texts.

Example Exercise 14-1   **objective** 1

A corporation has $200,000 of income before income taxes, a 40% tax rate, and $130,000 of taxable income. Provide the journal entry for the current year's taxes.

Follow My Example 14-1

Income Tax Expense	80,000	
Income Tax Payable		52,000
Deferred Income Tax Payable		28,000

Income tax expense based on $200,000 reported income at 40%	$80,000
Income tax payable based on $130,000 taxable income at 40%	52,000
Income tax deferred to future years	$28,000

For Practice: PE 14-1A, PE 14-1B

Reporting Unusual Items on the Income Statement

objective 2

Describe and illustrate the reporting of unusual items on the income statement.

Generally accepted accounting principles require that certain unusual items be reported separately on the current or prior period's income statement. These items can be classified into items affecting the current period income statement and those affecting prior period income statements as shown below.

> Unusual Items Affecting the Current Period's Income Statement
> > Fixed asset impairments
> > Restructuring charges
> > Discontinued operations
> > Extraordinary item
>
> Unusual Items Affecting the Prior Period's Income Statement
> > Errors
> > Change in accounting principles

The first category of unusual items affects the current period's income statement. However, the location of the disclosure on the income statement is different between these items. Fixed asset impairment and restructuring charges are reported above income from continuing operations as shown in item 1 of Exhibit 2. That is, fixed asset impairment and restructuring charges are subtracted in arriving at income from continuing operations. Although discontinued operations and extraordinary items affect net income, they are reported below income from continuing operations as shown in item 2 of Exhibit 2.

In the following paragraphs, we first describe and illustrate unusual items affecting the current period's income statement. We then discuss unusual items affecting prior period income statements as shown in item 3 of Exhibit 2.

UNUSUAL ITEMS AFFECTING THE CURRENT PERIOD'S INCOME STATEMENT

Unusual items affecting the current period's income statement include fixed asset impairments, restructuring charges, discontinued operations, and extraordinary items. Fixed asset impairments and restructuring charges, sometimes termed *special charges* when combined, will be discussed first. Following these, we will discuss discontinued operations and extraordinary items.

EXHIBIT 2	Reporting of Unusual Items on the Income Statement

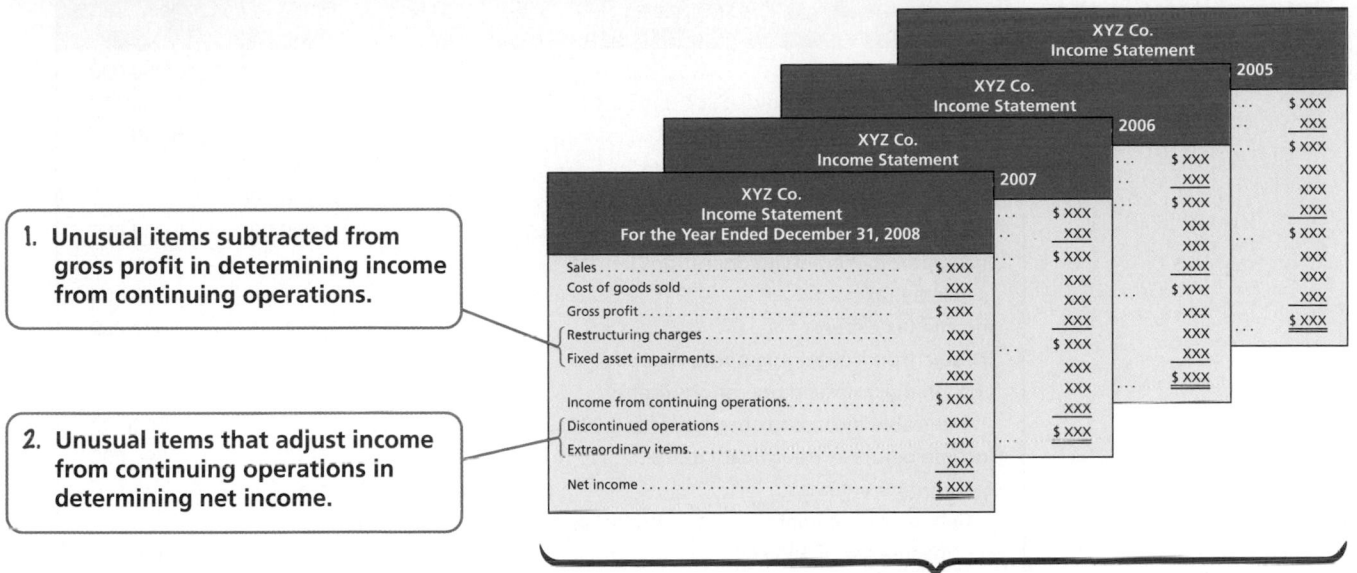

1. Unusual items subtracted from gross profit in determining income from continuing operations.

2. Unusual items that adjust income from continuing operations in determining net income.

3. Unusual items affecting prior period income statements.

Fixed Asset Impairments A **fixed asset impairment** occurs when the fair value of a fixed asset falls below its book value (cost less accumulated depreciation) and is not expected to recover.[8] Examples of events that might cause an asset impairment are (1) decreases in the market price of fixed assets, (2) significant changes in the business or regulations related to fixed assets, (3) adverse conditions affecting the use of fixed assets, or (4) expected cash flow losses from using fixed assets.[9] For example, on March 1, assume that Jones Corporation consolidates operations by closing a factory. As a result of the closing, plant and equipment is impaired by $750,000. The journal entry to record the impairment is as follows:

Mar.	1	Loss on Fixed Asset Impairment	750 0 0 0 00	
		Equipment		750 0 0 0 00

The loss on fixed asset impairment is reported as a separate expense item deducted from gross profit in determining income from continuing operations, as illustrated for Jones Corporation in Exhibit 3. In addition, note disclosure should describe the nature of the asset impaired and the cause of the impairment.

The loss reduces the book value of the fixed asset and thus reduces the depreciation expense for future periods. If the asset is later sold, the gain or loss on the sale would be based on the lower book value. Thus, asset impairment accounting recognizes the loss when it is first identified, rather than when the asset is later sold.

---

8 Fixed assets that are discontinued components, such as an operating segment, subsidiary, or asset group, should be treated as discontinued items, as discussed in a later section.
9 *Statement of Financial Accounting Standards No. 144,* "Accounting for the Impairment or Disposal of Long-Lived Assets" (Norwalk, CT: Financial Accounting Standards Board, 2001).

EXHIBIT 3

Unusual Items in the
Income Statement

Jones Corporation
Income Statement
For the Year Ended December 31, 2008

Net sales		$12,350,000
Cost of merchandise sold		5,800,000
Gross profit		$ 6,550,000
Selling and administrative expenses	$3,490,000	
Loss from asset impairment	750,000	
Restructuring charge	1,000,000	5,240,000
Income from continuing operations before		
income tax		$ 1,310,000
Income tax expense		620,000
Income from continuing operations		$ 690,000
Loss on discontinued operations (net of		
applicable income tax benefit of $50,000)		100,000
Income before extraordinary items		$ 590,000
Extraordinary item:		
Gain on condemnation of land (net of applicable		
income tax of $65,000)		150,000
Net income		$ 740,000

Integrity, Objectivity, and Ethics in Business

ETHICS

WHEN IS AN ASSET IMPAIRED?

The asset impairment principle is designed to reduce the subjectivity of timing asset write-downs. That is, write-downs should occur when the impairment is deemed permanent. In practice, however, judgment is still needed in determining when such impairment has occurred. Ethical managers will recognize asset write-downs when they occur, not when it is most convenient. For example, the SEC investigated Avon Products, Inc., for delaying the write-off of a computer software project. In settling the formal investigation, Avon had to restate its earnings to reflect the earlier write-off date.

Restructuring Charges **Restructuring charges** are costs incurred with actions such as canceling contracts, laying off or relocating employees, and combining operations. Often, these events incur initial one-time costs in order to obtain long-term savings. For example, terminated employees often receive a one-time termination or severance benefit at the time of their dismissal. Employee termination benefits are normally the most significant restructuring charges; thus, they will be the focus of this section.

Employee termination benefits arise when a plan specifying the number of terminated employees, the benefit, and the benefit timing has been authorized by senior management and communicated to the employees.[10] To illustrate, assume that the management of Jones Corporation communicates a plan to terminate 200 employees from the closed manufacturing plant on March 1. The plan calls for a termination benefit of $5,000 per employee. Once the plan is communicated to employees, they have the legal right to work for 60 days but may elect to leave the firm earlier. That is, employees may be paid severance at the end of 60 days or at any time in between.

---

10 *Statement of Financial Accounting Standards No. 146*, "Accounting for Costs Associated with Exit or Disposal Activities" (Norwalk, CT: Financial Accounting Standards Board, 2002).

The expense and liability to provide employee benefits should be recognized at fair value on the plan communication date.[11] The fair value of this plan would be $1,000,000 (200 employees × $5,000), which is the aggregate expected cost of terminating the employees. Thus, the $1,000,000 restructuring charge would be recorded as follows:

Mar.	1	Restructuring Charge	1000 00000	
		Employee Termination Obligation		1000 00000

The restructuring charge is reported as a separate expense deducted from gross profit in determining income from continuing operations, as shown in Exhibit 3. The employee termination obligation would be shown as a current liability. If the plan called for expected severance payments beyond one year, then a long-term liability would be recognized. In addition, a note should disclose the nature and cause of the restructuring event and the costs associated with the type of restructuring event.

The actual benefits paid to terminated employees should be debited to the liability as employees leave the firm. For example, assume that 25 employees find other employment and leave the company on March 25. The entry to record the severance payment to these employees would be as follows:

Mar.	25	Employee Termination Obligation	125 00000	
		Cash		125 00000

Example Exercise 14-2

objective

On December 20 of the current year, Torre Corporation determined that equipment had been impaired so that the book value of the equipment was reduced by $180,000. In addition, the senior management of the company communicated an employee severance plan whereby 80 employees could receive a termination benefit of $7,000 per employee. Provide the journal entry for the asset impairment and the restructuring charge.

Follow My Example 14-2

Dec. 20	Loss on Fixed Asset Impairment	180,000	
	Equipment		180,000
	Restructuring Charge	560,000*	
	Employee Termination Obligation		560,000
	*80 employees × $7,000		

For Practice: PE 14-2A, PE 14-2B

Discontinued Operations A gain or loss from disposing of a business segment or component of an entity is reported on the income statement as a gain or loss from **discontinued operations**. The term *business segment* refers to a major line of business for a company, such as a division, department, or certain class of customer. A *component* of an entity is the lowest level at which the operations and cash flows can be clearly distinguished, operationally and for financial reporting purposes, from the rest of the

---

11 For long-term severance agreements, present value concepts may be required to determine fair value. We will assume short-term agreements where the time value of money is assumed to be immaterial. Present value concepts are discussed in Chapter 15.

entity.[12] Examples would be a store for a retailer, a territory for a sales organization, or a product category for a consumer products company.

To illustrate the disclosure, assume that Jones Corporation has separate divisions that produce electrical products, hardware supplies, and lawn equipment. Jones sells its electrical products division at a loss. As shown in Exhibit 3 on page 616, this loss is deducted from Jones's income from continuing operations (income from its hardware and lawn equipment divisions). In addition, a note should disclose the identity of the segment sold, the disposal date, a description of the segment's assets and liabilities, and the manner of disposal.

Extraordinary Items   An **extraordinary item** results from events and transactions that (1) are significantly different (unusual) from the typical or the normal operating activities of the business *and* (2) occur infrequently. The gains and losses resulting from natural disasters that occur infrequently, such as floods, earthquakes, and fires, are extraordinary items. Gains or losses from condemning land or buildings for public use are also extraordinary. Such gains and losses, other than those from disposing of a business segment, should be reported in the income statement as extraordinary items, as shown in Exhibit 3.

Sometimes, extraordinary items result in unusual financial results. For example, Delta Air Lines once reported an extraordinary gain of over $5.5 million as the result of the crash of one of its 727s. The plane that crashed was insured for $6.5 million, but its book value in Delta's accounting records was $962,000. Gains and losses on the disposal of fixed assets are *not* extraordinary items. This is because (1) they are not unusual and (2) they recur from time to time in the normal operations of a business. Likewise, gains and losses from the sale of investments are usual and recurring for most businesses.

UNUSUAL ITEMS AFFECTING THE PRIOR PERIOD'S INCOME STATEMENT

In addition to unusual items impacting the income statement, there are two major items that require a retroactive restatement of prior period earnings. These two items are:

1. Errors in the recognition, measurement, presentation, or disclosure of financial statements, and
2. Changes from one generally accepted accounting principle to another generally accepted accounting principle.[13]

A retroactive restatement requires previously issued financial statements to be adjusted for the impact of errors and changes in accounting principle. If an error is discovered that impacts a prior period financial statement, the prior period statement, and all following statements, should be restated to reflect the correction. If there is a change from one generally accepted accounting principle to another generally accepted accounting principle, then the change is applied to prior period financial statements. That is, the prior period financial statements are restated as if the new accounting principle had always been used.[14] Thus, in both cases, these changes do *not* impact current period earnings, but will impact the earnings reported in past periods. As a result, the present Retained Earnings and other balance sheet accounts will be restated to reflect these prior period changes. Illustrations of these types of adjustments are provided in advanced accounting courses.

---

12 *Statement of Financial Accounting Standards No. 144*, op. cit., par. 41.
13 *Statement of Financial Accounting Standards No. 154*, "Accounting Changes and Error Corrections" (Norwalk, CT: Financial Accounting Standards Board, 2005).
14 Changes from one acceptable depreciation method to another acceptable depreciation method are an exception to this general rule and are to be treated prospectively as a change in estimate, as discussed in Chapter 10.

Earnings per Common Share

objective **3**

Prepare an income statement reporting earnings per share data.

The amount of net income is often used by investors and creditors in evaluating a company's profitability. However, net income by itself is difficult to use in comparing companies of different sizes. Also, trends in net income may be difficult to evaluate, using only net income, if there have been significant changes in a company's stockholders' equity. Thus, the profitability of companies is often expressed as earnings per share. **Earnings per common share (EPS)**, sometimes called *basic earnings per share*, is the net income per share of common stock outstanding during a period.

Because of its importance, earnings per share is reported in the financial press and by various investor services, such as Moody's and Standard & Poor's. Changes in earnings per share can lead to significant changes in the price of a corporation's stock in the marketplace. For example, the stock of eBay Inc. fell by over 19% to $83 per share after the company announced earnings per share of 33¢ as compared to Wall Street analysts' estimate of 34¢ per share.

Corporations whose stock is traded in a public market must report earnings per common share on their income statements.[15] If no preferred stock is outstanding, the earnings per common share is calculated as follows:

$$\text{Earnings per Common Share} = \frac{\text{Net Income}}{\text{Number of Common Shares Outstanding}}$$

When the number of common shares outstanding has changed during the period, a weighted average number of shares outstanding is used. If a company has preferred stock outstanding, the net income must be reduced by the amount of any preferred dividends, as shown below.

$$\text{Earnings per Common Share} = \frac{\text{Net Income} - \text{Preferred Stock Dividends}}{\text{Number of Common Shares Outstanding}}$$

Comparing the earnings per share of two or more years, based on only the net incomes of those years, could be misleading. For example, assume that Jones Corporation, whose partial income statement was presented in Exhibit 3, reported $700,000 net income for 2007. Also assume that no extraordinary or other unusual items were reported in 2007. Jones has no preferred stock outstanding and has 200,000 common shares outstanding in 2007 and 2008. The earnings per common share is $3.50 ($700,000/200,000 shares) for 2007 and $3.70 ($740,000/200,000 shares) for 2008. Comparing the two earnings per share amounts suggests that operations have improved. However, the 2008 earnings per share comparable to the $3.50 is $3.45, which is the income from continuing operations of $690,000 divided by 200,000 shares. The latter amount indicates a slight downturn in normal earnings.

When unusual items reported *below* income from continuing operations exist, earnings per common share should be reported for those items. To illustrate, a partial income statement for Jones Corporation, showing earnings per common share, is shown in Exhibit 4. In this income statement, Jones reports all the earnings per common share amounts on the face of the income statement. However, only earnings per share amounts for income from continuing operations and net income are required to be presented on the face of the statement. The other per share amounts may be presented in the notes to the financial statements.[16]

In the preceding paragraphs, we have assumed a simple capital structure with only common stock or common stock and preferred stock outstanding. Often, however, corporations have complex capital structures with various types of securities outstanding, such as convertible preferred stock, options, warrants, and contingently

---

15 *Statement of Financial Accounting Standards No. 128*, "Earnings per Share" (Norwalk, CT: Financial Accounting Standards Board, 1997).
16 Ibid., pars. 36 and 37.

EXHIBIT 4

Income Statement
with Earnings
per Share

Jones Corporation
Income Statement
For the Year Ended December 31, 2008

Earnings per common share:	
Income from continuing operations.	$ 3.45
Loss on discontinued operations, net of $50,000 tax benefit	0.50
Income before extraordinary items	$ 2.95
Extraordinary item:	
Gain on condemnation of land, net of applicable income	
tax of $65,000	0.75
Net income	$ 3.70

issuable shares. In such cases, the possible effects of converting such securities to common stock must be calculated and reported as *earnings per common share assuming dilution* or *diluted earnings per share.*[17] This topic is discussed further in advanced accounting texts.

Example Exercise 14-3   **objective** 3

Manning Company had net income of $250,000 during the year. There were 580,000 common shares and 2,000 shares of $100 par value, 9% preferred stock outstanding during the year. Determine the basic earnings per share.

Follow My Example 14-3

Earnings per share: $\dfrac{\$250{,}000 - \$18{,}000^*}{580{,}000} = \$0.40$ per share

*2,000 shares × $100 par value × 9% = $18,000

For Practice: PE 14-3A, PE 14-3B

Comprehensive Income

objective 4

Describe the concept and the reporting of comprehensive income.

Comprehensive income is defined as all changes in stockholders' equity during a period, except those resulting from dividends and stockholders' investments. Companies must report traditional net income plus or minus other comprehensive income items to arrive at comprehensive income.

Other comprehensive income items include foreign currency items, pension liability adjustments, and unrealized gains and losses on investments. Generally accepted accounting principles (GAAP) require these items to be disclosed separately from earnings. To the extent that other comprehensive income items give rise to tax effects, the taxes should be allocated to these items similar to that illustrated in Exhibit 4 for extraordinary items. The cumulative effects of other comprehensive income items must be reported separately from retained earnings and paid-in capital, on the balance sheet, as **accumulated other comprehensive income**. When other comprehen-

---

17 Ibid., pars. 11–39.

In the 2005 edition of *Accounting Trends & Techniques*, over 95% of the surveyed companies reported other comprehensive income, and the majority of these companies disclosed it in the statement of stockholders' equity.

sive income items are not present, the income statement and balance sheet formats are similar to those we have illustrated in this and preceding chapters.

Companies may report comprehensive income on the income statement, in a separate statement of comprehensive income, or in the statement of stockholders' equity. In addition, companies may use terms other than comprehensive income, such as "total nonowner changes in equity."

To illustrate reporting for comprehensive income, assume that Triple-A Enterprises Inc. reported comprehensive income on a separate statement, called the *statement of comprehensive income*, as follows:

Triple-A Enterprises Inc. Statement of Comprehensive Income For the Year Ended December 31, 2008	
Net income	$8 5 0 0 00
Other comprehensive income, net of tax	9 0 00
Total comprehensive income	$8 5 9 0 00

The Stockholders' Equity section of the balance sheet for Triple-A Enterprises is as follows:

Triple-A Enterprises Inc. Stockholders' Equity December 31, 2008 and 2007	2008	2007
Stockholders' equity:		
Common stock	$ 20 0 0 0 00	$ 20 0 0 0 00
Paid-in capital in excess of par	36 0 0 0 00	36 0 0 0 00
Retained earnings	165 5 0 0 00	157 0 0 0 00
Accumulated other comprehensive income	1 2 9 0 00	1 2 0 0 00
Total stockholders' equity	$222 7 9 0 00	$214 2 0 0 00

Accumulated other comprehensive income is the cumulative effect of other comprehensive income items. Thus, the additional other comprehensive income of $90 for 2008 is added to the accumulated other comprehensive income on December 31, 2007, to yield the December 31, 2008, balance of $1,290.

You should note that comprehensive income does not affect net income or retained earnings. In the next section, we will illustrate the determination of other comprehensive income, using unrealized gains and losses on investments.

Example Exercise 14-4   objective 4

Myers Company had a net income of $74,000 and other comprehensive income of $12,500 for 2008. On January 1, 2008, the Retained Earnings balance was $425,000, and the Accumulated Other Comprehensive Income balance was $57,000. Determine the (a) comprehensive income for 2008, (b) Retained Earnings balance on December 31, 2008, and (c) Accumulated Other Comprehensive Income balance on December 31, 2008.

(continued)

Follow My Example 14-4

  a. $86,500 = $74,000 + $12,500
  b. $499,000 = $425,000 + $74,000
  c. $69,500 = $57,000 + $12,500

For Practice: PE 14-4A, PE 14-4B

Accounting for Investments in Stocks

objective   **5**

Describe the accounting for investments in stocks.

Corporations not only issue stock, but they also purchase stocks of other companies for investment purposes. Like individuals, businesses have a variety of reasons for investing in stocks, called **equity securities**. A business may purchase stocks as a means of earning a return (income) on excess cash that it does not need for its normal operations. Such investments are usually for a short period of time. In other cases, a business may purchase the stock of another company as a long-term investment. Such investments can be as a means of developing or maintaining business relationships with another company. Sometimes, a business will purchase most, if not all, of the common stock of another company for purposes of owning and controlling another entity. This is termed a *business combination*. In this section, we will discuss short-term investments in equity securities, long-term investments in equity securities, sales of investments, and business combinations. First, however, we will introduce two major equity security classifications according to generally accepted accounting principles.

The equity securities in which a business invests may be classified as trading securities or available-for-sale securities. **Trading securities** are securities that management intends to actively trade for profit. Businesses holding trading securities are those whose normal operations involve buying and selling securities. Examples of such businesses include banks and insurance companies. **Available-for-sale securities** are securities that management expects to sell in the future but which are not actively traded for profit. For example, Warren Buffett, one of the wealthiest men in the world, invests through a public company called Berkshire Hathaway Inc. In a recent annual report, Berkshire Hathaway reported over $35 billion of equity investment holdings listed on its balance sheet as available-for-sale securities. Some of these investments include The Coca-Cola Company, McDonald's, and American Express Company. In this section, we describe and illustrate the accounting for available-for-sale equity securities. The accounting for trading securities is described and illustrated in advanced accounting texts.

SHORT-TERM INVESTMENTS IN STOCKS

Rather than allow excess cash to be idle until it is needed, a business may invest in available-for-sale securities. These investments are classified as **temporary investments** or *marketable securities*. Although such investments may be retained for several years,

Integrity, Objectivity, and Ethics in Business

WHAT DOES IT TAKE TO SUCCEED IN LIFE?

The answer to this question, according to Warren Buffett, the noted investment authority, is three magic ingredients: intelligence, energy, and integrity. According to Buffett, "If you lack the third ingredient, the other two will kill you." In other words, without integrity, your intelligence and energy may very well misguide you.

Source: Eric Clifford, *University of Tennessee Torchbearer,* Summer 2002.

they continue to be classified as temporary, provided they meet two conditions. First, the securities are readily marketable and can be sold for cash at any time. Second, management intends to sell the securities when the business needs cash for operations.

Temporary investments in available-for-sale securities are recorded in a current asset account, *Marketable Securities*, at their cost. This cost includes all amounts spent to acquire the securities, such as broker's commissions. Any dividends received on the investment are recorded as a debit to *Cash* and a credit to *Dividend Revenue*.[18]

To illustrate, assume that on June 1 Crabtree Co. purchased 2,000 shares of Inis Corporation common stock at $89.75 per share plus a brokerage fee of $500. On October 1, Inis declared a $0.90 per share cash dividend payable on November 30. Crabtree's entries to record the stock purchase and the receipt of the dividend are as follows:

June	1	Marketable Securities	180 0 0 0 00	
		Cash		180 0 0 0 00
		Purchased 2,000 shares of Inis Corporation		
		common stock [($89.75 × 2,000 shares) +		
		$500].		
Nov.	30	Cash	1 8 0 0 00	
		Dividend Revenue		1 8 0 0 00
		Received dividend on Inis Corporation		
		common stock (2,000 shares × $0.90).		

On the balance sheet, temporary investments are reported at their fair market value. Market values are normally available from stock quotations in financial newspapers, such as *The Wall Street Journal*. Any difference between the fair market values of the securities and their cost is an **unrealized holding gain or loss**. This gain or loss is termed "unrealized" because a transaction (the sale of the securities) is necessary before a gain or loss becomes real (realized).

To illustrate, assume that Crabtree Co.'s portfolio of temporary investments was purchased during 2008 and has the following fair market values and unrealized gains and losses on December 31, 2008:

Common Stock	Cost	Market	Unrealized Gain (Loss)
Edwards Inc.	$150,000	$190,000	$ 40,000
SWS Corp.	200,000	200,000	—
Inis Corporation	180,000	210,000	30,000
Bass Co.	160,000	150,000	(10,000)
Total	$690,000	$750,000	$ 60,000

If income taxes of $18,000 are allocated to the unrealized gain, Crabtree's temporary investments should be reported at their total cost of $690,000, plus the unrealized gain (net of applicable income tax) of $42,000 ($60,000 − $18,000), as shown in Exhibit 5.

The unrealized gain (net of applicable taxes) of $42,000 should also be reported as an *other comprehensive income item*, as we mentioned in the preceding section. For example, assume that Crabtree Co. has net income of $720,000 for the year ended December 31, 2008. Crabtree elects to report comprehensive income in the *statement of comprehensive income*, as shown in Exhibit 6. In addition, the accumulated other comprehensive income on the balance sheet would also be $42,000, representing the beginning balance of zero plus other comprehensive income of $42,000, as shown in Exhibit 5.

---

18 Stock dividends received on an investment are not journalized, since they have no effect on the investor's assets and revenues.

EXHIBIT 5

Temporary
Investments on the
Balance Sheet

Crabtree Co.
Balance Sheet (selected items)
December 31, 2008

Assets

Current assets:

Cash		$119,500
Temporary investments in marketable		
securities at cost	$690,000	
Unrealized gain (net of applicable		
income tax of $18,000)	42,000	732,000

Stockholders' Equity

Accumulated other comprehensive income		$ 42,000

EXHIBIT 6

Statement of
Comprehensive
Income

Crabtree Co.
Statement of Comprehensive Income
For the Year Ended December 31, 2008

Net income		$720,000
Other comprehensive income:		
Unrealized gain on temporary investments in marketable		
securities (net of applicable income tax of $18,000)		42,000
Comprehensive income		$762,000

Unrealized losses are reported in a similar manner. Unrealized gains and losses are reported as other comprehensive income items until the related securities are sold. When temporary securities are sold, the unrealized gains or losses become realized and are included in determining net income.

Example Exercise 14-5   objective **5**

Drew Company began operations on January 1, 2008, and purchased temporary investments in marketable securities during the year at a cost of $75,000. The end-of-period market value for these investments was $110,000. Net income was $180,000 for 2008. Determine (a) the reported amount of marketable securities on the December 31, 2008, balance sheet and (b) the comprehensive income for 2008. Assume a tax rate of 40%.

Follow My Example 14-5

a.	Initial cost		$ 75,000
	Unrealized gain ($110,000 − $75,000)	$35,000	
	Less: Tax on unrealized gain ($35,000 × 40%)	14,000	
	Unrealized gain, net of tax		21,000
	Reported amount of marketable securities		$ 96,000
b.	Net income		$180,000
	Unrealized gain ($110,000 − $75,000)	$35,000	
	Less: Tax on unrealized gain ($35,000 × 40%)	14,000	
	Other comprehensive income, net of tax		21,000
	Comprehensive income		$201,000

For Practice: PE 14-5A, PE 14-5B

LONG-TERM INVESTMENTS IN STOCKS

Long-term investments in stocks are not intended as a source of cash in the normal operations of the business. Rather, such investments are often held for their income, long-term gain potential, or influence over another business entity. They are reported in the balance sheet under the caption **Investments**, which usually follows the Current Assets section.

Long-term investments in stock are treated as available-for-sale securities, as we illustrated previously for short-term available-for-sale securities. Thus, a long-term investment treated as an available-for-sale security is recorded at cost and reported at fair market value net of any applicable income tax effects. In addition, any unrealized gains and losses are reported as part of the comprehensive income.[19] For example, Delta Air Lines disclosed investments in Priceline.com preferred stock as a noncurrent investment at the appraised fair market value.

Accounting for Long-Term Stock Investments

Is there a significant influence over the investee?

No → Account for the investment as an available-for-sale security

Yes → Account for the investment by using the equity method

However, if the investor (the buyer of the stock) has significant influence over the operating and financing activities of the investee (company whose stock is owned), the **equity method** is used. When the equity method is used, a stock purchase is recorded at cost, as shown previously. Evidence of significant influence includes the percentage of ownership, the existence of intercompany transactions, and the interchange of managerial personnel. Generally, if the investor owns 20% or more of the voting stock of the investee, it is assumed that the investor has significant influence over the investee.

Under the equity method, the investment is *not* subsequently adjusted to fair value. Rather, the book value of the investment is adjusted as follows:

1. The investor's share of the periodic net income of the investee is recorded as an *increase in the investment account* and as *income for the period*. Likewise, the investor's share of an investee's net loss is recorded as a *decrease in the investment account* and as a *loss for the period*.
2. The investor's share of cash dividends from the investee is recorded as an *increase in the cash account* and a *decrease in the investment account*.

To illustrate, assume that on January 2, Hally Inc. pays cash of $350,000 for 40% of the common stock and net assets of Brock Corporation. Assume also that, for the year ending December 31, Brock Corporation reports net income of $105,000 and declares and pays $45,000 in dividends. Using the equity method, Hally Inc. (the investor) records these transactions as follows:

Jan.	2	Investment in Brock Corporation Stock	350 000 00	
		Cash		350 000 00
		Purchased 40% of Brock Corporation stock.		
Dec.	31	Investment in Brock Corporation Stock	42 000 00	
		Income of Brock Corporation		42 000 00
		Recorded 40% share of Brock Corporation		
		net income of $105,000.		
Dec.	31	Cash	18 000 00	
		Investment in Brock Corporation Stock		18 000 00
		Recorded 40% share of Brock Corporation		
		dividends.		

---

19 An exception to reporting unrealized gains and losses as part of comprehensive income is made if the decrease in the market value for a stock is considered permanent. In this case, the cost of the individual stock is written down (decreased), and the amount of the write-down is included in net income.

The combined effect of recording 40% of Brock Corporation's net income and dividends is to increase Hally's interest in the net assets of Brock by $24,000 ($42,000 − $18,000), as shown below.

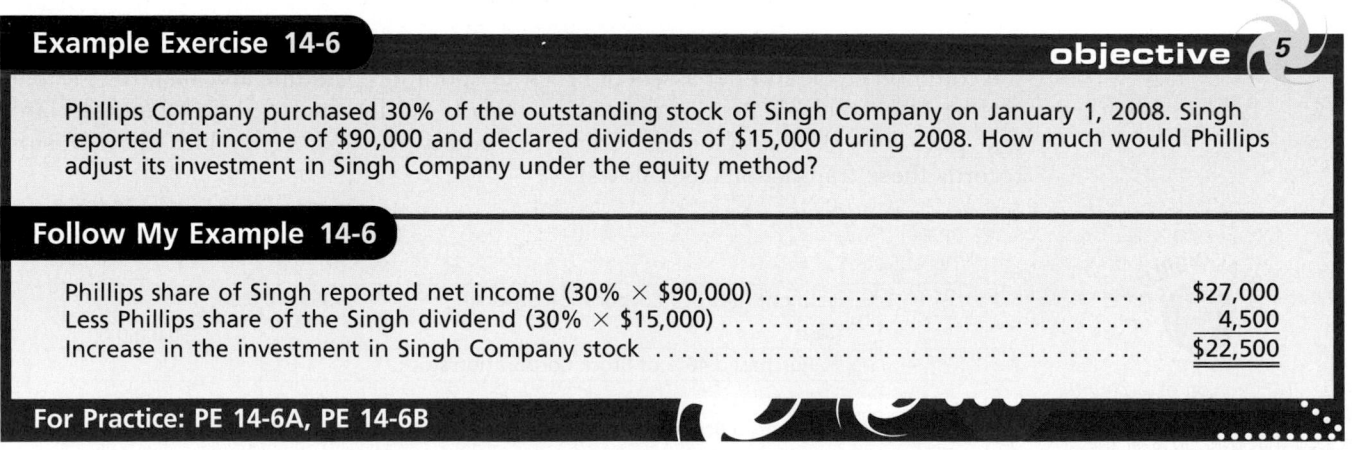

Investment and Dividends

The equity method causes the investment account to mirror the proportional changes in the book value of the investee. Thus, Brock Corporation's book value increased by $60,000 ($105,000 − $45,000), while the investment in Brock Corporation stock account increased by Hally's proportional share of that increase, or $24,000 ($60,000 × 40%). Thus, both the book value of Brock Corporation and Hally's investment in Brock increased at the same rate from the original cost.

Example Exercise 14-6   objective 5

Phillips Company purchased 30% of the outstanding stock of Singh Company on January 1, 2008. Singh reported net income of $90,000 and declared dividends of $15,000 during 2008. How much would Phillips adjust its investment in Singh Company under the equity method?

Follow My Example 14-6

Phillips share of Singh reported net income (30% × $90,000)	$27,000
Less Phillips share of the Singh dividend (30% × $15,000)	4,500
Increase in the investment in Singh Company stock	$22,500

For Practice: PE 14-6A, PE 14-6B

SALE OF INVESTMENTS IN STOCKS

Accounting for the sale of stock is the same for both short- and long-term investments. When shares of stock are sold, the investment account is credited for the carrying amount (book value) of the shares sold. The cash or receivables account is debited for the proceeds (sales price less commission and other selling costs). Any difference between the proceeds and the carrying amount is recorded as a gain or loss on the sale and is included in determining net income.

To illustrate, assume that an investment in Drey Inc. stock has a carrying amount of $15,700 when it is sold on March 1. If the proceeds from the sale of the stock are $17,500, the entry to record the transaction is as follows:

Mar.	1	Cash		17 5 0 0 00	
		Investment in Drey Inc. Stock			15 7 0 0 00
		Gain on Sale of Investments			1 8 0 0 00

BUSINESS COMBINATIONS

A business may make an investment in another business by acquiring a controlling share, often greater than 50%, of the outstanding voting stock of another corporation by paying cash or exchanging stock. This is termed a **business combination**. Businesses may combine in order to produce more efficiently, diversify product lines, expand geographically, or acquire know-how.

A corporation owning all or a majority of the voting stock of another corporation is called a **parent company**. The corporation that is controlled is called the **subsidiary company**. For example, PayPal became a subsidiary of eBay Inc. when eBay exchanged eBay common stock for all the outstanding common stock of PayPal. Although parent and subsidiary corporations may operate as a single economic unit, they continue to maintain separate accounting records and prepare their own periodic financial statements.

At the end of the year, the financial statements of the parent and subsidiary are combined and reported as a single company.[20] These combined financial statements are called **consolidated financial statements**. Such statements are usually identified by adding "and subsidiary(ies)" to the name of the parent corporation or by adding "consolidated" to the statement title. For example, eBay's income statement is titled, "Consolidated Statement of Income." To the stockholders of the parent company, consolidated financial statements are more meaningful than separate statements for each corporation. This is because the parent company, in substance, controls the subsidiaries, even though the parent and its subsidiaries are separate entities. Accounting for business combinations and preparing consolidated financial statements are discussed in greater detail in advanced accounting courses.

Business Connections

1 + 1 = 3

Companies merge in order to create synergy, which occurs when the value of the companies as a single unit is greater than their value as separate companies. How do mergers create synergy? The four basic strategies for creating value in a merger are explained below.

1. *Reduce costs:* When two companies combine, they may be able to eliminate duplicate administrative expenses. For example, the combined company does not need two CEOs or two CFOs, or the company can run on a single computer system or distribution network. Hewlett-Packard Company, identified cost savings such as these in justifying its acquisition of Compaq Computer Corporation.
2. *Replace management:* If the target company has been suffering from mismanagement, the acquirer can purchase the target for a low price and replace the target company's management.

3. *Horizontal integration:* The acquirer may purchase the target company because it has a complementary product line, territory, or customer base to its own. The new combined entity is able to serve customers with a broader reach than were two separate entities. For example, The Walt Disney Company purchased Pixar in order to reestablish its presence as the premier animation movie studio in the era of digital animation.
4. *Vertical integration:* A vertical integration occurs when a business acquires a supplier or customer. Acquiring a supplier may provide a more stable source of supply of a strategic resource and reduce coordination costs. For example, Delta Air Lines acquired Comair Holdings Inc., a regional jet carrier, to supply passengers from smaller cities into its large city hub system.

---

20 When a parent company owns less than 100% of the subsidiary stock, the amount owned by the outsiders is often termed a minority interest and is reported immediately following the consolidated total liabilities. Accounting for the minority interest is covered in advanced accounting texts.

Financial Analysis and Interpretation

A firm's growth potential and future earnings prospects are indicated by how much the market is willing to pay per dollar of a company's earnings. This ratio, called the **price-earnings ratio**, or *P/E ratio*, is commonly included in stock market quotations reported by the financial press. A high P/E ratio indicates that the market expects high growth and earnings in the future. Likewise, a low P/E ratio indicates lower growth and earnings expectations.

The price-earnings ratio on common stock is computed by dividing the stock's market price per share at a specific date by the company's annual earnings per share, as shown below.

$$\text{Price-Earnings Ratio} = \frac{\text{Market Price per Share of Common Stock}}{\text{Earnings per Share of Common Stock}}$$

Investors that invest in high price-earnings ratio companies are often referred to as *growth* investors. Growth investors pay a high price for shares because they expect the company to grow and provide a superior return. That is, high price-earnings ratios can be related to investor optimism. Examples of growth companies are Google (P/E 87), eBay Inc. (P/E 54), and Genentech, Inc. (P/E 72). Growth companies are considered risky because high growth expectations are already reflected in the market price. Thus, if the company's high growth expectations are not realized, the stock price will likely fall.

In contrast, investors in low price-earnings ratio companies are often referred to as *value* investors. Value investors invest in companies with stable and predictable earnings. The value investor believes that the low price-earnings ratio investment is safer than a high price-earnings investment, since the stock is priced at a "bargain" level. Value investing is generally considered the "tortoise" strategy to the growth investor's "hare" strategy. Examples of value stocks are Bank of America Corporation (P/E 11), H.J. Heinz Company (P/E 16), and Ford Motor Company (P/E 9).

To illustrate the calculation of the price-earnings ratio, assume that Harper Inc. reported earnings per share of $1.64 in 2008 and $1.35 in 2007. The market prices per common share are $24.60 at the end of 2008 and $16.20 at the end of 2007. The price-earnings ratio on this stock is computed as follows:

	Price-Earnings Ratio
Year 2008	15 ($24.60/$1.64)
Year 2007	12 ($16.20/$1.35)

The price-earnings ratio indicates that a share of Harper Inc.'s common stock was selling for 12 times the amount of earnings per share at the end of 2007. At the end of 2008, the common stock was selling for 15 times the amount of earnings per share. These results would indicate a generally improving expectation of growth and earnings for Harper Inc. However, a prospective investor should also consider the price-earnings ratios for competing firms in the same industry.

At a Glance

1. Journalize the entries for corporate income taxes, including deferred income taxes.

Key Points	Key Learning Outcomes	Example Exercises	Practice Exercises
Corporations are subject to income tax and are required to make estimated payments throughout the year. The effects of temporary differences between taxable income and income before income taxes must be allocated between periods.	• Journalize estimated tax payments. • Journalize and interpret temporary differences that give rise to deferred taxes.	14-1	14-1A, 14-1B

2. Describe and illustrate the reporting of unusual items on the income statement.

Key Points	Key Learning Outcomes	Example Exercises	Practice Exercises
Fixed asset impairments and restructuring charges are separately disclosed and deducted as part of operating expenses in determining income from continuing operations. The gain or loss from disposal of a business and gains and losses from unusual and infrequent (extraordinary) events are disclosed separately below income from continuing operations. Errors and changes from one generally accepted accounting method to another are treated as restatements of prior period financial statements.	• Identify, journalize, and report fixed asset impairments and restructuring charges. • Identify and report gains and losses from discontinued operations and extraordinary items. • Describe unusual items affecting prior period financial statements.	**14-2**	14-2A, 14-2B

3. Prepare an income statement reporting earnings per share data.

Key Points	Key Learning Outcomes	Example Exercises	Practice Exercises
Earnings per share is a required disclosure. Basic earnings per share removes preferred dividends in the numerator of the calculation. Earnings per share should be separately disclosed for discontinued operations and extraordinary items.	• Calculate basic earnings per share. • Prepare earnings per share disclosures for discontinued operations and extraordinary items.	**14-3**	14-3A, 14-3B

4. Describe the concept and the reporting of comprehensive income.

Key Points	Key Learning Outcomes	Example Exercises	Practice Exercises
Comprehensive income is all the changes in stockholders' equity during a period except those resulting from dividends and stockholders' investments. Total comprehensive income includes other comprehensive income, which consists of items excluded from net income, such as unrealized gains and losses on certain investments in debt or equity securities. Accumulated other comprehensive income is separately reported in the Stockholders' Equity section of the balance sheet.	• Prepare a statement of comprehensive income. • Determine and report accumulated other comprehensive income.	**14-4** **14-4**	14-4A, 14-4B 14-4A, 14-4B

5. Describe the accounting for investments in stocks.

Key Points	Key Learning Outcomes	Example Exercises	Practice Exercises
Short- and long-term investments in marketable securities may be accounted for as available-for-sale securities. Available-for-sale securities are recognized at fair value on the balance sheet, with changes in fair value being recognized as other comprehensive income. Long-term investments in equity securities in which there is a significant influence are accounted for under the equity method. Investments as the result of a business combination are accounted for as consolidations.	• Identify, journalize, and report changes in market value for available-for-sale securities. • Identify, journalize, and report investments under the equity method. • Define and describe the accounting for a business combination.	**14-5** **14-6**	14-5A, 14-5B 14-6A, 14-6B

Key Terms

accumulated other comprehensive income (620)
available-for-sale securities (622)
business combinations (627)
comprehensive income (620)
consolidated financial statements (627)
discontinued operations (617)
earnings per common share (EPS) (619)

equity method (625)
equity securities (622)
extraordinary item (618)
fixed asset impairment (615)
investments (625)
other comprehensive income items (620)
parent company (627)
permanent differences (613)
price-earnings ratio (628)

restructuring charges (616)
subsidiary company (627)
taxable income (611)
temporary differences (612)
temporary investments (622)
trading securities (622)
unrealized holding gain or loss (623)

Illustrative Problem

The following data were selected from the records of Botanica Greenhouses Inc. for the current fiscal year ended August 31:

Administrative expenses	$ 82,200
Cost of merchandise sold	750,000
Fixed asset impairment	115,000
Gain on condemnation of land	25,000
Income tax:	
Applicable to continuing operations	27,200
Applicable to gain on condemnation of land	10,000
Applicable to loss on discontinued operations (reduction)	24,000
Interest expense	15,200
Loss on discontinued operations	60,200
Restructuring charge	40,000
Sales	1,252,500
Selling expenses	182,100

Instructions
Prepare a multiple-step income statement, concluding with a section for earnings per share in the form illustrated in this chapter. There were 10,000 shares of common stock (no preferred) outstanding throughout the year. Assume that the gain on condemnation of land is an extraordinary item.

Solution

Botanica Greenhouses Inc. Income Statement For the Year Ended August 31, 2008		
Sales.		$1,252,500
Cost of merchandise sold.		750,000
Gross profit.		$ 502,500
Operating expenses:		
Selling expenses	$182,100	
Administrative expenses	82,200	
Fixed asset impairment.	115,000	
Restructuring charge	40,000	
Total operating expenses.		419,300
Income from operations		$ 83,200
Other expense:		
Interest expense		15,200
Income from continuing operations before		
income tax		$ 68,000
Income tax expense.		27,200
Income from continuing operations		$ 40,800
Loss on discontinued operations	$ 60,200	
Less applicable income tax	24,000	36,200
Income before extraordinary item.		$ 4,600
Extraordinary Item:		
Gain on condemnation of land	$ 25,000	
Less applicable income tax	10,000	15,000
Net Income		$ 19,600
Earnings per share:		
Income from continuing operations		$4.08
Loss on discontinued operations		3.62
Income before extraordinary item		$0.46
Extraordinary item		1.50
Net income		$1.96

Self-Examination Questions

(Answers at End of Chapter)

1. During its first year of operations, a corporation elected to use the straight-line method of depreciation for financial reporting purposes and MACRS in determining taxable income. If the income tax rate is 40% and the amount of depreciation expense is $60,000 under the straight-line method and $100,000 under MACRS, what is the amount of income tax deferred to future years?
   A. $16,000   C. $40,000
   B. $24,000   D. $60,000

2. A material gain resulting from condemning land for public use would be reported on the income statement as a(n):
   A. extraordinary item.
   B. other income item.
   C. restructuring charge.
   D. fixed asset impairment.

3. Gwinnett Corporation's temporary investments cost $100,000 and have a market value of $120,000 at the end of the accounting period. Assuming a tax rate of

40%, the difference between the cost and market value would be reported as a:

A. $12,000 realized gain.
B. $12,000 unrealized gain.
C. $20,000 realized gain.
D. $20,000 unrealized gain.

4. Cisneros Corporation owns 75% of Harrell Inc. During the current year, Harrell Inc. reported net income of $150,000 and declared dividends of $40,000. How much would Cisneros Corporation increase Investment in Harrell Inc. Stock for the current year?

A. $0   C. $82,500
B. $30,000   D. $112,500

5. Harkin Company has a market price of $60 per share on December 31. The total stockholders' equity is $2,400,000, and the net income is $800,000. There are 200,000 shares outstanding. Preferred dividends are $50,000. The price-earnings ratio would be:

A. 3.
B. 15.
C. 16.
D. 20.

Eye Openers

1. How would the amount of deferred income tax payable be reported in the balance sheet if (a) it is payable within one year and (b) it is payable beyond one year?
2. Darnell Company owns plant and equipment that has a book value of $120 million. Due to a permanent decline in consumer demand for the products produced by this plant, the market value of the plant and equipment is appraised at $20 million. Describe the accounting treatment for this impairment.
3. How should the severance costs of terminated employees be accounted for?
4. During the current year, 40 acres of land that cost $200,000 were condemned for construction of an interstate highway. Assuming that an award of $320,000 in cash was received and that the applicable income tax on this transaction is 40%, how would this information be presented in the income statement?
5. Mann Corporation realized a material gain when its facilities at a designated floodway were acquired by the urban renewal agency. How should the gain be reported in the income statement?
6. An annual report of Ford Motor Company disclosed the sale of its ownership interest in Visteon Corporation, a major automotive components manufacturer. The estimated after-tax loss on disposal of these operations was $2.3 billion. Indicate how the loss from discontinued operations should be reported by Ford on its income statement.
7. How is the change from one acceptable accounting principle to another acceptable accounting principle shown on the income statement?
8. A corporation reports earnings per share of $1.38 for the most recent year and $1.10 for the preceding year. The $1.38 includes a $0.40-per-share gain from insurance proceeds related to a fully depreciated asset that was destroyed by fire.
   a. Should the composition of the $1.38 be disclosed in the financial reports?
   b. On the basis of the limited information presented, would you conclude that operations had improved or declined?
9. a. List some examples of other comprehensive income items.
   b. Does the reporting of other comprehensive income affect the determination of net income and retained earnings?
10. Why might a business invest in another company's stock?
11. How are temporary investments in marketable securities reported on the balance sheet?
12. How are unrealized gains and losses on temporary investments in marketable securities reported on the statement of comprehensive income?
13. a. What method of accounting is used for long-term investments in stock in which there is significant influence over the investee?
    b. Under what caption are long-term investments in stock reported on the balance sheet?
14. Glover Inc. received a $0.20-per-share cash dividend on 50,000 shares of Gestalt Corporation common stock, which Glover Inc. carries as a long-term investment. Assuming that Glover Inc. uses the equity method of accounting for its investment in Gestalt Corporation, what account would be credited for the receipt of the $10,000 dividend?

15. An annual report of The Campbell Soup Company reported on its income statement $2.4 million as "equity in earnings of affiliates." Journalize the entry that Campbell would have made to record this equity in earnings of affiliates.
16. How is an investment as the result of a business combination reported?

Practice Exercises

PE 14-1A
Deferred tax entries
obj. 1

A corporation has $540,000 of income before income taxes, a 35% tax rate, and $480,000 of taxable income. Provide the journal entry for the current year's taxes.

PE 14-1B
Deferred tax entries
obj. 1

Bismark Corp. has $90,000 of income before income taxes, a 40% tax rate, and $76,000 of taxable income. Provide the journal entry for the current year's taxes.

PE 14-2A
Journalize fixed asset impairment and restructuring charge
obj. 2

On December 15 of the current year, Adams Corporation determined that equipment had been impaired so that the book value of the equipment was reduced by $46,000. In addition, the senior management of the company communicated an employee severance plan whereby 15 employees could receive a termination benefit of $4,000 per employee. Provide the journal entry for the asset impairment and the restructuring charge.

PE 14-2B
Journalize fixed asset impairment and restructuring charge
obj. 2

On December 23 of the current year, Dallas Corporation determined that land had been impaired so that the book value of the land was reduced by $320,000. In addition, the senior management of the company communicated an employee severance plan whereby 45 employees could receive a termination benefit of $9,000 per employee. Provide the journal entry for the asset impairment and the restructuring charge.

PE 14-3A
Calculate earnings per share
obj. 3

Wyoming Company had net income of $2,430,000 during the year. There were 240,000 common shares and 30,000 shares of $100 par value, 9% preferred stock outstanding during the year. Determine the basic earnings per share.

PE 14-3B
Calculate earnings per share
obj. 3

Broad Plain Inc. had net income of $350,000 during the year. There were 420,000 common shares and 5,000 shares of $100 par value, 7% preferred stock outstanding during the year. Determine the basic earnings per share.

PE 14-4A
Comprehensive income
obj. 4

Zorba Company had a net income of $104,000 and other comprehensive income of $13,400 for 2008. On January 1, 2008, the Retained Earnings balance was $565,000, and the Accumulated Other Comprehensive Income balance was $71,000. Determine the (a) comprehensive income for 2008, (b) Retained Earnings balance on December 31, 2008, and (c) Accumulated Other Comprehensive Income balance on December 31, 2008.

PE 14-4B
Comprehensive income
obj. 4

Manitoba Company had a net income of $856,000 and other comprehensive income of $123,500 for 2008. On January 1, 2008, the Retained Earnings balance was $3,460,000, and the Accumulated Other Comprehensive Income balance was $624,000. Determine the (a) comprehensive income for 2008, (b) Retained Earnings balance on December 31, 2008, and (c) Accumulated Other Comprehensive Income balance on December 31, 2008.

PE 14-5A
Temporary investments
obj. 5

Mansfield Company began operations on January 1, 2008, and purchased temporary investments in marketable securities during the year at a cost of $123,000. The end-of-period market value for these investments was $137,000. Net income was $151,000 for 2008. Determine (a) the reported amount of marketable securities on the December 31, 2008, balance sheet and (b) the comprehensive income for 2008. Assume a tax rate of 40%.

PE 14-5B
Temporary investments
obj. 5

Aaron Company began operations on January 1, 2008, and purchased temporary investments in marketable securities during the year at a cost of $56,000. The end-of-period market value for these investments was $49,700. Net income was $97,500 for 2008. Determine (a) the reported amount of marketable securities on the December 31, 2008, balance sheet and (b) the comprehensive income for 2008. Assume a tax rate of 35%.

PE 14-6A
Equity method
obj. 5

Gilliam Company purchased 35% of the outstanding stock of Forrester Company on January 1, 2008. Forrester reported net income of $675,000 and declared dividends of $155,000 during 2008. How much would Gilliam adjust its investment in Forrester Company under the equity method?

PE 14-6B
Equity method
obj. 5

Miranda Company purchased 25% of the outstanding stock of Orson Company on January 1, 2008. Orson reported a net loss of $300,000 and declared dividends of $40,000 during 2008. How much would Miranda adjust its investment in Orson Company under the equity method?

Exercises

EX 14-1
Income tax entries
obj. 1

Journalize the entries to record the following selected transactions of Lone Star Leather Co.:

Apr. 15. Paid the first installment of the estimated income tax for the current fiscal year ending December 31, $90,000. No entry had been made to record the liability.
June 15. Paid the second installment of $90,000.
Sept. 15. Paid the third installment of $90,000.
Dec. 31. Recorded the estimated income tax liability for the year just ended and the deferred income tax liability, based on the transactions above and the following data:

Income tax rate	40%
Income before income tax	$950,000
Taxable income according to tax return	$800,000

Jan. 15. Paid the fourth installment of $50,000.

EX 14-2
Deferred income taxes
obj. 1

Storage Systems Inc. recognized service revenue of $420,000 on its financial statements in 2007. Assume, however, that the Tax Code requires this amount to be recognized for tax purposes in 2008. The taxable income for 2007 and 2008 is $2,600,000 and $3,000,000, respectively. Assume a tax rate of 40%.

Prepare the journal entries to record the tax expense, deferred taxes, and taxes payable for 2007 and 2008, respectively.

EX 14-3
Deferred income taxes
obj. 1

Eason Company began operations on January 1, 2007, and reported net income of $260,000 during the year. Eason had a taxable income of $350,000 for 2007. The difference between the reported net income and taxable income will reverse in 2008. The reported net income for 2008 was $405,000. There were no other temporary differences. The tax rate is 35% for both years. Prepare the journal entries to record the tax expense, deferred taxes, and taxes payable for 2007 and 2008, respectively.

EX 14-4
Fixed asset impairment
obj. 2

✓ a. $74,000,000

Laser Pulse Communications Inc. spent $90 million expanding its fiber optic communication network between Chicago and Los Angeles during 2006. The fiber optic network was assumed to have a 10-year life, with a $10 million salvage value, when it was put into service on January 1, 2007. The network is depreciated using the straight-line method. At the end of 2008, the expected traffic volume on the fiber optic network was only 60% of what was originally expected. The reduced traffic volume caused the fair market value of the asset to be estimated at $50 million on December 31, 2008. The loss is not expected to be recoverable.

a. Determine the book value of the network on December 31, 2008, prior to the impairment adjustment.
b. Provide the journal entry to record the fixed asset impairment on December 31, 2008.
c. Provide the balance sheet disclosure for fixed assets on December 31, 2008.

EX 14-5
Fixed asset impairment
obj. 2

Harmony Resorts Inc. owns and manages resort properties. On January 15, 2008, one of its properties was found to be adjacent to a toxic chemical disposal site. As a result of the negative publicity, this property's bookings dropped 40% during 2008. On December 31, 2008, the accounts of the company showed the following details regarding the impaired property:

Land	$ 30,000,000
Buildings and improvements (net)	120,000,000
Equipment (net)	25,000,000
Total	$175,000,000

Management decides that closing the resort is the only option. As a result, it is estimated that the buildings and improvements will be written off completely. The land can be sold for other uses for $17 million, while the equipment can be disposed of for $6 million, net of disposal costs.

a. Provide the journal entry to record the asset impairment on December 31, 2008.
b. ➤ Provide the note disclosure for the impairment.

EX 14-6
Restructuring charge
obj. 2

✓ a. Restructuring charge, $4,680,000

Morton Company's board of directors approved and communicated an employee severance plan in response to a decline in demand for the company's products. The plan called for the elimination of 180 headquarters positions by providing a severance equal to 5% of the annual salary multiplied by the number of years of service. The average annual salary of the eliminated positions is $65,000. The average tenure of terminated employees is eight years. The plan was communicated to employees on November 1, 2008. Actual termination notices will be distributed over the period between December 1, 2008, and April 1, 2009. On December 21, 2008, 50 employees received a lay-off notice and were terminated with severance.

a. Provide the appropriate journal entry for the restructuring charge.
b. Provide the journal entry to record the severance payment on December 21, 2008, assuming that the actual tenure and salary of terminated employees were consistent with the overall average.
c. Provide the balance sheet and note disclosures on December 31, 2008.

EX 14-7
Restructuring charge
obj. 2

✓ a. Restructuring charge, $3,774,000

Kiwi Juice Company has been suffering a downturn in its juice business due to adverse publicity regarding the caffeine content of its drink products. As a result, the company has been required to restructure operations. The board of directors approved and communicated a plan on July 1, 2008, calling for the following actions:

1. Close a juice plant on October 15, 2008. Closing, equipment relocation, and employee relocation costs are expected to be $600,000 during October.
2. Eliminate 300 plant positions. A severance will be paid to the terminated employees equal to 400% of their estimated monthly earnings payable in four quarterly installments on October 15, 2008; January 15, 2009; April 15, 2009; and July 15, 2009.

3. Terminate a juice supply contract, activating a $150,000 cancellation penalty, payable upon notice of termination. The notice will be formally delivered to the supplier on August 15, 2008.

The 300 employees earn an average of $14 per hour. The average employee works 180 hours per month.

a. Determine the total restructuring charge for 2008.
b. Provide the journal entry for the restructuring charge on July 1, 2008. (*Note:* Use Restructuring Obligation as the liability account, since the charges involve more than just employee terminations.)
c. Provide the journal entry for the October 15, 2008, employee severance payment.
d. Provide the balance sheet disclosure for December 31, 2008.
e. ⬤▬▶ Provide a note disclosure for December 31, 2008.

EX 14-8
Restructuring charges and asset impairments
obj. 2

✓ *a. Severance restructuring charge, $780,000*

TransCo Inc. has suffered losses due to increased competition in its service market from low-cost independent truckers. As a result, on December 31, 2008, the board of directors of the company approved and communicated a restructuring plan that calls for selling 50 tractor-trailers out of a fleet of 400. In addition, the plan calls for the elimination of 50 driver positions and 15 staff support positions. The market price for used tractor-trailers is depressed due to general overcapacity in the transportation industry. As a result, the market value of tractor-trailers is estimated to be only 60% of the book value of these assets. It is not believed that the impairment in fixed assets is recoverable. The cost and accumulated depreciation of the total tractor-trailer fleet on December 31 are $48 million and $14 million, respectively. The restructuring plan will provide a severance to the drivers and staff totaling $12,000 per employee, payable on March 14, 2009, which is the expected employee termination date.

a. Provide the journal entries on December 31, 2008, for the fixed asset impairment and the employee severance costs.
b. ⬤▬▶ Provide the balance sheet and note disclosure on December 31, 2008.
c. Provide the journal entry for March 14, 2009.

EX 14-9
Extraordinary item
obj. 2

A company received life insurance proceeds on the death of its president before the end of its fiscal year. It intends to report the amount in its income statement as an extraordinary item.

⬤▬▶ Would this reporting be in conformity with generally accepted accounting principles? Discuss.

EX 14-10
Extraordinary item
obj. 2

REAL WORLD

For the year ended December 31, 2002, Delta Air Lines, provided the following note to its financial statements:

> *On September 22, 2001, the Air Transportation Safety and System Stabilization Act (Stabilization Act) became effective. The Stabilization Act is intended to preserve the viability of the U.S. air transportation system following the terrorist attacks on September 11, 2001 by, among other things, (1) providing for payments from the U.S. Government totaling $5 billion to compensate U.S. air carriers for losses incurred from September 11, 2001, through December 31, 2001, as a result of the September 11 terrorist attacks and (2) permitting the Secretary of Transportation to sell insurance to U.S. air carriers.*
>
> *Our allocated portion of compensation under the Stabilization Act was $668 million. Due to uncertainties regarding the U.S. government's calculation of compensation, we recognized $634 million of this amount in our 2001 Consolidated Statement of Operations. We recognized the remaining $34 million of compensation in our 2002 Consolidated Statement of Operations. We received $112 million and $556 million in cash for the years ended December 31, 2002 and 2001, respectively, under the Stabilization Act.*

⬤▬▶ Do you believe that the income related to the Stabilization Act should be reported as an extraordinary item on the income statement of Delta Air Lines?

EX 14-11
Extraordinary items

obj. 2

Below are three separate historical incidents giving rise to losses for three different companies.

a. In 1980, Weyerhaeuser, a major wood products company, lost $36 million in timber, logs, and building equipment as a result of the volcanic eruption of Mount St. Helens in the state of Washington.

b. In 2001, Dow Jones & Company, Inc., the publisher of *The Wall Street Journal*, suffered $1.7 million in losses due to damage in its headquarters building as a result of the 9/11 terrorist incident.

c. In 2005, Northrop Grumman Corporation, a major defense contractor, reported significant losses in its shipbuilding yards along the Gulf Coast as a result of Hurricane Katrina. The losses were sufficient to cut its projected earnings in half for the year.

In each case, identify whether the loss should be reported as extraordinary.

EX 14-12
Identifying extraordinary items

obj. 2

Assume that the amount of each of the following items is material to the financial statements. Classify each item as either normally recurring (NR) or extraordinary (E).

a. Restructuring charge related to employee termination benefits.
b. Loss on sale of fixed assets.
c. Uninsured flood loss. (Flood insurance is unavailable because of periodic flooding in the area.)
d. Interest revenue on notes receivable.
e. Loss on disposal of equipment considered to be obsolete because of development of new technology.
f. Uninsured loss on building due to hurricane damage. The firm was organized in 1920 and had not previously incurred hurricane damage.
g. Uncollectible accounts expense.
h. Gain on sale of land condemned for public use.

EX 14-13
Income statement

objs. 2, 3

✓Net income, $126,600

Wind Surfer Inc. produces and distributes equipment for sailboats. On the basis of the following data for the current fiscal year ended June 30, 2008, prepare a multiple-step income statement for Wind Surfer, including an analysis of earnings per share in the form illustrated in this chapter. There were 20,000 shares of $150 par common stock outstanding throughout the year.

Administrative expenses	$ 104,000
Cost of merchandise sold	467,500
Gain on condemnation of land (extraordinary item)	58,000
Income tax applicable to gain on condemnation of land	23,200
Income tax reduction applicable to loss from discontinued operations	32,000
Income tax applicable to income from continuing operations	93,200
Loss on discontinued operations	80,000
Loss from fixed asset impairment	120,000
Restructuring charge	50,000
Sales	1,100,000
Selling expenses	125,500

EX 14-14
Income statement

objs. 2, 3

✓ Correct EPS for net income, $0.47

Audio Affection Inc. sells automotive and home stereo equipment. It has 50,000 shares of $100 par common stock outstanding and 10,000 shares of $2, $100 par cumulative preferred stock outstanding as of December 31, 2008. List the errors you find in the following income statement for the year ended December 31, 2008.

(continued)

Audio Affection Inc.
Income Statement
For the Year Ended December 31, 2008

Net sales		$967,000
Cost of merchandise sold		578,000
Gross profit		$389,000
Operating expenses:		
Selling expenses	$127,000	
Administrative expenses	142,000	269,000
Income from continuing operations before income tax		$120,000
Income tax expense		48,000
Income from continuing operations		$ 72,000
Fixed asset impairment		(24,000)
Income before condemnation of land, restructuring charge, and discontinued operations		$ 48,000
Extraordinary items:		
Gain on condemnation of land, net of applicable income tax of $20,000		30,000
Restructuring charge, net of applicable income tax of $8,000		(12,000)
Loss on discontinued operations (net of applicable income tax of $15,000)		(22,500)
Net income		$ 43,500
Earnings per common share:		
Income from continuing operations		$ 1.44
Fixed asset impairment		(0.48)
Income before extraordinary item and discontinued operations		$ 0.96
Extraordinary items:		
Gain on condemnation of land		0.60
Restructuring charge		(0.24)
Loss on discontinued operations		(0.45)
Net income		$ 0.87

EX 14-15
Earnings per share with preferred stock
obj. 3

FirstLight Lighting Company had earnings for 2008 of $150,600. The company had 90,000 shares of common stock outstanding during the year. In addition, the company issued 2,000 shares of $100 par value preferred stock on January 5, 2008. The preferred stock has a dividend of $6 per share. There were no transactions in either common or preferred stock during 2008.

Determine the basic earnings per share for FirstLight.

EX 14-16
Comprehensive income
obj. 4
a. $1,693,000

The statement of comprehensive income for Lancaster Company was as follows:

Lancaster Company
Statement of Comprehensive Income
For the Year Ended December 31, 2008

Net income	$460,000
Other comprehensive income:	
Unrealized loss on temporary investments in marketable equity securities (net of $25,000 tax benefit)	(45,000)
Total comprehensive income	$415,000

The balance sheet dated December 31, 2007, showed a Retained Earnings balance of $1,483,000 and an Accumulated Other Comprehensive Income balance of $171,000. The company paid $250,000 in dividends during 2008.

a. Determine the December 31, 2008, Retained Earnings balance.
b. Determine the December 31, 2008, Accumulated Other Comprehensive Income (Loss) balance.

EX 14-17
Comprehensive income and temporary investments

objs. 4, 5

✓ c. $84,000

The statement of comprehensive income for the years ended December 31, 2008 and 2009, plus selected items from comparative balance sheets of Johnson Wholesalers Inc. are as follows:

Johnson Wholesalers Inc.
Statement of Comprehensive Income
For the Years Ended December 31, 2008 and 2009

	2008	2009
Net income	a.	$100,000
Other comprehensive income (loss), net of tax	b.	4,000
Total comprehensive income	c.	e.

Johnson Wholesalers Inc.
Selected Balance Sheet Items
December 31, 2007, 2008, and 2009

	Dec. 31, 2007	Dec. 31, 2008	Dec. 31, 2009
Temporary investments in marketable securities at fair market value, net of taxes on unrealized gains or losses	$ 32,000	d.	f.
Retained earnings	175,000	$250,000	g.
Accumulated other comprehensive income or (loss)	(8,000)	1,000	h.

There were no dividends or purchases or sales of temporary investments. Other comprehensive items included only after tax unrealized gains and losses on investments. Determine the missing lettered items.

EX 14-18
Comprehensive income and temporary investments

objs. 4, 5

✓ a. Total comprehensive income, $205,000

During 2008, Mango Corporation held a portfolio of available-for-sale securities having a cost of $260,000. There were no purchases or sales of investments during the year. The market values after adjusting for the impact of taxes, at the beginning and end of the year, were $215,000 and $270,000, respectively. The net income for 2008 was $150,000, and no dividends were paid during the year. The Stockholders' Equity section of the balance sheet was as follows on December 31, 2007:

Mango Corporation
Stockholders' Equity
December 31, 2007

Common stock	$ 35,000
Paid-in capital in excess of par value	350,000
Retained earnings	435,000
Accumulated other comprehensive loss	(45,000)
Total	$775,000

a. Prepare a statement of comprehensive income for 2008.
b. Prepare the stockholders' equity section of the balance sheet for December 31, 2008.

EX 14-19
Temporary investments and other comprehensive income

objs. 4, 5

✓ a. 2009 unrealized gain, $54,000

The temporary investments of Catalyst Inc. only include 10,000 shares of Bristol Inc. common stock purchased on January 10, 2008, for $20 per share. As of the December 31, 2008, balance sheet date, assume that the share price declined to $16 per share. As of the December 31, 2009, balance sheet date, assume that the share price rose to $25 per share. The investment was held through December 31, 2009. Assume a tax rate of 40%.

a. Determine the net after-tax unrealized gain or loss from holding the Bristol common stock for 2008 and 2009.
b. What is the balance of Accumulated Other Comprehensive Income or Loss for December 31, 2008, and December 31, 2009?
c. Where is Accumulated Other Comprehensive Income or Deficit disclosed on the financial statements?

EX 14-20
Temporary investments in marketable securities

obj. 5

During 2008, its first year of operations, Geo-Metrics Corporation purchased the following securities as a temporary investment:

Security	Shares Purchased	Cost	Cash Dividends Received
M-Labs Inc.	1,000	$19,000	$ 750
Spectrum Corp.	2,500	38,000	1,400

a. Record the purchase of the temporary investments for cash.
b. Record the receipt of the dividends.

EX 14-21
Financial statement reporting of temporary investments

objs. 4, 5

✓ *b. Comprehensive income, $101,800*

Using the data for Geo-Metrics Corporation in Exercise 14-20, assume that as of December 31, 2008, the M-Labs Inc. stock had a market value of $25 per share and the Spectrum Corp. stock had a market value of $14 per share. For the year ending December 31, 2008, Geo-Metrics Corporation had net income of $100,000. Its tax rate is 40%.

a. Prepare the balance sheet presentation for the temporary investments.
b. Prepare a statement of comprehensive income presentation for the temporary investments.

EX 14-22
Entries for investment in stock, receipt of dividends, and sale of shares

obj. 5

On February 27, Ball Corporation acquired 4,000 shares of the 50,000 outstanding shares of Bat Co. common stock at 40.75 plus commission charges of $200. On July 8, a cash dividend of $1.75 per share and a 2% stock dividend were received. On December 7, 1,000 shares were sold at 53, less commission charges of $65. Record the entries to record (a) the purchase of the stock, (b) the receipt of dividends, and (c) the sale of the 1,000 shares.

EX 14-23
Entries using equity method for stock investment

obj. 5

At a total cost of $1,960,000, Turner Corporation acquired 70,000 shares of May Corp. common stock as a long-term investment. Turner Corporation uses the equity method of accounting for this investment. May Corp. has 280,000 shares of common stock outstanding, including the shares acquired by Turner Corporation. Journalize the entries by Turner Corporation to record the following information:

a. May Corp. reports net income of $3,000,000 for the current period.
b. A cash dividend of $3.80 per common share is paid by May Corp. during the current period.

EX 14-24
Equity method for stock investment

obj. 5

Sweet Company's balance sheet disclosed its long-term investment in Sour Company for comparative years as follows:

	Dec. 31, 2008	Dec. 31, 2007
Investment in Sour Company stock (in millions)	$146	$135

In addition, the 2008 Sweet Company income statement disclosed equity earnings in the Sour Company investment as $15 million. Sweet Company neither purchased nor sold Sour Company stock during 2008. The market value of Sour Company stock on December 31, 2008, was $154.

▬▬▶ Explain the change in the Investment in Sour Company Stock from December 31, 2007, to December 31, 2008.

EX 14-25
Price-earnings ratio

Goodman Company had a net income of $672,000 for 2008. Goodman Company's balance sheet disclosed the stockholders' equity on December 31, 2008, as follows:

Preferred stock, 8,000 shares of $100 par value, 6% stock	$ 800,000
Common stock, 120,000 shares of $1 par value stock issued and outstanding	120,000
Paid-in capital in excess of par value	2,400,000
Total stockholders' equity	$3,320,000

The price of Goodman common stock was $72.80 per share on December 31, 2008. Determine the price-earnings ratio for Goodman Company.

EX 14-26
Price-earnings ratio calculations

FAI

✓ a. 2005: 9.7

ExxonMobil Corporation is one of the largest companies in the world. The company explores, develops, refines, and markets petroleum products. The basic earnings per share for three comparative years were as follows:

	Years Ended Dec. 31,		
	2005	**2004**	**2003**
Basic earnings per share	$5.76	$3.91	$3.24

The market prices at the end of each year were $56, $51, and $41 for December 31, 2005, 2004, and 2003, respectively.

a. Determine the price-earnings ratio for 2005, 2004, and 2003, using end-of-year prices. Round to one decimal place.
b. Interpret your results over the three years.

Problems Series A

PR 14-1A
Income tax allocation

obj. 1

✓ 1. Year-end balance, 3rd year, $12,000

Differences between the accounting methods applied to accounts and financial reports and those used in determining taxable income yielded the following amounts for the first four years of a corporation's operations:

	First Year	Second Year	Third Year	Fourth Year
Income before income taxes	$250,000	$300,000	$500,000	$400,000
Taxable income	200,000	280,000	540,000	430,000

The income tax rate for each of the four years was 40% of taxable income, and each year's taxes were promptly paid.

Instructions
1. Determine for each year the amounts described by the following captions, presenting the information in the form indicated:

Year	Income Tax Deducted on Income Statement	Income Tax Payments for the Year	Deferred Income Tax Payable	
			Year's Addition (Deduction)	Year-End Balance

2. Total the first three amount columns.

PR 14-2A
Income tax; income statement

objs. 2, 3, 4

✓ Net income, $34,300

The following data were selected from the records of Xtreme World Inc. for the current fiscal year ended June 30, 2008:

Advertising expense	$ 57,000
Cost of merchandise sold	345,000
Depreciation expense—office equipment	16,000
Depreciation expense—store equipment	45,000
Gain on discontinued operations	38,000
Income tax:	
Applicable to continuing operations	10,500
Applicable to gain on disposal of business segment	11,400
Applicable to loss on condemnation of land (reduction)	7,200
Insurance expense	9,000
Interest expense	18,000
Loss from condemnation of land	24,000

(continued)

Loss from fixed asset impairment	$ 40,000
Miscellaneous administrative expense	11,000
Miscellaneous selling expense	14,000
Office salaries expense	70,000
Rent expense	25,000
Restructuring charge	50,000
Sales	865,000
Sales commissions expense	130,000
Unrealized gain on temporary investments	35,000

Instructions

Prepare a multiple-step income statement, concluding with a section for earnings per share in the form illustrated in this chapter. There were 5,000 shares of common stock (no pre-ferred) outstanding throughout the year. Assume that the loss on the condemnation of land is an extraordinary item.

PR 14-3A

*Income statement;
retained earnings
statement; balance sheet*

objs. 1, 2, 3, 4

✓ *Net income, $67,200*

The following data were taken from the records of Amana Bread Corporation for the year ended October 31, 2008:

Income statement data:

Administrative expenses	$ 80,000
Cost of merchandise sold	458,000
Gain on condemnation of land	80,000
Income tax:	
Applicable to continuing operations	36,800
Applicable to loss from discontinued business segment	24,000
Applicable to gain on condemnation of land	32,000
Interest expense	5,000
Interest revenue	4,000
Loss from discontinued operations	60,000
Loss from fixed asset impairment	35,000
Restructuring charge	65,000
Sales	955,000
Selling expenses	224,000

Retained earnings and balance sheet data:

Accounts payable	$ 47,800
Accounts receivable	185,000
Accumulated depreciation	465,000
Accumulated other comprehensive loss	28,000
Allowance for doubtful accounts	5,400
Cash	165,300
Common stock, $1 par (100,000 shares authorized; 82,000 shares issued)	82,000
Deferred income taxes payable (current portion, $5,400)	28,300
Dividends:	
Cash dividends for common stock	35,000
Cash dividends for preferred stock	16,000
Stock dividends for common stock	12,000
Dividends payable	12,750
Employee termination obligation (current)	45,000
Equipment	1,958,000
Income tax payable	11,200
Interest receivable	2,500
Merchandise inventory (October 31, 2008), at lower of cost (FIFO) or market	122,000
Notes receivable	42,500
Paid-in capital from sale of treasury stock	16,000
Paid-in capital in excess of par—common stock	451,000
Paid-in capital in excess of par—preferred stock	8,000
Patents	14,000
Preferred 8% stock, $100 par (10,000 shares authorized; 2,000 shares issued)	200,000
Prepaid expenses	2,600
Retained earnings, November 1, 2007	1,277,250
Temporary investment in marketable equity securities	122,000
Treasury stock (2,000 shares of common stock at cost of $20 per share)	40,000
Unrealized loss on temporary equity securities (net of taxes)	28,000

Instructions

1. Prepare a multiple-step income statement for the year ended October 31, 2008, concluding with earnings per share. In computing earnings per share, assume that the average number of common shares outstanding was 80,000 and preferred dividends were $16,000. Assume that the gain on condemnation of land is an extraordinary item.
2. Prepare a retained earnings statement for the year ended October 31, 2008.
3. Prepare a balance sheet in report form as of October 31, 2008.

PR 14-4A
Entries for investments in stock
obj. 5

Samson Company is a wholesaler of men's hair products. The following transactions relate to certain securities acquired by Samson Company, which has a fiscal year ending on December 31:

2006

Jan. 3. Purchased 4,000 shares of the 100,000 outstanding common shares of Nichols Corporation at 55 plus commission and other costs of $480.

July 2. Received the regular cash dividend of $1.25 a share on Nichols Corporation stock.

Dec. 5. Received the regular cash dividend of $1.25 a share plus an extra dividend of $0.10 a share on Nichols Corporation stock.

(Assume that all intervening transactions have been recorded properly and that the number of shares of stock owned have not changed from December 31, 2006, to December 31, 2008.)

2009

Jan. 2. Purchased controlling interest in Telico Inc. for $540,000 by purchasing 32,000 shares directly from the estate of the founder of Telico. There are 128,000 shares of Telico Inc. stock outstanding.

July 6. Received the regular cash dividend of $1.25 a share and a 4% stock dividend on the Nichols Corporation stock.

Oct. 23. Sold 800 shares of Nichols Corporation stock at 68. The broker deducted commission and other costs of $140, remitting the balance.

Dec. 10. Received a cash dividend at the new rate of $1.50 a share on the Nichols Corporation stock.

31. Received $38,000 of cash dividends on Telico Inc. stock. Telico Inc. reported net income of $260,000 in 2009. Samson uses the equity method of accounting for its investment in Telico Inc.

Instructions
Record the entries for the preceding transactions.

Problems Series B

PR 14-1B
Income tax allocation
obj. 1

✓1. Year-end balance,
3rd year, $4,200

Differences between the accounting methods applied to accounts and financial reports and those used in determining taxable income yielded the following amounts for the first four years of a corporation's operations:

	First Year	Second Year	Third Year	Fourth Year
Income before income taxes	$50,000	$65,000	$90,000	$100,000
Taxable income	35,000	60,000	98,000	112,000

The income tax rate for each of the four years was 35% of taxable income, and each year's taxes were promptly paid.

Instructions

1. Determine for each year the amounts described by the following captions, presenting the information in the form indicated:

(continued)

	Income Tax Deducted on Income Statement	Income Tax Payments for the Year	Deferred Income Tax Payable	
Year			Year's Addition (Deduction)	Year-End Balance

2. Total the first three amount columns.

PR 14-2B
Income tax; income statement

objs. 2, 3, 4

✓ *Net income, $203,000*

ATV Inc. sells off-road motorcycles and vehicles. The following data were selected from the records of ATV Inc. for the current fiscal year ended March 31, 2008:

Advertising expense	$ 36,000
Cost of merchandise sold	1,640,000
Depreciation expense—office equipment	32,000
Depreciation expense—store equipment	145,000
Gain on condemnation of land	54,000
Income tax:	
Applicable to continuing operations	94,200
Applicable to loss from discontinued operations (reduction)	23,400
Applicable to gain on condemnation of land	16,200
Interest revenue	25,000
Loss from disposal of business segment	78,000
Loss from fixed asset impairment	32,000
Miscellaneous administrative expense	41,000
Miscellaneous selling expense	25,000
Office salaries expense	230,000
Rent expense	100,000
Restructuring charge	70,000
Sales	2,800,000
Sales salaries expense	160,000
Unrealized loss on temporary investments	40,000

Instructions

Prepare a multiple-step income statement, concluding with a section for earnings per share in the form illustrated in this chapter. There were 20,000 shares of common stock (no preferred) outstanding throughout the year. Assume that the gain on the condemnation of land is an extraordinary item.

PR 14-3B
Income statement; retained earnings statement; balance sheet

objs. 1, 2, 3, 4

✓ *Net income, $128,700*

The following data were taken from the records of Disk N' Dat Corporation for the year ended August 31, 2008.

Income statement data:

Administrative expenses	$ 23,000
Cost of merchandise sold	232,000
Gain on condemnation of land	75,000
Income tax:	
Applicable to continuing operations	70,200
Applicable to loss from discontinued operation	14,400
Applicable to gain on condemnation of land	30,000
Interest expense	3,000
Interest revenue	2,500
Loss from disposal of discontinued operation	36,000
Loss from fixed asset impairment	14,000
Restructuring charge	45,000
Sales	550,000
Selling expenses	60,000

Retained earnings and balance sheet data:

Accounts payable	$ 12,000
Accounts receivable	28,000
Accumulated depreciation	145,000

Accumulated other comprehensive income	$ 9,000
Allowance for doubtful accounts	2,500
Cash	87,500
Common stock, $1 par (100,000 shares authorized; 46,000 shares issued)	46,000
Deferred income taxes payable (current portion, $4,700)	12,800
Dividends:	
Cash dividends for common stock	21,000
Cash dividends for preferred stock	9,000
Stock dividends for common stock	5,000
Dividends payable	7,500
Employee termination obligation (current)	30,000
Equipment	1,350,000
Income tax payable	21,450
Interest receivable	500
Merchandise inventory (August 31, 2008), at lower of cost (FIFO) or market	87,000
Paid-in capital from sale of treasury stock	5,000
Paid-in capital in excess of par—common stock	820,000
Paid-in capital in excess of par—preferred stock	20,000
Patents	40,000
Preferred 6% stock, $100 par (30,000 shares authorized; 1,500 shares issued)	150,000
Prepaid expenses	15,900
Retained earnings, September 1, 2007	397,950
Temporary investments in marketable equity securities (at cost)	125,000
Treasury stock (1,000 shares of common stock at cost of $30 per share)	30,000
Unrealized gain on marketable equity securities	9,000

Instructions

1. Prepare a multiple-step income statement for the year ended August 31, 2008, concluding with earnings per share. In computing earnings per share, assume that the average number of common shares outstanding was 45,000 and preferred dividends were $9,000. Assume that the gain on the condemnation of land is an extraordinary item.
2. Prepare a retained earnings statement for the year ended August 31, 2008.
3. Prepare a balance sheet in report form as of August 31, 2008.

PR 14-4B
Entries for investments in stock

obj. 5

Encore Design Inc. produces and sells theater set designs and costumes. The following transactions relate to certain securities acquired by Encore Design Inc., which has a fiscal year ending on December 31:

2006
Feb. 10. Purchased 8,000 shares of the 150,000 outstanding common shares of Mode Corporation at 36 plus commission and other costs of $864.
July 15. Received the regular cash dividend of $1.10 a share on Mode Corporation stock.
Dec. 15. Received the regular cash dividend of $1.10 a share plus an extra dividend of $0.05 a share on Mode Corporation stock.

    (Assume that all intervening transactions have been recorded properly and that the number of shares of stock owned have not changed from December 31, 2006, to December 31, 2008.)

2009
Jan. 3. Purchased controlling interest in Applause Inc. for $675,000 by purchasing 30,000 shares directly from the estate of the founder of Applause. There are 100,000 shares of Applause Inc. stock outstanding.
Apr. 14. Received the regular cash dividend of $1.10 a share and a 2% stock dividend on the Mode Corporation stock.
July 26. Sold 1,000 shares of Mode Corporation stock at 32. The broker deducted commission and other costs of $125, remitting the balance.
Dec. 15. Received a cash dividend at the new rate of $1.20 a share on the Mode Corporation stock.
    31. Received $12,500 of cash dividends on Applause Inc. stock. Applause Inc. reported net income of $325,000 in 2009. Encore Design uses the equity method of accounting for its investment in Applause Inc.

Instructions
Journalize the entries for the preceding transactions.

Special Activities

SA 14-1
Equity method disclosure

The following note to the consolidated financial statements for Goodyear Tire & Rubber Company relates to the principles of consolidation used in preparing the financial statements:

> *The Company's investments in 20% to 50% owned companies in which it has the ability to exercise significant influence over operating and financial policies are accounted for by the equity method. Accordingly, the Company's share of the earnings of these companies is included in consolidated net income.*

Is it a requirement that Goodyear use the equity method in this situation? Explain.

SA 14-2
Special charges analysis

The two-year comparative income statements and a note disclosure for Mercury Shoes Inc. were as follows:

Income Statement
Mercury Shoes Inc.
For the Years Ended December 31, 2008 and 2007

	2008	2007
Sales	$510,000	$430,000
Cost of merchandise sold	224,400	193,500
Gross profit	$285,600	$236,500
Selling and administrative expenses	122,400	107,500
Loss on fixed asset impairment	127,500	—
Income from operations	$ 35,700	$129,000
Income tax expense	14,280	51,600
Net income	$ 21,420	$ 77,400

Note: A fixed asset impairment of $127,500 was recognized in 2008 as the result of abandoning an order management software system. The system project was started in early 2007 and ran into significant delays and performance problems throughout 2008. It was determined that there was no incremental benefit from completing the system. Thus, the accumulated costs associated with the system were written off.

1. Divide each amount in the 2008 and 2007 income statements by total sales for the given year.
2. Interpret the performance of the company in 2008.

SA 14-3
Comprehensive income

The Stockholders' Equity section of Yum! Brands, Inc., the operator of Pizza Hut, KFC, and Taco Bell restaurants, for two recent comparative dates was as follows:

Yum! Brands, Inc.
Stockholders' Equity (selected items)
December 31, 2005 and December 31, 2004
(in millions)

	Dec. 31, 2005	Dec. 31, 2004
Common stock, no par value	$ 0	$ 659
Retained earnings	1,619	1,067
Accumulated other comprehensive income (loss)	(170)	(131)
Total stockholders' equity	$1,449	$1,595

1. What is the "other" comprehensive income or loss for the year ended December 31, 2005?
2. Explain the concept of other comprehensive income.

SA 14-4
Ethics and professional conduct in business

ETHICS

Dillon Osborn is the president and chief operating officer of Dollars N' Sense Corporation, a developer of personal financial planning software. During the past year, Dollars N' Sense Corporation was forced to sell 10 acres of land to the city of Houston for expansion of a freeway exit. The corporation fought the sale; but after condemnation hearings, a judge ordered it to sell the land. Because of the land's location and the fact that Dollars N' Sense Corporation had purchased the land over 15 years ago, the corporation recorded a $0.20-per-share gain on the sale. Always looking to turn a negative into a positive, Dillon has decided to announce the corporation's earnings per share of $1.05, without identifying the $0.20 impact of selling the land. Although he will retain majority ownership, Dillon plans on selling 20,000 of his shares in the corporation sometime within the next month.

➤ Are Dillon's plans to announce earnings per share of $1.05 without mentioning the $0.20 impact of selling the land ethical and professional?

SA 14-5
Reporting extraordinary item

Sunshine Fruit Co. is in the process of preparing its annual financial statements. Sunshine Fruit is a large citrus grower located in central Florida. The following is a discussion between Curtis Kirk, the controller, and Liz Gwinn, the chief executive officer and president of Sunshine Fruit Co.

Liz: Curtis, I've got a question about your rough draft of this year's income statement.
Curtis: Sure, Liz. What's your question?
Liz: Well, your draft shows a net loss of $750,000.
Curtis: That's right. We'd have had a profit, except for this year's frost damage. I figured that the frost destroyed over 30% of our crop. We had a good year otherwise.
Liz: That's my concern. I estimated that if we eliminate the frost damage, we'd show a profit of . . . let's see . . . about $250,000.
Curtis: That sounds about right.
Liz: This income statement seems misleading. Why can't we show the loss on the frost damage separately? That way the bank and our outside investors will be able to see that this year's loss is just temporary. I'd hate to get them upset over nothing.
Curtis: Maybe we can do something. I recall from my accounting courses something about showing unusual items separately. Let's see . . . yes, I remember. They're called extraordinary items.
Liz: Well, we haven't had any frost damage in over five years. This year's damage is certainly extraordinary. Let's do it!

➤ Discuss the appropriateness of revising Sunshine Fruit's income statement to report the frost damage separately as an extraordinary item.

SA 14-6
Extraordinary items and discontinued operations

REAL WORLD

Group Project

Internet Project

In groups of three or four, search company annual reports, news releases, or the Internet for extraordinary items and announcements of discontinued operations. Identify the most unusual extraordinary item in your group. Also, select a discontinued operation of a well-known company that might be familiar to other students or might interest them.

Prepare a brief analysis of the earnings per share impact of both the extraordinary item and the discontinued operation. Estimate the *potential* impact on the company's market price by multiplying the current price-earnings ratio by the earnings per share amount of each item.

One Internet site that has annual reports is EDGAR (Electronic Data Gathering, Analysis, and Retrieval), the electronic archives of financial statements filed with the Securities and Exchange Commission. SEC documents can be retrieved using the EdgarScan service from PricewaterhouseCoopers at **http://edgarscan.pwcglobal.com**.

To obtain annual report information, type in a company name in the appropriate space. EdgarScan will list the reports available to you for the company you've selected. Select the most recent annual report filing, identified as a 10-K or 10-K405. EdgarScan provides an outline of the report, including the separate financial statements. You can double click the income statement and balance sheet for the selected company into an Excel™ spreadsheet for further analysis.

Answers to Self-Examination Questions

1. **A**   The amount of income tax deferred to future years is $16,000 (answer A), determined as follows:

Depreciation expense, MACRS	$100,000
Depreciation expense, straight-line method	60,000
Excess expense in determining taxable income	$ 40,000
Income tax rate	× 40%
Income tax deferred to future years	$ 16,000

2. **A**   Events and transactions that are distinguished by their unusual nature and by the infrequency of their occurrence, such as a gain on condemning land for public use, are reported in the income statement as extraordinary items (answer A). A restructuring charge (answer C) and fixed asset impairment (answer D) are unusual items that are related to different accounting events than land condemnation.

3. **B**   The difference between the cost of temporary investments held as available-for-sale securities and their market value is reported as an unrealized gain, net of applicable income taxes, as shown below.

Market value of investments	$120,000
Cost of investments	100,000
	$ 20,000
Applicable taxes (40%)	8,000
Unrealized gain, net of taxes	$ 12,000

The unrealized gain of $12,000 (answer B) is reported on the balance sheet as an addition to the cost of the investments and as part of other comprehensive income.

4. **C**   Under the equity method of accounting for investments in stocks, Cisneros Corporation records its share of both net income and dividends of Harrell Inc. in Investment in Harrell Inc. Stock. Thus, Investment in Harrell Inc. Stock would increase by $82,500 [($150,000 × 75%) − ($40,000 × 75%)] for the current year. $30,000 (answer B) is only Cisneros Corporation's share of Harrell's dividends for the current year. $112,500 (answer D) is only Cisneros Corporation's share of Harrell's net income for the year.

5. **C**   Price-Earnings Ratio =

$$\frac{\text{Market Price per Common Share}}{\text{Earnings per Share}}, \text{ or}$$

$$\frac{\$60}{(\$800,000 - \$50,000)/200,000} = 16$$

Bonds Payable and Investments in Bonds

objectives

After studying this chapter, you should be able to:

1 **Compute the potential impact of long-term borrowing on earnings per share.**

2 **Describe the characteristics, terminology, and pricing of bonds payable.**

3 **Journalize entries for bonds payable.**

4 **Describe and illustrate the payment and redemption of bonds payable.**

5 **Journalize entries for the purchase, interest, discount and premium amortization, and sale of bond investments.**

6 **Prepare a corporation balance sheet.**

Under Armour®

Most of us don't have enough money in our bank accounts to buy a house or a car by simply writing a check. Just imagine if you had to save the complete purchase price of a house before you could buy it! To help us make these types of purchases, banks will typically lend us the money, as long as we agree to repay the loan along with interest in smaller payments in the future. Loans such as this, or long-term debt, allow us to purchase assets such as houses and cars today, which benefit us over the long term.

The use of debt can also help a business reach its objectives. Most businesses have to borrow money in order to acquire assets that they will use to generate income. For example, Under Armour®, a maker of performance athletic clothing, uses debt to acquire assets that it needs to manufacture and sell its prod-

ucts. Since it began in 1995, the company has used long-term debt to transform itself from a small business to a leading athletic wear company. The company now sells products in over 8,000 retail stores across the world. In addition, Under Armour® products are used by a number of teams in the National Football League, Major League Baseball, the National Hockey League, and in Olympic sports.

While debt can help companies like Under Armour® grow to achieve financial success, too much debt can be a financial burden that may even lead to bankruptcy. Just like individuals, businesses must manage debt wisely. In this chapter, we will discuss the nature of, accounting for, analysis of, and investments in long-term debt.

Financing Corporations

objective *1*

Compute the potential impact of long-term borrowing on earnings per share.

As discussed above, both individuals and corporations use debt to purchase assets or resources today that they might otherwise be unable to afford. Corporations often finance their operations by purchasing on credit and issuing notes or bonds. We have discussed accounts payable and notes payable in earlier chapters. A **bond** is simply a form of an interest-bearing note. Like a note, a bond requires periodic interest payments, and the face amount must be repaid at the maturity date. Bondholders are creditors of the issuing corporation, and their claims on the assets of the corporation rank ahead of stockholders.

One of the many factors that influence the decision to issue debt or equity is the effect of each alternative on earnings per share. To illustrate the possible effects, assume that a corporation's board of directors is considering the following alternative plans for financing a $4,000,000 company:

	Plan 1	Plan 2	Plan 3
Issue 12% bonds	—	—	$2,000,000
Issue 9% preferred stock, $50 par value	—	$2,000,000	1,000,000
Issue common stock, $10 par value	$4,000,000	2,000,000	1,000,000
	$4,000,000	$4,000,000	$4,000,000

In each case, we assume that the stocks or bonds are issued at their par or face amount. The corporation is expecting to earn $800,000 annually, before deducting interest on the bonds and income taxes estimated at 40% of income. Exhibit 1 shows the effect of the three plans on the income of the corporation and the earnings per share on common stock.

EXHIBIT 1

Effect of Alternative Financing Plans— $800,000 Earnings

	Plan 1	Plan 2	Plan 3
12% bonds	—	—	$2,000,000
Preferred 9% stock, $50 par	—	$2,000,000	1,000,000
Common stock, $10 par	$4,000,000	2,000,000	1,000,000
Total	$4,000,000	$4,000,000	$4,000,000
Earnings before interest and income tax	$ 800,000	$ 800,000	$ 800,000
Deduct interest on bonds	—	—	240,000
Income before income tax	$ 800,000	$ 800,000	$ 560,000
Deduct income tax	320,000	320,000	224,000
Net income	$ 480,000	$ 480,000	$ 336,000
Dividends on preferred stock	—	180,000	90,000
Available for dividends on common stock	$ 480,000	$ 300,000	$ 246,000
Shares of common stock outstanding	÷ 400,000	÷ 200,000	÷ 100,000
Earnings per share on common stock	$ 1.20	$ 1.50	$ 2.46

When interest rates are low, corporations usually finance their operations with debt. For example, as interest rates fell in recent years, corporations issued large amounts of new debt.

Exhibit 1 indicates that Plan 3 yields the highest earnings per share on common stock and is thus the most attractive for common stockholders. If the estimated earnings are more than $800,000, the difference between the earnings per share to common stockholders under Plan 1 and Plan 3 is even greater.[1] However, if smaller earnings occur, Plans 2 and 3 become less attractive to common stockholders. To illustrate, the effect of earnings of $440,000 rather than $800,000 is shown in Exhibit 2.

In addition to the effect on earnings per share, the board of directors should consider other factors in deciding whether to issue debt or equity. For example, once bonds are issued, periodic interest payments and repayment of the face value of the bonds are beyond the control of the corporation. That is, if these payments are not made, the bondholders could seek court action and force the company into bankruptcy. In contrast, a corporation is not legally obligated to pay dividends.

EXHIBIT 2

Effect of Alternative Financing Plans— $440,000 Earnings

	Plan 1	Plan 2	Plan 3
12% bonds	—	—	$2,000,000
Preferred 9% stock, $50 par	—	$2,000,000	1,000,000
Common stock, $10 par	$4,000,000	2,000,000	1,000,000
Total	$4,000,000	$4,000,000	$4,000,000
Earnings before interest and income tax	$ 440,000	$ 440,000	$ 440,000
Deduct interest on bonds	—	—	240,000
Income before income tax	$ 440,000	$ 440,000	$ 200,000
Deduct income tax	176,000	176,000	80,000
Net income	$ 264,000	$ 264,000	$ 120,000
Dividends on preferred stock	—	180,000	90,000
Available for dividends on common stock	$ 264,000	$ 84,000	$ 30,000
Shares of common stock outstanding	÷ 400,000	÷ 200,000	÷ 100,000
Earnings per share on common stock	$ 0.66	$ 0.42	$ 0.30

---

1 The higher earnings per share under Plan 3 is due to a finance concept known as *leverage*. This concept is discussed further in a later chapter.

Example Exercise 15-1

objective 1

Gonzales Co. is considering the following alternative plans for financing its company:

	Plan 1	Plan 2
Issue 10% bonds (at face value)	—	$2,000,000
Issue common stock, $10 par	$3,000,000	1,000,000

Income tax is estimated at 40% of income.

   Determine the earnings per share of common stock under the two alternative financing plans, assuming income before bond interest and income tax is $750,000.

Follow My Example 15-1

	Plan 1	Plan 2
Earnings before bond interest and income tax	$750,000	$750,000
Bond interest	0	200,000[2]
Balance	$750,000	$550,000
Income tax	300,000[1]	220,000[3]
Net income	$450,000	$330,000
Dividends on preferred stock	0	0
Earnings available for common stock	$450,000	$330,000
Number of common shares	/300,000	/100,000
Earnings per share on common stock	$ 1.50	$ 3.30

[1]$750,000 × 40%   [2]$2,000,000 × 10%   [3]$550,000 × 40%

For Practice: PE 15-1A, PE 15-1B

Characteristics, Terminology, and Pricing of Bonds Payable

objective 2

Describe the characteristics, terminology, and pricing of bonds payable.

In addition to their face values, interest rates, interest payment dates, and maturity dates, bonds may differ in a variety of ways. In this section, we describe the common characteristics of bonds and how bonds may differ from one another. In doing so, we introduce common terms used to describe types of bonds. In addition, we describe and illustrate how the price investors are willing to pay for a bond is determined.

BOND CHARACTERISTICS AND TERMINOLOGY

A corporation that issues bonds enters into a contract, called a **bond indenture** or *trust indenture*, with the bondholders. A bond issue is normally divided into a number of individual bonds. Usually, the face value of each bond, called the *principal*, is $1,000 or a multiple of $1,000. The interest on bonds may be payable annually, semiannually, or quarterly. Most bonds pay interest semiannually.

   The prices of bonds are quoted as a percentage of the bonds' face value. Thus, investors could purchase or sell Wal-Mart bonds quoted at 113.84 for $1,138.40. Likewise, bonds quoted at 109 could be purchased or sold for $1,090.

   When all bonds of an issue mature at the same time, they are called *term bonds*. If the maturities are spread over several dates, they are called *serial bonds*. For example, one-tenth of an issue of $1,000,000 bonds, or $100,000, may mature 16 years from the issue date, another $100,000 in the 17th year, and so on, until the final $100,000 matures in the 25th year.

   Bonds that may be exchanged for other securities, such as common stock, are called *convertible bonds*. Bonds that a corporation reserves the right to redeem before their maturity are called *callable bonds*. Bonds issued on the basis of the general credit of the corporation are called *debenture bonds*.

REAL WORLD

Time Inc. 7.625% bonds maturing in 2031 were listed as selling for 112.1081 on January 24, 2006.

PRICING OF BONDS PAYABLE

When a corporation issues bonds, the price that buyers are willing to pay for the bonds depends upon the following three factors:

1. The face amount of the bonds, which is the amount due at the maturity date.
2. The periodic interest to be paid on the bonds.
3. The market rate of interest.

Market = Contract Rate

Selling price of bond = $1,000

$1,000 BOND

Market Rate > Contract Rate

Selling price of bond < $1,000

$1,000 BOND — Discount

Market Rate < Contract Rate

Selling price of bond > $1,000

$1,000 BOND + Premium

The face amount and the periodic interest to be paid on the bonds are identified in the bond indenture. The periodic interest is expressed as a percentage of the face amount of the bond. This percentage or rate of interest is called the **contract rate** or *coupon rate*.

The *market* or **effective rate of interest** is determined by transactions between buyers and sellers of similar bonds. The market rate of interest is affected by a variety of factors, including investors' assessment of current economic conditions as well as future expectations.

If the contract rate of interest equals the market rate of interest, the bonds will sell at their face amount. If the market rate is higher than the contract rate, the bonds will sell at a **discount**, or less than their face amount. Why is this the case? Buyers are not willing to pay the face amount for bonds whose contract rate is lower than the market rate. The discount, in effect, represents the amount necessary to make up for the difference in the market and the contract interest rates. In contrast, if the market rate is lower than the contract rate, the bonds will sell at a **premium**, or more than their face amount. In this case, buyers are willing to pay more than the face amount for bonds whose contract rate is higher than the market rate.

The face amount of the bonds and the periodic interest on the bonds represent cash to be received by the buyer in the future. The buyer determines how much to pay for the bonds by computing the present value of these future cash receipts, using the market rate of interest. The concept of present value is based on the time value of money.

The time value of money concept recognizes that an amount of cash to be received today is worth more than the same amount of cash to be received in the future. For example, what would you rather have: $100 today or $100 one year from now? You would rather have the $100 today because it could be invested to earn income. For example, if the $100 could be invested to earn 10% per year, the $100 will accumulate to $110 ($100 plus $10 earnings) in one year. In this sense, you can think of the $100 in hand today as the **present value** of $110 to be received a year from today. This present value is illustrated in the following time line:

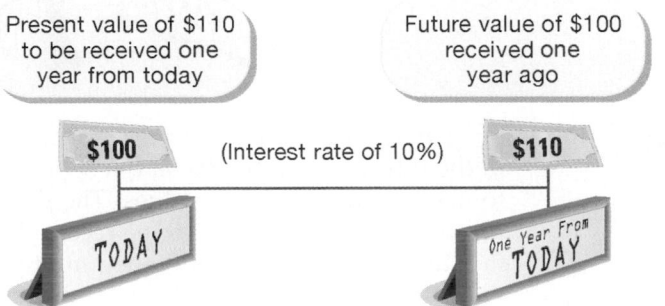

Present value of $110 to be received one year from today

Future value of $100 received one year ago

$100 (Interest rate of 10%) $110

TODAY

One Year From TODAY

A related concept to present value is **future value**. In the preceding illustration, the $110 to be received a year from today is the future value of $100 today, assuming an interest rate of 10%.

Present Value of the Face Amount of Bonds The present value of the face amount of bonds is the value today of the amount to be received at a future maturity date. For

Integrity, Objectivity, and Ethics in Business

CREDIT QUALITY

The market rate of interest for a corporate bond is influenced by a number of factors, including the credit quality of the issuer. In June 2002, WorldCom disclosed a massive accounting fraud within the company, prompting credit rating agencies and bond investors to drastically lower their assessment of the company's credit quality. As a result, the price of WorldCom's $30 billion in bond debt dropped to 15 cents on the dollar, or $4.5 billion in a few short weeks.

example, assume that you are to receive the face value of a $1,000 bond in one year. If the market rate of interest is 10%, the present value of the face value of the $1,000 bond is $909.09 ($1,000/1.10). This present value is illustrated in the following time line:

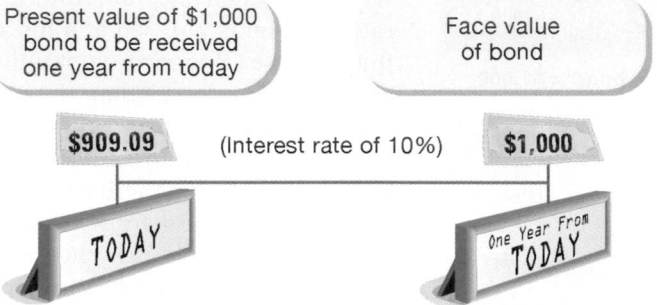

If you are to receive the face value of a $1,000 bond in two years, with interest of 10% compounded at the end of the first year, the present value is $826.45 ($909.09/1.10).[2] We illustrate this present value in the following time line:

Spreadsheet software with built-in present value functions can be used to calculate present values.

You can determine the present value of the face amount of bonds to be received in the future by a time line and a series of divisions. In practice, however, it is easier to use a table of present values. The *present value of $1 table* can be used to find the present value factor for $1 to be received after a number of periods in the future. The face amount of the bonds is then multiplied by this factor to determine its present value. Exhibit 3 is a partial table of the present value of $1.[3]

---

2 Note that the future value of $826.45 in two years, at an interest rate of 10% compounded annually, is $1,000.

3 To simplify the illustrations and homework assignments, the tables presented in this chapter are limited to 10 periods for a small number of interest rates, and the amounts are carried to only five decimal places. Computer programs are available for determining present value factors for any number of interest rates, decimal places, or periods. More complete interest tables are presented in Appendix A.

EXHIBIT 3   Present Value of $1 at Compound Interest

Periods	5%	5½%	6%	6½%	7%	10%	11%	12%	13%	14%
1	0.95238	0.94787	0.94340	0.93897	0.93458	0.90909	0.90090	0.89286	0.88496	0.87719
2	0.90703	0.89845	0.89000	0.88166	0.87344	0.82645	0.81162	0.79719	0.78315	0.76947
3	0.86384	0.85161	0.83962	0.82785	0.81630	0.75132	0.73119	0.71178	0.69305	0.67497
4	0.82270	0.80722	0.79209	0.77732	0.76290	0.68301	0.65873	0.63552	0.61332	0.59208
5	0.78353	0.76513	0.74726	0.72988	0.71299	0.62092	0.59345	0.56743	0.54276	0.51937
6	0.74622	0.72525	0.70496	0.68533	0.66634	0.56447	0.53464	0.50663	0.48032	0.45559
7	0.71068	0.68744	0.66506	0.64351	0.62275	0.51316	0.48166	0.45235	0.42506	0.39964
8	0.67684	0.65160	0.62741	0.60423	0.58201	0.46651	0.43393	0.40388	0.37616	0.35056
9	0.64461	0.61763	0.59190	0.56735	0.54393	0.42410	0.39092	0.36061	0.33288	0.30751
10	0.61391	0.58543	0.55840	0.53273	0.50835	0.38554	0.35218	0.32197	0.29459	0.26974

Exhibit 3 indicates that the present value of $1 to be received in two years with a market rate of interest of 10% a year is 0.82645. Multiplying the $1,000 face amount of the bond in the preceding example by 0.82645 yields $826.45.

In Exhibit 3, the Periods column represents the number of compounding periods, and the percentage columns represent the compound interest rate per period. For example, 10% for two years compounded *annually*, as in the preceding example, is 10% for two periods. Likewise, 10% for two years compounded *semiannually* would be 5% (10% per year/2 semiannual periods) for four periods (2 years × 2 semiannual periods). Similarly, 10% for three years compounded semiannually would be 5% (10%/2) for six periods (3 years × 2 semiannual periods).

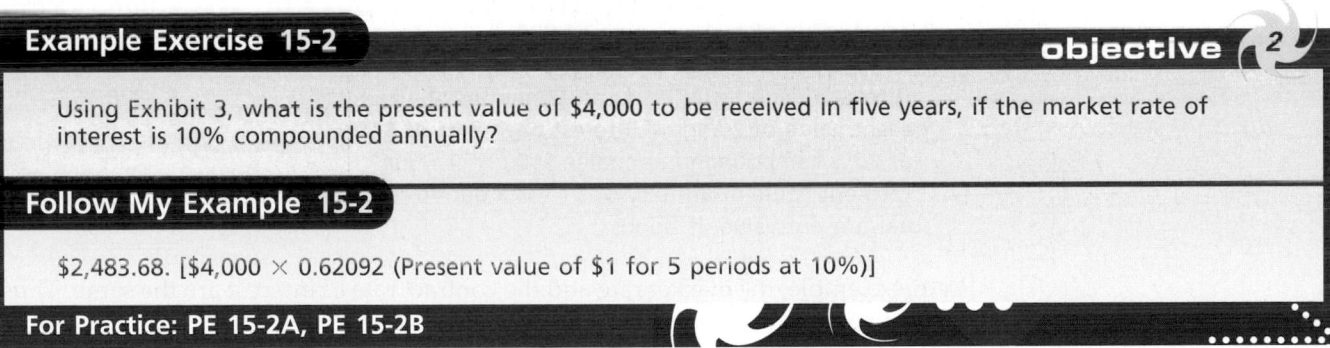

Example Exercise 15-2   objective ②

Using Exhibit 3, what is the present value of $4,000 to be received in five years, if the market rate of interest is 10% compounded annually?

Follow My Example 15-2

$2,483.68. [$4,000 × 0.62092 (Present value of $1 for 5 periods at 10%)]

For Practice: PE 15-2A, PE 15-2B

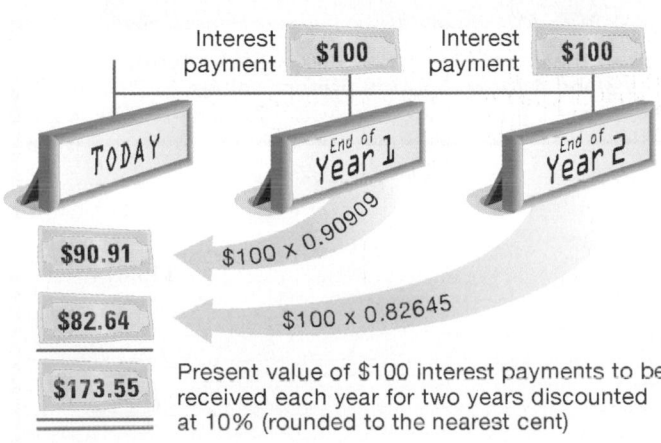

Interest payment **$100**   Interest payment **$100**

TODAY   End of Year 1   End of Year 2

$90.91 $100 × 0.90909

$82.64 $100 × 0.82645

$173.55   Present value of $100 interest payments to be received each year for two years discounted at 10% (rounded to the nearest cent)

Present Value of the Periodic Bond Interest Payments
The present value of the periodic bond interest payments is the value today of the amount of interest to be received at the end of each interest period. Such a series of equal cash payments at fixed intervals is called an **annuity**.

The **present value of an annuity** is the sum of the present values of each cash flow. To illustrate, assume that the $1,000 bond in the preceding example pays interest of 10% annually and that the market rate of interest is also 10%. In addition, assume that the bond matures at the end of two years. The present value of the two interest payments of $100 ($1,000 × 10%) is $173.55, as shown in the time line to the left. It can be determined by using the present value table shown in Exhibit 3.

Instead of using present value of amount tables, such as Exhibit 3, separate present value tables are normally used for annuities. Exhibit 4 is a partial table of the *present value of an annuity of $1* at compound interest. It shows the present value of $1 to be received at the end of each period for various compound rates of interest. For example, the present value of $100 to be received at the end of each of the next two years at 10% compound interest per period is $173.55 ($100 × 1.73554). This amount is the same amount that we computed previously.

EXHIBIT 4   **Present Value of Annuity of $1 at Compound Interest**

Periods	5%	5½%	6%	6½%	7%	10%	11%	12%	13%	14%
1	0.95238	0.94787	0.94340	0.93897	0.93458	0.90909	0.90090	0.89286	0.88496	0.87719
2	1.85941	1.84632	1.83339	1.82063	1.80802	1.73554	1.71252	1.69005	1.66810	1.64666
3	2.72325	2.69793	2.67301	2.64848	2.62432	2.48685	2.44371	2.40183	2.36115	2.32163
4	3.54595	3.50515	3.46511	3.42580	3.38721	3.16987	3.10245	3.03735	2.97447	2.91371
5	4.32948	4.27028	4.21236	4.15568	4.10020	3.79079	3.69590	3.60478	3.51723	3.43308
6	5.07569	4.99553	4.91732	4.84101	4.76654	4.35526	4.23054	4.11141	3.99755	3.88867
7	5.78637	5.68297	5.58238	5.48452	5.38929	4.86842	4.71220	4.56376	4.42261	4.28830
8	6.46321	6.33457	6.20979	6.08875	5.97130	5.33493	5.14612	4.96764	4.79677	4.63886
9	7.10782	6.95220	6.80169	6.65610	6.51523	5.75902	5.53705	5.32825	5.13166	4.94637
10	7.72174	7.53763	7.36009	7.18883	7.02358	6.14457	5.88923	5.65022	5.42624	5.21612

As we stated earlier, the amount buyers are willing to pay for a bond is the sum of the present value of the face value and the periodic interest payments, calculated by using the market rate of interest. In our example, this calculation is as follows:

Present value of face value of $1,000 due in 2 years, at 10% compounded annually: $1,000 × 0.82645 (present value factor of $1 for 2 periods at 10%)	$ 826.45
Present value of 2 annual interest payments of $100, at 10% compounded annually: $100 × 1.73554 (present value of annuity of $1 for 2 periods at 10%)	173.55
Total present value of bonds	$1,000.00

In this example, the market rate and the contract rate of interest are the same. Thus, the present value is the same as the face value.

Example Exercise 15-3   **objective 2**

Calculate the present value of a $20,000, 5%, five-year bond that pays $1,000 ($20,000 × 5%) interest annually, if the market rate of interest is 5%. Use Exhibits 3 and 4 for computing present values.

Follow My Example 15-3

Present value of face amount of $20,000 due in 5 years, at 5% compounded annually: $20,000 × 0.78353 (present value factor of $1 for 5 periods at 5%)	$15,671*
Present value of 5 annual interest payments of $1,000, at 5% interest compounded annually: $1,000 × 4.32948 (present value of annuity of $1 for 5 periods at 5%)	4,329*
Total present value of bonds	$20,000

*Rounded to the nearest dollar.

For Practice: PE 15-3A, PE 15-3B

Accounting for Bonds Payable

objective **3**

Journalize entries for bonds payable.

In the preceding section, we described and illustrated how present value concepts are used in determining how much buyers are willing to pay for bonds. In this section, we describe and illustrate how corporations record the issuance of bonds and the payment of bond interest.

BONDS ISSUED AT FACE AMOUNT

To illustrate the journal entries for issuing bonds, assume that on January 1, 2007, a corporation issues for cash $100,000 of 12%, five-year bonds, with interest of $6,000 payable *semiannually*. The market rate of interest at the time the bonds are issued is 12%. Since the contract rate and the market rate of interest are the same, the bonds will sell at their face amount. This amount is the sum of (1) the present value of the face amount of $100,000 to be repaid in five years and (2) the present value of 10 *semi-annual* interest payments of $6,000 each. This computation and a time line are shown below.

Present value of face amount of $100,000 due in 5 years,
   at 12% compounded semiannually: $100,000 × 0.55840
   (present value of $1 for 10 periods at 6%) .... $ 55,840
Present value of 10 semiannual interest payments of $6,000,
   at 12% compounded semiannually: $6,000 × 7.36009
   (present value of annuity of $1 for 10 periods at 6%) 44,160*
Total present value of bonds $100,000

*Because the present value tables are rounded to five decimal places, minor rounding differences may appear in the illustrations.

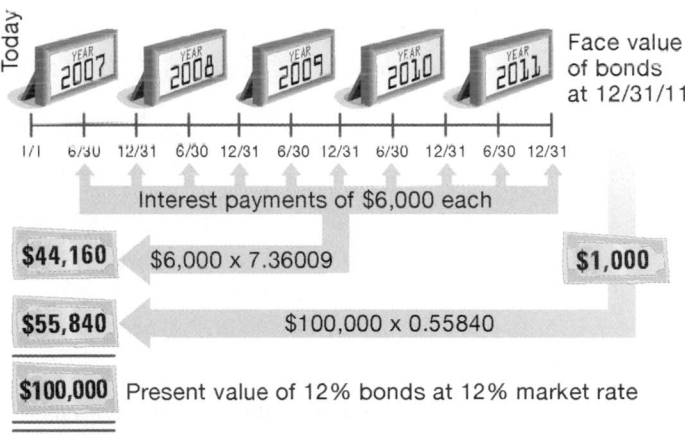

The following entry records the issuing of the $100,000 bonds at their face amount:

2007 Jan.	1	Cash		100 0 0 0 00		
		Bonds Payable			100 0 0 0 00	
		Issued $100,000 bonds payable at				
		face amount.				

Every six months after the bonds have been issued, interest payments of $6,000 are made. The first interest payment is recorded as shown at the top of the following page.

June	30	Interest Expense		6 0 0 0 00	
		Cash			6 0 0 0 00
		Paid six months' interest on bonds.			

At the maturity date, the payment of the principal of $100,000 is recorded as follows:

2011 Dec.	31	Bonds Payable		100 0 0 0 00	
		Cash			100 0 0 0 00
		Paid bond principal at maturity date.			

BONDS ISSUED AT A DISCOUNT

What if the market rate of interest is higher than the contract rate of interest? If the market rate of interest is 13% and the contract rate is 12% on the five-year, $100,000 bonds, the bonds will sell at a discount. The present value of these bonds is calculated as follows:

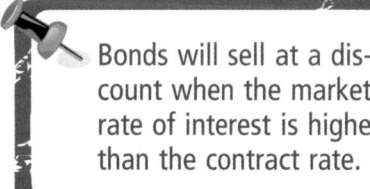

Bonds will sell at a discount when the market rate of interest is higher than the contract rate.

> Present value of face amount of $100,000 due in 5 years,
> at 13% compounded semiannually: $100,000 × 0.53273
> (present value of $1 for 10 periods at 6½%) $53,273
> Present value of 10 semiannual interest payments of $6,000,
> at 13% compounded semiannually: $6,000 × 7.18883
> (present value of an annuity of $1 for 10 periods at 6½%)   43,133
> Total present value of bonds $96,406

The two present values that make up the total are both less than the related amounts in the preceding example. This is because the market rate of interest was 12% in the first example, while the market rate of interest is 13% in this example. The present value of a future amount becomes less and less as the interest rate used to compute the present value increases.

The entry to record the issuing of the $100,000 bonds at a discount is shown below.

2007 Jan.	1	Cash		96 4 0 6 00	
		Discount on Bonds Payable		3 5 9 4 00	
		Bonds Payable			100 0 0 0 00
		Issued $100,000 bonds at discount.			

The $3,594 discount may be viewed as the amount that is needed to entice investors to accept a contract rate of interest that is below the market rate. You may think of the discount as the market's way of adjusting a bond's contract rate of interest to the higher market rate of interest. Using this logic, generally accepted accounting principles require that bond discounts be amortized as interest expense over the life of the bond.

Example Exercise 15-4   objective

On the first day of the fiscal year, a company issues a $1,000,000, 6%, five-year bond that pays semiannual interest of $30,000 ($1,000,000 × 6% × ½), receiving cash of $845,562. Journalize the entry to record the issuance of the bonds.

(continued)

AMORTIZING A BOND DISCOUNT

There are two methods of amortizing a bond discount: (1) the *straight-line method* and (2) the **effective interest rate method**, often called the *interest method*. Both methods amortize the same total amount of discount over the life of the bonds. The interest method is required by generally accepted accounting principles. However, the straight-line method is acceptable if the results obtained do not materially differ from the results that would be obtained by using the interest method. Because the straight-line method illustrates the basic concept of amortizing discounts and is simpler, we will use it in this chapter. We illustrate the interest method in an appendix to this chapter.

The straight-line method of amortizing a bond discount provides for amortization in equal periodic amounts. Applying this method to the preceding example yields amortization of $^{1}/_{10}$ of $3,594, or $359.40, each half year. The amount of the interest expense on the bonds is the same, $6,359.40 ($6,000 + $359.40), for each half year. The entry to record the first interest payment and the amortization of the related discount follows.

2007 June	30	Interest Expense	6 3 5 9 40		
		Discount on Bonds Payable			3 5 9 40
		Cash			6 0 0 0 00
		Paid semiannual interest and amortized $^{1}/_{10}$ of bond discount.			

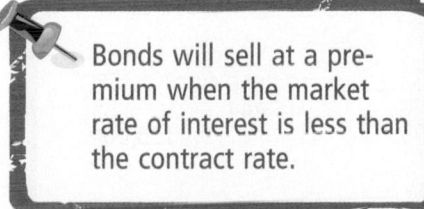

Bonds will sell at a premium when the market rate of interest is less than the contract rate.

BONDS ISSUED AT A PREMIUM

If the market rate of interest is 11% and the contract rate is 12% on the five-year, $100,000 bonds, the bonds will sell at a premium. The present value of these bonds is computed as shown at the top of the following page.

Present value of face amount of $100,000 due in 5 years,
at 11% compounded semiannually: $100,000 × 0.58543
(present value of $1 for 10 periods at 5½%) . . . . $ 58,543
Present value of 10 semiannual interest payments of $6,000,
at 11% compounded semiannually: $6,000 × 7.53763
(present value of an annuity of $1 for 10 periods at 5½%)   45,226
Total present value of bonds $103,769

The entry to record the issuing of the bonds is as follows:

2007 Jan.	1	Cash	103 7 6 9 00		
		Bonds Payable		100 0 0 0 00	
		Premium on Bonds Payable		3 7 6 9 00	
		Issued $100,000 bonds at a premium.			

Example Exercise 15-6   objective 3

A company issues a $2,000,000, 12%, five-year bond that pays semiannual interest of $120,000 ($2,000,000 × 12% × ½), receiving cash of $2,154,435. Journalize the bond issuance.

Follow My Example 15-6

Cash   2,154,435
    Premium on Bonds Payable   154,435
    Bonds Payable   2,000,000

For Practice: PE 15-6A, PE 15-6B

AMORTIZING A BOND PREMIUM

The amortization of bond premiums is basically the same as that for bond discounts, except that interest expense is decreased. In the above example, the straight-line method yields amortization of ¹/₁₀ of $3,769, or $376.90, each half year. The entry to record the first interest payment and the amortization of the related premium is as follows:

2007 June	30	Interest Expense	5 6 2 3 10		
		Premium on Bonds Payable	3 7 6 90		
		Cash		6 0 0 0 00	
		Paid semiannual interest and amortized ¹/₁₀ of bond premium.			

Example Exercise 15-7   objective 3

Using the bond from Example Exercise 15-6, journalize the first interest payment and the amortization of the related bond premium.

Follow My Example 15-7

Interest Expense   104,556
Premium on Bonds Payable   15,444
    Cash   120,000
        Paid interest bond and amortized the bond premium ($154,435/10).

For Practice: PE 15-7A, PE 15-7B

ZERO-COUPON BONDS

Some corporations issue bonds that provide for only the payment of the face amount at the maturity date. Such bonds are called *zero-coupon bonds*. Because they do not provide for interest payments, these bonds sell at a large discount. For example, Merrill Lynch & Co. Inc.'s zero-coupon bonds maturing in 2028 were selling for 21.50.

The issuing price of zero-coupon bonds is the present value of their face amount. To illustrate, if the market rate of interest is 13%, the present value of $100,000 zero-coupon, five-year bonds is calculated as follows:

> Present value of $100,000 due in 5 years, at 13%
>   compounded semiannually: $100,000 × 0.53273
>   (present value of $1 for 10 periods at 6½%) $53,273

The accounting for zero-coupon bonds is similar to that for interest-bearing bonds that have been sold at a discount. The discount is amortized as interest expense over the life of the bonds. The entry to record the issuing of the bonds is as follows:

2007					
Jan.	1	Cash		53 2 7 3 00	
		Discount on Bonds Payable		46 7 2 7 00	
		Bonds Payable			100 0 0 0 00
		Issued $100,000 zero-coupon			
		bonds			

Business Connections

CH-CH-CH-CHANGES IN BOND TRENDS

How would you like to tune into some of the royalties from your favorite rock star or song? In the past decade, several well-known rock stars have offered bonds backed by future royalties from their hit songs and albums. These include rock icons like James Brown, Rod Stewart, and Iron Maiden.

The trend toward linking music royalties to bonds began when rock star David Bowie packaged royalties from his 25-album catalog of over 300 songs as a $55 million bond issue. These "Bowie Bonds" had an average maturity of 10 years and paid 7.9% annual interest. On the issue date, Moody's Investors Service gave the bonds its highest rating, AAA. Potential investors were confident in the bonds, knowing that Bowie never sold fewer than

a million albums a year prior to the bond issuance. In addition, Bowie reportedly had a steady cash flow of $1 million per year from his existing music catalog. However, in recent years, investor confidence in these bonds has eroded. In May 2004, Moody's Investors Service downgraded the bonds to Baa3. This rating indicates that Moody's is skeptical of the catalog's ability to satisfy bond interest and principal payments.

While Bowie Bonds have fallen on hard times in recent years, they did give rise to a variety of similar bonds that were backed by the future earnings of intellectual property. These include intangibles like copyrights from music and films, patents from prescription drugs and technology, trade secrets, and Internet Web site names.

Payment and Redemption of Bonds Payable

The face value of bonds payable should be paid at the maturity date of the bonds. The entry to record the payment of bonds at their maturity date is a debit to Bonds Payable and a credit to Cash.

The bond indenture may require that funds for the payment of the face value of the bonds at maturity be set aside over the life of the bond issue. A bond indenture may restrict dividend payments to stockholders as a means of increasing the likelihood that the bonds will be paid at maturity. Finally, the bond indenture may allow for the early payment or redemption of the bond issue.

BOND SINKING FUNDS

Since the payment of bonds normally involves a large amount of cash, a bond indenture may require that cash be periodically transferred into a special cash fund over the life of the bond issue. Doing so ensures that an adequate amount of cash will be available at the maturity date for the payment of the face amount of the bonds. This special type of cash fund is called a **sinking fund**.

When cash is transferred to the sinking fund, it is recorded in an account called *Sinking Fund Cash*. When investments are purchased with the sinking fund cash, they are recorded in an account called *Sinking Fund Investments*. As income (interest or dividends) is received, it is recorded in an account called *Sinking Fund Revenue*.

Sinking fund revenue represents earnings of the corporation and is reported in the income statement as other income. The cash and the securities making up the sinking fund are reported in the balance sheet as investments, immediately below the Current Assets section.

A bond indenture may restrict dividend payments to stockholders as a means of increasing the likelihood that the bonds will be paid at maturity. In addition to or instead of this restriction, the bond indenture may require that funds for the payment of the face value of the bonds at maturity be set aside over the life of the bond issue. The amounts set aside are kept separate from other assets in the sinking fund.

BOND REDEMPTION

Pacific Bell issued 7.5% bonds, maturing in 2033 but callable in 2023.

A corporation may call or redeem bonds before they mature. This is often done if the market rate of interest declines significantly after the bonds have been issued. In this situation, the corporation may sell new bonds at a lower interest rate and use the funds to redeem the original bond issue. The corporation can thus save on future interest expenses.

A corporation often issues callable bonds to protect itself against significant declines in future interest rates. However, callable bonds are more risky for investors, who may not be able to replace the called bonds with investments paying an equal amount of interest.

Callable bonds can be redeemed by the issuing corporation within the period of time and at the price stated in the bond indenture. Normally, the call price is above the face value. A corporation may also redeem its bonds by purchasing them on the open market.

A corporation usually redeems its bonds at a price different from that of the carrying amount (or book value) of the bonds. The **carrying amount** of bonds payable is the balance of the bonds payable account (face amount of the bonds) less any unamortized discount or plus any unamortized premium. If the price paid for redemption is below the bond carrying amount, the difference in these two amounts is recorded as a gain. If the price paid for the redemption is above the carrying amount, a loss is recorded. Gains and losses on the redemption of bonds are reported in the Other Income and Expense section of the income statement.

To illustrate, assume that on June 30 a corporation has a bond issue of $100,000 outstanding, on which there is an unamortized premium of $4,000. Assuming that the corporation purchases one-fourth ($25,000) of the bonds for $24,000 on June 30, the entry to record the redemption is as follows:

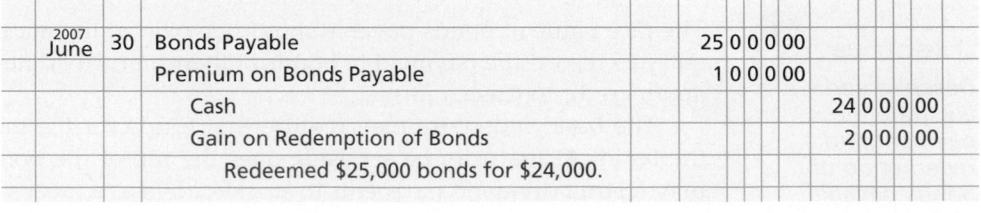

2007 June	30	Bonds Payable	25 0 0 0 00	
		Premium on Bonds Payable	1 0 0 0 00	
		Cash		24 0 0 0 00
		Gain on Redemption of Bonds		2 0 0 00
		Redeemed $25,000 bonds for $24,000.		

In the preceding entry, only a portion of the premium relating to the redeemed bonds is written off. The difference between the carrying amount of the bonds purchased, $26,000 ($25,000 + $1,000), and the price paid for the redemption, $24,000, is recorded as a gain.

If the corporation calls the entire bond issue for $105,000 on June 30, the entry to record the redemption is as follows:

2007 June	30	Bonds Payable	100 0 0 0 00	
		Premium on Bonds Payable	4 0 0 0 00	
		Loss on Redemption of Bonds	1 0 0 0 00	
		Cash		105 0 0 0 00
		Redeemed $100,000 bonds for $105,000.		

Example Exercise 15-8 objective 4

A $500,000 bond issue on which there is an unamortized discount of $40,000 is redeemed for $475,000. Journalize the redemption of the bonds.

Follow My Example 15-8

Bonds Payable	500,000	
Loss on Redemption of Bonds	15,000	
Discount on Bonds Payable		40,000
Cash		475,000

For Practice: PE 15-8A, PE 15-8B

Investments in Bonds

objective 5

Journalize entries for the purchase, interest, discount and premium amortization, and sale of bond investments.

The Walt Disney Company's 5.875% bonds maturing in 2017 were listed as selling for 103.375 on January 20, 2006.

Throughout this chapter, we have discussed bonds and the related transactions of the issuing corporation (the debtor). However, these transactions also affect investors. In this section, we discuss the accounting for bonds from the point of view of investors, and assume that the investor uses the cost principle to account for these investments.

ACCOUNTING FOR BOND INVESTMENTS—PURCHASE, INTEREST, AND AMORTIZATION

Bonds may be purchased either directly from the issuing corporation or through an organized bond exchange. Bond exchanges publish daily bond quotations. These quotations normally include the bond interest rate, maturity date, volume of sales, and the high, low, and closing prices for each corporation's bonds traded during the day. Prices for bonds are quoted as a percentage of the face amount. Thus, the price of a $1,000 bond quoted at 99.5 would be $995, while the price of a bond quoted at 104.25 would be $1,042.50.

As with other assets, the cost of a bond investment includes all costs related to the purchase. For example, for bonds purchased through an exchange, the amount paid as a broker's commission should be included as part of the cost of the investment.

When bonds are purchased between interest dates, the buyer normally pays the seller the interest accrued from the last interest payment date to the date of purchase. The amount of the interest paid is normally debited to *Interest Revenue*, since it is an offset against the amount that will be received at the next interest date.

To illustrate, assume that an investor purchases a $1,000 bond at 102 plus a brokerage fee of $5.30 and accrued interest of $10.20. The investor records the transaction as shown at the top of the following page.

	2007 Apr.	2	Investment in Lewis Co. Bonds		1 0 2 5 30		
			Interest Revenue		1 0 20		
			Cash			1 0 3 5 50	

> A premium or discount on a bond investment is recorded in the investment account and is amortized over the remaining life of the bonds.

The cost of the bond is recorded in a single investment account. The face amount of the bond and the premium (or discount) are normally not recorded in separate accounts. This is different from the accounting for bonds payable. Separate premium and discount accounts are usually not used by investors, because they usually do not hold bond investments until the bonds mature.

When bonds held as long-term investments are purchased at a price other than the face amount, the premium or discount should be amortized over the remaining life of the bonds. The amortization of premiums and discounts affects the investment and interest accounts as shown below.

Premium Amortization:			*Discount Amortization:*	
Interest Revenue	XXX		Investment in Bonds	XXX
Investment in Bonds		XXX	Interest Revenue		XXX

The amount of the amortization can be determined by using either the straight-line or interest methods. Unlike bonds payable, the amortization of premiums and discounts on bond investments is usually recorded at the end of the period, rather than when interest is received.

To illustrate the accounting for bond investments, assume that on July 1, 2007, Crenshaw Inc. purchases $50,000 of 8% bonds of Deitz Corporation, due in $8\frac{3}{4}$ years. Crenshaw Inc. purchases the bonds directly from Deitz Corporation to yield an effective interest rate of 11%. The purchase price is $41,706 plus interest of $1,000 ($50,000 × 8% × $\frac{3}{12}$) accrued from April 1, 2007, the date of the last semiannual interest payment. Entries in the accounts of Crenshaw Inc. at the time of purchase and for the remainder of the fiscal period ending December 31, 2007, are as follows:

Calculations:

Cost of $50,000 of Deitz
  Corporation bonds $41,706
Interest accrued
  ($50,000 × 8% × $\frac{3}{12}$)   1,000
Total $42,706

$50,000 × 8% × $\frac{6}{12}$ = $2,000

$50,000 × 8% × $\frac{3}{12}$ = $1,000

Face value of bonds $50,000
Cost of bond invest.   41,706
Discount on bond
  investment $ 8,294

Number of months
  to maturity
  ($8\frac{3}{4}$ years × 12)   105 months
Monthly amortization
  ($8,294/105 months,
  rounded to nearest
  dollar) $79 per mo.
Amortization for
  6 months ($79 × 6) $474

	2007 July	1	Investment in Deitz Corporation Bonds		41 7 0 6 00		
			Interest Revenue		1 0 0 0 00		
			Cash			42 7 0 6 00	
			Purchased investment in bonds, plus				
			accrued interest.				
	Oct.	1	Cash		2 0 0 0 00		
			Interest Revenue			2 0 0 0 00	
			Received semiannual interest for				
			April 1 to October 1.				
	Dec.	31	Interest Receivable		1 0 0 0 00		
			Interest Revenue			1 0 0 0 00	
			Accrued interest from October 1				
			to December 31.				
		31	Investment in Deitz Corporation Bonds		4 7 4 00		
			Interest Revenue			4 7 4 00	
			Amortization of discount from July 1				
			to December 31.				

The effect of these entries on the interest revenue account is shown below.

Interest Revenue

July 1	1,000	Oct. 1		2,000
		Dec. 31 Adj.		1,000
		31 Adj.		474
		Adj. Bal.		2,474

ACCOUNTING FOR BOND INVESTMENTS—SALE

Many long-term investments in bonds are sold before their maturity date. When this occurs, the seller receives the sales price (less commissions and other selling costs) plus any accrued interest since the last interest payment date. Before recording the cash proceeds, the seller should amortize any discount or premium for the current period up to the date of sale. Any gain or loss on the sale is then recorded when the cash proceeds are recorded. Such gains and losses are normally reported in the Other Income and Expense section of the income statement.

To illustrate, assume that the Deitz Corporation bonds in the preceding example are sold for $47,350 plus accrued interest on June 30, 2014. The *carrying amount* of the bonds (cost plus amortized discount) as of January 1, 2014 (78 months after their purchase) is $47,868 [$41,706 + ($79 per month × 78 months)]. The entries to amortize the discount for the current year and to record the sale of the bonds are as follows:

Calculations:

$79 × 6 months

Carrying amount of bonds on
Jan. 1, 2014 $47,868
Discount amortized,
Jan. 1 to
June 30, 2014   474
Carrying amount of bonds on
June 30, 2014 $48,342
Proceeds of sale   47,350
Loss on sale $ 992

2014					
June	30	Investment in Deitz Corporation Bonds		474 00	
		Interest Revenue			474 00
		Amortized discount for current year.			
	30	Cash		48 350 00	
		Loss on Sale of Investments		992 00	
		Interest Revenue			1 000 00
		Investment in Deitz Corporation Bonds			48 342 00
		Received interest and proceeds			
		from sale of bonds.			
		Interest for April 1 to June 30 =			
		$50,000 × 8% × 3/12 = $1,000			

Example Exercise 15-9   objective 5

On October 1, 2008, Viewtec Corporation purchases $10,000 of 6% bonds of Watson Corporation, due in 9¼ years. The bonds were purchased at a price of $8,341 plus interest of $150 ($10,000 × 6% × 3/12) accrued from July 1, 2008, the date of the last semiannual interest payment.

a. Journalize the purchase of the bonds plus accrued interest.
b. Journalize the entry to record the amortization of the discount on December 31. (Round to the nearest dollar.)

Follow My Example 15-9

a. 2008
    Oct. 1   Investment in Watson Corporation Bonds   8,341
             Interest Revenue   150
                 Cash   8,491

b. 2008   Investment in Watson Corporation Bonds 45*
    Dec. 1   Interest Revenue   45
             *[($10,000 − $8,341)/111 months] × 3 months

For Practice: PE 15-9A, PE 15-9B

Corporation Balance Sheet

objective

6

Prepare a corporation balance sheet.

In previous chapters, we illustrated the income statement and retained earnings statement for a corporation. The consolidated balance sheet in Exhibit 5 illustrates the presentation of many of the items discussed in this and preceding chapters. These items include bond sinking funds, investments in bonds, goodwill, deferred income taxes, and bonds payable and unamortized discount.

BALANCE SHEET PRESENTATION OF BONDS PAYABLE

In Exhibit 5, Escoe Corporation's bonds payable are reported as long-term liabilities. If there were two or more bond issues, the details of each would be reported on the balance sheet or in a supporting schedule or note. Separate accounts are normally maintained for each bond issue.

When the balance sheet date is within one year of the maturity date of the bonds, the bonds may be classified as a current liability. This would be the case if the bonds are to be paid out of current assets. If the bonds are to be paid from a sinking fund or if they are to be refinanced with another bond issue, they should remain in the noncurrent category. In this case, the details of the retirement of the bonds are normally disclosed in a note to the financial statements.

The balance in Escoe's discount on bonds payable account is reported as a *deduction* from the bonds payable. Conversely, the balance in a bond premium account would be reported as an *addition* to the related bonds payable. Either on the face of the financial statements or in accompanying notes, a description of the bonds (terms, due date, and effective interest rate) and other relevant information such as sinking fund requirements should be disclosed.[4] Finally, the market (fair) value of the bonds payable should also be disclosed.

BALANCE SHEET PRESENTATION OF BOND INVESTMENTS

Investments in bonds or other debt securities that management intends to hold to their maturity are called **held-to-maturity securities**. Such securities are classified as long-term investments under the caption Investments. These investments are reported at their cost less any amortized premium or plus any amortized discount. In addition, the market (fair) value of the bond investments should be disclosed, either on the face of the balance sheet or in an accompanying note.

---

4 *Statement of Financial Accounting Standards No. 129,* "Disclosure Information About Capital Structure," Financial Accounting Standards Board (Norwalk, Connecticut: 1997).

EXHIBIT 5	Balance Sheet of a Corporation

Escoe Corporation and Subsidiaries
Consolidated Balance Sheet
December 31, 2008

Assets

Current assets:

Cash and cash equivalents		$ 407,500	
Accounts and notes receivable	$ 722,000		
Less allowance for doubtful receivables	37,000	685,000	
Inventories, at lower of cost (first-in, first-out) or market		917,500	
Prepaid expenses		70,000	
Total current assets			$2,080,000

Investments:

Bond sinking fund (market value, $473,000)		$ 422,500	
Investment in bonds of Dalton (market value, $231,000)		240,000	
Total investments			662,500

	Cost	Accumulated Depreciation	Book Value	
Property, plant, and equipment (depreciated by the straight-line method):				
Land	$ 250,000	—	$ 250,000	
Buildings	920,000	$ 379,955	540,045	
Machinery and equipment	2,764,400	766,200	1,998,200	
Total property, plant, and equipment	$3,934,400	$1,146,155		2,788,245

Intangible assets:

Goodwill		350,000
Total assets		$5,880,745

Liabilities

Current liabilities:

Accounts payable		$ 623,810	
Income tax payable		120,500	
Dividends payable		94,000	
Accrued liabilities		81,400	
Deferred income tax payable		10,000	
Total current liabilities			$ 929,710

Long-term liabilities:

Debenture 8% bonds payable, due December 31, 2026		
(market value, $950,000)	$1,000,000	
Less unamortized discount	60,000	
Total long-term liabilities		940,000

Deferred credits:

Deferred income tax payable		85,500
Total liabilities		$1,955,210

Stockholders' Equity

Paid-in capital:

Common stock, $20 par (250,000 shares authorized,		
100,000 shares issued)	$2,000,000	
Excess of issue price over par	320,000	
Total paid-in capital	$2,320,000	
Retained earnings	1,605,535	
Total stockholders' equity		3,925,535
Total liabilities and stockholders' equity		$5,880,745

Financial Analysis and Interpretation

Analysts often assess the relative risk of the bondholders in terms of the **number of times interest charges are earned** during the year. The higher the ratio, the greater the chance that interest payments will continue to be made if earnings decrease.

The amount available to make interest payments is not affected by taxes on income. This is because interest is deductible in determining taxable income. To illustrate, the following data were taken from the 2005 annual report of Briggs & Stratton Corporation:

Interest expense	$36,883,000
Income before income tax	$174,315,000

The number of times interest charges are earned, 5.73, is calculated below.

$$\text{Number of Times Interest Charges Are Earned} = \frac{\text{Income Before Income Tax} + \text{Interest Expense}}{\text{Interest Expense}}$$

$$\text{Number of Times Interest Charges Are Earned} = \frac{\$174,315,000 + \$36,883,000}{\$36,883,000} = 5.73$$

The number of times interest charges are earned indicates that the debtholders of Briggs & Stratton Corporation have adequate protection against a potential drop in earnings jeopardizing their receipt of interest payments. However, a final assessment should include a review of trends of past years and a comparison with industry averages.

Appendix

Effective Interest Rate Method of Amortization

The effective interest rate method of amortizing discounts and premiums provides for a constant rate of interest on the carrying amount of the bonds at the beginning of each period. This is in contrast to the straight-line method, which provides for a constant amount of interest expense.

The interest rate used in the interest method of amortization is the market rate on the date the bonds are issued. The carrying amount of the bonds to which the interest rate is applied is the face amount of the bonds minus any unamortized discount or plus any unamortized premium. Under the interest method, the interest expense to be reported on the income statement is computed by multiplying the effective interest rate by the carrying amount of the bonds. The difference between the interest expense computed in this way and the periodic interest payment is the amount of discount or premium to be amortized for the period.

AMORTIZATION OF DISCOUNT BY THE INTEREST METHOD

To illustrate the interest method for amortizing bond discounts, we assume the following data from the chapter illustration of issuing $100,000 bonds at a discount:

Face value of 12%, 5-year bonds, interest compounded semiannually	$100,000
Present value of bonds at effective (market) rate of interest of 13%	96,406
Discount on bonds payable	$ 3,594

Applying the interest method to these data yields the amortization table in Exhibit 6. You should note the following items in this table:

1. The interest paid (Column A) remains constant at 6% of $100,000, the face amount of the bonds.
2. The interest expense (Column B) is computed at 6½% of the bond carrying amount at the beginning of each period. This results in an increasing interest expense each period.
3. The excess of the interest expense over the interest payment of $6,000 is the amount of discount to be amortized (Column C).
4. The unamortized discount (Column D) decreases from the initial balance, $3,594, to a zero balance at the maturity date of the bonds.
5. The carrying amount (Column E) increases from $96,406, the amount received for the bonds, to $100,000 at maturity.

EXHIBIT 6   **Amortization of Discount on Bonds Payable**

Interest Payment	A Interest Paid (6% of Face Amount)	B Interest Expense (6½% of Bond Carrying Amount)	C Discount Amortization (B − A)	D Unamortized Discount (D − C)	E Bond Carrying Amount ($100,000 − D)
				$3,594	$ 96,406
1	$6,000	$6,266 (6½% of $96,406)	$266	3,328	96,672
2	6,000	6,284 (6½% of $96,672)	284	3,044	96,956
3	6,000	6,302 (6½% of $96,956)	302	2,742	97,258
4	6,000	6,322 (6½% of $97,258)	322	2,420	97,580
5	6,000	6,343 (6½% of $97,580)	343	2,077	97,923
6	6,000	6,365 (6½% of $97,923)	365	1,712	98,288
7	6,000	6,389 (6½% of $98,288)	389	1,323	98,677
8	6,000	6,414 (6½% of $98,677)	414	909	99,091
9	6,000	6,441 (6½% of $99,091)	441	468	99,532
10	6,000	6,470 (6½% of $99,532)	468*	—	100,000

*Cannot exceed unamortized discount.

The entry to record the first interest payment on June 30, 2007, and the related discount amortization is as follows:

2007 June	30	Interest Expense		6 2 6 6 00		
		Discount on Bonds Payable			2 6 6 00	
		Cash			6 0 0 0 00	
		Paid semiannual interest and amortized				
		bond discount for ½ year.				

If the amortization is recorded only at the end of the year, the amount of the discount amortized on December 31 would be $550. This is the sum of the first two semiannual amortization amounts ($266 and $284) from Exhibit 6.

AMORTIZATION OF PREMIUM BY THE INTEREST METHOD

To illustrate the interest method for amortizing bond premiums, we assume the following data from the chapter illustration of issuing $100,000 bonds at a premium:

Present value of bonds at effective (market) rate of interest of 11%	$103,769
Face value of 12%, 5-year bonds, interest compounded semiannually	100,000
Premium on bonds payable	$ 3,769

Using the interest method to amortize the above premium yields the amortization table in Exhibit 7. You should note the following items in this table:

1. The interest paid (Column A) remains constant at 6% of $100,000, the face amount of the bonds.
2. The interest expense (Column B) is computed at 5½% of the bond carrying amount at the beginning of each period. This results in a decreasing interest expense each period.
3. The excess of the periodic interest payment of $6,000 over the interest expense is the amount of premium to be amortized (Column C).
4. The unamortized premium (Column D) decreases from the initial balance, $3,769, to a zero balance at the maturity date of the bonds.
5. The carrying amount (Column E) decreases from $103,769, the amount received for the bonds, to $100,000 at maturity.

EXHIBIT 7   Amortization of Premium on Bonds Payable

Interest Payment	A Interest Paid (6% of Face Amount)	B Interest Expense (5½% of Bond Carrying Amount)	C Premium Amortization (A − B)	D Unamortized Premium (D − C)	E Bond Carrying Amount ($100,000 + D)
				$3,769	$103,769
1	$6,000	$5,707 (5½% of $103,769)	$293	3,476	103,476
2	6,000	5,691 (5½% of $103,476)	309	3,167	103,167
3	6,000	5,674 (5½% of $103,167)	326	2,841	102,841
4	6,000	5,656 (5½% of $102,841)	344	2,497	102,497
5	6,000	5,637 (5½% of $102,497)	363	2,134	102,134
6	6,000	5,617 (5½% of $102,134)	383	1,751	101,751
7	6,000	5,596 (5½% of $101,751)	404	1,347	101,347
8	6,000	5,574 (5½% of $101,347)	426	921	100,921
9	6,000	5,551 (5½% of $100,921)	449	472	100,472
10	6,000	5,526 (5½% of $100,472)	472*	—	100,000

*Cannot exceed unamortized premium.

The entry to record the first interest payment on June 30, 2007, and the related premium amortization is as follows:

2007					
June	30	Interest Expense	5 7 0 7 00		
		Premium on Bonds Payable	2 9 3 00		
		Cash		6 0 0 0 00	
		Paid semiannual interest and amortized			
		bond premium for ½ year.			

If the amortization is recorded only at the end of the year, the amount of the premium amortized on December 31, 2007, would be $602. This is the sum of the first two semiannual amortization amounts ($293 and $309) from Exhibit 7.

At a Glance

1. Compute the potential impact of long-term borrowing on earnings per share.

Key Points	Key Learning Outcomes	Example Exercises	Practice Exercises
Corporations can finance their operations by issuing bonds or additional equity. A bond is simply a form of an interest-bearing note. One of the many factors that influence a corporation's decision on whether it should issue debt or equity is the effect each alternative has on earnings per share.	• Define the concept of a bond. • Calculate and compare the effect of alternative financing plans on earnings per share.	15-1	15-1A, 15-1B

2. Describe the characteristics, terminology, and pricing of bonds payable.

Key Points	Key Learning Outcomes	Example Exercises	Practice Exercises
A corporation that issues bonds enters into a contract, or bond indenture. The characteristics of a bond depend on the type of bonds issued by a corporation. When a corporation issues bonds, the price that buyers are willing to pay for the bonds depends upon (1) the face amount of the bonds, (2) the periodic interest to be paid on the bonds, and (3) the market rate of interest. The price that a buyer is willing to pay for a bond is the sum of (1) the present value of the face amount and (2) the present value of the periodic interest payments.	• Define the characteristics of a bond. • Describe the various types of bonds. • Describe the factors that determine the price of a bond. • Define a bond discount or premium. • Calculate the present value of the face amount of a bond. • Calculate the present value of the periodic bond interest payments.	15-2 15-3	15-2A, 15-2B 15-3A, 15-3B

3. Journalize entries for bonds payable.

Key Points	Key Learning Outcomes	Example Exercises	Practice Exercises
The journal entry for issuing bonds payable debits Cash for the proceeds received and credits Bonds Payable for the face amount of the bonds. Any difference between the face amount of the bonds and the proceeds is debited to Discount on Bonds Payable or credited to Premium on Bonds Payable. A discount or premium on bonds payable is amortized to interest expense over the life of the bonds.	• Calculate the price of a bond. • Journalize the issuance of bonds at face value and the payment of periodic interest. • Journalize the issuance of bonds at a discount. • Journalize the amortization of a bond discount or premium. • Journalize the issuance of bonds at a premium. • Journalize the amortization of a bond premium.	15-4 15-5 15-6 15-7	15-4A, 15-4B 15-5A, 15-5B 15-6A, 15-6B 15-7A, 15-7B

(continued)

4. Describe and illustrate the payment and redemption of bonds payable.

Key Points	Key Learning Outcomes	Example Exercises	Practice Exercises
At the maturity date, the entry to record the payment at face value of a bond is a debit to Bonds Payable and a credit to Cash. Since the payment of bonds normally involves a large amount of cash, a bond indenture may require that cash be periodically transferred into a sinking fund. When a corporation redeems bonds, bonds payable is debited for the face amount of the bonds, the premium (discount) on bonds payable account is debited (credited) for its balance, Cash is credited, and any gain or loss on the redemption is recorded.	• Explain bond redemptions. • Journalize the redemption of bonds payable.	15-8	15-8A, 15-8B

5. Journalize entries for the purchase, interest, discount and premium amortization, and sale of bond investments.

Key Points	Key Learning Outcomes	Example Exercises	Practice Exercises
A long-term investment in bonds is recorded by debiting Investments in Bonds. When bonds are purchased between interest dates, the amount of interest paid should be debited to Interest Revenue. Any discount or premium on bond investments should be amortized, using the straight-line or effective interest rate methods. When bonds held as long-term investments are sold, any discount or premium for the current period should first be amortized.	• Journalize the purchase of bond investments. • Prepare the journal entry to record the receipt of periodic interest from bond investments. • Prepare the adjusting journal entry to accrue interest on bond investments and amortization of discounts and premiums on bond investments. • Journalize the sale of bond investments.	15-9	15-9A, 15-9B

6. Prepare a corporation balance sheet.

Key Points	Key Learning Outcomes	Example Exercises	Practice Exercises
Bonds payable are usually reported as long-term liabilities. A discount on bonds should be reported as deduction from the related bonds payable. A premium on bonds should be reported as an addition to related bonds payable. Investments in bonds that are held-to-maturity securities are reported as investments at cost less any amortized premium or plus any amortized discount.	• Illustrate the balance sheet presentation of bond investments and bonds payable.		

Key Terms

annuity (655)
bond (650)
bond indenture (652)
carrying amount (662)
contract rate (653)
discount (653)

effective interest rate method (659)
effective rate of interest (653)
future value (653)
held-to-maturity securities (666)
number of times interest charges
   are earned (668)

premium (653)
present value (653)
present value of an annuity (655)
sinking fund (662)

Illustrative Problem

The fiscal year of Russell Inc., a manufacturer of acoustical supplies, ends December 31. Selected transactions for the period 2007 through 2014, involving bonds payable issued by Russell Inc., are as follows:

2007
June 30. Issued $2,000,000 of 25-year, 7% callable bonds dated June 30, 2007, for cash of $1,920,000. Interest is payable semiannually on June 30 and December 31.
Dec. 31. Paid the semiannual interest on the bonds.
    31. Recorded straight-line amortization of $1,600 of discount on the bonds.
    31. Closed the interest expense account.

2008
June 30. Paid the semiannual interest on the bonds.
Dec. 31. Paid the semiannual interest on the bonds.
    31. Recorded straight-line amortization of $3,200 of discount on the bonds.
    31. Closed the interest expense account.

2014
June 30. Recorded the redemption of the bonds, which were called at 101.5. The balance in the bond discount account is $57,600 after the payment of interest and amortization of discount have been recorded. (Record the redemption only.)

Instructions

1. Journalize entries to record the preceding transactions.
2. Determine the amount of interest expense for 2007 and 2008.
3. Determine the carrying amount of the bonds as of December 31, 2008.

Solution

1.

2007 June	30	Cash	1,920 0 0 0 00	
		Discount on Bonds Payable	80 0 0 0 00	
		Bonds Payable		2,000 0 0 0 00
Dec.	31	Interest Expense	70 0 0 0 00	
		Cash		70 0 0 0 00
Dec.	31	Interest Expense	1 6 0 0 00	
		Discount on Bonds Payable		1 6 0 0 00
		Amortization of discount from July 1		
		to December 31.		
	31	Income Summary	71 6 0 0 00	
		Interest Expense		71 6 0 0 00

(continued)

2008 June	30	Interest Expense		70 0 0 0 00	
		Cash			70 0 0 0 00
Dec.	31	Interest Expense		70 0 0 0 00	
		Cash			70 0 0 0 00
	31	Interest Expense		3 2 0 0 00	
		Discount on Bonds Payable			3 2 0 0 00
		Amortization of discount from			
		January 1 to December 31.			
	31	Income Summary		143 2 0 0 00	
		Interest Expense			143 2 0 0 00
2014 June	30	Bonds Payable		2,000 0 0 0 00	
		Loss on Redemption of Bonds Payable		87 6 0 0 00	
		Discount on Bonds Payable			57 6 0 0 00
		Cash			2,030 0 0 0 00

2. a. 2007—$71,600
   b. 2008—$143,200

3. Initial carrying amount of bonds $1,920,000
   Discount amortized on December 31, 2007 1,600
   Discount amortized on December 31, 2008 3,200
   Carrying amount of bonds, December 31, 2008 .... $1,924,800

Self-Examination Questions

(Answers at End of Chapter)

1. If a corporation plans to issue $1,000,000 of 12% bonds at a time when the market rate for similar bonds is 10%, the bonds can be expected to sell at:
   A. their face amount.
   B. a premium.
   C. a discount.
   D. a price below their face amount.

2. If the bonds payable account has a balance of $900,000 and the discount on bonds payable account has a balance of $72,000, what is the carrying amount of the bonds?
   A. $828,000
   B. $900,000
   C. $972,000
   D. $580,000

3. The cash and securities that make up the sinking fund established for the payment of bonds at maturity are classified on the balance sheet as:
   A. current assets.
   B. investments.
   C. long-term liabilities.
   D. current liabilities.

4. If a firm purchases $150,000 of bonds of X Company at 101 plus accrued interest of $2,000 and pays broker's commissions of $50, the amount debited to Investment in X Company Bonds would be:
   A. $150,000.
   B. $151,550.
   C. $153,500.
   D. $153,550.

5. The balance in the discount on bonds payable account would usually be reported in the balance sheet in the:
   A. Current Assets section.
   B. Current Liabilities section.
   C. Long-Term Liabilities section.
   D. Investments section.

Eye Openers

1. Describe the two distinct obligations incurred by a corporation when issuing bonds.
2. Explain the meaning of each of the following terms as they relate to a bond issue: (a) convertible, (b) callable, and (c) debenture.

3. What is meant by the phrase "time value of money"?
4. What has the higher present value: (a) $18,000 to be received at the end of two years, or (b) $9,000 to be received at the end of each of the next two years?
5. If you asked your broker to purchase for you a 9% bond when the market interest rate for such bonds was 10%, would you expect to pay more or less than the face amount for the bond? Explain.
6. A corporation issues $5,000,000 of 7% bonds to yield interest at the rate of 5%. (a) Was the amount of cash received from the sale of the bonds greater or less than $5,000,000? (b) Identify the following terms related to the bond issue: (1) face amount, (2) market or effective rate of interest, (3) contract rate of interest, and (4) maturity amount.
7. If bonds issued by a corporation are sold at a premium, is the market rate of interest greater or less than the contract rate?
8. The following data relate to a $2,000,000, 8% bond issue for a selected semiannual interest period:

Bond carrying amount at beginning of period	$2,125,000
Interest paid during period	160,000
Interest expense allocable to the period	148,750

(a) Were the bonds issued at a discount or at a premium? (b) What is the unamortized amount of the discount or premium account at the beginning of the period? (c) What account was debited to amortize the discount or premium?
9. Assume that Smith Co. amortizes premiums and discounts on bonds payable at the end of the year rather than when interest is paid. What accounts would be debited and credited to record (a) the amortization of a discount on bonds payable and (b) the amortization of a premium on bonds payable?
10. Would a zero-coupon bond ever sell for its face amount?
11. What is the purpose of a bond sinking fund?
12. Assume that two 30-year, 10% bond issues are identical, except that one bond issue is callable at its face amount at the end of five years. Which of the two bond issues do you think will sell for a lower value?
13. Bonds Payable has a balance of $500,000, and Discount on Bonds Payable has a balance of $22,000. If the issuing corporation redeems the bonds at 97, is there a gain or loss on the bond redemption?
14. Where are investments in bonds that are classified as held-to-maturity securities reported on the balance sheet?
15. At what amount are held-to-maturity investments in bonds reported on the balance sheet?

Practice Exercises

PE 15-1A
Determining the effect of alternative financing plans on earnings per share

obj. 1

Wilkinson Co. is considering the following alternative financing plans.

	Plan 1	Plan 2
Issue 12% bonds (at face value)	$1,000,000	$500,000
Issue preferred $2 stock, $10 per share	—	700,000
Issue common stock, $10 par	1,000,000	800,000

Income tax is estimated at 40% of income.
Determine the earnings per share of common stock, assuming income before bond interest and income tax is $400,000.

PE 15-1B
Determining the effect of alternative financing plans on earnings per share

obj. 1

Knight Co. is considering the following alternative financing plans.

	Plan 1	Plan 2
Issue 9% bonds (at face value)	$3,000,000	$2,400,000
Issue preferred $2.50 stock, $25 per share	—	1,200,000
Issue common stock, $20 par	3,000,000	2,400,000

Income tax is estimated at 40% of income.

Determine the earnings per share of common stock, assuming income before bond interest and income tax is $500,000.

PE 15-2A
Determine the present value of a future amount
obj. 2

Using Exhibit 3, what is the present value of $7,000 to be received in 10 years, if the market rate of interest is 7% compounded annually?

PE 15-2B
Determine the present value of a future amount
obj. 2

Using Exhibit 3, what is the present value of $3,000 to be received in seven years, if the market rate of interest is 12% compounded annually?

PE 15-3A
Determine the present value of a bond
obj. 2

Calculate the present value of a $150,000, 7%, 10-year bond that pays $10,500 ($150,000 × 7%) interest annually, if the market rate of interest is 7%. Use Exhibits 3 and 4 for computing present values.

PE 15-3B
Determine the present value of a bond
obj. 2

Calculate the present value of an $80,000, 10%, five-year bond that pays $8,000 ($80,000 × 10%) interest annually, if the market rate of interest is 10%. Use Exhibits 3 and 4 for computing present values.

PE 15-4A
Record the issuance of bonds payable
obj. 3

On the first day of the fiscal year, a company issues a $500,0000, 10%, 10-year bond that pays semiannual interest of $25,000 ($500,000 × 10% × ½), receiving cash of $463,202. Journalize the bond issuance.

PE 15-4B
Record the issuance of bonds payable
obj. 3

On the first day of the fiscal year, a company issues a $1,500,000, 8%, five-year bond that pays semiannual interest of $60,000 ($1,500,000 × 8% × ½), receiving cash of $1,330,403. Journalize the bond issuance.

PE 15-5A
Record the interest for bonds payable
obj. 3

Using the bond from Practice Exercise 15-4A, journalize the first interest payment and the amortization of the related bond discount.

PE 15-5B
Record the interest for bonds payable
obj. 3

Using the bond from Practice Exercise 15-4B, journalize the first interest payment and the amortization of the related bond discount.

PE 15-6A
Record the issuance of bonds payable
obj. 3

A company issues a $2,000,000, 12%, five-year bond that pays semiannual interest of $120,000 ($2,000,000 × 12% × ½), receiving cash of $2,154,429. Journalize the bond issuance.

PE 15-6B
Record the issuance of bonds payable
obj. 3

A company issues a $1,000,000, 10%, ten-year bond that pays semiannual interest of $50,000 ($1,000,000 × 10% × ½), receiving cash of $1,065,040. Journalize the bond issuance.

PE 15-7A
Record the interest for bonds payable
obj. 3

Using the bond from Practice Exercise 15-6A, journalize the first interest payment and the amortization of the related bond premium.

PE 15-7B
Record the interest for bonds payable
obj. 3

Using the bond from Practice Exercise 15-6B, journalize the first interest payment and the amortization of the related bond premium.

PE 15-8A
Record the redemption of bonds payable
obj. 4

A $700,000 bond issue on which there is an unamortized discount of $60,000 is redeemed for $685,000. Journalize the redemption of the bonds.

PE 15-8B
Record the redemption of bonds payable
obj. 4

A $250,000 bond issue on which there is an unamortized premium of $20,000 is redeemed for $245,000. Journalize the redemption of the bonds.

PE 15-9A
Record the purchase of a bond investment
obj. 5

On September 1, 2008, Wilkerson Corporation purchases $70,000 of 8% bonds of Maxtech Corporation, due in $9\frac{1}{4}$ years. The bonds were purchased at a price of $56,000 plus interest of $1,400 ($70,000 × 8% × $\frac{3}{12}$) accrued from June 1, 2008, the date of the last semiannual interest payment. (a) Journalize the purchase of the bonds plus accrued interest. (b) Journalize the entry to record the amortization of the discount on December 31.

PF 15-9B
Record the purchase of a bond investment
obj. 5

On March 1, 2008, Gordon Corporation purchases $50,000 of 10% bonds of PUA-Tech Corporation, due in $9\frac{1}{4}$ years. The bonds were purchased at a price of $40,000 plus interest of $1,250 ($50,000 × 10% × $\frac{3}{12}$) accrued from December 1, 2007, the date of the last semiannual interest payment. (a) Journalize the purchase of the bonds plus accrued interest. (b) Journalize the entry to record the amortization of the discount on December 31.

Exercises

EX 15-1
Effect of financing on earnings per share
obj. 1
✓ a. $0.68

Bliss Co., which produces and sells skiing equipment, is financed as follows:

Bonds payable, 6% (issued at face amount)	$4,000,000
Preferred $2 stock (nonparticipating), $25 par	4,000,000
Common stock, $20 par	4,000,000

Income tax is estimated at 40% of income.

Determine the earnings per share of common stock, assuming that the income before bond interest and income tax is (a) $1,000,000, (b) $1,800,000, and (c) $3,200,000.

EX 15-2
Evaluate alternative financing plans
obj. 1

▬▬▶ Based upon the data in Exercise 15-1, discuss factors other than earnings per share that should be considered in evaluating such financing plans.

EX 15-3
Corporate financing
obj. 1

The financial statements for Williams-Sonoma, Inc., are presented in Appendix D at the end of the text. What is the major source of financing for Williams-Sonoma?

EX 15-4
Present value of amounts due
obj. 2

Determine the present value of $200,000 to be received in three years, using an interest rate of 7%, compounded annually, as follows:

a. By successive divisions. (Round to the nearest dollar.)
b. By using the present value table in Exhibit 3.

EX 15-5
Present value of an annuity
obj. 2

Determine the present value of $75,000 to be received at the end of each of four years, using an interest rate of 5%, compounded annually, as follows:

a. By successive computations, using the present value table in Exhibit 3.
b. By using the present value table in Exhibit 4.

EX 15-6
Present value of an annuity
obj. 2
✓ *$24,924,420*

On January 1, 2008, you win $40,000,000 in the state lottery. The $40,000,000 prize will be paid in equal installments of $2,000,000 over 20 years. The payments will be made on December 31 of each year, beginning on December 31, 2008. If the current interest rate is 5%, determine the present value of your winnings. Use the present value tables in Appendix A.

EX 15-7
Present value of an annuity
obj. 2

Assume the same data as in Exercise 15-6, except that the current interest rate is 10%.
➤ Will the present value of your winnings using an interest rate of 10% be one-half the present value of your winnings using an interest rate of 5%? Why or why not?

EX 15-8
Present value of bonds payable; discount
objs. 2, 3

Caps Co. produces and sells bottle capping equipment for soft drink and spring water bottlers. To finance its operations, Caps Co. issued $20,000,000 of five-year, 9% bonds with interest payable semiannually at an effective interest rate of 10%. Determine the present value of the bonds payable, using the present value tables in Exhibits 3 and 4. Round to the nearest dollar.

EX 15-9
Present value of bonds payable; premium
objs. 2, 3
✓ *$15,565,317*

Clowney Co. issued $15,000,000 of five-year, 12% bonds with interest payable semiannually, at an effective interest rate of 11%. Determine the present value of the bonds payable, using the present value tables in Exhibits 3 and 4. Round to the nearest dollar.

EX 15-10
Bond price
objs. 2, 3

REAL WORLD

McDonald's 6.375% bonds due in 2028 were reported as selling for 108.89.
➤ Were the bonds selling at a premium or at a discount? Explain.

EX 15-11
Entries for issuing bonds
obj. 3

Wolfe Co. produces and distributes fiber optic cable for use by telecommunications companies. Wolfe Co. issued $12,000,000 of 10-year, 8% bonds on May 1 of the current year, with interest payable on May 1 and November 1. The fiscal year of the company is the calendar year. Journalize the entries to record the following selected transactions for the current year:

May   1. Issued the bonds for cash at their face amount.
Nov. 1. Paid the interest on the bonds.
Dec. 31. Recorded accrued interest for two months.

EX 15-12
Entries for issuing bonds and amortizing discount by straight-line method
obj. 3

On the first day of its fiscal year, Ellis Company issued $12,000,000 of five-year, 10% bonds to finance its operations of producing and selling home improvement products. Interest is payable semiannually. The bonds were issued at an effective interest rate of 12%, resulting in Ellis Company receiving cash of $11,116,854.

✓ *b. $1,376,629*

a. Journalize the entries to record the following:
 1. Sale of the bonds.
 2. First semiannual interest payment. (Amortization of discount is to be recorded annually.)
 3. Second semiannual interest payment.
 4. Amortization of discount at the end of the first year, using the straight-line method. (Round to the nearest dollar.)
b. Determine the amount of the bond interest expense for the first year.

EX 15-13
Computing bond proceeds, entries for issuing bonds and amortizing premium by straight-line method
objs. 2, 3

Hemby Corporation wholesales oil and grease products to equipment manufacturers. On March 1, 2008, Hemby Corporation issued $4,000,000 of five-year, 13% bonds at an effective interest rate of 11%. Interest is payable semiannually on March 1 and September 1. Journalize the entries to record the following:

a. Sale of bonds on March 1, 2008. (Use the tables of present values in Exhibits 3 and 4 to determine the bond proceeds. Round to the nearest dollar.)
b. First interest payment on September 1, 2008, and amortization of bond premium for six months, using the straight-line method. (Round to the nearest dollar.)

EX 15-14
Entries for issuing and calling bonds; loss
objs. 3, 4

Farrar Corp., a wholesaler of office furniture, issued $7,000,000 of 20-year, 9% callable bonds on April 1, 2008, with interest payable on April 1 and October 1. The fiscal year of the company is the calendar year. Journalize the entries to record the following selected transactions:

2008
Apr.   1. Issued the bonds for cash at their face amount.
Oct.   1. Paid the interest on the bonds.

2012
Oct.   1. Called the bond issue at 103, the rate provided in the bond indenture. (Omit entry for payment of interest.)

EX 15-15
Entries for issuing and calling bonds; gain
objs. 3, 4

Rolfes Corp. produces and sells designer clothing. To finance its operations, Rolfes Corp. issued $4,000,000 of 30-year, 7% callable bonds on January 1, 2008, with interest payable on January 1 and July 1. The fiscal year of the company is the calendar year. Journalize the entries to record the following selected transactions:

2008
Jan.   1. Issued the bonds for cash at their face amount.
July   1. Paid the interest on the bonds.

2014
July   1. Called the bond issue at 96, the rate provided in the bond indenture. (Omit entry for payment of interest.)

EX 15-16
Reporting bonds
objs. 4, 6

At the beginning of the current year, two bond issues (X and Y) were outstanding. During the year, bond issue X was redeemed and a significant loss on the redemption of bonds was reported as an extraordinary item on the income statement. At the end of the year, bond issue Y was reported as a current liability because its maturity date was early in the following year. A sinking fund of cash and securities sufficient to pay the series Y bonds was reported in the balance sheet as *Investments*.

▬▬▶ Identify the flaws in the reporting practices related to the two bond issues.

EX 15-17
Amortizing discount on bond investment
obj. 5

A company purchased a $5,000, 25-year zero-coupon bond for $820 to yield 8.5% to maturity. How is the interest revenue computed?

EX 15-18
Entries for purchase and sale of investment in bonds; loss
obj. 5

Nanotech Innovations Co. sells orthopedic supplies to hospitals. Journalize the entries to record the following selected transactions of Nanotech Innovations Co.:

a. Purchased for cash $600,000 of Sanhueza Co. 7% bonds at 102 plus accrued interest of $10,500.
b. Received first semiannual interest.
c. At the end of the first year, amortized $960 of the bond premium.
d. Sold the bonds at 98 plus accrued interest of $3,500. The bonds were carried at $606,720 at the time of the sale.

EX 15-19
Entries for purchase and sale of investment in bonds; gain
obj. 5

Burtard Company develops and sells graphics software for use by architects. Journalize the entries to record the following selected transactions of Burtard Company:

a. Purchased for cash $450,000 of Blaga Co. 8% bonds at 97 plus accrued interest of $9,000.
b. Received first semiannual interest.
c. Amortized $1,080 of the bond investment at the end of the first year.
d. Sold the bonds at 101 plus accrued interest of $3,000. The bonds were carried at $442,440 at the time of the sale.

EX 15-20
Number of times interest charges earned

The following data were taken from recent annual reports of Southwest Airlines, which operates a low-fare airline service to over 50 cities in the United States.

	Current Year	Preceding Year
Interest expense	$ 88,000,000	$ 91,000,000
Income before income tax	489,000,000	708,000,000

a. Determine the number of times interest charges were earned for the current and preceding years. Round to one decimal place.
b. ➤ What conclusions can you draw?

APPENDIX EX 15-21
Amortize discount by interest method
✓ *b. $1,179,806*

On the first day of its fiscal year, Pedro Dynamite Company issued $11,000,000 of five-year, 9% bonds to finance its operations of producing and selling home electronics equipment. Interest is payable semiannually. The bonds were issued at an effective interest rate of 12%, resulting in Pedro Dynamite Company receiving cash of $9,785,645.

a. Journalize the entries to record the following:
   1. Sale of the bonds.
   2. First semiannual interest payment. (Amortization of discount is to be recorded annually.)
   3. Second semiannual interest payment.
   4. Amortization of discount at the end of the first year, using the interest method. (Round to the nearest dollar.)
b. Compute the amount of the bond interest expense for the first year.

APPENDIX EX 15-22
Amortize premium by interest method
✓ *b. $294,923*

Jarhead Corporation wholesales oil and grease products to equipment manufacturers. On March 1, 2008, Jarhead Corporation issued $2,500,000 of five-year, 13% bonds at an effective interest rate of 11%, receiving cash of $2,688,440. Interest is payable semiannually on March 1 and September 1. Jarhead Corporation's fiscal year begins on March 1.

a. Journalize the entries to record the following:
   1. Sale of the bonds.
   2. First interest payment on September 1, 2008. (Amortization of premium is to be recorded annually.)
   3. Second interest payment on March 1, 2009.
   4. Amortization of premium at the end of the first year, using the interest method. (Round to the nearest dollar.)
b. Determine the bond interest expense for the first year.

APPENDIX EX 15-23
Compute bond proceeds, amortizing premium by interest method, and interest expense

✓ a. $24,487,410
✓ c. $203,818

Ti-Pod Co. produces and sells advanced electronic equipment. On the first day of its fiscal year, Ti-Pod Co. issued $22,000,000 of five-year, 14% bonds at an effective interest rate of 11%, with interest payable semiannually. Compute the following, presenting figures used in your computations.

a. The amount of cash proceeds from the sale of the bonds. (Use the tables of present values in Exhibits 3 and 4. Round to the nearest dollar.)
b. The amount of premium to be amortized for the first semiannual interest payment period, using the interest method. (Round to the nearest dollar.)
c. The amount of premium to be amortized for the second semiannual interest payment period, using the interest method. (Round to the nearest dollar.)
d. The amount of the bond interest expense for the first year.

APPENDIX EX 15-24
Compute bond proceeds, amortizing discount by interest method, and interest expense

✓ a. $25,376,439
✓ b. $168,822

Little Chicken Co. produces and sells restaurant equipment. On the first day of its fiscal year, Little Chicken Co. issued $27,500,000 of five-year, 8% bonds at an effective interest rate of 10%, with interest payable semiannually. Compute the following, presenting figures used in your computations.

a. The amount of cash proceeds from the sale of the bonds. (Use the tables of present values in Exhibits 3 and 4.)
b. The amount of discount to be amortized for the first semiannual interest payment period, using the interest method. (Round to the nearest dollar.)
c. The amount of discount to be amortized for the second semiannual interest payment period, using the interest method. (Round to the nearest dollar.)
d. The amount of the bond interest expense for the first year.

Problems Series A

PR 15-1A
Effect of financing on earnings per share
obj. 1

✓ 1. Plan 3: $10.64

Three different plans for financing a $30,000,000 corporation are under consideration by its organizers. Under each of the following plans, the securities will be issued at their par or face amount, and the income tax rate is estimated at 40% of income.

	Plan 1	Plan 2	Plan 3
8% bonds	—	—	$20,000,000
Preferred $2 stock, $50 par	—	$20,000,000	10,000,000
Common stock, $10 par	$40,000,000	20,000,000	10,000,000
Total	$40,000,000	$40,000,000	$40,000,000

Instructions
1. Determine for each plan the earnings per share of common stock, assuming that the income before bond interest and income tax is $20,000,000.
2. Determine for each plan the earnings per share of common stock, assuming that the income before bond interest and income tax is $2,600,000.
3. ▬▬▶ Discuss the advantages and disadvantages of each plan.

PR 15-2A
Present value; bond premium; entries for bonds payable transactions
objs. 2, 3

✓ 3. $53,796

Atlantis Inc. produces and sells voltage regulators. On July 1, 2007, Atlantis Inc. issued $800,000 of 10-year, 14% bonds at an effective interest rate of 13%. Interest on the bonds is payable semiannually on December 31 and June 30. The fiscal year of the company is the calendar year.

Instructions
1. Journalize the entry to record the amount of the cash proceeds from the sale of the bonds. Use the tables of present values in Appendix A to compute the cash proceeds, rounding to the nearest dollar.

(continued)

2. Journalize the entries to record the following:
   a. The first semiannual interest payment on December 31, 2007, including the amortization of the bond premium, using the straight-line method. (Round to the nearest dollar.)
   b. The interest payment on June 30, 2008, and the amortization of the bond premium, using the straight-line method. (Round to the nearest dollar.)
3. Determine the total interest expense for 2007.
4. ▬▬▶ Will the bond proceeds always be greater than the face amount of the bonds when the contract rate is greater than the market rate of interest? Explain.

PR 15-3A

Present value; bond discount; entries for bonds payable transactions

objs. 2, 3

✓ 3. $723,347

On July 1, 2007, Iaket Equipment Inc. issued $12,500,000 of 10-year, 11% bonds at an effective interest rate of 12%. Interest on the bonds is payable semiannually on December 31 and June 30. The fiscal year of the company is the calendar year.

Instructions

1. Journalize the entry to record the amount of the cash proceeds from the sale of the bonds. Use the tables of present values in Appendix A to compute the cash proceeds, rounding to the nearest dollar.
2. Journalize the entries to record the following:
   a. The first semiannual interest payment on December 31, 2007, and the amortization of the bond discount, using the straight-line method. (Round to the nearest dollar.)
   b. The interest payment on June 30, 2008, and the amortization of the bond discount, using the straight-line method. (Round to the nearest dollar.)
3. Determine the total interest expense for 2007.
4. ▬▬▶ Will the bond proceeds always be less than the face amount of the bonds when the contract rate is less than the market rate of interest? Explain.

PR 15-4A

Entries for bonds payable transactions

objs. 3, 4

✓ 2. a. $1,005,659

Kornet Co. produces and sells graphite for golf clubs. The following transactions were completed by Kornet Co., whose fiscal year is the calendar year:

2007
July   1. Issued $19,000,000 of seven-year, 12% callable bonds dated July 1, 2007, at an effective rate of 10%, receiving cash of $20,880,780. Interest is payable semiannually on December 31 and June 30.
Dec. 31. Paid the semiannual interest on the bonds.
       31. Recorded bond premium amortization of $134,341, which was determined by using the straight-line method.
       31. Closed the interest expense account.

2008
June 30. Paid the semiannual interest on the bonds.
Dec. 31. Paid the semiannual interest on the bonds.
Dec. 31. Recorded bond premium amortization of $268,682, which was determined by using the straight-line method.
       31. Closed the interest expense account.

2009
July   1. Recorded the redemption of the bonds, which were called at 101.5. The balance in the bond premium account is $1,343,416 after the payment of interest and amortization of premium have been recorded. (Record the redemption only.)

Instructions

1. Journalize the entries to record the foregoing transactions.
2. Indicate the amount of the interest expense in (a) 2007 and (b) 2008.
3. Determine the carrying amount of the bonds as of December 31, 2008.

PR 15-5A

Entries for bond investments

obj. 5

The following selected transactions relate to certain securities acquired by Wildflower Blueprints Inc., whose fiscal year ends on December 31:

2007
Sept. 1. Purchased $600,000 of Wilson Company 20-year, 10% bonds dated July 1, 2007, directly from the issuing company, for $578,580 plus accrued interest of $10,000.

Dec. 31. Received the semiannual interest on the Wilson Company bonds.
    31. Recorded bond discount amortization of $360 on the Wilson Company bonds. The amortization amount was determined by using the straight-line method.

(Assume that all intervening transactions and adjustments have been properly recorded and that the number of bonds owned has not changed from December 31, 2007, to December 31, 2011.)

2012
June 30. Received the semiannual interest on the Wilson Company bonds.
Oct. 31. Sold one-half of the Wilson Company bonds at 97 plus accrued interest. The broker deducted $400 for commission, etc., remitting the balance. Prior to the sale, $450 of discount on one-half of the bonds was amortized, reducing the carrying amount of those bonds to $292,080.
Dec. 31. Received the semiannual interest on the Wilson Company bonds.
    31. Recorded bond discount amortization of $540 on the Wilson Company bonds.

Instructions
Journalize the entries to record the foregoing transactions.

APPENDIX PR 15-6A
Entries for bonds payable transactions; interest method of amortizing bond premium

✓2. $54,865

Atlantis Inc. produces and sells voltage regulators. On July 1, 2007, Atlantis Inc. issued $800,000 of 10-year, 14% bonds at an effective interest rate of 13%, receiving proceeds of $844,077. Interest on the bonds is payable semiannually on December 31 and June 30. The fiscal year of the company is the calendar year.

Instructions
1. Journalize the entries to record the following:
   a. The first semiannual interest payment on December 31, 2007, and the amortization of the bond premium, using the interest method. (Round to the nearest dollar.)
   b. The interest payment on June 30, 2008, and the amortization of the bond premium, using the interest method. (Round to the nearest dollar.)
2. Determine the total interest expense for 2007.

APPENDIX PR 15-7A
Entries for bonds payable transactions; interest method of amortizing bond discount

✓2. $706,984

On July 1, 2007, Iaket Equipment Inc. issued $12,500,000 of 10-year, 11% bonds at an effective interest rate of 12%, receiving proceeds of $11,783,070. Interest on the bonds is payable semiannually on December 31 and June 30. The fiscal year of the company is the calendar year.

Instructions
1. Journalize the entries to record the following:
   a. The first semiannual interest payment on December 31, 2007, and the amortization of the bond discount, using the interest method.
   b. The interest payment on June 30, 2008, and the amortization of the bond discount, using the interest method.
2. Determine the total interest expense for 2007.

Problems Series B

PR 15-1B
Effect of financing on earnings per share
obj. 1

✓1. Plan 3: $9.06

Three different plans for financing a $30,000,000 corporation are under consideration by its organizers. Under each of the following plans, the securities will be issued at their par or face amount, and the income tax rate is estimated at 40% of income.

	Plan 1	Plan 2	Plan 3
8% bonds	—	—	$15,000,000
Preferred 4% stock, $100 par	—	$15,000,000	7,500,000
Common stock, $4 par	$30,000,000	15,000,000	7,500,000
Total	$30,000,000	$30,000,000	$30,000,000

Instructions

1. Determine for each plan the earnings per share of common stock, assuming that the income before bond interest and income tax is $30,000,000.
2. Determine for each plan the earnings per share of common stock, assuming that the income before bond interest and income tax is $1,800,000.
3. ▭▭▶ Discuss the advantages and disadvantages of each plan.

PR 15-2B
Present value; bond premium; entries for bonds payable transactions

objs. 2, 3

✓ 3. $870,307

Bobblehead Corporation produces and sells basketball jerseys. On July 1, 2008, Bobblehead Corporation issued $16,000,000 of seven-year, 13% bonds at an effective interest rate of 10%. Interest on the bonds is payable semiannually on December 31 and June 30. The fiscal year of the company is the calendar year.

Instructions

1. Journalize the entry to record the amount of the cash proceeds from the sale of the bonds. Use the tables of present values in Appendix A to compute the cash proceeds, rounding to the nearest dollar.
2. Journalize the entries to record the following:
    a. The first semiannual interest payment on December 31, 2008, and the amortization of the bond premium, using the straight-line method. (Round to the nearest dollar.)
    b. The interest payment on June 30, 2009, and the amortization of the bond premium, using the straight-line method. (Round to the nearest dollar.)
3. Determine the total interest expense for 2008.
4. ▭▭▶ Will the bond proceeds always be greater than the face amount of the bonds when the contract rate is greater than the market rate of interest? Explain.

PR 15-3B
Present value; bond discount; entries for bonds payable transactions

objs. 2, 3

✓ 3. $1,251,378

On July 1, 2007, Austin Corporation, a wholesaler of electronic circuits, issued $22,000,000 of 20-year, 11% bonds at an effective interest rate of 12%. Interest on the bonds is payable semiannually on December 31 and June 30. The fiscal year of the company is the calendar year.

Instructions

1. Journalize the entry to record the amount of the cash proceeds from the sale of the bonds. Use the tables of present values in Appendix A to compute the cash proceeds, rounding to the nearest dollar.
2. Journalize the entries to record the following:
    a. The first semiannual interest payment on December 31, 2007, and the amortization of the bond discount, using the straight-line method. (Round to the nearest dollar.)
    b. The interest payment on June 30, 2008, and the amortization of the bond discount, using the straight-line method. (Round to the nearest dollar.)
3. Determine the total interest expense for 2007.
4. ▭▭▶ Will the bond proceeds always be less than the face amount of the bonds when the contract rate is less than the market rate of interest? Explain.

PR 15-4B
Entries for bonds payable transactions

objs. 3, 4

✓ 2. a. $577,386

The following transactions were completed by Michura Inc., whose fiscal year is the calendar year:

2007
July   1. Issued $12,000,000 of 10-year, 9% callable bonds dated July 1, 2007, at an effective rate of 11%, receiving cash of $11,252,273. Interest is payable semiannually on December 31 and June 30.
Dec. 31. Paid the semiannual interest on the bonds.
        31. Recorded bond discount amortization of $37,386, which was determined by using the straight-line method.
        31. Closed the interest expense account.

2008
June 30. Paid the semiannual interest on the bonds.
Dec. 31. Paid the semiannual interest on the bonds.
        31. Recorded bond discount amortization of $74,772, which was determined by using the straight-line method.
        31. Closed the interest expense account.

2009
June 30. Recorded the redemption of the bonds, which were called at 98. The balance in the bond discount account is $598,183 after payment of interest and amortization of discount have been recorded. (Record the redemption only.)

Instructions
1. Journalize the entries to record the foregoing transactions.
2. Indicate the amount of the interest expense in (a) 2007 and (b) 2008.
3. Determine the carrying amount of the bonds as of December 31, 2008.

PR 15-5B
Entries for bond investments

obj. 5

Valent Inc. leases motor vehicles. The following selected transactions relate to certain securities acquired as a long-term investment by Valent Inc., whose fiscal year ends on December 31:

2007
Sept. 1. Purchased $800,000 of Ivan Company 10-year, 9% bonds dated July 1, 2007, directly from the issuing company, for $853,100 plus accrued interest of $12,000.
Dec. 31. Received the semiannual interest on the Ivan Company bonds.
     31. Recorded bond premium amortization of $1,800 on the Ivan Company bonds. The amortization amount was determined by using the straight-line method.

(Assume that all intervening transactions and adjustments have been properly recorded and that the number of bonds owned has not changed from December 31, 2007, to December 31, 2012.)

2013
June 30. Received the semiannual interest on the Ivan Company bonds.
Aug. 31. Sold one-half of the Ivan Company bonds at 102 plus accrued interest. The broker deducted $500 for commission, etc., remitting the balance. Prior to the sale, $1,800 of premium on one-half of the bonds is to be amortized, reducing the carrying amount of those bonds to $405,600.
Dec. 31. Received the semiannual interest on the Ivan Company bonds.
     31. Recorded bond premium amortization of $2,700 on the Ivan Company bonds.

Instructions
Journalize the entries to record the foregoing transactions.

APPENDIX PR 15-6B
Entries for bonds payable transactions; interest method of amortizing bond premium

✓ 2. $918,785

Bobblehead Corporation produces and sells basketball jerseys. On July 1, 2008, Bobblehead Corporation issued $16,000,000 of seven-year, 13% bonds at an effective interest rate of 10%, receiving proceeds of $18,375,706. Interest on the bonds is payable semiannually on December 31 and June 30. The fiscal year of the company is the calendar year.

Instructions
1. Journalize the entries to record the following:
   a. The first semiannual interest payment on December 31, 2008, and the amortization of the bond premium, using the interest method. (Round to the nearest dollar.)
   b. The interest payment on June 30, 2009, and the amortization of the bond premium, using the interest method. (Round to the nearest dollar.)
2. Determine the total interest expense for 2008.

APPENDIX PR 15-7B
Entries for bonds payable transactions; interest method of amortizing bond discount

✓ 2. $1,220,692

On July 1, 2007, Austin Corporation, a wholesaler of electronic circuits, issued $22,000,000 of 20-year, 11% bonds at an effective interest rate of 12%, receiving proceeds of $20,344,863. Interest on the bonds is payable semiannually on December 31 and June 30. The fiscal year of the company is the calendar year.

Instructions
1. Journalize the entries to record the following:
   a. The first semiannual interest payment on December 31, 2007, and the amortization of the bond discount, using the interest method. (Round to the nearest dollar.)
   b. The interest payment on June 30, 2008, and the amortization of the bond discount, using the interest method. (Round to the nearest dollar.)
2. Determine the total interest expense for 2007.

Comprehensive Problem 4

✓ 2.a. Net income,
$229,000

Selected transactions completed by Delhome Products Inc. during the fiscal year ending July 31, 2008, were as follows:

a. Issued 12,500 shares of $30 par common stock at $65, receiving cash.

b. Issued 10,000 shares of $125 par preferred 8% stock at $160, receiving cash.

c. Issued $15,000,000 of 10-year, 12% bonds at an effective interest rate of 10%, with interest payable semiannually. Use the present value tables in Appendix A to determine the bond proceeds. (Round to the nearest dollar.)

d. Declared a dividend of $0.25 per share on common stock and $2.50 per share on preferred stock. On the date of record, 125,000 shares of common stock were outstanding, no treasury shares were held, and 18,750 shares of preferred stock were outstanding.

e. Paid the cash dividends declared in (d).

f. Redeemed $500,000 of 8-year, 15% bonds at 101. The balance in the bond premium account is $6,150 after the payment of interest and amortization of premium have been recorded. (Record only the redemption of the bonds payable.)

g. Purchased 6,250 shares of treasury common stock at $62.50 per share.

h. Declared a 2% stock dividend on common stock and a $2.50 cash dividend per share on preferred stock. On the date of declaration, the market value of the common stock was $63.75 per share. On the date of record, 125,000 shares of common stock had been issued, 6,250 shares of treasury common stock were held, and 18,750 shares of preferred stock had been issued. (Round to the nearest dollar.)

i. Issued the stock certificates for the stock dividends declared in (h) and paid the cash dividends to the preferred stockholders.

j. Purchased $150,000 of Lewis Sports Inc. 10-year, 15% bonds, directly from the issuing company, for $145,500 plus accrued interest of $5,625.

k. Sold, at $72.50 per share, 3,750 shares of treasury common stock purchased in (g).

l. Recorded the payment of semiannual interest on the bonds issued in (c) and the amortization of the premium for six months. The amortization was determined using the straight-line method. (Round the amortization to the nearest dollar.)

m. Accrued interest for four months on the Lewis Sports Inc. bonds purchased in (j). Also recorded amortization of $120.

Instructions

1. Journalize the selected transactions.

2. After all of the transactions for the year ended July 31, 2008, had been posted (including the transactions recorded in (1) and all adjusting entries), the data below and on the following page were taken from the records of Delhome Products Inc.

   a. Prepare a multiple-step income statement for the year ended July 31, 2008, concluding with earnings per share. In computing earnings per share, assume that the average number of common shares outstanding was 125,000 and preferred dividends were $131,250. (Round earnings per share to the nearest cent.)

   b. Prepare a retained earnings statement for the year ended July 31, 2008.

   c. Prepare a balance sheet in report form as of July 31, 2008.

Income statement data:	
Advertising expense	$ 150,000
Cost of merchandise sold	3,498,750
Delivery expense	27,000
Depreciation expense—office buildings and equipment	25,000
Depreciation expense—store buildings and equipment	90,000
Gain on redemption of bonds	1,150
Income tax:	
Applicable to continuing operations	247,509
Applicable to loss from discontinued operations	100,000
Applicable to gain from redemption of bonds	150
Interest expense	778,266
Interest revenue	2,025
Loss from disposal of discontinued operations	250,000

Loss from fixed asset impairment	$ 187,500
Miscellaneous administrative expenses	7,500
Miscellaneous selling expenses	13,750
Office rent expense	50,000
Office salaries expense	170,000
Office supplies expense	10,000
Restructuring charges	93,750
Sales	6,300,000
Sales commissions	195,000
Sales salaries expense	360,000
Store supplies expense	20,000
Retained earnings and balance sheet data:	
Accounts payable	212,000
Accounts receivable	562,500
Accumulated depreciation—office buildings and equipment	1,670,650
Accumulated depreciation—store buildings and equipment	4,428,750
Allowance for doubtful accounts	43,750
Bonds payable, 11%, due 2018	14,500,000
Cash	250,000
Common stock, $30 par (400,000 shares authorized;	
124,875 shares outstanding)	3,746,250
Deferred income tax payable (current portion, $17,500)	51,375
Dividends:	
Cash dividends for common stock	122,815
Cash dividends for preferred stock	187,500
Stock dividends for common stock	151,406
Dividends payable	37,500
Employee termination obligation (current)	81,250
Goodwill	540,000
Income tax payable	40,000
Interest receivable	7,500
Investment in Lewis Sports Inc. bonds (long-term)	145,620
Merchandise Inventory (July 31, 2008), at lower of	
cost (fifo) or market	850,000
Notes receivable	156,250
Office buildings and equipment	7,412,500
Paid-in capital from sale of treasury stock	37,500
Paid-in capital in excess of par—common stock	700,000
Paid-in capital in excess of par—preferred stock	300,000
Preferred 8% stock, $125 par (30,000 shares authorized;	
18,750 shares issued)	2,343,750
Premium on bonds payable	1,769,722
Prepaid expenses	31,250
Retained earnings, August 1, 2007	2,302,970
Store buildings and equipment	21,920,876
Treasury stock (2,500 shares of common stock at cost	
of $62.50 per share)	156,250

Special Activities

SA 15-1
General Electric bond issuance

ETHICS   REAL WORLD

General Electric Capital, a division of General Electric, uses long-term debt extensively. In early 2002, GE Capital issued $11 billion in long-term debt to investors, then within days filed legal documents to prepare for another $50 billion long-term debt issue. As a result of the $50 billion filing, the price of the initial $11 billion offering declined (due to higher risk of more debt).

Bill Gross, a manager of a bond investment fund, "denounced a 'lack in candor' related to GE's recent debt deal. 'It was the most recent and most egregious example of how bondholders are mistreated.' Gross argued that GE was not forthright when GE Capital recently issued $11 billion

in bonds, one of the largest issues ever from a U.S. corporation. What bothered Gross is that three days after the issue the company announced its intention to sell as much as $50 billion in additional debt, warrants, preferred stock, guarantees, letters of credit and promissory notes at some future date."

> In your opinion, did GE Capital act unethically by selling $11 billion of long-term debt without telling those investors that a few days later it would be filing documents to prepare for another $50 billion debt offering?

Source: Jennifer Ablan, "Gross Shakes the Bond Market; GE Calms It, a Bit," *Barron's*, March 25, 2002.

SA 15-2
Ethics and professional conduct in business

ETHICS

Jenkins Pharmaceuticals develops and produces prescription medications primarily for use in hospitals. The company has an outstanding $100,000,000, 30-year, 12% bond issued dated July 1, 2001. The bond issue is due June 30, 2031. The bond indenture requires a bond sinking fund, which has a balance of $12,000,000 as of July 1, 2007. The company is currently experiencing a shortage of funds due to a recent acquisition. Bob Snapple, the company's treasurer, is considering using the funds from the bond sinking fund to cover payroll and other bills that are coming due at the end of the month. Bob's brother-in-law is a trustee in a sinking fund, who has indicated willingness to allow Bob to use the funds from the sinking fund to temporarily meet the company's cash needs.

> Discuss whether Bob's proposal is appropriate.

SA 15-3
Present values

Kristen Nash recently won the jackpot in the New Jersey lottery while she was visiting her parents. When she arrived at the lottery office to collect her winnings, she was offered the following three payout options:

a. Receive $5,000,000 in cash today.
b. Receive $2,000,000 today and $600,000 per year for 10 years, with the first $600,000 payment being received one year from today.
c. Receive $1,000,000 per year for 10 years, with the first payment being received one year from today.

> Assuming that the effective rate of interest is 9%, which payout option should Kristen select? Explain your answer and provide any necessary supporting calculations.

SA 15-4
Preferred stock vs. bonds

Beacon Inc. has decided to expand its operations to owning and operating long-term health care facilities. The following is an excerpt from a conversation between the chief executive officer, Terry Clark, and the vice president of finance, Frank Mills.

Terry: Frank, have you given any thought to how we're going to finance the acquisition of St. Seniors Health Care?
Frank: Well, the two basic options, as I see it, are to issue either preferred stock or bonds. The equity market is a little depressed right now. The rumor is that the Federal Reserve Bank's going to increase the interest rates either this month or next.
Terry: Yes, I've heard the rumor. The problem is that we can't wait around to see what's going to happen. We'll have to move on this next week if we want any chance to complete the acquisition of St. Seniors.
Frank: Well, the bond market is strong right now. Maybe we should issue debt this time around.
Terry: That's what I would have guessed as well. St. Seniors's financial statements look pretty good, except for the volatility of its income and cash flows. But that's characteristic of the industry.

> Discuss the advantages and disadvantages of issuing preferred stock versus bonds.

SA 15-5
Investing in bonds

REAL WORLD

During fiscal year 2004, Georgia-Pacific called the following bond issuances:

$243 million	9.875% bonds	due November 1, 2021
$250 million	9.625% bonds	due March 15, 2022
$250 million	9.500% bonds	due May 15, 2022

Group Project

$240 million   9.125% bonds   due July 1, 2022
$250 million   8.250% bonds   due March 1, 2023
$250 million   8.125% bonds   due June 15, 2023

In groups of three or four:

1. Identify the face value, coupon rate, and maturity of each bond issue.
2. Discuss some of the potential reasons that Georgia-Pacific may have had for deciding to call these bond issues early.

SA 15-6
Investing in bonds

Group Project

Select a bond from listings that appear daily in *The Wall Street Journal*, and summarize the information related to the bond you select. Include the following information in your summary:

1. Contract rate of interest
2. Year when the bond matures
3. Current yield (effective rate of interest)
4. Closing price of bond (indicate date)
5. Other information noted about the bond, such as whether it is a zero-coupon bond (see the Explanatory Notes to the listings)

In groups of three or four, share the information you developed about the bond you selected. As a group, select one bond to invest $100,000 in and prepare a justification for your choice for presentation to the class. For example, your justification should include a consideration of risk and return.

SA 15-7
Financing business expansion

You hold a 25% common stock interest in the family-owned business, a vending machine company. Your sister, who is the manager, has proposed an expansion of plant facilities at an expected cost of $5,000,000. Two alternative plans have been suggested as methods of financing the expansion. Each plan is briefly described as follows:

Plan 1. Issue $5,000,000 of 20-year, 7% notes at face amount.
Plan 2. Issue an additional 87,500 shares of $5 par common stock at $20 per share, and $3,250,000 of 20-year, 7% notes at face amount.

The balance sheet as of the end of the previous fiscal year is as follows:

Vendco, Inc.
Balance Sheet
December 31, 2008

Assets	
Current assets	$2,350,000
Property, plant, and equipment	5,150,000
Total assets	$7,500,000

Liabilities and Stockholders' Equity	
Liabilities	$2,000,000
Common stock, $5	800,000
Paid-in capital in excess of par	80,000
Retained earnings	4,620,000
Total liabilities and stockholders' equity	$7,500,000

Net income has remained relatively constant over the past several years. The expansion program is expected to increase yearly income before bond interest and income tax from $500,000 in the previous year to $700,000 for this year. Your sister has asked you, as the company treasurer, to prepare an analysis of each financing plan.

1. Prepare a table indicating the expected earnings per share on the common stock under each plan. Assume an income tax rate of 40%. Round to the nearest cent.
2. a. ▭▭▭▶ Discuss the factors that should be considered in evaluating the two plans.
   b. ▭▭▭▶ Which plan offers the greater benefit to the present stockholders? Give reasons for your opinion.

SA 15-8
Bond ratings

Internet Project

Moody's Investors Service maintains a Web site at **http://www.Moodys.com**. One of the services offered at this site is a listing of announcements of recent bond rating changes. Visit this site and read over some of these announcements. Write down several of the reasons provided for rating downgrades and upgrades. If you were a bond investor or bond issuer, would you care if Moody's changed the rating on your bonds? Why or why not?

SA 15-9
Bonds payable in the financial statements

FAI

Refer to the financial statements of Williams-Sonoma, Inc., given in Appendix D at the end of this book.

1. How much interest expense did Williams-Sonoma record in 2003, 2004, and 2005?
2. What is the number of times interest charges are earned for Williams-Sonoma in 2003, 2004, and 2005? Evaluate this ratio for Williams-Sonoma. (Round your answer to one decimal place.)

Answers to Self-Examination Questions

1. **B**   Since the contract rate on the bonds is higher than the prevailing market rate, a rational investor would be willing to pay more than the face amount, or a premium (answer B), for the bonds. If the contract rate and the market rate were equal, the bonds could be expected to sell at their face amount (answer A). Likewise, if the market rate is higher than the contract rate, the bonds would sell at a price below their face amount (answer D) or at a discount (answer C).

2. **A**   The bond carrying amount is the face amount plus unamortized premium or less unamortized discount. For this question, the carrying amount is $900,000 less $72,000, or $828,000 (answer A).

3. **B**   Although the sinking fund may consist of cash as well as securities, the fund is listed on the balance sheet as an investment (answer B) because it is to be used to pay the long-term liability at maturity.

4. **B**   The amount debited to the investment account is the cost of the bonds, which includes the amount paid to the seller for the bonds (101% × $150,000) plus broker's commissions ($50), or $151,550 (answer B). The $2,000 of accrued interest that is paid to the seller should be debited to Interest Revenue, since it is an offset against the amount that will be received as interest at the next interest date.

5. **C**   The balance of Discount on Bonds Payable is usually reported as a deduction from Bonds Payable in the Long-Term Liabilities section (answer C) of the balance sheet. Likewise, a balance in a premium on bonds payable account would usually be reported as an addition to Bonds Payable in the Long-Term Liabilities section of the balance sheet.

Statement of Cash Flows

© ELAINE THOMPSON/ASSOCIATED PRESS

objectives

After studying this chapter, you should be able to:

1 *Summarize the types of cash flow activities reported in the statement of cash flows.*

2 *Prepare a statement of cash flows, using the indirect method.*

3 *Prepare a statement of cash flows, using the direct method.*

Jones Soda Co.

uppose you were to receive $100 as a result of some event. Would it make a difference what the event was? Yes, it would! If you received $100 for your birthday, then it's a gift. If you received $100 as a result of working part time for a week, then it's the result of your effort. If you received $100 as a loan, then it's money that you will have to pay back in the future. If you received $100 as a result of selling your CD player, then it's the result of giving up something tangible. Thus, the same $100 received can be associated with different types of events, and these events have different meanings to you. You would much rather receive a $100 gift than take out a $100 loan. Likewise, company stakeholders would also view events such as these differently.

Companies are required to report information about the events causing a change in cash over a period time. This information is reported in the statement of cash flows. One such company is Jones Soda Co. Jones began in the late 1980s as an alternative beverage company, known for its customer provided labels, unique flavors, and support for extreme sports. You have probably seen Jones Soda at Barnes & Noble, Panera Bread, or Starbucks, or maybe sampled some of its unique flavors, such as Fufu Berry®, Blue Bubblegum®, or Lemon Drop®. As with any company, cash is important to Jones Soda. Without cash, Jones would be unable to expand its brands, distribute its product, support extreme sports, or provide a return for its owners. Thus, its managers are concerned about the sources and uses of cash.

In previous chapters, we have used the income statement, balance sheet, retained earnings statement, and other information to analyze the effects of management decisions on a business's financial position and operating performance. In this chapter, we focus on the events causing a change in cash by presenting the preparation and use of the statement of cash flows.

Reporting Cash Flows

objective **1**

Summarize the types of cash flow activities reported in the statement of cash flows.

In Chapter 1, we introduced the statement of cash flows as one of the basic financial statements of a business. The **statement of cash flows** reports a firm's major cash inflows and outflows for a period.[1] It provides useful information about a firm's ability to generate cash from operations, maintain and expand its operating capacity, meet its financial obligations, and pay dividends. As a result, it is used by managers in evaluating past operations and in planning future investing and financing activities. It is also used by investors, creditors, and others in assessing a firm's profit potential. In addition, it is a basis for assessing the firm's ability to pay its maturing debt.

The statement of cash flows reports cash flows by three types of activities:

1. **Cash flows from operating activities** are cash flows from transactions that affect net income. Examples of such transactions include the purchase and sale of merchandise by a retailer.
2. **Cash flows from investing activities** are cash flows from transactions that affect the investments in noncurrent assets. Examples of such transactions include the sale and purchase of fixed assets, such as equipment and buildings.
3. **Cash flows from financing activities** are cash flows from transactions that affect the debt and equity of the business. Examples of such transactions include issuing or retiring equity and debt securities.

---

1 As used in this chapter, *cash* refers to cash and cash equivalents. Examples of cash equivalents include short-term, highly liquid investments, such as money market funds, certificates of deposit, and commercial paper.

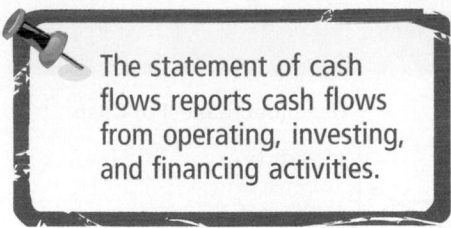

The statement of cash flows reports cash flows from operating, investing, and financing activities.

netsolutions

The cash flows from operating activities are normally presented first, followed by the cash flows from investing activities and financing activities. The total of the net cash flow from these activities is the net increase or decrease in cash for the period. The cash balance at the beginning of the period is added to the net increase or decrease in cash, resulting in the cash balance at the end of the period. The ending cash balance on the statement of cash flows equals the cash reported on the balance sheet. Exhibit 1 illustrates a simple statement of cash flows that is reproduced from Chapter 1 (Exhibit 6) for NetSolutions.

▶ EXHIBIT 1

Statement of Cash Flows—NetSolutions

NetSolutions Statement of Cash Flows For the Month Ended November 30, 2007		
Cash flows from operating activities:		
Cash received from customers	$ 7,500	
Deduct cash payments for expenses and		
payments to creditors	4,600	
Net cash flow from operating activities		$ 2,900
Cash flows from investing activities:		
Cash payments for purchase of land		(20,000)
Cash flows from financing activities:		
Cash received as owner's investment	$25,000	
Deduct cash withdrawal by owner	2,000	
Net cash flow provided by financing activities		23,000
Net cash flow and November 30, 2007, cash balance		$ 5,900

We have not discussed the statement of cash flows since introducing the statement in Chapter 1. We did this because a more complete understanding of operating, investing, and financing activities is helpful prior to developing and interpreting this statement. Previous chapters have introduced and described these activities so that you now have a foundation for the discussion that follows.

Exhibit 2 shows the major sources and uses of cash according to the three cash flow activities reported in the statement of cash flows. A *source* of cash causes the cash flow to increase, also called a *cash inflow*. For example, in Exhibit 1, the $25,000 cash received as owner's investment from Chris Clark is a financing activity that is a source of cash. A *use* of cash causes cash flow to decrease, also called a *cash outflow*. In Exhibit 1, NetSolutions' $20,000 cash payment for purchase of land is a use of cash. By reporting cash flows by operating, investing, and financing activities, significant relationships within and among the activities can be evaluated. For example, the cash receipts from issuing bonds can be related to repayments of borrowings when both are reported as financing activities. Also, the impact of each of the three activities (operating, investing, and financing) on cash flows can be identified. This allows investors and creditors to evaluate the effects of a firm's profits on cash flows and its ability to generate cash flows for dividends and for paying debts.

CASH FLOWS FROM OPERATING ACTIVITIES

The most important cash flows of a business often relate to operating activities. There are two alternative methods for reporting cash flows from operating activities in the statement of cash flows. These methods are (1) the direct method and (2) the indirect method.

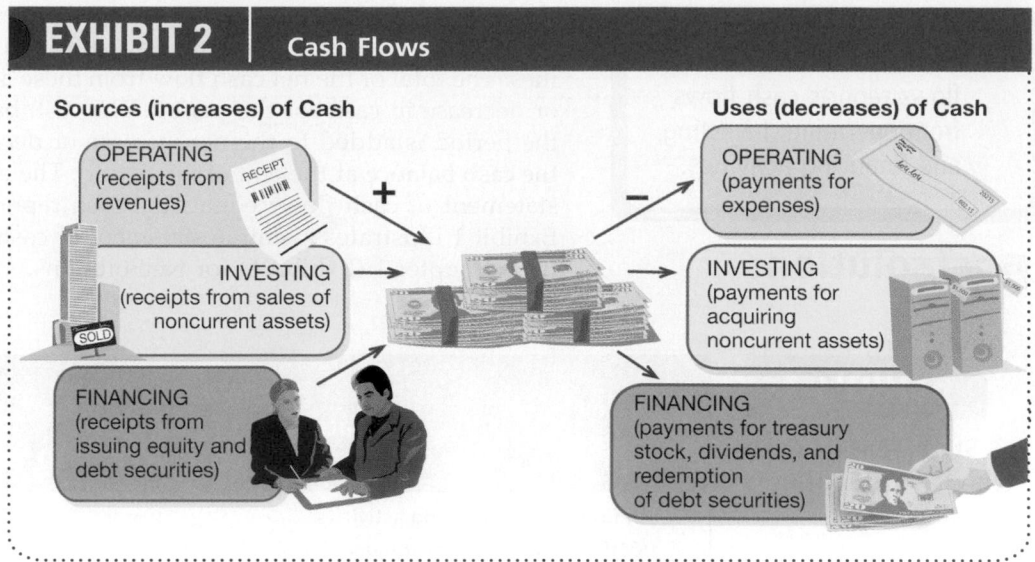

EXHIBIT 2 | Cash Flows

Sources (increases) of Cash   Uses (decreases) of Cash

OPERATING
(receipts from
revenues)   OPERATING
                                                     (payments for
                                        +   expenses)   −

INVESTING
(receipts from sales of
noncurrent assets)   INVESTING
                                                     (payments for
                                                     acquiring
                                                     noncurrent assets)

FINANCING
(receipts from
issuing equity and
debt securities)   FINANCING
                                                     (payments for treasury
                                                     stock, dividends, and
                                                     redemption
                                                     of debt securities)

Cash Flows from Operating Activities

Direct Method = Indirect Method

The **direct method** reports the sources of operating cash and the uses of operating cash. The major source of operating cash is cash received from customers. The major uses of operating cash include cash paid to suppliers for merchandise and services and cash paid to employees for wages. The difference between these operating cash receipts and cash payments is the net cash flow from operating activities. The direct method is illustrated in Exhibit 1 for NetSolutions.

The primary advantage of the direct method is that it reports the sources and uses of operating cash flows in the statement of cash flows. Its primary disadvantage is that the necessary data may not be readily available and may be costly to gather.

The **indirect method** reports the operating cash flows by beginning with net income and adjusting it for revenues and expenses that do not involve the receipt or payment of cash. In other words, accrual net income is adjusted to determine the net amount of cash flows from operating activities.

A major advantage of the indirect method is that it focuses on the differences between net income and cash flows from operations. Thus, it shows the relationship between the income statement, the balance sheet, and the statement of cash flows. Because the data are readily available, the indirect method is normally less costly to use than the direct method. Because of these advantages, over 99% of all firms use the indirect method to report cash flows from operations.[2] We have not discussed the indirect method until this point, because it assumes an understanding of the accrual accounting concepts discussed in the prior chapters.

Exhibit 3 illustrates the cash flows from operating activities section of the statement of cash flows under the direct and indirect methods. Both statements are for NetSolutions for the month ended November 2007. The methods show the same amount of net cash flow from operating activities, regardless of the method. We will illustrate both methods in detail later in this chapter.

REAL WORLD

The Walt Disney Company recently invested $1.4 billion in parks, resorts, and other properties, including the development of Hong Kong Disneyland.

CASH FLOWS FROM INVESTING ACTIVITIES

Cash inflows from investing activities normally arise from selling fixed assets, investments, and intangible assets. Cash outflows normally include payments to acquire fixed assets, investments, and intangible assets.

---

2 *Accounting Trends & Techniques*, AICPA, 2005 edition.

EXHIBIT 3	**Cash Flow from Operations: Direct and Indirect Methods—NetSolutions**

Direct Method (from Exhibit 1)		**Indirect Method**	
Cash flows from operating activities:		Cash flows from operating activities:	
Cash received from customers	$7,500	Net income	$3,050
Deduct cash payments for expenses		Add increase in accounts payable	400
and payments to creditors	4,600		$3,450
		Deduct increase in supplies	550
Net cash flow from operating activities	$2,900	Net cash flow from operating activities	$2,900

the same

Cash flows from investing activities are reported on the statement of cash flows by first listing the cash inflows. The cash outflows are then presented. If the inflows are greater than the outflows, *net cash flow provided by investing activities* is reported. If the inflows are less than the outflows, *net cash flow used for investing activities* is reported.

The cash flows from investing activities section in the statement of cash flows for NetSolutions from Exhibit 1 is shown below.

Cash flows from investing activities:
Cash payments for purchase of land . . . . $(20,000)

CASH FLOWS FROM FINANCING ACTIVITIES

Cash inflows from financing activities normally arise from issuing debt or equity securities. Examples of such inflows include issuing bonds, notes payable, and preferred and common stocks. Cash outflows from financing activities include paying cash dividends, repaying debt, and acquiring treasury stock.

Cash flows from financing activities are reported on the statement of cash flows by first listing the cash inflows. The cash outflows are then presented. If the inflows are greater than the outflows, *net cash flow provided by financing activities* is reported. If the inflows are less than the outflows, *net cash flow used for financing activities* is reported.

The cash flows from financing activities section in the statement of cash flows for NetSolutions from Exhibit 1 is shown below.

Cash flows from financing activities:
Cash received as owner's investment $25,000
Deduct cash withdrawal by owner   2,000
Net cash flow provided by financing activities $23,000

NONCASH INVESTING AND FINANCING ACTIVITIES

A business may enter into investing and financing activities that do not directly involve cash. For example, it may issue common stock to retire long-term debt. Such a transaction does not have a direct effect on cash. However, the transaction does eliminate the need for future cash payments to pay interest and retire the bonds. Thus, because of their future effect on cash flows, such transactions should be reported to readers of the financial statements.

When noncash investing and financing transactions occur during a period, their effect is reported in a separate schedule. This schedule usually appears at the bottom of the statement of cash flows. For example, in such a schedule, Google recently disclosed the issuance of over $25 million in common stock for business acquisitions. Other examples of noncash investing and financing transactions include acquiring fixed assets by issuing bonds or capital stock and issuing common stock in exchange for convertible preferred stock.

Business Connections

REAL WORLD

TOO MUCH CASH!

Is it possible to have too much cash? Clearly, most of us would answer no. However, a business views cash differently than an individual. Naturally, a business needs cash to develop and launch new products, expand markets, purchase plant and equipment, and acquire other businesses. However, some businesses have built up huge cash balances beyond even these needs. For example, both Microsoft Corporation and Dell Inc. have accumulated billions of dollars in cash and temporary investments, totaling in excess of 60% of their total assets. Such large cash balances can lower the return on total assets. As stated by one analyst, "When a company sits on cash (which earns 1% or 2%) and leaves equity outstanding . . . , it is tantamount to taking a loan at 15% and investing in a passbook savings account that earns 2%—it destroys value." So while having too much cash is a good problem to have, companies like Microsoft, Cisco Systems, Inc., IBM, Apple Computer Inc., and Dell are under pressure to pay dividends or repurchase common stock. For example, Microsoft recently declared a $32 billion special dividend to return cash to its shareholders.

NO CASH FLOW PER SHARE

The term *cash flow per share* is sometimes reported in the financial press. Often, the term is used to mean "cash flow from operations per share." Such reporting may be misleading to users of the financial statements. For example, users might interpret cash flow per share as the amount available for dividends. This would not be the case if most of the cash generated by operations is required for repaying loans or for reinvesting in the business. Users might also think that cash flow per share is equivalent or perhaps superior to earnings per share. For these reasons, the financial statements, including the statement of cash flows, should not report cash flow per share.

Example Exercise 16-1
objective 1

Identify whether each of the following would be reported as an operating, investing, or financing activity in the statement of cash flows.

a. Purchase of patent
b. Payment of cash dividend
c. Disposal of equipment

d. Cash sales
e. Purchase of treasury stock
f. Payment of wages expense

Follow My Example 16-1

a. Investing
b. Financing
c. Investing

d. Operating
e. Financing
f. Operating

For Practice: PE 16-1A, PE 16-1B

Statement of Cash Flows—The Indirect Method

objective 2

Prepare a statement of cash flows, using the indirect method.

The indirect method of reporting cash flows from operating activities is normally less costly and more efficient than the direct method. In addition, when the direct method is used, the indirect method must also be used in preparing a supplemental reconciliation of net income with cash flows from operations. The 2005 edition of *Accounting Trends & Techniques* reported that 99% of the companies surveyed used the indirect method. For these reasons, we will first discuss the indirect method of preparing the statement of cash flows.

To collect the data for the statement of cash flows, all the cash receipts and cash payments for a period could be analyzed. However, this procedure is expensive and time consuming. A more efficient approach is to analyze the changes in the noncash balance sheet accounts. The logic of this approach is that a change in any balance sheet account (including cash) can be analyzed in terms of changes in the other balance sheet accounts. To illustrate, the accounting equation is rewritten below to focus on the cash account.

Assets = Liabilities + Stockholders' Equity
Cash + Noncash Assets = Liabilities + Stockholders' Equity
Cash = Liabilities + Stockholders' Equity − Noncash Assets

Any change in the cash account results in a change in one or more noncash balance sheet accounts. That is, if the cash account changes, then a liability, stockholders' equity, or noncash asset account must also change.

Additional data are also obtained by analyzing the income statement accounts and supporting records. For example, since the net income or net loss for the period is closed to *Retained Earnings*, a change in the retained earnings account can be partially explained by the net income or net loss reported on the income statement.

There is no order in which the noncash balance sheet accounts must be analyzed. However, it is usually more efficient to analyze the accounts in the reverse order in which they appear on the balance sheet. Thus, the analysis of retained earnings provides the starting point for determining the cash flows from operating activities, which is the first section of the statement of cash flows.

The comparative balance sheet for Rundell Inc. on December 31, 2008 and 2007, is used to illustrate the indirect method. This balance sheet is shown in Exhibit 4. Selected ledger accounts and other data are presented as needed.[3]

RETAINED EARNINGS

The comparative balance sheet for Rundell Inc. shows that retained earnings increased $80,000 during the year. Analyzing the entries posted to the retained earnings account indicates how this change occurred. The retained earnings account for Rundell Inc. is shown below.

ACCOUNT Retained Earnings					**ACCOUNT NO.**		
						Balance	
Date		**Item**	**Debit**	**Credit**	**Debit**	**Credit**	
2008 Jan.	1	Balance				202 3 0 0 00	
Dec.	31	Net income		108 0 0 0 00		310 3 0 0 00	
	31	Cash dividends	28 0 0 0 00			282 3 0 0 00	

The retained earnings account must be carefully analyzed because some of the entries to retained earnings may not affect cash. For example, a decrease in retained earnings resulting from issuing a stock dividend does not affect cash. Such transactions are not reported on the statement of cash flows.

For Rundell Inc., the retained earnings account indicates that the $80,000 change resulted from net income of $108,000 and cash dividends declared of $28,000. The effect of each of these items on cash flows is discussed in the following sections.

CASH FLOWS FROM OPERATING ACTIVITIES—INDIRECT METHOD

The net income of $108,000 reported by Rundell Inc. normally is not equal to the amount of cash generated from operations during the period. This is because net income is determined using the accrual method of accounting.

---

3 An appendix that discusses using a spreadsheet (work sheet) as an aid in assembling data for the statement of cash flows is presented at the end of this chapter. This appendix illustrates the use of this spreadsheet in reporting cash flows from operating activities using the indirect method.

EXHIBIT 4

Comparative
Balance Sheet

Rundell Inc.
Comparative Balance Sheet
December 31, 2008 and 2007

Assets	2008	2007	Increase Decrease*
Cash.	$ 97,500	$ 26,000	$ 71,500
Accounts receivable (net).	74,000	65,000	9,000
Inventories.	172,000	180,000	8,000*
Land.	80,000	125,000	45,000*
Building.	260,000	200,000	60,000
Accumulated depreciation—building.	(65,300)	(58,300)	7,000
Total assets.	$618,200	$537,700	$ 80,500
Liabilities			
Accounts payable (merchandise			
creditors).	$ 43,500	$ 46,700	$ 3,200*
Accrued expenses payable			
(operating expenses).	26,500	24,300	2,200
Income taxes payable.	7,900	8,400	500*
Dividends payable.	14,000	10,000	4,000
Bonds payable.	100,000	150,000	50,000*
Total liabilities.	$191,900	$239,400	$ 47,500*
Stockholders' Equity			
Common stock ($2 par).	$ 24,000	$ 16,000	$ 8,000
Paid-in capital in excess of par.	120,000	80,000	40,000
Retained earnings.	282,300	202,300	80,000
Total stockholders' equity.	$426,300	$298,300	$128,000
Total liabilities and stockholders' equity. . . .	$618,200	$537,700	$ 80,500

Under the accrual method of accounting, revenues and expenses are recorded at different times from when cash is received or paid. For example, merchandise may be sold on account and the cash received at a later date. Likewise, insurance expense represents the amount of insurance expired during the period. The premiums for the insurance may have been paid in a prior period.

Under the indirect method, these differences are used to reconcile the net income to cash flows from operating activities. The typical adjustments to net income under the indirect method are reported in the statement of cash flows, as shown in Exhibit 5.[4]

In practice, the list of adjustments often begins with expenses that do not affect cash. Common examples are depreciation of fixed assets and amortization of intangible assets. Thus, in Exhibit 5, these two items are *added* to net income in determining cash flows from operating activities.

Typically, the next adjustments to net income are for gains and losses from disposal of assets. These adjustments arise because cash flows from operating activities should not include investing or financing transactions. For example, assume that land costing $50,000 was sold for $90,000 (a gain of $40,000). The sale should be reported as an investing activity: "Cash receipts from the sale of land, $90,000." However, the $40,000 gain on the disposal of the land is included in net income on the income statement. Thus, the $40,000 gain is *deducted* from net income in determining cash flows from operations to

---

4 Other items that also require adjustments to net income to obtain cash flows from operating activities include amortization of bonds payable discounts (add), losses on debt retirement (add), amortization of bonds payable premium (deduct), and gains on retirement of debt (deduct).

EXHIBIT 5

Adjustments to Net Income (Loss) Using the Indirect Method

	Increase (Decrease)
Net income (loss)	$ XXX
Adjustments to reconcile net income to net cash flow from operating activities:	
Depreciation of fixed assets	XXX
Amortization of intangible assets	XXX
Losses on disposal of assets	XXX
Gains on disposal of assets	(XXX)
Changes in current operating assets and liabilities:	
Increases in noncash current operating assets	(XXX)
Decreases in noncash current operating assets	XXX
Increases in current operating liabilities	XXX
Decreases in current operating liabilities	(XXX)
Net cash flow from operating activities	$ XXX
	or
	$(XXX)

Subtract	Add
Increases in accounts receivable	Decreases in accounts receivable
Increases in inventory	Decreases in inventory
Increases in prepaid expenses	Decreases in prepaid expenses
Decreases in accounts payable	Increases in accounts payable
Decreases in accrued expenses payable	Increases in accrued expenses payable

avoid "double counting" the cash flow from the gain. Likewise, losses from the disposal of fixed assets are *added* to net income in determining cash flows from operations.

Net income is also adjusted for changes in noncash current assets and current liabilities that support operations. Under the indirect method, these items are often listed last as "changes in current operating assets and liabilities." Under this heading, current assets are listed first, followed by current liabilities. Changes in noncash current assets and current liabilities are the result of revenue or expense transactions that may or may not affect cash flow. For example, a sale of $10,000 on account increases accounts receivable by $10,000. However, cash is not affected. Thus, the increase in accounts receivable of $10,000 between two balance sheet dates is *deducted* from net income in arriving at cash flows from operating activities. In contrast, a decrease in accounts receivable indicates the collection of cash that may have been reported as revenues in a prior period. Thus, a decrease in accounts receivable is added to net income in arriving at cash flows from operating activities.

Similar adjustments to net income are required for the changes in the other current asset and liability accounts supporting operations, such as inventory, prepaid expenses, accounts payable, and other accrued expenses. The direction of the adjustment is shown at the bottom of Exhibit 5. For example, an increase in accounts payable from the beginning to the end of the period would be added to net income in determining cash flows from operating activities.

The effect of dividends payable, though a current liability, is not included in the operating activity section of the statement of cash flows. Dividends payable is omitted from Exhibit 5 because dividends are not an operating activity that affects net income. Later in the chapter, we will discuss how dividends are reported in the statement of cash flows as a part of financing activities. In the following paragraphs, we will discuss each of the adjustments that convert Rundell Inc.'s net income to "Cash flows from operating activities."

Depreciation The comparative balance sheet in Exhibit 4 indicates that Accumulated Depreciation—Building increased by $7,000. As shown at the top of the following page, this account indicates that depreciation for the year was $7,000 for the building.

ACCOUNT *Accumulated Depreciation—Building*					ACCOUNT NO.	
					Balance	
Date	**Item**	**Debit**	**Credit**	**Debit**	**Credit**	
2008 Jan. 1	Balance				58 3 0 0 00	
Dec. 31	Depreciation for year		7 0 0 0 00		65 3 0 0 00	

The $7,000 of depreciation expense reduced net income but did not require an outflow of cash. Thus, the $7,000 is added to net income in determining cash flows from operating activities, as follows:

Cash flows from operating activities:
Net income $108,000
Add depreciation   7,000 $115,000

Gain on Sale of Land   The ledger or income statement of Rundell Inc. indicates that the sale of land resulted in a gain of $12,000. As we discussed previously, the sale proceeds, which include the gain and the carrying value of the land, are included in cash flows from investing activities.[5] The gain is also included in net income. Thus, to avoid double reporting, the gain of $12,000 is deducted from net income in determining cash flows from operating activities, as shown below.

Cash flows from operating activities:
Net income $108,000
Deduct gain on sale of land   12,000

Example Exercise 16-2   objective 2

Omni Corporation's accumulated depreciation increased by $12,000, while patents decreased by $3,400 between balance sheet dates. There were no purchases or sales of depreciable or intangible assets during the year. In addition, the income statement showed a gain of $4,100 from the sale of land. Reconcile a net income of $50,000 to net cash flow from operating activities.

Follow My Example 16-2

Net income $50,000
Adjustments to reconcile net income to net cash flow from operating activities:
    Depreciation   12,000
    Amortization   3,400
    Gain from sale of land . . . .   (4,100)
Net cash flow from operating activities $61,300

For Practice: PE 16-2A, PE 16-2B

Changes in Current Operating Assets and Liabilities   As shown in Exhibit 5, decreases in noncash current assets and increases in current liabilities are added to net income. In contrast, increases in noncash current assets and decreases in current liabilities are deducted from net income. The current asset and current liability accounts of Rundell Inc. are as follows:

---

5 The reporting of the proceeds (cash flows) from the sale of land as part of investing activities is discussed later in this chapter.

Accounts	December 31 2008	December 31 2007	Increase Decrease*
Accounts receivable (net)	$ 74,000	$ 65,000	$9,000
Inventories	172,000	180,000	8,000*
Accounts payable (merchandise creditors)	43,500	46,700	3,200*
Accrued expenses payable (operating expenses) ..	26,500	24,300	2,200
Income taxes payable	7,900	8,400	500*

REAL WORLD

Continental Airlines had a net loss of $363 million but a positive cash flow from operating activities of $373 million. This difference was mostly due to $414 million of depreciation expenses and $417 million from changes in operating assets and liabilities.

As discussed previously, the $9,000 increase in *accounts receivable* indicates that the sales on account during the year are $9,000 more than collections from customers on account. The amount reported as sales on the income statement therefore includes $9,000 that did not result in a cash inflow during the year. Thus, $9,000 is deducted from net income.

The $8,000 decrease in *inventories* indicates that the merchandise sold exceeds the cost of the merchandise purchased by $8,000. The amount deducted as cost of merchandise sold on the income statement therefore includes $8,000 that did not require a cash outflow during the year. Thus, $8,000 is added to net income.

The $3,200 decrease in *accounts payable* indicates that the amount of cash payments for merchandise exceeds the merchandise purchased on account by $3,200. The amount reported on the income statement for cost of merchandise sold therefore excludes $3,200 that required a cash outflow during the year. Thus, $3,200 is deducted from net income.

The $2,200 increase in *accrued expenses payable* indicates that the amount incurred during the year for operating expenses exceeds the cash payments by $2,200. The amount reported on the income statement for operating expenses therefore includes $2,200 that did not require a cash outflow during the year. Thus, $2,200 is added to net income.

The $500 decrease in *income taxes payable* indicates that the amount paid for taxes exceeds the amount incurred during the year by $500. The amount reported on the income statement for income tax therefore is less than the amount paid by $500. Thus, $500 is deducted from net income.

Example Exercise 16-3

objective **2**

Victor Corporation's comparative balance sheet for current assets and liabilities was as follows:

	Dec. 31, 2009	Dec. 31, 2008
Accounts receivable	$ 6,500	$ 4,900
Inventory	12,300	15,000
Accounts payable	4,800	5,200
Dividends payable	5,000	4,000

Adjust net income of $70,000 for changes in operating assets and liabilities to arrive at cash flows from operating activities.

Follow My Example 16-3

Net income	$70,000
Adjustments to reconcile net income to net cash flow from operating activities:	
Changes in current operating assets and liabilities:	
Increase in accounts receivable	(1,600)
Decrease in inventory	2,700
Decrease in accounts payable	(400)
Net cash flow from operating activities	$70,700

For Practice: PE 16-3A, PE 16-3B

Integrity, Objectivity, and Ethics in Business

CREDIT POLICY AND CASH FLOW

One would expect customers to pay for products and services sold on account. Unfortunately, that is not always the case. Collecting accounts receivable efficiently is the key to turning a current asset into positive cash flow. Most entrepreneurs would rather think about the exciting aspects of their business—such as product development, marketing, sales, and advertising—rather than credit collection. This can be a mistake. Hugh McHugh of Overhill Flowers, Inc., decided that he would have no more trade accounts after dealing with Christmas orders that weren't paid for until late February, or sometimes not paid at all. As stated by one collection service, "One thing business owners always tell me is that they never thought about [collections] when they started their own business." To the small business owner, the collected receivable is often their paycheck, so it pays to pay attention.

Source: Paulette Thomas, "Making Them Pay: The Last Thing Most Entrepreneurs Want to Think About Is Bill Collection; It Should Be One of the First Things," *The Wall Street Journal*, September 19, 2005, p. R6.

Reporting Cash Flows from Operating Activities   We have now presented all the necessary adjustments to convert the net income to cash flows from operating activities for Rundell Inc. These adjustments are summarized in Exhibit 6 for the statement of cash flows.

EXHIBIT 6   Cash Flows from Operating Activities—Indirect Method

Cash flows from operating activities:		
Net income	$108,000	
Adjustments to reconcile net income to net cash flow from operating activities:		
Depreciation	7,000	
Gain on sale of land	(12,000)	
Changes in current operating assets and liabilities:		
Increase in accounts receivable	(9,000)	
Decrease in inventory	8,000	
Decrease in accounts payable	(3,200)	
Increase in accrued expenses	2,200	
Decrease in income taxes payable	(500)	
Net cash flow from operating activities		$100,500

Example Exercise 16-4

objective

Omicron Inc. reported the following data:

Net income	$120,000
Depreciation expense	12,000
Loss on disposal of equipment	15,000
Increase in accounts receivable	5,000
Decrease in accounts payable	2,000

Prepare the cash flows from operating activities section of the statement of cash flows using the indirect method.

(continued)

Follow My Example 16-4

Cash flows from operating activities:	
Net income	$120,000
Adjustments to reconcile net income to net cash flow from operating activities:	
Depreciation	12,000
Loss from disposal of equipment	15,000
Changes in current operating assets and liabilities:	
Increase in accounts receivable	(5,000)
Decrease in accounts payable	(2,000)
Net cash flow from operating activities	$140,000

For Practice: PE 16-4A, PE 16-4B

CASH FLOWS USED FOR PAYMENT OF DIVIDENDS

According to the retained earnings account of Rundell Inc., shown earlier in the chapter, cash dividends of $28,000 were declared during the year. However, the dividends payable account, shown below, indicates that dividends of only $24,000 were paid during the year.

ACCOUNT Dividends Payable   **ACCOUNT NO.**

					Balance	
Date		Item	Debit	Credit	Debit	Credit
2008 Jan.	1	Balance				10 0 0 0 00
	10	Cash paid	10 0 0 0 00		—	—
June	20	Dividends declared		14 0 0 0 00		14 0 0 0 00
July	10	Cash paid	14 0 0 0 00		—	—
Dec.	20	Dividends declared		14 0 0 0 00		14 0 0 0 00

The $24,000 of dividend payments represents a cash outflow that is reported in the financing activities section as follows:

Cash flows from financing activities:	
Cash paid for dividends	$24,000

COMMON STOCK

The common stock account increased by $8,000, and the paid-in capital in excess of par—common stock account increased by $40,000, as shown below. These increases result from issuing 4,000 shares of common stock for $12 per share.

ACCOUNT Common Stock   **ACCOUNT NO.**

					Balance	
Date		Item	Debit	Credit	Debit	Credit
2008 Jan.	1	Balance				16 0 0 0 00
Nov.	1	4,000 shares issued for cash		8 0 0 0 00		24 0 0 0 00

ACCOUNT Paid-In Capital in Excess of Par—Common Stock   **ACCOUNT NO.**

					Balance	
Date		Item	Debit	Credit	Debit	Credit
2008 Jan.	1	Balance				80 0 0 0 00
Nov.	1	4,000 shares issued for cash		40 0 0 0 00		120 0 0 0 00

This cash inflow is reported in the financing activities section as follows:

> Cash flows from financing activities:
>   Cash received from sale of common stock $48,000

BONDS PAYABLE

The bonds payable account decreased by $50,000, as shown below. This decrease results from retiring the bonds by a cash payment for their face amount.

ACCOUNT Bonds Payable				ACCOUNT NO.	
				Balance	
Date	Item	Debit	Credit	Debit	Credit
2008 Jan. 1	Balance				150 0 0 0 00
June 30	Retired by payment of cash				
	at face amount	50 0 0 0 00			100 0 0 0 00

This cash outflow is reported in the financing activities section as follows:

> Cash flows from financing activities:
>   Cash paid to retire bonds payable $50,000

BUILDING

The building account increased by $60,000, and the accumulated depreciation—building account increased by $7,000, as shown below.

ACCOUNT Building				ACCOUNT NO.	
				Balance	
Date	Item	Debit	Credit	Debit	Credit
2008 Jan. 1	Balance			200 0 0 0 00	
Dec. 27	Purchased for cash	60 0 0 0 00		260 0 0 0 00	

ACCOUNT Accumulated Depreciation—Building				ACCOUNT NO.	
				Balance	
Date	Item	Debit	Credit	Debit	Credit
2008 Jan. 1	Balance				58 3 0 0 00
Dec. 31	Depreciation for the year		7 0 0 0 00		65 3 0 0 00

The purchase of a building for cash of $60,000 is reported as an outflow of cash in the investing activities section, as follows:

> Cash flows from investing activities:
>   Cash paid for purchase of building $60,000

The credit in the accumulated depreciation—building account, shown earlier, represents depreciation expense for the year. This depreciation expense of $7,000 on the building has already been considered as an addition to net income in determining cash flows from operating activities, as reported in Exhibit 6.

LAND

The $45,000 decline in the land account resulted from two separate transactions, as shown below.

	Date		Item	Debit	Credit	Balance Debit	Balance Credit
ACCOUNT *Land*						**ACCOUNT NO.**	
	2008 Jan.	1	Balance			125 0 0 0 00	
	June	8	Sold for $72,000 cash		60 0 0 0 00	65 0 0 0 00	
	Oct.	12	Purchased for $15,000 cash	15 0 0 0 00		80 0 0 0 00	

The first transaction is the sale of land with a cost of $60,000 for $72,000 in cash. The $72,000 proceeds from the sale are reported in the investing activities section, as follows:

> Cash flows from investing activities:
>   Cash received from sale of land (includes
> $12,000 gain reported in net income) $72,000

The proceeds of $72,000 include the $12,000 gain on the sale of land and the $60,000 cost (book value) of the land. As shown in Exhibit 6, the $12,000 gain is also deducted from net income in the cash flows from operating activities section. This is necessary so that the $12,000 cash inflow related to the gain is not included twice as a cash inflow.

The second transaction is the purchase of land for cash of $15,000. This transaction is reported as an outflow of cash in the investing activities section, as follows:

> Cash flows from investing activities:
>   Cash paid for purchase of land $15,000

Example Exercise 16-5   objective 2

Alpha Corporation purchased land for $125,000. Later in the year, the company sold land with a book value of $165,000 for $200,000. How are the effects of these transactions reported on the statement of cash flows?

Follow My Example 16-5

The gain on sale of land is deducted from net income as shown below:
Gain on sale of land . . . . $ (35,000)

The purchase and sale of land is reported as part of cash flows from investing activities as shown below:
Cash received for sale of land   200,000
Cash paid for purchase of land . . . .   (125,000)

For Practice: PE 16-5A, PE 16-5B

PREPARING THE STATEMENT OF CASH FLOWS

The statement of cash flows for Rundell Inc. is prepared from the data assembled and analyzed above, using the indirect method. Exhibit 7 shows the statement of cash flows prepared by Rundell Inc. The statement indicates that the cash position increased by $71,500 during the year. The most significant increase in net cash flows, $100,500, was from operating activities. The most significant use of cash, $26,000, was for financing activities.

EXHIBIT 7		
Statement of Cash Flows—Indirect Method		

Rundell Inc.
Statement of Cash Flows
For the Year Ended December 31, 2008

Cash flows from operating activities:			
Net income		$108,000	
Adjustments to reconcile net income to net cash flow from operating activities:			
Depreciation		7,000	
Gain on sale of land		(12,000)	
Changes in current operating assets and liabilities:			
Increase in accounts receivable		(9,000)	
Decrease in inventory		8,000	
Decrease in accounts payable		(3,200)	
Increase in accrued expenses		2,200	
Decrease in income taxes payable		(500)	
Net cash flow from operating activities			$100,500
Cash flows from investing activities:			
Cash from sale of land		$ 72,000	
Less: Cash paid to purchase land	$ 15,000		
Cash paid for purchase of building	60,000	75,000	
Net cash flow used for investing activities			(3,000)
Cash flows from financing activities:			
Cash received from sale of common stock		$ 48,000	
Less: Cash paid to retire bonds payable	$ 50,000		
Cash paid for dividends	24,000	74,000	
Net cash flow used for financing activities			(26,000)
Increase in cash			$ 71,500
Cash at the beginning of the year			26,000
Cash at the end of the year			$ 97,500

Statement of Cash Flows—The Direct Method

objective **3**

Prepare a statement of cash flows, using the direct method.

As we discussed previously, the manner of reporting cash flows from investing and financing activities is the same under the direct and indirect methods. In addition, the direct method and the indirect method will report the same amount of cash flows from operating activities. However, the methods differ in how the cash flows from operating activities data are obtained, analyzed, and reported.

To illustrate the direct method, we will use the comparative balance sheet and the income statement for Rundell Inc. In this way, we can compare the statement of cash flows under the direct method and the indirect method.

Exhibit 8 shows the changes in the current asset and liability account balances for Rundell Inc. The income statement in Exhibit 8 shows additional data for Rundell Inc.

The direct method reports cash flows from operating activities by major classes of operating cash receipts and operating cash payments. The difference between the major classes of total operating cash receipts and total operating cash payments is the net cash flow from operating activities.

CASH RECEIVED FROM CUSTOMERS

The $1,180,000 of sales for Rundell Inc. is reported by using the accrual method. To determine the cash received from sales to customers, the $1,180,000 must be adjusted.

EXHIBIT 8

Balance Sheet and Income Statement Data for Direct Method

Rundell Inc.
Schedule of Changes in Current Accounts

Accounts	December 31 2008	December 31 2007	Increase Decrease*
Cash	$ 97,500	$ 26,000	$71,500
Accounts receivable (net)	74,000	65,000	9,000
Inventories	172,000	180,000	8,000*
Accounts payable (merchandise creditors)	43,500	46,700	3,200*
Accrued expenses payable (operating expenses)	26,500	24,300	2,200
Income taxes payable	7,900	8,400	500*
Dividends payable	14,000	10,000	4,000

Rundell Inc.
Income Statement
For the Year Ended December 31, 2008

Sales		$1,180,000
Cost of merchandise sold		790,000
Gross profit		$ 390,000
Operating expenses:		
Depreciation expense	$ 7,000	
Other operating expenses	196,000	
Total operating expenses		203,000
Income from operations		$ 187,000
Other income:		
Gain on sale of land	$ 12,000	
Other expense:		
Interest expense	8,000	4,000
Income before income tax		$ 191,000
Income tax expense		83,000
Net income		$ 108,000

The adjustment necessary to convert the sales reported on the income statement to the cash received from customers is summarized below.

For Rundell Inc., the cash received from customers is $1,171,000, as shown below.

Sales	$1,180,000
Less increase in accounts receivable	9,000
Cash received from customers	$1,171,000

The additions to *accounts receivable* for sales on account during the year were $9,000 more than the amounts collected from customers on account. Sales reported on the income statement therefore included $9,000 that did not result in a cash inflow during the year. In other words, the increase of $9,000 in accounts receivable during 2008 indicates that sales on account exceeded cash received from customers by $9,000. Thus, $9,000 is deducted from sales to determine the cash received from customers. The $1,171,000 of cash received from customers is reported in the cash flows from operating activities section of the cash flow statement.

Example Exercise 16-6
objective 3

Sales reported on the income statement were $350,000. The accounts receivable balance declined $8,000 over the year. Determine the amount of cash received from customers.

Follow My Example 16-6

Sales	$350,000
Add decrease in accounts receivable	8,000
Cash received from customers	$358,000

For Practice: PE 16-6A, PE 16-6B

CASH PAYMENTS FOR MERCHANDISE

The $790,000 of cost of merchandise sold is reported on the income statement for Rundell Inc., using the accrual method. The adjustments necessary to convert the cost of merchandise sold to cash payments for merchandise during 2008 are summarized below.

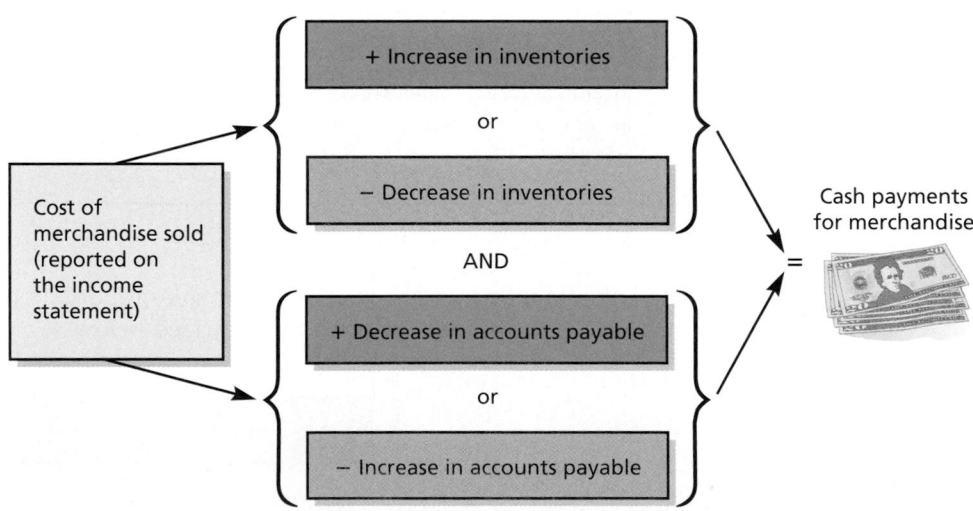

For Rundell Inc., the amount of cash payments for merchandise is $785,200, as determined below.

Cost of merchandise sold	$790,000
Deduct decrease in inventories	(8,000)
Add decrease in accounts payable	3,200
Cash payments for merchandise	$785,200

The $8,000 decrease in *inventories* indicates that the merchandise sold exceeded the cost of the merchandise purchased by $8,000. The amount reported on the income statement for cost of merchandise sold therefore includes $8,000 that did not require a cash outflow during the year. Thus, $8,000 is deducted from the cost of merchandise sold in determining the cash payments for merchandise.

The $3,200 decrease in *accounts payable* (merchandise creditors) indicates a cash outflow that is excluded from cost of merchandise sold. That is, the decrease in accounts payable indicates that cash payments for merchandise were $3,200 more than the purchases on account during 2008. Thus, $3,200 is added to the cost of merchandise sold in determining the cash payments for merchandise.

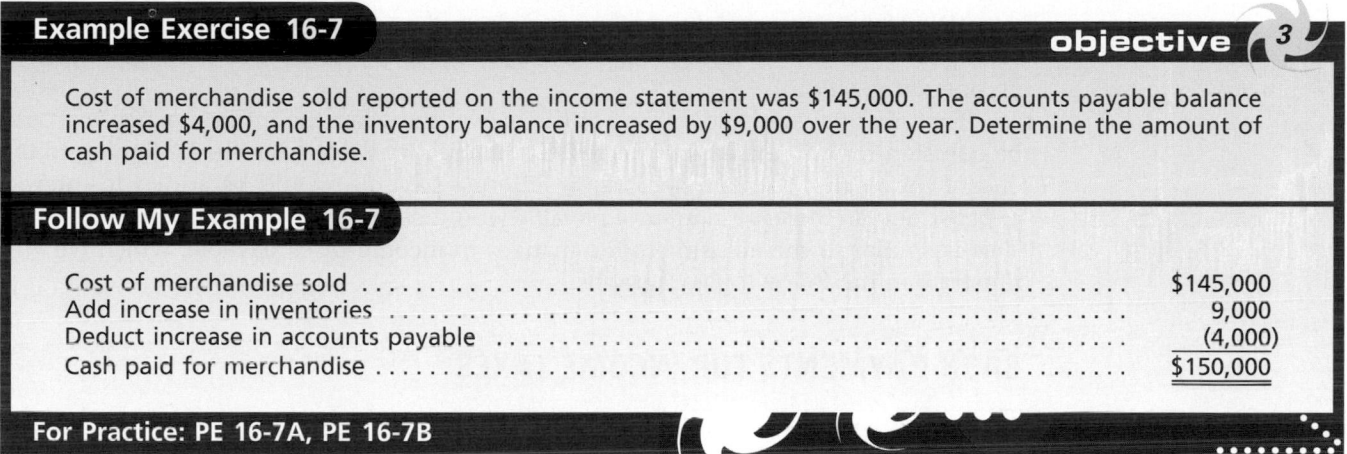

Example Exercise 16-7 · objective 3

Cost of merchandise sold reported on the income statement was $145,000. The accounts payable balance increased $4,000, and the inventory balance increased by $9,000 over the year. Determine the amount of cash paid for merchandise.

Follow My Example 16-7

Cost of merchandise sold	$145,000
Add increase in inventories	9,000
Deduct increase in accounts payable	(4,000)
Cash paid for merchandise	$150,000

For Practice: PE 16-7A, PE 16-7B

CASH PAYMENTS FOR OPERATING EXPENSES

The $7,000 of depreciation expense reported on the income statement did not require a cash outflow. Thus, under the direct method, it is not reported on the statement of cash flows. The $196,000 reported for other operating expenses is adjusted to reflect the cash payments for operating expenses, as summarized below.

For Rundell Inc., the amount of cash payments for operating expenses is $193,800, determined as follows:

Operating expenses other than depreciation	$196,000
Deduct increase in accrued expenses	2,200
Cash payments for operating expenses	$193,800

The increase in *accrued expenses* (operating expenses) indicates that operating expenses include $2,200 for which there was no cash outflow (payment) during the year. That is, the increase in accrued expenses indicates that the cash payments for operating expenses were $2,200 less than the amount reported as an expense during the year. Thus, $2,200 is deducted from the operating expenses on the income statement in determining the cash payments for operating expenses.

GAIN ON SALE OF LAND

The income statement for Rundell Inc. in Exhibit 8 reports a gain of $12,000 on the sale of land. As we discussed previously, the gain is included in the proceeds from the sale of land, which is reported as part of the cash flows from investing activities.

INTEREST EXPENSE

The income statement for Rundell Inc. in Exhibit 8 reports interest expense of $8,000. The interest expense is related to the bonds payable that were outstanding during the year. We assume that interest on the bonds is paid on June 30 and December 31. Thus, $8,000 cash outflow for interest expense is reported on the statement of cash flows as an operating activity.

If interest payable had existed at the end of the year, the interest expense would be adjusted for any increase or decrease in interest payable from the beginning to the end of the year. That is, a decrease in interest payable would be added to interest expense and an increase in interest payable would be subtracted from interest expense. This is similar to the adjustment for changes in income taxes payable, which we will illustrate in the following paragraphs.

CASH PAYMENTS FOR INCOME TAXES

The adjustment to convert the income tax reported on the income statement to the cash basis is summarized below.

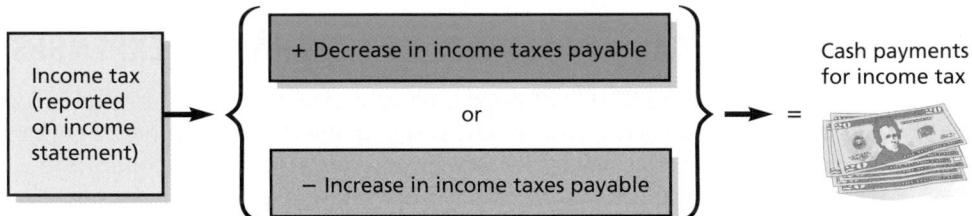

For Rundell Inc., cash payments for income tax are $83,500, determined as follows:

Income tax	$83,000
Add decrease in income taxes payable	500
Cash payments for income tax	$83,500

The cash outflow for income taxes exceeded the income tax deducted as an expense during the period by $500. Thus, $500 is added to the amount of income tax reported on the income statement in determining the cash payments for income tax.

REPORTING CASH FLOWS FROM OPERATING ACTIVITIES—DIRECT METHOD

Exhibit 9 is a complete statement of cash flows for Rundell Inc., using the direct method for reporting cash flows from operating activities. The portions of this statement that differ from the indirect method are highlighted in color. Exhibit 9 also includes the separate schedule reconciling net income and net cash flow from operating activities. This schedule must accompany the statement of cash flows when the direct method is used. This schedule is similar to the cash flows from operating activities section of the statement of cash flows prepared using the indirect method.

EXHIBIT 9

Statement of Cash Flows—Direct Method

Rundell Inc.
Statement of Cash Flows
For the Year Ended December 31, 2008

Cash flows from operating activities:			
Cash received from customers		$1,171,000	
Deduct: Cash payments for merchandise.	$785,200		
Cash payments for operating expenses. . . .	193,800		
Cash payments for interest	8,000		
Cash payments for income taxes	83,500	1,070,500	
Net cash flow from operating activities			$100,500
Cash flows from investing activities:			
Cash from sale of land		$ 72,000	
Less: Cash paid to purchase land	$ 15,000		
Cash paid for purchase of building	60,000	75,000	
Net cash flow used for investing activities			(3,000)
Cash flows from financing activities:			
Cash received from sale of common stock		$ 48,000	
Less: Cash paid to retire bonds payable	$ 50,000		
Cash paid for dividends	24,000	74,000	
Net cash flow used for financing activities			(26,000)
Increase in cash			$ 71,500
Cash at the beginning of the year			26,000
Cash at the end of the year			$ 97,500

Schedule Reconciling Net Income with Cash
Flows from Operating Activities:

Cash flows from operating activities:	
Net income	$108,000
Adjustments to reconcile net income to net cash flow from operating activities:	
Depreciation	7,000
Gain on sale of land	(12,000)
Changes in current operating assets and liabilities:	
Increase in accounts receivable	(9,000)
Decrease in inventory	8,000
Decrease in accounts payable	(3,200)
Increase in accrued expenses	2,200
Decrease in income taxes payable	(500)
Net cash flow from operating activities	$100,500

Financial Analysis and Interpretation

A valuable tool for evaluating the cash flows of a business is free cash flow. **Free cash flow** is a measure of operating cash flow available for corporate purposes after providing sufficient fixed asset additions to maintain current productive capacity and dividends. Thus, free cash flow can be calculated as follows:

Cash flow from operating activities	$XXX
Less: Investments in fixed assets to maintain current production	XXX
Free cash flow	$XXX

Analysts often use free cash flow, rather than cash flows from operating activities, to measure the financial strength of a business. Many high-technology firms must aggressively reinvest in new technology to remain competitive. This can reduce free cash flow. For example, Motorola Inc.'s free cash flow is less than 10% of the cash flow from operating activities. In contrast, The Coca-Cola Company's free cash flow is approximately 75% of the cash flow from operating activities. The top three nonfinancial companies with the largest free cash flows for a recent year were as follows:

	Free Cash Flow (in millions)
General Electric Company	$25,598
ExxonMobil Corporation	18,705
Microsoft Corporation	14,289

To illustrate, the cash flow from operating activities for Intuit Inc., the developer of TurboTax®, was $590 million in a recent fiscal year. The statement of cash flows indicated that the cash invested in property, plant, and equipment was $38 million. Assuming that the amount invested in property, plant, and equipment maintained existing operations, free cash flow would be calculated as follows (in millions):

Cash flow from operating activities	$590
Less: Investments in fixed assets to maintain current production	38
Free cash flow	$552

During this period, Intuit generated free cash flow in excess of $500 million, which was 94% of cash flows from operations and over 27% of sales.

Positive free cash flow is considered favorable. A company that has free cash flow is able to fund internal growth, retire debt, pay dividends, and enjoy financial flexibility. A company with no free cash flow is unable to maintain current productive capacity. Lack of free cash flow can be an early indicator of liquidity problems. As stated by one analyst, "Free cash flow gives the company firepower to reduce debt and ultimately generate consistent, actual income."[6]

Source: "CFO Free Cash Flow Scorecard," *CFO Magazine*, January 1, 2005.

Appendix

Spreadsheet (Work Sheet) for Statement of Cash Flows—The Indirect Method

A spreadsheet (work sheet) may be useful in assembling data for the statement of cash flows. Whether or not a spreadsheet (work sheet) is used, the concepts of cash flow and the statements of cash flows presented in this chapter are not affected. In this appendix, we will describe and illustrate the use of the spreadsheet (work sheet) for the indirect method.

6 Jill Krutick, *Fortune*, March 30, 1998, p. 106.

We will use the data for Rundell Inc., presented in Exhibit 4, as a basis for illustrating the spreadsheet (work sheet) for the indirect method. The procedures used in preparing this spreadsheet (work sheet), shown in Exhibit 10, are outlined below.

1. List the title of each balance sheet account in the Accounts column. For each account, enter its balance as of December 31, 2007, in the first column and its balance as of December 31, 2008, in the last column. Place the credit balances in parentheses. The column totals should equal zero, since the total of the debits in a column should equal the total of the credits in a column.
2. Analyze the change during the year in each account to determine the net increase (decrease) in cash and the cash flows from operating activities, investing activities, financing activities, and the noncash investing and financing activities. Show the effect of the change on cash flows by making entries in the Transactions columns.

ANALYZING ACCOUNTS

An efficient method of analyzing cash flows is to determine the type of cash flow activity that led to changes in balance sheet accounts during the period. As we analyze each noncash account, we will make entries on the spreadsheet (work sheet) for specific types of cash flow activities related to the noncash accounts. After we have analyzed all the noncash accounts, we will make an entry for the increase (decrease) in cash during the period. These entries, however, are not posted to the ledger. They only aid in assembling the data on the spreadsheet.

The order in which the accounts are analyzed is unimportant. However, it is more efficient to begin with the retained earnings account and proceed upward in the account listing.

RETAINED EARNINGS

The spreadsheet (work sheet) shows a Retained Earnings balance of $202,300 at December 31, 2007, and $282,300 at December 31, 2008. Thus, Retained Earnings increased $80,000 during the year. This increase resulted from two factors: (1) net income of $108,000 and (2) declaring cash dividends of $28,000. To identify the cash flows by activity, we will make two entries on the spreadsheet. These entries also serve to account for or explain, in terms of cash flows, the increase of $80,000.

In closing the accounts at the end of the year, the retained earnings account was credited for the net income of $108,000. The $108,000 is reported on the statement of cash flows as "cash flows from operating activities." The following entry is made in the Transactions columns on the spreadsheet. This entry (1) accounts for the credit portion of the closing entry (to Retained Earnings) and (2) identifies the cash flow in the bottom portion of the spreadsheet.

(a)	Operating Activities—Net Income	108,000	
	Retained Earnings		108,000

In closing the accounts at the end of the year, the retained earnings account was debited for dividends declared of $28,000. The $28,000 is reported as a financing activity on the statement of cash flows. The following entry on the spreadsheet (1) accounts for the debit portion of the closing entry (to Retained Earnings) and (2) identifies the cash flow in the bottom portion of the spreadsheet.

(b)	Retained Earnings	28,000	
	Financing Activities—Declared Cash Dividends		28,000

The $28,000 of declared dividends will be adjusted later for the actual amount of cash dividends paid during the year.

EXHIBIT 10   End-of-Period Spreadsheet (Work Sheet) for Statement of Cash Flows—Indirect Method

	A	B	C	D	E	F	G	
		Rundell Inc.						
		End-of-Period Spreadsheet (Work Sheet) for Statement of Cash Flows						
		For the Year Ended December 31, 2008						
	Accounts	Balance, Dec. 31, 2007		Transactions Debit		Credit	Balance, Dec. 31, 2008	
1	Cash	26,000	(o)	71,500			97,500	1
2	Accounts receivable (net)	65,000	(n)	9,000			74,000	2
3	Inventories	180,000			(m)	8,000	172,000	3
4	Land	125,000	(k)	15,000	(l)	60,000	80,000	4
5	Building	200,000	(j)	60,000			260,000	5
6	Accumulated depreciation—building	(58,300)			(i)	7,000	(65,300)	6
7	Accounts payable (merchandise creditors)	(46,700)	(h)	3,200			(43,500)	7
8	Accrued expenses payable (operating expenses)	(24,300)			(g)	2,200	(26,500)	8
9	Income taxes payable	(8,400)	(f)	500			(7,900)	9
10	Dividends payable	(10,000)			(e)	4,000	(14,000)	10
11	Bonds payable	(150,000)	(d)	50,000			(100,000)	11
12	Common stock	(16,000)			(c)	8,000	(24,000)	12
13	Paid-in capital in excess of par	(80,000)			(c)	40,000	(120,000)	13
14	Retained earnings	(202,300)	(b)	28,000	(a)	108,000	(282,300)	14
15	Totals	0		237,200		237,200	0	15
16	Operating activities:							16
17	Net income		(a)	108,000				17
18	Depreciation of building		(i)	7,000				18
19	Gain on sale of land				(l)	12,000		19
20	Increase in accounts receivable				(n)	9,000		20
21	Decrease in inventories		(m)	8,000				21
22	Decrease in accounts payable				(h)	3,200		22
23	Increase in accrued expenses		(g)	2,200				23
24	Decrease in income taxes payable				(f)	500		24
25	Investing activities:							25
26	Sale of land		(l)	72,000				26
27	Purchase of land				(k)	15,000		27
28	Purchase of building				(j)	60,000		28
29	Financing activities:							29
30	Issued common stock		(c)	48,000				30
31	Retired bonds payable				(d)	50,000		31
32	Declared cash dividends				(b)	28,000		32
33	Increase in dividends payable		(e)	4,000				33
34	Net increase in cash				(o)	71,500		34
35	Totals			249,200		249,200		35

OTHER ACCOUNTS

The entries for the other accounts are made in the spreadsheet in a manner similar to entries (a) and (b). A summary of these entries is as follows:

(c)	Financing Activities—Issued Common Stock	48,000	
	Common Stock		8,000
	Paid-In Capital in Excess of Par—Common Stock		40,000
(d)	Bonds Payable	50,000	
	Financing Activities—Retired Bonds Payable		50,000
(e)	Financing Activities—Increase in Dividends Payable	4,000	
	Dividends Payable		4,000
(f)	Income Taxes Payable	500	
	Operating Activities—Decrease in Income Taxes Payable		500

(g)	Operating Activities—Increase in Accrued Expenses	2,200	
	Accrued Expenses Payable		2,200
(h)	Accounts Payable	3,200	
	Operating Activities—Decrease in Accounts Payable		3,200
(i)	Operating Activities—Depreciation of Building	7,000	
	Accumulated Depreciation—Building		7,000
(j)	Building	60,000	
	Investing Activities—Purchase of Building		60,000
(k)	Land	15,000	
	Investing Activities—Purchase of Land		15,000
(l)	Investing Activities—Sale of Land	72,000	
	Operating Activities—Gain on Sale of Land		12,000
	Land		60,000
(m)	Operating Activities—Decrease in Inventories	8,000	
	Inventories		8,000
(n)	Accounts Receivable	9,000	
	Operating Activities—Increase in Accounts Receivable		9,000
(o)	Cash	71,500	
	Net Increase in Cash		71,500

After we have analyzed all the balance sheet accounts and made the entries on the spreadsheet (work sheet), all the operating, investing, and financing activities are identified in the bottom portion of the spreadsheet. The accuracy of the spreadsheet entries is verified by the equality of each pair of the totals of the debit and credit Transactions columns.

PREPARING THE STATEMENT OF CASH FLOWS

The statement of cash flows prepared from the spreadsheet is identical to the statement in Exhibit 7. The data for the three sections of the statement are obtained from the bottom portion of the spreadsheet.

At a Glance

1. Summarize the types of cash flow activities reported in the statement of cash flows.

Key Points	Key Learning Outcomes	Example Exercises	Practice Exercises
The statement of cash flows reports cash receipts and cash payments by three types of activities: operating activities, investing activities, and financing activities. Investing and financing for a business may be affected by transactions that do not involve cash. The effect of such transactions should be reported in a separate schedule accompanying the statement of cash flows.	• Classify transactions that either provide or use cash into either operating, investing, or financing activities.	16-1	16-1A, 16-1B

(continued)

2. Prepare a statement of cash flows, using the indirect method.

Key Points	Key Learning Outcomes	Example Exercises	Practice Exercises
The changes in the noncash balance sheet accounts are used to develop the statement of cash flows, beginning with the cash flows from operating activities.			
Determine the cash flows from operating activities using the indirect method by adjusting net income for expenses that do not require cash and for gains and losses from disposal of fixed assets.	• Adjust net income for non-cash expenses and gains and losses from asset disposals under the indirect method.	**16-2**	16-2A, 16-2B
Determine the cash flows from operating activities using the indirect method by adjusting net income for changes in current operating assets and liabilities.	• Adjust net income for changes in current operating assets and liabilities under the indirect method.	**16-3**	16-3A, 16-3B
Report cash flows from operating activities under the indirect method.	• Prepare the cash flows from operating activities under the indirect method in proper form.	**16-4**	16-4A, 16-4B
Report investing and financing activities on the statement of cash flows.	• Prepare the remainder of the statement of cash flows by reporting investing and financing activities.	**16-5**	16-5A, 16-5B

3. Prepare a statement of cash flows, using the direct method.

Key Points	Key Learning Outcomes	Example Exercises	Practice Exercises
The direct method reports cash flows from operating activities by major classes of operating cash receipts and cash payments. The difference between the major classes of total operating cash receipts and total operating cash payments is the net cash flow from operating activities. The investing and financing activities sections of the statement are the same as under the indirect method.	• Prepare the cash flows from operating activities and the remainder of the statement of cash flows under the direct method.	**16-6** **16-7**	16-6A, 16-6B 16-7A, 16-7B

Key Terms

cash flows from financing
  activities (692)
cash flows from investing
  activities (692)

cash flows from operating
  activities (692)
direct method (694)
free cash flow (712)

indirect method (694)
statement of cash flows (692)

Illustrative Problem

The comparative balance sheet of Dowling Company for December 31, 2008 and 2007, is as follows:

Dowling Company Comparative Balance Sheet December 31, 2008 and 2007		
Assets	**2008**	**2007**
Cash	$ 140,350	$ 95,900
Accounts receivable (net)	95,300	102,300
Inventories	165,200	157,900
Prepaid expenses	6,240	5,860
Investments (long-term)	35,700	84,700
Land	75,000	90,000
Buildings	375,000	260,000
Accumulated depreciation—buildings	(71,300)	(58,300)
Machinery and equipment	428,300	428,300
Accumulated depreciation—machinery and equipment	(148,500)	(138,000)
Patents	58,000	65,000
Total assets	$1,159,290	$1,093,660
Liabilities and Stockholders' Equity		
Accounts payable (merchandise creditors)	$ 43,500	$ 46,700
Accrued expenses (operating expenses)	14,000	12,500
Income taxes payable	7,900	8,400
Dividends payable	14,000	10,000
Mortgage note payable, due 2019	40,000	0
Bonds payable	150,000	250,000
Common stock, $30 par	450,000	375,000
Excess of issue price over par—common stock	66,250	41,250
Retained earnings	373,640	349,810
Total liabilities and stockholders' equity	$1,159,290	$1,093,660

The income statement for Dowling Company is shown here:

Dowling Company Income Statement For the Year Ended December 31, 2008		
Sales		$1,100,000
Cost of merchandise sold		710,000
Gross profit		$ 390,000
Operating expenses:		
Depreciation expense	$ 23,500	
Patent amortization	7,000	
Other operating expenses	196,000	
Total operating expenses		226,500
Income from operations		$ 163,500
Other income:		
Gain on sale of investments	$ 11,000	
Other expense:		
Interest expense	26,000	(15,000)
Income before income tax		$ 148,500
Income tax expense		50,000
Net income		$ 98,500

An examination of the accounting records revealed the following additional information applicable to 2008:

a. Land costing $15,000 was sold for $15,000.
b. A mortgage note was issued for $40,000.
c. A building costing $115,000 was constructed.
d. 2,500 shares of common stock were issued at 40 in exchange for the bonds payable.
e. Cash dividends declared were $74,670.

Instructions

1. Prepare a statement of cash flows, using the indirect method of reporting cash flows from operating activities.
2. Prepare a statement of cash flows, using the direct method of reporting cash flows from operating activities.

Solution

1.

Dowling Company
Statement of Cash Flows—Indirect Method
For the Year Ended December 31, 2008

Cash flows from operating activities:			
Net income		$ 98,500	
Adjustments to reconcile net income to net cash flow from operating activities:			
Depreciation		23,500	
Amortization of patents		7,000	
Gain on sale of investments		(11,000)	
Changes in current operating assets and liabilities:			
Decrease in accounts receivable		7,000	
Increase in inventories		(7,300)	
Increase in prepaid expenses		(380)	
Decrease in accounts payable		(3,200)	
Increase in accrued expenses		1,500	
Decrease in income taxes payable		(500)	
Net cash flow from operating activities			$115,120
Cash flows from investing activities:			
Cash received from sale of:			
Investments	$60,000		
Land	15,000	$ 75,000	
Less: Cash paid for construction of building		115,000	
Net cash flow used for investing activities			(40,000)
Cash flows from financing activities:			
Cash received from issuing mortgage note payable		$ 40,000	
Less: Cash paid for dividends		70,670	
Net cash flow used for financing activities			(30,670)
Increase in cash			$ 44,450
Cash at the beginning of the year			95,900
Cash at the end of the year			$140,350
Schedule of Noncash Investing and Financing Activities:			
Issued common stock to retire bonds payable			$100,000

2.

Dowling Company
Statement of Cash Flows—Direct Method
For the Year Ended December 31, 2008

Cash flows from operating activities:			
Cash received from customers[1]		$1,107,000	
Deduct: Cash paid for merchandise[2]	$720,500		
Cash paid for operating expenses[3]	194,880		
Cash paid for interest expense	26,000		
Cash paid for income tax[4]	50,500	991,880	
Net cash flow from operating activities			$115,120
Cash flows from investing activities:			
Cash received from sale of:			
Investments	$ 60,000		
Land	15,000	$ 75,000	
Less: Cash paid for construction of building . . .		115,000	
Net cash flow used for investing activities			(40,000)
Cash flows from financing activities:			
Cash received from issuing mortgage			
note payable	$ 40,000		
Less: Cash paid for dividends[5]	70,670		
Net cash flow used for financing activities			(30,670)
Increase in cash			$ 44,450
Cash at the beginning of the year			95,900
Cash at the end of the year			$140,350

Schedule of Noncash Investing and
Financing Activities:

Issued common stock to retire bonds payable . .	$100,000

Schedule Reconciling Net Income with Cash Flows
from Operating Activities[6]

Computations:
[1]$1,100,000 + $7,000 = $1,107,000
[2]$710,000 + $3,200 + $7,300 = $720,500
[3]$196,000 + $380 − $1,500 = $194,880
[4]$50,000 + $500 = $50,500

[5]$74,670 + $10,000 − $14,000 = $70,670
[6]The content of this schedule is the same as the operating activities section of Part 1 of this solution and is not reproduced here for the sake of brevity.

Self-Examination Questions

(Answers at End of Chapter)

1. An example of a cash flow from an operating activity is:
   A. receipt of cash from the sale of stock.
   B. receipt of cash from the sale of bonds.
   C. payment of cash for dividends.
   D. receipt of cash from customers on account.

2. An example of a cash flow from an investing activity is:
   A. receipt of cash from the sale of equipment.
   B. receipt of cash from the sale of stock.
   C. payment of cash for dividends.
   D. payment of cash to acquire treasury stock.

3. An example of a cash flow from a financing activity is:
   A. receipt of cash from customers on account.
   B. receipt of cash from the sale of equipment.

C. payment of cash for dividends.
D. payment of cash to acquire land.

4. Which of the following methods of reporting cash flows from operating activities adjusts net income for revenues and expenses not involving the receipt or payment of cash?
   A. Direct method   C. Reciprocal method
   B. Purchase method   D. Indirect method

5. The net income reported on the income statement for the year was $55,000, and depreciation of fixed assets for the year was $22,000. The balances of the current asset and current liability accounts at the beginning and end of the year are shown at the top of the following page.

	End	Beginning
Cash	$ 65,000	$ 70,000
Accounts receivable	100,000	90,000
Inventories	145,000	150,000
Prepaid expenses	7,500	8,000
Accounts payable		
(merchandise creditors)	51,000	58,000

The total amount reported for cash flows from operating activities in the statement of cash flows, using the indirect method, is:

A. $33,000.   C. $65,500.
B. $55,000.   D. $77,000.

Eye Openers

1. What is the principal disadvantage of the direct method of reporting cash flows from operating activities?
2. What are the major advantages of the indirect method of reporting cash flows from operating activities?
3. A corporation issued $300,000 of common stock in exchange for $300,000 of fixed assets. Where would this transaction be reported on the statement of cash flows?
4. a. What is the effect on cash flows of declaring and issuing a stock dividend?
   b. Is the stock dividend reported on the statement of cash flows?
5. A retail business, using the accrual method of accounting, owed merchandise creditors (accounts payable) $290,000 at the beginning of the year and $315,000 at the end of the year. How would the $25,000 increase be used to adjust net income in determining the amount of cash flows from operating activities by the indirect method? Explain.
6. If salaries payable was $75,000 at the beginning of the year and $60,000 at the end of the year, should $15,000 be added to or deducted from income to determine the amount of cash flows from operating activities by the indirect method? Explain.
7. A long-term investment in bonds with a cost of $75,000 was sold for $84,000 cash. (a) What was the gain or loss on the sale? (b) What was the effect of the transaction on cash flows? (c) How should the transaction be reported in the statement of cash flows if cash flows from operating activities are reported by the indirect method?
8. A corporation issued $4,000,000 of 20-year bonds for cash at 105. How would the transaction be reported on the statement of cash flows?
9. Fully depreciated equipment costing $65,000 was discarded. What was the effect of the transaction on cash flows if (a) $12,000 cash is received, (b) no cash is received?
10. For the current year, Bearings Company decided to switch from the indirect method to the direct method for reporting cash flows from operating activities on the statement of cash flows. Will the change cause the amount of net cash flow from operating activities to be (a) larger, (b) smaller, or (c) the same as if the indirect method had been used? Explain.
11. Name five common major classes of operating cash receipts or operating cash payments presented on the statement of cash flows when the cash flows from operating activities are reported by the direct method.
12. In a recent annual report, eBay Inc. reported that during the year it issued stock of $128 million for acquisitions. How would this be reported on the statement of cash flows?

Practice Exercises

PE 16-1A
Classifying cash flows
obj. 1

Identify whether each of the following would be reported as an operating, investing, or financing activity in the statement of cash flows.

a. Issuance of bonds payable
b. Collection of accounts receivable
c. Purchase of investments

d. Disposal of equipment
e. Payment for selling expenses
f. Cash sales

PE 16-1B
Classifying cash flows
obj. 1

Identify whether each of the following would be reported as an operating, investing, or financing activity in the statement of cash flows.

a. Payment for administrative expenses
b. Retirement of bonds payable
c. Purchase of land

d. Issuance of common stock
e. Cash received from customers
f. Payment of accounts payable

PE 16-2A
Adjustments to net income—indirect method
obj. 2

Zale Corporation's accumulated depreciation—equipment increased by $8,000, while patents decreased by $5,200 between balance sheet dates. There were no purchases or sales of depreciable or intangible assets during the year. In addition, the income statement showed a loss of $6,000 from the sale of investments. Reconcile a net income of $90,000 to net cash flow from operating activities.

PE 16-2B
Adjustments to net income—indirect method
obj. 2

Nordic Corporation's accumulated depreciation—furniture increased by $3,500, while patents decreased by $1,800 between balance sheet dates. There were no purchases or sales of depreciable or intangible assets during the year. In addition, the income statement showed a gain of $12,500 from the sale of land. Reconcile a net income of $125,000 to net cash flow from operating activities.

PE 16-3A
Changes in current operating assets and liabilities—indirect method
obj. 2

Sage Corporation's comparative balance sheet for current assets and liabilities was as follows:

	Dec. 31, 2008	Dec. 31, 2007
Accounts receivable	$12,000	$14,000
Inventory	9,000	6,500
Accounts payable	8,500	7,200
Dividends payable	24,000	26,000

Adjust net income of $110,000 for changes in operating assets and liabilities to arrive at cash flows from operating activities.

PE 16-3B
Changes in current operating assets and liabilities—indirect method
obj. 2

Lanier Corporation's comparative balance sheet for current assets and liabilities was as follows:

	Dec. 31, 2008	Dec. 31, 2007
Accounts receivable	$32,500	$25,000
Inventory	69,000	48,000
Accounts payable	51,500	32,000
Dividends payable	15,000	16,400

Adjust net income of $290,000 for changes in operating assets and liabilities to arrive at cash flows from operating activities.

PE 16-4A
Reporting cash flows from operating activities—indirect method
obj. 2

Texas Holdem Inc. reported the following data:

Net income	$85,000
Depreciation expense	14,000
Gain on disposal of equipment	10,500
Decrease in accounts receivable	6,000
Decrease in accounts payable	1,800

Prepare the cash flows from operating activities section of the statement of cash flows using the indirect method.

PE 16-4B
Reporting cash flows from operating activities—indirect method
obj. 2

Pier Inc. reported the following data:

Net income	$150,000
Depreciation expense	25,000
Loss on disposal of equipment	14,300
Increase in accounts receivable	9,400
Increase in accounts payable	4,300

Prepare the cash flows from operating activities section of the statement of cash flows using the indirect method.

PE 16-5A
Reporting land transactions on the statement of cash flows
obj. 2

Gamma Corporation purchased land for $200,000. Later in the year, the company sold land with a book value of $105,000 for $90,000. How are the effects of these transactions reported on the statement of cash flows?

PE 16-5B
Reporting land transactions on the statement of cash flows
obj. 2

Sunrise Corporation purchased land for $500,000. Later in the year, the company sold land with a book value of $320,000 for $375,000. How are the effects of these transactions reported on the statement of cash flows?

PE 16-6A
Cash received from customers—direct method
obj. 3

Sales reported on the income statement were $623,000. The accounts receivable balance increased $48,000 over the year. Determine the amount of cash received from customers.

PE 16-6B
Cash received from customers—direct method
obj. 3

Sales reported on the income statement were $58,400. The accounts receivable balance decreased $2,100 over the year. Determine the amount of cash received from customers.

PE 16-7A
Cash payments for merchandise—direct method
obj. 3

Cost of merchandise sold reported on the income statement was $568,000. The accounts payable balance decreased $28,000, and the inventory balance decreased by $39,000 over the year. Determine the amount of cash paid for merchandise.

PE 16-7B
Cash payments for merchandise—direct method
obj. 3

Cost of merchandise sold reported on the income statement was $111,000. The accounts payable balance increased $5,700, and the inventory balance increased by $8,400 over the year. Determine the amount of cash paid for merchandise.

Exercises

EX 16-1
Cash flows from operating activities—net loss
obj. 1

REAL WORLD

On its income statement for a recent year, Northwest Airlines Corporation reported a net loss of $862 million from operations. On its statement of cash flows, it reported $271 million of cash flows from operating activities.
➤ Explain this apparent contradiction between the loss and the positive cash flows.

EX 16-2
Effect of transactions on cash flows
obj. 1
✓ *b. Cash receipt, $36,000*

State the effect (cash receipt or payment and amount) of each of the following transactions, considered individually, on cash flows:

a. Sold 5,000 shares of $30 par common stock for $90 per share.
b. Sold equipment with a book value of $42,500 for $36,000.
c. Purchased land for $250,000 cash.
d. Purchased 5,000 shares of $30 par common stock as treasury stock at $60 per share.
e. Sold a new issue of $100,000 of bonds at 98.
f. Paid dividends of $1.50 per share. There were 40,000 shares issued and 5,000 shares of treasury stock.

g. Retired $500,000 of bonds, on which there was $2,500 of unamortized discount, for $500,500.

h. Purchased a building by paying $40,000 cash and issuing a $90,000 mortgage note payable.

EX 16-3
Classifying cash flows
obj. 1

Identify the type of cash flow activity for each of the following events (operating, investing, or financing):

a. Issued preferred stock.
b. Net income.
c. Sold equipment.
d. Purchased treasury stock.
e. Purchased buildings.
f. Purchased patents.

g. Issued bonds.
h. Issued common stock.
i. Sold long-term investments.
j. Paid cash dividends.
k. Redeemed bonds.

EX 16-4
Cash flows from operating activities—indirect method
obj. 2

Indicate whether each of the following would be added to or deducted from net income in determining net cash flow from operating activities by the indirect method:

a. Gain on retirement of long-term debt
b. Increase in merchandise inventory
c. Amortization of patent
d. Decrease in accounts receivable
e. Depreciation of fixed assets
f. Decrease in prepaid expenses
g. Decrease in salaries payable

h. Increase in notes receivable due in 90 days from customers
i. Decrease in accounts payable
j. Loss on disposal of fixed assets
k. Increase in notes payable due in 90 days to vendors

EX 16-5
Cash flows from operating activities—indirect method
obj. 2

✓ *Net cash flow from operating activities, $111,700*

The net income reported on the income statement for the current year was $92,000. Depreciation recorded on store equipment for the year amounted to $18,600. Balances of the current asset and current liability accounts at the beginning and end of the year are as follows:

	End of Year	Beginning of Year
Cash	$46,700	$44,200
Accounts receivable (net)	32,300	31,100
Merchandise inventory	54,800	56,700
Prepaid expenses	4,000	3,500
Accounts payable (merchandise creditors)	46,000	42,900
Wages payable	21,400	23,600

Prepare the cash flows from operating activities section of the statement of cash flows, using the indirect method.

EX 16-6
Cash flows from operating activities—indirect method
objs. 1, 2

✓ *a. Cash flows from operating activities, $203,100*

The net income reported on the income statement for the current year was $165,300. Depreciation recorded on equipment and a building amounted to $46,700 for the year. Balances of the current asset and current liability accounts at the beginning and end of the year are as follows:

	End of Year	Beginning of Year
Cash	$ 42,000	$ 43,500
Accounts receivable (net)	65,400	69,200
Inventories	125,900	115,100
Prepaid expenses	5,800	6,400
Accounts payable (merchandise creditors)	61,400	64,200
Salaries payable	8,300	8,000

a. Prepare the cash flows from operating activities section of the statement of cash flows, using the indirect method.

b. ▬▬▶ If the direct method had been used, would the net cash flow from operating activities have been the same? Explain.

EX 16-7
Cash flows from operating activities—indirect method
objs. 1, 2

The income statement disclosed the following items for 2008:

Depreciation expense	$ 24,500
Gain on disposal of equipment	10,200
Net income	186,000

Balances of the current assets and current liability accounts changed between December 31, 2007, and December 31, 2008, as follows:

Accounts receivable	$4,400
Inventory	2,000*
Prepaid insurance	800*
Accounts payable	2,700*
Income taxes payable	900
Dividends payable	500

*Decrease

Prepare the cash flows from operating activities section of the statement of cash flows, using the indirect method.

EX 16-8
Determining cash payments to stockholders
obj. 2

The board of directors declared cash dividends totaling $120,000 during the current year. The comparative balance sheet indicates dividends payable of $35,000 at the beginning of the year and $30,000 at the end of the year. What was the amount of cash payments to stockholders during the year?

EX 16-9
Reporting changes in equipment on statement of cash flows
obj. 2

An analysis of the general ledger accounts indicates that office equipment, which cost $60,000 and on which accumulated depreciation totaled $15,000 on the date of sale, was sold for $41,000 during the year. Using this information, indicate the items to be reported on the statement of cash flows.

EX 16-10
Reporting changes in equipment on statement of cash flows
obj. 2

An analysis of the general ledger accounts indicates that delivery equipment, which cost $45,000 and on which accumulated depreciation totaled $32,000 on the date of sale, was sold for $15,000 during the year. Using this information, indicate the items to be reported on the statement of cash flows.

EX 16-11
Reporting land transactions on statement of cash flows
obj. 2

On the basis of the details of the following fixed asset account, indicate the items to be reported on the statement of cash flows:

ACCOUNT *Land* **ACCOUNT NO.**

Date		Item	Debit	Credit	Balance Debit	Balance Credit
2008						
Jan.	1	Balance			900,000	
Feb.	5	Purchased for cash	400,000		1,300,000	
Oct.	30	Sold for $365,000		250,000	1,050,000	

EX 16-12
Reporting stockholders' equity items on statement of cash flows
obj. 2

On the basis of the following stockholders' equity accounts, indicate the items, exclusive of net income, to be reported on the statement of cash flows. There were no unpaid dividends at either the beginning or the end of the year.

ACCOUNT *Common Stock, $10 par* **ACCOUNT NO.**

Date		Item	Debit	Credit	Balance Debit	Balance Credit
2008						
Jan.	1	Balance, 70,000 shares				700,000
Feb.	11	16,000 shares issued for cash		160,000		860,000
June	30	4,100-share stock dividend		41,000		901,000

ACCOUNT *Paid-In Capital in Excess of Par—Common Stock*					ACCOUNT NO.
2008					
Jan.	1	Balance			140,000
Feb.	11	16,000 shares issued for cash		336,000	476,000
June	30	Stock dividend		102,500	578,500

ACCOUNT *Retained Earnings*					ACCOUNT NO.
2008					
Jan.	1	Balance			1,000,000
June	30	Stock dividend	143,500		856,500
Dec.	30	Cash dividend	124,000		732,500
	31	Net income		630,000	1,362,500

EX 16-13
Reporting land acquisition for cash and mortgage note on statement of cash flows

obj. 2

On the basis of the details of the following fixed asset account, indicate the items to be reported on the statement of cash flows:

ACCOUNT *Land*					ACCOUNT NO.	
					Balance	
Date		Item	Debit	Credit	Debit	Credit
2008						
Jan.	1	Balance			160,000	
Feb.	10	Purchased for cash	326,000		486,000	
Nov.	20	Purchased with long-term mortgage note	400,000		886,000	

EX 16-14
Reporting issuance and retirement of long-term debt

obj. 2

On the basis of the details of the following bonds payable and related discount accounts, indicate the items to be reported in the financing section of the statement of cash flows, assuming no gain or loss on retiring the bonds:

ACCOUNT *Bonds Payable*					ACCOUNT NO.	
					Balance	
Date		Item	Debit	Credit	Debit	Credit
2008						
Jan.	1	Balance				150,000
Jan.	3	Retire bonds	70,000			80,000
July	30	Issue bonds		350,000		430,000

ACCOUNT *Discount on Bonds Payable*					ACCOUNT NO.	
2008						
Jan.	1	Balance			12,000	
Jan.	3	Retire bonds		5,600	6,400	
July	30	Issue bonds	20,000		26,400	
Dec.	31	Amortize discount		1,600	24,800	

EX 16-15
Determining net income from net cash flow from operating activities

obj. 2

Emerald Golf Inc. reported a net cash flow from operating activities of $86,700 on its statement of cash flows for the year ended December 31, 2008. The following information was reported in the cash flows from operating activities section of the statement of cash flows, using the indirect method:

Decrease in income taxes payable	$2,000
Decrease in inventories	5,600
Depreciation	8,500
Gain on sale of investments	3,400
Increase in accounts payable	1,200
Increase in prepaid expenses	700
Increase in accounts receivable	4,300

Determine the net income reported by Emerald Golf Inc. for the year ended December 31, 2008.

EX 16-16
Cash flows from operating activities—indirect method
obj. 2

✓ *Net cash flow used in operating activities, ($773)*

Selected data derived from the income statement and balance sheet of Jones Soda Co. for a recent year are as follows:

Income statement data (in thousands):	
Net earnings	$1,330
Depreciation expense	193
Stock-based compensation expense (noncash)	20
Balance sheet data (in thousands):	
Increase in accounts receivable	$1,328
Increase in inventory	1,550
Increase in prepaid expenses	124
Increase in accounts payable	686

a. Prepare the cash flows from operating activities section of the statement of cash flows using the indirect method for Jones Soda Co. for the year.
b. ⬤▬▬▷ Interpret your results in part (a).

EX 16-17
Statement of cash flows—indirect method
obj. 2

✓ *Net cash flow from operating activities, $50*

The comparative balance sheet of Alliance Structures Inc. for December 31, 2008 and 2007, is as follows:

	Dec. 31, 2008	Dec. 31, 2007
Assets		
Cash	$ 90	$ 23
Accounts receivable (net)	30	27
Inventories	24	21
Land	35	55
Equipment	32	22
Accumulated depreciation—equipment	(9)	(5)
Total	$202	$143
Liabilities and Stockholders' Equity		
Accounts payable (merchandise creditors)	$ 17	$ 10
Dividends payable	1	—
Common stock, $1 par	6	3
Paid-in capital in excess of par—common stock	30	10
Retained earnings	148	120
Total	$202	$143

The following additional information is taken from the records:

a. Land was sold for $15.
b. Equipment was acquired for cash.
c. There were no disposals of equipment during the year.
d. The common stock was issued for cash.
e. There was a $40 credit to Retained Earnings for net income.
f. There was a $12 debit to Retained Earnings for cash dividends declared.

Prepare a statement of cash flows, using the indirect method of presenting cash flows from operating activities.

EX 16-18
Statement of cash flows—indirect method
obj. 2

List the errors you find in the following statement of cash flows. The cash balance at the beginning of the year was $83,600. All other amounts are correct, except the cash balance at the end of the year.

Whole Life Nutrition Products Inc.
Statement of Cash Flows
For the Year Ended December 31, 2008

Cash flows from operating activities:			
Net income		$123,400	
Adjustments to reconcile net income to net cash flow from operating activities:			
Depreciation		35,000	
Gain on sale of investements		6,000	
Changes in current operating assets and liabilities:			
Increase in accounts receivable		9,500	
Increase in inventories		(12,300)	
Increase in accounts payable		(3,700)	
Decrease in accrued expenses		(900)	
Net cash flow from operating activities			$157,000
Cash flows from investing activities:			
Cash received from sale of investments		$ 85,000	
Less: Cash paid for purchase of land	$ 90,000		
Cash paid for purchase of equipment	150,100	240,100	
Net cash flow used for investing activities			(155,100)
Cash flows from financing activities:			
Cash received from sale of common stock		$107,000	
Cash paid for dividends		45,000	
Net cash flow provided by financing activities			152,000
Increase in cash			$153,900
Cash at the end of the year			105,300
Cash at the beginning of the year			$259,200

EX 16-19
Cash flows from operating activities—direct method

obj. 3

✓ a. $471,000

The cash flows from operating activities are reported by the direct method on the statement of cash flows. Determine the following:

a. If sales for the current year were $450,000 and accounts receivable decreased by $21,000 during the year, what was the amount of cash received from customers?

b. If income tax expense for the current year was $35,000 and income tax payable decreased by $3,100 during the year, what was the amount of cash payments for income tax?

EX 16-20
Cash paid for merchandise purchases

obj. 3

The cost of merchandise sold for Kohl's Corporation for a recent year was $8,639 million. The balance sheet showed the following current account balances (in millions):

	Balance, End of Year	Balance, Beginning of Year
Merchandise inventories	$2,238	$1,947
Accounts payable	830	705

Determine the amount of cash payments for merchandise.

EX 16-21
Determining selected amounts for cash flows from operating activities—direct method

obj. 3

✓ b. $59,900

Selected data taken from the accounting records of Extravaganza Inc. for the current year ended December 31 are as follows:

	Balance, December 31	Balance, January 1
Accrued expenses (operating expenses)	$ 4,300	$ 4,700
Accounts payable (merchandise creditors)	32,100	35,400
Inventories	59,500	64,700
Prepaid expenses	2,500	3,000

During the current year, the cost of merchandise sold was $345,000, and the operating expenses other than depreciation were $60,000. The direct method is used for presenting the cash flows from operating activities on the statement of cash flows.

Determine the amount reported on the statement of cash flows for (a) cash payments for merchandise and (b) cash payments for operating expenses.

EX 16-22
Cash flows from operating activities—direct method

obj. 3

✓ *Net cash flow from operating activities, $87,200*

The income statement of Country Kitchen Bakeries Inc. for the current year ended June 30 is as follows:

Sales		$456,000
Cost of merchandise sold		259,000
Gross profit		$197,000
Operating expenses:		
Depreciation expense	$35,000	
Other operating expenses	92,400	
Total operating expenses		127,400
Income before income tax		$ 69,600
Income tax expense		19,300
Net income		$ 50,300

Changes in the balances of selected accounts from the beginning to the end of the current year are as follows:

	Increase Decrease*
Accounts receivable (net)	$10,500*
Inventories	3,500
Prepaid expenses	3,400*
Accounts payable (merchandise creditors)	7,200*
Accrued expenses (operating expenses)	1,100
Income tax payable	2,400*

Prepare the cash flows from operating activities section of the statement of cash flows, using the direct method.

EX 16-23
Cash flows from operating activities—direct method

obj. 3

✓ *Net cash flow from operating activities, $47,600*

The income statement for Wholly Bagel Company for the current year ended June 30 and balances of selected accounts at the beginning and the end of the year are as follows:

Sales		$184,000
Cost of merchandise sold		67,000
Gross profit		$117,000
Operating expenses:		
Depreciation expense	$14,500	
Other operating expenses	49,000	
Total operating expenses		63,500
Income before income tax		$ 53,500
Income tax expense		15,400
Net income		$ 38,100

	End of Year	Beginning of Year
Accounts receivable (net)	$14,800	$12,900
Inventories	38,100	33,100
Prepaid expenses	6,000	6,600
Accounts payable (merchandise creditors)	27,900	25,900
Accrued expenses (operating expenses)	7,900	8,600
Income tax payable	1,500	1,500

Prepare the cash flows from operating activities section of the statement of cash flows, using the direct method.

EX 16-24
Free cash flow

Mediterranean Tile Company has cash flows from operating activities of $120,000. Cash flows used for investments in property, plant, and equipment totaled $45,000, of which 60% of this investment was used to replace existing capacity.

Determine the free cash flow for Mediterranean Tile Company.

EX 16-25
Free cash flow

The financial statements for Williams-Sonoma, Inc., are provided in Appendix D at the end of the text.

Determine the free cash flow for the year ended January 29, 2006. Assume that 70% of purchases of property and equipment were for new store openings, and the remaining was for remodeling and updating existing stores.

Problems Series A

PR 16-1A
Statement of cash flows—indirect method

obj. 2

✓ *Net cash flow from operating activities, $72,200*

The comparative balance sheet of Oak and Tile Flooring Co. for June 30, 2008 and 2007, is as follows:

	June 30, 2008	June 30, 2007
Assets		
Cash	$ 34,700	$ 23,500
Accounts receivable (net)	101,600	92,300
Inventories	146,300	142,100
Investments	0	50,000
Land	145,000	0
Equipment	215,000	175,500
Accumulated depreciation	(48,600)	(41,300)
	$594,000	$442,100
Liabilities and Stockholders' Equity		
Accounts payable (merchandise creditors)	$100,900	$ 95,200
Accrued expenses (operating expenses)	15,000	13,200
Dividends payable	12,500	10,000
Common stock, $1 par	56,000	50,000
Paid-in capital in excess of par—common stock	220,000	100,000
Retained earnings	189,600	173,700
	$594,000	$442,100

The following additional information was taken from the records of Oak and Tile Flooring Co.:

a. Equipment and land were acquired for cash.
b. There were no disposals of equipment during the year.
c. The investments were sold for $45,000 cash.
d. The common stock was issued for cash.
e. There was a $65,900 credit to Retained Earnings for net income.
f. There was a $50,000 debit to Retained Earnings for cash dividends declared.

Instructions
Prepare a statement of cash flows, using the indirect method of presenting cash flows from operating activities.

PR 16-2A
Statement of cash flows—indirect method

obj. 2

The comparative balance sheet of Portable Luggage Company at December 31, 2008 and 2007, is as follows:

✓ *Net cash flow from operating activities, $221,700*

	Dec. 31, 2008	Dec. 31, 2007
Assets		
Cash	$ 175,900	$ 143,200
Accounts receivable (net)	264,100	235,000
Inventories	352,300	405,800
Prepaid expenses	12,500	10,000
Land	120,000	120,000
Buildings	680,000	450,000
Accumulated depreciation—buildings	(185,000)	(164,500)
Machinery and equipment	310,000	310,000
Accumulated depreciation—machinery & equipment	(85,000)	(76,000)
Patents	42,500	48,000
	$1,687,300	$1,481,500
Liabilities and Stockholders' Equity		
Accounts payable (merchandise creditors)	$ 332,300	$ 367,900
Dividends payable	13,000	10,000
Salaries payable	30,200	34,600
Mortgage note payable, due 2015	90,000	—
Bonds payable	—	154,000
Common stock, $1 par	24,000	20,000
Paid-in capital in excess of par—common stock	200,000	50,000
Retained earnings	997,800	845,000
	$1,687,300	$1,481,500

An examination of the income statement and the accounting records revealed the following additional information applicable to 2008:

a. Net income, $204,800.
b. Depreciation expense reported on the income statement: buildings, $20,500; machinery and equipment, $9,000.
c. Patent amortization reported on the income statement, $5,500.
d. A building was constructed for $230,000.
e. A mortgage note for $90,000 was issued for cash.
f. 4,000 shares of common stock were issued at $38.50 in exchange for the bonds payable.
g. Cash dividends declared, $52,000.

Instructions

Prepare a statement of cash flows, using the indirect method of presenting cash flows from operating activities.

PR 16-3A
Statement of cash flows—indirect method

obj. 2

✓ *Net cash flow from operating activities, $4,100*

The comparative balance sheet of Reston Supply Co. at December 31, 2008 and 2007, is as follows:

	Dec. 31, 2008	Dec. 31, 2007
Assets		
Cash	$ 45,500	$ 51,200
Accounts receivable (net)	106,700	92,400
Inventories	139,200	131,200
Prepaid expenses	2,800	4,000
Land	150,000	210,000
Buildings	300,000	150,000
Accumulated depreciation—buildings	(60,200)	(55,500)
Equipment	100,100	80,300
Accumulated depreciation—equipment	(20,200)	(24,500)
	$763,900	$639,100
Liabilities and Stockholders' Equity		
Accounts payable (merchandise creditors)	$ 90,000	$ 95,600
Income tax payable	4,000	3,200
Bonds payable	50,000	0
Common stock, $1 par	33,000	30,000
Paid-in capital in excess of par—common stock	180,000	120,000
Retained earnings	406,900	390,300
	$763,900	$639,100

The noncurrent asset, noncurrent liability, and stockholders' equity accounts for 2008 are as follows:

ACCOUNT *Land*   ACCOUNT NO.

Date		Item	Debit	Credit	Balance Debit	Balance Credit
2008						
Jan.	1	Balance			210,000	
Apr.	20	Realized $69,000 cash from sale		60,000	150,000	

ACCOUNT *Buildings*   ACCOUNT NO.

Date		Item	Debit	Credit	Balance Debit	Balance Credit
2008						
Jan.	1	Balance			150,000	
Apr.	20	Acquired for cash	150,000		300,000	

ACCOUNT *Accumulated Depreciation—Buildings*   ACCOUNT NO.

Date		Item	Debit	Credit	Balance Debit	Balance Credit
2008						
Jan.	1	Balance				55,500
Dec.	31	Depreciation for year		4,700		60,200

ACCOUNT *Equipment*   ACCOUNT NO.

Date		Item	Debit	Credit	Balance Debit	Balance Credit
2008						
Jan.	1	Balance			80,300	
	26	Discarded, no salvage		10,000	70,300	
Aug.	11	Purchased for cash	29,800		100,100	

ACCOUNT *Accumulated Depreciation—Equipment*   ACCOUNT NO.

Date		Item	Debit	Credit	Balance Debit	Balance Credit
2008						
Jan.	1	Balance				24,500
	26	Equipment discarded	10,000			14,500
Dec.	31	Depreciation for year		5,700		20,200

ACCOUNT *Bonds Payable*   ACCOUNT NO.

Date		Item	Debit	Credit	Balance Debit	Balance Credit
2008						
May	1	Issued 20-year bonds		50,000		50,000

ACCOUNT *Common Stock, $1 par*   ACCOUNT NO.

Date		Item	Debit	Credit	Balance Debit	Balance Credit
2008						
Jan.	1	Balance				30,000
Dec.	7	Issued 3,000 shares of common stock for $21 per share		3,000		33,000

ACCOUNT *Paid-In Capital in Excess of Par—Common Stock*   ACCOUNT NO.

Date		Item	Debit	Credit	Balance Debit	Balance Credit
2008						
Jan.	1	Balance				120,000
Dec.	7	Issued 3,000 shares of common stock for $21 per share		60,000		180,000

ACCOUNT *Retained Earnings*   ACCOUNT NO.

Date		Item	Debit	Credit	Balance Debit	Balance Credit
2008						
Jan.	1	Balance				390,300
Dec.	31	Net income		28,600		418,900
	31	Cash dividends	12,000			406,900

Instructions

Prepare a statement of cash flows, using the indirect method of presenting cash flows from operating activities.

PR 16-4A
Statement of cash flows—direct method

obj. 3

✓ *Net cash flow from operating activities, $107,900*

The comparative balance sheet of Green Earth Lawn and Garden Inc. for December 31, 2008 and 2009, is as follows:

	Dec. 31, 2009	Dec. 31, 2008
Assets		
Cash	$ 137,900	$142,300
Accounts receivable (net)	206,800	190,500
Inventories	290,500	284,100
Investments	0	90,000
Land	200,000	0
Equipment	255,000	205,000
Accumulated depreciation	(100,300)	(76,700)
	$ 989,900	$835,200
Liabilities and Stockholders' Equity		
Accounts payable (merchandise creditors)	$ 224,900	$201,400
Accrued expenses (operating expenses)	14,100	16,500
Dividends payable	21,000	19,000
Common stock, $1 par	10,000	8,000
Paid-in capital in excess of par—common stock	200,000	100,000
Retained earnings	519,900	490,300
	$ 989,900	$835,200

The income statement for the year ended December 31, 2009, is as follows:

Sales		$940,000
Cost of merchandise sold		489,300
Gross profit		$450,700
Operating expenses:		
Depreciation expense	$ 23,600	
Other operating expenses	278,900	
Total operating expenses		302,500
Operating income		$148,200
Other income:		
Gain on sale of investments		32,000
Income before income tax		$180,200
Income tax expense		62,300
Net income		$117,900

The following additional information was taken from the records:

a. Equipment and land were acquired for cash.
b. There were no disposals of equipment during the year.
c. The investments were sold for $122,000 cash.
d. The common stock was issued for cash.
e. There was a $88,300 debit to Retained Earnings for cash dividends declared.

Instructions
Prepare a statement of cash flows, using the direct method of presenting cash flows from operating activities.

PR 16-5A
Statement of cash flows—direct method applied to PR 16-1A

obj. 3

✓ *Net cash flow from operating activities, $72,200*

The comparative balance sheet of Oak and Tile Flooring Co. for June 30, 2008 and 2007, is as follows:

	June 30, 2008	June 30, 2007
Assets		
Cash	$ 34,700	$ 23,500
Accounts receivable (net)	101,600	92,300
Inventories	146,300	142,100
Investments	0	50,000
Land	145,000	0
Equipment	215,000	175,500
Accumulated depreciation	(48,600)	(41,300)
	$594,000	$442,100

Liabilities and Stockholders' Equity

Accounts payable (merchandise creditors)	$100,900	$ 95,200
Accrued expenses (operating expenses)	15,000	13,200
Dividends payable	12,500	10,000
Common stock, $1 par	56,000	50,000
Paid-in capital in excess of par—common stock	220,000	100,000
Retained earnings	189,600	173,700
	$594,000	$442,100

The income statement for the year ended June 30, 2008, is as follows:

Sales		$963,400
Cost of merchandise sold		662,100
Gross profit		$301,300
Operating expenses:		
Depreciation expense	$ 7,300	
Other operating expenses	195,000	
Total operating expenses		202,300
Operating income		$ 99,000
Other expenses:		
Loss on sale of investments		(5,000)
Income before income tax		$ 94,000
Income tax expense		28,100
Net income		$ 65,900

The following additional information was taken from the records:

a. Equipment and land were acquired for cash.
b. There were no disposals of equipment during the year.
c. The investments were sold for $45,000 cash.
d. The common stock was issued for cash.
e. There was a $50,000 debit to Retained Earnings for cash dividends declared.

Instructions
Prepare a statement of cash flows, using the direct method of presenting cash flows from operating activities.

Problems Series B

PR 16-1B
Statement of cash flows—indirect method
obj. 2

✓ *Net cash flow from operating activities, $61,900*

The comparative balance sheet of Gold Medal Sporting Goods Inc. for December 31, 2008 and 2007, is shown as follows:

	Dec. 31, 2008	Dec. 31, 2007
Assets		
Cash	$ 391,100	$ 366,200
Accounts receivable (net)	142,400	130,600
Inventories	401,100	385,700
Investments	0	150,000
Land	205,000	0
Equipment	440,700	345,700
Accumulated depreciation—equipment	(104,000)	(92,500)
	$1,476,300	$1,285,700
Liabilities and Stockholders' Equity		
Accounts payable (merchandise creditors)	$ 267,800	$ 253,100
Accrued expenses (operating expenses)	26,400	32,900
Dividends payable	15,000	12,000
Common stock, $10 par	80,000	60,000
Paid-in capital in excess of par—common stock	300,000	175,000
Retained earnings	787,100	752,700
	$1,476,300	$1,285,700

The following additional information was taken from the records:

a. The investments were sold for $175,000 cash.
b. Equipment and land were acquired for cash.
c. There were no disposals of equipment during the year.
d. The common stock was issued for cash.
e. There was a $94,400 credit to Retained Earnings for net income.
f. There was a $60,000 debit to Retained Earnings for cash dividends declared.

Instructions

Prepare a statement of cash flows, using the indirect method of presenting cash flows from operating activities.

PR 16-2B

Statement of cash flows—indirect method

obj. **2**

✓ *Net cash flow from operating activities, $108,500*

The comparative balance sheet of Air Glide Athletic Apparel Co. at December 31, 2008 and 2007, is as follows:

	Dec. 31, 2008	Dec. 31, 2007
Assets		
Cash	$ 45,800	$ 56,200
Accounts receivable (net)	70,200	75,600
Merchandise inventory	100,500	93,500
Prepaid expenses	4,200	3,000
Equipment	204,700	167,800
Accumulated depreciation—equipment	(53,400)	(41,300)
	$372,000	$354,800
Liabilities and Stockholders' Equity		
Accounts payable (merchandise creditors)	$ 78,200	$ 74,300
Mortgage note payable	0	105,000
Common stock, $1 par	15,000	10,000
Paid-in capital in excess of par—common stock	180,000	100,000
Retained earnings	98,800	65,500
	$372,000	$354,800

Additional data obtained from the income statement and from an examination of the accounts in the ledger for 2008 are as follows:

a. Net income, $81,300.
b. Depreciation reported on the income statement, $26,100.
c. Equipment was purchased at a cost of $50,900, and fully depreciated equipment costing $14,000 was discarded, with no salvage realized.
d. The mortgage note payable was not due until 2011, but the terms permitted earlier payment without penalty.
e. 5,000 shares of common stock were issued at $17 for cash.
f. Cash dividends declared and paid, $48,000.

Instructions

Prepare a statement of cash flows, using the indirect method of presenting cash flows from operating activities.

PR 16-3B

Statement of cash flows—indirect method

obj. **2**

✓ *Net cash flow from operating activities, ($68,400)*

The comparative balance sheet of Rise N' Shine Juice Co. at December 31, 2008 and 2007, is as follows:

	Dec. 31, 2008	Dec. 31, 2007
Assets		
Cash	$ 392,300	$ 412,300
Accounts receivable (net)	354,200	325,600
Inventories	542,100	497,000
Prepaid expenses	12,500	15,000
Land	135,000	205,000
Buildings	625,000	385,000
Accumulated depreciation—buildings	(174,600)	(163,400)
Equipment	218,900	194,300
Accumulated depreciation—equipment	(60,400)	(67,800)
	$2,045,000	$1,803,000

Liabilities and Stockholders' Equity

Accounts payable (merchandise creditors)	$ 394,200	$ 409,500
Bonds payable	115,000	0
Common stock, $1 par	58,000	50,000
Paid-in capital in excess of par—common stock	400,000	240,000
Retained earnings	1,077,800	1,103,500
	$2,045,000	$1,803,000

The noncurrent asset, noncurrent liability, and stockholders' equity accounts for 2008 are as follows:

ACCOUNT *Land*   **ACCOUNT NO.**

					Balance	
Date		Item	Debit	Credit	Debit	Credit
2008						
Jan.	1	Balance			205,000	
Apr.	20	Realized $64,000 cash from sale		70,000	135,000	

ACCOUNT *Buildings*   **ACCOUNT NO.**

					Balance	
2008						
Jan.	1	Balance			385,000	
Apr.	20	Acquired for cash	240,000		625,000	

ACCOUNT *Accumulated Depreciation—Buildings*   **ACCOUNT NO.**

					Balance	
2008						
Jan.	1	Balance				163,400
Dec.	31	Depreciation for year		11,200		174,600

ACCOUNT *Equipment*   **ACCOUNT NO.**

					Balance	
2008						
Jan.	1	Balance			194,300	
	26	Discarded, no salvage		20,000	174,300	
Aug.	11	Purchased for cash	44,600		218,900	

ACCOUNT *Accumulated Depreciation—Equipment*   **ACCOUNT NO.**

					Balance	
2008						
Jan.	1	Balance				67,800
	26	Equipment discarded	20,000			47,800
Dec.	31	Depreciation for year		12,600		60,400

ACCOUNT *Bonds Payable*   **ACCOUNT NO.**

					Balance	
2008						
May	1	Issued 20-year bonds		115,000		115,000

ACCOUNT *Common Stock, $1 Par*   **ACCOUNT NO.**

					Balance	
2008						
Jan.	1	Balance				50,000
Dec.	7	Issued 8,000 shares of common stock for $21 per share		8,000		58,000

ACCOUNT *Paid-In Capital in Excess of Par—Common Stock*   **ACCOUNT NO.**

					Balance	
2008						
Jan.	1	Balance				240,000
Dec.	7	Issued 8,000 shares of common stock for $21 per share		160,000		400,000

(continued)

ACCOUNT Retained Earnings					ACCOUNT NO.		
						Balance	
Date		Item	Debit	Credit	Debit	Credit	
2008							
Jan.	1	Balance				1,103,500	
Dec.	31	Net loss	11,700			1,091,800	
	31	Cash dividends	14,000			1,077,800	

Instructions

Prepare a statement of cash flows, using the indirect method of presenting cash flows from operating activities.

PR 16-4B
Statement of cash flows—direct method

obj. 3

✓ *Net cash flow from operating activities, $193,600*

The comparative balance sheet of Home and Hearth Inc. for December 31, 2009 and 2008, is as follows:

	Dec. 31, 2009	Dec. 31, 2008
Assets		
Cash	$ 402,100	$ 424,600
Accounts receivable (net)	354,200	342,100
Inventories	631,900	614,200
Investments	0	150,000
Land	325,000	0
Equipment	550,000	425,000
Accumulated depreciation	(152,700)	(125,300)
	$2,110,500	$1,830,600
Liabilities and Stockholders' Equity		
Accounts payable (merchandise creditors)	$ 482,400	$ 467,800
Accrued expenses (operating expenses)	39,600	44,200
Dividends payable	5,500	4,000
Common stock, $1 par	24,000	20,000
Paid-in capital in excess of par—common stock	260,000	120,000
Retained earnings	1,299,000	1,174,600
	$2,110,500	$1,830,600

The income statement for the year ended December 31, 2009, is as follows:

Sales		$3,745,700
Cost of merchandise sold		1,532,500
Gross profit		$2,213,200
Operating expenses:		
Depreciation expense	$ 27,400	
Other operating expenses	1,936,800	
Total operating expenses		1,964,200
Operating income		$ 249,000
Other expense:		
Loss on sale of investments		(40,000)
Income before income tax		$ 209,000
Income tax expense		63,000
Net income		$ 146,000

The following additional information was taken from the records:

a. Equipment and land were acquired for cash.
b. There were no disposals of equipment during the year.
c. The investments were sold for $110,000 cash.
d. The common stock was issued for cash.
e. There was a $21,600 debit to Retained Earnings for cash dividends declared.

Instructions
Prepare a statement of cash flows, using the direct method of presenting cash flows from operating activities.

PR 16-5B
Statement of cash flows—direct method applied to PR 16-1B

obj. 3

✓ *Net cash flow from operating activities, $61,900*

The comparative balance sheet of Gold Medal Sporting Goods Inc. for December 31, 2008 and 2007, is as follows:

	Dec. 31, 2008	Dec. 31, 2007
Assets		
Cash	$ 391,100	$ 366,200
Accounts receivable (net)	142,400	130,600
Inventories	401,100	385,700
Investments	0	150,000
Land	205,000	0
Equipment	440,700	345,700
Accumulated depreciation—equipment	(104,000)	(92,500)
	$1,476,300	$1,285,700
Liabilities and Stockholders' Equity		
Accounts payable (merchandise creditors)	$ 267,800	$ 253,100
Accrued expenses (operating expenses)	26,400	32,900
Dividends payable	15,000	12,000
Common stock, $10 par	80,000	60,000
Paid-in capital in excess of par—common stock	300,000	175,000
Retained earnings	787,100	752,700
	$1,476,300	$1,285,700

The income statement for the year ended December 31, 2008, is as follows:

Sales		$1,632,500
Cost of merchandise sold		908,300
Gross profit		$ 724,200
Operating expenses:		
Depreciation expense	$ 11,500	
Other operating expenses	609,000	
Total operating expenses		620,500
Operating income		$ 103,700
Other income:		
Gain on sale of investments		25,000
Income before income tax		$ 128,700
Income tax expense		34,300
Net income		$ 94,400

The following additional information was taken from the records:

a. The investments were sold for $175,000 cash.
b. Equipment and land were acquired for cash.
c. There were no disposals of equipment during the year.
d. The common stock was issued for cash.
e. There was a $60,000 debit to Retained Earnings for cash dividends declared.

Instructions
Prepare a statement of cash flows, using the direct method of presenting cash flows from operating activities.

Special Activities

SA 16-1
Ethics and professional conduct in business

ETHICS

Linda Stern, president of Venician Fashions Inc., believes that reporting operating cash flow per share on the income statement would be a useful addition to the company's just completed financial statements. The following discussion took place between Linda Stern and Venician Fashions' controller, Ben Trotter, in January, after the close of the fiscal year.

Linda: I have been reviewing our financial statements for the last year. I am disappointed that our net income per share has dropped by 10% from last year. This is not going to look good to our shareholders. Isn't there anything we can do about this?

Ben: What do you mean? The past is the past, and the numbers are in. There isn't much that can be done about it. Our financial statements were prepared according to generally accepted accounting principles, and I don't see much leeway for significant change at this point.

Linda: No, no. I'm not suggesting that we "cook the books." But look at the cash flow from operating activities on the statement of cash flows. The cash flow from operating activities has increased by 20%. This is very good news—and, I might add, useful information. The higher cash flow from operating activities will give our creditors comfort.

Ben: Well, the cash flow from operating activities is on the statement of cash flows, so I guess users will be able to see the improved cash flow figures there.

Linda: This is true, but somehow I feel that this information should be given a much higher profile. I don't like this information being "buried" in the statement of cash flows. You know as well as I do that many users will focus on the income statement. Therefore, I think we ought to include an operating cash flow per share number on the face of the income statement—someplace under the earnings per share number. In this way users will get the complete picture of our operating performance. Yes, our earnings per share dropped this year, but our cash flow from operating activities improved! And all the information is in one place where users can see and compare the figures. What do you think?

Ben: I've never really thought about it like that before. I guess we could put the operating cash flow per share on the income statement, under the earnings per share. Users would really benefit from this disclosure. Thanks for the idea—I'll start working on it.

Linda: Glad to be of service.

How would you interpret this situation? Is Ben behaving in an ethical and professional manner?

SA 16-2
Using the statement of cash flows

You are considering an investment in a new start-up company, Aspen Technologies Inc., an Internet service provider. A review of the company's financial statements reveals a negative retained earnings. In addition, it appears as though the company has been running a negative cash flow from operating activities since the company's inception.

How is the company staying in business under these circumstances? Could this be a good investment?

SA 16-3
Analysis of cash flow from operations

The Retailing Division of Bargain Buyer Inc. provided the following information on its cash flow from operations:

Net income	$ 450,000
Increase in accounts receivable	(540,000)
Increase in inventory	(600,000)
Decrease in accounts payable	(90,000)
Depreciation	100,000
Cash flow from operating activities	$(680,000)

The manager of the Retailing Division provided the accompanying memo with this report:

From: Senior Vice President, Retailing Division

I am pleased to report that we had earnings of $450,000 over the last period. This resulted in a return on invested capital of 10%, which is near our targets for this division. I have been aggressive in building the revenue volume in the division. As a result, I am happy to report that we have increased the number of new credit card customers as a result of an aggressive marketing campaign. In addition, we have found some excellent merchandise opportunities. Some of our suppliers have made some of their apparel merchandise available at a deep discount. We have purchased as much of these goods as possible in order to improve profitability. I'm also happy to report that our vendor payment problems have improved. We are nearly caught up on our over-due payables balances.

➤ Comment on the senior vice president's memo in light of the cash flow information.

SA 16-4
Analysis of statement of cash flows

Jabari Daniels is the president and majority shareholder of Cabinet Craft Inc., a small retail store chain. Recently, Daniels submitted a loan application for Cabinet Craft Inc. to Montvale National Bank. It called for a $200,000, 9%, 10-year loan to help finance the construction of a building and the purchase of store equipment, costing a total of $250,000, to enable Cabinet Craft Inc. to open a store in Montvale. Land for this purpose was acquired last year. The bank's loan officer requested a statement of cash flows in addition to the most recent income statement, balance sheet, and retained earnings statement that Daniels had submitted with the loan application.

As a close family friend, Daniels asked you to prepare a statement of cash flows. From the records provided, you prepared the following statement.

Cabinet Craft Inc.
Statement of Cash Flows
For the Year Ended December 31, 2008

Cash flows from operating activities:		
Net income		$ 94,500
Adjustments to reconcile net income to net cash flow from operating activities:		
Depreciation		26,000
Gain on sale of investments		(8,000)
Changes in current operating assets and liabilities:		
Decrease in accounts receivable		5,000
Increase in inventories		(12,000)
Increase in accounts payable		8,500
Decrease in accrued expenses		(1,200)
Net cash flow from operating activities		$112,800
Cash flows from investing activities:		
Cash received from investments sold	$ 50,000	
Less cash paid for purchase of store equipment	(30,000)	
Net cash flow provided by investing activities		20,000
Cash flows from financing activities:		
Cash paid for dividends	$ 35,000	
Net cash flow used for financing activities		(35,000)
Increase in cash		$ 97,800
Cash at the beginning of the year		34,800
Cash at the end of the year		$132,600

Schedule of Noncash Financing and Investing Activities:		
Issued common stock for land		$ 75,000

After reviewing the statement, Daniels telephoned you and commented, "Are you sure this statement is right?" Daniels then raised the following questions:

1. "How can depreciation be a cash flow?"
2. "Issuing common stock for the land is listed in a separate schedule. This transaction has nothing to do with cash! Shouldn't this transaction be eliminated from the statement?"

(continued)

3. "How can the gain on sale of investments be a deduction from net income in determining the cash flow from operating activities?"
4. "Why does the bank need this statement anyway? They can compute the increase in cash from the balance sheets for the last two years."

After jotting down Daniels' questions, you assured him that this statement was "right." However, to alleviate Daniels' concern, you arranged a meeting for the following day.

a. ◖▬▬▶ How would you respond to each of Daniels' questions?
b. ◖▬▬▶ Do you think that the statement of cash flows enhances the chances of Cabinet Craft Inc. receiving the loan? Discuss.

SA 16-5
Statement of cash flows

Group Project

Internet Project

This activity will require two teams to retrieve cash flow statement information from the Internet. One team is to obtain the most recent year's statement of cash flows for Johnson & Johnson, and the other team the most recent year's statement of cash flows for AMR Corp. (American Airlines).

The statement of cash flows is included as part of the annual report information that is a required disclosure to the Securities and Exchange Commission (SEC). The SEC, in turn, provides this information online through its EDGAR service. EDGAR (Electronic Data Gathering, Analysis, and Retrieval) is the electronic archive of financial statements filed with the Securities and Exchange Commission (SEC). SEC documents can be retrieved using the EdgarScan service from PricewaterhouseCoopers at **http://edgarscan.pwcglobal.com**.

To obtain annual report information, type in a company name in the appropriate space. EdgarScan will list the reports available to you for the company you've selected. Select the most recent annual report filing, identified as a 10-K or 10-K405. EdgarScan provides an outline of the report, including the separate financial statements. You can double-click the income statement and balance sheet for the selected company into an Excel™ spreadsheet for further analysis.

As a group, compare the two statements of cash flows.

a. How are Johnson & Johnson and AMR similar or different regarding cash flows?
b. Compute and compare the free cash flow for each company, assuming additions to property, plant, and equipment replace current capacity.

Answers to Self-Examination Questions

1. **D**   Cash flows from operating activities affect transactions that enter into the determination of net income, such as the receipt of cash from customers on account (answer D). Receipts of cash from the sale of stock (answer A) and the sale of bonds (answer B) and payments of cash for dividends (answer C) are cash flows from financing activities.

2. **A**   Cash flows from investing activities include receipts from the sale of noncurrent assets, such as equipment (answer A), and payments to acquire noncurrent assets. Receipts of cash from the sale of stock (answer B) and payments of cash for dividends (answer C) and to acquire treasury stock (answer D) are cash flows from financing activities.

3. **C**   Payment of cash for dividends (answer C) is an example of a financing activity. The receipt of cash from customers on account (answer A) is an operating activity. The receipt of cash from the sale of equipment (answer B) is an investing activity. The payment of cash to acquire land (answer D) is an example of an investing activity.

4. **D**   The indirect method (answer D) reports cash flows from operating activities by beginning with net income and adjusting it for revenues and expenses not involving the receipt or payment of cash.

5. **C**   The cash flows from operating activities section of the statement of cash flows would report net cash flow from operating activities of $65,500, determined as follows:

Cash flows from operating activities:	
Net income	$ 55,000
Adjustments to reconcile net income to net cash flow from operating activities:	
Depreciation	22,000
Changes in current operating assets and liabilities:	
Increase in accounts receivable	(10,000)
Decrease in inventories	5,000
Decrease in prepaid expenses	500
Decrease in accounts payable	(7,000)
Net cash flow from operating activities	$65,500

Financial Statement Analysis

© CHITOSE SUZUKI/ASSOCIATED PRESS

objectives

After studying this chapter, you should be able to:

1 *List basic financial statement analytical procedures.*

2 *Apply financial statement analysis to assess the solvency of a business.*

3 *Apply financial statement analysis to assess the profitability of a business.*

4 *Describe the contents of corporate annual reports.*

Williams-Sonoma, Inc.

During a recent year, Williams-Sonoma, Inc., reported revenues of over $3.1 billion and net income of over $190 million. The common stock of Williams-Sonoma is traded on the New York Stock Exchange (symbol WSM) and closed on February 17, 2006, at $39.80 per share. Based upon current market values, Williams-Sonoma is worth almost $4.6 billion. Do you wish you could have invested in Williams-Sonoma 15 years ago?

Williams-Sonoma is a specialty retailer in the United States, well-known for its home furnishings. The company began in 1956, when owner Chuck Williams opened a store selling restaurant-quality cookware from France in Sonoma, California. The business expanded quickly, and Williams soon moved his store to Sutter Street in San Francisco. From there, the company expanded into catalogs, the Internet, and additional brands, such as Pottery Barn.

The success of Williams-Sonoma shows that reputation and the popularity of a company's product are important indicators of success. However, these are not the *only* factors that determine a company's success. A business needs to combine product offerings with proper financial, marketing, and sales

strategies to be successful. Clearly, Williams-Sonoma has accomplished this. If you had invested in its common stock back in 1990, the stock price would have risen from $3 per share to nearly $40 per share today.

How, then, should you select companies in which to invest? Like any significant purchase, you should do some research to guide your investment decision. If you were buying a car, for example, you might go to Edmunds.com to obtain reviews, ratings, prices, specifications, options, and fuel economy across a number of vehicle alternatives. In deciding whether to invest in a company, you can use financial analysis to gain insight into a company's past performance and future prospects. This chapter describes and illustrates common financial data that can be analyzed to assist you in making investment decisions such as whether or not to invest in Williams-Sonoma stock. The contents of corporate annual reports are also discussed.

Source: Walter Nicholls, "The 90-Year-Old Pioneer Behind Williams-Sonoma," *The Seattle Times,* October 5, 2005.

Basic Analytical Procedures

objective 1

List basic financial statement analytical procedures.

The basic financial statements provide much of the information users need to make economic decisions about businesses. In this chapter, we illustrate how to perform a complete analysis of these statements by integrating individual analytical measures.

Analytical procedures may be used to compare items on a current statement with related items on earlier statements. For example, cash of $150,000 on the current balance sheet may be compared with cash of $100,000 on the balance sheet of a year earlier. The current year's cash may be expressed as 1.5 or 150% of the earlier amount, or as an increase of 50% or $50,000.

Analytical procedures are also widely used to examine relationships within a financial statement. To illustrate, assume that cash of $50,000 and inventories of $250,000 are included in the total assets of $1,000,000 on a balance sheet. In relative terms, the cash balance is 5% of the total assets, and the inventories are 25% of the total assets.

In this chapter, we will illustrate a number of common analytical measures. The measures are not ends in themselves. They are only guides in evaluating financial and operating data. Many other factors, such as trends in the industry and general economic conditions, should also be considered.

HORIZONTAL ANALYSIS

The percentage analysis of increases and decreases in related items in comparative financial statements is called **horizontal analysis**. The amount of each item on the most recent statement is compared with the related item on one or more earlier statements. The amount of increase or decrease in the item is listed, along with the percent of increase or decrease.

Horizontal analysis may compare two statements. In this case, the earlier statement is used as the base. Horizontal analysis may also compare three or more statements. In this case, the earliest date or period may be used as the base for comparing all later dates or periods. Alternatively, each statement may be compared to the immediately preceding statement. Exhibit 1 is a condensed comparative balance sheet for two years for Lincoln Company, with horizontal analysis.

EXHIBIT 1

Comparative Balance Sheet—Horizontal Analysis

Lincoln Company
Comparative Balance Sheet
December 31, 2008 and 2007

	2008	2007	Increase (Decrease) Amount	Percent
Assets				
Current assets	$ 550,000	$ 533,000	$ 17,000	3.2%
Long-term investments	95,000	177,500	(82,500)	(46.5%)
Property, plant, and				
equipment (net)	444,500	470,000	(25,500)	(5.4%)
Intangible assets	50,000	50,000	—	—
Total assets	$1,139,500	$1,230,500	$ (91,000)	(7.4%)
Liabilities				
Current liabilities	$ 210,000	$ 243,000	$ (33,000)	(13.6%)
Long-term liabilities	100,000	200,000	(100,000)	(50.0%)
Total liabilities	$ 310,000	$ 443,000	$(133,000)	(30.0%)
Stockholders' Equity				
Preferred 6% stock, $100 par . . .	$ 150,000	$ 150,000	—	—
Common stock, $10 par	500,000	500,000	—	—
Retained earnings	179,500	137,500	$ 42,000	30.5%
Total stockholders' equity	$ 829,500	$ 787,500	$ 42,000	5.3%
Total liabilities and				
stockholders' equity	$1,139,500	$1,230,500	$ (91,000)	(7.4%)

We cannot fully evaluate the significance of the various increases and decreases in the items shown in Exhibit 1 without additional information. Although total assets at the end of 2008 were $91,000 (7.4%) less than at the beginning of the year, liabilities were reduced by $133,000 (30%), and stockholders' equity increased $42,000 (5.3%). It appears that the reduction of $100,000 in long-term liabilities was achieved mostly through the sale of long-term investments.

The balance sheet in Exhibit 1 may be expanded to include the details of the various categories of assets and liabilities. An alternative is to present the details in separate schedules. Exhibit 2 is a supporting schedule with horizontal analysis.

The decrease in accounts receivable may be due to changes in credit terms or improved collection policies. Likewise, a decrease in inventories during a period of increased sales may indicate an improvement in the management of inventories.

EXHIBIT 2

Comparative Schedule
of Current Assets—
Horizontal Analysis

Lincoln Company
Comparative Schedule of Current Assets
December 31, 2008 and 2007

	2008	2007	Increase (Decrease) Amount	Percent
Cash	$ 90,500	$ 64,700	$ 25,800	39.9%
Marketable securities	75,000	60,000	15,000	25.0%
Accounts receivable (net)	115,000	120,000	(5,000)	(4.2%)
Inventories	264,000	283,000	(19,000)	(6.7%)
Prepaid expenses	5,500	5,300	200	3.8%
Total current assets	$550,000	$533,000	$ 17,000	3.2%

The changes in the current assets in Exhibit 2 appear favorable. This assessment is supported by the 24.8% increase in net sales shown in Exhibit 3.

EXHIBIT 3

Comparative Income
Statement—
Horizontal Analysis

Lincoln Company
Comparative Income Statement
For the Years Ended December 31, 2008 and 2007

	2008	2007	Increase (Decrease) Amount	Percent
Sales	$1,530,500	$1,234,000	$296,500	24.0%
Sales returns and allowances . . .	32,500	34,000	(1,500)	(4.4%)
Net sales	$1,498,000	$1,200,000	$298,000	24.8%
Cost of goods sold	1,043,000	820,000	223,000	27.2%
Gross profit	$ 455,000	$ 380,000	$ 75,000	19.7%
Selling expenses	$ 191,000	$ 147,000	$ 44,000	29.9%
Administrative expenses	104,000	97,400	6,600	6.8%
Total operating expenses	$ 295,000	$ 244,400	$ 50,600	20.7%
Income from operations	$ 160,000	$ 135,600	$ 24,400	18.0%
Other income	8,500	11,000	(2,500)	(22.7%)
	$ 168,500	$ 146,600	$ 21,900	14.9%
Other expense (interest)	6,000	12,000	(6,000)	(50.0%)
Income before income tax	$ 162,500	$ 134,600	$ 27,900	20.7%
Income tax expense	71,500	58,100	13,400	23.1%
Net income	$ 91,000	$ 76,500	$ 14,500	19.0%

An increase in net sales may not have a favorable effect on operating performance. The percentage increase in Lincoln Company's net sales is accompanied by a greater percentage increase in the cost of goods (merchandise) sold.[1] This has the effect of reducing gross profit as a percentage of sales. Selling expenses increased significantly, and administrative expenses increased slightly. Overall, operating expenses increased by 20.7%, whereas gross profit increased by only 19.7%.

The increase in income from operations and in net income is favorable. However, a study of the expenses and additional analyses and comparisons should be made before reaching a conclusion as to the cause.

Exhibit 4 illustrates a comparative retained earnings statement with horizontal analysis. It reveals that retained earnings increased 30.5% for the year. The increase is due to net income of $91,000 for the year, less dividends of $49,000.

---

1 The term *cost of goods sold* is often used in practice in place of *cost of merchandise sold*. Such usage is followed in this chapter.

EXHIBIT 4

Comparative Retained
Earnings Statement—
Horizontal Analysis

Lincoln Company
Comparative Retained Earnings Statement
December 31, 2008 and 2007

	2008	2007	Increase (Decrease) Amount	Percent
Retained earnings, January 1.....	$137,500	$100,000	$37,500	37.5%
Net income for the year.........	91,000	76,500	14,500	19.0%
Total........................	$228,500	$176,500	$52,000	29.5%
Dividends:				
On preferred stock..........	$ 9,000	$ 9,000	—	—
On common stock...........	40,000	30,000	$10,000	33.3%
Total........................	$ 49,000	$ 39,000	$10,000	25.6%
Retained earnings, December 31 ...	$179,500	$137,500	$42,000	30.5%

Example Exercise 17-1   objective ①

The comparative cash and accounts receivable balances for a company are provided below.

	2008	2007
Cash	$62,500	$50,000
Accounts receivable (net)	74,400	80,000

Based on this information, what is the amount and percentage of increase or decrease that would be shown in a balance sheet with horizontal analysis?

Follow My Example 17-1

Cash	$12,500 increase ($62,500 − $50,000), or 25%
Accounts receivable	$5,600 decrease ($74,400 − $80,000), or −7%

For Practice: PE 17-1A, PE 17-1B

VERTICAL ANALYSIS

A percentage analysis may also be used to show the relationship of each component to the total within a single statement. This type of analysis is called **vertical analysis**. Like horizontal analysis, the statements may be prepared in either detailed or condensed form. In the latter case, additional details of the changes in individual items may be presented in supporting schedules. In such schedules, the percentage analysis may be based on either the total of the schedule or the statement total. Although vertical analysis is limited to an individual statement, its significance may be improved by preparing comparative statements.

In vertical analysis of the balance sheet, each asset item is stated as a percent of the total assets. Each liability and stockholders' equity item is stated as a percent of the total liabilities and stockholders' equity. Exhibit 5 is a condensed comparative balance sheet with vertical analysis for Lincoln Company.

The major percentage changes in Lincoln Company's assets are in the current asset and long-term investment categories. Current assets increased from 43.3% to 48.3% of total assets, and long-term investments decreased from 14.4% to 8.3% of total assets. In the Liabilities and Stockholders' Equity sections of the balance sheet, the greatest percentage changes are in long-term liabilities and retained earnings. Stockholders' equity increased from 64% to 72.8% of total liabilities and stockholders' equity in 2008. There is a comparable decrease in liabilities.

EXHIBIT 5

Comparative Balance
Sheet—Vertical
Analysis

Lincoln Company
Comparative Balance Sheet
December 31, 2008 and 2007

	2008		2007	
	Amount	Percent	Amount	Percent
Assets				
Current assets	$ 550,000	48.3%	$ 533,000	43.3%
Long-term investments	95,000	8.3	177,500	14.4
Property, plant, and				
equipment (net)	444,500	39.0	470,000	38.2
Intangible assets	50,000	4.4	50,000	4.1
Total assets	$1,139,500	100.0%	$1,230,500	100.0%
Liabilities				
Current liabilities	$ 210,000	18.4%	$ 243,000	19.7%
Long-term liabilities	100,000	8.8	200,000	16.3
Total liabilities	$ 310,000	27.2%	$ 443,000	36.0%
Stockholders' Equity				
Preferred 6% stock, $100 par	$ 150,000	13.2%	$ 150,000	12.2%
Common stock, $10 par	500,000	43.9	500,000	40.6
Retained earnings	179,500	15.7	137,500	11.2
Total stockholders' equity	$ 829,500	72.8%	$ 787,500	64.0%
Total liabilities and				
stockholders' equity	$1,139,500	100.0%	$1,230,500	100.0%

In a vertical analysis of the income statement, each item is stated as a percent of net sales. Exhibit 6 is a condensed comparative income statement with vertical analysis for Lincoln Company.

EXHIBIT 6

Comparative Income
Statement—Vertical
Analysis

Lincoln Company
Comparative Income Statement
For the Years Ended December 31, 2008 and 2007

	2008		2007	
	Amount	Percent	Amount	Percent
Sales	$1,530,500	102.2%	$1,234,000	102.8%
Sales returns and allowances	32,500	2.2	34,000	2.8
Net sales	$1,498,000	100.0%	$1,200,000	100.0%
Cost of goods sold	1,043,000	69.6	820,000	68.3
Gross profit	$ 455,000	30.4%	$ 380,000	31.7%
Selling expenses	$ 191,000	12.8%	$ 147,000	12.3%
Administrative expenses	104,000	6.9	97,400	8.1
Total operating expenses	$ 295,000	19.7%	$ 244,400	20.4%
Income from operations	$ 160,000	10.7%	$ 135,600	11.3%
Other income	8,500	0.6	11,000	0.9
	$ 168,500	11.3%	$ 146,600	12.2%
Other expense (interest).	6,000	0.4	12,000	1.0
Income before income tax	$ 162,500	10.9%	$ 134,600	11.2%
Income tax expense	71,500	4.8	58,100	4.8
Net income	$ 91,000	6.1%	$ 76,500	6.4%

The percentages of gross profit and net income to sales for a recent fiscal year for Target and Wal-Mart are shown below.

	Target	Wal-Mart
Gross profit to sales	31.2%	22.9%
Net income to sales	6.8%	3.6%

Wal-Mart has a significantly lower gross profit margin percentage than does Target, which is likely due to Wal-Mart's aggressive pricing strategy. However, Target's gross profit margin advantage shrinks when comparing the net income to sales ratio. Target must have larger selling and administrative expenses to sales than does Wal-Mart. Even so, Target's net income to sales is still 3.2 percentage points better than Wal-Mart's net income to sales.

We must be careful when judging the significance of differences between percentages for the two years. For example, the decline of the gross profit rate from 31.7% in 2007 to 30.4% in 2008 is only 1.3 percentage points. In terms of dollars of potential gross profit, however, it represents a decline of approximately $19,500 (1.3% × $1,498,000).

COMMON-SIZE STATEMENTS

Horizontal and vertical analyses with both dollar and percentage amounts are useful in assessing relationships and trends in financial conditions and operations of a business. Vertical analysis with both dollar and percentage amounts is also useful in comparing one company with another or with industry averages. Such comparisons are easier to make with the use of common-size statements. In a **common-size statement**, all items are expressed in percentages.

Common-size statements are useful in comparing the current period with prior periods, individual businesses, or one business with industry percentages. Industry data are often available from trade associations and financial information services. Exhibit 7 is a comparative common-size income statement for two businesses.

Exhibit 7 indicates that Lincoln Company has a slightly higher rate of gross profit than Madison Corporation. However, this advantage is more than offset by Lincoln Company's higher percentage of selling and administrative expenses. As a result, the income from operations of Lincoln Company is 10.7% of net sales, compared with 14.4% for Madison Corporation—an unfavorable difference of 3.7 percentage points.

EXHIBIT 7

Common-Size Income Statement

Lincoln Company and Madison Corporation
Condensed Common-Size Income Statement
For the Year Ended December 31, 2008

	Lincoln Company	Madison Corporation
Sales	102.2%	102.3%
Sales returns and allowances	2.2	2.3
Net sales	100.0%	100.0%
Cost of goods sold	69.6	70.0
Gross profit	30.4%	30.0%
Selling expenses	12.8%	11.5%
Administrative expenses	6.9	4.1
Total operating expenses	19.7%	15.6%
Income from operations	10.7%	14.4%
Other income	0.6	0.6
	11.3%	15.0%
Other expense (interest)	0.4	0.5
Income before income tax	10.9%	14.5%
Income tax expense	4.8	5.5
Net income	6.1%	9.0%

OTHER ANALYTICAL MEASURES

In addition to the preceding analyses, other relationships may be expressed in ratios and percentages. Often, these items are taken from the financial statements and thus are a type of vertical analysis. Comparing these items with items from earlier periods is a type of horizontal analysis.

Example Exercise 17-2   objective ①

Income statement information for Lee Corporation is provided below.

Sales	$100,000
Cost of goods sold	65,000
Gross profit	$ 35,000

Prepare a vertical analysis of the income statement for Lee Corporation.

Follow My Example 17-2

	Amount	Percentage	
Sales	$100,000	100%	($100,000/$100,000)
Cost of goods sold	65,000	65	($65,000/$100,000)
Gross profit	$ 35,000	35%	($35,000/$100,000)

For Practice: PE 17-2A, PE 17-2B

Solvency Analysis

objective ②

Apply financial statement analysis to assess the solvency of a business.

Two popular printed sources for industry ratios are *Annual Statement Studies* from Robert Morris Associates and *Industry Norms & Key Business Ratios* from Dun's Analytical Services. Online analysis is available from Zacks Investment Research site or Market Guide's site, both of which are linked to the text's Web site at **www.thomson edu.com/accounting/warren**.

Some aspects of a business's financial condition and operations are of greater importance to some users than others. However, all users are interested in the ability of a business to pay its debts as they are due and to earn income. The ability of a business to meet its financial obligations (debts) is called **solvency**. The ability of a business to earn income is called **profitability**.

The factors of solvency and profitability are interrelated. A business that cannot pay its debts on a timely basis may experience difficulty in obtaining credit. A lack of available credit may, in turn, lead to a decline in the business's profitability. Eventually, the business may be forced into bankruptcy. Likewise, a business that is less profitable than its competitors is likely to be at a disadvantage in obtaining credit or new capital from stockholders.

In the following paragraphs, we discuss various types of financial analyses that are useful in evaluating the solvency of a business. In the next section, we discuss various types of profitability analyses. The examples in both sections are based on Lincoln Company's financial statements presented earlier. In some cases, data from Lincoln Company's financial statements of the preceding year and from other sources are also used. These historical data are useful in assessing the past performance of a business and in forecasting its future performance. The results of financial analyses may be even more useful when they are compared with those of competing businesses and with industry averages.

Solvency analysis focuses on the ability of a business to pay or otherwise satisfy its current and noncurrent liabilities. It is normally assessed by examining balance sheet relationships, using the following major analyses:

1. Current position analysis
2. Accounts receivable analysis
3. Inventory analysis
4. The ratio of fixed assets to long-term liabilities
5. The ratio of liabilities to stockholders' equity
6. The number of times interest charges are earned

CURRENT POSITION ANALYSIS

To be useful in assessing solvency, a ratio or other financial measure must relate to a business's ability to pay or otherwise satisfy its liabilities. Using measures to assess a

> Solvency analysis focuses on the ability of a business to pay or otherwise satisfy its current and noncurrent liabilities.

business's ability to pay its current liabilities is called *current position analysis*. Such analysis is of special interest to short-term creditors.

An analysis of a firm's current position normally includes determining the working capital, the current ratio, and the quick ratio. The current and quick ratios are most useful when analyzed together and compared to previous periods and other firms in the industry.

Working Capital The excess of the current assets of a business over its current liabilities is called *working capital*. The working capital is often used in evaluating a company's ability to meet currently maturing debts. It is especially useful in making monthly or other period-to-period comparisons for a company. However, amounts of working capital are difficult to assess when comparing companies of different sizes or in comparing such amounts with industry figures. For example, working capital of $250,000 may be adequate for a small kitchenware store, but it would be inadequate for all of Williams-Sonoma, Inc.

Current Ratio Another means of expressing the relationship between current assets and current liabilities is the **current ratio**. This ratio is sometimes called the *working capital ratio* or *bankers' ratio*. The ratio is computed by dividing the total current assets by the total current liabilities. For Lincoln Company, working capital and the current ratio for 2008 and 2007 are as follows:

	2008	2007
a. Current assets	$550,000	$533,000
b. Current liabilities	210,000	243,000
Working capital (a − b)	$340,000	$290,000
Current ratio (a/b)	2.6	2.2

Microsoft Corporation maintains a high current ratio—4.7 for a recent year. Microsoft's stable and profitable software business has allowed it to develop a strong cash position coupled with no short-term notes payable.

The current ratio is a more reliable indicator of solvency than is working capital. To illustrate, assume that as of December 31, 2008, the working capital of a competitor is much greater than $340,000, but its current ratio is only 1.3. Considering these facts alone, Lincoln Company, with its current ratio of 2.6, is in a more favorable position to obtain short-term credit than the competitor, which has the greater amount of working capital.

Quick Ratio The working capital and the current ratio do not consider the makeup of the current assets. To illustrate the importance of this consideration, the current position data for Lincoln Company and Jefferson Corporation as of December 31, 2008, are as follows:

	Lincoln Company	Jefferson Corporation
Current assets:		
Cash	$ 90,500	$ 45,500
Marketable securities	75,000	25,000
Accounts receivable (net)	115,000	90,000
Inventories	264,000	380,000
Prepaid expenses	5,500	9,500
a. Total current assets	$550,000	$550,000
b. Current liabilities	210,000	210,000
Working capital (a − b)	$340,000	$340,000
Current ratio (a/b)	2.6	2.6

Both companies have a working capital of $340,000 and a current ratio of 2.6. But the ability of each company to pay its current debts is significantly different. Jefferson Corporation has more of its current assets in inventories. Some of these inventories must be sold and the receivables collected before the current liabilities can be paid in full. Thus, a large amount of time may be necessary to convert these inventories into cash. Declines in market prices and a reduction in demand could also impair its ability to pay current liabilities. In contrast, Lincoln Company has cash and current assets (marketable securities and accounts receivable) that can generally be converted to cash rather quickly to meet its current liabilities.

A ratio that measures the "instant" debt-paying ability of a company is called the **quick ratio** or *acid-test ratio*. It is the ratio of the total quick assets to the total current liabilities. **Quick assets** are cash and other current assets that can be quickly converted to cash. Quick assets normally include cash, marketable securities, and receivables. The quick ratio data for Lincoln Company are as follows:

	2008	2007
Quick assets:		
Cash	$ 90,500	$ 64,700
Marketable securities	75,000	60,000
Accounts receivable (net)	115,000	120,000
a. Total quick assets	$280,500	$244,700
b. Current liabilities	$210,000	$243,000
Quick ratio (a/b)	1.3	1.0

Example Exercise 17-3   objective 2

The following items are reported on a company's balance sheet:

Cash	$300,000
Marketable securities	100,000
Accounts receivable (net)	200,000
Inventory	200,000
Accounts payable	400,000

Determine (a) the current ratio and (b) the quick ratio.

Follow My Example 17-3

a.   Current Ratio = Current Assets /Current Liabilities
     Current Ratio = ($300,000 + $100,000 + $200,000 + $200,000)/$400,000
     Current Ratio = 2.0

b.   Quick Ratio = Quick Assets /Current Liabilities
     Quick Ratio = ($300,000 + $100,000 + $200,000)/$400,000
     Quick Ratio = 1.5

For Practice: PE 17-3A, PE 17-3B

ACCOUNTS RECEIVABLE ANALYSIS

The size and makeup of accounts receivable change constantly during business operations. Sales on account increase accounts receivable, whereas collections from customers decrease accounts receivable. Firms that grant long credit terms usually have larger accounts receivable balances than those granting short credit terms. Increases or decreases in the volume of sales also affect the balance of accounts receivable.

It is desirable to collect receivables as promptly as possible. The cash collected from receivables improves solvency. In addition, the cash generated by prompt collections from customers may be used in operations for such purposes as purchasing merchandise in large quantities at lower prices. The cash may also be used for payment of dividends to stockholders or for other investing or financing purposes. Prompt collection also lessens the risk of loss from uncollectible accounts.

Accounts Receivable Turnover The relationship between sales and accounts receivable may be stated as the **accounts receivable turnover**. This ratio is computed by dividing net sales by the average net accounts receivable.[2] It is desirable to base the average on monthly balances, which allows for seasonal changes in sales. When such data are not available, it may be necessary to use the average of the accounts receivable balance at the beginning and the end of the year. If there are trade notes receivable as well as accounts, the two may be combined. The accounts receivable turnover data for Lincoln Company are as follows.

	2008	2007
a. Net sales	$1,498,000	$1,200,000
Accounts receivable (net):		
Beginning of year	$ 120,000	$ 140,000
End of year	115,000	120,000
Total	$ 235,000	$ 260,000
b. Average (Total/2)	$ 117,500	$ 130,000
Accounts receivable turnover (a/b)	12.7	9.2

The increase in the accounts receivable turnover for 2008 indicates that there has been an improvement in the collection of receivables. This may be due to a change in the granting of credit or in collection practices or both.

Number of Days' Sales in Receivables Another measure of the relationship between sales and accounts receivable is the **number of days' sales in receivables**. This ratio is computed by dividing the average accounts receivable by the average daily sales. Average daily sales is determined by dividing net sales by 365 days. The number of days' sales in receivables is computed for Lincoln Company as follows:

	2008	2007
a. Average (Total/2)	$ 117,500	$ 130,000
Net sales	$1,498,000	$1,200,000
b. Average daily sales (Sales/365)	$4,104	$3,288
Number of days' sales in receivables (a/b)	28.6	39.5

The number of days' sales in receivables is an estimate of the length of time (in days) the accounts receivable have been outstanding. Comparing this measure with the credit terms provides information on the efficiency in collecting receivables. For example, assume that the number of days' sales in receivables for Grant Inc. is 40. If Grant Inc.'s credit terms are n/45, then its collection process appears to be efficient. On the other hand, if Grant Inc.'s credit terms are n/30, its collection process does not appear to be efficient. A comparison with other firms in the same industry and with prior years also provides useful information. Such comparisons may indicate efficiency of collection procedures and trends in credit management.

---

2 If known, *credit* sales should be used in the numerator. Because credit sales are not normally known by external users, we use net sales in the numerator.

Example Exercise 17-4 **objective** 2

A company reports the following:

Net sales	$960,000
Average accounts receivable (net)	48,000

Determine (a) the accounts receivable turnover and (b) the number of days' sales in receivables. Round to one decimal place.

Follow My Example 17-4

a. Accounts Receivable Turnover = Sales/Average Accounts Receivable
     Accounts Receivable Turnover = $960,000/$48,000
     Accounts Receivable Turnover = 20.0

b. Number of Days' Sales in Receivables = Average Accounts Receivable/Average Daily Sales
     Number of Days' Sales in Receivables = $48,000/($960,000/365) = $48,000/$2,630
     Number of Days' Sales in Receivables = 18.3 days

For Practice: PE 17-4A, PE 17-4B

INVENTORY ANALYSIS

A business should keep enough inventory on hand to meet the needs of its customers and its operations. At the same time, however, an excessive amount of inventory reduces solvency by tying up funds. Excess inventories also increase insurance expense, property taxes, storage costs, and other related expenses. These expenses further reduce funds that could be used elsewhere to improve operations. Finally, excess inventory also increases the risk of losses because of price declines or obsolescence of the inventory. Two measures that are useful for evaluating the management of inventory are the inventory turnover and the number of days' sales in inventory.

Inventory Turnover   The relationship between the volume of goods (merchandise) sold and inventory may be stated as the **inventory turnover**. It is computed by dividing the cost of goods sold by the average inventory. If monthly data are not available, the average of the inventories at the beginning and the end of the year may be used. The inventory turnover for Lincoln Company is computed as follows:

	2008	2007
a. Cost of goods sold	$1,043,000	$820,000
Inventories:		
Beginning of year	$ 283,000	$311,000
End of year	264,000	283,000
Total	$ 547,000	$594,000
b. Average (Total/2)	$ 273,500	$297,000
Inventory turnover (a/b)	3.8	2.8

The inventory turnover improved for Lincoln Company because of an increase in the cost of goods sold and a decrease in the average inventories. Differences across inventories, companies, and industries are too great to allow a general statement on what is a good inventory turnover. For example, a firm selling food should have a higher turnover than a firm selling furniture or jewelry. Likewise, the perishable foods department of a supermarket should have a higher turnover than the soaps and cleansers department. However, for each business or each department within a business, there is a reasonable turnover rate. A turnover lower than this rate could mean that inventory is not being managed properly.

Number of Days' Sales in Inventory Another measure of the relationship between the cost of goods sold and inventory is the **number of days' sales in inventory**. This measure is computed by dividing the average inventory by the average daily cost of goods sold (cost of goods sold divided by 365). The number of days' sales in inventory for Lincoln Company is computed as follows:

	2008	2007
a. Average (Total/2)	$ 273,500	$297,000
Cost of goods sold	$1,043,000	$820,000
b. Average daily cost of goods sold (COGS/365 days)	$2,858	$2,247
Number of days' sales in inventory (a/b)	95.7	132.2

The number of days' sales in inventory is a rough measure of the length of time it takes to acquire, sell, and replace the inventory. For Lincoln Company, there is a major improvement in the number of days' sales in inventory during 2008. However, a comparison with earlier years and similar firms would be useful in assessing Lincoln Company's overall inventory management.

Example Exercise 17-5   objective 2

A company reports the following:

Cost of goods sold	$560,000
Average inventory	112,000

Determine (a) the inventory turnover and (b) the number of days' sales in inventory. Round to one decimal place.

Follow My Example 17-5

a.   Inventory Turnover = Cost of Goods Sold/Average Inventory
Inventory Turnover = $560,000/$112,000
Inventory Turnover = 5.0

b.   Number of Days' Sales in Inventory = Average Inventory/Average Daily Cost of Goods Sold
Number of Days' Sales in Inventory = $112,000/($560,000/365) = $112,000/$1,534
Number of Days' Sales in Inventory = 73.0 days

For Practice: PE 17-5A, PE 17-5B

RATIO OF FIXED ASSETS TO LONG-TERM LIABILITIES

Long-term notes and bonds are often secured by mortgages on fixed assets. The **ratio of fixed assets to long-term liabilities** is a solvency measure that indicates the margin of safety of the noteholders or bondholders. It also indicates the ability of the business to borrow additional funds on a long-term basis. The ratio of fixed assets to long-term liabilities for Lincoln Company is as follows:

	2008	2007
a. Fixed assets (net)	$444,500	$470,000
b. Long-term liabilities	$100,000	$200,000
Ratio of fixed assets to long-term liabilities (a/b)	4.4	2.4

The major increase in this ratio at the end of 2008 is mainly due to liquidating one-half of Lincoln Company's long-term liabilities. If the company needs to borrow additional funds on a long-term basis in the future, it is in a strong position to do so.

RATIO OF LIABILITIES TO STOCKHOLDERS' EQUITY

Claims against the total assets of a business are divided into two groups: (1) claims of creditors and (2) claims of owners. The relationship between the total claims of the creditors and owners—the **ratio of liabilities to stockholders' equity**—is a solvency measure that indicates the margin of safety for creditors. It also indicates the ability of the business to withstand adverse business conditions. When the claims of creditors are large in relation to the equity of the stockholders, there are usually significant interest payments. If earnings decline to the point where the company is unable to meet its interest payments, the business may be taken over by the creditors.

The ratio of liabilities to stockholders' equity varies across industries. For example, recent annual reports of some selected companies showed the following ratio of liabilities to stockholders' equity:

Continental Airlines	66.8
Procter & Gamble	2.5
Circuit City Stores, Inc.	0.8

The airline industry generally uses more debt financing than the consumer product or retail industries. Thus, the airline industry is generally considered more risky.

The relationship between creditor and stockholder equity is shown in the vertical analysis of the balance sheet. For example, the balance sheet of Lincoln Company in Exhibit 5 indicates that on December 31, 2008, liabilities represented 27.2% and stockholders' equity represented 72.8% of the total liabilities and stockholders' equity (100.0%). Instead of expressing each item as a percent of the total, this relationship may be expressed as a ratio of one to the other, as follows:

	2008	2007
a. Total liabilities	$310,000	$443,000
b. Total stockholders' equity	$829,500	$787,500
Ratio of liabilities to stockholders' equity (a/b)	0.4	0.6

The balance sheet of Lincoln Company shows that the major factor affecting the change in the ratio was the $100,000 decrease in long-term liabilities during 2008. The ratio at the end of both years shows a large margin of safety for the creditors.

Example Exercise 17-6

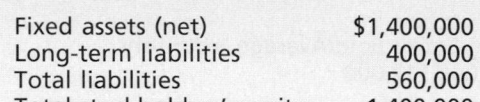

objective 2

The following information was taken from Acme Company's balance sheet:

Fixed assets (net)	$1,400,000
Long-term liabilities	400,000
Total liabilities	560,000
Total stockholders' equity	1,400,000

Determine the company's (a) ratio of fixed assets to long-term liabilities and (b) ratio of liabilities to total stockholders' equity.

Follow My Example 17-6

a. Ratio of Fixed Assets to Long-Term Liabilities = Fixed Assets/Long-Term Liabilities
    Ratio of Fixed Assets to Long-Term Liabilities = $1,400,000/$400,000
    Ratio of Fixed Assets to Long-Term Liabilities = 3.5

b. Ratio of Liabilities to Total Stockholders' Equity = Total Liabilities/Total Stockholders' Equity
    Ratio of Liabilities to Total Stockholders' Equity = $560,000/$1,400,000
    Ratio of Liabilities to Total Stockholders' Equity = 0.4

For Practice: PE 17-6A, PE 17-6B

NUMBER OF TIMES INTEREST CHARGES EARNED

Corporations in some industries, such as airlines, normally have high ratios of debt to stockholders' equity. For such corporations, the relative risk of the debtholders is normally measured as the **number of times interest charges are earned**, sometimes called the *fixed charge coverage ratio*, during the year. The higher the ratio, the lower the risk that interest payments will not be made if earnings decrease. In other words, the higher the ratio, the greater the assurance that interest payments will be made on a continuing basis. This measure also indicates the general financial strength of the business, which is of interest to stockholders and employees as well as creditors.

The amount available to meet interest charges is not affected by taxes on income. This is because interest is deductible in determining taxable income. Thus, the number of times interest charges are earned for Lincoln Company is computed as shown below, rounded to one decimal place.

	2008	2007
Income before income tax	$162,500	$134,600
a. Add interest expense	6,000	12,000
b. Amount available to meet interest charges	$168,500	$146,600
Number of times interest charges earned (b/a)	28.1	12.2

These calculations indicate Lincoln Company has very high coverage of its interest charges for both years. Analysis such as this can also be applied to dividends on preferred stock. In such a case, net income is divided by the amount of preferred dividends to yield the *number of times preferred dividends are earned*. This measure indicates the risk that dividends to preferred stockholders may not be paid.

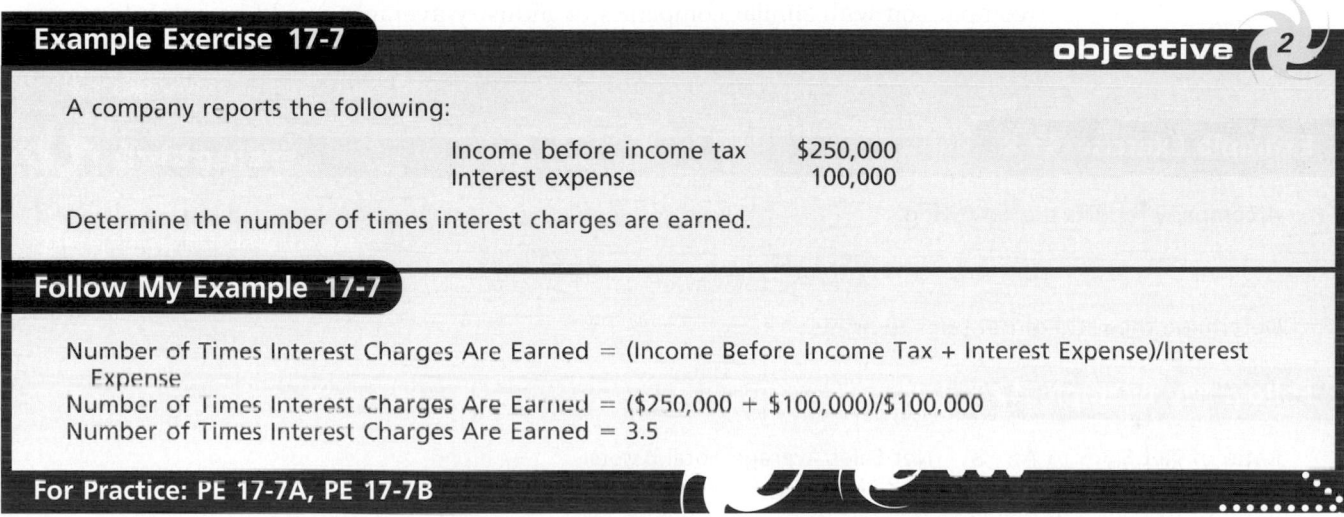

Example Exercise 17-7 objective 2

A company reports the following:

Income before income tax $250,000
Interest expense 100,000

Determine the number of times interest charges are earned.

Follow My Example 17-7

Number of Times Interest Charges Are Earned = (Income Before Income Tax + Interest Expense)/Interest Expense
Number of Times Interest Charges Are Earned = ($250,000 + $100,000)/$100,000
Number of Times Interest Charges Are Earned = 3.5

For Practice: PE 17-7A, PE 17-7B

Profitability Analysis

objective 3

Apply financial statement analysis to assess the profitability of a business.

The ability of a business to earn profits depends on the effectiveness and efficiency of its operations as well as the resources available to it. Profitability analysis, therefore, focuses primarily on the relationship between operating results as reported in the income statement and resources available to the business as reported in the balance sheet. Major analyses used in assessing profitability include the following:

1. Ratio of net sales to assets
2. Rate earned on total assets
3. Rate earned on stockholders' equity
4. Rate earned on common stockholders' equity
5. Earnings per share on common stock
6. Price-earnings ratio
7. Dividends per share
8. Dividend yield

> Profitability analysis focuses on the relationship between operating results and the resources available to a business.

RATIO OF NET SALES TO ASSETS

The ratio of net sales to assets is a profitability measure that shows how effectively a firm utilizes its assets. For example, two competing businesses have equal amounts of assets. If the sales of one are twice the sales of the other, the business with the higher sales is making better use of its assets.

In computing the ratio of net sales to assets, any long-term investments are excluded from total assets, because such investments are unrelated to normal operations involving the sale of goods or services. Assets may be measured as the total at the end of the year, the average at the beginning and end of the year, or the average of monthly totals. The basic data and the computation of this ratio for Lincoln Company are as follows:

	2008	2007
a. Net sales	$1,498,000	$1,200,000
Total assets (excluding long-term investments):		
Beginning of year	$1,053,000	$1,010,000
End of year	1,044,500	1,053,000
Total	$2,097,500	$2,063,000
b. Average (Total/2)	$1,048,750	$1,031,500
Ratio of net sales to assets (a/b)	1.4	1.2

This ratio improved during 2008, primarily due to an increase in sales volume. A comparison with similar companies or industry averages would be helpful in assessing the effectiveness of Lincoln Company's use of its assets.

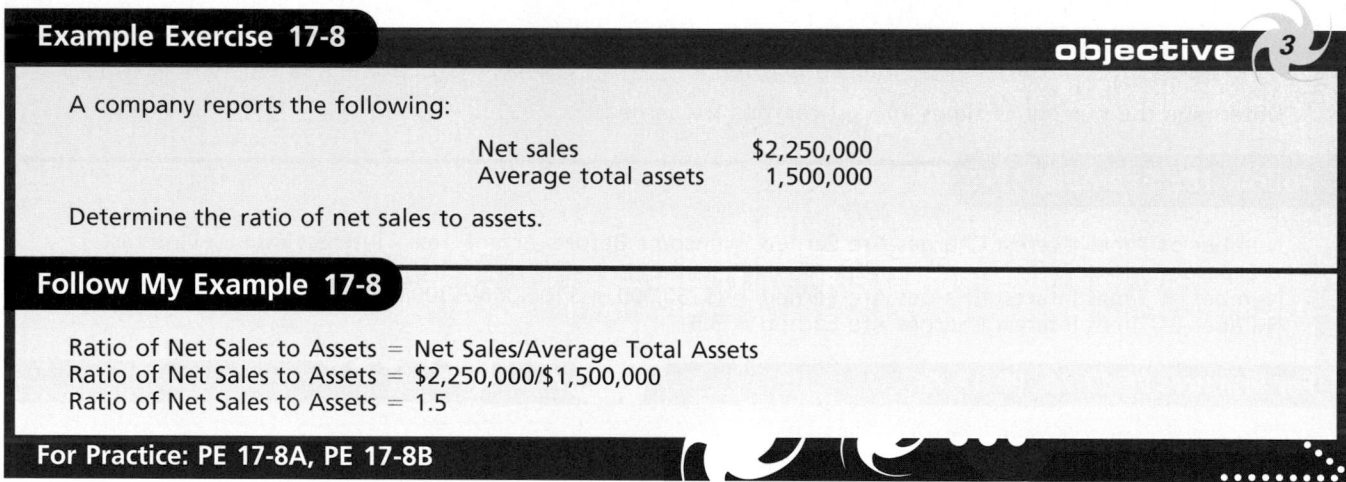

Example Exercise 17-8   objective **3**

A company reports the following:

Net sales	$2,250,000
Average total assets	1,500,000

Determine the ratio of net sales to assets.

Follow My Example 17-8

Ratio of Net Sales to Assets = Net Sales/Average Total Assets
Ratio of Net Sales to Assets = $2,250,000/$1,500,000
Ratio of Net Sales to Assets = 1.5

For Practice: PE 17-8A, PE 17-8B

RATE EARNED ON TOTAL ASSETS

The **rate earned on total assets** measures the profitability of total assets, without considering how the assets are financed. This rate is therefore not affected by whether the assets are financed primarily by creditors or stockholders.

The rate earned on total assets is computed by adding interest expense to net income and dividing this sum by the average total assets. Adding interest expense to net income eliminates the effect of whether the assets are financed by debt or equity. The rate earned by Lincoln Company on total assets is computed as follows:

	2008	2007
Net income	$ 91,000	$ 76,500
Plus interest expense	6,000	12,000
a. Total	$ 97,000	$ 88,500
Total assets:		
Beginning of year	$1,230,500	$1,187,500
End of year	1,139,500	1,230,500
Total	$2,370,000	$2,418,000
b. Average (Total/2)	$1,185,000	$1,209,000
Rate earned on total assets (a/b)	8.2%	7.3%

The rate earned on total assets of Lincoln Company during 2008 improved over that of 2007. A comparison with similar companies and industry averages would be useful in evaluating Lincoln Company's profitability on total assets.

Sometimes it may be desirable to compute the *rate of income from operations to total assets*. This is especially true if significant amounts of nonoperating income and expense are reported on the income statement. In this case, any assets related to the nonoperating income and expense items should be excluded from total assets in computing the rate. In addition, using income from operations (which is before tax) has the advantage of eliminating the effects of any changes in the tax structure on the rate of earnings. When evaluating published data on rates earned on assets, you should be careful to determine the exact nature of the measure that is reported.

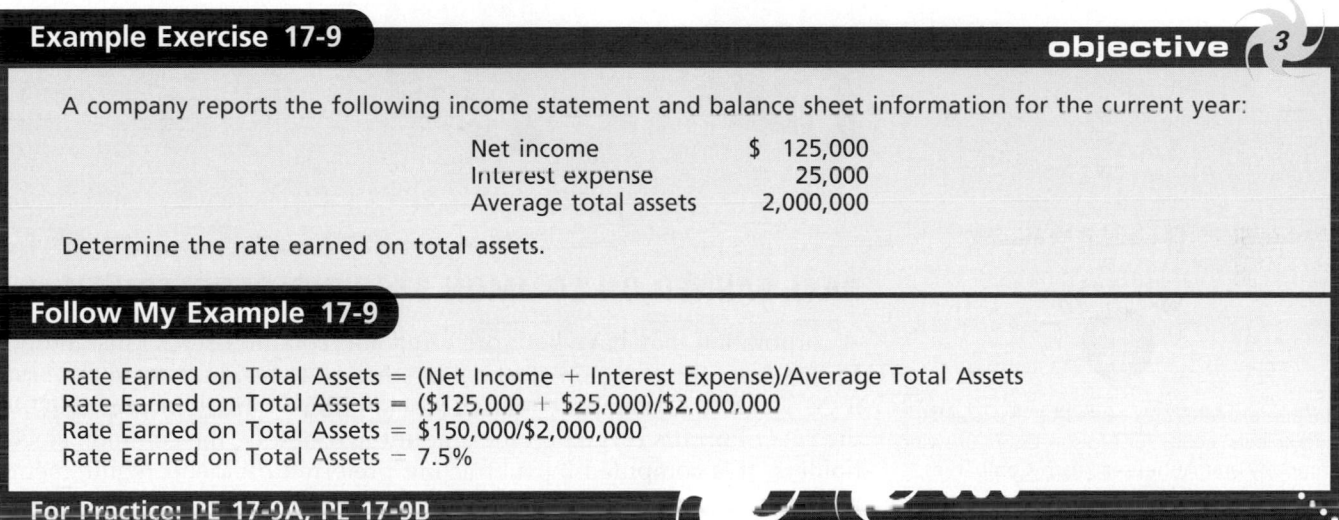

Example Exercise 17-9   objective **3**

A company reports the following income statement and balance sheet information for the current year:

Net income	$ 125,000
Interest expense	25,000
Average total assets	2,000,000

Determine the rate earned on total assets.

Follow My Example 17-9

Rate Earned on Total Assets = (Net Income + Interest Expense)/Average Total Assets
Rate Earned on Total Assets = ($125,000 + $25,000)/$2,000,000
Rate Earned on Total Assets = $150,000/$2,000,000
Rate Earned on Total Assets = 7.5%

For Practice: PE 17-9A, PE 17-9B

RATE EARNED ON STOCKHOLDERS' EQUITY

Another measure of profitability is the **rate earned on stockholders' equity**. It is computed by dividing net income by average total stockholders' equity. In contrast to the rate earned on total assets, this measure emphasizes the rate of income earned on the amount invested by the stockholders.

The total stockholders' equity may vary throughout a period. For example, a business may issue or retire stock, pay dividends, and earn net income. If monthly amounts are not available, the average of the stockholders' equity at the beginning and the end of the year is normally used to compute this rate. For Lincoln Company, the rate earned on stockholders' equity is computed as follows:

	2008	2007
a. Net income	$ 91,000	$ 76,500
Stockholders' equity:		
Beginning of year	$ 787,500	$ 750,000
End of year	829,500	787,500
Total	$1,617,000	$1,537,500
b. Average (Total/2)	$ 808,500	$ 768,750
Rate earned on stockholders' equity (a/b)	11.3%	10.0%

The rate earned by a business on the equity of its stockholders is usually higher than the rate earned on total assets. This occurs when the amount earned on assets acquired with creditors' funds is more than the interest paid to creditors. This difference in the rate on stockholders' equity and the rate on total assets is called **leverage**.

Lincoln Company's rate earned on stockholders' equity for 2008, 11.3%, is greater than the rate of 8.2% earned on total assets. The leverage of 3.1% (11.3% − 8.2%) for 2008 compares favorably with the 2.7% (10.0% − 7.3%) leverage for 2007. Exhibit 8 shows the 2008 and 2007 leverages for Lincoln Company.

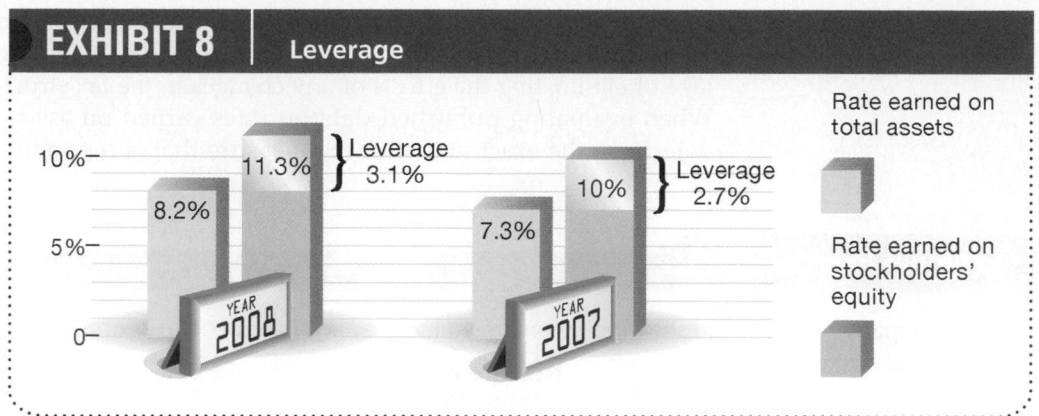

EXHIBIT 8 | Leverage

RATE EARNED ON COMMON STOCKHOLDERS' EQUITY

The approximate rates earned on assets and stockholders' equity for Molson Coors Brewing Company and Anheuser-Busch Companies, Inc., for a recent fiscal year are shown below.

	Molson Coors	Anheuser-Busch
Rate earned on assets	4%	15%
Rate earned on stockholders' equity	12%	83%

Anheuser-Busch has been more profitable and has benefited from a greater use of leverage than has Molson Coors.

A corporation may have both preferred and common stock outstanding. In this case, the common stockholders have the residual claim on earnings. The **rate earned on common stockholders' equity** focuses only on the rate of profits earned on the amount invested by the common stockholders. It is computed by subtracting preferred dividend requirements from the net income and dividing by the average common stockholders' equity.

Lincoln Company has $150,000 of 6% nonparticipating preferred stock outstanding on December 31, 2008 and 2007. Thus, the annual preferred dividend requirement is $9,000 ($150,000 × 6%). The common stockholders' equity equals the total stockholders' equity, including retained earnings, less the par of the preferred stock ($150,000). The basic data and the rate earned on common stockholders' equity for Lincoln Company are as follows:

	2008	2007
Net income	$ 91,000	$ 76,500
Preferred dividends	9,000	9,000
a. Remainder—identified with common stock	$ 82,000	$ 67,500
Common stockholders' equity:		
Beginning of year	$ 637,500	$ 600,000
End of year	679,500	637,500
Total	$1,317,000	$1,237,500
b. Average (Total/2)	$ 658,500	$ 618,750
Rate earned on common stockholders' equity (a/b)	12.5%	10.9%

The rate earned on common stockholders' equity differs from the rates earned by Lincoln Company on total assets and total stockholders' equity. This occurs if there are borrowed funds and also preferred stock outstanding, which rank ahead of the common shares in their claim on earnings. Thus, the concept of leverage, as we discussed in the preceding section, can also be applied to the use of funds from the sale of preferred stock as well as borrowing. Funds from both sources can be used in an attempt to increase the return on common stockholders' equity.

A company reports the following:

Net income	$ 125,000
Preferred dividends	5,000
Average stockholders' equity	1,000,000
Average common stockholders' equity	800,000

Determine (a) the rate earned on stockholders' equity and (b) the rate earned on common stockholders' equity.

Follow My Example 17-10

a. Rate Earned on Stockholders' Equity = Net Income/Average Stockholders' Equity
   Rate Earned on Stockholders' Equity = $125,000/$1,000,000
   Rate Earned on Stockholders' Equity = 12.5%

b. Rate Earned on Common Stockholders' Equity = (Net Income − Preferred Dividends)/Average
                                               Common Stockholders' Equity
   Rate Earned on Common Stockholders' Equity = ($125,000 − $5,000)/$800,000
   Rate Earned on Common Stockholders' Equity = 15%

For Practice: PE 17-10A, PE 17-10B

EARNINGS PER SHARE ON COMMON STOCK

One of the profitability measures often quoted by the financial press is **earnings per share (EPS) on common stock**. It is also normally reported in the income statement in corporate annual reports. If a company has issued only one class of stock, the earnings per share is computed by dividing net income by the number of shares of stock outstanding. If preferred and common stock are outstanding, the net income is first reduced by the amount of preferred dividend requirements.[3]

The data on the earnings per share of common stock for Lincoln Company are as follows:

	2008	2007
Net income	$91,000	$76,500
Preferred dividends	9,000	9,000
a. Remainder—identified with common stock	$82,000	$67,500
b. Shares of common stock outstanding	50,000	50,000
Earnings per share on common stock (a/b)	$1.64	$1.35

PRICE-EARNINGS RATIO

Another profitability measure quoted by the financial press is the **price-earnings (P/E) ratio** on common stock. The price-earnings ratio is an indicator of a firm's future earnings prospects. It is computed by dividing the market price per share of common stock at a specific date by the annual earnings per share. To illustrate, assume that the market prices per common share are 41 at the end of 2008 and 27 at the end of 2007. The price-earnings ratio on common stock of Lincoln Company is computed as follows:

	2008	2007
Market price per share of common stock	$41.00	$27.00
Earnings per share on common stock	÷ 1.64	÷ 1.35
Price-earnings ratio on common stock	25	20

---

3 Additional details related to earnings per share were discussed in Chapter 14.

The price-earnings ratio indicates that a share of common stock of Lincoln Company was selling for 20 times the amount of earnings per share at the end of 2007. At the end of 2008, the common stock was selling for 25 times the amount of earnings per share.

Example Exercise 17-11   objective 3

A company reports the following:

Net income	$250,000
Preferred dividends	$15,000
Shares of common stock outstanding	20,000
Market price per share of common stock	$35.00

a. Determine the company's earnings per share on common stock.
b. Determine the company's price-earnings ratio. Round to one decimal place.

Follow My Example 17-11

a. Earnings per Share on Common Stock = (Net Income − Preferred Dividends)/Shares of Common Stock Outstanding
    Earnings per Share = ($250,000 − $15,000)/20,000
    Earnings per Share = $11.75

b. Price-Earnings Ratio = Market Price per Share of Common Stock/Earnings per Share on Common Stock
    Price-Earnings Ratio = $35.00/$11.75
    Price-Earnings Ratio = 3.0

For Practice: PE 17-11A, PE 17-11B

REAL WORLD

The dividend per share, dividend yield, and P/E ratio of a common stock are normally quoted on the daily listing of stock prices in *The Wall Street Journal* and on Yahoo!'s finance Web site.

DIVIDENDS PER SHARE AND DIVIDEND YIELD

Since the primary basis for dividends is earnings, dividends per share and earnings per share on common stock are commonly used by investors in assessing alternative stock investments. The dividends per share for Lincoln Company were $0.80 ($40,000/50,000 shares) for 2008 and $0.60 ($30,000/50,000 shares) for 2007.

Dividends per share can be reported with earnings per share to indicate the relationship between dividends and earnings. Comparing these two per share amounts indicates the extent to which the corporation is retaining its earnings for use in operations. Exhibit 9 shows these relationships for Lincoln Company.

EXHIBIT 9   Dividends and Earnings per Share of Common Stock

The **dividend yield** on common stock is a profitability measure that shows the rate of return to common stockholders in terms of cash dividends. It is of special interest to investors whose main investment objective is to receive current returns (dividends) on an investment rather than an increase in the market price of the investment. The dividend yield is computed by dividing the annual dividends paid per share of common stock by the market price per share on a specific date. To illustrate, assume that the market price was 41 at the end of 2008 and 27 at the end of 2007. The dividend yield on common stock of Lincoln Company is as follows:

	2008	2007
Dividends per share of common stock	$ 0.80	$ 0.60
Market price per share of common stock	÷ 41.00	÷ 27.00
Dividend yield on common stock	2.0%	2.2%

SUMMARY OF ANALYTICAL MEASURES

Exhibit 10 presents a summary of the analytical measures that we have discussed. These measures can be computed for most medium-size businesses. Depending on the specific business being analyzed, some measures might be omitted or additional measures could be developed. The type of industry, the capital structure, and the diversity of the business's operations usually affect the measures used. For example, analysis for an airline might include revenue per passenger mile and cost per available seat as measures. Likewise, analysis for a hotel might focus on occupancy rates.

Percentage analyses, ratios, turnovers, and other measures of financial position and operating results are useful analytical measures. They are helpful in assessing a business's past performance and predicting its future. They are not, however, a substitute for sound judgment. In selecting and interpreting analytical measures, conditions peculiar to a business or its industry should be considered. In addition, the influence of the general economic and business environment should be considered.

In determining trends, the interrelationship of the measures used in assessing a business should be carefully studied. Comparable indexes of earlier periods should also be studied. Data from competing businesses may be useful in assessing the efficiency of operations for the firm under analysis. In making such comparisons, however, the effects of differences in the accounting methods used by the businesses should be considered.

EXHIBIT 10   Summary of Analytical Measures

	Method of Computation	Use
Solvency measures:		
Working Capital	Current Assets − Current Liabilities	To indicate the ability to meet currently maturing obligations
Current Ratio	$\dfrac{\text{Current Assets}}{\text{Current Liabilities}}$	
Quick Ratio	$\dfrac{\text{Quick Assets}}{\text{Current Liabilities}}$	To indicate instant debt-paying ability
Accounts Receivable Turnover	$\dfrac{\text{Net Sales}}{\text{Average Accounts Receivable}}$	To assess the efficiency in collecting receivables and in the management of credit
Numbers of Days' Sales in Receivables	$\dfrac{\text{Average Accounts Receivable}}{\text{Average Daily Sales}}$	
Inventory Turnover	$\dfrac{\text{Cost of Goods Sold}}{\text{Average Inventory}}$	To assess the efficiency in the management of inventory
Number of Days' Sales in Inventory	$\dfrac{\text{Average Inventory}}{\text{Average Daily Cost of Goods Sold}}$	
Ratio of Fixed Assets to Long-Term Liabilities	$\dfrac{\text{Fixed Assets (net)}}{\text{Long-Term Liabilities}}$	To indicate the margin of safety to long-term creditors
Ratio of Liabilities to Stockholders' Equity	$\dfrac{\text{Total Liabilities}}{\text{Total Stockholders' Equity}}$	To indicate the margin of safety to creditors
Number of Times Interest Charges Earned	$\dfrac{\text{Income Before Income Tax + Interest Expense}}{\text{Interest Expense}}$	To assess the risk to debtholders in terms of number of times interest charges were earned
Profitability measures:		
Ratio of Net Sales to Assets	$\dfrac{\text{Net Sales}}{\text{Average Total Assets (excluding long-term investments)}}$	To assess the effectiveness in the use of assets
Rate Earned on Total Assets	$\dfrac{\text{Net Income + Interest Expense}}{\text{Average Total Assets}}$	To assess the profitability of the assets
Rate Earned on Stockholders' Equity	$\dfrac{\text{Net Income}}{\text{Average Total Stockholders' Equity}}$	To assess the profitability of the investment by stockholders
Rate Earned on Common Stockholders' Equity	$\dfrac{\text{Net Income − Preferred Dividends}}{\text{Average Common Stockholders' Equity}}$	To assess the profitability of the investment by common stockholders
Earnings per Share on Common Stock	$\dfrac{\text{Net Income − Preferred Dividends}}{\text{Shares of Common Stock Outstanding}}$	
Price-Earnings Ratio	$\dfrac{\text{Market Price per Share of Common Stock}}{\text{Earnings per Share of Common Stock}}$	To indicate future earnings prospects, based on the relationship between market value of common stock and earnings
Dividends per Share of Common Stock	$\dfrac{\text{Dividends}}{\text{Shares of Common Stock Outstanding}}$	To indicate the extent to which earnings are being distributed to common stockholders
Dividend Yield	$\dfrac{\text{Dividends per Share of Common Stock}}{\text{Market Price per Share of Common Stock}}$	To indicate the rate of return to common stockholders in terms of dividends

Integrity, Objectivity, and Ethics in Business

ONE BAD APPLE

A recent survey by *CFO* magazine reported that 47% of chief financial officers have been pressured by the chief executive officer to use questionable accounting. In addition, only 38% of those surveyed feel less pressure to use aggressive accounting today than in years past, while 20% believe there is more pressure. Perhaps more troublesome is the chief financial officers' confidence in the quality of financial information, with only 27% being "very confident" in the quality of financial information presented by public companies.

Source: D. Durfee, "It's Better (and Worse) Than You Think," *CFO*, May 3, 2004.

Corporate Annual Reports

objective 4

Describe the contents of corporate annual reports.

Public corporations are required to issue annual reports to their stockholders and other interested parties. Such reports summarize the corporation's operating activities for the past year and plans for the future. There are many variations in the order and form for presenting the major sections of annual reports. However, one section of the annual report is devoted to the financial statements, including the accompanying notes. In addition, annual reports usually include the following sections:

1. Management discussion and analysis
2. Report on adequacy of internal control
3. Report on fairness of financial statements

In the following paragraphs, we describe these sections. Each section, as well as the financial statements, is illustrated in the annual report for Williams-Sonoma, Inc., in Appendix D.

MANAGEMENT DISCUSSION AND ANALYSIS

A required disclosure in the annual report filed with the Securities and Exchange Commission is the **Management's Discussion and Analysis (MD&A)**. The MD&A provides critical information in interpreting the financial statements and assessing the future of the company.

The MD&A includes an analysis of the results of operations and discusses management's opinion about future performance. It compares the prior year's income statement with the current year's to explain changes in sales, significant expenses, gross profit, and income from operations. For example, an increase in sales may be explained by referring to higher shipment volume or stronger prices.

The MD&A also includes an analysis of the company's financial condition. It compares significant balance sheet items between successive years to explain changes in liquidity and capital resources. In addition, the MD&A discusses significant risk exposure.

A new subsection of the MD&A required by the Sarbanes-Oxley Act must now include a section describing any "off-balance-sheet" arrangements. Such arrangements are discussed in advanced accounting courses.

REPORT ON ADEQUACY OF INTERNAL CONTROL

As discussed in Chapter 8, the Sarbanes-Oxley Act of 2002 requires management to provide a report stating their responsibility for establishing and maintaining internal control. In addition, the report must state management's conclusion concerning the effectiveness of internal controls over financial reporting. The act also requires a public accounting firm to examine and verify management's conclusions regarding internal control. Thus, public companies must provide two reports, one by management and one by a public accounting firm, certifying the management report as accurate. In some situations, the auditor may combine these reports into a single report. The combined report for Williams-Sonoma, Inc., is included in the annual report in Appendix D.

REPORT ON FAIRNESS OF FINANCIAL STATEMENTS

In addition to a public accounting firm's internal control report, all publicly held corporations are also required to have an independent audit (examination) of their financial statements. For the financial statements of most companies, the CPAs who conduct the audit render an opinion on the fairness of the statements. An opinion stating that the financial statements fairly represent the financial condition of a public company is said to be an unqualified, or "clean," opinion. The Independent Auditors' Report for Williams-Sonoma, Inc., is an unqualified opinion.

Business Connections

REAL WORLD

INVESTING STRATEGIES

How do people make investment decisions? Investment decisions, like any major purchase, must meet the needs of the buyer. For example, if you have a family of five and are thinking about buying a new car, you probably wouldn't buy a two-seat sports car. It just wouldn't meet your objectives or fit your lifestyle. Alternatively, if you are a young single person, a minivan might not meet your immediate needs. Investors buy stocks in the same way, buying stocks that match their investment style and their financial needs. Two common approaches are value and growth investing.

Value Investing

Value investors search for undervalued stocks. That is, the investor tries to find companies whose value is not reflected in their stock price. These are typically quiet, "boring" companies with excellent financial performance that are temporarily out of favor in the stock market. This investment approach assumes that the stock's price will eventually rise to match the company's value. The most successful investor of all time, Warren Buffett, uses this approach almost exclusively. Naturally, the key to successful value investing is to accurately determine a stock's value. This will often include analyzing a company's financial ratios, as discussed in this chapter, compared to target ratios and industry norms. For example,

the stock of Darden Restaurants, the operator of restaurant chains including Olive Garden and Red Lobster, was selling for $18.35 on May 25, 2003, a value relative to its earnings per share of $1.36. Over the next three years, the company's stock price more than doubled, reaching $41.44 on February 17, 2006.

Growth Investing

The growth investor tries to identify companies that have the potential to grow sales and earnings through new products, markets, or opportunities. Growth companies are often newer companies that are still unproven but that possess unique technologies or capabilities. The strategy is to purchase these companies before their potential becomes obvious, hoping to profit from relatively large increases in the company's stock price. This approach, however, carries the risk that the growth may not occur. Growth investors use many of the ratios discussed in this chapter to identify high-potential growth companies. For example, in March 2003, Research in Motion Limited, maker of the popular BlackBerry® handheld mobile device, reported earnings per share of −$0.96, and the company's stock price was trading near $5 per share. In the following two years, the company's sales increased by 340%, earnings increased to $1.14 per share, and the company's stock price rose above $75 per share.

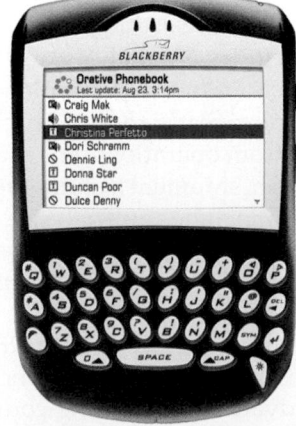

At a Glance

1. List basic financial statement analytical procedures.

Key Points	Key Learning Outcomes	Example Exercises	Practice Exercises
The basic financial statements provide much of the information users need to make economic decisions. Analytical procedures are used to compare items on a current financial statement with related items on earlier statements, or to examine relationships within a financial statement.	• Prepare a horizontal analysis from a company's financial statements. • Prepare a vertical analysis from a company's financial statements.	17-1	17-1A, 17-1B
	• Prepare common-size financial statements.	17-2	17-2A, 17-2B

2. Apply financial statement analysis to assess the solvency of a business.

Key Points	Key Learning Outcomes	Example Exercises	Practice Exercises
All users of financial statements are interested in the ability of a business to pay its debts (solvency) and earn income (profitability). Solvency and profitability are interrelated. Solvency analysis is normally assessed by examining the following balance sheet relationships: (1) current position analysis, (2) accounts receivable analysis, (3) inventory analysis, (4) the ratio of fixed assets to long term liabilities, (5) the ratio of liabilities to stockholders' equity, and (6) the number of times interest charges are earned.	• Determine working capital. • Calculate and interpret the current ratio.	17-3	17-3A, 17-3B
	• Calculate and interpret the quick ratio.	17-3	17-3A, 17-3B
	• Calculate and interpret accounts receivable turnover.	17-4	17-4A, 17-4B
	• Calculate and interpret number of days' sales in receivables.	17-4	17-4A, 17-4B
	• Calculate and interpret inventory turnover.	17-5	17-5A, 17-5B
	• Calculate and interpret number of days' sales in inventory.	17-5	17-5A, 17-5B
	• Calculate and interpret the ratio of fixed assets to long-term liabilities.	17-6	17-6A, 17-6B
	• Calculate and interpret the ratio of liabilities to stockholders' equity.	17-6	17-6A, 17-6B
	• Calculate and interpret the number of times interest charges are earned.	17-7	17-7A, 17-7B

(continued)

3. Apply financial statement analysis to assess the profitability of a business.

Key Points	Key Learning Outcomes	Example Exercises	Practice Exercises
Profitability analysis focuses mainly on the relationship between operating results (income statement) and resources available (balance sheet). Major analyses include (1) the ratio of net sales to assets, (2) the rate earned on total assets, (3) the rate earned on stockholders' equity, (4) the rate earned on common stockholders' equity, (5) earnings per share on common stock, (6) the price-earnings ratio, (7) dividends per share, and (8) dividend yield.	• Calculate and interpret the ratio of net sales to assets.	**17-8**	17-8A, 17-8B
	• Calculate and interpret the rate earned on total assets.	**17-9**	17-9A, 17-9B
	• Calculate and interpret the rate earned on stockholders' equity.	**17-10**	17-10A, 17-10B
	• Calculate and interpret the rate earned on common stockholders' equity.	**17-10**	17-10A, 17-10B
	• Calculate and interpret the earnings per share on common stock.	**17-11**	17-11A, 17-11B
	• Calculate and interpret the price-earnings ratio.	**17-11**	17-11A, 17-11B
	• Calculate and interpret the dividends per share and dividend yield.		
	• Describe the uses and limitations of analytical measures.		

4. Describe the contents of corporate annual reports.

Key Points	Key Learning Outcomes	Example Exercises	Practice Exercises
Corporations normally issue annual reports to their stockholders and other interested parties. Such reports summarize the corporation's operating activities for the past year and plans for the future.	• Describe the elements of a corporate annual report.		

Key Terms

accounts receivable turnover (751)
common-size statement (747)
current ratio (749)
dividend yield (761)
earnings per share (EPS) on common stock (759)
horizontal analysis (742)
inventory turnover (752)
leverage (757)
Management's Discussion and Analysis (MD&A) (763)
number of days' sales in inventory (753)

number of days' sales in receivables (751)
number of times interest charges are earned (754)
price-earnings (P/E) ratio (759)
profitability (748)
quick assets (750)
quick ratio (750)
rate earned on common stockholders' equity (758)
rate earned on stockholders' equity (757)
rate earned on total assets (756)

ratio of fixed assets to long-term liabilities (753)
ratio of liabilities to stockholders' equity (754)
solvency (748)
vertical analysis (745)

Illustrative Problem

Rainbow Paint Co.'s comparative financial statements for the years ending December 31, 2008 and 2007, are as follows. The market price of Rainbow Paint Co.'s common stock was $30 on December 31, 2007, and $25 on December 31, 2008.

Rainbow Paint Co.
Comparative Income Statement
For the Years Ended December 31, 2008 and 2007

	2008	2007
Sales	$5,125,000	$3,257,600
Sales returns and allowances	125,000	57,600
Net sales	$5,000,000	$3,200,000
Cost of goods sold	3,400,000	2,080,000
Gross profit	$1,600,000	$1,120,000
Selling expenses	$ 650,000	$ 464,000
Administrative expenses	325,000	224,000
Total operating expenses	$ 975,000	$ 688,000
Income from operations	$ 625,000	$ 432,000
Other income	25,000	19,200
	$ 650,000	$ 451,200
Other expense (interest)	105,000	64,000
Income before income tax	$ 545,000	$ 387,200
Income tax expense	300,000	176,000
Net income	$ 245,000	$ 211,200

Rainbow Paint Co.
Comparative Retained Earnings Statement
For the Years Ended December 31, 2008 and 2007

	2008	2007
Retained earnings, January 1	$723,000	$581,800
Add net income for year	245,000	211,200
Total	$968,000	$793,000
Deduct dividends:		
On preferred stock	$ 40,000	$ 40,000
On common stock	45,000	30,000
Total	$ 85,000	$ 70,000
Retained earnings, December 31	$883,000	$723,000

(continued)

	2008	2007
Rainbow Paint Co. Comparative Balance Sheet December 31, 2008 and 2007		
Assets		
Current assets:		
Cash	$ 175,000	$ 125,000
Marketable securities	150,000	50,000
Accounts receivable (net)	425,000	325,000
Inventories	720,000	480,000
Prepaid expenses	30,000	20,000
Total current assets	$1,500,000	$1,000,000
Long-term investments.	250,000	225,000
Property, plant, and equipment (net)	2,093,000	1,948,000
Total assets	$3,843,000	$3,173,000
Liabilities		
Current liabilities	$ 750,000	$ 650,000
Long-term liabilities:		
Mortgage note payable, 10%, due 2011	$ 410,000	—
Bonds payable, 8%, due 2014	800,000	$ 800,000
Total long-term liabilities	$1,210,000	$ 800,000
Total liabilities	$1,960,000	$1,450,000
Stockholders' Equity		
Preferred 8% stock, $100 par	$ 500,000	$ 500,000
Common stock, $10 par	500,000	500,000
Retained earnings	883,000	723,000
Total stockholders' equity	$1,883,000	$1,723,000
Total liabilities and stockholders' equity	$3,843,000	$3,173,000

Instructions

Determine the following measures for 2008:

1. Working capital
2. Current ratio
3. Quick ratio
4. Accounts receivable turnover
5. Number of days' sales in receivables
6. Inventory turnover
7. Number of days' sales in inventory
8. Ratio of fixed assets to long-term liabilities
9. Ratio of liabilities to stockholders' equity
10. Number of times interest charges earned
11. Number of times preferred dividends earned
12. Ratio of net sales to assets
13. Rate earned on total assets
14. Rate earned on stockholders' equity
15. Rate earned on common stockholders' equity
16. Earnings per share on common stock
17. Price-earnings ratio
18. Dividends per share of common stock
19. Dividend yield

Solution

(Ratios are rounded to the nearest single digit after the decimal point.)

1. Working capital: $750,000
   $1,500,000 − $750,000

2. Current ratio: 2.0
   $1,500,000/$750,000

3. Quick ratio: 1.0
   $750,000/$750,000

4. Accounts receivable turnover: 13.3
   $5,000,000/[($425,000 + $325,000)/2]

5. Number of days' sales in receivables: 27.4 days
   $5,000,000/365 = $13,699
   $375,000/$13,699

6. Inventory turnover: 5.7
   $3,400,000/[($720,000 + $480,000)/2]

7. Number of days' sales in inventory: 64.4 days
   $3,400,000/365 − $9,315
   $600,000/$9,315

8. Ratio of fixed assets to long-term liabilities: 1.7
   $2,093,000/$1,210,000

9. Ratio of liabilities to stockholders' equity: 1.0
   $1,960,000/$1,883,000

10. Number of times interest charges earned: 6.2
    ($545,000 + $105,000)/$105,000

11. Number of times preferred dividends earned: 6.1
    $245,000/$40,000

12. Ratio of net sales to assets: 1.5
    $5,000,000/[($3,593,000 + $2,948,000)/2]

13. Rate earned on total assets: 10.0%
    ($245,000 + $105,000)/[($3,843,000 + $3,173,000)/2]

14. Rate earned on stockholders' equity: 13.6%
    $245,000/[($1,883,000 + $1,723,000)/2]

15. Rate earned on common stockholders' equity: 15.7%
    ($245,000 − $40,000)/[($1,383,000 + $1,223,000)/2]

16. Earnings per share on common stock: $4.10
    ($245,000 − $40,000)/50,000

17. Price-earnings ratio: 6.1
    $25/$4.10

18. Dividends per share of common stock: $0.90
    $45,000/50,000 shares

19. Dividend yield: 3.6%
    $0.90/$25

Self-Examination Questions

(Answers at End of Chapter)

1. What type of analysis is indicated by the following?

	Amount	Percent
Current assets	$100,000	20%
Property, plant, and equipment	400,000	80
Total assets	$500,000	100%

   A. Vertical analysis   C. Profitability analysis
   B. Horizontal analysis   D. Contribution margin
                                               analysis

2. Which of the following measures indicates the ability of a firm to pay its current liabilities?
   A. Working capital   C. Quick ratio
   B. Current ratio   D. All of the above

3. The ratio determined by dividing total current assets by total current liabilities is:
   A. current ratio.   C. bankers' ratio.
   B. working capital ratio.   D. all of the above.

4. The ratio of the quick assets to current liabilities, which indicates the "instant" debt-paying ability of a firm, is the:
   A. current ratio.   C. quick ratio.
   B. working capital ratio.   D. bankers' ratio.

5. A measure useful in evaluating efficiency in the management of inventories is the:
   A. working capital ratio.
   B. quick ratio.
   C. number of days' sales in inventory.
   D. ratio of fixed assets to long-term liabilities.

Eye Openers

1. What is the difference between horizontal and vertical analysis of financial statements?
2. What is the advantage of using comparative statements for financial analysis rather than statements for a single date or period?
3. The current year's amount of net income (after income tax) is 20% larger than that of the preceding year. Does this indicate an improved operating performance? Discuss.
4. How would you respond to a horizontal analysis that showed an expense increasing by over 80%?
5. How would the current and quick ratios of a service business compare?
6. For Lindsay Corporation, the working capital at the end of the current year is $8,000 less than the working capital at the end of the preceding year, reported as follows:

	Current Year	Preceding Year
Current assets:		
Cash, marketable securities, and receivables	$35,000	$36,000
Inventories	55,000	42,000
Total current assets	$90,000	$78,000
Current liabilities	50,000	30,000
Working capital	$40,000	$48,000

Has the current position improved? Explain.
7. Why would the accounts receivable turnover ratio be different between Wal-Mart and Procter & Gamble?
8. A company that grants terms of n/45 on all sales has a yearly accounts receivable turnover, based on monthly averages, of 5. Is this a satisfactory turnover? Discuss.
9. a. Why is it advantageous to have a high inventory turnover?
   b. Is it possible for the inventory turnover to be too high? Discuss.
   c. Is it possible to have a high inventory turnover and a high number of days' sales in inventory? Discuss.
10. What do the following data taken from a comparative balance sheet indicate about the company's ability to borrow additional funds on a long-term basis in the current year as compared to the preceding year?

	Current Year	Preceding Year
Fixed assets (net)	$300,000	$300,000
Total long-term liabilities	100,000	120,000

11. a. How does the rate earned on total assets differ from the rate earned on stockholders' equity?

    b. Which ratio is normally higher? Explain.

12. a. Why is the rate earned on stockholders' equity by a thriving business ordinarily higher than the rate earned on total assets?

    b. Should the rate earned on common stockholders' equity normally be higher or lower than the rate earned on total stockholders' equity? Explain.

13. The net income (after income tax) of Choi Inc. was $15 per common share in the latest year and $60 per common share for the preceding year. At the beginning of the latest year, the number of shares outstanding was doubled by a stock split. There were no other changes in the amount of stock outstanding. What were the earnings per share in the preceding year, adjusted for comparison with the latest year?

14. The price-earnings ratio for the common stock of Cotter Company was 10 at December 31, the end of the current fiscal year. What does the ratio indicate about the selling price of the common stock in relation to current earnings?

15. Why would the dividend yield differ significantly from the rate earned on common stockholders' equity?

16. Favorable business conditions may bring about certain seemingly unfavorable ratios, and unfavorable business operations may result in apparently favorable ratios. For example, Trivec Company increased its sales and net income substantially for the current year, yet the current ratio at the end of the year is lower than at the beginning of the year. Discuss some possible causes of the apparent weakening of the current position, while sales and net income have increased substantially.

Practice Exercises

PE 17-1A
Horizontal analysis
obj. 1

The comparative marketable securities and inventory balances for a company are provided below.

	2008	2007
Marketable securities	$68,200	$55,000
Inventory	63,700	65,000

Based on this information, what is the amount and percentage of increase or decrease that would be shown in a balance sheet with horizontal analysis?

PE 17-1B
Horizontal analysis
obj. 1

The comparative accounts payable and long-term debt balances of a company are provided below.

	2008	2007
Accounts payable	$141,600	$120,000
Long-term debt	150,000	125,000

Based on this information, what is the amount and percentage of increase or decrease that would be shown in a balance sheet with horizontal analysis?

PE 17-2A
Common-size financial statements
obj. 1

Income statement information for Washburn Corporation is provided below.

Sales	$400,000
Cost of goods sold	340,000
Gross profit	$ 60,000

Prepare a vertical analysis of the income statement for Washburn Corporation.

PE 17-2B
Common-size financial statements
obj. 1

Income statement information for Lewis Corporation is provided below.

Sales	$250,000
Gross profit	100,000
Net income	50,000

Prepare a vertical analysis of the income statement for Lewis Corporation.

PE 17-3A
Current position analysis
obj. 2

The following items are reported on a company's balance sheet:

Cash	$125,000
Marketable securities	40,000
Accounts receivable (net)	30,000
Inventory	120,000
Accounts payable	150,000

Determine (a) the current ratio and (b) the quick ratio. Round to one decimal place.

PE 17-3B
Current position analysis
obj. 2

The following items are reported on a company's balance sheet:

Cash	$275,000
Marketable securities	200,000
Accounts receivable (net)	625,000
Inventory	300,000
Accounts payable	800,000

Determine (a) the current ratio and (b) the quick ratio. Round to one decimal place.

PE 17-4A
Accounts receivable analysis
obj. 2

A company reports the following:

Net sales	$450,000
Average accounts receivable (net)	37,500

Determine (a) the accounts receivable turnover and (b) the number of days' sales in receivables. Round to one decimal place.

PE 17-4B
Accounts receivable analysis
obj. 2

A company reports the following:

Net sales	$225,000
Average accounts receivable (net)	25,000

Determine (a) the accounts receivable turnover and (b) the number of days' sales in receivables. Round to one decimal place.

PE 17-5A
Inventory analysis
obj. 2

A company reports the following:

Cost of goods sold	$465,000
Average inventory	71,500

Determine (a) the inventory turnover and (b) the number of days' sales in inventory. Round to one decimal place.

PE 17-5B
Inventory analysis
obj. 2

A company reports the following:

Cost of goods sold	$330,000
Average inventory	55,000

Determine (a) the inventory turnover and (b) the number of days' sales in inventory. Round to one decimal place.

PE 17-6A
Ratio of fixed assets to long-term liabilities and ratio of liabilities to stockholders' equity
obj. 2

The following information was taken from Straub Company's balance sheet:

Fixed assets (net)	$700,000
Long-term liabilities	218,750
Total liabilities	235,000
Total stockholders' equity	940,000

Determine the company's (a) ratio of fixed assets to long-term liabilities and (b) ratio of liabilities to stockholders' equity.

PE 17-6B
Ratio of fixed assets to long-term liabilities and ratio of liabilities to stockholders' equity
obj. 2

The following information was taken from Tristar Company's balance sheet:

Fixed assets (net)	$900,000
Long-term liabilities	625,000
Total liabilities	850,000
Total stockholders' equity	500,000

Determine the company's (a) ratio of fixed assets to long-term liabilities and (b) ratio of liabilities to stockholders' equity.

PE 17-7A
Number of times interest charges are earned
obj. 2

A company reports the following:

Income before income tax	$375,000
Interest expense	120,000

Determine the number of times interest charges are earned.

PE 17-7B
Number of times interest charges are earned
obj. 2

A company reports the following:

Income before income tax	$625,000
Interest expense	160,000

Determine the number of times interest charges are earned.

PE 17-8A
Ratio of net sales to assets
obj. 3

A company reports the following:

Net sales	$1,170,000
Average total assets	650,000

Determine the ratio of net sales to assets.

PE 17-8B
Ratio of net sales to assets
obj. 3

A company reports the following:

Net sales	$1,520,000
Average total assets	950,000

Determine the ratio of net sales to assets.

PE 17-9A
Rate earned on total assets
obj. 3

A company reports the following income statement and balance sheet information for the current year:

Net income	$ 225,000
Interest expense	20,000
Average total assets	3,250,000

Determine the rate earned on total assets.

PE 17-9B
Rate earned on total assets
obj. 3

A company reports the following income statement and balance sheet information for the current year:

Net income	$ 115,000
Interest expense	10,000
Average total assets	1,250,000

Determine the rate earned on total assets.

PE 17-10A
Rate earned on stockholders' equity and rate earned on common stockholders' equity
obj. 3

A company reports the following:

Net income	$ 225,000
Preferred dividends	20,000
Average stockholders' equity	1,750,000
Average common stockholders' equity	1,000,000

Determine (a) the rate earned on stockholders' equity and (b) the rate earned on common stockholders' equity. Round to one decimal place.

PE 17-10B
Rate earned on stockholders' equity and rate earned on common stockholders' equity
obj. 3

A company reports the following:

Net income	$115,000
Preferred dividends	10,000
Average stockholders' equity	850,000
Average common stockholders' equity	750,000

Determine (a) the rate earned on stockholders' equity and (b) the rate earned on common stockholders' equity.

PE 17-11A
Earnings per share on common stock and price earnings ratio
obj. 3

A company reports the following:

Net income	$115,000
Preferred dividends	$15,000
Shares of common stock outstanding	20,000
Market price per share of common stock	$65.00

a. Determine the company's earnings per share on common stock.
b. Determine the company's price-earnings ratio.

PE 17-11B
Earnings per share on common stock and price earnings ratio
obj. 3

A company reports the following:

Net income	$525,000
Preferred dividends	$25,000
Shares of common stock outstanding	50,000
Market price per share of common stock	$75.00

a. Determine the company's earnings per share on common stock.
b. Determine the company's price-earnings ratio.

Exercises

EX 17-1
Vertical analysis of income statement
obj. 1

✓ a. 2008 net income: $37,500; 5% of sales

Revenue and expense data for Jazz-Tech Communications Co. are as follows:

	2008	2007
Sales	$750,000	$600,000
Cost of goods sold	450,000	312,000
Selling expenses	120,000	126,000
Administrative expenses	105,000	84,000
Income tax expense	37,500	30,000

a. Prepare an income statement in comparative form, stating each item for both 2008 and 2007 as a percent of sales. Round to one decimal place.

b. Comment on the significant changes disclosed by the comparative income statement.

EX 17-2
Vertical analysis of income statement
obj. 1

✓ *a. Fiscal year 2004 income from continuing operations, 26.7% of revenues*

The following comparative income statement (in thousands of dollars) for the fiscal years 2003 and 2004 was adapted from the annual report of Speedway Motorsports, Inc., owner and operator of several major motor speedways, such as the Atlanta, Texas, and Las Vegas Motor Speedways.

	Fiscal Year 2004	Fiscal Year 2003
Revenues:		
Admissions	$156,718	$150,253
Event-related revenue	137,074	127,055
NASCAR broadcasting revenue	110,016	90,682
Other operating revenue	42,711	36,539
Total revenue	$446,519	$404,529
Expenses and other:		
Direct expense of events	$ 81,432	$ 77,962
NASCAR purse and sanction fees	78,473	69,691
Other direct expenses	102,053	101,408
General and administrative	65,152	58,698
Total expenses and other	$327,110	$307,759
Income from continuing operations	$119,409	$ 96,770

a. Prepare a comparative income statement for fiscal years 2003 and 2004 in vertical form, stating each item as a percent of revenues. Round to one decimal place.

b. Comment on the significant changes.

EX 17-3
Common-size income statement
obj. 1

✓ *a. Jaribo net income: $85,000; 6.8% of sales*

Revenue and expense data for the current calendar year for Jaribo Communications Company and for the communications industry are as follows. The Jaribo Communications Company data are expressed in dollars. The communications industry averages are expressed in percentages.

	Jaribo Communications Company	Communications Industry Average
Sales	$1,265,000	101.0%
Sales returns and allowances	15,000	1.0
Cost of goods sold	450,000	41.0
Selling expenses	525,000	38.0
Administrative expenses	143,750	10.5
Other income	22,500	1.2
Other expense (interest)	18,750	1.7
Income tax expense	50,000	4.0

a. Prepare a common-size income statement comparing the results of operations for Jaribo Communications Company with the industry average. Round to one decimal place.

b. As far as the data permit, comment on significant relationships revealed by the comparisons.

EX 17-4
Vertical analysis of balance sheet
obj. 1

Balance sheet data for the Dover Hot Tub Company on December 31, the end of the fiscal year, are shown at the top of the following page.

**✓ Retained earnings,
Dec. 31, 2008, 47.5%**

	2008	2007
Current assets	$768,000	$250,000
Property, plant, and equipment	336,000	650,000
Intangible assets	96,000	100,000
Current liabilities	270,000	175,000
Long-term liabilities	300,000	255,000
Common stock	60,000	70,000
Retained earnings	570,000	500,000

Prepare a comparative balance sheet for 2008 and 2007, stating each asset as a percent of total assets and each liability and stockholders' equity item as a percent of the total liabilities and stockholders' equity. Round to one decimal place.

EX 17-5
Horizontal analysis of the income statement
obj. 1

✓ a. Net income decrease, 53.3%

Income statement data for Web-pics Company for the years ended December 31, 2008 and 2007, are as follows:

	2008	2007
Sales	$117,000	$150,000
Cost of goods sold	56,000	70,000
Gross profit	$ 61,000	$ 80,000
Selling expenses	$ 36,000	$ 37,500
Administrative expenses	12,500	10,000
Total operating expenses	$ 48,500	$ 47,500
Income before income tax	$ 12,500	$ 32,500
Income tax expense	2,000	10,000
Net income	$ 10,500	$ 22,500

a. Prepare a comparative income statement with horizontal analysis, indicating the increase (decrease) for 2008 when compared with 2007. Round to one decimal place.
b. What conclusions can be drawn from the horizontal analysis?

EX 17-6
Current position analysis
obj. 2

✓ a. 2008 working capital, $1,265,000

The following data were taken from the balance sheet of Outdoor Suppliers Company:

	Dec. 31, 2008	Dec. 31, 2007
Cash	$325,000	$300,000
Marketable securities	270,000	256,000
Accounts and notes receivable (net)	440,000	430,000
Inventories	675,000	557,000
Prepaid expenses	130,000	81,000
Accounts and notes payable (short-term)	425,000	450,000
Accrued liabilities	150,000	130,000

a. Determine for each year (1) the working capital, (2) the current ratio, and (3) the quick ratio. Round ratios to one decimal place.
b. What conclusions can be drawn from these data as to the company's ability to meet its currently maturing debts?

EX 17-7
Current position analysis
obj. 2

✓ a. (1) Dec. 25, 2004 current ratio, 1.2

PepsiCo, Inc., the parent company of Frito-Lay snack foods and Pepsi beverages, had the following current assets and current liabilities at the end of two recent years:

	Dec. 31, 2005 (in millions)	Dec. 25, 2004 (in millions)
Cash and cash equivalents	$1,716	$1,280
Short-term investments, at cost	3,166	2,165
Accounts and notes receivable, net	3,261	2,999
Inventories	1,693	1,541
Prepaid expenses and other current assets	618	654
Short-term obligations	2,889	1,054
Accounts payable and other current liabilities	5,971	5,999
Income taxes payable	546	99

a. Determine the (1) current ratio and (2) quick ratio for both years. Round to one decimal place.

b. What conclusions can you draw from these data?

EX 17-8
Current position analysis
obj. 2

The bond indenture for the 20-year, 11% debenture bonds dated January 2, 2007, required working capital of $560,000, a current ratio of 1.5, and a quick ratio of 1.2 at the end of each calendar year until the bonds mature. At December 31, 2008, the three measures were computed as follows:

1. Current assets:

Cash	$190,000
Marketable securities	95,000
Accounts and notes receivable (net)	171,000
Inventories	20,000
Prepaid expenses	4,500
Intangible assets	55,000
Property, plant & equipment	65,000
Total current assets (net)	$600,500
Current liabilities:	
Accounts and short-term notes payable	$250,000
Accrued liabilities	150,000
Total current liabilities	400,000
Working capital	$200,500

2. Current Ratio = 1.50 ($600,500/$400,000)
3. Quick Ratio = 2.04 ($511,000/$250,000)

a. List the errors in the determination of the three measures of current position analysis.
b. Is the company satisfying the terms of the bond indenture?

EX 17-9
Accounts receivable analysis
obj. 2

✓ *a. Accounts receivable turnover, 2008, 6.9*

The following data are taken from the financial statements of Creekside Technology Inc. Terms of all sales are 2/10, n/60.

	2008	2007	2006
Accounts receivable, end of year	$ 75,452	$ 85,500	$81,624
Monthly average accounts receivable (net)	78,261	80,645	—
Net sales	540,000	500,000	—

a. Determine for each year (1) the accounts receivable turnover and (2) the number of days' sales in receivables. Round to nearest dollar and one decimal place.
b. What conclusions can be drawn from these data concerning accounts receivable and credit policies?

EX 17-10
Accounts receivable analysis
obj. 2

✓ *a. (1) May's accounts receivable turnover, 7.1*

The May Department Stores Company (Marshall Field's, Hecht's, Lord & Taylor) and Federated Department Stores, Inc. (Macy's and Bloomingdale's) are two of the largest department store chains in the United States. Both companies offer credit to their customers through their own credit card operations. Information from the financial statements for both companies for two recent years is as follows (all numbers are in millions):

	May	Federated
Merchandise sales	$14,441	$15,630
Credit card receivables—beginning	2,294	3,418
Credit card receivables—ending	1,788	3,213

a. Determine the (1) accounts receivable turnover and (2) the number of days' sales in receivables for both companies. Round to one decimal place.
b. Compare the two companies with regard to their credit card policies.

EX 17-11
Inventory analysis
obj. 2

✓ *a. Inventory turnover, current year, 7.5*

The following data were extracted from the income statement of Clear View Systems Inc.:

	Current Year	Preceding Year
Sales	$756,000	$950,760
Beginning inventories	67,200	44,000
Cost of goods sold	492,000	528,200
Ending inventories	64,000	67,200

a. Determine for each year (1) the inventory turnover and (2) the number of days' sales in inventory. Round to nearest dollar and one decimal place.

b. ▭▬▶ What conclusions can be drawn from these data concerning the inventories?

EX 17-12
Inventory analysis
obj. 2

REAL WORLD

✓ *a. Dell inventory turnover, 88.2*

Dell Inc. and Hewlett-Packard Company (HP) compete with each other in the personal computer market. Dell's strategy is to assemble computers to customer orders, rather than for inventory. Thus, for example, Dell will build and deliver a computer within four days of a customer entering an order on a Web page. Hewlett-Packard, on the other hand, builds some computers prior to receiving an order, then sells from this inventory once an order is received. Below is selected financial information for both companies from a recent year's financial statements (in millions):

	Dell Inc.	Hewlett-Packard Company
Sales	$55,908	$86,696
Cost of goods sold	45,620	66,440
Inventory, beginning of period	459	7,071
Inventory, end of period	576	6,877

a. Determine for both companies (1) the inventory turnover and (2) the number of days' sales in inventory. Round to one decimal place.

b. ▭▬▶ Interpret the inventory ratios by considering Dell's and Hewlett-Packard's operating strategies.

EX 17-13
Ratio of liabilities to stockholders' equity and number of times interest charges earned
obj. 2

✓ *a. Ratio of liabilities to stockholders' equity, Dec. 31, 2008, 0.5*

The following data were taken from the financial statements of Quality Construction Inc. for December 31, 2008 and 2007:

	December 31, 2008	December 31, 2007
Accounts payable	$ 240,000	$ 224,000
Current maturities of serial bonds payable	320,000	320,000
Serial bonds payable, 10%, issued 2004, due 2014	1,600,000	1,920,000
Common stock, $1 par value	160,000	160,000
Paid-in capital in excess of par	800,000	800,000
Retained earnings	3,404,800	2,560,000

The income before income tax was $844,800 and $537,600 for the years 2008 and 2007, respectively.

a. Determine the ratio of liabilities to stockholders' equity at the end of each year. Round to one decimal place.

b. Determine the number of times the bond interest charges are earned during the year for both years. Round to one decimal place.

c. ▭▬▶ What conclusions can be drawn from these data as to the company's ability to meet its currently maturing debts?

EX 17-14
Ratio of liabilities to stockholders' equity and number of times interest charges earned
obj. 2

Hasbro and Mattel, Inc., are the two largest toy companies in North America. Condensed liabilities and stockholders' equity from a recent balance sheet are shown for each company as follows:

✓ a. Hasbro, 1.0

	Hasbro	Mattel, Inc.
Current liabilities	$1,148,611,000	$1,727,171,000
Long-term debt	302,698,000	400,000,000
Deferred liabilities	149,627,000	243,509,000
Total liabilities	$1,600,936,000	$2,370,680,000
Shareholders' equity:		
Common stock, $0.50 par value	$ 104,847,000	$ 441,369,000
Additional paid-in capital	380,745,000	1,594,332,000
Retained earnings	1,721,209,000	1,093,288,000
Accumulated other comprehensive loss and other equity items	82,290,000	(269,828,000)
Treasury stock, at cost	(649,367,000)	(473,349,000)
Total stockholders' equity	$1,639,724,000	$2,385,812,000
Total liabilities and stockholders' equity	$3,240,660,000	$4,756,492,000

The income from operations and interest expense from the income statement for both companies were as follows:

	Hasbro	Mattel, Inc.
Income from operations	$293,012,000	$730,817,000
Interest expense	31,698,000	77,764,000

a. Determine the ratio of liabilities to stockholders' equity for both companies. Round to one decimal place.

b. Determine the number of times interest charges are earned for both companies. Round to one decimal place.

c. ▭▭▶ Interpret the ratio differences between the two companies.

EX 17-15
Ratio of liabilities to stockholders' equity and ratio of fixed assets to long-term liabilities

obj. 2

✓ a. H.J. Heinz, 3.1

Recent balance sheet information for two companies in the food industry, H.J. Heinz Company and The Hershey Company, are as follows (in thousands of dollars):

	H.J. Heinz	Hershey
Net property, plant, and equipment	$2,163,938	$1,659,138
Current liabilities	2,587,068	1,518,223
Long-term debt	4,121,984	942,755
Other liabilities (pensions, deferred taxes)	1,266,093	813,182
Stockholders' equity	2,602,573	1,021,076

a. Determine the ratio of liabilities to stockholders' equity for both companies. Round to one decimal place.

b. Determine the ratio of fixed assets to long-term liabilities for both companies. Round to one decimal place.

c. ▭▭▶ Interpret the ratio differences between the two companies.

EX 17-16
Ratio of net sales to assets

obj. 3

✓ a. YRC Worldwide, 1.9

Three major segments of the transportation industry are motor carriers, such as YRC Worldwide; railroads, such as Union Pacific; and transportation arrangement services, such as C.H. Robinson Worldwide Inc. Recent financial statement information for these three companies is shown as follows (in thousands of dollars):

	YRC Worldwide	Union Pacific	C.H. Robinson Worldwide
Net sales	$6,767,485	$12,215,000	$4,341,538
Average total assets	3,545,199	34,041,500	994,423

a. Determine the ratio of net sales to assets for all three companies. Round to one decimal place.

b. ▭▭▶ Assume that the ratio of net sales to assets for each company represents their respective industry segment. Interpret the differences in the ratio of net sales to assets in terms of the operating characteristics of each of the respective segments.

EX 17-17
Profitability ratios

obj. 3

✔ *a. Rate earned on total assets, 2008, 11.6%*

The following selected data were taken from the financial statements of Berry Group Inc. for December 31, 2008, 2007, and 2006:

	December 31, 2008	December 31, 2007	December 31, 2006
Total assets	$1,160,000	$1,040,000	$880,000
Notes payable (10% interest)	150,000	150,000	150,000
Common stock	360,000	360,000	360,000
Preferred $8 stock, $100 par			
(no change during year)	160,000	160,000	160,000
Retained earnings	426,900	327,200	205,000

The 2008 net income was $112,500, and the 2007 net income was $135,000. No dividends on common stock were declared between 2006 and 2008.

a. Determine the rate earned on total assets, the rate earned on stockholders' equity, and the rate earned on common stockholders' equity for the years 2007 and 2008. Round to one decimal place.

b. ▭▭▶ What conclusions can be drawn from these data as to the company's profitability?

EX 17-18
Profitability ratios

obj. 3

✔ *a. 2005 rate earned on total assets, 6.0%*

Ann Taylor Retail, Inc., sells professional women's apparel through company-owned retail stores. Recent financial information for Ann Taylor is provided below (all numbers in thousands):

	Fiscal Year Ended	
	Jan. 28, 2006	Jan. 29, 2005
Net income	$81,872	$63,276
Interest expense	2,083	3,641

	Jan. 28, 2006	Jan. 29, 2005	Jan. 31, 2004
Total assets	$1,492,906	$1,327,338	$1,256,397
Total stockholders' equity	1,034,482	926,744	818,856

Assume the apparel industry average rate earned on total assets is 8.2%, and the average rate earned on stockholders' equity is 16.7% for fiscal 2005.

a. Determine the rate earned on total assets for Ann Taylor for the fiscal years ended January 28, 2006, and January 29, 2005. Round to one digit after the decimal place.

b. Determine the rate earned on stockholders' equity for Ann Taylor for the fiscal years ended January 28, 2006, and January 29, 2005. Round to one decimal place.

c. ▭▭▶ Evaluate the two-year trend for the profitability ratios determined in (a) and (b).

d. ▭▭▶ Evaluate Ann Taylor's profit performance relative to the industry.

EX 17-19
Six measures of solvency or profitability

objs. 2, 3

✔ *c. Ratio of net sales to assets, 1.5*

The following data were taken from the financial statements of Bendax Enterprises Inc. for the current fiscal year. Assuming that long-term investments totaled $240,000 throughout the year and that total assets were $2,525,000 at the beginning of the year, determine the following: (a) ratio of fixed assets to long-term liabilities, (b) ratio of liabilities to stockholders' equity, (c) ratio of net sales to assets, (d) rate earned on total assets, (e) rate earned on stockholders' equity, and (f) rate earned on common stockholders' equity. Round to one decimal place.

Property, plant, and equipment (net)		$1,200,000
Liabilities:		
Current liabilities	$ 60,000	
Mortgage note payable, 8%, issued 1997, due 2013	825,000	
Total liabilities		$ 885,000

Stockholders' equity:

Preferred $9 stock, $100 par (no change during year) ...			$ 250,000
Common stock, $20 par (no change during year)			800,000

Retained earnings:

Balance, beginning of year	$600,000		
Net income	216,000	$816,000	
Preferred dividends	$ 22,500		
Common dividends	57,600	80,100	
Balance, end of year			735,900
Total stockholders' equity			$1,785,900
Net sales			$3,600,000
Interest expense			$ 66,000

EX 17-20
Six measures of solvency or profitability
objs. 2, 3

✓d. Price-earnings ratio, 16.1

The balance sheet for Chaney Resources Inc. at the end of the current fiscal year indicated the following:

Bonds payable, 10% (issued in 1995, due in 2015)	$2,250,000
Preferred $25 stock, $200 par	500,000
Common stock, $10 par	2,500,000

Income before income tax was $625,000, and income taxes were $175,000 for the current year. Cash dividends paid on common stock during the current year totaled $125,000. The common stock was selling for $25 per share at the end of the year. Determine each of the following: (a) number of times bond interest charges are earned, (b) number of times preferred dividends are earned, (c) earnings per share on common stock, (d) price-earnings ratio, (e) dividends per share of common stock, and (f) dividend yield. Round to one decimal place except earnings per share, which should be rounded to two decimal places.

EX 17-21
Earnings per share, price-earnings ratio, dividend yield
obj. 3

✓b. Price-earnings ratio, 14.8

The following information was taken from the financial statements of Royer Medical Inc. for December 31 of the current fiscal year:

Common stock, $5 par value (no change during the year)	$1,500,000
Preferred $5 stock, $50 par (no change during the year)	450,000

The net income was $450,000, and the declared dividends on the common stock were $75,000 for the current year. The market price of the common stock is $20 per share.

For the common stock, determine (a) the earnings per share, (b) the price-earnings ratio, (c) the dividends per share, and (d) the dividend yield. Round to one decimal place except earnings per share, which should be rounded to two decimal places.

EX 17-22
Earnings per share
obj. 3

✓b. Earnings per share on common stock, $3.00

The net income reported on the income statement of Ground Hog Co. was $1,250,000. There were 250,000 shares of $40 par common stock and 50,000 shares of $10 preferred stock outstanding throughout the current year. The income statement included two extraordinary items: a $360,000 gain from condemnation of land and a $235,000 loss arising from flood damage, both after applicable income tax. Determine the per share figures for common stock for (a) income before extraordinary items and (b) net income.

EX 17-23
Price-earnings ratio; dividend yield
obj. 3

The table below shows the stock price, earnings per share, and dividends per share for three companies as of February 10, 2006:

	Price	Earnings per Share	Dividends per Share
Bank of America Corporation	$44.47	$4.15	$2.00
eBay Inc.	41.60	0.78	0.00
The Coca-Cola Company	41.19	2.04	1.12

a. Determine the price-earnings ratio and dividend yield for the three companies. Round to one decimal place.

b. Explain the differences in these ratios across the three companies.

Problems Series A

PR 17-1A
Horizontal analysis for income statement

obj. 1

✓ *1. Net sales, 25.1% increase*

For 2008, Doane Inc. reported its most significant increase in net income in years. At the end of the year, Jeff Newton, the president, is presented with the following condensed comparative income statement:

Doane Inc.
Comparative Income Statement
For the Years Ended December 31, 2008 and 2007

	2008	2007
Sales	$91,500	$73,200
Sales returns and allowances	1,440	1,200
Net sales	$90,060	$72,000
Cost of goods sold	50,400	42,000
Gross profit	$39,660	$30,000
Selling expenses	$16,560	$14,400
Administrative expenses	10,800	9,600
Total operating expenses	$27,360	$24,000
Income from operations	$12,300	$ 6,000
Other income	600	600
Income before income tax	$12,900	$ 6,600
Income tax expense	2,880	1,440
Net income	$10,020	$ 5,160

Instructions

1. Prepare a comparative income statement with horizontal analysis for the two-year period, using 2007 as the base year. Round to one decimal place.
2. To the extent the data permit, comment on the significant relationships revealed by the horizontal analysis prepared in (1).

PR 17-2A
Vertical analysis for income statement

obj. 1

✓ *1. Net income, 2007, 8.0%*

For 2008, Dusan Water Supplies Inc. initiated a sales promotion campaign that included the expenditure of an additional $21,000 for advertising. At the end of the year, Ivana Novatna, the president, is presented with the following condensed comparative income statement:

Dusan Water Supplies Inc.
Comparative Income Statement
For the Years Ended December 31, 2008 and 2007

	2008	2007
Sales	$255,000	$214,000
Sales returns and allowances	5,000	4,000
Net sales	$250,000	$210,000
Cost of goods sold	142,500	121,800
Gross profit	$107,500	$ 88,200
Selling expenses	$100,000	$ 50,400
Administrative expenses	20,000	16,800
Total operating expenses	$120,000	$ 67,200
Income from operations	$ (12,500)	$ 21,000
Other income	6,250	4,200
Income before income tax	$ (6,250)	$ 25,200
Income tax expense (benefit)	(2,500)	8,400
Net income (loss)	$ (3,750)	$ 16,800

Instructions

1. Prepare a comparative income statement for the two-year period, presenting an analysis of each item in relationship to net sales for each of the years. Round to one decimal place.
2. ▭▭▭▭▭▶ To the extent the data permit, comment on the significant relationships revealed by the vertical analysis prepared in (1).

PR 17-3A
Effect of transactions on current position analysis

obj. 2

✓*1. c. Quick ratio, 1.4*

Data pertaining to the current position of Tsali Industries, Inc., are as follows:

Cash	$195,000
Marketable securities	92,500
Accounts and notes receivable (net)	293,000
Inventories	357,500
Prepaid expenses	15,000
Accounts payable	295,000
Notes payable (short-term)	92,000
Accrued expenses	42,500

Instructions

1. Compute (a) the working capital, (b) the current ratio, and (c) the quick ratio. Round to one decimal place.
2. List the following captions on a sheet of paper:

Transaction	Working Capital	Current Ratio	Quick Ratio

Compute the working capital, the current ratio, and the quick ratio after each of the following transactions, and record the results in the appropriate columns. Consider each transaction separately and assume that only that transaction affects the data given above. Round to one decimal place.

a. Sold marketable securities at no gain or loss, $37,500.
b. Paid accounts payable, $84,000.
c. Purchased goods on account, $55,000.
d. Paid notes payable, $32,500.
e. Declared a cash dividend, $38,000.
f. Declared a common stock dividend on common stock, $21,500.
g. Borrowed cash from bank on a long-term note, $185,000.
h. Received cash on account, $93,500.
i. Issued additional shares of stock for cash, $175,000.
j. Paid cash for prepaid expenses, $15,000.

PR 17-4A
Nineteen measures of solvency and profitability

objs. 2, 3

✓*9. Ratio of liabilities to stockholders' equity, 0.5*

The comparative financial statements of Triad Images Inc. are as follows. The market price of Triad Images Inc. common stock was $55 on December 31, 2008.

Triad Images Inc.
Comparative Retained Earnings Statement
For the Years Ended December 31, 2008 and 2007

	Dec. 31, 2008	Dec. 31, 2007
Retained earnings, January 1	$1,006,500	$ 781,500
Add net income for year	430,000	277,500
Total	$1,436,500	$1,059,000
Deduct dividends:		
On preferred stock	$ 12,500	$ 12,500
On common stock	40,000	40,000
Total	$ 52,500	$ 52,500
Retained earnings, December 31	$1,384,000	$1,006,500

(continued)

Triad Images Inc.
Comparative Income Statement
For the Years Ended December 31, 2008 and 2007

	2008	2007
Sales	$3,395,000	$3,062,500
Sales returns and allowances	35,000	22,500
Net sales	$3,360,000	$3,040,000
Cost of goods sold	1,500,000	1,437,500
Gross profit	$1,860,000	$1,602,500
Selling expenses	$ 726,000	$ 718,750
Administrative expenses	486,000	475,000
Total operating expenses	$1,212,000	$1,193,750
Income from operations	$ 648,000	$ 408,750
Other income	48,000	37,500
	$ 696,000	$ 446,250
Other expense (interest)	98,000	50,000
Income before income tax	$ 598,000	$ 396,250
Income tax expense	168,000	118,750
Net income	$ 430,000	$ 277,500

Triad Images Inc.
Comparative Balance Sheet
December 31, 2008 and 2007

	Dec. 31, 2008	Dec. 31, 2007
Assets		
Current assets:		
Cash	$ 132,000	$ 120,000
Marketable securities	387,000	157,500
Accounts receivable (net)	260,000	196,500
Inventories	425,000	332,500
Prepaid expenses	27,500	35,000
Total current assets	$1,231,500	$ 841,500
Long-term investments	319,500	250,000
Property, plant, and equipment (net)	2,575,000	2,000,000
Total assets	$4,126,000	$3,091,500
Liabilities		
Current liabilities	$ 342,000	$ 285,000
Long-term liabilities:		
Mortgage note payable, 8%, due 2013	$ 600,000	—
Bonds payable, 10%, due 2017	500,000	$ 500,000
Total long-term liabilities	$1,100,000	$ 500,000
Total liabilities	$1,442,000	$ 785,000
Stockholders' Equity		
Preferred $2.50 stock, $100 par	$ 500,000	$ 500,000
Common stock, $20 par	800,000	800,000
Retained earnings	1,384,000	1,006,500
Total stockholders' equity	$2,684,000	$2,306,500
Total liabilities and stockholders' equity	$4,126,000	$3,091,500

Instructions

Determine the following measures for 2008, rounding to one decimal place:

1. Working capital
2. Current ratio
3. Quick ratio
4. Accounts receivable turnover
5. Number of days' sales in receivables
6. Inventory turnover
7. Number of days' sales in inventory
8. Ratio of fixed assets to long-term liabilities

9. Ratio of liabilities to stockholders' equity
10. Number of times interest charges earned
11. Number of times preferred dividends earned
12. Ratio of net sales to assets
13. Rate earned on total assets
14. Rate earned on stockholders' equity
15. Rate earned on common stockholders' equity
16. Earnings per share on common stock
17. Price-earnings ratio
18. Dividends per share of common stock
19. Dividend yield

PR 17-5A
Solvency and profitability trend analysis
objs. 2, 3

Shore Company has provided the following comparative information:

	2008	2007	2006	2005	2004
Net income	$ 42,000	$ 70,000	$ 140,000	$ 210,000	$ 210,000
Interest expense	142,800	133,000	119,000	112,000	105,000
Income tax expense	12,600	21,000	42,000	63,000	63,000
Total assets (ending balance)	2,240,000	2,100,000	1,890,000	1,680,000	1,400,000
Total stockholders' equity (ending balance)	812,000	770,000	700,000	560,000	350,000
Average total assets	2,170,000	1,995,000	1,785,000	1,540,000	1,260,000
Average stockholders' equity	791,000	735,000	630,000	455,000	315,000

You have been asked to evaluate the historical performance of the company over the last five years.

Selected industry ratios have remained relatively steady at the following levels for the last five years:

	2004–2008
Rate earned on total assets	11%
Rate earned on stockholders' equity	20%
Number of times interest charges earned	3.0
Ratio of liabilities to stockholders' equity	2.0

Instructions
1. Prepare four line graphs with the ratio on the vertical axis and the years on the horizontal axis for the following four ratios (rounded to one decimal place):
   a. Rate earned on total assets
   b. Rate earned on stockholders' equity
   c. Number of times interest charges earned
   d. Ratio of liabilities to stockholders' equity
   Display both the company ratio and the industry benchmark on each graph. That is, each graph should have two lines.
2. ▭▶ Prepare an analysis of the graphs in (1).

Problems Series B

PR 17-1B
Horizontal analysis for income statement
obj. 1

For 2008, Phoenix Technology Company reported its most significant decline in net income in years. At the end of the year, Hai Chow, the president, is presented with the following condensed comparative income statement:

✓ *1. Net sales, 11.8% increase*

Phoenix Technology Company
Comparative Income Statement
For the Years Ended December 31, 2008 and 2007

	2008	2007
Sales	$385,000	$343,200
Sales returns and allowances	4,800	3,200
Net sales	$380,200	$340,000
Cost of goods sold	180,000	144,000
Gross profit	$200,200	$196,000
Selling expenses	$ 87,400	$ 76,000
Administrative expenses	30,000	24,000
Total operating expenses	$117,400	$100,000
Income from operations	$ 82,800	$ 96,000
Other income	1,600	1,600
Income before income tax	$ 84,400	$ 97,600
Income tax expense	36,800	32,000
Net income	$ 47,600	$ 65,600

Instructions

1. Prepare a comparative income statement with horizontal analysis for the two-year period, using 2007 as the base year. Round to one decimal place.
2. ▬▬▶ To the extent the data permit, comment on the significant relationships revealed by the horizontal analysis prepared in (1).

PR 17-2B
Vertical analysis for income statement
obj. 1

✓ *1. Net income, 2008, 20.0%*

For 2008, Acedia Technology Company initiated a sales promotion campaign that included the expenditure of an additional $10,000 for advertising. At the end of the year, Gordon Kincaid, the president, is presented with the following condensed comparative income statement:

Acedia Technology Company
Comparative Income Statement
For the Years Ended December 31, 2008 and 2007

	2008	2007
Sales	$755,000	$676,000
Sales returns and allowances	5,000	6,000
Net sales	$750,000	$670,000
Cost of goods sold	292,500	274,700
Gross profit	$457,500	$395,300
Selling expenses	$172,500	$160,800
Administrative expenses	82,500	80,400
Total operating expenses	$255,000	$241,200
Income from operations	$202,500	$154,100
Other income	7,500	6,700
Income before income tax	$210,000	$160,800
Income tax expense	60,000	53,600
Net income	$150,000	$107,200

Instructions

1. Prepare a comparative income statement for the two-year period, presenting an analysis of each item in relationship to net sales for each of the years. Round to one decimal place.
2. ▬▬▶ To the extent the data permit, comment on the significant relationships revealed by the vertical analysis prepared in (1).

PR 17-3B
Effect of transactions on current position analysis
obj. 2

✓ *1. b. Current ratio, 2.1*

Data pertaining to the current position of Spruce Pine Medical Company are as follows:

Cash	$384,000
Marketable securities	176,000
Accounts and notes receivable (net)	608,000
Inventories	792,000
Prepaid expenses	48,000
Accounts payable	624,000
Notes payable (short-term)	240,000
Accrued expenses	80,000

Instructions

1. Compute (a) the working capital, (b) the current ratio, and (c) the quick ratio. Round to one decimal place.
2. List the following captions on a sheet of paper:

Transaction	Working Capital	Current Ratio	Quick Ratio

Compute the working capital, the current ratio, and the quick ratio after each of the following transactions, and record the results in the appropriate columns. Consider each transaction separately and assume that only that transaction affects the data given above. Round to one decimal place.

a. Sold marketable securities at no gain or loss, $65,000.
b. Paid accounts payable, $90,000.
c. Purchased goods on account, $120,000.
d. Paid notes payable, $65,000.
e. Declared a cash dividend, $32,500.
f. Declared a common stock dividend on common stock, $34,000.
g. Borrowed cash from bank on a long-term note, $160,000.
h. Received cash on account, $125,000.
i. Issued additional shares of stock for cash, $425,000.
j. Paid cash for prepaid expenses, $16,000.

PR 17-4B
*Nineteen measures of
solvency and profitability*
objs. 2, 3

✓5. Number of days'
sales in receivables, 50.8

The comparative financial statements of Dental Innovations Inc. are as follows. The market price of Dental Innovations Inc. common stock was $15 on December 31, 2008.

Dental Innovations Inc.
Comparative Retained Earnings Statement
For the Years Ended December 31, 2008 and 2007

	Dec. 31, 2008	Dec. 31, 2007
Retained earnings, January 1	$265,000	$ 31,000
Add net income for year	321,500	244,000
Total	$586,500	$275,000
Deduct dividends:		
On preferred stock	$ 10,000	$ 5,000
On common stock	7,000	5,000
Total	$ 17,000	$ 10,000
Retained earnings, December 31	$569,500	$265,000

Dental Innovations Inc.
Comparative Income Statement
For the Years Ended December 31, 2008 and 2007

	2008	2007
Sales	$1,055,000	$966,000
Sales returns and allowances	5,000	6,000
Net sales	$1,050,000	$960,000
Cost of goods sold	300,000	312,000
Gross profit	$ 750,000	$648,000
Selling expenses	$ 202,500	$220,000
Administrative expenses	146,250	132,000
Total operating expenses	$ 348,750	$352,000
Income from operations	$ 401,250	$296,000
Other income	15,000	12,000
	$ 416,250	$308,000
Other expense (interest)	64,000	40,000
Income before income tax	$ 352,250	$268,000
Income tax expense	30,750	24,000
Net income	$ 321,500	$244,000

(continued)

Dental Innovations Inc.
Comparative Balance Sheet
December 31, 2008 and 2007

	Dec. 31, 2008	Dec. 31, 2007
Assets		
Current assets:		
Cash	$ 165,000	$ 101,500
Marketable securities	335,000	205,500
Accounts receivable (net)	160,000	132,000
Inventories	67,500	41,500
Prepaid expenses	27,000	14,500
Total current assets	$ 754,500	$ 495,000
Long-term investments	310,000	160,000
Property, plant, and equipment (net)	950,000	610,000
Total assets	$2,014,500	$1,265,000
Liabilities		
Current liabilities	$ 225,000	$ 200,000
Long-term liabilities:		
Mortgage note payable, 10%, due 2013	$ 240,000	—
Bonds payable, 8%, due 2017	500,000	$ 500,000
Total long-term liabilities	$ 740,000	$ 500,000
Total liabilities	$ 965,000	$ 700,000
Stockholders' Equity		
Preferred $2.50 stock, $50 par	$ 200,000	$ 100,000
Common stock, $10 par	280,000	200,000
Retained earnings	569,500	265,000
Total stockholders' equity	$1,049,500	$ 565,000
Total liabilities and stockholders' equity	$2,014,500	$1,265,000

Instructions

Determine the following measures for 2008, rounding to one decimal place:

1. Working capital
2. Current ratio
3. Quick ratio
4. Accounts receivable turnover
5. Number of days' sales in receivables
6. Inventory turnover
7. Number of days' sales in inventory
8. Ratio of fixed assets to long-term liabilities
9. Ratio of liabilities to stockholders' equity
10. Number of times interest charges earned
11. Number of times preferred dividends earned
12. Ratio of net sales to assets
13. Rate earned on total assets
14. Rate earned on stockholders' equity
15. Rate earned on common stockholders' equity
16. Earnings per share on common stock
17. Price-earnings ratio
18. Dividends per share of common stock
19. Dividend yield

PR 17-5B
Solvency and profitability trend analysis

objs. 2, 3

Van DeKamp Company has provided the following comparative information:

	2008	2007	2006	2005	2004
Net income	$1,815,000	$1,200,000	$ 900,000	$ 600,000	$ 450,000
Interest expense	271,800	234,000	202,500	162,000	135,000
Income tax expense	635,250	420,000	315,000	210,000	157,500
Total assets (ending balance)	9,035,000	6,800,000	5,250,000	3,900,000	3,000,000
Total stockholders' equity (ending balance)	6,015,000	4,200,000	3,000,000	2,100,000	1,500,000
Average total assets	7,917,500	6,025,000	4,575,000	3,450,000	2,700,000
Average stockholders' equity	5,107,500	3,600,000	2,550,000	1,800,000	1,350,000

You have been asked to evaluate the historical performance of the company over the last five years.

Selected industry ratios have remained relatively steady at the following levels for the last five years:

	2004–2008
Rate earned on total assets	13%
Rate earned on stockholders' equity	20%
Number of times interest charges earned	4.0
Ratio of liabilities to stockholders' equity	1.3

Instructions

1. Prepare four line graphs with the ratio on the vertical axis and the years on the horizontal axis for the following four ratios (rounded to one decimal place):
   a. Rate earned on total assets
   b. Rate earned on stockholders' equity
   c. Number of times interest charges earned
   d. Ratio of liabilities to stockholders' equity
   Display both the company ratio and the industry benchmark on each graph. That is, each graph should have two lines.
2. ▱▱▱▱▸ Prepare an analysis of the graphs in (1).

Williams-Sonoma, Inc., Problem

FINANCIAL STATEMENT ANALYSIS

The financial statements for Williams-Sonoma, Inc., are presented in Appendix D at the end of the text. The following additional information (in thousands) is available:

Accounts receivable at February 1, 2004	$ 31,573
Inventories at February 1, 2004	404,100
Total assets at February 1, 2004	1,470,735
Stockholders' equity at February 1, 2004	804,591

Instructions

1. Determine the following measures for the fiscal years ended January 29, 2006 and January 30, 2005, rounding to one decimal place.
   a. Working capital
   b. Current ratio
   c. Quick ratio
   d. Accounts receivable turnover
   e. Number of days' sales in receivables
   f. Inventory turnover
   g. Number of days' sales in inventory
   h. Ratio of liabilities to stockholders' equity
   i. Ratio of net sales to average total assets
   j. Rate earned on average total assets
   k. Rate earned on average common stockholders' equity
   l. Price-earnings ratio, assuming that the market price was $40.62 per share on January 29, 2006 and $34.53 on January 30, 2005.
   m. Percentage relationship of net income to net sales
2. ▱▱▱▱▸ What conclusions can be drawn from these analyses?

Special Activities

SA 17-1
Analysis of financing corporate growth

Assume that the president of Ice Mountain Brewery made the following statement in the Annual Report to Shareholders:

"The founding family and majority shareholders of the company do not believe in using debt to finance future growth. The founding family learned from hard experience during Prohibition and the Great Depression that debt can cause loss of flexibility and eventual loss of corporate control. The company will not place itself at such risk. As such, all future growth will be financed either by stock sales to the public or by internally generated resources."

▸ As a public shareholder of this company, how would you respond to this policy?

SA 17-2
Receivables and inventory turnover

Roan Mountain Fitness Company has completed its fiscal year on December 31, 2008. The auditor, Steve Berry, has approached the CFO, Tony Brubaker, regarding the year-end receivables and inventory levels of Roan Mountain Fitness. The following conversation takes place:

Steve: We are beginning our audit of Roan Mountain Fitness and have prepared ratio analyses to determine if there have been significant changes in operations or financial position. This helps us guide the audit process. This analysis indicates that the inventory turnover has decreased from 4.5 to 2.1, while the accounts receivable turnover has decreased from 10 to 6. I was wondering if you could explain this change in operations.

Tony: There is little need for concern. The inventory represents computers that we were unable to sell during the holiday buying season. We are confident, however, that we will be able to sell these computers as we move into the next fiscal year.

Steve: What gives you this confidence?

Tony: We will increase our advertising and provide some very attractive price concessions to move these machines. We have no choice. Newer technology is already out there, and we have to unload this inventory.

Steve: . . . and the receivables?

Tony: As you may be aware, the company is under tremendous pressure to expand sales and profits. As a result, we lowered our credit standards to our commercial customers so that we would be able to sell products to a broader customer base. As a result of this policy change, we have been able to expand sales by 35%.

Steve: Your responses have not been reassuring to me.

Tony: I'm a little confused. Assets are good, right? Why don't you look at our current ratio? It has improved, hasn't it? I would think that you would view that very favorably.

▸ Why is Steve concerned about the inventory and accounts receivable turnover ratios and Tony's responses to them? What action may Steve need to take? How would you respond to Tony's last comment?

SA 17-3
Vertical analysis

The condensed income statements through income from operations for Dell Inc. and Apple Computer, Inc., are reproduced below for recent fiscal years (numbers in millions of dollars).

	Dell Inc.	Apple Computer, Inc.
Sales (net)	$55,908	$13,931
Cost of sales	45,958	9,888
Gross profit	$ 9,950	$ 4,043
Selling, general, and administrative expenses	$ 5,140	$ 1,859
Research and development	463	534
Operating expenses	$ 5,603	$ 2,393
Income from operations	$ 4,347	$ 1,650

▸ Prepare comparative common-size statements, rounding percents to one decimal place. Interpret the analyses.

SA 17-4
Profitability and stockholder ratios

Ford Motor Company is the second largest automobile and truck manufacturer in the United States. In addition to manufacturing motor vehicles, Ford also provides vehicle-related financing, insurance, and leasing services. Historically, people purchase automobiles when the economy is strong and delay automobile purchases when the economy is faltering. For this reason, Ford is considered a cyclical company. This means that when the economy does well, Ford usually prospers, and when the economy is down, Ford usually suffers.

The following information is available for three recent years (in millions except per-share amounts):

	2005	2004	2003
Net income (loss)	$2,024	$3,487	$495
Preferred dividends	$0	$0	$0
Shares outstanding for computing earnings per share	1,846	1,830	1,832
Cash dividend per share	$0.40	$0.40	$0.40
Average total assets	$287,669	$308,032	$293,678
Average stockholders' equity	$14,501	$13,848	$8,532
Average stock price per share	$11.22	$14.98	$11.95

1. Calculate the following ratios for each year:
   a. Rate earned on total assets
   b. Rate earned on stockholders' equity
   c. Earnings per share
   d. Dividend yield
   e. Price-earnings ratio
2. What is the ratio of average liabilities to average stockholders' equity for 2005?
3. Why does Ford have so much leverage?
4. Explain the direction of the dividend yield and price-earnings ratio in light of Ford's profitability trend.

SA 17-5
Projecting financial statements

REAL WORLD

Internet Project

Go to Microsoft Corporation's Web site at **http://www.microsoft.com** and click on the "Investor Relations" area under "About Microsoft." Select the menu item "Stock Info and Analysis." Select the "What-if?" tool. With this tool, use horizontal and vertical information to create a full-year projection of the Microsoft income statement. Make the following assumptions:

Revenue growth	12%
Cost of goods sold as a percent of revenue	15%
Research and development growth	10%
Sales and marketing as a percent of sales	18%
General and administrative as a percent of sales	6%
Tax rate	32%
Diluted shares outstanding	12,000

SA 17-6
Comprehensive profitability and solvency analysis

REAL WORLD

Marriott International, Inc., and Hilton Hotels Corporation are two major owners and managers of lodging and resort properties in the United States. Abstracted income statement information for the two companies is as follows for a recent year:

	Marriott (in millions)	Hilton (in millions)
Operating profit before other expenses and interest	$ 477	$ 658
Other income (expenses)	318	(19)
Interest expense	(99)	(274)
Income before income taxes	$ 696	$ 365
Income tax expense	100	127
Net income	$ 596	$ 238

Balance sheet information is as follows:

	Marriott (in millions)	Hilton (in millions)
Total liabilities	$4,587	$5,674
Total stockholders' equity	4,081	2,568
Total liabilties and stockholders' equity	$8,668	$8,242

The average liabilities, stockholders' equity, and total assets were as follows:

	Marriott	Hilton
Average total liabilities	$4,210	$5,809
Average total stockholders' equity	3,960	2,404
Average total assets	8,423	8,213

1. Determine the following ratios for both companies (round to one decimal place after the whole percent):
   a. Rate earned on total assets
   b. Rate earned on total stockholders' equity
   c. Number of times interest charges are earned
   d. Ratio of liabilities to stockholders' equity
2. ▭▭▭▶ Analyze and compare the two companies, using the information in (1).

Answers to Self-Examination Questions

1. **A**   Percentage analysis indicating the relationship of the component parts to the total in a financial statement, such as the relationship of current assets to total assets (20% to 100%) in the question, is called vertical analysis (answer A). Percentage analysis of increases and decreases in corresponding items in comparative financial statements is called horizontal analysis (answer B). An example of horizontal analysis would be the presentation of the amount of current assets in the preceding balance sheet, along with the amount of current assets at the end of the current year, with the increase or decrease in current assets between the periods expressed as a percentage. Profitability analysis (answer C) is the analysis of a firm's ability to earn income. Contribution margin analysis (answer D) is discussed in a later managerial accounting chapter.

2. **D**   Various solvency measures, categorized as current position analysis, indicate a firm's ability to meet currently maturing obligations. Each measure contributes to the analysis of a firm's current position and is most useful when viewed with other measures and when compared with similar measures for other periods and for other firms. Working capital (answer A) is the excess of current assets over current liabilities; the current ratio (answer B) is the ratio of current assets to current liabilities; and the quick ratio (answer C) is the ratio of the sum of cash, receivables, and marketable securities to current liabilities.

3. **D**   The ratio of current assets to current liabilities is usually called the current ratio (answer A). It is sometimes called the working capital ratio (answer B) or bankers' ratio (answer C).

4. **C**   The ratio of the sum of cash, receivables, and marketable securities (sometimes called quick assets) to current liabilities is called the quick ratio (answer C) or acid-test ratio. The current ratio (answer A), working capital ratio (answer B), and bankers' ratio (answer D) are terms that describe the ratio of current assets to current liabilities.

5. **C**   The number of days' sales in inventory (answer C), which is determined by dividing the average inventory by the average daily cost of goods sold, expresses the relationship between the cost of goods sold and inventory. It indicates the efficiency in the management of inventory. The working capital ratio (answer A) indicates the ability of the business to meet currently maturing obligations (debt). The quick ratio (answer B) indicates the "instant" debt-paying ability of the business. The ratio of fixed assets to long-term liabilities (answer D) indicates the margin of safety for long-term creditors.

Appendices

Appendix A

Interest Tables

Present Value of $1 at Compound Interest Due in n Periods: $p_{\overline{n}\backslash i} = \dfrac{1}{(1 + i)^n}$

$n \backslash i$	5%	5.5%	6%	6.5%	7%	8%
1	0.95238	0.94787	0.94334	0.93897	0.93458	0.92593
2	0.90703	0.89845	0.89000	0.88166	0.87344	0.85734
3	0.86384	0.85161	0.83962	0.82785	0.81630	0.79383
4	0.82270	0.80722	0.79209	0.77732	0.76290	0.73503
5	0.78353	0.76513	0.74726	0.72988	0.71290	0.68058
6	0.74622	0.72525	0.70496	0.68533	0.66634	0.63017
7	0.71068	0.68744	0.66506	0.64351	0.62275	0.58349
8	0.67684	0.65160	0.62741	0.60423	0.58201	0.54027
9	0.64461	0.61763	0.59190	0.56735	0.54393	0.50025
10	0.61391	0.58543	0.55840	0.53273	0.50835	0.46319
11	0.58468	0.55491	0.52679	0.50021	0.47509	0.42888
12	0.55684	0.52598	0.49697	0.46968	0.44401	0.39711
13	0.53032	0.49856	0.46884	0.44102	0.41496	0.36770
14	0.50507	0.47257	0.44230	0.41410	0.38782	0.34046
15	0.48102	0.44793	0.41726	0.38883	0.36245	0.31524
16	0.45811	0.42458	0.39365	0.36510	0.33874	0.29189
17	0.43630	0.40245	0.37136	0.34281	0.31657	0.27027
18	0.41552	0.38147	0.35034	0.32189	0.29586	0.25025
19	0.39573	0.36158	0.33051	0.30224	0.27651	0.23171
20	0.37689	0.34273	0.31180	0.28380	0.25842	0.21455
21	0.35894	0.32486	0.29416	0.26648	0.24151	0.19866
22	0.34185	0.30793	0.27750	0.25021	0.22571	0.18394
23	0.32557	0.29187	0.26180	0.23494	0.21095	0.17032
24	0.31007	0.27666	0.24698	0.22060	0.19715	0.15770
25	0.29530	0.26223	0.23300	0.20714	0.18425	0.14602
26	0.28124	0.24856	0.21981	0.19450	0.17211	0.13520
27	0.26785	0.23560	0.20737	0.18263	0.16093	0.12519
28	0.25509	0.22332	0.19563	0.17148	0.15040	0.11591
29	0.24295	0.21168	0.18456	0.16101	0.14056	0.10733
30	0.23138	0.20064	0.17411	0.15119	0.13137	0.09938
31	0.22036	0.19018	0.16426	0.14196	0.12277	0.09202
32	0.20987	0.18027	0.15496	0.13329	0.11474	0.08520
33	0.19987	0.17087	0.14619	0.12516	0.10724	0.07889
34	0.19036	0.16196	0.13791	0.11752	0.10022	0.07304
35	0.18129	0.15352	0.13010	0.11035	0.09366	0.06764
40	0.14205	0.11746	0.09722	0.08054	0.06678	0.04603
45	0.11130	0.08988	0.07265	0.05879	0.04761	0.03133
50	0.08720	0.06877	0.05429	0.04291	0.03395	0.02132

Present Value of $1 at Compound Interest Due in n Periods: $p_{\bar{n}|i} = \dfrac{1}{(1+i)^n}$

$n \backslash i$	9%	10%	11%	12%	13%	14%
1	0.91743	0.90909	0.90090	0.89286	0.88496	0.87719
2	0.84168	0.82645	0.81162	0.79719	0.78315	0.76947
3	0.77218	0.75132	0.73119	0.71178	0.69305	0.67497
4	0.70842	0.68301	0.65873	0.63552	0.61332	0.59208
5	0.64993	0.62092	0.59345	0.56743	0.54276	0.51937
6	0.59627	0.56447	0.53464	0.50663	0.48032	0.45559
7	0.54703	0.51316	0.48166	0.45235	0.42506	0.39964
8	0.50187	0.46651	0.43393	0.40388	0.37616	0.35056
9	0.46043	0.42410	0.39092	0.36061	0.33288	0.30751
10	0.42241	0.38554	0.35218	0.32197	0.29459	0.26974
11	0.38753	0.35049	0.31728	0.28748	0.26070	0.23662
12	0.35554	0.31863	0.28584	0.25668	0.23071	0.20756
13	0.32618	0.28966	0.25751	0.22917	0.20416	0.18207
14	0.29925	0.26333	0.23199	0.20462	0.18068	0.15971
15	0.27454	0.23939	0.20900	0.18270	0.15989	0.14010
16	0.25187	0.21763	0.18829	0.16312	0.14150	0.12289
17	0.23107	0.19784	0.16963	0.14564	0.12522	0.10780
18	0.21199	0.17986	0.15282	0.13004	0.11081	0.09456
19	0.19449	0.16351	0.13768	0.11611	0.09806	0.08295
20	0.17843	0.14864	0.12403	0.10367	0.08678	0.07276
21	0.16370	0.13513	0.11174	0.09256	0.07680	0.06383
22	0.15018	0.12285	0.10067	0.08264	0.06796	0.05599
23	0.13778	0.11168	0.09069	0.07379	0.06014	0.04911
24	0.12640	0.10153	0.08170	0.06588	0.05323	0.04308
25	0.11597	0.09230	0.07361	0.05882	0.04710	0.03779
26	0.10639	0.08390	0.06631	0.05252	0.04168	0.03315
27	0.09761	0.07628	0.05974	0.04689	0.03689	0.02908
28	0.08955	0.06934	0.05382	0.04187	0.03264	0.02551
29	0.08216	0.06304	0.04849	0.03738	0.02889	0.02237
30	0.07537	0.05731	0.04368	0.03338	0.02557	0.01963
31	0.06915	0.05210	0.03935	0.02980	0.02262	0.01722
32	0.06344	0.04736	0.03545	0.02661	0.02002	0.01510
33	0.05820	0.04306	0.03194	0.02376	0.01772	0.01325
34	0.05331	0.03914	0.02878	0.02121	0.01568	0.01162
35	0.04899	0.03558	0.02592	0.01894	0.01388	0.01019
40	0.03184	0.02210	0.01538	0.01075	0.00753	0.00529
45	0.02069	0.01372	0.00913	0.00610	0.00409	0.00275
50	0.01345	0.00852	0.00542	0.00346	0.00222	0.00143

Present Value of Ordinary Annuity of $1 per Period: $p_{\overline{n}|i} = \dfrac{1 - \dfrac{1}{(1+i)^n}}{i}$

$n \backslash i$	5%	5.5%	6%	6.5%	7%	8%
1	0.95238	0.94787	0.94340	0.93897	0.93458	0.92593
2	1.85941	1.84632	1.83339	1.82063	1.80802	1.78326
3	2.72325	2.69793	2.67301	2.64848	2.62432	2.57710
4	3.54595	3.50515	3.46511	3.42580	3.38721	3.31213
5	4.32948	4.27028	4.21236	4.15568	4.10020	3.99271
6	5.07569	4.99553	4.91732	4.84101	4.76654	4.62288
7	5.78637	5.68297	5.58238	5.48452	5.38923	5.20637
8	6.46321	6.33457	6.20979	6.08875	5.97130	5.74664
9	7.10782	6.95220	6.80169	6.65610	6.51523	6.24689
10	7.72174	7.53763	7.36009	7.18883	7.02358	6.71008
11	8.30641	8.09254	7.88688	7.68904	7.49867	7.13896
12	8.86325	8.61852	8.38384	8.15873	7.94269	7.53608
13	9.39357	9.11708	8.85268	8.59974	8.35765	7.90378
14	9.89864	9.58965	9.29498	9.01384	8.74547	8.22424
15	10.37966	10.03758	9.71225	9.40267	9.10791	8.55948
16	10.83777	10.46216	10.10590	9.76776	9.44665	8.85137
17	11.27407	10.86461	10.47726	10.11058	9.76322	9.12164
18	11.68959	11.24607	10.82760	10.43247	10.05909	9.37189
19	12.08532	11.60765	11.15812	10.73471	10.33560	9.60360
20	12.46221	11.95038	11.46992	11.01851	10.59401	9.81815
21	12.82115	12.27524	11.76408	11.28498	10.83553	10.01680
22	13.16300	12.58317	12.04158	11.53520	11.06124	10.20074
23	13.48857	12.87504	12.30338	11.77014	11.27219	10.37106
24	13.79864	13.15170	12.55036	11.99074	11.46933	10.52876
25	14.09394	13.41393	12.78336	12.19788	11.65358	10.67478
26	14.37518	13.66250	13.00317	12.39237	11.82578	10.80998
27	14.64303	13.89810	13.21053	12.57500	11.98671	10.93516
28	14.89813	14.12142	13.40616	12.74648	12.13711	11.05108
29	15.14107	14.33310	13.59072	12.90749	12.27767	11.15841
30	15.37245	14.53375	13.76483	13.05868	12.40904	11.25778
31	15.59281	14.72393	13.92909	13.20063	12.53181	11.34980
32	15.80268	14.90420	14.08404	13.33393	12.64656	11.43500
33	16.00255	15.07507	14.23023	13.45909	12.75379	11.51389
34	16.19290	15.23703	14.36814	13.57661	12.85401	11.58693
35	16.37420	15.39055	14.49825	13.68696	12.94767	11.65457
40	17.15909	16.04612	15.04630	14.14553	13.33171	11.92461
45	17.77407	16.54773	15.45583	14.48023	13.60552	12.10840
50	18.25592	16.93152	15.76186	14.72452	13.80075	12.23348

Present Value of Ordinary Annuity of \$1 per Period: $p_{\bar{n}|i} = \dfrac{1 - \dfrac{1}{(1 + i)^n}}{i}$

n \ i	9%	10%	11%	12%	13%	14%
1	0.91743	0.90909	0.90090	0.89286	0.88496	0.87719
2	1.75911	1.73554	1.71252	1.69005	1.66810	1.64666
3	2.53130	2.48685	2.44371	2.40183	2.36115	2.32163
4	3.23972	3.16986	3.10245	3.03735	2.97447	2.91371
5	3.88965	3.79079	3.69590	3.60478	3.51723	3.43308
6	4.48592	4.35526	4.23054	4.11141	3.99755	3.88867
7	5.03295	4.86842	4.71220	4.56376	4.42261	4.28830
8	5.53482	5.33493	5.14612	4.96764	4.79677	4.63886
9	5.99525	5.75902	5.53705	5.32825	5.13166	4.94637
10	6.41766	6.14457	5.88923	5.65022	5.42624	5.21612
11	6.80519	6.49506	6.20652	5.93770	5.68694	5.45273
12	7.16072	6.81369	6.49236	6.19437	5.91765	5.66029
13	7.48690	7.10336	6.74987	6.42355	6.12181	5.84236
14	7.78615	7.36669	6.96187	6.62817	6.30249	6.00207
15	8.06069	7.60608	7.19087	6.81086	6.46238	6.14217
16	8.31256	7.82371	7.37916	6.97399	6.60388	6.26506
17	8.54363	8.02155	7.54879	7.11963	6.72909	6.37286
18	8.75562	8.20141	7.70162	7.24967	6.83991	6.46742
19	8.95012	8.36492	7.83929	7.36578	6.93797	6.55037
20	9.12855	8.51356	7.96333	7.46944	7.02475	6.62313
21	9.29224	8.64869	8.07507	7.56200	7.10155	6.68696
22	9.44242	8.77154	8.17574	7.64465	7.16951	6.74294
23	9.58021	8.88322	8.26643	7.71843	7.22966	6.79206
24	9.70661	8.98474	8.34814	7.78432	7.28288	6.83514
25	9.82258	9.07704	8.42174	7.84314	7.32998	6.87293
26	9.92897	9.16094	8.48806	7.89566	7.37167	6.90608
27	10.02658	9.23722	8.54780	7.94255	7.40856	6.93515
28	10.11613	9.30657	8.60162	7.98442	7.44120	6.96066
29	10.19828	9.36961	8.65011	8.02181	7.47009	6.98304
30	10.27365	9.42691	8.69379	8.05518	7.49565	7.00266
31	10.34280	9.47901	8.73315	8.08499	7.51828	7.01988
32	10.40624	9.52638	8.76860	8.11159	7.53830	7.03498
33	10.46444	9.56943	8.80054	8.13535	7.55602	7.04823
34	10.51784	9.60858	8.82932	8.15656	7.57170	7.05985
35	10.56682	9.64416	8.85524	8.17550	7.58557	7.07005
40	10.75736	9.77905	8.95105	8.24378	7.63438	7.10504
45	10.88118	9.86281	9.00791	8.28252	7.66086	7.12322
50	10.96168	9.91481	9.04165	8.30450	7.67524	7.13266

Appendix B

Reversing Entries

Some of the adjusting entries recorded at the end of an accounting period have an important effect on otherwise routine transactions that occur in the following period. A typical example is accrued wages owed to employees at the end of a period. If there has been an adjusting entry for accrued wages expense, the first payment of wages in the following period will include the accrual. In the absence of some special provision, Wages Payable must be debited for the amount owed for the earlier period, and Wages Expense must be debited for the portion of the payroll that represents expense for the later period. However, an *optional* entry—the reversing entry—may be used to simplify the analysis and recording of this first payroll entry in a period. As the term implies, a *reversing entry* is the exact opposite of the adjusting entry to which it relates. The amounts and accounts are the same as the adjusting entry; the debits and credits are reversed.

@netsolutions

We will illustrate the use of reversing entries by using the data for NetSolutions' accrued wages, which were presented in Chapter 3. These data are summarized in Exhibit 1.

EXHIBIT 1

Accrued Wages

1. Wages are paid on the second and fourth Fridays for the two-week periods ending on those Fridays. The payments were $950 on December 13 and $1,200 on December 27.

2. The wages accrued for Monday and Tuesday, December 30 and 31, are $250.

3. Wages paid on Friday, January 10, total $1,275.

			December			
S	M	T	W	T	F	S
1	2	3	4	5	6	7
8	9	10	11	12	13	14
15	16	17	18	19	20	21
22	23	24	25	26	27	28
29	30	31				

Wages expense (paid), $950

Wages expense (paid), $1,200

Wages expense (accrued), $250

			January			
S	M	T	W	T	F	S
			1	2	3	4
5	6	7	8	9	10	11

Wages expense (paid), $1,275

The adjusting entry for the accrued wages of December 30 and 31 is as follows:

1							1
2	Dec.	31	Wages Expense	51	2 5 0 00		2
3			Wages Payable	22		2 5 0 00	3
4			Accrued wages.				4

After the adjusting entry has been posted, Wages Expense will have a debit balance of $4,525 ($4,275 + $250), as shown on the top of page B-3. Wages Payable will have a credit balance of $250, as shown at the bottom of this page. After the closing process is completed, Wages Expense will have a zero balance and will be ready for entries in the next period. Wages Payable, on the other hand, has a balance of $250. Without a reversing entry, it is necessary to record the $1,275 payroll on January 10 as follows:

1							1
2	2008 Jan.	10	Wages Payable	22	2 5 0 00		2
3			Wages Expense	51	1 0 2 5 00		3
4			Cash	11		1 2 7 5 00	4

The employee who records the January 10 entry must refer to the prior period's adjusting entry to determine the amount of the debits to Wages Payable and Wages Expense. Because the January 10 payroll is not recorded in the usual manner, there is a greater chance that an error may occur. This chance of error is reduced by recording a reversing entry as of the first day of the fiscal period. For example, the reversing entry for the accrued wages expense is as follows:

1							1
2	2008 Jan.	1	Wages Payable	22	2 5 0 00		2
3			Wages Expense	51		2 5 0 00	3
4			Reversing entry.				4

The reversing entry transfers the $250 liability from Wages Payable to the credit side of Wages Expense. The nature of the $250 is unchanged—it is still a liability. Because of its unusual nature, an explanation is normally written under the journal entry. When the payroll is paid on January 10, the following entry is recorded:

1							1
2	Jan.	31	Wages Expense	51	1 2 7 5 00		2
3			Cash	11		1 2 7 5 00	3

After this entry is posted, Wages Expense has a debit balance of $1,025. This amount is the wages expense for the period January 1–10. The sequence of entries, including adjusting, closing, and reversing entries, is illustrated in the following accounts:

ACCOUNT Wages Payable							ACCOUNT NO. 22	
			Post.			Balance		
Date		Item	Ref.	Debit	Credit	Debit	Credit	
2007 Dec.	31	Adjusting	5		2 5 0 00		2 5 0 00	
2008 Jan.	1	Reversing	7	2 5 0 00		—	—	

ACCOUNT *Wages Expense*							ACCOUNT NO. *51*	
		Post.				Balance		
Date	Item	Ref.	Debit	Credit		Debit	Credit	
2007 Nov. 30		1	2 1 2 5 00			2 1 2 5 00		
Dec. 13		3	9 5 0 00			3 0 7 5 00		
27		3	1 2 0 0 00			4 2 7 5 00		
31	Adjusting	5	2 5 0 00			4 5 2 5 00		
31	Closing	6		4 5 2 5 00		—	—	
2008 Jan. 1	Reversing	7		2 5 0 00			2 5 0 00	
10		7	1 2 7 5 00			1 0 2 5 00		

In addition to accrued expenses (accrued liabilities), reversing entries may be journalized for accrued revenues (accrued assets). For example, the following reversing entry could be recorded for NetSolutions' accrued fees earned:

1								1
2	Jan.	1	Fees Earned	41	5 0 0 00			2
3			Accounts Receivable	12		5 0 0 00		3
4			Reversing entry.					4

As we mentioned, the use of reversing entries is optional. However, with the increased use of computerized accounting systems, data entry personnel may be inputting routine accounting entries. In such an environment, reversing entries may be useful, since these individuals may not recognize the impact of adjusting entries on the related transactions in the following period.

EX B-1
Adjusting and reversing entries

On the basis of the following data, (a) journalize the adjusting entries at December 31, the end of the current fiscal year, and (b) journalize the reversing entries on January 1, the first day of the following year.

1. Sales salaries are uniformly $14,000 for a five-day workweek, ending on Friday. The last payday of the year was Friday, December 26.
2. Accrued fees earned but not recorded at December 31, $7,975.

EX B-2
Adjusting and reversing entries

On the basis of the following data, (a) journalize the adjusting entries at June 30, the end of the current fiscal year, and (b) journalize the reversing entries on July 1, the first day of the following year.

1. Wages are uniformly $9,375 for a five-day workweek, ending on Friday. The last payday of the year was Friday, June 27.
2. Accrued fees earned but not recorded at June 30, $6,100.

EX B-3
Entries posted to the wages expense account

Portions of the wages expense account of a business are shown at the top of the following page.

a. Indicate the nature of the entry (payment, adjusting, closing, reversing) from which each numbered posting was made.
b. Journalize the complete entry from which each numbered posting was made.

ACCOUNT	Wages Expense						ACCOUNT NO. 53
			Post.			Balance	
Date	Item		Ref.	Dr.	Cr.	Dr.	Cr.
2007							
Dec. 26		(1)	49	62,500		1,747,800	
31		(2)	50	12,500		1,760,300	
31		(3)	51		1,760,300	—	—
2008							
Jan. 1		(4)	52		12,500		12,500
2		(5)	53	60,000		47,500	

EX B-4
Entries posted to the salaries expense account

Portions of the salaries expense account of a business are shown below.

ACCOUNT	Salaries Expense						ACCOUNT NO. 53
			Post.			Balance	
Date	Item		Ref.	Dr.	Cr.	Dr.	Cr.
2007							
Dec. 26		(1)	29	30,000		1,500,000	
31		(2)	30	10,000		1,510,000	
31		(3)	31		1,510,000	—	—
2008							
Jan. 1		(4)	32		10,000		10,000
2		(5)	33	30,000		20,000	

a. Indicate the nature of the entry (payment, adjusting, closing, reversing) from which each numbered posting was made.
b. Journalize the complete entry from which each numbered posting was made.

Appendix C ●

End-of-Period Spreadsheet (Work Sheet) for a Merchandising Business

A merchandising business may use an end-of-period spreadsheet (work sheet) in assembling the data for preparing financial statements and adjusting and closing entries. In this appendix, we illustrate such a spreadsheet (work sheet) for the perpetual inventory system.

@netsolutions

The end-of-period spreadsheet (work sheet) in Exhibit 1 is for NetSolutions on December 31, 2009. In this spreadsheet (work sheet), we list all of the accounts, including the accounts that have no balances, in the order that they appear in Net-Solutions' ledger.

The data needed for adjusting the accounts of NetSolutions are as follows:

Physical merchandise inventory on December 31, 2009		$62,150
Office supplies on hand on December 31, 2009		480
Insurance expired during 2009		1,910
Depreciation during 2009 on Store equipment		3,100
Office equipment		2,490
Salaries accrued on December 31, 2009: Sales salaries	$780	
Office salaries	360	1,140
Rent earned during 2009		600

There is no specific order in which to analyze the accounts in the spreadsheet (work sheet), assemble the adjustment data, and make the adjusting entries. However, you can normally save time by selecting the accounts in the order in which they appear on the trial balance. Using this approach, the adjustment for merchandise inventory shrinkage is listed first as entry (a) on the spreadsheet (work sheet), followed by the adjustment for office supplies used as entry (b), and so on.

After all the adjustments have been entered on the spreadsheet (work sheet), the Adjustments columns are totaled to prove the equality of debits and credits. As we illustrated in Chapter 4, the adjusted amounts of the balances in the Trial Balance columns are extended to the Adjusted Trial Balance columns.[1] The Adjusted Trial Balance columns are then totaled to prove the equality of debits and credits.

The balances, as adjusted, are then extended to the statement columns. The four statement columns are totaled, and the net income or net loss is determined. For Net-Solutions, the difference between the credit and debit columns of the Income Statement section is $75,400, the amount of the net income. The difference between the debit and credit columns of the Balance Sheet section is also $75,400, which is the increase in owner's equity as a result of the net income. Agreement between the two balancing amounts is evidence of debit-credit equality and mathematical accuracy.

---

1 Some accountants prefer to eliminate the Adjusted Trial Balance columns and to extend the adjusted balances directly to the statement columns. Such a spreadsheet (work sheet) is often used if there are only a few adjustment items.

EXHIBIT 1	End-of-Period Spreadsheet (Work Sheet) for Merchandising Business Using Perpetual Inventory System

	A	B	C	D	E	F	G	H	I	J	K	
		NetSolutions										
		End-of-Period Spreadsheet (Work Sheet)										
		For the Year Ended December 31, 2009										
	Account Title	Unadjusted Trial Balance		Adjustments		Adjusted Trial Balance		Income Statement		Balance Sheet		
		Dr.	Cr.	Dr.	Cr.	Dr.	Cr.	Dr.	Cr.	Dr.	Cr.	
1	Cash	52,950				52,950				52,950		1
2	Accounts Receivable	91,080				91,080				91,080		2
3	Merchandise Inventory	63,950			(a)1,800	62,150				62,150		3
4	Office Supplies	1,090			(b) 610	480				480		4
5	Prepaid Insurance	4,560			(c)1,910	2,650				2,650		5
6	Land	20,000				20,000				20,000		6
7	Store Equipment	27,100				27,100				27,100		7
8	Accum. Depr.—Store Equipment		2,600		(d)3,100		5,700				5,700	8
9	Office Equipment	15,570				15,570				15,570		9
10	Accum. Depr.—Office Equipment		2,230		(e)2,490		4,720				4,720	10
11	Accounts Payable		22,420				22,420				22,420	11
12	Salaries Payable				(f)1,140		1,140				1,140	12
13	Unearned Rent		2,400	(g) 600			1,800				1,800	13
14	Notes Payable											14
15	(final payment due 2017)		25,000				25,000				25,000	15
16	Chris Clark, Capital		153,800				153,800				153,800	16
17	Chris Clark, Drawing	18,000				18,000				18,000		17
18	Sales		720,185				720,185		720,185			18
19	Sales Returns and Allowances	6,140				6,140		6,140				19
20	Sales Discounts	5,790				5,790		5,790				20
21	Cost of Merchandise Sold	523,505		(a)1,800		525,305		525,305				21
22	Sales Salaries Expense	52,650		(f) 780		53,430		53,430				22
23	Advertising Expense	10,860				10,860		10,860				23
24	Depr. Exp.—Store Equipment			(d)3,100		3,100		3,100				24
25	Delivery Expense	2,800				2,800		2,800				25
26	Miscellaneous Selling Expense	630				630		630				26
27	Office Salaries Expense	20,660		(f) 360		21,020		21,020				27
28	Rent Expense	8,100				8,100		8,100				28
29	Depr. Exp.—Office Equipment			(e)2,490		2,490		2,490				29
30	Insurance Expense			(c)1,910		1,910		1,910				30
31	Office Supplies Expense			(b) 610		610		610				31
32	Misc. Administrative Expense	760				760		760				32
33	Rent Revenue				(g) 600		600		600			33
34	Interest Expense	2,440				2,440		2,440				34
35		928,635	928,635	11,650	11,650	935,365	935,365	645,385	720,785	289,980	214,580	35
36	Net income							75,400			75,400	36
37								720,785	720,785	289,980	289,980	37
38												38

(a) Merchandise inventory shrinkage for period, $1,800 ($63,950 − $62,150).
(b) Office supplies used, $610 ($1,090 − $480).
(c) Insurance expired, $1,910.
(d) Depreciation of store equipment, $3,100.
(e) Depreciation of office equipment, $2,490.
(f) Salaries accrued but not paid (sales salaries, $780; office salaries, $360), $1,140.
(g) Rent earned from amount received in advance, $600.

The income statement, statement of owner's equity, and balance sheet can be prepared from the spreadsheet (work sheet). These financial statements are shown in Exhibits 1, 3, and 4 in Chapter 6. The Adjustments columns in the spreadsheet (work sheet) may be used as the basis for journalizing the adjusting entries. Net-Solutions' adjusting entries at the end of 2009 are shown at the top of the following page.

	Date		Description	Post. Ref.	Debit	Credit	
1	2009		Adjusting Entries				1
2	Dec.	31	Cost of Merchandise Sold	510	1 8 0 0 00		2
3			Merchandise Inventory	115		1 8 0 0 00	3
4			Inventory shrinkage.				4
5							5
6		31	Office Supplies Expense	534	6 1 0 00		6
7			Office Supplies	116		6 1 0 00	7
8			Supplies used.				8
9							9
10		31	Insurance Expense	533	1 9 1 0 00		10
11			Prepaid Insurance	117		1 9 1 0 00	11
12			Insurance expired.				12
13							13
14		31	Depr. Expense—Store Equipment	522	3 1 0 0 00		14
15			Accumulated Depr.—Store Equipment	124		3 1 0 0 00	15
16			Store equipment depreciation.				16
17							17
18		31	Depr. Expense—Office Equipment	532	2 4 9 0 00		18
19			Accumulated Depr.—Office Equipment	126		2 4 9 0 00	19
20			Office equipment depreciation.				20
21							21
22		31	Sales Salaries Expense	520	7 8 0 00		22
23			Office Salaries Expense	530	3 6 0 00		23
24			Salaries Payable	211		1 1 4 0 00	24
25			Accrued salaries.				25
26							26
27		31	Unearned Rent	212	6 0 0 00		27
28			Rent Revenue	610		6 0 0 00	28
29			Rent earned.				29

JOURNAL — Page 28

The Income Statement columns of the work sheet may be used as the basis for preparing the closing entries. The closing entries for NetSolutions at the end of 2009 are shown on page 271 of Chapter 6.

After the closing entries have been prepared and posted to the accounts, a post-closing trial balance may be prepared to verify the debit-credit equality. The only accounts that should appear on the post-closing trial balance are the asset, contra asset, liability, and owner's capital accounts with balances. These are the same accounts that appear on the end-of-period balance sheet.

PR C-1

End-of-period spreadsheet (work sheet), financial statements, and adjusting and closing entries for perpetual inventory system

✓ 2. Net income: $107,900

The accounts and their balances in the ledger of Stones Co. on December 31, 2008, are as follows:

Cash	$ 9,000	Sales	$775,000
Accounts Receivable	72,500	Sales Returns and Allowances	11,900
Merchandise Inventory	165,000	Sales Discounts	7,100
Prepaid Insurance	9,700	Cost of Merchandise Sold	457,200
Store Supplies	4,250	Sales Salaries Expense	76,400
Office Supplies	2,100	Advertising Expense	25,000
Store Equipment	160,000	Depreciation Expense—	
Accumulated Depreciation—		Store Equipment	—
Store Equipment	40,300	Store Supplies Expense	—
Office Equipment	70,000	Miscellaneous Selling Expense	1,600
Accumulated Depreciation—		Office Salaries Expense	34,000
Office Equipment	17,200	Rent Expense	16,000
Accounts Payable	66,700	Insurance Expense	—
Salaries Payable	—	Depreciation Expense—	
Unearned Rent	1,200	Office Equipment	—
Note Payable		Office Supplies Expense	—
(final payment due 2016)	125,000	Miscellaneous Administrative	
Chang Yu, Capital	134,600	Expense	1,650
Chang Yu, Drawing	25,000	Rent Revenue	—
Income Summary	—	Interest Expense	11,600

The data needed for year-end adjustments on December 31 are as follows:

Physical merchandise inventory on December 31		$159,000
Insurance expired during the year		3,700
Supplies on hand on December 31:		
Store supplies		1,100
Office supplies		600
Depreciation for the year:		
Store equipment		5,000
Office equipment		2,800
Salaries payable on December 31:		
Sales salaries	$2,600	
Office salaries	500	3,100
Unearned rent on December 31		600

Instructions

1. Prepare an end-of-period spreadsheet (work sheet) for the fiscal year ended December 31, 2008. List all accounts in the order given.
2. Prepare a multiple-step income statement.
3. Prepare a statement of owner's equity.
4. Prepare a report form of balance sheet, assuming that the current portion of the note payable is $25,000.
5. Journalize the adjusting entries.
6. Journalize the closing entries.

PR C-2

End-of-period spreadsheet (work sheet), financial statements, and adjusting and closing entries for perpetual inventory system

✓ 1. Net income: $49,750

The accounts and their balances in the ledger of LeClassic Sports Co. on December 31, 2008, are as follows:

Cash	$ 18,000	Sales Discounts	$ 7,100
Accounts Receivable	42,500	Cost of Merchandise Sold	557,000
Merchandise Inventory	215,000	Sales Salaries Expense	81,400
Prepaid Insurance	9,700	Advertising Expense	45,000
Store Supplies	4,250	Depreciation Expense—	
Office Supplies	2,100	Store Equipment	—
Store Equipment	182,000	Delivery Expense	6,000
Accumulated Depreciation—		Store Supplies Expense	—
Store Equipment	40,300	Miscellaneous Selling Expense	1,600
Office Equipment	60,000	Office Salaries Expense	44,000
Accumulated Depreciation—		Rent Expense	25,200
Office Equipment	17,200	Insurance Expense	—
Accounts Payable	56,700	Depreciation Expense—	
Salaries Payable	—	Office Equipment	—
Unearned Rent	1,200	Office Supplies Expense	—
Note Payable (final payment, 2013)	125,000	Miscellaneous Administrative	
Tanya Brill, Capital	217,600	Expense	1,650
Tanya Brill, Drawing	5,000	Rent Revenue	—
Sales	875,000	Interest Expense	11,600
Sales Returns and Allowances	13,900		

The data needed for year-end adjustments on December 31 are as follows:

Merchandise inventory on December 31		$210,000
Insurance expired during the year		6,800
Supplies on hand on December 31:		
Store supplies		1,200
Office supplies		750
Depreciation for the year:		
Store equipment		7,500
Office equipment...		3,800
Salaries payable on December 31:		
Sales salaries	$2,600	
Office salaries	1,500	4,100
Unearned rent on December 31		400

Instructions

1. Prepare an end-of-period spreadsheet (work sheet) for the fiscal year ended December 31, listing all accounts in the order given.
2. Prepare a multiple-step income statement.
3. Prepare a statement of owner's equity.
4. Prepare a report form of balance sheet, assuming that the current portion of the note payable is $15,000.
5. Journalize the adjusting entries.
6. Journalize the closing entries.

WILLIAMS-SONOMA, INC.

2 0 0 5 ANNUAL REPORT

Annual Meeting of Shareholders
May 23, 2006

ITEM 8. FINANCIAL STATEMENTS AND SUPPLEMENTARY DATA

Williams-Sonoma, Inc.
Consolidated Statements of Earnings

	Fiscal Year Ended		
Dollars and shares in thousands, except per share amounts	Jan. 29, 2006	Jan. 30, 2005	Feb. 1, 2004
Net revenues	$3,538,947	$3,136,931	$2,754,368
Cost of goods sold	2,103,465	1,865,786	1,643,791
Gross margin	1,435,482	1,271,145	1,110,577
Selling, general and administrative expenses	1,090,392	961,176	855,790
Interest income	(5,683)	(1,939)	(873)
Interest expense	1,975	1,703	22
Earnings before income taxes	348,798	310,205	255,638
Income taxes	133,932	118,971	98,427
Net earnings	$ 214,866	$ 191,234	$ 157,211
Basic earnings per share	$ 1.86	$ 1.65	$ 1.36
Diluted earnings per share	$ 1.81	$ 1.60	$ 1.32
Shares used in calculation of earnings per share:			
Basic	115,616	116,159	115,583
Diluted	118,427	119,347	119,016

See Notes to Consolidated Financial Statements.

38

Williams-Sonoma, Inc.
Consolidated Balance Sheets

Dollars and shares in thousands, except per share amounts	Jan. 29, 2006	Jan. 30, 2005
ASSETS		
Current assets		
Cash and cash equivalents	$ 360,982	$ 239,210
Accounts receivable (less allowance for doubtful accounts of $168 and $217)	51,020	42,520
Merchandise inventories – net	520,292	452,421
Prepaid catalog expenses	53,925	53,520
Prepaid expenses	31,847	38,018
Deferred income taxes	57,267	39,015
Other assets	7,831	9,061
Total current assets	1,083,164	873,765
Property and equipment – net	880,305	852,412
Other assets (less accumulated amortization of $679 and $2,066)	18,151	19,368
Total assets	$1,981,620	$1,745,545
LIABILITIES AND SHAREHOLDERS' EQUITY		
Current liabilities		
Accounts payable	$ 196,074	$ 173,781
Accrued salaries, benefits and other	93,434	86,767
Customer deposits	172,775	148,535
Income taxes payable	83,589	72,052
Current portion of long-term debt	18,864	23,435
Other liabilities	25,656	17,587
Total current liabilities	590,392	522,157
Deferred rent and lease incentives	218,254	212,193
Long-term debt	14,490	19,154
Deferred income tax liabilities	18,455	21,057
Other long-term obligations	14,711	13,322
Total liabilities	856,302	787,883
Commitments and contingencies – See Note L		
Shareholders' equity		
Preferred stock, $.01 par value, 7,500 shares authorized, none issued	—	—
Common stock, $.01 par value, 253,125 shares authorized, 114,779 shares issued and outstanding at January 29, 2006; 115,372 shares issued and outstanding at January 30, 2005	1,148	1,154
Additional paid-in capital	325,146	286,720
Retained earnings	791,329	664,619
Accumulated other comprehensive income	7,695	5,169
Total shareholders' equity	1,125,318	957,662
Total liabilities and shareholders' equity	$1,981,620	$1,745,545

See Notes to Consolidated Financial Statements.

Form 10-K

Williams-Sonoma, Inc.
Consolidated Statements of Shareholders' Equity

Dollars and shares in thousands	Common Stock Shares	Common Stock Amount	Additional Paid-in Capital	Retained Earnings	Accumulated Other Comprehensive Income (Loss)	Deferred Stock-Based Compensation	Total Shareholders' Equity	Comprehensive Income
Balance at February 2, 2003	114,317	$1,143	$196,259	$446,837	$ (11)	$(250)	$ 643,978	
Net earnings	—	—	—	157,211	—	—	157,211	$157,211
Foreign currency translation adjustment and related tax effect	—	—	—	—	3,298	—	3,298	3,298
Exercise of stock options and related tax effect	3,295	33	59,516	—	—	—	59,549	
Repurchase and retirement of common stock	(1,785)	(18)	(3,450)	(56,227)	—	—	(59,695)	
Amortization of deferred stock-based compensation	—	—	—	—	—	250	250	
Comprehensive income								$160,509
Balance at February 1, 2004	115,827	1,158	252,325	547,821	3,287	—	804,591	
Net earnings	—	—	—	191,234	—	—	191,234	$191,234
Foreign currency translation adjustment	—	—	—	—	1,882	—	1,882	1,882
Exercise of stock options and related tax effect	1,818	18	39,257	—	—	—	39,275	
Repurchase and retirement of common stock	(2,273)	(22)	(4,862)	(74,436)	—	—	(79,320)	
Comprehensive income								$193,116
Balance at January 30, 2005	115,372	1,154	286,720	664,619	5,169	—	957,662	
Net earnings	—	—	—	214,866	—	—	214,866	$214,866
Foreign currency translation adjustment	—	—	—	—	2,526	—	2,526	2,526
Exercise of stock options and related tax effect	1,829	18	43,727	—	—	—	43,745	
Repurchase and retirement of common stock	(2,422)	(24)	(5,741)	(88,156)	—	—	(93,921)	
Stock-based compensation expense	—	—	440	—	—	—	440	
Comprehensive income								$217,392
Balance at January 29, 2006	114,779	$1,148	$325,146	$791,329	$7,695	$ —	$1,125,318	

See Notes to Consolidated Financial Statements.

Williams-Sonoma, Inc.
Consolidated Statements of Cash Flows

	Fiscal Year Ended		
Dollars in thousands	Jan. 29, 2006	Jan. 30, 2005	Feb. 1, 2004
Cash flows from operating activities:			
Net earnings	$ 214,866	$ 191,234	$ 157,211
Adjustments to reconcile net earnings to net cash provided by operating activities:			
Depreciation and amortization	123,199	111,624	99,534
Loss on disposal/impairment of assets	12,050	1,080	2,353
Amortization of deferred lease incentives	(24,909)	(22,530)	(19,513)
Deferred income taxes	(20,791)	(6,254)	(6,472)
Tax benefit from exercise of stock options	15,743	13,085	20,429
Stock-based compensation expense	440	—	250
Other	—	335	—
Changes in:			
Accounts receivable	(6,829)	(10,900)	2,796
Merchandise inventories	(67,474)	(48,017)	(82,196)
Prepaid catalog expenses	(405)	(15,056)	(3,302)
Prepaid expenses and other assets	9,032	(19,702)	(15,161)
Accounts payable	14,365	17,773	(11,358)
Accrued salaries, benefits and other	15,950	9,955	(1,020)
Customer deposits	24,066	32,273	23,014
Deferred rent and lease incentives	27,661	42,080	34,800
Income taxes payable	11,409	7,457	7,986
Net cash provided by operating activities	348,373	304,437	209,351
Cash flows from investing activities:			
Purchases of property and equipment	(151,788)	(181,453)	(211,979)
Net cash used in investing activities	(151,788)	(181,453)	(211,979)
Cash flows from financing activities:			
Proceeds from bond issuance	—	15,000	—
Repayments of long-term obligations	(9,235)	(9,789)	(7,610)
Proceeds from exercise of stock options	28,002	26,190	39,120
Repurchase of common stock	(93,921)	(79,320)	(59,695)
Credit facility costs	(654)	(288)	(41)
Net cash used in financing activities	(75,808)	(48,207)	(28,226)
Effect of exchange rates on cash and cash equivalents	995	523	1,269
Net increase (decrease) in cash and cash equivalents	121,772	75,300	(29,585)
Cash and cash equivalents at beginning of year	239,210	163,910	193,495
Cash and cash equivalents at end of year	$ 360,982	$ 239,210	$ 163,910
Supplemental disclosure of cash flow information:			
Cash paid during the year for:			
Interest[1]	$ 3,352	$ 3,585	$ 2,367
Income taxes	130,766	105,910	79,184
Non-cash investing and financing activities:			
Assets acquired under capital lease obligations	—	—	1,275
Consolidation of Memphis-based distribution facilities:			
Fixed assets assumed	—	—	19,512
Long-term debt assumed	—	—	18,223
Other long-term liabilities assumed	—	—	1,289

[1] *Interest paid, net of capitalized interest, was $2.2 million, $1.9 million and $0.2 million in fiscal 2005, 2004 and 2003, respectively.*

See Notes to Consolidated Financial Statements.

41

Williams-Sonoma, Inc.
Notes to Consolidated Financial Statements

Note A: Summary of Significant Accounting Policies

We are a specialty retailer of products for the home. The retail segment of our business sells our products through our six retail store concepts (Williams-Sonoma, Pottery Barn, Pottery Barn Kids, Hold Everything, West Elm and Williams-Sonoma Home). The direct-to-customer segment of our business sells similar products through our eight direct-mail catalogs (Williams-Sonoma, Pottery Barn, Pottery Barn Kids, Pottery Barn Bed + Bath, PBteen, Hold Everything, West Elm and Williams-Sonoma Home) and six e-commerce websites (williams-sonoma.com, potterybarn.com, potterybarnkids.com, pbteen.com, westelm.com and holdeverything.com). The catalogs reach customers throughout the U.S., while the six retail concepts currently operate 570 stores in 43 states, Washington, D.C. and Canada.

In January 2006, we decided to transition the merchandising strategies of our Hold Everything brand into our other existing brands by the end of fiscal 2006. In connection with this transition, we incurred a pre-tax charge of approximately $13,500,000, or $0.07 per diluted share, in the fourth quarter of fiscal 2005. These costs primarily included the initial asset impairment and lease termination costs associated with the shutdown of the Hold Everything retail stores, the asset impairment of the e-commerce website, and the write-down of impaired merchandise inventories. Of this pre-tax charge, approximately $4,500,000 is included in cost of goods sold and approximately $9,000,000 is included in selling, general, and administrative expenses. We expect to incur an additional after-tax charge of $0.03 per diluted share in the first half of fiscal 2006.

Significant intercompany transactions and accounts have been eliminated.

Fiscal Year
Our fiscal year ends on the Sunday closest to January 31, based on a 52/53-week year. Fiscal years 2005, 2004 and 2003 ended on January 29, 2006 (52 weeks), January 30, 2005 (52 weeks) and February 1, 2004 (52 weeks), respectively. The Company's next 53-week fiscal year will be fiscal 2007, ending on February 3, 2008.

Use of Estimates
The preparation of financial statements in accordance with accounting principles generally accepted in the United States of America requires us to make estimates and assumptions that affect the reported amounts of assets, liabilities, revenues and expenses and related disclosures of contingent assets and liabilities. These estimates and assumptions are evaluated on an on-going basis and are based on historical experience and various other factors that we believe to be reasonable under the circumstances. Actual results could differ from these estimates.

Cash Equivalents
Cash equivalents include highly liquid investments with an original maturity of three months or less. Our policy is to invest in high-quality, short-term instruments to achieve maximum yield while maintaining a level of liquidity consistent with our needs. Book cash overdrafts issued but not yet presented to the bank for payment are reclassified to accounts payable.

Allowance for Doubtful Accounts
A summary of activity in the allowance for doubtful accounts is as follows:

Dollars in thousands	Fiscal 2005	Fiscal 2004	Fiscal 2003
Balance at beginning of year	$217	$207	$ 64
Provision for loss on accounts receivable	(49)	10	143
Accounts written off	—	—	—
Balance at end of year	$168	$217	$207

42

Merchandise Inventories

Merchandise inventories, net of an allowance for excess quantities and obsolescence, are stated at the lower of cost (weighted average method) or market. We estimate a provision for damaged, obsolete, excess and slow-moving inventory based on inventory aging reports and specific identification. We generally reserve, based on inventory aging reports, for 50% of the cost of all inventory between one and two years old and 100% of the cost of all inventory over two years old. If actual obsolescence is different from our estimate, we will adjust our provision accordingly. Specific reserves are also recorded in the event the cost of the inventory exceeds the fair market value. In addition, on a monthly basis, we estimate a reserve for expected shrinkage at the concept and channel level based on historical shrinkage factors and our current inventory levels. Actual shrinkage is recorded at year-end based on the results of our physical inventory count and can vary from our estimates due to such factors as changes in operations within our distribution centers, the mix of our inventory (which ranges from large furniture to small tabletop items) and execution against loss prevention initiatives in our stores, off-site storage locations, and our third party transportation providers.

Approximately 63%, 62% and 61% of our merchandise purchases in fiscal 2005, fiscal 2004 and fiscal 2003, respectively, were foreign-sourced, primarily from Asia and Europe.

Prepaid Catalog Expenses

Prepaid catalog expenses consist of third party incremental direct costs, including creative design, paper, printing, postage and mailing costs for all of our direct response catalogs. Such costs are capitalized as prepaid catalog expenses and are amortized over their expected period of future benefit. Such amortization is based upon the ratio of actual revenues to the total of actual and estimated future revenues on an individual catalog basis. Estimated future revenues are based upon various factors such as the total number of catalogs and pages circulated, the probability and magnitude of consumer response and the assortment of merchandise offered. Each catalog is generally fully amortized over a six to nine month period, with the majority of the amortization occurring within the first four to five months. Prepaid catalog expenses are evaluated for realizability on a monthly basis by comparing the carrying amount associated with each catalog to the estimated probable remaining future profitability (remaining net revenues less merchandise cost of goods sold, selling expenses and catalog related-costs) associated with that catalog. If the catalog is not expected to be profitable, the carrying amount of the catalog is impaired accordingly. Catalog advertising expenses were $321,610,000, $278,169,000 and $250,337,000 in fiscal 2005, fiscal 2004 and fiscal 2003, respectively.

Property and Equipment

Property and equipment is stated at cost. Depreciation is computed using the straight-line method over the estimated useful lives of the assets below. Any reduction in the estimated lives would result in higher depreciation expense in a given period for the related assets.

Leasehold improvements	Shorter of estimated useful life or lease term (generally 3 – 22 years)
Fixtures and equipment	2 – 20 years
Buildings and building improvements	12 – 40 years
Capitalized software	2 – 10 years
Corporate aircraft	20 years (20% salvage value)
Capital leases	Shorter of estimated useful life or lease term (generally 4 – 5 years)

Internally developed software costs are capitalized in accordance with the American Institute of Certified Public Accountants Statement of Position 98-1, "Accounting for the Costs of Computer Software Developed or Obtained for Internal Use."

Interest costs related to assets under construction, including software projects, are capitalized during the construction or development period. We capitalized interest costs of $1,200,000, $1,689,000 and $2,142,000 in fiscal 2005, fiscal 2004 and fiscal 2003, respectively.

Form 10-K

For any store closures where a lease obligation still exists, we record the estimated future liability associated with the rental obligation on the date the store is closed in accordance with Statement of Financial Accounting Standards ("SFAS") No. 146, "Accounting for Costs Associated with Exit or Disposal Activities." However, most store closures occur upon the lease expiration.

We review the carrying value of all long-lived assets for impairment whenever events or changes in circumstances indicate that the carrying value of an asset may not be recoverable. In accordance with SFAS No. 144, "Accounting for the Impairment or Disposal of Long-Lived Assets," we review for impairment all stores for which current cash flows from operations are negative, or the construction costs are significantly in excess of the amount originally expected. Impairment results when the carrying value of the assets exceeds the undiscounted future cash flows over the life of the lease. Our estimate of undiscounted future cash flows over the lease term (typically 5 to 22 years) is based upon our experience, historical operations of the stores and estimates of future store profitability and economic conditions. The future estimates of store profitability and economic conditions require estimating such factors as sales growth, employment rates, lease escalations, inflation on operating expenses and the overall economics of the retail industry for up to 20 years in the future, and are therefore subject to variability and difficult to predict. If a long-lived asset is found to be impaired, the amount recognized for impairment is equal to the difference between the carrying value and the asset's fair value. The fair value is estimated based upon future cash flows (discounted at a rate that approximates our weighted average cost of capital) or other reasonable estimates of fair market value.

Lease Rights and Other Intangible Assets
Lease rights, representing costs incurred to acquire the lease of a specific commercial property, are recorded at cost in other assets and are amortized over the lives of the respective leases. Other intangible assets include fees associated with the acquisition of our credit facility and are recorded at cost in other assets and amortized over the life of the facility.

Self-Insured Liabilities
We are primarily self-insured for workers' compensation, employee health benefits and product and general liability claims. We record self-insurance liabilities based on claims filed, including the development of those claims, and an estimate of claims incurred but not yet reported. Factors affecting this estimate include future inflation rates, changes in severity, benefit level changes, medical costs and claim settlement patterns. Should a different amount of claims occur compared to what was estimated, or costs of the claims increase or decrease beyond what was anticipated, reserves may need to be adjusted accordingly. We determine our workers' compensation liability and general liability claims reserves based on an actuarial analysis. Reserves for self-insurance liabilities are recorded within accrued salaries, benefits and other on our consolidated balance sheet.

Customer Deposits
Customer deposits are primarily comprised of unredeemed gift certificates and merchandise credits and deferred revenue related to undelivered merchandise. We maintain a liability for unredeemed gift certificates and merchandise credits until the earlier of redemption, escheatment or seven years. After seven years, the remaining unredeemed gift certificate or merchandise credit liability is relieved and recorded within selling, general and administrative expenses.

Deferred Rent and Lease Incentives
For leases that contain fixed escalations of the minimum annual lease payment during the original term of the lease, we recognize rental expense on a straight-line basis over the lease term, including the construction period, and record the difference between rent expense and the amount currently payable as deferred rent. Any rental expense incurred during the construction period is capitalized as a leasehold improvement within property and equipment and depreciated over the lease term. Deferred lease incentives include construction allowances received from landlords, which are amortized on a straight-line basis over the lease term, including the construction period. Beginning in fiscal 2006, in accordance with Financial Accounting Standards Board

("FASB") Staff Position ("FSP") FAS 13-1, "Accounting for Rental Costs Incurred During a Construction Period," we will expense any rental costs incurred during the construction period.

Contingent Liabilities

Contingent liabilities are recorded when it is determined that the outcome of an event is expected to result in a loss that is considered probable and reasonably estimable.

Fair Value of Financial Instruments

The carrying values of cash and cash equivalents, accounts receivable, investments, accounts payable and debt approximate their estimated fair values.

Revenue Recognition

We recognize revenues and the related cost of goods sold (including shipping costs) at the time the products are received by customers in accordance with the provisions of Staff Accounting Bulletin ("SAB") No. 101, "Revenue Recognition in Financial Statements" as amended by SAB No. 104, "Revenue Recognition." Revenue is recognized for retail sales (excluding home-delivered merchandise) at the point of sale in the store and for home-delivered merchandise and direct-to-customer sales when the merchandise is delivered to the customer. Discounts provided to customers are accounted for as a reduction of sales. We record a reserve for estimated product returns in each reporting period. Shipping and handling fees charged to the customer are recognized as revenue at the time the products are delivered to the customer.

Sales Returns Reserve

Our customers may return purchased items for an exchange or refund. We record a reserve for estimated product returns, net of cost of goods sold, based on historical return trends together with current product sales performance. If actual returns, net of cost of goods sold, are different than those projected by management, the estimated sales returns reserve will be adjusted accordingly. A summary of activity in the sales returns reserve is as follows:

Dollars in thousands	Fiscal 2005[1]	Fiscal 2004[1]	Fiscal 2003[1]
Balance at beginning of year	$ 13,506	$ 12,281	$ 10,292
Provision for sales returns	243,807	215,715	182,829
Actual sales returns	(243,631)	(214,490)	(180,840)
Balance at end of year	$ 13,682	$ 13,506	$ 12,281

[1]Amounts are shown net of cost of goods sold.

Vendor Allowances

We may receive allowances or credits from vendors for volume rebates. In accordance with Emerging Issues Task Force ("EITF") 02-16, "Accounting by a Customer (Including a Reseller) for Certain Consideration Received from a Vendor," our accounting policy is to treat such volume rebates as an offset to the cost of the product or services provided at the time the expense is recorded. These allowances and credits received are primarily recorded in cost of goods sold or in selling, general and administrative expenses.

Foreign Currency Translation

The functional currency of our Canadian subsidiary is the Canadian dollar. Assets and liabilities are translated into U.S. dollars using the current exchange rates in effect at the balance sheet date, while revenues and expenses are translated at the average exchange rates during the period. The resulting translation adjustments are recorded as other comprehensive income within shareholders' equity. Gains and losses resulting from foreign currency transactions have not been significant and are included in selling, general and administrative expenses.

Financial Instruments

As of January 29, 2006, we have 14 retail stores in Canada, which expose us to market risk associated with foreign currency exchange rate fluctuations. As necessary, we have utilized 30-day foreign currency contracts to minimize any currency remeasurement risk associated with intercompany assets and liabilities of our Canadian subsidiary. These contracts are accounted for by adjusting the carrying amount of the contract to market and recognizing any gain or loss in selling, general and administrative expenses in each reporting period. We did not enter into any new foreign currency contracts during fiscal 2005 or fiscal 2004. Any gain or loss associated with these types of contracts in prior years was not material to us.

Income Taxes

Income taxes are accounted for using the asset and liability method. Under this method, deferred income taxes arise from temporary differences between the tax basis of assets and liabilities and their reported amounts in the consolidated financial statements. We record reserves for estimates of probable settlements of foreign and domestic tax audits. At any one time, many tax years are subject to audit by various taxing jurisdictions. The results of these audits and negotiations with taxing authorities may affect the ultimate settlement of these issues. Our effective tax rate in a given financial statement period may be materially impacted by changes in the mix and level of earnings.

Earnings Per Share

Basic earnings per share is computed as net earnings divided by the weighted average number of common shares outstanding for the period. Diluted earnings per share is computed as net earnings divided by the weighted average number of common shares outstanding for the period plus common stock equivalents, consisting of shares subject to stock options and other stock compensation awards.

Stock-Based Compensation

We account for stock options and awards granted to employees using the intrinsic value method in accordance with Accounting Principles Board Opinion No. 25, "Accounting for Stock Issued to Employees." No compensation expense has been recognized in the consolidated financial statements for stock options, as we grant all stock options with an exercise price equal to the market price of our common stock at the date of grant, however, stock compensation expense is recognized in the consolidated financial statements for restricted stock unit awards. SFAS No. 123, "Accounting for Stock-Based Compensation," as amended by SFAS No. 148, "Accounting for Stock-Based Compensation – Transition and Disclosure," however, requires the disclosure of pro forma net earnings and earnings per share as if we had adopted the fair value method. Under SFAS No. 123, the fair value of stock-based awards to employees is calculated through the use of option pricing models. These models require subjective assumptions, including future stock price volatility and expected time to exercise, which affect the calculated values. Our calculations are based on a single option valuation approach, and forfeitures are recognized as they occur.

The following table illustrates the effect on net earnings and earnings per share as if we had applied the fair value recognition provisions of SFAS No. 123, as amended by SFAS No. 148, to all of our stock-based compensation arrangements.

	Fiscal Year Ended		
Dollars in thousands, except per share amounts	Jan. 29, 2006	Jan. 30, 2005	Feb. 1, 2004
Net earnings, as reported	$214,866	$191,234	$157,211
Add: Stock-based employee compensation expense included in reported net earnings, net of related tax effect	273	—	154
Deduct: Total stock-based employee compensation expense determined under fair value method for all awards, net of related tax effect	(16,788)	(17,059)	(16,780)
Pro forma net earnings	$198,351	$174,175	$140,585
Basic earnings per share			
As reported	$ 1.86	$ 1.65	$ 1.36
Pro forma	1.72	1.50	1.22
Diluted earnings per share			
As reported	$ 1.81	$ 1.60	$ 1.32
Pro forma	1.69	1.47	1.16

The fair value of each option grant was estimated on the date of the grant using the Black-Scholes option-pricing model with the following weighted average assumptions:

	Fiscal Year Ended		
	Jan. 29, 2006	Jan. 30, 2005	Feb. 1, 2004
Dividend yield	—	—	—
Volatility	59.2%	60.1%	63.9%
Risk-free interest rate	4.3%	3.9%	3.4%
Expected term (years)	6.5	6.8	6.7

In January 2006, we issued 840,000 restricted stock units of our common stock to certain employees. Fifty percent of the restricted stock units will vest on January 31, 2010, and the remaining fifty percent will vest on January 31, 2011 based upon the employees' continued employment throughout the vesting period. Accordingly, total compensation expense (based upon the fair market value of $42.18 on the issue date) of $35,431,000 will be recognized on a straight-line basis over the vesting period. In fiscal 2005, we recognized approximately $440,000 of compensation expense related to these restricted stock units.

During fiscal 2001, we entered into employment agreements with certain executive officers. All stock-based compensation expense related to these agreements was fully recognized as of our first quarter ended May 4, 2003. We recognized approximately zero, zero and $250,000 of stock-based compensation expense related to these employment agreements in fiscal 2005, fiscal 2004 and fiscal 2003, respectively.

New Accounting Pronouncements
In December 2004, the FASB issued SFAS No. 123R, "Share Based Payment." SFAS No. 123R will require us to measure and record compensation expense in our consolidated financial statements for all employee share-based compensation awards using a fair value method. In addition, the adoption of SFAS No. 123R requires additional accounting and disclosure related to the income tax and cash flow effects resulting from share-based payment arrangements. We expect to adopt this Statement using the modified prospective application transition method beginning in the first quarter of fiscal 2006. We anticipate the adoption of this Statement to result in a reduction to our diluted earnings per share of approximately $0.19 for fiscal 2006.

In March 2005, the FASB issued FASB Interpretation No. ("FIN") No. 47, "Accounting for Conditional Asset Retirement Obligations – An Interpretation of FASB Statement No. 143," which requires an entity to recognize a liability for the fair value of a conditional asset retirement obligation when incurred if the liability's fair value can be reasonably estimated. We adopted the provisions of FIN 47 as of January 29, 2006. The adoption of this Interpretation did not have a material impact on our consolidated financial position, results of operations or cash flows.

In October 2005, the FASB issued FSP No. FAS 13-1, "Accounting for Rental Costs Incurred during a Construction Period," which requires us, beginning on January 30, 2006, to expense all rental costs associated with our operating leases that are incurred during a construction period. Prior to this date, rental costs incurred during the construction period were capitalized until the store opening date. We anticipate the adoption of this Staff Position to result in a reduction to our diluted earnings per share of approximately $0.03 for fiscal 2006.

In September 2005, the EITF issued EITF No. 05-6, "Determining the Amortization Period for Leasehold Improvements Purchased after Lease Inception or Acquired in a Business Combination," which requires us to amortize leasehold improvements that are placed in service significantly after the beginning of a lease term over the shorter of the useful life of the assets, or a term that includes required lease periods and renewals that are deemed to be reasonably assumed at the date the leasehold improvement is purchased. This EITF did not have a material impact on our consolidated financial position, results of operations or cash flows.

Reclassifications
Certain items in the fiscal 2004 and fiscal 2003 consolidated financial statements have been reclassified to conform to the fiscal 2005 presentation.

Note B: Property and Equipment

Property and equipment consists of the following:

Dollars in thousands	Jan. 29, 2006	Jan. 30, 2005
Leasehold improvements	$ 651,498	$ 600,249
Fixtures and equipment	437,243	398,826
Land and buildings	131,484	131,471
Capitalized software	145,407	132,614
Corporate systems projects in progress[1]	98,398	77,077
Corporate aircraft	48,677	48,618
Construction in progress[2]	31,501	8,063
Capital leases	11,920	11,920
Total	1,556,128	1,408,838
Accumulated depreciation and amortization	(675,823)	(556,426)
Property and equipment – net	$ 880,305	$ 852,412

[1]*Corporate systems projects in progress is primarily comprised of a new merchandising, inventory management and order management system currently under development.*
[2]*Construction in progress is primarily comprised of leasehold improvements and furniture and fixtures related to new, unopened retail stores.*

48

Note C: Borrowing Arrangements

Long-term debt consists of the following:

Dollars in thousands	Jan. 29, 2006	Jan. 30, 2005
Senior notes	—	$ 5,716
Obligations under capital leases	$ 3,458	5,673
Memphis-based distribution facilities obligation	15,696	17,000
Industrial development bonds	14,200	14,200
Total debt	33,354	42,589
Less current maturities	18,864	23,435
Total long-term debt	$14,490	$19,154

Senior Notes

In August, 2005, we repaid the remaining outstanding balance of $5,716,000 on our unsecured senior notes, with interest payable semi-annually at 7.2% per annum.

Capital Leases

Our $3,458,000 of capital lease obligations consist primarily of in-store computer equipment leases with a term of 60 months. The in-store computer equipment leases include an early purchase option at 54 months for $2,496,000, which is approximately 25% of the acquisition cost. We have an end of lease purchase option to acquire the equipment at the greater of fair market value or 15% of the acquisition cost.

Subsequent to year-end, we exercised the early purchase option on three of these leases and expect to exercise this option on the remaining computer equipment leases during fiscal 2006.

See Note F for a discussion on our bond-related debt pertaining to our Memphis-based distribution facilities.

Industrial Development Bonds

In June 2004, in an effort to utilize tax incentives offered to us by the state of Mississippi, we entered into an agreement whereby the Mississippi Business Finance Corporation issued $15,000,000 in long-term variable rate industrial development bonds, the proceeds, net of debt issuance costs, of which were loaned to us to finance the acquisition and installation of leasehold improvements and equipment located in our newly leased Olive Branch distribution center (the "Mississippi Debt Transaction"). The bonds are marketed through a remarketing agent and are secured by a letter of credit issued under our $300,000,000 line of credit facility. The bonds mature on June 1, 2024. The bond rate resets each week based upon current market rates. The rate in effect at January 29, 2006 was 4.5%.

The bond agreement allows for each bondholder to tender their bonds to the trustee for repurchase, on demand, with seven days advance notice. In the event the remarketing agent fails to remarket the bonds, the trustee will draw upon the letter of credit to fund the purchase of the bonds. As of January 29, 2006, $14,200,000 remained outstanding on these bonds and was classified as current debt. The bond proceeds are restricted for use in the acquisition and installation of leasehold improvements and equipment located in our Olive Branch, Mississippi facility. As of January 29, 2006, we had acquired and installed $14,700,000 of leasehold improvements and equipment associated with the facility.

Form 10-K

The aggregate maturities of long-term debt at January 29, 2006 were as follows:

Dollars in thousands	
Fiscal 2006[1]	$18,864
Fiscal 2007	1,668
Fiscal 2008	1,584
Fiscal 2009	1,438
Fiscal 2010	1,462
Thereafter	8,338
Total	$33,354

[1]Includes $14.2 million related to the Mississippi Debt Transaction classified as current debt.

Credit Facility

As of January 29, 2006, we have a credit facility that provides for a $300,000,000 unsecured revolving line of credit that may be used for loans or letters of credit and contains certain financial covenants, including a maximum leverage ratio (funded debt adjusted for lease and rent expense to EBITDAR), and a minimum fixed charge coverage ratio. Prior to August 22, 2009, we may, upon notice to the lenders, request an increase in the credit facility of up to $100,000,000, to provide for a total of $400,000,000 of unsecured revolving credit. The credit facility contains events of default that include, among others, non-payment of principal, interest or fees, inaccuracy of representations and warranties, violation of covenants, bankruptcy and insolvency events, material judgments, cross defaults to certain other indebtedness and events constituting a change of control. The occurrence of an event of default will increase the applicable rate of interest by 2.0% and could result in the acceleration of our obligations under the credit facility, and an obligation of any or all of our U.S. subsidiaries to pay the full amount of our obligations under the credit facility. The credit facility matures on February 22, 2010, at which time all outstanding borrowings must be repaid and all outstanding letters of credit must be cash collateralized.

We may elect interest rates calculated at Bank of America's prime rate (or, if greater, the average rate on overnight federal funds plus one-half of one percent) or LIBOR plus a margin based on our leverage ratio. No amounts were borrowed under the credit facility during fiscal 2005 or fiscal 2004. However, as of January 29, 2006, $36,073,000 in issued but undrawn standby letters of credit were outstanding under the credit facility. The standby letters of credit were issued to secure the liabilities associated with workers' compensation, other insurance programs and certain debt transactions. As of January 29, 2006, we were in compliance with our financial covenants under the credit facility.

Letter of Credit Facilities

We have three unsecured commercial letter of credit reimbursement facilities for an aggregate of $145,000,000, each of which expires on September 9, 2006. As of January 29, 2006, an aggregate of $105,260,000 was outstanding under the letter of credit facilities. Such letters of credit represent only a future commitment to fund inventory purchases to which we had not taken legal title as of January 29, 2006. The latest expiration possible for any future letters of credit issued under the agreements is February 6, 2007.

Interest Expense

Interest expense was $1,975,000 (net of capitalized interest of $1,200,000), $1,703,000 (net of capitalized interest of $1,689,000), and $22,000 (net of capitalized interest of $2,142,000) for fiscal 2005, fiscal 2004 and fiscal 2003, respectively.

Note D: Income Taxes

The components of earnings before income taxes, by tax jurisdiction, are as follows:

	Fiscal Year Ended		
Dollars in thousands	Jan. 29, 2006	Jan. 30, 2005	Feb. 1, 2004
United States	$ 337,468	$ 303,986	$ 252,119
Foreign	11,330	6,219	3,519
Total earnings before income taxes	$ 348,798	$ 310,205	$ 255,638

The provision for income taxes consists of the following:

	Fiscal Year Ended		
Dollars in thousands	Jan. 29, 2006	Jan. 30, 2005	Feb. 1, 2004
Current payable			
Federal	$ 131,242	$ 105,096	$ 87,194
State	19,002	17,642	15,640
Foreign	4,479	2,487	2,065
Total current	154,723	125,225	104,899
Deferred			
Federal	(18,912)	(6,168)	(3,587)
State	(1,538)	(70)	(2,015)
Foreign	(341)	(16)	(870)
Total deferred	(20,791)	(6,254)	(6,472)
Total provision	$ 133,932	$ 118,971	$ 98,427

Except where required by U.S. tax law, no provision was made for U.S. income taxes on the cumulative undistributed earnings of our Canadian subsidiary, as we intend to utilize those earnings in the Canadian operations for an indefinite period of time and do not intend to repatriate such earnings.

Accumulated undistributed earnings of our Canadian subsidiary were approximately $13,440,000 as of January 29, 2006. It is currently not practical to estimate the tax liability that might be payable if these foreign earnings were repatriated.

A reconciliation of income taxes at the federal statutory corporate rate to the effective rate is as follows:

	Fiscal Year Ended		
	Jan. 29, 2006	Jan. 30, 2005	Feb. 1, 2004
Federal income taxes at the statutory rate	35.0%	35.0%	35.0%
State income tax rate, less federal benefit	3.4%	3.4%	3.5%
Total	38.4%	38.4%	38.5%

Form 10-K

Significant components of our deferred tax accounts are as follows:

Dollars in thousands	Jan. 29, 2006	Jan. 30, 2005
Deferred tax asset (liability)		
Current:		
Compensation	$ 15,362	$ 14,667
Inventory	11,580	11,357
Accrued liabilities	14,186	13,725
Customer deposits	36,079	19,342
Deferred catalog costs	(20,696)	(20,540)
Other	756	464
Total current	57,267	39,015
Non-current:		
Depreciation	(11,559)	(18,634)
Deferred rent	8,683	8,275
Deferred lease incentives	(16,506)	(11,595)
Other	927	897
Total non-current	(18,455)	(21,057)
Total	$ 38,812	$ 17,958

Note E: Accounting for Leases

Operating Leases

We lease store locations, warehouses, corporate facilities, call centers and certain equipment under operating and capital leases for original terms ranging generally from 3 to 22 years. Certain leases contain renewal options for periods up to 20 years. The rental payment requirements in our store leases are typically structured as either minimum rent, minimum rent plus additional rent based on a percentage of store sales if a specified store sales threshold is exceeded, or rent based on a percentage of store sales if a specified store sales threshold or contractual obligations of the landlord have not been met.

We have an operating lease for a 1,002,000 square foot retail distribution facility located in Olive Branch, Mississippi. The lease has an initial term of 22.5 years, expiring January 2022, with two optional five-year renewals. The lessor, an unrelated party, is a limited liability company. The construction and expansion of the distribution facility was financed by the original lessor through the sale of $39,200,000 Taxable Industrial Development Revenue Bonds, Series 1998 and 1999, issued by the Mississippi Business Finance Corporation. The bonds are collateralized by the distribution facility. As of January 29, 2006, approximately $31,249,000 was outstanding on the bonds. During fiscal 2005, we made annual rental payments of approximately $3,753,000, plus applicable taxes, insurance and maintenance expenses.

We have an operating lease for an additional 1,103,000 square foot retail distribution facility located in Olive Branch, Mississippi. The lease has an initial term of 22.5 years, expiring January 2023, with two optional five-year renewals. The lessor, an unrelated party, is a limited liability company. The construction of the distribution facility was financed by the original lessor through the sale of $42,500,000 Taxable Industrial Development Revenue Bonds, Series 1999, issued by the Mississippi Business Finance Corporation. The bonds are collateralized by the distribution facility. As of January 29, 2006, approximately $34,396,000 was outstanding on the bonds. During fiscal 2005, we made annual rental payments of approximately $4,181,000, plus applicable taxes, insurance and maintenance expenses.

In December 2003, we entered into an agreement to lease 780,000 square feet of a distribution facility located in Olive Branch, Mississippi. The lease has an initial term of six years, with two optional two-year renewals. The agreement includes an option to lease an additional 390,000 square feet of the same distribution center. We exercised this option during fiscal 2005, however, as of January 29, 2006, we had not occupied this space. During fiscal 2005, we made annual rental payments of approximately $1,927,000, plus applicable taxes, insurance and maintenance expenses.

On February 2, 2004, we entered into an agreement to lease 781,000 square feet of a distribution center located in Cranbury, New Jersey. The lease has an initial term of seven years, with three optional five-year renewals. The agreement requires us to lease an additional 219,000 square feet of the facility in the event the current tenant vacates the premises. As of January 29, 2006, the current tenant had not yet vacated the premises. During fiscal 2005, we made annual rental payments of approximately $3,339,000, plus applicable taxes, insurance and maintenance expenses.

On August 18, 2004, we entered into an agreement to lease a 500,000 square foot distribution facility located in Memphis, Tennessee. The lease has an initial term of four years, with one optional three-year and nine-month renewal. During fiscal 2005, we made annual rental payments of approximately $913,000, plus applicable taxes, insurance and maintenance expenses.

Total rental expense for all operating leases was as follows:

	Fiscal Year Ended		
Dollars in thousands	Jan. 29, 2006	Jan. 30, 2005	Feb. 1, 2004[1]
Minimum rent expense	$ 119,440	$ 110,618	$ 101,377
Contingent rent expense	33,529	26,724	21,796
Less: Sublease rental income	(62)	(59)	(90)
Total rent expense	$ 152,907	$ 137,283	$ 123,083

[1]*Includes rent expense for our Memphis-based distribution facilities which were consolidated by us on February 1, 2004. See Note F.*

The aggregate minimum annual rental payments under noncancelable operating leases (excluding the Memphis-based distribution facilities) in effect at January 29, 2006 were as follows:

Dollars in thousands	Minimum Lease Commitments[1]
Fiscal 2006	$ 178,846
Fiscal 2007	176,891
Fiscal 2008	170,041
Fiscal 2009	160,569
Fiscal 2010	149,092
Thereafter	672,358
Total	$ 1,507,797

[1]*Projected payments include only those amounts that are fixed and determinable as of the reporting date.*

Note F: Consolidation of Memphis-Based Distribution Facilities

Our Memphis-based distribution facilities include an operating lease entered into in July 1983 for a distribution facility in Memphis, Tennessee. The lessor is a general partnership ("Partnership 1") comprised of W. Howard Lester, Chairman of the Board of Directors and a significant shareholder, and James A. McMahan, a Director Emeritus and a significant shareholder. Partnership 1 does not have operations separate from the leasing of this distribution facility and does not have lease agreements with any unrelated third parties.

Partnership 1 financed the construction of this distribution facility through the sale of a total of $9,200,000 of industrial development bonds in 1983 and 1985. Annual principal payments and monthly interest payments are required through maturity in December 2010. The Partnership 1 industrial development bonds are collateralized by the distribution facility and the individual partners guarantee the bond repayments. As of January 29, 2006, $1,887,000 was outstanding under the Partnership 1 industrial development bonds.

During fiscal 2005, we made annual rental payments of approximately $618,000 plus interest on the bonds calculated at a variable rate determined monthly (3.5% in January 2006), applicable taxes, insurance and maintenance expenses. Although the current term of the lease expires in August 2006, we are obligated to renew the operating lease on an annual basis until these bonds are fully repaid.

Our other Memphis-based distribution facility includes an operating lease entered into in August 1990 for another distribution facility that is adjoined to the Partnership 1 facility in Memphis, Tennessee. The lessor is a general partnership ("Partnership 2") comprised of W. Howard Lester, James A. McMahan and two unrelated parties. Partnership 2 does not have operations separate from the leasing of this distribution facility and does not have lease agreements with any unrelated third parties.

Partnership 2 financed the construction of this distribution facility and related addition through the sale of a total of $24,000,000 of industrial development bonds in 1990 and 1994. Quarterly interest and annual principal payments are required through maturity in August 2015. The Partnership 2 industrial development bonds are collateralized by the distribution facility and require us to maintain certain financial covenants. As of January 29, 2006, $13,809,000 was outstanding under the Partnership 2 industrial development bonds.

During fiscal 2005, we made annual rental payments of approximately $2,600,000, plus applicable taxes, insurance and maintenance expenses. This operating lease has an original term of 15 years expiring in August 2006, with three optional five-year renewal periods. We are, however, obligated to renew the operating lease on an annual basis until these bonds are fully repaid.

As of February 1, 2004, the Company adopted FIN 46R, which requires existing unconsolidated variable interest entities to be consolidated by their primary beneficiaries if the entities do not effectively disperse risks among parties involved. The two partnerships described above qualify as variable interest entities under FIN 46R due to their related party relationship and our obligation to renew the leases until the bonds are fully repaid. Accordingly, the two related party variable interest entity partnerships from which we lease our Memphis-based distribution facilities were consolidated by us as of February 1, 2004. As of January 29, 2006, the consolidation resulted in increases to our consolidated balance sheet of $18,250,000 in assets (primarily buildings), $15,696,000 in debt, and $2,554,000 in other long-term liabilities. Consolidation of these partnerships did not have an impact on our net income. However, the interest expense associated with the partnerships' debt, shown as occupancy expense in fiscal 2003, is now recorded as interest expense. In fiscal 2005 and fiscal 2004, this interest expense approximated $1,462,000 and $1,525,000, respectively.

Note G: Earnings Per Share

The following is a reconciliation of net earnings and the number of shares used in the basic and diluted earnings per share computations:

Dollars and amounts in thousands, except per share amounts	Net Earnings	Weighted Average Shares	Per-Share Amount
2005			
Basic	$214,866	115,616	$1.86
Effect of dilutive stock options	—	2,811	
Diluted	$214,866	118,427	$1.81
2004			
Basic	$191,234	116,159	$1.65
Effect of dilutive stock options	—	3,188	
Diluted	$191,234	119,347	$1.60
2003			
Basic	$157,211	115,583	$1.36
Effect of dilutive stock options	—	3,433	
Diluted	$157,211	119,016	$1.32

Options with an exercise price greater than the average market price of common shares for the period were 320,000 in fiscal 2005, 196,000 in fiscal 2004 and 436,000 in fiscal 2003 and were not included in the computation of diluted earnings per share, as their inclusion would be anti-dilutive.

Note H: Common Stock

Authorized preferred stock consists of 7,500,000 shares at $0.01 par value of which none was outstanding during fiscal 2005 or fiscal 2004. Authorized common stock consists of 253,125,000 shares at $0.01 par value. Common stock outstanding at the end of fiscal 2005 and fiscal 2004 was 114,779,000 and 115,372,000 shares, respectively. Our Board of Directors is authorized to issue stock options for up to the total number of shares authorized and remaining available for grant under each plan.

In May 2005, our Board of Directors authorized a stock repurchase program to acquire up to 2,000,000 additional shares of our outstanding common stock. During the fourth quarter of fiscal 2005, we repurchased and retired 780,800 shares at a weighted average cost of $41.70 per share and a total cost of approximately $32,556,000. During fiscal 2005, we repurchased and retired a total of 2,422,300 shares at a weighted average cost of $38.77 per share and a total cost of approximately $93,921,000. As of fiscal year-end, the remaining authorized number of shares eligible for repurchase was 20,000. During the first quarter of fiscal 2006, we repurchased and retired these shares at a weighted average cost of $38.84 per share and a total cost of approximately $777,000, which completed all stock repurchase programs previously authorized by our Board of Directors.

In March 2006, our Board of Directors authorized a stock repurchase program to acquire up to an additional 2,000,000 shares of our outstanding common stock. Stock repurchases under this program may be made through open market and privately negotiated transactions at times and in such amounts as management deems appropriate. The timing and actual number of shares repurchased will depend on a variety of factors, including price, corporate and regulatory requirements, capital availability, and other market conditions. The stock repurchase program does not have an expiration date and may be limited or terminated at any time without prior notice.

Prior to March 2006, we had never declared or paid a cash dividend on our common stock. In March 2006, our Board of Directors authorized the initiation of a quarterly cash dividend. The quarterly dividend will be initiated at $0.10 per common share, payable on May 24, 2006, to shareholders of record as of the close of business on April 26, 2006. The aggregate quarterly dividend is estimated at approximately $11,500,000 based on the current number of common shares outstanding. The indicated annual cash dividend, subject to capital availability, is $0.40 per common share, or approximately $46,000,000 in fiscal 2006 based on the current number of common shares outstanding.

Note I: Stock Compensation

Our 1993 Stock Option Plan, as amended (the "1993 Plan"), provides for grants of incentive and nonqualified stock options up to an aggregate of 17,000,000 shares. Stock options may be granted under the 1993 Plan to key employees and Board members of the company and any parent or subsidiary. Annual grants are limited to options to purchase 200,000 shares on a per person basis under this plan. All stock option grants made under the 1993 Plan have a maximum term of ten years, except incentive stock options issued to shareholders with greater than 10% of the voting power of all of our stock, which have a maximum term of five years. The exercise price of these options is not less than 100% of the fair market value of our stock on the date of the option grant or not less than 110% of such fair market value for an incentive stock option granted to a 10% shareholder. Options granted to employees generally vest over five years. Options granted to non-employee Board members generally vest in one year.

Our 2000 Nonqualified Stock Option Plan, as amended (the "2000 Plan"), provides for grants of nonqualified stock options up to an aggregate of 3,000,000 shares. Stock options may be granted under the 2000 Plan to employees who are not officers or Board members. Annual grants are not limited on a per person basis under this plan. All nonqualified stock option grants under the 2000 Plan have a maximum term of ten years with an exercise price of 100% of the fair value of the stock at the option grant date. Options granted to employees generally vest over five years.

Our Amended and Restated 2001 Long-Term Incentive Plan (the "2001 Plan") provides for grants of incentive stock options, nonqualified stock options, restricted stock awards and deferred stock awards up to an aggregate of 8,500,000 shares. Awards may be granted under the 2001 Plan to officers, employee and non-employee Board

55

members of the company and any parent or subsidiary. Annual grants are limited to options to purchase 1,000,000 shares, 200,000 shares of restricted stock, and deferred stock awards of up to 200,000 shares on a per person basis. All stock option grants made under the 2001 Plan have a maximum term of ten years, except incentive stock options issued to 10% shareholders, which have a maximum term of five years. The exercise price of these stock options is not less than 100% of the fair market value of our stock on the date of the option grant or not less than 110% of such fair market value for an incentive stock option granted to a 10% shareholder. Options granted to employees generally vest over five years. Options granted to non-employee Board members generally vest in one year. Non-employee Board members automatically receive stock options on the date of their initial election to the Board and annually thereafter on the date of the annual meeting of shareholders (so long as they continue to serve as a non-employee Board member).

The following table reflects the aggregate activity under our stock option plans:

	Shares	Weighted Average Exercise Price
Balance at February 2, 2003	14,567,106	$14.77
Granted (weighted average fair value of $15.56)	1,596,075	24.37
Exercised	(3,294,478)	11.87
Canceled	(1,089,045)	18.07
Balance at February 1, 2004	11,779,658	16.58
Granted (weighted average fair value of $20.58)	1,626,811	32.57
Exercised	(1,817,308)	14.41
Canceled	(488,734)	20.81
Balance at January 30, 2005	11,100,427	19.08
Granted (weighted average fair value of $23.77)	1,754,990	39.07
Exercised	(1,829,082)	15.30
Canceled	(716,426)	26.81
Balance at January 29, 2006	10,309,909	22.63
Exercisable, February 1, 2004	5,077,371	$12.83
Exercisable, January 30, 2005	5,461,541	14.26
Exercisable, January 29, 2006	5,704,164	16.00

Options to purchase 2,424,858 shares were available for grant at January 29, 2006.

The following table summarizes information about stock options outstanding at January 29, 2006:

	Options Outstanding			*Options Exercisable*	
Range of exercise prices	Number Outstanding	Weighted Average Contractual Life (Years)	Weighted Average Exercise Price	Number Exercisable	Weighted Average Exercise Price
$ 4.50 – $ 9.50	1,651,008	2.71	$ 8.17	1,651,008	$ 8.17
$ 9.66 – $14.50	1,880,843	4.07	12.80	1,529,680	12.61
$15.00 – $22.47	2,006,335	5.68	19.56	1,282,100	18.26
$22.48 – $31.58	1,786,723	7.14	26.80	922,126	26.66
$32.01 – $43.85	2,985,000	8.82	36.39	319,250	32.92
$ 4.50 – $43.85	10,309,909	6.07	$22.63	5,704,164	$16.00

In January 2006, we issued 840,000 restricted stock units of our common stock to certain employees. Fifty percent of the restricted stock units will vest on January 31, 2010, and the remaining fifty percent will vest on January 31, 2011 based upon the employees' continued employment throughout the vesting period. As of January 29, 2006, 840,000 restricted stock units were outstanding.

Note J: Associate Stock Incentive Plan and Other Employee Benefits

We have a defined contribution retirement plan, the "Williams-Sonoma, Inc. Associate Stock Incentive Plan" (the "Plan"), for eligible employees, which is intended to be qualified under Internal Revenue Code Sections 401(a), 401(k) and 401(m). The Plan permits eligible employees to make salary deferral contributions in accordance with Internal Revenue Code Section 401(k) up to 15% of eligible compensation each pay period (4% for certain higher paid individuals). Employees designate the funds in which their contributions are invested. Each participant may choose to have his or her salary deferral contributions and earnings thereon invested in one or more investment funds, including investing in our company stock fund. Prior to November 1, 2005, all matching contributions were invested in our company stock fund. Effective November 1, 2005, participants were allowed to reallocate past matching contributions to one or more investment funds. Effective December 1, 2005, company contributions are invested in a similar manner as the participant's salary deferral contributions. Effective August 1, 2003, our matching contribution is equal to 50% of the participant's salary deferral contribution each pay period, taking into account only those contributions that do not exceed 6% of the participant's eligible pay for the pay period (4% for certain higher paid individuals). For the first five years of the participant's employment, all matching contributions generally vest at the rate of 20% per year of service, measuring service from the participant's hire date. Thereafter, all matching contributions vest immediately. Our contributions to the plan were $3,322,000 in fiscal 2005, $2,850,000 in fiscal 2004 and $3,540,000 in fiscal 2003.

We have a nonqualified executive deferred compensation plan that provides supplemental retirement income benefits for a select group of management and other certain highly compensated employees. This plan permits eligible employees to make salary and bonus deferrals that are 100% vested. We have an unsecured obligation to pay in the future the value of the deferred compensation adjusted to reflect the performance, whether positive or negative, of selected investment measurement options, chosen by each participant, during the deferral period. At January 29, 2006, $11,176,000 was included in other long-term obligations. Additionally, we have purchased life insurance policies on certain participants to potentially offset these unsecured obligations. The cash surrender value of these policies was $9,661,000 at January 29, 2006 and was included in other assets.

Note K: Financial Guarantees

We are party to a variety of contractual agreements under which we may be obligated to indemnify the other party for certain matters. These contracts primarily relate to our commercial contracts, operating leases, trademarks, intellectual property, financial agreements and various other agreements. Under these contracts, we may provide certain routine indemnifications relating to representations and warranties or personal injury matters. The terms of these indemnifications range in duration and may not be explicitly defined. Historically, we have not made significant payments for these indemnifications. We believe that if we were to incur a loss in any of these matters, the loss would not have a material effect on our financial condition or results of operations.

Note L: Commitments and Contingencies

On September 30, 2004, we entered into a five-year service agreement with IBM to host and manage certain aspects of our data center information technology infrastructure. The terms of the agreement require the payment of both fixed and variable charges over the life of the agreement. The variable charges are primarily based on CPU hours, storage capacity and support services that are expected to fluctuate throughout the term of the agreement.

Under the terms of the agreement, we are subject to a minimum charge over the five-year term of the agreement. This minimum charge is based on both a fixed and variable component calculated as a percentage of the total estimated service charges over the five-year term of the agreement. As of January 29, 2006, we estimate the remaining minimum charge to be approximately $21,000,000. The fixed component of this minimum charge will be paid annually not to exceed approximately $5,000,000, while the variable component will be based on usage. The agreement can be terminated at any time for cause and after 24 months for convenience. In the event the agreement is terminated for convenience, a graduated termination fee will be assessed based on the time period remaining in the contract term, not to exceed $9,000,000. During fiscal 2005, we recognized expense of approximately $12,000,000 relating to this agreement.

Form 10-K

In addition, we are involved in lawsuits, claims and proceedings incident to the ordinary course of our business. These disputes, which are not currently material, are increasing in number as our business expands and our company grows larger. Litigation is inherently unpredictable. Any claims against us, whether meritorious or not, could be time consuming, result in costly litigation, require significant amounts of management time and result in the diversion of significant operational resources. The results of these lawsuits, claims and proceedings cannot be predicted with certainty. However, we believe that the ultimate resolution of these current matters will not have a material adverse effect on our consolidated financial statements taken as a whole.

Note M: Segment Reporting

We have two reportable segments, retail and direct-to-customer. The retail segment has six merchandising concepts which sell products for the home (Williams-Sonoma, Pottery Barn, Pottery Barn Kids, Hold Everything, West Elm and Williams-Sonoma Home). The six retail merchandising concepts are operating segments, which have been aggregated into one reportable segment, retail. The direct-to-customer segment has seven merchandising concepts (Williams-Sonoma, Pottery Barn, Pottery Barn Kids, PBteen, Hold Everything, West Elm and Williams-Sonoma Home) and sells similar products through our eight direct-mail catalogs (Williams-Sonoma, Pottery Barn, Pottery Barn Kids, Pottery Barn Bed + Bath, PBteen, Hold Everything, West Elm and Williams-Sonoma Home) and six e-commerce websites (williams-sonoma.com, potterybarn.com, potterybarnkids.com, pbteen.com, westelm.com and holdeverything.com). Management's expectation is that the overall economics of each of our major concepts within each reportable segment will be similar over time.

These reportable segments are strategic business units that offer similar home-centered products. They are managed separately because the business units utilize two distinct distribution and marketing strategies. It is not practicable for us to report revenue by product group.

We use earnings before unallocated corporate overhead, interest and taxes to evaluate segment profitability. Unallocated costs before income taxes include corporate employee-related costs, depreciation expense, other occupancy expense and administrative costs, primarily in our corporate systems, corporate facilities and other administrative departments. Unallocated assets include corporate cash and cash equivalents, the net book value of corporate facilities and related information systems, deferred income taxes and other corporate long-lived assets.

Income tax information by segment has not been included as taxes are calculated at a company-wide level and are not allocated to each segment.

Segment Information

Dollars in thousands	Retail[1]	Direct-to-Customer	Unallocated	Total
2005				
Net revenues	$2,032,907	$1,506,040	—	$3,538,947
Depreciation and amortization expense	84,045	17,566	$ 21,588	123,199
Earnings (loss) before income taxes[2]	278,057	232,023	(161,282)	348,798
Assets[3]	986,222	295,200	700,198	1,981,620
Capital expenditures	96,918	20,984	33,886	151,788
2004				
Net revenues	$1,810,979	$1,325,952	—	$3,136,931
Depreciation and amortization expense	76,667	16,174	$ 18,783	111,624
Earnings (loss) before income taxes	253,038	210,809	(153,642)	310,205
Assets[3]	910,924	279,579	555,042	1,745,545
Capital expenditures	90,027	40,894	50,532	181,453
2003				
Net revenues	$1,622,383	$1,131,985	—	$2,754,368
Depreciation and amortization expense	68,800	15,472	$ 15,262	99,534
Earnings (loss) before income taxes	231,512	172,266	(148,140)	255,638
Assets[3]	822,340	218,603	429,792	1,470,735
Capital expenditures	121,759	11,845	78,375	211,979

[1]Net revenues include $64.6 million, $50.1 million and $42.7 million in fiscal 2005, 2004 and 2003, respectively, related to our foreign operations.

[2]Includes $11.4 million, $2.0 million, and $0.1 million in the retail, direct-to-customer, and corporate unallocated segments, respectively, related to the transitioning of the merchandising strategies of our Hold Everything brand into our other existing brands.

[3]Includes $26.5 million, $23.1 million and $22.5 million of long-term assets in fiscal 2005, 2004 and 2003, respectively, related to our foreign operations.

Form 10-K

59

Glossary

A

accelerated depreciation method A depreciation method that provides for a higher depreciation amount in the first year of the asset's use, followed by a gradually declining amount of depreciation. (444)

account An accounting form that is used to record the increases and decreases in each financial statement item. (49)

account form The form of balance sheet that resembles the basic format of the accounting equation, with assets on the left side and the liabilities and owner's equity sections on the right side. (21, 257)

account payable The liability created by a purchase on account. (14)

account receivable A claim against the customer created by selling merchandise or services on credit. (15, 63, 394)

accounting An information system that provides reports to stakeholders about the economic activities and condition of a business. (7)

accounting cycle The process that begins with analyzing and journalizing transactions and ends with the post-closing trial balance. (159)

accounting equation Assets = Liabilities + Owner's Equity (12)

accounting period concept The accounting concept that assumes that the economic life of the business can be divided into time periods. (104)

accounting system The methods and procedures used by a business to collect, classify, summarize, and report financial data for use by management and external users. (204)

accounts payable subsidiary ledger The subsidiary ledger containing the individual accounts with suppliers (creditors). (206)

accounts receivable subsidiary ledger The subsidiary ledger containing the individual accounts with customers. (206)

accounts receivable turnover The relationship between net sales and accounts receivable, computed by dividing the net sales by the average net accounts receivable; measures how frequently during the year the accounts receivable are being converted to cash. (409, 751)

accrual basis of accounting Under this basis of accounting, revenues and expenses are reported in the income statement in the period in which they are earned or incurred. (104)

accruals A revenue or expense that has not been recorded. (104)

accrued assets *See* **accrued revenues**. (106)

accrued expenses Expenses that have been incurred *but not recorded* in the accounts. (106)

accrued liabilities *See* **accrued expenses**. (106)

accrued revenues Revenues that have been earned *but not recorded* in the accounts. (106)

accumulated depreciation The contra asset account credited when recording the depreciation of a fixed asset. (115)

accumulated other comprehensive income The cumulative effects of other comprehensive income items reported separately in the stockholders' equity section of the balance sheet. (620)

adjusted trial balance The trial balance prepared after all the adjusting entries have been posted. (120)

adjusting entries The journal entries that bring the accounts up to date at the end of the accounting period. (105)

adjusting process An analysis and updating of the accounts when financial statements are prepared. (105)

administrative expenses (general expenses) Expenses incurred in the administration or general operations of the business. (254)

aging the receivables The process of analyzing the accounts receivable and classifying them according to various age groupings, with the due date being the base point for determining age. (401)

Allowance for Doubtful Accounts The contra asset account for accounts receivable. (397)

allowance method The method of accounting for uncollectible accounts that provides an expense for uncollectible receivables in advance of their write-off. (395)

amortization The periodic transfer of the cost of an intangible asset to expense. (453)

annuity A series of equal cash flows at fixed intervals. (655)

assets The resources owned by a business. (12, 51)

available-for-sale securities Securities that management expects to sell in the future but which are not actively traded for profit. (622)

average cost method The method of inventory costing that is based upon the assumption that costs should be charged against revenue by using the weighted average unit cost of the items sold. (310)

B

Bad Debt Expense The operating expense incurred because of the failure to collect receivables. (395)

balance of the account The amount of the difference between the debits and the credits that have been entered into an account. (50)

balance sheet A list of the assets, liabilities, and owner's equity *as of a specific date*, usually at the close of the last day of a month or a year. (18)

bank reconciliation The analysis that details the items responsible for the difference between the cash balance reported in the bank statement and the balance of the cash account in the ledger. (364)

bank statement A summary of all transactions mailed to the depositor or made available online by the bank each month. (360)

bond A form of an interest-bearing note used by corporations to borrow on a long-term basis. (650)

bond indenture The contract between a corporation issuing bonds and the bondholders. (652)

book value The cost of a fixed asset minus accumulated depreciation on the asset. (443)

book value of the asset (or net book value) The difference between the cost of a fixed asset and its accumulated depreciation. (115)

boot The amount a buyer owes a seller when a fixed asset is traded in on a similar asset. (449)

business An organization in which basic resources (inputs), such as materials and labor, are assembled and processed to provide goods or services (outputs) to customers. (2)

business combination A business making an investment in another business by acquiring a controlling share, often greater than 50%, of the outstanding voting stock of another corporation by paying cash or exchanging stock. (627)

business entity concept A concept of accounting that limits the economic data in the accounting system to data related directly to the activities of the business. (11)

business stakeholder A person or entity who has an interest in the economic performance of a business. (4)

business transaction An economic event or condition that directly changes an entity's financial condition or directly affects its results of operations. (12)

C

capital expenditures The costs of acquiring fixed assets, adding to a fixed asset, improving a fixed asset, or extending a fixed asset's useful life. (438)

capital leases Leases that include one or more provisions that result in treating the leased assets as purchased assets in the accounts. (439)

carrying amount The balance of the bonds payable account (face amount of the bonds) less any unamortized discount or plus any unamortized premium. (662)

cash Coins, currency (paper money), checks, money orders, and money on deposit that is available for unrestricted withdrawal from banks and other financial institutions. (357)

cash basis of accounting Under this basis of accounting, revenues and expenses are reported in the income statement in the period in which cash is received or paid. (104)

cash dividend A cash distribution of earnings by a corporation to its shareholders. (578)

cash equivalents Highly liquid investments that are usually reported with cash on the balance sheet. (368)

cash flows from financing activities The section of the statement of cash flows that reports cash flows from transactions affecting the equity and debt of the business. (692)

cash flows from investing activities The section of the statement of cash flows that reports cash flows from transactions affecting investments in noncurrent assets. (692)

cash flows from operating activities The section of the statement of cash flows that reports the cash transactions affecting the determination of net income. (692)

cash payments journal The special journal in which all cash payments are recorded. (214)

cash receipts journal The special journal in which all cash receipts are recorded. (210)

cash short and over account An account which has recorded errors in cash sales or errors in making change causing the amount of actual cash on hand to differ from the beginning amount of cash plus the cash sales for the day. (357)

Certified Management Accountant (CMA) A private accountant employed by companies, government, and not-for-profit entities, requiring a college degree, two years of experience, and successful completion of a two-day examination. (9)

Certified Public Accountant (CPA) Public accountants who have met a state's education, experience, and examination requirements. (10)

chart of accounts A list of the accounts in the ledger. (51)

clearing account Another name for the Income Summary account because it has the effect of clearing the revenue and expense accounts of their balances. (152)

closing entries The entries that transfer the balances of the revenue, expense, and drawing accounts to the owner's capital account. (152)

closing process The transfer process of converting temporary account balances to zero by transferring the revenue and expense account balances to Income Summary, transferring the Income Summary account balance to the owner's capital account, and transferring the owner's drawing account to the owner's capital account. (152)

common stock The stock outstanding when a corporation has issued only one class of stock. (572)

common-size statement A financial statement in which all items are expressed only in relative terms. (747)

compensating balance A requirement by some banks requiring depositors to maintain minimum cash balances in their bank accounts. (368)

comprehensive income All changes in stockholders' equity during a period, except those resulting from dividends and stockholders' investments. (620)

consolidated financial statements Financial statements resulting from combining parent and subsidiary statements. (627)

contra account (or contra asset account) An account offset against another account. (115)

contract rate The periodic interest to be paid on the bonds that is identified in the bond indenture; expressed as a percentage of the face amount of the bond. (653)

controlling account The account in the general ledger that summarizes the balances of the accounts in a subsidiary ledger. (206)

copyright An exclusive right to publish and sell a literary, artistic, or musical composition. (454)

corporation A business organized under state or federal statutes as a separate legal entity. (3)

cost concept A concept of accounting that determines the amount initially entered into the accounting records for purchases. (11)

cost of merchandise purchased The cost of net purchases plus transportation costs. (253)

cost of merchandise sold The cost that is reported as an expense when merchandise is sold. (251)

credit memorandum A form used by a seller to inform the buyer of the amount the seller proposes to credit to the account receivable due from the buyer. (261)

credit period The amount of time the buyer is allowed in which to pay the seller. (260)

credit terms Terms for payment on account by the buyer to the seller. (260)

credits Amounts entered on the right side of an account. (50)

current assets Cash and other assets that are expected to be converted to cash or sold or used up, usually within one year or less, through the normal operations of the business. (150)

current liabilities Liabilities that will be due within a short time (usually one year or less) and that are to be paid out of current assets. (150)

current ratio A financial ratio that is computed by dividing current assets by current liabilities. (749)

D

database The part of a computer system that collects, stores, and organizes information so it can be quickly retrieved. (219)

debit memorandum A form used by a buyer to inform the seller of the amount the buyer proposes to debit to the account payable due the seller. (264)

debits Amounts entered on the left side of an account. (50)

deferrals An asset or liability that is recorded when cash is received or paid that is expected to become a revenue or expense in a later period. (111)

deferred expenses Items that have been initially recorded as assets but are expected to become expenses over time or through the normal operations of the business. (106)

deferred revenues Items that have been initially recorded as liabilities but are expected to become revenues over time or through the normal operations of the business. (106)

deficiency The debit balance in the owner's equity account of a partner. (542)

deficit A debit balance in the retained earnings account. (572)

defined benefit plan A pension plan that promises employees a fixed annual pension benefit at retirement, based on years of service and compensation levels. (497)

defined contribution plan A pension plan that requires a fixed amount of money to be invested for the employee's behalf during the employee's working years. (496)

depletion The process of transferring the cost of natural resources to an expense account. (452)

depreciation The systematic periodic transfer of the cost of a fixed asset to an expense account during its expected useful life. (115, 440)

depreciation expense The portion of the cost of a fixed asset that is recorded as an expense each year of its useful life. (115)

direct method A method of reporting the cash flows from operating activities as the difference between the operating cash receipts and the operating cash payments. (694)

direct write-off method The method of accounting for uncollectible accounts that recognizes the expense only when accounts are judged to be worthless. (395)

discontinued operations Operations of a major line of business or component for a company, such as a division, a department, or a certain class of customer, that have been disposed of. (617)

discount The interest deducted from the maturity value of a note or the excess of the face amount of bonds over their issue price. (481, 574, 653)

discount rate The rate used in computing the interest to be deducted from the maturity value of a note. (481)

dishonored note receivable A note that the maker fails to pay on the due date. (406)

dividend yield A ratio, computed by dividing the annual dividends paid per share of common stock by the market price per share at a specific date, that indicates the rate of return to stockholders in terms of cash dividend distributions. (587, 760)

double-declining-balance method A method of depreciation that provides periodic depreciation expense based on the declining book value of a fixed asset over its estimated life. (443)

double-entry accounting system A system of accounting for recording transactions, based on recording increases and decreases in accounts so that debits equal credits. (58)

drawing The account used to record amounts withdrawn by an owner of a proprietorship. (51)

E

earnings per common share (EPS) Net income per share of common stock outstanding during a period. (619)

earnings per share (EPS) on common stock The profitability ratio of net income available to common shareholders to the number of common shares outstanding. (759)

e-commerce The use of the Internet for performing business transactions. (222)

effective interest rate method The method of amortizing discounts and premiums that provides for a constant rate of interest on the carrying amount of the bonds at the beginning of each period; often called simply the "interest method." (659)

effective rate of interest The market rate of interest at the time bonds are issued. (653)

electronic funds transfer (EFT) A system in which computers rather than paper (money, checks, etc.) are used to effect cash transactions. (358)

elements of internal control The control environment, risk assessment, control activities, information and communication, and monitoring. (351)

employee fraud The intentional act of deceiving an employer for personal gain. (350)

employee's earnings record A detailed record of each employee's earnings. (491)

end-of-period spreadsheet (work sheet) A tool that some accountants prepare in either manual or electronic form at the end of a period that illustrates the impact of adjustments on the financial statements. (146)

equity method A method of accounting for an investment in common stock by which the investment account is adjusted for the investor's share of periodic net income and cash dividends of the investee. (625)

equity securities   The common and preferred stock of a firm. (622)

ethics   Moral principles that guide the conduct of individuals. (4)

expenses   Assets used up or services consumed in the process of generating revenues. (15, 51)

extraordinary items   Events and transactions that (1) are significantly different (unusual) from the typical or the normal operating activities of a business and (2) occur infrequently. (618)

F

fees earned   Revenue from providing services. (15)

FICA tax   Federal Insurance Contributions Act tax used to finance federal programs for old-age and disability benefits (social security) and health insurance for the aged (Medicare). (485)

financial accounting   The branch of accounting that is concerned with recording transactions using generally accepted accounting principles (GAAP) for a business or other economic unit and with a periodic preparation of various statements from such records. (8)

Financial Accounting Standards Board (FASB)   The authoritative body that has the primary responsibility for developing accounting principles. (10)

financial statements   Financial reports that summarize the effects of events on a business. (17)

first-in, first-out (FIFO) method   The method of inventory costing based on the assumption that the costs of merchandise sold should be charged against revenue in the order in which the costs were incurred. (310)

fiscal year   The annual accounting period adopted by a business. (174)

fixed (plant) assets   Assets that depreciate over time, such as equipment, machinery, and buildings. (150)

fixed asset impairment   A condition when the fair value of a fixed asset falls below its book value and is not expected to recover. (615)

fixed asset turnover ratio   The number of dollars of sales that are generated from each dollar of average fixed assets during the year, computed by dividing the net sales by the average net fixed assets. (458)

fixed assets (or plant assets)   Long-term or relatively permanent tangible assets that are used in the normal business operations. (115, 435)

FOB (free on board) destination   Freight terms in which the seller pays the transportation costs from the shipping point to the final destination. (266)

FOB (free on board) shipping point   Freight terms in which the buyer pays the transportation costs from the shipping point to the final destination. (266)

free cash flow   The amount of operating cash flow remaining after replacing current productive capacity and maintaining current dividends. (712)

fringe benefits   Benefits provided to employees in addition to wages and salaries. (495)

future value   The estimated worth in the future of an amount of cash on hand today invested at a fixed rate of interest. (653)

G

general journal   The two-column form used for entries that do not "fit" in any of the special journals. (207)

general ledger   The primary ledger, when used in conjunction with subsidiary ledgers, that contains all of the balance sheet and income statement accounts. (206)

generally accepted accounting principles (GAAP)   Generally accepted guidelines for the preparation of financial statements. (10)

goodwill   An intangible asset that is created from such favorable factors as location, product quality, reputation, and managerial skill. (454)

gross pay   The total earnings of an employee for an employee for a payroll period. (483)

gross profit   Sales minus the cost of merchandise sold. (251)

gross profit method   A method of estimating inventory cost that is based on the relationship of gross profit to sales. (325)

H

held-to-maturity securities   Investments in bonds or other debt securities that management intends to hold to their maturity. (666)

horizontal analysis   Financial analysis that compares an item in a current statement with the same item in prior statements. (742)

I

income from operations (operating income)   Revenues less operating expenses and service department charges for a profit or investment center. (254)

income statement   A summary of the revenue and expenses *for a specific period of time*, such as a month or a year. (18)

Income Summary   An account to which the revenue and expense account balances are transferred at the end of a period. (152)

indirect method   A method of reporting the cash flows from operating activities as the net income from operations adjusted for all deferrals of past cash receipts and payments and all accruals of expected future cash receipts and payments. (694)

intangible assets   Long-term assets that are useful in the operations of a business, are not held for sale, and are without physical qualities. (453)

interest revenue   Money received for interest. (15)

internal controls   The policies and procedures used to safeguard assets, ensure accurate business information, and ensure compliance with laws and regulations. (205, 348)

inventory shrinkage   The amount by which the merchandise for sale, as indicated by the balance of the merchandise inventory account, is larger than the total amount of merchandise counted during the physical inventory. (270)

inventory turnover   The relationship between the volume of goods sold and inventory, computed by dividing the cost of goods sold by the average inventory. (326, 752)

investments   The balance sheet caption used to report long-term investments in stocks not intended as a source of cash in the normal operations of the business. (625)

invoice   The bill that the seller sends to the buyer. (260)

J

journal The initial record in which the effects of a transaction are recorded. (52)

journal entry The form of recording a transaction in a journal. (52)

journalizing The process of recording a transaction in the journal. (52)

L

last-in, first-out (LIFO) method A method of inventory costing based on the assumption that the most recent merchandise inventory costs should be charged against revenue. (310)

ledger A group of accounts for a business. (51)

leverage The amount of debt used by a firm to finance its assets; causes the rate earned on stockholders' equity to vary from the rate earned on total assets because the amount earned on assets acquired through the use of funds provided by creditors varies from the interest paid to these creditors. (757)

liabilities The rights of creditors that represent debts of the business. (12, 51)

limited liability company (LLC) A business form consisting of one or more persons or entities filing an operating agreement with a state to conduct business with limited liability to the owners, yet treated as a partnership for tax purposes. (4, 528)

liquidation The winding-up process when a partnership goes out of business. (539)

long-term liabilities Liabilities that usually will not be due for more than one year. (150)

lower-of-cost-or-market (LCM) method A method of valuing inventory that reports the inventory at the lower of its cost or current market value (replacement cost). (320)

M

management (or managerial) accounting The branch of accounting that uses both historical and estimated data in providing information that management uses in conducting daily operations, in planning future operations, and in developing overall business strategies. (9)

Management's Discussion and Analysis (MD&A) An annual report disclosure that provides management's analysis of the results of operations and financial condition. (763)

manufacturing business A type of business that changes basic inputs into products that are sold to individual customers. (3)

matching concept (or matching principle) A concept of accounting in which expenses are matched with the revenue generated during a period by those expenses. (18, 104)

materiality concept A concept of accounting that implies that an error may be treated in the easiest possible way. (73)

maturity value The amount that is due at the maturity or due date of a note. (406)

merchandise available for sale The cost of merchandise available for sale to customers. (254)

merchandise inventory Merchandise on hand (not sold) at the end of an accounting period. (251)

merchandising business A type of business that purchases products from other businesses and sells them to customers. (3)

multiple-step income statement A form of income statement that contains several sections, subsections, and subtotals. (252)

N

natural business year A fiscal year that ends when business activities have reached the lowest point in an annual operating cycle. (174)

net income or net profit The amount by which revenues exceed expenses. (18)

net loss The amount by which expenses exceed revenues. (18)

net pay Gross pay less payroll deductions; the amount the employer is obligated to pay the employee. (483)

net purchases Determined when purchases returns and allowances and the purchases discounts are deducted from the total purchases. (253)

net realizable value The estimated selling price of an item of inventory less any direct costs of disposal, such as sales commissions. (321, 397)

net sales Revenue received for merchandise sold to customers less any sales returns and allowances and sales discounts. (252)

notes receivable A customer's written promise to pay an amount and possibly interest at an agreed-upon rate. (150, 394)

number of days' sales in inventory The relationship between the volume of sales and inventory, computed by dividing the inventory at the end of the year by the average daily cost of goods sold. (326, 753)

number of days' sales in receivables The relationship between sales and accounts receivable, computed by dividing the net accounts receivable at the end of the year by the average daily sales. (409, 751)

number of times interest charges are earned A ratio that measures creditor margin of safety for interest payments, calculated as income before interest and taxes divided by interest expense. (668, 754)

O

objectivity concept A concept of accounting that requires accounting records and the data reported in financial statements be based on objective evidence. (11)

operating leases Leases that do not meet the criteria for capital leases and thus are accounted for as operating expenses. (439)

other comprehensive income Specified items that are reported separately from net income, including foreign currency items, pension liability adjustments, and unrealized gains and losses on investments. (620)

other expense Expenses that cannot be traced directly to operations. (255)

other income Revenue from sources other than the primary operating activity of a business. (255)

outstanding stock The stock in the hands of stockholders. (572)

owner's equity The owner's right to the assets of the business. (12, 51)

P

paid-in capital Capital contributed to a corporation by the stockholders and others. (571)

par The monetary amount printed on a stock certificate. (572)

parent company The corporation owning all or a majority of the voting stock of the other corporation. (627)

partnership An unincorporated business form consisting of two or more persons conducting business as co-owners for profit. (3, 527)

partnership agreement The formal written contract creating a partnership. (527)

patents Exclusive rights to produce and sell goods with one or more unique features. (453)

payroll The total amount paid to employees for a certain period. (482)

payroll register A multicolumn report used to assemble and summarize payroll data at the end of each payroll period. (488)

periodic system The inventory system in which the inventory records do not show the amount available for sale or sold during the period. (254)

permanent differences Differences between taxable and income (before taxes) reported on the income statement that may arise because certain revenues are exempt from tax and certain expenses are not deductible in determining taxable income. (613)

perpetual system The inventory system in which each purchase and sale of merchandise is recorded in an inventory account. (254)

petty cash fund A special cash fund to pay relatively small amounts. (367)

physical inventory A detailed listing of merchandise on hand. (309)

post-closing trial balance A summary listing of the titles and balances of accounts in the ledger after closing entries have been prepared to ensure the ledger is in balance at the beginning of the next period. (155)

posting The process of transferring the debits and credits from the journal entries to the accounts. (59)

preferred stock A class of stock with preferential rights over common stock. (573)

premium The excess of the issue price of a stock over its par value or the excess of the issue price of bonds over their face amount. (574, 653)

prepaid expenses Items such as supplies that will be used in the business in the future. *Also see* **deferred expenses**. (14, 106)

present value The estimated worth today of an amount of cash to be received (or paid) in the future. (653)

present value of an annuity The sum of the present values of a series of equal cash flows to be received at fixed intervals. (655)

price-earnings (P/E) ratio The ratio of the market price per share of common stock, at a specific date, to the annual earnings per share. (759)

price-earnings ratio The ratio computed by dividing a corporation's stock market price per share at a specific date by the company's annual earnings per share. (628)

prior period adjustments Corrections of material errors related to a prior period or periods, excluded from the determination of net income. (585)

private accounting The field of accounting whereby accountants are employed by a business firm or a not-for-profit organization. (9)

proceeds The net amount available from discounting a note payable. (481)

profit The difference between the amounts received from customers for goods or services provided and the amounts paid for the inputs used to provide the goods or services. (2)

profitability The ability of a firm to earn income. (748)

proprietorship A business owned by one individual. (3)

public accounting The field of accounting where accountants and their staff provide services on a fee basis. (9)

purchase return or allowance From the buyer's perspective, returned merchandise or an adjustment for defective merchandise. (252)

purchases discounts Discounts taken by the buyer for early payment of an invoice. (252)

purchases journal The journal in which all items purchased on account are recorded. (212)

Q

quick assets Cash and other current assets that can be quickly converted to cash, such as marketable securities and receivables. (501, 750)

quick ratio A financial ratio that measures the ability to pay current liabilities with quick assets (cash, marketable securities, accounts receivable). (501, 750)

R

rate earned on common stockholders' equity A measure of profitability computed by dividing net income, reduced by preferred dividend requirements, by common stockholders' equity. (758)

rate earned on stockholders' equity A measure of profitability computed by dividing net income by total stockholders' equity. (757)

rate earned on total assets A measure of the profitability of assets, without regard to the equity of creditors and stockholders in the assets. (756)

ratio of fixed assets to long-term liabilities A leverage ratio that measures the margin of safety of long-term creditors, calculated as the net fixed assets divided by the long-term liabilities. (753)

ratio of liabilities to stockholders' equity A comprehensive leverage ratio that measures the relationship of the claims of creditors to that stockholders' equity. (754)

real accounts Term for balance sheet accounts because they are relatively permanent and carried forward from year to year. (151)

realization   The sale of assets when a partnership is being liquidated. (539)

receivables   All money claims against other entities, including people, business firms, and other organizations. (394)

rent revenue   Money received for rent. (15)

report form   The form of balance sheet with the liabilities and owner's equity sections presented below the assets section. (21, 257)

residual value   The estimated value of a fixed asset at the end of its useful life. (440)

restrictions   Amounts of retained earnings that have been limited for use as dividends. (584)

restructuring charge   The costs associated with involuntarily terminating employees, terminating contracts, consolidating facilities, or relocating employees. (616)

retail inventory method   A method of estimating inventory cost that is based on the relationship of gross profit to sales. (324)

retained earnings   Net income retained in a corporation. (571)

retained earnings statement   A summary of the changes in the retained earnings in a corporation for a specific period of time, such as a month or a year. (584)

revenue expenditures   Costs that benefit only the current period or costs incurred for normal maintenance and repairs of fixed assets. (438)

revenue journal   The journal in which all sales and services on account are recorded. (208)

revenue recognition concept   The accounting concept that supports reporting revenues when the services are provided to customers. (104)

revenues   Increases in owner's equity as a result of selling services or products to customers. (14, 51)

S

sales   The total amount charged customers for merchandise sold, including cash sales and sales on account. (15, 252)

sales discounts   From the seller's perspective, discounts that a seller may offer the buyer for early payment. (252)

sales returns and allowances   From the seller's perspective, returned merchandise or an adjustment for defective merchandise. (252)

Sarbanes-Oxley Act of 2002   An act passed by Congress to restore public confidence and trust in the financial statements of companies. (348)

selling expenses   Expenses that are incurred directly in the selling of merchandise. (254)

service business   A business providing services rather than products to customers. (3)

single-step income statement   A form of income statement in which the total of all expenses is deducted from the total of all revenues. (255)

sinking fund   A fund in which cash or assets are set aside for the purpose of paying the face amount of the bonds at maturity. (662)

slide   An error in which the entire number is moved one or more spaces to the right or the left, such as writing $542.00 as $54.20 or $5,420.00. (74)

solvency   The ability of a firm to pay its debts as they come due. (748)

special journals   Journals designed to be used for recording a single type of transaction. (207)

special-purpose fund   A cash fund used for a special business need. (367)

stated value   A value, similar to par value, approved by the board of directors of a corporation for no-par stock. (572)

statement of cash flows   A summary of the cash receipts and cash payments *for a specific period of time*, such as a month or a year. (18, 692)

statement of members' equity   A summary of the changes in each member's equity in a limited liability corporation that have occurred during a specific period of time. (545)

statement of owner's equity   A summary of the changes in owner's equity that have occurred *during a specific period of time*, such as a month or a year. (18)

statement of partnership equity   A summary of the changes in each partner's capital in a partnership that have occurred during a specific period of time. (544)

statement of partnership liquidation   A summary of the liquidation process whereby cash is distributed to the partners based on the balances in their capital accounts. (540)

statement of stockholders' equity   A summary of the changes in the stockholders' equity in a corporation that have occurred during a specific period of time. (585)

stock   Shares of ownership of a corporation. (568)

stock dividend   A distribution of shares of stock to its stockholders. (580)

stock split   A reduction in the par or stated value of a common stock and the issuance of a proportionate number of additional shares. (586)

stockholders   The owners of a corporation. (568)

stockholders' equity   The owners' equity in a corporation. (571)

straight-line method   A method of depreciation that provides for equal periodic depreciation expense over the estimated life of a fixed asset. (442)

subsidiary company   The corporation that is controlled by a parent company. (627)

subsidiary ledger   A ledger containing individual accounts with a common characteristic. (205)

T

T account   The simplest form of an account. (49)

taxable income   The income according to the tax laws that is used as a base for determining the amount of taxes owed. (611)

temporary (nominal) accounts   Accounts that report amounts for only one period. (152)

temporary differences   Differences between taxable income and income before income taxes, created because items are recognized in one period for tax purposes and in another period for income statement purposes. Such differences reverse or turn around in later years. (612)

temporary investments   The balances sheet caption used to report investments in income-yielding securities that can be quickly sold and converted to cash as needed. (622)

trade discounts Discounts from the list prices in published catalogs or special discounts offered to certain classes of buyers. (268)

trade-in allowance The amount a seller allows a buyer for a fixed asset that is traded in for a similar asset. (449)

trademark A name, term, or symbol used to identify a business and its products. (454)

trading securities Securities that management intends to actively trade for profit. (622)

transportation in Costs of transportation. (253)

transposition An error in which the order of the digits is changed, such as writing $542 as $452 or $524. (74)

treasury stock Stock that a corporation has once issued and then reacquires. (581)

trial balance A summary listing of the titles and balances of accounts in the ledger. (72)

two-column journal An all-purpose journal. (59)

U

unadjusted trial balance A summary listing of the titles and balances of accounts in the ledger prior to the posting of adjusting entries. (72)

unearned revenue The liability created by receiving revenue in advance. (61)

unearned revenues *See* **deferred revenues**. (106)

unit of measure concept A concept of accounting requiring that economic data be recorded in dollars. (11)

units-of-production method A method of depreciation that provides for depreciation expense based on the expected productive capacity of a fixed asset. (442)

unrealized holding gain or loss The difference between the fair market value of the securities and their cost. (623)

V

vertical analysis An analysis that compares each item in a current statement with a total amount within the same statement. (745)

voucher A special form for recording relevant data about a liability and the details of its payment. (359)

voucher system A set of procedures for authorizing and recording liabilities and cash payments. (359)

W

working capital The excess of the current assets of a business over its current liabilities. (749)

Subject Index

Company Index

Abbreviations and Acronyms Commonly Used in Business and Accounting

AAA	American Accounting Association
ABC	Activity-based costing
AICPA	American Institute of Certified Public Accountants
CIA	Certified Internal Auditor
CIM	Computer-integrated manufacturing
CMA	Certified Management Accountant
CPA	Certified Public Accountant
Cr.	Credit
Dr.	Debit
EFT	Electronic funds transfer
EPS	Earnings per share
FAF	Financial Accounting Foundation
FASB	Financial Accounting Standards Board
FEI	Financial Executives International
FICA tax	Federal Insurance Contributions Act tax
FIFO	First-in, first-out
FOB	Free on board
GAAP	Generally accepted accounting principles
GASB	Governmental Accounting Standards Board
GNP	Gross National Product
IMA	Institute of Management Accountants
IRC	Internal Revenue Code
IRS	Internal Revenue Service
JIT	Just-in-time
LIFO	Last-in, first-out
Lower of C or M	Lower of cost or market
MACRS	Modified Accelerated Cost Recovery System
n/30	Net 30
n/eom	Net, end-of-month
P/E Ratio	Price-earnings ratio
POS	Point of sale
ROI	Return on investment
SEC	Securities and Exchange Commission
TQC	Total quality control

Classification of Accounts

Account Title	Account Classification	Normal Balance	Financial Statement
Accounts Payable	Current liability	Credit	Balance sheet
Accounts Receivable	Current asset	Debit	Balance sheet
Accumulated Depreciation	Contra fixed asset	Credit	Balance sheet
Accumulated Depletion	Contra fixed asset	Credit	Balance sheet
Advertising Expense	Operating expense	Debit	Income statement
Allowance for Doubtful Accounts	Contra current asset	Credit	Balance sheet
Amortization Expense	Operating expense	Debit	Income statement
Bonds Payable	Long-term liability	Credit	Balance sheet
Building	Fixed asset	Debit	Balance sheet
_____ Capital	Owner's equity	Credit	Statement of owner's equity/ Balance sheet
Capital Stock	Stockholders' equity	Credit	Balance sheet
Cash	Current asset	Debit	Balance sheet
Cash Dividends	Stockholders' equity	Debit	Retained earnings statement
Cash Dividends Payable	Current liability	Credit	Balance sheet
Common Stock	Stockholders' equity	Credit	Balance sheet
Cost of Merchandise (Goods) Sold	Cost of merchandise (goods sold)	Debit	Income statement
Deferred Income Tax Payable	Current liability/Long-term liability	Credit	Balance sheet
Depletion Expense	Operating expense	Debit	Income statement
Discount on Bonds Payable	Long-term liability	Debit	Balance sheet
Dividend Revenue	Other income	Credit	Income statement
Dividends	Stockholders' equity	Debit	Retained earnings statement
_____ Drawing	Owner's equity	Debit	Statement of owner's equity
Employees Federal Income Tax Payable	Current liability	Credit	Balance sheet
Equipment	Fixed asset	Debit	Balance sheet
Exchange Gain	Other income	Credit	Income statement
Exchange Loss	Other expense	Debit	Income statement
Factory Overhead (Overapplied)	Deferred credit	Credit	Balance sheet (interim)
Factory Overhead (Underapplied)	Deferred debit	Debit	Balance sheet (interim)
Federal Income Tax Payable	Current liability	Credit	Balance sheet
Federal Unemployment Tax Payable	Current liability	Credit	Balance sheet
Finished Goods	Current asset	Debit	Balance sheet
Gain on Disposal of Fixed Assets	Other income	Credit	Income statement
Gain on Redemption of Bonds	Other income	Credit	Income statement
Gain on Sale of Investments	Other income	Credit	Income statement
Goodwill	Intangible asset	Debit	Balance sheet
Income Tax Expense	Income tax	Debit	Income statement
Income Tax Payable	Current liability	Credit	Balance sheet
Insurance Expense	Operating expense	Debit	Income statement
Interest Expense	Other expense	Debit	Income statement
Interest Receivable	Current asset	Debit	Balance sheet
Interest Revenue	Other income	Credit	Income statement
Investment in Bonds	Investment	Debit	Balance sheet
Investment in Stocks	Investment	Debit	Balance sheet
Investment in Subsidiary	Investment	Debit	Balance sheet
Land	Fixed asset	Debit	Balance sheet
Loss on Disposal of Fixed Assets	Other expense	Debit	Income statement
Loss on Redemption of Bonds	Other expense	Debit	Income statement
Loss on Sale of Investments	Other expense	Debit	Income statement
Marketable Securities	Current asset	Debit	Balance sheet
Materials	Current asset	Debit	Balance sheet